Rereading America

Cultural Contexts for
Critical Thinking and Writing

Rereading America

Cultural Contexts for Critical Thinking and Writing

Third Edition

Edited by

Gary Colombo
LOS ANGELES CITY COLLEGE

Robert Cullen
SAN JOSE STATE UNIVERSITY

Bonnie Lisle
UNIVERSITY OF CALIFORNIA, LOS ANGELES

Bedford Books *of* St. Martin's Press · Boston

For Bedford Books

President and Publisher: Charles H. Christensen
General Manager and Associate Publisher: Joan E. Feinberg
Managing Editor: Elizabeth M. Schaaf
Developmental Editor: Jane Betz
Production Editor: Lori Chong
Production Associate: Heidi Hood
Production Assistant: Alanya Harter
Copyeditor: Anthony Perriello
Cover Design: Hannus Design Associates
Cover Art: Detail from a studio art quilt, *Squares and Bars,* Carol H. Gersen, © 1989. From a private collection.
Cover Photography: Susan Kahn. Courtesy of the Taunton Press, publisher of *The New Quilt 1,* © 1991.

Library of Congress Catalog Card Number: 94–65165

Manufactured in the United States of America.

9 8 7 6 5
f e d c b a

For information, write: St. Martin's Press, Inc.
175 Fifth Avenue, New York, NY 10010

Editorial Offices: Bedford Books *of* St. Martin's Press
75 Arlington Street, Boston, MA 02116

ISBN: 0–312–10139–2

Preface for Instructors

About *Rereading America*

Designed for first-year college writing and critical thinking courses, *Rereading America* anthologizes a diverse set of selections focused on the myths that dominate U.S. culture. This central theme brings together 76 readings on a broad range of topics—education, family life, gender, race, success, the environment, and freedom—topics that raise controversial issues meaningful to college students of all backgrounds. We've drawn these readings from many sources, both within the academy and outside of it; the selections are both multicultural and cross-curricular, and they therefore represent an unusual variety of voices, styles, and subjects.

The readings in this anthology speak directly to students' experiences and concerns. Every college student has had some brush with prejudice, and most have something to say about the environment, the family, or the stereotypes they see on film and television. The issues raised here help students to link their personal experiences with broader cultural perspectives and lead students to analyze, or "read," the cultural forces that have shaped and continue to shape their lives. By linking the personal and the cultural, students begin to recognize that they are not academic outsiders—that they do have knowledge, assumptions, and intellectual frameworks that give them authority in academic culture. Connecting personal knowledge and academic discourse helps students see that they are able to think, speak, and write academically and that they don't have to absorb passively what the "experts" say.

A Cultural Approach to Critical Thinking When the first edition of *Rereading America* appeared in 1989, many colleges were just beginning to respond to the concerns of an increasingly diverse student population. Since then, multiculturalism has become a burning issue on campuses across the country. Colleges have established programs to promote curricular diversity, and publishers have responded with a number of readers featuring a range of multicultural selections. Most of these anthologies, however, seek to integrate rather than transform the existing curriculum. In *Rereading America,* we go beyond simple representation of historically marginalized groups: we place cultural diversity at the heart of our approach to critical thinking, reading, and writing.

Critical analysis means asking tough questions—questions that arise from a dynamic interplay of ideas and perspectives. But many students find this kind of internal dialogue difficult to achieve. Traditional schooling is partly to blame: presenting ideas as commodities transmitted from teacher to student and conveying information as objective "fact," the traditional classroom gives students the impression that knowledge is static, not continually re-created through tension, struggle, and debate. Critical thinking is further impeded by dominant cultural myths: these collective and often unconsciously held beliefs influence our thinking, reading, and writing—conditioning our responses, determining the questions we ask and the questions we repress.

The selections in this edition ask students to explore the influence of our culture's dominant myths—our national beliefs about success, gender, race, freedom, and so forth. Each chapter introduces students to perspectives that challenge these deeply held ideals and values, asking them to confront difficult questions and encouraging them to work out their own answers. Thus, instead of treating cultural diversity as just another topic to be studied or "appreciated," *Rereading America* invites students to grapple with the real differences in perspectives that arise in a pluralistic society like ours. This method helps students to break through conventional assumptions and patterns of thought that hinder fresh critical responses and inhibit dialogue; it helps them to develop the intellectual independence essential to critical thinking, reading, and writing.

An extensive introductory essay, "Thinking Critically, Challenging Cultural Myths," offers students a thorough orientation to this distinctly social and dialogic approach to critical thinking. It introduces students to the relationships among thinking, cultural diversity, and the notion of dominant cultural myths, and shows how such myths can influence their academic performance. You'll also find a section devoted to active reading, which offers suggestions for prereading, prewriting, note taking, text marking, and keeping a reading journal.

The book is structured so that each chapter focuses on a myth that has played a dominant role in U.S. culture. In all, we address seven myths:

Learning power: the myth of educational empowerment
Harmony at home: the myth of the model family
Women and men in relationship: myths of gender
Created equal: the myth of the melting pot
Money and success: the myth of individual opportunity
Nature and technology: the myth of progress
Liberty and justice for all: the myth of freedom

Comprehensive chapter introductions offer students an overview of each cultural myth, placing it in historical context, raising some central questions, and orienting students to the structure of the chapter.

Extensive Apparatus . *Rereading America* offers a wealth of specific suggestions for class discussions, critical thinking activities, and writing assignments. We believe strongly in the generative power of collaborative work, and have included many activities that lend themselves to small-group work. The prereading exercises that follow each chapter introduction encourage students to reflect on what they already know of the cultural myth at hand before they begin reading selections addressing it; our purpose is to make them aware of the way that these dominant cultural forces shape the assumptions, ideas, and values they bring to their studies. The three groups of questions following each selection ask students to consider the piece carefully in several contexts: "Engaging the Text" focuses on close reading of the selection itself; "Exploring Connections" puts the selection into dialogue with other selections throughout the book; "Extending the Critical Context" invites students to connect the ideas they have read about here with sources of knowledge outside the anthology, including library research, personal experience, interviews, ethnographic-style observations, and so forth. In this edition we've also included a number of questions linking readings with contemporary feature films for instructors who want to address the interplay of cultural myths, the mass media, and critical analysis in greater depth.

The accompanying manual, *Resources for Teaching* REREADING AMERICA, provides detailed advice about ways to make the most of both the readings and the questions; it also offers further ideas for discussion, class activities, and writing assignments.

What's New in the Third Edition

Revision, as we constantly remind our students, is an intensely collaborative process: it requires us to discover fresh perspectives on our work—literally to see it with new eyes. Revision can also mean rededicating yourself to the original purpose—the vision—that inspired you to write. This third edition of *Rereading America* results from revision in both senses. In response to suggestions from instructors across the country, we have worked to make this edition of *Rereading America* more accessible for first-year students, and we have included timely new materials meant to spark student interest and classroom debate. In addition, we have used the third edition to renew our commitment to a vision of education as critical self-discovery in the context of America's many cultures.

New Chapter Sequence Over the years a number of faculty members have urged us to alter the sequence of chapters in *Rereading America* to make it easier for students to make personal connections with the myths we present. The Third Edition incorporates many of these suggestions: we've moved the chapters on education, family, gender, and the melting pot to the first half of the book, acknowledging the richness of student experience in these areas. Most first-year college students need little encouragement to "read" the cultural myths that inform our thinking about schools, families, male/female stereotypes, and racial categories. The second half of the book addresses topics that are more abstract and conceptual in nature: the myths of individual opportunity, progress, and—new in this edition—the myth of freedom. We hope that this organizational revision makes it easier for students to appreciate the direct impact that cultural myths have had on their personal lives and prepares them to explore the workings of such myths in cultural areas that might initially seem more removed from their immediate experience.

Media Essays and Visual Images We've eliminated the media chapter in this edition, because it didn't fit *Rereading America's* conceptual structure very comfortably, and because the media selections seemed more relevant when treated within the context of specific myths like gender, family, or race than as isolated chapters. Therefore, we have included media essays throughout the book.

Because many students discover new ideas and associations when they engage issues visually as well as in writing, in this edition we've also included a selection of photographs and cartoons. The photos that open each chapter are integrated into the prereading assignments found in the chapter introductions; the cartoons, offered as a bit of comic relief and an opportunity for some visual thinking, are paired with appropriate readings throughout the text.

Focus on Struggle and *Resistance* Most multicultural readers approach diversity in one of two ways: either they adopt a pluralist approach and conceive of American society as a kind of salad bowl of cultures, or, in response to recent worries about the lack of "objectivity" in the new multicultural curriculum, they take what might be called the "talk show" approach and present American culture as a series of pro-and-con debates on a number of social issues. The third edition of *Rereading America,* like its predecessors, follows neither of these approaches. Pluralist readers, we feel, make a promise that's impossible to keep: no single text, and no single course, can do justice to the many complex cultures that inhabit the United States. Thus, the materials selected for *Rereading America* aren't meant to offer a taste of what "family" means for Native Americans, or the flavor of gender relations among recent immigrants. Instead, we've included selections like Melvin Dixon's "Aunt Ida Pieces a Quilt" or James Weinrich and Walter Williams's description of bisexuality and the *berdache* tradition in tribal cultures, because they offer us fresh critical perspectives on the common myths that shape our ideas, values, and beliefs. Rather than seeing this anthology as a mosaic or kaleidoscope of cultural fragments that combine to form a beautiful picture, it's more accurate to think of *Rereading America* as a handbook that helps students explore the ways that the dominant culture shapes their ideas, values, and beliefs.

This notion of cultural dominance is studiously avoided in most recent multicultural anthologies. Salad bowl readers generally sidestep the issue of cultural dynamics: intent on celebrating America's cultural diversity, they offer a relatively static picture of a nation fragmented into a kind of cultural archipelago. Talk show readers admit the idea of conflict, but they distort the reality of cultural dynamics by presenting cultural conflict as matter of rational—and equally balanced—pro and con debate. All of the materials anthologized in *Rereading America* address the cultural struggles that animate American society—the tensions that result from the expections established by our dominant cultural myths and the diverse realities that these myths often contradict.

Ultimately, *Rereading America* is about resistance. In this new edition we have tried harder than ever to include readings that offer positive alternatives to the dilemmas of cultural conflict—from the students Robin Templeton describes in "Not For Sale," who organize to reject the presence of *Channel One* in their classrooms, to the teens who are rewriting the myth of the melting pot in Lynell George's "Gray Boys, Funky Aztecs, and Honorary Homegirls." To make this commitment to resistance as visible as possible, we've tried to conclude every chapter of this new edition with a suite of readings offering creative, and we hope empowering, examples of Americans who work together to redefine our national myths.

Acknowledgments

Editing *Rereading America* is always an act of national collaboration. Every new edition puts us in touch with teachers and students across the country who are eager to share their ideas and favorite readings. Occasionally we've received some less-than-inspiring reviews from other cultural guardians as well—folks like Lynne Cheney and Rush Limbaugh—but we assume it's always meant in good fun. Among our more serious colleagues and collaborators, we'd like to thank the following for their helpful criticism and advice: Perias Pillay, Los Angeles City College; Perrin Reid, Glendale Community College; Sheila Rhodes, University of California, Los Angeles; and Mike Rose, University of California, Los Angeles. We are also grateful to the following people for responding to a revision questionnaire: Katya Amato, Portland State University; Jeanne Anderson, University of Louisville; Julie Drew Anderson, University of South Florida; Sharon K. Anthony, Portland Community College; Rodney Ash, Western State College of Colorado; David Axelson, Western State College of Colorado; Valerie Babb, Georgetown University; Flavia Bacarella, Herbert H. Lehman College; Michael A. Balas, Nassau Community College; Gwen Barday, East Carolina University; Jim Baril, Western State College of Colorado; Richard Barney, University of Oklahoma; Jeannette Batz, Saint Louis University; Les Belikian, Los Angeles City College; Patricia Ann Bender, Rutgers University, Newark; Jon Bentley, Albuquerque Technical Vocational Institute; Sara Blake, El Camino College; Jean L. Blanning, Michigan Technological University; Maurice Blauf, Hutchins School of Liberal Studies; Joseph Bodziock, Clarion University; Will Bohnaker, Portland State University; Susan R. Bowers, Susquehanna University; Laura Brady, George Mason University; Eugenia M. Bragen, Baruch College; Byron Caminero-Santangelo, Saddleback College; Julianna de Magalhaes Castro, Highline Community College; Cheryl Christiansen, California State University, Stanislaus; Ann Christie, Goucher College; Stuart Christie, University of California, Santa Cruz; Renny Christopher, Cabrillo College; Gloria Collins, San Jose State University; Richard Conway, Lamar Community College; Harry James Cook, Dundalk Community College; Richard Courage, Westchester Community College; Cynthia Cox, Belmont University; Dulce M. Cruz, Indiana University; Wendy J. Cutler, Hocking Technical College; Patricia A. Daskivich, Los Angeles Harbor College; Anthony Dawahare, Loyola University, Chicago; Thomas Dean, Cardinal Stritch College; Elise Donovan, Union County College; Miriam Dow, George Washington University; Douglass T. Doyle, University of South Florida; Diana Dreyer, Slippery Rock University; Michele Driscoll, San Francisco State University; Cynthia Dubielak, Hocking Technical College; M. H. Dunlop, Iowa State University; Steve Dunn, Western State College of Colorado; Mary DuPree, University of Idaho; Harriet Dwinell, American University; K. C. Eapen, Clark Atlanta University; Iain J. W. Ellis, Bowling Green State University; Sharon Emmons, University of Portland; G. Euridge, Ohio State University; Rand Floren, Santa Rosa Junior College; Marie Foley, Santa Barbara City College; Barry Fruchter, Nassau Community College; Sandy Fugate, Western Michigan University; Arra M. Garab, Northern Illinois University; Peter Gardner, Berklee College of Music; Mary R. Georges, University of California, Los Angeles; Paul Gery, Western State College of Colorado; Michele Glazer, Portland Community College–Sylvania; William Gleason, University of California, Los Angeles; Sara Gogal, Portland Community College; Krystyna Golkowska, Ithaca College; Jim Gorman; Andrea Greenbaum, University of South Florida; Ervene Gulley, Bloomsburg University; James C. Hall, University of Iowa; Craig Hancock, State University of New York, Albany; Jan Hayhurst, Community College of Pittsburgh; G. Held, Queens College; Jay W. Helman, Western State College of Colorado; Penny L. Hirsch, Northwestern University; Roseanne L. Hoefel, Iowa State University; Carol Hovanec, Ramapo College; Allison A. Hutira, Youngstown State University; John M. Jakaitis, Indiana State University; Jeannette J. Jeneault, Syracuse University; Robert T. Kelley, Urstnus College; Kathleen Kelly, Northeastern University; Kathleen Kiehl, Cabrillo College; Frances E. Kino, Iona College, Yonkers Campus; Blanche Jamson, Southeastern Oklahoma State University; Ron Johnson, Skyline College; Elizabeth Mary Kirchen, University of Michigan, Dearborn; Judith Kirscht, University of California, Santa Barbara; Jeffrey A. Kisner, Waynesburg College; Phil Klingsmith, Western State College of Colorado; Philip A. Korth, Michigan State University; S. J. Kotz, Virginia Polytechnic Institute and State University; Joann Krieg, Hofstra University; Catherine W. Kroll, Sonoma State American Language Institute; Jim Krusoe, Santa Monica College; Frank La Ferriere, Los Angeles City College; Susan Latta, Purdue University; Sheila A. Lebo, University of California, Los Angeles;

D. Lebofsky, Temple University; Mitzi Lewellen, Normandale Community College; Lis Leyson, Fullerton College; Joseph Like, Beloit College; Don Lipman, Los Angeles City College; Solange Lira, Boston University; L. Loeffel, Syracuse University; Paul Loukides, Albion College; Bernadette Flynn Low, Dundalk Community College; Paul Lowdenslager, Western State College of Colorado; Susan G. Luck, Lorain County Community College; Janet Madden-Simpson, El Camino College; Annette March, Cabrillo College; Kathleen Marley, Fairleigh Dickerson University; Lorraine Mercer, Portland State University; Clifford Marks, University of Wyoming; Peggy Marron, University of Wyoming; David Martinez, University of California, Los Angeles; Laura McCall, Western State College of Colorado; K. Ann McCarthy, Shoreline Community College; Richard McGowan, St. Joseph's College; Grace McLaughlin, Portland Community College; Ann A. Merrill, Emory University; Dale Metcalfe, University of California, Davis; Charles Miller, Western State College of Colorado; Carol Porterfield Milowski, Bemidji State University; Ann Mine, Oregon State University; Kathy Molloy, Santa Barbara City College; Candace Montoya, University of Oregon; Amy Mooney, South Puget Sound Community College; Fred Moss, University of Wisconsin–Waukesha; Merlyn E. Mowrey, Central Michigan University; Denise Muller, San Jose State University; William Murphy, University of Maine, Machias; Susan Nance, Bowling Green State University; Patricia M. Naulty, Canisius College; Scott R. Nelson, Louisiana State University; Robert Newman, State University of New York at Buffalo; Thu Nguyen, Irvine Valley College; Todd T. Nilson, University of Kentucky; Fran O'Connor, Nassau Community College; Sarah-Hope Parmeter, University of California, Santa Cruz; Sandra Patterson, Western State College of Colorado; Marsha Penti, Michigan Technological University; Erik Peterson, University of Minnesota; Linda Peterson, Salt Lake Community College; Michele Peterson, Santa Barbara City College; Madeleine Picciotto, Oglethorpe University; Kirsten Pierce, Villanova University; Dan Pinti, Ohio State University; Fritz H. Pointer, Contra Costa College; Paige S. Price, University of Oregon; Teresa M. Redd, Howard University; Thomas C. Renzi, State University College at Buffalo; Geri Rhodes, Albuquerque Technical Vocational Institute Walter G. Rice, Dundalk Community College; Bruce Richardson, University of Wyoming; Randall Rightmire, Los Angeles Southwest College; Jeffrey Ritchie, Northern Kentucky University; Patricia Roberts, Allentown College of St. Francis de Sales; Marjorie Roemer, University of Cincinnati; Bonnie Ross, Los Angeles Valley College; Renee Ruderman, Metropolitan State College, Denver; Lillian Ruiz-Powell, Miracosta College; Geoffrey J. Sadock, Bergen Community College; Mollie Sandock, Valparaiso University; Bryan Scanlon, Western Michigan University; Wayne Scheer, Atlanta Metro College; Linda Scholer, College of San Mateo; Jurgen E. Schlunk, West Virginia University; Esther L. Schwartz, Allegheny County Community College; David Seitz, University of Illinois, Chicago; Jennifer A. Senft, University of California, Los Angeles; Ann Shapiro, State University of New York, Farmingdale;

Nancy Shaw, Ursinus College; Eric Shibuya, University of Oklahoma; Jeanette Shumaker, San Diego State University; Michele Moragne e Silva, St. Edward's University; Rashna B. Singh, Holyoke Community College; Craig Sirles, De Paul University; Bill Siverly, Portland Community College; Antony Sloan, Bowling Green State University; Susan Belasco Smith, Allegheny College; Cynthia Solem, Cabrillo College; Andrew M. Stauffer, University of Virginia; Joseph Steinbach, Purdue University; Skai Stelzer, University of Toledo; Susan Sterr, Santa Monica College; Mark Stiger, Western State College of Colorado; Ann Marie Stock, Hamline University; John B. Stoker, Kent State University; Ann Stolls, University of Illinois, Chicago; Brendan D. Strasser, Bowling Green State University; David Strong, Indiana University; Miriam Stuarts, Loyola University; Bonnie Surfus, University of South Florida; Karen Thomas, University of California, Los Angeles; Alice L. Trupe, Community College of Allegheny County; Eileen Turaff, Cleveland State University; Ruth Ann Thompson, Fordham University; Mark Todd, Western State College of Colorado; Michael Uebel, University of Virginia; James Varn, Morris College; Keith Walters, Ohio State University; Robert R. Watson, Grand Valley State University; Nola J. Wegman, Valparaiso University; Edwin Weihe, Seattle University; R. L. Welker, University of Virginia; Douglas Wixson, University of Missouri; Janice M. Wolff, Saginaw Valley State University; Brent Yaciw, University of South Florida; Nancy Young, Bentley, Curry, and Regis Colleges; and Naomi F. Zucker, University of Rhode Island.

We continue to owe Charles Christensen at Bedford Books a debt of gratitude for having the vision and the integrity to stand behind a book as challenging as *Rereading America.* Not every publisher would have backed this project with as much enthusiasm and faith. Jane Betz used her ample talents as an editor and psychologist to keep this edition on track, even when we had nearly lost sight of it amid the multiple distractions of academic life. At Bedford we also wish to thank Joan Feinberg for constantly reminding everyone how important this book really is; Lori Chong and Heidi Hood for guiding the manuscript through production on a very tight schedule; and Andrea Goldman, Kim Chabot, and Laura Arcari for valiant acts of research and manuscript preparation. We are grateful to Anthony Perriello for careful copyediting.

Finally, Elena Barcia, Liz Silver, and Roy Weitz deserve special thanks for tactfully not reminding us how we vowed we'd do this differently the next time and for surviving yet another edition.

Contents

2

Harmony at Home: *The Myth of the Model Family* 141

4

Created Equal: *The Myth of the Melting Pot* 328

7

Liberty and Justice for All: *The Myth of Freedom* 658

Rereading America

Cultural Contexts for Critical Thinking and Writing

Thinking Critically, Challenging Cultural Myths

Becoming a College Student

Beginning college can be a disconcerting experience. It may be the first time you've lived away from home and had to deal with the stresses and pleasures of independence. There's increased academic competition, increased temptation, and a whole new set of peer pressures. In the dorms you may find yourself among people whose backgrounds make them seem foreign and unapproachable. If you commute, you may be struggling against a feeling of isolation that you've never faced before. And then there are increased expectations. For an introductory history class you may read as many books as you covered in a year of high school coursework. In anthropology, you might be asked to conduct ethnographic research—when you've barely heard of an ethnography before, much less written one. In English you may tackle more formal analytic writing in a single semester than you've ever done in your life.

College typically imposes fewer rules than high school, but also gives you less guidance and makes greater demands — demands that affect the quality as well as the quantity of your work. By your first midterm exam, you may suspect that your previous academic experience is irrelevant, that nothing you've done in school has prepared you to think, read, or write in the ways your professors expect. Your sociology instructor says she doesn't care whether you can remember all the examples in the textbook as long as you can apply the theoretical concepts to real situations. In your composition class, the perfect five-paragraph essay you turn in for your first assignment is dismissed as "superficial, mechanical, and dull." Meanwhile, the lecturer in your political science or psychology course is rejecting ideas about country, religion, family, and self that have always been a part of your deepest beliefs. How can you cope with these new expectations and challenges?

There is no simple solution, no infallible five-step method that works for everyone. As you meet the personal challenges of college, you'll grow as a human being. You'll begin to look critically at your old habits, beliefs, and values, to see them in relation to the new world you're entering. You may have to re-examine your relationships to family, friends, neighborhood, and heritage. You'll have to sort out your strengths from your weaknesses and make tough choices about who you are and who you want to become. Your academic work demands the same process of serious self-examination. To excel in college work you need to grow intellectually—to become a critical thinker.

What Is Critical Thinking?

What do instructors mean when they tell you to think critically? Most would say that it involves asking questions rather than memorizing information. Instead of simply collecting the "facts," a critical thinker probes them, looking for underlying assumptions and ideas. Instead of focusing on dates and events in history or symptoms in psychology, she probes for motives, causes — an explanation of how these things came to be. A critical thinker cultivates the ability to imagine and value points of view different from her own — then strengthens, refines, enlarges, or reshapes her ideas in light of those other perspectives. She is at once open and skeptical: receptive to new ideas yet careful to test them against previous experience and knowledge. In short, a critical thinker is an active learner, someone with the ability to shape, not merely absorb, knowledge.

All this is difficult to put into practice, because it requires getting outside your own skin and seeing the world from multiple perspectives. To see why critical thinking doesn't come naturally, take another look at the cover of this book. Many would scan the title, *Rereading America,* take in the surface meaning — to reconsider America — and go on to page one. There isn't much to question here; it just "makes sense." But what happens with the student who brings a different perspective? For example, a student from El Salvador might justly complain that the title reflects an ethnocentric view of what it means to be an American. After all, since America encompasses all the countries of North, South, and Central America, he lived in "America" long before arriving in the United States. When this student reads the title, then, he actually does *reread* it; he reads it once in the "common sense" way but also from the perspective of someone who has lived in a country dominated by U.S. intervention and interests. This double vision or double perspective frees him to look beyond the "obvious" meaning of the book and to question its assumptions.

Of course, you don't have to be bicultural to become a proficient critical thinker. You can develop a genuine sensitivity to alternative perspectives even if you've never lived outside your hometown. But to do so you need to recognize that there are no "obvious meanings." The automatic equation that the native-born student makes between "America" and the United States seems to make sense only because our culture has traditionally endorsed the idea that the United States *is* America and, by implication, that other countries in this hemisphere are somehow inferior—not the genuine article. We tend to accept this equation and its unfortunate implications because we are products of our culture.

The Power of Cultural Myths

Culture shapes the way we think; it tells us what "makes sense." It holds people together by providing us with a shared set of customs, values, ideas, and beliefs, as well as a common language. We live enmeshed in this cultural web: it influences the way we relate to others, the way we look, our tastes, our habits; it enters our dreams and desires. But as culture binds us together it also selectively blinds us. As we grow up, we accept ways of looking at the world, ways of thinking and being that might best be characterized as cultural frames of reference or cultural myths. These myths help us understand our place in the world—our place as prescribed by our culture. They define our relationships to friends and lovers, to the past and future, to nature, to power, and to nation. Becoming a critical thinker means learning how to look beyond these cultural myths and the assumptions embedded in them.

You may associate the word "myth" primarily with the myths of the ancient Greeks. The legends of gods and heroes like Athena, Zeus, and Oedipus embodied the central ideals and values of Greek civilization — notions like civic responsibility, the primacy of male authority, and humility before the gods. The stories were "true" not in a literal sense but as reflections of important cultural beliefs. These myths assured the Greeks of the nobility of their origins; they provided models for the roles that Greeks would play in their public and private lives; they justified inequities in Greek society; they helped the Greeks understand human life and destiny in terms that "made sense" within the framework of that culture.

Our cultural myths do much the same. Take, for example, the myth of freedom. A strong belief in freedom unites us; we have only to reflect on the number of lives lost in wars fought "for freedom" to grasp its power as a cultural myth. However, look beneath the surface of our collective belief in freedom, and you'll find that we understand it in very different ways. Some see freedom as the right to participate in the electoral process by casting a ballot and electing representatives and leaders. Others say it's freedom of choice, or speech, or unlimited economic opportunity. One person will argue passionately that all government exists solely to guarantee the freedoms enjoyed by individual citizens. The next one will argue just as passionately that our obsession with freedom has become the single biggest problem in modern society. The list of possible definitions is endless, and so is the debate about whether each of us is genuinely free. But the power of myth lies in its ability to override these differences. Politicians and advertisers rely on our automatic emotional response to treasured cultural ideas: when they invoke the ideal of freedom, they expect us to feel a surge of patriotism and count on us not to ask whether the candidate or product really embodies the specific values we associate with freedom.

Cultural myths gain such enormous power over us by insinuating themselves into our thinking before we're aware of them. Most are learned at a deep, even unconscious level. Gender roles are a good example. As children we get gender role models from our families, our schools, our churches, and other important institutions. We see them acted out in the relationships between family members or portrayed on television, in the movies, or in song lyrics. Before long, the culturally determined roles we see for women and men appear to us as "self-evident": it seems "natural" for a man to be strong, responsible, competitive, and heterosexual, just as it may seem "unnatural" for a man to shun competitive activity or to take a romantic interest in other men. Our most dominant cultural myths shape the way we perceive the world and blind us to alternative ways of seeing and being. When something violates the expectations that such myths create, it may even be called unnatural, immoral, or perverse.

Cultural Myths as Obstacles to Critical Thinking

Cultural myths can have more subtle effects as well. In academic work they can reduce the complexity of our reading and thinking. Recently, a professor at Los Angeles City College noted that he and his students couldn't agree in their interpretations of the following poem by Theodore Roethke:

My Papa's Waltz

The whiskey on your breath
Could make a small boy dizzy;
But I hung on like death:
Such waltzing was not easy.

We romped until the pans
Slid from the kitchen shelf;
My mother's countenance
Could not unfrown itself.

The hand that held my wrist
Was battered on one knuckle;
At every step you missed
My right ear scraped a buckle.

You beat time on my head
With a palm caked hard by dirt,
Then waltzed me off to bed
Still clinging to your shirt.

The instructor read this poem as a clear expression of a child's love for his blue-collar father, a rough-and-tumble man who had worked hard all his life ("a palm caked hard by dirt"), who was not above taking a drink of whiskey to ease his mind, but who also found the time to "waltz" his son off to bed. The students didn't see this at all. They saw the poem as a story about an abusive father and heavy drinker. They seemed unwilling to look beyond the father's roughness and the whiskey on his breath, equating these with drunken violence. Although the poem does suggest an element of fear mingled with the boy's excitement ("I hung on like death"), the class ignored its complexity—the mixture of fear, love, and boisterous fun that colors the son's memory of his father. It's possible that some students might overlook the positive traits in the father in this poem because they have suffered child abuse themselves. But this couldn't be true for all the students in the class. The difference between these interpretations lies, instead, in the influence of cultural myths. After all, in a culture dominated by images of the family that emphasize "positive" parenting, middle-class values, and sensitive fathers, it's no wonder that students refused to see this father sympathetically. Our culture simply doesn't associate good, loving families with drinking or with even the suggestion of physical roughness.

Years of acculturation — the process of internalizing cultural values — leave us with a set of rigid categories for "good" and "bad" parents, narrow conceptions of how parents should look, talk, and behave toward their children. These categories work like mental pigeonholes: they help us sort out our experiences rapidly, almost unconsciously (obviously, we can't ponder every new situation we meet as if it were a puzzle or a philosophical problem). But while cultural categories help us make practical decisions in everyday life, they also impose their inherent rigidity on our thinking and thus limit our ability to understand the complexity of our experience. They reduce the world to dichotomies — simplified either/or choices: either women or men, either heterosexuals or homosexuals, either nature or culture, either animal or human, either American or "alien," either us or them.

Rigid cultural beliefs can present serious obstacles to success for first-year college students. For example, a student's cultural myths may so color her thinking that she finds it nearly impossible to comprehend Freud's ideas about infant sexuality. Her ingrained assumptions about childhood innocence and sexual guilt may make it impossible for her to see children as sexual beings—a concept absolutely basic to an understanding of the history of psychoanalytic theory. Yet college-level critical inquiry thrives on exactly this kind of revision of common sense: academics prize the unusual, the subtle, the ambiguous, the complex — and expect students to appreciate them as well. Good critical thinkers in all academic disciplines welcome the opportunity to challenge conventional ways of seeing the world; they seem to take delight in questioning everything that appears clear and self-evident.

Questioning: The Basis of Critical Thinking

By questioning the myths that dominate our culture, we can begin to resist the limits they impose on our vision. In fact, they invite such questioning. Often our personal experience fails to fit the images the myths project: a young woman's ambition to be a test pilot may clash with the ideal of femininity our culture promotes; a Cambodian immigrant who has suffered from racism in the United States may question our professed commitment to equality; a student in the vocational track may not see education as the road to success that we assume it is; and few of our families these days fit the mythic model of husband, wife, two kids, a dog, and a house in the suburbs.

Moreover, because cultural myths serve such large and varied needs, they're not always coherent or consistent. Powerful contradictory myths coexist in our society and our own minds. For example, while the myth of freedom celebrates equality, the myth of individual success pushes us to strive for inequality—to "get ahead" of everyone else. Likewise, our attitude toward the natural world is deeply paradoxical: we see nature simultaneously as a refuge from corrupt, urban society and as a resource to be exploited for the technological advancement of that society. These contradictions infuse our history, literature, and popular culture; they're so much a part of our thinking that we tend to take them for granted, unaware of their inconsistencies.

Learning to recognize contradictions lies at the very heart of critical thinking, for intellectual conflict inevitably generates questions: can both (or all) perspectives be true? What evidence do I have for the validity of each? Is there some way to reconcile them? Are there still other alternatives? Questions like these represent the beginning of serious academic analysis. They stimulate the reflection, discussion, and research that are the essence of good scholarship. Thus, whether we find contradictions between myth and lived experience, or between opposing myths, the wealth of powerful, conflicting material generated by our cultural mythology offers a particularly rich context for critical inquiry.

The Structure of *Rereading America*

We've designed this book to help you develop the habits of mind you'll need to become a critical thinker—someone who can look skeptically at the myths and cultural assumptions that shape your thinking, someone who can evaluate issues from multiple perspectives. Each of the seven chapters addresses one of the dominant myths of American culture. We begin with a topic that every student should have a lot to say about — the myth of educational empowerment. There's no better way to start thinking critically about American culture than to examine the "hidden curriculum" of schooling and to explore what school tells every student about the nature of learning. "Learning Power" gives you the chance to reflect on your own personal attitudes and ideas about education. The next three chapters address myths of the dominant culture that are also closely tied to our identities and personal experience. In "Harmony at Home" we look at the impact that the myth of the nuclear family has had on Americans who don't fit comfortably within its limitations. We also present some serious challenges to this time-honored definition of American family life. "Women and Men in Relationship" considers the socially created categories of gender — the traditional roles that enforce differences between women and men. This chapter also introduces individuals who defy these stereotypical gender boundaries. The fourth chapter, "Created Equal," ends the first section of the book by examining two myths that have powerfully affected racial and ethnic relations in the United States: the myth of the melting pot, which celebrates cultural homogenization, and the myth of racial and ethnic superiority, which promotes separateness and inequality. This chapter probes the nature of prejudice, explores the ways that prejudicial attitudes are created, and examines several alternatives to a race-divided society. Each of these chapters, then, questions how our culture divides and defines our world, how it artificially channels our experience into oppositions like Black and white, family and stranger, male and female, straight and gay.

The second section of *Rereading America* focuses on cultural myths that are more abstract — and perhaps, for that reason, less directly connected with personal experience. "Money and Success" addresses the myth of the American Dream—the idea of unlimited personal opportunity that brought millions of immigrants to our shores and set the story of America in motion. It invites you to weigh some of the human costs of the dream and to reconsider your own definitions of success. The book's sixth chapter, "Nature and Technology," explores the myth of progress and the idea that humans are essentially different from, and thus destined to control, the natural world. The final chapter concentrates on what is perhaps one of our most central and most revered cultural ideals—the myth of freedom. "Liberty and Justice for All" questions the health of freedom in the United States and examines some of the dilemmas that arise when individual rights come into conflict. Ultimately, this final chapter challenges you to reflect on the role that freedom plays in your own life as an American.

The Selections

Our identities — who we are and how we relate to others — are deeply entangled with the cultural values we have internalized since infancy. Cultural myths become so closely identified with our personal beliefs that rereading them actually means rereading ourselves, rethinking the way we see the world. Questioning long-held assumptions can be an exhilarating experience, but it can be distressing too. Thus, you may find certain selections in *Rereading America* difficult, controversial, or even downright offensive. They are meant to challenge you and to provoke classroom debate. But as you discuss the ideas you encounter in this book, remind yourself that your classmates may bring with them very different, and equally profound, beliefs. Keep an open mind, listen carefully, and treat other perspectives with the same respect you'd expect other people to show for your own. It's by encountering new ideas and engaging with others in open dialogue that we learn and grow.

Rereading America deliberately includes few traditional or conservative points of view, because such views seldom challenge the cultural myths that have surrounded us all our lives. And we have not tried to "balance" pro and con arguments, for we believe that doing so reinforces simplistic, "either/or" thinking. Instead, since it's often necessary to stand outside a culture to see it anew, we've included many strongly dissenting views: there are works by radical environmentalists, socialists, disabled activists, gay rights advocates, and more. You may find that their views confirm your own experience of what it means to be an American, or you may find that you bitterly disagree with them. We only hope that you will use the materials here to gain some insight into the values and beliefs that shape our thinking and our national identity. This book is meant to complicate the mental categories that our cultural myths have established for us. Our intention is not to present a new "truth" to replace the old but to expand the range of perspectives you bring to all your reading and writing in college. We believe that learning to see and value other perspectives will enable you to think more critically — to question, for yourself, the truth of any statement.

You may also note that several selections in *Rereading America* challenge the way you think writing is supposed to look or sound. You won't find many "classic" essays in this book, the finely crafted reflective essays on general topics that are often held up as models of "good writing." It's not that we reject this type of essay in principle. It's just that most writers who stand outside mainstream culture seem to have little use for it. The kind of writing that challenges dominant cultural values often comes out of scholarly research, so you can expect to cut your teeth on some serious academic analysis in this book. We also believe that unusual styles and uses of language, like unconventional ideas, offer points of entry into critical thinking. Thus, you will come across some selections—like Gloria Anzaldúa's "La conciencia de la mestiza"—that seem to violate all the conventions of writing and even include passages in another language or dialect. Although such readings may seem disorienting at first, we'll do our best to get you over the tough spots by offering help in chapter introductions, headnotes, and footnotes. We think these selections will reward the extra trouble it may take you to read them, because encountering new styles, besides being intellectually stimulating, can help you become a more flexible reader and writer.

Our selections come from a wide variety of sources—professional books and journals from many disciplines, popular magazines, college textbooks, autobiographies, oral histories, and literary works. We've included this variety partly for the very practical reason that you're likely to encounter texts like these in your college coursework. But we also see textual diversity, like ethnic and political diversity, as a way to multiply perspectives and stimulate critical analysis. For example, an academic article like Jean Anyon's study of social class and school curriculum might give you a new way of understanding Mike Rose's personal narrative about his classroom experiences. On the other hand, you may find that some of the teachers Rose encounters don't neatly fit Anyon's theoretical model: Do such discrepancies mean that Anyon's argument is invalid? That her analysis needs to be modified to account for these teachers? That the teachers are simply exceptions to the rule? You'll probably want to consider your own classroom experience as you wrestle with such questions. Throughout the book, we've chosen readings that "talk to each other" in this way and that draw on the cultural knowledge you bring with you. These readings invite you to join the conversation; we hope they raise difficult questions, prompt lively discussion, and stimulate critical inquiry.

The Power of Dialogue

Good thinking, like good writing and good reading, is an intensely social activity. Thinking, reading, and writing are all forms of relationship — when you read, you enter into dialogue with an author about the subject at hand; when you write, you address an imaginary reader, testing your ideas against probable responses, reservations, and arguments. Thus, you can't become an accomplished writer simply by declaring your right to speak or by criticizing as an act of principle: real authority comes when you enter into the discipline of an active exchange of opinions and interpretations. Critical thinking, then, is always a matter of dialogue and debate — discovering relationships between apparently unrelated ideas, finding parallels between your own experiences and the ideas you read about, exploring points of agreement and conflict between yourself and other people.

We've designed the readings and questions in this text to encourage you to make just these kinds of connections. You'll notice, for example, that we often ask you to divide into small groups to discuss readings, and we frequently suggest that you take part in projects that require you to collaborate with your classmates. We're convinced that the only way you can learn critical reading, thinking, and writing is by actively engaging others in an intellectual exchange. So we've built into the text many opportunities for listening, discussion, and debate.

The questions that follow each selection should guide you in critical thinking. Like the readings, they're intended to get you started, not to set limits; we strongly recommend that you also devise your own questions and pursue them either individually or in study groups. We've divided our questions into three categories. Here's what to expect from each:

- Those labeled "Engaging the Text" focus on the individual selection they follow. They're designed to highlight important issues in the reading, to help you begin questioning and evaluating what you've read, and sometimes to remind you to consider the author's choices of language, evidence, structure, and style.

- The questions labeled "Exploring Connections" will lead you from the selection you've just finished to one or more other readings in this book. It's hard to make sparks fly from just one stone; if you think hard about these connecting questions, though, you'll see some real collisions of ideas and perspectives, not just polite and predictable "differences of opinion."
- The final questions for each reading, "Extending the Critical Context," invite you to extend your thinking beyond the book—to your family, your community, your college, the media, or the more traditional research environment of the library. The emphasis here is on creating new knowledge by applying ideas from this book to the world around you and by testing these ideas in your world.

Active Reading

You've undoubtedly read many textbooks, but it's unlikely that you've had to deal with the kind of analytic, argumentative, and scholarly writing you'll find in college and in *Rereading America*. These different writing styles require a different approach to reading as well. In high school you probably read to "take in" information, often for the sole purpose of reproducing it later on a test. In college you'll also be expected to recognize larger issues, such as the author's theoretical slant, her goals and methods, her assumptions, and her relationship to other writers and researchers. These expectations can be especially difficult in the first two years of college, when you take introductory courses that survey large, complex fields of knowledge. With all these demands on your attention, you'll need to read actively to keep your bearings. Think of active reading as a conversation between you and the text: instead of listening passively as the writer talks, respond to what she says with questions and comments of your own. Here are some specific techniques you can practice to become a more active reader.

Prereading and Prewriting

It's best with most college reading to "preread" the text. In prereading, you briefly look over whatever information you have on the author and the selection itself. Reading chapter introductions and headnotes like those provided in this book can save you time and effort by giving you information about the author's background and concerns, the subject or thesis of the selection, and its place in the chapter as a whole. Also take a look at the title and at any headings or subheadings in the piece. These will give you further clues about an article's general scope and organization. Next, quickly skim the entire selection, paying a bit more attention to the first few paragraphs and the conclusion. Now you should have a pretty good sense of the author's position—what she's trying to say in this piece of writing.

At this point you may do one of several things before you settle down to in-depth reading. You may want to jot down in a few lines what you think the author is doing. Or you may want to make a list of questions you can ask about this topic based on your prereading. Or you may want to freewrite a page or so on the subject. Informally writing out your own ideas will prepare you for more in-depth reading by recalling what you already know about the topic.

We emphasize writing about what you've read because reading and writing are complementary activities: being an avid reader will help you as a writer by familiarizing you with a wide range of ideas and styles to draw on; likewise, writing about what you've read will give you a deeper understanding of your reading. In fact, the more actively you "process" or reshape what you've read, the better you'll comprehend and remember it. So you'll learn more effectively by marking a text as you read than by simply reading; taking notes as you read is even more effective than marking, and writing about the material for your own purposes (putting it in your own words and connecting it with what you already know) is better still.

Marking the Text and Taking Notes

After prereading and prewriting, you're ready to begin critical reading in earnest. As you read, be sure to highlight ideas and phrases that strike you as especially significant — those that seem to capture the gist of a particular paragraph or section, or those that relate directly to the author's purpose or argument. While prereading can help you identify central ideas, you may find that you need to reread difficult sections or flip back and skim an earlier passage if you feel yourself getting lost. Many students think of themselves as poor readers if they can't whip through an article at high speed without pausing. However, the best readers read recursively — that is, they shuttle back and forth, browsing, skimming, and rereading as necessary, depending on their interest, their familiarity with the subject, and the difficulty of the material. This shuttling actually parallels what goes on in your mind when you read actively, as you alternately recall prior knowledge or experience and predict or look for clues about where the writer is going next.

Keep a record of your mental shuttling by writing comments in the margins as you read. It's often useful to gloss the contents of each paragraph or section, to summarize it in a word or two written alongside the text. This note will serve as a reminder or key to the section when you return to it for further thinking, discussion, or writing. You may also want to note passages that puzzled you. Or you may want to write down personal reactions or questions stimulated by the reading. Take time to ponder why you felt confused or annoyed or affirmed by a particular passage. Let yourself wonder "out loud" in the margins as you read.

Presented below are one student's notes on a few stanzas of Inés Hernández-Ávila's "Para Teresa" (p. 74). In this example, you can see that the reader puts glosses or summary comments to the left of the poem and questions or personal responses to the right. You should experiment and create your own system of note taking, one that works best for the way you read. Just remember that your main goals in taking notes are to help you

Para Teresa[1]

Inés Hernández-Ávila

This poem explores and attempts to resolve an old conflict between its speaker and her schoolmate, two Chicanas at "Alamo which-had-to-be-its-name" Elementary School who have radically different ideas about what education means and does. Inés Hernández-Ávila (b. 1947) is a professor of Native American studies at the University of California, Davis. This poem appeared in her collection Con Razón, Corazón *(1987). Her forthcoming collection of poetry is entitled* Wardance/Danza Guerrera: For all the 'skins and all the Meskins *(expected in 1995).*

[Left margin: Writes to Teresa]
A tí-Teresa Compean
Te dedico las palabras estás [Right margin: Why in Spanish?]
que explotan de mi corazón[2] [Right margin: Why do her words explode?]

[Left margin: The day of their confrontation]
That day during lunch hour
at Alamo which-had-to-be-its-name [Right margin: ! Why?]
Elementary
my dear raza [Right margin: — Feels close to T. (?)]
That day in the bathroom
Door guarded
Myself cornered
I was accused by you, Teresa
Tú y las demás de tus amigas
Pachucas todas
Eran Uds. cinco.[3]

[Left margin: T.'s accusation]
Me gritaban que porque me creía tan grande[4]
What was I trying to do, you growled
Show you up?
Make the teachers like me, pet me, [Right margin: Teachers must be white / Anglo.]
Tell me what a credit to my people I was?
I was playing right into their hands, you challenged
And you would have none of it. [Right margin: Speaker is a "good student."]
I was to stop.

[1]For Teresa. [Author's note]
[2]To you, Teresa Compean, I dedicate these words that explode from my heart. [Author's note]
[3]You and the rest of your friends, all Pachucas, there were five of you. [Author's note]
[4]You were screaming at me, asking me why I thought I was so hot. [Author's note]

understand the author's overall position, to deepen and refine your responses to the selection, and to create a permanent record of those responses.

Keeping a Reading Journal

You may also want (or be required) to keep a reading journal in response to the selections you cover in *Rereading America*. In such a journal you'd keep all the freewriting that you do either before or after reading. Some students find it helpful to keep a double-entry journal, writing initial responses on the left side of the page and adding later reflections and reconsiderations on the right. You may want to use your journal as a place to explore personal reactions to your reading. You can do this by writing out imaginary dialogues — between two writers who address the same subject, between yourself and the writer of the selection, or between two parts of yourself. You can use the journal as a place to rewrite passages from a poem or essay in your own voice and from your own point of view. You can write letters to an author you particularly like or dislike (or to a character in a story or poem). You might even draw a cartoon that comments on one of the reading selections.

Many students don't write as well as they could because they're afraid to take risks. They may have been repeatedly penalized for breaking "rules" of grammar or essay form; their main concern in writing, then, becomes avoiding trouble, not exploring ideas or experimenting with style. But without risk and experimentation, there's little possibility of growth. One of the benefits of journal writing is that it gives you a place to experiment with ideas, free from worries about "correctness." Here are two examples of student journal entries, in response to "Para Teresa" (we reprint the entries as they were written):

Entry 1: Internal Dialogue

ME 1: I agree with Inés Hernández-Ávila's speaker. Her actions were justifiable in a way that if you can't fight'em, join'em. After all, Teresa Compean is just making the situation worse for her because not only is she sabotaging the teacher-student relationship, she's also destroying her chance for a good education.

ME 2: Hey, Teresa's action was justifiable. Why else would the speaker admit at the end of the poem that what Teresa did was fine thus she respects Teresa more.

ME 1: The reason the speaker respected Teresa was because she (Teresa) was still keeping her culture alive, although through different means. It wasn't her action that the speaker respected, it was the representation of it.

ME 2: The reason I think Teresa acted the way she did was because she felt she had something to prove to society. She wanted to show that no one could push her people around; that her people were tough.

Entry 2: Personal Response

"Con cố gắng học giỏi, cho Bá Má,
Rồi sau nầy đời sống của con sẽ thõai mái lắm.[5]
What if I don't want to?
What if I can't?
Sometimes I feel my parents don't understand what
I'm going through.
To them, education is money.
And money is success.
They don't see beyond that.
Sometimes I want to fail my classes purposely to
See their reaction, but that is too cruel.
They have taught me to value education.
Education makes you a person, makes you somebody, they say.
I agree.
They are proud I am going to UCLA.
They brag to their friends, our vietnamese community, people
I don't even know.

. . .

They believe in me, but I doubt myself. . . .

[5]"Daughter, study hard (for us, your Mom and Dad), so your future will be bright and easy."

You'll notice that neither of these students talks directly about "Para Teresa" as a poem. Instead, each uses it as a point of departure for her own reflections on ethnicity, identity, and education. Although we've included a number of literary works in *Rereading America*, we don't expect you to do literary analysis. We want you to use these pieces to stimulate your own thinking about the cultural myths they address. So don't feel you have to discuss imagery in Inés Hernández-Ávila's "Para Teresa" or characterization in Toni Cade Bambara's "The Lesson" in order to understand and appreciate them.

Finally, remember that the readings are just a starting point for discussion: you have access to a wealth of other perspectives and ideas among your family, friends, classmates; in your college library; in your personal experience; and in your own imagination. We urge you to consult them all as you grapple with the perspectives you encounter in this text.

1

Learning Power

The Myth of Education and Empowerment

Education is the engine that drives the American dream of success. The chance to learn, to gain the skills that pay off in upward mobility, has sustained the hope of millions of Americans. We're all familiar with the stories of sacrifice and success: the father who works two shifts a day to send his child to college; the older sister who cashes in her own dreams, leaving school to work and care for the family so her sisters and brothers will have a chance. As a nation we look up to figures like Abraham Lincoln and Frederick Douglass, who learned to see beyond poverty and slavery by learning to read. Education tells us that the American dream can work for anyone: it reassures us that the path to success lies through individual effort and talent, not through blind luck or birth. However, this powerful myth conceals as much as it reveals — it fails to capture the complex ways education shapes us.

School emphatically did not appear as a route to success to the leaders of the Six Nations in 1744. In that year, Benjamin Franklin reports, the government of Virginia offered to provide six American Indian youths with the best college education the colony could offer. The tribal leaders politely declined, pointing out that

> our ideas of this kind of education happen not to be the same with yours. We have had some experience of it; several of our young people were formerly brought up at the colleges of the northern provinces; they were instructed in all your sciences; but when they came back to us, they were bad runners; ignorant of every means of living in the woods; unable to bear either cold or hunger; knew neither how to build a cabin, take a deer, or kill an enemy; spoke our language imperfectly; were therefore neither fit for hunters, warriors, or counsellors: they were totally good for nothing.

It's not surprising that these leaders saw a colonial college education as useless. Education works to socialize young people — to teach them the values, beliefs, and skills central to their society; the same schooling that prepared students for life in Anglo-American culture made them singularly unfit for life in tribal culture.

Even within the same culture, the goals of education shift with the changing concerns of the larger society. The Puritans, for example, saw school as a force for spiritual rather than worldly advancement. Lessons were designed to reinforce moral and religious training and to teach children to read the Bible for themselves. But with the Revolutionary War came a new task for education. Following the overthrow of British rule, leaders sought to create a spirit of nationalism that would unify the former colonies. Differences were to be set aside, for, as George Washington pointed out, "the more homogeneous our citizens can be made . . . the greater will be our prospect of permanent union." The goal of schooling became the creation of uniformly loyal, patriotic Americans. In the words of Benjamin Rush, one of the signers of the Declaration of Independence, "Our schools of learning, by producing one general and uniform system of education, will render the mass of the people more homogeneous and thereby fit them more easily for uniform and peaceable government." For revolutionary leaders like Washington and Rush, education served the national interest first and individual development second.

The nineteenth century brought even greater pressures for uniformity and "homogenization" in educating young Americans. Massive immigration from eastern and southern Europe led to fears that non-English-speaking people would undermine the cultural identity of the United States. Many saw school as the first line of defense against this perceived threat, a place where the children of "foreigners" could become Americanized. The use of education to enforce cultural conformity was clearer still for American Indian children: beginning in the 1880s, government-supported schools taught them Anglo-American values and deliberately weaned them from tribal ways, just as the Six Nations' elders had foreseen and feared over a century before.

Industrialization gave rise to another kind of uniformity in nineteenth-century public education: the increasing demand for factory workers put a premium on young people who were obedient and able to work according to fixed schedules. Accordingly, in 1874, leading educators proposed a system of schooling that would meet the needs of the "modern industrial community" by stressing "punctuality, regularity, attention, and silence, as habits necessary through life." History complicates the myth of educational empowerment; as these few examples attest, school can bind as well as free us, enforce conformity as well as foster individual talent.

But history also supplies examples of education serving the idealistic goals of democracy, equality, and civic empowerment. Thomas Jefferson saw school as a training ground for democratic citizenship. Recognizing that an illiterate and ill-informed population would be unable to assume the responsibilities of self-government, in 1781 Jefferson laid out a comprehensive plan for public education in the state of Virginia. According to this plan, all children would be eligible for three years of free public instruction. Of those who could not afford further schooling, one promising "genius" from each school was to be "raked from the rubbish" and given six more years of free education. At the end of that time, ten boys would be selected to attend college at public expense. Jeffersonian Virginia may have been the first place in the United States where education so clearly offered the penniless boy a path to success. However, this path was open to very few, and Jefferson, like Washington and Rush, seemed more concerned with benefiting the state than serving the individual student: "we hope to avail the state of those talents which nature has sown as liberally among the poor as the rich, but which perish without use, if not sought for and cultivated."

Nineteenth-century educator and reformer Horace Mann worked to expand Jefferson's model of public education: not content to rescue a handful of "geniuses," he sought to give all students a chance for success. Mann believed that, with knowledge and hard work, anyone could prosper; thus, he maintained, universal education is "the great equalizer of the conditions of men," a virtual cure for poverty. At the turn of the century, educational theorist John Dewey made even greater claims for educational empowerment. Arguing that "education is the fundamental method of social progress and reform," Dewey proposed that schools strive to produce thinking citizens rather than obedient workers. The national interest, in his view, could be served only by developing fully the talents and abilities of all citizens: "only by being true to the full growth of all the individuals who make it up, can society by any chance be true to itself." Our current myths of education echo the optimism of Mann and Dewey, promising to help us not only achieve our private dreams of success but also perform our civic responsibilities — and perhaps even transform society.

Does education truly empower us, or are these empty promises? This chapter takes a critical look at education — what it can do and how it shapes our identities. The first two readings ask whether day-to-day life in American classrooms measures up to the myth. Theodore Sizer's "What High School Is" opens the chapter by comparing the idealistic goals of secondary education with the experience of an average high school student. In " 'I Just Wanna Be Average,' " Mike Rose gives a moving personal account of the power that teachers can exert, for good or ill, over their students' lives.

The next section explores how education works to define us — how it molds our perceptions and our destinies. In "Social Class and the Hidden Curriculum of Work," Jean Anyon suggests that schools virtually program students for success or failure according to their socioeconomic status. The autobiographical selection by Richard Rodriguez raises questions about the ambivalent role education plays in the life of many Americans who come from families new to the world of higher education. In her dramatic narrative poem "Para Teresa," Inés Hernández-Ávila asks whether academic achievement demands cultural conformity or whether it can become a form of protest against oppression and racism. "Learning to Read" closes this section with the moving story of Malcolm X's spiritual and political rebirth through his self-made education in prison.

The trio of selections that follows focuses more specifically on the experiences of women in the classroom. Myra Sadker and David Sadker's "Higher Education: Colder by Degrees" describes a variety of inequities and abuses suffered by women in higher education. "Connected Education for Women," by psychologist Blythe McVicker Clinchy and her three colleagues, offers an alternative to the traditional model of teaching and learning for women — a model that emphasizes cooperation and personal engagement. Maxine Hong Kingston's "Silence" shows how a cultural mismatch between student and school leads a Chinese American girl to doubt the power of her own voice.

The concluding section offers two selections highlighting examples of educational success. In "Secondary Schools, Primary Lessons," George H. Wood examines two innovative educational programs based on experiential learning. Robin Templeton's "Not for Sale," the media selection for this chapter, closes our exploration of schooling by reporting on students who have organized across the country to resist the growing commercialization of education in the United States.

Sources

John Dewey, "The School and Society" (1899) and "My Pedagogic Creed" (1897). In *John Dewey on Education.* New York: Modern Library, 1964.

Benjamin Franklin, "Remarks Concerning the Savages of North America." In *The Works of Dr. Benjamin Franklin.* Hartford: S. Andrus and Son, 1849.

Thomas Jefferson, *Notes on the State of Virginia.* Chapel Hill: University of North Carolina Press, 1955.

Leonard Pitt, *We Americans,* vol. 2, 3rd ed. Dubuque: Kendall/Hunt, 1987.

Edward Stevens and George H. Wood, *Justice, Ideology, and Education: An Introduction to the Social Foundations of Education.* New York: Random House, 1987.

Elizabeth Vallance, "Hiding the Hidden Curriculum: An Interpretation of the Language of Justification in Nineteenth-Century Educational Reform." *Curriculum Theory Network,* vol. 4, no. 1 (1973–74), pp. 5–21.

Before Reading

- Freewrite for fifteen or twenty minutes about your best and worst educational experiences. Then, working in groups, compare notes to see if you can find recurring themes or ideas in what you've written. What aspects of school seem to stand out most clearly in your memories? Do the best experiences have anything in common? How about the worst? What aspects of your school experience didn't show up in the freewriting?
- Work in small groups to draw a collective picture that expresses your experience of high school or college. Don't worry about your drawing skill—just load the page with imagery, feelings, and ideas. Then show your work to other class members and let them try to interpret it.
- Write a journal entry from the point of view of the girl pictured on the title page of this chapter (p. 15). Try to capture the thoughts that are going through her head. What has her day in school been like? What is she looking forward to? What is she dreading? Share your entries with your classmates and discuss your responses.

What High School Is

THEODORE SIZER

High school, as the one institution nearly every U.S. citizen participates in, may be the nation's most widely shared cultural experience. This selection contrasts the mythic aims of schooling with the realities of life in American high schools. Sizer begins by describing a day in the life of a typical student, actually a fictional composite of many students interviewed during his research. His analysis of the rather dispiriting scenario follows. Sizer (b. 1932) is director of the Annenberg Institute for School Reform at Brown University and chair of the Coalition of Essential Schools, a national organization devoted to educational reform. This selection is taken from Horace's Compromise: The Dilemma of the American High School *(1984). Sizer's more recent book,* Horace's School: Redesigning the American High School *(1992), should be available at your college library.*

Mark, sixteen and a genial eleventh-grader, rides a bus to Franklin High School, arriving at 7:25. It is an Assembly Day, so the schedule is adapted to allow for a meeting of the entire school. He hangs out with his friends, first outside school and then inside, by his locker. He carries a pile of textbooks and notebooks; in all, it weighs eight and a half pounds.

From 7:30 to 8:19, with nineteen other students, he is in Room 304 for English class. The Shakespeare play being read this year by the eleventh grade is *Romeo and Juliet.* The teacher, Ms. Viola, has various students in turn take parts and read out loud. Periodically, she interrupts the (usually halting) recitations to ask whether the thread of the conversation in the play is clear. Mark is entertained by the stumbling readings of some of his classmates. He hopes he will not be asked to be Romeo, particularly if his current steady, Sally, is Juliet. There is a good deal of giggling in class, and much attention paid to who may be called on next. Ms. Viola reminds the class of a test on this part of the play to be given next week.

The bell rings at 8:19. Mark goes to the boys' room, where he sees a classmate who he thinks is a wimp but who constantly tries to be a buddy. Mark avoids the leech by rushing off. On the way, he notices two boys engaged in some sort of transaction, probably over marijuana. He pays them no attention. 8:24. Typing class. The rows of desks that embrace big office machines are almost filled before the bell. Mark is uncomfortable here: typing class is girl country. The teacher constantly threatens what to Mark is a humiliatingly female future: "Your employer won't like these erasures." The minutes during the period are spent copying a letter from a handbook onto business stationery. Mark struggles to keep from looking at his work; the teacher wants him to watch only the material from which he is copying. Mark is frustrated, uncomfortable, and scared that he will not complete his letter by the class's end, which would be embarrassing.

Nine-tenths of the students present at school that day are assembled in the auditorium by the 9:18 bell. The dilatory[1] tenth still stumble in, running down aisles. Annoyed class deans try to get the mob settled. The curtains part; the program is a concert by a student rock group. Their electronic gear flashes under the lights, and the five boys and one girl in the group work hard at being casual. Their movements on stage are studiously at three-quarter time, and they chat with one another as though the tumultuous screaming of their schoolmates were totally inaudible. The girl balances on a stool; the boys crank up the music. It is very soft rock, the sanitized lyrics surely cleared with the assistant principal. The girl sings, holding the mike close to her mouth, but can scarcely be heard. Her light voice is tentative, and the lyrics indecipherable. The guitars, amplified, are tuneful, however, and the drums are played with energy.

5 The students around Mark — all juniors, since they are seated by class — alternately slouch in their upholstered, hinged seats, talking to one another, or sit forward, leaning on the chair backs in front of them, watching the band. A boy near Mark shouts noisily at the microphone-fondling singer, "Bite it . . . ohhh," and the area round Mark explodes in vulgar male laughter, but quickly subsides. A teacher walks down the aisle. Songs continue, to great applause. Assembly is over at 9:46, two minutes early.

9:53 and biology class. Mark was at a different high school last year and did not take this course there as a tenth-grader. He is in it now, and all but one of his classmates are a year younger than he. He sits on the side, not taking part in the chatter that goes on after the bell. At 9:57, the public address system goes on, with the announcements of the day. After a few words from the principal ("Here's today's cheers and jeers . . ." with a cheer for the winning basketball team and a jeer for the spectators who made a ruckus at the gymnasium), the task is taken over by officers of ASB (Associated Student Bodies). There is an appeal for "bat bunnies." Carnations are for sale by the Girls' League. Miss Indian American is coming. Students are auctioning off their services (background catcalls are heard) to earn money for the prom. Nominees are needed for the ballot for school bachelor and school bachelorette. The announcements end with a "thought for the day. When you throw a little mud, you lose a little ground."

At 10:04 the biology class finally turns to science. The teacher, Mr. Robbins, has placed one of several labeled laboratory specimens — some are pinned in frames, others swim in formaldehyde — on each of the classroom's eight laboratory tables. The three or so students whose chairs circle each of

[1]*dilatory:* Tending to delay or procrastinate.

these benches are to study the specimen and make notes about it or drawings of it. After a few minutes each group of three will move to another table. The teacher points out that these specimens are of organisms already studied in previous classes. He says that the period-long test set for the following day will involve observing some of these specimens — then to be without labels — and writing an identifying paragraph on each. Mr. Robbins points out that some of the printed labels ascribe the specimens names different from those given in the textbook. He explains that biologists often give several names to the same organism.

The class now falls to peering, writing, and quiet talking. Mr. Robbins comes over to Mark, and in whispered words asks him to carry a requisition form for science department materials to the business office. Mark, because of his "older" status, is usually chosen by Robbins for this kind of errand. Robbins gives Mark the form and a green hall pass to show to any teacher who might challenge him, on his way to the office, for being out of a classroom. The errand takes Mark four minutes. Meanwhile Mark's group is hard at work but gets to only three of the specimens before the bell rings at 10:42. As the students surge out, Robbins shouts a reminder about a "double" laboratory period on Thursday.

Between classes one of the seniors asks Mark whether he plans to be a candidate for schoolwide office next year. Marks says no. He starts to explain. The 10:47 bell rings, meaning that he is late for French class.

There are fifteen students in Monsieur Bates's language class. He hands 10
out tests taken the day before: *"C'est bien fait, Etienne . . . c'est mieux, Marie . . . tch, tch, Robert . . ."* Mark notes his C+ and peeks at the A− in front of Susanna, next to him. The class has been assigned seats by M. Bates; Mark resents sitting next to prissy, brainy Susanna. Bates starts by asking a student to read a question and give the correct answer. *"James, question un."* James haltingly reads the question and gives an answer that Bates, now speaking English, says is incomplete. In due course: *"Mark, question cinq."* Mark does his bit, and the sequence goes on, the eight quiz questions and answers filling about twenty minutes of time.

"Turn to page forty-nine. *Maintenant, lisez après moi . . .*" and Bates reads a sentence and has the class echo it. Mark is embarrassed by this and mumbles with a barely audible sound. Others, like Susanna, keep the decibel count up, so Mark can hide. This I-say-you-repeat drill is interrupted once by the public address system, with an announcement about a meeting for the cheerleaders. Bates finishes the class, almost precisely at the bell, with a homework assignment. The students are to review these sentences for a brief quiz the following day. Mark takes note of the assignment, because he knows that tomorrow will be a day of busy-work in French class. Much though he dislikes oral drills, they are better than the workbook stuff that Bates hands out. Write, write, write, for Bates to throw away, Mark thinks.

11:36. Down to the cafeteria, talking noisily, hanging out, munching. Getting to Room 104 by 12:17: U.S. history. The teacher is sitting cross-legged on his desk when Mark comes in, heatedly arguing with three students over the fracas that had followed the previous night's basketball game. The teacher, Mr. Suslovic, while agreeing that the spectators from their school certainly were provoked, argues that they should neither have been so obviously obscene in yelling at the opposing cheerleaders nor have allowed Coke cans to be rolled out on the floor. The three students keep saying that "it isn't fair." Apparently they and some others had been assigned "Saturday mornings" (detentions) by the principal for the ruckus.

At 12:34, the argument appears to subside. The uninvolved students, including Mark, are in their seats, chatting amiably. Mr. Suslovic climbs off his desk and starts talking: "We've almost finished this unit, chapters nine and ten . . ." The students stop chattering among themselves and turn toward Suslovic. Several slouch down in their chairs. Some open notebooks. Most have the five-pound textbook on their desks.

Suslovic lectures on the cattle drives, from north Texas to railroads west of St. Louis. He breaks up this narrative with questions ("Why were the railroad lines laid largely east to west?"), directed at nobody in particular and eventually answered by Suslovic himself. Some students take notes. Mark doesn't. A student walks in the open door, hands Mr. Suslovic a list, and starts whispering with him. Suslovic turns from the class and hears out this messenger. He then asks, "Does anyone know where Maggie Sharp is?" Someone answers, "Sick at home"; someone else says, "I thought I saw her at lunch." Genial consternation.[2] Finally Suslovic tells the messenger, "Sorry, we can't help you," and returns to the class: "Now, where were we?" He goes on for some minutes. The bell rings. Suslovic forgets to give the homework assignment.

1:11 and Algebra II. There is a commotion in the hallway: someone's 15
locker is rumored to have been opened by the assistant principal and a narcotics agent. In the five-minute passing time, Mark hears the story three times and three ways. A locker had been broken into by another student. It was Mr. Gregory and a narc. It was the cops, and they did it without Gregory's knowing. Mrs. Ames, the mathematics teacher, has not heard anything about it. Several of the nineteen students try to tell her and start arguing among themselves. "O.K., that's enough." She hands out the day's problem, one sheet to each student. Mark sees with dismay that it is a single, complicated "word" problem about some train that, while traveling at 84 mph, due west, passes a car that was going due east at 55 mph. Mark struggles: Is it $d = rt$ or $t = rd$? The class becomes quiet, writing, while Mrs. Ames writes some additional, short problems on the blackboard. "Time's up." A sigh; most students still writing. A muffled "Shit." Mrs. Ames frowns. "Come on, now." She collects papers, but it takes four minutes for her to corral them all.

[2]*genial consternation:* Good-humored confusion or bewilderment.

"Copy down the problems from the board." A minute passes. "William, try number one." William suggests an approach. Mrs. Ames corrects and cajoles, and William finally gets it right. Mark watches two kids to his right passing notes; he tries to read them, but the handwriting is illegible from his distance. He hopes he is not called on, and he isn't. Only three students are asked to puzzle out an answer. The bell rings at 2:00. Mrs. Ames shouts a homework assignment over the resulting hubbub.

Mark leaves his books in his locker. He remembers that he has homework, but figures that he can do it during English class the next day. He knows that there will be an in-class presentation of one of the *Romeo and Juliet* scenes and that he will not be in it. The teacher will not notice his homework writing, or won't do anything about it if she does.

Mark passes various friends heading toward the gym, members of the basketball teams. Like most students, Mark isn't an active school athlete. However, he is associated with the yearbook staff. Although he is not taking "Yearbook" for credit as an English course, he is contributing photographs. Mark takes twenty minutes checking into the yearbook staff's headquarters (the classroom of its faculty adviser) and getting some assignments of pictures from his boss, the senior who is the photography editor. Mark knows that if he pleases his boss and the faculty adviser, he'll take that editor's post for the next year. He'll get English credit for his work then.

After gossiping a bit with the yearbook staff, Mark will leave school by 2:35 and go home. His grocery market bagger's job is from 4:45 to 8:00, the rush hour for the store. He'll have a snack at 4:30, and his mother will save him some supper to eat at 8:30. She will ask whether he has any homework, and he'll tell her no. Tomorrow, and virtually every other tomorrow, will be the same for Mark, save for the lack of the assembly: each period then will be five minutes longer.

Most Americans have an uncomplicated vision of what secondary edu- 20
cation should be. Their conception of high school is remarkably uniform across the country, a striking fact, given the size and diversity of the United States and the politically decentralized character of the schools. This uniformity is of several generations' standing. It has, however, two appearances, each quite different from the other, one of words and the other of practice, a world of political rhetoric and Mark's world.

A California high school's general goals, set out in 1979, could serve equally well most of America's high schools, public and private. This school had as its ends:

- Fundamental scholastic achievement . . . to acquire knowledge and share in the traditionally accepted academic fundamentals . . . to develop the ability to make decisions, to solve problems, to reason independently, and to accept responsibility for self-evaluation and continuing self-improvement.

- Career and economic competence . . .
- Citizenship and civil responsibility . . .
- Competence in human and social relations . . .
- Moral and ethical values . . .
- Self-realization and mental and physical health . . .
- Aesthetic awareness . . .
- Cultural diversity . . .[3]

In addition to its optimistic rhetoric, what distinguishes this list is its comprehensiveness. The high school is to touch most aspects of an adolescent's existence — mind, body, morals, values, career. No one of these areas is given especial prominence. School people arrogate to themselves an obligation to all.

An example of the wide acceptability of these goals is found in the courts. Forced to present a detailed definition of "thorough and efficient education," elementary as well as secondary, a West Virginia judge sampled the best of conventional wisdom and concluded that

> there are eight general elements of a thorough and efficient system of education: (a) Literacy, (b) The ability to add, subtract, multiply, and divide numbers, (c) Knowledge of government to the extent the child will be equipped as a citizen to make informed choices among persons and issues that affect his own governance, (d) Self-knowledge and knowledge of his or her total environment to allow the child to intelligently choose life work — to know his or her options, (e) Work-training and advanced academic training as the child may intelligently choose, (f) Recreational pursuits, (g) Interests in all creative arts such as music, theater, literature, and the visual arts, and (h) Social ethics, both behavioral and abstract, to facilitate compatibility with others in this society.[4]

That these eight — now powerfully part of the debate over the purpose and practice of education in West Virginia — are reminiscent of the influential list, "The Seven Cardinal Principles of Secondary Education," promulgated in 1918 by the National Education Association, is no surprise.[5] The

[3]Shasta High School, Redding, California. An eloquent and analogous statement, "The Essentials of Education," one stressing explicitly the "interdependence of skills and content" that is implicit in the Shasta High School statement, was issued in 1980 by a coalition of education associations. Organizations for the Essentials of Education (Urbana, Illinois) [Author's note]

[4]Judge Arthur M. Recht, in his order resulting from *Pauley v. Kelly,* 1979, as reprinted in *Education Week,* May 26, 1982, p. 10. See also, in *Education Week,* January 16, 1983, pp. 21, 24, Jonathan P. Sher, "The Struggle to Fulfill a Judicial Mandate: How Not to 'Reconstruct' Education in W. Va." [Author's note]

[5]Bureau of Education, Department of the Interior, "Cardinal Principles of Secondary Education: A Report of the Commission on the Reorganization of Secondary Education, appointed by the National Education Association," *Bulletin,* no. 35 (Washington, U.S. Government Printing Office, 1918). [Author's note]

rhetoric of high school purpose has been uniform and consistent for decades. Americans agree on the goals for their high schools.

That agreement is convenient, but it masks the fact that virtually all the 25
words in these goal statements beg definition. Some schools have labored long to identify specific criteria beyond them; the result has been lists of daunting pseudospecificity and numbing earnestness. However, most leave the words undefined and let the momentum of traditional practice speak for itself. That is why analyzing how Mark spends his time is important: from watching him one uncovers the important purposes of education, the ones that shape practice. Mark's day is similar to that of other high school students across the country, as similar as the rhetoric of one goal statement to others'. Of course, there are variations, but the extent of consistency in the shape of school routine for a large and diverse adolescent population is extraordinary, indicating more graphically than any rhetoric the measure of agreement in America about what one does in high school, and, by implication, what it is for.

The basic organizing structures in schools are familiar. Above all, students are grouped by age (that is, freshman, sophomore, junior, senior) and all are expected to take precisely the same time — around 720 school days over four years, to be precise — to meet the requirements for a diploma. When one is out of his grade level, he can feel odd, as Mark did in his biology class. The goals are the same for all, and the means to achieve them are also similar.

Young males and females are treated remarkably alike; the schools' goals are the same for each gender. In execution, there are differences, as those pressing sex discrimination suits have made educators intensely aware. The students in metalworking classes are mostly male; those in home economics, mostly female. But it is revealing how much less sex discrimination there is in high schools than in other American institutions. For many young women, the most liberated hours of their week are in school.

School is to be like a job: you start in the morning and end in the afternoon, five days a week. You don't get much of a lunch hour, so you go home early, unless you are an athlete or are involved in some special school or extracurricular activity. School is conceived of as the children's workplace, and it takes young people off parents' hands and out of the labor market during prime-time work hours. Not surprisingly, many students see going to school as little more than a dogged necessity. They perceive the day-to-day routine, a Minnesota study reports, as one of "boredom and lethargy." One of the students summarizes: school is "boring, restless, tiresome, puts ya to sleep, tedious, monotonous, pain in the neck."[6]

The school schedule is a series of units of time: the clock is king. The

[6]Diane Hedin, Paula Simon, and Michael Robin, *Minnesota Youth Poll: Youth's Views on School and School Discipline*, Minnesota Report 184 (1983), Agricultural Experiment Station, University of Minnesota, p. 13. [Author's note]

base time block is about fifty minutes in length. Some schools, on what they call modular scheduling, split that fifty-minute block into two or even three pieces. Most schools have double periods for laboratory work, especially in the sciences, or four-hour units for the small numbers of students involved in intensive vocational or other work-study programs. The flow of all school activity arises from or is blocked by these time units. "How much time do I have with my kids?" is the teacher's key question.

30 Because there are many claims for those fifty-minute blocks, there is little time set aside for rest between them, usually no more than three to ten minutes, depending on how big the school is and, consequently, how far students and teachers have to walk from class to class. As a result, there is a frenetic[7] quality to the school day, a sense of sustained restlessness. For the adolescents, there are frequent changes of room and fellow students, each change giving tempting opportunities for distraction, which are stoutly resisted by teachers. Some schools play soft music during these "passing times," to quiet the multitude, one principal told me.

Many teachers have a chance for a coffee break. Few students do. In some city schools where security is a problem, students must be in class for seven consecutive periods, interrupted by a heavily monitored twenty-minute lunch period for small groups, starting as early as 10:30 A.M. and running to after 1:00 P.M. A high premium is placed on punctuality and on "being where you're supposed to be." Obviously, a low premium is placed on reflection and repose. The student rushes from class to class to collect knowledge. Savoring it, it is implied, is not to be done much in school, nor is such meditation really much admired. The picture that these familiar patterns yield is that of an academic supermarket. The purpose of going to school is to pick things up, in an organized and predictable way, the faster the better.

What is supposed to be picked up is remarkably consistent among all sorts of high schools. Most schools specifically mandate three out of every five courses a student selects. Nearly all of these mandates fall into five areas — English, social studies, mathematics, science, and physical education. On the average, English is required to be taken each year, social studies and physical education three out of the four high school years, and mathematics and science one or two years. Trends indicate that in the mid-eighties there is likely to be an increase in the time allocated to these last two subjects. Most students take classes in these four major academic areas beyond the minimum requirements, sometimes in such special areas as journalism and "yearbook," offshoots of English departments.[8]

Press most adults about what high school is for, and you hear these

[7]*frenetic:* Frantic; frenzied.

[8]I am indebted to Harold F. Sizer and Lyde E. Sizer for a survey of the diploma requirements of fifty representative secondary schools, completed for "A Study of High Schools." [Author's note]

subjects listed. *High school? That's where you learn English and math and that sort of thing.* Ask students, and you get the same answer. High school is to "teach" these "subjects."

What is often absent is any definition of these subjects or any rationale for them. They are just there, labels. Under those labels lie a multitude of things. A great deal of material is supposed to be "covered"; most of these courses are surveys, great sweeps of the stuff of their parent disciplines.

35 While there is often a sequence *within* subjects — algebra before trigonometry, "first-year" French before "second-year" French — there is rarely a coherent relationship or sequence *across* subjects. Even the most logically related matters — reading ability as a precondition for the reading of history books, and certain mathematical concepts or skills before the study of some of physics — are only loosely coordinated, if at all. There is little demand for a synthesis of it all; English, mathematics, and the rest are discrete items, to be picked up individually. The incentive for picking them up is largely through tests and, with success at these, in credits earned.

Coverage within subjects is the key priority. If some imaginative teacher makes a proposal to force the marriage of, say, mathematics and physics or to require some culminating challenges to students to use several subjects in the solution of a complex problem, and if this proposal will take "time" away from other things, opposition is usually phrased in terms of what may be thus forgone. If we do that, we'll have to give up colonial history. We won't be able to get to programming. We'll not be able to read *Death of a Salesman.*[9] There isn't time. The protesters usually win out.

The subjects come at a student like Mark in random order, a kaleidoscope of worlds: algebraic formulae to poetry to French verbs to Ping-Pong to the War of the Spanish Succession, all before lunch. Pupils are to pick up these things. Tests measure whether the picking up has been successful.

The lack of connection between stated goals, such as those of the California high school cited earlier, and the goals inherent in school practice is obvious and, curiously, tolerated. Most striking is the gap between statements about "self-realization and mental and physical growth" or "moral and ethical values" — common rhetoric in school documents — and practice. Most physical education programs have neither the time nor the focus really to ensure fitness. Mental health is rarely defined. Neither are ethical values, save at the negative extremes, such as opposition to assault or dishonesty. Nothing in the regimen of a day like Mark's signals direct or implicit teaching in this area. The "schoolboy code" (not ratting on a fellow student) protects the marijuana pusher, and a leechlike associate is shrugged off without concern. The issue of the locker search was pushed aside, as not appropriate for class time.

Most students, like Mark, go to class in groups of twenty to twenty-seven students. The expected attendance in some schools, particularly those

[9]*Death of a Salesman:* 1957 award-winning drama by American playwright Arthur Miller.

in low-income areas, is usually higher, often thirty-five students per class, but high absentee rates push the actual numbers down. About twenty-five per class is an average figure for expected attendance, and the actual numbers are somewhat lower. There are remarkably few students who go to class in groups much larger or smaller than twenty-five.[10]

A student such as Mark sees five or six teachers per day; their differing 40
styles and expectations are part of his kaleidoscope. High school staffs are highly specialized: guidance counselors rarely teach mathematics, mathematics teachers rarely teach English, principals rarely do any classroom instruction. Mark, then, is known a little bit by a number of people, each of whom sees him in one specialized situation. No one may know him as a "whole person"—unless he becomes a special problem or has special needs.

Save in extracurricular or coaching situations, such as in athletics, drama, or shop classes, there is little opportunity for sustained conversation between student and teacher. The mode is a one-sentence or two-sentence exchange: *Mark, when was Grover Cleveland president?* Let's see, was [it] 1890 . . . or something . . . wasn't he the one . . . he was elected twice, wasn't he? . . . *Yes . . . Gloria, can you get the dates right?* Dialogue is strikingly absent, and as a result the opportunity of teachers to challenge students' ideas in a systematic and logical way is limited. Given the rushed, full quality of the school day, it can seldom happen. One must infer that careful probing of students' thinking is not a high priority. How one gains (to quote the California school's statement of goals again) "the ability to make decisions, to solve problems, to reason independently, and to accept responsibility for self-evaluation and continuing self-improvement" without being challenged is difficult to imagine. One certainly doesn't learn these things merely from lectures and textbooks.

Most schools are nice places. Mark and his friends enjoy being in theirs. The adults who work in schools generally like adolescents. The academic pressures are limited, and the accommodations to students are substantial. For example, if many members of an English class have jobs after school, the English teacher's expectations for them are adjusted, downward. In a word, school is sensitively accommodating, as long as students are punctual, where they are supposed to be, and minimally dutiful about picking things up from the clutch of courses in which they enroll.

This characterization is not pretty, but it is accurate, and it serves to describe the vast majority of American secondary schools. "Taking subjects" in a systematized, conveyor-belt way is what one does in high school. That this process is, in substantial respects, not related to the rhetorical purposes of education is tolerated by most people, perhaps because they do not really either believe in those ill-defined goals or, in their heart of hearts, believe

[10]Education Research Service, Inc. *Class Size: A Summary of Research* (Arlington, Virginia, 1978); and *Class Size Research: A Critique of Recent Meta-Analyses* (Arlington, Virginia, 1980). [Author's note]

that schools can or should even try to achieve them. The students are happy taking subjects. The parents are happy, because that's what they did in high school. The rituals, the most important of which is graduation, remain intact. The adolescents are supervised, safely and constructively most of the time, during the morning and afternoon hours, and they are off the labor market. That is what high school is all about.

Engaging the Text

1. Sizer uses metaphors describing Mark's classes as a "kaleidoscope of worlds" and comparing his school to an "academic supermarket" or a "conveyor belt" from which students "pick up" ideas. What does Sizer mean by these metaphors? What do they suggest about the problems of high school education in the United States? What metaphor best describes your own high school education?
2. What kind of student is Mark? Imagine his background and home life. Why do you think Sizer chose him to illustrate his view of high school?
3. Would you say that Sizer's depiction of American high schools is accurate? How does it compare with your high school experience?
4. Debate Sizer's claim that "for most young women, the most liberated hours of their week are in school."

Exploring Connections

5. How might Sizer explain the humor in the two cartoons by Matt Groening (rhymes with "raining") that follow this selection?
6. Read Toni Cade Bambara's "The Lesson" (p. 482), and compare Mark's day with Sylvia's. Who learns more, and why? What does each style of education offer, and what does each lack? Does your comparison suggest any practicable changes that might be made in American high schools?

Extending the Critical Context

7. Work in groups to design a high school that would make a "supermarket" or "kaleidoscope" approach to education impossible. Describe one day of a student's life in this hypothetical school.
8. Some students find or construct a coherent curriculum in college, but for others college is just a bigger "supermarket" than high school was. What can students do in either high school or college to lessen the fragmentation of intellectual experience that Sizer describes?
9. If you feel your high school served you poorly, write an educational "Bill of Wrongs" — a manifesto detailing the shortcomings of education at the high school you attended and calling for specific reforms. Send this with a cover letter to your former principal.
10. Divide Mark's day into active and passive blocks of time. Then do a similar analysis of one day from your recent education. Write a journal entry on the problems of passive education and the possible solutions for them.

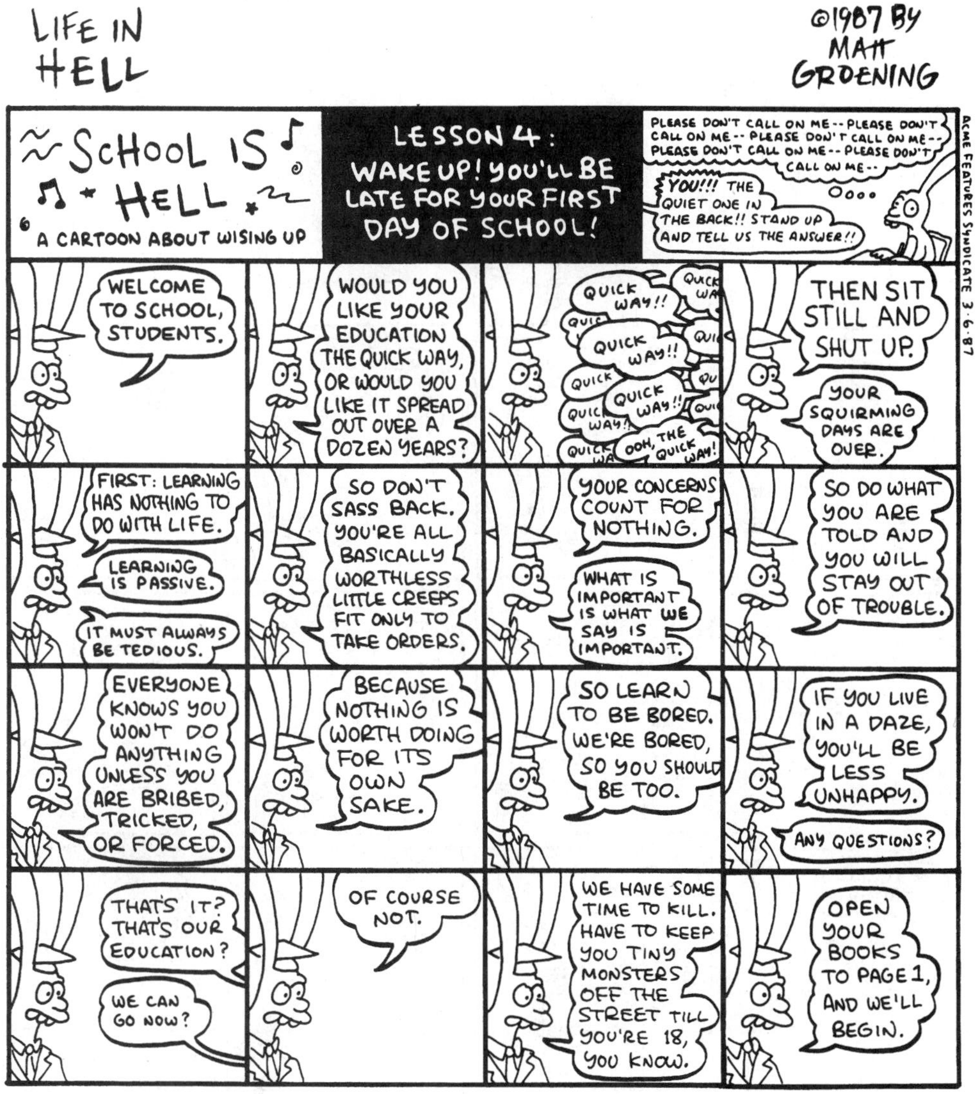

LIFE IN HELL

©1987 BY MATT GROENING

SCHOOL IS HELL

A CARTOON ABOUT WISING UP

LESSON 4: WAKE UP! YOU'LL BE LATE FOR YOUR FIRST DAY OF SCHOOL!

PLEASE DON'T CALL ON ME -- PLEASE DON'T CALL ON ME -- PLEASE DON'T CALL ON ME -- PLEASE DON'T CALL ON ME --

YOU!!! THE QUIET ONE IN THE BACK!! STAND UP AND TELL US THE ANSWER!!

OOOO

ACME FEATURES SYNDICATE 3·6·87

WELCOME TO SCHOOL, STUDENTS.

WOULD YOU LIKE YOUR EDUCATION THE QUICK WAY, OR WOULD YOU LIKE IT SPREAD OUT OVER A DOZEN YEARS?

QUICK WAY!!

QUICK WAY!!

QUICK WAY!!

OOH, THE QUICK WAY!

THEN SIT STILL AND SHUT UP.

YOUR SQUIRMING DAYS ARE OVER.

FIRST: LEARNING HAS NOTHING TO DO WITH LIFE.

LEARNING IS PASSIVE.

IT MUST ALWAYS BE TEDIOUS.

SO DON'T SASS BACK. YOU'RE ALL BASICALLY WORTHLESS LITTLE CREEPS FIT ONLY TO TAKE ORDERS.

YOUR CONCERNS COUNT FOR NOTHING.

WHAT IS IMPORTANT IS WHAT WE SAY IS IMPORTANT.

SO DO WHAT YOU ARE TOLD AND YOU WILL STAY OUT OF TROUBLE.

EVERYONE KNOWS YOU WON'T DO ANYTHING UNLESS YOU ARE BRIBED, TRICKED, OR FORCED.

BECAUSE NOTHING IS WORTH DOING FOR ITS OWN SAKE.

SO LEARN TO BE BORED. WE'RE BORED, SO YOU SHOULD BE TOO.

IF YOU LIVE IN A DAZE, YOU'LL BE LESS UNHAPPY.

ANY QUESTIONS?

THAT'S IT? THAT'S OUR EDUCATION?

WE CAN GO NOW?

OF COURSE NOT.

WE HAVE SOME TIME TO KILL. HAVE TO KEEP YOU TINY MONSTERS OFF THE STREET TILL YOU'RE 18, YOU KNOW.

OPEN YOUR BOOKS TO PAGE 1, AND WE'LL BEGIN.

LIFE IN SCHOOL
©1983 BY MATT GROENING
NOW, CLASS, WHO CAN TELL ME THE PURPOSE OF WHAT WE HAVE LEARNED TODAY?
ANYONE?
TO BE DULL LITTLE OBEDIENT SHEEP.
TO KNUCKLE UNDER TO PETTY AUTHORITY.
TO AVOID ALL FUNDAMENTAL CRITICISM OF THE POWERS THAT BE.
TO REGARD THOSE WHO ARE DIFFERENT WITH SUSPICION AND CONTEMPT.
TO GO ALONG WITH EVERY PREVAILING BELIEF.
I'M WAITING.
TO FILL OUR BRAINS WITH FACTS WITHOUT STIMULATING MENTAL ACTIVITY.
TO MAKE US GET USED TO MEANINGLESS BUSYWORK IN PREPARATION FOR OUR BORING ADULT JOBS.
TO KEEP US OFF THE STREETS TILL WE'RE EIGHTEEN.
WELL, HERE GOES.
YES--YOU THERE IN THE BACK.
TODAY WE LEARNED THE IMPORTANCE OF GOOD CITIZENSHIP, CIVIC PRIDE, AND KEEPING OUR DESKS TIDY.
THANK YOU, THAT WAS VERY GOOD.
AND TO BE DEVIOUS LITTLE WEASELS.

"I Just Wanna Be Average"

MIKE ROSE

Mike Rose (b. 1944) is anything but average: he has published poetry, scholarly research, a textbook, and a widely praised book on America's educationally underprivileged, Lives on the Boundary. *He is associate director of UCLA Writing Programs and has won awards from the National Academy of Education, the National Council of Teachers of English, and the John Simon Guggenheim Memorial Foundation. Below you'll read the story of how this highly successful teacher and writer started high school in the "vocational education" track, learning dead-end skills from teachers who were often underprepared or incompetent. Rose shows that students whom the system has written off can have tremendous unrealized potential, and his critique of the school system specifies several reasons for the "failure" of students who go through high school belligerent, fearful, stoned, frustrated, or just plain bored. This selection comes from* Lives on the Boundary *(1989). Rose is currently working on a new book that explores the possibilities and hopes for public education.*

It took two buses to get to Our Lady of Mercy. The first started deep in South Los Angeles and caught me at midpoint. The second drifted through neighborhoods with trees, parks, big lawns, and lots of flowers. The rides were long but were livened up by a group of South L.A. veterans whose parents also thought that Hope had set up shop in the west end of the county. There was Christy Biggars, who, at sixteen, was dealing and was, according to rumor, a pimp as well. There were Bill Cobb and Johnny Gonzales, grease-pencil artists extraordinaire, who left Nembutal-enhanced[1] swirls of "Cobb" and "Johnny" on the corrugated walls of the bus. And then there was Tyrrell Wilson. Tyrrell was the coolest kid I knew. He ran the dozens[2] like a metric halfback, laid down a rap that outrhymed and outpointed Cobb, whose rap was good but not great—the curse of a moderately soulful kid trapped in white skin. But it was Cobb who would sneak a radio onto the bus, and thus underwrote his patter with Little Richard, Fats Domino, Chuck Berry, the Coasters,[3] and Ernie K. Doe's mother-in-law, an awful woman who was "sent from down below." And so it was that Christy and

[1]*Nembutal:* Trade name for pentobarbital, a sedative drug.

[2]*the dozens:* A verbal game of African origin in which competitors try to top each other's insults.

[3]*Little Richard, Fats Domino, Chuck Berry, the Coasters:* Popular Black musicians of the 1950s.

Cobb and Johnny G. and Tyrrell and I and assorted others picked up along the way passed our days in the back of the bus, a funny mix brought together by geography and parental desire.

Entrance to school brings with it forms and releases and assessments. Mercy relied on a series of tests, mostly the Stanford-Binet,[4] for placement, and somehow the results of my tests got confused with those of another student named Rose. The other Rose apparently didn't do very well, for I was placed in the vocational track, a euphemism for the bottom level. Neither I nor my parents realized what this meant. We had no sense that Business Math, Typing, and English–Level D were dead ends. The current spate of reports on the schools criticizes parents for not involving themselves in the education of their children. But how would someone like Tommy Rose, with his two years of Italian schooling, know what to ask? And what sort of pressure could an exhausted waitress apply? The error went undetected, and I remained in the vocational track for two years. What a place.

My homeroom was supervised by Brother Dill, a troubled and unstable man who also taught freshman English. When his class drifted away from him, which was often, his voice would rise in paranoid accusations, and occasionally he would lose control and shake or smack us. I hadn't been there two months when one of his brisk, face-turning slaps had my glasses sliding down the aisle. Physical education was also pretty harsh. Our teacher was a stubby ex-lineman who had played old-time pro ball in the Midwest. He routinely had us grabbing our ankles to receive his stinging paddle across our butts. He did that, he said, to make men of us. "Rose," he bellowed on our first encounter; me standing geeky in line in my baggy shorts. " 'Rose'? What the hell kind of name is that?"

"Italian, sir," I squeaked.

"Italian! Ho. Rose, do you know the sound a bag of shit makes when it 5
hits the wall?"

"No, sir."

"Wop!"[5]

Sophomore English was taught by Mr. Mitropetros. He was a large, bejeweled man who managed the parking lot at the Shrine Auditorium. He would crow and preen and list for us the stars he'd brushed against. We'd ask questions and glance knowingly and snicker, and all that fueled the poor guy to brag some more. Parking cars was his night job. He had little training in English, so his lesson plan for his day work had us reading the district's required text, *Julius Caesar,* aloud for the semester. We'd finish the play way before the twenty weeks was up, so he'd have us switch parts again and again and start again: Dave Snyder, the fastest guy at Mercy, muscling through Caesar to the breathless squeals of Calpurnia, as interpreted by Steve Fusco, a surfer who owned the school's most envied paneled wagon.

[4] *Stanford-Binet:* An IQ test.

[5] *Wop:* Derogatory term for Italian.

Week ten and Dave and Steve would take on new roles, as would we all, and render a water-logged Cassius and a Brutus that are beyond my powers of description.

Spanish I — taken in the second year — fell into the hands of a new recruit. Mr. Montez was a tiny man, slight, five foot six at the most, soft-spoken and delicate. Spanish was a particularly rowdy class, and Mr. Montez was as prepared for it as a doily maker at a hammer throw. He would tap his pencil to a room in which Steve Fusco was propelling spitballs from his heavy lips, in which Mike Dweetz was taunting Billy Hawk, a half-Indian, half-Spanish, reed-thin, quietly explosive boy. The vocational track at Our Lady of Mercy mixed kids traveling in from South L.A. with South Bay surfers and a few Slavs and Chicanos from the harbors of San Pedro. This was a dangerous miscellany: surfers and hodads[6] and South-Central blacks all ablaze to the metronomic tapping of Hector Montez's pencil.

10 One day Billy lost it. Out of the corner of my eye I saw him strike out with his right arm and catch Dweetz across the neck. Quick as a spasm, Dweetz was out of his seat, scattering desks, cracking Billy on the side of the head, right behind the eye. Snyder and Fusco and others broke it up, but the room felt hot and close and naked. Mr. Montez's tenuous authority was finally ripped to shreds, and I think everyone felt a little strange about that. The charade was over, and when it came down to it, I don't think any of the kids really wanted it to end this way. They had pushed and pushed and bullied their way into a freedom that both scared and embarrassed them.

Students will float to the mark you set. I and the others in the vocational classes were bobbing in pretty shallow water. Vocational education has aimed at increasing the economic opportunities of students who do not do well in our schools. Some serious programs succeed in doing that, and through exceptional teachers — like Mr. Gross in *Horace's Compromise*[7] — students learn to develop hypotheses and troubleshoot, reason through a problem, and communicate effectively — the true job skills. The vocational track, however, is most often a place for those who are just not making it, a dumping ground for the disaffected. There were a few teachers who worked hard at education; young Brother Slattery, for example, combined a stern voice with weekly quizzes to try to pass along to us a skeletal outline of world history. But mostly the teachers had no idea of how to engage the imaginations of us kids who were scuttling along at the bottom of the pond.

And the teachers would have needed some inventiveness, for none of us was groomed for the classroom. It wasn't just that I didn't know things — didn't know how to simplify algebraic fractions, couldn't identify different kinds of clauses, bungled Spanish translations — but that I had developed various faulty and inadequate ways of doing algebra and making sense of Spanish. Worse yet, the years of defensive tuning out in elementary

[6]*hodads:* Nonsurfers.

[7]*Horace's Compromise:* A book on American education by Theodore Sizer. See p. 20.

school had given me a way to escape quickly while seeming at least half alert. During my time in Voc. Ed., I developed further into a mediocre student and a somnambulant problem solver, and that affected the subjects I did have the wherewithal to handle: I detested Shakespeare; I got bored with history. My attention flitted here and there. I fooled around in class and read my books indifferently — the intellectual equivalent of playing with your food. I did what I had to do to get by, and I did it with half a mind.

But I did learn things about people and eventually came into my own socially. I liked the guys in Voc. Ed. Growing up where I did, I understood and admired physical prowess, and there was an abundance of muscle here. There was Dave Snyder, a sprinter and halfback of true quality. Dave's ability and his quick wit gave him a natural appeal, and he was welcome in any clique, though he always kept a little independent. He enjoyed acting the fool and could care less about studies, but he possessed a certain maturity and never caused the faculty much trouble. It was a testament to his independence that he included me among his friends — I eventually went out for track, but I was no jock. Owing to the Latin alphabet and a dearth of *R*s and *S*s, Snyder sat behind Rose, and we started exchanging one-liners and became friends.

There was Ted Richard, a much-touted Little League pitcher. He was chunky and had a baby face and came to Our Lady of Mercy as a seasoned street fighter. Ted was quick to laugh and he had a loud, jolly laugh, but when he got angry he'd smile a little smile, the kind that simply raises the corner of the mouth a quarter of an inch. For those who knew, it was an eerie signal. Those who didn't found themselves in big trouble, for Ted was very quick. He loved to carry on what we would come to call philosophical discussions: What is courage? Does God exist? He also loved words, enjoyed picking up big ones like *salubrious* and *equivocal* and using them in our conversations — laughing at himself as the word hit a chuckhole rolling off his tongue. Ted didn't do all that well in school — baseball and parties and testing the courage he'd speculated about took up his time. His textbooks were *Argosy* and *Field and Stream,* whatever newspapers he'd find on the bus stop — from the *Daily Worker* to pornography — conversations with uncles or hobos or businessmen he'd meet in a coffee shop, *The Old Man and the Sea.* With hindsight, I can see that Ted was developing into one of those rough-hewn intellectuals whose sources are a mix of the learned and the apocryphal, whose discussions are both assured and sad.

15 And then there was Ken Harvey. Ken was good-looking in a puffy way and had a full and oily ducktail and was a car enthusiast . . . a hodad. One day in religion class, he said the sentence that turned out to be one of the most memorable of the hundreds of thousands I heard in those Voc. Ed. years. We were talking about the parable of the talents, about achievement, working hard, doing the best you can do, blah-blah-blah, when the teacher called on the restive Ken Harvey for an opinion. Ken thought about it, but just for a second, and said (with studied, minimal affect), "I just wanna be

average." That woke me up. Average? Who wants to be average? Then the athletes chimed in with the clichés that make you want to laryngectomize them, and the exchange became a platitudinous melee. At the time, I thought Ken's assertion was stupid, and I wrote him off. But his sentence has stayed with me all these years, and I think I am finally coming to understand it.

Ken Harvey was gasping for air. School can be a tremendously disorienting place. No matter how bad the school, you're going to encounter notions that don't fit with the assumptions and beliefs that you grew up with — maybe you'll hear these dissonant notions from teachers, maybe from the other students, and maybe you'll read them. You'll also be thrown in with all kinds of kids from all kinds of backgrounds, and that can be unsettling — this is especially true in places of rich ethnic and linguistic mix, like the L.A. basin. You'll see a handful of students far excel you in courses that sound exotic and that are only in the curriculum of the elite: French, physics, trigonometry. And all this is happening while you're trying to shape an identity, your body is changing, and your emotions are running wild. If you're a working-class kid in the vocational track, the options you'll have to deal with this will be constrained in certain ways: you're defined by your school as "slow"; you're placed in a curriculum that isn't designed to liberate you but to occupy you, or, if you're lucky, train you, though the training is for work the society does not esteem; other students are picking up the cues from your school and your curriculum and interacting with you in particular ways. If you're a kid like Ted Richard, you turn your back on all this and let your mind roam where it may. But youngsters like Ted are rare. What Ken and so many others do is protect themselves from such suffocating madness by taking on with a vengeance the identity implied in the vocational track. Reject the confusion and frustration by openly defining yourself as the Common Joe. Champion the average. Rely on your own good sense. Fuck this bullshit. Bullshit, of course, is everything you — and the others — fear is beyond you: books, essays, tests, academic scrambling, complexity, scientific reasoning, philosophical inquiry.

The tragedy is that you have to twist the knife in your own gray matter to make this defense work. You'll have to shut down, have to reject intellectual stimuli or diffuse them with sarcasm, have to cultivate stupidity, have to convert boredom from a malady into a way of confronting the world. Keep your vocabulary simple, act stoned when you're not or act more stoned than you are, flaunt ignorance, materialize your dreams. It is a powerful and effective defense — it neutralizes the insult and the frustration of being a vocational kid and, when perfected, it drives teachers up the wall, a delightful secondary effect. But like all strong magic, it exacts a price.

My own deliverance from the Voc. Ed. world began with sophomore biology. Every student, college prep to vocational, had to take biology, and unlike the other courses, the same person taught all sections. When teaching the vocational group, Brother Clint probably slowed down a bit or omitted a little of the fundamental biochemistry, but he used the same book and more or less the same syllabus across the board. If one class got tough, he could get tougher. He was young and powerful and very handsome, and looks and physical strength were high currency. No one gave him any trouble.

I was pretty bad at the dissecting table, but the lectures and the textbook were interesting: plastic overlays that, with each turned page, peeled away skin, then veins and muscle, then organs, down to the very bones that Brother Clint, pointer in hand, would tap out on our hanging skeleton. Dave Snyder was in big trouble, for the study of life — versus the living of it — was sticking in his craw. We worked out a code for our multiple-choice exams. He'd poke me in the back: once for the answer under *A*, twice for *B*, and so on; and when he'd hit the right one, I'd look up to the ceiling as though I were lost in thought. Poke: cytoplasm. Poke, poke: methane. Poke, poke, poke: William Harvey. Poke, poke, poke, poke: islets of Langerhans. This didn't work out perfectly, but Dave passed the course, and I mastered the dreamy look of a guy on a record jacket. And something else happened. Brother Clint puzzled over this Voc. Ed. kid who was racking up 98s and 99s on his tests. He checked the school's records and discovered the error. He recommended that I begin my junior year in the College Prep program. According to all I've read since, such a shift, as one report put it, is virtually impossible. Kids at that level rarely cross tracks. The telling thing is how chancy both my placement into and exit from Voc. Ed. was; neither I nor my parents had anything to do with it. I lived in one world during spring semester, and when I came back to school in the fall, I was living in another.

Switching to College Prep was a mixed blessing. I was an erratic student. 20
I was undisciplined. And I hadn't caught onto the rules of the game: why work hard in a class that didn't grab my fancy? I was also hopelessly behind in math. Chemistry was hard; toying with my chemistry set years before hadn't prepared me for the chemist's equations. Fortunately, the priest who taught both chemistry and second-year algebra was also the school's athletic director. Membership on the track team covered me; I knew I wouldn't get lower than a C. U.S. history was taught pretty well, and I did okay. But civics was taken over by a football coach who had trouble reading the textbook aloud — and reading aloud was the centerpiece of his pedagogy. College Prep at Mercy was certainly an improvement over the vocational program — at least it carried some status — but the social science curriculum was weak, and the mathematics and physical sciences were simply beyond me. I had a miserable quantitative background and ended up copying some assignments and finessing the rest as best I could. Let me try to explain how it feels to see again and again material you should once have learned but didn't.

You are given a problem. It requires you to simplify algebraic fractions or to multiply expressions containing square roots. You know this is pretty basic material because you've seen it for years. Once a teacher took some time with you, and you learned how to carry out these operations. Simple versions, anyway. But that was a year or two or more in the past, and these are more complex versions, and now you're not sure. And this, you keep telling yourself, is ninth- or even eighth-grade stuff.

Next it's a word problem. This is also old hat. The basic elements are as familiar as story characters: trains speeding so many miles per hour or shadows of buildings angling so many degrees. Maybe you know enough, have sat through enough explanations, to be able to begin setting up the problem: "If one train is going this fast . . ." or "This shadow is really one line of a triangle . . ." Then: "Let's see . . ." "How did Jones do this?" "Hmmmm." "No." "No, that won't work." Your attention wavers. You wonder about other things: a football game, a dance, that cute new checker at the market. You try to focus on the problem again. You scribble on paper for a while, but the tension wins out and your attention flits elsewhere. You crumple the paper and begin daydreaming to ease the frustration.

The particulars will vary, but in essence this is what a number of students go through, especially those in so-called remedial classes. They open their textbooks and see once again the familiar and impenetrable formulas and diagrams and terms that have stumped them for years. There is no excitement here. *No* excitement. Regardless of what the teacher says, this is not a new challenge. There is, rather, embarrassment and frustration and, not surprisingly, some anger in being reminded once again of long-standing inadequacies. No wonder so many students finally attribute their difficulties to something inborn, organic: "That part of my brain just doesn't work." Given the troubling histories many of these students have, it's miraculous that any of them can lift the shroud of hopelessness sufficiently to make deliverance from these classes possible.

Through this entire period, my father's health was deteriorating with cruel momentum. His arteriosclerosis progressed to the point where a simple nick on his shin wouldn't heal. Eventually it ulcerated and widened. Lou Minton would come by daily to change the dressing. We tried renting an oscillating bed — which we placed in the front room — to force blood through the constricted arteries in my father's legs. The bed hummed through the night, moving in place to ward off the inevitable. The ulcer continued to spread, and the doctors finally had to amputate. My grandfather had lost his leg in a stockyard accident. Now my father too was crippled. His convalescence was slow but steady, and the doctors placed him in the Santa Monica Rehabilitation Center, a sun-bleached building that opened out onto the warm spray of the Pacific. The place gave him some strength and some color and some training in walking with an artificial leg. He did pretty well for a year or so until he slipped and broke his hip. He was confined to a wheelchair after that, and the confinement contributed to the diminishing of his body and spirit.

I am holding a picture of him. He is sitting in his wheelchair and smiling 25
at the camera. The smile appears forced, unsteady, seems to quaver, though

it is frozen in silver nitrate. He is in his mid-sixties and looks eighty. Late in my junior year, he had a stroke and never came out of the resulting coma. After that, I would see him only in dreams, and to this day that is how I join him. Sometimes the dreams are sad and grisly and primal: my father lying in a bed soaked with his suppuration,[8] holding me, rocking me. But sometimes the dreams bring him back to me healthy: him talking to me on an empty street, or buying some pictures to decorate our old house, or transformed somehow into someone strong and adept with tools and the physical.

Jack MacFarland couldn't have come into my life at a better time. My father was dead, and I had logged up too many years of scholastic indifference. Mr. MacFarland had a master's degree from Columbia and decided, at twenty-six, to find a little school and teach his heart out. He never took any credentialing courses, couldn't bear to, he said, so he had to find employment in a private system. He ended up at Our Lady of Mercy teaching five sections of senior English. He was a beatnik who was born too late. His teeth were stained, he tucked his sorry tie in between the third and fourth buttons of his shirt, and his pants were chronically wrinkled. At first, we couldn't believe this guy, thought he slept in his car. But within no time, he had us so startled with work that we didn't much worry about where he slept or if he slept at all. We wrote three or four essays a month. We read a book every two to three weeks, starting with the *Iliad* and ending up with Hemingway. He gave us a quiz on the reading every other day. He brought a prep school curriculum to Mercy High.

MacFarland's lectures were crafted, and as he delivered them he would pace the room jiggling a piece of chalk in his cupped hand, using it to scribble on the board the names of all the writers and philosophers and plays and novels he was weaving into his discussion. He asked questions often, raised everything from Zeno's paradox to the repeated last line of Frost's "Stopping by Woods on a Snowy Evening." He slowly and carefully built up our knowledge of Western intellectual history — with facts, with connections, with speculations. We learned about Greek philosophy, about Dante, the Elizabethan world view, the Age of Reason, existentialism. He analyzed poems with us, had us reading sections from John Ciardi's *How Does a Poem Mean?*, making a potentially difficult book accessible with his own explanations. We gave oral reports on poems Ciardi didn't cover. We imitated the styles of Conrad, Hemingway, and *Time* magazine. We wrote and talked, wrote and talked. The man immersed us in language.

Even MacFarland's barbs were literary. If Jim Fitzsimmons, hung over and irritable, tried to smart-ass him, he'd rejoin with a flourish that would spark the indomitable Skip Madison—who'd lost his front teeth in a hapless tackle—to flick his tongue through the gap and opine, "good chop," drawing out the single "o" in stinging indictment. Jack MacFarland, this tobacco-

[8]*suppuration:* Discharge from wounds.

stained intellectual, brandished linguistic weapons of a kind I hadn't encountered before. Here was this *egghead,* for God's sake, keeping some pretty difficult people in line. And from what I heard, Mike Dweetz and Steve Fusco and all the notorious Voc. Ed. crowd settled down as well when MacFarland took the podium. Though a lot of guys groused in the schoolyard, it just seemed that giving trouble to this particular teacher was a silly thing to do. Tomfoolery, not to mention assault, had no place in the world he was trying to create for us, and instinctively everyone knew that. If nothing else, we all recognized MacFarland's considerable intelligence and respected the hours he put into his work. It came to this: the troublemaker would look foolish rather than daring. Even Jim Fitzsimmons was reading *On the Road* and turning his incipient alcoholism to literary ends.

There were some lives that were already beyond Jack MacFarland's ministrations, but mine was not. I started reading again as I hadn't since elementary school. I would go into our gloomy little bedroom or sit at the dinner table while, on the television, Danny McShane was paralyzing Mr. Moto with the atomic drop, and work slowly back through *Heart of Darkness,* trying to catch the words in Conrad's sentences. I certainly was not MacFarland's best student; most of the other guys in College Prep, even my fellow slackers, had better backgrounds than I did. But I worked very hard, for MacFarland had hooked me. He tapped my old interest in reading and creating stories. He gave me a way to feel special by using my mind. And he provided a role model that wasn't shaped on physical prowess alone, and something inside me that I wasn't quite aware of responded to that. Jack MacFarland established a literacy club, to borrow a phrase of Frank Smith's, and invited me — invited all of us — to join.

30 There's been a good deal of research and speculation suggesting that the acknowledgement of school performance with extrinsic rewards — smiling faces, stars, numbers, grades — diminishes the intrinsic satisfaction children experience by engaging in reading or writing or problem solving. While it's certainly true that we've created an educational system that encourages our best and brightest to become cynical grade collectors and, in general, have developed an obsession with evaluation and assessment, I must tell you that venal though it may have been, I loved getting good grades from MacFarland. I now know how subjective grades can be, but then they came tucked in the back of essays like bits of scientific data, some sort of spectroscopic readout that said, objectively and publicly, that I had made something of value. I suppose I'd been mediocre for too long and enjoyed a public redefinition. And I suppose the workings of my mind, such as they were, had been private for too long. My linguistic play moved into the world; . . . these papers with their circled, red B-pluses and A-minuses linked my mind to something outside it. I carried them around like a club emblem.

One day in the December of my senior year, Mr. MacFarland asked me where I was going to go to college. I hadn't thought much about it. Many of the students I teach today spent their last year in high school with a physics text in one hand and the Stanford catalog in the other, but I wasn't even aware of what "entrance requirements" were. My folks would say that they wanted me to go to college and be a doctor, but I don't know how seriously I ever took that; it seemed a sweet thing to say, a bit of supportive family chatter, like telling a gangly daughter she's graceful. The reality of higher education wasn't in my scheme of things: no one in the family had gone to college; only two of my uncles had completed high school. I figured I'd get a night job and go to the local junior college because I knew that Snyder and Company were going there to play ball. But I hadn't even prepared for that. When I finally said, "I don't know," MacFarland looked down at me — I was seated in his office — and said, "Listen, you can write."

My grades stank. I had A's in biology and a handful of B's in a few English and social science classes. All the rest were C's — or worse. MacFarland said I would do well in his class and laid down the law about doing well in the others. Still, the record for my first three years wouldn't have been acceptable to any four-year school. To nobody's surprise, I was turned down flat by USC and UCLA. But Jack MacFarland was on the case. He had received his bachelor's degree from Loyola University, so he made calls to old professors and talked to somebody in admissions and wrote me a strong letter. Loyola finally accepted me as a probationary student. I would be on trial for the first year, and if I did okay, I would be granted regular status. MacFarland also intervened to get me a loan, for I could never have afforded a private college without it. Four more years of religion classes and four more years of boys at one school, girls at another. But at least I was going to college. Amazing.

In my last semester of high school, I elected a special English course fashioned by Mr. MacFarland, and it was through this elective that there arose at Mercy a fledgling literati. Art Mitz, the editor of the school newspaper and a very smart guy, was the kingpin. He was joined by me and by Mark Dever, a quiet boy who wrote beautifully and who would die before he was forty. MacFarland occasionally invited us to his apartment, and those visits became the high point of our apprenticeship: we'd clamp on our training wheels and drive to his salon.

He lived in a cramped and cluttered place near the airport, tucked away in the kind of building that architectural critic Reyner Banham calls a *dingbat.* Books were all over: stacked, piled, tossed, and crated, underlined and dog eared, well worn and new. Cigarette ashes crusted with coffee in saucers or spilling over the sides of motel ashtrays. The little bedroom had, along two of its walls, bricks and boards loaded with notes, magazines, and oversized books. The kitchen joined the living room, and there was a stack of German newspapers under the sink. I had never seen anything like it: a great flophouse of language furnished by City Lights and Café le Metro. I read every title. I flipped through paperbacks and scanned jackets and memorized names: Gogol, *Finnegans Wake,* Djuna Barnes, Jackson Pollock, *A Coney Island of the Mind,* F. O. Matthiessen's *American Renaissance,* all sorts of Freud, *Troubled Sleep,* Man Ray, *The Education of Henry Adams,* Richard Wright, *Film as Art,* William Butler Yeats, Marguerite Duras, *Redburn, A Season in Hell, Kapital.* On the cover of Alain-Fournier's *The Wanderer* was an Edward Gorey drawing of a young man on a road winding into dark trees. By the hotplate sat a strange Kafka novel called *Amerika,* in which an adolescent hero crosses the Atlantic to find the Nature Theater of Oklahoma. Art and Mark would be talking about a movie or the school newspaper, and I would be consuming my English teacher's library. It was heady stuff. I felt like a Pop Warner[9] athlete on steroids.

35 Art, Mark, and I would buy stogies and triangulate from MacFarland's apartment to the Cinema, which now shows X-rated films but was then L.A.'s premier art theater, and then to the musty Cherokee Bookstore in Hollywood to hobnob with beatnik homosexuals — smoking, drinking bourbon and coffee, and trying out awkward phrases we'd gleaned from our mentor's bookshelves. I was happy and precocious and a little scared as well, for Hollywood Boulevard was thick with a kind of decadence that was foreign to the South Side. After the Cherokee, we would head back to the security of MacFarland's apartment, slaphappy with hipness.

Let me be the first to admit that there was a good deal of adolescent passion in this embrace of the avant-garde: self-absorption, sexually charged pedantry, an elevation of the odd and abandoned. Still it was a time during which I absorbed an awful lot of information: long lists of titles, images from expressionist paintings, new wave shibboleths,[10] snippets of philosophy, and names that read like Steve Fusco's misspellings — Goethe, Nietzsche, Kierkegaard. Now this is hardly the stuff of deep understanding. But it was an introduction, a phrase book, a Baedeker[11] to a vocabulary of ideas, and it felt good at the time to know all these words. With hindsight I realize how layered and important that knowledge was.

It enabled me to do things in the world. I could browse bohemian bookstores in far-off, mysterious Hollywood; I could go to the Cinema and see events through the lenses of European directors; and, most of all, I could share an evening, talk that talk, with Jack MacFarland, the man I most admired at the time. Knowledge was becoming a bonding agent. Within a year or two, the persona of the disaffected hipster would prove too cynical, too alienated to last. But for a time it was new and exciting: it provided a critical perspective on society, and it allowed me to act as though I were living beyond the limiting boundaries of South Vermont.[12]

[9]*Pop Warner:* A nationwide youth athletics organization.
[10]*new wave shibboleths:* Trendy phrases or jargon.
[11]*Baedeker:* Travel guide.
[12]*South Vermont:* A street in an economically depressed area of Los Angeles.

Engaging the Text

1. Describe Rose's life in Voc. Ed. What were his teachers like? Have you ever had experience with teachers like these?
2. What did Voc. Ed. do to Rose and his fellow students? How did it affect them intellectually, emotionally, and socially? Why was it subsequently so hard for Rose to catch up in math?
3. Why is high school so disorienting to students like Ken Harvey? How does he cope with it? What other strategies do students use to cope with the pressures and judgments they encounter in school?
4. What does Jack MacFarland offer Rose that finally helps him learn? Do you think it was inevitable that someone with Rose's intelligence would eventually succeed?

Exploring Connections

5. How does Rose's perception of educational ills differ from Theodore Sizer's in "What High School Is" (p. 20)? Explain how their arguments support or contradict each other. Whose ideas do you find more persuasive or important?
6. Draw a Groening-style cartoon (see pp. 31–32) or comic strip of Rose in the vocational track, or of Rose before and after his liberation from Voc. Ed.
7. Read Gregory Mantsios's "Rewards and Opportunities: The Politics and Economics of Class in the U.S." (p. 465) and write an imaginary dialogue between Rose and Mantsios about why some students, like Rose, seem to be able to break through social class barriers and others, like Dave Snyder, Ted Richard, and Ken Harvey, do not.

Extending the Critical Context

8. Rose explains that high school can be a "tremendously disorienting place" (para. 16). What, if anything, do you find disorienting about college? What steps can students at your school take to lessen feelings of disorientation? What could the college do to help them?
9. Review one or more of Rose's descriptions of his high school classmates; then write a description of one of your own high school classmates, trying to capture in a nutshell how that person coped or failed to cope with the educational system.
10. Watch *Stand and Deliver* or *Dead Poets Society* on videotape and compare the movie's depiction of the teacher to Rose's portrayal of Jack MacFarland. What do such charismatic teachers offer their students personally and intellectually? Do you see any disadvantages to classes taught by teachers like these?

From *Social Class and the Hidden Curriculum of Work*

Jean Anyon

It's no surprise that schools in wealthy communities are better than those in poor communities, or that they better prepare their students for desirable jobs. It may be shocking, however, to learn how vast the differences in schools are — not so much in resources as in teaching methods and philosophies of education. Jean Anyon observed five elementary schools over the course of a full school year and concluded that fifth-graders of different economic backgrounds are already being prepared to occupy particular rungs on the social ladder. In a sense, some whole schools are on the vocational education track, while others are geared to produce future doctors, lawyers, and business leaders. Anyon's main audience is professional educators, so you may find her style and vocabulary challenging, but, once you've read her descriptions of specific classroom activities, the more analytic parts of the essay should prove easier to understand. Anyon is chairperson of the Department of Education at Rutgers University, Newark; this essay first appeared in Journal of Education *in 1980.*

Scholars in political economy and the sociology of knowledge have recently argued that public schools in complex industrial societies like our own make available different types of educational experience and curriculum knowledge to students in different social classes. Bowles and Gintis[1] for example, have argued that students in different social-class backgrounds are rewarded for classroom behaviors that correspond to personality traits allegedly rewarded in the different occupational strata — the working classes for docility and obedience, the managerial classes for initiative and personal assertiveness. Basil Bernstein, Pierre Bourdieu, and Michael W. Apple,[2] focusing on school knowledge, have argued that knowledge and skills leading to social power and regard (medical, legal, managerial) are made available to the advantaged social groups but are withheld from the working classes, to whom a more "practical" curriculum is offered (manual skills, clerical

[1] S. Bowles and H. Gintis, *Schooling in Capitalist America: Educational Reform and the Contradictions of Economic Life* (New York: Basic Books, 1976). [Author's note]

[2] B. Bernstein, *Class, Codes and Control, Vol. 3. Towards a Theory of Educational Transmission,* 2d ed. (London: Routledge & Kegan Paul, 1977); P. Bourdieu and J. Passeron, *Reproduction in Education, Society and Culture* (Beverly Hills, Calif.: Sage, 1977); M. W. Apple, *Ideology and Curriculum* (Boston: Routledge & Kegan Paul, 1979). [Author's note]

knowledge). While there has been considerable argumentation of these points regarding education in England, France, and North America, there has been little or no attempt to investigate these ideas empirically in elementary or secondary schools and classrooms in this country.[3]

This article offers tentative empirical support (and qualification) of the above arguments by providing illustrative examples of differences in student *work* in classrooms in contrasting social class communities. The examples were gathered as part of an ethnographical[4] study of curricular, pedagogical, and pupil evaluation practices in five elementary schools. The article attempts a theoretical contribution as well and assesses student work in the light of a theoretical approach to social-class analysis. . . . It will be suggested that there is a "hidden curriculum" in schoolwork that has profound implications for the theory — and consequence — of everyday activity in education. . . .

The Sample of Schools

. . . The social-class designation of each of the five schools will be identified, and the income, occupation, and other relevant available social characteristics of the students and their parents will be described. The first three schools are in a medium-sized city district in northern New Jersey, and the other two are in a nearby New Jersey suburb.

The first two schools I will call *working-class schools*. Most of the parents have blue-collar jobs. Less than a third of the fathers are skilled, while the majority are in unskilled or semiskilled jobs. During the period of the study (1978–1979), approximately 15 percent of the fathers were unemployed. The large majority (85 percent) of the families are white. The following occupations are typical: platform, storeroom, and stockroom workers; foundrymen, pipe welders, and boilermakers; semiskilled and unskilled assembly-line operatives; gas station attendants, auto mechanics, maintenance workers, and security guards. Less than 30 percent of the women work, some part-time and some full-time, on assembly lines, in storerooms and stockrooms, as waitresses, barmaids, or sales clerks. Of the fifth-grade parents, none of the wives of the skilled workers had jobs. Approximately 15 percent of the families in each school are at or below the federal "poverty" level;[5] most of the rest of the family incomes are at or below $12,000, except some

[3]But see, in a related vein, M. W. Apple and N. King, "What Do Schools Teach?" *Curriculum Inquiry* 6 (1977): 341–58; R. C. Rist, *The Urban School: A Factory for Failure* (Cambridge, Mass.: MIT Press, 1973). [Author's note]

[4]*ethnographical:* Based on an anthropological study of cultures or subcultures — the "cultures" in this case being the five schools observed.

[5]The U.S. Bureau of the Census defines *poverty* for a nonfarm family of four as a yearly income of $6,191 a year or less. U.S. Bureau of the Census, *Statistical Abstract of the United States: 1978* (Washington, D.C.: U.S. Government Printing Office, 1978), p. 465, table 754. [Author's note]

of the skilled workers whose incomes are higher. The incomes of the majority of the families in these two schools (at or below $12,000) are typical of 38.6 percent of the families in the United States.[6]

The third school is called the *middle-class school,* although because of 5
neighborhood residence patterns, the population is a mixture of several social classes. The parents' occupations can be divided into three groups: a small group of blue-collar "rich," who are skilled, well-paid workers such as printers, carpenters, plumbers, and construction workers. The second group is composed of parents in working-class and middle-class white-collar jobs: women in office jobs, technicians, supervisors in industry, and parents employed by the city (such as firemen, policemen, and several of the school's teachers). The third group is composed of occupations such as personnel directors in local firms, accountants, "middle management," and a few small capitalists (owners of shops in the area). The children of several local doctors attend this school. Most family incomes are between $13,000 and $25,000, with a few higher. This income range is typical of 38.9 percent of the families in the United States.[7]

The fourth school has a parent population that is at the upper income level of the upper middle class and is predominantly professional. This school will be called the *affluent professional school.* Typical jobs are: cardiologist, interior designer, corporate lawyer or engineer, executive in advertising or television. There are some families who are not as affluent as the majority (the family of the superintendent of the district's schools, and the one or two families in which the fathers are skilled workers). In addition, a few of the families are more affluent than the majority and can be classified in the capitalist class (a partner in a prestigious Wall Street stock brokerage firm). Approximately 90 percent of the children in this school are white. Most family incomes are between $40,000 and $80,000. This income span represents approximately 7 percent of the families in the United States.[8]

In the fifth school the majority of the families belong to the capitalist class. This school will be called the *executive elite school* because most of the fathers are top executives (for example, presidents and vice-presidents) in major United States–based multinational corporations — for example, AT&T, RCA, Citibank, American Express, U.S. Steel. A sizable group of fathers are top executives in financial firms in Wall Street. There are also a number of fathers who list their occupations as "general counsel" to a par-

[6]U.S. Bureau of the Census, "Money Income in 1977 of Families and Persons in the United States," *Current Population Reports* Series P-60, no. 118 (Washington, D.C.: U.S. Government Printing Office, 1979), p. 2, table A. [Author's note]

[7]Ibid. [Author's note]

[8]This figure is an estimate. According to the Bureau of the Census, only 2.6 percent of families in the United States have money income of $50,000 or over. U.S. Bureau of the Census, *Current Population Reports* Series P-60. For figures on income at these higher levels, see J. D. Smith and S. Franklin, "The Concentration of Personal Wealth, 1922–1969," *American Economic Review* 64 (1974): 162–67. [Author's note]

ticular corporation, and these corporations are also among the large multinationals. Many of the mothers do volunteer work in the Junior League, Junior Fortnightly, or other service groups; some are intricately involved in town politics; and some are themselves in well-paid occupations. There are no minority children in the school. Almost all the family incomes are over $100,000, with some in the $500,000 range. The incomes in this school represent less than 1 percent of the families in the United States.[9]

Since each of the five schools is only one instance of elementary education in a particular social class context, I will not generalize beyond the sample. However, the examples of schoolwork which follow will suggest characteristics of education in each social setting that appear to have theoretical and social significance and to be worth investigation in a larger number of schools. . . .

The Working-Class Schools

In the two working-class schools, work is following the steps of a procedure. The procedure is usually mechanical, involving rote behavior and very little decision making or choice. The teachers rarely explain why the work is being assigned, how it might connect to other assignments, or what the idea is that lies behind the procedure or gives it coherence and perhaps meaning or significance. Available textbooks are not always used, and the teachers often prepare their own dittos or put work examples on the board. Most of the rules regarding work are designations of what the children are to do; the rules are steps to follow. These steps are told to the children by the teachers and are often written on the board. The children are usually told to copy the steps as notes. These notes are to be studied. Work is often evaluated not according to whether it is right or wrong but according to whether the children followed the right steps.

The following examples illustrate these points. In math, when two-digit 10
division was introduced, the teacher in one school gave a four-minute lecture on what the terms are called (which number is the divisor, dividend, quotient, and remainder). The children were told to copy these names in their notebooks. Then the teacher told them the steps to follow to do the problems, saying, "This is how you do them." The teacher listed the steps on the board, and they appeared several days later as a chart hung in the middle of the front wall: "Divide, Multiply, Subtract, Bring Down." The children often did examples of two-digit division. When the teacher went over the examples with them, he told them what the procedure was for each problem, rarely asking them to conceptualize or explain it themselves: "Three into twenty-two is seven; do your subtraction and one is left over." During the week that two-digit division was introduced (or at any other time), the investigator did not observe any discussion of the idea of grouping involved in division, any

[9] Smith and Franklin, "The Concentration of Personal Wealth." [Author's note]

use of manipulables, or any attempt to relate two-digit division to any other mathematical process. Nor was there any attempt to relate the steps to an actual or possible thought process of the children. The observer did not hear the terms *dividend, quotient,* and so on, used again. The math teacher in the other working-class school followed similar procedures regarding two-digit division and at one point her class seemed confused. She said, "You're confusing yourselves. You're tensing up. Remember, when you do this, it's the same steps over and over again — and that's the way division always is." Several weeks later, after a test, a group of her children "still didn't get it," and she made no attempt to explain the concept of dividing things into groups or to give them manipulables for their own investigation. Rather, she went over the steps with them again and told them that they "needed more practice."

In other areas of math, work is also carrying out often unexplained fragmented procedures. For example, one of the teachers led the children through a series of steps to make a 1-inch grid on their paper *without* telling them that they were making a 1-inch grid or that it would be used to study scale. She said, "Take your ruler. Put it across the top. Make a mark at every number. Then move your ruler down to the bottom. No, put it across the bottom. Now make a mark on top of every number. Now draw a line from . . ." At this point a girl said that she had a faster way to do it and the teacher said, "No, you don't; you don't even know what I'm making yet. Do it this way or it's wrong." After they had made the lines up and down and across, the teacher told them she wanted them to make a figure by connecting some dots and to measure that, using the scale of 1 inch equals 1 mile. Then they were to cut it out. She said, "Don't cut it until I check it."

In both working-class schools, work in language arts is mechanics of punctuation (commas, periods, question marks, exclamation points), capitalization, and the four kinds of sentences. One teacher explained to me, "Simple punctuation is all they'll ever use." Regarding punctuation, either a teacher or a ditto stated the rules for where, for example, to put commas. The investigator heard no classroom discussion of the aural context of punctuation (which, of course, is what gives each mark its meaning). Nor did the investigator hear any statement or inference that placing a punctuation mark could be a decision-making process, depending, for example, on one's intended meaning. Rather, the children were told to follow the rules. Language arts did not involve creative writing. There were several writing assignments throughout the year, but in each instance the children were given a ditto, and they wrote answers to questions on the sheet. For example, they wrote their "autobiography" by answering such questions as "Where were you born?" "What is your favorite animal?" on a sheet entitled "All About Me."

In one of the working-class schools, the class had a science period several times a week. On the three occasions observed, the children were not called upon to set up experiments or to give explanations for facts or concepts.

Rather, on each occasion the teacher told them in his own words what the book said. The children copied the teacher's sentences from the board. Each day that preceded the day they were to do a science experiment, the teacher told them to copy the directions from the book for the procedure they would carry out the next day and to study the list at home that night. The day after each experiment, the teacher went over what they had "found" (they did the experiments as a class, and each was actually a class demonstration led by the teacher). Then the teacher wrote what they "found" on the board, and the children copied that in their notebooks. Once or twice a year there are science projects. The project is chosen and assigned by the teacher from a box of 3-by-5-inch cards. On the card the teacher has written the question to be answered, the books to use, and how much to write. Explaining the cards to the observer, the teacher said, "It tells them exactly what to do, or they couldn't do it."

Social studies in the working-class schools is also largely mechanical, rote work that was given little explanation or connection to larger contexts. In one school, for example, although there was a book available, social studies work was to copy the teacher's notes from the board. Several times a week for a period of several months the children copied these notes. The fifth grades in the district were to study United States history. The teacher used a booklet she had purchased called "The Fabulous Fifty States." Each day she put information from the booklet in outline form on the board and the children copied it. The type of information did not vary: the name of the state, its abbreviation, state capital, nickname of the state, its main products, main business, and a "Fabulous Fact" ("Idaho grew twenty-seven billion potatoes in one year. That's enough potatoes for each man, woman, and . . ."). As the children finished copying the sentences, the teacher erased them and wrote more. Children would occasionally go to the front to pull down the wall map in order to locate the states they were copying, and the teacher did not dissuade them. But the observer never saw her refer to the map; nor did the observer ever hear her make other than perfunctory remarks concerning the information the children were copying. Occasionally the children colored in a ditto and cut it out to make a stand-up figure (representing, for example, a man roping a cow in the Southwest). These were referred to by the teacher as their social studies "projects."

Rote behavior was often called for in classroom work. When going over 15
math and language art skills sheets, for example, as the teacher asked for the answer to each problem, he fired the questions rapidly, staccato, and the scene reminded the observer of a sergeant drilling recruits: above all, the questions demanded that you stay at attention: "The next one? What do I put here? . . . Here? Give us the next." Or "How many commas in this sentence? Where do I put them . . . The next one?"

The four fifth-grade teachers observed in the working-class schools attempted to control classroom time and space by making decisions without consulting the children and without explaining the basis for their decisions.

The teacher's control thus often seemed capricious. Teachers, for instance, very often ignored the bells to switch classes—deciding among themselves to keep the children after the period was officially over to continue with the work or for disciplinary reasons or so they (the teachers) could stand in the hall and talk. There were no clocks in the rooms in either school, and the children often asked, "What period is this?" "When do we go to gym?" The children had no access to materials. These were handed out by teachers and closely guarded. Things in the room "belonged" to the teacher: "Bob, bring me my garbage can." The teachers continually gave the children orders. Only three times did the investigator hear a teacher in either working-class school preface a directive with an unsarcastic "please," or "let's" or "would you." Instead, the teachers said, "Shut up," "Shut your mouth," "Open your books," "Throw your gum away—if you want to rot your teeth, do it on your own time." Teachers made every effort to control the movement of the children, and often shouted, "Why are you out of your seat??!!" If the children got permission to leave the room, they had to take a written pass with the date and time. . . .

Middle-Class School

In the middle-class school, work is getting the right answer. If one accumulates enough right answers, one gets a good grade. One must follow the directions in order to get the right answers, but the directions often call for some figuring, some choice, some decision making. For example, the children must often figure out by themselves what the directions ask them to do and how to get the answer: what do you do first, second, and perhaps third? Answers are usually found in books or by listening to the teacher. Answers are usually words, sentences, numbers, or facts and dates; one writes them on paper, and one should be neat. Answers must be given in the right order, and one cannot make them up.

The following activities are illustrative. Math involves some choice: one may do two-digit division the long way or the short way, and there are some math problems that can be done "in your head." When the teacher explains how to do two-digit division, there is recognition that a cognitive process is involved; she gives you several ways and says, "I want to make sure you understand what you're doing—so you get it right"; and, when they go over the homework, she asks the *children* to tell how they did the problem and what answer they got.

In social studies the daily work is to read the assigned pages in the textbook and to answer the teacher's questions. The questions are almost always designed to check on whether the students have read the assignment and understood it: who did so-and-so; what happened after that; when did it happen, where, and sometimes, why did it happen? The answers are in the book and in one's understanding of the book; the teacher's hints when one doesn't know the answers are to "read it again" or to look at the picture or at the rest of the paragraph. One is to search for the answer in the "context," in what is given.

Language arts is "simple grammar, what they need for everyday life." 20
The language arts teacher says, "They should learn to speak properly, to write business letters and thank-you letters, and to understand what nouns and verbs and simple subjects are." Here, as well, actual work is to choose the right answers, to understand what is given. The teacher often says, "Please read the next sentence and then I'll question you about it." One teacher said in some exasperation to a boy who was fooling around in class, "If you don't know the answers to the questions I ask, then you can't stay in this *class!* [pause] You *never* know the answers to the questions I ask, and it's not fair to me — and certainly not to you!"

Most lessons are based on the textbook. This does not involve a critical perspective on what is given there. For example, a critical perspective in social studies is perceived as dangerous by these teachers because it may lead to controversial topics; the parents might complain. The children, however, are often curious, especially in social studies. Their questions are tolerated and usually answered perfunctorily. But after a few minutes the teacher will say, "All right, we're not going any farther. Please open your social studies workbook." While the teachers spend a lot of time explaining and expanding on what the textbooks say, there is little attempt to analyze how or why things happen, or to give thought to how pieces of a culture, or, say, a system of numbers or elements of a language fit together or can be analyzed. What has happened in the past and what exists now may not be equitable or fair, but (shrug) that is the way things are and one does not confront such matters in school. For example, in social studies after a child is called on to read a passage about the pilgrims, the teacher summarizes the paragraph and then says, "So you can see how strict they were about everything." A child asks, "Why?" "Well, because they felt that if you weren't busy you'd get into trouble." Another child asks, "Is it true that they burned women at the stake?" The teacher says, "Yes, if a woman did anything strange, they hanged them. [*sic*] What would a woman do, do you think, to make them burn them? [*sic*] See if you can come up with better answers than my other [social studies] class." Several children offer suggestions, to which the teacher nods but does not comment. Then she says, "Okay, good," and calls on the next child to read.

Work tasks do not usually request creativity. Serious attention is rarely given in school work on *how* the children develop or express their own feelings and ideas, either linguistically or in graphic form. On the occasions when creativity or self-expression is requested, it is peripheral to the main activity or it is "enrichment" or "for fun." During a lesson on what similes are, for example, the teacher explains what they are, puts several on the board, gives some other examples herself, and then asks the children if they can "make some up." She calls on three children who give similes, two of which are actually in the book they have open before them. The teacher does not comment on this and then asks several others to choose similes from the list of phrases in the book. Several do so correctly, and she says, "Oh good! You're picking them out! See how good we are?" Their homework is to pick out the rest of the similes from the list.

Creativity is not often requested in social studies and science projects, either. Social studies projects, for example, are given with directions to "find information on your topic" and write it up. The children are not supposed to copy but to "put it in your own words." Although a number of the projects subsequently went beyond the teacher's direction to find information and had quite expressive covers and inside illustrations, the teacher's evaluative comments had to do with the amount of information, whether they had "copied," and if their work was neat.

The style of control of the three fifth-grade teachers observed in this school varied from somewhat easygoing to strict, but in contrast to the working-class schools, the teachers' decisions were usually based on external rules and regulations—for example, on criteria that were known or available to the children. Thus, the teachers always honor the bells for changing classes, and they usually evaluate children's work by what is in the textbooks and answer booklets.

25 There is little excitement in schoolwork for the children, and the assignments are perceived as having little to do with their interests and feelings. As one child said, what you do is "store facts up in your head like cold storage—until you need it later for a test or your job." Thus, doing well is important because there are thought to be *other* likely rewards: a good job or college.[10]

Affluent Professional School

In the affluent professional school, work is creative activity carried out independently. The students are continually asked to express and apply ideas and concepts. Work involves individual thought and expressiveness, expansion and illustration of ideas, and choice of appropriate method and material. (The class is not considered an open classroom, and the principal explained that because of the large number of discipline problems in the fifth grade this year they did not departmentalize. The teacher who agreed to take part in the study said she is "more structured" this year than she usually is.) The products of work in this class are often written stories, editorials and essays, or representations of ideas in mural, graph, or craft form. The products of work should not be like everybody else's and should show individuality. They should exhibit good design, and (this is important) they must also fit empirical reality. Moreover, one's work should attempt to interpret or "make sense" of reality. The relatively few rules to be followed regarding work are

[10]A dominant feeling, expressed directly and indirectly by teachers in this school, was boredom with their work. They did, however, in contrast to the working-class schools, almost always carry out lessons during class times. [Author's note]

usually criteria for, or limits on, individual activity. One's product is usually evaluated for the quality of its expression and for the appropriateness of its conception to the task. In many cases, one's own satisfaction with the product is an important criterion for its evaluation. When right answers are called for, as in commercial materials like SRA (Science Research Associates) and math, it is important that the children decide on an answer as a result of thinking about the idea involved in what they're being asked to do. Teacher's hints are to "think about it some more."

The following activities are illustrative. The class takes home a sheet requesting each child's parents to fill in the number of cars they have, the number of television sets, refrigerators, games, or rooms in the house, and so on. Each child is to figure the average number of a type of possession owned by the fifth grade. Each child must compile the "data" from all the sheets. A calculator is available in the classroom to do the mechanics of finding the average. Some children decide to send sheets to the fourth-grade families for comparison. Their work should be "verified" by a classmate before it is handed in.

Each child and his or her family has made a geoboard. The teacher asks the class to get their geoboards from the side cabinet, to take a handful of rubber bands, and then to listen to what she would like them to do. She says, "I would like you to design a figure and then find the perimeter and area. When you have it, check with your neighbor. After you've done that, please transfer it to graph paper and tomorrow I'll ask you to make up a question about it for someone. When you hand it in, please let me know whose it is and who verified it. Then I have something else for you to do that's really fun. [pause] Find the average number of chocolate chips in three cookies. I'll give you three cookies, and you'll have to *eat* your way through, I'm afraid!" Then she goes around the room and gives help, suggestions, praise, and admonitions that they are getting noisy. They work sitting, or standing up at their desks, at benches in the back, or on the floor. A child hands the teacher his paper and she comments, "I'm not accepting this paper. Do a better design." To another child she says, "That's fantastic! But you'll never find the area. Why don't you draw a figure inside [the big one] and subtract to get the area?"

The school district requires the fifth grade to study ancient civilization (in particular, Egypt, Athens, and Sumer). In this classroom, the emphasis is on illustrating and re-creating the culture of the people of ancient times. The following are typical activities: the children made an 8mm film on Egypt, which one of the parents edited. A girl in the class wrote the script, and the class acted it out. They put the sound on themselves. They read stories of those days. They wrote essays and stories depicting the lives of the people and the societal and occupational divisions. They chose from a list of projects, all of which involved graphic representations of ideas: for example, "Make a mural depicting the division of labor in Egyptian society."

Each child wrote and exchanged a letter in hieroglyphics with a fifth 30 grader in another class, and they also exchanged stories they wrote in cuneiform. They made a scroll and singed the edges so it looked authentic. They each chose an occupation and made an Egyptian plaque representing that occupation, simulating the appropriate Egyptian design. They carved their design on a cylinder of wax, pressed the wax into clay, and then baked the clay. Although one girl did not choose an occupation but carved instead a series of gods and slaves, the teacher said, "That's all right, Amber, it's beautiful." As they were working the teacher said, "Don't cut into your clay until you're satisfied with your design."

Social studies also involves almost daily presentation by the children of some event from the news. The teacher's questions ask the children to expand what they say, to give more details, and to be more specific. Occasionally she adds some remarks to help them see connections between events.

The emphasis on expressing and illustrating ideas in social studies is accompanied in language arts by an emphasis on creative writing. Each child wrote a rebus story for a first grader whom they had interviewed to see what kind of story the child liked best. They wrote editorials on pending decisions by the school board and radio plays, some of which were read over the school intercom from the office and one of which was performed in the auditorium. There is no language arts textbook because, the teacher said, "The principal wants us to be creative." There is not much grammar, but there is punctuation. One morning when the observer arrived, the class was doing a punctuation ditto. The teacher later apologized for using the ditto. "It's just for review," she said. "I don't teach punctuation that way. We use their language." The ditto had three unambiguous rules for where to put commas in a sentence. As the teacher was going around to help the children with the ditto, she repeated several times, "Where you put commas depends on how you say the sentence; it depends on the situation and what you want to say." Several weeks later the observer saw another punctuation activity. The teacher had printed a five-paragraph story on an oak tag and then cut it into phrases. She read the whole story to the class from the book, then passed out the phrases. The group had to decide how the phrases could best be put together again. (They arranged the phrases on the floor.) The point was not to replicate the story, although that was not irrelevant, but to "decide what you think the best way is." Punctuation marks on cardboard pieces were then handed out, and the children discussed and then decided what mark was best at each place they thought one was needed. At the end of each paragraph the teacher asked, "Are you satisfied with the way the paragraphs are now? Read it to yourself and see how it sounds." Then she read the original story again, and they compared the two.

Describing her goals in science to the investigator, the teacher said, "We use ESS (Elementary Science Study). It's very good because it gives a hands-on experience — so they can make *sense* out of it. It doesn't matter whether it [what they find] is right or wrong. I bring them together and there's value in discussing their ideas."

The products of work in this class are often highly valued by the children and the teacher. In fact, this was the only school in which the investigator was not allowed to take original pieces of the children's work for her files. If the work was small enough, however, and was on paper, the investigator could duplicate it on the copying machine in the office.

The teacher's attempt to control the class involves constant negotiation. 35
She does not give direct orders unless she is angry because the children have been too noisy. Normally, she tries to get them to foresee the consequences of their actions and to decide accordingly. For example, lining them up to go see a play written by the sixth graders, she says, "I presume you're lined up by someone with whom you want to sit. I hope you're lined up by someone you won't get in trouble with." . . .

One of the few rules governing the children's movement is that no more than three children may be out of the room at once. There is a school rule that anyone can go to the library at any time to get a book. In the fifth grade I observed, they sign their name on the chalkboard and leave. There are no passes. Finally, the children have a fair amount of officially sanctioned say over what happens in the class. For example, they often negotiate what work is to be done. If the teacher wants to move on to the next subject, but the children say they are not ready, they want to work on their present projects some more, she very often lets them do it.

Executive Elite School

In the executive elite school, work is developing one's analytical intellectual powers. Children are continually asked to reason through a problem, to produce intellectual products that are both logically sound and of top academic quality. A primary goal of thought is to conceptualize rules by which elements may fit together in systems and then to apply these rules in solving a problem. Schoolwork helps one to achieve, to excel, to prepare for life.

The following are illustrative. The math teacher teaches area and perimeter by having the children derive formulas for each. First she helps them, through discussion at the board, to arrive at $A = W \times L$ as a formula (not *the* formula) for area. After discussing several, she says, "Can anyone make up a formula for perimeter? Can you figure that out yourselves? [pause] Knowing what we know, can we think of a formula?" She works out three children's suggestions at the board, saying to two, "Yes, that's a good one," and then asks the class if they can think of any more. No one volunteers. To prod them, she says, "If you use rules and good reasoning, you get many ways. Chris, can you think up a formula?"

She discusses two-digit division with the children as a decision-making process. Presenting a new type of problem to them, she asks, "What's the *first* decision you'd make if presented with this kind of example? What is the first thing you'd *think?* Craig?" Craig says, "To find my first partial quotient." She responds, "Yes, that would be your first decision. How would you do that?" Craig explains, and then the teacher says, "OK, we'll see how that works for you." The class tries his way. Subsequently, she comments on the merits and shortcomings of several other children's decisions. Later, she tells the investigator that her goals in math are to develop their reasoning and mathematical thinking and that, unfortunately, "there's no *time* for manipulables."

40 While right answers are important in math, they are not "given" by the book or by the teacher but may be challenged by the children. Going over some problems in late September the teacher says, "Raise your hand if you do not agree." A child says, "I don't agree with sixty-four." The teacher responds, "OK, there's a question about sixty-four. [to class] Please check it. Owen, they're disagreeing with you. Kristen, they're checking yours." The teacher emphasized this repeatedly during September and October with statements like "Don't be afraid to say you disagree. In the last [math] class, somebody disagreed, and they were right. Before you disagree, check yours, and if you still think we're wrong, then we'll check it out." By Thanksgiving, the children did not often speak in terms of right and wrong math problems but of whether they agreed with the answer that had been given.

There are complicated math mimeos with many word problems. Whenever they go over the examples, they discuss how each child has set up the problem. The children must explain it precisely. On one occasion the teacher said, "I'm more — just as interested in *how* you set up the problem as in what answer you find. If you set up a problem in a good way, the answer is *easy* to find."

Social studies work is most often reading and discussion of concepts and independent research. There are only occasional artistic, expressive, or illustrative projects. Ancient Athens and Sumer are, rather, societies to analyze. The following questions are typical of those that guide the children's independent research. "What mistakes did Pericles make after the war?" "What mistakes did the citizens of Athens make?" "What are the elements of a civilization?" "How did Greece build an economic empire?" "Compare the way Athens chose its leaders with the way we choose ours." Occasionally the children are asked to make up sample questions for their social studies tests. On an occasion when the investigator was present, the social studies teacher rejected a child's question by saying, "That's just fact. If I asked you that question on a test, you'd complain it was just memory! Good questions ask for concepts."

In social studies — but also in reading, science, and health — the teachers initiate classroom discussions of current social issues and problems. These discussions occurred on every one of the investigator's visits, and a teacher told me, "These children's opinions are important — it's important that they learn to reason things through." The classroom discussions always struck the observer as quite realistic and analytical, dealing with concrete social issues like the following: "Why do workers strike?" "Is that right or wrong?" "Why do we have inflation, and what can be done to stop it?" "Why do companies put chemicals in food when the natural ingredients are available?" and so on. Usually the children did not have to be prodded to give their opinions. In fact, their statements and the interchanges between them struck the observer as quite sophisticated conceptually and verbally, and well-informed. Occasionally the teachers would prod with statements such as, "Even if you don't know [the answers], if you think logically about it, you can figure it out." And "I'm asking you [these] questions to help you think this through."

Language arts emphasizes language as a complex system, one that should be mastered. The children are asked to diagram sentences of complex grammatical construction, to memorize irregular verb conjugations (he lay, he has lain, and so on . . .), and to use the proper participles, conjunctions, and interjections in their speech. The teacher (the same one who teaches social studies) told them, "It is not enough to get these right on tests; you must use what you learn [in grammar classes] in your written and oral work. I will grade you on that."

Most writing assignments are either research reports and essays for so- 45
cial studies or experiment analyses and write-ups for science. There is only an occasional story or other "creative writing" assignment. On the occasion observed by the investigator (the writing of a Halloween story), the points the teacher stressed in preparing the children to write involved the structural aspects of a story rather than the expression of feelings or other ideas. The teacher showed them a filmstrip, "The Seven Parts of a Story," and lectured them on plot development, mood setting, character development, consistency, and the use of a logical or appropriate ending. The stories they subsequently wrote were, in fact, well-structured, but many were also personal and expressive. The teacher's evaluative comments, however, did not refer to the expressiveness or artistry but were all directed toward whether they had "developed" the story well.

Language arts work also involved a large amount of practice in presentation of the self and in managing situations where the child was expected to be in charge. For example, there was a series of assignments in which each child had to be a "student teacher." The child had to plan a lesson in grammar, outlining, punctuation, or other language arts topic and explain the concept to the class. Each child was to prepare a worksheet or game and a homework assignment as well. After each presentation, the teacher and other children gave a critical appraisal of the "student teacher's" performance. Their criteria were: whether the student spoke clearly, whether the lesson was interesting, whether the student made any mistakes, and whether he or she kept control of the class. On an occasion when a child did not maintain control, the teacher said, "When you're up there, you have authority and you have to use it. I'll back you up." . . .

The executive elite school is the only school where bells do not demarcate the periods of time. The two fifth-grade teachers were very strict about changing classes on schedule, however, as specific plans for each session had been made. The teachers attempted to keep tight control over the children during lessons, and the children were sometimes flippant, boisterous, and occasionally rude. However, the children may be brought into line by reminding them that "It is up to you." "You must control yourself," "you are responsible for your work," you must "set your own priorities." One teacher told a child, "You are the only driver of your car—and only you can regulate your speed." A new teacher complained to the observer that she had thought "these children" would have more control.

While strict attention to the lesson at hand is required, the teachers make relatively little attempt to regulate the movement of the children at other times. For example, except for the kindergartners the children in this school do not have to wait for the bell to ring in the morning; they may go to their classroom when they arrive at school. Fifth graders often came early to read, to finish work, or to catch up. After the first two months of school, the fifth-grade teachers did not line the children up to change classes or to go to gym, and so on, but, when the children were ready and quiet, they were told they could go—sometimes without the teachers.

In the classroom, the children could get materials when they needed them and took what they needed from closets and from the teacher's desk. They were in charge of the office at lunchtime. During class they did not have to sign out or ask permission to leave the room; they just got up and left. Because of the pressure to get work done, however, they did not leave the room very often. The teachers were very polite to the children, and the investigator heard no sarcasm, no nasty remarks, and few direct orders. The teachers never called the children "honey" or "dear" but always called them by name. The teachers were expected to be available before school, after school, and for part of their lunchtime to provide extra help if needed. . . .

The foregoing analysis of differences in schoolwork in contrasting social 50
class contexts suggests the following conclusion: the "hidden curriculum" of schoolwork is tacit preparation for relating to the process of production in a particular way. Differing curricular, pedagogical, and pupil evaluation practices emphasize different cognitive and behavioral skills in each social setting and thus contribute to the development in the children of certain potential relationships to physical and symbolic capital,[11] to authority, and to the process of work. School experience, in the sample of schools discussed here, differed qualitatively by social class. These differences may not only contribute to the development in the children in each social class of certain types of economically significant relationships and not others but would thereby help to *reproduce* this system of relations in society. In the contribution to the reproduction of unequal social relations lies a theoretical meaning and social consequence of classroom practice.

The identification of different emphases in classrooms in a sample of

[11]*physical and symbolic capital:* Elsewhere Anyon defines *capital* as "property that is used to produce profit, interest, or rent"; she defines *symbolic capital* as the knowledge and skills that "may yield social and cultural power."

contrasting social class contexts implies that further research should be conducted in a large number of schools to investigate the types of work tasks and interactions in each to see if they differ in the ways discussed here and to see if similar potential relationships are uncovered. Such research could have as a product the further elucidation of complex but not readily apparent connections between everyday activity in schools and classrooms and the unequal structure of economic relationships in which we work and live.

ENGAGING THE TEXT

1. Examine the ways any single subject is taught in the four types of schools Anyon describes. What differences in teaching methods and in the student-teacher relationship do they reflect? What other differences do you note in the schools? What schools in your geographic region would closely approximate the working-class, middle-class, affluent professional, and executive elite schools of her article?
2. What attitudes toward knowledge and work are the four types of schools teaching their students? What kinds of jobs are students being prepared to do? Do you see any evidence that the schools in your community are producing particular kinds of workers?
3. What is the "hidden curriculum" of Anyon's title? How is this curriculum taught, and what social, cultural, or political purposes does it serve?

EXPLORING CONNECTIONS

4. What kind of a school — working class, middle class, affluent professional, or executive elite — does Mark attend in Theodore Sizer's "What High School Is" (p. 20)? On what do you base your judgment? How might Anyon interpret the "supermarket" mentality of the school Sizer describes?
5. Draw a Groening-like (see pp. 31–32) cartoon or comic strip about a classroom situation in a working-class, middle-class, professional, or elite school (but do not identify the type of school explicitly). Pool all the cartoons from the class. In small groups, sort the comics according to the type of school they represent.
6. Analyze the teaching styles that Mike Rose encounters at Our Lady of Mercy (p. 33). Which of Anyon's categories would they fit best? Do Rose's experiences at his high school tend to confirm or complicate Anyon's analysis?

EXTENDING THE CRITICAL CONTEXT

7. Should all schools be run like the professional or elite schools? What would be the advantages of making these schools models for all social classes? Do you see any possible disadvantages?
8. Choose a common elementary school task or skill that Anyon does not mention. Outline four ways it might be taught in the four types of schools.

The Achievement of Desire

RICHARD RODRIGUEZ

Hunger of Memory, *the autobiography of Richard Rodriguez and the source of the following selection, set off a storm of controversy in the Chicano community when it appeared in 1981. Some hailed it as an uncompromising portrayal of the difficulties of growing up between two cultures; others condemned it because it seemed to blame Mexican Americans for the difficulties they encountered assimilating into mainstream American society. Rodriguez was born in 1944 into an immigrant family outside San Francisco. Though he was unable to speak English when he entered school, his educational career can only be described as brilliant: undergraduate work at Stanford University, graduate study at Berkeley and Columbia, a Fulbright fellowship to study English literature in London, a subsequent grant from the National Endowment for the Humanities. In this selection, Rodriguez analyzes the motives that led him to abandon his study of Renaissance literature and return to live with his parents. He is currently an associate editor with the Pacific News Service in San Francisco, an essayist for the* MacNeil/Lehrer News Hour, *and a contributing editor for* Harper's *magazine and for the Opinion section of the Los Angeles* Times. *Recent books include* Mexico's Children *(1991) and* Days of Obligation: An Argument with My Mexican Father *(1993), which was nominated for the Pulitzer Prize in nonfiction.*

I stand in the ghetto classroom — "the guest speaker" — attempting to lecture on the mystery of the sounds of our words to rows of diffident students. "Don't you hear it? Listen! The music of our words. *'Sumer is i-cumen in.*[1] . . .' And songs on the car radio. We need Aretha Franklin's voice to fill plain words with music — her life." In the face of their empty stares, I try to create an enthusiasm. But the girls in the back row turn to watch some boy passing outside. There are flutters of smiles, waves. And someone's mouth elongates heavy, silent words through the barrier of glass. Silent words — the lips straining to shape each voiceless syllable: *"Meet meee late errr."* By the door, the instructor smiles at me, apparently hoping that I will be able to spark some enthusiasm in the class. But only one student seems to be listening. A girl, maybe fourteen. In this gray room her eyes shine with ambition. She keeps nodding and nodding at all that I say; she even takes notes. And each time I ask a question, she jerks up and down in her desk

[1]*Sumer is i-cumen in:* Opening line of a Middle English poem ("Summer has come").

like a marionette, while her hand waves over the bowed heads of her classmates. It is myself (as a boy) I see as she faces me now (a man in my thirties).

The boy who first entered a classroom barely able to speak English, twenty years later concluded his studies in the stately quiet of the reading room in the British Museum. Thus with one sentence I can summarize my academic career. It will be harder to summarize what sort of life connects the boy to the man.

With every award, each graduation from one level of education to the next, people I'd meet would congratulate me. Their refrain always the same: "Your parents must be very proud." Sometimes then they'd ask me how I managed it — my "success." (How?) After a while, I had several quick answers to give in reply. I'd admit, for one thing, that I went to an excellent grammar school. (My earliest teachers, the nuns, made my success their ambition.) And my brother and both my sisters were very good students. (They often brought home the shiny school trophies I came to want.) And my mother and father always encouraged me. (At every graduation they were behind the stunning flash of the camera when I turned to look at the crowd.)

As important as these factors were, however, they account inadequately for my academic advance. Nor do they suggest what an odd success I managed. For although I was a very good student, I was also a very bad student. I was a "scholarship boy," a certain kind of scholarship boy. Always successful, I was always unconfident. Exhilarated by my progress. Sad. I became the prized student — anxious and eager to learn. Too eager, too anxious — an imitative and unoriginal pupil. My brother and two sisters enjoyed the advantages I did, and they grew to be as successful as I, but none of them ever seemed so anxious about their schooling. A second-grade student, I was the one who came home and corrected the "simple" grammatical mistakes of our parents. ("Two negatives make a positive.") Proudly I announced — to my family's startled silence — that a teacher had said I was losing all trace of a Spanish accent. I was oddly annoyed when I was unable to get parental help with a homework assignment. The night my father tried to help me with an arithmetic exercise, he kept reading the instructions, each time more deliberately, until I pried the textbook out of his hands, saying, "I'll try to figure it out some more by myself."

When I reached the third grade, I outgrew such behavior. I became 5
more tactful, careful to keep separate the two very different worlds of my day. But then, with ever-increasing intensity, I devoted myself to my studies. I became bookish, puzzling to all my family. Ambition set me apart. When my brother saw me struggling home with stacks of library books, he would laugh, shouting: "Hey, Four Eyes!" My father opened a closet one day and was startled to find me inside, reading a novel. My mother would find me reading when I was supposed to be asleep or helping around the house or

playing outside. In a voice angry or worried or just curious, she'd ask: "What do you see in your books?" It became the family's joke. When I was called and wouldn't reply, someone would say I must be hiding under my bed with a book.

(How did I manage my success?)

What I am about to say to you has taken me more than twenty years to admit: *A primary reason for my success in the classroom was that I couldn't forget that schooling was changing me and separating me from the life I enjoyed before becoming a student.* That simple realization! For years I never spoke to anyone about it. Never mentioned a thing to my family or my teachers or classmates. From a very early age, I understood enough, just enough about my classroom experiences to keep what I knew repressed, hidden beneath layers of embarrassment. Not until my last months as a graduate student, nearly thirty years old, was it possible for me to think much about the reasons for my academic success. Only then. At the end of my schooling, I needed to determine how far I had moved from my past. The adult finally confronted, and now must publicly say, what the child shuddered from knowing and could never admit to himself or to those many faces that smiled at his every success. ("Your parents must be very proud. . . .")

At the end, in the British Museum (too distracted to finish my dissertation) for weeks I read, speed-read, books by modern educational theorists, only to find infrequent and slight mention of students like me. (Much more is written about the more typical case, the lower-class student who barely is helped by his schooling.) Then one day, leafing through Richard Hoggart's *The Uses of Literacy*, I found, in his description of the scholarship boy, myself. For the first time I realized that there were other students like me, and so I was able to frame the meaning of my academic success, its consequent price — the loss.

Hoggart's description is distinguished, at least initially, by deep understanding. What he grasps very well is that the scholarship boy must move between environments, his home and the classroom, which are at cultural extremes, opposed. With his family, the boy has the intense pleasure of intimacy, the family's consolation in feeling public alienation. Lavish emotions texture home life. *Then*, at school, the instruction bids him to trust lonely reason primarily. Immediate needs set the pace of his parents' lives. From his mother and father the boy learns to trust spontaneity and nonrational ways of knowing. *Then*, at school, there is mental calm. Teachers emphasize the value of a reflectiveness that opens a space between thinking and immediate action.

Years of schooling must pass before the boy will be able to sketch the 10
cultural differences in his day as abstractly as this. But he senses those differences early. Perhaps as early as the night he brings home an assignment from school and finds the house too noisy for study.

> He has to be more and more alone, if he is going to "get on." He will have, probably unconsciously, to oppose the ethos[2] of the hearth, the intense gregariousness of the working-class family group. Since everything centres upon the living-room, there is unlikely to be a room of his own; the bedrooms are cold and inhospitable, and to warm them or the front room, if there is one, would not only be expensive, but would require an imaginative leap—out of the tradition—which most families are not capable of making. There is a corner of the living-room table. On the other side Mother is ironing, the wireless is on, someone is singing a snatch of song or Father says intermittently whatever comes into his head. The boy has to cut himself off mentally, so as to do his homework, as well as he can.[3]

The next day, the lesson is as apparent at school. There are even rows of desks. Discussion is ordered. The boy must rehearse his thoughts and raise his hand before speaking out in a loud voice to an audience of classmates. And there is time enough, and silence, to think about ideas (big ideas) never considered at home by his parents.

Not for the working-class child alone is adjustment to the classroom difficult. Good schooling requires that any student alter early childhood habits. But the working-class child is usually least prepared for the change. And, unlike many middle-class children, he goes home and sees in his parents a way of life not only different but starkly opposed to that of the classroom. (He enters the house and hears his parents talking in ways his teachers discourage.)

Without extraordinary determination and the great assistance of others — at home and at school — there is little chance for success. Typically most working-class children are barely changed by the classroom. The exception succeeds. The relative few become scholarship students. Of these, Richard Hoggart estimates, most manage a fairly graceful transition. Somehow they learn to live in the two very different worlds of their day. There are some others, however, those Hoggart pejoratively terms "scholarship boys," for whom success comes with special anxiety. Scholarship boy: good student, troubled son. The child is "moderately endowed," intellectually mediocre, Hoggart supposes — though it may be more pertinent to note the special qualities of temperament in the child. High-strung child. Brooding. Sensitive. Haunted by the knowledge that one *chooses* to become a student. (Education is not an inevitable or natural step in growing up.) Here is a child who cannot forget that his academic success distances him from a life he loved, even from his own memory of himself.

Initially, he wavers, balances allegiance. ("The boy is himself [until he reaches, say, the upper forms[4]] very much of *both* the worlds of home and

[2]*ethos:* The fundamental spirit or character of a thing.

[3]All quotations are from Richard Hoggart, *The Uses of Literacy* (London: Chatto and Windus, 1957), chapter 10. [Author's note]

[4]*upper forms:* Upper grades or classes in British secondary schools.

school. He is enormously obedient to the dictates of the world of school, but emotionally still strongly wants to continue as part of the family circle.") Gradually, necessarily, the balance is lost. The boy needs to spend more and more time studying, each night enclosing himself in the silence permitted and required by intense concentration. He takes his first step toward academic success, away from his family.

From the very first days, through the years following, it will be with his 15
parents — the figures of lost authority, the persons toward whom he feels deepest love — that the change will be most powerfully measured. A separation will unravel between them. Advancing in his studies, the boy notices that his mother and father have not changed as much as he. Rather, when he sees them, they often remind him of the person he once was and the life he earlier shared with them. He realizes what some Romantics[5] also know when they praise the working class for the capacity for human closeness, qualities of passion and spontaneity, that the rest of us experience in like measure only in the earliest part of our youth. For the Romantic, this doesn't make working-class life childish. Working-class life challenges precisely because it is an *adult* way of life.

The scholarship boy reaches a different conclusion. He cannot afford to admire his parents. (How could he and still pursue such a contrary life?) He permits himself embarrassment at their lack of education. And to evade nostalgia for the life he has lost, he concentrates on the benefits education will bestow upon him. He becomes especially ambitious. Without the support of old certainties and consolations, almost mechanically, he assumes the procedures and doctrines of the classroom. The kind of allegiance the young student might have given his mother and father only days earlier, he transfers to the teacher, the new figure of authority. "[The scholarship boy] tends to make a father-figure of his form-master,"[6] Hoggart observes.

But Hoggart's calm prose only makes me recall the urgency with which I came to idolize my grammar school teachers. I began by imitating their accents, using their diction, trusting their every direction. The very first facts they dispensed, I grasped with awe. Any book they told me to read, I read — then waited for them to tell me which books I enjoyed. Their every casual opinion I came to adopt and to trumpet when I returned home. I stayed after school "to help" — to get my teacher's undivided attention. It was the nun's encouragement that mattered most to me. (She understood exactly what — my parents never seemed to appraise so well — all my achievements entailed.) Memory gently caressed each word of praise bestowed in the classroom so that compliments teachers paid me years ago come quickly to mind even today.

[5] *Romantics:* Adherents of the principles of romanticism — a literary and philosophical movement that emphasized the imagination, freedom, nature, the return to a simple life, and the ordinary individual.

[6] *form-master:* A teacher in a British secondary school.

The enthusiasm I felt in second-grade classes I flaunted before both my parents. The docile, obedient student came home a shrill and precocious son who insisted on correcting and teaching his parents with the remark: "My teacher told us. . . ."

I intended to hurt my mother and father. I was still angry at them for having encouraged me toward classroom English. But gradually this anger was exhausted, replaced by guilt as school grew more and more attractive to me. I grew increasingly successful, a talkative student. My hand was raised in the classroom; I yearned to answer any question. At home, life was less noisy than it had been. (I spoke to classmates and teachers more often each day than to family members.) Quiet at home, I sat with my papers for hours each night. I never forgot that schooling had irretrievably changed my family's life. That knowledge, however, did not weaken ambition. Instead, it strengthened resolve. Those times I remembered the loss of my past with regret, I quickly reminded myself of all the things my teachers could give me. (They could make me an educated man.) I tightened my grip on pencil and books. I evaded nostalgia. Tried hard to forget. But one does not forget by trying to forget. One only remembers. I remembered too well that education had changed my family's life. I would not have become a scholarship boy had I not so often remembered.

Once she was sure that her children knew English, my mother would 20
tell us, "You should keep up your Spanish." Voices playfully groaned in response. "*¡Pochos!*"[7] my mother would tease. I listened silently.

After a while, I grew more calm at home. I developed tact. A fourth-grade student, I was no longer the show-off in front of my parents. I became a conventionally dutiful son, politely affectionate, cheerful enough, even — for reasons beyond choosing — my father's favorite. And much about my family life was easy then, comfortable, happy in the rhythm of our living together: hearing my father getting ready for work; eating the breakfast my mother had made me; looking up from a novel to hear my brother or one of my sisters playing with friends in the backyard; in winter, coming upon the house all lighted up after dark.

But withheld from my mother and father was any mention of what most mattered to me: the extraordinary experience of first-learning. Late afternoon: in the midst of preparing dinner, my mother would come up behind me while I was trying to read. Her head just over mine, her breath warmly scented with food. "What are you reading?" Or, "Tell me all about your new courses." I would barely respond, "Just the usual things, nothing special." (A half smile, then silence. Her head moving back in the silence. Silence! Instead of the flood of intimate sounds that had once flowed smoothly between us, there was this silence.) After dinner, I would rush to a bedroom with papers and books. As often as possible, I resisted parental pleas to "save

[7] *pocho:* A derogatory Spanish word for a Mexican American who has adopted the attitudes, values, and lifestyle of Anglo culture.

lights" by coming to the kitchen to work. I kept so much, so often, to myself. Sad. Enthusiastic. Troubled by the excitement of coming upon new ideas. Eager. Fascinated by the promising texture of a brand-new book. I hoarded the pleasures of learning. Alone for hours. Enthralled. Nervous. I rarely looked away from my books — or back on my memories. Nights when relatives visited and the front rooms were warmed by Spanish sounds, I slipped quietly out of the house.

It mattered that education was changing me. It never ceased to matter. My brother and sisters would giggle at our mother's mispronounced words. They'd correct her gently. My mother laughed girlishly one night, trying not to pronounce *sheep* as *ship*. From a distance I listened sullenly. From that distance, pretending not to notice on another occasion, I saw my father looking at the title pages of my library books. That was the scene on my mind when I walked home with a fourth-grade companion and heard him say that his parents read to him every night. (A strange-sounding book — *Winnie the Pooh.*) Immediately, I wanted to know, "What is it like?" My companion, however, thought I wanted to know about the plot of the book. Another day, my mother surprised me by asking for a "nice" book to read. "Something not too hard you think I might like." Carefully I chose one, Willa Cather's[8] *My Antonia.* But when, several weeks later, I happened to see it next to her bed unread except for the first few pages, I was furious and suddenly wanted to cry. I grabbed up the book and took it back to my room and placed it in its place, alphabetically on my shelf.

"Your parents must be very proud of you." People began to say that to me about the time I was in sixth grade. To answer affirmatively, I'd smile. Shyly I'd smile, never betraying my sense of the irony: I was not proud of my mother and father. I was embarrassed by their lack of education. It was not that I ever thought they were stupid, though stupidly I took for granted their enormous native intelligence. Simply, what mattered to me was that they were not like my teachers.

25 But, "Why didn't you tell us about the award?" my mother demanded, her frown weakened by pride. At the grammar school ceremony several weeks after, her eyes were brighter than the trophy I'd won. Pushing back the hair from my forehead, she whispered that I had "shown" the *gringos.*[9] A few minutes later, I heard my father speak to my teacher and felt ashamed of his labored, accented words. Then guilty for the shame. I felt such contrary feelings. (There is no simple roadmap through the heart of the scholarship boy.) My teacher was so soft-spoken and her words were edged sharp and clean. I admired her until it seemed to me that she spoke too carefully. Sensing that she was condescending to them, I became nervous. Resentful. Protective. I tried to move my parents away. "You both must be very proud

[8]*Willa Cather:* American novelist (1876–1947).
[9]*gringos:* Anglos.

of Richard," the nun said. They responded quickly. (They were proud.) "We are proud of all our children." Then this afterthought: "They sure didn't get their brains from us." They all laughed. I smiled.

In fourth grade I embarked upon a grandiose reading program. "Give me the names of important books," I would say to startled teachers. They soon found out that I had in mind "adult books." I ignored their suggestion of anything I suspected was written for children. (Not until I was in college, as a result, did I read *Huckleberry Finn* or *Alice's Adventures in Wonderland.*) Instead, I read *The Scarlet Letter* and Franklin's *Autobiography.* And whatever I read I read for extra credit. Each time I finished a book, I reported the achievement to a teacher and basked in the praise my effort earned. Despite my best efforts, however, there seemed to be more and more books I needed to read. At the library I would literally tremble as I came upon whole shelves of books I hadn't read. So I read and I read and I read: *Great Expectations;* all the short stories of Kipling; *The Babe Ruth Story;* the entire first volume of the *Encyclopaedia Britannica* (A–ANSTEY) the *Iliad; Moby Dick; Gone with the Wind; The Good Earth; Ramona; Forever Amber; The Lives of the Saints; Crime and Punishment; The Pearl.* . . . Librarians who initially frowned when I checked out the maximum ten books at a time started saving books they thought I might like. Teachers would say to the rest of the class, "I only wish the rest of you took reading as seriously as Richard obviously does."

But at home I would hear my mother wondering, "What do you see in your books?" (Was reading a hobby like her knitting? Was so much reading even healthy for a boy? Was it the sign of "brains"? Or was it just a convenient excuse for not helping around the house on Saturday mornings?) Always, "What do you see . . . ?"

What *did* I see in my books? I had the idea that they were crucial for my academic success, though I couldn't have said exactly how or why. In the sixth grade I simply concluded that what gave a book its value was some major idea or theme it contained. If that core essence could be mined and memorized, I would become learned like my teachers. I decided to record in a notebook the themes of the books that I read. After reading *Robinson Crusoe,* I wrote that its theme was "the value of learning to live by oneself." When I completed *Wuthering Heights,* I noted the danger of "letting emotions get out of control." Rereading these brief moralistic appraisals usually left me disheartened. I couldn't believe that they were really the source of reading's value. But for many more years, they constituted the only means I had of describing to myself the educational value of books.

I entered high school having read hundreds of books. My habit of reading made me a confident speaker and writer of English. Reading also enabled me to sense something of the shape, the major concerns, of Western thought.

(I was able to say something about Dante[10] and Descartes[11] and Engels[12] and James Baldwin[13] in my high school term papers.) In these various ways, books brought me academic success as I hoped that they would. But I was not a good reader. Merely bookish, I lacked a point of view when I read. Rather, I read in order to acquire a point of view. I vacuumed books for epigrams, scraps of information, ideas, themes — anything to fill the hollow within me and make me feel educated. When one of my teachers suggested to his drowsy tenth-grade English class that a person could not have a "complicated idea" until he had read at least two thousand books, I heard the remark without detecting either its irony or its very complicated truth. I merely determined to compile a list of all the books I had ever read. Harsh with myself, I included only once a title I might have read several times. (How, after all, could one read a book more than once?) And I included only those books over a hundred pages in length. (Could anything shorter be a book?)

30 There was yet another high school list I compiled. One day I came across a newspaper article about the retirement of an English professor at a nearby state college. The article was accompanied by a list of the "hundred most important books of Western Civilization." "More than anything else in my life," the professor told the reporter with finality, "these books have made me all that I am." That was the kind of remark I couldn't ignore. I clipped out the list and kept it for the several months it took me to read all of the titles. Most books, of course, I barely understood. While reading Plato's *Republic,* for instance, I needed to keep looking at the book jacket comments to remind myself what the text was about. Nevertheless, with the special patience and superstition of a scholarship boy, I looked at every word of the text. And by the time I reached the last word, relieved, I convinced myself that I had read *The Republic.* In a ceremony of great pride, I solemnly crossed Plato off my list.

. . . The scholarship boy does not straddle, cannot reconcile, the two great opposing cultures of his life. His success is unromantic and plain. He sits in the classroom and offers those sitting beside him no calming reassurance about their own lives. He sits in the seminar room — a man with brown skin, the son of working-class Mexican immigrant parents. (Addressing the professor at the head of the table, his voice catches with nervousness.) There is no trace of his parents' accent in his speech. Instead he approximates the accents of teachers and classmates. Coming from *him* those sounds seem suddenly odd. Odd too is the effect produced when *he* uses academic jar-

[10]*Dante:* Dante Alighieri, Italian poet (1265–1321); author of the *Divine Comedy.*

[11]*Descartes:* René Descartes, French philosopher and mathematician (1596–1650).

[12]*Engels:* Friedrich Engels, German socialist (1820–1895); coauthor with Karl Marx of the *Communist Manifesto* in 1848.

[13]*James Baldwin:* American novelist and essayist (1924–1987).

gon — bubbles at the tip of his tongue: "*Topos* . . . negative capability . . . vegetation imagery in Shakespearean comedy."[14] He lifts an opinion from Coleridge, takes something else from Frye or Empson or Leavis.[15] He even repeats exactly his professor's earlier comment. All his ideas are clearly borrowed. He seems to have no thought of his own. He chatters while his listeners smile — their look one of disdain.

When he is older and thus when so little of the person he was survives, the scholarship boy makes only too apparent his profound lack of *self*-confidence. This is the conventional assessment that even Richard Hoggart repeats:

> [The scholarship boy] tends to over-stress the importance of examinations, of the piling-up of knowledge and of received opinions. He discovers a technique of apparent learning, of the acquiring of facts rather than of the handling and use of facts. He learns how to receive a purely literate education, one using only a small part of the personality and challenging only a limited area of his being. He begins to see life as a ladder, as a permanent examination with some praise and some further exhortation at each stage. He becomes an expert imbiber and dolerout; his competence will vary, but will rarely be accompanied by genuine enthusiasms. He rarely feels the reality of knowledge, of other men's thoughts and imaginings, on his own pulses . . . He has something of the blinkered pony about him. . . .

But this is criticism more accurate than fair. The scholarship boy is a very bad student. He is the great mimic; a collector of thoughts, not a thinker; the very last person in class who ever feels obliged to have an opinion of his own. In large part, however, the reason he is such a bad student is because he realizes more often and more acutely than most other students — than Hoggart himself—that education requires radical self-reformation. As a very young boy, regarding his parents, as he struggles with an early homework assignment, he knows this too well. That is why he lacks self-assurance. He does not forget that the classroom is responsible for remaking him. He relies on his teacher, depends on all that he hears in the classroom and reads in his books. He becomes in every obvious way the worst student, a dummy mouthing the opinions of others. But he would not be so bad — nor would he become so successful, a *scholarship* boy — if he did not accurately perceive that the best synonym for primary "education" is "imitation."

Like me, Hoggart's imagined scholarship boy spends most of his years in the classroom afraid to long for his past. Only at the very end of his schooling does the boy-man become nostalgic. In this sudden change of heart, Richard Hoggart notes:

[14] *topos . . . negative capability . . . :* Technical terms associated with the study of literary criticism.

[15] *Coleridge . . . Frye . . . Empson . . . Leavis:* Important literary critics.

> He longs for the membership he lost, "he pines for some Nameless Eden where he never was." The nostalgia is the stronger and the more ambiguous because he is really "in quest of his own absconded self yet scared to find it." He both wants to go back and yet thinks he has gone beyond his class, feels himself weighted with knowledge of his own and their situation, which hereafter forbids him the simpler pleasures of his father and mother. . . .

According to Hoggart, the scholarship boy grows nostalgic because he 35
remains the uncertain scholar, bright enough to have moved from his past, yet unable to feel easy, a part of a community of academics.

This analysis, however, only partially suggests what happened to me in my last years as a graduate student. When I traveled to London to write a dissertation on English Renaissance literature, I was finally confident of membership in a "community of scholars." But the pleasure that confidence gave me faded rapidly. After only two or three months in the reading room of the British Museum, it became clear that I had joined a lonely community. Around me each day were dour faces eclipsed by large piles of books. There were the regulars, like the old couple who arrived every morning, each holding a loop of the shopping bag which contained all their notes. And there was the historian who chattered madly to herself. ("Oh dear! Oh! Now, what's this? What? Oh, my!") There were also the faces of young men and women worn by long study. And everywhere eyes turned away the moment our glance accidentally met. Some persons I sat beside day after day, yet we passed silently at the end of the day, strangers. Still, we were united by a common respect for the written word and for scholarship. We did form a union, though one in which we remained distant from one another.

More profound and unsettling was the bond I recognized with those writers whose books I consulted. Whenever I opened a text that hadn't been used for years, I realized that my special interests and skills united me to a mere handful of academics. We formed an exclusive—eccentric!—society, separated from others who would never care or be able to share our concerns. (The pages I turned were stiff like layers of dead skin.) I began to wonder: Who, beside my dissertation director and a few faculty members, would ever read what I wrote? and: Was my dissertation much more than an act of social withdrawal? These questions went unanswered in the silence of the Museum reading room. They remained to trouble me after I'd leave the library each afternoon and feel myself shy—unsteady, speaking simple sentences at the grocer's or the butcher's on my way back to my bed-sitter.[16]

Meanwhile my file cards accumulated. A professional, I knew exactly how to search a book for pertinent information. I could quickly assess and summarize the usability of the many books I consulted. But whenever I started to write, I knew too much (and not enough) to be able to write anything but sentences that were overly cautious, timid, strained brittle un-

[16]*bed-sitter:* A one-room apartment.

der the heavy weight of footnotes and qualifications. I seemed unable to dare a passionate statement. I felt drawn by professionalism to the edge of sterility, capable of no more than pedantic, lifeless, unassailable prose.

Then nostalgia began.

40 After years spent unwilling to admit its attractions, I gestured nostalgically toward the past. I yearned for that time when I had not been so alone. I became impatient with books. I wanted experience more immediate. I feared the library's silence. I silently scorned the gray, timid faces around me. I grew to hate the growing pages of my dissertation on genre[17] and Renaissance literature. (In my mind I heard relatives laughing as they tried to make sense of its title.) I wanted something—I couldn't say exactly what. I told myself that I wanted a more passionate life. And a life less thoughtful. And above all, I wanted to be less alone. One day I heard some Spanish academics whispering back and forth to each other, and their sounds seemed ghostly voices recalling my life. Yearning became preoccupation then. Boyhood memories beckoned, flooded my mind. (Laughing intimate voices. Bounding up the front steps of the porch. A sudden embrace inside the door.)

For weeks after, I turned to books by educational experts. I needed to learn how far I had moved from my past—to determine how fast I would be able to recover something of it once again. But I found little. Only a chapter in a book by Richard Hoggart . . . I left the reading room and the circle of faces.

I came home. After the year in England, I spent three summer months living with my mother and father, relieved by how easy it was to be home. It no longer seemed very important to me that we had little to say. I felt easy sitting and eating and walking with them. I watched them, nevertheless, looking for evidence of those elastic, sturdy strands that bind generations in a web of inheritance. I thought as I watched my mother one night: of course a friend had been right when she told me that I gestured and laughed just like my mother. Another time I saw for myself: my father's eyes were much like my own, constantly watchful.

But after the early relief, this return, came suspicion, nagging until I realized that I had not neatly sidestepped the impact of schooling. My desire to do so was precisely the measure of how much I remained an academic. *Negatively* (for that is how this idea first occurred to me): my need to think so much and so abstractly about my parents and our relationship was in itself an indication of my long education. My father and mother did not pass their time thinking about the cultural meanings of their experience. It was I who described their daily lives with airy ideas. And yet, *positively:* the ability to consider experience so abstractly allowed me to shape into desire what would

[17]*genre:* A class or category of artistic work; e.g., the genre of poetry.

otherwise have remained indefinite, meaningless longing in the British Museum. If, because of my schooling, I had grown culturally separated from my parents, my education finally had given me ways of speaking and caring about that fact.

My best teachers in college and graduate school, years before, had tried to prepare me for this conclusion, I think, when they discussed texts of aristocratic pastoral literature. Faithfully, I wrote down all that they said. I memorized it: "The praise of the unlettered by the highly educated is one of the primary themes of 'elitist' literature." But, "the importance of the praise given the unsolitary, richly passionate and spontaneous life is that it simultaneously reflects the value of a reflective life." I heard it all. But there was no way for any of it to mean very much to me. I was a scholarship boy at the time, busily laddering my way up the rungs of education. To pass an examination, I copied down exactly what my teachers told me. It would require many more years of schooling (an inevitable miseducation) in which I came to trust the silence of reading and the habit of abstracting from immediate experience — moving away from a life of closeness and immediacy I remembered with my parents, growing older — before I turned unafraid to desire the past, and thereby achieved what had eluded me for so long — the end of education.

Engaging the Text

1. How does education affect Rodriguez's relationship to his family, his past, and his culture? Do you agree with him that education requires "radical self-reformation" (para. 33)?
2. What is a "scholarship boy"? Why does Rodriguez consider himself a bad student despite his academic success?
3. What happens to Rodriguez in London? Why does he ultimately abandon his studies there?
4. What drives Rodriguez to succeed? What does education represent to him? To his father and mother?
5. What is Rodriguez's final assessment of what he has gained and lost through his education? Do you agree with his analysis?

Exploring Connections

6. Compare Rodriguez's attitude toward education and success with that of Mike Rose (p. 33) in "'I Just Wanna Be Average.'"
7. Read "Stephen Cruz" (p. 460) and compare his attitudes toward education and success with those of Rodriguez.
8. To what extent do Rodriguez's experiences as a "scholarship boy" confirm or complicate Jean Anyon's analysis (p. 45) of the relationship between social class, education, and success?

Extending the Critical Context

9. What are your personal motives for academic success? How do they compare with those of Rodriguez?
10. Today many college students find that they're following in the footsteps of family members — not breaking ground as Rodriguez did. What special difficulties do such second- or third-generation college students face?

Para Teresa[1]

Inés Hernández-Ávila

This poem explores and attempts to resolve an old conflict between its speaker and her schoolmate, two Chicanas at "Alamo which-had-to-be-its-name" Elementary School who have radically different ideas about what education means and does. Inés Hernández-Ávila (b. 1947) is a professor of Native American studies at the University of California, Davis. This poem appeared in her collection Con Razón, Corazón *(1987). Her forthcoming collection of poetry is entitled* Wardance/Danza Guerrera: For all the 'skins and all the Meskins *(expected in 1995).*

A tí-Teresa Compean
Te dedico las palabras estás
que explotan de mi corazón[2]

That day during lunch hour
at Alamo which-had-to-be-its-name
Elementary
my dear raza
That day in the bathroom
Door guarded
Myself cornered
I was accused by you, Teresa
Tú y las demás de tus amigas
Pachucas todas
Eran Uds. cinco.[3]

[1]For Teresa. [Author's note]

[2]To you, Teresa Compean, I dedicate these words that explode from my heart. [Author's note]

[3]You and the rest of your friends, all Pachucas, there were five of you. [Author's note]

Me gritaban que porque me creía tan grande[4]
What was I trying to do, you growled
Show you up?
Make the teachers like me, pet me,
Tell me what a credit to my people I was?
I was playing right into their hands, you challenged
And you would have none of it.
I was to stop.

I was to be like you
I was to play your game of deadly defiance
Arrogance, refusal to submit.
The game in which the winner takes nothing
Asks for nothing
Never lets his weaknesses show.

But I didn't understand.
My fear salted with confusion
Charged me to explain to you
I did nothing *for the teachers.*
I studied for my parents and for my grandparents
Who cut out honor roll lists
Whenever their nietos'[5] names appeared
For my shy mother who mastered her terror
to demand her place in mother's clubs
For my carpenter-father who helped me patiently with my math.
For my abuelos que me regalaron lápices en la Navidad[6]
And for myself.

Porque reconocí en aquel entonces
una verdad tremenda
que me hizo a mi un rebelde
Aunque tú no te habías dadocuenta[7]
We were not inferior
You and I, y las demás de tus amigas
Y los demás de nuestra gente[8]
I knew it the way I knew I was alive
We were good, honorable, brave
Genuine, loyal, strong

[4]You were screaming at me, asking me why I thought I was so hot. [Author's note]

[5]Grandchildren's. [Author's note]

[6]Grandparents who gave me gifts of pencils at Christmas. [Author's note]

[7]Because I recognized a great truth then that made me a rebel, even though you didn't realize it. [Author's note]

[8]And the rest of your friends / And the rest of our people. [Author's note]

And smart.
Mine was a deadly game of defiance, also.
My contest was to prove
beyond any doubt
that we were not only equal but superior to them.
That was why I studied.
If I could do it, we all could.

You let me go then.
Your friends unblocked the way
I who-did-not-know-how-to-fight
was not made to engage with you-who-grew-up-fighting
Tu y yo, Teresa[9]
We went in different directions
Pero fuimos juntas.[10]

In sixth grade we did not understand
Uds. with the teased, dyed-black-but-reddening hair,
Full petticoats, red lipsticks
and sweaters with the sleeves
pushed up
Y yo conformándome con lo que deseaba mi mamá[11]
Certainly never allowed to dye, to tease, to paint myself
I did not accept your way of anger,
Your judgements
You did not accept mine.

But now in 1975, when I am twenty-eight
Teresa Compean
I remember you.
Y sabes —
Te comprendo,
Es más, te respeto.
Y, si me permites,
Te nombro — "hermana."[12]

[9]You and I. [Author's note]

[10]But we were together. [Author's note]

[11]And I conforming to my mother's wishes. [Author's note]

[12]And do you know what, I understand you. Even more, I respect you. And, if you permit me, I name you my sister. [Author's note]

Engaging the Text

1. The speaker says that she didn't understand Teresa at the time of the incident she describes. What didn't she understand, and why? How have her views of

Teresa and of herself changed since then? What seems to have brought about this change?

2. What attitudes toward school and the majority culture do Teresa and the speaker represent? What about the speaker's family? In what way are both girls playing a game of "deadly defiance"? What arguments can you make for each form of rebellion?
3. Why do you think Hernández-Ávila wrote this poem in both Spanish and English? What does doing so say about the speaker's life? About her change of attitude toward Teresa?

Exploring Connections

4. Compare and contrast the speaker's attitude toward school and family with those of Richard Rodriguez (p. 61). What motivates each of them? What tensions do they feel?
5. Write a dialogue between the speaker of this poem, who wants to excel, and Ken Harvey, the boy whom Mike Rose said just wanted to be average (p. 33). Explore the uncertainties, pressures, and desires that these students felt. In what ways are these two apparently contrasting students actually similar?

Extending the Critical Context

6. Was there a person or group you disliked, feared, or fought with in elementary school? Has your understanding of your adversary or of your own motives changed since them? If so, what brought about this change?

Learning to Read

Malcolm X

Born Malcolm Little on May 19, 1925, Malcolm X was one of the most articulate and powerful leaders of Black America during the 1960s. A street hustler convicted of robbery in 1946, he spent seven years in prison, where he educated himself and became a disciple of Elijah Muhammad, founder of the Nation of Islam. In the days of the civil rights movement, Malcolm X emerged as the leading spokesman for Black separatism, a philosophy that urged Black Americans to cut political, social, and economic ties with the white community. After a pilgrimage to Mecca, the capital of the Muslim world, in 1964, he became an orthodox Muslim, adopted the Muslim name El Hajj Malik El-Shabazz, and distanced himself from the teachings of the

Black Muslims. He was assassinated in 1965. In the following excerpt from his autobiography (1965) coauthored with Alex Haley and published the year of his death, Malcolm X describes his self-education.

It was because of my letters that I happened to stumble upon starting to acquire some kind of a homemade education.

I became increasingly frustrated at not being able to express what I wanted to convey in letters that I wrote, especially those to Mr. Elijah Muhammad.[1] In the street, I had been the most articulate hustler out there — I had commanded attention when I said something. But now, trying to write simple English, I not only wasn't articulate, I wasn't even functional. How would I sound writing in slang, the way I would *say* it, something such as, "Look, daddy, let me pull your coat about a cat, Elijah Muhammad — "

Many who today hear me somewhere in person, or on television, or those who read something I've said, will think I went to school far beyond the eighth grade. This impression is due entirely to my prison studies.

It had really begun back in the Charlestown Prison, when Bimbi[2] first made me feel envy of his stock of knowledge. Bimbi had always taken charge of any conversations he was in, and I had tried to emulate him. But every book I picked up had few sentences which didn't contain anywhere from one to nearly all of the words that might as well have been in Chinese. When I just skipped those words, of course, I really ended up with little idea of what the book said. So I had come to the Norfolk Prison Colony still going through only book-reading motions. Pretty soon, I would have quit even these motions, unless I had received the motivation that I did.

I saw that the best thing I could do was get hold of a dictionary — to 5
study, to learn some words. I was lucky enough to reason also that I should try to improve my penmanship. It was sad. I couldn't even write in a straight line. It was both ideas together that moved me to request a dictionary along with some tablets and pencils from the Norfolk Prison Colony school.

I spent two days just riffling uncertainly through the dictionary's pages. I'd never realized so many words existed! I didn't know *which* words I needed to learn. Finally, just to start some kind of action, I began copying.

In my slow, painstaking, ragged handwriting, I copied into my tablet everything printed on that first page, down to the punctuation marks.

I believe it took me a day. Then, aloud, I read back, to myself, everything I'd written on the tablet. Over and over, aloud, to myself, I read my own handwriting.

[1] *Elijah Muhammad:* American clergyman (1897–1975); leader of the Nation of Islam, 1935–1975.

[2] *Bimbi:* A fellow inmate whose encyclopedic learning and verbal facility greatly impressed Malcolm X.

I woke up the next morning, thinking about those words — immensely proud to realize that not only had I written so much at one time, but I'd written words that I never knew were in the world. Moreover, with a little effort, I also could remember what many of these words meant. I reviewed the words whose meanings I didn't remember. Funny thing, from the dictionary first page right now, that "aardvark" springs to my mind. The dictionary had a picture of it, a long-tailed, long-eared, burrowing African mammal, which lives off termites caught by sticking out its tongue as an anteater does for ants.

I was so fascinated that I went on — I copied the dictionary's next page. And the same experience came when I studied that. With every succeeding page, I also learned of people and places and events from history. Actually the dictionary is like a miniature encyclopedia. Finally the dictionary's A section had filled a whole tablet — and I went on into the B's. That was the way I started copying what eventually became the entire dictionary. It went a lot faster after so much practice helped me to pick up handwriting speed. Between what I wrote in my tablet, and writing letters, during the rest of my time in prison I would guess I wrote a million words.

I suppose it was inevitable that as my word-base broadened, I could for the first time pick up a book and read and now begin to understand what the book was saying. Anyone who has read a great deal can imagine the new world that opened. Let me tell you something: from then until I left that prison, in every free moment I had, if I was not reading in the library, I was reading on my bunk. You couldn't have gotten me out of books with a wedge. Between Mr. Muhammad's teachings, my correspondence, my visitors, . . . and my reading of books, months passed without my even thinking about being imprisoned. In fact, up to then, I never had been so truly free in my life.

The Norfolk Prison Colony's library was in the school building. A variety of classes was taught there by instructors who came from such places as Harvard and Boston universities. The weekly debates between inmate teams were also held in the school building. You would be astonished to know how worked up convict debaters and audiences would get over subjects like "Should Babies Be Fed Milk?"

Available on the prison library's shelves were books on just about every general subject. Much of the big private collection that Parkhurst[3] had willed to the prison was still in crates and boxes in the back of the library — thousands of old books. Some of them looked ancient: covers faded, old-time parchment-looking binding. Parkhurst . . . seemed to have been principally interested in history and religion. He had the money and the special interest to have a lot of books that you wouldn't have in a general circulation. Any college library would have been lucky to get that collection.

[3]*Parkhurst:* Charles Henry Parkhurst (1842–1933); American clergyman, reformer, and president of the Society for the Prevention of Crime.

As you can imagine, especially in a prison where there was heavy emphasis on rehabilitation, an inmate was smiled upon if he demonstrated an unusually intense interest in books. There was a sizable number of well-read inmates, especially the popular debaters. Some were said by many to be practically walking encyclopedias. They were almost celebrities. No university would ask any student to devour literature as I did when this new world opened to me, of being able to read and *understand.*

15 I read more in my room than in the library itself. An inmate who was known to read a lot could check out more than the permitted maximum number of books. I preferred reading in the total isolation of my own room.

When I had progressed to really serious reading, every night at about ten P.M. I would be outraged with the "lights out." It always seemed to catch me right in the middle of something engrossing.

Fortunately, right outside my door was a corridor light that cast a glow into my room. The glow was enough to read by, once my eyes adjusted to it. So when "lights out" came, I would sit on the floor where I could continue reading in that glow.

At one-hour intervals the night guards paced past every room. Each time I heard the approaching footsteps, I jumped into bed and feigned sleep. And as soon as the guard passed, I got back out of bed onto the floor area of that light-glow, where I would read for another fifty-eight minutes—until the guard approached again. That went on until three or four every morning. Three or four hours of sleep a night was enough for me. Often in the years in the streets I had slept less than that.

The teachings of Mr. Muhammad stressed how history had been "whitened"—when white men had written history books, the black man simply had been left out. Mr. Muhammad couldn't have said anything that would have struck me much harder. I had never forgotten how when my class, me and all of those whites, had studied seventh-grade United States history back in Mason, the history of the Negro had been covered in one paragraph, and the teacher had gotten a big laugh with his joke, "Negroes' feet are so big that when they walk, they leave a hole in the ground."

20 This is one reason why Mr. Muhammad's teachings spread so swiftly all over the United States, among *all* Negroes, whether or not they became followers of Mr. Muhammad. The teachings ring true—to every Negro. You can hardly show me a black adult in America—or a white one, for that matter—who knows from the history books anything like the truth about the black man's role. In my own case, once I heard of the "glorious history of the black man," I took special pains to hunt in the library for books that would inform me on details about black history.

I can remember accurately the very first set of books that really impressed me. I have since bought that set of books and I have it at home for my children to read as they grow up. It's called *Wonders of the World.* It's full of pictures of archeological finds, statues that depict, usually, non-European people.

I found books like Will Durant's[4] *Story of Civilization.* I read H. G. Wells'[5] *Outline of History. Souls of Black Folk* by W. E. B. Du Bois[6] gave me a glimpse into the black people's history before they came to this country. Carter G. Woodson's[7] *Negro History* opened my eyes about black empires before the black slave was brought to the United States, and the early Negro struggles for freedom.

J. A. Rogers'[8] three volumes of *Sex and Race* told about race-mixing before Christ's time; and Aesop being a black man who told fables; about Egypt's Pharaohs; about the great Coptic Christian Empires;[9] about Ethiopia, the earth's oldest continuous black civilization, as China is the oldest continuous civilization.

Mr. Muhammad's teaching about how the white man had been created led me to *Findings In Genetics* by Gregor Mendel.[10] (The dictionary's G section was where I had learned what "genetics" meant.) I really studied this book by the Austrian monk. Reading it over and over, especially certain sections, helped me to understand that if you started with a black man, a white man could be produced; but starting with a white man, you never could produce a black man — because the white chromosome is recessive. And since no one disputes that there was but one Original Man, the conclusion is clear.

During the last year or so, in the *New York Times,* Arnold Toynbee[11] 25
used the word "bleached" in describing the white man. His words were: "White (i.e., bleached) human beings of North European origin. . . ." Toynbee also referred to the European geographic area as only a peninsula of Asia. He said there is no such thing as Europe. And if you look at the globe, you will see for yourself that America is only an extension of Asia. (But at the same time Toynbee is among those who have helped to bleach history. He has written that Africa was the only continent that produced no history. He won't write that again. Every day now, the truth is coming to light.)

[4]*Will Durant:* American author and historian (1885–1981).

[5]*H. G. Wells:* English novelist and historian (1866–1946).

[6]*W. E. B. Du Bois:* William Edward Burghardt Du Bois, distinguished Black scholar, author, and activist (1868–1963). Du Bois was the first director of the NAACP and was an important figure in the Harlem Renaissance; his best-known book is *Souls of Black Folk.*

[7]*Carter G. Woodson:* Distinguished African American historian (1875–1950); considered the father of Black history.

[8]*J. A. Rogers:* African American historian and journalist (1883–1965).

[9]*Coptic Christian Empire:* The domain of the Coptic Church, a native Egyptian Christian church that retains elements of its African origins.

[10]*Gregor Mendel:* Austrian monk, botanist, and pioneer in genetic research (1822–1884).

[11]*Arnold Toynbee:* English historian (1889–1975).

I never will forget how shocked I was when I began reading about slavery's total horror. It made such an impact upon me that it later became one of my favorite subjects when I became a minister of Mr. Muhammad's. The world's most monstrous crime, the sin and the blood on the white man's hands, are almost impossible to believe. Books like the one by Frederick Olmsted[12] opened my eyes to the horrors suffered when the slave was landed in the United States. The European woman, Fanny Kemble,[13] who had married a Southern white slaveowner, described how human beings were degraded. Of course I read *Uncle Tom's Cabin.*[14] In fact, I believe that's the only novel I have ever read since I started serious reading.

Parkhurst's collection also contained some bound pamphlets of the Abolitionist[15] Anti-Slavery Society of New England. I read descriptions of atrocities, saw those illustrations of black slave women tied up and flogged with whips; of black mothers watching their babies being dragged off, never to be seen by their mothers again; of dogs after slaves, and of the fugitive slave catchers, evil white men with whips and clubs and chains and guns. I read about the slave preacher Nat Turner, who put the fear of God into the white slavemaster. Nat Turner wasn't going around preaching pie-in-the-sky and "non-violent" freedom for the black man. There in Virginia one night in 1831, Nat and seven other slaves started out at his master's home and through the night they went from one plantation "big house" to the next, killing, until by the next morning 57 white people were dead and Nat had about 70 slaves following him. White people, terrified for their lives, fled from their homes, locked themselves up in public buildings, hid in the woods, and some even left the state. A small army of soldiers took two months to catch and hang Nat Turner. Somewhere I have read where Nat Turner's example is said to have inspired John Brown[16] to invade Virginia and attack Harpers Ferry nearly thirty years later, with thirteen white men and five Negroes.

I read Herodotus,[17] "the father of History," or, rather, I read about him. And I read the histories of various nations, which opened my eyes gradually, then wider and wider, to how the whole world's white men had indeed acted like devils, pillaging and raping and bleeding and draining the whole world's non-white people. I remember, for instance, books such as Will Durant's

[12]*Frederick Olmsted:* Frederick Law Olmsted (1822–1903), American landscape architect, city planner, and opponent of slavery.

[13]*Fanny Kemble:* Frances Anne Kemble, English actress and author (1809–1893); best known for her autobiographical *Journal of a Residence on a Georgia Plantation,* published in 1863 to win support in Britain for the abolitionist cause.

[14]*Uncle Tom's Cabin:* Harriet Beecher Stowe's 1852 antislavery novel.

[15]*abolitionist:* Advocating the prohibition of slavery.

[16]*John Brown:* American abolitionist (1800–1859); leader of an attack on Harpers Ferry, West Virginia, in 1859.

[17]*Herodotus:* Early Greek historian (484?–425? B.C.).

The Story of Oriental Civilization, and Mahatma Gandhi's[18] accounts of the struggle to drive the British out of India.

Book after book showed me how the white man had brought upon the world's black, brown, red, and yellow peoples every variety of the suffering of exploitation. I saw how since the sixteenth century, the so-called "Christian trader" white man began to ply the seas in his lust for Asian and African empires, and plunder, and power. I read, I saw, how the white man never has gone among the non-white peoples bearing the Cross in the true manner and spirit of Christ's teachings — meek, humble, and Christlike.

30 I perceived, as I read, how the collective white man had been actually nothing but a piratical opportunist who used Faustian machinations[19] to make his own Christianity his initial wedge in criminal conquests. First, always "religiously," he branded "heathen" and "pagan" labels upon ancient non-white cultures and civilizations. The stage thus set, he then turned upon his non-white victims his weapons of war.

I read how, entering India — half a *billion* deeply religious brown people — the British white man, by 1759, through promises, trickery, and manipulations, controlled much of India through Great Britain's East India Company. The parasitical British administration kept tentacling out to half of the sub-continent. In 1857, some of the desperate people of India finally mutinied — and, excepting the African slave trade, nowhere has history recorded any more unnecessary bestial and ruthless human carnage than the British suppression of the non-white Indian people.

Over 115 million African blacks — close to the 1930's population of the United States — were murdered or enslaved during the slave trade. And I read how when the slave market was glutted, the cannibalistic white powers of Europe next carved up, as their colonies, the richest areas of the black continent. And Europe's chancelleries for the next century played a chess game of naked exploitation and power from Cape Horn to Cairo.

Ten guards and the warden couldn't have torn me out of those books. Not even Elijah Muhammad could have been more eloquent than those books were in providing indisputable proof that the collective white man had acted like a devil in virtually every contact he had with the world's collective non-white man. I listen today to the radio, and watch television, and read the headlines about the collective white man's fear and tension concerning China. When the white man professes ignorance about why the Chinese hate him so, my mind can't help flashing back to what I read, there in prison, about how the blood forebears of this same white man raped China at a time when China was trusting and helpless. Those original white "Christian traders" sent into China millions of pounds of opium. By 1839, so many

[18]*Mahatma Gandhi:* Hindu religious leader, social reformer, and advocate of nonviolence (1869–1948).

[19]*Faustian machinations:* Evil plots or schemes. Faust was a legendary character who sold his soul to the devil for knowledge and power.

of the Chinese were addicts that China's desperate government destroyed twenty thousand chests of opium. The first Opium War[20] was promptly declared by the white man. Imagine! Declaring *war* upon someone who objects to being narcotized! The Chinese were severely beaten, with Chinese-invented gunpowder.

The Treaty of Nanking made China pay the British white man for the destroyed opium; forced open China's major ports to British trade; forced China to abandon Hong Kong; fixed China's import tariffs so low that cheap British articles soon flooded in, maiming China's industrial development.

After a second Opium War, the Tientsin Treaties legalized the ravaging opium trade, legalized a British-French-American control of China's customs. China tried delaying that Treaty's ratification; Peking was looted and burned.

"Kill the foreign white devils!" was the 1901 Chinese war cry in the Boxer Rebellion.[21] Losing again, this time the Chinese were driven from Peking's choicest areas. The vicious, arrogant white man put up the famous signs, "Chinese and dogs not allowed."

Red China after World War II closed its doors to the Western white world. Massive Chinese agricultural, scientific, and industrial efforts are described in a book that *Life* magazine recently published. Some observers inside Red China have reported that the world never has known such a hate-white campaign as is now going on in this non-white country where, present birth-rates continuing, in fifty more years Chinese will be half the earth's population. And it seems that some Chinese chickens will soon come home to roost, with China's recent successful nuclear tests.

Let us face reality. We can see in the United Nations a new world order being shaped, along color lines — an alliance among the non-white nations. America's U.N. Ambassador Adlai Stevenson[22] complained not long ago that in the United Nations "a skin game"[23] was being played. He was right. He was facing reality. A "skin game" *is* being played. But Ambassador Stevenson sounded like Jesse James accusing the marshal of carrying a gun. Because who in the world's history ever has played a worse "skin game" than the white man?

Mr. Muhammad, to whom I was writing daily, had no idea of what a new world had opened up to me through my efforts to document his teachings in books.

[20] *Opium War:* 1839–1842 war between Britain and China that ended with China's cession of Hong Kong to British rule.

[21] *Boxer Rebellion:* The 1898–1900 uprising by members of a secret Chinese society who opposed foreign influence in Chinese affairs.

[22] *Adlai Stevenson:* American politician (1900–1965); Democratic candidate for the presidency in 1952 and 1956.

[23] *skin game:* A dishonest or fraudulent scheme, business operation, or trick, with the added reference in this instance to skin color.

When I discovered philosophy, I tried to touch all the landmarks of 40
philosophical development. Gradually, I read most of the old philosophers, Occidental and Oriental. The Oriental philosophers were the ones I came to prefer; finally, my impression was that most Occidental philosophy had largely been borrowed from the Oriental thinkers. Socrates, for instance, traveled in Egypt. Some sources even say that Socrates was initiated into some of the Egyptian mysteries. Obviously Socrates got some of his wisdom among the East's wise men.

I have often reflected upon the new vistas that reading opened to me. I knew right there in prison that reading had changed forever the course of my life. As I see it today, the ability to read awoke inside me some long dormant craving to be mentally alive. I certainly wasn't seeking any degree, the way a college confers a status symbol upon its students. My homemade education gave me, with every additional book that I read, a little bit more sensitivity to the deafness, dumbness, and blindness that was afflicting the black race in America. Not long ago, an English writer telephoned me from London, asking questions. One was, "What's your alma mater?" I told him, "Books." You will never catch me with a free fifteen minutes in which I'm not studying something I feel might be able to help the black man.

Yesterday I spoke in London, and both ways on the plane across the Atlantic I was studying a document about how the United Nations proposes to insure the human rights of the oppressed minorities of the world. The American black man is the world's most shameful case of minority oppression. What makes the black man think of himself as only an internal United States issue is just a catch-phrase, two words, "civil rights." How is the black man going to get "civil rights" before first he wins his *human* rights? If the American black man will start thinking about his *human* rights, and then start thinking of himself as part of one of the world's great peoples, he will see he has a case for the United Nations.

I can't think of a better case! Four hundred years of black blood and sweat invested here in America, and the white man still has the black man begging for what every immigrant fresh off the ship can take for granted the minute he walks down the gangplank.

But I'm digressing. I told the Englishman that my alma mater was books, a good library. Every time I catch a plane, I have with me a book that I want to read — and that's a lot of books these days. If I weren't out here every day battling the white man, I could spend the rest of my life reading, just satisfying my curiosity — because you can hardly mention anything I'm not curious about. I don't think anybody ever got more out of going to prison than I did. In fact, prison enabled me to study far more intensively than I would have if my life had gone differently and I had attended some college. I imagine that one of the biggest troubles with colleges is there are too many distractions, too much panty-raiding, fraternities, and boola-boola and all of that. Where else but in a prison could I have attacked my ignorance by being able to study intensely sometimes as much as fifteen hours a day?

ENGAGING THE TEXT

1. What motivated Malcolm X to educate himself?
2. What kind of knowledge did Malcolm X gain by learning to read? How did this knowledge free or empower him?
3. Would it be possible for public schools to empower students in the way that Malcolm X's self-education empowered him? If so, how? If not, why not?
4. Some readers are offended by the strength of Malcolm X's accusations and by his grouping of all members of a given race into "collectives." Given the history of racial injustice he recounts here, do you feel he is justified in taking such a position?

EXPLORING CONNECTIONS

5. Compare and contrast Malcolm X's views on the meaning and purpose of education — or on the value and nature of reading — with those of Richard Rodriguez (p. 61). How can you account for the differences in their attitudes?
6. Imagine that Theodore Sizer (p. 20), Mike Rose (p. 33), Richard Rodriguez (p. 61), and Malcolm X have been appointed to redesign American education. Working in groups, role-play a meeting in which the committee attempts to reach consensus on its recommendations. Report to the class the results of the committee's deliberations and discuss them.

EXTENDING THE CRITICAL CONTEXT

7. Survey some typical elementary or secondary school textbooks to test the currency of Malcolm X's charge that the educational establishment presents a "whitened" view of America. What view of America is presently being projected in public school history and social science texts?
8. Go to the library and read one page of the dictionary chosen at random. Study the meanings of any unfamiliar words and follow up on the information on your page by consulting encyclopedias, books, or articles. Let yourself be guided by chance and by your interests. After you've tried this experiment, discuss in class the benefits and drawbacks of an unsystematic self-education like Malcolm X's.

Higher Education: Colder by Degrees

MYRA SADKER AND DAVID SADKER

Following the civil rights movement, race- and gender-segregated colleges and universities across the country began to integrate their student populations. After decades of "separate-but-equal" schooling, women and ethnic minority groups were eager to compete as equals in college classrooms.

But recently, critics have questioned the effectiveness and equity of institutions that claim to offer color- and gender-blind education. In this selection from Failing at Fairness: How America's Schools Cheat Girls *(1994), the Sadkers document pervasive sexism in American colleges, from gender bias in the lecture hall to acquaintance rape on fraternity row. Professors of education at The American University in Washington, D.C., Myra Sadker (b. 1943) and David Sadker (b. 1942) have coauthored several publications on sexism in education.*

The Divided Campus

Graduation day is a family milestone, official recognition of full and active partnership in the American Dream. Parents crowd the bookstore to buy sweatshirts and baseball caps emblazoned with school insignia. Even the car shows its colors with a college decal affixed to the window, proclaiming to all the world previous accomplishments and future promise. Amid all this celebration it is easy to forget that little more than a century ago higher education was mainly a man's world.

In the late 1800s college was the place to be for rich young men; it was a source of social polish and a rollicking good time. Informal sporting events and athletic competitions were harbingers of today's lucrative college football and basketball seasons. Fraternities created a world without adult rules, a haven for males in their late teens and early twenties who drank, gambled, and talked about loose women. While a few focused on academics, most worked at fitting in and getting along, the marks of a successful student. In the vernacular of the 1800s, working to win the approval of the professor by class participation was ridiculed as "sticking your neck out" or "fishing." Cheaters were shielded by fraternities and secret societies, and peer loyalty was the measure of integrity.[1]

The first women to enter this male-ordered campus were venturing into unmapped terrain. True pioneers who defied conventions to settle in hostile territory, they were not greeted with open arms or the hospitality accorded welcome guests. At the University of Michigan after the Civil War, women could not join the campus newspaper or college yearbook staffs. Michigaum, the prestigious honor society, closed its doors to females and kept the portals shut throughout the century. Cornell's response to the newcomers was undisguised disgust, and the school excluded them from clubs and social activities. Even speaking to women on campus was an infraction of fraternity rules. At Wesleyan, male students beat other men who talked to women.

When they graduated, these pioneering women cultivated new careers.

[1]An interesting and lively discussion of this period is provided in Helen Lefkowitz Horowitz, *Campus Life: Undergraduate Cultures from the End of the Eighteenth Century to the Present* (New York: Alfred A. Knopf, 1987). [Authors' note]

Many worked in elementary schools or the recently created high schools. By 1918, 84 percent of the nation's teaching force were women, and in this profession they could earn more than unskilled men and could support themselves. Like Jane Addams[2] and her Hull House colleagues, some women became settlement workers in the new profession of social work, while others studied to become doctors. As this wave of college women surged into emerging careers, they often abandoned the traditional life-style of marriage and motherhood.

5 Many college administrators were not ecstatic about these new students. At Stanford, 102 men and 98 women graduated in 1901, but the women received more honors and awards. In 1904, Stanford corrected the problem by setting a quota for future enrollments of three males for every female admitted, a policy maintained until 1933.[3] But the rate of women flooding the nation's colleges could not be halted. In 1870, two out of three postsecondary institutions turned women away; only thirty years later, more than two out of three admitted them; and by 1900, 19 percent of college graduates were female. But as their numbers increased, they became more conventional and less courageous. . . .

The trickle of female pioneers fighting for admission to male universities in the 1870s eventually became a tidal wave. A century later most remaining holdouts, including many Ivy League schools, finally capitulated and opened their doors. Today, women are the majority, 53 percent of the nation's postsecondary students, and the barriers once separating the sexes seem to have been demolished. But appearances deceive. The brick walls have been replaced with those of glass; the partitions are so transparent that they are all but invisible. The campus remains a divided one; it channels women and men into different educations that lead to separate and unequal futures.

The "hard" sciences are still housed on the male side of the glass wall. Almost 70 percent of today's students who major in physics, chemistry, and computer science are male. Engineering tops all of these, however, with 85 percent of bachelor degrees going to men. The overwhelmingly male majority extends beyond the hard sciences and engineering to theology (75 percent male), philosophy (64 percent), agriculture (69 percent), and architecture (61 percent).[4]

[2] *Jane Addams:* American reformer (1860–1935), author, suffragist, and recipient of the 1931 Nobel Peace Prize. In 1889, with Ellen Gates Starr, Addams founded Hull House, a community center for Chicago's poor which became an internationally recognized symbol of social reform.

[3] Miriam K. Chamberlain (ed.), *Women in Academe: Progress and Prospects* (New York: Russell Sage Foundation, 1988), p. 4. [Authors' note]

[4] Thomas Snyder and Charlene Hoffman, *Digest of Education Statistics 1992* (Washington, DC: U.S. Department of Education, 1992), pp. 275, 277, 295, 296. Michael R. Ransom, "Gender Segregation by Field in Higher Education," *Research in Higher Education* 31:5 (October 5, 1990), pp. 477–94. Judith G. Touchton and Lynne Davis with the assistance of Vivian Parker Makosky, *Fact Book on Women in Higher Education* (New York: Macmillan, 1991). [Authors' note]

But it would be a mistake to view the male campus only in terms of academic courses because the heart of extracurricular life beats there, too. Male athletes enjoy an impressive array of "perks," including special meal allowances, exclusive living arrangements, lucrative scholarships, and at all too many institutions, academic dispensation when studies and game schedules conflict. This side of the campus also has valuable real estate, precious land that was turned over to fraternity row. In fact, this is the part of the campus where the lion's share of financial and educational resources are invested.

On the other side of the glass wall, the "soft" sciences and humanities are taught to classes populated mostly by women. On this second campus, females receive 90 percent of the bachelor degrees in home economics, 84 percent in health sciences, and 67 percent in general liberal arts. Here women are awarded three out of every four degrees in education and foreign language, and two out of three in psychology, communications, and the performing arts. On the women's side of the glass wall, class schedules are less likely to include advanced courses in mathematics, science, and technology. If graduation requirements insist on science courses, women typically opt for biology rather than physics or chemistry. Science, after all, is what many worked hard to avoid in high school. Although they pay the same tuition, study in the same libraries, reside in the same dorms, and receive diplomas with the name of the same college, the female students are less likely to take the courses that lead to lucrative and prestigious careers.

Women who move on to graduate and professional schools, where they 10
earn half as many doctorates as men, also discover the divided campus:[5] men receive 75 percent of the doctoral degrees in business and 91 percent of those in engineering, but women acquire more doctorates than men in education. Despite this, three out of every four professors are male, and nine out of ten are white and non-Hispanic. Even prestigious Ivy League schools, the ones with their pick of the most talented women, seem unable to find them. Only 10 percent to 13 percent of Ivy League faculties are female, and they earn on average almost $14,000 less annually than their male colleagues.[6] Nationally, 68 percent of male faculty members have tenure, while only 45 percent of the women enjoy this lifetime job security. It is no secret among faculty members who is valued, vested, and rewarded. Through comments, attitudes, and behavior, the message is clear that female faculty members have second-class citizenship on campus; and this message filters down to the students.

[5]Even in the social sciences and humanities, women earn only 46 percent of the doctoral degrees. In the life sciences, as in biology, women earn 37 percent of all doctorates. Although women acquire close to half of the bachelor's degrees in mathematics, their share drops to 40 percent at the master's level and less than 18 percent at the doctoral level. [Authors' note]

[6]Anthony DePalma, "Rare in Ivy League: Women Who Work as Full Professors," *New York Times* (January 24, 1993), pp. 1, 23. [Authors' note]

If students somehow miss the salary and tenure subtleties, the power of numbers overwhelms. Ninety-eight percent of the engineering faculty is male. While this is the most extreme imbalance, in every field students see mainly male professors: more than 60 percent in the humanities, 75 percent in business, fine arts, and the social sciences, and 83 percent in the natural sciences. Again, women are best represented in education, but even here, where they claim almost 58 percent of the doctorates, they are only 45 percent of the faculty.[7] Female students who are looking for role models, counselors, and mentors must search long and hard. With Hispanic and African-American women comprising only 1 percent of the faculty, students who are both minority and female receive an even stronger signal of their place on campus. Lacking role models and missing the mentoring connection, college women are less likely to pursue graduate work. The process becomes a continuing cycle: mainly male professors prepare men to become the faculty of the future, and the campus remains divided and unequal.

Every now and then the glass wall separating the two campuses is almost visible. For example, when we visited the school of education at one university, we entered a building and turned right. If we had turned left, we would have arrived at the physics department and met a faculty that was 100 percent male. As we observed students entering the building, it was like watching gender-segregated lines in elementary school: those who turned left for physics were male, those who turned right for the school of education were female.

Sometimes the differences between the two campuses is as simple as turning right or left in a building, but other differences can be observed in a different school: the community college. These two-year institutions offer a less expensive education, but they are also less prestigious. As the prestige factor dips, the proportion of women rises: women hold 47 percent of community college faculty positions and comprise 57 percent of the students.[8]

While females are more likely to attend community colleges, they are less likely to find themselves at the most highly selective schools. Harvard may not be able to list by name the students who will be admitted next year, but it does know that only 40 percent of them will be women. Since females face occupational and income barriers, they will probably earn less than men and therefore will have less to donate to the university. From this perspective, admitting more men who will earn more money may be seen as good business practice. So economic discrimination becomes grounds for admissions discrimination, which in turn leads to further economic discrimination.

Although there are now more female applicants to college, most Ivy 15
League schools also seem hard-pressed to locate acceptable female candi-

[7]Snyder and Hoffman, *Digest of Education Statistics, 1992*, p. 296. [Authors' note]

[8]Susan Klein and Karen Bogart, "Achieving Sex Equity in Education: A Comparison of Pre- and Post-Secondary Levels," *Equity and Excellence* 23:1–2 (Spring 1987), pp. 114–22. [Authors' note]

dates.[9] Only Columbia University accepts approximately equal numbers of female and male students. The frightening possibility of women comprising the majority of the student body can be reason enough to tinker with the admissions machinery.[10] In 1987, officials at the University of North Carolina noted that more than half of their new students were women. They recommended placing more weight on SAT tests and less on high school grades in order to achieve the "desirable" balance.

Although sex segregation on campus has become a way of life, there are times when students attend classes in equal numbers. The glass walls come down in general subjects required of everybody, courses such as English and political science. In these classrooms, parallel campuses converge, and all students sit in the same rooms, read the same texts, and are taught by the same professors. But even as men and women share the same space, they receive substantially different teaching.

In a Silent Voice

At the highest educational level, where the instructors are the most credentialed and the students the most capable, teaching is the most biased. We discovered this during a two-year grant in which we and a staff of trained raters observed and coded postsecondary classrooms. When we analyzed the data, we discovered how hidden lessons, rooted in elementary school and exacerbated in high school, emerged full-blown in the college classroom. Drawn from our research files, the following classroom scene offers more than a discussion of the Constitution; it shows how earlier subtle sexism has evolved and intensified.

> The course on the U.S. Constitution is required for graduation, and more than fifty students, approximately half male and half female, file in. The professor begins by asking if there are questions on next week's midterm. Several hands go up.
>
> BERNIE: Do we have to memorize names and dates in the book? Or will the test be more general?
>
> PROFESSOR: You do have to know those critical dates and people. Not every one but the important ones. If I were you, Bernie, I would spend time learning them. Ellen?
>
> ELLEN: What kind of short-answer questions will there be?
>
> PROFESSOR: All multiple choice.
>
> ELLEN: Will we have the whole class time?
>
> PROFESSOR: Yes, we'll have the whole class time. Anyone else?
>
> BEN (calling out): Will there be an extra-credit question?

[9] *The Insider's Guide to Colleges*, compiled and edited by the staff of the *Yale Daily News* (New York: St. Martin's Press, 1993). [Authors' note]

[10] Caroline Hodges Persell, Sophia Catsambis, and Peter W. Cookson, Jr., "Differential Asset Conversion: Class and Gendered Pathways to Selective Colleges," *Sociology of Education* 65:3 (July 1992), pp. 208–25. [Authors' note]

PROFESSOR: I hadn't planned on it. What do you think?

BEN: I really like them. They take some of the pressure off. You can also see who is doing extra work.

PROFESSOR: I'll take it under advisement. Charles?

CHARLES: How much of our final grade is this?

PROFESSOR: The midterm is 25 percent. But remember, class participation counts as well. Why don't we begin?

The professor lectures on the Constitution for twenty minutes before he asks a question about the electoral college. The electoral college is not as hot a topic as the midterm, so only four hands are raised. The professor calls on Ben.

BEN: The electoral college was created because there was a lack of faith in the people. Rather than have them vote for the president, they voted for the electors.

PROFESSOR: I like the way you think. (He smiles at Ben, and Ben smiles back.) Who could vote? (Five hands go up, five out of fifty.) Angie?

ANGIE: I don't know if this is right, but I thought only men could vote.

BEN (calling out): That was a great idea. We began going downhill when we let women vote. (Angie looks surprised but says nothing. Some of the students laugh, and so does the professor. He calls on Barbara.)

BARBARA: I think you had to be pretty wealthy, own property—

JOSH (not waiting for Barbara to finish, calls out): That's right. There was a distrust of the poor, who could upset the democracy. But if you had property, if you had something at stake, you could be trusted not to do something wild. Only property owners could be trusted.

PROFESSOR: Nice job, Josh. But why do we still have electors today? Mike?

MIKE: Tradition, I guess.

PROFESSOR: Do you think it's tradition? If you walked down the street and asked people their views of the electoral college, what would they say?

MIKE: Probably they'd be clueless. Maybe they would think that it elects the Pope. People don't know how it works.

PROFESSOR: Good, Mike. Judy, do you want to say something? (Judy's hand is at "half-mast," raised but just barely. When the professor calls her name, she looks a bit startled.)

JUDY (speaking very softly): Maybe we would need a whole new constitutional convention to change it. And once they get together to change that, they could change anything. That frightens people, doesn't it? (As Judy speaks, a number of students fidget, pass notes, and leaf through their books; a few even begin to whisper.)

A visit to the typical college class, which is a stop on the campus tour that most parents never make, shows that students behave as if they, too, are visitors. While 80 percent of pupils in elementary and secondary classes contribute at least one comment in each of their classes, approximately half of the college class says nothing at all. One in two sits through an entire class without ever answering a question, asking one, or making a comment. Women's silence is loudest at college, with twice as many females voiceless. Considering the rising cost of college tuition, the female rule of speech seems to be: the more you pay, the less you say.

At the other end of the college speech spectrum are the salient students who monopolize the discussion. Their hands shoot up for attention even before the professor finishes the question. Others don't bother to wave for recognition; they blurt out answers, sometimes way off the mark, before other students formulate their ideas. As in the class we described, these aggressive, Jeopardy-like players are usually male. In our research we have found that men are twice as likely to monopolize class discussions, and women are twice as likely to be silent. The college classroom is the finale of a twelve-year rehearsal, the culminating showcase for a manly display of verbal dominance.

Studying classrooms at Harvard, Catherine Krupnick also discovered this gender divide, one where males perform and females watch. Here were the most academically talented women in the nation, and even they were silenced. When they did speak, they were more likely to be interrupted. Males talked more often, and they talked longer. When the professor as well as most of the students were male, the stage was set for women to be minor players, a virtual Harvard underclass.[11]

Bernice Sandler and Roberta Hall found that professors give males more 20
nonverbal attention as well. They make more eye contact with men, wait longer for them to answer, and are more likely to remember their names. The result, Sandler and Hall concluded, is a "chilly classroom climate," one that silently robs women of knowledge and self-esteem.[12]

When females do volunteer comments, the impact of years of silence and self-devaluation becomes evident. In our class scenario above, Angie showed this loss. Like many women, she has learned to preface her speech with phrases like "I'm not sure if this is what you want" or "This probably isn't right but . . ." These female preambles of self-deprecation are a predictable part of the college classroom. In our coding system we called them "self-put-downs." In class after class we were disheartened at how many times women compromised superb comments: "I'm not really sure," "This is just a guess," "I don't know, but could the answer be . . ." Or like Judy

[11]Catherine Krupnick, "Unlearning Gender Roles," in Kenneth Winston and Mary Jo Bane (eds.), *Gender and Public Policy: Cases and Comments* (Boulder, CO: Westview Press, 1992). Catherine Krupnick, "Women and Men in the Classroom: Inequality and Its Remedies," *Teaching and Learning: Journal of the Harvard Danforth Center* 1:1 (May 1985), pp. 18–25. [Authors' note]

[12]Roberta Hall and Bernice Sandler, *The Classroom Climate: A Chilly One for Women?* (Washington, DC: Project on the Status and Education of Women, Association of American Colleges, 1982). For a summary of differences in women's and men's views of Harvard, see Richard Light, *The Harvard Assessment Seminars, First Report* (Cambridge, MA: Harvard University Press, 1990). [Authors' note]

they spoke in such a soft and tentative manner that their classmates don't even bother to listen.

When we asked college women why they neutralized the power of their own speech, they offered revealing explanations:

> I do it to lower expectations. If my answer is wrong, so what? I don't lose anything. I already said it might be wrong.
>
> I don't want to seem like I'm taking over the class or anything. If I disguise that I know the answers, then the other students won't resent me.
>
> I say I'm not sure because I'm really not sure. I'm not certain that I'm following the professor, and I'm just being honest about it.
>
> I didn't know I was talking like that.

The last one is the reaction we hear most frequently. Self-doubt has become part of women's public voice, and most are unaware it has happened.[13] This pattern of uncertain speech is reminiscent of the standardized science test taken in elementary and middle school, the exam where many girls selected the "I don't know" option rather than take a guess at the correct response. By the time these schoolgirls become college women, the "I don't know" option, the only one guaranteed not to garner any points, has insinuated itself into speech, a tacit acknowledgment of diminished status.

We also found that one-third of the college classrooms that contain both males and females are characterized by informally sex-segregated seating, patterns formed by the students themselves. The salient students, usually male, are well versed in the concept of strategic seating; they choose places where they can be spotted quickly by the professor. Those who want to hide, the silent students, who are more likely to be female, prize the corners, the unobtrusive areas, and the anonymity that grows with distance. It is as if a transparent gender divide was erected within the classroom.

While not as stark, the parallel with the sex segregation of elementary school is obvious. And teachers continue their patterns, too. The subtle bias in teacher reactions that we detected in lower grades resurfaces in college. Professors usually respond to student answers with neutral silence or a vague "Okay." But when praise is awarded, when criticism is leveled, or when help is given, the male student is more likely to be on the receiving end. In the class scene we described, Mike was challenged to improve his answer and then rewarded for the correction. In fact, the professor praised three male students: Ben, Josh, and Mike. Women's comments never received the professor's stamp of approval. At best they were merely acknowledged, at worst interrupted or ridiculed. So, like boys in elementary school, men in college

[13] For a discussion of how classroom communication is more compatible with male communication training, see Deborah Tannen, "Teachers' Classroom Strategies Should Recognize That Men and Women Use Language Differently," *Chronicle of Higher Education* 37 (June 19, 1991), pp. B1–B3. [Authors' note]

receive not only more attention from the professor but better attention as well.

The professor in the previous example did not intervene when Ben 25
poked fun at women and at Angie's comment, but he did not say anything sexist or sexual himself. But many professors do. At Iowa State, 65 percent of female students said they had been the target of sexist comments, and 43 percent said professors flirted with them. At Harvard University, almost half the women graduate students reported sexual harassment. This is how women described the incidents:

> He came into class, looked directly at me, and announced to everyone, "Your sweater is too tight." I felt terrible. The next week he whispered to me, "You look like you had a tough night." I just dropped his course and had to go to summer school.

> One day this professor requested that I come to his office to discuss a paper. When I arrived, he escorted me to a chair and closed the office door. He walked over to me, put his hands on either side of my face, and told me I was a very beautiful woman. Then he kissed my forehead. We never discussed any of my academic work. . . . I disregarded his constant requests to visit his office and hurriedly left his class. I received my lowest grade in his course.

Joseph Thorpe, a professor at the University of Missouri, knows just how bad it can get. He sent questionnaires to over one thousand women who were recent recipients of psychology doctorates and were members of the American Psychological Association. Thorpe found that many students had been propositioned by their professors. Most of these overtures were turned down, but almost half said they suffered academic penalties for refusing. The survey also revealed that one in every four or five women studying for their psychology doctorates was having sex with the teacher, adviser, or mentor responsible for her academic career.[14]

"These figures seem terribly high," we said in an interview with Thorpe. "Do you think they're inflated?"

"I think they underpredict what's going on," he said. "The study did not interview any of the women who dropped out, the ones who became so emotionally devastated that they never finished their programs. If we knew those numbers, the figures would be higher. In fact, for subgroups in our sample, the numbers were higher. When we looked at the responses from single, separated, or divorced female students, the sex-with-adviser rate climbed to 33 percent."

[14] Robert D. Glaser and Joseph S. Thorpe, "Unethical Intimacy: A Survey of Sexual Contact and Advances Between Psychology Educators and Female Graduate Students," *American Psychologist* 40 (January 1986), pp. 43–51. Billie Wright Dziech and Linda Weiner, *The Lecherous Professor: Sexual Harassment on Campus* (Boston: Beacon Press, 1984), pp. 13, 115–16. Claudia Dreifus, "Sex with Professors," *Glamour* (August 1986), pp. 264–65, 308–09, 311. [Authors' note]

Senior professors are overwhelmingly male and critically important. These professors distribute funds in the form of assistantships and fellowships. They can offer coauthorships on publications crucial to a fledgling career. With the right phone calls, they can land prestigious jobs for their students. Male students are more likely to be part of this mentoring relationship, but when women are mentored, the dynamics sometimes become sexual.

With grades and professional careers at stake, female students may feel vulnerable and powerless to object.[15] If a professor is a senior faculty member and distinguished in his field, it becomes even more difficult. When one of our students at The American University told us of harassment she was experiencing in a course, we urged her to bring charges. "It's useless," she told us. "This professor is a nationally known scholar. When I said I was going to report him, he laughed. 'No one would believe you,' he said. 'Do you know how many awards I have won? I'm like a god on this campus.' " This young woman did not report the professor; she dropped the course instead.

The alienation of female students on the male campus emerges even in 30
the quiet alcoves of the university library. Surrounded by books with few if any females, women continue to learn they are worth less.

Out of Sight, Out of Mind

The first grant we ever received was to investigate sex bias in college books. In the late 1970s, we spent more than a year examining the twenty-four best-selling teacher education textbooks. We read each line, evaluated every photo, and assessed the books from cover to cover — from the table of contents to the index. Twenty-three of the twenty-four texts gave the issue of gender equity less than 1 percent of book space. One-third never mentioned the topic. Those least likely to include girls and women were the books about how to teach mathematics and science courses. Not one of the twenty-four texts provided teachers with strategies or resources to eliminate sexism from the classroom.

Using these college texts, tomorrow's teachers would actually learn to be more sexist. One book offered a lengthy rationale for paying female teach-

[15]Patricia L. Bask, Joanne L. Jensen, and Jami Price, "Women's Graduate School Experiences, Professional Career Expectations and Their Relationship," paper presented at the American Educational Research Association, Chicago, Illinois, April 1991. S. Y. Jenkins, *Gender Differences in Graduate Student Relationships with Their Major Faculty Advisor*, unpublished doctoral dissertation, University of Oregon, 1985. Kenneth S. Pope, Hanna Levinson, and L. R. Schover, "Sexual Relationships in Psychology Training: Results and Implications of a National Survey," *American Psychologist* 34 (1979), pp. 682–89. Corinna A. Ethington and Rita Bode, "Differences in the Graduate Experience for Males and Females," paper presented at the American Educational Research Association, San Francisco, California, April 1991. [Authors' note]

ers less than male teachers. Another author advised prospective teachers to stock their classroom libraries with twice as many books about males as females. The author explained that "boys will not read 'girl books' but girls will read 'boy books.' " An educational psychology text offered this helpful tidbit to increase teacher efficiency: "If all the boys in a high school class routinely get distracted when a curvaceous and provocative coed undulates into the room to pick up attendance slips, tape the attendance slips to the outside of the door."[16]

A science textbook explained that girls "know less, do less, explore less, and are prone to be more superstitious than boys." Another education text emphasized the impact of technology with a fascinating analogy: if it were not for recent technological breakthroughs, "all women over twenty years of age in the United States would have to be telephone operators to handle all the phone calls." A reading textbook offered recommendations for bringing parent power into the classroom: "Some fathers could help the third-grade boys make birdhouses easier than the teacher could; some mothers could teach sixth-grade girls how to knit; many mothers would be glad to drive a carload of children to the airport, to the museum, or to the public library."[17]

Adding to the stereotyped narrative was the male world presented by the books. From the photographs to the index listings, education was pictured as populated and experienced by boys and men. One text highlighted seventy-three famous educators, seventy-two of whom were male. Another text featured the work of thirty renowned educators, all men. The message to tomorrow's teachers, most of whom are women, was clear: even in this female profession, it is the men who deserve to be remembered.

To turn this picture around, we developed a set of nonsexist guidelines, 35
suggestions for publishers interested in creating fairer college texts. Several publishers distributed our guidelines to their authors. A few publishers actually sent our research findings to the authors of the textbooks we had critiqued and requested that they "repair" their work in future editions.

Considering the job done, we turned our attention to classroom interaction, but in 1991 we were jolted back into the world of college books. The second edition of our own teacher education textbook had just been published, and we were sent an advance copy. We had taken special care to integrate women and minorities throughout the narrative of the book, but the outside of the book was something else. Without our knowledge the publisher had chosen a vibrant multicultural photograph, but it included four times more boys than girls. A call to the publisher cleared up the matter. It was all a "terrible mistake"; the photograph had been chosen to reflect cultural diversity, but the publisher, sensitive to racial representation, had not

[16] Myra Sadker and David Sadker, *Beyond Pictures and Pronouns: Sexism in Teacher Education Textbooks* (Washington, DC: Office of Education, 1980), pp. 8, 38. [Authors' note]

[17] Sadker and Sadker, *Beyond Pictures and Pronouns*, pp. 38, 39. [Authors' note]

noticed that girls were left out. We began calling other publishers about their guidelines. Here is a typical exchange:

"Guidelines? What guidelines?"

"The nonsexist guidelines you agreed to follow over a decade ago."

"Over a decade ago. That's way before I arrived here. I don't remember seeing any nonsexist guidelines."

Many college textbooks have withstood the winds of change. From phi- 40
losophy to psychology, from history to the sciences, students may still learn about a world of male accomplishment and female invisibility. Centuries of recorded history parade before today's college students, but women continue to make only a rare appearance. For example, a classic text in English literature survey courses is the two-volume *Norton Anthology*. Here the culture's great works are collected, and the literary canon is offered to the next generation. Norton has introduced students to centuries of literature: Chaucer, Shakespeare, Milton, Byron, Shelley, Keats, Matthew Arnold, T. S. Eliot; the showcase of male literary accomplishment is extensive. The 3,450 pages of the initial 1962 edition were expanded to 5,000 pages in the 1986 (fifth) edition, where the preface discusses efforts to reflect "contemporary culture." Less than 15 percent of these new pages included women writers. In fact, the percentage of women in the *Norton Anthology* was greater in 1962 than in 1986.[18]

Women in higher education are frequently aware that their lives are left out of books, and they feel excluded from a recorded culture that is not their own. As one student said: "In history we never talked about what women did; in geography it was always what was important to men; it was the same in our English class—we hardly ever studied women authors. I won't even talk about math and science. . . . I always felt as though I didn't belong. . . . Now I just deaden myself against it so I don't hear it anymore. But I really feel alienated."[19]

Centuries of bias cannot be undone in a single chapter or insert, but authors and publishers try nonetheless. The results of their efforts to rectify imbalance can be seen in chapters or boxes called "Women and Art," "Female Authors," "Famous Women Scientists," or "American Diversity: Founding Mothers." This last title came from a popular 1991 political science textbook that offers information about women's contributions during the revolution.[20] The authors tell how the "daughters of the revolution"

[18]William Sullivan, "The *Norton Anthology* and the Canon of English Literature," paper presented at the Annual Meeting of the College English Association, San Antonio, Texas, 1991. Jordan J. Titus, "Gender Messages in Education Foundations Textbooks," *Journal of Teacher Education* 44:1 (January–February 1993), pp. 38–44. [Authors' note]

[19]Magda Lewis, "Interrupting Patriarchy: Politics, Resistance, and Transformation in the Feminist Classroom," *Harvard Educational Review* 60:4 (November 1990), pp. 467–88. [Authors' note]

[20]Susan Welch et al., *Understanding American Government* (St. Paul, MN: West Publishing Co., 1991), p. 24. [Authors' note]

boycotted British goods, wrote political pamphlets, were leaders in the fight for independence, and fought in the Revolutionary War disguised as men. In fact, the only Revolutionary War veteran buried at West Point is a woman who took full advantage of the absence of pre-induction physicals and joined the Continental army. The "Founding Mothers" represents a step forward, but it is only one page long, which is the problem with boxes and chapters. The student is left with a fragmented world view: males are the main story and women are a sideshow, confined to a brief insert, anecdote, or biographical summary.

Sometimes women do not even make sideshow status. The controversy over generic male pronouns and nouns is a case in point. Some professors and students say that words such as "he" and "mankind" exclude women, while others charge that all the fuss is a tempest in a teapot, a case of semantic hypersensitivity. But studies show that words are powerful indeed. When a career or job is described using male pronouns, females find the job less appealing than when neutral terms are used. When a job applicant is referred to as a "girl" instead of a "woman," she is seen as less tough, less dignified, and of course less well paid.[21]

Despite studies showing that when "man" is said, in the mind's eye man is seen, many college texts persist in using these deceptive generics. Some authors even resort to creative strategies such as asking readers to imagine that inclusive language has been used, as if saying makes it so.

> Note that we have not made a distinction between the sexes. The theory is intended to apply to adolescent boys as well as adolescent girls. We have used the masculine gender in this report for convenience; it should be considered a neutral, general usage.[22]

When textbooks exclude them, some women develop their own defense. We were discussing generic words with our class when one of our students, Paul, showed us a copy of *Everyone Wins! A Citizen's Guide to Development,* a book about protecting the environment.[23] "This book belongs to my friend Connie at Portland State," he told us. "I want you to see what she did." As we leafed through the text, we saw how Connie had laboriously crossed out all the *he* and *him* pronouns and replaced them with *she* and *her.* "Connie

[21] Barbara Westbrook Eakins and R. Gene Eakins, *Sex Differences in Human Communication* (Boston: Houghton Mifflin, 1978). Joseph Schneider and Sally Hacker, "Sex Role Imagery and the Use of Generic 'Man' in Introductory Texts: A Case in the Sociology of Sociology," *American Sociologist* 8 (February 1973), pp. 12–18. Cheris Kramer, Barrie Thorne, and Nancy Henley, "Perspectives on Language and Communication," *Signs: Journal of Women in Culture and Society* 3:3 (1978), pp. 638–51. Robert Brannon, "The Consequences of Sexist Language," paper presented at the American Psychological Association, August 1978. [Authors' note]

[22] Martin Gold and David Mann, *Expelled to a Friendlier Place: A Study of Effective Alternative Schools* (Ann Arbor, MI: University of Michigan Press, 1984), p. 6. [Authors' note]

[23] Richard Klein, *Everyone Wins! A Citizen's Guide to Development* (Chicago: Planners Press, 1990). [Authors' note]

felt as though the book was talking to someone else," Paul said, "so as she read through it, she included herself."

We asked our students to analyze the content of their textbooks to see 45
how widespread sex bias was in the books read at our own university. They found psychology, economics, and sociology textbooks that rarely even mentioned a woman's name. One art book included 245 photographs, but only 18 depicted women. Other studies have also noted the slow pace of textbook change, but not all textbooks are frozen in time; several contain nonsexist language and include males and females in relatively equal numbers. Why such extremes? Unlike elementary and high schools, postsecondary schools do not have committees to evaluate and select books. At the college level, professors choose their own texts and call it academic freedom. For students, it's *caveat emptor.*[24]

The Girls Next Door

> When I entered college in North Carolina in the 1960s, I was given my official women's rule book, a thirty-four-page tome filled with guidelines and expectations for all coeds. (Female students were "coeds"; male students were "gentlemen.") The following are some of the rules:
>
> - No beer in the dorm, even to use as a hair rinse, as was the custom of the day. Men, of course, could have as much beer in their rooms as they wished.
> - No smoking while walking on campus since this was considered "unladylike" conduct.
> - No visiting a boy's apartment unless there was another couple present.
> - No dates outside the town line unless you were "signed out" to do so. Male students could go wherever they pleased.
>
> The rules went on and on. I don't believe male students had a rule book. To be fair, I should note that by the time I graduated in 1970, the rule book had been shortened to pamphlet length.

In the 1970s, when students reinvented dorm life, they abridged and then discarded the rule book completely. Almost overnight single-sex dorms seemed out of date and coeducational living became the arrangement of choice. Researchers found both positive and negative sides to these new coed dorms. Men told fewer off-color jokes, drank less, and talked with women more; women became more outgoing and were more likely to attend university events. Cross-sex friendships flourished as residents went to classes, meals, and university activities together. But there were problems as well as benefits. While men studied more, women in coed dorms took their academic work less seriously, held lower career aspirations, and

[24]*caveat emptor:* Latin for "let the buyer beware," this legal principle relieves sellers of responsibility for the quality of a product. Students are advised, then, to scrutinize their colleges as carefully as they would a used car.

dropped out of school more often. And stories of unwanted teasing and touching became increasingly frequent.[25]

Stories that surfaced in the 1970s have become commonplace on today's campus. A survey of Cornell students found that four out of five women experienced sexist comments and 68 percent received unwanted attention from men. At the Massachusetts Institute of Technology, 92 percent of the women reported receiving unwanted sexual attention. At the University of Rhode Island, seven out of ten women said they were sexually insulted by men. Sexual harassment can occur anywhere on campus, but students are especially vulnerable when it happens where they live.[26]

> My dorm at Stanford is composed of fifty men and women who reside on two coed hallways. We are all freshmen. Last week several of the girls, including me, discovered that the men on the second floor had posted in the men's room a "rating and ranking" sheet of the second-floor women. The ranking was obviously based on the relative physical attractiveness of the girls in the dorm and was accompanied by various and sundry disgusting comments. Naturally, many of the second-floor women were upset by this list. . . . I decided that this was something so fundamentally wrong, I couldn't ignore it.
>
> As the week progressed, I began to discuss "the list" with some of the second-floor men, explaining my objections. I felt that the list was dehumanizing and humiliating . . . immature and childish, a remnant of middle school days. How could these guys whom we'd been living with for eight months think of their closest friends in such superficial terms? How could they degrade us in that way? And most of all, how could they be sitting in front of me and defending themselves instead of apologizing for their actions?
>
> Eventually a male resident adviser decided to hold a house meeting to discuss the problem in a more formal setting. This meeting became a battle between me and the ten to twelve men on the second floor who could find nothing wrong with their "list." Amazingly enough, throughout the entire argument not one of the other second-floor women who had initially been so angered . . . had the strength to help validate my arguments with her support. In fact, several were so afraid to become embroiled in an argument that they pretended they knew nothing about the list. The men who were not part of the ranking and who I knew were opposed to it . . .

[25]Judith Corbett and Robert Sommer, "Anatomy of a Coed Residence Hall," *Journal of College Student Personnel* 13:3 (May 1972), pp. 215–17. Rudolf H. Moos and Jean Otto, "The Impact of Coed Living on Males and Females," *Journal of College Student Personnel* 16:6 (November 1975), pp 459–67. Robert Brown, John Winkworth, and Larry Brakskamp, "Student Development in a Coed Residence Hall: Promiscuity, Prophylactic, or Panacea?" *Journal of College Student Personnel* 14:2 (March 1973), pp. 98–104. Charles C. Schroeder and Morris LeMay, "The Impact of Coed Residence Halls on Self-Actualization," *Journal of College Student Personnel* 14:2 (March 1973), pp. 105–10. [Authors' note]

[26]"Harassing Women Becomes a Sick College Sport," *Utne Reader* (May–June 1990), pp. 70–71. Linda J. Rubin and Sherry B. Borgers, "Sexual Harassment in Universities During the 1980s," *Sex Roles* 23:7–8 (1990), pp. 397–411. [Authors' note]

> didn't attack my position, but they certainly were not willing to put themselves on the line to defend it. After this confrontation and for the next few days, however, many of the women in the dorm . . . came to me separately and thanked me for standing up for them and myself, and for trying to explain how disturbing and upsetting the situation was.

In this case, words created a psychological betrayal, shattering the veneer of honest communication. When the betrayal is physical instead of verbal, it is far more threatening.

> I was driving home from a bar with five guys who lived in my dorm. Most of them were drunk (I wasn't). I was sitting on the lap of one of my friends. He kept trying to touch me on my inner thighs or my buttocks. I was squirming and telling him to stop, but he ignored me. The other guys kept laughing. One kept grabbing my breasts while another whispered in my ear that I should go to his room tonight. I felt like Jodie Foster in *The Accused.* I was trapped in a car with no way to escape.

The young woman from The American University who described this incident to us said that the "guys were just messing around," and nothing else happened; but she felt "frightened, helpless, and violated." She said, "When I tell people the story, they say that being with five drunk guys is just asking for trouble. But they don't understand. These guys were my *friends.*" Another college student also described the frightening transformation of someone she considered a friend, the man who lived next door.

> John and I were friends in the same dorm. Just friends. He knew I had a boyfriend and that I saw him as a friend. One day I was in his room talking with him. We were always hanging out in each other's rooms, listening to music and watching TV. When I got up to leave, he blocked the door, grabbed my arms, and forcefully kissed me. I was shocked. I didn't know what to do. I mean, this was a pretty good friend of mine acting like this. He picked me up and threw me down on his bed. . . . He started kissing me and saying how much he wanted to make love to me. I said no. I was completely pinned down. I have never felt so lacking in control in my own life. I realized that something I didn't want to happen could—and I didn't have any say in the situation. He didn't care about my feelings. I must have said no about a thousand times. I kept struggling, and I finally convinced him to stop. . . .
>
> To this day (and I know this for sure because he lives next door to me) he doesn't feel as if he did anything wrong. I still haven't been able to make him understand how he affected me that day. Almost being raped . . . I can only begin to imagine what I would have felt like if a rape had really happened.

Baffled by the way her trusted friend treated her, this young woman keeps playing the incident over and over in her mind, trying to understand why it happened. But these terrifying experiences are not even distant possibilities in the minds of new students as they unload their cars and move into their dorms. And most parents, as they wave good-bye, have no inkling of the alarming extracurricular activities their tuition dollars may be buying.

The Years of Living Dangerously

During the 1980s fraternity and sorority membership grew, and by the 1990s over a million students were part of the resurgence of Greek associations on campus. Fraternities often set the social rhythm of undergraduate life because they have more and bigger houses for parties; sometimes they have the only location on campus.

Walk through the typical campus and you are far more likely to see a fraternity house than a sorority house. When we asked college students why fraternities were more likely to claim campus real estate, we often heard a rendition of the bordello story, which goes something like this: "It's an ancient law here in [the District of Columbia, St. Louis, Boston, or the city of your choice]. When three or four women rent or buy a house together, it's considered a brothel. Back then it was called a bordello. That's why sorority houses are illegal. It has nothing to do with campus inequality, it's just these stupid, outdated bordello laws."

The longer history of fraternities and their greater wealth and influence, 50
not bordello laws, have created the real estate gender gap. But we have heard this explanation at so many different colleges and universities, it qualifies as campus mythology.

Nationally there are more than twice as many fraternities as sororities. And on the typical campus, sorority row is a weak reflection of its male counterpart. On some campuses the sorority house is big enough only for meetings and parties; no one lives there. On others, there are no sorority houses, just dorm areas where sorority sisters live together. In many cases there is not even dorm space; all that is available is a meeting room in a university building.

This less well-appointed sorority life still produces enthusiastic supporters. As one woman said, "Living like sisters creates a lifelong bond. The sorority gave me friendship and support." Both fraternity and sorority members are quick to point out that they raise money for charitable causes and do good work for children, the poor, and the homeless. But it is the social activities — and scandals — that gain public attention, and these usually take place on the male side of the campus.

Fraternity row is home to an all-male society, one separate from the rest of the world where secret rituals bond new brothers into a surrogate family. Here the stage is set for life's last fling before the onset of work and family responsibilities. Alcohol, parties, good times, and close friendships characterize fraternity life. But along with horseplay and harmless fun, there exists a menacing, darker side:

> The theme for Dartmouth's winter carnival was *Camelot,* so a group of fraternity brothers built a snow sculpture for the event — a woman's breast

pierced by a sword and captioned GUINEVERE — THANKS FOR THE MAMMARIES, ARTHUR.[27]

At Middlebury, the 1988 toga party was hosted by one of the biggest fraternities on campus. As part of the decor, the torso of a female mannequin was hung from the balcony and splattered with red paint to look like blood. A sign underneath suggested the female body was available for sex.[28]

One fraternity sponsored a campus scavenger hunt. Points were awarded to those who could produce photocopies of female genitalia.

A fraternity on a New England college campus hosted "pig parties." Females from a nearby state teacher's college were imported, and the date of the one voted ugliest was the winner.

At UCLA a fraternity manual, forgotten in an apartment, found its way into a campus magazine. The fraternity's history, traditions, and bylaws were included, as well as a series of songs the pledges were supposed to memorize. Many of the lyrics described sexual scenes that were shockingly graphic, unbelievably bizarre, and revoltingly sadistic. For example, one song recounted the life of a Mexican girl named Lupe who performed any sexual act imaginable. She first had intercourse when she was eight years old, and even in death, "while maggots crawl[ed] out of her decomposed womb," the smile on her face signaled that she still wanted more sex.[29]

When fraternity members are involved in these pranks and songs, they create a mind-set that turns women into objects, animals, prey. Then the college campus becomes a setting of very real danger.

The young woman, newly arrived on campus, was seeking acceptance from her classmates. She looked forward to attending the fraternity party, a beginning event in her college social life. At the party she was encouraged to drink, and eventually she passed out. The brothers had a name for this practice: "working a Yes out." She was carried upstairs, stripped, and raped by a number of men. They lined up outside the door and took turns, an approach called "pulling train." Several times she regained consciousness and pleaded for them to stop. The university learned of the incident and punished those involved. Several were required to do community service projects. Some additional reading and writing projects were also assigned for the fraternity members involved. The woman who was gang-raped left without graduating.[30]

[27]Andrew Merton, "Return to Brotherhood," *Ms.* (September 1985), pp. 60–62.

[28]Beth Ann Krier, "Frat Row," *Los Angeles Times* (February 9, 1990), pp. E1, E7–9.

[29]For additional examples and analyses of these activities, see Jean O'Gorman Hughes and Bernice Sandler, *Peer Harassment: Hassles for Women on Campus* (Washington, DC: Project on the Status and Education of Women, Association of American Colleges, 1988). [Authors' note]

[30]Lis McMillen, "An Anthropologist's Disturbing Picture of Gang Rape on Campus," *Chronicle of Higher Education* 37 (September 19, 1990), p. A3. Peggy Reeves Sanday, *Fraternity Gang Rape: Sex, Brotherhood, and Privilege on Campus* (New York: New York University Press, 1990). [Authors' note]

> The police had a difficult time piecing together the sordid details. A gang rape was reported at the Pi Kappa Alpha house at Florida State University, and a witness alleged that a visiting brother from Auburn University helped dump the body of the unconscious woman at a neighboring fraternity house. Even though they were charged with obstructing justice, all the brothers kept their pledge of secrecy. Although two were on trial facing life sentences, no one would cooperate with the police.[31]

Campus rape is more common than college officials care to admit, and they are far less well equipped to deal with it than most parents realize. According to national studies, approximately one in four college women says she has been forced into having sex, and one in six reports having been raped.[32] While most people think of rape as an assault by a violent stranger, in nine out of ten college incidents, the sex is forced by a friend or acquaintance. Victims experience a maelstrom of emotions: shock, disbelief, fear, and depression. They also agonize over every nuance of their own behavior and are likely to find themselves at fault: "How could I have been so wrong about him?" "What did I do to lead him on?" When the perpetrator is a "friend," college women are not even sure they have a right to call the ordeal "rape."[33]

While the victim is at a loss to figure out how it happened, the perpetrator fits a predictable profile. Socialized into the aggressive male role, he believes that women tease and lead him on, that they provoke and enjoy sexual encounters and later cry rape falsely. To these men it is not rape at all but part of a game men and women play. More than one in every three college men believes that a woman who says "no" to sex really means "yes," or at least "maybe." According to one study, a shocking 30 percent of men admitted they would rape a woman if they thought they could get away with it.[34]

Drugs and alcohol trigger sexual violence. Intoxicated men are more 55
likely to be violent, and intoxicated women are less able to resist. This dangerous situation is viewed very differently by females and males. When

[31] Michael Hirschorn, "Two Colleges Drop Recognition of Fraternities, Sororities Amid Continuing Concern Over Groups' Behavior," *Chronicle of Higher Education* (May 11, 1988), pp. A27–28. [Authors' note]

[32] Mary P. Koss, Christine A. Gidycz, and Nadine Wisniewski, "The Scope of Rape: Incidence and Prevalence of Sexual Aggression and Victimization in a National Sample of Higher Education Students," *Journal of Consulting and Clinical Psychology* 55:2 (1987), pp. 162–70. [Authors' note]

[33] Aileen Adams and Gail Abarbanel, *Sexual Assault on Campus: What Colleges Can Do* (Santa Monica, CA: Rape Treatment Center, 1988). Diana E. H. Russell, *Sexual Exploitation: Rape, Child Sexual Assault, and Workplace Harassment* (Beverly Hills, CA: Sage, 1984). [Authors' note]

[34] Alan Berkowitz, "College Men as Perpetrators of Acquaintance Rape and Sexual Assault: A Review of Recent Research," *College Health* 40 (January 1992), pp. 175–81. Mary Koss, Thomas E. Dinero, Cynthia Seibel, and Susan Cox, "Stranger and Acquaintance Rape: Are There Differences in the Victim's Experience?," *Psychology of Women Quarterly* 12 (March 1988), pp. 1–24. [Authors' note]

asked, "If a woman is heavily intoxicated, is it okay to have sex with her?" only one in fifty women agreed. But one in four college men said that an intoxicated female was an appropriate target for sex. In addition to alcohol or drugs, location and date can be danger factors. Women who find themselves in a man's living quarters, at his party, or even in his car are more vulnerable.[35] So are women who go out with athletes.

Basking in status and popularity, male athletes are like campus nobility. In athletic events and on television, their physical exploits garner glory, network dollars, and alumni contributions. But off the field, physical exploits of a different nature can bring disgrace. The National Institute of Mental Health found athletes involved in one out of every three sexual assaults nationally. At Maryland's Towson State, athletes are five times more likely than others to be involved in gang rapes. A major southern university found that 27 percent of its athletes had threatened women into having sex against their will. In just one year, from 1989 to 1990, at least fifteen gang rapes were reported, involving fifty athletes. No one knows how many gang rapes went unreported.[36]

> Meg Davis called them her friends; she "buddied" with them. In the spring semester her "friends," all on the university's football team, sexually assaulted her. For three hours, seven to nine men took turns. She blacked out as she was being sodomized. Back at the dorm, she showered until the hot water ran out. "I felt so dirty. Even so, I didn't call what happened to me rape. These were guys I knew. It wasn't until I went to a women's center in town that someone explained I'd been gang-raped."[37]

After fraternities, athletic teams are most likely to be involved in gang rapes. Whether called "brotherhood," as in fraternity houses, or "teamwork," as in sports, the mind-set generated by male bonding can suppress independent thought and morality. A director of a rape treatment center described the impact of this bonding: "There has never been a single case in all the gang rapes we've seen where one man tried to stop it. . . . It's more important to be part of the group than to be the person who does what's right."[38]

At Carleton College in Northfield, Minnesota, women took matters into

[35]Charlene Muehlenhard and Melaney Linton, "Date Rape and Sexual Aggression in Dating Situations: Incidence and Risk Factors," *Journal of Counseling Psychology* 34:2 (1987), pp. 186–96. Kelly Elizabeth Naylor, *Gender Role Strain: A Contributing Factor to Acquaintance Rape in a College Population at Risk*, unpublished doctoral dissertation, DePaul University, 1991. [Authors' note]

[36]Thomas Jackson, "A University Athletic Department's Rape and Assault Experiences," *Journal of College Student Development* 32 (January 1991), pp. 77–78. Merrill Melnick, "Male Athletes and Sexual Assault," *Journal of Physical Education, Recreation and Dance* 63 (May–June 1992), pp. 32–35. [Authors' note]

[37]Jill Neimark, "Out of Bounds: The Truth About Athletes and Rape," *Mademoiselle* (May 1991), pp. 198, 244. [Authors' note]

[38]Gail Abarbanel quoted in Neimark, "The Truth About Athletes and Rape," p. 198. [Authors' note]

their own hands. As one woman said, "I had been on the campus for five weeks when I was raped. The college knew this man was a rapist, and they could have prevented this from happening."[39] After hearing the evidence, Carleton suspended the male offender for less than a year. When he returned to campus, he harassed the woman who had reported the rape. She and others sued the college, and then they did something else. On the wall of the women's bathroom at the university's library, as a warning to other women on campus, they posted an unofficial list of the names of Carleton men who had raped.

Colleges are not always slow to respond. Many institute special programs to sensitize the campus community, but when these programs are evaluated, the results are surprising. Female participants become more sensitive to the problem even before the training begins. Just responding to questions about rape on a survey changes their attitudes, heightens their level of concern, and causes them to become more sympathetic toward rape victims. Once in the program, they place even more importance on stopping college rape. But males respond differently. Traditional educational programs have little impact on their attitudes, and evaluation results show that many who continue to believe pro-rape myths blame the victim. These starkly different reactions to rape prevention reveal not only a profound gender gap in perception but also a fundamental difference in campus entitlement and power.[40]

[39]Michelle Collison, "Increase in Reports of Sexual Assaults Strains Campus Disciplinary Systems," *Chronicle of Higher Education* (May 15, 1991), pp. A29–A30. [Authors' note]

[40]Genie O. Lenihan et al., "Gender Differences in Rape Supportive Attitudes Before and After Date Rape Education Intervention," *Journal of College Student Development* 33:4 (July 1992), pp. 331–38. Patricia Yancey Martin and Robert A. Hummer, "Fraternities and Rape on Campus," *Gender and Society* 3:4 (December 1989), pp. 457–73. David Ellis, "Setting New Goals for the Greek System," *Educational Record* 70:3–4 (Summer–Fall 1989), pp. 48–53. *Status of the College Fraternity and Sorority, 1990* (Bloomington, IN: Center for the Study of the College Fraternity, 1990). Patrick J. Harrison, Jeanette Downes, and Michael D. Williams, "Date and Acquaintance Rape: Perceptions and Attitude Change Strategies," *Journal of College Student Development* 32 (March 1991), pp. 131–39. [Authors' note]

Engaging the Text

1. Working in groups, write up study notes for this selection, charting Sadker and Sadker's key claims and evidence in the following areas:
   - the history of women at the university
   - current structural/numerical biases
   - bias in the classroom
   - books
   - "campus life," including housing and extracurricular activities
   - sexual harassment/rape
2. Write a journal entry evaluating your own college experiences in light of Sadker

and Sadker's revelations about campus life. To what extent do your experiences and observations confirm or challenge their analysis of sexism in higher education?

3. Test the Sadkers' claims by closely observing one class on your campus. Take notes on all the things they analyzed: female vs. male seating, frequency and nature of speech, amount of attention received from the professor, and so on. Compare notes with students who observed other classes. What patterns, if any, do you see?

Exploring Connections

4. Theodore Sizer (p. 20) described the typical day of a male high school student. Based on your observations and reading, write your own description of the typical day of a female college student.
5. In examining social class and educational opportunities, Jean Anyon (p. 45) describes a "hidden curriculum." Compare and contrast Anyon's hidden curriculum with the one revealed in this selection.
6. Explain each panel of the "Doonesbury" cartoon that follows in light of Sadker and Sadker's observations about "a girl's education."

Extending the Critical Context

7. Ask your school's administration for data on the percentage of female and male faculty, tenured and untenured, by department. Also find out the number of male and female majors in various departments. (You may have to divide the work and approach department chairs directly.) Do your data support Sadker and Sadker's claims?
8. Read Leora Tanenbaum's review of *Failing at Fairness* in the February 28, 1994, edition of *The Nation* — a review which is in some respects severely critical of the book. Report to the class on the issues Tanenbaum raises. When experts disagree, how does the college student know whom to believe?
9. In recent years, there has been growing interest in returning to same-sex schooling at all educational levels. Working in groups, brainstorm the advantages and disadvantages of gender-segregated education.
10. Sadker and Sadker note that efforts at sensitivity education to stop rape appear to have little impact on male students. Research what your college does to address sexual harassment and rape. Beyond sensitivity training, what can institutions of higher education do to reduce the threat of violence to women on campus?

Doonesbury

BY GARRY TRUDEAU

Silence

Maxine Hong Kingston

To the Chinese immigrant, white Americans are "ghosts"—threatening and occasionally comical specters who speak an incomprehensible tongue. For many immigrants, becoming American means living among "ghosts," finding a new voice, adopting new values, defining a new self. This selection, from Maxine Hong Kingston's enormously popular autobiography, The Woman Warrior, *describes the conflicts experienced by a young Chinese girl as she struggles to adapt to new ways in her American school. Maxine Hong Kingston (b. 1940) teaches at the University of California, Berkeley.* The Woman Warrior *won the National Book Critics Circle Award for nonfiction in 1976 and was named by* Time *magazine as one of the top ten nonfiction works of the 1970s. Kingston has since published* China Men *(1980) and* Tripmaster Monkey *(1989), in addition to numerous poems, short stories, and articles in national magazines. The stage play* The Woman Warrior *debuted in Berkeley in 1994.*

Long ago in China, knot-makers tied string into buttons and frogs, and rope into bell pulls. There was one knot so complicated that it blinded the knot-maker. Finally an emperor outlawed this cruel knot, and the nobles could not order it anymore. If I had lived in China, I would have been an outlaw knot-maker.

Maybe that's why my mother cut my tongue. She pushed my tongue up and sliced the frenum. Or maybe she snipped it with a pair of nail scissors. I don't remember her doing it, only her telling me about it, but all during childhood I felt sorry for the baby whose mother waited with scissors or knife in hand for it to cry—and then, when its mouth was wide open like a baby bird's, cut. The Chinese say "a ready tongue is an evil."

I used to curl up my tongue in front of the mirror and tauten my frenum into a white line, itself as thin as a razor blade. I saw no scars in my mouth. I thought perhaps I had had two frena, and she had cut one. I made other children open their mouths so I could compare theirs to mine. I saw perfect pink membranes stretching into precise edges that looked easy enough to cut. Sometimes I felt very proud that my mother committed such a powerful act upon me. At other times I was terrified—the first thing my mother did when she saw me was to cut my tongue.

"Why did you do that to me, Mother?"

"I told you." 5

"Tell me again."

"I cut it so that you would not be tongue-tied. Your tongue would be able to move in any language. You'll be able to speak languages that are completely different from one another. You'll be able to pronounce anything. Your frenum looked too tight to do those things, so I cut it."

"But isn't 'a ready tongue an evil'?"

"Things are different in this ghost country."

"Did it hurt me? Did I cry and bleed?" 10

"I don't remember. Probably."

She didn't cut the other children's. When I asked cousins and other Chinese children whether their mothers had cut their tongues loose, they said, "What?"

"Why didn't you cut my brothers' and sisters' tongues?"

"They didn't need it."

"Why not? Were theirs longer than mine?" 15

"Why don't you quit blabbering and get to work?"

If my mother was not lying she should have cut more, scraped away the rest of the frenum skin, because I have a terrible time talking. Or she should not have cut at all, tampering with my speech. When I went to kindergarten and had to speak English for the first time, I became silent. A dumbness — a shame — still cracks my voice in two, even when I want to say "hello" casually, or ask any easy question in front of the check-out counter, or ask directions of a bus driver. I stand frozen, or I hold up the line with the complete, grammatical sentence that comes squeaking out at impossible length. "What did you say?" says the cab driver, or "Speak up," so I have to perform again, only weaker the second time. A telephone call makes my throat bleed and takes up that day's courage. It spoils my day with self-disgust when I hear my broken voice come skittering out into the open. It makes people wince to hear it. I'm getting better, though. Recently I asked the postman for special-issue stamps; I've waited since childhood for postmen to give me some of their own accord. I am making progress, a little every day.

My silence was thickest — total — during the three years that I covered my school paintings with black paint. I painted layers of black over houses and flowers and suns, and when I drew on the blackboard, I put a layer of chalk on top. I was making a stage curtain, and it was the moment before the curtain parted or rose. The teachers called my parents to school, and I saw they had been saving my pictures, curling and cracking, all alike and black. The teachers pointed to the pictures and looked serious, talked seriously too, but my parents did not understand English. ("The parents and teachers of criminals were executed," said my father.) My parents took the pictures home. I spread them out (so black and full of possibilities) and pretended the curtains were swinging open, flying up, one after another, sunlight underneath, mighty operas.

During the first silent year I spoke to no one at school, did not ask before going to the lavatory, and flunked kindergarten. My sister also said nothing for three years, silent in the playground and silent at lunch. There were other quiet Chinese girls not of our family, but most of them got over it sooner than we did. I enjoyed the silence. At first it did not occur to me

I was supposed to talk or to pass kindergarten. I talked at home and to one or two of the Chinese kids in the class. I made motions and even made some jokes. I drank out of a toy saucer when the water spilled out of the cup, and everybody laughed, pointing at me, so I did it some more. I didn't know that Americans don't drink out of saucers.

20 I liked the Negro students (Black Ghosts) best because they laughed the loudest and talked to me as if I were a daring talker too. One of the Negro girls had her mother coil braids over her ears Shanghai-style like mine; we were Shanghai twins except that she was covered with black like my paintings. Two Negro kids enrolled in Chinese school, and the teachers gave them Chinese names. Some Negro kids walked me to school and home, protecting me from the Japanese kids, who hit me and chased me and stuck gum in my ears. The Japanese kids were noisy and tough. They appeared one day in kindergarten, released from concentration camp,[1] which was a tic-tac-toe mark, like barbed wire, on the map.

It was when I found out I had to talk that school became a misery, that the silence became a misery. I did not speak and felt bad each time that I did not speak. I read aloud in first grade, though, and heard the barest whisper with little squeaks come out of my throat. "Louder," said the teacher, who scared the voice away again. The other Chinese girls did not talk either, so I knew the silence had to do with being a Chinese girl.

Reading out loud was easier than speaking because we did not have to make up what to say, but I stopped often, and the teacher would think I'd gone quiet again. I could not understand "I." The Chinese "I" has seven strokes, intricacies. How could the American "I," assuredly wearing a hat like the Chinese, have only three strokes, the middle so straight? Was it out of politeness that this writer left off strokes the way a Chinese has to write her own name small and crooked? No, it was not politeness; "I" is a capital and "you" is a lower-case. I stared at that middle line and waited so long for its black center to resolve into tight strokes and dots that I forgot to pronounce it. The other troublesome word was "here," no strong consonant to hang on to, and so flat, when "here" is two mountainous ideographs.[2] The teacher, who had already told me every day how to read "I" and "here," put me in the low corner under the stairs again, where the noisy boys usually sat.

When my second grade class did a play, the whole class went to the auditorium except the Chinese girls. The teacher, lovely and Hawaiian, should have understood about us, but instead left us behind in the classroom. Our voices were too soft or nonexistent, and our parents never signed the permission slips anyway. They never signed anything unnecessary. We

[1]*concentration camp:* Refers to one of the U.S. camps where Japanese Americans were imprisoned during World War II.

[2]*ideographs:* Composite characters in Chinese writing made by combining two or more other characters.

opened the door a crack and peeked out, but closed it again quickly. One of us (not me) won every spelling bee, though.

I remember telling the Hawaiian teacher, "We Chinese can't sing 'land where our fathers died.' " She argued with me about politics, while I meant because of curses. But how can I have that memory when I couldn't talk? My mother says that we, like the ghosts, have no memories.

After American school, we picked up our cigar boxes, in which we had 25
arranged books, brushes, and an inkbox neatly, and went to Chinese school, from 5:00 to 7:30 P.M. There we chanted together, voices rising and falling, loud and soft, some boys shouting, everybody reading together, reciting together and not alone with one voice. When we had a memorization test, the teacher let each of us come to his desk and say the lesson to him privately, while the rest of the class practiced copying or tracing. Most of the teachers were men. The boys who were so well behaved in the American school played tricks on them and talked back to them. The girls were not mute. They screamed and yelled during recess, when there were no rules; they had fistfights. Nobody was afraid of children hurting themselves or of children hurting school property. The glass doors to the red and green balconies with the gold joy symbols were left wide open so that we could run out and climb the fire escapes. We played capture-the-flag in the auditorium, where Sun Yat-sen[3] and Chiang Kai-shek's[4] pictures hung at the back of the stage, the Chinese flag on their left and the American flag on their right. We climbed the teak ceremonial chairs and made flying leaps off the stage. One flag headquarters was behind the glass door and the other on stage right. Our feet drummed on the hollow stage. During recess the teachers locked themselves up in their office with the shelves of books, copybooks, inks from China. They drank tea and warmed their hands at a stove. There was no play supervision. At recess we had the school to ourselves, and also we could roam as far as we could go — downtown, Chinatown stores, home — as long as we returned before the bell rang.

At exactly 7:30 the teacher again picked up the brass bell that sat on his desk and swung it over our heads, while we charged down the stairs, our cheering magnified in the stairwell. Nobody had to line up.

Not all of the children who were silent at American school found voice at Chinese school. One new teacher said each of us had to get up and recite in front of the class, who was to listen. My sister and I had memorized the lesson perfectly. We said it to each other at home, one chanting, one listening. The teacher called on my sister to recite first. It was the first time a teacher had called on the second-born to go first. My sister was scared. She glanced at me and looked away; I looked down at my desk. I hoped that she could do it because if she could, then I would have to. She opened her

[3] *Sun Yat-sen:* Chinese politician, intellectual, and revolutionary (1866–1925).

[4] *Chiang Kai-shek:* Military leader of the Chinese Revolution (1887–1975), later leader of the Nationalist government driven to Taiwan by their former allies, the Chinese Communists.

mouth and a voice came out that wasn't a whisper, but it wasn't a proper voice either. I hoped that she would not cry, fear breaking up her voice like twigs underfoot. She sounded as if she were trying to sing through weeping and strangling. She did not pause or stop to end the embarrassment. She kept going until she said the last word, and then she sat down. When it was my turn, the same voice came out, a crippled animal running on broken legs. You could hear splinters in my voice, bones rubbing jagged against one another. I was loud, though. I was glad I didn't whisper. There was one little girl who whispered.

Engaging the Text

1. Explain the significance of the first paragraph and Kingston's assertion that she "would have been an outlaw knot-maker."
2. Did Kingston's mother literally cut her tongue? If so, why, and what was the result? If not, why does Kingston create this elaborate and graphic story?
3. Why is the young Kingston silent in American school? What's the connection for her between being silent and being Chinese? Between being silent and being female?
4. Kingston writes that school became "a misery" (para. 21). Was this misery avoidable? What, if anything, could Kingston, her American school, her parents, or her Chinese school have done better?
5. Compare and contrast the two schools Kingston attended. Consider their activities, their rules, the behavior of the students and teachers, their probable goals. Why are the schools so different?

Exploring Connections

6. Compare and contrast Kingston's experience with that of the speaker in Inés Hernández-Ávila's "Para Teresa" (p. 74). Consider each girl's relationship to her family, her attitude toward school, and her strategy for coping with or fitting into Anglo society.
7. Richard Rodriguez (p. 61) also reports a period of silence and discomfort in school. How does his situation compare with Kingston's? Are the differences you see a matter of degree, or were the two students silent for different reasons?
8. How might the Sadkers (p. 86) explain Kingston's silence in school?
9. Write a scenario in which the silent young Kingston encounters a "connected teacher" (see "Connected Education for Women," p. 115). What would the teacher do, and how might the young Kingston respond? Read your scenario aloud in class.

Extending the Critical Context

10. Write a journal entry or essay about a time you felt silenced in school. Describe the situation in detail. How did you perceive yourself? How do you think others perceived you? What factors, both in and outside the classroom, led to the situation?

Connected Education for Women

BLYTHE MCVICKER CLINCHY,
MARY FIELD BELENKY,
NANCY GOLDBERGER,
AND JILL MATTUCK TARULE

Like Myra Sadker and David Sadker (p. 86), the authors of this excerpt believe that higher education in the United States unnecessarily intimidates and alienates women students, and that schools usually fail to teach in the productive and humane ways they should. They based their conclusions on extensive interviews with more than a hundred women in widely diverse colleges and adult education programs. In this brief selection, they explain how "connected education" might solve some of the problems women experience in school. The authors are all psychologists — Blythe Clinchy at Wellesley College, Mary Belenky at the University of Vermont, Nancy Goldberger at the Fielding Institute in Santa Barbara, and Jill Tarule at the University of Vermont, where she is dean of education. The article from which this reading is excerpted appeared in the Journal of Education *in 1985. In 1988 the same authors published* Women's Ways of Knowing: The Development of Self, Voice, and Mind, *which won the Distinguished Publication Award from the Association of Women in Psychology.*

Most of the institutions of higher education in this country were designed by men, and most continue to be run by men. In recent years feminist teachers and scholars have begun to question the structure, the curriculum, and the pedagogical practices of these institutions, and they have put forth useful proposals for change (e.g., Bowles & Duelli Klein, 1983; Martin, 1984; Nicholson, 1980; Rich, 1979; Spanier, Bloom, & Borovik, 1984). But in order to design an education appropriate for women we must learn about the academic experiences of ordinary women, women who are, in most cases, neither teachers nor scholars nor even feminists, but simply students.

In a project on "Education for Women's Development," supported by the Fund for the Improvement of Post-secondary Education, we asked 135 ordinary women to share their educational experiences with us. The women were drawn from three private liberal arts colleges (a women's college, an "early college" which admits younger students, and a progressive coeducational college), an inner-city community college, an urban public high school, two adult education programs, and three rural human service agencies which we call "invisible colleges." The women ranged in age from 16 to 65 and came from a variety of ethnic, class, and religious backgrounds. Some were single, some divorced, some married. Many had borne and raised children.

Connected Teaching

Not one of the women we interviewed advocated the traditional form of education characterized by Paulo Freire[1] as a "banking model," in which the teacher's role is "to 'fill' the students by making deposits of information which he considers to constitute true knowledge," and the student's job is merely to "store the deposits" (Freire, 1971, p. 60). Even a woman who, heavily dependent upon knowledge received from authorities, said, "I just want to listen to the instructor" said, in almost the next breath, "I don't really think that anybody can put something into someone that isn't there. It has to be there."

Many women expressed — some firmly, some shakily — this belief that they possessed latent knowledge. The kind of teacher they praised and the kind they yearned for was a teacher who would help them articulate and expand their latent knowledge: a midwife-teacher. The midwife-teacher is the opposite of the banker-teacher. While the bank clerk deposits knowledge in the learner's head, the midwife draws it out. She assists the students in giving birth to their own ideas, in making their own tacit knowledge explicit and elaborating it.

Here are some examples of women talking about their midwife-teachers: 5
"She helped me to be able to say what I wanted to say." "He said to me, 'What you're thinking is fine, but think more.' " "She let me do what I wanted to do [with my poetry] and helped me do it and pushed it further." "She told me, 'Go home and write what you feel, because then you can look at it and see how you felt.' " "I told her that I'd had this dream that inspired my painting, and she said, 'Keep drawing from that dream until you can't draw from it any more.' "

In Freire's banking model the teacher constructs knowledge in private and talks about it in public, so that the students may store it. In the connected education model, as in Freire's "problem-posing" model, teacher and students construct knowledge together. Several women cherished memories of classes like this. One woman told us about a connected class that had occurred by accident. Usually, she said, her English teacher "just hands you his thoughts," but on one memorable occasion he allowed a discussion to erupt.

> We were all raising our hands and talking about I forget what book, and some of the students brought up things that he hadn't thought about that made him see it in a whole different way, and he was really excited, and we all came to a conclusion that none of us had started out with. We came up with an answer to a question we thought was unanswerable in the be-

[1] *Paulo Freire:* Noted Brazilian educator, philosopher, and political activist (b. 1921).

> ginning, and it just made you all feel really good when you walked out of class. You felt you had accomplished something and that you understood the book. And he was pleased, too.

At the next class meeting, however, the teacher had reverted to the banking mode. "I guess he doesn't like that method," the student said.

The connected class provides a culture in which ideas can grow. It is, in the writer Peter Elbow's[2] (1973) words, a "yoghurt" class, as opposed to a "movie" class. Members of the connected class are not mere spectators; they actively nurture each other's ideas. A senior at the women's college tries to explain what goes on in her art history seminar: "Somebody will say, 'Well, do you mean . . . ?' and then somebody else says, 'No, I mean . . .' It's clarifying." The teacher has fostered a special atmosphere in the class.

> It's allowing everyone to voice things that they think are uncertain. It's allowing people to realize that they're not stupid for questioning things. It's okay to say, "Why" or "How" or "What." I think it's important to let everybody voice their uncertainties.

In a connected class no one apologizes for uncertainty. It is assumed that evolving thought must be tentative.

Connected classes seem to work best when members of the group meet over a long period of time and get to know each other well. The early college, a small college in which most classes are conducted as seminars, came closest to fulfilling these conditions. One of the women we interviewed attended the early college for two years and then transferred to a larger school. There she enrolled in a seminar on modern British poetry, one of her favorite topics. "It was awful," she says. "The people didn't know how to talk about anything. They didn't know how to share ideas. It was always an argument. It wasn't an idea to be developed, to be explored." At the early college, students came to know their classmates' styles of thinking. "It was like a family group trying to work out a family problem, except it was an idea." In most colleges there is no chance to form family groups. Each course starts with a new cast of characters, runs for 13 weeks or so, and then disperses.

In a community, unlike a hierarchy, people get to know each other. They do not act as representatives of positions to be attacked or defended or as occupants of roles but as individuals with particular modes of thinking. A first-year student remarked that her editing group composed of three classmates in a writing course was not working: "We just talk about commas and junk like that."

> I had a peer editing group in high school, and it was terrific. But we all knew each other inside out, so you knew what each person was trying to do in her writing, and you knew what kinds of criticisms helped her and what kind hurt her feelings. You can't really help if you don't know people.

[2]*Peter Elbow:* American educator (b. 1935) specializing in writing instruction.

Unless she knows the critic personally and the critic knows her personally, she says, she finds criticism of her work "hurtful, but not helpful."

Connected teaching is personal. Connected teachers present themselves 10
as genuine, flawed human beings. They allow students to observe the imperfect processes of their thinking. Connected teachers take a personal interest in their students. They want to know how each individual student is thinking. But connected teaching is not "soft." It is rigorous. And it is objective, although not coldly impersonal.

Connected teachers practice a sophisticated form of what we call "connected knowing," a "technique of *disciplined* subjectivity" (Erikson, 1964) requiring them to "systematically empathize" with their students (Wilson, 1977, p. 259). They try to practice what Peter Elbow (1973, p. 171) calls "projection in the good sense," using their own reactions to the material the class is studying to formulate hypotheses about the students' reactions.

Cynthia, an alumna quoted earlier, told us about an English teacher who could serve as an ideal prototype.

> This woman and her method of teaching and her attitude towards life moved me very much. She was so rigorous. She wanted things always to add up. You had to have a system and you had to make everything work. You had to assume that there was a purpose to everything the artist did. And if something seemed odd, you couldn't overlook it or ignore it or throw it out.

This teacher was thoroughly "objective" in treating the students' responses as real and independent of her own.

> She was intensely, genuinely interested in everybody's feelings about things. She asked a question and wanted to know what your response was. She wanted to know because she wanted to see what sort of effect this writing was having. She wasn't using us as a sounding board for her own feelings about things. She really wanted to know. . . .

Cynthia's English teacher does not treat her own experience of the material under study as primary, and she does not assume that her students experience the material as she does; this would be undisciplined subjectivity or, as Elbow (1973, p. 171) puts it, "projection in the bad sense." She "really wants to know" how the students are experiencing the material. . . .

Belief, Doubt, and Development

Midwives are believers. They trust their students' thinking and encour- 15
age them to expand it. But in the psychological literature concerning the factors promoting cognitive development, doubt has played a more prominent role than belief and the adversarial model has dominated institutions of higher education (Rich, 1979). In order to stimulate cognitive growth, according to this model, the teacher should point out flaws in the students' thinking, put forth opposing notions, encourage debate, and challenge students to defend their ideas. One should attempt to induce cognitive conflict

in students' minds. We do not deny that cognitive conflict can act as an impetus to growth, but in all our interviews only a handful of women described a powerful and positive learning experience in which a teacher challenged their ideas in this fashion. The women did mention such incidents, but they did not describe them as occasions for cognitive growth. On the whole, women found the experience of being doubted debilitating, rather than energizing.

Because so many women are already filled with self-doubt, doubts imposed from outside seem at best redundant ("I'm always reprimanding myself"), and at worst destructive, confirming their own sense of themselves as inadequate knowers. The doubting model, then, may be peculiarly inappropriate for women (although we are not convinced that it is appropriate for men, either).

We believe that most women want and need an education in which connection is emphasized over separation, understanding and acceptance over judgment and assessment, and collaboration over debate. They need a curriculum which accords respect to and allows time for the knowledge that emerges from firsthand experience. They need a system which, instead of imposing its own expectations and arbitrary requirements, helps them to define their own questions and evolve their own patterns of work for pursuing these questions. These are the lessons we think we have learned in listening to ordinary women.

References

Bowles, G., & Duelli Klein, R. (1983). *Theories of women's studies.* London: Routledge & Kegan Paul.

Elbow, P. (1973). *Writing without teachers.* London: Oxford University Press.

Erikson, E. (1964). On the nature of clinical evidence. In E. Erikson, *Insight and responsibility* (pp. 49–80). New York: Norton.

Freire, P. (1971). *Pedagogy of the oppressed.* New York: Seaview.

Martin, J. (1984). Bringing women into educational thought. *Educational Theory, 34,* 341–353.

Nicholson, L. (1980). Women and schooling. *Educational Theory, 30,* 225–233.

Rich, A. (1979). *On Lies, Secrets, and Silence: Selected prose: 1966–78.* New York: Norton.

Spanier, B., Bloom, A., & Borovik, D. (1984). *Toward a balanced curriculum: A source book for initiating gender integration projects.* Cambridge, MA: Schenkman.

Wilson, S. (1977). The use of ethnographic techniques in educational research. *Review of Educational Research, 47,* 245–265.

ENGAGING THE TEXT

1. Explain in your own words what is meant by the "banking model," by "midwife-teachers," by a "yoghurt class," and by "connected education."
2. Write an extended journal entry about a class you've taken, either in college or in the past, that illustrates the "banking model" of education. How would you

evaluate the experience? Do you agree with the suggestion that a traditional "banking" approach affects women more than men?

3. Write another journal entry, this time about your educational experience which most closely resembled "connected education." Was this experience as positive as Clinchy et al. portray it to be? Why do you think connected education is so rare?

Exploring Connections

4. To what extent does the model of connected education presented by Clinchy et al. address the gender inequities described by Myra Sadker and David Sadker (p. 86)? What more might be necessary to ensure equity for women?
5. In "Social Class and the Hidden Curriculum of Work" (p. 45), Jean Anyon links specific classroom practices with the social status and jobs different schools expect their students to hold later in life. Write your own analysis of how traditional practices in higher education relate to the expected social status and jobs of women.
6. Drawing on the analysis of traditional and connected teaching in this article, discuss which model best describes Jack MacFarland in Mike Rose's " 'I Just Wanna Be Average' " (p. 33).
7. Theodore Sizer (p. 20) and Clinchy et al. present a number of metaphors to describe different models of education: "academic supermarket," "conveyor belt," "banking model," "midwife-teachers," "yoghurt class." Brainstorm a list of your own metaphors that capture the experience of schooling.

Extending the Critical Context

8. Analyze your current classes for evidence of connected and traditional teaching techniques. Write a journal entry on your reactions to the teaching styles you observe, and compare notes with classmates.
9. When teachers attempt to practice connected teaching (peer editing groups, collaborative learning groups, small group discussions, and so on), they find that some students resist these efforts. Why do you think some students reject them?
10. Many contemporary writers — including scholars, poets, novelists, and political activists — suggest that women experience and respond to the world differently than men. Write a short narrative about a world in which "women's values" dominate. Share your story in class and discuss.

Secondary Schools, Primary Lessons

GEORGE H. WOOD

The stories of Mike Rose (p. 33), Richard Rodriguez (p. 61), and Malcolm X (p. 77) earlier in this chapter all showed individuals succeeding despite *the educational system they encountered. Now you will read about whole schools whose innovative methods have produced lots of successful students, sometimes where they would be least expected. As you learn about Harlem's "CPESS" and New Hampshire's Thayer, compare them to the schools you have attended. Your "tour guide" to these schools is himself the principal of a high school, a professor of education at Ohio State University, and a former elementary and middle school teacher. He has published many articles on education and democracy as well as the book from which this piece is taken,* Schools That Work: America's Most Innovative Public Education Programs *(1992).*

At Central Park East Secondary School in New York City's Harlem neighborhood, four students are crowded over a set of observation notes. They have been conducting a series of experiments and observations on the topic of nutrition. Their work has included measuring and calculating the calories in various foods, identifying parts of the tongue that respond to various tastes, and researching the differences in eating habits over generations.

Today the team is exploring how best to exhibit their findings. A slide-tape show is discarded because not enough people would see it. Posters are judged inadequate as well: too many posters are already on display. "What about flyers for preschools and things like senior centers?" Sherri, thirteen and ready to change the world, suggests. The group seizes on the idea and within minutes they've divided the tasks. Two students begin layout work, while Sherri and Loretta head out to get prices for printing and lists of possible distribution points.

Somewhere near Thayer Junior/Senior High School in Winchester, New Hampshire, a team of students with a video camera and notebooks walks slowly through an open field. The land is slated to become a hazardous-waste dump, and the kids are anxious to find out what it is the town would be covering up. A spring is discovered, filmed, and noted, as are several species of wildflowers and tracks and other signs of animals. These findings, analyzed back in the school's science room, become the basis for a communitywide hearing on the proposed dump — and its ultimate rejection.

Back at Central Park East yet another team of kids is tackling a complex math problem. They've been asked to construct their own instrument for measuring the movement of stars and planets. But first they have to come up with a formula that allows for the earth's movement as well. It's quite a puzzle, and they tackle it again and again, each false start seeming to redouble their determination. Finally they hit upon an idea, take what they already know about the speed of the earth, measure the movement of the sun, and begin computing the earth's effect on another object's movement through the sky. An imperfect start, but one that over time will reveal a great deal about mathematics, astronomy, and science.

In Rabun Gap, Georgia, a group of high school students publish the 5
quarterly *Foxfire* magazine. Over the past quarter-century they and their predecessors have also published nearly a dozen books — each researched, written, edited, and sold to publishers by the kids themselves. In class today there is a debate over whether to put a picture of a husband and wife who had not been traditionally well-respected in the community on the cover. A poor family, they supported themselves through doing odd jobs and producing unusual whirligigs for lawns — over one hundred of which occupied the lawn in front of their converted-boxcar home. Several of the students had taken an interest in the family and their work and had developed a deeper appreciation of their life and craft. But putting their picture on the cover of *Foxfire* magazine would raise more than a few eyebrows in the area. After a long discussion, the issue was put to rest when Kim rose to speak:

> Growing up in Rabun County and knowin' about the —— s, it's kinda like Polish jokes, a thing you take for granted. . . . But once I got into the article, I saw how his work is artistic, it's folk art, it's valuable. . . . He's a proud man, and he has lots of character . . . and they deserve some respect.

So do Kim and all of her colleagues, because they show us what kids can do if only given a chance. And giving every kid this chance is a measure of how well each of the schools discussed in this chapter works.

Harlem, New York City: Less Is More

On the corner of Madison Avenue and East 103rd Street stands a moderate-size, relatively unattractive brick school building. It is the Jackie Robinson School Building and it houses what many think is one of the best secondary schools in New York or perhaps the entire United States — Central Park East Secondary School (CPESS). This is not a likely location for such a school. The campus is run-down, hemmed in by busy Madison Avenue on one side, an elevated mass transit train track on the other, and the large towers of overcrowded subsidized housing projects all around. The view out any first- or second-floor window is impeded by metal screening over the windows to prevent breakins, and in case that fails, all the computers are wheeled every night to locked closets for which only teachers have keys.

To get to school students often negotiate piles of garbage, homeless people asleep on the sidewalk, and the occasional offer of illicit drugs.

Once inside the school it is as if you have entered another world. The halls are spotless. Science rooms bubble with ongoing student experiments, math rooms are cluttered with models and physical shapes, and humanities rooms hold back avalanches of books and ideas. Your attention is always drawn inward, and for a while you forget the street outside.

The students here are not those who come to mind for most of us when we think about school success. The makeup of the student body is a prototype of schools that fail. The school draws the majority of its students from east and central Harlem, two of New York's poorest neighborhoods. As is to be expected, approximately 75 percent of the children come from poor families. The students also come from ethnic groups that are not traditionally successful in the New York school system. Approximately 45 percent of the students are black and 30 percent are Hispanic, groups that in the city of New York have drop-out rates of 78 percent and 72 percent respectively.

And yet these children are succeeding at CPESS. One indication of that 10
success is that virtually no one drops out of school. Another is that CPESS students do as well or better than children in any other New York City school on citywide standardized tests. But there is yet another, more important indicator—the kids themselves. You notice first that they arrive early, some more than an hour before school, so that they can use the library or attend the optional foreign language classes. Follow them through the day and watch the excitement in their eyes as they prepare a video on executive power to show other students, or their concentration as they build instruments to measure the motion of the planets and stars, or their sorrow as Lennie brings George to his "farm" in the closing pages of Steinbeck's *Of Mice and Men*. In the halls the chatter is happy, friendly, good-natured—you are greeted with smiles and offers of help. Herb Rosenfeld, the teacher who doubles as assistant principal, tests your observational skills: "Have you found the place where the kids go off to hide and smoke during the day?" You admit that, no, maybe you're not such a good observer, you have not yet found such a spot. And Herb grins: "There isn't one."

How can this be? Amidst all the horror stories about inner-city schools, here is a school (and there are many others) that succeeds, both by conventional measures and by the clear indications kids themselves give. But this school doesn't have the back-to-the-basics, sit-in-the-desk-and-be-quiet environment that many have come to equate with teaching and learning. Instead, it is an active, busy place, with students coming and going, working in groups, seldom if ever reading a textbook, and engaged in a wide variety of tasks. Two things make this possible: a sense of community that is built here, and a narrowed yet richer curriculum. These two things lead to students who care about their learning, themselves, and each other.

The sense of community at CPESS is built through both the internal organization of the school and links to the community outside the school walls. CPESS was started in 1985, and Deborah Meier, the school's principal (called Debbie by staff and students alike), makes it clear that the desire to see kids more connected to a school was a driving force behind its founding. She and the staff wanted to be different from the "huge and impersonal" high schools that dot the city: "Places with thousands of kids, hundreds of teachers, a vast array of complex schedules, no cohesion, and little sense of community — where many kids get lost, lose hope, are uninspired."

To combat this alienation, CPESS is kept small and made smaller still by dividing it up into "houses." Each house of around 80 students and four teachers holds two grade levels, seventh/eighth, ninth/tenth, or eleventh/twelfth (also called the Senior Institute). The relatively low student/teacher ratio is accomplished by having *everyone* teach; you won't find teams of administrators huddled over coffee or behind closed office doors in this building.

To make the school even smaller and more personal, there is its basic building block — advisory. According to Herb, to understand CPESS you have to "start with what happens in advisory." Each teacher is assigned a group of about fourteen students (that's how many fit in a school-district van), all from the same grade level, all in his or her house. Unlike the usual homeroom setup, where kids show up in the morning, hear announcements, and leave, advisory groups meet for nearly three hours a week. The time is occupied with the usual housekeeping chores — attendance, announcements, materials to be sent home. But more important, advisory is where kids connect with the school through a single adult.

"The advisory is a group arrangement in which one adult develops a 15
relationship with a number of students that allows him to paint a complete picture of each of these students, at least in school," explains Herb. "In order to do that, you have to know what kids are feeling. So, through a variety of different devices — journal writing, small group discussion — kids are pushed to express themselves. Express themselves in detail and at length and to reach for what they may be thinking or feeling that normally they may not express." Advisory groups take trips together, and the advisor is the one who reports all academic progress to families and maintains contact with a child's home. This structure is a clear and deliberate attempt to create community, to support children and integrate them into the life of the school.

The students themselves speak most eloquently about the system. "Ricky [Harris, a teacher in the seventh/eighth grade house] cares about us. That's why he's always calling us at home when we're absent, and pushing us to get our work done to our best. He treats me like a little brother, and I love him like a brother, too." A tenth-grade student who attended another high school for two years echoes Debbie Meier's observation: "At [the other school] we were just numbers. Here everybody knows you, especially your advisor. We can go to Herb for help with school, home, whatever; he's always there." Small classes, houses, advisory: that is what community at CPESS is all about — someone is always there.

Of course, the danger with any tight-knit community is that it can turn in on itself to the exclusion of others, encouraging members not to build relationships with outsiders (say, for example, communities built on racism, religious intolerance, or age). Unfortunately, many of the "communities" to which our children belong do just that. Formally, think about single-sex organizations, religious groups of believers only, athletic teams from which many students are cut, and social groups based on academic criteria. Informally, think of the cliques children form which ostracize some students, making them untouchables who can socially contaminate any student who offers help or support. Then think of the school — when the door swings shut at the start of the day, virtually no one is let out without passes, in triplicate signed three days before, virtually no one comes in, and all life is segregated by age as teenagers find only other teens for models. Here the main form of interaction children have with other "communities" is to cheer for their defeat and humiliation on the athletic field. And we wonder why young people seem so unwilling to be "involved" in the community. How did adults get so dumb?

Students are not kept in isolation at CPESS. Every Monday through Thursday morning, if you stand outside the school, you see what seems to be a steady stream of truants, kids who stopped by to be counted as present but are now slipping back out for a day. In fact, these are some of the most responsible young people around: students on the way to their community service placement. For half a day each week every student works as a volunteer in one of over forty-five different community service placements throughout the Upper East and West Sides of New York City. Working as a teacher's aide, organizing games for children in a pediatric emergency unit, getting out a mailing for a community theater, writing for a neighborhood newspaper, talking, or more important, listening, to senior citizens at a nursing home, all these tasks and more are taken on by the students.

The school day is structured so that an entire house is gone from the school at the same time, so students do not miss classes and staff have extended planning time together. While students do not receive a grade for their work, it is a vital part of their educational experience that must be completed for graduation. The students are responsible for getting to and from the placement on their own — and they do, either walking, taking a subway, or riding a bus. Seldom, if ever, do they miss a day. There is a simple lesson here: give a student a real responsibility, and he or she will act responsibly.

Naomi Danzig, coordinator of the service program, was there at the 20
beginning when Debbie Meier suggested that it would be good if students left CPESS with a marketable skill and some real-life experience in the world of work. The program has developed in ways that go well beyond that original goal, as students have developed links to their own community that help them see the contribution they can make. Naomi puts it this way: "We want them to see how they are powerful people right now. That they can con-

tribute and be effective now, not at some far-off date in the future. In other words, this has very little to do with credentials. We live in a highly credentialed society that can only assess people on the basis of pieces of paper. We say all of our kids can contribute now, that they are all capable of understanding the difference they can make. The students are more spontaneous [in the program]; they are generally on their own so it allows them to be who they are, caring, warm, insightful; these are not attributes that normally early or middle adolescents praise in one another. The peer pressures are as strong here as anywhere else: how you dress, how you walk, what you do in or out of school. . . . We hope, we know, this gives them an opportunity to be themselves."

But does the academic agenda of the classroom get slighted in all this? Kids out of school, advisory meetings during the day, what about all the calls we hear for more "time on task," more hours in the school day? CPESS has an answer for its doubters on this agenda: less is more.

Unlike the comprehensive high schools so many of us know or knew in our hometowns, students at CPESS do not choose their courses from a list of electives. Every student takes the same core of courses. But it is not a core curriculum like that being touted by test-and-measure statehouse reformers. You won't find endless lists of names and dates to memorize, or sheets of math problems to work. The curriculum at CPESS is, in Herb's words, "thematically developed through essential questions, and learning and growth are assessed by kids doing things." The best way to look at the thematic and narrowed nature of the curriculum is to follow one student through a day at CPESS. Remember, though, there is no such thing as a typical day; some days start with advisory and some end with it; community service is scheduled once a week; and academic classes may take the entire morning, or afternoon, or both. We'll follow Jimi, a seventh grader in the East House of Division I (seventh and eighth graders). In other schools Jimi would be in a pull-out program for children with special needs. Living with his unemployed mother in one of the area's many housing projects, he came to CPESS after not finding success in several other New York City schools. Here, he began the year by attempting to burn down the school. Today, halfway through the school year, he's our tour guide and you would never have picked him out as a "problem" student.

Jimi's school day can begin as early at 8 A.M., when the school building opens. Jimi makes a point of arriving at 8:15, when the school is already buzzing with activity. He finds a corner in the library and spends about half an hour on his schoolwork. The next fifteen minutes are spent on the rapid-fire give and take that only another teenager could understand.

The academic day begins at 9, and today that means Jimi is in Ricky Harris's humanities/social studies class. This class meets for two hours, as do most of the classes, allowing extended time for real work. This year's theme is the emergence of contemporary political issues, with a focus on United States History. Next year, Jimi and his fellow seventh graders will study the peopling of America — the theme this year's eighth graders had last year. The two-year rotation of themes insures that every student in the multi-graded houses gets every theme. The eighth graders will move on to the ninth/tenth-grade themes of comparative systems of law and government and non-European traditions.

Today Ricky and his students are dealing with the news media and its 25
influence on political events. This particular topic is a spin-off of an earlier one in which the students followed the 1988 presidential election from the perspective of the issues in their community and the influence of people of color on electoral politics. Ricky has cast backward today, using the Boston Massacre and accounts of it to discuss propaganda. Listening in on the discussion you hear the same questions repeated several times — how do we know that, what evidence do you have, where would we find out? These and other questions have a familiar ring because versions of these same questions are posted in various places on the walls. On one wall are the "essential questions," which all of the humanities teachers utilize to organize the subject matter under consideration. They are:

- How do people achieve power?
- How do people respond to being deprived of power?
- How does power change hands?
- What gives laws their power?

Of course, these questions change each year as the humanities theme changes. Another set of questions is located near the door in every room in the school. These questions form the "Habits of Mind" that all teachers in all subject matters focus on:

- How do we know what we know?
- What's the evidence?
- What's the viewpoint?
- How else may it be considered?
- What difference does it make?

So when Ricky asks if Paul Revere's etching and poem about the Boston Massacre are accurate, it makes sense that these twelve- and thirteen-year-olds ask fairly sophisticated questions in response. For instance, what news accounts of the event are available, what did British papers report, and what would be a credible source for information about the actual events? And when students are grappling with the underlying issue here, it makes sense that they see propaganda as a tool some people use to get power. Building from one theme, they have not only developed a complex understanding of a historical event but have also begun to grasp a concept that will serve them well for their lives as citizens: propaganda and its uses.

At 11:00 Jimi and his friends move on to the two-hour math/science block. For the most part students receive an hour of each subject, changing rooms and teachers halfway through the period. However, the block does allow for the teachers to collaborate and extend the time as needed. In Bridget Bellettiere's math class students are working on a variety of tasks around the theme of patterns in numbers. All of them will make either a slide rule or an abacus as a way of presenting how number sets work. Their projects will be accompanied by reports on the principles behind their exhibits. Similar exhibitions are used in all subject areas to evaluate what students know. Several times during the class Bridget is approached by a student who has found an easier way to unlock the problems presented by the slide rule or abacus. Each time she smiles and responds that of course it's all right to use the "easier" way; after all, the students have just unlocked another pattern in math.

Science follows immediately, and the students quickly gather in groups to work on their exhibition in this area. For two years the science curriculum in Division I focuses on the human being, teaching basic biology through the questions of who and what we are, how we work, and how we fit into the environment. Utilizing scientific methods of inquiry, students explore issues in fitness, nutrition, reproduction, growth, the brain and senses, and ecology. Jimi's group is working on an exhibition that involves devising an experiment to determine the salt and sugar threshold for twenty other students. This work requires two additional skills, computer science and art, that we haven't seen earlier today and that seem to have been missing from the curriculum.

In fact, both of these subjects are woven into the core courses Jimi has 30
had today. Studio art is taught directly through a ten-week course that introduces students to a variety of media. But the real art instruction comes as students visit Joel Handorff's art room to integrate artistic endeavors into their exhibitions. And art and music appreciation are taught in the humanities classes as those topics naturally arise through the students' studies. Computer science is approached in a similar way, taught when the students need computer skills for computation, graphing, word processing, or similar tasks. Again, less is more. By taking just two or three subjects, utilizing a limited number of questions about them, and pursuing those questions thematically, students gain a wide range of skills that help them do something real with what they are learning.

At 1:00 Jimi is off to lunch. This is when the physical education program takes place as well, including a fair number of intramural sports. Jimi returns to Ricky's room for advisory for the last hour of the day. Advisory today deals with academics, in particular how often students are writing in their journals, what books they are reading for leisure, how well they are doing their homework. They also need to discuss how to raise money for their advisory trip. Ricky checks in with each young person and offers suggestions for improvement. Next time advisory may cover health and family education (including sex education and drug abuse), career exploration, or social and ethical concerns. Each advisor builds a program around these issues as his/her group needs them.

After school Jimi heads home. Other students linger in the library (open until 5:00), some stay for instrumental music, still others for team sports. Jimi and his colleagues have had another good day at a very special school. It's a place where people care about one another, where students gain in-depth understandings of the world around them, where what they do matters. It's a school where Lindsay, a tenth grader, claims she has "learned to learn for myself. I'll think of something that wasn't there; I'll figure it out my own way. I'm learning stuff that wasn't even asked." And it's the answers to those unasked questions that make all the difference—in this school and in our lives.

Winchester, New Hampshire: Getting the Climate Right

The New England states: picture-postcard perfect, a mecca for nature lovers of all sorts, fall foliage, winter skiing, spring maple sugaring, summer backpacking. Dotted with small villages distinguished by their general stores and village greens, parts of New England seem to be stuck in time; a simpler, slower, more genteel era of town meetings, yeoman farmers, small merchants, and face-to-face democracy. Indeed, these enduring traditions of communal life do still exist here, and at their best they remind us of what democratic life can promise. But the problems of the modern world know no geographic boundary—and they show up in the lives of New England's young people just as they do in New York City.

At the end of Park Street in the village of Winchester, New Hampshire, sits Thayer Junior/Senior High School. It is a school that only a decade ago had a drop-out rate of nearly 50 percent, and fewer than 15 percent of the graduates went on to higher education of any form. Underlying all this was a feeling that many students at Thayer just were not connected to the school. Faced with fairly limited employment possibilities when they left school, students saw few reasons to attend to the curriculum or the life of the school.

Into this setting entered Dennis Littky, an educator taking time out from 35
his career to rebuild a cabin and nurture a community newspaper. When the Thayer principalship came open in the summer of 1981, Littky applied and reentered the educational world. He came with a vision: "I knew that I wanted the kids to be good thinkers, to use their minds, to like school; I knew I wanted the relationship between teachers and kids to be good—I wanted us to not be fighting but to work together; so there was all that stuff that I knew. . . . But now the question was, how do you go about doing that?" The answer to that question presented itself as Dennis spent the summer meeting with every student, teacher, and most of the parents in the community. Simply put, says Dennis, "Everyone knew the atmosphere had to

get better. And that was my first thing. I don't think you can move on to other areas until you get the climate right."

Getting the climate right meant a number of things at Thayer. First it meant turning the physical space of the building into a place that invited students rather than repulsed them. The work started in the common spaces of the school—the cafeteria, the entryways, the halls. Not only were tables and ceilings repaired, walls painted, and floors patched, but a special project began as well. One student, a returning senior, had indicated little interest in school in his summer meeting with Dennis. Dennis searched to find an activity to keep the young man in school, and he found it in art. Dennis offered him a cafeteria wall as a canvas. After a summer of work, the Pegasus, a life-size mural exploding with color, emerged. Given Thayer's history it isn't surprising that bets were placed among the local townspeople as to when the Pegasus would be defaced. It watches over the cafeteria today, however, untouched, serving as the unofficial mascot for the school. Almost every year it is joined by another mural, just as dramatic, somewhere in the school, a mural always initiated and designed by a student (or students).

The message in this seemingly simple act of environmental enhancement (apparently not so obvious when we look at the drab, sterile, or often outright ugly school interiors in so many communities) was to tell students that someone cared about them, that someone was willing to take a risk to make their space more pleasant. But beauty wasn't enough, and the next move was to challenge and change the academic structures that create the inhospitable environments in so many schools. It was these changes that protected the murals as well as raised Thayer's graduation rate to nearly 95 percent, with over 60 percent of those graduates going on to some form of higher education.

Much of the conventional wisdom today is that school days need to be longer. Littky started in the other direction: "I figured it made no sense to do more of what we already weren't doing right. So one of the first things I did was to call the state [education office] to find out what the minimum amount of time was that we could spend in school." The answer was six and a half hours, so Thayer went to a six-period day, one hour per period, and *no* study halls. Then every student met with Littky to work out a schedule, and as needs arose—say students wanting to intern in a day-care center or a local senior citizen center—they were worked into the schedule.

When you visit Thayer you immediately pick up the relaxed tempo that hour-long class periods generate. Students are not lugging around seven sets of books, racing from room to room at thirty-seven minutes after, or eight minutes until, the hour. Rather, classes move easily into extended projects and teachers and students savor the time available to settle in, focus, read, discuss, or write about the topic at hand. At the end of the period there is not the usual flurry of books slapping shut, quickly scribbled assignments, work tossed on the desk, and a mad dash for the door. In fact, there are not even any bells ringing to mark the passing of a period, and more likely than not someone will forget to ring the only bell of the day, the one at the day's close.

Not satisfied, always seeing the school as "a living organism that has got 40
to be changing all the time," Littky and his staff have begun moving toward using even larger blocks of time for extended study. One of the most interesting of these projects, and something of a model for other parts of the school, is the Spectrum program. The idea behind Spectrum is simple: take a team of teachers from different subject areas, give them the first four hours of the day and the same number of students they would normally see during that time, and let them design their own program. What has emerged is a group of eleventh and twelfth graders of all abilities (admitted on a first come, first serve basis), three teachers (in natural history, English, and math), and a schedule that leaves you wondering why everyone doesn't do it this way.

Dan Bisaccio, Julie Gainsburg, and Val Cole are the Spectrum teachers. Every week they work with fifty-five students, the same students they have shared as a team all year. The students are divided into three subgroups and rotate between teachers, some days seeing all three, others seeing just one or two for extended periods of time. In addition, one period a day is set aside as a "coaching period," a time when the students are not formally scheduled into a room but can work in small groups on projects or meet one-on-one with a teacher for extra help. Often they learn from a curriculum that is woven together by a theme. Like their experience with Thoreau's *Walden*[1] — they first read the book in English class and then studied the pond's geologic origins in natural history class.

Aside from linking the curriculum together, there are two additional benefits from altering the usual schedule of the high school day. The first and most obvious is the ability to make the daily schedule respond to the curriculum, not the curriculum respond to the schedule. Dan, who teaches natural history, provides us with a simple example: "I wanted to go out collecting fossils at a place about a mile from here. It didn't make sense to bring all the kids to the site; it would be somewhat dangerous for one thing, and, two, a lot of people would get lost in the shuffle. So we were able to work out a schedule where for three days I was able to take one group of kids per day for the whole morning to the site. It didn't interfere with their academic schedule at all because the three of us just arranged it so the other two would take kids for longer periods of time." Time, such a precious commodity in a child's life; how important to be able to spend it wisely and with care. The second benefit is a by-product of the time issue, but an intended one. Spectrum makes the school smaller and gives the students another point of connection with it. While in some high schools students see

[1]*Walden:* The classic book about self-reliance and nature published by Henry David Thoreau in 1854.

seven or eight teachers a day, these kids spend virtually all of their time with three. While some high school students rotate through seven classes with upward of thirty different companions per session, these students spend most of their day with just several dozen people.

But the students' connection with the program is not left to chance. A special space — an abandoned barn behind the school — has become the group's "home" away from the school; group outings are a regular part of the program; and parents are involved in both social and planning activities. Spectrum provides a special place where kids and teachers have time not only to pursue subjects but also to get to know one another. It is a way of connecting the student with the school community, letting each student know that he or she counts.

But what of the other students at Thayer? Are they connected as well? Indeed, long before Spectrum [or the similar teaming efforts that are under way], Littky and his faculty had instituted an advisory system at Thayer. Similar in intent to the program at Central Park East, it was another part of Littky's agenda to get the climate right. Each Thayer staff member, including the principal and guidance counselor, is assigned a group of advisees. Since all faculty members are involved, each advisory group consists of only ten students. It stays together throughout the students' two junior high and four high school years at Thayer. Each advisor is responsible for all communication home about his/her students, arranging parent conferences, compiling report cards, and the general life of each advisee at school.

Don Weisberger, a special education teacher at Thayer, describes the 45
system's effect this way: "Advisory in one word is communication. It makes the school smaller. . . . [Students] know someone's there for them, they are not getting lost among all the other students. . . . In advisory we don't talk *at* kids, we talk *with* kids."

For Greg, a senior, the system has meant that an "advisor is there if we have problems, say, like with another teacher, or school, or whatever, or if we just need someone to talk to. [My advisor] wants to know as much as he can about each person so he knows their weaknesses and their strengths and he is always willing to help. . . . He looks out for us as much as he can."

Beyond these formal structures, the folks at Thayer challenge yet one more notion that often shapes the structures of schooling. Inherent in much school organization is the assumption that individuals cannot be responsible for their own behavior, that it takes suspensions, assistant principals, student handbooks, and grades to keep students in line.

The school Littky came to was plagued with discipline problems. Teachers felt they had no control; kids felt overwhelmed by the rules. The solution was, first, to assume that student misbehavior and teacher frustration weren't necessarily the "fault" of either party. Rather, as Dennis puts it, any time a student was in trouble, "I assumed it wasn't just the kid's fault but a problem of the environment." So the staff and the students took a long look at the school rules, giving here, taking there, but really looking at what is necessary to make a school run. Finally they came up with a few rules that everyone could agree on — at which point they were hardly needed. The cycle of mistrust and tension was broken merely by everyone "getting clear that the priority was the kids. That we would do whatever we could for the kids, and were doing it, through advisory and the schedule and all the other stuff. And when you treat them with respect, with dignity, they act responsibly." The gospel according to Littky.

And it works. Dan Bisaccio points out that one of the big differences between Thayer and other schools he knows of is that you "don't find the kids rowdy to the extent you might expect; there's virtually no vandalism or theft here." That explains why there are *no locks* on the lockers in the hall. Stephanie, a junior, explains that "kids here aren't into stealing and stuff. It just won't be right to do that to your friends." When I'm walking down the hall with Dennis I point out several locks on a row of lockers. "Oh, yeah," he chuckles, "those are seventh graders, they haven't figured out where they are yet."

The responsible nature of the students flows outside the school as well. 50
At one time, as hard as I find this to believe after my visits to Thayer, the kids at the school were apparently referred to by some as the "Thayer animals." Disaffected, angry, alienated, they were unwelcome in many places and feared in others. But now the name "Thayer" on a letter jacket or windbreaker marks a student as someone special. Thayer students are recognized as valuable members of the community, as people who make Winchester's junior and senior high schools among the best around. Dan mentioned this to me as we were traveling on the field trip to Walden. "Most of the time we are told that our students are some of the most knowledgeable and best-behaved students that the host has ever met." At the end of that days's visit as we were leaving Walden Pond, the naturalist who had been our guide caught up with Dan and me as we returned to our car. "You know," he said, "we get hundreds of groups through here every year. But I can't remember one that was this well-mannered, asked so many questions, and treated the place with such respect. Would you please thank your students for me?" Dan just looked at me and smiled.

Of course, changing a school's character and structure is never easy. In some ways it may be even harder to change in the often very conservative and close-knit communities of New England. Such was the case in Winchester, as Littky found when he was fired in 1987. It took several court challenges and the election of a new school board to reinstate him, but in the end of the majority of the community rallied around him. It wasn't an easy time for Dennis, his teachers, or the students. But he never entertained the thought of just walking away. He and his staff are driven by a vision that makes their work possible, and that makes coming to school every day a challenge they want to face: "When it all works, I'd like the kid to be an inquisitive learner. To be somebody who is excited about reading a book or learning something, or seeing something. A person who is strong enough to stand up and speak for what he or she wants. A person . . . who is continuing to learn and to grow. Somebody who understands him or herself and understands learning. That's what is important."

Engaging the Text

1. Review Wood's descriptions of Central Park East Secondary School (CPESS) and Thayer Junior/Senior High School and jot down, in your own words, a list of the central concepts that make these schools work (e.g., "Learning is active, not passive"). Compare notes with other students and discuss which of these concepts are most important. Has your own schooling been built on a similar or different philosophy of education? To extend the assignment, consider what students can do at your college to make sure higher education does not resemble a bad high school education.
2. What conditions (types of teacher, students, parents, resources, etc.) are needed to create the kinds of extraordinary schools that Wood describes? Do you think such schools can flourish anywhere?
3. Wood's descriptions of these schools are very positive. Do you see any potential problems with the education at CPESS and Thayer?

Exploring Connections

4. Compare and contrast Jimi's day at CPESS to Mark's day in Theodore Sizer's "What High School Is" (p. 20).
5. Jean Anyon describes four types of schools in "Social Class and the Hidden Curriculum of Work" (p. 45). Which of these four does CPESS most closely resemble, and why?
6. How closely do the classes in CPESS and Thayer resemble the model of connected education proposed by Blythe McVicker Clinchy et al. (p. 115)?

Extending the Critical Context

7. On the walls of CPESS one can find listed "essential questions" and "Habits of Mind" (paras. 25–26). Organize a group to draft and post key questions or principles for your writing class or other classes.
8. Drawing on concepts and models described in "Secondary Schools, Primary Lessons" and other selections you have read in this chapter, work in groups to draft a proposal for an ideal school. Make your proposal as detailed as possible, addressing the structure of the school day, the kinds of materials taught, teaching/learning methods, student and teacher roles and responsibilities—even the design and setting of the school building.

Not for Sale

Robin Templeton

No school is an island: even in our democratic society, schools have always promoted the values of the broader community. The political and cultural agenda of a classroom can be subtle, as in the "hidden curriculum" of class-based values and behaviors described above by Jean Anyon (p. 45); at other times the agenda is blatantly obvious, as when children in the Southwest were punished for speaking Spanish in the classroom. Many cultural analysts are alarmed at the introduction of commercial messages into schools. In the following essay, Robin Templeton explains some of the problems as well as a few cases of student resistance to classroom commercialism. Templeton is codirector of UNPLUG, a youth campaign for commercial-free education, and editor of Education for the People.

When it comes to public education in the United States, free markets and free minds are mutually exclusive. Recent commercial ventures in the classroom demonstrate that when corporations attempt to cash in on the crisis in education, they are more interested in youth as passive consumers —to be marketed to the highest bidder—than as active thinkers. The most glaring of these ventures is *Channel One*, a commercial TV program which Whittle Communications broadcasts into almost 12,000 junior high and high schools across the country. For each thirty-second commercial on *Channel One* (the program contains two minutes of commercials per broadcast), Whittle garners $195,455 from advertisers including Burger King, Procter & Gamble, and Reebok.

This lesson in classroom commercialism defines democracy — not as civic responsibility or community involvement—but as buyer's choice. Commercialism reduces education to a spectator event and students to a target audience. But students are defying marketers' vision of them as easy converts to brand loyalty. Youth are not just sitting back memorizing advertising jingles: increasingly, they are taking action against commercials in their schools.

Students at Coronado High School in Coronado, California, for instance, wrote an editorial in their school paper headlined "*Channel One* Invades Coronado High School" which asked: "Do you get the feeling that Big Brother will be watching? I do. . . . We must investigate [the makers of *Channel One*] more before we put such a huge amount of trust in their hands. . . . Selling advertising minutes out of our school day exploits the entire educational process. It cheapens it. Education no longer becomes a learning process, it becomes a billboard."

Many young people, however, feel that the issue is more about freedom than it is the motives of corporations that exploit education for advertising purposes. "We don't feel corrupted by watching commercials," said a student in Fargo, North Dakota. "But we do think we should have the choice of watching or turning them off."

5 Today, students at Fargo North High School do have this choice. Though *Channel One*'s contracts with subscriber schools stipulate that 80 percent of the student body watch the program 90 percent of the school year, at Fargo North the program is now shown before school starts. Viewing is, in effect, optional and as a result very few students watch the program.

Students won the right to choose through protest. Two years ago, Fargo students organized a two-day boycott of classes showing *Channel One*, involving over 600 of the 850 students at the school. Erika Hovland, a boycott leader, described: "*Channel One* has no educational value. The school gets $50,000 worth of free [video] equipment, but the students gain nothing." While Whittle spokespeople dismissed the Fargo protests as an "aberration," students in schools across the country are making it clear they don't want to be used as bargaining chips for TVs.

Channel One Is Bad News

Josh Fleming, a student at McCallum High School in Austin, says that "by subscribing to *Channel One*, [his school] condones the fact that teenagers are still being killed for Nike shoes that cost $100. . . . There are alternatives to forcing students to watch commercials. All it takes is a little initiative to find them."

Finding alternatives to *Channel One* is crucial in light of the realities facing students. The Center for Disease Control reported last year that one in four U.S. high school students had carried a weapon to school at least once during the month before they were surveyed. Karen Miller, a parent in Houston, is concerned that *Channel One* pushes products where students cannot afford them: "In Texas, where about half of our school population can't afford a dollar for lunch, *Channel One* is a constant reminder of the need for a new car or new clothes."

The CDC also found that one in twelve high school students has attempted suicide, while another 19 percent have planned to take their own lives. What does this have to with *Channel One?* Peggy Charren, founder of Action for Children's Television, explains: "Learning works when you feel good about yourself. And advertising works when you don't — you have to feel your hair isn't quite right, or wouldn't it be nice to have new sneakers or nicer clothes. The two ideas are in conflict."

10 Jennifer Morales, a high school student in Seattle agrees that "*Channel One* compromises a lot of values that high school tries to teach kids. Like that social pressure is not healthy. That you have your own mind."

Many students find both the advertising and the news on *Channel One* degrading. In fact, a 1992 University of Michigan study commissioned by Whittle found that *Channel One* was "too fast-paced and fragmented to deepen students' understanding of current events." *Channel One* is a ten-minute news and features program arranged around two minutes of advertising. These two minutes a day amount to one full school day a year in which students do nothing but watch commercials on school time. This translates into millions of wasted tax dollars in school districts across the country and a gross public subsidy of the private sector.

And *Channel One* isn't stopping at two minutes of compulsory advertising. According to *Education Daily,* "Whittle is pressing its nearly 12,000 subscriber schools to increase the show's advertising time from 2 to 2.5 minutes, purportedly for the time it did not sell during previous programs." In 1990, Christopher Whittle predicted that "within five years [*Channel One*] will be in 95 percent of all middle and high schools in the United States. In a sense, it will be a new institution in America's schools." So far, *Channel One* has penetrated 350,000 classrooms, institutionalizing advertising in 40 percent of secondary education.

Schools most in need of resources are also most susceptible to classroom hucksters pawning video equipment in exchange for the attention of future consumers. Whittle Communications insists it wants to improve education and help poor students. For low-income schools, however, *Channel One* is a double-edged sword. Arnold Fege of the National Parent Teacher Association explains: "Poor communities, as a condition of their impoverishment, get the privilege of being exploited by Whittle."

A case in point is the Pawtucket school district in Rhode Island. Pawtucket, the most financially strapped school district in the state, became the first district in Rhode Island to sign on with *Channel One,* despite a state law banning commercial advertising on school grounds.

15 Commercial ventures in the classroom set a dangerous precedent: that the private sector can make a profit from the public school system, even as the system itself crumbles fiscally. Furthermore, while Corporate America gives the appearance it is stepping in to bail out public education, major corporations — because of their impact on the economy at large — are in fact significantly implicated in the current crisis in education.

To Christopher Whittle, public education is simply invalid. In his view, market forces alone can make the school system viable. Whittle Communications' Edison Project, for instance, has planned to open a chain of private, for-profit U.S. schools in 1996. Whittle has compared the national public school system to East Berlin and says of the Edison Project: "In a sense, we're trying to build West Berlin. We want to build something different and better, so the old system, East Berlin, will want to copy it."[1] In an interview

[1]*East Berlin . . . will want to copy it:* Before the reunification of Germany, Western democracies poured money into West Berlin to show off their economic success just across the border from economically depressed East Germany.

with *USA Today,* Whittle also compared the Edison Project to Lithuania breaking away from the former Soviet Union.

Underlying Whittle's tired anticommunist rhetoric is the notion that U.S. public schools are a vestige of the social welfare state. Whittle feels that these schools must be torn down in order for the private sector to maximize its hold on people's education in this country.

Youth as Target Market

The average young person in the United States watches about twenty-five hours of television a week and almost one hour of TV commercials a day. According to *Advertising Age,* the annual spending power of 18- to 29-year-olds is $125 billion. In addition, kids influence over $130 billion of their parents' spending each year. Corporate advertisers are hustling to grab hold of the baby busters' spending dollars. *Channel One* emerges from this hustle, casting students as "good CPU" (Cost Per Unit) and therefore a sound financial investment for advertisers.

Channel One is not the only hustler. Modern, a Madison Avenue firm, advertises in an industry journal with a picture of a preteen school girl framed by the words: "Reach her before she gets credit. Modern product sampling

can help you develop brand loyalty even before she becomes a serious shopper." Another Modern ad features a preschooler dressed in a suit, briefcase at his side and the words: "His first day job is in kindergarten. Modern can put your sponsored educational materials in the lesson plan. If he's in your target market, call us." You can contact Modern at 1-800-237-7114 to let them know what you think.

Young people are letting the corporations in their classroom know what 20
they think. Mounting youth resistance to *Channel One* is making a statement that the profit motive, packaged as a charity giveaway, cannot take the place of a national commitment to justice and equality in education.

The Fargo, North Dakota, student struggle points to an important organizing strategy against commercialism as well as *Channel One*'s Achilles' heel: Christopher Whittle, founder and CEO of Whittle Communications, admits that if schools were not required to show the program and its commercials, he'd "be out of business tomorrow." *Channel One* makes a profit because it has assembled for advertisers a captive audience of youth unprecedented in its size and lack of distractions. As more students demonstrate they do not watch *Channel One*, the program's attractiveness to advertisers could plummet. Bettina Dobbs, president of Guardians for Education in Maine, considers *Channel One* "a lesson in the elevation of greed and materialism over real education." *Channel One* can also provide, however, a lesson in the power youth have to affect the practices of major corporations.

Engaging the Text

1. Take a few minutes to recount any experiences you have had with commercials in the classroom. What other forms of corporate presence, if any, are you aware of in high school or higher education?
2. This essay touches on many issues. Working in groups, list each claim made by Templeton and each claim made by a student quoted in the essay. Also list any evidence provided for each claim. Finally, select a few of the most interesting issues for a classroom debate.
3. If the average young person watches twenty-five hours of television a week and an hour of advertisements per day (para. 18), is the battle over a few minutes of commercials at school worth fighting? How does *Channel One* fit into the larger picture of commercialism in the United States?

Exploring Connections

4. In imitation of Theodore Sizer (p. 20), write a version of what "Mark's typical school day" would be like if Whittle Communications had its way. If possible, work in small groups with each group focusing on one part of Mark's day. Read the composite narrative aloud.
5. Review Jean Anyon's analysis of social class and schooling (p. 45). How might she interpret the developments Templeton discusses?

6. Which, if any, of Templeton's arguments are mirrored in the cartoon on page 138? How far-fetched is the cartoonist's vision of the American classroom of the future?

EXTENDING THE CRITICAL CONTEXT

7. Carefully watch six or seven commercials pitched at a young audience. (If possible, use a VCR and select a channel like MTV or ESPN2 or a show with young "demos" — that is, a demographically young audience.) What messages, hidden or obvious, are being conveyed in these advertisements? Do they contradict your notion of the values and attitudes schools should be promoting?
8. Templeton's essay highlights the activities of students who have organized themselves to improve the conditions of their classrooms and the quality of education they receive. Research your campus newspaper archives to learn about past student-led movements on your campus. What issues did they address, and how effective were they in achieving their goals? What issue(s) could students organize around to improve education or campus life today at your college? What might they do to achieve this goal?

2

Harmony at Home

The Myth of the Model Family

What would an American political campaign be without wholesome photographs of the candidates kissing babies and posing with their loving families? Politicians understand the cultural power of these symbols; they appreciate the family as one of our most sacred American institutions. The vision of the ideal nuclear family — Dad, Mom, a couple of kids, maybe a dog, and a spacious suburban home — is a cliché but also a potent myth, a dream that millions of Americans work to fulfill. The image is so compelling that it's easy to forget what a short time it's been around, especially compared with the long history of the family itself.

In fact, what we call the "traditional" family, headed by a breadwinner-father and a housewife-mother, has existed for little more than two hundred years, and the suburbs only came into being in the 1950s. But the family as a social institution was legally recognized in Western culture at least as far back as the Code of Hammurabi, published in ancient Mesopotamia some four thousand years ago. To appreciate how profoundly concepts of family life have changed, consider the absolute power of the Mesopotamian father, the patriarch: the law allowed him to use any of his dependents, including his wife, as collateral for loans or even to sell family members outright to pay his debts.

Although patriarchal authority was less absolute in Puritan America, fathers remained the undisputed heads of families. Seventeenth-century Connecticut, Massachusetts, and New Hampshire enacted laws condemning rebellious children to severe punishment and, in extreme cases, to death. In the early years of the American colonies, as in Western culture stretching back to Hammurabi's time, unquestioned authority within the family served as both the model for and the basis of state authority. Just as family members owed complete obedience to the father, so all citizens owed unquestioned loyalty to the king and his legal representatives. In his influential volume *Democracy in America* (1835), French aristocrat Alexis de Tocqueville describes the relationship between the traditional European family and the old political order:

> . . . Among aristocratic nations, social institutions recognize, in truth, no one in the family but the father; children are received by society at his hands; society governs him, he governs them. Thus, the parent not only has a natural right, but acquires a political right to command them; he is the author and the support of his family; but he is also its constituted ruler.

By the mid-eighteenth century, however, new ideas about individual freedom and democracy were stirring the colonies. And by the time Tocqueville visited the United States in 1831, they had evidently worked a revolution in the family as well as in the nation's political structure: he observes, "When the condition of society becomes democratic, and men adopt as their general principle that it is good and lawful to judge of all things for one's self, . . . the power which the opinions of a father exercise over those of his sons diminishes, as well as his legal power." To Tocqueville, this shift away from strict patriarchal rule signaled a change in the emotional climate of families: "in proportion as manners and laws become more democratic, the relation of father and son becomes more intimate and more affectionate; rules and authority are less talked of, confidence and tenderness are oftentimes increased, and it would seem that the natural bond is drawn closer. . . ." In his view, the American family heralded a new era in human relations. Freed from the rigid hierarchy of the past, parents and children could meet as near equals, joined by "filial love and fraternal affection."

This vision of the democratic family—a harmonious association of parents and children united by love and trust—has mesmerized popular culture in the United States. From the nineteenth century to the present, popular novels, magazines, music, and advertising images have glorified the comforts of loving domesticity. In recent years, we've probably absorbed our strongest impressions of the ideal family from television situation comedies. In the 1950s we had the Andersons on *Father Knows Best,* the Stones on *The Donna Reed Show,* and the real-life Nelson family on *The Adventures of Ozzie & Harriet.* Over the next three decades, the model stretched to include single parents, second marriages, and interracial adoptions on *My Three Sons, The Brady Bunch,* and *Diff'rent Strokes,* but the underlying ideal of wise, loving parents and harmonious, happy families remained unchanged. But today, America has begun to worry about the health of its families: even the families on TV no longer reflect the domestic tranquility of the Anderson clan. America is becoming increasingly ambivalent about the future of family life, and perhaps with good reason. The myth of the family scarcely reflects the complexities of modern American life. High divorce rates, the rise of the single-parent household, the impact of remarriage, and a growing frankness about domestic violence are transforming the way we see family life; many families must also contend with the stresses of urban life and economic hardship. Such pressures on and within the family can be particularly devastating to young people: the suicide rate among fifteen- to nineteen-year-olds has more than tripled in the last thirty years. In our world it's no longer clear whether the family is a blessing to be cherished or an ordeal to be survived.

This chapter examines the impact of the myth of the model family and explores alternative visions of family life. The first four selections raise questions about the myth itself. In "Looking for Work" Gary Soto recalls his boyhood desire to live the myth — and recounts his humorously futile attempts to transform his working-class Chicano family into a facsimile of the Cleavers on *Leave It to Beaver.* Anndee Hochman's painful memoir about her parents' response to her coming out as a lesbian invites you to consider the chilling idea that behind family unity lurks the demand for utter conformity. "Friends as Family" by Karen Lindsey offers a devastating critique of the patriarchal family and proposes that we jettison the biological family as a defunct institution. Josh Ozersky's "TV's Antifamilies: Married . . . with Malaise," this chapter's media essay, completes our tour of the mythic nuclear family with a critique of the toxic families that have become staple fare on prime-time TV.

The chapter's second half, exploring alternatives to the nuclear family, begins with Bebe Moore Campbell's "Envy," a lively personal account of growing up father-hungry in a female-dominated African American family. In "Black Women and Motherhood," Patricia Hill Collins presents another perspective on the many roles played by Black mothers and offers a model of the extended family that defies the narrow definitions prescribed by the Eurocentric family myth. Stephanie Coontz carries this idea farther in "We Always Stood on Our Own Two Feet" by suggesting that throughout its history the American family has been surrounded by networks of private and public support.

The chapter closes with two positive personal reflections on the meaning of family life. In "An Indian Story," Roger Jack paints a warm, magical portrait of the bond between a Native American boy and his caretaker aunt. Melvin Dixon's poem "Aunt Ida Pieces a Quilt" celebrates a woman, and a family, that rises above prejudice to commemorate a nephew lost to AIDS. Together with the rest of the selections in the chapter's second half, these personal reflections affirm the continuing power of families as sources of acceptance, love, and support.

Sources

Gerda Lerner, *The Creation of Patriarchy.* New York: Oxford University Press, 1986.

Steven Mintz and Susan Kellogg, *Domestic Revolutions: A Social History of American Family Life.* New York: Free Press, 1988.

Alexis de Tocqueville, *Democracy in America.* 1835; New York: Vintage Books, 1990.

Before Reading

- Spend ten minutes or so jotting down every word, phrase, or image you associate with the idea of "family." Write as freely as possible, without censoring your thoughts or worrying about grammatical correctness. Working in small groups, compare lists and try to categorize your responses. What assumptions about families do they reveal?
- Draw a visual representation of your family. This could take the form of a graph, chart, diagram, map, cartoon, symbolic picture, or literal portrait. Don't worry if you're not a skillful artist: the main point is to convey an idea, and even stick figures can speak eloquently. When you're finished, write a journal entry about your drawing. Was it easier to depict some feelings or ideas visually than it would have been to describe them in words? Did you find some things about your family difficult or im-

possible to convey visually? Does your drawing "say" anything that surprises you?

- Do a brief freewrite about the family pictured on the title page of this chapter (p. 141). What can you tell about this family, its values, and the relationships between its members? What seems attractive about this image? What questions does it raise for you? To what extent does this image express your own ideal of family life?

Looking for Work

GARY SOTO

"Looking for Work" is the narrative of a nine-year-old Mexican American boy who wants his family to imitate the "perfect families" he sees on TV. Much of the humor in this essay comes from the author's perspective as an adult looking back at his childhood self, but Soto also respects the child's point of view. In the marvelous details of this midsummer day, Soto captures the interplay of seductive myth and complex reality. Gary Soto (b. 1952), now a professor of English at the University of California, Berkeley, grew up "on the industrial side of Fresno, right smack against a junkyard and the junkyard's cross-eyed German shepherd." Having discovered poetry almost by chance in a city college library, he has now published several volumes of his own, including The Elements of San Joaquin *(1977),* Father Is a Pillow Tied to a Broom *(1980), and* Home Course in Religion *(1991). He has also published essays, prose memoirs, and novels for young readers. "Looking for Work" appeared in* Living Up the Street: Narrative Recollections *(1985).*

One July, while killing ants on the kitchen sink with a rolled newspaper, I had a nine-year-old's vision of wealth that would save us from ourselves. For weeks I had drunk Kool-Aid and watched morning reruns of *Father Knows Best,* whose family was so uncomplicated in its routine that I very much wanted to imitate it. The first step was to get my brother and sister to wear shoes at dinner.

"Come on, Rick — come on, Deb," I whined. But Rick mimicked me and the same day that I asked him to wear shoes he came to the dinner table in only his swim trunks. My mother didn't notice, nor did my sister, as we sat to eat our beans and tortillas in the stifling heat of our kitchen. We all gleamed like cellophane, wiping the sweat from our brows with the backs of our hands as we talked about the day: Frankie our neighbor was beat up by Faustino; the swimming pool at the playground would be closed for a day because the pump was broken.

Such was our life. So that morning, while doing-in the train of ants which arrived each day, I decided to become wealthy, and right away! After downing a bowl of cereal, I took a rake from the garage and started up the block to look for work.

We lived on an ordinary block of mostly working class people: warehousemen, egg candlers,[1] welders, mechanics, and a union plumber. And there were many retired people who kept their lawns green and the gutters uncluttered of the chewing gum wrappers we dropped as we rode by on our bikes. They bent down to gather our litter, muttering at our evilness.

At the corner house I rapped the screen door and a very large woman 5
in a muu-muu answered. She sized me up and then asked what I could do.

"Rake leaves," I answered smiling.

"It's summer, and there ain't no leaves," she countered. Her face was pinched with lines; fat jiggled under her chin. She pointed to the lawn, then the flower bed, and said: "You see any leaves there — or there?" I followed her pointing arm, stupidly. But she had a job for me and that was to get her a Coke at the liquor store. She gave me twenty cents, and after ditching my rake in a bush, off I ran. I returned with an unbagged Pepsi, for which she thanked me and gave me a nickel from her apron.

I skipped off her porch, fetched my rake, and crossed the street to the next block where Mrs. Moore, mother of Earl the retarded man, let me weed a flower bed. She handed me a trowel and for a good part of the morning my fingers dipped into the moist dirt, ripping up runners of Bermuda grass. Worms surfaced in my search for deep roots, and I cut them in halves, tossing them to Mrs. Moore's cat who pawed them playfully as they dried in the sun. I made out Earl whose face was pressed to the back window of the house, and although he was calling to me I couldn't understand what he was trying to say. Embarrassed, I worked without looking up, but I imagined his contorted mouth and the ring of keys attached to his belt — keys that jingled with each palsied step. He scared me and I worked quickly to finish the flower bed. When I did finish Mrs. Moore gave me a quarter and two peaches from her tree, which I washed there but ate in the alley behind my house.

I was sucking on the second one, a bit of juice staining the front of my T-shirt, when Little John, my best friend, came walking down the alley with a baseball bat over his shoulder, knocking over trash cans as he made his way toward me.

Little John and I went to St. John's Catholic School, where we sat among 10
the "stupids." Miss Marino, our teacher, alternated the rows of good students with the bad, hoping that by sitting side-by-side with the bright students the stupids might become more intelligent, as though intelligence were conta-

[1]*egg candler:* One who inspects eggs by holding them up to a light.

gious. But we didn't progress as she had hoped. She grew frustrated when one day, while dismissing class for recess, Little John couldn't get up because his arms were stuck in the slats of the chair's backrest. She scolded us with a shaking finger when we knocked over the globe, denting the already troubled Africa. She muttered curses when Leroy White, a real stupid but a great softball player with the gift to hit to all fields, openly chewed his host[2] when he made his First Communion; his hands swung at his sides as he returned to the pew looking around with a big smile.

Little John asked what I was doing, and I told him that I was taking a break from work, as I sat comfortably among high weeds. He wanted to join me, but I reminded him that the last time he'd gone door-to-door asking for work his mother had whipped him. I was with him when his mother, a New Jersey Italian who could rise up in anger one moment and love the next, told me in a polite but matter-of-fact voice that I had to leave because she was going to beat her son. She gave me a homemade popsicle, ushered me to the door, and said that I could see Little John the next day. But it was sooner than that. I went around to his bedroom window to suck my popsicle and watch Little John dodge his mother's blows, a few hitting their mark but many whirring air.

It was midday when Little John and I converged in the alley, the sun blazing in the high nineties, and he suggested that we go to Roosevelt High School to swim. He needed five cents to make fifteen, the cost of admission, and I lent him a nickel. We ran home for my bike and when my sister found out that we were going swimming, she started to cry because she didn't have the fifteen cents but only an empty Coke bottle. I waved for her to come and three of us mounted the bike — Debra on the cross bar, Little John on the handle bars and holding the Coke bottle which we would cash for a nickel and make up the difference that would allow all of us to get in, and me pumping up the crooked streets, dodging cars and pot holes. We spent the day swimming under the afternoon sun, so that when we got home our mom asked us what was darker, the floor or us? She feigned a stern posture, her hands on her hips and her mouth puckered. We played along. Looking down, Debbie and I said in unison, "Us."

That evening at dinner we all sat down in our bathing suits to eat our beans, laughing and chewing loudly. Our mom was in a good mood, so I took a risk and asked her if sometime we could have turtle soup. A few days before I had watched a television program in which a Polynesian tribe killed a large turtle, gutted it, and then stewed it over an open fire. The turtle, basted in a sugary sauce, looked delicious as I ate an afternoon bowl of cereal, but my sister, who was watching the program with a glass of Kool-Aid between her knees, said, "Caca."

[2] *his host:* The wafer that represents, in the Catholic sacrament of Communion, the bread of the Last Supper and the body of Christ.

My mother looked at me in bewilderment. "Boy, are you a crazy Mexican. Where did you get the idea that people eat turtles?"

"On television," I said, explaining the program. Then I took it a step further. "Mom, do you think we could get dressed up for dinner one of these days? David King does." 15

"Ay, Dios," my mother laughed. She started collecting the dinner plates, but my brother wouldn't let go of his. He was still drawing a picture in the bean sauce. Giggling, he said it was me, but I didn't want to listen because I wanted an answer from Mom. This was the summer when I spent the mornings in front of the television that showed the comfortable lives of white kids. There were no beatings, no rifts in the family. They wore bright clothes; toys tumbled from their closets. They hopped into bed with kisses and woke to glasses of fresh orange juice, and to a father sitting before his morning coffee while the mother buttered his toast. They hurried through the day making friends and gobs of money, returning home to a warmly lit living room, and then dinner. *Leave It to Beaver* was the program I replayed in my mind:

"May I have the mashed potatoes?" asks Beaver with a smile.

"Sure, Beav," replies Wally as he taps the corners of his mouth with a starched napkin.

The father looks on in his suit. The mother, decked out in earrings and a pearl necklace, cuts into her steak and blushes. Their conversation is politely clipped.

"Swell," says Beaver, his cheeks puffed with food. 20

Our own talk at dinner was loud with belly laughs and marked by our pointing forks at one another. The subjects were commonplace.

"Gary, let's go to the ditch tomorrow," my brother suggests. He explains that he has made a life preserver out of four empty detergent bottles strung together with twine and that he will make me one if I can find more bottles. "No way are we going to drown."

"Yeah, then we could have a dirt clod fight," I reply, so happy to be alive.

Whereas the Beaver's family enjoyed dessert in dishes at the table, our mom sent us outside, and more often than not I went into the alley to peek over the neighbor's fences and spy out fruit, apricot or peaches.

I had asked my mom and again she laughed that I was a crazy *chavalo*[3] as she stood in front of the sink, her arms rising and falling with suds, face glistening from the heat. She sent me outside where my brother and sister were sitting in the shade that the fence threw out like a blanket. They were talking about me when I plopped down next to them. They looked at one another and then Debbie, my eight-year-old sister, started in. 25

"What's this crap about getting dressed up?"

She had entered her *profanity* stage. A year later she would give up

[3]*chavalo:* Kid.

such words and slip into her Catholic uniform, and into squealing on my brother and me when we "cussed this" and "cussed that."

I tried to convince them that if we improved the way we looked we might get along better in life. White people would like us more. They might invite us to places, like their homes or front yards. They might not hate us so much.

My sister called me a "craphead," and got up to leave with a stalk of grass dangling from her mouth. "They'll never like us."

My brother's mood lightened as he talked about the ditch — the white 30
water, the broken pieces of glass, and the rusted car fenders that awaited our knees. There would be toads, and rocks to smash them.

David King, the only person we knew who resembled the middle class, called from over the fence. David was Catholic, of Armenian and French descent, and his closet was filled with toys. A bear-shaped cookie jar, like the ones on television, sat on the kitchen counter. His mother was remarkably kind while she put up with the racket we made on the street. Evenings, she often watered the front yard and it must have upset her to see us — my brother and I and others — jump from trees laughing, the unkillable kids of the very poor, who got up unshaken, brushed off, and climbed into another one to try again.

David called again. Rick got up and slapped grass from his pants. When I asked if I could come along he said no. David said no. They were two years older so their affairs were different from mine. They greeted one another with foul names and took off down the alley to look for trouble.

I went inside the house, turned on the television, and was about to sit down with a glass of Kool-Aid when Mom shooed me outside.

"It's still light," she said. "Later you'll bug me to let you stay out longer. So go on."

I downed my Kool-Aid and went outside to the front yard. No one was 35
around. The day had cooled and a breeze rustled the trees. Mr. Jackson, the plumber, was watering his lawn and when he saw me he turned away to wash off his front steps. There was more than an hour of light left, so I took advantage of it and decided to look for work. I felt suddenly alive as I skipped down the block in search of an overgrown flower bed and the dime that would end the day right.

Engaging the Text

1. Why is the narrator attracted to the kind of family life depicted on TV? What, if anything, does he think is wrong with his life? Why do his desires apparently have so little impact on his family?
2. Why does the narrator first go looking for work? How has the meaning of work changed by the end of the story, when he goes out again "in search of an overgrown flower bed and the dime that would end the day right"? Explain.
3. As Soto looks back on his nine-year-old self, he has a different perspective on

things than he had as a child. How would you characterize the mature Soto's thoughts about his childhood family life? (Was it "a good family"? What was wrong with Soto's thinking as a nine-year-old?) Back up your remarks with specific references to the narrative.

4. Review the story to find each mention of food or drink. Explain the role these references play.
5. Review the cast of "supporting characters" in this narrative—the mother, sister, brother, friends, and neighbors. What does each contribute to the story and in particular to the meaning of family within the story?

Exploring Connections

6. Read Bebe Moore Campbell's "Envy" (p. 182) or Roger Jack's "An Indian Story" (p. 225) and compare Soto's family to one of the families portrayed in these selections. In particular, consider gender roles, the household atmosphere, and the expectations placed on children and parents.
7. Compare and contrast the relationship of school and family in this narrative to that described by Mike Rose (p. 33), Richard Rodriguez (p. 61), Inés Hernández-Ávila (p. 74), or Maxine Hong Kingston (p. 110).
8. Like Soto's story, the cartoon on page 152 attests to the power of the media to shape our ideas about family. Write a journal entry describing the media family that most accurately reflects your image of family life. Discuss these entries, and the impact of media on your image of the family, with your classmates.

Extending the Critical Context

9. Write a journal entry about a time when you wished your family were somehow different. What caused your dissatisfaction? What did you want your family to be like? Was your dissatisfaction ever resolved?
10. "Looking for Work" is essentially the story of a single day. Write a narrative of one day when you were eight or nine or ten; use details as Soto does to give the events of the day broader significance.

Growing Pains: Beyond "One Big Happy Family"

Anndee Hochman

This narrative shows how life in what looks like "one big happy family" can be a lot more complicated when viewed from the inside. Hochman writes evocatively about her childhood and about how her emerging lesbian identity tested the boundaries of family love. Hochman (b. 1962) has worked as a reporter for the Washington Post, *a VISTA volunteer, a counselor for homeless teenagers, and a creative writing teacher. She is now a free-lance writer; "Growing Pains" comes from her book* Everyday Acts and Small Subversions: Women Reinventing Family, Community, and Home *(1994).*

I remember waking up to the smell of salt.

Each August when I was little, my parents loaded the car with Bermuda shorts and groceries, beach towels and Scrabble board, and drove to the New Jersey shore. My great-uncle Bernie Ochman had bought a $16,000 bay-front house there in the mid-1950s; he imagined it as a sort of free-wheeling compound, where all the aunts, grandparents, and cousins of my mother's large extended family could gather each summer.

Bernie died before my parents were married, but my mother carried out his vision with her usual zest. She made sure the taxes on the house were paid quarterly, the water valve was turned on each May, and there were enough hamburgers for everyone on Memorial Day and the Fourth of July.

In August, my parents worked feverishly for two weeks, then packed up and headed to the shore for what my father used to call, with some sarcasm, "a little peace and quiet." We left at night to avoid traffic on the Atlantic City Expressway. I always fell asleep in the car and always woke up as we came over the bay bridge, where the smell of salt, moist and thick, would touch me like a mitten dipped in the ocean.

"Are we there yet?" I'd mumble from the back seat. 5

"Almost," my mom would say, and my dad would turn left, then left again, and park the car as close as he could to the big white house.

I loved the shore house because it was so different from home. The front steps tilted a little. Gray paint flaked off the window frames. Two daybeds in the living room were draped with pea green spreads, and the loveseats wore crunchy plastic slipcovers. The picket fence was red.

Even the architecture broke rules. The front room had been added as an afterthought, a low-budget job. The carpenters never removed what had once been the house's front window, now ridiculous in the wall between the front room and the kitchen. I used to sit on the stairs, tapping on the kitchen window and making faces until my mother or my grandmother or Aunt Sadie looked up from the dishes and waved at me. Then I would collapse in giggles.

Upstairs, there was no hall, no doors on the bedrooms. In fact, the bedrooms were not really separate rooms at all, just thin-walled divisions of the upper floor. The front stairs climbed right into the middle of Aunt Charlotte and Uncle Freddie's room; you could stand on the top step and almost tickle Uncle Freddie's feet.

Walk through that bedroom, and the next one, and the next, and you 10

ROGER REALIZES A CHERISHED CHILDHOOD MEMORY IS ACTUALLY A SCENE FROM AN OLD MOVIE.

arrived at the bathroom, which had its own quirks — a white claw-foot tub, a hasty shower rigged up with red rubber tubing, and two doors. When I was older, I would check the sliding locks on both doors several times before I dared to unpeel my damp, sandy bathing suit.

Aunt Sadie and Uncle Izzy slept in the larger of the two rear bedrooms, in twin beds pushed together to make one. The very back room was long and narrow, like a single-lane swimming pool, with windows that let in wet salty air off the bay. My grandparents — Bubie and Pop-pop — slept here.

My mother loves to tell the story of my father's first visit to this family compound, during their courtship. He recoiled at the upstairs setup; a private motel room, with a door that locked, was more what he had in mind. My mother informed him firmly that she was a package deal; if he loved her, he would learn to love her family — the father who smoked terrible cigars, the sister who rolled her hair in Kotex sanitary pads, the mother who stewed bruised peaches in the hot, tiny kitchen. And he could start loving them here, in their peculiar summer habitat.

I thought the house was wonderful. The connecting rooms reminded me of a maze, the sort of place where surprises could hunch in old dressers, under beds. Later I realized how the physical space shaped our time there, dissolving the barriers that, in most houses, separate adults from children, private from communal space, eating from work. At the shore, my friends and I played jacks in the middle of the living room, hide and seek in the freestanding metal closets. When people got hungry, they helped themselves from one of the three refrigerators. If I wanted to be alone, I opened a book.

There was one last room upstairs, an odd sixth bedroom lodged in the center of the house. It was the only bedroom with a door, and it belonged to my parents. When I was younger, I assumed they took that room out of generosity. It was small and dark and hot, and you had to grope for the light switch behind a high wooden headboard. It was also the only room in the house in which two people could have a private talk, or take a nap, without somebody else clomping through on her way to the bathroom.

Much later, the summer I was twenty-two, I finally grasped the full 15
significance of that room and made love with Jon Feldstein in it one June weekend when the family wasn't there. "Do you want to have sex?" he had asked, without expectation in his voice, as if it were a foregone conclusion. Later he said, "Well, you know, it gets better with practice."

I did not practice with Jon Feldstein again. In fact, I didn't practice with anyone until more than two years later. By then, I had fallen into a deep and surprising infatuation with one of my closest friends, driven my Datsun cross-country alone, and settled in Portland.

Early in the summer of 1987, I flew back east to tell my parents I was in love with a woman and believed I was destined to be in love with women throughout the foreseeable future. It was Memorial Day weekend, the time we traditionally turned on the water valve and began to inhabit the house at the shore. My mother and I drove there in her blue Honda.

"I think that's how it's going to be for me. With women, I mean," I told her.

"Well, your father thought so," she said finally. "He thought so back in November. I told him that was ridiculous, that you'd always had boyfriends."

She said a lot of other things after that, about not having grandchildren 20
and what a hard path I'd chosen and how she and my father weren't going to be around forever and had hoped to see me taken care of. I concentrated on driving and on the way blood was beating in my ankles, my thumbs, my neck, my ears. I wanted to go to sleep and not wake up until I smelled salt. When we came close to the bay, my mother asked me to pull into a parking lot so she could cry for a while. "I'm sorry," I said, but it didn't seem to help.

At the house, I walked around, touching things, while my mother told my father that he was right, I *was* having an affair with a woman. I wanted to eat something, anything, off the familiar mismatched dishes, play Scrabble until the stars came out, stand on the back porch and watch boats slip under the bridge, tap on the kitchen window until someone waved at me. Instead I went into the bathroom and locked both doors.

About midnight, while I lay sleepless in Aunt Sadie and Uncle Izzy's room, my mother came in and crawled into the other twin bed. "I feel so empty," she said. "I feel empty inside. . . . I don't feel any joy anymore. I feel like the family is breaking apart. I remember how the family was when Uncle Bernie was alive, how this house was. . . ." And her voice, already thin, cracked like a bowl dropped on a tile floor — a splintering and then silence where something used to be.

2 A.M. 3 A.M. Everyone had trooped off to bed in pairs — cousins Joni and Gerry, cousins Debbie and Ralph. Except for my grandfather, who had always stayed up late to watch television and stayed up even later since my grandmother died three years before. Finally he switched off the set, and the house went dark and quiet.

"Don't you feel it's unnatural?" my mother asked. "Don't you feel it's just wrong, that it's weird?"

How can you ask me about being weird in this house, I wanted to shout. 25
This house, with its bedrooms barging into each other and its mismatched dishes, its double-doored bathroom and its red picket fence. When I used to complain that our family wasn't like other families, you laughed and said, "Well, we may not be normal, but we have a lot of fun."

I didn't say these things. I only thought them. And it wasn't until much later, until very recently, that I began to understand why my mother could tolerate the quirks in that house. The madcap shell at the shore housed a solid, predictable center. Relatives came and went in pairs. Someday, presumably, I would join the procession; one of my children would tap on the kitchen window and giggle when I waved. The house might be a little cracked, but the family was predictable, enduring.

I understand why you are so upset, I could tell my mother now. The world has gone crazy and all the walls are too thin and your mother is dead and your sister divorced and your daughter loves women and everything is coming unglued and nothing turns out the way we plan.

4 A.M. 5 A.M. My mother stayed in my room all night, talking and weep-

ing. Toward morning, as boats began to slosh in the bay, I fell into an exhausted, tear-stained sleep. When I woke up at noon, we ate tuna subs and drove back to Philadelphia.

The New Jersey beach house was never just a summertime shelter. It housed my family's favorite image of itself at our expansive best — gathered around the huge dining room table, traipsing through the bedrooms, one big happy family. Just like all the television shows I watched and worshipped.

It is no accident that this particular image clung. The picture of such 30
charmed and cheerful families took hold in the decade preceding my birth, a bit of postwar propaganda that paid homage to the supposedly idyllic families of Victorian times. Mass-marketed by television, the Cleaver clan and others were burned into our minds by millions of cathode-ray tubes.

The feminist movement challenged that postwar myth as women began to examine the contents inside the "happy family" cliché. Feminists of the late 1960s and 1970s urged their sisters to live authentic lives and to begin them at home. They insisted that personal choices had political import — that is, the daily, minute interactions of our lives *mattered*, not just for each of us alone, but potentially for everyone, for the world. "When a woman tells the truth," Adrienne Rich wrote, "she is creating the possibility for more truth around her."

Women pointed out that families maintained the illusion of happiness only by denying important facts — about adoptions, abortions, illness and illegitimate births, divorces and deaths. Some families devoted their lives to maintaining the secret of a son's homosexuality, a grandmother's alcoholism, a father's violent rage. Melancholy and despair split family members not only from outsiders but from each other; certain topics, one understood, were simply not discussed.

In consciousness-raising groups, women discovered the exhilaration of telling each other unvarnished stories of their bodies, relationships, and families. Back at home, in their kitchens and living rooms, they began to apply these feminist ideals: that *how* people talked meant as much as the conclusions they reached; that the only way to solve problems was to actively engage them; that keeping secrets cost too much.

It was feminism, in part, that prompted me to tell my own family a difficult truth, one I was sure would cause misunderstanding and pain. I was frightened to disturb the jovial peace that was a source of such family pride; at the same time, I could not visit that unpretentious house and pretend I was someone else. I wanted to be known, and seen, in the ways I had come to know and see myself.

I did it because I chose truth over tranquility. Because I had come to 35
believe that real families fight and resist, sob and explode, apologize and forgive. Beneath the fiction of happiness lies the raw, important tissue of human relationships.

And I did it because I had watched other women live without lying. For some, that meant no longer passing as heterosexual. For others, it meant acknowledging they did not want partners or children. Some urged their biological relatives and chosen kin to talk about subjects long considered taboo. Their example made my own convictions more fierce. Their bravery buoyed me.

"It's hard. We argue and struggle," Selma Miriam of the Bloodroot restaurant collective told me, with a glance around the room at her "cronies."

"You know each other's weaknesses," said Betsey Beaven, another Bloodroot member. "Love requires a lot of cultivation. It can be tenuous. You have to work on it all the time. It's very difficult at times, but so rewarding when you get through to the other side."

I remember my friend Susan's assessment, at the end of a long discussion about what separates family from friends. "Family," she said, "are the people I've struggled through things with."

Again, always, the personal becomes political. Women striving daily to 40
make plain the good and the bad of their lives also contribute to a larger change, the breakdown of fictions that divide us from each other — white from black, lesbian from straight, old from young. Women who refuse to act out lies at home can turn the same honest scrutiny outside, demanding truth in their work, their education, their politics.

Maybe happiness, I have come to think, is a limiting proposition, a flat summary of human emotion in the same way a sitcom is a flat summary of real life. "Happy families" don't account for the ways people are knit by sorrow, the way bonds grow stronger through anger and grief.

This is it, I tell myself now; this mess is as real as it gets. I try to cherish flux — the mercurial moods, the feelings that flood and recede, the infinite chaos in which families become families.

Two days after I came out to my parents at the beach house, I returned to Portland, with my bicycle packed in a United Airlines baggage carrier and my grandmother's cameo ring on the pinky finger of my left hand. I'd found the ring in a jewelry box in my bedroom. It was delicate, a filigree setting with a small oblong cameo, the ivory-faced woman profiled on a peach background.

The thin silver band barely eased over the knuckle on my pinky — lesbians' traditional ring-bearing finger. Wearing it, I felt marked, as though I were bringing contraband across the border in broad daylight, all my conflicting allegiances exposed.

My head ached. Would my relatives still love me if I failed to do my 45
part by marrying and enlarging the family with children? Could I ever bring a woman lover to the shore? Where would we sleep?

How would I reconcile my relatives with the various families I developed as a writer, a Jew, a lesbian, a social worker, an East Coast expatriate in the Northwest? How far could everyone stretch without snapping, refusing wholeness, flying apart like shrapnel?

I stumbled off the plane at midnight into a solid hug from Marian, a coworker at the social service agency where I counseled street youth. At work that week, I walked numbly through my routine. On Friday, while cleaning up the drop-in center after the last round of kids, I looked at my left hand. Where the cameo of my grandmother's ring had been, a little rectangle of skin showed through the filigree window. In the agency's dim basement, I leaned against a paneled wall and sobbed.

All the rest of that summer my parents and I exchanged letters, envelopes full of anger and accusation, concern and caution, guilt and grief. I had been such a good child, cheerful, diligent, and brainy — good citizen awards in ninth grade, acceptance to Yale, an internship, then a job, at *The Washington Post.* It was bad enough that I had left the *Post* after two years, moved 3,000 miles away and begun to work with homeless teenagers. Now this! Where had I gotten such subversive ideas?

Perhaps in a certain south Jersey beach house, in a maze of doorless rooms.

From the West Coast, I glanced anxiously over my shoulder: Were my relatives still there, with their shopping and their sweaters, their softening faces and their stiff resistance to change? If I returned, would I be swallowed up? If I stayed, would I be left adrift? Is that the brittle choice that, ultimately, forms the boundary line of every family: Be like us, or be alone?

I took off the empty ring and put it in a drawer. I spent that summer prowling my past, looking for signposts to help navigate the present. I heard voices, comforting and cautionary, joyous and pained, voices that chased in endless loops through my head.

"You can do anything you set your mind to."

"Don't leave."

"The world is full of interesting people and places."

"This family is the only safe spot on earth."

"Follow your dreams."

"Stay put."

I listened, and remembered, and wrote things down.

Engaging the Text

1. How do you explain the title of this piece? What tone does it set, and what message does it convey?
2. Throughout this essay, Hochman uses the shore house as a symbol of her family. Review her descriptions of the house and discuss in some detail what made the house special to her. To what extent is it an apt symbol for her family life?
3. Why does the revelation that Hochman is in love with a woman so disturb her family? How — and how well — do the author and her family deal with this situation?
4. What is Hochman's notion of "family"? Aside from the issue of homosexuality, does it differ from "mainstream" or "traditional" views, and if so, how?

5. Why did Hochman include the description of her brief "affair" with Jon Feldstein? How do you interpret this incident?

Exploring Connections

6. In the previous selection (p. 145), Gary Soto is frustrated because his parents won't or can't meet his expectations of what ideal parents should be. Brainstorm a list of qualities that both Soto and Hochman seem to expect in their ideal parents. Are these qualities that any child might desire in a parent? What other qualities would you add to this list?
7. Write a dialogue between Richard Rodriguez (p. 61) and Anndee Hochman on the costs of conformity to and rebellion against family traditions and values.

Extending the Critical Context

8. At the end of Hochman's essay she offers a brief sample of past family voices that continue to haunt her (para. 51). Make your own list of voices from your family's past. What do these voices tell you? What do they say about your family's beliefs, values, and attitudes?
9. Hochman's essay challenges us to consider the chilling idea that families demand that sons and daughters "be like us or be alone" (para. 50). To what extent do you agree that families are held together by conformity?
10. Think back to a particular time or place in your childhood that seemed as special or meaningful to you as her summer house seemed to Hochman. Try to describe this time or place in as much detail as possible, and then explain how it shaped your own view of family life.
11. Watch *The Wedding Banquet,* and compare the actions and reactions of the parents and children in this film with those of Hochman and her parents. What underlying values and assumptions about family unity do these responses suggest?

Friends as Family

Karen Lindsey

In this introduction to her book Friends as Family *(1981), Karen Lindsey offers a feminist critique of patriarchal family life and proposes a tantalizing and controversial thesis — that families need not be defined by biological relationships but may be "chosen." In clearing the ground to make this argument, she also offers some startling information about the history of the family. Lindsey (b. 1944) is a teacher, editor, and free-lance writer. She coauthored, with Susan M. Love,* Dr. Susan Love's Breast Book, *about breast cancer and disease;* Divorced, Beheaded, Survived, *a feminist analysis of the wives of Henry VIII, is due to be published in 1995.*

The traditional family isn't working. This should not come as a startling revelation to anyone who picks up this book: it may be the single fact on which every American, from the Moral Majority member through the radical feminist, agrees. Statistics abound: 50 percent of couples married since 1970 and 33 percent of those married since 1950 are divorced. One out of every six children under eighteen lives with only one parent. The number of children living in families headed by women more than doubled between 1954 and 1975.[1] The family no longer has room for aged parents. Increasing numbers of the elderly live alone or in nursing homes: only 11 percent live with their children or with other relatives.[2]

Even when the family stays together, it often does so under grim conditions. As many as 60 percent of all married women are beaten at least once by their husbands.[3] One in every hundred children is beaten, sexually molested, or severely neglected by parents.[4] And between 500,000 and one million elderly parents are abused each year by the adult offspring they live with.[5] Whatever the family in the United States is, it isn't *Father Knows Best.*[6]

There are a lot of people who refuse to believe this, who prefer to attribute both the problems within families and the increasing breakup of families to the "new narcissism" or the evils of the "me generation." This theory, promulgated by many conservatives and liberals, and legitimized by intellectual pseudo-leftists like Christopher Lasch,[7] suggests (Lasch, at least, is shrewd enough never to come out and say it) that if people would only stop worrying about their own personal fulfillment and return to the loving bosom of the patriarchal family, the world would be a happy place. Such apologists for the family tend to ignore the issue of intrafamily abuse, since it paints a somewhat different portrait of "those basic things we used to know."

[1]Susan Dworkin, "Carter Wants to Save the Family, but He Can't Even Save His Family Conference," *Ms.*, September 1987, pp. 62, 98. [Author's note]

[2]Beth B. Hess, *Growing Old in America* (New Brunswick, N.J.: Transaction Books, 1976), p. 26. [Author's note]

[3]Terry Davidson, *Conjugal Crime: Understanding and Changing the Wifebeating Pattern* (New York: Hawthorn, 1978), pp. 6–7. [Author's note]

[4]Naomi Feigelson Chase, *A Child Is Being Beaten* (New York: Holt, Rinehart, & Winston, 1975), p. 185. [Author's note]

[5]Lynn Langway, "Unveiling a Family Secret," *Newsweek*, Feb. 18, 1980, pp. 104–06. [Author's note]

[6]*Father Knows Best:* 1950s TV show featuring a highly idealized family.

[7]*Christopher Lasch:* American social critic and historian (1932–1994).

Lasch is totally remarkable in this regard: in neither his massively popular *The Culture of Narcissism* nor his earlier and even more reactionary *Haven in a Heartless World*[8] does he discuss wife abuse or child abuse. Indeed, to perpetuate the myth of the new narcissism, he can't *afford* to acknowledge family violence. The myth of the new narcissism is more than a myth. It's also a lie. And it's important to remember that, although we often confuse the two, "myth" and "lie" are not by definition synonyms. Myth, as the dictionary tells us, is "a traditional story of ostensible historical events that serves to unfold part of the world view of a people or explain a practice, belief, or natural phenomenon." Or, as the introduction to *World Mythology* says, it is "the spontaneous defense of the human mind faced with an unintelligible or hostile world."[9]

Objective reality neither affirms nor negates a myth. Athena and Zeus 5
never existed; Jesus existed but little is known about his life; George Washington, Florence Nightingale, and Bo Derek[10] are real people about whom a great deal is known. But all exist mythically, apart from their objective existence or nonexistence.

What is true of mythical people is true of mythical concepts. Heaven and hell, the nuclear family, the Russian Revolution: all are myths, though clearly two are also historical facts. They are myths because, apart from whatever reality they have, the way in which we view them helps clarify, even shape, our vision of the world. It is in this sense that I speak of the myth of the family.

The myth of the new narcissism bases itself on the myth of the family. As Lasch and others conceptualize it, the theory of the new narcissism is that nobody cares about social causes any more, nobody cares about anyone else, and everyone is single-mindedly devoted to self-fulfillment. People of the '70s took the liberation ideologies of the '60s and individualized them, creating a selfish and decadent society concerned only with material or psychological gain. This was symbolized most strongly by the breakdown of the family. The agenda of the '80s is thus clear: return to the good old days, before the breakdown of the nuclear family.

According to this new myth, the world is now divided into *Cosmopolitan* or *Redbook*:[11] you can have a life of sex clubs and high-powered careers or a life of Mommy staying home and cooking, Daddy going to work all day and spending the evening at home, and 2.4 happy and obedient kids. There is nothing else. The acceptance of these alternatives as the parameters of

[8]Christopher Lasch, *The Culture of Narcissism* (New York: Warner Books, 1979), and *Haven in a Heartless World* (New York: Basic Books, 1977). [Author's note]

[9]Pierre Grimal, ed., *Larousse World Mythology* (London: The Hamlin Publishing Group, 1965), p. 9. [Author's note]

[10]*Bo Derek:* American actor and model (b. 1956) once considered one of the world's most beautiful women.

[11]*Cosmopolitan or Redbook:* Two popular magazines for women, with two very different audiences, as Lindsey indicates.

human experience leaves us little real choice. If we wish to retain our humanity — to be caring, nurturing people and, by the same token, cared-for and nurtured people — we must opt for the traditional family. Whatever evils we perceive in the nuclear family, the freedom to live without human relationships is ultimately no freedom, but hell. And so the acceptance of the myth as truth has the very real possibility of turning us — at least women — into collaborators in our own oppression.

The myth of the new narcissism is a perfect example of what Mary Daly calls "false naming." False naming, Daly argues, creates a concept of reality which is a tool of oppression: it invents a definition of reality and forces us to live under the terms of that definition. Speaking specifically of the oppression of women, Daly writes: "Women have had the power of naming stolen from us. We have not been free to use our own power to name ourselves, the world, or god . . . women are now realizing that the universal imposing of names by men has been false because partial. That is, inadequate words have been taken as adequate."[12]

And so it is essential to our survival to name the lie, to look beyond the 10
words to the reality they obscure. To do this, we must start with the base of the myth — the notion that there was once an ideally happy family which has only recently been destroyed by the forces of organized selfishness. Whether that ideal family is supposed to have occurred in the confines of the historically recent nuclear family, or in the older extended family, it exists as a vision of that which has been destroyed, that to which we must return. As Will Rogers[13] said, things ain't the way they used to be, and maybe they never were.

When *was* the Golden Age of the happy family? Mythmakers vary on this question, but their most common image suggests it was sometime during the nineteenth century that the world was a Norman Rockwell[14] painting. (Lasch, perhaps the shrewdest of the Golden Age mythologizers, never places it in any historical period, though he repeatedly implies that it did indeed exist.) Was it in 1869, when John Stuart Mill[15] wrote *The Subjugation of Women,* decrying the fact that thousands of husbands routinely "indulge in the utmost habitual excesses of bodily violence towards the unhappy wife"?[16] Was it in 1878, when Frances Power Cobbe wrote of the area of Liverpool known as the "kicking district" because so many of its residents kicked their wives' faces with hobnailed boots?[17] Was it in 1890, when the *Encyclopaedia Britannica* noted that the "modern crime of infanticide shows

[12]Mary Daly, *Beyond God the Father: Toward a Philosophy of Women's Liberation* (Boston: Beacon Press, 1973), p. 8. [Author's note]

[13]*Will Rogers:* American humorist and actor (1879–1935).

[14]*Norman Rockwell:* American painter and illustrator (1894–1978), famous for idealized portraits of American life.

[15]*John Stuart Mill:* English philosopher and economist (1806–1873).

[16]Davidson, p. 108. [Author's note]

[17]Davidson, p. 110. [Author's note]

no symptoms of diminishing in the leading nations of Europe"?[18] Was it a little earlier—in the 1830s or '40s, when thousands of temperance societies sprang up throughout the United States in response to the growing number of abusive drunken men? "The drunken spouse could (and did) spend the family money as he chose, sell off his and his wife's property, apprentice their children, and assault wife and children alike."[19]

Perhaps, then, the nineteenth century is too late in history—perhaps the evils of industrialism had taken hold and destroyed the Golden Age. Perhaps we need to look back further to find our happy family—maybe to the Middle Ages, before the forces of industry had torn the family apart, when husband, wife, and children all worked the farm together in domestic harmony. The only problem is that during this period, "men were exhorted from the pulpit to beat their wives and their wives to kiss the rod that beat them. The deliberate teaching of domestic violence, combined with the doctrine that women and children by nature could have no human rights, had taken such hold by the late Middle Ages that men had come to treat their wives and children worse than their beasts."[20]

Well, there's always the Renaissance,[21] bringing light to the primitive mentality bred by the Middle Ages. The Spanish scholar Vives, so influential in the court of England under Henry VIII and his first wife, Katherine of Aragón, is usually viewed as one of the more enlightened intellects of the era: he was influential in spreading the theory that girls, as well as boys, should be well educated. He, like dozens of other scholars in the Tudor[22] era, published tracts on childrearing and domestic harmony. Vives wrote approvingly that he knew "many fathers to cut the throats of their daughters, bretheren of their sisters, and kinsmen of their kinswomen" when these unfortunate women were discovered to be unchaste.[23] He explained that his own mother had never "lightly laughed upon me, she never cockered me. . . . Therefore there was nobody that I did more flee, or was more loath to come nigh, than my mother, when I was a child." Showing affection, or "cherishing," he said, "marreth sons, but it utterly destroyeth daughters."[24]

It was perhaps fortunate for both daughters and sons that they *didn't* feel too comfortable at home, since they were likely to be betrothed at

[18]Chase, p. 17. Infanticide itself seems to have occurred chiefly among the poor—though as always there is reason to suspect its occurrence, discreetly covered up, in more affluent families as well. [Author's note]

[19]Judith Papachristou, *Women Together* (New York: Knopf, 1976), p. 19. [Author's note]

[20]Davidson, p. 98. [Author's note]

[21]*Renaissance:* The intellectual and artistic movement that spread from fourteenth-century Italy to the rest of Europe by the seventeenth century.

[22]*Tudor:* The Royal dynasty in England from 1485 to 1603.

[23]Lu Emily Pearson, *Elizabethans at Home* (Stanford, Calif.: Stanford University Press, 1957), p. 248. [Author's note]

[24]H. F. M. Prescott, *Mary Tudor* (New York: Macmillan, 1953), p. 26. [Author's note]

infancy and married off in adolescence — often, in the case of upperclass offspring, never to see their families again. Margaret Beaufort, grandmother of Henry VIII, was married off at 12, gave birth to Henry Tudor,[25] and never had another child — probably as a result of early childbirth. Her granddaughter, Margaret of Scotland, was also forced to marry at 12, and left her home to live with her husband, the King of Scotland; her letters home are filled with misery and homesickness.[26]

15 Wifebeating and childbeating were approved by most of the tractwriters of the time, though often the husband was advised to use physical abuse only as a last resort. Needless to say many husbands *didn't* obey these pious exhortations. On at least one occasion, the Duke of Norfolk (Anne Boleyn's uncle) had his servants help him beat his wife; they stopped only when blood began pouring out of her mouth.[27]

The statistics on physical abuse in various historical periods tell us something about family violence in the past. But they don't tell us about the nonviolent forms of misery in people's lives. We can make assumptions about the viability of marriage and family life today because divorce is permissible: people who leave their families are presumably unhappy in them. But how do we know what human misery (as well as human happiness) existed among people who had no option but to live together? How many parents despised the children they had no choice but to raise? How many wives loathed their husbands; how many husbands hated their wives? How many people lived together in a helpless toleration that later ages would call contentment? Such records as we have are usually diaries and letters written by members of privileged classes — people who could read and write, people who had the luxury of privacy in which to record their thoughts.

The story of Anne Askew, the sixteenth-century Protestant martyr who wrote about her life and religion as she awaited execution, and whose maid was able to smuggle the document to the exiled Bishop Bale, provides a terse but poignant picture of miserable cohabitation between a brilliant young woman and a cloddish, conservative husband.[28] How many other Anne Askews were there whose stories were never told, even to their closest friends? We have the words of Lady Jane Grey, the doomed child who was to briefly become England's queen in the same era, complaining to the scholar Roger Ascham of her parents' abuses and coldness. How many such children never voiced their complaints, or voiced them to less-concerned listeners than hers?[29] We are told by Martin Luther, the leading light of the

[25] Alison Plowden, *Tudor Women* (New York: Atheneum 1979), p. 8. [Author's note]

[26] Alison Plowden, *The House of Tudor* (New York: Stein & Day, 1976), p. 47. [Author's note]

[27] Lacey Baldwin Smith, *A Tudor Tragedy: The Life and Times of Catherine Howard* (New York: Pantheon, 1961), p. 28. [Author's note]

[28] John Bale, *Select Works* (London: Parker Society, 1849), pp. 140–240. [Author's note]

[29] Mary M. Luke, *A Crown for Elizabeth* (New York: Coward-McCann, 1970), p. 191. [Author's note]

Protestant Reformation, that his parents were severe and abusive, and his childhood miserable.[30] We have a chilling vision of intra-family hatred in the story of the 350 Lollard Heretics[31] discovered in Lincoln County in 1521. The reason so many were caught is that parents and children, husbands and wives, eagerly informed against each other.[32] How many people in how many eras would have left their husbands, wives, and parents if there had been any possibility of their doing so?

There is another aspect of family which the proponents of the Golden Age like to ignore: the family has always been a very different reality for each of its members. The father had absolute power over all the other members; the mother had some power over her sons and very much power over her daughters; the son was under his parents' control, but knew that one day he would probably be able to rule his own family and perhaps even the mother who now ruled him; the daughter had no power and could anticipate little. The family may well have been — and may well still be — a "haven from the heartless world" for many men. But for women and children, it has always been the very *center* of the heartless world, from which no haven existed. For man, the limits of the family have been tacitly recognized, and legitimate or quasi-legitimate institutions have been established to supplement their needs. Men have always been permitted mistresses, even if official morality has shaken its head; women have rarely been able to get by with taking lovers. The very existence of prostitution, which has always coexisted with the family, offers implicit approval of men's search for extrafamilial fulfillment. Both Saint Augustine and Saint Thomas Aquinas recognized this, when they likened prostitution to a sewer, ugly but necessary to keep the palace functioning.[33] Monogamous marriage, which the Golden Agers celebrate, has usually meant only monogamous wifehood.

I'm not trying to suggest that families have always been devoid of love, or caring, of the "cherishing" that Vives found so destructive. There are records of happy families, as there are records of unhappy ones. And in any event the human need for communication, for sharing, for love would certainly find a way to be satisfied in almost any situation. The very quality of shared experience, shared history, can build strong bonds of love and affection among people. In a family, in a commune, in a prison, people can make deep and indissoluble connections with one another. But if it isn't recognized that the family, historically, *was* a prison, which people entered not by choice but by necessity, the real happiness as well as the real misery becomes

[30]Philip Hughes, *A Popular History of the Reformation* (Garden City, N.Y.: Hanover House, 1957), p. 98. [Author's note]

[31]*Lollard Heretics:* Lollardry was a medieval English movement founded by John Wycliffe in the late fourteenth century. The heretics criticized the church's wealth amid widespread poverty, wanted to abolish celibacy for the clergy, condemned all wars, and called for personal interpretation of the Bible.

[32]A. G. Dickens, *The English Reformation* (New York: Schocken, p. 27). [Author's note]

[33]Simone de Beauvoir, *The Second Sex* (New York: Bantam, 1961), p. 96. [Author's note]

mythologized into something quite distinct from the reality. The family becomes, in Daly's words, a creation of false naming.

The false naming that creates the myth of the happy traditional family 20
has its corollary in the false naming that says life outside the family is miserable and empty, that people who choose childlessness have no real relationships with children or with the future, and that friends are never as fulfilling as family. In our culture, there is family, and there are friends. Sometimes friendship is deep, even heroic—especially, perhaps exclusively, among men. Damon and Pythias,[34] Jonathan and David.[35] But mostly, friendship is secondary: friends are who you pass pleasant time with, who you like but don't love, to whom you make minimal if any commitment. Above all, *friends are not family.* Blood is thicker than water. Your friends are always "other"; your family is who you are. Friends, in that most demeaning of phrases, are "just friends." And we have believed it; we have mystified it and mythologized it. We have taken the lie for the truth, and in doing so we have almost made it true.

But people are larger than the myths they try to live by. And the truth hidden by the myth is that people have always created larger families than the biological family—larger, and infinitely more diverse. It has been there for many of us, perhaps for most of us, and we have always said to ourselves, this is different, this is me and my life, this has nothing to do with the way things are.

Side by side with the language of our oppression, other phrases have evolved and been assimilated into our vocabulary without our understanding their importance. "She's been a second mother to me." "He's just like a brother." "You are the daughter I've never had." "We're all one big happy family." Why have we never suspected that these innocuous phrases contain as much revolutionary potential as anything Karl Marx[36] or Emma Goldman[37] or Mary Wollstonecraft[38] ever said? Such phrases suggest that the family is something more than your husband or wife and the offspring of you and your spouse and the people who are related to you because somebody somewhere has the same blood parent, that someone totally outside the limits of that kinship definition can be your family. The family isn't what we've been taught it is. Thus we are not trapped between the Scylla and Charybdis[39] that the lie of the new narcissism offers; we do not need to

[34]*Damon and Pythias:* In classical mythology, Damon pledged his life to help his friend Pythias.

[35]*Jonathan and David:* In the Old Testament, Jonathan was the son of King Saul of Israel. He saved David from Saul's jealous attack on David's life. (See 1 Samuel.)

[36]*Karl Marx:* German social and political theorist (1818–1883), founder of communism.

[37]*Emma Goldman:* Russian-born American anarchist, speaker, and publisher (1869–1940). She was imprisoned for obstructing the draft and for advocating birth control and was deported in 1919.

[38]*Mary Wollstonecraft:* English writer (1759–1797), one of the first to advocate equal rights for women and men.

[39]*Scylla and Charybdis:* A deadly pair of threats; in classical mythology, they were sea monsters identified with a rock and a whirlpool.

choose between living without human bondings, or with bondings not of our choice. We can create our own bondings, choose them as they meet our needs; we can define, with others we have chosen and who have chosen us, what the nature of our bondings will be.

I think that some of the power that marriage has had for us — at least for women, although possibly for men as well — lies in this concept of choice. In an era when half of all marriages end in divorce, when couples openly live together, when the taint of "illegitimacy" is fading, marriage still has a powerful hold on women. And the power isn't only over women of the mainstream. Radical and socialist feminists marry; women who have lived with their lovers marry; women who have lived with *many* lovers marry. Even women who eschew monogamy marry. Sometimes they marry to placate parents, sometimes to make life easier for the children they plan to have. But I suspect that often these are simply the surface explanations for far more fundamental, more mythic, reasons.

The mythic power of marriage is threefold. To begin with, it offers a feeling of protection, of economic security. Historically, this has been accurate. A woman without a husband to protect her was at the mercy of her relatives and of strangers. The only other economically viable option was the convent, and even here a woman might find herself the "poor relation" of nuns from more affluent or prestigious families. Even today in the United States, women earn 59 percent of what men earn, and the poor are largely made up of women and their children.[40]

The second, and related, mythic power of marriage rests in its promise 25
of permanence. The myth of true-love-forever may be comparatively recent, but a few centuries is long enough to embed a myth into a culture. Further, the permanence of marriage predates romantic love. A man might abuse his wife, he might take on mistresses, he might functionally desert her. But he — or his kin, when he fails to meet his obligations — must support her and their children, and abandonment of one's wife carries strong social censure. Henry VIII's fame as an historic ogre rests not on his dissolution of the monasteries and consequent impoverishment of thousands of monks, nuns, and the beggars who relied on them for charity, not on his arbitrary executions of hundreds of "papists" and "heretics," but on his open willingness to discard, through divorce and execution, four wives. Especially when a woman has children, she is given the right to expect that her husband, whose bloodline she has preserved, will continue to provide for her needs.

The third myth, and the one that is the concern of this book, is that of the spouse as chosen relative. It is true that only in very recent history has a woman had any actual choice in whom she marries, that it has historically been assumed that a spouse will be chosen by the parents of both men and

[40]Judy Foreman, "9 to 5 grows, so does its clout," *Boston Globe*, Sept. 28, 1979. [Author's note]

women. But alongside this reality has always existed the story of the woman who defies the rule — who chooses, or attempts to choose, her mate. Cleopatra[41] chose Marc Antony, Dido[42] chose Aeneas, and in so doing they destroyed both their empires and their lives.

This is a negative image of choice, and in any case most women don't have the options available to women who rule nations. But the stories of royalty have always provided the mythology of the lower classes, and at the very least these stories introduce the *concept* of choice into the selection of a mate. In recent centuries, the concept has significantly changed. The choice has been transmitted into a good one; it is worth losing everything to maintain the integrity of that choice, select one's true love, and reject the choice of others, even when that choice seems more sensible. Indeed, in contemporary mythology, that choice often *guarantees* happiness — marry Mr. Right and your troubles are over.

But however the myth varies, its power rests in the fact that except in the atypical instance of adoption, your spouse is the only relative you are ever permitted to choose. You are born to your parents and, by extension, to their kin, and you raise the children you give birth to. The young, modern woman who chooses her mate has behind her a string of spiritual ancestors as long as Banquo's ghost,[43] ancestors to whom, at least once, however briefly, the thought of choosing their own mates must have occurred. It is a thought so monumental that its very existence must have changed something in the mind of its thinker. Few women could have voiced this change, and even fewer could have acted on it. But we are the heirs of that change nonetheless.

Now an even greater concept has entered into our minds. We can choose most of our family. We can choose *all* of our family. In some ways, recognition of this possibility has begun to surface in popular culture. Recently, several magazines published articles about the need to create new, familial ways to celebrate holidays, and described festive scenes shared by former and current spouses, in-laws from both marriages, and offspring from the divorced parents' current and former marriages.

30 As far as it goes, this represents an important step in breaking through the oppressive definitions of family. For people who have shared history, who have loved each other and lived through major parts of each other's lives together, the concept of "family" should apply, in much the same way

[41]*Cleopatra:* Queen of Egypt (69–30 B.C.). After two marriages in Egypt and an affair with Caesar, Cleopatra married Marc Antony, a potential rival from Rome who fell in love with her. They eventually committed suicide after military defeats by Roman forces.

[42]*Dido:* In Roman mythology, the queen of Carthage. Virgil's *Aeneid* describes her love for Aeneas, a shipwrecked Trojan. When he continued his journey, she threw herself on a burning pyre.

[43]*Banquo's ghost:* A reference to Shakespeare's *Macbeth* (act 4, scene 1); Macbeth, who has murdered Banquo, sees an apparition of eight kings of Banquo's lineage.

as it applies to parents and grown siblings who no longer live together or share the same interests but who are indelibly part of one another's lives.

But it isn't only spouses who share or have shared each other's lives, who have created a common past with each other. Friends, neighbors, coworkers have often lived through as many experiences together as husbands and wives—have created, perhaps unconsciously, equally strong bonds. And slowly these bonds too are seeping into popular mythology.

A good barometer of the change is television, which is probably the most potent force in mid-twentieth-century American mythmaking. In the '50s, the model of the family was clear-cut. Mommy, Daddy, and the kids. *Father Knows Best. I Remember Mama. Ozzie and Harriet. Make Room for Daddy. I Love Lucy. Life of Riley.* Even *Burns and Allen,* miles ahead of the others in wit and sophistication, showed two nuclear families, and the Burnses had a son (though he never appeared till the later episodes). Only *My Little Margie,* saccharine sweet as it was, dared to veer from the accepted family norm: Daddy was a widower who lived with his grown daughter.

In the '60s, things began to change. Divorce was a social reality, but a fantasy taboo, so TV compromised. The mortality rate among television spouses soared: suddenly widows and widowers with kids were the norm. *The Diahann Carroll Show. The Doris Day Show. The Andy Griffith Show. The Partridge Family.* And then the crème de la crème, *The Brady Bunch:* widow with cute large brood marries widower with cute large brood, re-creating the two-parent family with a vengeance. It was an interesting attempt to cover up by half admitting what was happening to the family. Viewers who were divorced or separated could identify with the one-parent (or re-created two-parent) family, but could not have the validity of their own experience confirmed. Death is a tragedy, not a choice: the family still works until something more cosmic than human need disrupts it.

By the '70s even that wasn't enough, and the workplace family began to achieve some recognition. It started with *The Mary Tyler Moore Show.* Mary Richards, the character Moore played, had just broken off with her boyfriend and had come to Minneapolis to seek a job. Her coworkers and her best friend, Rhoda, became her family. This was no accident: the characters on the show *talked* about being a family. In one episode, Rhoda refused a job in New York because it would separate her from Mary. With little fanfare, *The Mary Tyler Moore Show* tastefully broke a taboo.

Then there was *Mod Squad,* the story of three stereotypically alienated kids who become cops, and in the process also become each other's family. Corny as that show was (and reactionary in its basic theme—three dropouts become narcs), a caring and commitment among the three came through as it never did in any other cop show. The relationship, in fact, may have scared some of its creators. A year or two ago, they aired a two-hour special, *Return of the Mod Squad,* in which the three, now living separate lives, are reunited essentially to establish that the old "family" was an adolescent phase and they have now outgrown each other.

But the model of on-the-job families continues—perhaps to reasure all the divorced people, the not-yet-married people, the not-in-romantic-relationship people, that they aren't totally alone. Good shows and bad, serious and silly, they are astoundingly numerous. The cops on *Barney Miller,* the soldiers on *M*A*S*H,* the radio personnel on *WKRP in Cincinnati.* Even on as vacuous a show as *Love Boat,* the workmates in more than one episode are described as a family. Last season, in fact, the Love Boat family was solidified by its adoption of a child—Captain Stuebing's illegitimate, ten-year-old daughter, Vicki. In the episode introducing Vicki's residence on board the ship, a social worker at first is reluctant to permit the girl to live in such an unstable environment, with no family but the captain. But she is soon persuaded that Vicki does indeed have a family on the ship. Vicki, she says, is "one lucky lady. . . . You have not one parent but five, all of them loving, caring people."[44]

In *M*A*S*H,* too, the family has been verbalized. At one point, fatherly Colonel Potter says, "The 4077 is not just a roster of people; it's my family. Not only that, but a loyal family." In another episode, Corporal Klinger, shattered by the news that his wife is divorcing him, comes to realize that "I may not have a family anymore in Toledo, but I sure have one here." In yet another, Margaret describes the unit as "like a family," and then corrects herself. "No," she says firmly, "it *is* a family." Sometimes the familial relationship among the characters is mirrored in the relationship of the actors. An interview with the cast of *M*A*S*H* brings up familial references. Gary Burghoff, who played the boyish Radar O'Reilly, told one writer that since the death of his own father, "I think of Harry [Morgan] as my new father."[45]

Some of TV's workplace families are more believable than others: the warmth of the *M*A*S*H* personnel comes through beautifully; the poke-in-the-ribs camaraderie of the *Love Boat* crew evokes little feeling of connection or commitment. But, however successful each is, TV has come to recognize, and institutionalize, the workplace family.

In 1978 a brief-lived show called *The Apple Family* attempted a truly radical idea — the story of unrelated people who came together with the idea of forming a consciously chosen family, not an office family or a thrown-together family. The show didn't last. It wasn't very good, and in any event lots of shows don't last, so maybe that doesn't mean anything. On the other hand, maybe it does. Maybe it means that television, which influences so much of our thinking, can't afford to tell us we can choose our own families. It is, after all, a very dangerous message. It will be interesting to see the fate of a fall 1981 program, *Love, Sidney,* in which a gay man lives with a het-

[44]The quotes from television shows came from the diligent research of Lisa Leghorn, one of my chosen-family members, who selflessly spent hours watching *M*A*S*H* and *Love Boat* to cull them for me. [Author's note]

[45]David S. Reiss, *M*A*S*H: The Exclusive Inside Story of TV's Most Popular Show* (New York: Bobbs-Merrill, 1980), p. 35. [Author's note]

erosexual woman and her daughter, forming, in the producer's words, a "surrogate family."[46]

In writing this book, I've had to make choices about terminology. This 40
is always sticky, since words inevitably attempt to pin down human experience, and human experience always exists in countless variations. What do we call the family as we know it? The nuclear family is only a recent phenomenon, springing out of the older extended family. "Family of origin" is inaccurate if it attempts to include grandparents, aunts, uncles, and cousins whom we may not even meet until we are five, ten, or thirty, but who are still part of that concept called family. "Biological family" comes closest, and I have chosen to use it, but not without trepidation, since both marriage and adoption are integral parts of it. I've chosen it because it seems to me to encompass not the whole reality, but the whole *myth:* blood is thicker than water. Much of the power of the patriarchy rests on the concept of biological kinship: a man needs a son to carry on his genes and his name; hence woman is forced into marriage and monogamy. Marriage historically is the integration of two bloodlines, and it is this, not the more recent myth of romance, that is the central mythical commitment of marriage: "She is the mother of my children." The stepmother in the fairy tale *must* be wicked, because her natural alliance is to the children of her own body, not those of her husband's body. Adoption of children not of one's own bloodline is always an adaptation. When one can't have children of "one's own," one creates a substitute, in effect pretending that the child is blood kin. The reality has changed; the myth remains untouched. Hence, I am using "biological family" to encompass the myth in all its facets, since it is the myth rather than the fact of genetical inheritance that governs our lives.

The same problem of terminology arises when I find myself defining the kinds of contemporary nonbiological family. Definition, the creation of categories — these are useful and necessary, but they are also dangerous. They are useful if, like clothing, they can be worn when they're comfortable and can stretch to fit whatever they cover, allowing themselves to be discarded when they no longer fit properly. If they become straitjackets, restricting and confining, they are destructive; they have become false naming. True naming is a process of infinite growth, infinite flexibility. And so I have drawn up categories of nonbiological family. I think they are useful categories, helping to put into focus a reality we've been taught not to see. But they are loose categories. A given relationship may fall into one, or two, or three categories. There may be — there must be — other categories. I've chosen mine because they fit my experience and my observations.

The three kinds of nonbiological family I've seen are the "honorary relative" family — the family friend who is your "uncle" or "aunt" as you

[46]Frank Swertlow, "TV Update," *TV Guide*, June 6, 1981, p. A-1. [Author's note] (*Love, Sidney* was canceled after two seasons on NBC.)

grow up; the workplace family; and, finally, the chosen family—the friends who, with no outside force throwing you together, you have consciously or unconsciously chosen to be your family. . . .

The chosen family isn't always an unmitigated good: I'm not attempting to erase *Father Knows Best* and replace it with an equally silly picture of happy little chosen families creating heaven on earth. Sometimes the chosen family mirrors the worst of biological families — the patriarchal power, the crippling dependency, the negation of the individual selves that can exist in a secure framework. Charles Manson[47] was the leader of a chosen family; so was Jim Jones.[48] Armies create families of men who are permitted and encouraged through their bonding to rape and kill. To expand definitions, to create choice, doesn't guarantee that the choices will be either wise or moral. But choice itself is good, and with it comes a greater potential for good than exists in its absence. . . .

[47]*Charles Manson:* Leader of the "family" that murdered actor Sharon Tate and six of her friends in 1969.

[48]*Jim Jones:* American-born head of a fanatical religious sect, some nine hundred members of which committed mass suicide in Guyana.

Engaging the Text

1. Is it possible to *choose* one's own family? Are the kinds of chosen families Lindsey describes really families, or "just" groups of friends?
2. Explain the concept of the "new narcissism." How, according to Lindsey, has it affected the American family?
3. Early in this selection, Lindsey draws a distinction between a myth and a lie. Explain and illustrate the difference between these two terms.
4. What, according to Lindsey, is the relationship between patriarchy and the traditional nuclear family?
5. Analyze the structure of Lindsey's argument. How persuasive is the evidence she provides in its defense?

Exploring Connections

6. How would Lindsey analyze Anndee Hochman's dilemma (p. 150)?
7. Look ahead to Gloria Naylor's story "The Two" (p. 319). Analyze the couple in the story as an example of a chosen family. Would Lindsey say they meet her criteria for a functional family? Would you?
8. The "Dysfunctional Family Greeting Cards" on page 172 reflect some of the abuses of the patriarchal family indicted by Lindsey. Can you suggest ideas for additional dysfunctional family greeting cards, perhaps composed from the parent's — not the child's — point of view?

Extending the Critical Context

9. Several recent books, like Robert Bly's *Iron John,* suggest that Americans are experiencing a deep psychological hunger for a strong father — the need for a firm but kind embodiment of authority and male power. Do you share this perception? How might Lindsey argue against it?
10. At the end of this selection, Lindsey suggests that chosen families may have some negative as well as positive aspects. What, in your opinion, might be the negative implications of a society composed primarily of voluntary families?
11. Do you know any example of nonbiological or chosen families? How do they differ from the biological families you know? Are there purposes each serves that the other cannot?
12. Watch *Longtime Companion* or *Paris Is Burning* and discuss the alternate or chosen families these films depict. What needs do such families fulfill?

TV's Antifamilies: Married . . . with Malaise

Josh Ozersky

The history of the patriarchal family may conceal generations of dysfunctionality, as Karen Lindsey claims in the previous selection (p. 158), but in recent years the media have made toxic families the norm. This essay charts America's growing obsession with TV families that explode the myth of harmony at home and suggests that we're attracted to hip caricatures of family life because laughing at our problems is easier than trying to solve them. A critic of American popular culture and author of several articles on the subject, Ozersky (b. 1967) is currently pursuing graduate studies at Notre Dame University.

It's an odd thing when a cartoon series is praised as one of the most trenchant and "realistic" programs on TV, but there you are. Never mind the Cosby-size ratings: if merchandising says anything about American culture, and it does, then America was utterly infatuated with *The Simpsons* in 1990. "Utterly," because unlike other big winners in the industry such as the Teenage Mutant Ninja Turtles and the New Kids on the Block, the Simpsons graced not only T-shirts for the clamoring young, but T-shirts (and sweatshirts and posters and mugs) that went out in droves to parents, who rivaled kids for viewer loyalty.

The animated series chronicles the life of the Simpson family: father Homer, who works in a nuclear power plant and reads bowling-ball catalogs; mother Marge, with her blue beehive hairdo and raspy voice; misunderstood-Bohemian daughter Lisa; baby Maggie; and bratty son Bart, the anti-everything star of the series. Bart appeals to kids, who see a flattering image of themselves, and to their parents, who, even as they identify with

Bart against his lumpkin parents, enjoy Bart's caricature of their own children, with his incomprehensible sloganeering ("Don't have a cow, man!") and bad manners. Nor, tellingly, has the popularity of the show stopped with the white mainstream: a black Bart soon began to turn up in unlicensed street paraphernalia.

In the first of the unauthorized shirts, Bart was himself, only darkened. The novelty soon wore off, however, and in successive generations Bart found himself ethnicized further: "Air Bart" had him flying toward a basketball hoop exclaiming, "In your face, home boy." Another shirt had Bart leering at zaftig black women, loutishly yelling, "Big Ole Butt!" at their retreating figures. And in later versions, Bart has a gold tooth, a razor cut, and an angry snarl—the slogan "I got the power!" juts overhead in an oversized balloon.

The "I got the power!" Bart is barely recognizable, disfigured by rancor. But even more jarring than his appearance is his vitriol, so out of keeping with the real Bart's laid-back, ironic demeanor — an endemic condition among TV characters. The naked discontent on that shirt is jarring, disturbing. It lacks the light touch. TV does not—but then the playful suppression of unhappiness has always been one of TV's great strengths; and in its latest, ugliest form, it subtly discourages alarm at the decline of the family, its own complicity in that decline, and the resulting effects on a disintegrating society.

The success in the last few seasons of new, "antifamily" sitcoms, such 5
as Fox's *Married . . . with Children* and *The Simpsons* and ABC's *Roseanne,* began a trend that has made waves in television. "Whether it's the influence of Bart Simpson and those cheeky sitcoms from Fox," wrote *TV Guide* in September [1990] "or ABC's artsy antisoap *Twin Peaks,*[1] unconventionality is in; slick and safe are out." The "cheeky sitcoms" began that trend. *Roseanne,* about an obese and abrasive proletarian mom, and *Married . . . with Children,* a half hour of pure viciousness, represented along with *The Simpsons* a new development of the situation comedy, TV's definitive genre. Each program (as well as its inevitable imitators) focuses on a family marked by visual styles and characterization as bleak and miserable as those of former TV families had been handsome or cheerful.

The innovation received a lot of attention in the mass media, most of it favorable. Richard Zoglin in *Time* hailed the "real-world grit these shows provide," produced psychological authorities, and quoted Barbara Ehrenreich's wide-eyed "Zeitgeist Goddess" piece in the *New Republic.* The *New York Times*'s Caryl Rivers wrote approvingly of the new realism, although she noted perfunctorily that gays, minorities, and women were less visible

[1]*Twin Peaks:* A popular 1990 TV mystery show renowned for its bizarrely complicated plot and ironic detachment.

than they should have been. What all sides had in common, however, was a willingness to point out the improvement over other forms of TV. "The antifamily shows aren't against the family, exactly, just scornful of the romantic picture TV has often painted of it," Zoglin pointed out. "We're like a mutant Ozzie and Harriet," Simpsons creator Matt Groening boasted in *Newsweek,* which went on to point out that the show was "hardly the stuff of Saturday-morning children's programming." "Thankfully, we are past the days of perfect Mom and all-wise Dad and their twin beds," wrote the *New York Times*'s Rivers, speaking for reviewers and feature writers everywhere. And this was prior to the advent of the "unconventional" mystery serial *Twin Peaks,* which still has feature writers striving for superlatives to describe its "innovations" and "departures."

This unanimous juxtaposition of the "antifamilies" to the stern TV households of yesteryear is a specious comparison designed to amuse and flatter. Not as the result of any conspiracy—writers in the commercial mass media generally write to please, and what they say is true enough if you have as your entire frame of reference the past and present of TV. But far from the "authenticity" it pretends to, the "grit" for the new shows is merely an improved artifice, a challenge only to the verisimilitude of art directors and casting companies. By pretending to realism, TV only extends its own hegemony,[2] in which every standard of comparison points back to another sham. "Gosh," gushed *TV Guide* of Bart, "can you imagine Bud Anderson[3] being so . . . *disrespectful* to Dad?" As if the lead of *Father Knows Best* had only recently become a figure of fun.

It is through this sort of pseudo–self-deprecation that TV tries to ingratiate itself with Americans, who in an age marked by pervasive irony want to run with the hare and hunt with the hound—to feel superior to TV and yet keep watching it. TV offers this target audience an abundance of self-images that will permit them this trick. The target viewers may be enlightened, making the "choice of a new generation" by seeing through *My Little Margie,*[4] or avant-garde, on the cutting edge, for watching *Twin Peaks,* which, like *Hill Street Blues* before it, supposedly "breaks all the rules." They are in utter harmony with the very mechanics of TV production, which has no secrets from us, as we know from David Letterman's insider gags, such as the "Late Night Danger Cam."

As for discrediting paternalistic authority figures, Mark Crispin Miller has pointed out that the imperious Dads of fifties TV, now such a rich source of burlesque, were overturned by a maturing medium very early on. The "grim old abstinence" of the Puritan patriarch stood in the way of the "grim new self-indulgence" of consumer culture and was hence banished. Dads turned into "pleasant nullities," like Dick York in *Bewitched* and Timothy

[2]*hegemony:* Dominance.
[3]*Bud Anderson:* Son in the 1950s TV series *Father Knows Best.*
[4]*My Little Margie:* Popular 1950s TV situation comedy.

Busfield in *thirtysomething,* or unenlightened butts of knowing and self-flattering jokes, like Archie Bunker and Homer Simpson.

The downfall of Dad, however, saw no concomitant rise of Mom or the kids. Rather, it was advertisers and corporations that benefited from the free-spending self-indulgence of all parties, liberated from patriarchal discipline. And the networks, of course, cashed in and sold advertisers airtime. In the world beyond the screen, the family has disintegrated into epidemic divorces and deteriorating marriages, latchkey children, and working parents reduced to spending "quality time" with their children, as though they were hospital visitors or the lovelorn spouses of soldiers on leave. Meanwhile, the TV world — not only in sitcoms but in endless "special reports" and talk shows and (particularly) commercials — insists again and again that we are hipper, more "open," more enlightened, and facing changing "relationships" in a new and better way. Mom, often divorced and underpaid, has her new "independence," a standard theme of programming, and Dad and the kids, faced with other losses and hardships, are offered the bold new "grittiness" of prime-time entertainment. TV has absorbed the American family's increasing sense of defeat and estrangement and presented it as an ironic in-joke.

This dynamic is seldom noted, although the mere *fact* of watching is noted by critics and commentators everywhere, and nowhere more visibly than on TV itself. The opening credits of *The Simpsons* end with the family, assembled at the end of the day, jumping mutely into fixed position on the sofa and clicking on the TV set. This absorption of criticism is and has been, except for sheer distraction, TV's greatest weapon against criticism. The transformation of the hearth into an engine of negation, after all, should have caused *some* stir. And so it would have, if TV were no more than the yammering salesman it has caricatured itself as in satirical moments. But, as Miller demonstrates, TV has never shown us TV; rather, it shows itself to us as a laughable, absurd, and harmless entity, much like the characters on its shows.

When not played for background noise — whooping Indians in older shows, unctuous game-show hosts or newsmen in newer ones — depictions of the TV set on TV itself render it invisible and omnipresent. TV itself, its conventions and production, may be the crucial point of reference for the sophisticated appeal it enjoys today, but the set as household centerpiece is seldom seen, and then only as a joke, as on *The Simpsons.* Instead, the set most often poses as a portal to the outer world: hence its constant stream of images that tease us with alluring beaches, blue waters, busy city streets. Even in its living rooms, where we know its presence to be inescapable, the TV is often missing. This effect is accomplished by a simple trick of photography when the family watches TV in *All in the Family,* in *Good Times,* in *Married . . . with Children,* etc., the scene is shot from behind the TV set. As the family sits facing us, with the screen nowhere in sight, the illusion exists for a moment that the TV really is, if not a portal, then a mirror or reflection of us. A close look at these families, and at our own, soon banishes this impression. We are not like these TV families at all; and the TV set is obtrusive, ideological, and tendentious.

When speaking of the "antifamily" sitcoms, most of the commentators seem to have in mind *Married . . . with Children.* No other show so luridly plays up the sheer negativity of the current "authenticity" trend, nor does any other show do so with such predictable regularity. The series portrays the Bundys, a lower-middle-class family with two children and a dog. Father Al (Ed O'Neill) only has "knotted bowels" to show for his life supporting the family. Peg (Katey Sagal) is Al's castrating wife. There is also the inevitable sharp-tongued teenage son, who singles out for special heckling his brainless and sleazy sister. The relentlessly ironic quality of a happy family turned thoroughly upside-down flatters the audience for their enlightenment (no *Donna Reed,*[5] this) even as it invites them to enjoy the ongoing frenzy of spite in which the show indulges. And frenzy is indeed the word. Every member of the family despises everyone else, and any given program consists of little more than continuous insults, interspersed with snide loathing or occasional expressions of despair.

FATHER (to son): Did I ever tell you not to get married?
SON: Yeah, Dad.
FATHER: Did I ever tell you not to become a shoe salesman?
SON: Yeah, Dad.
FATHER: Well, then I've told you everything I know.

This sort of resigned and paralytic discontent dominates the tone of *Married . . . with Children;* it lacks even the dim rays of hope that occasionally lifted Ralph Kramden's or Riley's[6] gloomy existence. Every show is devoted to a new kind of humiliation: to earn extra money, Al becomes a burger-flipper; when son Bud falls victim to a practical joke perpetrated by an old flame his slutty sister Kelly comes to his defense by crucifying the girl against a locker; wife Peg belittles Al's manhood in front of strangers. Again and again, the unrelenting negativity of the show finds new ways to expand, purifying itself of any nonironic, positive content. Lovebird neighbors intended for contrast in the first season soon divorce, adding to the show's already vast reserve of bitterness. Christina Applegate, the young actress who plays Kelly, filled out during the first two years, adding a missing element of nasty prurience to the show.

The result of this hermetic exclusion of all warmth, say a number of 15
apologists for the show, is positive: "With these new programs," says Barbara Cadow, a psychologist at USC, "we see we're doing all right by comparison."

[5]*Donna Reed:* Star of the 1950s *Donna Reed Show* and archetype of the perfect nuclear-family mother.

[6]*Ralph Kramden . . . Riley:* Leading characters on the 1950s situation comedies *The Honeymooners* and *The Life of Riley.*

Yet at the same time, it is the very "realism" of these shows that won them praise again and again. This "realism" appeals to a cynical element in us — no one would ever admit to resembling Roseanne Barr or her family, but they are eminently "realistic" portraits of the losers next door. Roseanne Barr is shrewish and miserable to the point of self-parody, and this is seen as the great strength of her series. "Mom" (who Roseanne, it is assumed, represents) "is no longer interested in being a human sacrifice on the altar of 'pro-family' values," says Barbara Ehrenreich in the *New Republic.*

The praise of the same style of TV both for its realism and for its horrific exaggeration, while apparently contradictory, is based on a common assumption. In each case, the pervasive unhappiness and derision on TV sitcoms is assumed to be a reflection, albeit a negative one, of the unhappiness of real families. Cadow assumes that it is caricature, and Ehrenreich that it is a manifesto, but neither woman doubts that both shows offer some kind of corrective to real life for their viewers, and that this explains their popularity. This congratulatory view of hit TV shows contains a fundamental error: the old network executive's rationale that TV "gives people what they want," in response to their Nielsen-measured "choice."

The concentration of mass media into a few corporate hands invalidates that idea even more today than in the past. Given TV's entirely corporate nature, it is unreasonable to assume that the channels are referenda, since almost every channel, at least until recently, offered almost identical options. What succeeds with the public makes it, yes. But that "success" is determined by TV's agenda — which now, as always, is more than selling dog biscuits. Consumption must be encouraged psychologically; sectors and tendencies in American society have to be identified and exploited. "Since the major broadcasters are no longer winning the big numbers," observes *TV Guide,* "they're now fighting for the youthful demographics that bring in the highest revenues. That's why everyone is hyping bold, hip shows."

Of course, the success of a culture based on mass consumption depends on the creation of boundless needs; boundless needs presuppose boundless discontent. Boundless discontent must begin with the family, where social patterns are first internalized. If, latchkey in hand, TV can flatter a kinless and dispossessed child into adulthood and at the same time kid his or her parents about it, perfect consumers are thereby made. The family becomes a breeding ground for easygoing and independent citizens of the marketplace, transported beyond the inner struggle and deep feeling of family life, and bound in their place by the laws of supply and demand, consumer "choices," and a continual negation of their truest selves.

By presenting unhappy families to viewers, TV achieves many gains. First, as Cadow rightly points out, mocking the traditional family does flatter the distorted family of our times. However, this does not necessarily lift spirits. On the contrary, it lowers expectations; it stupefies discontent instead of healing it. *Married . . . with Children* is the prototype of this strategy. The petty or profound resentments of real families do not rival those of the Bundys, but then neither does their ability to punish and humiliate each other. By making our problems "seem all right by comparison," the series trivializes them rather than taking them seriously. It in fact worsens them by its counsel of despair.

Secondly, the dysfunctional TV family aids advertisers in their perennial 20
quest for credibility by creating a supersaturated atmosphere of irony, which atrophies our ability to believe in anything. Commercials themselves work on a principle of pseudorebelliousness. Burger King — now officially touted by the Simpsons — proudly sports the "radical" motto, "Sometimes you've gotta break the rules." Swallowing these giant absurdities relies not on credulity, but on an ironic, self-assured disbelief. *Roseanne,* with its trademark sarcasm, and *Twin Peaks,* with its tongue-in-cheek grotesqueries, are good examples.

Third, and most insidious, is the stability of TV's dysfunctional families, and their passive acceptance of their fate. A successful cast is the source of "ensemble acting," which has been the formula for success for some time now on TV. Since TV characters now move in herds, they do not get divorced, move out, have devastating affairs, or anything else that would disrupt the fabric of the show's format. Implicitly, these shows assure us that family life is largely a nightmare, but one that is self-perpetuating and only requires handling with a deft, protective irony. This irony, the antithesis of deep feeling, is the essential assault on the family and on all human relationships, reducing them to problems of managerial acumen. Thus, while remaining intact in their own impoverished world, sitcom families undermine the stability of real families, discrediting the embarrassingly earnest, often abject bonds of kin while hermetically sealing themselves off from the possibility of familial collapse. And this while they consume the increasingly rare time in which American families are actually together.

The Simpsons, the most popular of the group and certainly the least ironic and "antifamily," is TV's most effective reinforcer. This paradox begins with the fact that the show is a cartoon: With their yellow skin, bulging eyes, and comical motions, the Simpsons are funny just to look at, and hence relieve the audience of the need to continually jeer at them. The Bundy family of *Married . . . with Children,* like all sitcom characters, aspire to the televisual purity of cartoon characters, but are stuck in rubbery bags of protoplasm with nothing but one-liners and a laugh track to hide behind. The Simpsons, oddly, are freer than other TV families to act human.

And so they do. There is an element of family loyalty and principle to be found in the Simpsons, often combined with witty and valid social criticism. Brother Bart and sister Lisa petulantly demand of baby Maggie to "come to the one you love most," to which the infant responds by crawling lovingly to the TV. Or again, when father Homer's sinister boss inquires disbelievingly, "You'd give up a job and a raise for your principles?" Homer responds (with almost none of the usual sitcom character's irony), "When you put it that way, it does sound farfetched — but that's the lunk you're lookin' at!" "Hmm," the boss replies. "You're not as dumb as you look. Or sound. Or as our best testing indicates."

With pointed jokes such as these, *The Simpsons* might prompt us to conclude the same about its vast audience. The harmlessness of these jokes can be taken for granted; no one who watches TV is going to stop because they see TV criticized. We criticize it ourselves as a matter of course. On the contrary, we feel flattered, and less inclined to stop watching.

And we are that much less inclined to object to the continuing presence 25
of unsafe workplaces, vast corporations, the therapy racket, and all the other deserving targets of the Simpsons' harmless barbs. The genial knowingness of shows like *The Simpsons* subverts criticism through an innocuous pseudocriticism, just as the familial discontents of TV shows subvert alarm at graver discontents in real life. Criticism is further weakened by the show's irony, which although less than some other programs is still pervasive and fundamental to its humor. No one in an ironic show can get too far out of line. For example, in one episode, misunderstood Lisa meets that well-worn figure of Caucasian lore, the wise and virtuous old colored bluesman, ever ready to act as mentor to young white people in their search for self-knowledge. *The Simpsons* is far too hip to hand us such a hackneyed cliché. The Virtuous Old Blues Man is as empty a conceit as the Perfect Family — so on the show, he is named "Bleeding Gums Murphy" (Why? "I haven't brushed my teeth in thirty years, that's why.") In place of the usual soulful laments, he sings the "I Don't Have an Italian Suit Blues."

Such undercutting is typical of TV as a whole; attempts to transcend the flattened-out emotional landscape of TV are almost invariably punished by some droll comeuppance. But since as bizarre cartoons there is little need to belittle them, the Simpsons get a little more than most and are occasionally allowed moments of earnestness unmitigated by the selfishness of *thirtysomething*, the weirdness of *Twin Peaks*, or the inevitable "comic relief" — the stock entrances of deadpan tots and witty oldsters, etc. — used to terminate the maudlin embraces of nonanimated sitcomites. None of this is to be had on *The Simpsons*, but the picture it presents is still fundamentally hopeless. The Simpsons are basically boobs, and their occasional bursts of tenderness or insight are buried under biting irony and superior, if affectionate, mockery. More than any of the other "antifamily" shows, *The Simpsons* seems to come close to our lives; more than any of the other shows, as a result, it commits us to a shared vision of pessimism and self-deprecation.

Because the TV screen is neither a mirror, reflecting ourselves paralyzed in chairs in front of it, nor a window, through which we observe the antics of distant players, it is an implicit invitation to participate in a vision of "society" largely designed to flatter us in sinister ways, manipulate our attention, and commit us to the status quo. In discrediting "yesterday's" family values in its various "breakthrough" shows (ostensibly defining *A Different*

World for us, as the title of one series has it), TV seeks only to impose its own values — which is to say, the values of the marketplace. Bart Simpson, master sneerer, is the prototype of the modern series character who — by the social scripts of TV — reflects us. Small, ridiculous, and at the same time admirable for his sarcasm and enlightened self-interest, Bart is the child of the culture of TV, his parents mere intermediaries.

Paradoxically, that is why the most powerless sector of American society has adopted him, fitting him with their own wishful slogan — "I got the power!" Though black Bart's anger may be incongruous with TV, his proclamation is not, since TV is so successful an invitation to impotent posturing. At the moment, the rage of the underclass cannot be appropriated by TV, yet in black Bart, in the fatal joining of ironic hipness and earnest wrath, we see perhaps a glimpse of the future (and in fact there are already a spate of new black shows — for example, *Fresh Prince of Bel Air, In Living Color*). "I got the power!" says black Bart. But in the world of the TV family, no one has power. Empty fantasies of might, like cynical, knowing giggles, are terminal symptoms of our capitulation to TV's vision.

Life outside of that vision *is* ugly and is becoming uglier as ties, familial and societal, dissolve and decay. But the only power we do have is the power of our own real selves to reject the defensive posture of materialist or ironist or cynic, and the soullessness of TV's "hip, bold," antilife world. Bart and his aspirants exist in that world, and their example serves only to impoverish us.

Engaging the Text

1. According to Ozersky, what do TV critics mean when they say that TV antifamilies "reflect" reality? What does Ozersky think of this idea? Do you agree?
2. How does Ozersky explain the popularity of TV antifamilies? How would you account for their appeal?
3. In Ozersky's view, what led to the rise of the antifamily on TV?
4. To what extent do you agree with Ozersky's position that TV's negativity encourages us to accept declining family values and a decaying society?
5. Ozersky notes that TV has been seen as a window, a portal, and a mirror. Why does he reject these interpretations of TV's function? What role does he see TV playing in our society? What metaphor do you think most accurately describes TV's social role?

Exploring Connections

6. Write an imaginary dialogue between Bart Simpson and the nine-year-old Gary Soto on the experience of American family life. Which of their views, would you say, is more realistic?
7. In "Friends as Family" (p. 158), Karen Lindsey offers a brief sketch of TV portrayals of family life, from the happy nuclear families of the 1950s to the rise

of the "workplace" family of the 1970s. Do current "chosen" TV families represent an alternative to the antifamily? What might Ozersky say about the cultural vision that is implied in contemporary "workplace" or "chosen" family shows like *Northern Exposure, Murphy Brown, Seinfeld,* and *Love and War?*

8. How does Robin Templeton's account of student opposition to *Channel One* (p. 135) complicate Ozersky's analysis of the impact of TV on American society?

Extending the Critical Context

9. Test Ozersky's claims about TV's antifamilies by viewing a segment of *The Simpsons* or *Roseanne* in class. To what extent do you agree that such shows have "absorbed the American family's increasing sense of defeat and estrangement and presented it as an ironic in-joke" (para. 10)?
10. Survey recent TV representations of family life (*Home Improvement, Family Matters, Grace Under Fire, Me and the Boys,* etc.) and discuss the current state of the TV antifamily. Are TV families still filled with "unrelenting negativity" and meaningless rebellion?
11. Ozersky offers a stinging critique of the social nihilism of TV's antifamilies, but he gives us little sense of what the alternative might be. Working in groups, draft a brief proposal for a half-hour TV show featuring a realistic family that does not reflect the hip cynicism Ozersky describes. Is it possible to depict a positive family on TV without returning to *Father Knows Best?*

Envy

Bebe Moore Campbell

What would make a schoolgirl who is afraid to chew gum in class threaten to stab her teacher? In this narrative, at least, it's not grammar drills or sentence diagrams — it's anger, frustration, and envy caused by an absentee father. Like Gary Soto's "Looking for Work" (p. 145), this personal recollection of childhood combines the authenticity of actual experience with the artistry of expert storytelling. Bebe Moore Campbell (b. 1950) has published articles in many national newspapers and magazines, including The New York Times Magazine, Ebony, Working Mother, Ms., *and the* Los Angeles Times. *Her books include* Your Blues Ain't Like Mine *(1992);* Sweet Summer: Growing Up with and Without My Dad *(1989), from which this selection is taken; and her new novel,* Brothers and Sisters.

The red bricks of 2239 North 16th Street melded into the uniformity of look-alike doors, windows, and brownstone-steps. From the outside our rowhouse looked the same as any other. When I was a toddler, the similarity was unsettling. The family story was that my mother and I were out walking on the street one day when panic rumbled through me. "Where's our house? Where's our house?" I cried, grabbing my mother's hand.

My mother walked me to our house, pointed to the numbers painted next to the door. "Twenty-two thirty-nine," she said, slapping the wall. "This is our house."

Much later I learned that the real difference was inside.

In my house there was no morning stubble, no long johns or Fruit of the Loom on the clothesline, no baritone hollering for keys that were sitting on the table. There was no beer in the refrigerator, no ball game on TV, no loud cussing. After dark the snores that emanated from the bedrooms were subtle, ladylike, little moans really.

Growing up, I could have died from overexposure to femininity. Women 5
ruled at 2239. A grandmother, a mother, occasionally an aunt, grown-up girlfriends from at least two generations, all the time rubbing up against me, fixing my food, running my bathwater, telling me to sit still and be good in those grown-up, girly-girl voices. Chanel and Prince Matchabelli wafting through the bedrooms. Bubble bath and Jergens came from the bathroom, scents unbroken by aftershave, macho beer breath, a good he-man funk. I remember a house full of 'do rags and rollers, the soft, sweet allure of Dixie peach and bergamot;[1] brown-skinned queens wearing pastel housecoats and worn-out size six-and-a-half flip-flops that slapped softly against the wood as the royal women climbed the stairs at night carrying their paperbacks to bed.

The outside world offered no retreat. School was taught by stern, old-maid white women with age spots and merciless gray eyes; ballet lessons, piano lessons, Sunday school, and choir were all led by colored sisters with a hands-on-their-hips attitude who cajoled and screeched in distaff[2] tongues.

And what did they want from me, these Bosoms? Achievement! This desire had nothing to do with the pittance they collected from the Philadelphia Board of Education or the few dollars my mother paid them. Pushing little colored girls forward was in their blood. They made it clear: a life of white picket fences and teas was for other girls to aspire to. I was to *do* something. And if I didn't climb willingly up their ladder, they'd drag me to the top. Rap my knuckles hard for not practicing. Make me lift my leg until I wanted to die. Stay after school and write "I will listen to the teacher" five hundred times. They were not playing. "Obey them," my mother commanded.

When I entered 2B — the Philadelphia school system divided grades into A and B — in September 1957, I sensed immediately that Miss Bradley was not a woman to be challenged. She looked like one of those evil old

[1]*bergamot:* A citrus tree with a fragrant fruit.
[2]*distaff:* Female, maternal.

spinsters Shirley Temple[3] was always getting shipped off to live with; she was kind of hefty, but so tightly corseted that if she happened to grab you or if you fell against her during recess, it felt as if you were bouncing into a steel wall. In reality she was a sweet lady who was probably a good five years past her retirement age when I wound up in her class. Miss Bradley remained at Logan for one reason and one reason only: she was dedicated. She wanted her students to learn! learn! learn! Miss Bradley was halfway sick, hacking and coughing her lungs out through every lesson, spitting the phlegm into fluffy white tissues from the box on her desk, but she was *never* absent. Each day at three o'clock she kissed each one of her "little pupils" on the cheek, sending a faint scent of Emeraude home with us. Her rules for teaching children seemed to be: love them; discipline them; reward them; and make sure they are clean.

Every morning she ran a hygiene check on the entire class. She marched down the aisle like a stormtrooper, rummaging through the ears of hapless students, checking for embedded wax. She looked under our fingernails for dirt. Too bad on you if she found any. Once she made David, a stringy-haired white boy who thought Elvis Presley was a living deity and who was the most notorious booger-eater in the entire school, go to the nurse's office to have the dirt cleaned from under his fingernails. Everybody knew that what was under David's fingernails was most likely dried-up boogies and not dirt, but nobody said anything.

10 If she was death on dirt and earwax, Miss Bradley's specialty was head-lice patrol. Down the aisles she stomped in her black Enna Jettick shoes,[4] stopping at each student to part strands of blond, brown, or dark hair, looking for cooties. Miss Bradley would flip through plaits, curls, kinks—the woman was relentless. I always passed inspection. Nana put enough Nu Nile in my hair to suffocate any living creature that had the nerve to come tipping up on my scalp. Nu Nile was the official cootie killer. I was clean, wax-free, bug-free, and smart. The folder inside my desk contained a stack of spelling and arithmetic papers with A's emblazoned across the top, gold stars in the corner. Miss Bradley always called on me. She sent me to run errands for her too. I was her pet.

When Mrs. Clark, my piano teacher and my mother's good friend, told my mother that Logan Elementary School was accepting children who didn't live in the neighborhood, my mother immediately enrolled Michael and later me. "It's not crowded and it's mixed," she told a nodding, smiling Nana. The fact that Logan was integrated was the main reason Michael and I were sent there. Nana and Mommy, like most upwardly mobile colored women, believed that to have the same education as a white child was the first step up the rocky road to success. This viewpoint was buttressed by the fact that

[3]*Shirley Temple:* Famous child actor (b. 1928); later, Shirley Temple Black, U.S. ambassador.

[4]*Enna Jettick shoes:* Brand name of "sensible" women's shoes.

George Washington Carver, my neighborhood school, was severely overcrowded. Logan was just barely integrated, with only a handful of black kids thrown in with hordes of square-jawed, pale-eyed second-generation Ukrainians whose immigrant parents and grandparents populated the neighborhood near the school. There were a few dark-haired Jews and aristocratic-looking WASPs too. My first day in kindergarten it was Nana who enthusiastically grabbed Michael's and my hands, pulling us away from North Philly's stacked-up rowhouses, from the hucksters whose wagons bounced down the streets with trucks full of ripe fruits and vegetables, from the street-corner singers and jitterbugs who filled my block with all-day doo-wahs. It was Nana who resolutely walked me past the early-morning hordes of colored kids heading two blocks away to Carver Elementary School, Nana who pulled me by the hand and led me in another direction.

We went underground at the Susquehanna and Dauphin subway station, leaving behind the unremitting asphalt and bricks and the bits of paper strewn in the streets above us. We emerged at Logan station, where sunlight, brilliant red and pink roses and yellow chrysanthemums, and neatly clipped lawns and clean streets startled me. There were robins and blue jays flying overhead. The only birds in my neighborhood were sparrows and pigeons. Delivering me at the schoolyard, Nana firmly cupped my chin with her hand as she bent down to instruct me. "Your mother's sending you up here to learn, so you do everything your teacher tells you to, okay?" To Michael she turned and said, "You're not up here to be a monkey on a stick." Then to both of us: "Don't talk. Listen. Act like you've got some home training. You've got as much brains as anybody up here. Do you know that? All right now. Make Nana proud of you."

A month after I returned from Pasquotank County,[5] I sat in Miss Bradley's classroom on a rainy Monday watching her write spelling words on the blackboard. The harsh sccurr, sccurr of Miss Bradley's chalk and the tinny sound the rain made against the window took my mind to faraway places. I couldn't get as far away as I wanted. Wallace, the bane of the whole class, had only moments earlier laid the most gigunda fart in history, one in a never-ending series, and the air was just clearing. His farts were silent wonders. Not a hint, not the slightest sound. You could be in the middle of a sentence and then wham! bam! Mystery Funk would knock you down.

Two seats ahead of me was Leonard, a lean colored boy from West Philly who always wore suits and ties to school, waving his hand like a crazy man. A showoff if ever there was one.

I was bored that day. I looked around at the walls. Miss Bradley had 15
decorated the room with pictures of the ABCs in cursive. Portraits of the presidents were hanging in a row on one wall above the blackboard. On the bulletin board there was a display of the Russian satellite, *Sputnik I,* and

[5] *Pasquotank County:* County in North Carolina where Campbell's father lived; she visited him there every summer.

the American satellite, *Explorer I.* Miss Bradley was satellite-crazy. She thought it was just wonderful that America was in the "space race" and she constantly filled our heads with space fantasies. "Boys and girls," she told us, "one day man will walk on the moon." In the far corner on another bulletin board there was a Thanksgiving scene of turkeys and pilgrims. And stuck in the corner was a picture of Sacajawea.[6] Sacajawea, Indian Woman Guide. I preferred looking at Sacajawea over satellites any day.

Thinking about the bubble gum that lay in my pocket, I decided to sneak a piece, even though gum chewing was strictly forbidden. I rarely broke the rules. Could anyone hear the loud drumming of my heart, I wondered, as I slid my hand into my skirt pocket and felt for the Double Bubble? I peeked cautiously to either side of me. Then I managed to unwrap it without even rustling the paper; I drew my hands to my lips, coughed, and popped the gum in my mouth. Ahhh! Miss Bradley's back was to the class. I chomped down hard on the Double Bubble. Miss Bradley turned around. I quickly packed the gum under my tongue. My hands were folded on top of my desk. "Who can give me a sentence for 'birthday'?" Leonard just about went nuts. Miss Bradley ignored him, which she did a lot. "Sandra," Miss Bradley called.

A petite white girl rose obediently. I liked Sandra. She had shared her crayons with me once when I left mine at home. I remember her drawing: a white house with smoke coming out of the chimney, a little girl with yellow hair like hers, a mommy, a daddy, a little boy, and a dog standing in front of the house in a yard full of flowers. Her voice was crystal clear when she spoke. There were smiles in that voice. She said, "My father made me a beautiful dollhouse for my birthday."

The lump under my tongue was suddenly a stone and when I swallowed, the taste was bitter. I coughed into a piece of tablet paper, spit out the bubble gum, and crumpled up the wad and pushed it inside my desk. The center of my chest was burning. I breathed deeply and slowly. Sandra sat down as demurely as a princess. She crossed her ankles. Her words came back to me in a rush. "Muuuy fatha made me a bee-yoo-tee-ful dollhouse." Miss Bradley said, "Very good," and moved on to the next word. Around me hands were waving, waving. Pick me! Pick me! Behind me I could hear David softly crooning, "You ain't nothin' but a hound dog, cryin' all the time." Sometimes he would stick his head inside his desk, sing Elvis songs, and pick his boogies at the same time. Somebody was jabbing pins in my chest. Ping! Ping! Ping! I wanted to holler, "Yowee! Stop!" as loud as I could, but I pressed my lips together hard.

"Now who can give me a sentence?" Miss Bradley asked. I put my head down on my desk and when Miss Bradley asked me what was wrong I told her that I didn't feel well and that I didn't want to be chosen. When Leonard

[6] *Sacajawea:* A Shoshone Indian woman (1786–1812), captured and sold to a white man; she became the famous guide of the 1804 Lewis and Clark expedition.

collected the homework, I shoved mine at him so hard all the papers he was carrying fell on the floor.

Bile was still clogging my throat when Miss Bradley sent me into the 20
cloakroom to get my lunchbox. The rule was, only one student in the cloakroom at a time. When the second one came in, the first one had to leave. I was still rummaging around in my bookbag when I saw Sandra.

"Miss Bradley said for you to come out," she said. She was smiling. That dollhouse girl was always smiling. I glared at her.

"Leave when I get ready to," I said, my words full of venom.

Sandra's eyes darted around in confusion. "Miss Bradley said . . ." she began again, still trying to smile as if she expected somebody to crown her Miss America or something and come take her picture any minute.

In my head a dam broke. Terrible waters rushed out. "I don't care about any Miss Bradley. If she messes with me I'll, I'll . . . I'll take my butcher knife and stab her until she bleeds." What I lacked in props I made up for in drama. My balled-up hand swung menacingly in the air. I aimed the invisible dagger toward Sandra. Her Miss America smile faded instantly. Her eyes grew round and frightened as she blinked rapidly. "Think I won't, huh? Huh?" I whispered, enjoying my meanness, liking the scared look on Sandra's face. Scaredy cat! Scaredy cat! Muuuy fatha made me a bee-yoo-tee-full dollhouse. "What do you think about that?" I added viciously, looking into her eyes to see the total effect of my daring words.

But Sandra wasn't looking at me. Upon closer inspection, I realized that 25
she was looking *over* me with sudden relief in her face. I turned to see what was so interesting, and my chin jammed smack into the Emeraude-scented iron bosom of Miss Bradley. Even as my mind scrambled for an excuse, I knew I was lost.

Miss Bradley had a look of horror on her face. For a minute she didn't say anything, just stood there looking as though someone had slapped her across the face. Sandra didn't say anything. I didn't move. Finally, "Would you mind repeating what you just said, Bebe."

"I didn't say anything, Miss Bradley." I could feel my dress sticking to my body.

"Sandra, what did Bebe say?"

Sandra was crying softly, little delicate tears streaming down her face. For just a second she paused, giving a tiny shudder. I rubbed my ear vigorously, thinking, "Oh, please . . ."

"She said, she said, if you bothered with her she would cut you with her 30
knife."

"Unh unh, Miss Bradley, I didn't say that. I didn't. I didn't say anything like that."

Miss Bradley's gray eyes penetrated mine. She locked me into her gaze until I looked down at the floor. Then she looked at Sandra.

"Bebe, you and I had better go see the principal."

The floor blurred. The principal!! Jennie G., the students called her with awe and fear. As Miss Bradley wrapped her thick knuckles around my forearm and dutifully steered me from the cloakroom and out the classroom door, I completely lost what little cool I had left. I began to cry, a jerky, hiccuping, snot-filled cry for mercy. "I didn't say it. I didn't say it," I moaned.

Miss Bradley was nonplussed. Dedication and duty overruled compas- 35
sion. Always. "Too late for that now," she said grimly.

Jennie G.'s office was small, neat, and dim. The principal was dwarfed by the large brown desk she sat behind, and when she stood up she wasn't much bigger than I. But she was big enough to make me tremble as I stood in front of her, listening to Miss Bradley recount the sordid details of my downfall. Jennie G. was one of those pale, pale vein-showing white women. She had a vocabulary of about six horrible phrases, designed to send chills of despair down the spine of any young transgressor. Phrases like "We'll just see about that" or "come with me, young lady," spoken ominously. Her face was impassive as she listened to Miss Bradley. I'd been told that she had a six-foot paddle in her office used solely to beat young transgressors. Suppose she tried to beat me? My heart gave a lurch. I tugged rapidly at my ears. I longed to suck my thumb.

"Well, Bebe, I think we'll have to call your mother."

My mother! I wanted the floor to swallow me up and take me whole. My mother! As Jennie G. dialed the number, I envisioned my mother's face, clouded with disappointment and shame. I started crying again as I listened to the principal telling my mother what had happened. They talked for a pretty long time. When she hung up, ole Jennie G. flipped through some paper on her desk before looking at me sternly.

"You go back to class and watch your mouth, young lady."

As I was closing the door to her office I heard her say to Miss Bradley, 40
"What can you expect?"

"Ooooh, you're gonna get it girl," is how Michael greeted me after school. Logan's colored world was small, and news of my demise had blazed its way through hallways and classrooms, via the brown-skinned grapevine. Everyone from North Philly, West Philly, and Germantown knew about my crime. The subway ride home was depressing. My fellow commuters kept coming up to me and asking, "Are you gonna get in trouble?" Did they think my mother would give me a reward or something? I stared at the floor for most of the ride, looking up only when the train came to a stop and the doors hissed open. Logan. Wyoming. Hunting Park. Each station drew me closer to my doom, whatever that was going to be. "What can you expect?" I mulled over those words. What did she mean? My mother rarely spanked, although Nana would give Michael or me, usually Michael, a whack across the butt from time to time. My mother's social-worker instincts were too strong for such undignified displays; Doris believed in talking things out, which was sometimes worse than a thousand beatings. As the train drew closer to Susquehanna and Dauphin I thought of how much I hated for my mother to be disappointed in me. And now she would be. "What can you expect?"

Of me? Didn't Jennie G. know that I was riding a subway halfway across town as opposed to walking around the corner to Carver Elementary School, for a reason: the same reason I was dragged away from Saturday cartoons and pulled from museum to museum, to Judimar School of Dance for ballet (art class for Michael), to Mrs. Clark for piano. The Bosoms wanted me to Be Somebody, to be the second generation to live out my life as far away from a mop and scrub brush and Miss Ann's floors as possible.

My mother had won a full scholarship to the University of Pennsylvania. The story of that miracle was a treasured family heirloom. Sometimes Nana told the tale and sometimes my mother described how the old Jewish counselor at William Penn High School approached her and asked why a girl with straight E's (for "excellent") was taking the commercial course. My mother replied that Nana couldn't afford to send her to college, that she planned to become a secretary. "Sweetheart, you switch to academic," the woman told her. "You'll get to college." When her graduation day approached, the counselor pulled her aside. "I have two scholarships for you. One to Cheyney State Teacher's College and the other to the University of Pennsylvania." Cheyney was a small black school outside of Philadelphia, My mother chose Penn. I had been born to a family of hopeful women. One miracle had already taken place. They expected more. And now I'd thrown away my chance. Michael, who was seated next to me on the subway and whose generosity of spirit had lasted a record five subway stops, poked me in my arm. "Bebe," he told me gleefully, "your ass is grass."

Nana took one look at my guilty face, scowled at me, and sucked her teeth until they whistled. My mother had called her and told her what happened and now she was possessed by a legion of demons. I had barely entered the room when she exploded. "Don't. Come. In. Here. Crying," Nana said, her voice booming, her lips quivering and puffy with anger. When Nana talked in staccato language she was beyond pissed off. Waaaay beyond. "What. Could. Possess. You. To. Say. Such. A. Thing? Embarrassingyourmotherlikethatinfrontof *those people!*" Before I could answer she started singing some Dinah Washington[7] song, real loud. Volume all the way up. With every word she sang I sank deeper and deeper into gloom.

Later that evening, when my mother got home and Aunt Ruth, Mi- 45
chael's mother, came to visit, the three women lectured me in unison. The room was full of flying feathers. Three hens clucking away at me, their breasts heaving with emotion. Cluck! Cluck! Cluck! How could I have said such a thing? What on earth was I thinking about? Cluck! Cluck! Cluck! A knife, such a *colored* weapon.

"But I didn't do anything," I wailed, the tears that had been trickling all day now falling in full force.

[7]*Dinah Washington:* Blues singer, born Ruth Jones (1924–1963).

"Umph, umph, umph," Nana said, and started singing. Billie Holiday[8] this time.

"You call threatening somebody with a knife nothing?" Aunt Ruth asked. Ruth was Nana's middle girl. She was the family beauty, as pretty as Dorothy Dandridge[9] or Lena Horne.[10] Now her coral lips were curled up in disdain and her Maybelline eyebrows were raised in judgment against me. "They expect us to act like animals and you have to go and say that. My God."

Animals. Oh. Oh. Oh.

50 My mother glared at her sister, but I looked at Aunt Ruth in momentary wonder and appreciation. Now I understood. The unspoken rule that I had sensed all my life was that a colored child had to be on her best behavior whenever she visited the white world. Otherwise, whatever opportunity was being presented would be snatched away. I had broken the rule. I had committed the unpardonable sin of embarrassing my family in front of *them.* Sensing my remorse and shame, Mommy led me out of the kitchen. We sat down on the living room sofa; my mother took my hand, "Bebe, I want you to go to your room and think about what you've done. I don't understand your behavior. It was very hard for me to get you in Logan." She drew a breath. I drew a breath and looked into the eyes of a social worker. "I'm extremely disappointed in you."

I didn't go straight to my room. Instead I sneaked into Michael's room, which overlooked Mole Street, the tiny, one-sided alley of narrow rowhouses that faced the backyards of 16th Street. Michael and I usually played on the "back street." Alone in Michael's room with the window open, I could hear Mr. Watson, our neighbor, hollering at one of his kids. Why had I said what I said? What had possessed me? Then I remembered. "Muuuy fatha made me a bee-yoo-tee-ful dollhouse for muuuuy birthday." Something pinched me inside my chest when I heard those words. Pain oozed from my heart like a tube of toothpaste bursting open, going every whichaway. Blue-eyes kept yapping away with her golden hair and her goofy little smile. Who cared what her fatha did? Who cared? I couldn't help it. When she came into the cloakroom I got mad all over again. When I said I had a knife, she looked just like Grandma Mary's chickens. Scared. And my chest stopped hurting. Just stopped.

Mr. Watson's baritone voice was a seismic rumble echoing with the threat of upheaval, violence. His words floated over Mole Street and into the bedroom window. Whoever was in trouble over there was really gonna get it. None of this "go to your room" stuff. None of this corny "I'm disappointed in you" stuff. Mr. Watson was getting ready to beat somebody's ass.

Adam's. He was the youngest and one of my playmates. I could tell by

[8] *Billie Holiday:* Celebrated jazz singer (1915–1959).

[9] *Dorothy Dandridge:* Glamorous film star (1923–1965).

[10] *Lena Horne:* Singer, actor (b. 1917); first Black woman vocalist to be featured with a white band.

his pleading voice. "Please, Daddy. I won't do it anymore, Daddy. I'm sorry, Daddy."

Michael came into the room. "What are you doing?" he whispered.

"Shhh. Adam's getting a whipping." 55

"You better go to your room before Aunt Doris comes upstairs."

"Shhhh."

My playmate's misery took my mind off my own. His father's exotic yelling hypnotized me. From downstairs I could hear the hens, still clucking away. Michael and I sat quietly, not making a sound. Mr. Watson's voice sounded so foreign coming into our house. For a moment I pretended that his anger was emanating from Michael's bedroom, and I remembered how only last year he got mad and ran after all of us kids — Jackie, Jane, and Adam, his own three, and me. His face was covered with shaving cream and he held a razor in one hand and a thick leather belt in the other. I don't recall what we had done, but I remember him chasing us and yelling ferociously, "This belt's got your name on it too, Miss Bebe!" And I recall that I was thrilled when the leather grazed my hiney with the vengeance of a father's wrath.

My mind drifted back a few years. The memory was vague and fuzzy. When I was four or five I was playing on Mole Street when my ten-year-old neighbor, a boy named Buddy, asked me to come inside his yard. He was sitting on an old soda crate. "Come closer," he told me. "Wanna play doctor?"

"Uh huh." 60

"You can examine me."

I told my mother, prattling on about the "game" I had played. She sat me down on her bed. "Did he touch your private parts?"

"Nope." Why was Mommy's face so serious?

"Did you touch his?"

"I touched his zipper." Had I done something wrong? 65

Nana went into hysterics, singing and screeching like a wild woman. "Mother, just calm down," Mommy told her.

Mommy was cool, every inch the social worker; she took my hand and we walked down the street to Buddy's house. He was in his yard making a scooter out of the crate. "Buddy," my mother said softly. When he saw the two of us, he dropped his hammer. "Buddy, I want to talk with you."

My mother questioned him. Calmly put the fear of God in him. Warned him of penalties for a repeat performance. And that was that. Not quite. Weeks, maybe months later, my father came to visit me, one of his pop-in, no-real-occasion visits. My mother, my father, and I were sitting in his car and she told him about my playing doctor. His leg shot out in wild, uncontrollable spasms. His face became contorted and he started yelling. Nana's screeching paled in contrast. This was rage that my mother and Nana could not even begin to muster. And it was in my honor. This energy was for my avengement, my protection. Or should have been. But the sound of his fury frightened me. I remember angling away from my father, this man who was yelling like an animal in pain. I leaned toward my mother, and she put one arm around me and with her other hand tried to pat my father's shoulder, only he snatched [it] away. He learned forward and started reaching for his chair.[11] "I may not be able to walk, goddammit, but I can tear that little son of a bitch's ass up."

My mother kept talking very softly, saying, "No, no, no. It's all right. He's just a kid. I took care of it. It's okay." I leaned away from my father's anger, his determination. He frightened me. But the rage was fascinating too. And after a while, when my father was shouting only a little, I moved closer to him. I wanted to see the natural progression of his hot words. If he snatched his wheelchair out of the backseat and rolled up to Buddy's house, what would he do? What would he do in my honor? My mother calmed my father. His shouting subsided. I was relieved. I was disappointed.

"Hey" — I suddenly heard Michael's persistent voice — "ain't you glad 70
Mr. Watson ain't your father?" I felt Michael's hands, shaking my shoulder. "Ain't you?"

I didn't answer. I was thinking about Miss Bradley, Jennie G., Aunt Ruth, Nana, and Mommy. All these women with power over me. I could hear Mrs. Watson telling her husband that enough was enough and then the baritone telling her he knew when to stop and Adam letting out another feeble little yelp. "Muuuy fatha made me a bee-yoo-tee-ful dollhouse." Maybe my mother would write my daddy and tell him how bad I had been. Maybe he would get so mad he would get into his car and drive all the way to Philly just to whip my behind. Or tell me he was disappointed in me. Either one.

The Bosoms decided to forgive me. My mother woke me up with a kiss and a snuggle and then a crisp, "All right, Bebe. It's a brand-new day. Forget about yesterday." When I went to get a bowl of cereal that morning, my Aunt Ruth was sitting in the kitchen drinking coffee and reading the newspaper. She had spent the night. "Did you comb your hair?" she asked me.

I nodded.

"That's not what I call combed. Go get me the comb and brush."

She combed out my hair and braided it all over again. This time there 75
were no wispy little ends sticking out. "Now you look nice," she said. "Now you look like a pretty girl, and when you go to school today, act like a pretty girl. All right?"

I nodded.

Last night Nana had hissed at me between her teeth. "If you want to behave like a little *heathen,* if you want go up there acting like a, a . . . *monkey on a stick* . . . well, thenyoucangotoschoolrightaroundthecornerandI'llwalk youbackhomeandI'llcomeandgetyouforlunchnowyou*behave*yourself!" But

[11]*his chair:* Campbell's father had lost the use of his legs in an automobile accident.

today she was sanguine, even jovial, as she fixed my lunch. She kissed me when I left for school.

On my way out the door my mother handed me two elegant letters, one to Miss Bradley and the other to Jennie G., assuring them that I had an overactive imagination, that I had no access to butcher knives or weapons of any kind, that she had spoken to me at length about my unfortunate outburst, and that henceforth my behavior would be exemplary. These letters were written on her very best personalized stationery. The paper was light pink and had "D.C.M." in embossed letters across the top. Doris C. knew lots of big words and she had used every single one of them in those letters. I knew that all of her *i*'s were dotted and all of her *t*'s were crossed. I knew the letters were extremely dignified. My mother was very big on personal dignity. Anyone who messed with her dignity was in serious trouble.

I was only five when an unfortunate teller at her bank called her by her first name loud enough for the other customers to hear. My mother's body stiffened when she heard, "Doris, oh Doris," coming from a girl almost young enough to be her child.

"Are you talking to *me*, dear?" Her English was so clipped, her words 80
so razor sharp she could have taken one, stabbed the teller, and drawn blood. The girl nodded, her speckled green eyes wide and gaping, aware that something was going on, not quite sure what, and speechless because she was no match at all for this imperious little brown-skinned woman. "The people in *my* office all call me *Mrs. Moore.*"

And she grabbed me by the hand and we swept out of the bank. Me and Bette Davis.[12] Me and Claudia McNeil.[13] People stepped aside to let us pass.

So I knew my mother's letters not only would impress Miss Bradley and Jennie G. but also would go a long way toward redeeming me. After Miss Bradley read the note she told me I have a very nice mother and let me know that if I was willing to be exemplary she would let bygones be bygones and I could get back into her good graces. She was, after all, a dedicated teacher. And I had learned my lesson.

My mother wrote my father about the knife incident. I waited anxiously to hear from him. Would he suddenly appear? I searched the street in front of the school every afternoon. At home I jumped up nervously whenever I heard a horn beep. Finally, a letter from my dad arrived — one page of southpaw scribble.

> Dear Bebe,
> Your mother told me what happened in school about the knife. That wasn't a good thing to say. I think maybe you were joking. Remember, a lot of

[12]*Bette Davis:* Actor (1908–1989) known for her portrayals of strong, beautiful, intelligent women.

[13]*Claudia McNeil:* Emmy-winning actor (b. 1917).

times white people don't understand how colored people joke, so you have to be careful what you say around them. Be a good girl.

Lots of love,
Daddy.

The crumpled letter hit the edge of the wastepaper basket in my mother's room and landed in front of her bureau. I picked it up and slammed it into the basket, hitting my hand in the process. I flung myself across the bed, buried my face into my pillow, and howled with pain, rage, and sadness. "It's not fair," I wailed. Ole Blondie had her dollhouse-making daddy whenever she wanted him. "Muuuy fatha . . ." Jackie, Jane, and Adam had their wild, ass-whipping daddy. All they had to do was walk outside their house, look under a car, and there he was, tinkering away. Ole ugly grease-monkey man. Why couldn't I have my daddy all the time too? I didn't want a letter signed "Lots of love," I wanted my father to come and yell at me for acting like a monkey on a stick. I wanted him to come and beat my butt or shake his finger in my face, or tell me that what I did wasn't so bad after all. Anything, I just wanted him to come.

Engaging the Text

1. Why does Sandra's sentence in Miss Bradley's class so upset Bebe?
2. The family in "Envy" is clearly matriarchal: "Women ruled at 2239" (para. 5). What positive and negative effects did this matriarchal family have on the author when she was a child?
3. How did the matriarchs groom young Bebe for success? What lessons were taught in this family? Do you think the women's methods of raising the child were the best possible?
4. What does the young Bebe think she is missing with her father's absence? What might he provide that the women do not? Do you think the mature author sees the situation much differently than she did as a child?
5. What traditionally male roles do the women in Bebe's family play? How well do you think they perform these roles?

Exploring Connections

6. Write an imaginary dialogue between Karen Lindsey (p. 158) and Bebe Moore Campbell on the importance of fathers.
7. Compare and contrast the mother-daughter relationships portrayed in this story, in Anndee Hochman's "Growing Pains" (p. 150), and in Maxine Hong Kingston's "Silence" (p. 110). Which relationship is closest to your ideal, and why?

Extending the Critical Context

8. If you have ever felt the lack of a father, mother, sister, brother, or grandparent in your family, write a journal entry or narrative memoir exploring your memories and emotions.

9. At the end of *Sweet Summer,* Campbell decides that, while she saw her father only during the summer, her extended family, including uncles, boarders, and family friends, had provided her with plenty of healthy male influences. Read the rest of the book and report to the class on Campbell's portrayal of her relationship with her immediate and extended family.

Black Women and Motherhood

PATRICIA HILL COLLINS

For decades many American sociologists failed to understand African American families because their assumption that Western European families were "normal" made any different families seem flawed or deficient. Even today, politicians and religious leaders sometimes criticize family relationships and parenting styles that fall outside the norm of the nuclear family. This essay by Patricia Hill Collins, focusing on women within the Black family, offers a close look at the positive roles that Black women have played in American family and community life. Collins (b. 1948) is an associate professor of African American studies at the University of Cincinnati. This selection is taken from her book Black Feminist Thought: Knowledge, Consciousness, and the Politics of Empowerment *(1991).*

The institution of Black motherhood consists of a series of constantly renegotiated relationships that African-American women experience with one another, with Black children, with the larger African-American community, and with self. These relationships occur in specific locations such as the individual households that make up African-American extended family networks, as well as in Black community institutions (Martin and Martin 1978; Sudarkasa 1981b). Moreover, just as Black women's work and family experiences varied during the transition from slavery to the post–World War II political economy, how Black women define, value, and shape Black motherhood as an institution shows comparable diversity.

Black motherhood as an institution is both dynamic and dialectical.[1] An ongoing tension exists between efforts to mold the institution of Black motherhood to benefit systems of race, gender, and class oppression and efforts

[1]*dialectical:* Based on opposition or tension between competing "truths" or viewpoints. An example follows in Collins's text: the stereotype of the Black "mammy" versus the image of a self-reliant, independent mother.

by African-American women to define and value our own experiences with motherhood. The controlling images of the mammy, the matriarch, and the welfare mother and the practices they justify are designed to oppress. In contrast, motherhood can serve as a site where Black women express and learn the power of self-definition, the importance of valuing and respecting ourselves, the necessity of self-reliance and independence, and a belief in Black women's empowerment. This tension leads to a continuum of responses. Some women view motherhood as a truly burdensome condition that stifles their creativity, exploits their labor, and makes them partners in their own oppression. Others see motherhood as providing a base for self-actualization, status in the Black community, and a catalyst for social activism. These alleged contradictions can exist side by side in African-American communities and families and even within individual women.

Embedded in these changing relationships are [a number of] enduring themes that characterize a Black women's standpoint on Black motherhood. For any given historical moment, the particular form that Black women's relationships with one another, children, community, and self actually take depends on how this dialectical relationship between the severity of oppression facing African-American women and our actions in resisting that oppression is expressed.

Bloodmothers, Othermothers, and Women-Centered Networks

In African-American communities, fluid and changing boundaries often distinguish biological mothers from other women who care for children. Biological mothers, or bloodmothers, are expected to care for their children. But African and African-American communities have also recognized that vesting one person with full responsibility for mothering a child may not be wise or possible. As a result, othermothers—women who assist bloodmothers by sharing mothering responsibilities—traditionally have been central to the institution of Black motherhood (Troester 1984).

5 The centrality of women in African-American extended families reflects both a continuation of West African cultural values and functional adaptations to race and gender oppression (Tanner 1974; Stack 1974; Aschenbrenner 1975; Martin and Martin 1978; Sudarkasa 1981b; Reagon 1987). This centrality is not characterized by the absence of husbands and fathers. Men may be physically present and/or have well-defined and culturally significant roles in the extended family and the kin unit may be woman-centered. Bebe Moore Campbell's (1989) parents separated when she was small. Even though she spent the school year in the North Philadelphia household maintained by her grandmother and mother, Campbell's father assumed an important role in her life. "My father took care of me," Campbell remembers. "Our separation didn't stunt me or condemn me to a lesser humanity. His absence never made me a fatherless child. I'm not fatherless now" (p. 271).

In woman-centered kin units such as Campbell's — whether a mother-child household unit, a married couple household, or a larger unit extending over several households — the centrality of mothers is not predicated on male powerlessness (Tanner 1974, 133).

Organized, resilient, women-centered networks of bloodmothers and othermothers are key in understanding this centrality. Grandmothers, sisters, aunts, or cousins act as othermothers by taking on child-care responsibilities for one another's children. When needed, temporary child-care arrangements can turn into long-term care or informal adoption (Stack 1974; Gutman 1976). Despite strong cultural norms encouraging women to become biological mothers, women who choose not to do so often receive recognition and status from othermother relationships that they establish with Black children.

In African-American communities these women-centered networks of community-based child care often extend beyond the boundaries of biologically related individuals and include "fictive kin" (Stack 1974). Civil rights activist Ella Baker describes how informal adoption by othermothers functioned in the rural southern community of her childhood:

> My aunt who had thirteen children of her own raised three more. She had become a midwife, and a child was born who was covered with sores. Nobody was particularly wanting the child, so she took the child and raised him . . . and another mother decided she didn't want to be bothered with two children. So my aunt took one and raised him . . . they were part of the family. (Cantarow 1980, 59)

Even when relationships are not between kin or fictive kin, African-American community norms traditionally were such that neighbors cared for one anothers' children. Sara Brooks, a southern domestic worker, describes the importance that the community-based child care a neighbor offered her daughter had for her: "She kept Vivian and she didn't charge me nothin' either. You see, people used to look after each other, but now it's not that way. I reckon it's because we all was poor, and I guess they put theirself in the place of the person that they was helpin'" (Simonsen 1986, 181). Brooks's experiences demonstrate how the African-American cultural value placed on cooperative child care traditionally found institutional support in the adverse conditions under which so many Black women mothered.

Othermothers are key not only in supporting children but also in helping bloodmothers who, for whatever reason, lack the preparation or desire for motherhood. In confronting racial oppression, maintaining community-based child care and respecting othermothers who assume child-care responsibilities serve a critical function in African-American communities. Children orphaned by sale or death of their parents under slavery, children conceived through rape, children of young mothers, children born into extreme poverty or to alcoholic or drug-addicted mothers, or children who for other reasons cannot remain with their bloodmothers have all been supported by othermothers, who, like Ella Baker's aunt, take in additional children even when they have enough of their own.

Young women are often carefully groomed at an early age to become othermothers. As a ten-year-old, civil rights activist Ella Baker learned to be an othermother by caring for the children of a widowed neighbor: "Mama would say, 'You must take the clothes to Mr. Powell's house, and give so-and-so a bath.' The children were running wild. . . . The kids . . . would take off across the field. We'd chase them down, and bring them back, and put 'em in the tub, and wash 'em off, and change clothes, and carry the dirty ones home, and wash them. Those kind of things were routine" (Cantarow 1980, 59).

Many Black men also value community-based child care but exercise these values to a lesser extent. Young Black men are taught how to care for children (Young 1970; Lewis 1975). During slavery, for example, Black children under age ten experienced little division of labor. They were dressed alike and performed similar tasks. If the activities of work and play are any indication of the degree of gender role differentiation that existed among slave children, "then young girls probably grew up minimizing the difference between the sexes while learning far more about the differences between the races" (D. White 1985, 94). Differences among Black men and women in attitudes toward children may have more to do with male labor force patterns. As Ella Baker observes, "my father took care of people too, but . . . my father had to work" (Cantarow 1980, 60).

Historically, community-based child care and the relationships among bloodmothers and othermothers in women-centered networks have taken diverse institutional forms. In some polygynous West African societies, the children of the same father but different mothers referred to one another as brothers and sisters. While a strong bond existed between the biological mother and her child—one so strong that, among the Ashanti for example, "to show disrespect towards one's mother is tantamount to sacrilege" (Fortes 1950, 263)—children could be disciplined by any of their other "mothers." Cross-culturally, the high status given to othermothers and the cooperative nature of child-care arrangements among bloodmothers and othermothers in Caribbean and other Black societies gives credence to the importance that people of African descent place on mothering (Clarke 1966; Shimkin et al. 1978; Sudarkasa 1981a, 1981b).

Although the political economy of slavery brought profound changes to enslaved Africans, cultural values concerning the importance of motherhood and the value of cooperative approaches to child care continued. While older women served as nurses and midwives, their most common occupation was caring for the children of parents who worked (D. White 1985). Informal adoption of orphaned children reinforced the importance of social motherhood in African-American communities (Gutman 1976).

The relationship between bloodmothers and othermothers survived the transition from a slave economy to postemancipation southern rural agriculture. Children in southern rural communities were not solely the responsibility of their biological mothers. Aunts, grandmothers, and others who had time to supervise children served as othermothers (Young 1970; Dougherty 1978). The significant status women enjoyed in family networks and in African-American communities continued to be linked to their bloodmother and othermother activities.

The entire community structure of bloodmothers and othermothers is 15
under assault in many inner-city neighborhoods, where the very fabric of African-American community life is being eroded by illegal drugs. But even in the most troubled communities, remnants of the othermother tradition endure. Bebe Moore Campbell's 1950s North Philadelphia neighborhood underwent some startling changes when crack cocaine flooded the streets in the 1980s. Increases in birth defects, child abuse, and parental neglect left many children without care. But some residents, such as Miss Nee, continue the othermother tradition. After raising her younger brothers and sisters and five children of her own, Miss Nee cares for three additional children whose families fell apart. Moreover, on any given night Miss Nee's house may be filled by up to a dozen children because she has a reputation for never turning away a needy child ("Children of the Underclass" 1989).

Traditionally, community-based child care certainly has been functional for African-American communities and for Black women. Black feminist theorist Bell Hooks suggests that the relationships among bloodmothers and othermothers may have greater theoretical importance than currently recognized:

> This form of parenting is revolutionary in this society because it takes place in opposition to the ideas that parents, especially mothers, should be the only childrearers. . . . This kind of shared responsibility for child care can happen in small community settings where people know and trust one another. It cannot happen in those settings if parents regard children as their "property," their possession. (1984, 144)

The resiliency of women-centered family networks illustrates how traditional cultural values — namely, the African origins of community-based child care — can help people cope with and resist oppression. By continuing community-based child care, African-American women challenge one fundamental assumption underlying the capitalist system itself: that children are "private property" and can be disposed of as such. Notions of property, child care, and gender differences in parenting styles are embedded in the institutional arrangements of any given political economy. Under the property model stemming from capitalist patriarchal families, parents may not literally assert that their children are pieces of property, but their parenting may reflect assumptions analogous to those they make in connection with property (J. Smith 1983). For example, the exclusive parental "right" to discipline children as parents see fit, even if discipline borders on abuse, parallels the widespread assumption that property owners may dispose of their property without consulting members of the larger community. By seeing the larger community as responsible for children and by giving othermothers and other nonparents "rights" in child rearing, African-Americans challenge prevailing property relations. It is in this sense that traditional bloodmother/othermother relationships in women-centered networks are "revolutionary."

Mothers, Daughters, and Socialization for Survival

Black mothers of daughters face a troubling dilemma. On one hand, to ensure their daughters' physical survival, mothers must teach them to fit into systems of oppression. For example, as a young girl Black activist Ann Moody questioned why she was paid so little for the domestic work she began at age nine, why Black women domestics were sexually harassed by their white male employers, why no one would explain the activities of the National Association for the Advancement of Colored People to her, and why whites had so much more than Blacks. But her mother refused to answer her questions and actually chastised her for questioning the system and stepping out of her "place" (Moody 1968). Like Ann Moody, Black daughters learn to expect to work, to strive for an education so they can support themselves, and to anticipate carrying heavy responsibilities in their families and communities because these skills are essential to their own survival and those for whom they will eventually be responsible (Ladner 1972; Joseph 1981). New Yorker Michele Wallace recounts: "I can't remember when I first learned that my family expected me to work, to be able to take care of myself when I grew up. . . . It had been drilled into me that the best and only sure support was self-support" (1978, 89–90). Mothers also know that if their daughters uncritically accept the limited opportunities offered Black women, they become willing participants in their own subordination. Mothers may have ensured their daughters' physical survival, but at the high cost of their emotional destruction.

On the other hand, Black daughters with strong self-definitions and self-valuations who offer serious challenges to oppressive situations may not physically survive. When Ann Moody became active in the early 1960s in sit-ins and voter registration activities, her mother first begged her not to participate and then told her not to come home because she feared the whites in Moody's hometown would kill her. Despite the dangers, mothers routinely encourage Black daughters to develop skills to confront oppressive conditions. Learning that they will work and that education is a vehicle for advancement can also be seen as ways of enhancing positive self-definitions and self-valuations in Black girls. Emotional strength is essential, but not at the cost of physical survival.

Historian Elsa Barkley Brown captures this delicate balance Black mothers negotiate by pointing out that her mother's behavior demonstrated the "need to teach me to live my life one way and, at the same time, to provide all the tools I would need to live it quite differently" (1989, 929). Black daughters must learn how to survive in interlocking structures of race, class, and gender oppression while rejecting and transcending those same structures. In order to develop these skills in their daughters, mothers demonstrate varying combinations of behaviors devoted to ensuring their daughters' survival—such as providing them with basic necessities and protecting them in dangerous environments — to helping their daughters go further than mothers themselves were allowed to go.

This special vision of Black mothers may grow from the nature of work 20
women have done to ensure Black children's survival. These work experiences have provided Black women with a unique angle of vision, a particular perspective on the world to be passed on to Black daughters. African and African-American women have long integrated economic self-reliance with mothering. In contrast to the cult of true womanhood,[2] in which work is defined as being in opposition to and incompatible with motherhood, work for Black women has been an important and valued dimension of Afrocentric definitions of Black motherhood. Sara Brooks describes the powerful connections that economic self-reliance and mothering had in her childhood: "When I was about nine I was nursin' my sister Sally— I'm about seven or eight years older than Sally. And when I would put her to sleep, instead of me goin' somewhere and sit down and play, I'd get my little old hoe and get out there and work right in the field around the house" (in Simonsen 1986, 86).

Mothers who are domestic workers or who work in proximity to whites may experience a unique relationship with the dominant group. For example, African-American women domestics are exposed to all the intimate details of the lives of their white employers. Working for whites offers domestic workers a view from the inside and exposes them to ideas and resources that might aid in their children's upward mobility. In some cases domestic workers form close, long-lasting relationships with their employers. But domestic workers also encounter some of the harshest exploitation confronting women of color. The work is low paid, has few benefits, and exposes women to the threat and reality of sexual harassment. Black domestics could see the dangers awaiting their daughters.

Willi Coleman's mother used a Saturday-night hair-combing ritual to impart a Black women's standpoint on domestic work to her daughters:

> Except for special occasions mama came home from work early on Saturdays. She spent six days a week mopping, waxing, and dusting other women's houses and keeping out of reach of other women's husbands. Saturday nights were reserved for "taking care of them girls" hair and the telling of stories. Some of which included a recitation of what she had endured and how she had triumphed over "folks that were lower than dirt" and "no-

[2]*cult of true womanhood:* The nineteenth-century ideal of women as saintly, even angelic, beings — passive and innocent creatures who should be sheltered from the rough world of men.

> good snakes in the grass." She combed, patted, twisted, and talked, saying things which would have embarrassed or shamed her at other times. (Coleman 1987, 34)

Bonnie Thornton Dill's (1980) study of the child-rearing goals of domestic workers illustrates how African-American women see their work as both contributing to their children's survival and instilling values that will encourage their children to reject their proscribed "place" as Blacks and strive for more. Providing a better chance for their children was a dominant theme among Black women. Domestic workers described themselves as "struggling to give their children the skills and training they did not have; and as praying that opportunities which had not been open to them would be open to their children" (p. 110). But the women also realized that while they wanted to communicate the value of their work as part of the ethics of caring and personal accountability, the work itself was undesirable. Bebe Moore Campbell's (1989) grandmother and college-educated mother stressed the importance of education. Campbell remembers, "[they] wanted me to Be Somebody, to be the second generation to live out my life as far away from a mop and scrub brush and Miss Ann's floors as possible" (p. 83).

Understanding this goal of balancing the need for the physical survival of their daughters with the vision of encouraging them to transcend the boundaries confronting them explains many apparent contradictions in Black mother-daughter relationships. Black mothers are often described as strong disciplinarians and overly protective; yet these same women manage to raise daughters who are self-reliant and assertive. To explain this apparent contradiction, Gloria Wade-Gayles suggests that Black mothers:

> do not socialize their daughters to be "passive" or "irrational." Quite the contrary, they socialize their daughters to be independent, strong, and self-confident. Black mothers are suffocatingly protective and domineering precisely because they are determined to mold their daughters into whole and self-actualizing persons in a society that devalues Black women. (1984, 12)

African-American mothers place a strong emphasis on protection, either by trying to shield their daughters as long as possible from the penalties attached to their race, class, and gender status or by teaching them skills of independence and self-reliance so that they will be able to protect themselves. Consider the following verse from a traditional blues song:

> I ain't good lookin' and ain't got waist-long hair
> I say I ain't good lookin' and I ain't got waist-long hair
> But my mama gave me something that'll take me anywhere.
> (Washington 1984, 144)

Unlike white women, symbolized by "good looks" and "waist-long hair," Black women have been denied male protection. Under such conditions it becomes essential that Black mothers teach their daughters skills that will "take them anywhere."

Black women's autobiographies and fiction can be read as texts revealing 25
the multiple ways that African-American mothers aim to shield their daughters from the demands of being Black women in oppressive conditions. Michele Wallace describes her growing understanding of how her mother viewed raising Black daughters in Harlem: "My mother has since explained to me that since it was obvious her attempt to protect me was going to prove a failure, she was determined to make me realize that as a black girl in white America I was going to find it an uphill climb to keep myself together" (1978, 98). In discussing the mother-daughter relationship in Paule Marshall's *Brown Girl, Brownstones,* Rosalie Troester catalogues the ways mothers have aimed to protect their daughters and the impact this may have on relationships themselves:

> Black mothers, particularly those with strong ties to their community, sometimes build high banks around their young daughters, isolating them from the dangers of the larger world until they are old and strong enough to function as autonomous women. Often these dikes are religious, but sometimes they are built with education, family, or the restrictions of a close-knit and homogeneous community. . . . This isolation causes the currents between Black mothers and daughters to run deep and the relationship to be fraught with an emotional intensity often missing from the lives of women with more freedom. (1984, 13)

Michele Wallace's mother built banks around her headstrong adolescent daughter by institutionalizing her in a Catholic home for troubled girls. Wallace went willingly, believing "I thought at the time that I would rather live in hell than be with my mother" (1978, 98). But years later Wallace's evaluation of her mother's decision changed: "Now that I know my mother better, I know that her sense of powerlessness made it all the more essential to her that she take radical action" (p. 98).

African-American mothers try to protect their daughters from the dangers that lie ahead by offering them a sense of their own unique self-worth. Many contemporary Black women writers report the experience of being singled out, of being given a sense of specialness at an early age which encouraged them to develop their talents. My own mother marched me to the public library at age five, helped me get my first library card, and told me that I could do anything if I learned how to read. In discussing the works of Paule Marshall, Dorothy West, and Alice Walker, Mary Helen Washington observes that all three writers make special claims about the roles their mothers played in the development of their creativity: "The bond with their mothers is such a fundamental and powerful source that the term 'mothering the mind' might have been coined specifically to define their experiences as writers" (1984, 144).

Black women's efforts to provide a physical and psychic base for their children can affect mothering styles and the emotional intensity of Black mother-daughter relationships. As Gloria Wade-Gayles points out, "mothers in Black Women's fiction are strong and devoted . . . they are rarely affectionate" (1984, 10). For example, in Toni Morrison's *Sula* (1974), Eva Peace's husband ran off, leaving her with three small children and no money. Despite her feelings, "the demands of feeding her three children were so acute she had to postpone her anger for two years until she had both the time and energy for it" (p. 32). Later in the novel Eva's daughter Hannah asks, "Mamma, did you ever love us?" (p. 67). Eva angrily replies, "What you talkin' bout did I love you girl I stayed alive for you" (p. 69). For far too many Black mothers, the demands of providing for children in interlocking systems of oppression are sometimes so demanding that they have neither the time nor the patience for affection. And yet most Black daughters love and admire their mothers and are convinced that their mothers truly love them (Joseph 1981).

Black daughters raised by mothers grappling with hostile environments have to come to terms with their feelings about the difference between the idealized versions of maternal love extant in popular culture and the strict and often troubled mothers in their lives. For a daughter, growing up means developing a better understanding that even though she may desire more affection and greater freedom, her mother's physical care and protection are acts of maternal love. Ann Moody describes her growing awareness of the cost her mother paid as a domestic worker who was a single mother of three. Watching her mother sleep after the birth of another child, Moody remembers:

> For a long time I stood there looking at her. I didn't want to wake her up. I wanted to enjoy and preserve that calm, peaceful look on her face, I wanted to think she would always be that happy. . . . Adline and Junior were too young to feel the things I felt and know the things I knew about Mama. They couldn't remember when she and Daddy separated. They had never heard her cry at night as I had or worked and helped as I had done when we were starving. (1968, 57)

Moody initially sees her mother as a strict disciplinarian, a woman who tries to protect her daughter by withholding information. But as Moody matures and better understands the oppression in her community, her ideas change. On one occasion Moody left school early the day after a Black family had been brutally murdered by local whites. Moody's description of her mother's reaction reflects her deepening understanding: "When I walked in the house Mama didn't even ask me why I came home. She just looked at me. And for the first time I realized she understood what was going on within me or was trying to anyway" (1968, 136).

Another example of a daughter's efforts to understand her mother is offered in Renita Weems's account of coming to grips with maternal desertion. In the following passage Weems struggles with the difference between the stereotypical image of the superstrong Black mother and her own alcoholic mother's decision to leave her children: "My mother loved us. I must believe that. She worked all day in a department store bakery to buy shoes and school tablets, came home to curse out neighbors who wrongly accused her children of any impropriety (which in an apartment complex usually meant stealing), and kept her house cleaner than most sober women" (1984, 26). Weems concludes that her mother loved her because she provided for her to the best of her ability.

30 Othermothers often help to defuse the emotional intensity of relationships between bloodmothers and their daughters. In recounting how she dealt with the intensity of her relationship with her mother, Weems describes the women teachers, neighbors, friends, and othermothers she turned to — women who, she observes, "did not have the onus of providing for me, and so had the luxury of talking to me" (1984, 27). Cheryl West's household included her brother, her lesbian mother, and Jan, her mother's lover. Jan became an othermother to West: "Yellow-colored, rotund and short in stature, Jan was like a second mother. . . . Jan braided my hair in the morning, mother worked two jobs and tucked me in at night. Loving, gentle, and fastidious in the domestic arena, Jan could be a rigid disciplinarian. . . . To the outside world . . . she was my 'aunt' who happened to live with us. But she was much more involved and nurturing than any of my 'real' aunts" (1987, 43).

June Jordan offers an eloquent analysis of one daughter's realization of the high personal cost African-American women can pay in providing an economic and emotional foundation for their children. In the following passage Jordan offers a powerful testament of how she came to see that her mother's work was an act of love:

> As a child I noticed the sadness of my mother as she sat alone in the kitchen at night. . . . Her woman's work never won permanent victories of any kind. It never enlarged the universe of her imagination or her power to influence what happened beyond the front door of our house. Her woman's work never tickled her to laugh or shout or dance. But she did raise me to respect her way of offering love and to believe that hard work is often the irreducible factor for survival, not something to avoid. Her woman's work produced a reliable home base where I could pursue the privileges of books and music. Her woman's work invented the potential for a completely different kind of work for us, the next generation of Black women: huge, rewarding hard work demanded by the huge, new ambitions that her perfect confidence in us engendered. (1985, 105)

Community Othermothers and Political Activism

Black women's experiences as othermothers provide a foundation for Black women's political activism. Nurturing children in Black extended family networks stimulates a more generalized ethic of caring and personal accountability among African-American women who often feel accountable to all the Black community's children.

This notion of Black women as community othermothers for all Black children traditionally allowed African-American women to treat biologically unrelated children as if they were members of their own families. For example, sociologist Karen Fields describes how her grandmother, Mamie Garvin Fields, draws on her power as a community othermother when dealing with unfamiliar children: "She will say to a child on the street who looks up to no good, picking out a name at random, 'Aren't you Miz Pinckney's boy?' in that same reproving tone. If the reply is, 'No, *ma'am*, my mother is Miz Gadsden,' whatever threat there was dissipates" (Fields and Fields 1983, xvii).

The use of family language in referring to members of the African-American community also illustrates this dimension of Black motherhood. In the following passage, Mamie Garvin Fields describes how she became active in surveying substandard housing conditions among African-Americans in Charleston. Note her explanation of why she uses family language:

> I was one of the volunteers they got to make a survey of the places where we were paying extortious rents for indescribable property. I said "we," although it wasn't Bob and me. We had our own home, and so did many of the Federated Women. Yet we still felt like it really was "we" living in those terrible places, and it was up to us to do something about them. (Fields and Fields 1983, 195)

Black women frequently describe Black children using family language. In recounting her increasingly successful efforts to teach a boy who had given other teachers problems, my daughter's kindergarten teacher stated, "You know how it can be—the majority of children in the learning disabled classes are *our children*. I know he didn't belong there, so I volunteered to take him." In their statements both women use family language to describe the ties that bind them as Black women to their responsibilities as members of an African-American community/family.

In explaining why the South Carolina Federation of Colored Women's 35
Clubs founded a home for girls, Mrs. Fields observes, "We all could see that we had a responsibility for those girls: they were the daughters of our community coming up" (Fields and Fields 1983, 197). Ms. Fields's activities as a community othermother on behalf of the "daughters" of her community represent an established tradition among educated Black women. Serving as othermothers to women in the Black community has a long history. A study of 108 of the first generation of Black club women found that three-quarters were married, three-quarters worked outside the home, but only one-fourth had children (Giddings 1984). These women emphasized self-support for Black women, whether married or not, and realized that self-sufficient community othermothers were important. "Not all women are intended for mothers," declares an 1894 edition of the *Woman's Era*. "Some of us have not the temperment for family life. . . . Clubs will make women think seri-

ously of their future lives, and not make girls think their only alternative is to marry" (Giddings 1984, 108).

Black women writers also explore this theme of the African-American community othermother who nurtures the Black community. One of the earliest examples is found in Frances Ellen Watkins Harper's 1892 novel *Iola Leroy.* By rejecting an opportunity to marry a prestigious physician and dissociate herself from the Black community, nearly white Iola, the main character, chooses instead to serve the African-American community. Similarly, in Alice Walker's *Meridian* (1976), the main character rejects the controlling image of the "happy slave," the self-sacrificing Black mother, and chooses to become a community othermother. Giving up her biological child to the care of an othermother, Meridian gets an education, works in the civil rights movement, and eventually takes on responsibility for the children of a small southern town. She engages in a "quest that will take her beyond the society's narrow meaning of the word *mother* as a physical state and expand its meaning to those who create, nurture, and save life in social and psychological as well as physical terms" (Christian 1985, 242).

Sociologist Cheryl Gilkes (1980, 1982, 1983b) suggests that community othermother relationships can be key in stimulating Black women's decisions to become community activists. Gilkes asserts that many of the Black women community activists in her study became involved in community organizing in response to the needs of their own children and of those in their communities. The following comment is typical of how many of the Black women in Gilkes's study relate to Black children: "There were alot of summer programs springing up for kids, but they were exclusive . . . and I found that most of *our kids* were excluded" (1980, 219). For many women what began as the daily expression of their obligations as community othermothers, as was the case for the kindergarten teacher, developed into full-fledged actions as community leaders.

This community othermother tradition also explains the "mothering the mind" relationships that can develop between Black women teachers and their Black women students. Unlike the traditional mentoring so widely reported in educational literature, this relationship goes far beyond that of providing students with either technical skills or a network of academic and professional contacts. Bell Hooks shares the special vision that teachers who see our work in community othermother terms can pass on to our students: "I understood from the teachers in those segregated schools that the work of any teacher committed to the full self-realization of students was necessarily and fundamentally radical, that ideas were not neutral, that to teach in a way that liberates, that expands consciousness, that awakens, is to challenge domination at its very core" (1989, 50). Like the mother-daughter relationship, this "mothering the mind" among Black women seeks to move toward the mutuality of a shared sisterhood that binds African-American women as community othermothers.

Community othermothers have made important contributions in building a different type of community in often hostile political and economic surroundings (Reagon 1987). Community othermothers' actions demonstrate a clear rejection of separateness and individual interest as the basis of either community organization or individual self-actualization. Instead, the connectedness with others and common interest expressed by community othermothers models a very different value system, one whereby Afrocentric feminist ethics of caring and personal accountability move communities forward.

Motherhood as a Symbol of Power

40 Motherhood—whether bloodmother, othermother, or community othermother—can be invoked by African-American communities as a symbol of power. Much of Black women's status in African-American communities stems not only from actions as mothers in Black family networks but from contributions as community othermothers.

Black women's involvement in fostering African-American community development forms the basis for community-based power. This is the type of power many African-Americans have in mind when they describe the "strong Black women" they see around them in traditional African-American communities. Community othermothers work on behalf of the Black community by expressing ethics of caring and personal accountability which embrace conceptions of transformative power and mutuality (Kuykendall 1983). Such power is transformative in that Black women's relationships with children and other vulnerable community members is not intended to dominate or control. Rather, its purpose is to bring people along, to — in the words of late-nineteenth-century Black feminists — "uplift the race" so that vulnerable members of the community will be able to attain the self-reliance and independence essential for resistance.

When older African-American women invoke their power as community othermothers, the results can be quite striking. Karen Fields recounts a telling incident:

> One night . . . as Grandmother sat crocheting alone at about two in the morning, a young man walked into the living room carrying the portable TV from upstairs. She said, "Who are you looking for *this* time of night?" As Grandmother [described] the incident to me over the phone, I could hear a tone of voice that I know well. It said, "Nice boys don't do that." So I imagine the burglar heard his own mother or grandmother at that moment. He joined in the familial game just created: "Well, he told me that I could borrow it." "*Who* told you?" "John." "Um um, no *John* lives here. You got the wrong house." (Fields and Fields 1983, xvi)

After this dialogue, the teenager turned around, went back upstairs, and returned the television.

In local African-American communities, community othermothers become identified as powerful figures through furthering the community's well-being. Sociologist Charles Johnson (1934/1979) describes the behavior of an elderly Black woman at a church service in rural 1930s Alabama. Even though she was not on the program, the woman stood up to speak. The master of ceremonies rang for her to sit down, but she refused to do so claiming, "I am the mother of this church, and I will say what I please" (p. 172). The master of ceremonies offered the following explanation to the congregation as to why he let the woman continue: "Brothers, I know you all honor Sister Moore. Course our time is short but she has acted as a mother to me. . . . Any time old folks get up I give way to them" (p. 173).

References

Aschenbrenner, Joyce. 1975. *Lifelines, Black Families in Chicago.* Prospect Heights, IL: Waveland Press.

Brown, Elsa Barkley. 1989. "African-American Women's Quilting: A Framework for Conceptualizing and Teaching African-American Women's History." *Signs* 14 (4): 921–29.

Campbell, Bebe Moore. 1989. *Sweet Summer: Growing Up with and Without My Dad.* New York: Putnam.

Cantarow, Ellen. 1980. *Moving the Mountain: Women Working for Social Change.* Old Westbury, NY: Feminist Press.

Christian, Barbara. 1985. *Black Feminist Criticism, Perspectives on Black Women Writers.* New York: Pergamon.

Clarke, Edith. 1966. *My Mother Who Fathered Me.* 2d ed. London: Allen and Unwin.

Coleman, Willi. 1987. "Closets and Keepsakes." *Sage: A Scholarly Journal on Black Women* 4 (2): 34–35.

Dill, Bonnie Thornton. 1980. "'The Means to Put My Children Through': Child-Rearing Goals and Strategies among Black Female Domestic Servants." In *The Black Woman,* edited by La Frances Rodgers-Rose, 107–23. Beverly Hills, CA: Sage.

Dougherty, Molly C. 1978. *Becoming a Woman in Rural Black Culture.* New York: Holt, Rinehart and Winston.

Fields, Mamie Garvin, and Karen Fields. 1983. *Lemon Swamp and Other Places: A Carolina Memoir.* New York: Free Press.

Fortes, Meyer. 1950. "Kinship and Marriage among the Ashanti." In *African Systems of Kinship and Marriage,* edited by A. R. Radcliffe-Brown and Daryll Forde, 252–84. New York: Oxford University Press.

Giddings, Paula. 1984. *When and Where I Enter . . . The Impact of Black Women on Race and Sex in America.* New York: William Morrow.

Gilkes, Cheryl Townsend. 1980. "'Holding Back the Ocean with a Broom': Black Women and Community Work." In *The Black Woman,* edited by La Frances Rodgers-Rose, 217–32. Beverly Hills, CA: Sage.

———. 1982. "Successful Rebellious Professionals: The Black Woman's Professional Identity and Community Commitment." *Psychology of Women Quarterly* 6 (3): 289–311.

———. 1983b. "Going Up for the Oppressed: The Career Mobility of Black Women Community Workers." *Journal of Social Issues* 39 (3): 1115–39.

Gutman, Herbert. 1976. *The Black Family in Slavery and Freedom, 1750–1925.* New York: Random House.

Hooks, Bell. 1984. *From Margin to Center.* Boston: South End Press.
———. 1989. *Talking Back: Thinking Feminist, Thinking Black.* Boston: South End Press.
Johnson, Charles S. [1934] 1979. *Shadow of the Plantation.* Chicago: University of Chicago Press.
Jordan, June. 1985. *On Call.* Boston: South End Press.
Joseph, Gloria. 1981. "Black Mothers and Daughters: Their Roles and Functions in American Society." In *Common Differences,* edited by Gloria Joseph and Jill Lewis, 75–126. Garden City, NY: Anchor.
Kuykendall, Eleanor H. 1983. "Toward an Ethic of Nurturance: Luce Irigaray on Mothering and Power." In *Motherhood: Essays in Feminist Theory,* edited by Joyce Treblicot, 263–74. Totowa, NJ: Rowman & Allanheld.
Ladner, Joyce. 1972. *Tomorrow's Tomorrow.* Garden City, NY: Doubleday.
Lewis, Diane K. 1975. "The Black Family: Socialization and Sex Roles." *Phylon* 36 (3): 221–37.
Martin, Elmer, and Joanne Mitchell Martin. 1978. *The Black Extended Family.* Chicago: University of Chicago Press.
Moody, Ann. 1968. *Coming of Age in Mississippi.* New York: Dell.
Morrison, Toni. 1974. *Sula.* New York: Random House.
Reagon, Bernice Johnson. 1987. "African Diaspora Women: The Making of Cultural Workers." In *Women in Africa and the African Diaspora,* edited by Rosalyn Terborg-Penn, Sharon Harley, and Andrea Benton Rushing, 167–80. Washington, DC: Howard University Press.
Shimkin, Demitri B., Edith M. Shimkin, and Dennis A. Frate, eds. 1978. *The Extended Family in Black Societies.* Chicago: Aldine.
Simonsen, Thordis, ed. 1986. *You May Plow Here: The Narrative of Sara Brooks.* New York: Touchstone.
Smith, Janet Farrell. 1983. "Parenting as Property." In *Mothering: Essays in Feminist Theory,* edited by Joyce Trebilcot, 199–212. Totowa, NJ: Rowman & Allanheld.
Stack, Carol D. 1974. *All Our Kin: Strategies for Survival in a Black Community.* New York: Harper & Row.
Sudarkasa, Niara. 1981a. "Female Employment and Family Organization in West Africa." In *The Black Woman Cross-Culturally,* edited by Filomina Chioma Steady, 49–64. Cambridge, MA: Schenkman.
———. 1981b. "Interpreting the African Heritage in Afro-American Family Organization." In *Black Families,* edited by Harriette Pipes McAdoo, 37–53. Beverly Hills, CA: Sage.
Tanner, Nancy. 1974. "Matrifocality in Indonesia and Africa and among Black Americans." In *Woman, Culture, and Society,* edited by Michelle Z. Rosaldo and Louise Lamphere, 129–56. Stanford: Stanford University Press.
Troester, Rosalie Riegle. 1984. "Turbulence and Tenderness: Mothers, Daughters, and 'Othermothers' in Paule Marshall's *Brown Girl, Brownstones.*" *Sage: A Scholarly Journal on Black Women* 1 (2): 13–16.
Wade-Gayles, Gloria. 1984. "The Truths of Our Mothers' Lives: Mother-Daughter Relationships in Black Women's Fiction." *Sage: A Scholarly Journal on Black Women* 1 (2): 8–12.
Walker, Alice. 1976. *Meridian.* New York: Pocket Books.
Wallace, Michele. 1978. *Black Macho and the Myth of the Superwoman.* New York: Dial Press.

Washington, Mary Helen. 1984. "I Sign My Mother's Name: Alice Walker, Dorothy West and Paule Marshall." In *Mothering the Mind: Twelve Studies of Writers and Their Silent Partners,* edited by Ruth Perry and Martine Watson Brorонley, 143–63. New York: Holmes & Meier.

Weems, Renita. 1984. "'Hush. Mama's Gotta Go Bye Bye': A Personal Narrative." *Sage: A Scholarly Journal on Black Women* 1 (2): 25–28.

West, Cheryl. 1987. "Lesbian Daughter." *Sage: A Scholarly Journal on Black Women* 4 (2): 42–44.

White, Deborah Gray. 1985. *Ar'n't I a Woman? Female Slaves in the Plantation South.* New York: W. W. Norton.

Young, Virginia Heyer. 1970. "Family and Childhood in a Southern Negro Community." *American Anthropologist* 72 (32): 269–88.

Engaging the Text

1. In what ways do the African American families described by Collins differ from traditional Eurocentric views of family structure?
2. Define "othermother" and "fictive kin." Why are these roles important to the African American family? Can you think of similar roles in families that are not African American?
3. What explanations does Collins give for the centrality of women in extended African American families?
4. Explain what Collins means by "socialization for survival" (para. 17) and define the dilemma it presents to Black mothers. Do you think this dilemma still exists?
5. Explain the connections Collins sees between African American family life and political struggle.

Exploring Connections

6. How might Collins respond to Karen Lindsey's critique (p. 158) of the limitations and abuses of the nuclear family?
7. Apply Collins's terms and ideas to Bebe Moore Campbell's "Envy" (p. 182). To what extent does Collins's analysis help explain Campbell's narrative? Does it change your understanding of "Envy"?
8. Read Toni Cade Bambara's "The Lesson" (p. 482) and discuss how Collins's description of community othermothers might illuminate Miss Moore's attitude toward Sylvia and her friends.

Extending the Critical Context

9. Survey several depictions of African American family life on recent TV shows. To what extent do the mothers on these shows display the attitudes, values, and behaviors that Collins describes? What images of Black motherhood does TV create?
10. As a class, watch Spike Lee's *Crooklyn* and explore the roles that African American women are given in this film. To what extent do their portrayals confirm or

complicate Collins's analysis of the roles typically played by African American women?

11. Write a paper exploring the dynamics of a particular family relationship (e.g., father-son, sisters) within some group in American society *other than* African American. Following Collins's example, you may wish to include anecdotal support as well as published research. In any case, try to identify the definitive characteristics or patterns of the chosen relationship. How does this relationship connect to the family, the community, or one's sense of self?

We Always Stood on Our Own Two Feet: Self-reliance and the American Family

STEPHANIE COONTZ

Like most heroic figures in America's mythology, the mythic American family is characterized by autonomy and independence. Think of those legendary Puritans, who "civilized" a continent with the values of hard work and self-reliance; then, too, there were the homesteaders, families of rugged individualists who "tamed" the Old West. The irony, as Stephanie Coontz documents in this selection, is that the American family succeeded only with generous doses of outside assistance. Coontz (b. 1944) teaches history and women's studies at Evergreen State College in Olympia, Washington; much of her work is devoted to correcting misconceptions about the American family. This selection is taken from the most recent of her books, The Way We Never Were: American Families and the Nostalgia Trap *(1992).*

"They never asked for handouts," my grandfather used to say whenever he and my grandmother regaled me with stories about pioneer life in Puget Sound[1] after George Washington Bush and Michael T. Simmons defied the British and founded the first American settlement in the area. But the homesteaders didn't turn down handouts either during that hard winter of 1852, when speculators had cornered almost all the already low supply of wheat. Fortunately, Bush refused to sell his grain for the high prices the market offered, reserving most of what he did not use himself to feed his neighbors and stake them to the next spring's planting.

[1]*Puget Sound:* The arm of the Pacific that links Seattle, Tacoma, and other Washington State ports to the sea.

The United States' successful claim to Puget Sound was based on the Bush-Simmons settlement. Ironically, once Bush had helped his community become part of the Oregon territory, he became subject to Oregon's exclusionary law prohibiting African Americans from residing in the Territory. His neighbors spearheaded passage of a special legislative bill in 1854, exempting Bush and his family from the law. Bush's descendants became prominent members of what was to become Washington state, and the story of Bush's generosity in 1852 has passed into local lore.[2] Neither my grandparents' paternalistic attitudes toward blacks nor their fierce hatred of charity led them to downplay how dependent the early settlers had been on Bush's aid, but the knowledge of that dependence did not modify their insistence that decent families were "beholden to no one."

When I was older, I asked my grandfather about the apparent contradiction. "Well," he said, "that was an exception; and they paid him back by getting that bill passed, didn't they? It's not like all these people nowadays, sitting around waiting for the government to take care of them. The government never gave us anything, and we never counted on help from anybody else, either." Unless, of course, they were family. "Blood's thicker than water, after all," my grandparents used to say.

My grandparents are not the only Americans to allow the myth of self-reliance to obscure the reality of their own life histories. Politicians are especially likely to fall prey to the convenient amnesia that permits so much self-righteous posturing about how the "dependent poor" ought to develop the self-reliance and independence that "the rest of us" have shown. Sen. Phil Gramm, for example, coauthor of the 1985 Gramm-Rudman-Hollings balanced budget amendment, is well known for his opposition to government handouts. However, his personal history is quite different from his political rhetoric.

5 Born in Georgia in 1942, to a father who was living on a federal veterans disability pension, Gramm attended a publicly funded university on a grant paid for by the federal War Orphans Act. His graduate work was financed by a National Defense Education Act fellowship, and his first job was at Texas A&M University, a federal land-grant institution. Yet when Gramm finally struck out on his own, the first thing he did was set up a consulting business where he could be, in his own words, "an advocate of fiscal responsibility and free enterprise." From there he moved on to Congress, where he has consistently attempted to slash federal assistance programs for low-income people.[3]

Self-reliance is one of the most cherished American values, although there is some ambiguity about what the smallest self-reliant unit is. For some

[2]For more on Bush's history and that of other black pioneers, see William Loren Katz, *The Black West* (Seattle: Open Hand Publishers, 1987). [Author's note]

[3]David Broder, "Phil Gramm's Free Enterprise," *Washington Post*, 16 February 1983; Marian Wright Edelman, *Families in Peril: An Agenda for Social Change* (Cambridge: Harvard University Press, 1987), pp. 27–28. [Author's note]

it is the rugged individualist; for most it is the self-sufficient family of the past, in which female nurturing sustained male independence vis-à-vis the outside world. While some people believe that the gender roles within this traditional family were unfair, and others that they were beneficial, most Americans agree that prior to federal "interference" in the 1930s, the self-reliant family was the standard social unit of our society. Dependencies used to be cared for within the "natural family economy," and even today the healthiest families "stand on their own two feet."[4]

The fact is, however, that depending on support beyond the family has been the rule rather than the exception in American history, despite recurring myths about individual achievement and family enterprise. It is true that public aid has become less local and more impersonal over the past two centuries . . . but Americans have been dependent on collective institutions beyond the family, including government, from the very beginning.

A Tradition of Dependence on Others

The tendency of Americans to overestimate what they have accomplished on their own and deny how much they owe to others has been codified in the myth that the colonists came on an "errand into the wilderness" and built a land of plenty out of nothing. In reality, however, the abundant concentrations of game, plants, and berries that so astonished Eastern colonists were not "natural"; they had been produced by the co-operative husbandry and collective land-use patterns of Native Americans. In the Northwest, the valuable Douglas fir forests and plentiful herds of deer and elk found by early settlers existed only because Native American burning practices had created sustained-yield succession forests that maximized use of these resources without exhausting them.[5]

Even after they confiscated the collective work of others, though, European settlers did not suddenly form a society of independent, self-reliant families. Recent research in social history demonstrates that early American families were dependent on a large network of neighbors, church institutions, courts, government officials, and legislative bodies for their sustenance. It is true that in colonial days, the poor or disabled were generally cared for in families, but not, normally, in their *own* families. Families who did not have enough money to pay their passage to America or establish their own farms were split up, with their members assigned to be educated,

[4]Allan Carlson, "How Uncle Sam Got in the Family's Way," *Wall Street Journal*, 20 April 1988, and "Is Social Security Pro-Family?" *Policy Studies* (Fall 1987): 49. [Author's note]

[5]James Axtell, *The European and the Indian: Essays in the Ethnohistory of Colonial North America* (New York: Oxford University Press, 1982), pp. 292–93; William Cronon, *Changes in the Land: Indians, Colonists, and the Ecology of New England* (New York: Hill and Wang, 1983), pp. 37–53; Richard White, *Land Use, Environment, and Social Change: The Shaping of Island County, Washington* (Seattle: University of Washington Press, 1980), pp. 20–26. [Author's note]

fed, and trained for work in various propertied households. Elderly, ill, or orphaned dependents were taken care of in other people's families, and city officials gave allowances in money or kind to faciliate such care. The home-care system, however, soon buckled under the weight of population growth and increasing economic stratification. By the mid-eighteenth century, governments had begun to experiment with poorhouses and outdoor relief.[6]

10 It was not a colonial value to avoid being beholden to others, even among the nonpoor. Borrowing and lending among neighbors were woven into the very fabric of life. The presence of outstanding accounts assured the continuing circulation of goods, services, and social interactions through the community: being under obligation to others and having favors owed was the mark of a successful person. Throughout the colonies, life was more corporate than individualistic or familial. People operated within a tight web of obligation, debt, dependence, "treating," and the calling in of favors.[7]

As America made the transition to a wage-earning society in the 1800s, patterns of personal dependence and local community assistance gave way to more formal procedures for organizing work and taking care of those who were unable to work, either temporarily or permanently. But the rise of a generalized market economy did not lessen dependency, nor did it make the family more able to take care of its own, in any sector of society.

Within the upper classes, family partnerships, arranged marriages, dowries, and family loans no longer met the need for capital, recruitment of trusted workers, and exploration of new markets. The business class developed numerous extrafamilial institutions: mercantile associations; credit-pooling consortia; new legal bodies for raising capital, such as corporations or limited liability partnerships; and chambers of commerce. Middle-class fraternal organizations, evangelical groups, and maternal associations also reached beyond kinship ties and local community boundaries to create a vast network of mutual aid organizations. The first half of the nineteenth century is usually called not the age of the family but the age of association.[8]

[6]Lorena Walsh, "Till Death Do Us Part," in *Growing Up in America: Historical Experience,* ed. Harvey Graff (Detroit: Wayne State University Press, 1987); Edmund Morgan, *The Puritan Family: Religion and Domestic Relations in Seventeenth-Century New England* (New York: Harper & Row, 1966); John Demos, *A Little Commonwealth: Family Life in Plymouth Colony* (New York: Oxford University Press, 1970); Lawrence Cremin, *American Education: The Colonial Experience, 1607–1783* (New York: Harper & Row, 1970), pp. 124–37. [Author's note]

[7]Laurel Thatcher Ulrich, "Housewife and Gadder: Themes of Self-sufficiency and Community in Eighteenth-Century New England," in *"To Toil the Livelong Day": America's Women at Work, 1780–1980,* ed. Carol Groneman and Mary Beth Norton (Ithaca, N.Y.: Cornell University Press, 1987); James Henretta, "Families and Farms: *Mentalite* in Pre-Industrial America," *William and Mary Quarterly* 35 (1978); Rhys Isaac, *The Transformation of Virginia, 1740–1790* (Chapel Hill: University of North Carolina Press, 1982), pp. 11–138. [Author's note]

[8]James Henretta, *The Evolution of American Society, 1700–1815* (Lexington, Mass.: Heath, 1973), p. 212; Stuart Blumin, *The Urban Threshold: Growth and Change in a Nineteenth-Century American Community* (Chicago: University of Chicago Press, 1976), p. 46;

For the working class throughout the nineteenth century, dependence was "a structural," almost inevitable, part of life. Among workers as well, accordingly, blood was not always thicker than neighborhood, class, ethnicity, or religion. Black, immigrant, and native-born white workers could not survive without sharing and assistance beyond family networks.[9]

Working-class and ethnic subcommunities evolved around mutual aid in finding jobs, surviving tough times, and pooling money for recreation. Immigrants founded lodges to provide material aid and foster cooperation. Laborers formed funeral aid societies and death or sick benefit associations; they held balls and picnics to raise money for injured workers, widows, or orphans, and took collections at the mills or plant gates nearly every payday. Recipients showed the same lack of embarrassment about accepting such help as did colonial families. Reformer Margaret Byington, observing working-class life at the end of the nineteenth century, noted that a gift of money to a fellow worker who was ill or simply down on his luck was "accepted . . . very simply, almost as a matter of course." Among the iron- and steelworkers of Pittsburgh, "Innumerable acts of benevolence passed between the residents of the rows and tenements, . . . rarely remarked upon except for their absence." Some workers' cultures revolved around religious institutions, some around cooperative societies or militant unionism — but all extended beyond the family. Indeed, historian Michael Katz has found that in parts of early-twentieth-century Philadelphia, "Neighbors seemed more reliable and willing to help one another than did kin."[10]

15 Among Catholic populations, godparenting was one way of institutionalizing such obligations beyond the family. In traditional Mexican and Mexican-American communities, for example, rites of baptism cut across divisions between rich and poor, Native American, mestizo, and Spanish. Godparents became *comadres* or *copadres*[11] with the biological parents, providing discipline and love as needed. They were morally obliged to give

---

Paul Johnson, *A Shopkeeper's Millennium: Society and Revivals in Rochester, New York, 1815–1837* (New York: Hill and Wang, 1978). [Author's note]

[9]Michael Katz, *Poverty and Policy in American History* (New York: Academic Press, 1983), p. 183. [Author's note]

[10]S. J. Kleinberg, *The Shadow of the Mills: Working-Class Families in Pittsburgh, 1870–1907* (Pittsburgh: University of Pittsburgh Press, 1989), pp. 270–75; Herbert Gutman, *Work, Culture, and Society in Industrializing America* (New York: Knopf, 1976); John Bodnar, *Natives and Newcomers: Ethnicity in an American Mill Town* (Pittsburgh: University of Pittsburgh Press, 1977); Margaret Byington, *Homestead: The Households of a Mill Town* (Pittsburgh: University of Pittsburgh Press, 1974), p. 16; James Borchert, *Alley Life in Washington: Family, Community, Religion, and Folklife in the City, 1850–1970* (Urbana: University of Illinois Press, 1980); Jacquelyn Dowd Hall et al., *Like a Family: The Making of a Southern Cotton Mill World* (Chapel Hill: University of North Carolina Press, 1987); David Montgomery, *The Fall of the House of Labor* (New York: Cambridge University Press, 1989); David Goldberg, *A Tale of Three Cities: Labor Organization and Protest in Paterson, Passaic, and Lawrence, 1916–1921* (New Brunswick: Rutgers University Press, 1989); Katz, *Poverty and Policy*, p. 49. [Author's note]

[11]*comadres or copadres:* Comothers or cofathers.

financial assistance in times of need or to take on full parental responsibilities if the biological parents should die. Irish and Italian districts had similar customs. Some Native American groups had special "blood brother" rituals; the notion of "going for sisters"[12] has long and still thriving roots in black communities.[13]

Yet even ties of expanded kinship, class, neighborhood, and ethnicity were never enough to get many families by. Poor Americans, for example, have always needed support from the public purse, even if that support has often been inadequate. Indeed, notes one welfare historian, the history of dependence and assistance in America is marked by "the early and pervasive role of the state. There has never been a golden age of volunteerism."[14]

By the end of the nineteenth century, neither poorhouses, outdoor relief, nor private charity could cope with the dislocations of industrial business cycles. As late as 1929, after nearly a decade of prosperity, the Brookings Institute found that the "natural family economy" was not working for most Americans: three-fifths of American families earned $2,000 or less a year and were unable to save anything to help them weather spells of unemployment or illness. The Great Depression, of course, left many more families unable to make it on their own.[15]

Even aside from times of depression, the inability of families to survive without public assistance has never been confined to the poor. Middle-class and affluent Americans have been every bit as dependent on public support. In fact, comparatively affluent families have received considerably *more* public subsidy than those in modest circumstances, while the costs of such subsidies have often been borne by those who derived the least benefit from them.

To illustrate the pervasiveness of dependence in American family history, I will examine in greater detail the two main family types that are usually held up as models of traditional American independence: the frontier family, archetype of American self-reliance, and the 1950s suburban family, whose strong moral values and work ethic are thought to have enabled so many to lift themselves up by their bootstraps. In fact, these two family types probably tie for the honor of being the most heavily subsidized in American history, as well as for the privilege of having had more of their advantages paid for by minorities and the lower classes.

[12]*"going for sisters":* Acting as sisters despite no blood relationship.

[13]Richard Griswold Del Castillo, *La Familia: Chicano Families in the Urban Southwest, 1848 to the Present* (Notre Dame: University of Notre Dame Press, 1984), pp. 42–43, 118; Carol Stack, *All Our Kin: Strategies for Survival in a Black Community* (New York: Harper & Row, 1974). [Author's note]

[14]Michael B. Katz, *In the Shadow of the Poorhouse: A Social History of Welfare in America* (New York: Basic Books, 1986), pp. 190, 240. [Author's note]

[15]Abraham Epstein, *Insecurity: A Challenge to Americans: A Study of Social Insurance in the United States and Abroad* (New York: H. Smith and R. Hass, 1933); Katz, *Poverty and Policy,* pp. 121, 126, 244. [Author's note]

Self-reliance and the American West

20 Our image of the self-reliant pioneer family has been bequeathed to us by the *Little House on the Prairie* books and television series, which almost every American has read or seen. What is less well known is that these stories, based on the memoirs of Laura Ingalls Wilder, were extensively revised by her daughter as an ideological attack on government programs. When Wilder's daughter, Rose Wilder Lane, failed to establish a secure income as a freelance writer in the 1930s, she returned to her family home in the Ozarks. Here, historian Linda Kerber reports, "Lane announced that she would no longer write so that she would not have to pay taxes to a New Deal government." However, "she *rewrote* the rough drafts of her mother's memoirs, . . . turning them into the *Little House* books in which the isolated family is pitted against the elements and makes it — or doesn't — with no help from the community."[16]

In reality, prairie farmers and other pioneer families owed their existence to massive federal land grants, government-funded military mobilizations that dispossessed hundreds of Native American societies and confiscated half of Mexico, and state-sponsored economic investment in the new lands. Even "volunteers" expected federal pay: much of the West's historic "antigovernment" sentiment originated in discontent when settlers did not get such pay or were refused government aid for unauthorized raids on Native American territory. It would be hard to find a Western family today or at any time in the past whose land rights, transportation options, economic existence, and even access to water were not dependent on federal funds. "Territorial experience got Westerners in the habit of federal subsidies," remarks Western historian Patricia Nelson Limerick, "and the habit persisted long after other elements of the Old West had vanished."[17]

It has been an expensive habit, in more ways than one. The federal government spent $15 million on the Louisiana Purchase in 1803 and then engaged in three years of costly fighting against the British in order to gain more of Florida. In the 1830s, state governments funded outright or financially guaranteed three-fourths of the $200 million it cost to build canals linking the Atlantic seaboard trading centers with new settlements around the Great Lakes and the Ohio and Mississippi rivers. The government got a bargain in the 1830s when it forced the Cherokees to "sell" their land for $9 million and then deducted $6 million from that for the cost of removing them along "The Trail of Tears," where almost a quarter of the 15,000 Native Americans died. Acquiring northern Mexico was even more expensive: the war of annexation cost $97 million; then, as victor, the United States was

[16]Linda Kerber, "Women and Individualism in American History," *The Massachusetts Review* (Winter 1989): 604–05. [Author's note]

[17]Patricia Nelson Limerick, *Legacy of Conquest: The Unbroken Past of the American West* (New York: Norton, 1987), p. 82. [Author's note]

able to "buy" Texas, California, southern Arizona, and New Mexico from Mexico for only an additional $25 million.

The land acquired by government military action or purchase, both funded from the public purse, was then sold — at a considerable loss — to private individuals. The Preemption Act of 1841 allowed settlers to buy land at $125 an acre, far below the actual acquisition cost; in 1854, the Graduation Act permitted lands that had been on the market for some time to be sold for even less. The Homestead Act of 1862 provided that a settler could buy 160 acres for $10 if the homesteader lived on the land for five years and made certain improvements. The federal government also gave each state 30,000 acres to help finance colleges that could improve agricultural education and techniques. These land-grant colleges made vital contributions to Western economic expansion.

Even after this generous, government-funded head start, pioneer families did not normally become self-sufficient. The stereotypical solitary Western family, isolated from its neighbors and constantly on the move, did exist, but it was also generally a failure. Economic success in nineteenth-century America, on the frontier as well as in the urban centers, was more frequently linked to persistence and involvement in a community than to family self-reliance or the restless "pioneering spirit."[18]

As historian John Mack Farragher describes frontier life in Sugar Creek, 25
Illinois, between 1820 and 1850, for example, "self-sufficiency" was not a family quality but "a community experience. . . . Sharing work with neighbors at cabin raisings, log rollings, hayings, husking, butchering, harvesting or threshing were all traditionally communal affairs." The prairie was considered common land for grazing, and a "'borrowing system' allowed scarce tools, labor and products to circulate to the benefit of all." As one contemporary explained to prospective settlers: "Your wheel-barrows, your shovels, your utensils of all sorts, belong not to yourself, but to the public who do not think it necessary even to *ask* a loan, but take it for granted." This community, it must be stressed, was not necessarily egalitarian: one traveler characterized Illinois as "heaven for men and horses, but a very different place for women and oxen." But "mutuality" and "suppression of self-centered behavior," not rugged individualism or even the carving out of a familial "oasis," were what created successful settlements as America moved West, while the bottom line of westward expansion was federal funding of exploration, development, transportation, and communication systems.[19]

[18]Stephen Thernstrom, *Poverty and Progress: Social Mobility in a Nineteenth-Century City* (Cambridge: Harvard University Press, 1964); Peter Knights, *The Plain People of Boston: A Study in City Growth* (New York: Oxford University Press, 1971); Lilian Schlissel, Byrd Gibbens, and Elizabeth Hampsten, *Far From Home: Families of the Westward Journey* (New York: Schocken, 1989); John Farragher and Christine Stansell, *Women and Men on the Overland Trail* (New Haven: Yale University Press, 1979). [Author's note]

[19]John Mack Farragher, "Open-Country Community: Sugar Creek, Illinois, 1820–1850," in *The Countryside in the Age of Capitalistic Transformation*, ed. Steven Hahmond and Jona-

In the early twentieth century, a new form of public assistance became crucial to Westerners' existence: construction of dams and other federally subsidized irrigation projects. During the Depression, government electrification projects brought pumps, refrigeration, and household technology to millions of families who had formerly had to hand pump and carry their water and who had lacked the capacity to preserve or export their farm produce. Small farmers depended on the government to slow down foreclosures and protect them from the boom and bust of overproduction, soil exhaustion, and cutthroat competition.[20]

Without public subsidies, the maintenance of independent family farms would have been impossible. Yet even with all this help from government and neighbors, small family enterprises did not turn out to be the major developers of the West. Their dependence on government subsidization, it turned out, produced a political constituency and ideological cover for policies that channeled much greater benefits to wealthy individuals and corporations. Of the billion acres of western land distributed by the end of the century, for example, only 147 million acres became homesteads, and even many of these ended up in speculators' hands. Sociologists Scott and Sally McNall estimate that "probably only one acre in nine went to the small pioneers." One hundred and eighty-three million acres of the public domain were given to railroad companies, generally in alternating square-mile sections to a depth of ten miles on either side of the line. These federal giveaways, not family enterprise, were what built most major western logging companies. Environmental historian John Opie and rural geographer Imhoff Vogeler argue that for 200 years, federal policy has promoted the myth of the independent family farm at the same time it has encouraged waste or misuse of land and water and subsidized huge, though not necessarily efficient, agribusinesses. Yet trying to solve such inequity by simply cutting federal subsidies, as in the 1990 Farm Bill, flies in the face of 200 years of experience: the existence of family farms and diversified agriculture has always depended on public subsidy.[21]

---

thon Prude (Chapel Hill: University of North Carolina Press, 1985), p. 245; John Mack Faragher, *Sugar Creek: Life on the Illinois Prairie* (New Haven: Yale University Press, 1986), pp. 132–33, 114; Michael Cassity, *Defending a Way of Life: An American Community in the Nineteenth Century* (Albany: State University of New York Press, 1989). [Author's note]

[20]Steven Mintz and Susan Kellogg, *Domestic Revolutions: A Social History of American Family Life* (New York: Free Press, 1988), pp. 146–47. [Author's note]

[21]Limerick, *Legacy of Conquest*, pp. 45–47, 82, 136; Scott and Sally Ann McNall, *Plains Families: Exploring Sociology Through Social History* (New York: St. Martin's, 1983), p. 9; Willard Cochrane, *The Development of American Agriculture: A Historical Analysis* (Minneapolis: University of Minnesota Press, 1979); "Lincoln Policy Shaped Local Forest Landscape," *Seattle Post-Intelligencer*, 20 April 1990; John Opie, *The Law of the Land: Two Hundred Years of American Farmland Policy* (Lincoln: University of Nebraska Press, 1987); Imhoff Vogeler, *The Myth of the Family Farm: Agribusiness Dominance of U.S. Agriculture* (Boulder: Westview Press, 1981). [Author's note]

Self-reliance and the Suburban Family

Another oft-cited example of familial self-reliance is the improvement in living standards experienced by many Americans during the 1950s. The surge in homeownership at that time, most people believe, occurred because families scraped together down payments, paid their mortgages promptly, raised their children to respect private property, and always "stood on their own two feet." An entire generation of working people thereby attained middle-class status, graduating from urban tenements to suburban homeownership, just as Lucille Ball and Desi Arnaz did in their television series.

The 1950s suburban family, however, was far more dependent on government handouts than any so-called "underclass" in recent U.S. history. Historian William Chafe estimates that "most" of the upward mobility at this time was subsidized in one form or another by government spending. Federal GI benefits, available to 40 percent of the male population between the ages of twenty and twenty-four, permitted a whole generation of men to expand their education and improve their job prospects without foregoing marriage and children. The National Defense Education Act retooled science education, subsidizing both American industry and the education of individual scientists. In addition, the surge in productivity during the 1950s was largely federally financed. More than $50 billion of government-funded wartime inventions and production processes were turned over to private companies after the war, creating whole new fields of employment.[22]

Even more directly, suburban homeownership depended on an un- 30
precedented enlargement of federal regulation and financing. The first steps were taken in the Great Depression, when the Home Owners Loan Corporation (HOLC) set up low-interest loans to allow people to refinance homes lost through foreclosure. The government began to underwrite the real estate industry by insuring private homeownership lenders, loaning directly to long-term buyers, and subsidizing the extension of electricity to new residential areas. But the real transformation of attitudes and intervention came in the 1950s, with the expansion of the Federal Housing Authority and Veterans' Administration loans.

Before the Second World War, banks often required a 50 percent down payment on homes and normally issued mortgages for only five to ten years. In the postwar period, however, the Federal Housing Authority (FHA), supplemented by the GI Bill, put the federal government in the business of insuring and regulating private loans for single-home construction. FHA policy required down payments of only 5 to 10 percent of the purchase price and guaranteed mortgages of up to thirty years at interest rates of just 2 to

[22]William Chafe, *The Unfinished Journey: America Since World War II* (New York: Oxford University Press, 1986), pp. 113, 143; Susan Hartmann, *The Home Front and Beyond: American Women in the 1940s* (Boston: Twayne Publishers, 1982), p. 165; Michael Parenti, *Democracy for the Few* (New York: St. Martin's, 1988), pp. 82–83. [Author's note]

3 percent on the balance. The Veterans Administration asked a mere dollar down from veterans. At the same time, government tax policies were changed to provide substantial incentives for savings and loan institutions to channel their funds almost exclusively into low-interest, long-term mortgages. Consequently, millions of Americans purchased homes with artificially low down payments and interest rates, courtesy of Uncle Sam.[23]

It was not family savings or individual enterprise, but federal housing loans and education payments (along with an unprecedented expansion of debt), that enabled so many 1950s American families to achieve the independence of homeownership. Almost *half* the housing in suburbia depended on such federal financing. As philosopher Alan Wolfe points out: "Even the money that people borrowed to pay for their houses was not lent to them on market principles; fixed-rate mortgages, for example, absolved an entire generation from inflation for thirty years."[24]

Yet this still understates the extent to which suburbia was a creation of government policy and federal spending. True, it was private real estate agents and construction companies who developed the suburban projects and private families who bought the homes. But it was government-funded research that developed the aluminum clapboards, prefabricated walls and ceilings, and plywood paneling that composed the technological basis of the postwar housing revolution. And few buyers would have been forthcoming for suburban homes without new highways to get them out to the sites, new sewer systems, utilities services, and traffic control programs — all of which were not paid for by the families who used them, but by the general public.

In 1947, the government began a project to build 37,000 miles of new highway. In 1956, the Interstate Highway Act provided for an additional 42,500 miles. Ninety percent of this construction was financed by the government. The prime beneficiaries of this postwar road-building venture, which one textbook calls "the greatest civil engineering project of world history," were suburbanites. Despite arguments that road building served "national interests," urban interstates were primarily "turned into commuter roads serving suburbia."[25]

[23]Dwight Lee, "Government Policy and the Distortions in Family Housing," in *The American Family and the State,* ed. Joseph Peden and Fred Glahe (San Francisco: Pacific Research Institute for Public Policy, 1986), p. 312. [Author's note]

[24]Kenneth Jackson, *Crabgrass Frontier: The Suburbanization of the United States* (New York: Oxford University Press, 1985), pp. 196–204, 215; Chafe, *Unfinished Journey,* p. 113; Henretta et al., *America's History,* vol. 2, pp. 849–50; Alan Wolfe, *Whose Keeper?: Social Science and Moral Obligation* (Berkeley: University of California Press, 1989), p. 62. [Author's note]

[25]James A. Henretta et al., *America's History,* vol. 2 (Chicago: Dorsey Press, 1987), p. 848; Jackson, *Crabgrass Frontier,* pp. 248–50; Neal Pierce, "New Highways Next Big Issue to Divide Nation," *The Olympian,* 28 May 1990, p. 8A. [Author's note]

Such federal patronage might be unobjectionable, even laudable — 35
though hardly a demonstration of self-reliance — if it had been available to all Americans equally. But the other aspect of federal subsidization of suburbia is that it worsened the plight of public transportation, the inner cities, poor families in general, and minority ones in particular.

Debating Family Policy: Why It's So Hard

Attempts to sustain the myth of family self-reliance in the face of all the historical evidence to the contrary have led policymakers into theoretical convolutions and practical miscalculations that are reminiscent of efforts by medieval philosophers to maintain that the earth, not the sun, was the center of the planetary system. In the sixteenth century, leading European thinkers insisted that the sun and all the planets revolved around the earth, much as Americans insist that our society revolves around family self-reliance. When evidence to the contrary mounted, defenders of the Ptolemaic universe postulated all sorts of elaborate planetary orbits, changes of direction, and even periodic loop-de-loops in order to reconcile observed reality with their cherished theory. Similarly, rather than admit that all families need public support, we have constructed ideological loop-de-loops that explain away each instance of dependence as an "exception," an "abnormality," or even an illusion. We have distributed public aid to families through convoluted bureaucratic orbits that have become impossible to track; and in some cases — most notably in the issue of subsidized homeownership — the system has become so cumbersome that it threatens to collapse around our ears.

Today, for example, economist Isabel Sawhill points out, purchases of new homes "absorb more than 100 percent of personal savings in the United States, compared to less than 25 percent as recently as 1970. Encouraging such purchases drains savings away from investments in the modernization of factories and equipment." Sawhill suggests that we either provide people with direct grants for purchases, a practice that would quickly expose how many of our housing subsidies go to the rich, or remove housing subsidies entirely and use them to reduce the deficit and/or increase low-income housing.[26]

We urgently need a debate about the best ways of supporting families in modern America, without blinders that prevent us from seeing the full extent of dependence and interdependence in American life. As long as we pretend that only poor or abnormal families need outside assistance, we will shortchange poor families, overcompensate rich ones, and fail to come up with effective policies for helping families in the middle.

[26]Isabel Sawhill, "Escaping the Fiscal Trap," *The American Prospect* (Spring 1990): pp. 21–22. [Author's note]

Engaging the Text

1. Using two columns, labeled "Myth" and "Reality," jot down some rough notes on the history of the American family that Coontz provides early in this reading. What's the point of this information? Do you accept Coontz's conclusions?
2. Do Coontz's portraits of colonial families, frontier families, and 1950s suburban families conflict with the ideas you have most often seen in books, films, and TV shows? How, and *why?* Why would the history of the American family get ignored, distorted, or mythologized?
3. Based on the portion of Coontz's book that you see here, what kind of government policies do you think she might endorse? What kinds of broader social or political arguments would the information in this excerpt support?

Exploring Connections

4. Sketch the myth of the model family as described by Anndee Hochman (p. 150), Karen Lindsey (p. 158), and Coontz. Also summarize the main challenges they pose to the myth.
5. Review Patricia Hill Collins's "Black Women and Motherhood" (p. 195) and compare the network of mutual support she describes in the Black family with the different sources of support enjoyed by the white nuclear family from colonial times until the present.

Extending the Critical Context

6. Research "self-reliance" in your own family history. Talk to parents and grandparents about how the family has prospered or struggled. After reviewing the array of outside assistance Coontz identifies, find out what kinds of help your own family may have received from the government or other sources. To what extent does your research support or challenge Coontz's thesis?
7. Think carefully about the area you live in. What major government-subsidized projects or businesses can you see (e.g., logging, mining, or skiing operations on national forest land; irrigation and flood-control projects; public roads, housing, open space reserves)? Who in your area derives the most benefit from government programs?
8. Investigate the cost of your education and the extent to which it is being financed from beyond the family's budget. (Your tuition and fees may not come close to covering the college's expenses.) What will your higher education cost, and who is paying the bill?

An Indian Story

Roger Jack

Like the earlier selection by Bebe Moore Campbell (p. 182), this story concerns growing up away from one's father—this time in one of the Indian cultures of the Pacific Northwest. It's also an intimate view of a nonnuclear family; the author is interested in the family not as a static set of defined relationships but as a social network that adapts to the ever-changing circumstances and needs of its members. Roger Jack's work has been published in several journals and anthologies, including Spawning the Medicine River, Earth Power Coming, *and* The Clouds Threw This Light. *"An Indian Story" appeared in* Dancing on the Rim of the World: An Anthology of Contemporary Northwest Native American Writing *(1990), edited by Andrea Lerner.*

Aunt Greta was always a slow person. Grandpa used to say she was like an old lady out of the old days who never hurried herself for anything, no matter what. She was only forty-five, heavyset, dark-complexioned, and very knowledgeable of the old ways, which made her seem even older. Most of the time she wore her hair straight up or in a ponytail that hung below her beltline. At home she wore pants and big, baggy shirts, but at ritual gatherings she wore her light blue calico dress, beaded moccasins, hair braided and clasped with beaded barrettes. Sometimes she wore a scarf on her head like ladies older than she. She said we emulate those we love and care for. I liked seeing her dressed for ceremonials. Even more, I liked seeing her stand before crowds of tribal members and guests translating the old language to the new for our elders, or speaking on behalf of the younger people who had no understanding of the Indian language. It made me proud to be her nephew and her son.

My mom died when I was little. Dad took care of me as best he could after that. He worked hard and earned good money as an accountant at the agency. But about a year after Mom died he married a half-breed Indian and this made me feel very uncomfortable. Besides, she had a child of her own who was white. We fought a lot—me and Jeffrey Pine—and then I'd get into trouble because I was older and was supposed to know better than to misbehave.

I ran away from home one day when everyone was gone—actually, I walked to Aunt Greta's and asked if I could move in with her since I had already spent so much time with her anyway. Then after I had gone to bed that night, Dad came looking for me and Aunt Greta told him what I had told her about my wanting to move in with her. He said it would be all right for a while, then we would decide what to do about it later. That was a long time ago. Now I am out of high school and going to college. Meanwhile, Jeffrey Pine is a high-school dropout and living with the folks.

Aunt Greta was married a long time ago. She married a guy named Mathew who made her very happy. They never had children, but when persistent people asked either of them what was wrong, they would simply reply they were working on it. Then Mathew died during their fifth year of marriage. No children. No legacy. After that Aunt Greta took care of Grandpa, who had moved in with them earlier when Grandma died. Grandpa wasn't too old, but sometimes he acted like it. I guess it came from that long, drawn-out transition from horse riding and breeding out in the wild country to reservation life in buggies, dirt roads, and cars. He walked slowly everywhere he went; he and Aunt Greta complemented each other that way.

Eventually, Aunt Greta became interested in tribal politics and threat- 5
ened to run for tribal council, so Grandpa changed her Indian name from Little Girl Heart to Old Woman Walking, which he had called Grandma when she was alive. Aunt Greta didn't mind. In fact, she was proud of her new name. Little Girl Heart was her baby name, she said. When Grandpa died a couple of years later she was all alone. She decided tribal politics wasn't for her but began teaching Indian culture and language classes. That's when I walked into her life like a newborn Mathew or Grandpa or the baby she never had. She had so much love and knowledge to share, which she passed on to me naturally and freely; she received wages for teaching others. But that was gesticulation, she said.

My home and academic life improved a lot after I had moved in with Aunt Greta. Dad and his wife had a baby boy, and then a girl, but I didn't see too much of them. It was like we were strangers living a quarter mile from one another. Aunt Greta and I went on vacations together from the time I graduated from the eighth grade. We were trailblazers, she said, because our ancestors never traveled very far from the homeland.

The first year we went to Maryhill, Washington, which is about a ten-hour drive from our reservation home in Park City, and saw the imitation Stonehenge Monument. We arrived there late in the evening because we had to stop off in every other town along the road to eat, whether or not we were hungry, because that was Aunt Greta's way and Grandma's and all the other old ladies of the tribe. You have to eat to survive, they would say. It was almost dark when we arrived at the park. We saw the huge outlines of the massive hewn stones placed in a circular position and towering well over our heads. We stood small and in awe of their magnificence, especially seeing darkness fall upon us. Stars grew brighter and we saw them more keenly as time passed. Then they started falling, dropping out of the sky to meet us where we stood. I could see the power of Aunt Greta protruding through her eyes; if I had power I wouldn't have to explore, physically, the sensation I imagined her feeling. She said nothing for a long time. Then, barely audible, she murmured something like, "I have no teepee. I need no cover. This moment has been waiting for me here all this time." She paused. Then, "I wasn't sure what I would find here, but I'm glad we came. I was going to say something goofy like 'we should have brought the teepee and we could call upon Coyote to come and knock over these poles so we could drape our canvas over the skeleton and camp!' But I won't. I'm just glad we came here."

"Oh no, you aren't flipping out on me, are you?" I ribbed her. She always said good Indians remember two things: their humor and their history. These are the elements that dictate our culture and our survival in this crazy world. If these are somehow destroyed or forgotten, we would be doomed to extinction. Our power gone. And she had the biggest, silliest grin on her face. She said, "I want to camp right here!" and I knew she was serious.

We camped in the car, in the parking lot, that night. But neither of us slept until nearly daybreak. She told me Coyote stories and Indian stories and asked me what I planned to do with my life. "I want to be like you," I told her. Then she reminded me that I had a Dad to think about, too, and that maybe I should think about taking up his trade. I thought about a lot of stories I had heard about boys following in their father's footsteps — good or bad — and I told Aunt Greta that I wasn't too sure about living on the reservation and working at the agency all my life. Then I tried to sleep, keeping in mind everything we had talked about. I was young, but my Indian memory was good and strong.

On our way home from Maryhill we stopped off at Coyote's Sweat-house 10
down by Soap Lake. I crawled inside the small cavernous stone structure and Aunt Greta said to make a wish for something good. She tossed a coin inside before we left the site. Then we drove through miles of desert country and basalt cliffs and canyons, but we knew we were getting closer to home when the pine trees starting weeding out the sagebrush, and the mountains overrode the flatland.

Our annual treks after that brought us to the Olympic Peninsula on the coast and the Redwood Forest in northern California; Yellowstone National Park in Wyoming and Glacier Park in Montana; and the Crazy Horse / Mount Rushmore Monuments in South Dakota. We were careful in coordinating our trips with pow-wows too. Then we talked about going all the way to Washington, D.C., and New York City to see the sights and how the other half lived, but we never did.

After high-school graduation we went to Calgary for a pow-wow and I got into trouble for drinking and fighting with some local Indians I had met. They talked me into it. The fight occurred when a girlfriend of one of the guys started acting very friendly toward me. Her boyfriend got jealous and started pushing me around and calling me names; only after I defended myself did the others join in the fight. Three of us were thrown into the tribe's makeshift jail. Aunt Greta was not happy when she came to pay my bail. As a matter of fact, I had never seen her angry before. Our neighbors at the campground thought it was funny that I had been arrested and thrown into jail and treated the incident as an everyday occurrence. I sat in the car imagining my own untimely death. I was so sick.

After dropping the ear poles, I watched Aunt Greta take down the rest of the teepee with the same meticulousness with which we had set it up. She went around the radius of the teepee removing wooden stakes from the ground that held fast the teepee's body to the earth. Then she stood on a folding chair to reach the pins that held the face of the teepee together. She folded the teepee into halves as it hung, still, on the center pole. She folded it again and again until it grew clumsy and uneven, then she motioned for me to come and drop the pole so she could untie the fastener that made the teepee our home. Meanwhile, I had to drop all skeletal poles from the sky and all that remained were a few holes in the ground and flattened patches of grass that said we had been there. I stood looking over the crowd. Lots of people had come from throughout Canada and the northern states for the pow-wow. Hundreds of people sat watching the war dance. Other people watched the stick-games and card games. But what caught my attention were the obvious drunks in the crowd. I was "one of them" now.

Aunt Greta didn't talk much while we drove home. It was a long, lonely drive. We stopped only twice to eat cold, tasteless meals. Once in Canada and once stateside. When we finally got home, Aunt Greta said, "Good night," and went to bed. It was only eight o'clock in the evening. I felt a heavy calling to go talk to Dad about what had happened. So I did.

He was alone when I arrived at his house. As usual I walked through the front door without knocking, but immediately heard him call out, "Son?"

"Yeah," I said as I went to sit on a couch facing him. "How did you know it was me?"

He smiled, said hello, and told me a father is always tuned in to his son. Then he sensed my hesitation to speak and asked, "What's wrong?"

"I got drunk in Calgary." My voice cracked. "I got into a fight and thrown in jail too. Aunt Greta had to bail me out. Now she's mad at me. She hasn't said much since we packed to come home."

"Did you tell her you were sorry for screwing up?" Dad asked.

"Yeah. I tried to tell her. But she clammed up on me."

"I wouldn't worry about it," Dad said. "This was bound to happen sooner or later. You really feel guilty when you take that first drink and get caught doing it. Hell, when I got drunk the first time, my Mom and Dad took turns preaching to me about the evils of drinking, fornication, and loose living. It didn't stop me though. I was one of those smart asses who had to have his own way. What you have to do is come up with some sort of reparation. Something that will get you back on Greta's good side."

"I guess that's what got to me. She didn't holler or preach to me. All the while I was driving I could feel her staring at me." My voice strengthened, "But she wouldn't say anything."

"Well, Son. You have to try to imagine what's going through her mind too. As much as I love you, you have been Greta's boy since you were knee-high to a grasshopper. She has done nothing but try to provide all the love and proper caring that she can for you. Maybe she thinks she has done something wrong in your upbringing. She probably feels more guilty about what happened than you. Maybe she hasn't said anything because she isn't handling this very well either." Dad became a little less serious before adding. "Of course, Greta's been around the block a time or two herself."

Stunned, I asked, "What do you mean?"

"Son, as much as Greta's life has changed, there are some of us who 25
remember her younger days. She liked drinking, partying, and loud music along with war dancing, stick-games, and pow-wows. She got along wherever she went looking for a good time. She was one of the few who could do that. The rest of us either took to drinking all the time, or we hit the pow-wow circuit all straight-faced and sober, never mixing up the two. Another good thing about Greta was that when she found her mate and decided to settle down, she did it right. After she married Mathew she quit running around." Dad smiled, "Of course, Mathew may have had some influence on her behavior, since he worked for the alcohol program."

"I wonder why she never remarried?" I asked.

"Some women just don't," Dad said authoritatively. "But she never had a shortage of men to take care of. She had your Grandpa—and YOU!" We laughed. Then he continued, "Greta could have had her pick of any man on the reservation. A lot of men chased after her before she married, and a lot of them chased after her after Mathew died. But she never had time for them."

"I wonder if she would have gotten married again if I hadn't moved in on her?"

"That's a question only Greta can answer. You know, she may work in tribal programs and college programs, but if she had to give it all up for one reason in the world, it would be you." Dad became intent, "You are her bloodline. You know that? Otherwise I wouldn't have let you stay with her all these years. The way her family believes is that two sisters coming from the same mother and father are the same. Especially blood. After your Mother died and you asked to go and live with your Aunt, that was all right. As a matter of fact, according to her way, we were supposed to have gotten married after our period of mourning was over."

"You—married to Aunt Greta!" I half-bellowed and again we laughed. 30

"Yeah. We could have made a hell of a family, don't you think?" Dad tried steadying his mood. "But, you know, maybe Greta's afraid of losing you too. Maybe she's afraid that you're entering manhood and that you'll be leaving her. Like when you go away to college. You are still going to college, aren't you?"

"Yeah. But I never thought of it as leaving her. I thought it more like going out and doing what's expected of me. Ain't I supposed to strike out on my own one day?"

"Yeah. Your leaving your family and friends behind may be expected, but like I said, 'you are everything to Greta,' and maybe she has other plans for you." Dad looked down to the floor and I caught a glimpse of graying streaks of hair on top of his head. Then he asked me which college I planned on attending.

"One in Spokane," I answered. "I ain't decided which one yet."

Then we talked about other things and before we knew it his missus 35
and the kids were home. Junior was nine, Anna Lee eight; they had gone to the last day of the tribe's celebration and carnival in Nespelem, which was what Aunt Greta and I had gone to Calgary to get away from for once. I sat quietly and wondered what Aunt Greta must have felt for my wrongdoing. The kids got louder as they told Dad about their carnival rides and games and prizes they had won. They shared their goodies with him and he looked to be having a good time eating popcorn and cotton candy.

I remembered a time when Mom and Dad brought me to the carnival. Grandpa and Grandma were with us. Mom and Dad stuck me on a big, black merry-go-round horse with flaming red nostrils and fiery eyes. Its long, dangling tongue hung out of its mouth. I didn't really want to ride that horse, but I felt I had to because Grandpa kept telling Mom and Dad that I belonged on a real horse and not some wooden thing. I didn't like the horse, when it hit certain angles it jolted and scared me even more. Mom and Dad offered me another ride on it, but I refused.

"Want some cotton candy?" Junior brought me back to reality. "We had fun going on the rides and trying to win some prizes. Here, you can have this one." He handed me one of his prizes. And, "Are you gonna stay with us tonight?"

I didn't realize it was after eleven o'clock.

"You can sleep in my bed," Junior offered.

"Yeah. Maybe I will, Little Brother." Junior smiled. I bade everyone 40
good night and went to his room and pulled back his top blanket revealing his Star Wars sheets. I chuckled at the sight of them before lying down and trying to sleep on them. This would be my first time sleeping away from Aunt Greta in a long time. I still felt tired from my drinking and the long drive home, but I was glad to have talked to Dad. I smiled in thinking that he said he loved me, because Indian men hardly ever verbalize their emotions. I went to sleep thinking how alone Aunt Greta must have felt after I had left home and promised myself to return there as early as I could.

I ate breakfast with the family before leaving. Dad told me one last thing that he and Aunt Greta had talked about sometime before. "You know, she talked about giving you an Indian name. She asked me if you had one and I said 'no.' She talked about it and I thought maybe she would go ahead and do it too, but her way of doing this is: boys are named for their father's side and girls are named for their mother's. Maybe she's still waiting for me to give you a name. I don't know."

"I remember when Grandpa named her, but I never thought of having a name myself. What was the name?" I asked.

"I don't remember. Something about stars."

Aunt Greta was sitting at the kitchen table drinking coffee and listening to an Elvis album when I got home. Elvis always made her lonesome for the old days or it cheered her up when she felt down. I didn't know what to say, but showed her the toy totem pole Junior had given me.

"That's cute," she said. "So you spent the night at the carnival?" 45

"No. Junior gave it to me," I explained. "I camped at Dad's."

"Are you hungry?" she was about to get up from the table.

"No. I've eaten." I saw a stack of pancakes on the stove. I hesitated another moment before asking, "What's with Elvis?"

"He's dead!" she said and smiled, because that's what I usually said to her. "Oh well, I just needed a little cheering up, I guess."

I remember hearing a story about Aunt Greta that happened a long time 50
ago. She was a teenager when the Elvis craze hit the reservation. Back then hardly any families had television sets, so they couldn't see Elvis. But when his songs hit the airwaves on the radio the girls went crazy. The guys went kind of crazy too — but they were pissed off crazy. A guy can't be that good looking and talented too, they claimed. They were jealous of Elvis. Elvis had a concert in Seattle and my Mom and Aunt Greta and a couple other girls went to it. Legend said that Elvis kissed Aunt Greta on the cheek during his performance and she took to heart the old "ain't never going to wash that cheek again" promissory and never washed her cheek for a long time and it got chapped and cracked until Grandpa and Grandma finally had to order her to go to the clinic to get some medicine to clean up her face. She hated them for a while, still swearing Elvis would be her number one man forever.

"How's your Dad?"

"He's all right. The kids were at the carnival when I got to his house, so we had a nice, long visit." I paused momentarily before adding, "And he told me some stories about you too."

"Oh?" she acted concerned even though her crow's feet showed.

"Yeah. He said you were quite a fox when you were young. And he said you probably could have had any man you wanted before you married Uncle Mathew, and you could have had any man after Uncle Mathew died. So, how come you never snagged yourself another husband?"

Aunt Greta sat quietly for a moment. I could see her slumping into the 55
old way of doing things which said you thought things through before saying them. "I suppose I could have had my pick of the litter. It's just that after my old man died I didn't want anyone else. He was so good to me that I didn't think I could find any better. Besides, I had you and Grandpa to care for, didn't I? Have I ever complained about that?"

"Yeah," I persisted, "but haven't you ever thought about what might have happened if you had gotten married again? You might have done like Dad and started a whole new family. Babies, even!"

Aunt Greta was truly embarrassed. "Will you get away from here with talk like that. I don't need babies. Probably won't be long now and you'll be bringing them home for me to take care of anyhow."

Now I was embarrassed. We got along great after that initial conversation. It was like we had never gone to Calgary and I had never gotten on to her wrong side at all. We were like kids rediscovering what it was worth to have a real good friend go away for a while and then come back. To be appreciative of each other, I imagined Aunt Greta might have said.

Our trip to Calgary happened in July. August and September found me dumbfounded as to what to do with myself college-wise. I felt grateful that Indian parents don't throw out their offspring when they reach a certain age. Aunt Greta said it was too late for fall term and that I should rest my brain for a while and think about going to college after Christmas. So I explored different schools in the area and talked to people who had gone to them. Meanwhile, some of my friends were going to Haskell Indian Junior College in Kansas. Aunt Greta frowned upon my going there. She said it was too far away from home, people die of malaria there, and if you're not drunk, you're just crazy. So I stuck with the Spokane plan.

That fall Aunt Greta was invited to attend a language seminar in Portland. She taught Indian language classes when asked to. So we decided to take a side trip to our old campsite at Stonehenge. This time we arrived early in the morning and it was foggy and drizzling rain. The sight of the stones didn't provide the feeling we had experienced earlier. To us, the sight seemed to be just a bunch of rocks standing, overlooking the Columbia River, a lot of sagebrush, and two state highways. It didn't offer us feelings of mysticism and power anymore. Unhappy with the mood, Aunt Greta said we might as well leave; her words hung heavy on the air.

We stayed in Portland for a week and then made it a special point to leave late in the afternoon so we could stop by Stonehenge again at dusk. So with careful planning we arrived with just enough light to take a couple pictures and then darkness began settling in. We sat in the car eating baloney sandwiches and potato chips and drinking pop because we were tired of restaurant food and we didn't want people staring at us when we ate. That's where we were when an early evening star fell. Aunt Greta's mouth fell open, potato chip crumbs clung to the sides of her mouth. "This is it!" she squealed in English, Indian, and English again. "Get out of the car, Son," and she half pushed me out the door. "Go and stand in the middle of the circle and pray for something good to happen to you." I ran out and stood waiting and wondering what was supposed to happen. I knew better than to doubt Aunt Greta's wishes or superstitions. Then the moment came to pass.

"Did you feel it?" she asked as she led me back to the car.

"I don't know," I told her because I didn't think anything had happened.

"I guess it just takes some people a little longer to realize," she said.

I never quite understood what was supposed to have happened that day. 65
A couple months later I was packing up to move to Spokane. I decided to go into the accounting business, like Dad. Aunt Greta quizzed me hourly before I was to leave whether I was all right and if I would be all right in the city. "Yeah, yeah," I heard myself repeating. So by the time I really was to leave she clued me in on her new philosophy: it wasn't that I was leaving her, it was just that she wouldn't be around to take care of me much anymore. She told me, "Good Indians stick together," and that I should search out our people who were already there, but not forget those who were still at home.

After I arrived in Spokane and settled down I went home all too frequently to actually experience what Aunt Greta and everyone told me. Then my studies got so intense that I didn't think I could travel home as much anymore. So I stayed in Spokane a lot more than before. Finally it got so I didn't worry as much about the folks at home. I would be out walking in the evening and know someone's presence was with me. I never bothered telephoning Dad at his office at the agency; and I never knew where or when Aunt Greta worked. She might have been at the agency or school. Then one day Dad telephoned me at school. After asking how I was doing, he told me why he was calling. "Your Aunt Greta is sick. The doctors don't know what's wrong with her yet. They just told me to advise her family of the possibility that it could be serious." I only half heard what he was saying, "Son, are you there?"

"Yeah."

"Did you hear me? Did you hear what I said?"

"Yeah. I don't think you have to worry about Aunt Greta though. She'll be all right. Like the old timers used to say, 'she might go away for a while, but she'll be back,'" and I hung up the telephone unalarmed.

Engaging the Text

1. Give specific examples of how the narrator's extended family or kinship structure works to solve family problems. What problems does it seem to create or make worse?
2. What key choices does the narrator make in this story? How are these choices influenced by family members or family considerations?
3. Is the family portrayed here matriarchal, patriarchal, egalitarian, or something else? Explain. To what extent is parenting influenced by gender roles?
4. What events narrated in this story might threaten the survival of a nuclear family? How well does the extended family manage these crises?
5. How strong an influence does the narrator's father have on him? How can you explain the father's influence given how rarely the two see each other?
6. How do you interpret the narrator's reaction when he hears about Aunt Greta's failing health? What is implied in the story's closing lines?

Exploring Connections

7. Compare and contrast Roger Jack's family with Bebe Moore Campbell's in "Envy" (p. 182). In what ways and for what reasons does each depart from the structure of the western European nuclear family?
8. Review Patricia Hill Collins's "Black Women and Motherhood" (p. 195). To what extent does Aunt Greta fulfill the roles of "othermother" and "community othermother" as defined by Collins? In what ways does her parenting depart from the African American models Collins describes?

Extending the Critical Context

9. This story celebrates the power of stories to connect people and to shape or affirm one's identity. Throughout, the narrator relates family stories about his father and his aunt that give him a clearer sense of himself and his relationship to those he loves. In a journal entry or essay, relate one or two family stories that are important to you and explain how they help you define who you are.

Aunt Ida Pieces a Quilt

Melvin Dixon

This is an extraordinary poem about AIDS, love, and family life. Its author, Melvin Dixon (b. 1950), received his Ph.D. from Brown University; in addition to teaching English at Queens College in New York, he published poetry, literary criticism, translations, and two novels. "Aunt Ida" appeared in Brother to Brother: New Writings by Black Gay Men *(1991). Dixon died of complications from AIDS in 1992.*

You are right, but your patch isn't big enough.
— Jesse Jackson

When a cure is found and the last panel is
sewn into place, the Quilt will be displayed
in a permanent home as a national monument
to the individual, irreplaceable people lost to AIDS —
and the people who knew and loved them most.
— Cleve Jones, *founder, The NAMES Project*

They brought me some of his clothes. The hospital gown,
those too-tight dungarees, his blue choir robe
with the gold sash. How that boy could sing!

His favorite color in a necktie. A Sunday shirt.
What I'm gonna do with all this stuff?
I can remember Junie without this business.
My niece Francine say they quilting all over the country.
So many good boys like her boy, gone.

At my age I ain't studying no needle and thread.
My eyes ain't so good now and my fingers lock in a fist,
they so eaten up with arthritis. This old back
don't take kindly to bending over a frame no more.
Francine say ain't I a mess carrying on like this.
I could make two quilts the time I spend running my mouth.

Just cut his name out the cloths, stitch something nice
about him. Something to bring him back. You can do it,
Francine say. Best sewing our family ever had.
Quilting ain't that easy, I say. Never was easy.
Y'all got to help me remember him good.

Most of my quilts was made down South. My mama
and my mama's mama taught me. Popped me on the tail
if I missed a stitch or threw the pattern out of line.
I did "Bright Star" and "Lonesome Square" and "Rally Round,"
what many folks don't bother with nowadays. Then Elmo and me
married and came North where the cold in Connecticut
cuts you like a knife. We was warm, though.
We had sackcloth and calico and cotton, 100% pure.
What they got now but polyester rayon. Factory made.

Let me tell you something. In all my quilts there's a secret
nobody knows. Every last one of them got my name Ida
stitched on the back side in red thread.
That's where Junie got his flair. Don't let nobody fool you.
When he got the Youth Choir standing up and singing
the whole church would rock. He'd throw up his hands
from them wide blue sleeves and the church would hush
right down to the funeral parlor fans whisking the air.
He'd toss his head back and holler and we'd all cry holy.

And nevermind his too-tight dungarees.
I caught him switching down the street one Saturday night,
and I seen him more than once. I said, Junie,
you ain't got to let the world know all your business.
Who cared where he went when he wanted to have fun.
He'd be singing his heart out come Sunday morning.

When Francine say she gonna hang this quilt in the church
I like to fall out. A quilt ain't no showpiece,

it's to keep you warm. Francine say it can do both.
Now I ain't so old-fashioned I can't change,
but I made Francine come over and bring her daughter
Belinda. We cut and tacked his name, *JUNIE.*
Just plain and simple, *"JUNIE, our boy."*
Cut the *J* in blue, the *U* in gold. *N* in dungarees
just as tight as you please. The *I* from the hospital gown
and the white shirt he wore First Sunday. Belinda
put the necktie in *E* in the cross stitch I showed her.

Wouldn't you know we got to talking about Junie.
We could smell him in the cloth.
Underarm. Afro Sheen pomade.[1] Gravy stains.
I forgot all about my arthritis.
When Francine left me to finish up, I swear
I heard Junie giggling right along with me
as I stitched Ida on the back side in red thread.

Francine say she gonna send this quilt to Washington
like folks doing from all 'cross the country,
so many good people gone. Babies, mothers, fathers
and boys like our Junie. Francine say
they gonna piece this quilt to another one,
another name and another patch
all in a larger quilt getting larger and larger.

Maybe we all like that, patches waiting to be pieced.
Well, I don't know about Washington.
We need Junie here with us. And Maxine,
she cousin May's husband's sister's people,
she having a baby and here comes winter already.
The cold cutting like knives. Now where did I put that needle?

[1]*Afro Sheen pomade:* Hair-care product for African Americans.

Engaging the Text

1. Identify all of the characters and their relationships in the poem. Then retell the story of the poem in your own words.
2. Discuss the movement of Aunt Ida's mind and her emotions as we move from stanza to stanza. What happens to Aunt Ida in the poem? What is the dominant feeling at the end of the poem?
3. Junie's clothes take on symbolic weight in the quilt and, of course, in the poem as well. What do the hospital gown, the dungarees, the choir robe, and the white shirt and necktie represent?
4. What is Aunt Ida about to make at the end of the poem, and what is its significance?

Exploring Connections

5. Discuss the actions of the women in this poem in light of Patricia Hill Collins's discussion of African American families (p. 195). To what extent do the authors share similar beliefs about Black families?
6. How might Melvin Dixon and Roger Jack (p. 225) respond to Anndee Hochman's suggestion (p. 150) that belonging to a family requires complete conformity? Which vision of family membership seems the most realistic to you?

Extending the Critical Context

7. Write a screenplay or dramatic script to "translate" the story of "Aunt Ida Pieces a Quilt" into dramatic form. Time permitting, organize a group to read or perform the piece for the class.
8. Throughout this chapter, families have been portrayed through a variety of metaphors: they have appeared as a nuclear unit, a house with many connecting rooms, a network of relationships, and a quilt with many parts. What are the implications of each of these metaphors? How do they affect our view of family? What other metaphors might capture your vision of American family life?
9. Watch the documentary *Common Threads: Stories from the Quilt* and write a poem based on the life of one of the people profiled in this film.

3

Women and Men in Relationship

Myths of Gender

Common sense tells us that there are obvious differences between females and males: after all, biology, not culture, determines whether or not you're able to bear children. But culture and cultural myths do shape the roles men and women play in our public and private relationships: we are born female and male, but we are made women and men. Sociologists distinguish between sex and gender — between one's biological identity and the conventional patterns of behavior we learn to associate with each sex. While biological sex remains a constant, the definition of "appropriate" gender behavior varies dramatically from one cultural group or historical period to the next. The variations show up markedly in the way we dress. For example, among many American Indian tribes, men who lived and dressed as women were respected as people who possessed special powers, whereas in contemporary Anglo-American culture, cross-dressers are usually seen as deviant or ridiculous. Male clothing in late-seventeenth- and early-eighteenth-century England would also have failed our current "masculinity" tests: in that period, elaborate laces, brocades, wigs, and even makeup signaled wealth, status, and sexual attractiveness for men and women alike.

History shows us how completely our gender derives from cultural myths about what is proper for men and women to think, enjoy, and do. And history is replete with examples of how the apparent "naturalness" of gender has been used to regulate political, economic, and personal relations between the sexes.

In his classic 1832 treatise on American democracy, for instance, James Fenimore Cooper remarked that women's domestic role and "necessary" subordination to men made them unsuitable for participation in the nation's public life. Thus, he argued, denying women the right to vote was perfectly consistent with the principles of American democracy:

> In those countries where the suffrage is said to be universal, exceptions exist, that arise from the necessity of things. . . . The interests of women being thought to be so identified with those of their male relatives as to become, in a great degree, inseparable, females are, almost generally, excluded from the possession of political rights. There can be no doubt that society is greatly the gainer, by thus excluding one half its members, and the half that is best adapted to give a tone to its domestic happiness, from the strife of parties, and the fierce struggles of political controversies. . . . These exceptions, however, do not very materially affect the principle of political equality. (*The American Democrat*)

Such beliefs have been remarkably persistent in the United States. It took over seventy years of hard political work by both black and white women's organizations to win the right to vote. But while feminists gained the vote for women in 1920 and the legal right to equal educational and employment opportunities in the 1970s, attitudes change even more slowly than laws. Contemporary antifeminist campaigns voice some of the same anxieties as their nineteenth-century counterparts over the "loss" of femininity and domesticity.

Women continue to suffer economic inequities based on cultural assumptions about gender. What's defined as "women's work" — nurturing, feeding, caring for family and home — is devalued and largely uncompensated; a 1980 study by the World Labor Organization showed that while women do two-thirds of the world's work, they receive only 10 percent of its income. But men, too, pay a high price for their culturally imposed roles. Studies of men's mental and physical health suggest that social pressure to "be a man" (that is, to be emotionally controlled, powerful, and successful) can contribute to isolation, anxiety, stress, and illness, and may be partially responsible for men's shorter life span.

This chapter focuses on cultural myths of gender and the influence they wield over human development and personal relationships. Selections in the first half of the chapter examine the way dominant American culture has defined female and male gender roles — and how those roles have in turn defined us. Jamaica Kincaid's "Girl" suggests, through a mother's advice to her daughter, what it means to be raised a woman. Holly Devor's "Becoming Members of Society" presents the idea that gender is a socially constructed "category" and discusses the psychological processes that underlie gender role acquisition. The oral history that follows, "Nora Quealey," provides an example of a woman torn between the roles she's been socially conditioned to play as a wife and mother and the realities of life on a blue-collar job. Michael Kimmel's provocatively titled "Clarence, William, Iron Mike, Senator Packwood, Spur Posse, Magic, . . . and Us" explores the social construction of masculinity and raises questions about the causes and cures for male violence.

The second half of the chapter presents strong rereadings of traditional gender roles and male-female relationships. In the chapter's media essay, "Sexism and Misogyny: Who Takes the Rap?" bell hooks probes the association between Black masculinity and violence and suggests that the misogyny of rap lyrics actually reflects the sexist aggression that is rampant in the dominant culture. Next, Judith Ortiz Cofer's personal reflection, "The Story of My Body," traces the shifting meanings of gender and identity for a woman of color who moves among different social and cultural contexts. In "Appearances" Carmen Vázquez offers another perspective on the idea of gender categorization: analyzing homophobia as the result of "gender betrayal," Vázquez documents case after case of violence directed against both gay and straight couples simply because they appeared to be homosexual. In "Strange Customs, Familiar Lives," two scholars challenge the restrictions of the male-female dichotomy by comparing definitions of gender and homosexuality across cultures.

The chapter closes with two positive redefinitions of gender and gendered relationships. In the essay "Where I Come from Is Like This" Paula Gunn Allen counters dominant American myths of gender with an eloquent description of the powerful roles played by women in Native American cultures. "The Two," Gloria Naylor's short story about a lesbian couple, invites you to reconsider the power of gender categories and the real meaning of relationship.

Sources

James Fenimore Cooper, *The American Democrat.* N.p.: Minerva Press, 1969.

Marilyn French, *Beyond Power: On Women, Men, and Morals.* New York: Ballantine Books, 1985.

Paula Giddings, *When and Where I Enter: The Impact of Black Women on Race and Sex in America.* New York: Bantam Books, 1984.

Leonard Pitt, *We Americans*, vol. 2, 3rd ed. Dubuque: Kendall/Hunt, 1987.

Will Roscoe, ed., *Living the Spirit: A Gay American Indian Anthology.* New York: St. Martin's Press, 1988.

Before Reading

- Working in single-sex groups, make an inventory of gender role characteristics: what attitudes, values, and abilities are usually ascribed to women, men, lesbians, gays, heterosexuals? Share your lists in class, looking for points of consensus and disagreement. Are there differences in the ways women and men perceive their own or each other's roles? Do you see larger differences between individual groups' responses or between women's and men's as a whole?
- Do a brief freewrite focusing on the performer in the frontispiece to this chapter (p. 238). How would you describe this person's gender? In what ways does this image challenge traditional ideas about maleness and femaleness?

Girl

Jamaica Kincaid

Although she now lives in New England, Jamaica Kincaid (b. 1949) retains strong ties, including citizenship, to her birthplace — the island of Antigua in the West Indies. After immigrating to the United States to attend college, she ended up educating herself instead, and did a good enough job to become a staff writer for The New Yorker *and the author of several books. About the influence of parents on children she says, "The magic is they carry so much you don't know about. They know you in a way you don't know yourself." Some of that magic is exercised in the story "Girl," which was first published in Kincaid's award-winning collection* At the Bottom of the River *(1983). Her latest novel is entitled* Autobiography of My Mother.

Wash the white clothes on Monday and put them on the stone heap; wash the color clothes on Tuesday and put them on the clothesline to dry; don't walk barehead in the hot sun; cook pumpkin fritters[1] in very hot sweet oil; soak your little cloths right after you take them off; when buying cotton to make yourself a nice blouse, be sure that it doesn't have gum[2] on it, because that way it won't hold up well after a wash; soak salt fish overnight before you cook it; is it true that you sing benna[3] in Sunday school?; always eat your food in such a way that it won't turn someone else's stomach; on Sundays try to walk like a lady and not like the slut you are so bent on becoming; don't sing benna in Sunday school; you mustn't speak to wharf-rat boys, not even to give directions; don't eat fruits on the street—flies will follow you; *but I don't sing benna on Sundays at all and never in Sunday school;* this is how to sew on a button; this is how to make a buttonhole for the button you have just sewed on; this is how to hem a dress when you see the hem coming down and so to prevent yourself from looking like the slut I know you are so bent on becoming; this is how you iron your father's khaki shirt so that it doesn't have a crease; this is how you iron your father's khaki pants so that they don't have a crease; this is how you grow okra—far from the house, because okra[4] tree harbors red ants; when you are growing dasheen,[5] make sure it gets plenty of water or else it makes your throat itch when you are eating it; this is how you sweep a corner; this is how you sweep a whole house; this is how you sweep a yard; this is how you smile to someone you don't like too much; this is how you smile to someone you don't like at all; this is how you smile to someone you like completely; this is how you set a table for tea; this is how you set a table for dinner; this is how you set a table for dinner with an important guest; this is how you set a table for lunch; this is how you set a table for breakfast; this is how to behave in the presence of men who don't know you very well, and this way they won't recognize immediately the slut I have warned you against becoming; be sure to wash every day, even if it is with your own spit; don't squat down to play marbles—you are not a boy, you know; don't pick people's flowers—you might catch something; don't throw stones at blackbirds, because it might not be a blackbird at all; this is how to make a bread pudding; this is how to

[1]*fritters:* Small fried cakes of batter, often containing vegetables, fruit, or other fillings.
[2]*gum:* Plant residue on cotton.
[3]*sing benna:* Sing popular music (not appropriate for Sunday school).
[4]*okra:* A shrub whose pods are used in soups, stews, and gumbo.
[5]*dasheen:* The taro plant, cultivated, like the potato, for its edible tuber.

make doukona;[6] this is how to make pepper pot;[7] this is how to make a good medicine for a cold; this is how to make a good medicine to throw away a child before it even becomes a child; this is how to catch a fish; this is how to throw back a fish you don't like, and that way something bad won't fall on you; this is how to bully a man; this is how a man bullies you; this is how to love a man, and if this doesn't work there are other ways, and if they don't work don't feel too bad about giving up; this is how to spit up in the air if you feel like it, and this is how to move quick so that it doesn't fall on you; this is how to make ends meet; always squeeze bread to make sure it's fresh; *but what if the baker won't let me feel the bread?*; you mean to say that after all you are really going to be the kind of woman who the baker won't let near the bread?

[6]*doukona:* Plaintain pudding; the plantain fruit is similar to the banana.
[7]*pepper pot:* A spicy West Indian stew.

Engaging the Text

1. What are your best guesses as to the time and place of the story? Who is telling the story? What does this dialogue tell you about the relationship between the characters, their values and attitudes? What else can you surmise about these people (for instance, ages, occupation, social status)? On what evidence in the story do you base these conclusions?
2. Why does the story juxtapose advice on cooking and sewing, for example, with the repeated warning not to act like a slut?
3. Explain the meaning of the last line of the story: "You mean to say that after all you are really going to be the kind of woman who the baker won't let near the bread?"
4. What does the story tell us about male-female relationships? According to the speaker, what roles are women and men expected to play?

Exploring Connections

5. Chapter One, "Learning Power," contains several pieces that describe "a girl's education," among them the cartoon by Garry Trudeau (p. 109), "Colder by Degrees" (p. 86), "Silence" (p. 110), and "Connected Education for Women" (p. 115). Compare and contrast the young girl's education in this story with the education described in one or more of the earlier selections. Differences will be easy to spot, so look carefully for similarities that may link the different times, places, and cultures.
6. To what extent does Patricia Hill Collins's "Black Women and Motherhood" (p. 195) help explain the mother's attitude and advice in this story?
7. What does it mean to be a successful mother in "Girl"? How does this compare to being a good mother or parent in "Growing Pains" (p. 150), "Envy" (p. 182), "An Indian Story" (p. 225), or "Looking for Work" (p. 145)? Of all the parents in these narratives, which do you consider most successful, which least, and why?

Extending the Critical Context

8. Write an imitation of the story. If you are a woman, record some of the advice or lessons your mother or another woman gave you; if you are a man, put down advice received from your father or from another male. Read what you have written aloud in class, alternating between male and female speakers, and discuss the results: How does parental guidance vary according to gender?
9. Write a page or two recording what the daughter might be thinking as she listens to her mother's advice; then compare notes with classmates.

Becoming Members of Society: Learning the Social Meanings of Gender

Holly Devor

Gender is the most transparent of all socially created ideas: we acquire gender roles so early in life and so thoroughly that it's hard to see them as the result of lessons taught and learned. Maleness and femaleness seem "natural," not the product of socialization. In this wide-ranging scholarly essay, Holly Devor suggests that many of our notions of what it means to be female or male are socially constructed. She also touches on the various ways that different cultures define gender. Devor moves quickly and assumes a well-educated audience, so be prepared to slow your reading pace to handle the material. Devor (b. 1951) teaches sociology at the University of Victoria in British Columbia. This selection is taken from her book Gender Blending: Confronting the Limits of Duality *(1989).*

The Gendered Self

The task of learning to be properly gendered members of society only begins with the establishment of gender identity. Gender identities act as cognitive filtering devices guiding people to attend to and learn gender role behaviors appropriate to their statuses. Learning to behave in accordance with one's gender identity is a lifelong process. As we move through our lives, society demands different gender performances from us and rewards, tolerates, or punishes us differently for conformity to, or digression from, social norms. As children, and later adults, learn the rules of membership in society, they come to see themselves in terms they have learned from the people around them.

Children begin to settle into a gender identity between the age of eighteen months and two years.[1] By the age of two, children usually understand that they are members of a gender grouping and can correctly identify other members of their gender.[2] By age three they have a fairly firm and consistent concept of gender. Generally, it is not until children are five to seven years old that they become convinced that they are permanent members of their gender grouping.[3]

Researchers test the establishment, depth, and tenacity of gender identity through the use of language and the concepts mediated by language. The language systems used in populations studied by most researchers in this field conceptualize gender as binary and permanent. All persons are either male or female. All males are first boys and then men; all females are first girls and then women. People are believed to be unable to change genders without sex change surgery, and those who do change sex are considered to be both disturbed and exceedingly rare.

This is by no means the only way that gender is conceived in all cultures. Many aboriginal cultures have more than two gender categories and accept the idea that, under certain circumstances, gender may be changed without changes being made to biological sex characteristics. Many North and South American native peoples had a legitimate social category for persons who wished to live according to the gender role of another sex. Such people were sometimes revered, sometimes ignored, and occasionally scorned. Each culture had its own word to describe such persons, most commonly translated into English as "berdache." Similar institutions and linguistic concepts have also been recorded in early Siberian, Madagascan, and Polynesian societies, as well as in medieval Europe.[4]

Very young children learn their culture's social definitions of gender and 5

[1] Much research has been devoted to determining when gender identity becomes solidified in the sense that a child knows itself to be unequivocally either male of female. John Money and his colleagues have proposed eighteen months of age because it is difficult or impossible to change a child's gender identity once it has been established around the age of eighteen months. Money and Ehrhardt, p. 243. [Author's note]

[2] Mary Driver Leinbach and Beverly I. Fagot, "Acquisition of Gender Labels: A Test for Toddlers," *Sex Roles* 15 (1986), pp. 655–66. [Author's note]

[3] Maccoby, pp. 225–29; Kohlberg and Ullian, p. 211. [Author's note]

[4] See Susan Baker, "Biological Influences on Human Sex and Gender," in *Women: Sex and Sexuality*, ed. Catherine R. Stimpson and Ethel S. Person (Chicago: University of Chicago Press, 1980), p. 186; Evelyn Blackwood, "Sexuality and Gender in Certain Native American Tribes: The Case of Cross-Gender Females," *Signs* 10 (1984), pp. 27–42; Vern L. Bullough, "Transvestites in the Middle Ages," *American Journal of Sociology* 79 (1974), 1381–89; J. Cl. DuBois, "Transsexualisme et Anthropologie Culturelle," *Gynecologie Practique* 6 (1969), pp. 431–40; Donald C. Forgey, "The Institution of Berdache among the North American Plains Indians," *Journal of Sex Research* 11 (Feb. 1975), pp. 1–15; Walter L. Williams, *The Spirit and the Flesh: Sexual Diversity in American Indian Culture* (Boston: Beacon, 1986). [Author's note]

gender identity at the same time that they learn what gender behaviors are appropriate for them. But they only gradually come to understand the meaning of gender in the same way as the adults of their society do. Very young children may learn the words which describe their gender and be able to apply them to themselves appropriately, but their comprehension of their meaning is often different from that used by adults. Five year olds, for example, may be able to accurately recognize their own gender and the genders of the people around them, but they will often make such ascriptions on the basis of role information, such as hair style, rather than physical attributes, such as genitals, even when physical cues are clearly known to them. One result of this level of understanding of gender is that children in this age group often believe that people may change their gender with a change in clothing, hair style, or activity.[5]

The characteristics most salient to young minds are the more culturally specific qualities which grow out of gender role prescriptions. In one study, young school age children, who were given dolls and asked to identify their gender, overwhelmingly identified the gender of the dolls on the basis of attributes such as hair length or clothing style, in spite of the fact that the dolls were anatomically correct. Only 17 percent of the children identified the dolls on the basis of their primary or secondary sex characteristics.[6] Children, five to seven years old, understand gender as a function of role rather than as a function of anatomy. Their understanding is that gender (role) is supposed to be stable but that it is possible to alter it at will. This demonstrates that although the standard social definition of gender is based on genitalia, this is not the way that young children first learn to distinguish gender. The process of learning to think about gender in an adult fashion is one prerequisite to becoming a full member of society. Thus, as children grow older, they learn to think of themselves and others in terms more like those used by adults.

Children's developing concepts of themselves as individuals are necessarily bound up in their need to understand the expectations of the society of which they are a part. As they develop concepts of themselves as individuals, they do so while observing themselves as reflected in the eyes of others. Children start to understand themselves as individuals separate from others during the years that they first acquire gender identities and gender roles. As they do so, they begin to understand that others see them and respond to them as particular people. In this way they develop concepts of themselves as individuals, as an "I" (a proactive subject) simultaneously with self-images of themselves as individuals, as a "me" (a member of society, a subjective object). Children learn that they are both as they see themselves and as others see them.[7]

[5]Maccoby, p. 255. [Author's note]

[6]Ibid., p. 227. [Author's note]

[7]George Herbert Mead, "Self," in *The Social Psychology of George Herbert Mead*, ed. Anselm Strauss (Chicago: Phoenix Books, 1962, 1934), pp. 212–60. [Author's note]

To some extent, children initially acquire the values of the society around them almost indiscriminately. To the degree that children absorb the generalized standards of society into their personal concept of what is correct behavior, they can be said to hold within themselves the attitude of the "generalized other."[8] This "generalized other" functions as a sort of monitoring or measuring device with which individuals may judge their own actions against those of their generalized conceptions of how members of society are expected to act. In this way members of society have available to them a guide, or an internalized observer, to turn the more private "I" into the object of public scrutiny, the "me." In this way, people can monitor their own behavioral impulses and censor actions which might earn them social disapproval or scorn. The tension created by the constant interplay of the personal "I" and the social "me" is the creature known as the "self."

But not all others are of equal significance in our lives, and therefore not all others are of equal impact on the development of the self. Any person is available to become part of one's "generalized other," but certain individuals, by virtue of the sheer volume of time spent in interaction with someone, or by virtue of the nature of particular interactions, become more significant in the shaping of people's values. These "significant others" become prominent in the formation of one's self-image and one's ideals and goals. As such they carry disproportionate weight in one's personal "generalized other."[9] Thus, children's individualistic impulses are shaped into a socially acceptable form both by particular individuals and by a more generalized pressure to conformity exerted by innumerable faceless members of society. Gender identity is one of the most central portions of that developing sense of self. . . .

Gender Role Behaviors and Attitudes

The clusters of social definitions used to identify persons by gender are 10
collectively known as femininity and masculinity. Masculine characteristics are used to identify persons as males, while feminine ones are used as signifiers for femaleness. People use femininity or masculinity to claim and communicate their membership in their assigned, or chosen, sex or gender. Others recognize our sex or gender more on the basis of these characteristics than on the basis of sex characteristics, which are usually largely covered by clothing in daily life.

These two clusters of attributes are most commonly seen as mirror images of one another with masculinity usually characterized by dominance and aggression, and femininity by passivity and submission. A more evenhanded description of the social qualities subsumed by femininity and mas-

[8]G. H. Mead. [Author's note]

[9]Hans Gerth and C. Wright Mills, *Character and Social Structure: The Psychology of Social Institutions* (New York: Harcourt, Brace and World, 1953), p. 96. [Author's note]

culinity might be to label masculinity as generally concerned with egoistic dominance and femininity as striving for cooperation or communion.[10] Characterizing femininity and masculinity in such a way does not portray the two clusters of characteristics as being in a hierarchical relationship to one another but rather as being two different approaches to the same question, that question being centrally concerned with the goals, means, and use of power. Such an alternative conception of gender roles captures the hierarchical and competitive masculine thirst for power, which can, but need not, lead to aggression, and the feminine quest for harmony and communal well-being, which can, but need not, result in passivity and dependence.

Many activities and modes of expression are recognized by most members of society as feminine. Any of these can be, and often are, displayed by persons of either gender. In some cases, cross gender behaviors are ignored by observers, and therefore do not compromise the integrity of a person's gender display. In other cases, they are labeled as inappropriate gender role behaviors. Although these behaviors are closely linked to sexual status in the minds and experiences of most people, research shows that dominant persons of either gender tend to use influence tactics and verbal styles usually associated with men and masculinity, while subordinate persons, of either gender, tend to use those considered to be the province of women.[11] Thus it seems likely that many aspects of masculinity and femininity are the result, rather than the cause, of status inequalities.

Popular conceptions of femininity and masculinity instead revolve around hierarchical appraisals of the "natural" roles of males and females. Members of both genders are believed to share many of the same human characteristics, although in different relative proportions; both males and females are popularly thought to be able to do many of the same things, but most activities are divided into suitable and unsuitable categories for each gender class. Persons who perform the activities considered appropriate for another gender will be expected to perform them poorly; if they succeed adequately, or even well, at their endeavors, they may be rewarded with ridicule or scorn for blurring the gender dividing line.

The patriarchal gender schema[12] currently in use in mainstream North

[10]Egoistic dominance is a striving for superior rewards for oneself or a competitive striving to reduce the rewards for one's competitors even if such action will not increase one's own rewards. Persons who are motivated by desires for egoistic dominance not only wish the best for themselves but also wish to diminish the advantages of others whom they may perceive as competing with them. See Maccoby, p. 217. [Author's note]

[11]Judith Howard, Philip Blumstein, and Pepper Schwartz, "Sex, Power, and Influence Tactics in Intimate Relationships," *Journal of Personality and Social Psychology* 51 (1986), pp. 102–09; Peter Kollock, Philip Blumstein, and Pepper Schwartz, "Sex and Power in Interaction: Conversational Privileges and Duties," *American Sociological Review* 50 (1985), pp. 34–46. [Author's note]

[12]*schema:* A mental framework, scheme, or pattern that helps us make sense of experience.

American society reserves highly valued attributes for males and actively supports the high evaluation of any characteristics which might inadverently become associated with maleness. The ideology which the schema grows out of postulates that the cultural superiority of males is a natural outgrowth of the innate predisposition of males toward aggression and dominance, which is assumed to flow inevitably from evolutionary and biological sources. Female attributes are likewise postulated to find their source in innate predispositions acquired in the evolution of the species. Feminine characteristics are thought to be intrinsic to the female facility for childbirth and breastfeeding. Hence, it is popularly believed that the social position of females is biologically mandated to be intertwined with the care of children and a "natural" dependency on men for the maintenance of mother-child units. Thus the goals of femininity and, by implication, of all biological females are presumed to revolve around heterosexuality and maternity.[13]

Femininity, according to this traditional formulation, "would result in 15
warm and continued relationships with men, a sense of maternity, interest in caring for children, and the capacity to work productively and continuously in female occupations."[14] This recipe translates into a vast number of proscriptions and prescriptions. Warm and continued relations with men and an interest in maternity require that females be heterosexually oriented. A heterosexual orientation requires women to dress, move, speak, and act in ways that men will find attractive. As patriarchy has reserved active expressions of power as a masculine attribute, femininity must be expressed through modes of dress, movement, speech, and action which communicate weakness, dependency, ineffectualness, availability for sexual or emotional service, and sensitivity to the needs of others.

Some, but not all, of these modes of interrelation also serve the demands of maternity and many female job ghettos. In many cases, though, femininity is not particularly useful in maternity or employment. Both mothers and workers often need to be strong, independent, and effectual in order to do their jobs well. Thus femininity, as a role, is best suited to satisfying a masculine vision of heterosexual attractiveness.

Body postures and demeanors which communicate subordinate status and vulnerability to trespass through a message of "no threat" make people appear to be feminine. They demonstrate subordination through a minimizing of spatial use: people appear feminine when they keep their arms closer to their bodies, their legs closer together, and their torsos and heads less vertical then do masculine-looking individuals. People also look feminine when they point their toes inward and use their hands in small or childlike gestures. Other people also tend to stand closer to people they see as fem-

[13]Chodorow, p. 134. [Author's note]

[14]Jon K. Meyer and John E. Hoopes, "The Gender Dysphoria Syndromes: A Position Statement on So-Called 'Transsexualism'," *Plastic and Reconstructive Surgery* 54 (Oct. 1974), pp. 444–51. [Author's note]

inine, often invading their personal space, while people who make frequent appeasement gestures, such as smiling, also give the appearance of femininity. Perhaps as an outgrowth of a subordinate status and the need to avoid conflict with more socially powerful people, women tend to excel over men at the ability to correctly interpret, and effectively display, nonverbal communication cues.[15]

Speech characterized by inflections, intonations, and phrases that convey nonaggression and subordinate status also make a speaker appear more feminine. Subordinate speakers who use more polite expressions and ask more questions in conversation seem more feminine. Speech characterized by sounds of higher frequencies are often interpreted by listeners as feminine, childlike, and ineffectual.[16] Feminine styles of dress likewise display subordinate status through greater restriction of the free movement of the body, greater exposure of the bare skin, and an emphasis on sexual characteristics. The more gender distinct the dress, the more this is the case.

Masculinity, like femininity, can be demonstrated through a wide variety of cues. Pleck has argued that it is commonly expressed in North American society through the attainment of some level of proficiency at some, or all, of the following four main attitudes of masculinity. Persons who display success and high status in their social group, who exhibit "a manly air of toughness, confidence, and self-reliance" and "the aura of aggression, violence, and daring," and who conscientiously avoid anything associated with femininity are seen as exuding masculinity.[17] These requirements reflect the patriarchal ideology that masculinity results from an excess of testosterone, the assumption being that androgens supply a natural impetus toward aggression, which in turn impels males toward achievement and success. This vision of masculinity also reflects the ideological stance that ideal maleness (masculinity) must remain untainted by female (feminine) pollutants.

Masculinity, then, requires of its actors that they organize themselves 20
and their society in a hierarchical manner so as to be able to explicitly quantify the achievement of success. The achievement of high status in one's social group requires competitive and aggressive behavior from those who wish to obtain it. Competition which is motivated by a goal of individual achievement, or egoistic dominance, also requires of its participants a degree of emotional insensitivity to feelings of hurt and loss in defeated others, and

[15]Erving Goffman, *Gender Advertisements* (New York: Harper Colophon Books, 1976); Judith A. Hall, *Non-Verbal Sex Differences: Communication Accuracy and Expressive Style* (Baltimore: Johns Hopkins University Press, 1984); Nancy M. Henley, *Body Politics: Power, Sex and Non-Verbal Communication* (Englewood Cliffs, New Jersey: Prentice Hall, 1979); Marianne Wex, *"Let's Take Back Our Space": "Female" and "Male" Body Language as a Result of Patriarchal Structures* (Berlin: Frauenliteraturverlag Hermine Fees, 1979). [Author's note]

[16]Karen L. Adams, "Sexism and the English Language: The Linguistic Implications of Being a Woman," in *Women: A Feminist Perspective*, 3rd edition, ed. Jo Freeman (Palo Alto, Calif.: Mayfield, 1984), pp. 478–91; Hall, pp. 37, 130–37. [Author's note]

[17]Pleck, p. 139. [Author's note]

a measure of emotional insularity to protect oneself from becoming vulnerable to manipulation by others. Such values lead those who subscribe to them to view feminine persons as "born losers" and to strive to eliminate any similarities to feminine people from their own personalities. In patriarchally organized societies, masculine values become the ideological structure of the society as a whole. Masculinity thus becomes "innately" valuable and femininity serves a contrapuntal function to delineate and magnify the hierarchical dominance of masculinity.

Body postures, speech patterns, and styles of dress which demonstrate and support the assumption of dominance and authority convey an impression of masculinity. Typical masculine body postures tend to be expansive and aggressive. People who hold their arms and hands in positions away from their bodies, and who stand, sit, or lie with their legs apart — thus maximizing the amount of space that they physically occupy— appear most physically masculine. Persons who communicate an air of authority or a readiness for aggression by standing erect and moving forcefully also tend to appear more masculine. Movements that are abrupt and stiff, communicating force and threat rather than flexibility and cooperation, make an actor look masculine. Masculinity can also be conveyed by stern or serious facial expressions that suggest minimal receptivity to the influence of others, a characteristic which is an important element in the attainment and maintenance of egoistic dominance.[18]

Speech and dress which likewise demonstrate or claim superior status are also seen as characteristically masculine behavior patterns. Masculine speech patterns display a tendency toward expansiveness similar to that found in masculine body postures. People who attempt to control the direction of conversations seem more masculine.[19] Those who tend to speak more loudly, use less polite and more assertive forms, and tend to interrupt the conversations of others more often also communicate masculinity to others. Styles of dress which emphasize the size of upper body musculature, allow freedom of movement, and encourage an illusion of physical power and a look of easy physicality all suggest masculinity. Such appearances of strength and readiness to action serve to create or enhance an aura of aggressiveness and intimidation central to an appearance of masculinity. Expansive postures and gestures combine with these qualities to insinuate that a position of secure dominance is a masculine one.

Gender role characteristics reflect the ideological contentions underlying the dominant gender schema in North American society. That schema leads us to believe that female and male behaviors are the result of socially directed hormonal instructions which specify that females will want to have children and will therefore find themselves relatively helpless and dependent on males for support and protection. The schema claims that males are

[18]Goffman, *Gender Advertisements;* Hall; Henley; Wex. [Author's note]

[19]Adams; Hall, pp. 37, 130–37. [Author's note]

innately aggressive and competitive and therefore will dominate over females. The social hegemony[20] of this ideology ensures that we are all raised to practice gender roles which will confirm this vision of the nature of the sexes. Fortunately, our training to gender roles is neither complete nor uniform. As a result, it is possible to point to multitudinous exceptions to, and variations on, these themes. Biological evidence is equivocal about the source of gender roles,[21] psychological androgyny[22] is a widely accepted concept.[23] It seems most likely that gender roles are the result of systematic power imbalances based on gender discrimination.[24]

[20]*hegemony:* System of preponderant influence, authority, or dominance.
[21]See chapter 1. [Author's note]
[22]*androgyny:* The state of having both male and female characteristics.
[23]See chapter 2. [Author's note]
[24]Howard, Blumstein, and Schwartz; Kollock, Blumstein, and Schwartz. [Author's note]

Engaging the Text

1. Devor charges that most languages present gender as "binary and permanent" (para. 3). Has this been your own view? How does Devor challenge this idea — that is, what's the alternative to gender being binary and permanent — and how persuasive do you find her evidence?
2. How, according to Devor, do children "acquire" gender roles? What are the functions of the "generalized other" and the "significant other" in this process?
3. Explain the distinction Devor makes between the "I" and the "me" (para. 7 and 8). Write a journal entry describing some of the differences between your own "I" and "me."
4. Using examples from Devor and from other reading or observation, list some "activities and modes of expression" (para. 12) that society considers characteristically female and characteristically male. Which are acceptable cross-gender behaviors, and which not? Search for a "rule" that defines what types of cross-gender behaviors are tolerated.

Exploring Connections

5. Review Bebe Moore Campbell's "Envy" (p. 182). What evidence of gender role socialization do you find in this story? To what extent do Moore's childhood experiences complicate Devor's presentation of gender role acquisition?
6. Drawing on Devor's discussion of gender role formation, analyze the difference between the "I" and the "me" of the girl in Jamaica Kincaid's story (p. 241).

Extending the Critical Context

7. Working in groups, collect ads and photos from popular magazines and newspapers to make a collage of either male or female gender images. Compare and discuss your results. What values, attitudes, and beliefs do these media images teach about gender roles?

8. Watch *The Crying Game* on video and discuss how this film confirms and/or complicates traditional gender categories.

Nora Quealey

JEAN REITH SCHROEDEL

This interview reveals the thoughts of a woman who has encountered sexism in a traditionally male occupation — assembly line work on trucks. Quealey is proud, strong, insightful—and she thinks she would prefer being a housewife. Jean Reith Schroedel (b. 1951) began collecting oral histories of blue-collar working women when she was an undergraduate at the University of Washington; she published these interviews in Alone in a Crowd *(1985). She has worked as a machinist and a union organizer, and, fittingly, she supported her work on the book by driving a bus. She now holds a Ph.D. from the Massachusetts Institute of Technology and is a professor at the Claremont Graduate School in California.*

I was a housewife until five years ago. The best part was being home when my three kids came in from school. Their papers and their junk that they made from kindergarten on up — they were my total, whole life. And then one day I realized when they were grown up and gone, graduated and married, I was going to be left with nothing. I think there's a lot of women that way, housewives, that never knew there were other things and people outside of the neighborhood. I mean the block got together once a week for coffee and maybe went bowling, but that was it. My whole life was being there when the kids came home from school.

I never disliked anything. It was just like everything else in a marriage, there never was enough money to do things that you wanted—never to take a week's vacation away from the kids. If we did anything, it was just to take the car on Saturday or Sunday for a little, short drive. But there was never enough money. The extra money was the reason I decided to go out and get a job. The kids were getting older, needed more, wanted more, and there was just not enough.

See, I don't have a high school diploma, so when I went to Boeing and put an application in, they told me not to come back until I had a diploma or a G.E.D.[1] On the truck line they didn't mind that I hadn't finished school. I put an application in and got hired on the spot.

[1]*G.E.D.:* A high school equivalency certificate.

My dad works over at Bangor[2] in the ammunition depot, so I asked him what it would be like working with all men. The only thing he told me was if I was gonna work with a lot of men, that I would have to *listen* to swear words and some of the obscene things, but still *act* like a lady, or I'd never fit in. You can still be treated like a lady and act like a lady and work like a man. So I just tried to fit in. It's worked, too. The guys come up and they'll tell me jokes and tease me and a lot of them told me that I'm just like one of the guys. Yet they like to have me around because I wear make-up and I do curl my hair, and I try to wear not really frilly blouses, see-through stuff, but nice blouses.

We had one episode where a gal wore a tank top and when she bent 5
over the guys could see her boobs or whatever you call it, all the way down. Myself and a couple other women went and tried to complain about it. We wanted personnel to ask her to please wear a bra, or at least no tank tops. We were getting a lot of comebacks from the guys like, "When are you gonna dress like so-and-so," or "When are *you* gonna go without a bra," and "We wanna see what *you've* got." And I don't feel any need to show off; you know, I know what I've got. There were only a few women there, so that one gal made a very bad impression. But personnel said there was nothing they could do about it.

But in general the guys were really good. I started out in cab building hanging radio brackets and putting heaters in. It was all hand work, and at first I really struggled with the power screwdrivers and big reamers, but the guy training me was super neato. I would think, "Oh, dear, can I ever do this, can I really prove myself or come up to their expectations?" But the guys never gave me the feeling that I was taking the job from a man or food from his family's mouth. If I needed help, I didn't even have to ask, if they saw me struggling, they'd come right over to help.

I've worked in a lot of different places since I went to work there. I was in cab build for I don't know how long, maybe six months, eight months. Then they took me over to sleeper boxes, where I stayed for about two-and-one-half years. I put in upholstery, lined the head liners and the floor mats. After that I went on the line and did air conditioning. When the truck came to me, it had hoses already on it, and I'd have to hook up a little air-condition-pump-type thing and a suction that draws all the dust and dirt from the lines. Then you close that off, put Freon in, and tie down the line. Then I'd tie together a bunch of color-coded electrical wires with tie straps and electrical tape to hook the firewall to the engine. Sometimes I also worked on the sleeper boxes by crawling underneath and tightening down big bolts and washers. Next they sent me over to the radiator shop. I was the first woman ever to do radiators. That I liked. A driver would bring in the radiators, and you'd put it on a hoist, pick it up and put it on a sling, and work on one side

[2]*Bangor:* Site of a Trident nuclear submarine base in the state of Washington.

putting your fittings on and wiring and putting in plugs. Then they bounced me back to sleeper boxes for a while and finally ended up putting me in the motor department, where I am now. The motors are brought in on a dolly. The guy behind me hangs the transmission and I hang the pipe with the shift levers and a few other little things and that's about it. Except that we have to work terribly fast.

I was moved into the motor department after the big layoff. At that time we were doing ten motors a day. Now we're up to fourteen without any additional help. When we were down, the supervisor came to me and said we had to help fill in and give extra help to the other guys, which is fine. But the minute production went up, I still had to do my own job plus putting on parts for three different guys. These last two weeks have been really tough. I've been way behind. They've got two guys that are supposed to fill in when you get behind, but I'm stubborn enough that I won't go over and ask for help. The supervisor should be able to see that I'm working super-duper hard while some other guys are taking forty-five minutes in the can and having a sandwich and two cups of coffee. Sometimes I push myself so hard that I'm actually in a trance. And I have to stop every once in a while and ask, "What did I do?" I don't even remember putting parts on, I just go from one to the other, just block everything out — just go, go, go, go. And that is bad, for myself, my own sanity, my own health. I don't take breaks. I don't go to the bathroom. There's so much pressure on me, physical and mental stress. It's hard to handle because then I go home and do a lot of crying and that's bad for my kids because I do a lot of snapping and growling at them. When I'm down, depressed, aching, and sore, to come home and do that to the kids is not fair at all. The last couple of days the attitude I've had is, I don't care whether I get the job done or not. If they can't see I'm going under, then I don't care. And I'll take five or ten minutes to just go to the bathroom, sit on the floor, and take a couple of deep breaths, just anything to get away.

The company doesn't care about us at all. Let me give you an example. When we were having all this hot weather, I asked them please if we couldn't get some fans in here. Extension cords even, because some guys had their own fans. I wasn't just asking for myself, but those guys over working by the oven. They've got a thermometer there and it gets to a hundred and fifteen degrees by that oven! They've got their mouths open, can hardly breathe, and they're barely moving. So I said to the supervisor, "Why can't we have a fan to at least circulate the air?" "Oh, yeah, we'll look at it," was as far as it went. We're human. We have no right to be treated like animals. I mean you go out to a dairy farm and you've got air conditioning and music for those cows. I'm a person, and I don't like feeling weak and sick to my stomach and not feel like eating. Then to have the supervisor expect me to put out production as if I was mechanical — a thing, just a robot. I'm human.

You know, I don't even know what my job title is. I'm not sure if it's 10
trainee or not. But I do know I'll never make journeyman. I'll never make anything. I tried for inspection — took all the classes they offered at the plant, went to South Seattle Community College on my own time, studied blueprinting, and worked in all the different areas like they said I had to. I broke ground for the other girls, but they won't let me move up. And it all comes down to one thing, because I associated with a black man. I've had people in personnel tell me to stop riding to work with the man, even if it meant taking the bus to and from work. I said no one will make my decisions as to who I ride with and who my friends are. Because you walk into a building with a person, have lunch with him, let him buy you a cup of coffee, people condemn you. They're crazy, because when I have a friend, I don't turn my back on them just because of what people think. What I do outside the plant after quitting time is my own business. If they don't like it, that's their problem. But in that plant I've conducted myself as a lady and have nothing to be ashamed of. I plant my feet firmly and I stand by it.

Early on, I hurt my neck, back, and shoulder while working on sleeper boxes. When I went into the motor department I damaged them more by working with power tools above my head and reaching all day long. I was out for two weeks and then had a ten-week restriction. Personnel said I had to go back to my old job, and if I couldn't handle it I would have to go home. They wouldn't put me anywhere else, which is ridiculous, with all the small parts areas that people can sit down and work in while they are restricted. My doctor said if I went back to doing what I was doing when I got hurt, I had a fifty-fifty chance of completely paralyzing myself from the waist down. But like a fool I went back. Some of the guys helped me with the bending and stooping over. Then the supervisor borrowed a ladder with three steps and on rollers from the paint department. He wanted me to stand on the top step while working on motors which are on dollies on a moving chain. I'd be using two press-wrenches to tighten fittings down while my right knee was on the transmission and the left leg standing up straight. All this from the top step of a ladder on rollers. One slip and it would be all over. I backed off and said it wouldn't work. By this time I'd gotten the shop steward there, but he didn't do anything. In fact, the next day he left on three weeks' vacation without doing anything to help me. I called the union hall and was told they'd send a business rep down the next day. I never saw or heard from the man.

Anyhow, I'm still doing the same job as when I got hurt. I can feel the tension in my back and shoulder coming up. I can feel the spasms start and muscles tightening up. Things just keep gettin' worse and they don't care. People could be rotated and moved rather than being cramped in the same position, like in the sleeper boxes, where you never stand up straight and stretch your neck out. It's eight, ten, twelve hours a day all hunched over. In the next two years I've got to quit. I don't know what I'll do. If I end up

Drawing by Roz Chast. © 1988 The New Yorker Magazine, Inc.

paralyzed from the neck down, the company doesn't give a damn, the union doesn't give a damn, who's gonna take care of me? Who's gonna take care of my girls? I'm gonna be put in some moldy, old, stinkin' nursing home. I'm thirty-seven years old. I could live another thirty, forty years. And who's gonna really care about me?

I mean my husband left me. He was very jealous of my working with a lot of men and used to follow me to work. When I joined the bowling team,

I tried to get him to come and meet the guys I worked with. He came but felt left out because there was always an inside joke or something that he couldn't understand. He resented that and the fact that I made more money than he did. And my not being home bothered him. But he never said, "I want you to quit," or "We'll make it on what I get." If he had said that I probably would have quit. Instead we just muddled on. With me working, the whole family had to pitch in and help. When I come home at night my daughter has dinner waiting, and I do a couple loads of wash and everybody folds their own clothes. My husband pitched in for a while. Then he just stopped coming home. He found another lady that didn't work, had four kids, and was on welfare.

It really hurt and I get very confused still. I don't have the confidence and self-assurance I used to have. I think, "Why did I do that," or "Maybe I shouldn't have done it," and I have to force myself to say, "Hey, I felt and said what I wanted to and there's no turning back." It came out of me and I can't be apologizing for everything that I do. And, oh, I don't know, I guess I'm in a spell right now where I'm tired of being dirty. I want my fingernails long and clean. I want to not go up to the bathroom and find a big smudge of grease across my forehead. I want to sit down and be pampered and pretty all day. Maybe that wouldn't satisfy me, but I just can't imagine myself at fifty or sixty or seventy years old trying to climb on these trucks. I've been there for five years. I'm thirty-seven and I want to be out of there before I'm forty. And maybe I will. I've met this nice guy and he's talking of getting married. At the most, I would have to work for one more year and then I could stay at home, go back to being a housewife.

Engaging the Text

1. What are Nora Quealey's attitudes toward domesticity? Toward work? Toward money and success? Is she a traditional woman or a feminist?
2. Quealey's life is in some ways tragic. What are the greatest blows she has suffered? Do you think she could have avoided any of them? How — and at what price?
3. What motivates Quealey to persevere in the face of the difficulties she encounters? List as many possible motivations as you can, and review the text to find evidence of them.

Exploring Connections

4. How might Holly Devor (p. 244) explain the conflicts that Nora Quealey experiences in relation to her work, her male coworkers, and her sense of herself as a woman?
5. Write an imaginary dialogue among Nora Quealey, Anndee Hochman (p. 150), and Karen Lindsey (p. 158) in which they discuss their attitudes toward family life.

6. How do you think Nora Quealey would respond to the cartoon on page 257? Create a cartoon of your own that reflects Quealey's attitudes about her identity as a woman.

Extending the Critical Context

7. When male workers ask "When are *you* gonna go without a bra" or say "We wanna see what *you've* got," does their speech constitute sexual harassment? How do you think a female employee should respond to such comments? Do you think different standards should apply in different work settings, for example, industrial versus clerical versus professional? Find guidelines defining sexual harassment in your library or Student Affairs office and discuss these in class.
8. Play Ann Landers. Imagine that Quealey has written you a long letter—namely, the text you've just read. Write a confidential response giving advice, encouragement, or an analysis of her situation or feelings, as you see fit. Then write a separate paragraph stating the rationale for your response.

Clarence, William, Iron Mike, Tailhook, Senator Packwood, Spur Posse, Magic, . . . and Us

Michael S. Kimmel

What do the people in the title have in common besides the fact that they are biologically male? According to Michael Kimmel, they are all victims of socially constructed notions of masculinity—notions that inevitably lead to aggression in the bedroom or the boardroom. Kimmel (b. 1951) is one of the nation's foremost educators on men and masculinity. He is an associate professor of sociology at the State University of New York (Stony Brook campus), national spokesperson for the National Organization for Men Against Sexism, and author of many books and articles on sexuality and in particular on profeminist men. The selection here is excerpted from the anthology Transforming a Rape Culture *(1993), edited by Emilie Buchwald, Pamela R. Fletcher, and Martha Roth.*

The 1990s may be remembered as the decade in which America took a crash course on male sexuality. From the national teach-in on sexual harassment that emerged from Clarence Thomas's confirmation hearings, to accusations about sexual harassment against Senator Robert Packwood, to the

U.S. Navy Tailhook scandal, to Magic Johnson's revelation that he is infected with the HIV virus, to William Kennedy Smith and Mike Tyson's date rape trials, to the trials of lacrosse players at St. John's University and high school athletes at Glen Ridge, New Jersey, we've had a steady discussion about male sexuality, about a sexuality that is more about predatory conquest than pleasure and connection.

And there's no end in sight — which explains the title of this essay. In the immediate aftermath of the Clarence Thomas confirmation hearings, the media claimed, as if with one voice, that the hearings would have a "chilling effect" on American women — that women would be far less likely to come forward and report incidents of sexual harassment for fear that they would be treated in the same shameful way as Anita Hill was by the Senate Judiciary Committee. Have the media ever been more wrong?

Since then, we've had less of a "chilling effect," and more of a national thaw, as women have come forward in record numbers to report cases of sexual harassment, date rape, and acquaintance rape. "Every woman has her Clarence Thomas," commented one woman, sadly surveying the workplace over the past two decades. In an op-ed essay in the *New York Times,* novelist Mary Lee Settle commented that Anita Hill had, "by her heroic stance, given not only me but thousands of women who have been silenced by shame the courage and the need to speak out about what we have tried for so long to bury and forget."

Currently, corporations, state and local governments, universities, and law firms are scrambling to implement procedures to handle sexual harassment. Most seem motivated more out of fear of lawsuits than out of general concern for women's experiences; thus, they are more interested in adjudicating harassment *after the fact* than in developing mechanisms to prevent it. In the same way, colleges and universities are developing strategies to handle the remarkable rise in date and acquaintance rape, although only a few are developing programs on prevention.

With more women coming forward now than ever before, many men 5
have reacted defensively; "Men on Trial" has been the common headline linking Smith and Thomas in the media. But it's not *men* on trial here, it's *masculinity,* or, rather, a definition of masculinity that leads to certain behaviors that we now see as problematic and often physically threatening. Under prevailing definitions, men have been and are the "politically incorrect" sex.

But why have these issues emerged now? And why are issues such as sexual harassment and date rape the particular issues we're facing? Since it is certain that we will continue to face these issues for the rest of the decade, how can we understand these changes? And, most important, what can we do about it? How can we change the meanings of masculinity so that sexual harassment and date rape will disappear from our workplaces and our relationships?

The Social Construction of Male Sexuality

To speak of transforming masculinity is to begin with the way men are sexual in our culture. As social scientists now understand, sexuality is less a product of biological urges and more about the meanings that we attach to those urges, meanings that vary dramatically across cultures, over time, and among a variety of social groups within any particular culture. Sexual beings are made, not born. John Gagnon, a well-known theoretician of this approach, argues in his book *Human Sexualities* that

> People learn when they are quite young a few of the things that they are expected to be, and continue slowly to accumulate a belief in who they are and ought to be through the rest of childhood, adolescence, and adulthood. Sexual conduct is learned in the same ways and through the same processes; it is acquired and assembled in human interaction, judged and performed in specific cultural and historical worlds.

And the major item in that assemblage, the chief building block in the social construction of sexuality, is gender. We experience our sexual selves through a gendered prism. The meanings of sex to women and to men are very, very different. There really are a "his" and "hers" when it comes to sex. Just one example: think about the difference in the way we view a man or a woman who has a lot of different partners—the difference, say, between a stud and a slut.

The rules of masculinity and femininity are strictly enforced. And difference equals power. The difference between male and female sexuality reproduces men's power over women, and, simultaneously, the power of some men over other men, especially of the dominant, hegemonic[1] form of manhood—white, straight, middle-class—over marginalized masculinities. Those who dare to cross over—women who are sexually adventurous and men who are sexually passive—risk being seen as *gender*, not sexual, nonconformists. And we all know how homophobia links gender nonconformity to homosexuality. The stakes are high if you don't play along.

10 Sexual behavior confirms manhood. It makes men feel manly. Robert Brannon has identified the four traditional rules of American manhood: (1) No Sissy Stuff: Men can never do anything that even remotely suggests femininity. Manhood is a relentless repudiation and devaluation of the feminine. (2) Be a Big Wheel: Manhood is measured by power, wealth, and success. Whoever has the most toys when he dies, wins. (3) Be a Sturdy Oak: Manhood depends on emotional reserve. Dependability in a crisis requires that men not reveal their feelings. (4) Give 'em Hell: Exude an aura of manly daring and aggression. Go for it. Take risks.

These four rules lead to a sexuality built around accumulating partners

[1] *hegemonic:* Characterized by dominance or overbearing authority or influence.

(scoring), emotional distance, and risk taking. In locker rooms and on playgrounds across the country, men are taught that the goal of every encounter with women is to score. Men are supposed to be ever ready for sex, constantly seeking sex, and constantly seeking to escalate every encounter so that intercourse will result, since, as one of my students once noted, "It doesn't count unless you put it in."

The emotional distancing of the sturdy oak is considered necessary for adequate male sexual functioning, but it leads to some strange behaviors. For example, to keep from ejaculating "too soon," men may devise a fascinating array of distractions, such as counting, doing multiplication tables in their heads, or thinking about sports.

Risk taking is a centerpiece of male sexuality. Sex is about adventure, excitement, danger. Taking chances. Responsibility is a word that seldom turns up in male sexual discourse. And this of course has serious medical side effects; the possibilities include STDs,[2] impregnation, and AIDS—currently the most gendered disease in American history.

To rein in this constructed male "appetite," women have been assigned the role of asexual gatekeeper; women decide, metaphorically and literally, who enters the desired garden of earthly delights, and who doesn't. Women's sexual agency, women's sense of entitlement to desire, is drowned out by the incessant humming of male desire, propelling him ever forward. A man's job is to wear down her resistance. One fraternity at a college I was lecturing at last year offered seminars to pledges on dating etiquette that appropriated the book of business advice called *Getting to Yes.*

Sometimes that hum can be so loud that it drowns out the actual voice 15
of the real live woman that he's with. Men suffer from socialized deafness, a hearing impairment that strikes only when women say "no."

Who Are the Real Sexual Revolutionaries?

Of course, a lot has changed along the frontiers of the sexual landscape in the past two decades. We've had a sexual revolution, after all. But as the dust is settling from the sexual revolution, what emerges in unmistakably fine detail is that it's been women, not men, who are our era's real sexual pioneers. Of course, we men like to think that the sexual revolution, with its promises of more access to more partners with less emotional commitment, was tailor-made for male sexuality's fullest flowering. But in fact it's been women's sexuality that's changed in the past two decades, not men's. Women now feel capable, even *entitled,* to sexual pleasure. They have learned to say "yes" to their own desires, claiming their own sexual agency.

And men? We're still dancing the same tired dance of the sexual conquistadors. Look, for a minute, at that new late-night game show "Studs."

[2]*STDs:* Sexually transmitted diseases.

Here are the results of the sexual revolution in media miniature. The men and women all date one another, and from implicit innuendo to explicit guffaws, one assumes that every couple has gone to bed. What's not news is that the men are joking about it; what *is* news is that the women are equally capable of it.

Now some might argue that this simply confirms that women can have "male sex," that male sexuality was victorious because we've convinced women to be more like us. But then why are so many men wilting in the face of desiring women? Why are the offices of sex therapists crammed with men who complain not of premature ejaculation (the most common sexual problem twenty years ago — a sexual problem that involves being a bit overeager) but of what therapists euphemistically call "inhibited desire." That is, these men don't want to have sex now that all these women are able to claim their sexual rights.

Date Rape and Sexual Predation, Aggression, and Entitlement

As women have claimed the right to say "yes," they've also begun to assert their rights to say "no." Women are now demanding that men be more sexually responsible and are holding men accountable for their sexual behaviors. It is women who have changed the rules of sexual conduct. What used to be (and in many places still is) called male sexual etiquette—forcing a woman to have sex when she says no, conniving, coercing, pushing, ignoring efforts to get you to stop, getting her so drunk that she loses the ability (or consciousness) that one needs to give consent—is now defined as date rape.

In one recent study, by psychologist Mary Koss at the University of 20
Arizona, 45 percent of all college women said that they had had some form of sexual contact against their will. A full 25 percent had been pressed or forced to have sexual intercourse against their will. And Patricia Bowman, who went home with William Kennedy Smith from Au Bar in Palm Beach, Florida, knows all about those statistics. She testified that when she told Smith that she'd called her friends, and she was going to call the police, he responded, "You shouldn't have done that. Nobody's going to believe you." And, indeed, the jury didn't. I did.

I also believed that the testimony of three other women who claimed they were sexually assaulted by Smith should have been allowed in the trial. Such testimony would have established a pattern not of criminal assault, but of Smith's obvious belief in sexual *entitlement,* that he was entitled to press his sexual needs on women despite their resistance, because he didn't particularly care what they felt about it.

And Desiree Washington knows all about men who don't listen when a woman says no. Mike Tyson's aggressive masculinity in the boxing ring was sadly translated into a vicious misogyny with his ex-wife Robin Givens and a predatory sexuality, as evidenced by his behavior with Desiree Washington.

Tyson's "grandiose sense of entitlement, fueled by the insecurities and emotions of adolescence," as writer Joyce Carol Oates put it, led to a behavior with women that was as out of control as his homosocial[3] behavior inside the ring.

Tyson's case underscores our particular fascination with athletes, and the causal equation we make between athletes and sexual aggression. From the St. John's University lacrosse team, to Glen Ridge, New Jersey, high school athletes, to dozens of athletic teams and individual players at campuses across the nation, we're getting the message that our young male athletes, trained for fearless aggression on the field, are translating that into a predatory sexual aggression in relationships with women. Columnist Robert Lipsyte calls it the "varsity syndrome — winner take all, winning at any cost, violence as a tool, aggression as a mark of masculinity." The very qualities we seek in our athletes are exactly the qualities we do not want in young men today. Rather, we want to encourage respect for others, compassion, the ability to listen, and attention to process rather than the end goal. Our task is to make it clear that what we want from our athletes when they are on the playing field is *not* the same as what we want from them when they are playing the field.

I think, though, that athletes only illustrate a deeper problem: the problem of men in groups. Most athletes play on teams, so much of their social life and much of a player's public persona is constructed through association with his teammates. Another homosocial preserve, fraternities, are the site of most gang rapes that occur on college campuses, according to psychologist Chris O'Sullivan, who has been studying gang rape for several years. At scores of campus and corporate workshops over the past five years, women have shared the complaint that, while individual men may appear sympathetic when they are alone with women, they suddenly turn out to be macho louts capable of the vilest misogynistic statements when they are in groups of men. The members of the U.S. Navy Tailhook Association are quite possibly decent, law-abiding family men when they are alone or with their families. But put them together at a convention, and they become a marauding gang of hypermasculine thugs who should be prosecuted for felonious assault, not merely slapped on their collective wrists.

25 I suppose it's true that the members of Spur Posse, a group of relatively affluent southern California adolescent boys, are also "regular guys." Which makes their sexual predation and homosocial competition as chilling as it is revealing of something at the heart of American masculinity. Before a large group of young women and girls — one as young as ten! — came forward to claim that members of Spur Posse had sexually assaulted and raped them, these guys would have been seen as typical high school fellas. Members of the group competed with one another to have sex with the most girls and

[3]*homosocial:* Describing social interaction within the same sex — as in boxing, fraternity life, a boys' club, etc.

kept elaborately coded scores of their exploits by referring to various athletes' names as a way of signifying the number of conquests. Thus a reference to "Reggie Jackson" would refer to forty-four, the number on his jersey, while "David Robinson" would signify fifty different conquests. In this way, the boys could publicly compete with one another without the young women understanding that they were simply the grounds for homosocial competition.

When some of these young women accused the boys of assault and rape, many residents of their affluent suburb were shocked. The boys' mothers, particularly, winced when they heard that their fifteen-year-old sons had had sex with forty-four or fifty girls. A few expressed outrage. But the boys' fathers glowed with pride. "That's my boy," they declared in chorus. They accused the girls of being sluts. And we wonder where the kids get it from?

Spur Posse is only the most recent example of the way masculine sexual entitlement is offered to boys as part of their birthright. Transforming a rape culture is going to mean transforming a view of women as the vessels through which men can compete with one another, trying to better their positions on the homosocial ladders of success and status.

What is it about groups that seems to bring out the worst in men? I think it is because the animating condition for most American men is a deeply rooted fear of other men — a fear that other men will view us as less than manly. The fear of humiliation, of losing in a competitive ranking among men, of being dominated by other men — these are the fears that keep men in tow and that reinforce traditional definitions of masculinity as a false definition of safety. Homophobia (which I understand as more than the fear of homosexual men; it's also the fear of other men) keeps men acting like men, keeps men exaggerating their adherence to traditional norms, so that no other men will get the idea that we might really be that most dreaded person: the sissy.

Men's fear of being judged a failure as a man in the eyes of other men leads to a certain homosocial element within the heterosexual encounter: men often will use their sexual conquest as a form of currency to gain status among other men. Such homosocial competition contributes to the strange hearing impairment that men experience in any sexual encounter, a socialized deafness that leads us to hear "no" as "yes," to escalate the encounter, to always go for it, to score. And this is occurring just at the moment when women are, themselves, learning to say "yes" to their own sexuality, to say "yes" to their own desire for sexual pleasure. Instead of our socialized deafness, we need to become what Langston Hughes[4] called "articulate listeners": we need to trust women when they tell us what they want, and when they want it, and what they don't want as well. If we listen when women say "no," then they will feel more trusting and open to saying "yes" when they

[4]*Langston Hughes:* Poet (1902–1967) and major figure in the Harlem Renaissance, which was a flowering of African American art, music, and writing in the 1920s. See p. 756.

feel that. And we need to listen to our own inner voices, our own desires and needs. Not the voices that are about compulsively proving something that cannot be proved, but the voices that are about connection with another and the desires and passions that may happen between two equals.

30 Escalating a sexual encounter beyond what a woman may want is date rape, not sex; it is one of the most important issues we will face in the 1990s. It is transforming the sexual landscape as earlier sexual behaviors are being reevaluated in light of new ideas about sexual politics. We have to explore the meaning of the word *consent,* explore our own understandings, and make sure that these definitions are in accord with women's definitions.

From the Bedroom to the Boardroom

Just as women have been claiming the right to say "yes" and demanding the right to say "no" and have it listened to and respected in the sexual arena, they've also transformed the public arena, the workplace. As with sexuality, the real revolution in the past thirty years has been women's dramatic entry into the labor force in unprecedented numbers. Almost half of the labor force is female. I often demonstrate this point to my classes by asking the women who intend to have careers to raise their hands. All do. Then I ask them to keep their hands raised if their mothers have had a career outside the home for more than ten years. Half put their hands down. Then I ask them to keep their hands raised if their grandmothers had a career for ten years. Virtually no hands remain raised. In three generations, they can visibly see the difference in women's working lives. Women are in the work force to stay, and men had better get used to having them around.

That means that the cozy boy's club—another homosocial arena—has been penetrated by women. And this, just when that arena is more suffused with doubt and anxieties than ever before. We are, after all, a downwardly mobile culture. Most Americans are less successful now than their parents were at the same age. It now takes two incomes to provide the same standard of living that one income provided about a generation ago. And most of us in the middle class cannot afford to buy the houses in which we were brought up. Since men derive their identity in the public sphere, and the primary public arena where masculinity is demonstrated is the workplace, this is an important issue. There are fewer and fewer big wheels and more and more men who will feel as though they haven't made the grade, who will feel damaged, injured, powerless — men who will need to demonstrate their masculinity all over again. Suddenly, men's fears of humiliation and domination are out in the open, and there's a convenient target at which to vent those anxieties.

And now, here come women into the workplace in unprecedented numbers. It now seems virtually impossible that a man will go through his entire working life without having a woman colleague, coworker, or boss. Just when men's economic breadwinner status is threatened, women appear on the scene as easy targets for men's anger. Thus sexual harassment in the workplace is a distorted effort to put women back in their place, to remind women that they are not equal to men in the workplace, that they are still just women, even if they are in the workplace.

It seems to me that this is the context in which to explore the meaning of sexual harassment in our society. The Clarence Thomas confirmation hearings afford men a rare opportunity to do some serious soul searching. What is sexual harassment about? And why should men help put an end to it?

One thing that sexual harassment is usually *not* about, although you 35
couldn't convince the Senate Judiciary Committee of this, is a matter of one person telling the truth and the other person lying. Sexual harassment cases are difficult and confusing precisely because there are often a multiplicity of truths. "His" truth might be what appears to him as an innocent indication of sexual interest by harmless joking with the "boys in the office" (even if those "boys" happen to include women workers). "Her" truth is that those seemingly innocent remarks cause stress and anxiety about promotion, firing, and sexual pressure.

Judge Thomas asserted during the course of his testimony that "at no time did I become aware, either directly or indirectly, that she felt I had said or done anything to change the cordial nature of our relationship." And there is no reason to assume that he would have been aware of it. But that doesn't mean his words or actions did not have the effect that Professor Hill states, only that she was successful in concealing the resulting trauma from him — a concealment that women have carefully developed over the years in the workplace.

Why should this surprise us? Women and men experience the same event differently. Men experience their behavior from the perspective of those who have power, women from the perspective of those upon whom that power is exercised.

If an employer asks an employee for a date, and she declines, perhaps he has forgotten about it by the time he gets to the parking lot. No big deal, he says to himself. You ask someone out, and she says "no." You forget about it. In fact, repairing a wounded male ego often *requires* that you forget about it. But the female employee? She's now frozen, partly with fear. What if I said yes? Would I have gotten promoted? Would he have expected more than a date? Will I now get fired? Will someone else get promoted over me? What should I do? And so, she will do what millions of women do in that situation: she calls her friends, who counsel her to let the matter rest and get on with her work. And she remembers for a long, long time. Who, therefore, is likely to have a better memory: those in power or those against whom that power is deployed?

This is precisely the divergence in experience that characterizes the controversies spinning around Senator Bob Packwood. Long a public supporter of women's causes, Senator Packwood also apparently chased numerous women around office desks, clumsily trying to have affairs with them. He claims, now, that alcoholism caused this behavior and that he doesn't remember. It's a good thing that the women remember. They often do.

Sexual harassment is particularly volatile because it often fuses two levels 40
of power: the power of employers over employees and the power of men over women. Thus what may be said or intended as a man to a woman is also experienced in the context of superior and subordinate, or vice versa. Sexual harassment in the workplace results from men using their public position to demand or exact social relationships. It is the confusion of public and private, bringing together two arenas of men's power over women. Not only are men in positions of power in the workplace, but we are socialized to be the sexual initiators and to see sexual prowess as a confirmation of masculinity.

Sexual harassment is also a way to remind women that they are not yet equals in the workplace, that they really don't belong there. Harassment is most frequent in those occupations and workplaces where women are new and in the minority, like surgeons, firefighters, and investment bankers. "Men see women as invading a masculine environment," says Louise Fitzgerald, a University of Illinois psychologist. "These are guys whose sexual harassment has nothing whatever to do with sex. They're trying to scare women off a male preserve."

When the power of men is augmented by the power of employer over employee, it is easy to understand how humiliating and debilitating sexual harassment can be, and how individual women would be frightened about seeking redress. The workplace is not a level playing field. Subordinates rarely have the resources to complain against managers, whatever the problem.

Some men were confused by Professor Hill's charges, others furious about sexual harassment because it feels as though women are changing the rules. What used to be routine behavior for men in the workplace is now being called sexual harassment. "Clarence Thomas didn't do anything wrong that any American male hasn't done," commented Dale Whitcomb, a thirty-two-year-old machinist. How right he was. The fact that two-thirds of men surveyed said they would be complimented if they were propositioned by a woman at work gives some idea of the vast gulf between women's and men's perceptions of workplace sexual conduct.

Although men surely do benefit from sexual harassment, I believe that we also have a stake in ending it. First, our ability to form positive and productive relationships with women colleagues in the workplace is undermined by it. So long as sexual harassment is a daily occurrence and women are afraid of their superiors in the workplace, innocent men's behaviors may be misinterpreted. Second, men's ability to develop social and sexual relationships that are both ethical and exciting is also compromised. If a male boss dates a subordinate, can he really trust that the reason she is with him is because she *wants* to be? Or will there always be a lingering doubt that she is there because she is afraid not to be or because she seeks to please him because of his position?

Currently, law firms and corporations all over the country are scrambling 45
to implement sexual harassment policies, to make sure that sexual harassment will be recognized and punished. But our challenge is greater than admonition and post hoc counseling. Our challenge will be to prevent sexual harassment *before* it happens. And that means working with men. Men must come to see that these are not women who happen to be in the workplace (where, by this logic, they actually don't belong), but workers who happen to be women. And we'll need to change the meaning of success so that men don't look back at their careers when they retire and wonder what it was all for, whether any of it was worth it. Again, we'll need to change the definition of masculinity, dislodging it from these misshapen public enactments, including the capacity to embrace others as equals within it, because of an inner security and confidence that can last a lifetime. It is more important than ever to begin to listen to women, to listen with a compassion that understands that women's and men's experiences are different, and an understanding that men, too, can benefit from the elimination of sexual harassment.

Engaging the Text

1. Kimmel's opening statement is that "the 1990s may be remembered as the decade in which America took a crash course on male sexuality." To what extent do you think this is true? What has America really learned, and when, where, and how?
2. Discuss what Kimmel means when he says that "it's been women, not men, who are our era's real sexual pioneers" (para. 16) and that "it is women who have changed the rules of sexual conduct" (para. 19). Do you agree?
3. Debate Kimmel's claim that groups bring out the worst in men, perhaps because men fear that they will be "judged a failure as a man in the eyes of other men" (para. 29).
4. What connection does Kimmel make between masculinity and America's "downwardly mobile culture" (para. 32)? Explain why you do, or do not, find his hypothesis plausible.

Exploring Connections

5. Kimmel's explanation of how masculinity is socially constructed echoes Holly Devor's explanation of gender in "Becoming Members of Society" (p. 244). Review both readings to identify what points they make in common. Then analyze how Devor and Kimmel adjust their language, tone, and evidence to suit their different audiences.
6. Analyze Nora Quealey's narrative (p. 253) in light of Kimmel's claims about masculinity and sexual harassment.

7. Review Mike Rose's "'I Just Wanna Be Average'" (p. 33). How well does Kimmel's analysis of male gender roles account for the attitudes and actions of the young men Rose describes?

Extending the Critical Context

8. Find out the definitions and policies at your school concerning sexual harassment. Discuss these in class, paying special attention to Kimmel's claim that most universities "are more interested in adjudicating harassment *after the fact* than in developing mechanisms to prevent it" (para. 4). What mechanisms, if any, exist on your campus to prevent harassment? When were they implemented, and how effective do you think they are?
9. Many people would endorse the goals Kimmel sets out in his closing paragraph. How might some of these be achieved?

Sexism and Misogyny: Who Takes the Rap?

BELL HOOKS

This essay links Jane Campion's Academy Award–winning film The Piano *to "gangsta rap" by such artists as Snoop Doggy Dogg. While this may seem an unlikely combination, bell hooks argues that these seemingly different artistic expressions arise from a single sexist ideology. Without absolving rappers, she "contextualizes" their sexism, viewing it from a broader perspective. This perspective might just transform the way you see rap music, not to mention* The Piano. *bell hooks is the pen name of Gloria Watkins (b. 1952), who teaches English and women's studies at Oberlin College.* Ain't I a Woman: Black Women and Feminism, *one of her several books on race and feminism, was named one of the "twenty most influential women's books of the last twenty years" in a* Publishers Weekly *poll. The essay reprinted here appeared in* Z Magazine *in February 1994.*

For the past several months white mainstream media has been calling me to hear my views on gangsta rap. Whether major television networks, or small independent radio shows, they seek me out for the black and feminist "take" on the issue. After I have my say, I am never called back, never invited to do the television shows or the radio spots. I suspect they call, confident that when we talk they will hear the hard-core "feminist" trash of gangsta rap. When they encounter instead the hard-core feminist critique of white-supremacist capitalist patriarchy, they lose interest.

To white-dominated mass media, the controversy over gangsta rap makes great spectacle. Besides the exploitation of these issues to attract audiences, a central motivation for highlighting gangsta rap continues to be the sensationalist drama of demonizing black youth culture in general and the contributions of young black men in particular. It is a contemporary remake of *Birth of a Nation*[1] only this time we are encouraged to believe it is not just vulnerable white womanhood that risks destruction by black hands but everyone. When I counter this demonization of black males by insisting that gangsta rap does not appear in a cultural vacuum, but, rather, is expressive of the cultural crossing, mixings, and engagement of black youth culture with the values, attitudes, and concerns of the white majority, some folks stop listening.

The sexist, misogynist,[2] patriarchal[3] ways of thinking and behaving that are glorified in gangsta rap are a reflection of the prevailing values in our society, values created and sustained by white-supremacist capitalist patriarchy. As the crudest and most brutal expression of sexism, misogynistic attitudes tend to be portrayed by the dominant culture as an expression of male deviance. In reality they are part of a sexist continuum, necessary for the maintenance of patriarchal social order. While patriarchy and sexism continue to be the political and cultural norm in our society, feminist movement has created a climate where crude expressions of male domination are called into question, especially if they are made by men in power. It is useful to think of misogyny as a field that must be labored in and maintained both to sustain patriarchy but also to serve as an ideological antifeminist backlash. And what better group to labor on this "plantation" than young black men.

To see gansta rap as a reflection of dominant values in our culture rather than as an aberrant "pathological" standpoint does not mean that a rigorous feminist critique of the sexism and misogyny expressed in this music is not needed. Without a doubt black males, young and old, must be held politically accountable for their sexism. Yet this critique must always be contextualized or we risk making it appear that the behaviors this thinking supports and condones—rape, male violence against women, etc.—is a black male thing. And this is what is happening. Young black males are forced to take the "heat" for encouraging, via their music, the hatred of and violence against women that is a central core of patriarchy.

Witness the recent piece by Brent Staples in the *New York Times* titled 5
"The Politics of Gangster Rap: A Music Celebrating Murder and Misogyny."

[1]*Birth of a Nation:* 1915 silent movie by D. W. Griffith that has been acclaimed as one of America's greatest films and condemned as a piece of racist propaganda.

[2]*misogynist:* Women-hating.

[3]*patriarchal:* Describing a system in which authority and power belong primarily to males.

Defining the turf, Staples writes: "For those who haven't caught up, gangster rap is that wildly successful music in which all women are 'bitches' and 'whores' and young men kill each other for sport." No mention of white-supremacist capitalist patriarchy in this piece, not a word about the cultural context that would need to exist for young males to be socialized to think differently about gender. Staples assumes that black males are writing their lyrics off in the "jungle," away from the impact of mainstream socialization and desire. At no point in his piece does he ask why huge audiences, especially young white male consumers, are so turned on by this music, by the misogyny and sexism, by the brutality. Where is the anger and rage at females expressed in this music coming from, the glorification of all acts of violence? These are the difficult questions that Staples feels no need to answer.

One cannot answer them honestly without placing accountability on larger structures of domination and the individuals (often white, usually male but not always) who are hierarchically placed to maintain and perpetuate the values that uphold these exploitative and oppressive systems. That means taking a critical look at the politics of hedonistic[4] consumerism, the values of the men and women who produce gangsta rap. It would mean considering the seduction of young black males who find that they can make more money producing lyrics that promote violence, sexism, and misogyny than with any other content. How many disenfranchised black males would not surrender to expressing virulent forms of sexism, if they knew the rewards would be unprecedented material power and fame?

More than anything gangsta rap celebrates the world of the "material," the dog-eat-dog world where you do what you gotta do to make it. In this worldview, killing is necessary for survival. Significantly, the logic here is a crude expression of the logic of white-supremacist capitalist patriarchy. In his new book *Sexy Dressing Etc.* privileged white male law professor Duncan Kennedy gives what he calls "a set of general characterizations of U.S. culture" explaining that "It is individual (cowboys), material (gangsters), and philistine.[5]" Using this general description of mainstream culture would lead us to place "gangsta rap" not on the margins of what this nation is about, but at the center. Rather than being viewed as a subversion or disruption of the norm we would need to see it as an embodiment of the norm.

That viewpoint was graphically highlighted in the film *Menace II Society*, which dramatized not only young black males killing for sport, but also mass audiences voyeuristically watching and, in many cases, "enjoying" the kill. Significantly, at one point in the movie we see that the young black males have learned their "gangsta" values from watching television and movies — shows where white male gangsters are center stage. This scene undermines any notion of "essentialist" blackness that would have viewers believe the gangsterism these young black males embraced emerged from some unique black cultural experience.

[4]*hedonistic:* Based on the principle that pleasure is the chief good in life.
[5]*philistine:* Unappreciative of artistic values.

When I interviewed rap artist Ice Cube for *Spin* magazine last year, he talked about the importance of respecting black women and communication across gender. He spoke against male violence against women, even as he lapsed into a justification for anti-woman rap lyrics by insisting on the madonna/whore split where some females "carry" themselves in a manner that determines how they will be treated. When this interview was published, it was cut to nothing. It was a mass-media set-up. Folks (mostly white and male) had thought if the hard-core feminist talked with the hardened black man, sparks would fly; there would be a knock-down, drag-out spectacle. When Brother Cube and I talked to each other with respect about the political, spiritual, and emotional self-determination of black people, it did not make good copy. Clearly folks at the magazine did not get the darky show[6] they were looking for.

After this conversation, and talking with rappers and folks who listen to 10
rap, it became clear that while black male sexism is a serious problem in our communities and in black music, some of the more misogynist lyrics were there to stir up controversy and appeal to audiences. Nowhere is this more evident than in Snoop Doggy Dogg's record *Doggystyle.* A black male music and cultural critic called me to ask if I had checked this image out, to share that for one of the first times in his music buying life he felt he was seeing an image so offensive in its sexism and misogyny that he did not want to take that image home. That image (complete with doghouse, beware-the-dog sign, with a naked black female head in a doghouse, naked butt sticking out) was reproduced, "uncritically," in the November 29, 1993, issue of *Time* magazine. The positive music review of this album, written by Christopher John Farley and titled "Gangsta Rap, Doggystyle," makes no mention of sexism and misogyny, makes no reference to the cover. I wonder if a naked white female body had been inside the doghouse, presumably waiting to be fucked from behind, if *Time* would have reproduced an image of the cover along with their review. When I see the pornographic cartoon that graces the cover of *Doggystyle,* I do not think simply about the sexism and misogyny of young black men, I think about the sexist and misogynist politics of the powerful white adult men and women (and folks of color) who helped produce and market this album.

In her book *Misogynies* Joan Smith shares her sense that while most folks are willing to acknowledge unfair treatment of women, discrimination on the basis of gender, they are usually reluctant to admit that hatred of women is encouraged because it helps maintain the structure of male dominance. Smith suggests: "Misogyny wears many guises, reveals itself in different forms which are dictated by class, wealth, education, race, religion and other factors, but its chief characteristic is its pervasiveness." This point reverberated in my mind when I saw Jane Campion's widely acclaimed film *The Piano,* which I saw in the midst of mass-media focus on sexism and

[6]*darky show:* Demeaning term for a show featuring Blacks, such as a minstrel show.

misogyny in "gangsta rap." I had been told by many friends in the art world that this was "an incredible film, a truly compelling love story, etc." Their responses were echoed by numerous positive reviews. No one speaking about this film mentions misogyny and sexism or white-supremacist capitalist patriarchy.

The nineteenth-century world of the white invasion of New Zealand is utterly romanticized in this film (complete with docile happy darkies — Maori natives — who appear to have not a care in the world). And when the film suggests they care about white colonizers digging up the graves of their dead ancestors, it is the sympathetic poor white male who comes to the rescue. Just as the conquest of natives and lands is glamorized in this film, so is the conquest of femininity, personified by white womanhood, by the pale speechless corpselike Scotswoman, Ada, who journeys into this dark wilderness because her father has arranged for her to marry the white colonizer Stewart. Although mute, Ada expresses her artistic ability, the intensity of her vision and feelings, through piano playing. This passion attracts Baines, the illiterate white settler who wears the facial tattoos of the Maori — an act of appropriation that makes him (like the traditional figure of Tarzan) appear both dangerous and romantic. He is Norman Mailer's "white negro," seducing Ada by promising to return the piano that Stewart has exchanged with him for land. The film leads us to believe that Ada's passionate piano playing has been a substitution for repressed eroticism. When she learns to let herself go sexually, she ceases to need the piano. We watch the passionate climax of Baines's seduction as she willingly seeks him sexually. And we watch her husband Stewart in the role of voyeur, standing with dog outside the cabin where they fuck, voyeuristically consuming their pleasure. Rather than being turned off by her love for Baines, it appears to excite Stewart's passion; he longs to possess her all the more. Unable to win her back from Baines, he expresses his rage, rooted in misogyny and sexism, by physically attacking her and chopping off her finger with an ax. This act of male violence takes place with Ada's daughter, Flora, as a witness. Though traumatized by the violence she witnesses, she is still about to follow the white male patriarch's orders and take the bloody finger to Baines, along with the message that each time he sees Ada she will suffer physical mutilation.

Violence against land, natives, and women in this film, unlike that of gangsta rap, is portrayed uncritically, as though it is "natural," the inevitable climax of conflicting passions. The outcome of this violence is positive. Ultimately, the film suggests Stewart's rage was only an expression of irrational sexual jealousy, that he comes to his senses and is able to see "reason." In keeping with male exchange of women, he gives Ada and Flora to Baines. They leave the wilderness. On the voyage home Ada demands that her piano be thrown overboard because it is "soiled," tainted with horrible memories. Surrendering it she lets go of her longing to display passion through artistic expression. A nuclear family now, Baines, Ada, and Flora resettle and live happily-ever-after. Suddenly, patriarchal order is restored. Ada becomes a modest wife, wearing a veil over her mouth so that no one will see her lips struggling to speak words. Flora has no memory of trauma and is a happy child turning somersaults. Baines is in charge, even making Ada a new finger.

The Piano seduces and excites audiences with its uncritical portrayal of sexism and misogyny. Reviewers and audiences alike seem to assume that Campion's gender, as well as her breaking of traditional boundaries that inhibit the advancement of women in film, indicate that her work expresses a feminist standpoint. And, indeed, she does employ feminist "tropes,"[7] even as her work betrays feminist visions of female actualization, celebrates and eroticizes male domination. In Smith's discussion of misogyny she emphasizes that woman-hating is not solely the province of men: "We are all exposed to the prevailing ideology of our culture, and some women learn early on that they can prosper by aping the misogyny of men; these are the women who win provisional favor by denigrating other women, by playing on male prejudices, and by acting the 'man's woman'." Since this is not a documentary film that needs to remain faithful to the ethos of its historical setting, why is it that Campion does not resolve Ada's conflicts by providing us with an imaginary landscape where a woman can express passionate artistic commitment and find fulfillment in a passionate relationship? This would be no more farfetched than her cinematic portrayal of Ada's miraculous transformation from muteness into speech. Ultimately, Campion's *The Piano* advances the sexist assumption that heterosexual women will give up artistic practice to find "true love." That "positive" surrender is encouraged by the "romantic" portrayal of sexism and misogyny.

15 While I do not think that young black male rappers have been rushing in droves to see *The Piano,* there is a bond between those folks involved with high culture who celebrate and condone the sexist ideas and values upheld in this film and those who celebrate and condone "gangsta rap." Certainly Kennedy's description of the United States as a "cowboy, gangster, philistine" culture would also accurately describe the culture evoked in *The Piano.* Popular movies that are seen by young black males, for example *Indecent Proposal, Mad Dog and Glory, True Romance,* and *One False Move,* all eroticize male domination expressed via the exchange of women, as well as the subjugation of other men, through brutal violence.

Contrary to a racist white imagination which assumes that most young black males, especially those who are poor, live in a self-created cultural vacuum, uninfluenced by mainstream, cultural values, it is the application of those values, largely learned through passive uncritical consumption of mass media, that is revealed in "gangsta rap." Brent Staples is willing to challenge the notion that "urban primitivism is romantic" when it suggests that black males become "real men" by displaying the will to do violence, yet he remains resolutely silent about that world of privileged white culture that has

[7]*trope:* Originally a figure of speech such as metaphor or irony; here, "feminist 'tropes' " refers to language or visual images which suggest women's power or independence.

historically romanticized primitivism and eroticized male violence. Contemporary films like *Reservoir Dogs* and *Bad Lieutenant* celebrate urban primitivism and many less well done films (*Trespass, Rising Sun*) create and/or exploit the cultural demand for depictions of hard-core blacks who are willing to kill for sport.

To take "gangsta rap" to task for its sexism and misogyny while critically accepting and perpetuating those expressions of that ideology which reflect bourgeois standards (no rawness, no vulgarity) is not to call for a transformation of the culture of patriarchy. Ironically, many black male ministers, themselves sexist and misogynist, are leading the attacks against gangsta rap. Like the mainstream world that supports white-supremacist capitalist patriarchy, they are most concerned with calling attention to the vulgar obscene portrayals of women to advance the cause of censorship. For them, rethinking and challenging sexism, both in the dominant culture and in black life, is not the issue.

Mainstream white culture is not concerned about black male sexism and misogyny, particularly when it mainly is unleashed against black women and children. It is concerned when young white consumers utilize black vernacular popular culture to disrupt bourgeois values, whether it be the young white boy who expresses his rage at his mother by aping black male vernacular speech (a true story) or the masses of young white males (and middle-class men of color) seeking to throw off the constraints of bourgeois[8] bondage who actively assert in their domestic households via acts of aggression their rejection of the call to be "civilized." These are the audiences who feel such a desperate need for gangsta rap. It is much easier to attack gangsta rap than to confront the culture that produces that need.

Gangsta rap is part of the antifeminist backlash that is the rage right now. When young black males labor in the plantations of misogyny and sexism to produce gangsta rap, their right to speak this violence and be materially rewarded is extended to them by white-supremacist capitalist patriarchy. Far from being an expression of their "manhood," it is an expression of their own subjugation and humiliation by more powerful, less-visible forces of patriarchal gangsterism. They give voice to the brutal raw anger and rage against women that it is taboo for "civilized" adult men to speak. No wonder then that they have the task of tutoring the young, teaching them to eroticize and enjoy the brutal expressions of that rage (teaching them language and acts) before they learn to cloak it in middle-class decorum or Robert Bly[9] style reclaimings of lost manhood. The tragedy for young black males is that they are so easily duped by a vision of manhood that can only lead to their destruction.

[8]*bourgeois:* Middle-class, with the connotations here of blandness, materialism, and mediocrity.

[9]*Robert Bly:* Contemporary poet and writer best known as a central figure in the contemporary "men's movement."

Feminist critiques of the sexism and misogyny in gangsta rap, and in all aspects of popular culture, must continue to be bold and fierce. Black females must not be duped into supporting shit that hurts us under the guise of standing beside our men. If black men are betraying us through acts of male violence, we save ourselves and the race by resisting. Yet, our feminist critiques of black male sexism fail as meaningful political intervention if they seek to demonize black males and do not recognize that our revolutionary work is to transform white-supremacist capitalist patriarchy in the multiple areas of our lives where it is made manifest, whether in gangsta rap, the black church, or the Clinton administration. 20

Engaging the Text

1. Having read the full essay, return to the first paragraph and explain what bell hooks thinks the media expected her to say about gangsta rap and why they didn't want to hear what she *did* have to say.
2. Examine bell hooks's claim that brutal sexism is not "male deviance" (para. 3) but rather "part of a sexist continuum, necessary for the maintenance of patriarchal social order." How does this hypothesis account for the attitudes of the young Black men who produce gangsta rap?
3. Why does bell hooks discuss *The Piano* in the same essay with gangsta rap? Summarize in your own words the argument that links them, and discuss whether or not you find the argument persuasive.

Exploring Connections

4. To what extent do you think bell hooks's political and cultural agendas would be compatible with those of Michael S. Kimmel as outlined in the previous essay (p. 259)? Identify specific areas in which the two writers' ideas about our culture are similar, and specific areas where they seem to disagree.
5. This chapter opens with a story, "Girl" (p. 241), in which a mother gives her daughter advice and teaches her how to live. Based on this essay, what do you think bell hooks would like to teach young Black women? What about young Black men? What about other young people?

Extending the Critical Context

6. Watch *The Piano* and test bell hooks's claims. To what extent do you agree with bell hooks that the film "excites audiences with its uncritical portrayal of sexism and misogyny" (para. 14)? If you had seen the film before, did reading "Sexism and Misogyny" radically change your understanding of it or your reaction to it?
7. Carefully watch and listen to some current rap videos. How prevalent are sexism and misogyny? Do you find anything in these performances to support or contradict bell hooks's analysis?

The Story of My Body

JUDITH ORTIZ COFER

Accepting the idea that gender roles are socially constructed might not be too difficult, but it may come as a shock to realize that even the way we see our bodies is filtered through the lens of social values and beliefs. In this personal essay, Judith Ortiz Cofer reflects on the different roles her own body has assumed in different contexts and cultures—the ways that different societies have "read" the meanings of her physical appearance. The story of her body becomes, to some extent, the story of her life, and woven into the tale are intriguing comments on gender and on cross-cultural perception. A native of Puerto Rico, Ortiz Cofer (b. 1952) now lives in Georgia and is an associate instructor at the Bread Loaf Writers' Conference. Her publications include The Line of the Sun *(1989), a novel;* Silent Dancing *(1990), a collection of poetry and prose; and* The Latin Deli *(1993), in which "The Story of My Body" first appeared.*

Migration is the story of my body.
—VICTOR HERNÁNDEZ CRUZ

Skin

I was born a white girl in Puerto Rico but became a brown girl when I came to live in the United States. My Puerto Rican relatives called me tall; at the American school, some of my rougher classmates called me Skinny Bones, and the Shrimp because I was the smallest member of my classes all through grammar school until high school, when the midget Gladys was given the honorary post of front row center for class pictures and scorekeeper, bench warmer, in P.E. I reached my full stature of five feet in sixth grade.

I started out life as a pretty baby and learned to be a pretty girl from a pretty mother. Then at ten years of age I suffered one of the worst cases of chicken pox I have ever heard of. My entire body, including the inside of my ears and in between my toes, was covered with pustules which in a fit of panic at my appearance I scratched off my face, leaving permanent scars. A cruel school nurse told me I would always have them—tiny cuts that looked as if a mad cat had plunged its claws deep into my skin. I grew my hair long and hid behind it for the first years of my adolescence. This was when I learned to be invisible.

Color

In the animal world it indicates danger: the most colorful creatures are often the most poisonous. Color is also a way to attract and seduce a mate. In the human world color triggers many more complex and often deadly reactions. As a Puerto Rican girl born of "white" parents, I spent the first years of my life hearing people refer to me as *blanca,* white. My mother insisted that I protect myself from the intense island sun because I was more prone to sunburn than some of my darker, *trigueño*[1] playmates. People were always commenting within my hearing about how my black hair contrasted so nicely with my "pale" skin. I did not think of the color of my skin consciously except when I heard the adults talking about complexion. It seems to me that the subject is much more common in the conversation of mixed-race peoples than in mainstream United States society, where it is a touchy and sometimes even embarrassing topic to discuss, except in a political context. In Puerto Rico I heard many conversations about skin color. A pregnant woman could say, "I hope my baby doesn't turn out *prieto*" (slang for "dark" or "black") "like my husband's grandmother, although she was a good-looking *negra*[2] in her time." I am a combination of both, being olive-skinned—lighter than my mother yet darker than my fair-skinned father. In America, I am a person of color, obviously a Latina. On the Island I have been called everything from a *paloma blanca,*[3] after the song (by a black suitor), to *la gringa.*[4]

My first experience of color prejudice occurred in a supermarket in Paterson, New Jersey. It was Christmastime, and I was eight or nine years old. There was a display of toys in the store where I went two or three times a day to buy things for my mother, who never made lists but sent for milk, cigarettes, a can of this or that, as she remembered from hour to hour. I enjoyed being trusted with money and walking half a city block to the new, modern grocery store. It was owned by three good-looking Italian brothers. I liked the younger one with the crew-cut blond hair. The two older ones watched me and the other Puerto Rican kids as if they thought we were going to steal something. The oldest one would sometimes even try to hurry me with my purchases, although part of my pleasure in these expeditions came from looking at everything in the well-stocked aisles. I was also teaching myself to read English by sounding out the labels in packages: L&M cigarettes, Borden's homogenized milk, Red Devil potted ham, Nestle's chocolate mix, Quaker oats, Bustelo coffee, Wonder bread, Colgate toothpaste, Ivory soap, and Goya (makers of products used in Puerto Rican dishes)

[1]*trigueño:* Brown-skinned.
[2]*negra:* Black.
[3]*paloma blanca:* White dove.
[4]*la gringa:* A white, non-Latina woman.

everything — these are some of the brand names that taught me nouns. Several times this man had come up to me, wearing his blood-stained butcher's apron, and towering over me had asked in a harsh voice whether there was something he could help me find. On the way out I would glance at the younger brother who ran one of the registers and he would often smile and wink at me.

It was the mean brother who first referred to me as "colored." It was a 5
few days before Christmas, and my parents had already told my brother and me that since we were in Los Estados[5] now, we would get our presents on December 25 instead of Los Reyes, Three Kings Day, when gifts are exchanged in Puerto Rico. We were to give them a wish list that they would take to Santa Claus, who apparently lived in the Macy's store downtown — at least that's where we had caught a glimpse of him when we went shopping. Since my parents were timid about entering the fancy store, we did not approach the huge man in the red suit. I was not interested in sitting on a stranger's lap anyway. But I did covet Susie, the talking schoolteacher doll that was displayed in the center aisle of the Italian brothers' supermarket. She talked when you pulled a string on her back. Susie had a limited repertoire of three sentences: I think she could say: "Hello, I'm Susie Schoolteacher," "Two plus two is four," and one other thing I cannot remember. The day the older brother chased me away, I was reaching to touch Susie's blond curls. I had been told many times, as most children have, not to touch anything in a store that I was not buying. But I had been looking at Susie for weeks. In my mind, she was my doll. After all, I had put her on my Christmas wish list. The moment is frozen in my mind as if there were a photograph of it on file. It was not a turning point, a disaster, or an earth-shaking revelation. It was simply the first time I considered — if naively — the meaning of skin color in human relations.

I reached to touch Susie's hair. It seems to me that I had to get on tiptoe, since the toys were stacked on a table and she sat like a princess on top of the fancy box she came in. Then I heard the booming "Hey, kid, what do you think you're doing!" spoken very loudly from the meat counter. I felt caught, although I knew I was not doing anything criminal. I remember not looking at the man, but standing there, feeling humiliated because I knew everyone in the store must have heard him yell at me. I felt him approach, and when I knew he was behind me, I turned around to face the bloody butcher's apron. His large chest was at my eye level. He blocked my way. I started to run out of the place, but even as I reached the door I heard him shout after me: "Don't come in here unless you gonna buy something. You PR kids put your dirty hands on stuff. You always look dirty. But maybe dirty brown is your natural color." I heard him laugh and someone else too in the back. Outside in the sunlight I looked at my hands. My nails needed a little cleaning as they always did, since I liked to paint with watercolors, but I took

[5]*Los Estados:* "The States" — that is, the United States.

a bath every night. I thought the man was dirtier than I was in his stained apron. He was also always sweaty — it showed in big yellow circles under his shirt-sleeves. I sat on the front steps of the apartment building where we lived and looked closely at my hands, which showed the only skin I could see, since it was bitter cold and I was wearing my quilted play coat, dungarees, and a knitted navy cap of my father's. I was not pink like my friend Charlene and her sister Kathy, who had blue eyes and light brown hair. My skin is the color of the coffee my grandmother made, which was half milk, *leche con café* rather than *café con leche.*[6] My mother is the opposite mix. She has a lot of café in her color. I could not understand how my skin looked like dirt to the supermarket man.

I went in and washed my hands thoroughly with soap and hot water, and borrowing my mother's nail file, I cleaned the crusted watercolors from underneath my nails. I was pleased with the results. My skin was the same color as before, but I knew I was clean. Clean enough to run my fingers through Susie's fine gold hair when she came home to me.

Size

My mother is barely four feet eleven inches in height, which is average for women in her family. When I grew to five feet by age twelve, she was amazed and began to use the word tall to describe me, as in "Since you are tall, this dress will look good on you." As with the color of my skin, I didn't consciously think about my height or size until other people made an issue of it. It is around the preadolescent years that in America the games children play for fun become fierce competitions where everyone is out to "prove" they are better than others. It was in the playground and sports fields that my size-related problems began. No matter how familiar the story is, every child who is the last chosen for a team knows the torment of waiting to be called up. At the Paterson, New Jersey, public schools that I attended, the volleyball or softball game was the metaphor for the battlefield of life to the inner city kids — the black kids versus the Puerto Rican kids, the whites versus the blacks versus the Puerto Rican kids; and I was 4F,[7] skinny, short, bespectacled, and apparently impervious to the blood thirst that drove many of my classmates to play ball as if their lives depended on it. Perhaps they did. I would rather be reading a book than sweating, grunting, and running the risk of pain and injury. I simply did not see the point in competitive sports. My main form of exercise then was walking to the library, many city blocks away from my barrio.

Still, I wanted to be wanted. I wanted to be chosen for the team. Physical education was compulsory, a class where you were actually given a grade.

[6]*leche con café . . . café con leche:* Milk with coffee (light brown) . . . coffee with milk (dark brown).

[7]*4F:* Draft-board classification meaning "unfit for military service;" hence, not physically fit.

On my mainly all A report card, the C for compassion I always received from the P.E. teachers shamed me the same as a bad grade in a real class. Invariably, my father would say: "How can you make a low grade for *playing games?*" He did not understand. Even if I had managed to make a hit (it never happened) or get the ball over that ridiculously high net, I already had a reputation as a "shrimp," a hopeless nonathlete. It was an area where the girls who didn't like me for one reason or another — mainly because I did better than they on academic subjects — could lord it over me; the playing field was the place where even the smallest girl could make me feel powerless and inferior. I instinctively understood the politics even then; how the *not* choosing me until the teacher forced one of the team captains to call my name was a coup of sorts — there, you little show-off, tomorrow you can beat us in spelling and geography, but this afternoon you are the loser. Or perhaps those were only my own bitter thoughts as I sat or stood in the sidelines while the big girls were grabbed like fish and I, the little brown tadpole, was ignored until Teacher looked over in my general direction and shouted, "Call Ortiz," or, worse, "Somebody's *got* to take her."

10 No wonder I read Wonder Woman comics and had Legion of Super Heroes daydreams. Although I wanted to think of myself as "intellectual," my body was demanding that I notice it. I saw the little swelling around my once-flat nipples, the fine hairs growing in secret places; but my knees were still bigger than my thighs, and I always wore long- or half-sleeve blouses to hide my bony upper arms. I wanted flesh on my bones — a thick layer of it. I saw a new product advertised on TV. Wate-On. They showed skinny men and women before and after taking the stuff, and it was a transformation like the ninety-seven-pound-weakling-turned-into-Charles-Atlas ads that I saw on the back covers of my comic books. The Wate-On was very expensive. I tried to explain my need for it in Spanish to my mother, but it didn't translate very well, even to my ears — and she said with a tone of finality, eat more of my good food and you'll get fat — anybody can get fat. Right. Except me. I was going to have to join a circus someday as Skinny Bones, the woman without flesh.

Wonder Woman was stacked. She had a cleavage framed by the spread wings of a golden eagle and a muscular body that has become fashionable with women only recently. But since I wanted a body that would serve me in P.E., hers was my ideal. The breasts were an indulgence I allowed myself. Perhaps the daydreams of bigger girls were more glamorous, since our ambitions are filtered through our needs, but I wanted first a powerful body. I daydreamed of leaping up above the gray landscape of the city to where the sky was clear and blue, and in anger and self-pity, I fantasized about scooping my enemies up by their hair from the playing fields and dumping them on a barren asteroid. I would put the P.E. teachers each on their own rock in space too, where they would be the loneliest people in the universe, since I knew they had no "inner resources," no imagination, and in outer space, there would be no air for them to fill their deflated volleyballs with. In my mind all P.E. teachers have blended into one large spiky-haired woman with a whistle on a string around her neck and a volleyball under one arm. My Wonder Woman fantasies of revenge were a source of comfort to me in my early career as a shrimp.

I was saved from more years of P.E. torment by the fact that in my sophomore year of high school I transferred to a school where the midget, Gladys, was the focal point of interest for the people who must rank according to size. Because her height was considered a handicap, there was an unspoken rule about mentioning size around Gladys, but of course, there was no need to say anything. Gladys knew her place: front row center in class photographs. I gladly moved to the left or to the right of her, as far as I could without leaving the picture completely.

Looks

Many photographs were taken of me as a baby by my mother to send to my father, who was stationed overseas during the first two years of my life. With the army in Panama when I was born, he later traveled often on tours of duty with the navy. I was a healthy, pretty baby. Recently, I read that people are drawn to big-eyed round-faced creatures, like puppies, kittens, and certain other mammals and marsupials, koalas, for example, and, of course, infants. I was all eyes, since my head and body, even as I grew older, remained thin and small-boned. As a young child I got a lot of attention from my relatives and many other people we met in our barrio. My mother's beauty may have had something to do with how much attention we got from strangers in stores and on the street. I can imagine it. In the pictures I have seen of us together, she is a stunning young woman by Latino standards: long, curly black hair, and round curves in a compact frame. From her I learned how to move, smile, and talk like an attractive woman. I remember going into a bodega[8] for our groceries and being given candy by the proprietor as a reward for being *bonita,* pretty.

I can see in the photographs, and I also remember, that I was dressed in the pretty clothes, the stiff, frilly dresses, with layers of crinolines underneath, the glossy patent leather shoes, and, on special occasions, the skull-hugging little hats and the white gloves that were popular in the late fifties and early sixties. My mother was proud of my looks, although I was a bit too thin. She could dress me up like a doll and take me by the hand to visit relatives, or go to the Spanish mass at the Catholic church and show me off. How was I to know that she and the others who called me "pretty" were representatives of an aesthetic that would not apply when I went out into the mainstream world of school?

In my Paterson, New Jersey, public schools there were still quite a few 15
white children, although the demographics of the city were changing rapidly. The original waves of Italian and Irish immigrants, silk-mill workers, and

[8]*bodega:* Market.

laborers in the cloth industries had been "assimilated." Their children were now the middle-class parents of my peers. Many of them moved their children to the Catholic schools that proliferated enough to have leagues of basketball teams. The names I recall hearing still ring in my ears: Don Bosco High versus St. Mary's High, St. Joseph's versus St. John's. Later I too would be transferred to the safer environment of a Catholic school. But I started school at Public School Number 11. I came there from Puerto Rico, thinking myself a pretty girl, and found that the hierarchy for popularity was as follows: pretty white girl, pretty Jewish girl, pretty Puerto Rican girl, pretty black girl. Drop the last two categories; teachers were too busy to have more than one favorite per class, and it was simply understood that if there was a big part in the school play, or any competition where the main qualification was "presentability" (such as escorting a school visitor to or from the principal's office), the classroom's public address speaker would be requesting the pretty and/or nice-looking white boy or girl. By the time I was in the sixth grade, I was sometimes called by the principal to represent my class because I dressed neatly (I knew this from a progress report sent to my mother, which I translated for her) and because all the "presentable" white girls had moved to the Catholic schools (I later surmised this part). But I was still not one of the popular girls with the boys. I remember one incident where I stepped out into the playground in my baggy gym shorts and one Puerto Rican boy said to the other: "What do you think?" The other one answered: "Her face is OK, but look at the toothpick legs." The next best thing to a compliment I got was when my favorite male teacher, while handing out the class pictures, commented that with my long neck and delicate features I resembled the movie star Audrey Hepburn. But the Puerto Rican boys had learned to respond to a fuller figure: long necks and a perfect little nose were not what they looked for in a girl. That is when I decided I was a "brain." I did not settle into the role easily. I was nearly devastated by what the chicken pox episode had done to my self-image. But I looked into the mirror less often after I was told that I would always have scars on my face, and I hid behind my long black hair and my books.

After the problems at the public school got to the point where even nonconfrontational little me got beaten up several times, my parents enrolled me at St. Joseph's High School. I was then a minority of one among the Italian and Irish kids. But I found several good friends there — other girls who took their studies seriously. We did our homework together and talked about the Jackies. The Jackies were two popular girls, one blonde and the other red-haired, who had women's bodies. Their curves showed even in the blue jumper uniforms with straps that we all wore. The blonde Jackie would often let one of the straps fall off her shoulder, and although she, like all of us, wore a white blouse underneath, all the boys stared at her arm. My friends and I talked about this and and practiced letting our straps fall off our shoulders. But it wasn't the same without breasts or hips.

My final two and a half years of high school were spent in Augusta,

Georgia, where my parents moved our family in search of a more peaceful environment. Then we became part of a little community of our army-connected relatives and friends. School was yet another matter. I was enrolled in a huge school of nearly two thousand students that had just that year been forced to integrate. There were two black girls and there was me. I did extremely well academically. As to my social life, it was, for the most part, uneventful — yet it is in my memory blighted by one incident. In my junior year, I became wildly infatuated with a pretty white boy. I'll call him Ted. Oh, he was pretty: yellow hair that fell over his forehead, a smile to die for — and he was a great dancer. I watched him at Teen Town, the youth center at the base where all the military brats gathered on Saturday nights. My father had retired from the navy, and we had all our base privileges — one other reason we moved to Augusta. Ted looked like an angel to me. I worked on him for a year before he asked me out. This meant maneuvering to be within the periphery of his vision at every possible occasion. I took the long way to my classes in school just to pass by his locker, I went to football games, which I detested, and I danced (I too was a good dancer) in front of him at Teen Town — this took some fancy footwork, since it involved subtly moving my partner toward the right spot on the dance floor. When Ted finally approached me, "A Million to One" was playing on the jukebox, and when he took me into his arms, the odds suddenly turned in my favor. He asked me to go to a school dance the following Saturday. I said yes, breathlessly. I said yes, but there were obstacles to surmount at home. My father did not allow me to date casually. I was allowed to go to major events like a prom or a concert with a boy who had been properly screened. There was such a boy in my life, a neighbor who wanted to be a Baptist missionary and was practicing his anthropological skills on my family. If I was desperate to go somewhere and needed a date, I'd resort to Gary. This is the type of religious nut that Gary was: when the school bus did not show up one day, he put his hands over his face and prayed to Christ to get us a way to get to school. Within ten minutes a mother in a station wagon, on her way to town, stopped to ask why we weren't in school. Gary informed her that the Lord had sent her just in time to find us a way to get there in time for roll call. He assumed that I was impressed. Gary was even good-looking in a bland sort of way, but he kissed me with his lips tightly pressed together. I think Gary probably ended up marrying a native woman from wherever he may have gone to preach the Gospel according to Paul. She probably believes that all white men pray to God for transportation and kiss with their mouths closed. But it was Ted's mouth, his whole beautiful self, that concerned me in those days. I knew my father would say no to our date, but I planned to run away from home if necessary. I told my mother how important this date was. I cajoled and pleaded with her from Sunday to Wednesday. She listened to my arguments and must have heard the note of desperation in my voice. She said very gently to me: "You better be ready for disappointment." I did not ask what she meant. I did not want her fears for me to taint my happiness.

I asked her to tell my father about my date. Thursday at breakfast my father looked at me across the table with his eyebrows together. My mother looked at him with her mouth set in a straight line. I looked down at my bowl of cereal. Nobody said anything. Friday I tried on every dress in my closet. Ted would be picking me up at six on Saturday: dinner and then the sock hop at school. Friday night I was in my room doing my nails or something else in preparation for Saturday (I know I groomed myself nonstop all week) when the telephone rang. I ran to get it. It was Ted. His voice sounded funny when he said my name, so funny that I felt compelled to ask: "Is something wrong?" Ted blurted it all out without a preamble. His father had asked who he was going out with. Ted had told him my name. "Ortiz? That's Spanish, isn't it?" the father had asked. Ted had told him yes, then shown him my picture in the yearbook. Ted's father had shaken his head. No. Ted would not be taking me out. Ted's father had known Puerto Ricans in the army. He had lived in New York City while studying architecture and had seen how the spics lived. Like rats. Ted repeated his father's words to me as if I should understand *his* predicament when I heard why he was breaking our date. I don't remember what I said before hanging up. I do recall the darkness of my room that sleepless night and the heaviness of my blanket in which I wrapped myself like a shroud. And I remember my parents' respect for my pain and their gentleness toward me that weekend. My mother did not say "I warned you," and I was grateful for her understanding silence.

In college, I suddenly became an "exotic" woman to the men who had survived the popularity wars in high school, who were not practicing to be worldly: they had to act liberal in their politics, in their lifestyles, and in the women they went out with. I dated heavily for a while, then married young. I had discovered that I needed stability more than social life. I had brains for sure and some talent in writing. These facts were a constant in my life. My skin color, my size, and my appearance were variables — things that were judged according to my current self-image, the aesthetic values of the time, the places I was in, and the people I met. My studies, later my writing, the respect of people who saw me as an individual person they cared about, these were the criteria for my sense of self-worth that I would concentrate on in my adult life.

Engaging the Text

1. Ortiz Cofer writes a good deal about how people perceived her and about how their perceptions changed according to time and place. Trace the stages Ortiz Cofer lived through, citing examples from the text, and discuss in each instance how her self-image was affected by people around her. What main point(s) do you think Ortiz Cofer may be trying to make with this narrative?
2. Which of the difficulties Ortiz Cofer faces are related specifically to gender (or made more serious by gender)? Do boys face comparable problems?
3. In your opinion, did Ortiz Cofer make the right decisions throughout her story?

Is there anything she or her parents could have done to avoid or resist the various mistreatments she describes?

4. What role do media images play in Ortiz Cofer's story?
5. Was Ortiz Cofer's a happy, healthy family? What were its strengths, and in what ways, if any, did it let her down?
6. Does everyone have a similar story to Ortiz Cofer's, or not? Other people may be overweight, wear braces, mature very early or very late, have big noses or unusual voices, and so on. What, if anything, sets Ortiz Cofer's experience apart from the usual "traumas" of childhood?

Exploring Connections

7. Review Holly Devor's "Becoming Members of Society" (p. 244). How do Ortiz Cofer's experiences support and/or complicate Devor's explanation of gender role socialization?
8. Compare and contrast the young Ortiz Cofer with the young Maxine Hong Kingston in "Silence" (p. 110). What similarities do you see in their circumstances, their personalities, and their strategies for dealing with a less-than-friendly environment? Are there important differences between the two?
9. Several authors in Chapter One, "Learning Power," write about how education cheats girls. Discuss what authors like Myra Sadker and David Sadker (p. 86) and Blythe McVicker Clinchy et al. (p. 115) might say about Ortiz Cofer's experience in the schools. What, if anything, might schools do to reduce the kinds of problems Ortiz Cofer encountered?

Extending the Critical Context

10. In her self-analysis, Ortiz Cofer discusses the "variables" in her physical appearance — the socially determined values that influence her perception of her body. She also reflects on personal "facts" or "constants" — more durable features, like her writing and her need for stability—that contribute to her identity. Write a series of journal entries that tell the story of your own body. What "variables" have influenced your perception of your appearance? What "facts" about yourself have become "constants"?

Appearances

Carmen Vázquez

Have you ever gone for a walk in the evening, ridden a city bus, or gone out dancing? Did these activities make you fear for your life? In this essay, Vázquez writes about what can happen in such everyday situations when the pedestrian, commuter, or dancer is perceived as gay or lesbian. She also discusses some possible causes of homophobia, and she pleads for change. Vázquez (b. 1949) was born in Bayamon, Puerto Rico, and grew up in Harlem, New York. She has been active in the lesbian/gay movement for many years and is currently cochair of the Lesbian Agenda for Action as well as coordinator of Lesbian/Gay Health Services for the San Francisco Department of Public Health. She has published essays and book reviews in a number of publications. "Appearances" comes from an anthology entitled Homophobia: How We All Pay the Price *(1992).*

North of Market Street and east of Twin Peaks, where you can see the white fog mushroom above San Francisco's hills, is a place called the Castro. Gay men, lesbians, and bisexuals stroll leisurely up and down the bustling streets. They jaywalk with abandon. Night and day they fill the cafés and bars, and on weekends they line up for a double feature of vintage classics at their ornate and beloved Castro theater.

The 24 bus line brings people into and out of the Castro. People from all walks of life ride the electric-powered coaches. They come from the opulence of San Francisco's Marina and the squalor of Bayview projects. The very gay Castro is in the middle of its route. Every day, boys in pairs or gangs from either end of the city board the bus for a ride through the Castro and a bit of fun. Sometimes their fun is fulfilled with passionately obscene derision: "Fucking cocksucking faggots." "Dyke cunts." "Diseased butt fuckers." Sometimes, their fun is brutal.

Brian boarded the 24 Divisadero and handed his transfer to the driver one late June night. Epithets were fired at him the moment he turned for a seat. He slid his slight frame into an empty seat next to an old woman with silver blue hair who clutched her handbag and stared straight ahead. Brian stuffed his hands into the pockets of his worn brown bomber jacket and stared with her. He heard the flip of a skateboard in the back. The taunting shouts grew louder. "Faggot!" From the corner of his eye, he saw a beer bottle hurtling past the window and crash on the street. A man in his forties, wearing a Giants baseball cap and warmup jacket, yelled at the driver to stop the bus and get the hoodlums off. The bus driver ignored him and pulled out.

Brian dug his hands deeper into his pockets and clenched his jaw. It was just five stops to the top of the hill. When he got up to move toward the exit, the skate board slammed into his gut and one kick followed another until every boy had got his kick in. Despite the plea of the passengers, the driver never called the police.

5 Brian spent a week in a hospital bed, afraid that he would never walk again. A lawsuit filed by Brian against the city states, "As claimant lay crumpled and bleeding on the floor of the bus, the bus driver tried to force claimant off the bus so that the driver could get off work and go home.

Claimant was severely beaten by a gang of young men on the #24 Divisadero Bus who perceived that he was gay."

On the south side of Market Street, night brings a chill wind and rough trade. On a brisk November night, men with sculptured torsos and thighs wrapped in leather walked with precision. The clamor of steel on the heels of their boots echoed in the darkness. Young men and women walked by the men in leather, who smiled in silence. They admired the studded bracelets on Mickey's wrists, the shine of his flowing hair, and the rise of his laughter. They were, each of them, eager to be among the safety of like company where they could dance with abandon to the pulse of hard rock, the hypnotism of disco, or the measured steps of country soul. They looked forward to a few drinks, flirting with strangers, finding Mr. or Ms. Right or, maybe, someone to spend the night with.

At the end of the street, a lone black street lamp shone through the mist. The men in leather walked under the light and disappeared into the next street. As they reached the corner, Mickey and his friends could hear the raucous sounds of the Garden spill onto the street. They shimmied and rocked down the block and through the doors.

The Garden was packed with men and women in sweat-stained shirts. Blue smoke stung the eyes. The sour and sweet smell of beer hung in the air. Strobe lights pulsed over the dancers. Mickey pulled off his wash-faded black denim jacket and wrapped it around his waist. An iridescent blue tank top hung easy on his shoulders. Impatient with the wait for a drink, Mickey steered his girlfriend onto the crowded dance floor.

Reeling to the music and immersed in the pleasure of his rhythms, Mickey never saw the ice pick plunge into this neck. It was just a bump with a drunk yelling, "Lame-assed faggot." "Faggot. Faggot. Faggot. Punk faggot." Mickey thought it was a punch to the neck. He ran after the roaring drunk man for seven steps, then lurched and fell on the dance floor, blood gushing everywhere. His girlfriend screamed. The dance floor spun black.

Mickey was rushed to San Francisco General Hospital, where thirty-six 10
stitches were used by trauma staff to close the wound on his neck. Doctors said the pick used in the attack against him was millimeters away from his spinal cord. His assailant, charged with attempted murder, pleaded innocent.

Mickey and Brian were unfortunate stand-ins for any gay man. Mickey was thin and wiry, a great dancer clad in black denim, earrings dangling from his ear. Brian was slight of build, wore a leather jacket, and boarded a bus in the Castro. Dress like a homo, dance like a homo, must be a homo. The homophobic fury directed at lesbians, gay men, and bisexuals in America most often finds its target. Ironclad evidence of sexual orientation, however, is not necessary for someone to qualify as a potential victim of deadly fury. Appearances will do.

The incidents described above are based on actual events reported to the San Francisco Police and Community United Against Violence (CUAV), an agency serving victims of antilesbian and antigay violence where I worked for four years. The names of the victims have been changed. Both men assaulted were straight.

Incidents of antilesbian and antigay violence are not uncommon or limited to San Francisco. A *San Francisco Examiner* survey estimates that over one million hate-motivated physical assaults take place each year against lesbians, gays, and bisexuals. The National Gay and Lesbian Task Force conducted a survey in 1984 that found that 94 percent of all lesbians and gay men surveyed reported being physically assaulted, threatened, or harassed in an antigay incident at one time or another. The great majority of these incidents go unreported.

To my knowledge, no agency other than CUAV keeps track of incidents of antigay violence involving heterosexuals as victims. An average of 3 percent of the over three hundred victims seen by CUAV each year identify as heterosexuals. This may or may not be an accurate gauge of the actual prevalence of antigay violence directed at heterosexuals. Most law enforcement agencies, including those in San Francisco, have no way of documenting this form of assault other than under a generic "harassment" code. The actual incidence of violence directed at heterosexuals that is motivated by homophobia is probably much higher than CUAV's six to nine victims a year. Despite the official paucity of data, however, it is a fact that incidents of antigay and antilesbian violence in which straight men and women are victimized do occur. Shelters for battered women are filled with stories of lesbian baiting of staff and of women whose husbands and boyfriends repeatedly called them "dykes" or "whores" as they beat them.[1] I have personally experienced verbal abuse while in the company of a straight friend, who was assumed to be my lover.

15 Why does it happen? I have no definitive answers to that question. Understanding homophobic violence is no less complex than understanding racial violence. The institutional and ideological reinforcements of homophobia are myriad and deeply woven into our culture. I offer one perspective that I hope will contribute to a better understanding of how homophobia works and why it threatens all that we value as humane.

At the simplest level, looking or behaving like the stereotypical gay man or lesbian is reason enough to provoke a homophobic assault. Beneath the veneer of the effeminate gay male or the butch dyke, however, is a more basic trigger for homophobic violence. I call it *gender betrayal.*

The clearest expression I have heard of this sense of gender betrayal comes from Doug Barr, who was acquitted of murder in an incident of gay bashing in San Francisco that resulted in the death of John O'Connell, a gay man. Barr is currently serving a prison sentence for related assaults on the

[1] See Suzanne Pharr, *Homophobia: A Weapon of Sexism* (Inverness, Calif.: Chardon, 1988). [Author's note]

same night that O'Connor was killed. He was interviewed for a special report on homophobia produced by ABC's *20/20* (10 April 1986). When asked what he and his friends thought of gay men, he said, "We hate homosexuals. They degrade our manhood. We was brought up in a high school where guys are football players, mean and macho. Homosexuals are sissies who wear dresses. I'd rather be seen as a football player."

Doug Barr's perspective is one shared by many young men. I have made about three hundred presentations to high school students in San Francisco, to boards of directors and staff of nonprofit organizations, and at conferences and workshops on the topic of homophobia or "being lesbian or gay." Over and over again, I have asked, "Why do gay men and lesbians bother you?" The most popular response to the question is, "Because they act like girls," or, "Because they think they're men." I have even been told, quite explicitly, "I don't care what they do in bed, but they shouldn't act like that."

They shouldn't act like that. Women who are not identified by their relationship to a man, who value their female friendships, who like and are knowledgeable about sports, or work as blue-collar laborers and wear what they wish are very likely to be "lesbian baited" at some point in their lives. Men who are not pursuing sexual conquests of women at every available opportunity, who disdain sports, who choose to stay at home and be a househusband, who are employed as hairdressers, designers, or housecleaners, or who dress in any way remotely resembling traditional female attire (an earring will do) are very likely to experience the taunts and sometimes the brutality of "fag bashing."

The straitjacket of gender roles suffocates many lesbians, gay men, and 20
bisexuals, forcing them into closets without an exit and threatening our very existence when we tear the closet open. It also, however, threatens all heterosexuals unwilling to be bound by their assigned gender identity. Why, then, does it persist?

Suzanne Pharr's examination of homophobia as a phenomenon based in sexism and misogyny offers a succinct and logical explanation for the virulence of homophobia in Western civilization:

> It is not by chance that when children approach puberty and increased sexual awareness they begin to taunt each other by calling these names: "queer," "faggot," "pervert." It is at puberty that the full force of society's pressure to conform to heterosexuality and prepare for marriage is brought to bear. Children know what we have taught them, and we have given clear messages that those who deviate from standard expectations are to be made to get back in line. . . .
>
> To be named as lesbian threatens all women, not just lesbians, with great loss. And any woman who steps out of role risks being called a lesbian. To understand how this is a threat to all women, one must understand that any woman can be called a lesbian and there is no real way she can defend herself: there is no real way to credential one's sexuality. (*The Children's Hour*, a Lillian Hellman play, makes this point when a student asserts two

> teachers are lesbians and they have no way to disprove it.) She may be married or divorced, have children, dress in the most feminine manner, have sex with men, be celibate — but there are lesbians who do all these things. *Lesbians look like all women and all women look like lesbians.*[2]

I would add that gay men look like all men and all men look like gay men. There is no guaranteed method for identifying sexual orientation. Those small or outrageous deviations we sometimes take from the idealized mystique of "real men" and "real women" place all of us — lesbians, gay men, bisexuals, and heterosexuals alike — at risk of violence, derision, isolation, and hatred.

It is a frightening reality. Dorothy Ehrlich, executive director of the Northern California American Civil Liberties Union (ACLU), was the victim of a verbal assault in the Castro several years ago. Dorothy lives with her husband, Gary, and her two children, Jill and Paul, in one of those worn and comfortable Victorian homes that grace so many San Francisco neighborhoods. Their home is several blocks from the Castro, but Dorothy recalls the many times she and Gary could hear, from the safety of their bedroom, shouts of "faggot" and men running in the streets.

When Jill was an infant, Gary and Dorothy had occasion to experience for themsevles how frightening even the threat of homophobic violence can be. One foggy, chilly night they decided to go for a walk in the Castro. Dorothy is a small woman whom some might call petite; she wore her hair short at the time and delights in the comfort of jeans and oversized wool jackets. Gary is very tall and lean, a bespectacled and bearded cross between a professor and a basketball player who wears jean jackets and tweed jackets with the exact same slouch. On this night they were crossing Castro Street, huddled close together with Jill in Dorothy's arms. As they reached the corner, their backs to the street, they heard a truck rev its engine and roar up Castro, the dreaded "faggot" spewing from young men they could not see in the fog. They looked around them for the intended victims, but there was no one else on the corner with them. They were the target that night: Dorothy and Gary and Jill. They were walking on "gay turf," and it was reason enough to make them a target. "It was so frightening," Dorothy said. "So frightening and unreal."

But it is real. The *20/20* report on homophobia ends with the story of Tom and Jan Matarrase, who are married, have a child, and lived in Brooklyn, New York, at the time of their encounter with homophobic violence. On camera, Tom and Jan are walking down a street in Brooklyn lined with brown townhouses and black wrought-iron gates. It is snowing, and, with hands entwined, they walk slowly down the street where they were assaulted. Tom is wearing a khaki trenchcoat, slacks, and loafers. Snowflakes melt into the tight dark curls on his head. Jan is almost his height, her short bobbed hair

[2]Ibid., 17–19. [Author's note]

moving softly as she walks. She is wearing a black leather jacket, a red scarf, and burnt orange cords. The broadness of her hips and softness of her face belie the tomboy flavor of her carriage and clothes, and it is hard to believe that she was mistaken for a gay man. But she was.

They were walking home, holding hands and engrossed with each other. 25
On the other side of the street, Jan saw a group of boys moving toward them. As the gang approached, Jan heard a distinct taunt meant for her and Tom: "Aw, look at the cute gay couple." Tom and Jan quickened their step, but it was too late. Before they could say anything. Tom was being punched in the face and slammed against a car. Jan ran toward Tom and the car, screaming desperately that Tom was her husband. Fists pummeled her face as well. Outnumbered and in fear for their lives, Tom yelled at Jan to please open her jacket and show their assailants that she was a woman. The beating subsided only when Jan was able to show her breasts.

For the *20/20* interview, Jan and Tom sat in the warmth of their living room, their infant son in Jan's lap. The interviewer asked them how they felt when people said they looked like a gay couple. "We used to laugh," they said. "But now we realize how heavy the implications are. Now we know what the gay community goes through. We had no idea how widespread it was. It's on every level."

Sadly, it *is* on every level. Enforced heterosexism and the pressure to conform to aggressive masculine and passive feminine roles place fag bashers and lesbian baiters in the same psychic prison with their victims, gay or straight. Until all children are free to realize their full potential, until all women and men are free from the stigma, threats, alienation, or violence that come from stepping outside their roles, we are all at risk.

The economic and ideological underpinnings of enforced heterosexism and sexism or any other form of systematic oppression are formidable foes and far too complex for the scope of this essay. It is important to remember, however, that bigots are natural allies and that poverty or the fear of it has the power to seduce us all into conformity. In Castro graffiti, *faggot* appears right next to *nigger* and *kike.* Race betrayal or any threat to the sanctimony of light-skinned privilege engenders no less a rage than gender betrayal, most especially when we have a great stake in the elusive privilege of proper gender roles or the right skin color. *Queer lover* and *fag hag* are cut from the same mold that gave us *nigger lover,* a mold forged by fears of change and a loss of privilege.

Unfortunately, our sacrifices to conformity rarely guarantee the privilege or protection we were promised. Lesbians, gay men, and bisexuals who have tried to pass know that. Heterosexuals who have been perceived to be gay know that. Those of us with a vision of tomorrow that goes beyond tolerance to a genuine celebration of humanity's diversity have innumerable fronts to fight on. Homophobia is one of them.

But how will this front be won? With a lot of help, and not easily. 30
Challenges to homophobia and the rigidity of gender roles must go beyond

the visible lesbian and gay movement. Lesbians, gay men, and bisexuals alone cannot defuse the power of stigmatization and the license it gives to frighten, wound, or kill. Literally millions of us are needed on this front, straight and gay alike. We invite any heterosexual unwilling to live with the damage that "real men" or "real women" messages wreck on them, on their children, and on lesbians, gay men, and bisexuals to join us. We ask that you not let queer jokes go unchallenged at work, at home, in the media, or anywhere. We ask that you foster in your children a genuine respect for themselves and their right to be who and what they wish to be, regardless of their gender. We ask that you embrace your daughter's desire to swing a bat or be a

carpenter, that you nurture your son's efforts to express affection and sentiment. We ask that you teach your children how painful and destructive words like *faggot* or *bulldyke* are. We ask that you invite your lesbian, gay, and bisexual friends and relatives into the routine of your lives without demanding silence or discretion from them. We invite you to study our history, read the literature written by our people, patronize our businesses, come into our homes and neighborhoods. We ask that you give us your vote when we need it to protect our privacy or to elect open lesbians, gay men, and bisexuals to office. We ask that you stand with us in public demonstrations to demand our right to live as free people, without fear. We ask that you respect our dignity by acting to end the poison of homophobia.

Until individuals are free to choose their roles and be bound only by the limits of their own imagination, *faggot, dyke,* and *pervert* will continue to be playground words and adult weapons that hurt and limit far many more people than their intended victims. Whether we like it or not, the romance of virile men and dainty women, of Mother, Father, Dick, Jane, Sally, and Spot is doomed to extinction and dangerous in a world that can no longer meet the expectations conjured by history. There is much to be won and so little to lose in the realization of a world where the dignity of each person is worthy of celebration and protection. The struggle to end homophobia can and must be won, for all our sakes. Personhood is imminent.

Engaging the Text

1. Do you think violent events like the ones described above are fairly common or quite rare? How aware of this problem are people in your community? How much attention have you seen paid to gay-bashing in the newspapers, on TV, in books or films, or in everyday conversation?
2. Vázquez waits a while to disclose that "Brian" and "Mickey" were actually straight men, but she *does* disclose this fact. Why does she wait? Why does she disclose it? Does the issue of antigay violence change in any way when we recognize that its victims are sometimes heterosexual?
3. Vázquez cites "gender betrayal" as a possible cause of antigay violence. Explain gender betrayal in your own words; discuss how it works and how well it explains the violence described in the narratives Vázquez recounts.
4. According to Vázquez, Suzanne Pharr links homophobia to misogyny, the hatred of women: the "lesbian" label, she says, can be used to threaten all women. Review and discuss this argument; then discuss how well it can be applied to men, as Vázquez suggests it might be.
5. How do you explain the essay's closing sentence, "Personhood is imminent"?

Exploring Connections

6. Compare and contrast the harassment of gays and lesbians to the sexual harassment of women described in Kimmel's essay earlier in this chapter (p. 259).

7. To what extent does Vázquez's concept of "gender betrayal" (para. 16) explain the attitudes and behavior encountered by Nora Quealey (p. 253) and Lorraine and Theresa in "The Two" (p. 319)?
8. Look at the cartoon on page 294, Alison Bechdel's "Public Display of Affection" (part of her "Dykes to Watch Out For" series). Discuss the cartoon in light of Vázquez's essay. Write an imaginary dialogue between Vázquez and Bechdel on the subject of gay and lesbian harassment.

Extending the Critical Context

9. Vázquez writes that "the institutional and ideological reinforcements of homophobia are myriad and deeply woven into our culture" (para. 15). Over a period of days, keep track of all references to gays, lesbians, or homosexuality in casual conversations, news reports, TV programs, and other media. To what extent do you agree with Vázquez that homophobia is deeply ingrained in our culture?
10. San Francisco, the city in which the incidents described took place, is known as one of the most tolerant in the United States. Research your own community's history of assaults on gay and lesbian people. You might begin by talking to gay and lesbian organizations; police or public health departments may also have pertinent information. Report to the class or write a formal paper presenting your findings.

Strange Customs, Familiar Lives: Homosexualities in Other Cultures

James D. Weinrich and Walter L. Williams

In this selection, two researchers report on perceptions of gender and homosexuality in cultures around the world, and what they report may astound you. Beyond describing modes of thought and behavior unfamiliar to most Americans, the authors raise questions about the nature of gender itself and the adequacy of previous theories of gender. Weinrich (b. 1950) is a psychobiologist in the Department of Psychiatry at the University of California, San Diego. He has written and lectured extensively on sex, gender, and evolutionary biology and is the author of Sexual Landscapes: Why We Are What We Are, Why We Love Whom We Love *(1987). Walter Williams (b. 1948) is a professor of anthropology at the University of Southern California. In addition to dozens of scholarly papers, he has published* The Spirit and the Flesh: Sexual Diversity in American Indian Culture *(1986) and* Javanese Lives: Women and Men in Modern Indonesian Society *(1991).*

"Strange Customs, Familiar Lives" originally appeared in Homosexuality: Research Implications for Public Policy *(1991), edited by Weinrich and John C. Gonsiorek.*

Studies of other cultures offer an impressive contrast to the American notion that homosexuals are always scorned, abnormal, acting like the opposite sex, dangerous, likely to molest innocent children, and easily distinguishable from normal heterosexuals. Yet since American popular culture is for the most part ethnocentric,[1] when it interprets sexuality in other cultures the result has often been disastrously inaccurate. Typical heterosexual American tourists who see two Italian men or two Greek women walking down the street arm in arm or holding hands might get upset, since they know how to interpret such behaviors only in terms of homosexuality. When typical homosexual American tourists visit gay bars in countries like Japan or Mexico, they are often surprised to discover that most if not all of the patrons are married or plan to marry and have children — and so they wonder why so many homosexuals in those countries are still "in the closet" and not facing up to what is supposed to be their true nature.

In the context of this ethnocentrism, it is not surprising that early cross-cultural research on homosexuality emphasized the differences that are apparent when other cultures are described in their own terms. Intellectually, this point of view culminated in the *social constructionist* school, which, when applied to homosexuality research, views the nature of sexual orientation as constructed within a particular society as opposed to reflecting a fixed, underlying essence. Social constructionists have pointed to bisexuality, historical variation, and cross-cultural differences to support the notion that homosexuality is not merely an objectively observed trait. Instead, they claim that in an important sense the concept of a person "being a homosexual" does not really exist as an independent, fixed entity. It "exists" only in the minds of Westerners.

There is now a growing literature on homosexual behavior in other cultures, both modern ones and those that existed in past eras. Most important, several societies have been investigated in far more detail concerning their attitudes toward "homosexuality," whatever that is, than typically was reported in the early cross-cultural studies. We can now begin to compare the *diversity* of homosexual behavior patterns in different studies and see if the range of behaviors falling into these categories is similar or different across cultures and across time.

The result is surprising: the more a culture is studied, the more different

We thank John Boswell, John Gonsiorek, Ralph Hexter, and Richard Pillard for comments on early versions of the manuscript. [Authors' note]

[1]*ethnocentric:* Characterized by thinking that one's own ethnic group is superior.

patterns of homosexuality or homosexual behavior turn up in it, and the more this range of behavior seems similar to the range (if not the proportions) observed in other cultures, including Western culture. Yet each culture maintains its own way of interpreting this range of behavior, plucking out certain patterns as modal or "normal," ignoring but not denying the existence of others, and stigmatizing or trying to wish away the existence of yet other patterns. In doing so, most cultures subject their members to a unique combination of pressures, and construct concepts and terminologies that tend to make their members unaware of certain patterns and unable or unlikely to understand patterns that fall outside of the socially recognized ones.

5 In contrast, we believe that in order to arrive at a more complete understanding of human sexuality, including what our culture calls homosexuality, we need not only to include a social constructionist approach but also to go further. In particular, we have the following goals . . . :

- To help readers steeped in our culture's view of homosexuality to realize that this point of view is a distorted one in many ways, and to describe the positive contributions of the social constructionist movement.
- To show how social constructionism is inadequate as a model to describe the full diversity of findings now emerging from detailed investigations of same-sex eroticism in other cultures and at other times.
- Finally, to draw conclusions about how to use these insights in understanding "the modern homosexual identity" in America today.

Homosexuality as a Social Construction

The *social constructionist* view was first applied to the study of homosexuality by Mary McIntosh, when she wrote:

> The current conceptualization of homosexuality as a condition is a false one, resulting from ethnocentric bias. Homosexuality should be seen rather as a social role. Anthropological evidence shows that the role does not exist in all societies, and where it does it is not always the same as in modern western societies. Historical evidence shows that the role did not emerge in England until towards the end of the seventeenth century. Evidence from the "Kinsey Reports" shows that . . . the polarization between the heterosexual man and the homosexual man is far from complete. (McIntosh, 1968, p. 182)

Asserting that social constructionism is the *only* valid tool for this area of analysis, McIntosh's paper has been enormously influential. Note that it explicitly cites cross-cultural evidence, cross-historical evidence, and the existence of bisexuality in its support. A milder social constructionist view was defended by anthropologist Joseph Carrier, who did fieldwork in Mexico:

> What is considered homosexuality in one culture may be considered appropriate behavior within prescribed gender roles in another, a homosexual act only on the part of one participant in another, or a ritual act involving

> growth and masculinity in still another. Care must therefore be taken when judging sexual behavior cross-culturally with such culture-bound labels as "homosexual" and "homosexuality." . . . From whatever causes that homosexual impulses originate, whether they be biological or psychological, culture provides an additional dimension that cannot be ignored. (Carrier, 1980, p. 120)

Though Carrier alleges that cultural factors are important, he stops short of saying that other factors (such as biological ones) are not. Another position was defended by Erich Goode, who buttressed McIntosh's position with facts about ancient Greece:

> By focusing on same-gender sexual preference exclusively we may fail to notice differences that may be far more remarkable. . . . For instance, in ancient Greece, men who preferred the sexual company of other men . . . were of a type quite unlike our contemporary versions: most were married, had at least occasional sex with their wives, and they sired children. (Goode, 1981, p. 62)

And finally, Jonathan Katz, who used to talk about "gay people" in history (a nonconstructionist usage), has with his most recent book given up the term and adopted an openly hostile attitude toward it:

> In recent years, it has become common . . . to speak of "homosexual behavior" as universal. As allegedly universal, this "homosexual behavior" was the same, for example, in the American colonies in the 1680s as it is in Greenwich Village in the 1980s. I don't think so. It is only the most one-dimensional, mechanical "behaviorism" that suggests that that act of male with male called "sodomy" in the early colonies was identical to that behavior of males called "homosexual" in the 1980s. (Katz, 1983, pp. 17–18)

The notion common to all these social constructionist views is that sexual 10
orientation cannot be properly or completely understood apart from the social milieu in which it is embedded. The most extreme proponents of this point of view claim that "homosexuality" did not really exist until the term was coined in the modern West (by a German sexual reformer, Károly Kertbeny, in 1869): that the construction of sexuality is so important that it is improper to talk about "gay people in the Middle Ages," for example, or about "lesbians in ancient Greece."

It is important to realize that this point of view is far stronger than just pointing out how wrong it would be to assume that the "ancient French," for example, spoke "French." Social constructionists claim that the very term *homosexuality* skews the discussion in a Western direction in ways that we Westerners have trouble comprehending. Imagine, for example, a hypothetical society that attached a great deal of importance to the question of whether its citizens were dog lovers or cat lovers. Imagine that scientists constructed complicated psychological questionnaires to determine whether someone was a "feliphile" or a "caniphile," scored people on scales of "petual orientation," and received or were denied tenure on the basis of whether they could prove the existence of "bipetuality." Those allegedly scientific terms have a bizarre ring to us, in a society that cares little about whether someone prefers to spend time with dogs, cats, both, or neither. But someone raised in such a society might very well come into ours and make gross misinterpretations of our social patterns.

This is, according to the social constructionists, exactly the point. "Homosexuality" has no more of a real existence than "caniphilia" does. Our society makes the definition and shows concern only because it wants to differentiate and thereby control people who display variation in that trait. These are terms, they say, no more applicable outside their time and place than "French culture" is.

Homosexuality in Other Cultures

Let us now discuss some specific examples of the variations we see around the world and throughout history in people's constructions of and attitudes toward sexual behavior between males or between females. For reasons of space, we will focus on only two categories of variation, exemplified by ancient Greece and by various mixed-gender institutions in a variety of societies.

In ancient Greece, attitudes toward what we now call "homosexuality" varied from time to time and from place to place. It would be inaccurate to write as if these attitudes were uniform, just as it would be incorrect to talk about "the American view of sex" as if this view were uniform from coast to coast and from 1776 to 1999! Nevertheless, many Greek writers in ancient times wrote as if they considered the pleasures of one sex as opposed to the other to be morally equivalent, and as if a particular person could find pleasure in one sex one day and the other sex the next. Plutarch, for example wrote:

> The noble lover of beauty engages in love wherever he sees excellence and splendid natural endowment without regard for any difference in physiological detail. The lover of human beauty [will] be fairly and equably disposed toward both sexes, instead of supposing that males and females are as different in the matter of love as they are in their clothes. (Translation from Boswell, 1982)

As it happens, the Greeks had a word for each of several specific sexual 15
tastes, but no word at all for what might be called today's generic "homosexual." Plutarch saw sexual orientation in terms that would please the social constructionists. Indeed, Goode (quoted above) made nearly this point.

Moreover, the ancient Greeks often had attitudes toward same-sex sexual relations that were stunningly different from those even imagined today. In Plato's *Symposium*, for example, the dinner guests are each asked to give a brief speech about love. Amazingly to modern observers, each guest talks about love *between men;* not only is this form of love taken in stride, it seems to be the unspoken basis of discussion. This attitude is not anomalous; various city-states in ancient Greece had rules and regulations about how a male should go about courting another male, specified particular gifts that ought to be given at particular stages of the relationship, and so on.

In ancient Greece, homosexuality was not at all associated with an identification with the opposite sex. In fact, quite the opposite was true; it seemed logical, for example, for them to assume that the most masculine men would want to associate with and have sex with other males. Sappho, whose famous poetry expressed her love for young women, was not considered anything but feminine, as her society defined femininity. In contrast, in today's society, it is a stereotype that lesbians are masculine (some excessively so), and that gay men are effeminate (some to the point of parody or pity). Gay civil rights groups often point out that most homosexuals today do not cross-dress, that many transvestites are heterosexual, and so on.

What is sometimes hard to convey to Western citizens, however, is the fact that in some cultures cross-dressing and androgynous gender behavior were or are indeed statistically correlated with homosexual behavior, but *in a way that was appropriate or even approved for the culture* in which they took place. This is difficult because Westerners usually cannot imagine how ordinary heterosexuals could take such behaviors in stride. After all, isn't such gender-nonconformist behavior inherently upsetting to the heterosexual majority?

Not necessarily. In Thailand, for example, there is the institution of the effeminate *kathoey* (Jackson, 1989). It is their gender role that sets them apart from ordinary men (they enjoy dressing in women's clothes), as well as their sexual orientation (they like having sex with heterosexual men).

It is important to realize that *kathoey* are accepted in Thai culture. 20
Nearly every town has its annual *kathoey* beauty pageant, for example, which townspeople of all ages attend approvingly. And every town has many heterosexual men who have sex with *kathoey* and report enjoying it. Perhaps most important of all, these sex partners of *kathoey* are not considered unusual or deviant in any way.

In fact, there are many cultures today, and there have been many others in the past, in which some people of one sex dress as or, to a greater or lesser extent, take the role of members of the other sex, and with which homosexuality is often involved.

Among certain Eskimo and American Indian tribes, this type of person is called a berdache by anthropologists. Among the Chukchee in Siberia (Bogoras, 1904–1909), berdache males acquired magical or shamanistic gifts as the result of their transformation. Among the Chukchee, there were three levels of transformed shamans. Those at the lowest level just arranged their hair as women did, sometimes only every now and then. Those at the middle level dressed as women at the commands of the spirits, and for longer periods of time. And those at the highest level had the greatest powers, dressed as women full-time, spoke using the female linguistic forms, and formally got married to men — unlike the other two types, who married women.

Many North American Indian tribes had similar institutions, although the exact details differed from tribe to tribe (see Williams, 1986). Each tribe had its own name for berdaches. For example, the Sioux term is *winkte.* The Sioux traditional medicine man, Lame Deer, said:

> We think that if a woman has two little ones growing inside her, if she is going to have twins, sometimes instead of giving birth to two babies they have formed up in her womb into just one, into a half man–half woman kind of being. We call such a person a winkte. . . . In the old days a winkte dressed like a woman, cooked and did bead work. He behaved like a squaw and did not go to war. . . . There are good men among the winktes and they have been given certain powers. . . . [one] winkte . . . told me that if nature puts a burden on a man by making him different, it also gives him a power. He told me that a winkte has a gift of prophecy. (Lame Deer and Erdoes, 1972, pp. 149–150)

Among most American Indian tribes, as hinted in the passage above, being a berdache was not just a sexual matter: it has an important spiritual component. A berdache had a spiritual personality, and this spirituality was reflected in the roles his society assigned to him. Rather than being seen as a *cross*-dresser — namely, someone who dresses convincingly in the clothes of the opposite sex — berdaches are usually more accurately viewed as *gender mixers,* or people who combine aspects of both masculine and feminine styles in a single person, or who even have personality traits or behaviors that are associated with neither the masculine nor feminine averages. Often, this gave berdaches the right to arrange marriages, or made them especially useful to the rest of society by acting as go-betweens in gender matters or affairs of the heart.

In parallel fashion, many Native American cultures also gave social rec- 25
ognition to the fact that some females were inclined toward activities usually performed by men. They might mix these occupations with some traditional feminine pursuits, while other females made a nearly complete social transformation to masculine activities. For example, in 1576 the Portuguese explorer Pedro de Magalhaes de Gandavo wrote about a remarkable group of female warriors when he visited the Tupinamba Indians of northeastern Brazil:

> There are some Indian women who determine to remain chaste: these have no [sexual] commerce with men in any manner, nor would they consent to it even if refusal meant death. They give up all the duties of women and imitate men, and follow men's pursuits as if they were not women. They wear the hair cut in the same way as the men, and go to war with bows and arrows and pursue game, always in company with men; each has a woman to serve her, to whom she says she is married, and they treat each other and speak with each other as man and wife. (Quoted in Williams, 1986, p. 233)

With such a person it is usually a mistake to assume that "he" "really" "is" a man or a woman. Usually the members of the tribe viewed a berdache, in a way that seems very strange to Westerners, as both masculine and feminine, and neither! There is no better illustration of this than the following quote about berdaches in the Tewa tribe, who are called *quethos* (Jacobs, 1983):

> Although the Tewa elders with whom I have spoken would not assign a male or female sex to quetho, I pushed the point further on a number of occasions, asking if women were ever quethos. The answer was no. Then I asked if men were the only ones who were quethos. Again, the answer was no[!]. In trying to force a categorization of quethos as women or men . . . , I only exasperated my Tewa friends.

In the Arabic culture of Oman, it is hard to imagine an environment more hostile to "homosexuality" as the West sees it. Islam prescribes the death penalty for homosexual behavior, and many aspects of one's life are completely determined just by one's sex. For example, the sexes are rigidly separated. Men are not permitted to be in the presence of a woman for even a moment unless a man related to the woman—preferably her husband—is present as a chaperone. There are, however, exceptions. The anthropologist Unni Wikan reported about her fieldwork in Oman:

> I had completed four months of fieldwork when one day a friend of mine asked me to go visiting with her. Observing the rules of decency, we made our way through the back streets away from the market, where we met a man, dressed in a pink dishdasha, with whom my friend stopped to talk. I was highly astonished, as no decent woman stops to talk with a man in the street. So I reasoned he must be her very close male relative. But their interaction was too intimate. I began to suspect my friend's virtue. Could the man be her secret lover? No sooner had we left him than she identified him. "That one is a *xanith,*" she said. In the twenty-minute walk that followed, she pointed out four more. (Wikan, 1982, p. 169)

In Oman, men wear white dishdashas, women wear something else entirely, and *xaniths* wear a pastel-colored dishdasha. *Xaniths* do not in this sense "cross-dress," even though many of them take up stereotypically feminine occupations. In a sense, men and women in Oman are not each others' "opposite sex," but are instead "the other sex" (or perhaps even "another sex"). It is difficult to explain this to Westerners, whose conceptions of manhood and womanhood are so closely tied to the genitals, and are seen as two, and only two, "opposite sexes."

In Hinduism, there is the *hijra* caste, made up of genetic males who worship a female goddess, and who wish to change their sex to female (Nanda, 1984, 1990). When hijras are ready they undergo a castration and penectomy (penis-removing) operation that finalizes their status in the caste. Many *hijras* earn their living performing songs and dances at marriages and other heterosexual rites, and by performing free-lance shows in various places, such as college campuses. Their welcome at the locations where they entertain is sometimes ambivalent; *hijras* who have not been paid (or paid well enough) after their sometimes uninvited performances have been known to lift their skirts and show off to the crowd what they have underneath. Since one of the rules of the sect forbids underwear, this is a display most hosts want to avoid! In Indian culture, *hijras* are considered among the outcastes, yet even so they have managed to work their way into a begrudging acknowledgment by society.

All these examples of intermediate-gender status show, according to the 30
social constructionists, that culture is an overwhelmingly important force in determining the different forms that homosexual behavior takes in society. We agree that merely to describe this variability in cross-cultural terms overlooks the importance of the social construction of the very terms used in categorizing same-sex eroticism. On the other hand, it is a mistake to assert that these enormous differences are the end of the matter or the only important matter. Let us now turn to some similarities across cultures.

Cross-Cultural Similarities

The ancient Greeks had no single word for what we now call "homosexuality" — a fact that is interpreted by the social constructionists as evidence that "homosexuality" did not then exist. They do not claim that same-sex acts did not take place; just that it is nonsensical to apply our twentieth-century term to a pattern of behavior that is constructed under completely different conditions.

However that may be, consider the following creation myth recounted in Plato's *Symposium:*

> Formerly the natural state of man was not what it is now, but quite different. For at first there were three sexes, not two as at present, male and female, but also a third having a male-female sex . . . , [All these humans] had four arms and an equal number of legs, and two faces [and twice the usual number of the various parts of the body], and two privy members. . . . They had terrible strength and force, and great were their ambitions; they attacked the gods. . . .
>
> So Zeus and the other gods held council what they should do. . . . "I will tell you what I'll do now," says [Zeus], "I will slice each of them down through the middle!" . . . and then he sliced men through the middle. . . . So when the original body was cut through, each half wanted the other. . . .
>
> Then each of us is [half] of a man; he is sliced like a flatfish, and two made of one. So each one seeks his other [half]. Then all men who are a cutting of the old common sex which was called manwoman are [erotically] fond of women. . . . The women who are a cutting of the ancient [double] women do not care much about men, but are more attracted to women. . . . But those which are a cutting of the [double] male pursue the male. . . . So when one of these meets his own [matching] half, . . . then they are wonderfully overwhelmed by affection and intimacy and love, and . . . never wish to be apart for a moment. (Plato, reprinted 1956, pp. 86–88)

There are several striking things about this creation myth — things that are just as striking even if we take account of the possibility that Plato was joking instead of seriously recounting a myth already familiar to his listeners and readers. First, the myth suggests that the speaker believes that there are three kinds of people: females who are attracted to females, males who are attracted to males, and people who are attracted to the other sex. This is inconsistent with the notion, so popular among social constructionists, that these categories were literally unrecognizable and unknown before the seventeenth or the nineteenth century. Second, the myth completely turns on its head the Western stereotype that homosexuals resemble the opposite sex; it attributes heterosexuality, not homosexuality, to a kind of hermaphroditism.[2] Third, the ancient Greek pattern is commonly interpreted as one in which there was always, or ideally, a significant age difference between sex partners (i.e., that men courted youths, who in turn courted boys) — yet if one is yearning, according to this myth, for one's matching twin, it follows that one is yearning for someone of exactly the same age! And fourth, notice how all the really "positive" words — like "wonderfully," "affection," and "love" — are reserved for the men who pursue men. This is quite the opposite of the mainstream view in modern Western society, where some critics of homosexual relationships can actually get away with claiming that the love that homosexuals feel for each other is not "real" love.

In fact, ancient Greek society did recognize differences between people who were attracted to their own sex, people who were attracted to the other sex, and people who were attracted to both. But they didn't make a big deal about these differences. In fact, they probably made about as much of them as we nowadays make about the differences between introverts and extroverts, or between dog lovers and cat lovers. We have humorous books and monologues (e.g., Dizick and Bly, 1985) in which dog lovers and cat lovers cast aspersions on each other's personalities. But no one makes any particular "petual orientation" illegal! It is likely that Plato would not comprehend how some Americans could believe that certain kinds of homosexual sex are crimes worse than murder.

Now let us move on to the mixed-gender institutions like the *kathoey*, 35
the amazon, the berdache, the *xanith*, and the *hijra*. Here, anthropologists point out how much cross-cultural variation has been revealed by their studies of these kinds of people, and emphasize all the differences between these institutions and our own society. Berdaches, for example, had a specifically spiritual vocation, and often had a respected place in their tribes. The *kathoey* in Thailand are well respected for their particular talents, and are taken so much in stride by the common people that there is an Ann Landers–style advice column written for them that is published in a major national newspaper (the columnist's name translates as "Uncle Go"). *Hijras* are only

[2]*hermaphroditism:* The state of having both male and female reproductive organs.

grudgingly respected, if at all, hold very particular religious beliefs, and cannot return to the male sex after their castration operation. *Xaniths* were neither revered nor reviled, were trusted to be around women, and occasionally were known to switch back to the ordinary man's role later in life. In all four cultures, males in these mixed-gender categories have sex almost exclusively with ordinary "heterosexual" men in their tribes or villages, and those other men are not regarded as deviant or special. Similarly, American Indian amazons married women, and those women were seen as ordinary wives. How could these institutions be more different from each other? And just think of the enormous differences separating these kinds of social constructs from the ancient Greek pattern. What could be more ridiculous than to claim that all these diverse kinds of people could be called "homosexual"? The term seems enormously inappropriate.

To arrive at a more complex explanation of the world, however, we must allow ourselves to be dazzled not only by differences, but also by subtle similarities. Both diamonds and coal are made of carbon, and because of that fact, if you heat them they will burn. Although coal and diamonds are extremely dissimilar substances, they are also alike in a subtle and interesting way.

The better we get to know ancient Greece, and the more we learn about same-sex erotic behavior patterns in other cultures, the more we are discovering that the *range* of these patterns is far more similar from culture to culture than it might at first seem. In ancient Greece, there were effeminate men, but homosexuality in such men was not the common pattern of homosexuality seen in that culture, and so it is usually not the first or most often described pattern in the literature. In modern Thailand, terms are emerging to describe types of homosexuals that are more familiar to modern Westerners, but it would be a mistake (and an insult to the intelligence of Thais) to claim that Thais were unaware of these kinds of people before Western culture provided them with a vocabulary to describe them. In Mexico, where for reasons of machismo it is extremely important to declare oneself in the male world as either "butch" (inserting) or "fem" (inserted into), a considerable proportion of homosexual men actually take both roles (the butch role with someone who is more fem than they are, and the fem role with someone more butch). This makes their pattern a lot more similar than it would otherwise appear to American gay men, who typically play down butch-fem distinctions and are flexible in their insertor/insertee patterns. One of us (Williams, 1986, pp. 99–100) reports that particular berdaches were known to prefer partners much older than themselves, much younger, or about their same age. And Jacobs claims that the *quethos* among the Tewa resembled "contemporary gay males" to her in important respects (Jacobs, 1983, p. 460).

What may have appeared to be cross-cultural variation is in part variation in anthropologists, not variation in the cultures the anthropologists are describing. . . . This is not to deny that there is actual underlying variation in the cultures themselves, nor is it to deny that there are significant variations in the social constructions of those underlying patterns (obviously, such variation is enormous). Nor do we wish to propose that one particular culture's point of view is the "real" or "correct" or "best" way of interpreting observations. After all, from a chemist's point of view the most important fact about coal and diamonds is that they are both made of carbon; from the jeweler's point of view it is that one sparkles and the other does not. Neither viewpoint invalidates the other.

We believe, therefore, that there is a need to go beyond a social constructionist view. We suggest that an *interactionist* view can contribute even more to the study of human sexuality, by emphasizing the interaction of numerous factors in producing human eroticism. There is no need to deny similarities across cultures any more than there is a need to deny individual variation within a single culture.

Discussion and Conclusions

The terms *sexual orientation* and *sexual preference* are sometimes used 40
interchangeably and at other times hotly debated. When debated, it is usually over the issue of choice. *Orientation* is used more often by those who think there is little choice involved, and *preference* is used by those who think choice is important. This element of choice can be highlighted by comparing it with religion.

At some level, people can choose to be Catholic, say, or Anglican, or Islamic, and a society can choose to make Catholicism or Anglicanism or Islam a state religion. Of course, most people choose to believe what the state has mandated. Of course, there is social value in announcing one's conformity in such a society, and in some sense there is a de facto enshrining of heterosexuality in modern Western societies as if it were the state sexual preference. Thomas Szasz (1970, chap. 13), for example, compares homosexuality and heresy, homosexuals in his view having the role of sexual heretics dissenting from the heterosexuality mandated by the state.

This is an argument that helps fight antigay prejudice in a culture that takes religious pluralism seriously. In present-day Iran, in contrast, Szasz's argument would probably be just as applicable, logically speaking, but would promote the execution of homosexuals, not their liberation. As we scholars debate such matters, we must be careful not to overlook how societies will try to apply our findings in political debates. On the other hand, we should not become overly concerned when someone points out how some extremist government might use a scholarly or scientific finding in support of its oppressive policies; it is usually the tail that wags the dog in such instances. Although an oppressive power will often look to the ivory tower for intellectual justification for its oppression, residents in the tower (and their critics!) should not fool themselves into thinking that their ideas are causally involved in creating the oppression in the first place. They should only feel guilty if they have encouraged or helped along the oppression or the misuse of their ideas.

Most people are trained in childhood for the religion that they will come to believe in as adults, just as most children in our society are trained for the heterosexuality they will ultimately find stimulating. But think also of the people who convert to a religion other than the one they were raised in, or those who adopt a sexual orientation label for themselves different from the heterosexual one. In both these situations, the adult identity label is taken on as a result of deep thought (or even inner conflict) over a long period of time. The label results from deep inner emotions — emotions that in many people are susceptible to socialization, but not always in a simple way. (This is one reason why Szasz's [1970] insights about homosexuality and heresy make sense.)

In fact, people can "be" Catholic even if they don't go to Mass or practice Catholic rituals, or even if they know logically that this or that story about this or that saint is false. People can "be" defined as Catholics if they believe in their deepest feelings that certain statements about Christ and God are true. If they don't believe those statements in their heart of hearts, then they are not really Catholic, no matter how often they go to Mass or how hard they consciously try to pretend they believe them.

Likewise, people can be defined as "homosexual" even if they do not 45
perform any homosexual acts, or even if they despise the gay world or their homosexual feelings. People are homosexual if they experience romantic and/or sexual arousal repeatedly and consistently in the presence of some members of their own sex, but not with members of the other sex. A homosexual person can exist in a society that has no name for the trait. In a society that does not categorize individuals according to their sexual inclinations, homosexually inclined persons are unlikely to set themselves apart by choosing distinctive social arrangements or by calling themselves distinctive names. But the more perceptive people in such a society will, if the occasion arises, be able to discern the existence of these different patterns and comment upon them. This is, indeed, exactly what happened in certain medieval and ancient Greek debates about whether same-sex or other-sex love was better. Some people like Plato understood that different people have different sexual orientations, but because their society did not attach as much significance to these traits, they could be discussed in an offhanded way.

Just as psychologists can go to other cultures and, presumably, classify individuals as "introverts" or "extroverts," even if the cultures themselves have no names for those traits, so can sexologists go to other cultures and pick out individuals as "homosexual," "heterosexual," "bisexual," or "asexual." It is important to note that this does *not* imply that our Western sexual taxonomy is the best one, or that all persons in such a society will fit into our molds. Perhaps a majority will not. Yet it is quite misleading for us to declare, as some social constructionists have done, that there is no such thing as homosexuality or homosexuals in such cultures.

When different cultures give different reasons for an apple falling to earth, that does not demonstrate that gravity works differently in different societies. A culture that says the fall was "because of gravity" is not necessarily more right than one that says it fell "because it was ripe." In fact, we would be at least as intrigued if we could resurrect Plato or Sappho and have them classify members of our society in ancient Greek terms, or have a Native American berdache or Thai *kathoey* classify our friends using their native taxonomies. This cultural exploration becomes culturally imperialistic only if someone insists that our point of view is the best way, the only way, or the only interesting or intellectually respectable way, of classifying people.

If we were to do this exercise, we would discover some fascinating and subtle similarities in the ways that different societies have divided the sexual spectrum. For example, in the societies we have discussed so far, each culture considers the origins of the alternative gender trait to be important enough to merit an explanation. In each case it is alleged that the origins are beyond the control of the individual exhibiting the trait. Plato's myth alleges that we were ripped apart from our other halves against our will. Amazons were often believed to be masculine as a result of a dream instruction from the spirit world. The Sioux medicine man Lame Deer said that *winktes* were twins merged prenatally into psychic hermaphrodites. *Quethos* were alleged to have had their genitals exposed to the moon during infancy. The Chukchee *berdache* went on a vision quest and had dreams revealing his status to him. In most gender-mixing institutions, the trait could be recognized in children, even when the children themselves might be unaware of it.

We conclude that the spectrum of gender-role variability in other cultures is not too different from the spectrum in our own, even though there are different emphases in each society. Indeed, the younger generation of anthropologists, less worried about asking sexual questions than their predecessors and more knowledgeable about the various sexual predilections known (or unknown) to science, will more likely manage to ask the right questions of the younger generation of native informants, who may well be less worried about answering them. As a result, variability in anthropologists may decrease, and we might get a better estimate of the true amount of variability among cultures.

The homosexualities we see in the modern West bear some striking 50
resemblances to the homosexualities we see everywhere else on the globe, and saw throughout history. There are similarities running through them, and there are also important differences. In ancient Greece, and in parts of the Middle Ages, there were societies that paid relatively little attention to the question of whether it was men or women people found themselves falling in love with. Even so, from both time periods debates have

survived — fictional works, and presumably entertaining ones — in which someone saying homosexual love was better debated someone who said heterosexual love was better (for example, pseudo-Lucian,[3] 1967). As Boswell (1982) points out, those differences were recognized at those times; they were not invented in the seventeenth (according to McIntosh) or nineteenth (according to Katz) century.[4]

At the same time, society's attitudes toward those (real) traits were very different from those of our own society, and this had enormously important consequences. Our society has taken a natural kind of sexuality and made it taboo, in a way that is completely unnecessary for its stability or its values. It is time for us to learn from other cultures that uniform sameness is not a desirable goal for society. We can learn to appreciate and value diversity, and realize that with work and good will, we can love our homosexual and bisexual members, our *quethos,* our *xaniths* and *hijras,* our butches and our fems, as we love all the other members of our human family.

References

Bogoras, W. (1904–1909). The Chukchee. *Memoirs of the American Museum of Natural History, 11,* 1–732.

Boswell, J. (1982). Revolutions, universals, and sexual categories. *Salmagundi, 58–59,* 89–113.

Carrier, J. M. (1980). Homosexual behavior in cross-cultural perspective. In J. Marmor (Ed.), *Homosexual behavior: A modern reappraisal* (pp. 100–122). New York: Basic Books.

Dizick, M., & Bly, M. (1985). *Dogs are better than cats.* New York: Dolphin/Doubleday.

Goode, E. (1981). Comments on the homosexual role. *Journal of Sex Research, 17,* 54–65.

Jackson, P. A. (1989). *Male homosexuality in Thailand: An interpretation of contemporary Thai sources.* Elmhurst, NY: Global Academic Publishers.

Jacobs, S. (1983). Comments. *Current Anthropology, 24,* 459–460.

Katz, J. N. (1983). *Gay/lesbian almanac: A new documentary.* New York: Harper & Row.

Lame Deer, J. F., & Erdoes, R. (1972). *Lame Deer: Seeker of visions.* New York: Simon & Schuster.

McIntosh, M. (1968). The homosexual role. *Social Problems, 16,* 182–192.

Plato. (1956). The symposium. In E. H. Warmington & P. G. Rouse (Eds.) (W. H. D. Rouse, Trans.), *Great dialogs of Plato* (pp. 69–117). New York: New American Library.

pseudo-Lucian. (1967). Affairs of the heart. In M. D. Macleod (Trans.), *Lucian* (pp. 205–207), *8,* 150–235. Cambridge, MA: Loeb Classics.

[3]*pseudo-Lucian:* The "false" Lucian, that is, an anonymous writer whose works were once attributed to Lucian, a Greek writer of the second century A.D.

[4]In fairness to these authors, we should point out that McIntosh was talking about England, and Katz was talking about the British North American colonies. [Author's note]

Wikan, U. (1982). *Behind the veil in Arabia: Women in Oman.* Baltimore, MD: Johns Hopkins University Press.

Williams, W. L. (1986). *The spirit and the flesh: Sexual diversity in American Indian culture.* Boston: Beacon.

Engaging the Text

1. Reread the opening section of this essay (paras. 1–5) and discuss why Weinrich and Williams begin as they do. What are their key points? Discuss with classmates any statements you do not fully understand. Did the authors achieve the three goals they set out in paragraph 5?
2. Distinguish between the "social constructionist" view of homosexuality that Weinrich and Williams challenge and the "interactionist" view that they propose. What's wrong with the social constructionist hypothesis, and how does the interactionist model attempt to correct these flaws? How compelling do you find the authors' evidence?
3. Discuss the intent and the effectiveness of the following analogies used by Weinrich and Williams: the comparison of sexual orientation to "petual" orientation (paras. 11–12), and the comparison of gender socialization to religious training (paras. 41–44).

Exploring Connections

4. Use criticism of the limits of stereotypical gender roles in the essays by Holly Devor (p. 244), Michael Kimmel (p. 259), and Weinrich and Williams to construct alternative definitions of masculinity and femininity. Is it possible to construct any definition for male and female gender roles that isn't restrictive?
5. Like Carmen Vázquez (p. 287), Weinrich and Williams ask readers to be open-minded about homosexuality. What strategies do the writers of each selection employ to educate and persuade? Which approach do you think is more effective? Why?
6. To what extent does Weinrich and Williams's research support or complicate the notion presented by Holly Devor (p. 244) that gender is socially constructed and not, like sex, biologically determined?

Extending the Critical Context

7. Write a definition of "homosexuality" based on what you've learned in this selection. Then find several definitions in dictionaries, psychology textbooks, or other sources. How well do the published definitions hold up to your own?
8. The collection in which this essay appeared is subtitled "Research Implications for Public Policy." What implications for public policy do you see in Weinrich and Williams's research?

Where I Come from Is Like This

Paula Gunn Allen

Paula Gunn Allen was born in 1939 in Cubero, New Mexico, a Spanish-Mexican land grant village; where she comes from is life as a Laguna Pueblo–Sioux–Lebanese woman. In this essay she discusses some of the ways traditional images of women in American Indian cultures differ from images in mainstream American culture. Allen is a professor of English and American Indian literature at the University of California, Los Angeles. In addition to her scholarly work, Allen is widely recognized for her books of poetry and for her novel The Woman Who Owned the Shadows *(1983).*

In her most recent book, Grandmothers of the Light *(1991), she collects and weaves together a variety of stories drawn from the female spiritual traditions of Native America.*

This piece appeared in Allen's collection of essays The Sacred Hoop: Recovering the Feminine in American Indian Traditions *(1986).*

I

Modern American Indian women, like their non-Indian sisters, are deeply engaged in the struggle to redefine themselves. In their struggle they must reconcile traditional tribal definitions of women with industrial and postindustrial non-Indian definitions. Yet while these definitions seem to be more or less mutually exclusive, Indian women must somehow harmonize and integrate both in their own lives.

An American Indian woman is primarily defined by her tribal identity. In her eyes, her destiny is necessarily that of her people, and her sense of herself as a woman is first and foremost prescribed by her tribe. The definitions of woman's roles are as diverse as tribal cultures in the Americas. In some she is devalued, in others she wields considerable power. In some she is a familial/clan adjunct, in some she is as close to autonomous as her economic circumstances and psychological traits permit. But in no tribal definitions is she perceived in the same way as are women in western industrial and postindustrial cultures.

In the west, few images of women form part of the cultural mythos, and these are largely sexually charged. Among Christians, the madonna is the female prototype, and she is portrayed as essentially passive: her contribution is simply that of birthing. Little else is attributed to her and she certainly possesses few of the characteristics that are attributed to mythic figures among Indian tribes. This image is countered (rather than balanced) by the witch-goddess/whore characteristics designed to reinforce cultural beliefs about women, as well as western adversarial and dualistic perceptions of reality.

The tribes see women variously, but they do not question the power of femininity. Sometimes they see women as fearful, sometimes peaceful, sometimes omnipotent and omniscient, but they never portray women as mindless, helpless, simple, or oppressed. And while the women in a given tribe, clan, or band may be all these things, the individual woman is provided with a variety of images of women from the interconnected supernatural, natural, and social worlds she lives in.

As a half-breed American Indian woman, I cast about in my mind for 5
negative images of Indian women, and I find none that are directed to Indian women alone. The negative images I do have are of Indians in general and in fact are more often of males than of females. All these images come to me from non-Indian sources, and they are always balanced by a positive image. My ideas of womanhood, passed on largely by my mother and grandmothers, Laguna Pueblo women, are about practicality, strength, reasonableness, intelligence, wit, and competence. I also remember vividly the women who came to my father's store, the women who held me and sang to me, the women at Feast Day, at Grab Days,[1] the women in the kitchen of my Cubero home, the women I grew up with; none of them appeared weak or helpless, none of them presented herself tentatively. I remember a certain reserve on those lovely brown faces; I remember the direct gaze of eyes framed by bright-colored shawls draped over their heads and cascading down their backs. I remember the clean cotton dresses and carefully pressed hand-embroidered aprons they always wore; I remember laughter and good food, especially the sweet bread and the oven bread they gave us. Nowhere in my mind is there a foolish woman, a dumb woman, a vain woman, or a plastic woman, though the Indian women I have known have shown a wide range of personal style and demeanor.

My memory includes the Navajo woman who was badly beaten by her Sioux husband; but I also remember that my grandmother abandoned her Sioux husband long ago. I recall the stories about the Laguna woman beaten regularly by her husband in the presence of her children so that the children would not believe in the strength and power of femininity. And I remember the women who drank, who got into fights with other women and with the men, and who often won those battles. I have memories of tired women, partying women, stubborn women, sullen women, amicable women, selfish women, shy women, and aggressive women. Most of all I remember the women who laugh and scold and sit uncomplaining in the long sun on feast days and who cook wonderful food on wood stoves, in beehive mud ovens, and over open fires outdoors.

[1]*Grab Days:* Laguna ritual in which women throw food and small items (like pieces of cloth) to those attending.

Among the images of women that come to me from various tribes as well as my own are White Buffalo Woman, who came to the Lakota long ago and brought them the religion of the Sacred Pipe which they still practice; Tinotzin the goddess who came to Juan Diego to remind him that she still walked the hills of her people and sent him with her message, her demand and her proof to the Catholic bishop in the city nearby. And from Laguna I take the images of Yellow Woman, Coyote Woman, Grandmother Spider (Spider Old Woman), who brought the light, who gave us weaving and medicine, who gave us life. Among the Keres she is known as Thought Woman who created us all and who keeps us in creation even now. I remember Iyatiku, Earth Woman, Corn Woman, who guides and counsels the people to peace and who welcomes us home when we cast off this coil of flesh as huskers cast off the leaves that wrap the corn. I remember Iyatiku's sister, Sun Woman, who held metals and cattle, pigs and sheep, highways and engines and so many things in her bundle, who went away to the east saying that one day she would return.

II

Since the coming of the Anglo-Europeans beginning in the fifteenth century, the fragile web of identity that long held tribal people secure has gradually been weakened and torn. But the oral tradition has prevented the complete destruction of the web, the ultimate disruption of tribal ways. The oral tradition is vital; it heals itself and the tribal web by adapting to the flow of the present while never relinquishing its connection to the past. Its adaptability has always been required, as many generations have experienced. Certainly the modern American Indian woman bears slight resemblance to her forebears — at least on superficial examination — but she is still a tribal woman in her deepest being. Her tribal sense of relationship to all that is continues to flourish. And though she is at times beset by her knowledge of the enormous gap between the life she lives and the life she was raised to live, and while she adapts her mind and being to the circumstances of her present life, she does so in tribal ways, mending the tears in the web of being from which she takes her existence as she goes.

My mother told me stories all the time, though I often did not recognize them as that. My mother told me stories about cooking and childbearing; she told me stories about menstruation and pregnancy; she told me stories about gods and heroes, about fairies and elves, about goddesses and spirits; she told me stories about the land and the sky, about cats and dogs, about snakes and spiders; she told me stories about climbing trees and exploring the mesas; she told me stories about going to dances and getting married; she told me stories about dressing and undressing, about sleeping and waking; she told me stories about herself, about her mother, about her grandmother. She told me stories about grieving and laughing, about thinking and doing; she told me stories about school and about people; about darning and mending; she told me stories about turquoise and about gold; she told me European stories and Laguna stories; she told me Catholic stories and Presbyterian stories; she told me city stories and country stories; she told me political stories and religious stories. She told me stories about living and stories about dying. And in all of those stories she told me who I was, who I was supposed to be, whom I came from, and who would follow me. In this way she taught me the meaning of the words she said, that all life is a circle and everything has a place within it. That's what she said and what she showed me in the things she did and the way she lives.

Of course, through my formal, white, Christian education, I discovered 10
that other people had stories of their own — about women, about Indians, about fact, about reality — and I was amazed by a number of startling suppositions that others made about tribal customs and beliefs. According to the un-Indian, non-Indian view, for instance, Indians barred menstruating women from ceremonies and indeed segregated them from the rest of the people, consigning them to some space specially designed for them. This showed that Indians considered menstruating women unclean and not fit to enjoy the company of decent (nonmenstruating) people, that is, men. I was surprised and confused to hear this because my mother had taught me that white people had strange attitudes toward menstruation: they thought something was bad about it, that it meant you were sick, cursed, sinful, and weak and that you had to be very careful during that time. She taught me that menstruation was a normal occurrence, that I could go swimming or hiking or whatever else I wanted to do during my period. She actively scorned women who took to their beds, who were incapacitated by cramps, who "got the blues."

As I struggled to reconcile these very contradictory interpretations of American Indians' traditional beliefs concerning menstruation, I realized that the menstrual taboos were about power, not about sin or filth. My conclusion was later borne out by some tribes' own explanations, which, as you may well imagine, came as quite a relief to me.

The truth of the matter as many Indians see it is that women who are at the peak of their fecundity are believed to possess power that throws male power totally out of kilter. They emit such force that, in their presence, any male-owned or -dominated ritual or sacred object cannot do its usual task. For instance, the Lakota say that a menstruating woman anywhere near a yuwipi man, who is a special sort of psychic, spirit-empowered healer, for a day or so before he is to do his ceremony will effectively disempower him. Conversely, among many if not most tribes, important ceremonies cannot be held without the presence of women. Sometimes the ritual woman who empowers the ceremony must be unmarried and virginal so that the power she channels is unalloyed, unweakened by sexual arousal and penetration by a male. Other ceremonies require tumescent women, others the presence of mature women who have borne children, and still others depend for empowerment on postmenopausal women. Women may be segregated from the company of the whole band or village on certain occasions, but on certain occasions men are also segregated. In short, each ritual depends on a certain balance of power, and the positions of women within the phases of womanhood are used by tribal people to empower certain rites. This does not derive from a male-dominant view; it is not a ritual observance imposed on women by men. It derives from a tribal view of reality that distinguishes tribal people from feudal and industrial people.

Among the tribes, the occult power of women, inextricably bound to our hormonal life, is thought to be very great; many hold that we possess innately the blood-given power to kill — with a glance, with a step, or with a judicious mixing of menstrual blood into somebody's soup. Medicine women among the Pomo of California cannot practice until they are sufficiently mature; when they are immature, their power is diffuse and is likely to interfere with their practice until time and experience have it under control. So women of the tribes are not especially inclined to see themselves as poor helpless victims of male domination. Even in those tribes where something akin to male domination was present, women are perceived as powerful, socially, physically, and metaphysically. In times past, as in times present, women carried enormous burdens with aplomb. We were far indeed from the "weaker sex," the designation that white aristocratic sisters unhappily earned for us all.

I remember my mother moving furniture all over the house when she wanted it changed. She didn't wait for my father to come home and help — she just went ahead and moved the piano, a huge upright from the old days, the couch, the refrigerator. Nobody had told her she was too weak to do such things. In imitation of her, I would delight in loading trucks at my father's store with cases of pop or fifty-pound sacks of flour. Even when I was quite small I could do it, and it gave me a belief in my own physical strength that advancing middle age can't quite erase. My mother used to tell me about the Acoma Pueblo women she had seen as a child carrying huge ollas (water pots) on their heads as they wound their way up the tortuous stairwell carved into the face of the "Sky City" mesa, a feat I tried to imitate with books and tin buckets. ("Sky City" is the term used by the Chamber of Commerce for the mother village of Acoma, which is situated atop a high sandstone table mountain.) I was never very successful, but even the attempt reminded me that I was supposed to be strong and balanced to be a proper girl.

Of course, my mother's Laguna people are Keres Indian, reputed to be 15
the last extreme mother-right people on earth. So it is no wonder that I got notably nonwhite notions about the natural strength and prowess of women. Indeed, it is only when I am trying to get non-Indian approval, recognition, or acknowledgement that my "weak sister" emotional and intellectual ploys get the better of my tribal woman's good sense. At such times I forget that I just moved the piano or just wrote a competent paper or just completed a financial transaction satisfactorily or have supported myself and my children for most of my adult life.

Nor is my contradictory behavior atypical. Most Indian women I know are in the same bicultural bind: we vacillate between being dependent and strong, self-reliant and powerless, strongly motivated and hopelessly insecure. We resolve the dilemma in various ways: some of us party all the time; some of us drink to excess; some of us travel and move around a lot; some of us land good jobs and then quit them; some of us engage in violent exchanges; some of us blow our brains out. We act in these destructive ways because we suffer from the societal conflicts caused by having to identify with two hopelessly opposed cultural definitions of women. Through this destructive dissonance we are unhappy prey to the self-disparagement common to, indeed demanded of, Indians living in the United States today. Our situation is caused by the exigencies of a history of invasion, conquest, and colonization whose searing marks are probably ineradicable. A popular bumper sticker on many Indian cars proclaims: "If You're Indian You're In," to which I always find myself adding under my breath, "Trouble."

III

No Indian can grow to any age without being informed that her people were "savages" who interfered with the march of progress pursued by respectable, loving, civilized white people. We are the villains of the scenario when we are mentioned at all. We are absent from much of white history except when we are calmly, rationally, succinctly, and systematically dehumanized. On the few occasions we are noticed in any way other than as howling, bloodthirsty beings, we are acclaimed for our noble quaintness. In this definition, we are exotic curios. Our ancient arts and customs are used to draw tourist money to state coffers, into the pocketbooks and bank accounts of scholars, and into support of the American-in-Disneyland promoters' dream.

As a Roman Catholic child I was treated to bloody tales of how the savage Indians martyred the hapless priests and missionaries who went among them in an attempt to lead them to the one true path. By the time I was through high school I had the idea that Indians were people who had benefited mightily from the advanced knowledge and superior morality of the Anglo-Europeans. At least I had, perforce, that idea to lay beside the other one that derived from my daily experience of Indian life, an idea less dehumanizing and more accurate because it came from my mother and the other Indian people who raised me. That idea was that Indians are a people who don't tell lies, who care for their children and their old people. You never see an Indian orphan, they said. You always know when you're old that someone will take care of you — one of your children will. Then they'd list the old folks who were being taken care of by this child or that. No child is ever considered illegitimate among the Indians, they said. If a girl gets pregnant, the baby is still part of the family, and the mother is too. That's what they said, and they showed me real people who lived according to those principles.

Of course the ravages of colonization have taken their toll; there are orphans in Indian country now, and abandoned, brutalized old folks; there are even illegitimate children, though the very concept still strikes me as absurd. There are battered children and neglected children, and there are battered wives and women who have been raped by Indian men. Proximity to the "civilizing" effects of white Christians has not improved the moral quality of life in Indian country, though each group, Indian and white, explains the situation differently. Nor is there much yet in the oral tradition that can enable us to adapt to these inhuman changes. But a force is growing in that direction, and it is helping Indian women reclaim their lives. Their power, their sense of direction and of self will soon be visible. It is the force of the women who speak and work and write, and it is formidable.

20 Through all the centuries of war and death and cultural and psychic destruction have endured the women who raise the children and tend the fires, who pass along the tales and the traditions, who weep and bury the dead, who are the dead, and who never forget. There are always the women, who make pots and weave baskets, who fashion clothes and cheer their children on at powwow, who make fry bread and piki bread, and corn soup and chili stew, who dance and sing and remember and hold within their hearts the dream of their ancient peoples — that one day the woman who thinks will speak to us again, and everywhere there will be peace. Meanwhile we tell the stories and write the books and trade tales of anger and woe and stories of fun and scandal and laugh over all manner of things that happen every day. We watch and we wait.

My great-grandmother told my mother: never forget you are Indian. And my mother told me the same thing. This, then, is how I have gone about remembering, so that my children will remember too.

Engaging the Text

1. Outline how Allen's views of women differ from traditional Anglo-American views. Do you see any difference between Allen's perspective and "feminism" as you understand the term?
2. What does Allen mean by "bicultural bind" (para. 16)? How has it affected her, and how does she deal with it?
3. How does Allen represent relationships between American Indian women and men?
4. Why is remembering so important to Allen? What roles does it play in helping her live in a world dominated by an alien culture? How does it help her define herself as a woman?
5. Allen's essay includes much personal recollection. Try to "translate" some of this information into more abstract statements of theme or message. (For instance, you might write, "Women's roles in American Indian cultures are maintained through example, through oral tradition, and through ceremonial tribal practices.") What is gained, what lost in such "translations"?

6. Review how Allen uses the image of the web to explain tribal identity. In what ways is this an appropriate and effective metaphor? Have you encountered this image in other writing about women's social lives?

Exploring Connections

7. Drawing on Allen's discussion of the roles played by women and men in Indian society and Weinrich and Williams's discussion of the *berdache* in tribal cultures (p. 296), write an essay comparing Euro-American and Native American attitudes toward gender roles.
8. Allen's focus here is rather different from Roger Jack's in "An Indian Story" (p. 225); do you nevertheless see similarities in the two authors' ideas about family or tribal identity?
9. Review "Black Women and Motherhood" (p. 195) by Patricia Hill Collins. By what means and with what success are African American and Native American women resisting Anglo-European roles?

Extending the Critical Context

10. Are you struggling to reconcile different definitions of what you should be? Write an essay or journal entry exploring this issue. (For example, are family, friends, and school pushing you in different directions?)
11. Working in single-sex groups, create collages of male or female images drawn from a range of popular publications. What qualities, values, and attitudes do these images project? Are they consistent, or do you see contradictions and tensions within them? What myths about each gender do you see emerging?

The Two

Gloria Naylor

This story from Gloria Naylor's The Women of Brewster Place *(1982) paints a fictional portrait of a Black lesbian couple as their neighbors begin to discover their secret. As they emerge in the story, Lorraine and Theresa prompt us to reconsider stereotypes of homosexual people. Gloria Naylor (b. 1950) holds a master's degree in Afro-American Studies from Yale University.* The Women of Brewster Place *brought her national recognition and critical acclaim when it won the American Book Award for First Fiction. Naylor has also published a work of nonfiction,* Centennial *(1986), and three other novels:* Linden Hills *(1985),* Mama Day *(1988), and* Bailey's Cafe *(1992).*

At first they seemed like such nice girls. No one could remember exactly when they had moved into Brewster. It was earlier in the year before Ben[1] was killed — of course, it had to be before Ben's death. But no one remembered if it was in the winter or spring of that year that the two had come. People often came and went on Brewster Place like a restless night's dream, moving in and out in the dark to avoid eviction notices or neighborhood bulletins about the dilapidated condition of their furnishings. So it wasn't until the two were clocked leaving in the mornings and returning in the evenings at regular intervals that it was quietly absorbed that they now claimed Brewster as home. And Brewster waited, cautiously prepared to claim them, because you never knew about young women, and obviously single at that. But when no wild music or drunken friends careened out of the corner building on weekends, and especially, when no slightly eager husbands were encouraged to linger around that first-floor apartment and run errands for them, a suspended sigh of relief floated around the two when they dumped their garbage, did their shopping, and headed for the morning bus.

The women of Brewster had readily accepted the lighter, skinny one. There wasn't much threat in her timid mincing walk and the slighty protruding teeth she seemed so eager to show everyone in her bell-like good mornings and evenings. Breaths were held a little longer in the direction of the short dark one — too pretty, and too much behind. And she insisted on wearing those thin Qiana dresses that the summer breeze molded against the maddening rhythm of the twenty pounds of rounded flesh that she swung steadily down the street. Through slitted eyes, the women watched their men watching her pass, knowing the bastards were praying for a wind. But since she seemed oblivious to whether these supplications went answered, their sighs settled around her shoulders too. Nice girls.

And so no one even cared to remember exactly when they had moved into Brewster Place, until the rumor started. It had first spread through the block like a sour odor that's only faintly perceptible and easily ignored until it starts growing in strength from the dozen mouths it had been lying in, among clammy gums and scum-coated teeth. And then it was everywhere — lining the mouth and whitening the lips of everyone as they wrinkled up their noses at its pervading smell, unable to pinpoint the source or time of its initial arrival. Sophie could — she had been there.

It wasn't that the rumor had actually begun with Sophie. A rumor needs no true parent. It only needs a willing carrier, and it found one in Sophie. She had been there — on one of those August evenings when the sun's absence is a mockery because the heat leaves the air so heavy it presses the naked skin down on your body, to the point that a sheet becomes unbearable and sleep impossible. So most of Brewster was outside that night when the two had come in together, probably from one of those air-conditioned mov-

[1] *Ben:* The resident caretaker for the apartments in Brewster Place.

ies downtown, and had greeted the ones who were loitering around their building. And they had started up the steps when the skinny one tripped over a child's ball and the darker one had grabbed her by the arm and around the waist to break her fall. "Careful, don't wanna lose you now." And the two of them had laughed into each other's eyes and went into the building.

The smell had begun there. It outlined the image of the stumbling 5
woman and the one who had broken her fall. Sophie and a few other women sniffed at the spot and then, perplexed, silently looked at each other. Where had they seen that before? They had often laughed and touched each other — held each other in joy or its dark twin — but where had they seen *that* before? It came to them as the scent drifted down the steps and entered their nostrils on the way to their inner mouths. They had seen that — done that — with their men. That shared moment of invisible communion reserved for two and hidden from the rest of the world behind laughter or tears or a touch. In the days before babies, miscarriages, and other broken dreams, after stolen caresses in barn stalls and cotton houses, after intimate walks from church and secret kisses with boys who were now long forgotten or permanently fixed in their lives — that was where. They could almost feel the odor moving about in their mouths, and they slowly knitted themselves together and let it out into the air like a yellow mist that began to cling to the bricks on Brewster.

So it got around that the two in 312 were *that* way. And they had seemed like such nice girls. Their regular exits and entrances to the block were viewed with a jaundiced eye. The quiet that rested around their door on the weekends hinted of all sorts of secret rituals, and their friendly indifference to the men on the street was an insult to the women as a brazen flaunting of unnatural ways.

Since Sophie's apartment windows faced theirs from across the air shaft, she became the official watchman for the block, and her opinions were deferred to whenever the two came up in conversation. Sophie took her position seriously and was constantly alert for any telltale signs that might creep out around their drawn shades, across from which she kept a religious vigil. An entire week of drawn shades was evidence enough to send her flying around with reports that as soon as it got dark they pulled their shades down and put on the lights. Heads nodded in knowing unison — a definite sign. If doubt was voiced with a "But I pull my shades down at night too," a whispered "yeah, but you're not *that* way" was argument enough to win them over.

Sophie watched the lighter one dumping their garbage, and she went outside and opened the lid. Her eyes darted over the crushed tin cans, vegetable peelings, and empty chocolate chip cookie boxes. What do they do with all them chocolate chip cookies? It was surely a sign, but it would take some time to figure that one out. She saw Ben go into their apartment, and she waited and blocked his path as he came out, carrying his toolbox.

"What ya see?" She grabbed his arm and whispered wetly in his face.

Ben stared at her squinted eyes and drooping lips and shook his head 10
slowly. "Uh, uh, uh, it was terrible."

"Yeah?" She moved in a little closer.

"Worst busted faucet I seen in my whole life." He shook her hand off his arm and left her standing in the middle of the block.

"You old sop bucket," she muttered, as she went back up on her stoop. A broken faucet, huh? Why did they need to use so much water?

Sophie had plenty to report that day. Ben had said it was terrible in there. No, she didn't know exactly what he had seen, but you can imagine — and they did. Confronted with the difference that had been thrust into their predictable world, they reached into their imaginations and, using an ancient pattern, weaved themselves a reason for its existence. Out of necessity they stitched all of their secret fears and lingering childhood nightmares into this existence, because even though it was deceptive enough to try and look as they looked, talk as they talked, and do as they did, it had to have some hidden stain to invalidate it — it was impossible for them both to be right. So they leaned back, supported by the sheer weight of their numbers and comforted by the woven barrier that kept them protected from the yellow mist that enshrouded the two as they came and went on Brewster Place.

Lorraine was the first to notice the change in the people on Brewster 15
Place. She was a shy but naturally friendly woman who got up early, and had read the morning paper and done fifty sit-ups before it was time to leave for work. She came out of her apartment eager to start her day by greeting any of her neighbors who were outside. But she noticed that some of the people who had spoken to her before made a point of having something else to do with their eyes when she passed, although she could almost feel them staring at her back as she moved on. The ones who still spoke only did so after an uncomfortable pause, in which they seemed to be peering through her before they begrudged her a good morning or evening. She wondered if it was all in her mind and she thought about mentioning it to Theresa, but she didn't want to be accused of being too sensitive again. And how would Tee even notice anything like that anyway? She had a lousy attitude and hardly ever spoke to people. She stayed in that bed until the last moment and rushed out of the house fogged-up and grumpy, and she was used to being stared at — by men at least — because of her body.

Lorraine thought about these things as she came up the block from work, carrying a large paper bag. The group of women on her stoop parted silently and let her pass.

"Good evening," she said, as she climbed the steps.

Sophie was standing on the top step and tried to peek into the bag. "You been shopping, huh? What ya buy?" It was almost an accusation.

"Groceries." Lorraine shielded the top of the bag from view and squeezed past her with a confused frown. She saw Sophie throw a knowing glance to the others at the bottom of the stoop. What was wrong with this old woman? Was she crazy or something?

Lorraine went into her apartment. Theresa was sitting by the window, 20
reading a copy of *Mademoiselle.* She glanced up from her magazine. "Did you get my chocolate chip cookies?"

"Why good evening to you, too, Tee. And how was my day? Just wonderful." She sat the bag down on the couch. "The little Baxter boy brought in a puppy for show-and-tell, and the damn thing pissed all over the floor and then proceeded to chew the heel off my shoe, but, yes, I managed to hobble to the store and bring you your chocolate chip cookies."

Oh, Jesus, Theresa thought, she's got a bug up her ass tonight.

"Well, you should speak to Mrs. Baxter. She ought to train her kid better than that." She didn't wait for Lorraine to stop laughing before she tried to stretch her good mood. "Here, I'll put those things away. Want me to make dinner so you can rest? I only worked half a day, and the most tragic thing that went down was a broken fingernail and that got caught in my typewriter."

Lorraine followed Theresa into the kitchen. "No, I'm not really tired, and fair's fair, you cooked last night. I didn't mean to tick off like that; it's just that . . . well, Tee, have you noticed that people aren't as nice as they used to be?"

Theresa stiffened. Oh, God, here she goes again. "What people, Lor- 25
raine? Nice in what way?"

"Well, the people in this building and on the street. No one hardly speaks anymore. I mean, I'll come in and say good evening — and just silence. It wasn't like that when we first moved in. I don't know, it just makes you wonder; that's all. What are they thinking?"

"I personally don't give a shit what they're thinking. And their good evenings don't put any bread on my table."

"Yeah, but you didn't see the way that woman looked at me out there. They must feel something or know something. They probably — "

"They, they, they!" Theresa exploded. "You know, I'm not starting up with this again, Lorraine. Who in the hell are they? And where in the hell are we? Living in some dump of a building in this God-forsaken part of town around a bunch of ignorant niggers with the cotton still under their fingernails because of you and your theys. They knew something in Linden Hills, so I gave up an apartment for you that I'd been in for the last four years. And then they knew in Park Heights, and you made me so miserable there we had to leave. Now these mysterious theys are on Brewster Place. Well, look out that window, kid. There's a big wall down that block, and this is the end of the line for me. I'm not moving anymore, so if that's what you're working yourself up to — save it!"

When Theresa became angry she was like a lump of smoldering coal, 30
and her fierce bursts of temper always unsettled Lorraine.

"You see, that's why I didn't want to mention it." Lorraine began to pull at her fingers nervously. "You're always flying up and jumping to conclusions — no one said anything about moving. And I didn't know your life has been so miserable since you met me. I'm sorry about that," she finished tearfully.

Theresa looked at Lorraine, standing in the kitchen door like a wilted leaf, and she wanted to throw something at her. Why didn't she ever fight back? The very softness that had first attracted her to Lorraine was now a frequent cause for irritation. Smoked honey. That's what Lorraine had reminded her of, sitting in her office clutching that application. Dry autumn days in Georgia woods, thick bloated smoke under a beehive, and the first glimpse of amber honey just faintly darkened about the edges by the burning twigs. She had flowed just that heavily into Theresa's mind and had stuck there with a persistent sweetness.

But Theresa hadn't known then that this softness filled Lorraine up to the very middle and that she would bend at the slightest pressure, would be constantly seeking to surround herself with the comfort of everyone's goodwill, and would shrivel up at the least touch of disapproval. It was becoming a drain to be continually called upon for this nurturing and support that she just didn't understand. She had supplied it at first out of love for Lorraine, hoping that she would harden eventually, even as honey does when exposed to the cold. Theresa was growing tired of being clung to — of being the one who was leaned on. She didn't want a child — she wanted someone who could stand toe to toe with her and be willing to slug it out at times. If they practiced that way with each other, then they could turn back to back and beat the hell out of the world for trying to invade their territory. But she had found no such sparring partner in Lorraine, and the strain of fighting alone was beginning to show on her.

"Well, if it was that miserable, I would have been gone a long time ago," she said, watching her words refresh Lorraine like a gentle shower.

"I guess you think I'm some sort of a sick paranoid, but I can't afford to have people calling my job or writing letters to my principal. You know I've already lost a position like that in Detroit. And teaching is my whole life, Tee."

"I know," she sighed, not really knowing at all. There was no danger of that ever happening on Brewster Place. Lorraine taught too far from this neighborhood for anyone here to recognize her in that school. No, it wasn't her job she feared losing this time, but their approval. She wanted to stand out there and chat and trade makeup secrets and cake recipes. She wanted to be secretary of their block association and be asked to mind their kids while they ran to the store. And none of that was going to happen if they couldn't even bring themselves to accept her good evenings.

Theresa silently finished unpacking the groceries. "Why did you buy cottage cheese? Who eats that stuff?"

"Well, I thought we should go on a diet."

"If *we* go on a diet, then you'll disappear. You've got nothing to lose but your hair."

"Oh, I don't know. I thought that we might want to try and reduce our hips or something." Lorraine shrugged playfully. 40

"No, thank you. We are very happy with our hips the way they are," Theresa said, as she shoved the cottage cheese to the back of the refrigerator. "And even when I lose weight, it never comes off there. My chest and arms just get smaller, and I start looking like a bottle of salad dressing."

The two women laughed, and Theresa sat down to watch Lorraine fix dinner. "You know, this behind has always been my downfall. When I was coming up in Georgia with my grandmother, the boys used to promise me penny candy if I would let them pat my behind. And I used to love those jawbreakers — you know, the kind that lasted all day and kept changing colors in your mouth. So I was glad to oblige them, because in one afternoon I could collect a whole week's worth of jawbreakers."

"Really. That's funny to you? Having some boy feeling all over you."

Theresa sucked her teeth. "We were only kids, Lorraine. You know, you remind me of my grandmother. That was one straight-laced old lady. She had a fit when my brother told her what I was doing. She called me into the smokehouse and told me in this real scary whisper that I could get pregnant from letting little boys pat my butt and that I'd end up like my cousin Willa. But Willa and I had been thick as fleas, and she had already given me a step-by-step summary of how she'd gotten into her predicament. But I sneaked around to her house that night just to double-check her story, since that old lady had seemed so earnest. 'Willa, are you sure?' I whispered through her bedroom window. 'I'm tellin' ya, Tee,' she said. 'Just keep both feet on the ground and you home free.' Much later I learned that advice wasn't too biologically sound, but it worked in Georgia because those country boys didn't have much imagination."

Theresa's laughter bounced off of Lorraine's silent, rigid back and died in her throat. She angrily tore open a pack of the chocolate chip cookies. "Yeah," she said, staring at Lorraine's back and biting down hard into the cookie, "it wasn't until I came up north to college that I found out there's a whole lot of things that a dude with a little imagination can do to you even with both feet on the ground. You see, Willa forgot to tell me not to bend over or squat or — " 45

"Must you!" Lorraine turned around from the stove with her teeth clenched tightly together.

"Must I what, Lorraine? Must I talk about things that are as much a part of life as eating or breathing or growing old? Why are you always so uptight about sex or men?"

"I'm not uptight about anything. I just think its disgusting when you go on and on about — "

"There's nothing disgusting about it, Lorraine. You've never been with a man, but I've been with quite a few — some better than others. There were a couple who I still hope to this day will die a slow, painful death, but then there were some who were good to me — in and out of bed."

"If they were so great, then why are you with me?" Lorraine's lips were 50
trembling.

"Because — " Theresa looked steadily into her eyes and then down at the cookie she was twirling on the table. "Because," she continued slowly, "you can take a chocolate chip cookie and put holes in it and attach it to your ears and call it an earring, or hang it around your neck on a silver chain and pretend it's a necklace — but it's still a cookie. See — you can toss it in the air and call it a Frisbee or even a flying saucer, if the mood hits you, and it's still just a cookie. Send it spinning on a table — like this — until it's a wonderful blur of amber and brown light that you can imagine to be a topaz or rusted gold or old crystal, but the law of gravity has got to come into play, sometime, and it's got to come to rest — sometime. Then all the spinning and pretending and hoopla is over with. And you know what you got?"

"A chocolate chip cookie," Lorraine said.

"Uh-huh." Theresa put the cookie in her mouth and winked. "A lesbian." She got up from the table. "Call me when dinner's ready, I'm going back to read." She stopped at the kitchen door. "Now, why are you putting gravy on that chicken, Lorraine? You know it's fattening."

Engaging the Text

1. What type of community does Naylor describe in her opening two paragraphs, and how, specifically, does she create this atmosphere? Why is this important to the theme of the story?
2. Why does Naylor shift the story's point of view from that of the community to that of Lorraine and Theresa? How does this change of perspective affect the reader?
3. Why does Naylor make a point of details like drawn shades, chocolate chip cookies, and the broken faucet?
4. How important is sexuality in Lorraine and Theresa's relationship? What do they share besides lovemaking?
5. This story is now more than ten years old. Does its treatment of its main theme hold up well over time? Might a neighborhood today react in the same way to the presence of a homosexual couple? Do you think the story would be as well received today as it was in 1982? Explain.

Exploring Connections

6. To what extent does Weinrich and Williams's analysis of homosexuality in other cultures (p. 296) support Theresa's assertion that "a cookie is still a cookie" (para. 51)?
7. Analyze the couple in this story as an example of a "chosen family" as described by Karen Lindsey (p. 158). Would Lindsey say that Lorraine and Theresa are a functional family? Do you agree?
8. Compare and contrast the tribal women in this selection with the matriarchs in "Envy" by Bebe Moore Campbell (p. 182).

Extending the Critical Context

9. Find one or more psychology texts or articles authored before 1960 that cover homosexuality. How is it defined, described, and classified? How often is lesbianism specifically included in the discussion?
10. Investigate the policies and practices regarding homosexual teachers at various schools in your locale. Are there restrictions, explicit or implicit, against homosexual teachers? Are there restrictions on their behavior or appearance? Report to the class on your findings. Your sources might include interviews with teachers as well as school documents, newspaper stories, or legal cases.

4

Created Equal

The Myth of the Melting Pot

The myth of the melting pot predates the drafting of the U.S. Constitution. In 1782, a year before the Peace of Paris formally ended the Revolutionary War, Hector St. Jean de Crèvecoeur envisioned the young American republic as a crucible that would forge its disparate immigrant population into a vigorous new society with a grand future:

> What, then, is the American, this new man? He is either an European, or the descendant of an European. . . . He is an American, who leaving behind him all his ancient prejudices and manners, receives new ones from the new mode of life he has embraced, the new government he obeys, and the new rank he holds. . . . Here individuals of all nations are melted into a new race of men, whose labours and posterity will one day cause great changes in the world.

Crèvecoeur's metaphor has remained a powerful ideal for many generations of American scholars, politicians, artists, and ordinary citizens. Ralph Waldo Emerson, writing in his journal in 1845, celebrated the national vitality produced by the mingling of immigrant cultures: "in this continent — asylum of all nations, — the energy of . . . all the European tribes, — of the Africans, and of the Polynesians — will construct a new race, a new religion, a new state, a new literature." An English Jewish writer named Israel Zangwill, himself an immigrant, popularized the myth in his 1908 drama, *The Melting Pot.* In the play, the hero rhapsodizes, "Yes East and West, and North and South, the palm and the pine, the pole and the equator, the crescent and the cross — how the great Alchemist melts and fuses them with his purging flame! Here shall they all unite to build the Republic of Man and the Kingdom of God." The myth was perhaps most vividly dramatized, though, in a pageant staged by Henry Ford in the early 1920s. Decked out in the costumes of their native lands, Ford's immigrant workers sang traditional songs from their homelands as they danced their way into an enormous replica of a cast-iron pot. They then emerged from the other side wearing identical "American" business suits, waving miniature American flags, and singing "The Star-Spangled Banner."

The drama of becoming an American has deep roots: immigrants take on a new identity — and a new set of cultural myths — because they want to become members of the community, equal members with all the rights, responsibilities, and opportunities of their fellow citizens. The force of the melting pot myth lies in this implied promise that all Americans are indeed "created equal." However, the myth's promises of openness, harmony, unity, and equality were deceptive from the beginning. Crèvecoeur's exclusive concern with the mingling of *European* peoples (he lists the "English, Scotch, Irish, French, Dutch, Germans, and Swedes") utterly ignored the presence of some three-quarters of a million Africans and African Americans who then lived in this country, as well as the tribal peoples who had lived on the land for thousands of years before European contact. Crèvecoeur's vision of a country embracing "all nations" clearly applied only to northern European nations. Benjamin Franklin, in a 1751 essay, was more blunt; since Africa,

Asia, and most of America were inhabited by dark-skinned people, he argued, the American colonies should consciously try to increase the white population and keep out the rest: "Why increase the Sons of Africa, by Planting them in America, where we have so fair an opportunity, by excluding Blacks and Tawneys, of increasing the lovely White . . . ?" If later writers like Emerson and Zangwill saw a more inclusive cultural mix as a source of hope and renewal for the United States, others throughout this country's history have, even more than Franklin, feared that mix as a threat.

The fear of difference underlies another, equally powerful American myth — the myth of racial supremacy. This is the negative counterpart of the melting pot ideal: instead of the equal and harmonious blending of cultures, it proposes a racial and ethnic hierarchy based on the "natural superiority" of Anglo-Americans. Under the sway of this myth, differences become signs of inferiority, and "inferiors" are treated as childlike or even subhuman. This myth has given rise to some of the most shameful passages in our national life: slavery, segregation, and lynching; the near extermination of tribal peoples and cultures; the denial of citizenship and constitutional rights to African Americans, American Indians, Chinese and Japanese immigrants; the brutal exploitation of Mexican and Asian laborers . . . the catalog of injustices is long and painful. The melting pot ideal itself has often masked the myth of racial and ethnic superiority. "Inferiors" are expected to "melt" into conformity with Anglo-American behavior and values. Henry Ford's pageant conveys the message that ethnic identity is best left behind — exchanged for something "better," more uniform, less threatening.

This chapter explores the interaction between these two related cultural myths: the myth of unity and the myth of difference and hierarchy. It examines how the categories of race and ethnicity are defined and how they operate to divide us. These issues become crucial as the population of the United States grows increasingly diverse: the selections here challenge you to reconsider the fate of the melting pot myth as we enter the era of multiethnic, multicultural America. Can we learn to accept and honor our differences?

The first section of the chapter focuses on the myth of racial superiority. The introductory selection by Ronald Takaki offers a thumbnail sketch of ethnic relations in American history — from the first encounter of the English and the Powhatan Indians to the crisis of identity we suffer as a nation in the "post–Rodney King era." The poems that follow, by Wendy Rose and Janice Mirikitani, affirm the vitality of America's minority cultures despite a history of exploitation and racist violence. Next, "Racial Formation," by Michael Omi and Howard Winant, presents the idea that racial categories are not biologically determined but socially constructed. In the autobiographical essay "Split at the Root," Adrienne Rich reflects on the inner conflict she suffered as a woman torn between multiple, competing ethnic identities. The following selection by Vincent N. Parrillo outlines the most common sociological and psychological theories explaining the causes of prejudiced behavior. The account of C. P. Ellis's transformation from Ku Klux Klan member to union activist examines racism from the inside and raises questions about how, on a larger scale, we can combat the myth of racial superiority. Ed Guerrero's "Slaves, Monsters, and Others," the media essay for the chapter, rounds off our discussion with an ingenious and provocative interpretation of the complex messages about race encoded in popular science-fiction movies like *E.T.*, *Little Shop of Horrors,* and *Gremlins.*

The chapter's concluding section examines the emerging myth of the "new melting pot" of multicultural America. Shelby Steele's "I'm Black, You're White, Who's Innocent?" asks pointed questions about the forces that inhibit constructive dialogue between the races. Lynell George's essay "Gray Boys, Funky Aztecs, and Honorary Homegirls" counters Steele by suggesting that a new wave of cultural assimilation is already underway. The chapter ends with Gloria Anzaldúa's visionary call for a new way of looking at the world: a *mestiza,* or mixed, consciousness that liberates us from outworn and dangerous myths of difference. Aurora Levins Morales's poem "Child of the Americas" pays tribute both to cultural difference and the enduring power of the melting pot myth.

Sources

John Hope Franklin, *Race and History: Selected Essays,* 1938–1988. Baton Rouge: Louisiana State University Press, 1989, pp. 321–331.

Milton M. Gordon, *Assimilation in American Life: The Role of Race, Religion, and National Origins.* New York: Oxford University Press, 1964.

Itabari Njeri, "Beyond the Melting Pot." *Los Angeles Times,* January 13, 1991, pp. E1, E8–9.

Leonard Pitt, *We Americans,* vol. 2, 3rd ed. Dubuque: Kendall/Hunt, 1987.

Ronald Takaki, "Reflections on Racial Patterns in America." In *From Different Shores: Perspectives on Race and Ethnicity in America,* Ronald Takaki, ed. New York: Oxford University Press, 1987, pp. 26–37.

Before Reading

- Survey images in the popular media (newspapers, magazines, TV shows, movies, and pop music) for evidence of the myth of the melting pot. Do you find any figures in popular culture who seem to endorse the idea of a "new melting pot" in the United States? How closely do these images reflect your understanding of your own and other ethnic and racial groups? Explore these questions in a journal entry, then discuss in class.
- Alternatively, you might investigate the metaphors that are being used to describe racial and ethnic group relations or interactions between members of different groups on your campus and in your community.

Consult local news sources and campus publications, and keep your ears open for conversations that touch on these issues. Do some freewriting about what you discover and compare notes with classmates.

- Why do you think the people in the photo on page 328 are demonstrating? Write a narrative detailing the events that you imagine led up to the demonstration, its purpose, and its outcome. If you like, write the story from the perspective of one of the participants. Share stories in small groups and discuss why you came to the conclusions that you did about the origin and nature of the procession.

A Different Mirror

RONALD TAKAKI

The myth of the melting pot was cultivated by generations of historians who portrayed the American story as the saga of a single people. During the past decade, however, scholars have begun to recognize that the distinct, and sometimes conflicting, experiences woven into the tapestry of American history cannot be told as a single narrative with a unified point of view. Ronald Takaki is one of America's foremost new historians. In this excerpt from A Different Mirror: A History of Multicultural America, *Takaki challenges us to look at our history as a chorus of voices or a vast national anthology of stories. The grandson of Japanese immigrant plantation workers in Hawaii, Takaki (b. 1939) is a leading figure in the study of American race relations. His books include* From a Different Shore *(1989) and* Iron Cages: Race and Culture in Nineteenth-Century America *(1990). He currently teaches ethnic studies at the University of California, Berkeley.*

I had flown from San Francisco to Norfolk and was riding in a taxi to my hotel to attend a conference on multiculturalism. Hundreds of educators from across the country were meeting to discuss the need for greater cultural diversity in the curriculum. My driver and I chatted about the weather and the tourists. The sky was cloudy, and Virginia Beach was twenty minutes away. The rearview mirror reflected a white man in his forties. "How long have you been in this country?" he asked. "All my life," I replied, wincing. "I was born in the United States." With a strong southern drawl, he remarked: "I was wondering because your English is excellent!" Then, as I had many times before, I explained: "My grandfather came here from Japan in the 1880s. My family has been here, in America, for over a hundred years." He glanced at me in the mirror. Somehow I did not look "American" to him; my eyes and complexion looked foreign.

Suddenly, we both became uncomfortably conscious of a racial divide separating us. An awkward silence turned my gaze from the mirror to the passing landscape, the shore where the English and the Powhatan Indians first encountered each other. Our highway was on land that Sir Walter Raleigh[1] had renamed "Virginia" in honor of Elizabeth I, the Virgin Queen. In the English cultural appropriation of America, the indigenous peoples themselves would become outsiders in their native land. Here, at the eastern edge of the continent, I mused, was the site of the beginning of multicultural America. Jamestown, the English settlement founded in 1607, was nearby: the first twenty Africans were brought here a year before the Pilgrims arrived at Plymouth Rock. Several hundred miles offshore was Bermuda, the "Bermoothes" where William Shakespeare's Prospero had landed and met the native Caliban in *The Tempest.* Earlier, another voyager had made an Atlantic crossing and unexpectedly bumped into some islands to the south. Thinking he had reached Asia, Christopher Columbus mistakenly identified one of the islands as "Cipango" (Japan). In the wake of the admiral, many peoples would come to America from different shores, not only from Europe but also Africa and Asia. One of them would be my grandfather. My mental wandering across terrain and time ended abruptly as we arrived at my destination. I said good-bye to my driver and went into the hotel, carrying a vivid reminder of why I was attending this conference.

Questions like the one my taxi driver asked me are always jarring, but I can understand why he could not see me as American. He had a narrow but widely shared sense of the past—a history that has viewed American as European in ancestry. "Race," Toni Morrison[2] explained, has functioned as a "metaphor" necessary to the "construction of Americanness": in the creation of our national identity, "American" has been defined as "white."[3]

But America has been racially diverse since our very beginning on the Virginia shore, and this reality is increasingly becoming visible and ubiquitous. Currently, one-third of the American people do not trace their origins to Europe; in California, minorities are fast becoming a majority. They already predominate in major cities across the country—New York, Chicago, Atlanta, Detroit, Philadelphia, San Francisco, and Los Angeles.

This emerging demographic diversity has raised fundamental questions 5
about America's identity and culture. In 1990, *Time* published a cover story

[1]*Sir Walter Raleigh:* English explorer, statesman, courtier, historian, and poet (1552?–1618).

[2]*Toni Morrison:* Nobel Prize–winning African American novelist (b. 1931).

[3]Toni Morrison, *Playing in the Dark: Whiteness in the Literary Imagination* (Cambridge, Mass., 1992), p. 47. [Author's note]

on "America's Changing Colors." "Someday soon," the magazine announced, "white Americans will become a minority group." How soon? By 2056, most Americans will trace their descent to "Africa, Asia, the Hispanic world, the Pacific Islands, Arabia — almost anywhere but white Europe." This dramatic change in our nation's ethnic composition is altering the way we think about ourselves. "The deeper significance of America's becoming a majority nonwhite society is what it means to the national psyche, to individuals' sense of themselves and their nation — their idea of what it is to be American."[4]

Indeed, more than ever before, as we approach the time when whites become a minority, many of us are perplexed about our national identity and our future as one people. This uncertainty has provoked Allan Bloom to reaffirm the preeminence of Western civilization. Author of *The Closing of the American Mind,* he has emerged as a leader of an intellectual backlash against cultural diversity. In his view, students entering the university are "uncivilized," and the university has the responsibility to "civilize" them. Bloom claims he knows what their "hungers" are and "what they can digest." Eating is one of his favorite metaphors. Noting the "large black presence" in major universities, he laments the "one failure" in race relations — black students have proven to be "indigestible." They do not "melt as have *all* other groups." The problem, he contends, is that "blacks have become blacks": they have become "ethnic." This separatism has been reinforced by an academic permissiveness that has befouled the curriculum with "Black Studies" along with "Learn Another Culture." The only solution, Bloom insists, is "the good old Great Books approach."[5]

Similarly, E. D. Hirsch[6] worries that America is becoming a "tower of Babel," and that this multiplicity of cultures is threatening to rend our social fabric. He, too, longs for a more cohesive culture and a more homogeneous America: "If we *had* to make a choice between the *one* and the *many,* most Americans would choose the principle of unity, since we cannot function as a nation without it." The way to correct this fragmentization, Hirsch argues, is to acculturate "disadvantaged children." What do they need to know? "Only by accumulating shared symbols, and the shared information that symbols represent," Hirsch answers, "can we learn to communicate effectively with one another in our national community." Though he concedes the value of multicultural education, he quickly dismisses it by insisting that it "should not be allowed to supplant or interfere with our schools' responsibility to ensure our children's mastery of American literate culture."

[4]William A. Henry III, "Beyond the Melting Pot," in "America's Changing Colors," *Time,* vol. 135, no. 15 (April 9, 1990), pp. 28–31. [Author's note]

[5]Allan Bloom, *The Closing of the American Mind: How Higher Education Has Failed Democracy and Impoverished the Souls of Today's Students* (New York, 1987), pp. 19, 91–93, 340–341, 344. [Author's note]

[6]*E. D. Hirsch:* American literary and social critic (b. 1928).

In *Cultural Literacy: What Every American Needs to Know,* Hirsch offers a long list of terms that excludes much of the history of minority groups.[7]

While Bloom and Hirsch are reacting defensively to what they regard as a vexatious balkanization of America, many other educators are responding to our diversity as an opportunity to open American minds. In 1990, the Task Force on Minorities for New York emphasized the importance of a culturally diverse education. "Essentially," the *New York Times* commented, "the issue is how to deal with both dimensions of the nation's motto: 'E pluribus unum' — 'Out of many, one.' " Universities from New Hampshire to Berkeley have established American cultural diversity graduation requirements. "Every student needs to know," explained University of Wisconsin's chancellor Donna Shalala,[8] "much more about the origins and history of the particular cultures which, as Americans, we will encounter during our lives." Even the University of Minnesota, located in a state that is 98 percent white, requires its students to take ethnic studies courses. Asked why multiculturalism is so important, Dean Fred Lukermann answered: As a national university, Minnesota has to offer a national curriculum — one that includes all of the peoples of America. He added that after graduation many students move to cities like Chicago and Los Angeles and thus need to know about racial diversity. Moreover, many educators stress, multiculturalism has an intellectual purpose. By allowing us to see events from the viewpoints of different groups, a multicultural curriculum enables us to reach toward a more comprehensive understanding of American history.[9]

What is fueling this debate over our national identity and the content of our curriculum is America's intensifying racial crisis. The alarming signs and symptoms seem to be everywhere — the killing of Vincent Chin[10] in Detroit, the black boycott of a Korean grocery store in Flatbush,[11] the hysteria in Boston over the Carol Stuart murder,[12] the battle between white sportsmen and Indians over tribal fishing rights in Wisconsin, the Jewish-black clashes in Brooklyn's Crown Heights, the black-Hispanic competition for jobs and educational resources in Dallas, which *Newsweek* described as

[7] E. D. Hirsch, Jr., *Cultural Literacy: What Every American Needs to Know* (Boston, 1987), pp. xiii, xvii, 2, 18, 96. See also "The List," pp. 152–215. [Author's note]

[8] *Donna Shalala:* Appointed Secretary of Housing, Economy, and Welfare in 1993 (b. 1941).

[9] Edward Fiske, "Lessons," *New York Times,* February 7, 1990; "University of Wisconsin–Madison: The Madison Plan," February 9, 1988; interview with Dean Fred Lukermann, University of Minnesota, 1987. [Author's note]

[10] *Vincent Chin:* Chinese American killed by whites angered by competition from the Japanese auto industry during the 1980s.

[11] *Flatbush:* A predominantly African American area of New York.

[12] *Carol Stuart murder:* In this 1989 case, Stuart (a white woman) was murdered by her husband, who then convinced Boston police and the media that she had been killed by a Black assailant.

"a conflict of the have-nots," and the Willie Horton campaign commercials,[13] which widened the divide between the suburbs and the inner cities.[14]

This reality of racial tension rudely woke America like a fire bell in the 10
night on April 29, 1992. Immediately after four Los Angeles police officers were found not guilty of brutality against Rodney King,[15] rage exploded in Los Angeles. Race relations reached a new nadir. During the nightmarish rampage, scores of people were killed, over two thousand injured, twelve thousand arrested, and almost a billion dollars' worth of property destroyed. The live televised images mesmerized America. The rioting and the murderous melee on the streets resembled the fighting in Beirut and the West Bank. The thousands of fires burning out of control and the dark smoke filling the skies brought back images of the burning oil fields of Kuwait during Desert Storm. Entire sections of Los Angeles looked like a bombed city. "Is this America?" many shocked viewers asked. "Please, can we get along here," pleaded Rodney King, calling for calm. "We all can get along. I mean, we're all stuck here for a while. Let's try to work it out."[16]

But how should "we" be defined? Who are the people "stuck here" in America? One of the lessons of the Los Angeles explosion is the recognition of the fact that we are a multiracial society and that race can no longer be defined in the binary terms of white and black. "We" will have to include Hispanics and Asians. While blacks currently constitute 13 percent of the Los Angeles population, Hispanics represent 40 percent. The 1990 census revealed that South Central Los Angeles, which was predominantly black in 1965 when the Watts rebellion occurred, is now 45 percent Hispanic. A majority of the first 5,438 people arrested were Hispanic, while 37 percent were black. Of the fifty-eight people who died in the riot, more than a third were Hispanic, and about 40 percent of the businesses destroyed were Hispanic-owned. Most of the other shops and stores were Korean-owned. The dreams of many Korean immigrants went up in smoke during the riot: two thousand Korean-owned businesses were damaged or demolished, totaling about $400 million in losses. There is evidence indicating they were targeted. "After all," explained a black gang member, "we didn't burn our community, just *their* stores."[17]

[13]*Willie Horton campaign commercials:* Commercials supporting former President George Bush's 1988 election, widely criticized for playing on racist fears.

[14]"A Conflict of the Have-Nots," *Newsweek*, December 12, 1988, pp. 28–29. [Author's note]

[15]*Rodney King:* African American motorist severely beaten by four white Los Angeles police officers whose subsequent acquittal sparked the 1992 L.A. uprising.

[16]Rodney King's statement to the press, *New York Times*, May 2, 1992, p. 6. [Author's note]

[17]Tim Rutten, "A New Kind of Riot," *New York Review of Books*, June 11, 1992, pp. 52–53; Maria Newman, "Riots Bring Attention to Growing Hispanic Presence in South-Central Area," *New York Times*, May 11, 1992, p. A10; Mike Davis, "In L.A. Burning All Illusions," *The Nation*, June 1, 1992, pp. 744–745; Jack Viets and Peter Fimrite, "S.F. Mayor Visits Riot-Torn Area to Buoy Businesses," *San Francisco Chronicle*, May 6, 1992, p. A6. [Author's note]

"I don't feel like I'm in America anymore," said Denisse Bustamente as she watched the police protecting the firefighters. "I feel like I am far away." Indeed, Americans have been witnessing ethnic strife erupting around the world — the rise of neo-Nazism and the murder of Turks in Germany, the ugly "ethnic cleansing" in Bosnia, the terrible and bloody clashes between Muslims and Hindus in India. Is the situation here different, we have been nervously wondering, or do ethnic conflicts elsewhere represent a prologue for America? What is the nature of malevolence? Is there a deep, perhaps primordial, need for group identity rooted in hatred for the other? Is ethnic pluralism possible for America? But answers have been limited. Television reports have been little more than thirty-second sound bites. Newspaper articles have been mostly superficial descriptions of racial antagonisms and the current urban malaise. What is lacking is historical context; consequently, we are left feeling bewildered.[18]

How did we get to this point, Americans everywhere are anxiously asking. What does our diversity mean, and where is it leading us? *How* do we work it out in the post–Rodney King era?

Certainly one crucial way is for our society's various ethnic groups to develop a greater understanding of each other. For example, how can African Americans and Korean Americans work it out unless they learn about each other's cultures, histories, and also economic situations? This need to share knowledge about our ethnic diversity has acquired new importance and has given new urgency to the pursuit for a more accurate history.

More than ever before, there is a growing realization that the established 15
scholarship has tended to define America too narrowly. For example, in his prize-winning study *The Uprooted,* Harvard historian Oscar Handlin presented — to use the book's subtitle — "the Epic Story of the Great Migrations That Made the American People." But Handlin's "epic story" excluded the "uprooted" from Africa, Asia, and Latin America — the other "Great Migrations" that also helped to make "the American People." Similarly, in *The Age of Jackson,* Arthur M. Schlesinger, Jr., left out blacks and Indians. There is not even a mention of two marker events — the Nat Turner[19] insurrection and Indian removal,[20] which Andrew Jackson[21] himself would have been surprised to find omitted from a history of his era.[22]

Still, Schlesinger and Handlin offered us a refreshing revisionism, paving the way for the study of common people rather than princes and presidents.

[18]Rick DelVecchio, Suzanne Espinosa, and Carl Nolte, "Bradley Ready to Lift Curfew," *San Francisco Chronicle,* May 4, 1992, p. A1. [Author's note]

[19]*Nat Turner:* African American slave and leader of a slave revolt (1800–1831).

[20]*Indian removal:* Nineteenth-century U.S. government policy that forced American Indian peoples onto reservations from their native lands.

[21]*Andrew Jackson:* Seventh president of the United States (1767–1845).

[22]Oscar Handlin, *The Uprooted: The Epic Story of the Great Migrations That Made the American People* (New York, 1951); Arthur M. Schlesinger, Jr., *The Age of Jackson* (Boston, 1945). [Author's note]

They inspired the next generation of historians to examine groups such as the artisan laborers of Philadelphia and the Irish immigrants of Boston. "Once I thought to write a history of the immigrants in America," Handlin confided in his introduction to *The Uprooted.* "I discovered that the immigrants *were* American history." This door, once opened, led to the flowering of a more inclusive scholarship as we began to recognize that ethnic history was American history. Suddenly, there was a proliferation of seminal works such as Irving Howe's *World of Our Fathers: The Journey of the East European Jews to America,* Dee Brown's *Bury My Heart at Wounded Knee: An Indian History of the American West,* Albert Camarillo's *Chicanos in a Changing Society,* Lawrence Levine's *Black Culture and Black Consciousness,* Yuji Ichioka's *The Issei: The World of the First Generation Japanese Immigrants,* and Kerby Miller's *Emigrants and Exiles: Ireland and the Irish Exodus to North America.*[23]

But even this new scholarship, while it has given us a more expanded understanding of the mosaic called America, does not address our needs in the post–Rodney King era. These books and others like them fragment American society, studying each group separately, in isolation from the other groups and the whole. While scrutinizing our specific pieces, we have to step back in order to see the rich and complex portrait they compose. What is needed is a fresh angle, a study of the American past from a comparative perspective.

While all of America's many groups cannot be covered in one book, the English immigrants and their descendants require attention, for they possessed inordinate power to define American culture and make public policy. What men like John Winthrop,[24] Thomas Jefferson, and Andrew Jackson thought as well as did mattered greatly to all of us and was consequential for everyone. A broad range of groups has been selected: African Americans, Asian Americans, Chicanos, Irish, Jews, and Indians. While together they help to explain general patterns in our society, each has contributed to the making of the United States.

African Americans have been the central minority throughout our country's history. They were initially brought here on a slave ship in 1619. Actually, these first twenty Africans might not have been slaves; rather, like most of the white laborers, they were probably indentured servants.[25] The

[23]Handlin, *The Uprooted,* p. 3; Irving Howe, *World of Our Fathers: The Journey of the East European Jews to America and the Life They Found and Made* (New York, 1983); Dee Brown, *Bury My Heart at Wounded Knee: An Indian History of the American West* (New York, 1970); Albert Camarillo, *Chicanos in a Changing Society: From Mexican Pueblos to American Barrios in Santa Barbara and Southern California, 1848–1930* (Cambridge, Mass., 1979); Lawrence W. Levine, *Black Culture and Black Consciousness: Afro-American Folk Thought from Slavery to Freedom* (New York, 1977); Yuji Ichioka, *The Issei: The World of the First Generation Japanese Immigrants* (New York, 1988); Kerby A. Miller, *Emigrants and Exiles: Ireland and the Irish Exodus to North America* (New York, 1985). [Author's note]

[24]*John Winthrop:* First governor of the Massachusetts Bay Colony (1588–1649).

[25]*indentured servants:* Servants who had sold their labor and were bound to a household for a specified period of time.

transformation of Africans into slaves is the story of the "hidden" origins of slavery. How and when was it decided to institute a system of bonded black labor? What happened, while freighted with racial significance, was actually conditioned by class conflicts within white society. Once established, the "peculiar institution" would have consequences for centuries to come. During the nineteenth century, the political storm over slavery almost destroyed the nation. Since the Civil War and emancipation, race has continued to be largely defined in relation to African Americans — segregation, civil rights, the underclass, and affirmative action. Constituting the largest minority group in our society, they have been at the cutting edge of the Civil Rights Movement. Indeed, their struggle has been a constant reminder of America's moral vision as a country committed to the principle of liberty. Martin Luther King clearly understood this truth when he wrote from a jail cell: "We will reach the goal of freedom in Birmingham and all over the nation, because the goal of America is freedom. Abused and scorned though we may be, our destiny is tied up with America's destiny."[26]

Asian Americans have been here for over one hundred and fifty years, 20
before many European immigrant groups. But as "strangers" coming from a "different shore," they have been stereotyped as "heathen," exotic, and unassimilable. Seeking "Gold Mountain," the Chinese arrived first, and what happened to them influenced the reception of the Japanese, Koreans, Filipinos, and Asian Indians as well as the Southeast Asian refugees like the Vietnamese and the Hmong. The 1882 Chinese Exclusion Act was the first law that prohibited the entry of immigrants on the basis of nationality. The Chinese condemned this restriction as racist and tyrannical. "They call us 'Chink,'" complained a Chinese immigrant, cursing the "white demons." "They think we no good! America cuts us off. No more come now, too bad!" This precedent later provided a basis for the restriction of European immigrant groups such as Italians, Russians, Poles, and Greeks. The Japanese painfully discovered that their accomplishments in America did not lead to acceptance, for during World War II, unlike Italian Americans and German Americans, they were placed in internment camps. Two-thirds of them were citizens by birth. "How could I as a six-month-old child born in this country," asked Congressman Robert Matsui years later, "be declared by my own Government to be an enemy alien?" Today, Asian Americans represent the fastest-growing ethnic group. They have also become the focus of much mass media attention as "the Model Minority" not only for blacks and Chicanos, but also for whites on welfare and even middle-class whites experiencing economic difficulties.[27]

[26]Abraham Lincoln, "The Gettysburg Address," in *The Annals of America,* vol. 9, *1863–1865: The Crisis of the Union* (Chicago, 1968), pp. 462–463; Martin Luther King, *Why We Can't Wait* (New York, 1964), pp. 92–93. [Author's note]

[27]Interview with old laundryman, in "Interviews with Two Chinese," circa 1924, Box 326, folder 325, Survey of Race Relations, Stanford University, Hoover Institution Archives; Congressman Robert Matsui, speech in the House of Representatives on the 442 bill for redress

Chicanos represent the largest group among the Hispanic population, which is projected to outnumber African Americans. They have been in the United States for a long time, initially incorporated by the war against Mexico. The treaty had moved the border between the two countries, and the people of "occupied" Mexico suddenly found themselves "foreigners" in their "native land." As historian Albert Camarillo pointed out, the Chicano past is an integral part of America's westward expansion, also known as "manifest destiny."[28] But while the early Chicanos were a colonized people, most of them today have immigrant roots. Many began the trek to El Norte[29] in the early twentieth century. "As I had heard a lot about the United States," Jesus Garza recalled, "it was my dream to come here." "We came to know families from Chihuahua, Sonora, Jalisco, and Durango," stated Ernesto Galarza. "Like ourselves, our Mexican neighbors had come this far moving step by step, working and waiting, as if they were feeling their way up a ladder." Nevertheless, the Chicano experience has been unique, for most of them have lived close to their homeland — a proximity that has helped reinforce their language, identity, and culture. This migration to El Norte has continued to the present. Los Angeles has more people of Mexican origin than any other city in the world, except Mexico City. A mostly mestizo[30] people of Indian as well as African and Spanish ancestries, Chicanos currently represent the largest minority group in the Southwest, where they have been visibly transforming culture and society.[31]

The Irish came here in greater numbers than most immigrant groups. Their history has been tied to America's past from the very beginning. Ireland represented the earliest English frontier: the conquest of Ireland occurred before the colonization of America, and the Irish were the first group that the English called "savages." In this context, the Irish past foreshadowed the Indian future. During the nineteenth century, the Irish, like the Chinese, were victims of British colonialism. While the Chinese fled from the ravages of the Opium Wars, the Irish were pushed from their homeland by "English tyranny." Here they became construction workers and factory operatives as well as the "maids" of America. Representing a Catholic group seeking to settle in a fiercely Protestant society, the Irish immigrants were targets of

---

and reparations, September 17, 1987, *Congressional Record* (Washington, D.C., 1987), p. 7584. [Author's note]

[28]*manifest destiny:* Popular nineteenth-century belief that the United States was "destined" to rule the land west of the Mississippi.

[29]*El Norte:* The North (the United States and Canada).

[30]*mestizo:* Mixed race.

[31]Camarillo, *Chicanos in a Changing Society,* p. 2; Juan Nepomuceno Seguín, in David J. Weber (ed.), *Foreigners in Their Native Land: Historical Roots of the Mexican Americans* (Albuquerque, N. Mex., 1973), p. vi; Jesus Garza, in Manuel Gamio, *The Mexican Immigrant: His Life Story* (Chicago, 1931), p. 15; Ernesto Galarza, *Barrio Boy: The Story of a Boy's Acculturation* (Notre Dame, Ind., 1986), p. 200. [Author's note]

American nativist hostility. They were also what historian Lawrence J. McCaffrey called "the pioneers of the American urban ghetto," "previewing" experiences that would later be shared by the Italians, Poles, and other groups from southern and eastern Europe. Furthermore, they offer contrast to the immigrants from Asia. The Irish came about the same time as the Chinese, but they had a distinct advantage: the Naturalization Law of 1790 had reserved citizenship for "whites" only. Their compatible complexion allowed them to assimilate by blending into American society. In making their journey successfully into the mainstream, however, these immigrants from Erin pursued an Irish "ethnic" strategy: they promoted "Irish" solidarity in order to gain political power and also to dominate the skilled blue-collar occupations, often at the expense of the Chinese and blacks.[32]

Fleeing pogroms[33] and religious persecution in Russia, the Jews were driven from what John Cuddihy[34] described as the "Middle Ages into the Anglo-American world of the *goyim*[35] 'beyond the pale.' " To them, America represented the Promised Land. This vision led Jews to struggle not only for themselves but also for other oppressed groups, especially blacks. After the 1917 East St. Louis race riot, the Yiddish *Forward* of New York compared this anti-black violence to a 1903 pogrom in Russia: "Kishinev and St. Louis — the same soil, the same people." Jews cheered when Jackie Robinson broke into the Brooklyn Dodgers in 1947. "He was adopted as the surrogate hero by many of us growing up at the time," recalled Jack Greenberg of the NAACP Legal Defense Fund. "He was the way we saw ourselves triumphing against the forces of bigotry and ignorance." Jews stood shoulder to shoulder with blacks in the Civil Rights Movement: two-thirds of the white volunteers who went south during the 1964 Freedom Summer were Jewish. Today Jews are considered a highly successful "ethnic" group. How did they make such great socioeconomic strides? This question is often reframed by neoconservative intellectuals like Irving Kristol and Nathan Glazer to read: if Jewish immigrants were able to lift themselves from poverty into the mainstream through self-help and education without welfare and affirmative action, why can't blacks? But what this thinking overlooks is the unique history of Jewish immigrants, especially the initial advantages of many of them as literate and skilled. Moreover, it minimizes the virulence of racial prejudice rooted in American slavery.[36]

[32]Lawrence J. McCaffrey, *The Irish Diaspora in America* (Washington, D.C., 1984), pp. 6, 62. [Author's note]

[33]*pogroms:* Organized attacks in which Jews were terrorized and killed and their property stolen or destroyed.

[34]*John Cuddihy:* American sociologist.

[35]*goyim:* Gentiles.

[36]John Murray Cuddihy, *The Ordeal of Civility: Freud, Marx, Levi Strauss, and the Jewish Struggle with Modernity* (Boston, 1987), p. 165; Jonathan Kaufman, *Broken Alliance: The Turbulent Times between Blacks and Jews in America* (New York, 1989), pp. 28, 82, 83–84, 91, 93, 106. [Author's note]

Indians represent a critical contrast, for theirs was not an immigrant experience. The Wampanoags were on the shore as the first English strangers arrived in what would be called "New England." The encounters between Indians and whites not only shaped the course of race relations, but also influenced the very culture and identity of the general society. The architect of Indian removal, President Andrew Jackson told Congress: "Our conduct toward these people is deeply interesting to the national character." Frederick Jackson Turner[37] understood the meaning of this observation when he identified the frontier as our transforming crucible. At first, the European newcomers had to wear Indian moccasins and shout the war cry. "Little by little," as they subdued the wilderness, the pioneers became "a new product" that was "American." But Indians have had a different view of this entire process. "The white man," Luther Standing Bear of the Sioux explained, "does not understand the Indian for the reason that he does not understand America." Continuing to be "troubled with primitive fears," he has "in his consciousness the perils of this frontier continent. . . . The man from Europe is still a foreigner and an alien. And he still hates the man who questioned his path across the continent." Indians questioned what Jackson and Turner trumpeted as "progress." For them, the frontier had a different "significance": their history was how the West was lost. But their story has also been one of resistance. As Vine Deloria[38] declared, "Custer died for your sins."[39]

25 By looking at these groups from a multicultural perspective, we can comparatively analyze their experiences in order to develop an understanding of their differences and similarities. Race, we will see, has been a social construction that has historically set apart racial minorities from European immigrant groups. Contrary to the notions of scholars like Nathan Glazer and Thomas Sowell,[40] race in America has not been the same as ethnicity. A broad comparative focus also allows us to see how the varied experiences of different racial and ethnic groups occurred within shared contexts.

During the nineteenth century, for example, the Market Revolution employed Irish immigrant laborers in New England factories as it expanded cotton fields worked by enslaved blacks across Indian lands toward Mexico. Like blacks, the Irish newcomers were stereotyped as "savages," ruled by

[37] *Frederick Jackson Turner:* American historian (1861–1932).

[38] *Vine Deloria:* American Indian historian, writer, and activist (b. 1933); author of the influential *Custer Died for Your Sins* (1969).

[39] Andrew Jackson, First Annual Message to Congress, December 8, 1829, in James D. Richardson (ed.), *A Compilation of the Messages and Papers of the Presidents, 1789–1897* (Washington, D.C., 1897), vol. 2, p. 457; Frederick Jackson Turner, "The Significance of the Frontier in American History," in *The Early Writings of Frederick Jackson Turner* (Madison, Wis., 1938), pp. 185ff.; Luther Standing Bear, "What the Indian Means to America," in Wayne Moquin (ed.), *Great Documents in American Indian History* (New York, 1973), p. 307; Vine Deloria, Jr., *Custer Died for Your Sins: An Indian Manifesto* (New York, 1969). [Author's note]

[40] *Nathan Glazer and Thomas Sowell:* Conservative U.S. sociologists (b. 1923 and 1930, respectively).

passions rather than "civilized" virtues such as self-control and hard work. The Irish saw themselves as the "slaves" of British oppressors, and during a visit to Ireland in the 1840s, Frederick Douglass found that the "wailing notes" of the Irish ballads reminded him of the "wild notes" of slave songs. The United States annexation of California, while incorporating Mexicans, led to trade with Asia and the migration of "strangers" from Pacific shores. In 1870, Chinese immigrant laborers were transported to Massachusetts as scabs to break an Irish immigrant strike; in response, the Irish recognized the need for interethnic working-class solidarity and tried to organize a Chinese lodge of the Knights of St. Crispin. After the Civil War, Mississippi planters recruited Chinese immigrants to discipline the newly freed blacks. During the debate over an immigration exclusion bill in 1882, a senator asked: If Indians could be located on reservations, why not the Chinese?[41]

Other instances of our connectedness abound. In 1903, Mexican and Japanese farm laborers went on strike together in California: their union officers had names like Yamaguchi and Lizarras, and strike meetings were conducted in Japanese and Spanish. The Mexican strikers declared that they were standing in solidarity with their "Japanese brothers" because the two groups had toiled together in the fields and were now fighting together for a fair wage. Speaking in impassioned Yiddish during the 1909 "uprising of twenty thousand" strikers in New York, the charismatic Clara Lemlich compared the abuse of Jewish female garment workers to the experience of blacks: "[The bosses] yell at the girls and 'call them down' even worse than I imagine the Negro slaves were in the South." During the 1920s, elite universities like Harvard worried about the increasing number of Jewish students, and new admissions criteria were instituted to curb their enrollment. Jewish students were scorned for their studiousness and criticized for their "clannishness." Recently, Asian-American students have been the targets of similar complaints: they have been called "nerds" and told there are "too many" of them on campus.[42]

Indians were already here, while blacks were forcibly transported to America, and Mexicans were initially enclosed by America's expanding border. The other groups came here as immigrants: for them, America represented liminality—a new world where they could pursue extravagant urges and do things they had thought beyond their capabilities. Like the land itself, they found themselves "betwixt and between all fixed points of classifica-

[41] Nathan Glazer, *Affirmative Discrimination: Ethnic Inequality and Public Policy* (New York, 1978); Thomas Sowell, *Ethnic America: A History* (New York, 1981); David R. Roediger, *The Wages of Whiteness: Race and the Making of the American Working Class* (London, 1991), pp. 134–136; Dan Caldwell, "The Negroization of the Chinese Stereotype in California," *Southern California Quarterly*, vol. 33 (June 1971), pp. 123–131. [Author's note]

[42] Tomas Almaguer, "Racial Domination and Class Conflict in Capitalist Agriculture: The Oxnard Sugar Beet Workers' Strike of 1903," *Labor History*, vol. 25, no. 3 (summer 1984), p. 347; Howard M. Sachar, *A History of the Jews in America* (New York, 1992), p. 183. [Author's note]

tion." No longer fastened as fiercely to their old countries, they felt a stirring to become new people in a society still being defined and formed.[43]

These immigrants made bold and dangerous crossings, pushed by political events and economic hardships in their homelands and pulled by America's demand for labor as well as by their own dreams for a better life. "By all means let me go to America," a young man in Japan begged his parents. He had calculated that in one year as a laborer here he could save almost a thousand yen — an amount equal to the income of a governor in Japan. "My dear Father," wrote an immigrant Irish girl living in New York, "Any man or woman without a family are fools that would not venture and come to this plentyful Country where no man or woman ever hungered." In the shtetls[44] of Russia, the cry "To America!" roared like "wild-fire." "America was in everybody's mouth," a Jewish immigrant recalled. "Businessmen talked [about] it over their accounts; the market women made up their quarrels that they might discuss it from stall to stall; people who had relatives in the famous land went around reading their letters." Similarly, for Mexican immigrants crossing the border in the early twentieth century, El Norte became the stuff of overblown hopes. "If only you could see how nice the United States is," they said, "that is why the Mexicans are crazy about it."[45]

The signs of America's ethnic diversity can be discerned across the con- 30
tinent — Ellis Island, Angel Island,[46] Chinatown, Harlem, South Boston, the Lower East Side, places with Spanish names like Los Angeles and San Antonio or Indian names like Massachusetts and Iowa. Much of what is familiar in America's cultural landscape actually has ethnic origins. The Bing cherry was developed by an early Chinese immigrant named Ah Bing. American Indians were cultivating corn, tomatoes, and tobacco long before the arrival of Columbus. The term *okay* was derived from the Choctaw word *oke,* meaning "it is so." There is evidence indicating that the name *Yankee* came from Indian terms for the English — from *eankke* in Cherokee and *Yankwis* in Delaware. Jazz and blues as well as rock and roll have African American origins. The "Forty-Niners" of the Gold Rush learned mining techniques from the Mexicans; American cowboys acquired herding skills from Mexican *vaqueros* and adopted their range terms — such as *lariat* from *la reata, lasso*

[43]For the concept of liminality, see Victor Turner, *Dramas, Fields, and Metaphors: Symbolic Action in Human Society* (Ithaca, N.Y., 1974), pp. 232, 237; and Arnold Van Gennep, *The Rites of Passage* (Chicago, 1960). What I try to do is to apply liminality to the land called America. [Author's note]

[44]*shtetls:* Villages.

[45]Kazuo Ito, *Issei: A History of Japanese Immigrants in North America* (Seattle, 1973), p. 33; Arnold Schrier, *Ireland and the American Emigration, 1850–1900* (New York, 1970), p. 24; Abraham Cahan, *The Rise of David Levinsky* (New York, 1960; originally published in 1917), pp. 59–61; Mary Antin, quoted in Howe, *World of Our Fathers,* p. 27; Lawrence A. Cardoso, *Mexican Emigration to the United States, 1897–1931* (Tucson, Ariz., 1981), p. 80. [Author's note]

[46]*Ellis Island, Angel Island:* Ports of entry for immigrants on the East and West Coasts.

from *lazo,* and *stampede* from *estampida.* Songs like "God Bless America," "Easter Parade," and "White Christmas" were written by a Russian-Jewish immigrant named Israel Baline, more popularly known as Irving Berlin.[47]

Furthermore, many diverse ethnic groups have contributed to the building of the American economy, forming what Walt Whitman[48] saluted as "a vast, surging, hopeful army of workers." They worked in the South's cotton fields, New England's textile mills, Hawaii's canefields, New York's garment factories, California's orchards, Washington's salmon canneries, and Arizona's copper mines. They built the railroad, the great symbol of America's industrial triumph. Laying railroad ties, black laborers sang:

Down the railroad, um-huh
Well, raise the iron, um-huh
Raise the iron, um-huh.

Irish railroad workers shouted as they stretched an iron ribbon across the continent:

Then drill, my Paddies, drill —
Drill, my heroes, drill,
Drill all day, no sugar in your tay
Workin' on the U.P. railway.

Japanese laborers in the Northwest chorused as their bodies fought the fickle weather:

A railroad worker —
That's me!
I am great.
Yes, I am a railroad worker.
Complaining:
"It is too hot!"
"It is too cold!"
"It rains too often!"
"It snows too much!"
They all ran off.
I alone remained.
I am a railroad worker!

Chicano workers in the Southwest joined in as they swore at the punishing work:

[47] Ronald Takaki, *Strangers from a Different Shore: A History of Asian Americans* (Boston, 1989), pp. 88–89; Jack Weatherford, *Native Roots: How the Indians Enriched America* (New York, 1991), pp. 210, 212; Carey McWilliams, *North from Mexico: The Spanish-Speaking People of the United States* (New York, 1968), p. 154; Stephan Thernstrom (ed.), *Harvard Encyclopedia of American Ethnic Groups* (Cambridge, Mass., 1980), p. 22; Sachar, *A History of the Jews in America,* p. 367. [Author's note]

[48] *Walt Whitman:* American poet (1819–1892).

Some unloaded rails
Others unloaded ties,
And others of my companions
Threw out thousands of curses.[49]

Moreover, our diversity was tied to America's most serious crisis: the Civil War was fought over a racial issue — slavery. In his "First Inaugural Address," presented on March 4, 1861, President Abraham Lincoln declared: "One section of our country believes slavery is *right* and ought to be extended, while the other believes it is *wrong* and ought not to be extended." Southern secession, he argued, would be anarchy. Lincoln sternly warned the South that he had a solemn oath to defend and preserve the Union. Americans were one people, he explained, bound together by "the mystic chords of memory, stretching from every battlefield and patriot grave to every living heart and hearthstone all over this broad land." The struggle and sacrifices of the War for Independence had enabled Americans to create a new nation out of thirteen separate colonies. But Lincoln's appeal for unity fell on deaf ears in the South. And the war came. Two and a half years later, at Gettysburg, President Lincoln declared that "brave men" had fought and "consecrated" the ground of this battlefield in order to preserve the Union. Among the brave were black men. Shortly after this bloody battle, Lincoln acknowledged the military contribution of blacks. "There will be some black men," he wrote in a letter to an old friend, James C. Conkling, "who can remember that with silent tongue, and clenched teeth, and steady eye, and well-poised bayonet, they have helped mankind on to this great consummation. . . ." Indeed, 186,000 blacks served in the Union Army, and one-third of them were listed as missing or dead. Black men in blue, Frederick Douglass[50] pointed out, were "on the battlefield mingling their blood with that of white men in one common effort to save the country." Now the mystic chords of memory stretched across the new battlefields of the Civil War, and black soldiers were buried in "patriot graves." They, too, had given their lives to ensure that the "government of the people, by the people, for the people shall not perish from the earth."[51]

Like these black soldiers, the people in our study have been actors in

[49]Walt Whitman, *Leaves of Grass* (New York, 1958), p. 284; Mathilde Bunton, "Negro Work Songs" (1940), 1 typescript in Box 91 ("Music"), Illinois Writers Project, U.S.W.P.A., in James R. Grossman, *Land of Hope: Chicago, Black Southerners, and the Great Migration* (Chicago, 1989), p. 192; Carl Wittke, *The Irish in America* (Baton Rouge, La., 1956), p. 39; Ito, *Issei*, p. 343; Manuel Gamio, *Mexican Immigration to the United States* (Chicago, 1930), pp. 84–85. [Author's note]

[50]*Frederick Douglass:* Former slave, abolitionist, orator, and writer (1817?–1895).

[51]Abraham Lincoln, "First Inaugural Address," in *The Annals of America,* vol. 9, *1863–1865: The Crisis of the Union* (Chicago, 1968), p. 255; Lincoln, "The Gettysburg Address," pp. 462–463; Abraham Lincoln, letter to James C. Conkling, August 26, 1863, in *Annals of America,* p. 439; Frederick Douglass, in Herbert Aptheker (ed.), *A Documentary History of the Negro People in the United States* (New York, 1951), vol. 1, p. 496. [Author's note]

history, not merely victims of discrimination and exploitation. They are entitled to be viewed as subjects — as men and women with minds, wills, and voices.

> In the telling and retelling
>   of their stories,
> They create communities
>   of memory.

They also re-vision history. "It is very natural that the history written by the victim," said a Mexican in 1874, "does not altogether chime with the story of the victor." Sometimes they are hesitant to speak, thinking they are only "little people." "I don't know why anybody wants to hear my history," an Irish maid said apologetically in 1900. "Nothing ever happened to me worth the tellin'."[52]

But their stories are worthy. Through their stories, the people who have lived America's history can help all of us, including my taxi driver, understand that Americans originated from many shores, and that all of us are entitled to dignity. "I hope this survey do a lot of good for Chinese people," an immigrant told an interviewer from Stanford University in the 1920s. "Make American people realize that Chinese people are humans. I think very few American people really know anything about Chinese." But the remembering is also for the sake of the children. "This story is dedicated to the descendants of Lazar and Goldie Glauberman," Jewish immigrant Minnie Miller wrote in her autobiography. "My history is bound up in their history and the generations that follow should know where they came from to know better who they are." Similarly, Tomo Shoji, an elderly Nisei[53] woman, urged Asian Americans to learn more about their roots: "We got such good, fantastic stories to tell. All our stories are different." Seeking to know how they fit into America, many young people have become listeners; they are eager to learn about the hardships and humiliations experienced by their parents and grandparents. They want to hear their stories, unwilling to remain ignorant or ashamed of their identity and past.[54]

The telling of stories liberates. By writing about the people on Mango 35
Street, Sandra Cisneros[55] explained, "the ghost does not ache so much." The place no longer holds her with "both arms. She sets me free." Indeed, stories

[52]Weber (ed.), *Foreigners in Their Native Land*, p. vi; Hamilton Holt (ed.), *The Life Stories of Undistinguished Americans as Told by Themselves* (New York, 1906), p. 143. [Author's note]

[53]*Nisei:* Second-generation Japanese Americans.

[54]"Social Document of Pany Lowe, interviewed by C. H. Burnett, Seattle, July 5, 1924," p. 6, Survey of Race Relations, Stanford University, Hoover Institution Archives; Minnie Miller, "Autobiography," private manuscript, copy from Richard Balkin; Tomo Shoji, presentation, Ohana Cultural Center, Oakland, California, March 4, 1988. [Author's note]

[55]*Sandra Cisneros:* Contemporary Mexican American writer (b. 1954).

may not be as innocent or simple as they seem to be. Native American novelist Leslie Marmon Silko cautioned:

> I will tell you something about stories . . .
> They aren't just entertainment.
>   Don't be fooled.

Indeed, the accounts given by the people in this study vibrantly re-create moments, capturing the complexities of human emotions and thoughts. They also provide the authenticity of experience. After she escaped from slavery, Harriet Jacobs wrote in her autobiography: "[My purpose] is not to tell you what I have heard but what I have seen — and what I have suffered." In their sharing of memory, the people in this study offer us an opportunity to see ourselves reflected in a mirror called history.[56]

In his recent study of Spain and the New World, *The Buried Mirror,* Carlos Fuentes[57] points out that mirrors have been found in the tombs of ancient Mexico, placed there to guide the dead through the underworld. He also tells us about the legend of Quetzalcoatl, the Plumed Serpent: when this god was given a mirror by the Toltec deity Tezcatlipoca, he saw a man's face in the mirror and realized his own humanity. For us, the "mirror" of history can guide the living and also help us recognize who we have been and hence are. In *A Distant Mirror,* Barbara W. Tuchman[58] finds "phenomenal parallels" between the "calamitous 14th century" of European society and our own era. We can, she observes, have "greater fellow-feeling for a distraught age" as we painfully recognize the "similar disarray," "collapsing assumptions," and "unusual discomfort."[59]

But what is needed in our own perplexing times is not so much a "distant" mirror, as one that is "different." While the study of the past can provide collective self-knowledge, it often reflects the scholar's particular perspective or view of the world. What happens when historians leave out many of America's peoples? What happens, to borrow the words of Adrienne Rich,[60] "when someone with the authority of a teacher" describes our society, and "you are not in it"? Such an experience can be disorienting — "a moment of psychic disequilibrium, as if you looked into a mirror and saw nothing."[61]

[56] Sandra Cisneros, *The House on Mango Street* (New York, 1991), pp. 109–110; Leslie Marmon Silko, *Ceremony* (New York, 1978), p. 2; Harriet A. Jacobs, *Incidents in the Life of a Slave Girl, written by herself* (Cambridge, Mass., 1987; originally published in 1857), p. xiii. [Author's note]

[57] *Carlos Fuentes:* Mexican writer (b. 1928).

[58] *Barbara W. Tuchman:* English historian (1912–1989).

[59] Carlos Fuentes, *The Buried Mirror: Reflections on Spain and the New World* (Boston, 1992), pp. 10, 11, 109; Barbara W. Tuchman, *A Distant Mirror: The Calamitous 14th Century* (New York, 1978), pp. xiii, xiv. [Author's note]

[60] *Adrienne Rich:* Jewish American feminist, scholar, writer, and poet (b. 1929). See p. 365.

[61] Adrienne Rich, *Blood, Bread, and Poetry: Selected Prose, 1979–1985* (New York, 1986), p. 199. [Author's note]

Through their narratives about their lives and circumstances, the people of America's diverse groups are able to see themselves and each other in our common past. They celebrate what Ishmael Reed[62] has described as a society "unique" in the world because "the world is here"—a place "where the cultures of the world crisscross." Much of America's past, they point out, has been riddled with racism. At the same time, these people offer hope, affirming the struggle for equality as a central theme in our country's history. At its conception, our nation was dedicated to the proposition of equality. What has given concreteness to this powerful national principle has been our coming together in the creation of a new society. "Stuck here" together, workers of different backgrounds have attempted to get along with each other.

> People harvesting
> Work together unaware
> Of racial problems,

wrote a Japanese immigrant describing a lesson learned by Mexican and Asian farm laborers in California.[63]

Finally, how do we see our prospects for "working out" America's racial crisis? Do we see it as through a glass darkly? Do the televised images of racial hatred and violence that riveted us in 1992 during the days of rage in Los Angeles frame a future of divisive race relations—what Arthur Schlesinger, Jr.,[64] has fearfully denounced as the "disuniting of America"? Or will Americans of diverse races and ethnicities be able to connect themselves to a larger narrative? Whatever happens, we can be certain that much of our society's future will be influenced by which "mirror" we choose to see ourselves. America does not belong to one race or one group, the people in this study remind us, and Americans have been constantly redefining their national identity from the moment of first contact on the Virginia shore. By sharing their stories, they invite us to see ourselves in a different mirror.[65]

[62] *Ishmael Reed:* African American novelist (b. 1938).

[63] Ishmael Reed, "America: The Multinational Society," in Rick Simonson and Scott Walker (eds.), *Multi-cultural Literacy* (St. Paul, 1988), p. 160; Ito, *Issei,* p. 497. [Author's note]

[64] *Arthur Schlesinger, Jr.:* American historian (b. 1917).

[65] Arthur M. Schlesinger, Jr., *The Disuniting of America: Reflections on a Multicultural Society* (Knoxville, Tenn., 1991); Carlos Bulosan, *America Is in the Heart: A Personal History* (Seattle, 1981), pp. 188–189. [Author's note]

Engaging the Text

1. What, according to Takaki, are some illustrations that racial tension has become increasingly apparent in American society? Can you think of any others? Do you agree with Takaki that America faces an "intensifying racial crisis" (para. 9)?
2. Takaki suggests that American identity is changing rapidly. Working in small groups, brainstorm a list of qualities that are currently associated with American

identity. Then create a similar list for American identity in the year 2000. Overall, which portrait strikes you as more attractive? Why?

3. List the criticisms Takaki levels against traditional historical treatments of the American story. Then think back to the way you were taught American history. To what extent do you agree with Takaki's critique?
4. What kinds of connections does Takaki highlight between the racial and ethnic groups he discusses? What differences does he note?
5. Overall, what does Takaki think of the melting pot myth? How would you describe his vision of American society?

Exploring Connections

6. Read Paula Gunn Allen (p. 312) and Malcolm X (p. 77) as examples of the historical revision that Takaki is arguing for in this selection. To what extent do these selections fulfill Takaki's assertion that multicultural approaches will give us a "more comprehensive understanding of American history"? What do these revisions of American history add to your understanding of America?
7. Read Haunani-Kay Trask's "From a Native Daughter" (p. 571) as an example of the kind of sharing of stories that Takaki advocates as an alternative to traditional historical narratives. In what ways do the stories Trask tells "liberate" her?

8. The woman in the cartoon on the opposite page is criticized for fragmenting "good old American history" by highlighting the experiences of particular groups. Could this charge be made of Takaki? Do you think his approach advocates the "balkanization" of America? Why or why not?

Extending the Critical Context

9. Research textbooks currently used in American history courses on your campus. Do they represent the experiences of different groups or do they take a melting pot approach?
10. Research one of the historical events, figures, or ideas mentioned by Takaki. Consult several sources (standard encyclopedias, historical abstracts, indexes of ethnic history, etc.). Synthesize the information you gather in a brief report, and, in your conclusion, comment on the differences of content, emphasis, or bias you noted in the information presented by each source.
11. After interviewing family members, write your own personal history (or histories) describing your family's experience dealing with the diversity of American culture. You might focus on a family member's immigration experience or on a time when your family had to deal with new cultural attitudes, values, or customs. Share these stories in small groups of students and report back to the class on the similarities and differences you discovered.

Three Thousand Dollar Death Song

Wendy Rose

Many Native American writers have noted and decried the tendency to treat their heritage as something dead and gone, something to be studied like the fossil record of extinct animals. This poem is a proud song of protest against such dehumanization. Wendy Rose (b. 1948) is a Hopi-Miwok poet, visual artist, editor, and anthropologist. She currently serves as coordinator of American Indian studies at Fresno City College. She is the author of Going to War with All My Relations: New and Selected Poems *(1993);* Bone Dance: New and Selected Poems 1965–1993 *(1994); and* Now Poof She Is Gone *(due in 1994). This poem is from the most acclaimed collection of her poetry,* Lost Copper *(1980), which was nominated for an American Book Award.*

Nineteen American Indian Skeletons from Nevada
. . . valued at $3000 . . .
— Museum invoice, 1975

Is it in cold hard cash? the kind
that dusts the insides of men's pockets
lying silver-polished surface along the cloth.
Or in bills? papering the wallets of they
who thread the night with dark words. Or
checks? paper promises weighing the same
as words spoken once on the other side
of the grown grass and damned rivers
of history. However it goes, it goes
Through my body it goes
assessing each nerve, running its edges
along my arteries, planning ahead
for whose hands will rip me
into pieces of dusty red paper,
whose hands will smooth or smatter me
into traces of rubble. Invoiced now,
it's official how our bones are valued
that stretch out pointing to sunrise
or are flexed into one last foetal bend,[1]
that are removed and tossed about,
catalogued, numbered with black ink
on newly-white foreheads.
As we were formed to the white soldier's voice,
so we explode under white students' hands.
Death is a long trail of days
in our fleshless prison.

From this distant point we watch our bones
auctioned with our careful beadwork,
our quilled medicine bundles, even the bridles
of our shot-down horses. You: who have
priced us, you who have removed us: at what cost?
What price the pits where our bones share
a single bit of memory, how one century
turns our dead into specimens, our history
into dust, our survivors into clowns.
Our memory might be catching, you know;
picture the mortars,[2] the arrowheads, the labrets[3]
shaking off their labels like bears
suddenly awake to find the seasons have ended
while they slept. Watch them touch each other,

[1] *foetal bend:* Throughout history, many cultures have buried their dead in a curled position resembling that of a fetus.

[2] *mortars:* Bowl-shaped vessels.

[3] *labrets:* Ornaments of wood or bone worn in holes pierced through the lip.

measure reality, march out the museum door!
Watch as they lift their faces
and smell about for us; watch our bones rise
to meet them and mount the horses once again!
The cost, then, will be paid
for our sweetgrass-smelling having-been
in clam shell beads and steatite,[4]
dentalia[5] and woodpecker scalp, turquoise
and copper, blood and oil, coal
and uranium, children, a universe
of stolen things.

[4]*steatite:* A soft, easily carved stone; soapstone.
[5]*dentalia:* A type of mollusk shell resembling a tooth.

Engaging the Text

1. What do the Indian skeletons mentioned in the epigraph represent?
2. What is the "distant point" Rose mentions in the second stanza?
3. What item seems unusual or out of place in the catalog of "stolen things" that ends the poem? Why does Rose include it in the list? In what way were all these things stolen from the Indians?
4. How do time, place, and point of view shift in the poem? How do these shifts contribute to the poem's meaning?
5. A cynical reader might dismiss lines 36–51 as an empty threat: after all, the bones of slain warriors will not literally rise again and remount their horses. What symbolic or rhetorical purposes might these lines serve?

Exploring Connections

6. Working in pairs, write an imaginary dialogue between Ronald Takaki (p. 332) and Wendy Rose on the topic of the scholarly study of minority group cultures. How might Rose respond to the idea of multicultural history?
7. Imagine that Kevin Costner is about to make another film involving Native Americans, to follow up on the success of *Dances with Wolves.* Draft a letter to Costner from Wendy Rose or Paula Gunn Allen (p. 312) critiquing *Dances with Wolves,* suggesting ideas or issues for the sequel, warning of common misconceptions about Native American life, and so on. To extend the assignment, work in small groups to draft a brief statement of principles regarding the portrayal of native peoples in film.

Extending the Critical Context

8. Play the role of museum director. Write a letter to the *Reno Times* explaining and defending your museum's purchase of the skeletons. Make up any circumstances you think plausible. Then evaluate the effectiveness of your defense.

9. Investigate a museum in your area with an American Indian collection. What is displayed for public view, and how? What further materials are reserved for research or special exhibits? Has there been any controversy over rightful ownership of skeletons or artifacts? Report your findings to the class.

We, the Dangerous

JANICE MIRIKITANI

Janice Mirikitani is a third-generation Japanese American who was born in 1942, when the United States and Japan were at war. In this poem she presents a sobering catalog of the injustice, oppression, and violence that the United States has inflicted on Asian and Asian American people. Yet this poem also celebrates the persistence, pride, and courage that have enabled them to endure. Mirikitani is an editor, teacher, and community activist (in San Francisco) as well as a poet. Her collections of prose and poetry are Shedding Silence *(1987) and* Awake in the River *(1978), from which "We, the Dangerous" is reprinted.*

I swore
it would not devour me
I swore
it would not humble me
I swore
it would not break me.

  And they commanded we dwell in the desert
  Our children be spawn of barbed wire and barracks

We, closer to the earth,
squat, short thighed,
knowing the dust better.

  And they would have us make the garden
  Rake the grass to soothe their feet

We, akin to the jungle,
plotting with the snake,
tails shedding in civilized America.

  And they would have us skin their fish
  deft hands like blades/sliding back flesh/bloodless

We, who awake in the river
Ocean's child
Whale eater.

And they would have us strange scented women,
Round shouldered/strong and yellow/like the moon
to pull the thread to the cloth
to loosen their backs massaged in myth

We, who fill the secret bed,
the sweat shops
the laundries.

And they would dress us in napalm,
Skin shred to clothe the earth,
Bodies filling pock marked fields.
Dead fish bloating our harbors.

We, the dangerous,
Dwelling in the ocean.
Akin to the jungle.
Close to the earth.

Hiroshima
Vietnam
Tule Lake[1]

And yet we were not devoured.
And yet we were not humbled
And yet we are not broken.

[1] *Tule Lake:* The largest of the camps where Japanese immigrants and their children were imprisoned in the United States during World War II.

Engaging the Text

1. List the images associated with Asian people in the poem. What values and characteristics do these images suggest, and why are they "dangerous"?
2. Who are "they," and what values and characteristics does Mirikitani associate with them?
3. Discuss the significance of the shift from "I" to "we" between stanzas one and two.
4. What does the poem suggest about the social and economic status of Asians in the United States?
5. Explain the structure of the poem. Be sure to comment on the similarity of the first and last stanzas, on the way the two distinct types of stanzas in the rest of the poem play off each other, and on the poem's use of repetition.

Exploring Connections

6. Compare the roles of the speakers in Wendy Rose's "Three Thousand Dollar Death Song" (p. 351) and "We, the Dangerous." What are their relationships — historical, political, economic, cultural, emotional — to the people they are talking about? How do they portray the people who are the focus of these poems?
7. At the end of "A Different Mirror" (p. 332), Ronald Takaki says, "We can be certain that much of our society's future will be influenced by which 'mirror' we chose to see ourselves. America does not belong to one race or one group." How would you describe the America that is reflected in the "mirrors" held up by Wendy Rose and Janice Mirikitani? Are these poems healing or divisive?

Extending the Critical Context

8. Choose a marginalized group in American culture besides Asian Americans — for example, some other ethnic group, lesbians or gays, hearing-impaired people, the aged. Write at least two stanzas in imitation of Mirikitani's poem, keeping your structure identical to Mirikitani's but changing the actual words and ideas. For example, if you wrote from the point of view of a neglected parent, the lines "And they would dress us in napalm / Skin shred to clothe the earth" might become "And they would lock us in nursing homes / Bodies drugged to ease their consciences." Share your effort with classmates.
9. After reading Wendy Rose (p. 351) and Janice Mirikitani, write a poem based on one or more historical incidents involving some marginalized group.

Racial Formation

Michael Omi and Howard Winant

This selection sets the stage for an analysis of race issues in the United States. Michael Omi and Howard Winant provide a broad overview of the subject, arguing in particular that race is more social myth than biological fact. They also have a keen sense of the contradictions, ironies, and paradoxes that permeate racial consciousness in our culture. Omi is a professor of Asian American Studies at the University of California, Berkeley; Winant is a political sociologist at Temple University. The essay comes from their book, Racial Formation in the United States: From the 1960s to the 1980s *(1986).*

In 1982–83, Susie Guillory Phipps unsuccessfully sued the Louisiana Bureau of Vital Records to change her racial classification from black to white. The descendant of an eighteenth-century white planter and a black slave, Phipps was designated "black" in her birth certificate in accordance with a 1970 state law which declared anyone with at least one-thirty-second "Negro blood" to be black. The legal battle raised intriguing questions about the concept of race, its meaning in contemporary society, and its use (and abuse) in public policy. Assistant Attorney General Ron Davis defended the law by pointing out that some type of racial classification was necessary to comply with federal recordkeeping requirements and to facilitate programs for the prevention of genetic diseases. Phipps's attorney, Brian Begue, argued that the assignment of racial categories on birth certificates was unconstitutional and that the one-thirty-second designation was inaccurate. He called on a retired Tulane University professor who cited research indicating that most whites have one-twentieth "Negro" ancestry. In the end, Phipps lost. The court upheld a state law which quantified racial identity, and in so doing affirmed the legality of assigning individuals to specific racial groupings.[1]

The Phipps case illustrates the continuing dilemma of defining race and establishing its meaning in institutional life. Today, to assert that variations in human physiognomy are racially based is to enter a constant and intense debate. *Scientific* interpretations of race have not been alone in sparking heated controversy; *religious* perspectives have done so as well.[2] Most centrally, of course, race has been a matter of *political* contention. This has been particularly true in the United States, where the concept of race has varied enormously over time without ever leaving the center stage of U.S. history.

What Is Race?

Race consciousness, and its articulation in theories of race, is largely a modern phenomenon. When European explorers in the New World "discovered" people who looked different than themselves, these "natives" challenged then existing conceptions of the origins of the human species, and raised disturbing questions as to whether *all* could be considered in the same "family of man."[3] Religious debates flared over the attempt to reconcile the

[1]*San Francisco Chronicle,* 14 September 1982, 19 May 1983. Ironically, the 1970 Louisiana law was enacted to supersede an old Jim Crow statute which relied on the idea of "common report" in determining an infant's race. Following Phipps's unsuccessful attempt to change her classification and have the law declared unconstitutional, a legislative effort arose which culminated in the repeal of the law. See *San Francisco Chronicle,* 23 June 1983. [Authors' note]

[2]The Mormon church, for example, has been heavily criticized for its doctrine of black inferiority. [Authors' note]

[3]Thomas F. Gossett notes:

> Race theory . . . had up until fairly modern times no firm hold on European thought. On the other hand, race theory and race prejudice were by no means unknown at the time when the English colonists came to North America. Undoubtedly, the age

Bible with the existence of "racially distinct" people. Arguments took place over creation itself, as theories of polygenesis questioned whether God had made only one species of humanity ("monogenesis"). Europeans wondered if the natives of the New World were indeed human beings with redeemable souls. At stake were not only the prospects for conversion, but the types of treatment to be accorded them. The expropriation of property, the denial of political rights, the introduction of slavery and other forms of coercive labor, as well as outright extermination, all presupposed a worldview which distinguished Europeans — children of God, human beings, etc. — from "others." Such a worldview was needed to explain why some should be "free" and others enslaved, why some had rights to land and property while others did not. Race, and the interpretation of racial differences, was a central factor in that worldview.

. . . Many scholars in the eighteenth and nineteenth centuries dedicated themselves to the identification and ranking of variations in humankind. Race was thought of as a *biological* concept, yet its precise definition was the subject of debates which . . . continue to rage today. Despite efforts ranging from Dr. Samuel Morton's studies of cranial capacity[4] to contemporary attempts to base racial classification on shared gene pools,[5] the concept of race has defied biological definition.

> of exploration led many to speculate on race differences at a period when neither Europeans nor Englishmen were prepared to make allowances for vast cultural diversities. Even though race theories had not then secured wide acceptance or even sophisticated formulation, the first contacts of the Spanish with the Indians in the Americas can now be recognized as the beginning of a struggle between conceptions of the nature of primitive peoples which has not yet been wholly settled. (Thomas F. Gossett, *Race: The History of an Idea in America* [New York: Schocken Books, 1965], p. 16.)

Winthrop Jordan provides a detailed account of early European colonialists' attitudes about color and race in *White over Black: American Attitudes Toward the Negro, 1550–1812* (New York: Norton, 1977 [1968]), pp. 3–43. [Authors' note]

[4]Pro-slavery physician Samuel George Morton (1799–1851) compiled a collection of 800 crania from all parts of the world which formed the sample for his studies of race. Assuming that the larger the size of the cranium translated into greater intelligence, Morton established a relationship between race and skull capacity. Gossett reports that

> In 1849, one of his studies included the following results: the English skulls in his collection proved to be the largest, with an average cranial capacity of 96 cubic inches. The Americans and Germans were rather poor seconds, both with cranial capacities of 90 cubic inches. At the bottom of the list were the Negroes with 83 cubic inches, the Chinese with 82, and the Indians with 79. (Ibid., p. 74.)

On Morton's methods, see Stephen J. Gould, "The Finagle Factor," *Human Nature* (July 1978). [Authors' note]

[5]Definitions of race founded upon a common pool of genes have not held up when confronted by scientific research which suggests that the differences *within* a given human population are greater than those *between* populations. See L. L. Cavalli-Sforza, "The Genetics of Human Populations," *Scientific American* (September 1974), pp. 81–89. [Authors' note]

None of the ostensibly "objective" measures to determine and define racial categories were free from the invidious elements of racial ideology. 5
The eighteenth century saw the popular acceptance of a concept with roots in classical Greek thought — the "Great Chain of Being." Posing a grand hierarchy starting with inanimate objects, up through the lowliest forms of life, through "man," and culminating with God the Creator, the "Great Chain of Being" framed discussion about the gradations which existed among humankind. Which races were closer to God and which to apes? In a period where hierarchical arrangements in society were being questioned, the notion of a "Great Chain of Being" legitimated status differences and inequality with appeals to the "naturalness" of distinctions between human beings. To challenge this order would be tantamount to challenging God him/herself.[6]

In the nineteenth century, Count Arthur de Gobineau drew upon the most respected scientific studies of his day to compose his four-volume *Essay on the Inequality of Races* (1853–55). He not only greatly influenced the racial thinking of the period, but his themes were to be echoed in the racist ideologies of the next hundred years: beliefs that superior races produce superior cultures and that racial intermixtures result in the degradation of the superior racial stock. These themes found expression, for instance, in the eugenics movement inspired by Darwin's cousin, Francis Galton,[7] which had an immense impact on scientific and sociopolitical thought in Europe and the United States.[8]

Attempts to discern the *scientific meaning* of race continue to the present day. Although most physical anthropologists and biologists have abandoned the quest for a scientific basis to determine racial categories, controversies have recently flared in the area of genetics and educational psychology. For instance, an essay by Arthur Jensen[9] which argued that hereditary factors shape intelligence not only revived the "nature or nurture" controversy, but raised highly volatile questions about racial equality itself.[10] Clearly the attempt to establish a *biological* basis of race has not been swept into the dustbin of history, but is being resurrected in various scientific arenas. . . .

[6]Winthrop D. Jordan, op. cit., pp. 219–28. [Authors' note]

[7]*eugenics . . . Galton:* Francis Galton (1822–1911) coined the term "eugenics" (literally "good genes") for the science of improving a species by influencing or controlling reproduction. Promoted as a way of minimizing birth defects and congenital illnesses, eugenics has also led to sperm banks for geniuses, proposals to castrate sex offenders, and a call for tax incentives to lower African American birthrates.

[8]Two recent histories of eugenics are Allen Chase, *The Legacy of Malthus* (New York: Knopf, 1977); Daniel J. Kelves, *In the Name of Eugenics: Genetics and the Uses of Human Heredity* (New York: Knopf, 1985). [Authors' note]

[9]*Arthur Jensen:* Professor (b. 1923) whose theories of genetic determinism, suggesting that African Americans have lower IQs than whites, have been criticized as racist.

[10]Arthur Jensen, "How Much Can We Boost IQ and Scholastic Achievement?" *Harvard Educational Review*, vol. 39 (1969), pp. 1–123. [Authors' note]

Race as a Social Concept

The social sciences have come to reject biologistic notions of race in favor of an approach which regards race as a *social* concept. Beginning in the eighteenth century, this trend has been slow and uneven, but its direction clear. In the nineteenth century Max Weber[11] discounted biological explanations for racial conflict and instead highlighted the social and political factors which engendered such conflict.[12] The work of pioneering cultural anthropologist Franz Boas was crucial in refuting the scientific racism of the early twentieth century by rejecting the connection between race and culture, and the assumption of a continuum of "higher" and "lower" cultural groups. Within the contemporary social science literature, race is assumed to be a variable which is shaped by broader societal forces.

Race is indeed a pre-eminently *sociohistorical* concept. Racial categories and the meaning of race . . . have varied tremendously over time and between different societies.

In the United States, the black/white color line has historically been 10
rigidly defined and enforced. White is seen as a "pure" category. Any racial intermixture makes one "nonwhite." In the movie *Raintree County,* Elizabeth Taylor describes the worst of fates to befall whites as "havin' a little Negra blood in ya'—just one little teeny drop and a person's all Negra."[13] This thinking flows from what Marvin Harris[14] has characterized as the principle of *hypo-descent:*

> By what ingenious computation is the genetic tracery of a million years of evolution unraveled and each man [*sic*] assigned his proper social box? In the United States, the mechanism employed is the rule of hypo-descent. This descent rule requires Americans to believe that anyone who is known to have had a Negro ancestor is a Negro. We admit nothing in between. . . . "Hypo-descent" means affiliation with the subordinate rather than the superordinate group in order to avoid the ambiguity of intermediate identity. . . . The rule of hypo-descent is, therefore, an invention, which we in the United States have made in order to keep biological facts from intruding into our collective racist fantasies.[15]

The Susie Guillory Phipps case represents the contemporary expression of this racial logic.

By contrast, a striking feature of race relations in the lowland areas of

[11] *Max Weber:* (pronounced VAY-ber). German sociologist and political economist (1864–1920).

[12] Ernst Moritz Manasse, "Max Weber on Race," *Social Research,* vol. 14 (1947), pp. 191–221. [Authors' note]

[13] Quoted in Edward D. C. Campbell, Jr., *The Celluloid South: Hollywood and the Southern Myth* (Knoxville: University of Tennessee Press, 1981), pp. 168–70. [Authors' note]

[14] *Marvin Harris:* Contemporary cultural anthropologist (b. 1927).

[15] Marvin Harris, *Patterns of Race in the Americas* (New York: Norton, 1964), p. 56. [Authors' note]

Latin America since the abolition of slavery has been the relative absence of sharply defined racial groupings. No such rigid descent rule characterizes racial identity in many Latin American societies. Brazil, for example, has historically had less rigid conceptions of race, and thus a variety of "intermediate" racial categories exist. Indeed, as Harris notes, "One of the most striking consequences of the Brazilian system of racial identification is that parents and children and even brothers and sisters are frequently accepted as representatives of quite opposite racial types."[16] Such a possibility is incomprehensible within the logic of racial categories in the United States.

To suggest another example: the notion of "passing" takes on new meaning if we compare various American cultures' means of assigning racial identity. In the United States, individuals who are actually "black" by the logic of hypo-descent have attempted to skirt the discriminatory barriers imposed by law and custom by attempting to "pass" for white.[17] Ironically, these same individuals would not be able to pass for "black" in many Latin American societies.

Consideration of the term "black" illustrates the diversity of racial meanings which can be found among different societies and historically within a given society. In contemporary British politics the term "black" is used to refer to all nonwhites. Interestingly this designation has not arisen through the racist discourse of groups such as the National Front. Rather, in political and cultural movements, Asian as well as Afro-Caribbean youth are adopting the term as an expression of self-identity.[18] The wide-ranging meanings of "black" illustrate the manner in which racial categories are shaped politically.[19]

The meaning of race is defined and contested throughout society, in both collective action and personal practice. In the process, racial categories themselves are formed, transformed, destroyed, and reformed. We use the term *racial formation* to refer to the process by which social, economic, and political forces determine the content and importance of racial categories, and by which they are in turn shaped by racial meanings. . . .

[16]Ibid., p. 57. [Authors' note]

[17]After James Meredith had been admitted as the first black student at the University of Mississippi, Harry S. Murphy announced that he, and not Meredith, was the first black student to attend "Ole Miss." Murphy described himself as black but was able to pass for white and spent nine months at the institution without attracting any notice (ibid., p. 56). [Authors' note]

[18]A. Sivanandan, "From Resistance to Rebellion: Asian and Afro-Caribbean Struggles in Britain," *Race and Class*, vol. 23, nos. 2–3 (Autumn–Winter 1981). [Authors' note]

[19]Consider the contradictions in racial status which abound in the country with the most rigidly defined racial categories — South Africa. There a race classification agency is employed to adjudicate claims for upgrading of official racial identity. This is particularly necessary for the "colored" category. The apartheid system considers Chinese as "Asians" while the Japanese are accorded the status of "honorary whites." This logic nearly detaches race from any grounding in skin color and other physical attributes and nakedly exposed race as a juridicial category subject to economic, social, and political influences. (We are indebted to Steve Talbot for clarification of some of these points.) [Authors' note]

Racial Ideology and Racial Identity

The seemingly obvious, "natural" and "common sense" qualities which the existing racial order exhibits themselves testify to the effectiveness of the racial formation process in constructing racial meanings and racial identities. 15

One of the first things we notice about people when we meet them (along with their sex) is their race. We utilize race to provide clues about *who* a person is. This fact is made painfully obvious when we encounter someone whom we cannot conveniently racially categorize — someone who is, for example, racially "mixed" or of an ethnic/racial group with which we are not familiar. Such an encounter becomes a source of discomfort and momentarily a crisis of racial meaning. Without a racial identity, one is in danger of having no identity.

Our compass for navigating race relations depends on preconceived notions of what each specific racial group looks like. Comments such as, "Funny, you don't look black," betray an underlying image of what black should be. We also become disoriented when people do not act "black," "Latino," or indeed "white." The content of such stereotypes reveals a series of unsubstantiated beliefs about who these groups are and what "they" are like.[20]

In U.S. society, then, a kind of "racial etiquette" exists, a set of interpretative codes and racial meanings which operate in the interactions of daily life. Rules shaped by our perception of race in a comprehensively racial society determine the "presentation of self,"[21] distinctions of status, and appropriate modes of conduct. "Etiquette" is not mere universal adherence to the dominant group's rules, but a more dynamic combination of these rules with the values and beliefs of subordinated groupings. This racial "subjection" is quintessentially ideological. Everybody learns some combination, some version, of the rules of racial classification, and of their own racial identity, often without obvious teaching or conscious inculcation. Race becomes "common sense" — a way of comprehending, explaining, and acting in the world.

Racial beliefs operate as an "amateur biology," a way of explaining the variations in "human nature."[22] Differences in skin color and other obvious physical characteristics supposedly provide visible clues to differences lurking underneath. Temperament, sexuality, intelligence, athletic ability, aes-

[20] Gordon W. Allport, *The Nature of Prejudice* (Garden City, New York: Doubleday, 1958), pp. 184–200. [Authors' note]

[21] We wish to use this phrase loosely, without committing ourselves to a particular position on such social psychological approaches as symbolic interactionism, which are outside the scope of this study. An interesting study on this subject is S. M. Lyman and W. A Douglass, "Ethnicity: Strategies of Individual and Collective Impression Management," *Social Research,* vol. 40, no. 2 (1973). [Authors' note]

[22] Michael Billig, "Patterns of Racism: Interviews with National Front Members," *Race and Class,* vol. 20, no. 2 (Autumn 1978), pp. 161–79. [Authors' note]

thetic preferences, and so on are presumed to be fixed and discernible from the palpable mark of race. Such diverse questions as our confidence and trust in others (for example, clerks or salespeople, media figures, neighbors), our sexual preferences and romantic images, our tastes in music, films, dance, or sports, and our very ways of talking, walking, eating, and dreaming are ineluctably[23] shaped by notions of race. Skin color "differences" are thought to explain perceived differences in intellectual, physical, and artistic temperaments, and to justify distinct treatment of racially identified individuals and groups.

20 The continuing persistence of racial ideology suggests that these racial myths and stereotypes cannot be exposed as such in the popular imagination. They are, we think, too essential, too integral, to the maintenance of the U.S. social order. Of course, particular meanings, stereotypes, and myths can change, but the presence of a *system* of racial meanings and stereotypes, of racial ideology, seems to be a permanent feature of U.S. culture.

Film and television, for example, have been notorious in disseminating images of racial minorities which establish for audiences what people from these groups look like, how they behave, and "who they are."[24] The power of the media lies not only in their ability to reflect the dominant racial ideology, but in their capacity to shape that ideology in the first place. D. W. Griffith's epic *Birth of a Nation,* a sympathetic treatment of the rise of the Ku Klux Klan during Reconstruction, helped to generate, consolidate, and "nationalize" images of blacks which had been more disparate (more regionally specific, for example) prior to the film's appearance.[25] In U.S. television, the necessity to define characters in the briefest and most condensed manner has led to the perpetuation of racial caricatures, as racial stereotypes serve as shorthand for scriptwriters, directors, and actors, in commercials, etc. Television's tendency to address the "lowest common denominator" in

[23]*ineluctably:* Inescapably.

[24]"Miss San Antonio USA, Lisa Fernandez, and other Hispanics auditioning for a role in a television soap opera did not fit the Hollywood image of real Mexicans and had to darken their faces before filming." Model Aurora Garza said that their faces were bronzed with powder because they looked too white. " 'I'm a real Mexican [Garza said] and very dark anyway. I'm even darker right now because I have a tan. But they kept wanting me to make my face darker and darker' " (*San Francisco Chronicle,* 21 September 1984). A similar dilemma faces Asian American actors who feel that Asian character lead roles inevitably go to white actors who make themselves up to be Asian. Scores of Charlie Chan films, for example, have been made with white leads (the last one was the 1981 *Charlie Chan and the Curse of the Dragon Queen*). Roland Winters, who played in six Chan features, was asked by playwright Frank Chin to explain the logic of casting a white man in the role of Charlie Chan: " 'The only thing I can think of is, if you want to cast a homosexual in a show, and you get a homosexual, it'll be awful. It won't be funny . . . and maybe there's something there . . .' " (Frank Chin, "Confessions of the Chinatown Cowboy," *Bulletin of Concerned Asian Scholars,* vol. 4, no. 3 [Fall 1972]). [Authors' note]

[25]Melanie Martindale-Sikes, "Nationalizing 'Nigger' Imagery Through 'Birth of a Nation,' " paper prepared for the 73rd Annual Meeting of the American Sociological Association, 4–8 September 1978 in San Francisco. [Authors' note]

order to render programs "familiar" to an enormous and diverse audience leads it regularly to assign and reassign racial characteristics to particular groups, both minority and majority.

These and innumerable other examples show that we tend to view race as something fixed and immutable — something rooted in "nature." Thus we mask the historical construction of racial categories, the shifting meaning of race, and the crucial role of politics and ideology in shaping race relations. Races do not emerge full-blown. They are the results of diverse historical practices and are continually subject to challenge over their definition and meaning.

Engaging the Text

1. Why, according to Omi and Winant, did modern "race consciousness" arise? What examples do they offer of its historical influence?
2. How do Omi and Winant distinguish between biological and social definitions of race? What difference does it make which definition one accepts?
3. Explain the concept of "hypo-descent" (para. 10). How has it functioned to maintain racial categories?
4. Explain Omi and Winant's assertion that racial categories seem to be a matter of "common sense" (para. 15). Brainstorm a list of American "racial beliefs" about the "temperament, sexuality, intelligence, athletic ability, aesthetic preferences, and so on" (para. 19) of different racial groups. To what extent do you believe that the system of racist beliefs underlying these stereotypes is "a permanent feature of U.S. culture" (para. 20)? How might this system be changed?

Exploring Connections

5. Compare Omi and Winant's analysis of the social construction of racial categories with James Weinrich and Walter Williams's discussion of gender roles (p. 295). What similarities can you find between the ways that racial and gender role categories shape our beliefs, expectations, and responses? Are there any significant differences between the mental categories we construct for race and for gender?
6. Review Judith Ortiz Cofer's "The Story of My Body" (p. 278) and examine her reflections on her physical appearance for evidence of the racial beliefs and categories she learned as a child.

Extending the Critical Context

7. Analyze the racial and ethnic makeup of your class. How many nationalities, "races," and ethnic groups are represented, even if only minutely (for instance, "one sixty-fourth Welsh on my father's side")? After exploring such data, try to draw some conclusions about the status of race in the United States as a biological and as a social concept.

8. Omi and Winant suggest that television plays an important role in creating and maintaining racial categories because TV generally presents racial and cultural stereotypes in order to define characters "in the most condensed manner" possible. Working in small groups, describe the current state of racial categories on TV for African Americans, Latinos, Asian Americans, and Native Americans. Are these groups still represented stereotypically? What racial beliefs are associated with them in current TV programming? Is there a racial category with a corresponding set of racial beliefs on TV for white Americans?

Split at the Root: An Essay on Jewish Identity

ADRIENNE RICH

Academic discussions of race are relatively easy to handle when abstracted from personal experience. But the realities of life in a racist society can be devastating. In the following selection, Adrienne Rich assesses the personal costs of growing up in a world divided by prejudice. Rich (b. 1929) is one of America's premier poets and an ardent feminist. Her poetry, which has appeared in numerous collections over the past forty years, often addresses themes of social injustice, women's consciousness, and the need for an authentic human community. In 1974, she won the National Book Award for poetry for Diving into the Wreck. *She has also published* The Dream of a Common Language *(1978),* An Atlas of the Difficult Life *(1991), and* What Is Found There: Notebooks on Poetry and Politics *(1993). "Split at the Root" is taken from* Blood, Bread, and Poetry: Selected Prose, 1979–1985. *She has been a member of the Department of Literature of the American Academy and Institute of Arts and Letters since 1990.*

For about fifteen minutes I have been sitting chin in hand in front of the typewriter, staring out at the snow. Trying to be honest with myself, trying to figure out why writing this seems to be so dangerous an act, filled with fear and shame, and why it seems so necessary. It comes to me that in order to write this I have to be willing to do two things: I have to claim my father, for I have my Jewishness from him and not from my gentile mother; and I have to break his silence, his taboos; in order to claim him I have in a sense to expose him.

And there is, of course, the third thing: I have to face the sources and the flickering presence of my own ambivalence as a Jew; the daily, mundane anti-Semitisms of my entire life.

These are stories I have never tried to tell before. Why now? Why, I asked myself sometime last year, does this question of Jewish identity float so impalpably, so ungraspably around me, a cloud I can't quite see the outlines of, which feels to me to be without definition?

And yet I've been on the track of this longer than I think.

In a long poem written in 1960, when I was thirty-one years old, I 5
described myself as "Split at the root, neither Gentile nor Jew, / Yankee nor Rebel."[1] I was still trying to have it both ways: to be neither/nor, trying to live (with my Jewish husband and three children more Jewish in ancestry than I) in the predominantly gentile Yankee academic world of Cambridge, Massachusetts.

But this begins, for me, in Baltimore, where I was born in my father's workplace, a hospital in the Black ghetto, whose lobby contained an immense white marble statue of Christ.

My father was then a young teacher and researcher in the department of pathology at the Johns Hopkins Medical School, one of the very few Jews to attend or teach at that institution. He was from Birmingham, Alabama; his father, Samuel, was Ashkenazic,[2] an immigrant from Austria-Hungary, and his mother, Hattie Rice, a Sephardic[3] Jew from Vicksburg, Mississippi. My grandfather had had a shoe store in Birmingham, which did well enough to allow him to retire comfortably and to leave my grandmother income on his death. The only souvenirs of my grandfather, Samuel Rich, were his ivory flute, which lay on our living-room mantel and was not to be played with; his thin gold pocket watch, which my father wore; and his Hebrew prayer book, which I discovered among my father's books in the course of reading my way through his library. In this prayer book there was a newspaper clipping about my grandparents' wedding, which took place in a synagogue.

My father, Arnold, was sent in adolescence to a military school in the North Carolina mountains, a place for training white southern Christian gentlemen. I suspect that there were few, if any, other Jewish boys at Colonel Bingham's, or at "Mr. Jefferson's university" in Charlottesville, where he studied as an undergraduate. With whatever conscious forethought, Samuel and Hattie sent their son into the dominant southern WASP culture to become an "exception," to enter the professional class. Never, in describing these experiences, did he speak of having suffered — from loneliness, cultural alienation, or outsiderhood. Never did I hear him use the word *anti-Semitism.*

[1] Adrienne Rich, "Readings of History," in *Snapshots of a Daughter-in-Law* (New York: W. W. Norton, 1967), pp. 35–40. [Author's note]

[2] *Ashkenazic:* Pertaining to descendants of the Jews who settled in middle and northern Europe after the Babylonian captivity (597–538 B.C.)

[3] *Sephardic:* Pertaining to descendants of the Jews who settled in Spain and Portugal.

It was only in college, when I read a poem by Karl Shapiro beginning "To hate the Negro and avoid the Jew / is the curriculum," that it flashed on me that there was an untold side to my father's story of his student years. He looked recognizably Jewish, was short and slender in build with dark wiry hair and deep-set eyes, high forehead and curved nose.

10 My mother is a gentile. In Jewish law I cannot count myself a Jew. If it is true that "we think back through our mothers if we are women" (Virginia Woolf[4]) — and I myself have affirmed this — then even according to lesbian theory, I cannot (or need not?) count myself a Jew.

The white southern Protestant woman, the gentile, has always been there for me to peel back into. That's a whole piece of history in itself, for my gentile grandmother and my mother were also frustrated artists and intellectuals, a lost writer and a lost composer between them. Readers and annotators of books, note takers, my mother a good pianist still, in her eighties. But there was also the obsession with ancestry, with "background," the southern talk of family, not as people you would necessarily know and depend on, but as heritage, the guarantee of "good breeding." There was the inveterate romantic heterosexual fantasy, the mother telling the daughter how to attract men (my mother often used the word "fascinate"); the assumption that relations between the sexes could only be romantic, that it was in the woman's interest to cultivate "mystery," conceal her actual feelings. Survival tactics of a kind, I think today, knowing what I know about the white woman's sexual role in the southern racist scenario. Heterosexuality as protection, but also drawing white women deeper into collusion with white men.

It would be easy to push away and deny the gentile in me — that white southern woman, that social christian. At different times in my life I have wanted to push away one or the other burden of inheritance, to say merely *I am a woman; I am a lesbian.* If I call myself a Jewish lesbian, do I thereby try to shed some of my southern gentile white woman's culpability? If I call myself only through my mother, is it because I pass more easily through a world where being a lesbian often seems like outsiderhood enough?

According to Nazi logic, my two Jewish grandparents would have made me a *Mischling, first-degree* — nonexempt from the Final Solution.[5]

The social world in which I grew up was christian virtually without needing to say so — christian imagery, music, language, symbols, assumptions everywhere. It was also a genteel, white, middle-class world in which "common" was a term of deep opprobrium. "Common" white people might speak

[4]*Virginia Woolf:* English feminist, critic, and innovator in modern British fiction (1882–1941), best known for her novels *Mrs. Dalloway* and *To the Lighthouse.*

[5]*Final Solution:* Euphemistic name for the Nazi plan to execute Jews in "death camps" like Auschwitz and Dachau.

of "niggers"; *we* were taught never to use that word — *we* said "Negroes" (even as we accepted segregation, the eating taboo, the assumption that Black people were simply of a separate species). Our language was more polite, distinguishing us from the "rednecks" or the lynch-mob mentality. But so charged with negative meaning was even the word "Negro" that as children we were taught never to use it in front of Black people. We were taught that any mention of skin color in the presence of colored people was treacherous, forbidden ground. In a parallel way, the word "Jew" was not used by polite gentiles. I sometimes heard my best friend's father, a Presbyterian minister, allude to "the Hebrew people" or "people of the Jewish faith." The world of acceptable folk was white, gentile (christian, really), and had "ideals" (which colored people, white "common" people, were not supposed to have). "Ideals" and "manners" included not hurting someone's feelings by calling her or him a Negro or a Jew — naming the hated identity. This is the mental framework of the 1930s and 1940s in which I was raised.

(Writing this, I feel dimly like the betrayer; of my father, who did not 15
speak the word; of my mother, who must have trained me in the messages; of my caste and class; of my whiteness itself.)

Two memories: I am in a play reading at school of *The Merchant of Venice.* Whatever Jewish law says, I am quite sure I was *seen* as Jewish (with a reassuringly gentile mother) in that double vision that bigotry allows. I am the only Jewish girl in the class, and I am playing Portia.[6] As always, I read my part aloud for my father the night before, and he tells me to convey, with my voice, more scorn and contempt with the word "Jew": "Therefore, Jew . . ." I have to say the word out, and say it loudly. I was encouraged to pretend to be a non-Jewish child acting a non-Jewish character who has to speak the word "Jew" emphatically. Such a child would not have had trouble with the part. But *I* must have had trouble with the part, if only because the word itself was really taboo. I can see that there was a kind of terrible, bitter bravado about my father's way of handling this. And who would not dissociate from Shylock[7] in order to identify with Portia? As a Jewish child who was also a female, I loved Portia — and, like every other Shakespearean heroine, she proved a treacherous role model.

A year or so later I am in another play, *The School for Scandal,* in which a notorious spendthrift is described as having "many excellent friends . . . among the Jews." In neither case was anything explained, either to me or to the class at large, about this scorn for Jews and the disgust surrounding Jews and money. Money, when Jews wanted it, had it, or lent it to others, seemed to take on a peculiar nastiness; Jews and money had some peculiar and unspeakable relation.

At this same school — in which we had Episcopalian hymns and prayers, and read aloud through the Bible morning after morning — I gained the

[6]*Portia:* The heroine of Shakespeare's *The Merchant of Venice.*
[7]*Shylock:* The Jewish moneylender and villain of *The Merchant of Venice.*

impression that Jews were in the Bible and mentioned in English literature, that they had been persecuted centuries ago by the wicked Inquisition, but that they seemed not to exist in everyday life. These were the 1940s, and we were told a great deal about the Battle of Britain, the noble French Resistance fighters, the brave, starving Dutch — but I did not learn of the resistance of the Warsaw ghetto until I left home.

I was sent to the Episcopal church, baptized and confirmed, and attended it for about five years, though without belief. That religion seemed to have little to do with belief or commitment; it was liturgy that mattered, not spiritual passion. Neither of my parents ever entered that church, and my father would not enter *any* church for any reason — wedding or funeral. Nor did I enter a synagogue until I left Baltimore. When I came home from church, for a while, my father insisted on reading aloud to me from Thomas Paine's *The Age of Reason* — a diatribe against institutional religion. Thus, he explained, I would have a balanced view of these things, a choice. He — they — did not give me the choice to be a Jew. My mother explained to me when I was filling out forms for college that if any question was asked about "religion," I should put down "Episcopalian" rather than "none" — to seem to have no religion was, she implied, dangerous.

But it was white social christianity, rather than any particular christian 20
sect, that the world was founded on. The very word *Christian* was used as a synonym for virtuous, just, peace-loving, generous, etc., etc.[8] The norm was christian: "religion: none" was indeed not acceptable. Anti-Semitism was so intrinsic as not to have a name. I don't recall exactly being taught that the Jews killed Jesus — "Christ killer" seems too strong a term for the bland Episcopal vocabulary — but certainly we got the impression that the Jews had been caught out in a terrible mistake, failing to recognize the true Messiah, and were thereby less advanced in moral and spiritual sensibility. The Jews had actually allowed *moneylenders in the Temple* (again, the unexplained obsession with Jews and money). They were of the past, archaic, primitive, as older (and darker) cultures are supposed to be primitive; christianity was lightness, fairness, peace on earth, and combined the feminine appeal of "The meek shall inherit the earth" with the masculine stride of "Onward, Christian Soldiers."

Sometime in 1946, while still in high school, I read in the newspaper that a theater in Baltimore was showing films of the Allied liberation of the Nazi concentration camps. Alone, I went downtown after school one afternoon and watched the stark, blurry, but unmistakable newsreels. When I try to go back and touch the pulse of that girl of sixteen, growing up in many ways so precocious and so ignorant, I am overwhelmed by a memory of despair, a sense of inevitability more enveloping than any I had ever known.

[8]In a similar way the phrase "That's white of you" implied that you were behaving with the superior decency and morality expected of white but not of Black people. [Author's note]

Anne Frank's diary and many other personal narratives of the Holocaust were still unknown or unwritten. But it came to me that every one of those piles of corpses, mountains of shoes and clothing had contained, simply, individuals, who had believed, as I now believed of myself, that they were intended to live out a life of some kind of meaning, that the world possessed some kind of sense and order; yet *this* had happened to them. And I, who believed my life was intended to be so interesting and meaningful, was connected to those dead by something — not just mortality but a taboo name, a hated identity. Or was I — did I really have to be? Writing this now, I feel belated rage that I was so impoverished by the family and social worlds I lived in, that I had to try to figure out by myself what this did indeed mean for me. That I had never been taught about resistance, only about passing. That I had no language for anti-Semitism itself.

When I went home and told my parents where I had been, they were not pleased. I felt accused of being morbidly curious, not healthy, sniffing around death for the thrill of it. And since, at sixteen, I was often not sure of the sources of my feelings or of my motives for doing what I did, I probably accused myself as well. One thing was clear: there was nobody in my world with whom I could discuss those films. Probably at the same time, I was reading accounts of the camps in magazines and newspapers; what I remember were the films and having questions that I could not even phrase, such as *Are those men and women "them" or "us"?*

To be able to ask even the child's astonished question *Why do they hate us so?* means knowing how to say "we." The guilt of not knowing, the guilt of perhaps having betrayed my parents or even those victims, those survivors, through mere curiosity — these also froze in me for years the impulse to find out more about the Holocaust.

1947: I left Baltimore to go to college in Cambridge, Massachusetts, left (I thought) the backward, enervating South for the intellectual, vital North. New England also had for me some vibration of higher moral rectitude, of moral passion even, with its seventeenth-century Puritan self-scrutiny, its nineteenth-century literary "flowering," its abolitionist righteousness, Colonel Shaw and his Black Civil War regiment depicted in granite on Boston Common. At the same time, I found myself, at Radcliffe, among Jewish women. I used to sit for hours over coffee with what I thought of as the "real" Jewish students, who told me about middle-class Jewish culture in America. I described my background — for the first time to strangers — and they took me on, some with amusement at my illiteracy, some arguing that I could never marry into a strict Jewish family, some convinced I didn't "look Jewish," others that I did. I learned the names of holidays and foods, which surnames are Jewish and which are "changed names"; about girls who had had their noses "fixed," their hair straightened. For these young Jewish women, students in the late 1940s, it was acceptable, perhaps even necessary, to strive to look as gentile as possible; but they stuck proudly to being Jewish, expected to marry a Jew, have children, keep the holidays, carry on the culture.

I felt I was testing a forbidden current, that there was danger in these 25
revelations. I bought a reproduction of a Chagall[9] portrait of a rabbi in striped prayer shawl and hung it on the wall of my room. I was admittedly young and trying to educate myself, but I was also doing something that *is* dangerous: I was flirting with identity.

One day that year I was in a small shop where I had bought a dress with a too-long skirt. The shop employed a seamstress who did alterations, and she came in to pin up the skirt on me. I am sure that she was a recent immigrant, a survivor. I remember a short, dark woman wearing heavy glasses, with an accent so foreign I could not understand her words. Something about her presence was very powerful and disturbing to me. After marking and pinning up the skirt, she sat back on her knees, looked up at me, and asked in a hurried whisper: "You Jewish?" Eighteen years of training in assimilation sprang into the reflex by which I shook my head, rejecting her, and muttered, "No."

What was I actually saying "no" to? She was poor, older, struggling with a foreign tongue, anxious; she had escaped the death that had been intended for her, but I had no imagination of her possible courage and foresight, her resistance — I did not see in her a heroine who had perhaps saved many lives, including her own. I saw the frightened immigrant, the seamstress hemming the skirts of college girls, the wandering Jew. But I was an American college girl having her skirt hemmed. And I was frightened myself, I think, because she had recognized me ("It takes one to know one," my friend Edie at Radcliffe had said) even if I refused to recognize myself or her, even if her recognition was sharpened by loneliness or the need to feel safe with me.

But why should she have felt safe with me? I myself was living with a false sense of safety.

There are betrayals in my life that I have known at the very moment were betrayals: this was one of them. There are other betrayals committed so repeatedly, so mundanely, that they leave no memory trace behind, only a growing residue of misery, of dull, accreted self-hatred. Often these take the form not of words but of silence. Silence before the joke at which everyone is laughing; the anti-woman joke, the racist joke, the anti-Semitic joke. Silence and then amnesia. Blocking it out when the oppressor's language starts coming from the lips of one we admire, whose courage and eloquence have touched us: *She didn't really mean that; he didn't really say that.* But the accretions build up out of sight, like scale inside a kettle.

[9]*Chagall:* Marc Chagall, Russian painter (1887–1985), famous for surreal, dreamlike works inspired by his Jewish heritage.

1948: I come home from my freshman year at college, flaming with new 30
insights, new information. I am the daughter who has gone out into the world, to the pinnacle of intellectual prestige, Harvard, fulfilling my father's hopes for me, but also exposed to dangerous influences. I have already been reproved for attending a rally for Henry Wallace[10] and the Progressive party. I challenge my father: "Why haven't you told me that I am Jewish? Why do you never talk about being a Jew?" He answers measuredly, "You know that I have never denied that I am a Jew. But it's not important to me. I am a scientist, a deist.[11] I have no use for organized religion. I choose to live in a world of many kinds of people. There are Jews I admire and others whom I despise. I am a person, not simply a Jew." The words are as I remember them, not perhaps exactly as spoken. But that was the message. And it contained enough truth — as all denial drugs itself on partial truth — so that it remained for the time being unanswerable, leaving me high and dry, split at the root, gasping for clarity, for air.

At that time Arnold Rich was living in suspension, waiting to be appointed to the professorship of pathology at Johns Hopkins. The appointment was delayed for years, no Jew ever having held a professional chair in that medical school. And he wanted it badly. It must have been a very bitter time for him, since he had believed so greatly in the redeeming power of excellence, of being the most brilliant, inspired man for the job. With enough excellence, you could presumably make it stop mattering that you were Jewish; you could become the *only* Jew in the gentile world, a Jew so "civilized," so far from "common," so attractively combining southern gentility with European cultural values that no one would ever confuse you with the raw, "pushy" Jews of New York, the "loud, hysterical" refugees from eastern Europe, the "overdressed" Jews of the urban South.

We — my sister, mother, and I — were constantly urged to speak quietly in public, to dress without ostentation, to repress all vividness or spontaneity, to assimilate with a world which might see us as too flamboyant. I suppose that my mother, pure gentile though she was, could be seen as acting "common" or "Jewish" if she laughed too loudly or spoke aggressively. My father's mother, who lived with us half the year, was a model of circumspect behavior, dressed in dark blue or lavender, retiring in company, ladylike to an extreme, wearing no jewelry except a good gold chain, a narrow brooch, or a string of pearls. A few times, within the family, I saw her anger flare, felt the passion she was repressing. But when Arnold took us out to a restaurant or on a trip, the Rich women were always tuned down to some WASP level my father believed, surely, would protect us all — maybe also make us unrecognizable to the "real Jews" who wanted to seize us, drag us back to the *shtetl,* the ghetto, in its many manifestations.

[10] *Henry Wallace:* American journalist (1888–1965), politician, and agriculturalist who was the Progressive party's candidate for the presidency in 1948.

[11] *deist:* One who believes that human reason, not divine power, underlies the laws of the universe.

For, yes, that *was* a message—that some Jews would be after you, once they "knew," to rejoin them, to re-enter a world that was messy, noisy, unpredictable, maybe poor—"even though," as my mother once wrote me, criticizing my largely Jewish choice of friends in college, "some of them will be the most brilliant, fascinating people you'll ever meet." I wonder if that isn't one message of assimilation — of America — that the unlucky or the unachieving want to pull you backward, that to identify with them is to court downward mobility, lose the precious chance of passing, of token existence. There was always within this sense of Jewish identity a strong class discrimination. Jews might be "fascinating" as individuals but came with huge unruly families who "poured chicken soup over everyone's head" (in the phrase of a white southern male poet). Anti-Semitism could thus be justified by the bad behavior of certain Jews; and if you did not effectively deny family and community, there would always be a remote cousin claiming kinship with you who was the "wrong kind" of Jew.

I have always believed his attitude toward other Jews depended on who they were. . . . It was my impression that Jews of this background looked down on Eastern European Jews, including Polish Jews and Russian Jews, who generally were not as well educated. This from a letter written to me recently by a gentile who had worked in my father's department, whom I had asked about anti-Semitism there and in particular regarding my father. This informant also wrote me that it was hard to perceive anti-Semitism in Baltimore because the racism made so much more intense an impression: *I would almost have to think that blacks went to a different heaven than the whites, because the bodies were kept in a separate morgue, and some white persons did not even want blood transfusions from black donors.* My father's mind was predictably racist and misogynist;[12] yet as a medical student he noted in his journal that southern male chivalry stopped at the point of any white man in a streetcar giving his seat to an old, weary Black woman standing in the aisle. Was this a Jewish insight—an outsider's insight, even though the outsider was striving to be on the inside?

35 Because what isn't named is often more permeating than what is, I believe that my father's Jewishness profoundly shaped my own identity and our family existence. They were shaped both by external anti-Semitism and my father's self-hatred, and by his Jewish pride. What Arnold did, I think, was call his Jewish pride something else: achievement, aspiration, genius, idealism. Whatever was unacceptable got left back under the rubric of Jewishness or the "wrong kind" of Jews — uneducated, aggressive, loud. The message I got was that we were really superior: nobody else's father had collected so many books, had traveled so far, knew so many languages. Baltimore was a musical city, but for the most part, in the families of my school friends, culture was for women. My father was an amateur musician, read poetry, adored encyclopedic knowledge. He prowled and pounced over my school papers, insisting I use "grownup" sources; he criticized my poems for

[12]*misogynist:* A person who hates women.

faulty technique and gave me books on rhyme and meter and form. His investment in my intellect and talent was egotistical, tyrannical, opinionated, and terribly wearing. He taught me, nevertheless, to believe in hard work, to mistrust easy inspiration, to write and rewrite; to feel that I *was* a person of the book, even though a woman; to take ideas seriously. He made me feel, at a very young age, the power of language and that I could share in it.

The Riches were proud, but we also had to very careful. Our behavior had to be more impeccable than other people's. Strangers were not to be trusted, nor even friends; family issues must never go beyond the family; the world was full of potential slanderers, betrayers, *people who could not understand.* Even within the family, I realize that I never in my whole life knew what my father was really feeling. Yet he spoke—monologued—with driving intensity. You could grow up in such a house mesmerized by the local electricity, the crucial meanings assumed by the merest things. This used to seem to me a sign that we were all living on some high emotional plane. It was a difficult force field for a favored daughter to disengage from.

Easy to call that intensity Jewish; and I have no doubt that passion is one of the qualities required for survival over generations of persecution. But what happens when passion is rent from its original base, when the white gentile world is softly saying "Be more like us and you can be almost one of us"? What happens when survival seems to mean closing off one emotional artery after another? His forebears in Europe had been forbidden to travel or expelled from one country after another, had special taxes levied on them if they left the city walls, had been forced to wear special clothes and badges, restricted to the poorest neighborhoods. He had wanted to be a "free spirit," to travel widely, among "all kinds of people." Yet in his prime of life he lived in an increasingly withdrawn world, in his house up on a hill in a neighborhood where Jews were not supposed to be able to buy property, depending almost exclusively on interactions with his wife and daughters to provide emotional connectedness. In his home, he created a private defense system so elaborate that even as he was dying, my mother felt unable to talk freely with his colleagues or others who might have helped her. Of course, she acquiesced in this.

The loneliness of the "only," the token, often doesn't feel like loneliness but like a kind of dead echo chamber. Certain things that ought to don't resonate. Somewhere Beverly Smith writes of women of color "inspiring the behavior" in each other. When there's nobody to "inspire the behavior," act out of the culture, there is an atrophy, a dwindling, which is partly invisible.

Sometimes I feel I have seen too long from too many disconnected angles: white, Jewish, anti-Semite, racist, anti-racist, once-married, lesbian, middle-class, feminist, exmatriate southerner, *split at the root*—that I will never bring them whole. I would have liked, in this essay, to bring together the meanings of anti-Semitism and racism as I have experienced them and as I believe they intersect in the world beyond my life. But I'm not able to do this yet. I feel the tension as I think, make notes: *If you really look at the one reality, the other will waver and disperse.* Trying in one week to read Angela Davis and Lucy Davidowicz;[13] trying to hold throughout to a feminist, a lesbian, perspective — what does this mean? Nothing has trained me for this. And sometimes I feel inadequate to make any statement as a Jew; I feel the history of denial within me like an injury, a scar. For assimilation has affected *my* perceptions; those early lapses in meaning, those blanks, are with me still. My ignorance can be dangerous to me and to others.

Yet we can't wait for the undamaged to make our connections for us; 40
we can't wait to speak until we are perfectly clear and righteous. There is no purity and, in our lifetimes, no end to this process.

This essay, then, has no conclusions: it is another beginning for me. Not just a way of saying, in 1982 Right Wing America, *I, too, will wear the yellow star.*[14] It's a moving into accountability, enlarging the range of accountability. I know that in the rest of my life, the next half century or so, every aspect of my identity will have to be engaged. The middle-class white girl taught to trade obedience for privilege. The Jewish lesbian raised to be a heterosexual gentile. The woman who first heard oppression named and analyzed in the Black Civil Rights struggle. The woman with three sons, the feminist who hates male violence. The woman limping with a cane, the woman who has stopped bleeding are also accountable. The poet who knows that beautiful language can lie, that the oppressor's language sometimes sounds beautiful. The woman trying, as part of her resistance, to clean up her act.

[13]Angela Y. Davis, *Woman, Race and Class* (New York: Random House, 1981); Lucy S. Davidowicz, *The War against the Jews 1933–1945* (1975; New York: Bantam, 1979). [Author's note]

[14]*the yellow star:* The Star of David, used by Nazis during World War II to identify people who were Jewish.

Engaging the Text

1. In this personal reminiscence, Rich dissects her identity, analyzing her consciousness into separate, often antagonistic selves that compete for recognition. Work through her essay to identify these various selves and discuss how and why they conflict with one another.
2. Analyze the motives that underlie Arnold Rich's racism and his denial of his own Jewish heritage.
3. Why are other ethnic minority groups important to Rich?
4. When Rich mentions buying a Chagall portrait of a rabbi (para. 25), she writes, "but I was also doing something that *is* dangerous: I was flirting with identity." What does she mean? Why is exploring her own identity a "dangerous" act?

EXPLORING CONNECTIONS

5. Review Michael Omi and Howard Winant's notion of "racial categories" (p. 356) and use it to analyze the beliefs, values, and attitudes that Rich grew up with. What qualities and ideas did her family associate with Gentiles, Jews, and people of color? How and why did she redefine these categories for herself? What, according to Rich, were the personal costs of this redefinition of her values and beliefs?
6. Discuss the ways in which one or more of the following people or characters might be considered — like Rich — "split at the root":

the speaker of "Para Teresa" (p. 74)	Gary Soto (p. 145)
Richard Rodriguez (p. 61)	Nora Quealey (p. 253)
Anndee Hochman (p. 150)	Paula Gunn Allen (p. 312)
	Stephen Cruz (p. 460)

EXTENDING THE CRITICAL CONTEXT

7. Try your hand at writing your own self-analysis. How many separate selves do you contain? What demands do they make of you? How do they conflict? What does it mean for you to be "accountable" to them?

Causes of Prejudice

VINCENT N. PARRILLO

What motivates the creation of racial categories? In the following selection, Vincent Parrillo reviews several theories that seek to explain the motives for prejudiced behavior—from socialization theory to economic competition. As Parrillo indicates, prejudice cannot be linked to any single cause: a whole network of forces and frustrations underlies the reasons for this complex behavior. Parrillo (b. 1938) is chairperson of the Department of Sociology at William Paterson College in New Jersey. His other books include Contemporary Social Problems *(1990) and* Rethinking Today's Minorities *(1991). This excerpt originally appeared in* Strangers to These Shores *(1994).*

There appears to be no single cause of prejudice but, rather, many causes that are frequently interrelated. Because fear and suspicion of outgroups[1] are so widespread, scholars and scientists once believed that prej-

[1]*outgroups:* Social groups defined as "outsiders" from a given group's point of view. See "ingroups," p. 379.

udice was a natural or biological human attribute. Today, because of increased knowledge about the growth of prejudices in children and about the varying patterns of interaction throughout world history, behavioral scientists realize that prejudices are socially determined. A great many theories exist concerning exactly how we become prejudiced.

Socialization

In the socialization process individuals acquire the values, attitudes, beliefs, and perceptions of their culture or subculture, including religion, nationality, and social class. Generally, the child conforms to the parents' expectations in acquiring an understanding of the world and its people. Being young and therefore impressionable and knowing of no alternative conceptions of the world, the child usually accepts these concepts without questioning. We thus learn the prejudices of our parents and others, and they subtly become a part of our values and beliefs. Even if they are based on false stereotypes, prejudices shape our perceptions of various peoples and influence our attitudes and actions toward particular groups. For example, if we develop negative attitudes about Jews because we are taught that they are shrewd, acquisitive, and clannish — all-too-familiar stereotypes — as adults we may refrain from business or social relationships with them. We may not even realize the reason for such avoidance, so subtle has been the prejudice instilled within us.

People may learn certain prejudices because of their pervasiveness. The cultural screen that we develop and through which we view the world around us is not always accurate, but it does reflect shared values and attitudes, which are reinforced by others. Prejudice, like cultural values, is taught and learned through the socialization process. The prevailing prejudicial attitudes and actions often are deeply embedded in custom or law (for example, Jim Crow laws), and the new generation may accept them as proper, maintaining them in their adult lives.

Although socialization explains how prejudicial attitudes may be transmitted from one generation to the next, it does not explain their origin or why they intensify or diminish over the years. These aspects of prejudice must be explained in another way.

5 Herbert Blumer suggests that prejudice always involves the notion of group position in society.[2] Prejudiced people believe that one group is inferior to another, and they place each group in a hierarchical position in society. This perception of group position is an outgrowth of the individual's experiences and understanding of them. The group stereotypes are socially approved images held by members of one group about another.[3]

[2]Herbert Blumer, "Race Prejudice as a Sense of Group Position," *Pacific Sociological Review* 1 (1958), 3–7. [Author's note]

[3]William M. Newman, *American Pluralism*, Harper & Row, New York, 1973, p. 197. [Author's note]

Self-justification

Through self-justification, we denigrate a person or group to justify our maltreatment of them. In this situation, self-justification leads to prejudice and discrimination against another's group.

Some philosophers argue that we are not so much rational creatures as we are rationalizing creatures. We require reassurance that the things we do and the lives we live are proper, that good reasons for our actions exist. If we are able to convince ourselves that another group is inferior, immoral, or dangerous, then we can feel justified in discriminating against them, enslaving them, or even killing them.

History is filled with examples of people who thought their maltreatment of others was just and necessary: As defenders of the "true faith," the Crusaders killed "Christ-killers" (Jews) and "infidels" (Moslems). Participants in the Spanish Inquisition imprisoned, tortured, and executed "heretics," "the disciples of the Devil." The Puritans burned witches, whose refusal to confess "proved" they were evil. Indians were "heathen savages," blacks were "an inferior species," and thus both could be mistreated, enslaved, or killed. The civilians in the Vietnamese village of My Lai were "probably" aiding the Vietcong, so the soldiers felt justified in slaughtering the old men, women, and children they found there.

Some sociologists believe that self-justification works the other way around.[4] That is, instead of self-justification serving as a basis for subjugation of a people, the subjugation occurs first and the self-justification follows, resulting in prejudice and continued discrimination. The evolvement of racism as a concept after the establishment of the African slave trade would seem to support this idea. Philip Mason offers an insight into this view:

> A specialized society is likely to defeat a simpler society and provide a lower tier still of enslaved and conquered peoples. The rulers and organizers sought security for themselves and their children; to perpetuate the power, the esteem, and the comfort they had achieved, it was necessary not only that the artisans and labourers should work contentedly but that the rulers should sleep without bad dreams. No one can say with certainty how the myths originated, but it is surely relevant that when one of the founders of Western thought set himself to frame an ideal state that would embody social justice, he — like the earliest city dwellers — not only devised a society stratified in tiers but believed it would be necessary to persuade the traders and work-people that, by divine decree, they were made from brass and iron, while the warriors were made of silver and the rulers of gold.[5]

[4]See Marvin B. Scott and Stanford M. Lyman, "Accounts," *American Sociological Review* 33 (February 1988), 40–62. [Author's note]

[5]Philip Mason, *Patterns of Dominance,* Oxford University Press, New York, 1970, p. 7. Also, Philip Mason, *Race Relations,* Oxford University Press, New York, 1970, pp. 17–29. [Author's note]

Another example of self-justification serving as a cause of prejudice is 10
the dominant group's assumption of an attitude of superiority over other groups. In this respect establishing a prestige hierarchy—ranking the status of various ethnic groups—results in differential association. To enhance or maintain one's own self-esteem, one may avoid social contact with groups deemed inferior and associate only with those identified as being of high status. Through such behavior self-justification may come to intensify the social distance between groups. *Social distance* refers to the degree to which ingroup[6] members do not engage in social or primary relationships with members of various outgroups.

Personality

In 1950 T. W. Adorno and his colleagues reported a correlation between individuals' early childhood experiences of harsh parental discipline and their development of authoritarian personalities as adults.[7] If parents assume an excessively domineering posture in their relations with a child, exercising stern measures and threatening the withdrawal of love if the child does not respond with weakness and submission, then the child tends to be very insecure, nurturing much latent hostility against the parents. When such children become adults, they may demonstrate displaced aggression, directing their hostility against a powerless group as compensation for feelings of insecurity and fear. Highly prejudiced individuals tend to come from families that emphasize obedience.

The authors identified authoritarianism by the use of a measuring instrument called an F scale (the F standing for potential fascism). Other tests included the A-S (anti-Semitism) and E (ethnocentrism) scales, the latter measuring attitudes toward various minorities. One of their major findings was that people who scored high on authoritarianism also consistently showed a high degree of prejudice against all minority groups. These highly prejudiced persons were characterized by rigidity of viewpoint, dislike for ambiguity, strict obedience to leaders, and intolerance of weakness in themselves or others.

No sooner did *The Authoritarian Personality* appear than controversy began. H. H. Hyman and P. B. Sheatsley challenged the methodology and analysis.[8] Solomon Asch questioned the assumptions that the F scale responses represented a belief system and that structural variables, such as ideologies, stratification, mobility, and other social factors, do not play a role

[6]*ingroups:* Social groups whose members are united by a shared identity and a sense of their separateness from the "outgroups" surrounding them.

[7]T. W. Adorno, Else Frankel-Brunswik, Daniel J. Levinson, and R. Nevitt Sanford, *The Authoritarian Personality,* Harper & Row, New York, 1950. [Author's note]

[8]H. H. Hyman and P. B. Sheatsley, "The Authoritarian Personality: A Methodological Critique," in *Studies in the Scope and Method of "The Authoritarian Personality,"* ed. R. Christie and M. Jahoda, Free Press, Glencoe, IL, 1954. [Author's note]

in shaping personality.[9] E. A. Shils argued that the authors were interested only in measuring authoritarianism of the political right while ignoring such tendencies in those at the other end of the political spectrum.[10] Other investigators sought alternative explanations for the authoritarian personality. D. Stewart and T. Hoult extended the framework beyond family childhood experiences to include other social factors.[11] H. C. Kelman and Janet Barclay demonstrated that substantial evidence exists showing that lower intelligence and less education also correlate with high authoritarianism scores on the F scale.[12]

Despite the critical attacks, the underlying conceptions of *The Authoritarian Personality* were important, and research on personality as a factor in prejudice has continued. Subsequent investigators have refined and modified the original study. Correcting scores for response bias, they have conducted cross-cultural studies. Respondents in Germany and Near East countries, where a more authoritarian social structure exists, scored higher on authoritarianism. In Japan, Germany, and the United States, authoritarianism and social distance were moderately related. Other studies frequently have shown that an inverse relationship exists between social class and F scale scores.[13]

15 Although the authoritarian-personality studies have been helpful in the understanding of some aspects of prejudice, they have not provided a causal explanation. Most of the findings in this area show a correlation, but the findings do not prove, for example, that harsh discipline of children causes them to become prejudiced adults. Perhaps the strict parents were themselves prejudiced, and the child learned those attitudes from them. Or, as George Simpson and J. Milton Yinger say:

> One must be careful not to assume too quickly that a certain tendency—rigidity of mind, for example—that is correlated with prejudice necessarily causes that prejudice. . . . The sequence may be the other way around. . . . It is more likely that both are related to more basic factors.[14]

For some people prejudice may indeed be rooted in subconscious childhood tensions, but we simply do not know whether these tensions directly

[9] Solomon E. Asch, *Social Psychology*, Prentice-Hall, Englewood Cliffs, NJ, 1952, p. 545. [Author's note]

[10] E. A. Shils, "Authoritarianism: Right and Left," in *Studies in the Scope and Method of "The Authoritarian Personality."* [Author's note]

[11] D. Stewart and T. Hoult, "A Social-Psychological Theory of 'The Authoritarian Personality.'" *American Journal of Sociology* 65 (1959), 274. [Author's note]

[12] H. C. Kelman and Janet Barclay, "The F Scale as a Measure of Breadth of Perspective," *Journal of Abnormal and Social Psychology* 67 (1963), 608–615.

[13] For an excellent summary of authoritarian studies and literature, see John P. Kirscht and Ronald C. Dillehay, *Dimensions of Authoritarianism: A Review of Research and Theory*, University of Kentucky Press, Lexington, 1967. [Author's note]

[14] George E. Simpson and J. Milton Yinger, *Racial and Cultural Minorities: An Analysis of Prejudice and Discrimination*, Harper & Row, New York, 1953, p. 91. [Author's note]

cause a high degree of prejudice in the adult or whether other powerful social forces are the determinants. Whatever the explanation, authoritarianism is a significant phenomenon worthy of continued investigation. Recent research, however, has stressed social and situation factors, rather than personality, as important causes of prejudice and discrimination.[15]

Yet another dimension to the personality component is that people with low self-esteem are more prejudiced than those who feel good about themselves. Some researchers have argued that individuals with low self-esteem deprecate others to enhance their feelings about themselves.[16] A recent study suggests "low self-esteem individuals seem to have a generally negative view of themselves, their ingroup, outgroups, and perhaps the world," and thus their tendency to be more prejudiced is not due to rating the outgroup negatively in comparison to their ingroup.[17]

Frustration

Frustration is the result of relative deprivation in which expectations remain unsatisfied. Relative deprivation refers to a lack of resources, or rewards, in one's standard of living in comparison with others in the society. A number of investigators have suggested that frustrations tend to increase aggression toward others.[18] Frustrated people may easily strike out against the perceived cause of their frustration. However, this reaction is not always possible because the true source of the frustration is often too nebulous to be identified or too powerful to act against. In such instances the result may be a displaced or free-floating aggression; in this situation the frustrated individual or group usually redirects the aggressiveness against a more visible, vulnerable, and socially sanctioned target, one unable to strike back. Minorities meet these criteria and are thus frequently the recipients of displaced aggression by the dominant group.

Placing blame on others for something that is not their fault is known as scapegoating. The term comes from the ancient Hebrew custom of using

[15]Ibid., pp. 62–79. [Author's note]

[16]H. J. Ehrlich, *The Social Psychology of Prejudice,* Wiley, New York, 1974; G. Sherwood, "Self-Serving Biases in Person Perception," *Psychological Bulletin* 90 (1981), 445–459; T. A. Wills, "Downward Comparison Principles in Social Psychology," *Psychological Bulletin* 90 (1981), 245–271. [Author's note]

[17]Jennifer Crocker and Ian Schwartz, "Prejudice and Ingroup Favoritism in a Minimal Intergroup Situation: Effects of Self-Esteem," *Personality and Social Psychology Bulletin* Vol. 11, No. 4 (December 1985), 379–386. [Author's note]

[18]John Dollard, Leonard W. Doob, Neal E. Miller, O. H. Mowrer, and Robert P. Sears, *Frustration and Aggression,* Yale University Press, New Haven, CT, 1939; A. F. Henry and J. F. Short, Jr., *Suicide and Homicide,* Free Press, New York, 1954; Neal Miller and Richard Bugelski, "Minor Studies in Aggression: The Influence of Frustration Imposed by the Ingroup on Attitudes Expressed Toward Outgroups," *Journal of Psychology* 25 (1948), 437–442; Stuart Palmer, *The Psychology of Murder,* T. Y. Crowell, New York, 1960; Brenden C. Rule and Elizabeth Percival, "The Effects of Frustration and Attack on Physical Aggression," *Journal of Experimental Research on Personality* 5 (1971), 111–188.

a goat during the Day of Atonement as a symbol of the sins of the people. In an annual ceremony a priest placed his hands on the head of a goat and listed the people's sins in a symbolic transference of guilt; he then chased the goat out of the community, thereby freeing the people of sin.[19] Since those times the powerful group has usually punished the scapegoat group rather than allowing it to escape.

20 There have been many instances throughout world history of minority groups serving as scapegoats, including the Christians in ancient Rome, the French Huguenots, the Jews, the Chinese, the Irish, the Japanese, and the Quakers. Gordon Allport suggests that certain characteristics are necessary for a group to become a suitable scapegoat.[20] The group must be (1) highly visible in physical appearance or observable customs and actions; (2) not strong enough to strike back; (3) situated within easy access of the dominant group or, ideally, concentrated in one area, (4) a past target of hostility for whom latent hostility still exists; and (5) the symbol of an unpopular concept.

Some groups fit this typology better than others, but minority racial and ethnic groups have continually been a favorite choice. Irish, Italians, Catholics, Jews, Quakers, Mormons, Chinese, Japanese, blacks, Puerto Ricans, Chicanos, and Koreans have all been, at one time or another, the scapegoat in the United States. Especially in times of economic hardship, there seems to be a tendency to blame some group for the general conditions, often leading to aggressive action against the group as an expression of frustration. For example, a study by Carl Hovland and Robert Sears found that between 1882 and 1930, a definite correlation existed between a decline in the price of cotton and an increase in the number of lynchings of blacks.[21]

In several controlled experiments sociologists have attempted to measure the validity of the scapegoat theory. Neal Miller and Richard Bugelski tested a group of young men aged eighteen to twenty working in a government camp about their feelings toward various minority groups.[22] They were reexamined about these feelings after experiencing frustration by being obliged to take a long, difficult test and denied an opportunity to see a film at a local theater. This group showed some evidence of increased prejudicial feelings, whereas a control group, which did not experience any frustration, showed no change in prejudicial attitudes.

Donald Weatherley conducted an experiment with a group of college students to measure the relationship between frustration and aggression

[19] Leviticus 16:5–22. [Author's note]

[20] Gordon W. Allport, "The ABC's of Scapegoating," 5th rev. ed., Anti-Defamation League pamphlet, New York. [Author's note]

[21] Carl I. Hovland and Robert R. Sears, "Minor Studies of Aggression: Correlation of Lynchings with Economic Indices," *Journal of Psychology* 9 (Winter 1940), 301–310. [Author's note]

[22] Miller and Bugelski, "Minor Studies of Aggression," pp. 437–442. [Author's note]

against a specific disliked group.[23] After identifying students who were or were not highly anti-Semitic and subjecting them to a strong frustrating experience, he asked the students to write stories about pictures shown to them. Some of the students were shown pictures of people who had been given Jewish names; other students were presented with pictures of unnamed people. When the pictures were unidentified, no difference appeared between the stories of the anti-Semitic students and those of other students. However, when the pictures were identified, the anti-Semitic students wrote stories reflecting much more aggression against the Jews in the pictures than did the other students.

For over twenty years Leonard Berkowitz and his associates have studied and experimented with aggressive behavior. Their conclusions are that, confronted with equally frustrating situations, highly prejudiced individuals are more likely to seek scapegoats than are nonprejudiced individuals. Another intervening variable is that certain kinds of frustrations — personal (marital failure, injury, or mental illness) rather than shared (dangers of flood or hurricane) — make people more likely to seek scapegoats.[24]

25 Some experiments have shown that aggression does not increase if the frustration is understandable.[25] Other experimenters have found that people become aggressive *only* if the aggression directly relieves that frustration.[26] Still other studies have shown that anger is a more likely result if the person frustrating us could have acted otherwise.[27] Clearly, the results are mixed, depending on the variables within a given social situation.

Talcott Parsons suggests that the family and the occupational system are both likely to produce anxieties and insecurities that create frustration.[28] According to this view, the growing-up process (gaining parental affection and approval, identifying with and imitating sexual role models, and competing with others in adulthood) may involve severe emotional strain. The result is an adult personality with a large reservoir of repressed aggression

[23]Donald Weatherley, "Anti-Semitism and the Expression of Fantasy Aggression," *Journal of Abnormal and Social Psychology* 62 (1961), 454–457. [Author's note]

[24]See Leonard Berkowitz, "Whatever Happened to the Frustration-Aggression Hypothesis?" *American Behavioral Scientist* 21 (1978), 691–708; L. Berkowitz, *Aggression: A Social Psychological Analysis,* McGraw-Hill, New York, 1962. [Author's note]

[25]D. Zillman, *Hostility and Aggression,* Lawrence Erlbaum, Hillsdale, NJ, 1979; R. A. Baron, *Human Aggression,* Plenum Press, New York, 1977; N. Pastore, "The Role of Arbitrariness in the Frustration-Aggression Hypothesis," *Journal of Abnormal and Social Psychology* 47 (1952), 728–731. [Author's note]

[26]A. H. Buss, "Instrumentality of Aggression, Feedback, and Frustration as Determinants of Physical Aggression," *Journal of Personality and Social Psychology* 3 (1966), 153–162. [Author's note]

[27]J. R. Averill, "Studies on Anger and Aggression: Implications for Theories of Emotion," *American Psychologist* 38 (1983), 1145–1160. [Author's note]

[28]Talcott Parsons, "Certain Primary Sources and Patterns of Aggression in the Social Structure of the Western World," *Essays in Sociological Theory,* Free Press, New York, 1964, pp. 298–322. [Author's note]

that becomes free-floating — susceptible to redirection against convenient scapegoats. Similarly, the occupational system is a source of frustration: Its emphasis on competitiveness and individual achievement, its function of conferring status, its requirement that people inhibit their natural impulses at work, and its relationship to the state of the economy are but a few of the factors that generate emotional anxieties. Parsons pessimistically concludes that minorities fulfill a functional "need" as targets for displaced aggression and will therefore remain targets.[29]

Frustration-aggression theory, although helpful, is not completely satisfactory. It ignores the role of culture and the reality of actual social conflict, while failing to show a causal relationship. Most of the responses measured in these studies were of people already biased. Why did one group rather than another become the object of the aggression? Moreover, frustration does not necessarily precede aggression, and aggression does not necessarily flow from frustration.

Competition

People tend to be more hostile toward others when they feel their security is threatened; thus many social scientists conclude that economic competition and conflict breed prejudice. Certainly a great amount of evidence shows that negative stereotyping, prejudice, and discrimination increase strongly whenever competition for a limited number of jobs increases.

An excellent illustration concerns the Chinese sojourners in the nineteenth century. Prior to the 1870s the transcontinental railroad was being built, and the Chinese filled many of the jobs made available by this project in the sparsely populated West. Although they were expelled from the gold mines and schools and had no redress of grievances in the courts, they managed to convey to some whites an image of a clean, hard-working, law-abiding people. The completion of the railroad, the flood of former Civil War soldiers into the job market, and the economic depression of 1873 worsened their situation. The Chinese were even more frequently the victims of open discrimination and hostility. Their positive stereotype among some whites became more commonly a negative one: They were now "conniving," "crafty," "criminal," "the yellow menace." Only after they retreated into Chinatowns and entered specialty occupations not in competition with whites did the intense hostility abate.

One of the early pioneers in the scientific study of prejudice, John Dol- 30
lard, demonstrated how prejudice against the Germans, which had been virtually nonexistent, came about in a small American industrial town when times got bad.

[29]For an excellent review of Parsonian theory in this area, see Stanford M. Lyman, *The Black American in Sociological Thought: A Failure of Perspective*, Putnam, New York, 1972, pp. 145–169. [Author's note]

> Local whites largely drawn from the surrounding farms manifested considerable direct aggression toward the newcomers. Scornful and derogatory opinions were expressed about the Germans, and the native whites had a satisfying sense of superiority toward them. . . . The chief element in the permission to be aggressive against the Germans was rivalry for jobs and status in the local woodenware plants. The native whites felt definitely crowded for their jobs by the entering German groups and in case of bad times had a chance to blame the Germans who by their presence provided more competitors for the scarcer jobs. There seemed to be no traditional pattern of prejudice against Germans unless the skeletal suspicion of all out-groupers (always present) be invoked in this place.[30]

Both experimental studies and historical analyses have added credence to the economic-competition theory. Muzafer Sherif directed several experiments showing how intergroup competition at a boys' camp leads to conflict and escalating hostility.[31] Donald Young has shown that, throughout American history, in times with high unemployment and thus intense job competition, strong nativist movements against minorities have existed.[32] This pattern has held true regionally — with the Asians on the West Coast, the Italians in Louisiana, and the French Canadians in New England — and nationally, with the antiforeign movements always peaking during periods of depression. So it was with the Native American Party in the 1830s, the Know-Nothing Party in the 1850s, the American Protective Association in the 1890s, and the Ku Klux Klan after World War I. Since the passage of civil rights laws on employment in the twentieth century, researchers have consistently detected the strongest antiblack prejudice among whites who are closest to blacks on the socioeconomic ladder.[33] It seems that any group applying the pressure of job competition most directly on another group becomes its prejudicial target.

Once again, a theory offers some excellent insights into prejudice — there is a correlation between economic conditions and hostility toward minorities — but it also has some serious shortcomings. Not all groups who

[30] John Dollard, "Hostility and Fear in Social Life," *Social Forces* 17 (1938), 15–26. [Author's note]

[31] Muzafer Sherif, O. J. Harvey, B. Jack White, William Hood, and Carolyn Sherif, *Intergroup Conflict and Cooperation: The Robbers Cave Experiment,* University of Oklahoma Institute of Intergroup Relations, Norman, OK, 1961. See also M. Sherif, "Experiments in Group Conflict," *Scientific American* 195 (1956), 54–58. [Author's note]

[32] Donald Young, *Research Memorandum on Minority Peoples in the Depression,* Social Science Research Council, New York, 1937, pp. 133–141. [Author's note]

[33] Andrew Greeley and Paul Sheatsley, "The Acceptance of Desegregation Continues to Advance," *Scientific American* 210 (1971), 13–19; T. F. Pettigrew, "Three Issues in Ethnicity: Boundaries, Deprivations, and Perceptions," in M. Yinger and S. J. Cutler (eds.), *Major Social Issues: A Multidisciplinary View,* Free Press, New York, 1978; R. D. Vanneman and T. F. Pettigrew, "Race and Relative Deprivation in the United States," *Race* 13 (1972), 461–486. [Author's note]

have been objects of hostility have been economic competitors (for example, Quakers and Mormons). Moreover, why is there greater hostility against some groups than against others? Why do the negative feelings in some communities run against groups whose numbers are so small that they cannot possibly be an economic threat? It would appear that other values besides economic ones cause people to be antagonistic to a group perceived as an actual or potential threat.

Social Norms

Some sociologists have suggested that a relationship exists between prejudice and a person's tendency to conform to societal expectations.[34] Social norms—the norms of one's culture—provide the generally shared rules of what is and is not proper behavior; by learning and automatically accepting the prevailing prejudices, the individual is simply conforming to those norms. This theory says that there is a direct relationship between degree of conformity and degree of prejudice. If this is true, then people's prejudices would decrease or increase significantly when they move into areas where the prejudicial norm is either lesser or greater. Evidence supports this view. Thomas Pettigrew found that Southerners in the 1950s became less prejudiced against blacks when they interacted with them in the army, where the social norms were less prejudicial.[35] In another study Jeanne Watson found that people moving into an anti-Semitic neighborhood in New York City became more anti-Semitic.[36]

In 1937 John Dollard published his major study, *Caste and Class in a Southern Town,* providing an in-depth look into the emotional adjustment of whites and blacks to rigid social norms.[37] In his study of the processes, functions, and maintenance of accommodation, Dollard shows how the "carrot-and-stick" method is employed. Intimidation, or sometimes even severe reprisals for going against social norms, ensures compliance. However, such actions usually are unnecessary. The advantages whites and blacks gain in psychological, economic, or behavioral terms serve to perpetuate the caste order. These gains in personal security and stability set in motion a vicious circle. They encourage a way of life that reinforces the rationale of the social system in this community.

The problem with the social-norms theory is that although it explains 35

[34]See Harry H. L. Kitano, "Passive Discrimination in the Normal Person," *Journal of Social Psychology* 70 (1966), 23–31. [Author's note]

[35]Thomas Pettigrew, "Regional Differences in Anti-Negro Prejudice," *Journal of Abnormal and Social Psychology* 59 (1959), 28–36. [Author's note]

[36]Jeanne Watson, "Some Social and Psychological Situations Related to Change in Attitude," *Human Relations* 3 (1950), 15–56. [Author's note]

[37]John Dollard, *Caste and Class in a Southern Town,* 3d ed., Doubleday Anchor Books, Garden City, NY, 1957. [Author's note]

prevailing attitudes, it explains neither their origins nor the reasons for the development of new prejudices when other groups move into an area. In addition the theory does not explain why prejudicial attitudes against a particular group continue to rise and fall in cyclical fashion over the years.

Although many social scientists have attempted to identify the causes of prejudice, no single factor has proven to be an adequate explanation. Prejudice is a complex phenomenon, and it is most likely to be the product of more than one causal agent. Sociologists now tend either to emphasize multiple-causation explanations or else to stress social forces at work in specific and similar situations, such as economic conditions, stratification, or hostility toward an outgroup.

ENGAGING THE TEXT

1. What, according to Parrillo, is the "socialization process"? In what different ways can socialization instill prejudice?
2. How can prejudice arise from self-justification? Offer some examples of how a group can assume an attitude of superiority in order to justify ill-treatment of others.
3. How, according to Parrillo, might personal factors like authoritarian attitudes, low self-esteem, or frustration promote the growth of prejudice?
4. What is the relationship between economic competition and prejudice? Do you think prejudice would continue to exist if everyone had a good job with a comfortable income?

Exploring Connections

5. Review Ronald Takaki's "A Different Mirror" (p. 332), Wendy Rose's "Three Thousand Dollar Death Song" (p. 351), and Janice Mirikitani's "We, the Dangerous" (p. 354). What evidence can you find in these selections to support Parrillo's theory of economic competition?
6. What connections can you find between the theories of prejudice that Parrillo presents and Adrienne Rich's description of her father (p. 365)? Which of these theories best explains Arnold Rich's attitudes, values, and behavior?
7. Compare Parrillo's explanations of the relationship between authoritarianism, aggression, and prejudice and Michael Kimmel's discussion of the role that aggression plays in defining male identity (p. 258). Do you think that prejudicial attitudes are more common among men than among women?
8. Review Carmen Vázquez's "Appearances" (p. 287) to determine how useful Parrillo's theories are in analyzing prejudice against gays and lesbians. To what extent can theories like the socialization process, self-justification, authoritarianism, frustration, and economic competition help us understand antigay attitudes?
9. Look at the "Prejudice Workship" cartoon that appears on page 387. Do you agree with the cartoonist's suggestion that the young blond man is prejudiced? If so, which of the theories that Parrillo presents best accounts for his attitude? If not, why not?

Extending the Critical Context

10. List the various groups (racial, economic, cultural, social, familial, etc.) that you belong to and arrange them in a status hierarchy. Which groups were you born into? Which groups did you join voluntarily? Which have had the greatest impact on your socialization? Which groups isolate you the most from contact with outsiders?
11. Working in small groups, research recent news stories for examples of incidents involving racism or prejudice. Which of the theories described by Parrillo seem most useful for analyzing the motives underlying these events?

C. P. Ellis

Studs Terkel

The following oral history brings us uncomfortably close to unambiguous, deadly prejudice: C. P. Ellis is a former Ku Klux Klan member who claims to have overcome his racist (and sexist) attitudes; he speaks here as a union leader who feels an alliance to other workers, including Blacks and women. Studs Terkel (b. 1912) is probably the best-known practitioner of oral history in the United States. He has compiled several books by interviewing dozens of widely varying people — ordinary people for the most part — about important subjects like work, social class, race, and the Great Depression. The edited versions of these interviews are often surprisingly powerful crystallizations of American social history: Terkel's subjects give voice to the frustrations and hopes of whole generations of Americans. Terkel won a Pulitzer Prize in 1985 for "The Good War": An Oral History of World War II. *His most recent work is* Race: How Blacks and Whites Think and Feel About the American Obsession *(1993). "C. P. Ellis" first appeared in* American Dreams: Lost and Found *(1980).*

We're in his office in Durham, North Carolina. He is the business manager of the International Union of Operating Engineers. On the wall is a plaque: "Certificate of Service, in recognition to C. P. Ellis, for your faithful service to the city in having served as a member of the Durham Human Relations Council. February 1977."

At one time, he had been president (exalted cyclops) of the Durham chapter of the Ku Klux Klan. . . .

He is fifty-two years old.

My father worked in a textile mill in Durham. He died at forty-eight years old. It was probably from cotton dust. Back then, we never heard of brown lung. I was about seventeen years old and had a mother and sister depending on somebody to make a livin'. It was just barely enough insurance to cover his burial. I had to quit school and go to work. I was about eighth grade when I quit.

5 My father worked hard but never had enough money to buy decent clothes. When I went to school, I never seemed to have adequate clothes to wear. I always left school late afternoon with a sense of inferiority. The other kids had nice clothes, and I just had what Daddy could buy. I still got some of those inferiority feelin's now that I have to overcome once in a while.

I loved my father. He would go with me to ball games. We'd go fishin' together. I was really ashamed of the way he'd dress. He would take this money and give it to me instead of putting it on himself. I always had the feeling about somebody looking at him and makin' fun of him and makin' fun of me. I think it had to do somethin' with my life.

My father and I were very close, but we didn't talk about too many intimate things. He did have a drinking problem. During the week, he would work every day, but weekends he was ready to get plastered. I can understand when a guy looks at his paycheck and looks at his bills, and he's worked hard all the week, and his bills are larger than his paycheck. He'd done the best he could the entire week, and there seemed to be no hope. It's an illness thing. Finally you just say: "The heck with it. I'll just get drunk and forget it."

My father was out of work during the depression, and I remember going with him to the finance company uptown, and he was turned down. That's something that's always stuck.

My father never seemed to be happy. It was a constant struggle with him just like it was for me. It's very seldom I'd see him laugh. He was just tryin' to figure out what he could do from one day to the next.

After several years pumping gas at a service station, I got married. We 10
had to have children. Four. One child was born blind and retarded, which was a real additional expense to us. He's never spoken a word. He doesn't know me when I go to see him. But I see him, I hug his neck. I talk to him, tell him I love him. I don't know whether he knows me or not, but I know he's well taken care of. All my life, I had work, never a day without work, worked all the overtime I could get and still could not survive financially. I began to say there's somethin' wrong with this country. I worked my butt off and just never seemed to break even.

I had some real great ideas about this great nation. (Laughs.) They say to abide by the law, go to church, do right and live for the Lord, and everything'll work out. But it didn't work out. It just kept gettin' worse and worse.

I was workin' a bread route. The highest I made one week was seventy-five dollars. The rent on our house was about twelve dollars a week. I will never forget: outside of this house was a 265-gallon oil drum, and I never did get enough money to fill up that oil drum. What I would do every night, I would run up to the store and buy five gallons of oil and climb up the ladder and pour it in that 265-gallon drum. I could hear that five gallons when it hits the bottom of that oil drum, splatters, and it sounds like it's nothin' in there. But it would keep the house warm for the night. Next day you'd have to do the same thing.

I left the bread route with fifty dollars in my pocket. I went to the bank and borrowed four thousand dollars to buy the service station. I worked seven days a week, open and close, and finally had a heart attack. Just about two months before the last payments of that loan. My wife had done the best she could to keep it runnin'. Tryin' to come out of that hole, I just couldn't do it.

I really began to get bitter. I didn't know who to blame. I tried to find somebody. I began to blame it on black people. I had to hate somebody. Hatin' America is hard to do because you can't see it to hate it. You gotta have somethin' to look at to hate. (Laughs.) The natural person for me to hate would be black people, because my father before me was a member of the Klan. As far as he was concerned, it was the savior of the white people. It was the only organization in the world that would take care of the white people. So I began to admire the Klan.

I got active in the Klan while I was at the service station. Every Monday 15
night, a group of men would come by and buy a Coca-Cola, go back to the car, take a few drinks, and come back and stand around talkin'. I couldn't

help but wonder: Why are these dudes comin' out every Monday? They said they were with the Klan and have meetings close-by. Would I be interested? Boy, that was an opportunity I really looked forward to! To be part of somethin'. I joined the Klan, went from member to chaplain, from chaplain to vice-president, from vice-president to president. The title is exalted cyclops.

The first night I went with the fellas, they knocked on the door and gave the signal. They sent some robed Klansmen to talk to me and give me some instructions. I was led into a large meeting room, and this was the time of my life! It was thrilling. Here's a guy who's worked all his life and struggled all his life to be something, and here's the moment to be something. I will never forget it. Four robed Klansmen led me into the hall. The lights were dim, and the only thing you could see was an illuminated cross. I knelt before the cross. I had to make certain vows and promises. We promised to uphold the purity of the white race, fight communism, and protect white womanhood.

After I had taken my oath, there was loud applause goin' throughout the building', musta been at least four hundred people. For this one little ol' person. It was a thrilling moment for C. P. Ellis.

It disturbs me when people who do not really know what it's all about are so very critical of individual Klansmen. The majority of 'em are low-income whites, people who really don't have a part in something. They have been shut out as well as the blacks. Some are not very well educated either. Just like myself. We had a lot of support from doctors and lawyers and police officers.

Maybe they've had bitter experiences in this life and they had to hate somebody. So the natural person to hate would be the black person. He's beginnin' to come up, he's beginnin' to learn to read and start votin' and run for political office. Here are white people who are supposed to be superior to them, and we're shut out.

20 I can understand why people join extreme right-wing or left-wing groups. They're in the same boat I was. Shut out. Deep down inside, we want to be part of this great society. Nobody listens, so we join these groups.

At one time, I was state organizer of the National Rights party. I organized a youth group for the Klan. I felt we were getting old and our generation's gonna die. So I contacted certain kids in schools. They were havin' racial problems. On the first night, we had a hundred high school students. When they came in the door, we had "Dixie" playin'. These kids were just thrilled to death. I begin to hold weekly meetin's with 'em, teachin' the principles of the Klan. At that time, I believed Martin Luther King had Communist connections. I began to teach that Andy Young[1] was affiliated with the Communist party.

[1] *Andy Young:* Andrew Jackson Young, Jr. (b. 1932), prominent Black leader and politician. Young was a friend and adviser of Martin Luther King, Jr., and served as President Jimmy Carter's ambassador to the United Nations. In the 1980s, he was twice elected mayor of Atlanta.

I had a call one night from one of our kids. He was about twelve. He said: "I just been robbed downtown by two niggers." I'd had a couple of drinks and that really teed me off. I go downtown and couldn't find the kid. I got worried. I saw two young black people. I had the .32 revolver with me. I said: "Nigger, you seen a little young white boy up here? I just got a call from him and was told that some niggers robbed him of fifteen cents." I pulled my pistol out and put it right at his head. I said: "I've always wanted to kill a nigger and I think I'll make you the first one." I nearly scared the kid to death, and he struck off.

This was the time when the civil rights movement was really beginnin' to peak. The blacks were beginnin' to demonstrate and picket downtown stores. I never will forget some black lady I hated with a purple passion. Ann Atwater. Every time I'd go downtown, she'd be leadin' a boycott. How I hated—pardon the expression, I don't use it much now—how I just hated the black nigger. (Laughs.) Big, fat, heavy woman. She'd pull about eight demonstrations, and first thing you know they had two, three blacks at the checkout counter. Her and I have had some pretty close confrontations.

I felt very big, yeah. (Laughs.) We're more or less a secret organization. We didn't want anybody to know who we were, and I began to do some thinkin'. What am I hidin' for? I've never been convicted of anything in my life. I don't have any court record. What am I, C. P. Ellis, as a citizen and a member of the United Klansmen of America? Why can't I go the city council meeting and say: "This is the way we feel about the matter? We don't want you to purchase mobile units to set in our schoolyards. We don't want niggers in our schools."

We began to come out in the open. We would go to the meetings, and 25
the blacks would be there and we'd be there. It was a confrontation every time. I didn't hold back anything. We began to make some inroads with the city councilmen and county commissioners. They began to call us friend. Call us at night on the telephone: "C. P., glad you came to that meeting last night." They didn't want integration either, but they did it secretively, in order to get elected. They couldn't stand up openly and say it, but they were glad somebody was sayin' it. We visited some of the city leaders in their home and talk to 'em privately. It wasn't long before councilmen would call me up: "The blacks are comin' up tonight and makin' outrageous demands. How about some of you people showin' up and have a little balance?" I'd get on the telephone. "The niggers is comin' to the council meeting tonight. Persons in the city's called me and asked us to be there."

We'd load up our cars and we'd fill up half the council chambers, and the blacks the other half. During these times, I carried weapons to the meetings, outside my belt. We'd go there armed. We would wind up just hollerin' and fussin' at each other. What happened? As a result of our fightin' one another, the city council still had their way. They didn't want to give up control to the blacks nor the Klan. They were usin' us.

I began to realize this later down the road. One day I was walkin' downtown and a certain city council member saw me comin'. I expected him to shake my hand because he was talkin' to me at night on the telephone. I had been in his home and visited with him. He crossed the street. Oh shit, I began to think, somethin's wrong here. Most of 'em are merchants or maybe an attorney, an insurance agent, people like that. As long as they kept low-income whites and low-income blacks fightin', they're gonna maintain control.

I began to get that feeling after I was ignored in public. I thought: Bullshit, you're not gonna use me any more. That's when I began to do some real serious thinkin'.

The same thing is happening in this country today. People are being used by those in control, those who have all the wealth. I'm not espousing communism. We got the greatest system of government in the world. But those who have it simply don't want those who don't have it to have any part of it. Black and white. When it comes to money, the green, the other colors make no difference. (Laughs.)

I spent a lot of sleepless nights. I still didn't like blacks. I didn't want to 30
associate with 'em. Blacks, Jews, or Catholics. My father said: "don't have anything to do with 'em." I didn't until I met a black person and talked with him, eyeball to eyeball, and met a Jewish person and talked to him, eyeball to eyeball. I found out they're people just like me. They cried, they cussed, they prayed, they had desires. Just like myself. Thank God, I got to the point where I can look past labels. But at that time, my mind was closed.

I remember one Monday night Klan meeting. I said something was wrong. Our city fathers were using us. And I didn't like to be used. The reactions of the others was not too pleasant: "Let's just keep fightin' them niggers."

I'd go home at night and I'd have to wrestle with myself. I'd look at a black person walkin' down the street, and the guy'd have ragged shoes or his clothes would be worn. That began to do somethin' to me inside. I went through this for about six months. I felt I just had to get out of the Klan. But I wouldn't get out.

Then something happened. The state AFL–CIO[2] received a grant from the Department of HEW,[3] a $78,000 grant: how to solve racial problems in the school system. I got a telephone call from the president of the state AFL–CIO. "We'd like to get some people together from all walks of life." I said: "All walks of life? Who you talkin' about?" He said: "Blacks, whites, liberals, conservatives, Klansmen, NAACP[4] people."

[2]*AFL–CIO:* American Federation of Labor and Congress of Industrial Organizations — a huge federation of independent labor unions in the United States, Canada, Mexico, Panama, and elsewhere.

[3]*HEW:* Health, Education, and Welfare — at the time, a department of the federal government.

[4]*NAACP:* National Association for the Advancement of Colored People.

I said: "No way am I comin' with all those niggers. I'm not gonna be associated with those type of people." A White Citizens Council guy said: "Let's go up there and see what's goin' on. It's tax money bein' spent." I walk in the door, and there was a large number of blacks and white liberals. I knew most of 'em by face 'cause I seen 'em demonstratin' around town. Ann Atwater was there. (Laughs.) I just forced myself to go in and sit down.

The meeting was moderated by a great big black guy who was bushy-headed. (Laughs.) That turned me off. He acted very nice. He said: "I want you all to feel free to say anything you want to say." Some of the blacks stand up and say it's white racism. I took all I could take. I asked for the floor and cut loose. I said: "No, sir, it's black racism. If we didn't have niggers in the schools, we wouldn't have the problems we got today."

I will never forget. Howard Clements, a black guy, stood up. He said: "I'm certainly glad C. P. Ellis come because he's the most honest man here tonight." I said: "What's that nigger tryin' to do?" (Laughs.) At the end of that meeting, some blacks tried to come up shake my hand, but I wouldn't do it. I walked off.

Second night, same group was there. I felt a little more easy because I got some things off my chest. The third night, after they elected all the committees, they want to elect a chairman. Howard Clements stood up and said: "I suggest we elect two co-chairpersons." Joe Beckton, executive director of the Human Relations Commission, just as black as he can be, he nominated me. There was a reaction from some blacks. Nooo. And, of all things, they nominated Ann Atwater, that big old fat black gal that I had just hated with a purple passion, as co-chairman. I thought to myself: Hey, ain't no way I can work with that gal. Finally, I agreed to accept it, 'cause at this point, I was tired of fightin', either for survival or against black people or against Jews or against Catholics.

A Klansman and a militant black woman, co-chairmen of the school committee. It was impossible. How could I work with her? But after about two or three days, it was in our hands. We had to make it a success. This give me another sense of belongin', a sense of pride. This helped this inferiority feelin' I had. A man who has stood up publicly and said he despised black people, all of a sudden he was willin' to work with 'em. Here's a chance for a low-income white man to be somethin'. In spite of all my hatred for blacks and Jews and liberals, I accepted the job. Her and I began to reluctantly work together. (Laughs.) She had as many problems workin' with me as I had workin' with her.

One night, I called her: "Ann, you and I should have a lot of differences and we got 'em now. But there's somethin' laid out here before us, and if it's gonna be a success, you and I are gonna have to make it one. Can we lay aside some of these feelin's?" She said: "I'm willing if you are." I said: "Let's do it."

My old friends would call me at night: "C. P., what the hell is wrong 40
with you? You're sellin' out the white race." This begin to make me have guilt feelin's. Am I doin' right? Am I doin' wrong? Here I am all of a sudden makin' an about-face and tryin' to deal with my feelin's, my heart. My mind was beginnin' to open up. I was beginnin' to see what was right and what was wrong. I don't want the kids to fight forever.

We were gonna go ten nights. By this time, I had went to work at Duke University, in maintenance. Makin' very little money. Terry Sanford give me this ten days off with pay. He was president of Duke at the time. He knew I was a Klansman and realized the importance of blacks and whites getting along.

I said: "If we're gonna make this thing a success, I've got to get to my kind of people." The low-income whites. We walked the streets of Durham, and we knocked on doors and invited people. Ann was goin' into the black community. They just wasn't respondin' to us when we made these house calls. Some of 'em were cussin' us out. "You're sellin' us out, Ellis, get out of my door. I don't want to talk to you." Ann was gettin' the same response from blacks. "What are you doin' messin' with that Klansman?"

One day, Ann and I went back to the school and we sat down. We began to talk and just reflect. Ann said: "My daughter came home cryin' every day. She said her teacher was makin' fun of me in front of the other kids." I said: "Boy, the same thing happened to my kid. White liberal teacher was makin' fun of Tim Ellis's father, the Klansman. In front of other peoples. He came home cryin'." At this point — (he pauses, swallows hard, stifles a sob) — I begin to see, here we are, two people from the far ends of the fence, havin' identical problems, except hers bein' black and me bein' white. From that moment on, I tell ya, that gal and I worked together good. I begin to love the girl, really. (He weeps.)

The amazing thing about it, her and I, up to that point, had cussed each other, bawled each other, we hated each other. Up to that point, we didn't know each other. We didn't know we had things in common.

We worked at it, with the people who came to these meetings. They 45
talked about racism, sex education, about teachers not bein' qualified. After seven, eight nights of real intense discussion, these people, who'd never talked to each other before, all of a sudden came up with resolutions. It was really somethin', you had to be there to get the tone and feelin' of it.

At that point, I didn't like integration, but the law says you do this and I've got to do what the law says, okay? We said: "Let's take these resolutions to the school board." The most disheartening thing I've ever faced was the school system refused to implement any one of these resolutions. These were recommendations from the people who pay taxes and pay their salaries. (Laughs.)

I thought they were good answers. Some of 'em I didn't agree with, but

I been in this thing from the beginning, and whatever comes of it, I'm gonna support it. Okay, since the school board refused, I decided I'd just run for the school board.

I spent eighty-five dollars on the campaign. The guy runnin' against me spent several thousand. I really had nobody on my side. The Klan turned against me. The low-income whites turned against me. The liberals didn't particularly like me. The blacks were suspicious of me. The blacks wanted to support me, but they couldn't muster up enough to support a Klansman on the school board. (Laughs.) But I made up my mind that what I was doin' was right, and I was gonna do it regardless what anybody said.

It bothered me when people would call and worry my wife. She's always supported me in anything I wanted to do. She was changing, and my boys were too. I got some of my youth corps kids involved. They still followed me.

I was invited to the Democratic women's social hour as a candidate. 50
Didn't have but one suit to my name. Had it six, seven, eight years. I had it cleaned, put on the best shirt I had and a tie. Here were all this high-class wealthy candidates shakin' hands. I walked up to the mayor and stuck out my hand. He give me that handshake with that rag type of hand. He said: "C. P., I'm glad to see you." But I could tell by his handshake he was lyin' to me. This was botherin' me. I know I'm a low-income person. I know I'm not wealthy. I know they were sayin': "What's this little ol' dude runnin' for school board?" Yet they had to smile and make like they're glad to see me. I begin to spot some black people in that room. I automatically went to 'em and that was a firm handshake. They said: "I'm glad to see you, C. P." I knew they meant it — you can tell about a handshake.

Every place I appeared, I said I will listen to the voice of the people. I will not make a major decision until I first contacted all the organizations in the city. I got 4,640 votes. The guy beat me by two thousand. Not bad for eighty-five bucks and no constituency.

The whole world was openin' up, and I was learnin' new truths that I had never learned before. I was beginnin' to look at a black person, shake hands with him, and see him as a human bein'. I hadn't got rid of all this stuff, I've still got a little bit of it. But somethin' was happenin' to me.

It was almost like bein' born again. It was a new life. I didn't have these sleepless nights I used to have when I was active in the Klan and slippin' around at night. I could sleep at night and feel good about it. I'd rather live now than at any other time in history. It's a challenge.

Back at Duke, doin' maintenance, I'd pick up my tools, fix the commode, unstop the drains. But this got in my blood. Things weren't right in this country, and what we done in Durham needs to be told. I was so miserable at Duke, I could hardly stand it. I'd go to work every morning just hatin' to go.

My whole life had changed. I got an eighth-grade education, and I 55
wanted to complete high school. Went to high school in the afternoons on

a program called PEP — Past Employment Progress. I was about the only white in class, and the oldest. I begin to read about biology. I'd take my books home at night, 'cause I was determined to get through. Sure enough, I graduated. I got the diploma at home.

I come to work one mornin' and some guy says: "We need a union." At this time I wasn't pro-union. My daddy was anti-labor, too. We're not gettin' paid much, we're havin' to work seven days in a row. We're all starvin' to death. The next day, I meet the international representative of the Operating Engineers. He give me authorization cards. "Get these cards out and we'll have an election." There was eighty-eight for the union and seventeen no's. I was elected chief steward for the union.

Shortly after, a union man come down from Charlotte and says we need a full-time rep. We've got only two hundred people at the two plants here. It's just barely enough money comin' in to pay your salary. You'll have to get out and organize more people. I didn't know nothin' about organizin' unions, but I knew how to organize people, stir people up. (Laughs.) That's how I got to be business agent for the union.

When I began to organize, I began to see far deeper. I began to see people again bein' used. Blacks against whites. I say this without any hesitancy: management is vicious. There's two things they want to keep: all the money and all the say-so. They don't want these poor workin' folks to have none of that. I begin to see management fightin' me with everything they had. Hire anti-union law firms, badmouth unions. The people were makin' a dollar ninety-five an hour, barely able to get through weekends. I worked as a business rep for five years and was seein' all this.

Last year, I ran for business manager of the union. He's elected by the workers. The guy that ran against me was black, and our membership is seventy-five percent black. I thought: Claiborne, there's no way you can beat that black guy. People know your background. Even though you've made tremendous strides, those black people are not gonna vote for you. You know how much I beat him? Four to one. (Laughs).

The company used my past against me. They put out letters with a 60
picture of a robe and a cap: would you vote for a Klansman? They wouldn't deal with the issues. I immediately called for a mass meeting. I met with the ladies at an electric component plant. I said: "Okay, this is Claiborne Ellis. This is where I come from. I want you to know right now, you black ladies here, I was at one time a member of the Klan. I want you to know, because they'll tell you about it."

I invited some of my old black friends. I said: "Brother Joe, Brother Howard, be honest now and tell these people how you feel about me." They done it. (Laughs.) Howard Clements kidded me a little bit. He said: "I don't know what I'm doin' here, supportin' an ex-Klansman." (Laughs.) He said: "I know what C. P. Ellis come from. I knew him when he was. I knew him as he grew, and growed with him. I'm tellin' you now: follow, follow this Klansman." (He pauses, swallows hard.) "Any questions?" "No," the black ladies said. "Let's get on with the meeting, we need Ellis." (He laughs and weeps.) Boy, black people sayin' that about me. I won one thirty-four to forty-one. Four to one.

It makes you feel good to go into a plant and butt heads with professional union busters. You see black people and white people join hands to defeat the racist issues they use against people. They're tryin' the same things with the Klan. It's still happenin' today. Can you imagine a guy who's got an adult high school diploma runnin' into professional college graduates who are union busters? I gotta compete with 'em. I work seven days a week, nights and on Saturday and Sunday. The salary's not that great, and if I didn't care, I'd quit. But I care and I can't quit. I got a taste of it. (Laughs.)

I tell people there's a tremendous possibility in this country to stop wars, the battles, the struggles, the fights between people. People say: "That's an impossible dream. You sound like Martin Luther King." An ex-Klansman who sounds like Martin Luther King. (Laughs.) I don't think it's an impossible dream. It's happened in my life. It's happened in other people's lives in America.

I don't know what's ahead of me. I have no desire to be a big union official. I want to be right out here in the field with the workers. I want to walk through their factory and shake hands with that man whose hands are dirty. I'm gonna do all that one little ol' man can do. I'm fifty-two years old, and I ain't got many years left, but I want to make the best of 'em.

When the news came over the radio that Martin Luther King was as- 65
sassinated, I got on the telephone and begin to call other Klansmen. We just had a real party at the service station. Really rejoicin' 'cause that son of a bitch was dead. Our troubles are over with. They say the older you get, the harder it is for you to change. That's not necessarily true. Since I changed, I've set down and listened to tapes of Martin Luther King. I listen to it and tears come to my eyes 'cause I know what he's sayin' now. I know what's happenin'.

POSTSCRIPT:

The phone rings. A conversation.

"This was a black guy who's director of Operation Breakthrough in Durham. I had called his office. I'm interested in employin' some young black person who's interested in learnin' the labor movement. I want somebody who's never had an opportunity, just like myself. Just so he can read and write, that's all."

Engaging the Text

1. How does Ellis battle the racism he finds in himself? What gives him the motivation and strength to change? What specific changes does he undergo, and how successful is he in abandoning racist attitudes?

2. Would Ellis say that economic class is more important than race in determining job placement and occupational mobility? Find specific passages that reveal Ellis's beliefs about the connections between economic class, race, and success in American society. What do you believe?
3. How well does Ellis seem to understand himself, his feelings, his motives? Give evidence for your assertions.
4. What is Terkel's role in this selection? Is he unconsciously helping to rationalize or justify the actions of the Ku Klux Klan?

Exploring Connections

5. How well does the theory of racial formation spelled out by Michael Omi and Howard Winant (p. 356) account for Ellis's racism or his reform? Explain how you think those authors would interpret Ellis's history.
6. To what extent does Ellis's experience illustrate the theories of prejudice described by Vincent N. Parrillo (p. 376)? Does any one of these theories best account for Ellis's racism and his eventual transformation?
7. Review the account of Malcolm X's self-education (p. 77). How does the dramatic self-transformation he experiences compare with C. P. Ellis's rebirth? What relationships can you find between the circumstances that led to their initial attitudes, the conditions or events that fostered their transformations, and the effects that these transformations had on their characters?

Extending the Critical Context

8. Interview a friend, family member, or fellow student in another class to create your own oral history on the subject of racial attitudes. Ask your subject to describe a time when he or she was forced to re-evaluate his or her thoughts or feelings about someone from a different racial or ethnic group. Try to include as many relevent details as possible in your retelling of the story. Share and edit these oral histories in small groups, and then assemble them into a class anthology.
9. Several movies in the past decade portrayed white characters who discovered and began to fight against racism in their own societies. Watch *The Long Walk Home* or *A Dry White Season* and compare the transformation the central character undergoes with C. P. Ellis's. What motives lead them to challenge the racism of their ingroup? Are their transformations convincing? Do these films, and Ellis's story, offer a credible way of overcoming misunderstanding and hatred between races? Given the explanations Omi and Winant and Parrillo offer for the persistence of racism, do you think such "solutions" would be workable on a large scale? Why or why not?

Slaves, Monsters, and Others

Ed Guerrero

When Hollywood was still an orange grove, the U.S. film industry had already discovered the usefulness of stereotypes on the screen. Movie moguls were among the first media leaders to recognize that the socially constructed racial categories that shape thinking could also be exploited to control audience responses and elicit easy laughs. As Ed Guerrero points out in this selection, race even plays a major role in contemporary science-fiction movie fare. Decoding the racial stereotypes and race anxiety hidden in films like E.T., Little Shop of Horrors, *and* Gremlins, *Guerrero argues that many popular science-fiction films are actually symbolic critiques of the racist tensions submerged in American culture. Guerrero (b. 1944) teaches film and literature at the University of Delaware, is an accomplished documentary filmmaker, and has written extensively on Black and Third-World cinema. "Slaves, Monsters, and Others" originally appeared in* Framing Blackness: The African American Image in Film *(1993).*

> The idea of freedom is born, not in the consciousness of the master, but in the reality of the slave's condition. Freedom can mean nothing positive to the master; only control is meaningful. For the slave, freedom begins with the consciousness that real life comes with the negation of his social death.
>
> — Orlando Patterson, *Slavery and Social Death*

Once many plantations grew cotton; today, some grow movies. But the imperatives remain pretty much the same. As evidence of the incessant need to control black folks' dreams, commercial cinema in the United States, from its inception in Thomas Edison's 1890 "peepshows" to the megabudget entertainment packages of present-day Hollywood, has pretty consistently devalued the image of African Americans and other racial minorities by confining their representations within an ideological web of myths, stereotypes, and caricatures. That this practice exists and prevails can be easily confirmed by a quick trip to any video store or mall multiplex theater where Indiana Jones loots the Third World and subdues its people with whip and gun; where one can view the antiblack, anti-Asian allegory of *Gremlins* (1984) or the exotic-primitive Mr. T. as he grunts and intimidates; or where race is erased from the lily-white worlds of suburban America in, say, *Roxanne* (1987) and *Home Alone* (1990). It is also evident that the workings of this ideology of racial subordination and difference are not produced in a formal, aesthetic vacuum devoid of political concerns or historical influences. Instead, it is part of a broad cultural hegemony[1] structured into the fabric of dominant cinema at all levels, its production and content "overdetermined"[2] by Hollywood's profit-making strategies, the oppositional pressures of black political consciousness and activism, and the historical conditions at the moment of a given film's production.

. . . The social construction and representation of race, *otherness,* and nonwhiteness is an ongoing process, working itself out in many symbolic, cinematic forms of expression, but particularly in the abundant racialized metaphors and allegories of the fantasy, sci-fi, and horror genres. This practice can be explained by several mutually reinforcing factors including these genres' dependence on *difference* or *otherness* in the form of the monster in order to drive or energize their narratives; the now vast technological possibilities of imagining and rendering of all kinds of simulacra for aliens, monsters, mutant outcasts, and the like; and the infinite, fantastic narrative horizons and story worlds possible in these productions. Taken together, these themes and techniques give free associative range and symbolic play to the pent-up energies of society's repressed racial discourse. Because the representational and narrative conventions of sci-fi, fantasy, and horror films almost always defy or transcend dominant cinema's illusionist, linear style of depicting a naturalized "realism," the genre is open to subversive politics. Set in fantastic, often future worlds, these films can project the outcomes of failed institutional policies, nuclear wars, or exhausted ecosystems, and many of them offer quite sharp countercultural critiques of the dominant social policies and values of the present. In this regard, recall Jack Nicholson's portrayal of the Joker in *Batman* (1989) as he ridicules bourgeois aesthetics and trashes the "Fluggenhiem" Museum, or the bleak, dystopian vistas of *Soylent Green* (1973) and *Escape from New York* (1981), or both *Terminator* films (1984, 1991). These genres, then, hold great possibility for imagining *difference* and transcoding present-day social anxieties and are potentially powerful vehicles for doing so because they are so popular, accounting for over a third of Hollywood's box-office income during the 1980s.[3]

In the film that dictated the intense, gory style of the new wave of horror movies, George Romero's cult classic *Night of the Living Dead* (1968), the protagonist Ben, because his blackness is so understated and yet so obvious, well illustrates the power and complexity of racial imaging in the peak year of the turbulent 1960s. In *Night,* the black protagonist battles a multitude

[1] *hegemony:* Dominance.

[2] Robert B. Ray, *A Certain Tendency of the Hollywood Cinema, 1930–1980* (Princeton: Princeton University Press, 1985), p. 6. Here I follow Ray's interpretation of the work of Louis Althusser when Ray points out that "cinema as a whole, and even more emphatically, any individual movie, is massively overdetermined. No film results from a single cause, even if its maker thinks it does; as a discourse, the cinema, especially the commercial cinema, is simply too exposed, too public, to permit such circumspection." [Author's note]

[3] "Horror Sci-Fi Pix Earn 37% of Rentals — Big Rise During 10-Year Period," *Variety* (January 1981). [Author's note]

of white zombies that, in contrast to his energetic, heroic struggle for survival, signify an infectious, suffocating sense of culturally dead whiteness. At the film's ironic close, Ben, who has survived the zombies, is gunned down by a sheriff's posse of good ol' boys in a scene that is powerfully multivalent, alluding to the "search and destroy" operations of Vietnam as well as the violence of the civil rights years and racist lynch mobs of the nation's recent past. Moreover, this thematic contrast of black as "living," as opposed to the white "dead," is socially relevant and potent enough for Romero to extend its exploration in the other two films of the *Dead* trilogy, *Dawn of the Dead* (1978) and *Day of the Dead* (1985), with their respective black protagonists Peter and John.[4]

Inscribing racial difference in another manner, Steven Spielberg's endearing alien character of *E.T.: The Extraterrestrial* (1982) represents the ideal immigrant, the model minority from the dominant cultural perspective. Despite E.T.'s hairlessness, brown skin, and grotesque humanoid form, he has the compensations of being from an advanced technological civilization and of having blue eyes, signifying sensitivity, intelligence, and a spark of biological "whiteness."[5] But best of all, unlike Brother in *The Brother from Another Planet,* E.T. arrived alone, cannot reproduce, and has no intention of seeking citizenship; the film's plot is driven by E.T.'s desire to return home. Conversely, in the sci-fi, cop-buddy thriller *Alien Nation* (1988), images of racial otherness and a sustained allegory for nonwhite immigration with a clear mention of slavery are as obvious as they are socially urgent. In the near-future 1990s, a giant flying saucer, a rebellious slave ship in fact, lands off a Los Angeles beach and disembarks a community of runaway slave-aliens that quickly grows into a huge population inhabiting its own vast *barrio* in Los Angeles. Signifying our culture's reflex suspicion and contempt for racial *otherness,* as well as its need for clearly marked categories and boundaries so intrinsic to hegemonic racial order, the extraterrestrial new arrivals are quickly labeled "Slags" and their community "Slagtown." Thus the film's setting and historical moment, combined with the rapid growth of its newcomer population, their containment in a ghetto, and their begrudging acceptance on the urban scene, form a specific and complex mediation of the social tensions and concerns over undocumented and uncontrolled Latino immigration into Los Angeles.[6]

5 These same persistent anxieties over race and immigration are inflected in a more comic vein in *Little Shop of Horrors* (1986), specifically in the imaging of Audrey II, the flesh-eating giant green plant from outer space

[4]Richard Dyer, "White," *Screen* 23, no. 4 (Autumn 1988). [Author's note]

[5]It is interesting to note that blue eyes as racial metonymy for intelligence is perfectly constructed in Whoopi Goldberg's *Burglar* (1987), when in a full-face close-up featuring a spark of recognition in her blue eyes (provided by contact lenses), she solves the mystery of the film's plot. [Author's note]

[6]Charles Ramirez Berg, "Immigrants, Aliens, and Extraterrestrials: Science Fiction's Alien "Other" as (Among Other Things) New Hispanic Imagery," *Cineaction!* no. 18 (Fall 1989): 3–17. [Author's note]

with huge red lips and the black, bass soul voice of Levi Stubbs of the Four Tops. Audrey II's growth from a seedling to a twelve-foot-high avaricious monster suckled on human blood and singing "I'm a mean, green mother from outer space and I'm bad!" plays on white suburbanite and neoconservative anxieties that expanding nonwhite immigrant populations will become as large, demanding, and assertive as indigenous blacks are already perceived to be. Enacting these concerns, Audrey II's main refrain throughout the film is "Feed me!" as it continues to grow bigger, hungrier, and more threatening. The resonant, distinctly black voice of Levi Stubbs, who executes his role with the cunning and wit of a street-smart hustler, images Audrey II as dangerous but simultaneously entertaining and likeable. Thus the audience comes to perceive Audrey II with the same ambivalence that the dominant culture in all its racialized projections has historically framed the presence of black people in America, extending back to such traditional, stereotypical dichotomies of blacks as the child or savage, Sambo or brute.

While *Little Shop* ends happily, in a conventional, dominant cinema resolution, with Audrey II destroyed and the boy (Rick Moranis) getting the girl (Ellen Greene) and moving to a house in the suburbs, the film's final scene shrewdly acknowledges the intractable nature of the social-political problems that it so brilliantly casts in comic metaphor. For if, as argued, the monster in the horror, sci-fi, and fantasy genres is the incessant return of those repressed fears and problems that society cannot articulate or cope with openly, and if the film's symbolized issues—race, immigration, and the unchecked growth of nonwhite populations — are as yet unresolved, one would expect some sign of tension or dissonance at the film's end. Additionally, such an ending would be consonant with the multitude of apocalyptic, pessimistic endings prevailing in sci-fi and horror films such as *Planet of the Apes* (1969), *The Omen* (1976), and both remakes of *Invasion of the Body Snatchers* (1978) and *The Thing* (1982), all of which seem to be unable to envision a survivable, optimistic future for humankind or contemporary society.[7] Thus, outside the cartoonish little suburban house, unnoticed in the flower bed, there grows a new insurgent seedling generation of floral invaders. *Little Shop of Horrors* closes with the realization of its ultimate social threat. The "mean green mother from outer space" not only manages to immigrate but has taken root and will proliferate.

Of all the recent films constructing fantastic images of racial anxiety, perhaps Joe Dante's *Gremlins* (1984) and *Gremlins 2: The New Batch* (1990) stand out most for their sustained allegorical exploration of the themes of racial difference, proliferation, and transformation in America. The original feature, in all its complex, layered meanings, definitely caught the imagina-

[7]Fredric Jameson, "Progress versus Utopia; Or, Can We Imagine the Future?" *Science Fiction Studies* 9, no. 2 (1982); H. Bruce Franklin, "Don't Look Where We're Going: Visions of the Future in Science-Fiction Films, 1970–82," *Science-Fiction Studies* 10 (1983): 70–80; Pam Rosenthal, "Jacked In: Fordism, Cyberpunk, Marxism," *Socialist Review* 21, no. 1 (January–March 1991): 79–103. [Author's note]

tion and patronage of a broad popular audience. Made for a mere $11 million and grossing more than $148 million in receipts its first year, *Gremlins* was the third-most-popular film at the box office in 1984.[8] Set in small-town America, in clear allusion to the locales of such 1950s sci-fi horror movies as *Invasion of the Body Snatchers* (1956), *Invaders from Mars* (1953), and *The Blob* (1958), *Gremlins* evokes the well-worked paradigm of "small town USA" invaded or subverted by monsters or extraterrestrial aliens symbolizing contemporary threats to traditional American cultural values. Yet because the director is removed by a couple of generations from the politically paranoid monster movies of the 1950s,[9] Joe Dante's view of traditional small-town values as representative of the American norm is at best ironic or askance and more akin to that of David Lynch's kinky rendering of 1950s small-town life in the gothic *Blue Velvet* (1986). In one of the film's many comic moments, *Gremlins* illustrates its distance from a more innocent 1950s outlook when the protagonist's girl friend, Kate, explains that she does not like the holiday season because her father was discovered dead, wedged halfway down a chimney, on Christmas day.

Falling into the standard formula of the horror narrative, the film tells of a small, exotic creature, a "mogwai" named Gizmo, procured in an urban Chinatown and brought home as a gift for the prototypical American family at that most traditional and sentimental time of year, Christmas. The disruption of this idyllic setting and season arises when the three critical rules for the care and feeding of mogwais (don't expose to light, don't expose to water, and never feed after midnight) are predictably violated. Moreover, the creature's cinematic, horrific power and appeal are the result of its mode of exponential reproduction along with its ability to metamorphose from a domestic pet into a more mischievous and finally dangerous category of monster. Contrariwise, communal order is restored in the narrative with the systematic, violent eradication of the little demons, and the return of the original mogwai, the lovable Gizmo, to Chinatown.

Clearly established in *Gremlins'* opening, with little distance between metaphor and its social reference, the fantasy creature, the mogwai, is framed by its filmic context and the social concerns at its historical moment of production as an Asian immigrant. The mogwai is kept in a Chinatown shop stocked with other imported curiosities of the "Orient" by a grossly stereotypical old Chinese sage with a milky glass eye who spouts Charlie Chan aphorisms[10] but who, nonetheless, is circumspect about letting the

[8] *Magill's Cinema Annual 1985* (Englewood Cliffs, N.J.: Salem Press, 1985), p. 230. [Author's note]

[9] For an in-depth discussion of the shift from political threats of the 1950s to the biological threats of the 1980s onward, see Edward Guerrero, "AIDS as Monster in Science Fiction and Horror Cinema," *Journal of Popular Film and Television* 18, no. 3 (Fall 1990): 86–94. [Author's note]

[10] Margo Skinner, "NAATA Denounces Stereotypes," *Asian Week,* August 10, 1984. This article notes that the stereotypic racial nature of the film was not missed by the National Asian American Telecommunications Association. Furthermore, one member of the organization's

creature fall into the hands of an ignorant Westerner. Commenting on the generational erosion of even Chinese traditional values, however, the shopkeeper's grandson, operating on a cash-and-carry basis, secretly sells the mogwai to the film's bumbling father figure (Hoyt Axton) for a few hundred dollars. Once situated in the American family context as an entertaining pet, Gizmo, very much like E.T., becomes yet another figuration of the model minority.[11] Marking its powerlessness in the hierarchy of domination, Gizmo is isolated, passive, diminutive, and aims to entertain and please the family with strains of song and dance from the repertoire of its exotic, imported culture. Gizmo's only leverage in its new context is derived from its cuteness and obedience, attributes that the creature diligently strives to perfect.

Predictably, all is not as it appears. For the real threat and latent power 10
of the mogwai, as metaphor for Asian immigrant, is the potential menace of all monsters, carrying varied social meanings, in a range of sci-fi movies from *Them!* (1954) to *The Thing* (1982) and *Aliens* (1986).[12] This threat comes down to the power and politics of demographics, of reproducing one's own kind, expanding one's numbers and influence, which when considered in the political frame of a "one man, one vote" system, is possibly the most accessible route to political leverage for all marginalized collectivities, be they racial, class based, sexual, gendered, or just plain fantastic, multiplying monsters. So, when water is accidentally spilled on Gizmo, violating the first of the three prohibitions, the creature reproduces by popping several mogwai hatchlings out of its back. While this new breed resembles Gizmo, because of the strength and security in numbers, they are far more assertive and mischievous. And although Gizmo remains faithful to the narrative's small-town family and its normative values throughout the film, creating a distinct subject position for dominant sensibilities planted among the insurgents, this new generation takes on a self-focused, political consciousness analogous to the sort of political development that all second-generation immigrant

board, John Esaki, is very aware of the director's racial insensitivity, noting Joe Dante's comment about the Chinese shopkeeper that "he spouts aphorisms and all that old Charlie Chan stuff." [Author's note]

[11]Here I feel that it is important to note Steven Spielberg's connection to a whole string of cinematic figurations and films dealing with the themes of racial otherness and racial minorities. These films range from his construction of alien others in *Close Encounters of the Third Kind* and *E.T.* to the imperial subjugation of people of color in the *Indiana Jones* series, and the exploration of blackness in *The Color Purple.* And while Spielberg did not direct *Gremlins,* as the film's executive producer he collaborated closely with Joe Dante on all details of the script. [Author's note]

[12]Clearly, social anxiety over the increase of domestic and immigrant black and nonwhite populations due to their supposed higher than white populations' birthrates has been an abiding theme in the intellectual history of racism, whether articulated as white homogeneity, exclusionism, deportation, Social Darwinism, or eugenics. See Thomas F. Gossett, *Race: The History of an Idea in America* (New York: Schocken Books, 1973); George M. Fredrickson, *The Black Image in the White Mind* (Middletown, Conn.: Wesleyan University Press, 1987), pp. 228–255; Ronald T. Takaki, *Iron Cages: Race and Culture in Nineteenth-Century America* (Seattle: University of Washington Press, 1979), pp. 215–249. [Author's note]

groups experience in some form or another. Consequently, this new generation of mogwais is not "grateful" to the film's normative whites and has no need for Gizmo's subservient, accommodationist outlook.

What is more, if Gizmo represents a sort of groveling "Uncle Tom" attitude toward the relations of domination, as marked by its pet status within the all-American family, then the oppositional dynamic of *Gremlins'* racial, political allegory is filled in with the appearance of the creature's alter ego in the figuration of the new generation's militant leader, Stripe. Replete with a distinctive skunk's stripe down the middle of its head, emblematic of a sort of punk rocker's rejection of social norms, Stripe is definitely not an accommodationist or anyone's pet. Once hatched, he very quickly communicates his militant consciousness by biting the protagonist Billy's hand, bullying Gizmo into submission, and leading the new wave on a mischievous rampage throughout the house. At this point *Gremlins* turns from kiddie fantasy entertainment toward the menace of an all-out horror movie, when, in violation of rule 3, the mogwais are accidentally fed after midnight. This induces a total metamorphosis in the mogwais as they retreat into the ominous, slime-covered pods or cocoons reminiscent of the pod or nest scenes in *Alien* (1979) and *Aliens* (1986).

With this shift into a more horrific mood, *Gremlins'* racial allegory also starts to congeal and intensify in its social implications. For, significantly, a fundamental racial metamorphosis has occurred with the emergence from these primeval cocoons of a batch of small, scaly, reptilian gargoyles with upright, anthropomorphic postures and a coloration ranging from dark brown to the distinctly threatening, militant blackness of their leader, Stripe. Thus the mogwais come to represent a series of political, generational, and racial changes ranging from the submissive Asian immigrant model minority, Gizmo, to an assertive, politically conscious second generation of Asians organized around the militant leadership of Stripe, to a violent, insurgent mob of black and brown monsters, signifying indigenous populations of African Americans and Latinos, that fully realize the label of the film's title, *Gremlins.*[13]

Complications and intensifications of horror and allegory arise with this last phase of the creatures' metamorphosis when Stripe survives being destroyed at the Pheltzers' house only to escape and wind up falling into the swimming pool at the town YMCA. In one of the movie's most brilliant sequences, the pool steams, boils, and bubbles as the monster reproduces exponentially, thus quantifying the menace and horror of its social reference. For if Stripe is the dangerous issue of the passive Gizmo, then the resultant offspring from Stripe's "dip at the Y" represent a violence of fantastic, geometric proportions. The pool sequence ends with thousands of Gremlins

[13]Clearly marking the final stage of Stripe's evolution, the broad, unified anger and actions of blacks and Latinos during the 1992 Los Angeles rebellion well illustrates the anxieties of a white-dominated social order about its crumbling hegemony in the face of an unassimilated, dissatisfied Third World within the nation. [Author's note]

surging down nighttime Main Street USA in a horrific parody of the swarming youth gang scenes that were so impressive in *The Warriors* (1979). In a more historicized frame, this scene is reminiscent of the "roving bands of Negro youth," the worn description so often deployed by a nervous news media during the black urban rebellions of the late 1960s.

The exponential proliferation of the Gremlins results in murder, mayhem, and chaos for this small town at the height of the Christmas season, as the ultimate import of the film's racial allegory surfaces in all its complex referents, icons, and symbols in a series of distinctive scenes. The most noteworthy of these scenes occurs when the creatures invade the town bar and commence to party. The Gremlins drink themselves silly, swing from the overhead fan, fight, and generally carouse and riot, totally wrecking the establishment in the process. This rowdy saloon sequence proves to be a fertile setting for the images and cultural emblems of a threatening, inner-city, racial *otherness,* which are explored in a full range of grotesque caricatures. In a series of intricately worked tableaus and cameos, Gremlins parody inner-city youth break-dancing, depict urban black males playing cards, singing the blues, or as they are rendered in cool portraiture, sullenly hunched over drinks, decorated in sunglasses and stingy-brim hats. But the dramatic focus of the whole barroom sequence crystallizes when the film's heroine, Kate (Phoebe Cates), becomes trapped in the midst of this chaos and is forced to serve drinks, accommodating the Gremlins as a barmaid.

Besides a phantasmagorical display of racial puppetry, the sequence also 15
deploys the mechanics of both the rescue paradigm and the rape motif by evoking the specter of the vulnerable white woman alone, surrounded and threatened by the monstrosity of black *otherness.* This Manichaean conflict[14] between the antipodes of light and dark, usually most intensely expressed as a sexual threat, goes back to the beginnings of narrative cinema à la *The Birth of a Nation* and extends to its latest manifestation in the horror film *Candyman* (1992). For the white woman as the essence of whiteness, the most prized possession of the white man and the object of desire of all other races, is a powerful representational current running through Western literature and cinema and is one of the generic sources of race imagery in this century. It is the threat of the white woman's rape by the monstrous, black *other* that gives white-black contrasts much of their social charge and meaning.[15] The unconscious, driving power of this trope is made all too clear in the barroom sequence's climaxing image, when the ultimate menace of urban blackness erupts in the image of a ski-masked Gremlin that threatens Kate with a "Saturday night special."

The other large-scale *mise-en-scène* of intricate racial spectacle is set in

[14]*Manichaean conflict:* A conflict between good and evil. Believers in seventh-century Manichaeism saw the universe as divided equally between the forces of light (God) and darkness (Satan).

[15]Richard Dyer, *Heavenly Bodies, Film Stars and Society* (New York: St. Martin's, 1986), p. 43. [Author's note]

the town movie theater, which, predictably, becomes infested with rampaging Gremlins in an obvious parody of the out-of-control Saturday kiddie matinee. The point here is more subtle but holds equally revealing import. In a clever irony, as the feature comes on and the Gremlins settle down, they are captivated by Walt Disney's *Snow White and the Seven Dwarfs* (1937). Thus the Gremlins, themselves constructions of racial fantasy, sit transfixed by their binary contrast in the symbolic racial order, the perfect icon of whiteness and beauty, Snow White. But because in dominant cinema ideology "beauty and whiteness" cannot be articulated without reference to "grotesqueness and blackness," the Gremlins also share a subject position, within the text, with the figures of the seven dwarfs, as well as the "blackness" of the wicked queen. Thus in total identification with their spectator position in the film, the Gremlins sing "Heigh-ho, heigh-ho, it's off to work we go" along with the dwarfs. Equally revealing, this total scene of contemporary racial fantasy figures of the present viewing those of the past tells us something about the tenacity of such racist iconography in the popular mind and the temporal distance over which this whole system of racial constructions has traveled. So, much like *Gremlins* in terms of popular box-office appeal, in its own historical moment *Snow White and the Seven Dwarfs* was a film of vast influence, being the second-top moneymaking film of the 1930s and falling between those other two great signifiers of race and *otherness, Gone With the Wind* (1939) in first place and *King Kong* (1933) in third.[16] This riotous parody of the kiddie matinee gone berserk ends with genocidal clarity as Billy and Kate fill the theater with gas and blow the little demons up.

Following on the success of the first production, Gizmo returns in *Gremlins 2: The New Batch* (1990) to recast repressed social fears and, again, multiply uncontrollably. While the basic representations and social allusions remain in place, the allegorical impulse is not so sustained, and the story world has shifted from small-town USA to New York City. This time, director Joe Dante explores the issues of race and difference through fragmented moments of parody within the overall frame of a satire spoofing the business culture of a megacorporation headed by Daniel Clamp, an obvious amalgam of Donald Trump and Ted Turner. Because the social tensions that the movie transcodes are still with us, however, the overriding metaphor of Gremlins as nonwhite or Asian immigrants generally persists. Only this time the film's socially repressed fears have to do with nonwhite minorities gaining political power, as *Gremlins 2* satirizes the political subtleties of an increasingly influential "minority discourse" in contemporary American life[17] more than it plays upon latent anxieties over racial otherness. This, in part, explains the shift in *Gremlins 2*'s mix of genres more toward comedy and away from

[16]Cobbett Steinberg, *Reel Facts, The Movie Book of Records* (New York: Vintage, 1982), p. 15. [Author's note]

[17]Philip Gleason, "Minorities (Almost) All: The Minority Concept in American Social Thought," *American Quarterly* 43, no. 3 (September 1991): 392–424. [Author's note]

the final emphasis on horror in the original feature. After multiplying and rampaging through the giant Clamp office tower, the Gremlins manage to develop a collective, politicized minority consciousness, replete with an intellectual spokesperson (voiced brilliantly by Tony Randall) to articulate the goals and aspirations of their "ethnic group" on a television talk show. Ultimately, the Gremlins' goal is assimilation, to compete in the bustling urban culture of Manhattan, which is quintessentially an immigrant city. This is best revealed in the film's climactic resolution when the whole horde of Gremlins meet in the lobby of the building to do the city's theme song, "New York, New York," led by their intellectual leader in horn-rimmed glasses and cosmopolitan dress, before being let out on the streets, where they wish to "make it there" as the song suggests.

As in the first film, *Gremlins 2* predictably ends with the little monsters destroyed by the light of day. Also as in the first film, the endearing pet Gizmo survives, thus leaving open the opportunity for yet another sequel, as well as signifying the uncontainable persistence of those issues and anxieties that both films fantastically engage.

Certainly, because of a brilliant, ever-advancing studio technology, now able to render our most fantastic conceptualizations into the most convincing simulacra, we find ourselves, cinematically at least, in the same position as Dr. Morbius and the Krel in the sci-fi masterpiece *Forbidden Planet* (1956), who through their high technology were able to materialize anything that they could conceptualize. One hopes we will not meet an end analogous to theirs, that is, being destroyed by Id monsters emergent from our own racist, cinematic psyches. But it is fair to say that as national cultural life further diversifies and that unstable dominant social construct known as "whiteness" increasingly shrinks under the pressure of the multicultural wave, to become one minority among many by the year 2000, the idea and place of "the norm" in cinema will further erode, thus inspiring a more radical understanding and complex explorations of *difference(s)*. As for the genres of fantasy, science fiction, and horror, I believe that something like this shift, which started as a minuscule, dialectial countercurrent to the majority wave of politically paranoid monster movies of the 1950s, has long been under way and has been gaining momentum. This is evinced by a long trajectory of films containing sympathetic figures of social and psychic *otherness* at the repressed core of alien monstrosity, from *The Boy with Green Hair* (1948) and *The Day the Earth Stood Still* (1951) to *Close Encounters of the Third Kind* (1977), *E.T.: The Extraterrestrial* and *Swamp Thing* (both 1982), *Edward Scissorhands* (1990), and *The Applegates* and *People under the Stairs* (both 1991).

Engaging the Text

1. What, according to Guerrero, is the monster's role in horror, sci-fi, and fantasy movies?
2. What does Guerrero mean by "otherness"? Review the examples of symbolically

embodied "otherness" he refers to in films; can you offer examples from more-recent movies?

3. One of Guerrero's interpretive strategies is to search for relationships between the films he decodes and the historical events and social conditions current at the time of the film's making. Find several examples of Guerrero's use of history as an interpretive tool. Do the films he discusses do more than passively reflect the social realities of their historical contexts?
4. In what sense can sci-fi, horror, and fantasy films be seen as subverting traditional American values? Why do these particular film genres seem to welcome subversive messages?
5. Do you feel Guerrero "goes too far" in his interpretations? Write a journal entry exploring and responding to some of his claims.
6. Overall, do you think that Guerrero approves or disapproves of the use of racial images in these films?

Exploring Connections

7. How might the concepts of displaced aggression, group position, self-justification, and economic competition described by Vincent N. Parrillo (p. 376) help explain the racial stereotypes in the *Gremlins* movies?
8. To what extent does Guerrero's analysis of the racial messages and cultural criticism hidden in sci-fi movies complicate Michael Omi and Howard Winant's view (p. 356) of how television and film "disseminate" images of racial minorities?
9. Compare Guerrero's symbolic interpretation of sci-fi, horror, and fantasy films with bell hooks's reading of the messages about gender hidden in *The Piano* (p. 270). Do the films that Guerrero discusses also contain messages about the sexual anxieties of American culture? To what extent do they support or subvert traditional American gender-related values and attitudes?

Extending the Critical Context

10. Choose one of the films discussed by Guerrero that you, as a class, feel may not support his claims. Watch this film together and use it to test the accuracy and plausibility of Guerrero's arguments.
11. Apply Guerrero's technique of discovering hidden racial images and cultural anxieties to a recent sci-fi, horror, or fantasy film. How well does his thesis appear to hold for other movies in this genre?
12. The identification of monsters, aliens, and gremlins with specific racial and ethnic groups might strike some readers as offensive, regardless of the "subversive" intentions that may or may not be implicit within the films Guerrero analyzes. Do you think that Guerrero is mistakenly dignifying movies that simply may be pandering to audience prejudices? Why or why not?

I'm Black, You're White, Who's Innocent?

SHELBY STEELE

This essay comes from one of the most controversial American books of the past decade—The Content of Our Character: A New Vision of Race in America. *Shelby Steele (b. 1946) believes that Black Americans have failed to seize opportunities which would lead to social equality; he is also an outspoken critic of affirmative action, arguing that instead of promoting equality it locks its recipients into second-class status. Angry critics accuse him of underestimating the power of racism, of blaming victims for their predicament, of being a traitor to his race. In this selection, Steele offers his observations on why African and white Americans have not been able to sustain the kind of dialogue that would make mutual understanding possible. His essays have garnered a number of awards, including a National Book Critics Circle Award. Steele's writings have appeared in* Harper's, The American Scholar, The New Republic, *and many other journals and magazines.*

It is a warm, windless California evening, and the dying light that covers the redbrick patio is tinted pale orange by the day's smog. Eight of us, not close friends, sit in lawn chairs sipping chardonnay. A black engineer and I (we had never met before) integrate the group. A psychologist is also among us, and her presence encourages a surprising openness. But not until well after the lovely twilight dinner has been served, when the sky has turned to deep black and the drinks have long since changed to scotch, does the subject of race spring awkwardly upon us. Out of nowhere the engineer announces, with a coloring of accusation in his voice, that it bothers him to send his daughter to a school where she is one of only three black children. "I didn't realize my ambition to get ahead would pull me into a world where my daughter would lose touch with her blackness," he says.

Over the course of the evening we have talked about money, past and present addictions, child abuse, even politics. Intimacies have been revealed, fears named. But this subject, race, sinks us into one of those shaming silences where eye contact terrorizes. Our host looks for something in the bottom of his glass. Two women stare into the black sky as if to locate the Big Dipper and point it out to us. Finally, the psychologist seems to gather herself for a challenge, but it is too late. "Oh, I'm sure she'll be just fine," says our hostess, rising from her chair. When she excuses herself to get the coffee, the psychologist and two sky gazers offer to help.

With four of us now gone, I am surprised to see the engineer still silently holding his ground. There is a willfulness in his eyes, an inner pride. He knows he has said something awkward, but he is determined not to give a damn. His unwavering eyes intimidate even me. At last the host's head snaps erect. He has an idea. "The hell with coffee," he says. "How about some of the smoothest brandy you've ever tasted?" An idea made exciting by the escape it offers. Gratefully, we follow him back into the house, quickly drink his brandy, and say our good-byes.

An autopsy of this party might read: death induced by an abrupt and lethal injection of the American race issue. An accurate if superficial assessment. Since it has been my fate to live a rather integrated life, I have often witnessed sudden deaths like this. The threat of them, if not the reality, is a part of the texture of integration. In the late 1960s, when I was just out of college, I took a delinquent's delight in playing the engineer's role, and actually developed a small reputation for playing it well. Those were the days of flagellatory white guilt: it was such great fun to pinion some professor or housewife or, best of all, a large group of remorseful whites, with the knowledge of both their racism and their denial of it. The adolescent impulse to sneer at convention, to startle the middle-aged with doubt, could be indulged under the guise of racial indignation. And how could I lose? My victims—earnest liberals for the most part—could no more crawl out from under my accusations than Joseph K. in Kafka's *Trial*[1] could escape the amorphous charges brought against him. At this odd moment in history the world was aligned to facilitate my immaturity.

About a year of this was enough: the guilt that follows most cheap thrills 5
caught up to me, and I put myself in check. But the impulse to do it faded more slowly. It was one of those petty talents that is tied to vanity, and when there were ebbs in my self-esteem the impulse to use it would come alive again. In integrated situations I can still feel the faint itch. But then there are many youthful impulses that still itch and now, just inside the door of midlife, this one is least precious to me.

In the literature classes I teach I often see how the presence of whites all but seduces some black students into provocation. When we come to a novel by a black writer, say Toni Morrison, the white students can easily discuss the human motivations of the black characters. But, inevitably, a black student, as if by reflex, will begin to set in relief the various racial problems that are the background of these characters' lives. This student's tone will carry a reprimand: the class is afraid to confront the reality of racism. Classes cannot be allowed to die like dinner parties, however. My latest strategy is to thank that student for his or her moral vigilance and then appoint the young man or woman as the class's official racism monitor. But even if I get a laugh—I usually do, but sometimes the student is particularly

[1]*Kafka's* Trial: Austrian writer Franz Kafka (1883–1924) is famous for his dreamlike and ominous stories. In his novel *The Trial*, the character known only as Joseph K. battles an intricate legal and police system that never specifies his alleged crime.

indignant, and it gets uncomfortable — the strategy never quite works. Our racial division is suddenly drawn in neon. Overcaution spreads like spilled paint. And, in fact, the black student who started it all does become a kind of monitor. The very presence of this student imposes a new accountability on the class.

I think those who provoke this sort of awkwardness are operating out of a black identity that obliges them to badger white people about race almost on principle. Content hardly matters. (For example, it made little sense for the engineer to expect white people to anguish terribly much over his decision to send his daughter to school with *white* children.) Race indeed remains a source of white shame; the goal of these provocations is to put whites, no matter how indirectly, in touch with this collective guilt. In other words, these provocations I speak of are *power* moves, little shows of power that try to freeze the "enemy" in self-consciousness. They gratify and inflate the provocateur. They are the underdog's bite. And whites, far more secure in their power, respond with self-contained and tolerant silence that is itself a show of power. What greater power than that of nonresponse, the power to let a small enemy sizzle in his own juices, to even feel a little sad at his frustration just as one is also complimented by it. Black anger always, in a way, flatters white power. In America, to know that one is not black is to feel an extra grace, a little boost of impunity.

I think the real trouble between the races in America is that the races are not just races but competing power groups — a fact that is easily minimized, perhaps because it is so obvious. What is not so obvious is that this is true quite apart from the issue of class. Even the well-situated middle-class (or wealthy) black is never completely immune to that peculiar contest of power that his skin color subjects him to. Race is a separate reality in American society, an entity that carries its own potential for power, a mark of fate that class can soften considerably but not eradicate.

The distinction of race has always been used in American life to sanction each race's pursuit of power in relation to the other. The allure of race as a human delineation is the very shallowness of the delineation it makes. Onto this shallowness — mere skin and hair — men can project a false depth, a system of dismal attributions, a series of malevolent or ignoble stereotypes that skin and hair lack the substance to contradict. These dark projections then rationalize the pursuit of power. Your difference from me makes you bad, and your badness justifies, even demands, my pursuit of power over you — the oldest formula for aggression known to man. Whenever much importance is given to race, power is the primary motive.

But the human animal almost never pursues power without first con- 10
vincing himself that he is *entitled* to it. And this feeling of entitlement has its own precondition: to be entitled one must first believe in one's innocence, at least in the area where one wishes to be entitled. By innocence I mean a feeling of essential goodness in relation to others and, therefore, superiority to others. Our innocence always inflates us and deflates those we seek power

over. Once inflated we are entitled; we are in fact licensed to go after the power our innocence tells us we deserve. In this sense, *innocence is power.* Of course, innocence need not be genuine or real in any objective sense, as the Nazis demonstrated not long ago. Its only test is whether or not we can convince ourselves of it.

I think the racial struggle in America has always been primarily a struggle for innocence. White racism from the beginning has been a claim of white innocence and therefore of white entitlement to subjugate blacks. And in the sixties, as went innocence so went power. Blacks used the innocence that grew out of their long subjugation to seize more power, while whites lost some of their innocence and so lost a degree of power over blacks. Both races instinctively understand that to lose innocence is to lose power (in relation to each other). To be innocent someone else must be guilty, a natural law that leads the races to forge their innocence on each other's backs. The inferiority of the black always makes the white man superior; the evil might of whites makes blacks good. This pattern means that both races have a hidden investment in racism and racial disharmony despite their good intentions to the contrary. Power defines their relations, and power requires innocence, which, in turn, requires racism and racial division.

I believe it was his hidden investment that the engineer was protecting when he made his remark — the white "evil" he saw in a white school "depriving" his daughter of her black heritage confirmed his innocence. Only the logic of power explained his emphasis — he bent reality to show that he was once again a victim of the white world and, as a victim, innocent. His determined eyes insisted on this. And the whites, in their silence, no doubt protected their innocence by seeing him as an ungracious troublemaker, his bad behavior underscoring their goodness. What none of us saw was the underlying game of power and innocence we were trapped in, or how much we needed a racial impasse to play that game.

When I was a boy of about twelve, a white friend of mine told me one day that his uncle, who would be arriving the next day for a visit, was a racist. Excited by the prospect of seeing such a man, I spent the following afternoon hanging around the alley behind my friend's house, watching from a distance as this uncle worked on the engine of his Buick. Yes, here was evil and I was compelled to look upon it. And I saw evil in the sharp angle of his elbow as he pumped his wrench to tighten nuts. I saw it in the blade-sharp crease of his chinos, in the pack of Lucky Strikes that threatened to slip from his shirt pocket as he bent, and in the way his concentration seemed to shut out the human world. He worked neatly and efficiently, wiping his hands constantly, and I decided that evil worked like this.

I felt a compulsion to have this man look upon me so that I could see evil — so that I could see the face of it. But when he noticed me standing beside his toolbox, he said only, "If you're looking for Bobby, I think he went up to the school to play baseball." He smiled nicely and went back to work.

I was stunned for a moment, but then I realized that evil could be sly as well, could smile when it wanted to trick you.

Need, especially hidden need, puts a strong pressure on perception, and 15
my need to have this man embody white evil was stronger than any contravening evidence. As a black person you always hear about racists but rarely meet any who will let you know them as such. And I needed to incarnate this odious category of humanity, those people who hated Martin Luther King, Jr., and thought blacks should "go slow" or not at all. So, in my mental dictionary, behind the term "white racist," I inserted this man's likeness. I would think of him and say to myself, "There is no reason for him to hate black people. Only evil explains unmotivated hatred." And this thought soothed me; I felt innocent. If I hated white people, which I did not, at least I had a reason. His evil commanded me to assert in the world the goodness he made me confident of in myself.

In looking at this man I was *seeing for innocence* — a form of seeing that has more to do with one's hidden need for innocence (and power) than with the person or group one is looking at. It is quite possible, for example, that the man I saw that day was not a racist. He did absolutely nothing in my presence to indicate that he was. I invested an entire afternoon in seeing not the man but in seeing my innocence through the man. *Seeing for innocence* is, in this way, the essence of racism — the use of others as a means to our own goodness and superiority.

The loss of innocence has always to do with guilt, Kierkegaard[2] tells us, and it has never been easy for whites to avoid guilt where blacks are concerned. For whites, *seeing for innocence* means seeing themselves and blacks in ways that minimize white guilt. Often this amounts to a kind of white revisionism,[3] as when President Reagan declared himself "color-blind" in matters of race. The President, like many of us, may have aspired to racial color blindness, but few would grant that he ever reached this sublimely guiltless state. His statement clearly revised reality, moved it forward into some heretofore unknown America where all racial determinism would have vanished. I do not think that Ronald Reagan was a racist, as that term is commonly used, but neither do I think that he was capable of seeing color without making attributions, some of which may have been negative — nor am I, or anyone else I've ever met.

So why make such a statement? I think Reagan's claim of color blindness with regard to race was really a claim of racial innocence and guiltlessness — the preconditions for entitlement and power. This was the claim that grounded Reagan's campaign against special entitlement programs — affirmative action, racial quotas, and so on — that black power had won in the sixties. Color blindness was a strategic assumption of innocence that licensed Reagan's use of government power against black power. . . .

[2] *Kierkegaard:* Danish philosopher and religious thinker Søren Kierkegaard (1813–1855).

[3] *revisionism:* The reinterpretation or revising of reality to suit one's current purposes.

Black Americans have had to find a way to handle white society's presumption of racial innocence whenever they have sought to enter the American mainstream. Louis Armstrong's[4] exaggerated smile honored the presumed innocence of white society—*I will not bring you your racial guilt if you will let me play my music.* Ralph Ellison[5] calls this "masking"; I call it bargaining. But whatever it's called, it points to the power of white society to enforce its innocence. I believe this power is greatly diminished today. Society has reformed and transformed — Miles Davis[6] never smiles. Nevertheless, this power has not faded altogether and blacks must still contend with it.

Historically, blacks have handled white society's presumption of inno- 20
cence in two ways: they have bargained with it, granting white society its innocence in exchange for entry into the mainstream, or they have challenged it, holding that innocence hostage until their demand for entry (or other concessions) was met. A bargainer says, *I already believe you are innocent (good, fair-minded) and have faith that you will prove it.* A challenger says, *If you are innocent, then prove it.* Bargainers *give* in hope of receiving; challengers *withhold* until they receive. Of course, there is risk in both approaches, but in each case the black is negotiating his own self-interest against the presumed racial innocence of the larger society.

Clearly, the most visible black bargainer on the American scene today is Bill Cosby. His television show has been a perfect formula for black bargaining in the eighties. The remarkable Huxtable family—with its doctor/lawyer parent combination, its drug-free, college-bound children, and its wise yet youthful grandparents — is a blackface version of the American dream. Cosby is a subscriber to the American identity, and his subscription confirms his belief in its fair-mindedness. His vast audience knows this, knows that Cosby will never assault their innocence with racial guilt. Racial controversy is all but banished from the show. The Huxtable family never discusses affirmative action.

The bargain Cosby offers his white viewers—*I will confirm your racial innocence if you accept me*—is a good deal for all concerned. Not only does it allow whites to enjoy Cosby's humor with no loss of innocence, but it actually enhances their innocence by implying that race is not the serious problem for blacks that it once was. If anything, the success of this handsome, affluent black family points to the fair-mindedness of whites who, out of their essential goodness, changed society so that black families like the Huxtables could succeed. Whites can watch *The Cosby Show* and feel complimented on a job well done.

The power that black bargainers wield is the power of absolution. On

[4]*Louis Armstrong:* American jazz trumpet virtuoso and singer (1900–1971).

[5]*Ralph Ellison:* American novelist (b. 1914), best known for *Invisible Man,* the account of a nameless Black youth coming of age in a hostile society.

[6]*Miles Davis:* Jazz musician and trumpeter (1926–1991).

Thursday nights, Cosby, like a priest, absolves his white viewers, forgives and forgets the sins of the past. And for this he is rewarded with an almost sacrosanct[7] status. Cosby benefits from what might be called the gratitude factor. His continued number-one rating may have something to do with the (white) public's gratitude at being offered a commodity so rare in our time; he tells his white viewers each week that they are okay, and that this black man is not going to challenge them.

When a black bargains, he may invoke the gratitude factor and find himself cherished beyond the measure of his achievement; when he challenges, he may draw the dark projections of whites and become a source of irritation to them. If he moves back and forth between these two options, as I think many blacks do today, he will likely baffle whites. It is difficult for whites either to accept or reject such blacks. It seems to me that Jesse Jackson is such a figure—many whites see Jackson as a challenger by instinct and a bargainer by political ambition. They are uneasy with him, more than a little suspicious. His powerful speech at the 1984 Democratic Convention was a masterpiece of bargaining. In it he offered a King-like[8] vision of what America could be, a vision that presupposed Americans had the fair-mindedness to achieve full equality — an offer in hope of a return. A few days after this speech, looking for rest and privacy at a lodge in Big Sur,[9] he and his wife were greeted with standing ovations three times a day when they entered the dining room for meals. So much about Jackson is deeply American — his underdog striving, his irrepressible faith in himself, the daring of his ambition, and even his stubbornness. These qualities point to his underlying faith that Americans can respond to him despite race, and this faith is a compliment to Americans, an offer of innocence.

But Jackson does not always stick to the terms of his bargain as Cosby 25
does on TV. When he hugs Arafat,[10] smokes cigars with Castro,[11] refuses to repudiate Farrakhan,[12] threatens a boycott of major league baseball or, more recently, talks of "corporate barracudas," "pension-fund socialism," and "economic violence," he looks like a challenger in bargainer's clothing, and his positions on the issues look like familiar protests dressed in white-paper formality. At these times he appears to be revoking the innocence so much else about him seems to offer. The old activist seems to come out of hiding once again to take white innocence hostage until whites prove they deserve to have it. In his candidacy there is a suggestion of protest, a fierce insistence

[7]*sacrosanct:* Sacred.

[8]*King-like:* Like that of Martin Luther King, Jr.

[9]*Big Sur:* Section of the California coast known for its natural beauty.

[10]*Arafat:* Yasir Arafat (b. 1929), leader of the Palestine Liberation Organization, or PLO.

[11]*Castro:* Fidel Castro (b. 1926), president of Cuba.

[12]*Farrakhan:* Louis Farrakhan (b. 1933), Nation of Islam leader, often accused of making anti-Semitic remarks. Many African American politicians carefully distance themselves from Farrakhan.

on his *right* to run, that sends whites a message that he may secretly see them as a good bit less than innocent. His dilemma is to appear the bargainer while his campaign itself seems to be a challenge.

There are, of course, other problems that hamper Jackson's bid for the Democratic presidential nomination. He has held no elective office, he is thought too flamboyant and opportunistic by many, there are rather loud whispers of "character" problems. As an individual, he may not be the best test of a black man's chances for winning so high an office. Still, I believe it is the aura of challenge surrounding him that hurts him most. Whether it is right or wrong, fair or unfair, I think no black candidate will have a serious chance at his party's nomination, much less the presidency, until he can convince white Americans that he can be trusted to preserve their sense of racial innocence. Such a candidate will have to use his power of absolution; he will have to flatly forgive and forget. He will have to bargain with white innocence out of genuine belief that it really exists. There can be no faking it. He will have to offer a vision that is passionately raceless, a vision that strongly condemns any form of racial politics. This will require the most courageous kind of leadership, leadership that asks all the people to meet a new standard.

Now the other side of America's racial impasse: how do blacks lay claim to their racial innocence?

The most obvious and unarguable source of black innocence is the victimization that blacks endured for centuries at the hands of a race that insisted on black inferiority as a means to its own innocence and power. Like all victims, what blacks lost in power they gained in innocence — innocence that, in turn, entitled them to pursue power. This was the innocence that fueled the civil rights movement of the sixties and that gave blacks their first real power in American life — victimization metamorphosed into power via innocence. But this formula carries a drawback that I believe is virtually as devastating to blacks today as victimization once was. It is a formula that binds the victim to his victimization by linking his power to his status as a victim. And this, I'm convinced, is the tragedy of black power in America today. It is primarily a victim's power, grounded too deeply in the entitlement derived from past injustice and in the innocence that Western/Christian tradition has always associated with poverty.

Whatever gains this power brings in the short run through political action, it undermines in the long run. Social victims may be collectively entitled, but they are all too often individually demoralized. Since the social victim has been oppressed by society, he comes to feel that his individual life will be improved more by changes in society than by his own initiative. Without realizing it, he makes society rather than himself the agent of change. The power he finds in his victimization may lead him to collective action against society, but it also encourages passivity within the sphere of his personal life.

30 Not long ago, I saw a television documentary that examined life in Detroit's inner city on the twentieth anniversary of the riots there in which forty-three people were killed. A comparison of the inner city then and now showed a decline in the quality of life. Residents feel less safe, drug trafficking is far worse, crimes by blacks against blacks are more frequent, housing remains substandard, and the teenage pregnancy rate has skyrocketed. Twenty years of decline and demoralization, even as opportunities for blacks to better themselves have increased. This paradox is not peculiar to Detroit. By many measures, the majority of blacks — those not yet in the middle class — are further behind whites today than before the victories of the civil rights movement. But there is a reluctance among blacks to examine this paradox, I think, because it suggests that racial victimization is not our real problem. If conditions have worsened for most of us as racism has receded, then much of the problem must be of our own making. To admit this fully would cause us to lose the innocence we derive from our victimization. And we would jeopardize the entitlement we've always had to challenge society. We are in the odd and self-defeating position in which taking responsibility for bettering ourselves feels like a surrender to white power.

So we have a hidden investment in victimization and poverty. These distressing conditions have been the source of our own real power, and there is an unconscious sort of gravitation toward them, a complaining celebration of them. One sees evidence of this in the near happiness with which certain black leaders recount the horror of Howard Beach,[13] Bensonhurst,[14] and other recent instances of racial tension. As one is saddened by these tragic events, one is also repelled at the way some black leaders — agitated to near hysteria by the scent of victim power inherent in them — leap forward to exploit them as evidence of black innocence and white guilt. It is as though they sense the decline of black victimization as a loss of standing and dive into the middle of these incidents as if they were reservoirs of pure black innocence swollen with potential power.

Seeing for innocence pressures blacks to focus on racism and to neglect the individual initiative that would deliver them from poverty — the only thing that finally delivers *anyone* from poverty. With our eyes on innocence we see racism everywhere and miss opportunity even as we stumble over it. About 70 percent of black students at my university drop out before graduation — a flight from opportunity that racism cannot explain. It is an injustice that whites can see for innocence with more impunity than blacks can. The price whites pay is a certain blindness to themselves. Moreover, for whites seeing for innocence continues to engender the bad faith of a long-

[13] *Howard Beach:* Scene in Queens, New York, of a December 1986 racial confrontation in which several young African American men were severely beaten and one died.

[14] *Bensonhurst:* Location in Brooklyn, New York, where the racially motivated murder of sixteen-year-old Yusuf Hawkins took place in August 1989.

disgruntled minority. But the price blacks pay is an ever-escalating poverty that threatens to make the worst off a permanent underclass. Not fair, but real.

Challenging works best for the collective, while bargaining is more the individual's suit. From this point on, the race's advancement will come from the efforts of its individuals. True, some challenging will be necessary for a long time to come. But bargaining is now — today — a way for the black individual to *join* the larger society, to make a place for himself or herself.

"Innocence is ignorance," Kierkegaard says, and if this is so, the claim of innocence amounts to an insistence on ignorance, a refusal to know. In their assertions of innocence both races carve out very functional areas of ignorance for themselves — territories of blindness that license a misguided pursuit of power. Whites gain superiority by not knowing blacks; blacks gain entitlement by not seeing their own responsibility for bettering themselves. The power each race seeks in relation to the other is grounded in a double-edged ignorance of the self as well as of the other.

The original sin that brought us to an impasse at the dinner party I 35
mentioned occurred centuries ago, when it was first decided to exploit racial difference as a means to power. It was a determinism that flowed karmically from this sin that dropped over us like a net that night. What bothered me most was our helplessness. Even the engineer did not know how to go forward. His challenge hadn't worked, and he'd lost the option to bargain. The marriage of race and power depersonalized us, changed us from eight people to six whites and two blacks. The easiest thing was to let silence blanket our situation, our impasse. . . .

What both black and white Americans fear are the sacrifices and risks that true racial harmony demands. This fear is the measure of our racial chasm. And though fear always seeks a thousand justifications, none is ever good enough, and the problems we run from only remain to haunt us. It would be right to suggest courage as an antidote to fear, but the glory of the word might only intimidate us into more fear. I prefer the word effort — relentless effort, moral effort. What I like most about this word are its connotations of everydayness, earnestness, and practical sacrifice. No matter how badly it might have gone for us that warm summer night, we should have talked. We should have made the effort.

Engaging the Text

1. What does Steele mean by "innocence" and by "seeing for innocence"? How does he apply these terms to racial conflict and struggles for power in the United States? How do Blacks and whites claim innocence through racial conflict? What does Steele mean when he says that "innocence is power?"

2. According to Steele, what strategies have African Americans employed to handle "white society's presumption of racial innocence" (para. 19)? How does he account for public reactions to figures like Bill Cosby and Jesse Jackson in terms of these strategies? Are there other possible explanations of their appeal?
3. Steele believes that "bargaining is now — today — a way for the Black individual to *join* the larger society" (para. 33). Do you agree? Is bargaining an available and acceptable alternative for all African Americans?
4. Steele writes that when the issue of race comes up in classes, "overcaution spreads like spilled paint" (para. 6). If you have observed this phenomenon in class or in other circumstances, write a journal entry describing one such incident and analyzing the behavior of the people involved.

EXPLORING CONNECTIONS

5. How might Michael Omi and Howard Winant (p. 356) and Vincent N. Parrillo (p. 376) evaluate Steele's assertion that racism grows out of the desire to claim "innocence"?
6. Compare Steele's notions of bargaining and challenging with Ronald Takaki's idea of sharing stories (p. 332) as strategies for improving race relations. Which seems like the more fruitful or more realistic model for interethnic communication, and why?
7. Write an imaginary dialogue between C. P. Ellis (p. 388), Malcolm X (p. 77), and Shelby Steele on American racism. What might they each say about the causes of racist thinking and behavior? About the chances for curbing racism? How would they respond to each other's ideas and strategies for change?

EXTENDING THE CRITICAL CONTEXT

8. Watch Spike Lee's film *Do the Right Thing* on video. Choose one or two scenes that are most interesting in terms of guilt, innocence, and "seeing for innocence." Watch these scenes repeatedly and write a careful analysis of how guilt, innocence, and seeing for innocence operate in the characters' (or filmmaker's) psychology.
9. Find out the graduation rate for African American students at your school. Then interview a faculty member or administrator to get her or his perceptions of why your school does or does not graduate Black students in proportionate numbers. If several students do this assignment, you can begin to analyze prevailing attitudes on campus.
10. At the end of this essay, Steele says, "No matter how badly it might have gone for us . . . we should have talked. We should have made the effort." Working in groups, role-play the conversation that might have occurred that night. How might you initiate such conversations on your campus? Is talk the only or best solution to the kinds of tensions Steele describes?

Gray Boys, Funky Aztecs, and Honorary Homegirls

LYNELL GEORGE

A quarter of a century after the civil rights movement some Americans, like Shelby Steele (p. 411), worry about the future of race relations in the United States while others, like the students Lynell George describes in this essay, feel ready to leave old definitions of race behind. According to George, teens in cities like Los Angeles are living on the edge of a new way of looking at race and ethnicity: they're part of a new melting pot that's merging their varied backgrounds into a new, composite culture. Although George expresses reservations about this cultural ideal, she clearly sees hope that a new generation of Americans has already begun learning how to bridge racial divides. George (b. 1962) was born and raised in Los Angeles where she writes for the LA Weekly *and the* Los Angeles Times, *the source of this essay. In addition to her work in journalism, she has published* No Crystal Stair: African Americans in the City of Angels *(1992).*

Let's call him "Perry."

If you grew up in Los Angeles (back when it was still hip to dub the mix "melting pot") and sat through a homeroom roll call sandwiching you somewhere between a Martinez, Masjedi, Matsuda, and Meizel, you knew one — but more than likely two. This Culver City "Perry," a classmate of mine, had Farrah Fawcett–feathered blond hair, moist blue-gray eyes, and a *Tiger Beat* dimple in his chin. Tall and gregarious, at first glimpse he seemed destined for the surfers' corner in the cafeteria — that tight tangle of dreamy adolescents who, in wet suits under their hooded Bajas, made their way down to Zuma Beach on slate-gray February mornings. Blaring Led Zeppelin, Boston, or Aerosmith, they trailed westward, away from the sun.

In broad-lapel Qianna shirts and denim flares, Perry, who looked less like Peter Frampton than Barry Gibb, embraced the electronic trickery of Parliament-Funkadelic, the East Coast soul of the Isley Brothers, or some Ohio Players midnight jam swelling from the boombox. He certainly never surfed. He shadowed the intricate steps of the Soul Train dancers, sat with the black basketball players in the back of the bus and attempted to chat up their little sisters in a sonorous baritone carefully fashioned after (who else but) Barry White.

"Oh, man, he's like K.C., you know, in the Sunshine Band," those who knew him would tease. But new faces would take a second look, then bristle and inevitably inquire: "Hasn't anybody told him he ain't black?"

"Chill out," Perry's best partner, the tallest, most imposing BMOC would always defend. "He's OK. He's gray. . . ." 5

After a while, most everyone forgot what Perry wasn't — even forgot that he was "gray": the hard-won badge worn by those white kids who seemed much more comfortable hovering in the space between.

It often worked other ways, too. White kids, honorary homeboys and homegirls who dressed like *cholos* and talked the grand talk about *mi vida loca.* Blue-blood black kids who surfed and played mean, tireless sets of country club tennis. Japanese kids who saved their lunch money to buy Forum floor seats for Earth, Wind and Fire spectaculars and were slipping everyone hallway high-fives during passing period long before it became pro-ball decorum.

Over the years, L.A.'s mix has only evolved into a much more complex jumble as immigration patterns shift and swell, as blurred neighborhood boundaries subdivide or change hands. However, Los Angeles (as shown by the chaos last spring)[1] is still a segregated city, despite such "border towns" as Culver City, Echo Park, or Carson and the disparate bodies that inhabit them, blending and sharing their cultural trappings and identifiers. These contiguous neighborhoods inspire intercultural dialogue. And those living at the fringes have (not without incident) found it necessary to learn something about adaptation. Dealing not in dualities but in pluralities, survival in this city requires a cultural dexterity heretofore unimagined.

L.A. has metamorphosed into a crazy incubator, and the children who live on these streets and submit to their rhythm rise up as exquisite hothouse flowers. They beget their own language, style, codes — a shorthand mode of communication and identification. It's more than learning a handy salutation in Tagalog, being conversant in street slang or sporting hip-hop-inspired styles. This sort of cultural exchange requires active participation and demands that one press past the superficial toward a more meaningful discourse and understanding.

By no means a full-blown movement, these young people, a small coterie, exhibit large-scale possibilities. Unaware and without fanfare, they are compelling examples of how effortless and yet edifying reaching out can be. 10

Their free-form amalgamation billows up in street style (like the "Gangsta"/*cholo*-style baggy chinos and Pendletons that hit the mainstream fashion pages a few months back) as well as in street music. Latino rapper Kid Frost shook it up with his icy, tough-as-nails Public Enemy delivery, then sharpened the edges with staccato snatches in Spanish. For raw power, post-punk badboys the Red Hot Chili Peppers don't have a thing on their counterparts, the Badbrains.

Recently, the Funky Aztecs have taken the baton. Their new recording, "Chicano Blues," offers samples from soul crooner Bill Withers while vamp-

[1]*the chaos last spring:* The L.A. uprising of 1992 following the acquittal of four police officers in the Rodney King beating case.

ing on traditional twelve-bar delta blues. When not dipping into reggae dub-style or funk, Merciless, Indio, and Loco pay homage to the rich California melange with the raucous single, "Salsa *con* Soul Food."

For Merciless, who's nineteen, the mixing was almost inevitable. His family moved to an all-black neighborhood in Vallejo when he was nine, and before he shaved his head a year ago, "I had real curly hair," he says. "Just, I guess, by the way I dress, a lot of people mix me up with either being black or mixed with black." And the rhythms of hip-hop were a break from the street. "My Chicano partners they were all into their little gangs, you know, their little Notre XIV. Everyone was talking about gangster stuff: 'I'ma kill you,' 'I gotta gun,' 'this bitch is my "ho."' But I wasn't into that, I was more like expressing myself politically. It was mainly my black friends who were into rapping and deejaying and stuff like that.

"It's a trip because my own race trips off me. I even got chased out of my own barrio. But the brothers are real cool with me. It's not that I side on them or whatever because my race always puts me down. It's not like that, but if you're cool to me, I don't care what color you are — I'm going to give you that love right back."

Lives and attitudes like that wreak havoc with stubborn stereotypes and 15
archaic notions about what it is to be African-American, Latino, Asian-American, or Anglo in a quickly transfiguring metropolitan center. In a recent Village Voice Literary Supplement, L.A. expatriate Paul Beatty eloquently shared a vision of home: "Growing up in Los Angeles," writes Beatty, "I couldn't help noticing that language was closely tied to skin color" but not exclusively. "Black folks was either 'fittin'' or 'fixin'' to go to Taco Bell. . . . The four Asian kids I knew talked black. . . . When I started writing, I realized that me and my friends had difficulty processing the language. We felt like foreigners because no one understood us. We were a gang of verbal mulattoes. Black kids with black brains but white mouths — inbred with some cognitively dissonant Mexicans who didn't speak Spanish and looked crazy at anyone who thought they did."

Some argue that this sort of mixing dilutes culture and creates innumerable lost souls; but many of those who live it see this sharing as realistically inclusive and ultimately enriching — so long as one holds on to integral bits and pieces of one's own. Those more optimistic hear rumblings in and of this New Age patois as harbingers; these young people are well-equipped bellwethers of the new cultural hybrids of Los Angeles.

The mixing starts earlier and earlier, as Jai Lee Wong of the L.A. County Human Relations Commission points out: "My child is four and a half and is fluent in Spanish because his baby-sitter teaches it to him." He tends, she explains, to identify people by the language they speak, not by their racial or ethnic designations. "If they speak English, they are English or American. If they speak Korean, they're Korean," Wong says. "And even though his father is Chinese and speaks only English, my son thinks he's American. For him it's not based on race or ethnicity. He hears me and his father sitting around identifying people by race and it confuses him. Then one day he started talking about that 'green kid over there.' Turns out that he was talking about a white kid wearing a green shirt." Race is a concept not beyond but perhaps already behind him, Wong realizes; a clumsy piece of baggage that already weighs him down.

The new world view? "It's a people thing," Merciless says. "It's not a black or brown or white or red or orange thing. It's a people thing. We all just need to grow up."

On a recent postcard-bright Saturday afternoon, performance artist Danny Tisdale, assuming his flashy alter ego, Tracey Goodman, sets up a folding table with a matte-black cassette deck and a small P.A. system. Microphone in hand, he begins "hawking" a few specialty products for people of color: skin bleach, rainbow-hued hair extensions, and the "new" Contours Sculpting System ("used for refining the nose, lips and buttocks") to inquisitive Santa Barbara Paseo Nuevo mall denizens. Eyes concealed behind inky black shades, Tisdale/Goodman shouts out carnival-barker style: "Transitions, Incorporated!" just above Frank Sinatra's live, over-the-top rendition of "New York, New York." He promises "the ticket to success" as he displays photos of Michael Jackson, the smiling and yet-unaltered preteen juxtaposed with the blanched and angular post-"Thriller" visage.

Taking the proceedings as the real thing, an African-American woman 20
in a pin-striped suit and patent-leather sling-back heels breaks free from the circle, approaching the display at a quick clip. Interrupting the pitch, she requests a card, asks if surgery is at all involved. For a moment, most everyone gathered around the table incorrectly assumes she's a clever plant, a perfect foil. But as the woman becomes more insistent, arms flailing, voice ascending several octaves, Tisdale's manner appears less certain. He's fresh out of snappy retorts; smiles vanish slowly from the surrounding faces. "But will this really work for me?" she wants to know. "Will it truly help?" She's tried so many others.

The piece makes some people angry and renders others silent and bewildered. On a basic level it forces participants to confront, on the spot, the scope and texture of that uncomfortable quandary: What should one give up to achieve success in contemporary American society? The varied responses of those critiquing from the sidelines mirror the real-life incertitude of people enmeshed in this cultural gamble. A prime place in the mainstream isn't won without a price, or without compromise.

What happens when what was carried over from the Old Country becomes cumbersome, archaic, better to be swept under the rug lest anyone see? It is that loss of organic culture that sits at the heart of many debates about cultural accommodation. Most frequently, we see the conflict in terms of whitewash assimilation versus the "who stole the soul"–style wholesale cultural appropriation. Shelby Steele and Clarence Thomas[2] are trotted around (depending on the camp) as products or "victims" of the former. And rappers the Beastie Boys, Vanilla Ice, or Young Black Teenagers (an all-white rap crew) are seen as the latter: opportunists who pilfer the million-dollar beats and mimic the belligerent stance of this black urban art form without having the cultural understanding or sensitivity to carry it off effectively.

But even the most seemingly clear-cut examples of cultural compromise — like the mainstream-bound black woman tugging at Danny Tisdale's coat — are shaded or haunted by a wide array of weighty ramifications based on that choice, the consequences of turning one's back on one's culture. ". . . Blacks who imitate whites continue to regard whiteness with suspicion, fear, and even hatred," says professor and culture critic Bell Hooks in her latest book, *Black Looks,* revealing just one nuance in the many hues of assimilation — this one with a conditional cultural safety net woven in. And Hooks suggests that what appears to be, at face, an embrace, is something much more complex, even duplicitous; an ingenious, sophisticated tool fashioned especially for urban survival.

L.A., after all, is not at all the Shangri-La it often presents itself as being, especially when it comes to ethnic/cultural relations. Hate crimes, cross-cultural gang violence, ethnic "nationalists" such as skinheads, randomly hurled racial epithets along city byways are all a part of the city's fiber, woven in among flashes of accord and affinity. Xenophobia fueled by ignorance, rigid class stratification and skewed and outmoded media representations have all played a part in stoking interracial tensions in this city as well as across the nation.

That has helped make assimilation, for people of color, a weighty cul- 25
tural gamble, a risky compromise in the journey toward success within the American status quo. Nowadays, asking one to assume bits and pieces of another's culture at the expense of one's own is viewed as an exercise out of the question, especially when attacks from without are so pointed and regaining what was lost in the past has been so painful.

But alternative forms of assimilation — for example, that of slipping in and out of multiple cultural identities — don't demand that people reject their own identifiers. They stress inclusion. In light of L.A.'s rapidly metamorphosing demographics, this drift is likely to become not the exception but the rule.

The mere fact of L.A.'s diversity makes the contentious concept of assimilation far less cut-and-dried than it was in the past, when widespread use of the term *melting pot* suggested that a soul branded with "minority" status in the United States had to "melt down" his or her cultural trap-

[2] *Shelby Steele and Clarence Thomas:* African American author (see p. 411) and Supreme Court justice who have been criticized by some as cultural sell-outs.

pings—language, dress, religious ritual or even body type—to aspire to the American ideal.

Here, where Central and South America meet the Pacific Rim and West Indies, the definitions of what it means to be black, white, brown, or yellow blur, and fitting in requires an entirely different set of tools and techniques. Paule Cruz Takash, a UC San Diego anthropologist and ethnic studies professor, notes that "assimilation is not a one-way street," with everyone striving to adopt Anglo culture. As the phrase "Ellis Island West" spices news reports about the growing lines winding around the city's Immigration and Naturalization Service office, the question of assimilation becomes broader, takes on new definitions.

Ironically enough, in the past two decades, the media and other information arteries, traditional tools for stratifying cultures with the uncomplicated, and erroneous, shorthand of stereotypes, have been invaluable tools for breaking down stereotypes and reworking prevailing theories about cultural identity. New mixes take shape at monster movie-plexes, superbookstores, and the alternative glitz of underground clubs (and the easy access to them). The ears and eyes take it all in—and the brain then reassembles it, gives it new form.

And an increasing number of L.A. newcomers embody and advance the 30
recombinant culture. Nahom Tassew, a seventeen-year-old Ethiopian who's a junior at Belmont High, came to the United States knowing "just what I saw on movies and TV" about African-Americans. "I thought if I came here, I'd have to become a thief," he says, "or that was what people would think I was." After two and a half years, he has a new attitude ("I saw that [African-Americans at Belmont] were people . . . that there were good people and bad people, that every race has good people") as well as friends from Mexico, Guatemala, El Salvador, Japan, and China. And he's studying Spanish. "I need some Spanish words," he says. Just what will emerge from these admixtures is difficult to say. Tassew, at least, will acquire an early-age sophistication, learning classroom English along with the street Spanish of his neighborhood, finding astonishing cultural parallels (from salutation rituals to food) with his Chinese friends. In that environment, he and others have found, there is no room for xenophobia.

Principals and their support staffs at high schools around the city have been looking closely at their campuses' rapidly altering idiosyncratic mixes and the way students like Tassew work within them. At Carson's Banning High, principal Augustine Herrera has watched the numbers shift dramatically over the past six years. Upon his arrival, the school was 57 percent Latino. That ratio has changed drastically: Banning's population is now 72 percent Latino, 20 percent African-American, and 8 percent Asian/Pacific Islander. "For the most part they get along but I don't want to sugarcoat it." Herrera says: "We have the same problems that the city faces. We have kids who don't get along. What goes on in the city goes on on campus . . . a mindless name-calling that sometimes degenerates into a fight."

Race riots on L.A. high school campuses last fall were physical manifestations of city frictions at the boiling point. Students battling over abstracts or what, at face, seems frivolous — like the kind of music played at a Friday night dance.

"For many, it is the first time they have to mix," Herrera says, and conflicts and more positive exchanges are inevitable. "One feeder junior high is predominantly Latino, one is predominantly black — they must interact. At first there is a sense of distrust, so being in this environment is a good experience for them."

Assistant principal Bea Lamothe has noticed that the hip-hop-inspired cross colors, usually associated with black students, have caught on with the Samoans and Latinos this year, and she's carefully observed what is a quieter form of cultural exchange and communication as well. "There are a few African-Americans who live on the Eastside in Wilmington who wear white T-shirts and khakis and speak Spanish." Students are often unaware that they are mixing codes or modes, she says. They're living their lives, just trying to fit in.

At this age, these adolescents — native-born or immigrant — are not 35
looking for, or relying on, words to describe or define their lives. They prefer action over theory. For many of them, it's working. And like the music that fuels them and serves as an anthem: It's all in the mix.

The students have unfurled a cloth banner and hung it high above the stage of Belmont High School's cavernous auditorium. In electric, wild-style lettering it proclaims: La Raza Unida (The United Race). As the SRO crowd mills around her, principal Martha Bin stands on the sidelines, blond hair folded into an elegant updo, her walkie-talkie poised in a freshly manicured hand. This year, voting to pass on the usual Columbus Day assembly, the student body, Bin explains, chose instead to pay homage to the campus's Latin cultural mix — spanning several countries and continents.

In what looks like an elaborate show-and-tell, students bring bits and pieces of their culture to Belmont's stage. Since the auditorium won't accommodate the 4,000-plus student body at one seating, there are two assemblies — one morning, another in the afternoon. The second performance begins with several girls in frothy turquoise dresses, their partners in dark, pressed suits, displaying *rancheras.* Later come the *cumbias,* a mambo and an elaborate dance performed with lit candles that originated in Peru. Capping the show is a trio in below-the-knee, extra-large baggy shorts, who rap and joke in English, Spanish, and French.

"We are a school of immigrants," says Bin, sitting down for a moment in a quiet classroom next to the auditorium, her walkie-talkie close by. "Many of the black kids are Hispanic. We have Chinese-Cubans. We have Koreans who speak Portuguese." Belmont, one of the largest high schools in the nation, with 4,500 students on campus, buses out another 3,000 to accommodate the crush of the Temple/Beaudry/Echo Park district youth population from which it draws. Bin says 78 percent of the student body is Latino; the rest is a mix that includes citizens of Romania, Colombia, Armenia, Ethiopia, and Biafra. "You sit them together," Bin says, "they just have to get along — *conjunto* — together."

William Han, an eighteen-year-old Belmont senior, thinks he knows why. "Students who attend Belmont," he says, "are first-generation American students, whereas at other schools they are second or third. We are immigrants. This is our first experience." Han knows the struggle to adjust. It was just four years ago that he and his Korean parents moved here from their home in Brazil. A bright and talkative "American" teen, he wears an oversized jersey with "William" embroidered in green, green-gray pressed slacks, and black sneakers. His black hair is close-cropped and sticks up like the bristles of a stiff brush. Like many of the kids around him, he's something of a citizen of the world — he speaks Portuguese, Spanish, English, and Korean. "Things at Belmont are honest," he says. In the common fight to cope with a new culture, "people accept you for who you are."

40 Because of the intricate cultural mix surrounding the school, there are concerns and needs that are unique to Belmont. "Our ESL students tend to be Spanish speaking, but a lot of Asians speak Spanish before English on our campus because they hear it in their neighborhood," says assistant principal Rosa Morley, herself an embodiment of ethnic and cultural blending. (She has Chinese parents but grew up in Cuba. Fluent in Spanish, she feels most connected to Cuban culture.)

"The kids feel that the whole world is like this," Bin says, and that can be a problem later on. "They have some difficulty when they move out of this environment and are no longer the majority."

"We don't tell them this isn't the real world," Morley says. "They will find out sooner or later. We are sheltering them in a sense but cannot control what life will bring for them."

By college, one doesn't see as many "Culver City Perrys." The university, for those who make it, is often the startling baptism, a reawakening or first-awakening of self. Students moving out of ethnically/racially diverse environments and into the austere university setting come face to face with cultural stratification. It is, for many, the first time that they are called upon to choose sides or feel a need to become politically active.

The Institute for the Study of Social Change, based at UC Berkeley, reported on diversity at the university level a year ago in a study called the Diversity Project. The study's goal was to address "a vital and constantly unfolding development emerging in American social life," focusing primarily on demographic changes in the country and how they affect interpersonal communication on college campuses. There would be no solution to the problems of diversity, the report stressed, as long as we think in polar terms. The extremes of "assimilation to a single dominant culture where differences merge and disappear vs. a situation where isolated and self-segregated groups [retreat] into . . . enclaves" don't work, researchers concluded. The report was based on sixty-nine focus-group interviews with 291 UC Berkeley students.

The report advises a "third and more viable" option: "the simultaneous 45
possibility of strong ethnic and racial identities (including ethnically homogeneous affiliations and friendships) *alongside* a public participation of multiracial and multiethnic contacts that enriches the public and social sphere of life."

In testimonials in the Diversity Project, students spoke frankly about the problems of bridging two worlds and the inexorable pressure to fit in. An Asian-American male was traumatized when presented with a completely alien environment: "I was totally unaccustomed to being in [a] social situation where only Asians were there. So I was completely lost. . . . I got so frustrated, I rejected . . . my Asian-American identity and had a lot of Hispanic friends."

In this period of self-searching, what will help these students realize this "third experience"—recognizing diversity while maintaining their own distinctive cultural identity—is to develop the cultural equivalent of achieving bilingual or multilingual proficiency, to be sensitive enough to adapt to one's surroundings without losing sight of self.

This concept of cultural pluralism—where each group makes an influential and duly recognized contribution to American society—may seem naive or merely whimsical, but in light of the tremendous cultural shift, it is tenable. "Racial and ethnic identities are always formed in dialogue with one another," says George Lipsitz, professor of ethnic studies at UC San Diego and author of "Time Passages," a collection of essays on diversity and contemporary pop culture. "So to be Chicano in L.A. means to have a long engagement with black culture. What kind of Anglo you are depends on what group of color you're in dialogue with."

Lipsitz has noted that this mixing once was a more class-based phenomenon, but that drift has altered dramatically in recent years. "When I see desegregated groups of graffiti writers, one of the things that strikes me is that they're also mixed by class," he says. "Style leaders are working-class kids who present themselves as poorer than they are but they have a suburban following. One writer told me: 'Y'know, I go down to the Belmont Tunnel, I go out to the motor yard in Santa Monica, I meet a guy who lives in Beverly Hills, I meet someone who went to Europe last summer.' It's the way they expand what's open to them."

Lipsitz doesn't see this mixing as a grievous threat or as diluting culture, 50
as some nationalists do. People find allies wherever they find them, he believes. "For example, there is a group of graffiti writers who call themselves 'ALZA'—which stands for African, Latino, Zulu, and Anglo. ALZA, Lipsitz says, is Chicano slang for *rise up*. They found each other. Nobody set this up. Nobody put an ad in the paper. They look for spaces that are what we

call 'multicultural.' I don't think that they ever think to look at it in those ways. But there's a sense of interest and excitement and delight in difference that makes them look for more complexity."

But painting this phenomena as some sort of "we are the world" harmonious culture fest would be erroneous. Like those in the Diversity Project, Lipsitz has witnessed some of the more painful outcomes of "fitting nowhere," what isolation and alienation can do to a young person's spirit and soul. "I've talked to many students who are either from racially mixed backgrounds or who have what they consider to be an odd history—maybe they were the only black student in a white high school or something like that," he explains. "Then at the university it seems that there is an inside that they are not part of, and there is no obvious subgroup that they can join.

"They don't feel comfortable maybe with African-American culture. Or there are Chicanos who come in but they don't speak Spanish well enough for MEChA [a college-level Latino political organization]; or there are Asian-Americans who are Korean or Vietnamese, and the campus is dominated by Japanese- or Chinese-Americans." It is their love of difference, danger, and heterogeneity that brings them together. When a singer like George Clinton comes along—who's too black for the whites, too white for the blacks—"in a way he's talking to people whose lives are like that."

Susan Straight titled her first short-story collection after one of her favorite herky-jerky, George Clinton–sired Parliament-Funkadelic jams, "Aqua Boogie." Maybe it was something about the rhythm. But probably it was the music's quicksilver spirit—arrogantly individual and all over the map. When Straight's "Aquaboogie" hit the stores, book reviews, and small journals almost two years ago, she inspired quite a few double takes. In her stark, sober portrait, her blond hair framed a steely face out of which light eyes stared boldly into the camera. A novel in short stories, *Aquaboogie* finds its center in a depressed Southern California locale called Rio Seco and its characters among the working-class blacks who live and die there.

The writing—eloquent, sensitive, and honest—wouldn't have riled so many except for the fact that Susan Straight is white, one of the few white artists giving voice to what's considered to be a black experience. "If I was a lousy writer and I was trying to write about a neighborhood like the one I'm writing about and had all these details wrong . . . then I don't think I deserve to be published," Straight says. "I know my little corner of the world and that's what I write about. And I think I do a good job. I don't fit into a box," she adds with that same tough, unblinking stare, "and see this is a big problem for people. It's like everywhere I go, which box do I fit into? I don't. Sorry."

Straight, who balances a UC Riverside lecturing position with writing, 55
leading various local writing workshops and household duties, was born in Riverside. She still makes her home there with her husband (her high school

sweetheart, who is black) and two daughters in a sunny, rambling California Craftsman on a wide, tree-lined street. For Straight, fitting in was more of an issue once she left her Riverside friends and environs.

"I went to USC straight from high school. I got a scholarship—my Dad was unemployed at the time. I loved going to USC — once I found some friends," she recalls with a laugh. "When I first got there it was like I talked funny, I came from a bad neighborhood, I had a T-shirt that said 'Itsy-Bit' on the back in that Gothic writing. USC was a really scary place for me coming from Riverside, where everything was country."

She ended up hanging out with athletes—mostly black football players from places like Pomona and Inglewood. "Those were my friends," she says. The problem didn't end at USC's boundaries. It shadowed her cross-country, shot up at the University of Massachusetts, Amherst, where she was constantly embroiled in fiction workshop debates, then later took shape and form in the publishing world when she sent stories to *The New Yorker* and *The Atlantic*. "Of course everybody thought I was black, which I didn't know, but I understand," says Straight. "They just didn't want to read about that kind of stuff. They had problems with the dialect, they had problems with the subject. It was a little bit 'harsh.' One person wrote back: 'Your world view is very bleak. . . .' I thought, 'Man, I'm sorry. Fix the world, and then my view won't be so bleak.' "

What Straight was attempting to do with her body of work made some blacks angry, some whites a shade of uncomfortable that some found difficult to articulate—people like her first agent, who took it upon herself to chastise her client soundly. "She said: 'I didn't know you were white.' And then she said: 'I think you're deceiving people.' She sent all my stories back and wrote me a big, old long letter about '. . . the American public isn't ready for something like me. . . .' She really thought that I should be writing about something different," she says with a shrug, palms upturned. "So what am I supposed to do? Go back and get born again? Have different parents? Grow up in a different place? Marry a different man? Then I'll be writing about different things, right? That's a big order." Confronting her "bleak world view," Straight started writing mostly out of a sense of frustration and a need to take some sort of definitive action.

"Look at me," she says. "I weigh ninety-nine pounds. I mean what can I do? I can't bring my friends back from the dead. I can't stop people from doing what they're doing. Drugs have been a big problem. I've so many friends who have no brains left, and that's not from rock, that's from angel dust. I thought: 'Well I can go home and just write these little stories.' " Her "little" stories deal with enormous and grave issues—death, drug addiction, poverty, abandonment — but they also speak to nurturing aspects, the strength of black family structure, about love, about relationships between fathers and sons, mothers and daughters, community resilience. Not *the* black experience, Straight stresses, but a "particular" black experience.

What rests at the core of understanding, Straight believes, is reaching 60
out and treating others with respect. "People have always said that black

people know white people much better than white people know black people, because it's a matter of survival. And that's what I grew up hearing," says Straight. "Now being black is in vogue as far as the movies and stuff. Maybe it should be a matter of survival for white people to know how black people live now." As UC San Diego's Lipsitz notes, "You look around to see who has something to teach you," a new Golden Rule that can be looked upon as an informal paradigm for Twenty-first–Century survival. Kids on the borders of several cultures are "trying to be honest in a dishonest world," he says. "I think if something good were to happen, it would come from them. I think that they're trying to live a life that's not a lie."

Those who might be viewed by some as having "odd histories" because they've spent their lives juggling codes or responding to the various influences within them are breaking down walls and erecting sturdy bridges through the mere act of living their lives. Granted, this vision appears mere chimera, almost utopian. But it is, for them, proving to be an integral component of psychic survival. In this period of uneasy transition, complicated by overwhelmingly rapid change, young people ride the periphery, and their lives do impressive battle with notions of a now-archaic "norm." But their quiet revolution is fueled by much more than simply the adolescent ache to belong. It is a more honest, eyes-wide-open way to reach out and greet a world as confounding as they are.

Engaging the Text

1. What, according to George, does it mean to be "gray"? How does someone become a "gray boy," a "funky aztec," or an "honorary homegirl"?
2. Review several examples of the kind of "recombinant culture" that George describes. Can you think of examples of this new cultural style you have observed in your neighborhood, on campus, or in the media?
3. Working in small groups discuss whether or not it is possible to adopt multiple cultural styles, as George suggests, without losing your own cultural identity.
4. How does George explain the increase in racially motivated conflict within the new urban melting pot? Can you offer any additional explanations for the increase of racial tension within the new "recombinant culture"?
5. What, according to George, is the impact of college on the complex cultural identities of many entering students?

Exploring Connections

6. Review the theories of prejudice outlined by Michael Omi and Howard Winant (p. 356) and Vincent N. Parrillo (p. 376). How might they respond to George's assertion that the "concept of race" is already "behind" some young Americans — already a "clumsy piece of baggage" from the past that weighs them down?
7. Write a letter from Adrienne Rich (p. 365) to any one of the teens that George

mentions in which she offers her observations and advice about living with multiple identities. How might George's teens respond to Rich?

8. Write a dialogue between Shelby Steele (p. 411) and Lynell George on the future of race relations in the United States.

Extending the Critical Context

9. Collect as many media images (from films, TV shows, ads, music videos and lyrics, etc.) as you can that reflect the "recombinant culture" George discusses. Are these images evidence of a genuine cultural shift occurring in the United States or is all this talk of a "new melting pot" just a marketing ploy, a matter of fashion? What evidence do you find, if any, that America's "racial categories" are actually changing?
10. Write a journal entry describing your personal experience of moving from the culture(s) of your neighborhood to the culture of college. To what extent does your experience confirm George's claims that students in college often must deal with "cultural stratification" for the first time in their lives and that they are often forced to "choose sides"? Share your experiences in small groups and discuss whether you feel college works to polarize the racial, cultural, and economic differences between students.
11. Recently there has been growing controversy about whether it is possible or appropriate to speak with authority about the experience of a group whose sexual, racial, economic, and cultural background differs from one's own. In this selection, George presents the case of Susan Straight, a white writer who has published a collection of stories featuring the experiences of African American characters. Do you agree that Straight represents a "quiet revolution" in American society? Would it be equally possible for a white professor to teach African American studies? For a man to write with authority about the experiences of women?

La conciencia de la mestiza[1]/ *Towards a New Consciousness*

Gloria Anzaldúa

When Gloria Anzaldúa speaks of a "new consciousness," she's talking about creating a new self, about experiencing the world in a different way. She envisions a cultural evolution bringing new understandings of race, gender, class, and nationality. And in writing of the mestiza *consciousness and the multiple cultures from which it arises, she uses a new language — a*

[1] *la conciencia de la mestiza: Mestiza* consciousness; consciousness of the *mestiza* (a woman of mixed racial heritage).

hybrid of English, Castilian Spanish, a North Mexican dialect, Tex-Mex, and the Indian language Nahuatl. Anzaldúa is editor of Haciendo Caras: Making Face/Making Soul *(1990) and coeditor of* This Bridge Called My Back: Writings by Radical Women of Color *(1983). This selection is from her book* Borderlands = La Frontera: The New Mestiza *(1987). Although we've provided translations, we suggest that you not consult these in your first reading. Concentrate instead on Anzaldúa's main points and on her innovative blend of argument and poetry, of myth and manifesto.*

Por la mujer de mi raza
hablará el espíritu.[2]

José Vasconcelos, Mexican philosopher, envisaged *una raza mestiza, una mezcla de razas afines, una raza de color — la primera raza síntesis del globo.*[3] He called it a cosmic race, *la raza cósmica,* a fifth race embracing the four major races of the world.[4] Opposite to the theory of the pure Aryan,[5] and to the policy of racial purity that white America practices, his theory is one of inclusivity. At the confluence of two or more genetic streams, with chromosomes constantly "crossing over," this mixture of races, rather than resulting in an inferior being, provides hybrid progeny, a mutable, more malleable species with a rich gene pool. From this racial, ideological, cultural, and biological cross-pollinization, an "alien" consciousness is presently in the making — a new *mestiza* consciousness, *una conciencia de mujer.*[6] It is a consciousness of the Borderlands.

Una lucha de fronteras / A Struggle of Borders

Because I, a *mestiza,*
continually walk out of one culture
and into another,
because I am in all cultures at the same time,
alma entre dos mundos, tres, cuatro,
me zumba la cabeza con lo contradictorio.
Estoy norteada por todas las voces que me hablan
simultáneamente.[7]

[2]This is my own "take off" on José Vasconcelos's idea. José Vasconcelos, *La Raza Cósmica: Misión de la Raza Ibero-Americana* (México: Aguilar S.A. de Ediciones, 1961). [Author's note] *Por la mujer de mi raza . . . :* The Spirit shall speak through the women of my race.

[3]*una raza mestiza . . . :* A multiracial race, a mixture of kindred races, a race of color, the first synthetic race of the world.

[4]Vasconcelos. [Author's note]

[5]*the theory of the pure Aryan:* The myth espoused by Adolf Hitler and others of the racial superiority of white northern Europeans.

[6]*una conciencia de mujer:* A female consciousness.

[7]*alma entre dos mundos . . . :* A soul caught between two, three, four worlds. My head aches with contradictions. I'm led north by all the voices that speak to me simultaneously.

The ambivalence from the clash of voices results in mental and emotional states of perplexity. Internal strife results in insecurity and indecisiveness. The mestiza's dual or multiple personality is plagued by psychic restlessness.

In a constant state of mental nepantilism, an Aztec word meaning torn between ways, *la mestiza* is a product of the transfer of the cultural and spiritual values of one group to another. Being tricultural, monolingual, bilingual, or multilingual, speaking a patois,[8] and in a state of perpetual transition, the *mestiza* faces the dilemma of the mixed breed: which collectivity does the daughter of a darkskinned mother listen to?

El choque de un alma atrapado entre el mundo del espíritu y el mundo de la técnica a veces la deja entullada.[9] Cradled in one culture, sandwiched between two cultures, straddling all three cultures and their value systems, *la mestiza* undergoes a struggle of flesh, a struggle of borders, an inner war. Like all people, we perceive the version of reality that our culture communicates. Like others having or living in more than one culture, we get multiple, often opposing messages. The coming together of two self-consistent but habitually incompatible frames of reference[10] causes *un choque,* a cultural collision.

5 Within us and within *la cultura chicana,*[11] commonly held beliefs of the white culture attack commonly held beliefs of the Mexican culture, and both attack commonly held beliefs of the indigenous culture. Subconsciously, we see an attack on ourselves and our beliefs as a threat and we attempt to block with a counterstance.

But it is not enough to stand on the opposite river bank, shouting questions, challenging patriarchal, white conventions. A counterstance locks one into a duel of oppressor and oppressed; locked in mortal combat, like the cop and the criminal, both are reduced to a common denominator of violence. The counterstance refutes the dominant culture's views and beliefs, and, for this, it is proudly defiant. All reaction is limited by, and dependent on, what it is reacting against. Because the counterstance stems from a problem with authority — outer as well as inner — it's a step towards liberation from cultural domination. But it is not a way of life. At some point, on our way to a new consciousness, we will have to leave the opposite bank, the split between the two mortal combatants somehow healed so that we are on both shores at once and, at once, see through serpent and eagle eyes.[12] Or

[8]*patois:* Nonstandard dialect.

[9]*El choque de una alma atrapado . . . :* The struggle of a soul trapped between the world of the spirit and the world of technology sometimes leaves it paralyzed.

[10]Arthur Koestler termed this "bisociation." Albert Rothenberg, *The Creative Process in Art, Science, and Other Fields* (Chicago, IL: University of Chicago Press, 1979), 12. [Author's note]

[11]*la cultura chicana:* Chicana culture. Elsewhere in *Borderlands,* Anzaldúa writes, "*La Cultura chicana* identifies with the mother (Indian) rather than with the father (Spanish). Our faith is rooted in indigenous attributes, images, symbols, magic, and myth" (Chapter 3).

[12]*see through serpent and eagle eyes:* "The eagle symbolizes the spirit (as the sun, the

perhaps we will decide to disengage from the dominant culture, write it off altogether as a lost cause, and cross the border into a wholly new and separate territory. Or we might go another route. The possibilities are numerous once we decide to act and not react.

A Tolerance for Ambiguity

These numerous possibilities leave *la mestiza* floundering in uncharted seas. In perceiving conflicting information and points of view, she is subjected to a swamping of her psychological borders. She has discovered that she can't hold concepts or ideas in rigid boundaries. The borders and walls that are supposed to keep the undesirable ideas out are entrenched habits and patterns of behavior; these habits and patterns are the enemy within. Rigidity means death. Only by remaining flexible is she able to stretch the psyche[13] horizontally and vertically. *La mestiza* constantly has to shift out of habitual formations; from convergent thinking, analytical reasoning that tends to use rationality to move toward a single goal (a Western mode), to divergent thinking,[14] characterized by movement away from set patterns and goals and toward a more whole perspective, one that includes rather than excludes.

The new *mestiza* copes by developing a tolerance for contradictions, a tolerance for ambiguity. She learns to be an Indian in Mexican culture, to be Mexican from an Anglo point of view. She learns to juggle cultures. She has a plural personality, she operates in a pluralistic mode—nothing is thrust out, the good the bad and the ugly, nothing rejected, nothing abandoned. Not only does she sustain contradictions, she turns the ambivalence into something else.

She can be jarred out of ambivalence by an intense, and often painful, emotional event which inverts or resolves the ambivalence. I'm not sure exactly how. The work takes place underground—subconsciously. It is work that the soul performs. That focal point or fulcrum, that juncture where the *mestiza* stands, is where phenomena tend to collide. It is where the possibility of uniting all that is separate occurs. This assembly is not one where severed or separated pieces merely come together. Nor is it a balancing of opposing powers. In attempting to work out a synthesis, the self has added a third element which is greater than the sum of its severed parts. That third element is a new consciousness — a *mestiza* consciousness — and though it is a source of intense pain, its energy comes from continual creative motion that keeps breaking down the unitary aspect of each new paradigm.

---

father); the serpent symbolizes the soul (as the earth, the mother). Together, they symbolize the struggle between the spiritual/celestial/male and the underworld/earth/feminine" (*Borderlands*, Chapter 1).

[13]*the psyche:* The soul or self.

[14]In part, I derive my definitions for "convergent" and "divergent" thinking from Rothenberg, 12–13. [Author's note]

En unas pocas centurias,[15] the future will belong to the *mestiza.* Because 10
the future depends on the breaking down of the paradigms, it depends on the straddling of two or more cultures. By creating a new mythos — that is, a change in the way we perceive reality, the way we see ourselves, and the ways we behave — *la mestiza* creates a new consciousness.

The work of *mestiza* consciousness is to break down the subject-object duality that keeps her a prisoner and to show in the flesh and through the images in her work how duality is transcended. The answer to the problem between the white race and the colored, between males and females, lies in healing the split that originates in the very foundation of our lives, our culture, our languages, our thoughts. A massive uprooting of dualistic thinking in the individual and collective consciousness is the beginning of a long struggle, but one that could, in our best hopes, bring us to the end of rape, of violence, of war. . . .

El camino de la mestiza
The Mestiza Way

> Caught between the sudden contraction, the breath sucked in and the endless space, the brown woman stands still, looks at the sky. She decides to go down, digging her way along the roots of trees. Sifting through the bones, she shakes them to see if there is any marrow in them. Then, touching the dirt to her forehead, to her tongue, she takes a few bones, leaves the rest in their burial place.
>
> She goes through her backpack, keeps her journal and address book, throws away the muni-bart metromaps.[16] The coins are heavy and they go next, then the greenbacks flutter through the air. She keeps her knife, can opener, and eyebrow pencil. She puts bones, pieces of bark, *hierbas,*[17] eagle feather, snakeskin, tape recorder, the rattle and drum in her pack and she sets out to become the complete *tolteca.*[18]

Her first step is to take inventory. *Despojando, desgranando, quitando paja.*[19] Just what did she inherit from her ancestors? This weight on her back — which is the baggage from the Indian mother, which the baggage from the Spanish father, which the baggage from the Anglo?

Pero es difícil[20] differentiating between *lo heredado, lo adquirido, lo impuesto.*[21] She puts history through a sieve, winnows out the lies, looks at

[15]*En unas pocas centurias:* In a few centuries.

[16]*muni-bart metromaps:* Maps of bus and rail transportation in the San Francisco Bay area.

[17]*hierbas:* Herbs.

[18]Gina Valdés, *Puentes y Fronteras: Coplas Chicanas* (Los Angeles, CA: Castle Lithograph, 1982), 2. [Author's note] *tolteca:* The Toltec empire predates the Aztec in ancient Mexico. Anzaldúa associates the Toltecs with more woman-centered culture and religion than those of the warlike, patriarchal Aztecs.

[19]*Despojando, desgranando, quitando paja:* Stripping, removing the grain or the straw.

[20]*Pero es difícil:* But it is difficult.

[21]*le heredado, lo adquirido, lo impuesto:* The inherited, the acquired, the imposed.

the forces that we as a race, as women, have been a part of. *Luego bota lo que no vale, los desmientos, los desencuentos, el embrutecimiento. Aguarda el juicio, hondo y enraízado, de la gente antigua.*[22] This step is a conscious rupture with all oppressive traditions of all cultures and religions. She communicates that rupture, documents the struggle. She reinterprets history and, using new symbols, she shapes new myths. She adopts new perspectives toward the darkskinned, women, and queers. She strengthens her tolerance (and intolerance) for ambiguity. She is willing to share, to make herself vulnerable to foreign ways of seeing and thinking. She surrenders all notions of safety, of the familiar. Deconstruct, construct. She becomes a *nahual*,[23] able to transform herself into a tree, a coyote, into another person. She learns to transform the small "I" into the total Self. *Se hace moldeadora de su alma. Según la concepción que tiene de sí misma, así será.*[24]

Que no se nos olvide los hombres[25]

> *"Tú no sirves pa' nada*[26] —
> you're good for nothing.
> *Eres pura vieja."*[27]

"You're nothing but a woman" means you are defective. Its opposite is to be *un macho.* The modern meaning of the word "machismo," as well as the concept, is actually an Anglo invention. For men like my father, being "macho" meant being strong enough to protect and support my mother and us, yet being able to show love. Today's macho has doubts about his ability to feed and protect his family. His "machismo" is an adaptation to oppression and poverty and low self-esteem. It is the result of hierarchical male dominance. The Anglo, feeling inadequate and inferior and powerless, displaces or transfers these feelings to the Chicano by shaming him. In the Gringo[28] world, the Chicano suffers from excessive humility and self-effacement, shame of self and self-deprecation. Around Latinos he suffers from a sense of language inadequacy and its accompanying discomfort; with Native Americans he suffers from a racial amnesia which ignores our common blood, and from guilt because the Spanish part of him took their land and oppressed them. He has an excessive compensatory hubris[29] when around Mexicans from the other side. It overlays a deep sense of racial shame.

[22] *Luego bota lo que no vale . . . :* Then she discards whatever is useless, falsehoods and brutality. She waits for the deep, probing common sense of the ancient people.

[23] *nahual:* Sorceress.

[24] *Se hace moldeadora . . . :* She is able to mold her soul. Whatever image she has of herself, so she will be.

[25] *Que no se nos olvide los hombres:* Let us not forget men.

[26] *Tú no sirves pa' nada:* You're good for nothing.

[27] *Eres pura vieja:* You're nothing but a woman.

[28] *Gringo:* Anglo.

[29] *hubris:* Exaggerated pride or self-confidence.

The loss of a sense of dignity and respect in the macho breeds a false 15
machismo which leads him to put down women and even to brutalize them. Coexisting with his sexist behavior is a love for the mother which takes precedence over that of all others. Devoted son, macho pig. To wash down the shame of his acts, of his very being, and to handle the brute in the mirror, he takes to the bottle, the snort, the needle, and the fist.

Though we "understand" the root causes of male hatred and fear, and the subsequent wounding of women, we do not excuse, we do not condone, and we will no longer put up with it. From the men of our race, we demand the admission/acknowledgment/disclosure/testimony that they wound us, violate us, are afraid of us and of our power. We need them to say they will begin to eliminate their hurtful put-down ways. But more than the words, we demand acts. We say to them: We will develop equal power with you and those who have shamed us.

It is imperative that *mestizas* support each other in changing the sexist elements in the Mexican-Indian culture. As long as woman is put down, the Indian and the Black in all of us is put down. The struggle of the *mestiza* is above all a feminist one. As long as *los hombres* think they have to *chingar mujeres*[30] and each other to be men, as long as men are taught that they are superior and therefore culturally favored over *la mujer,*[31] as long as to be a *vieja*[32] is a thing of derision, there can be no real healing of our psyches. We're halfway there — we have such love of the Mother, the good mother. The first step is to unlearn the *puta/virgen*[33] dichotomy and to see *Coatlapopeuh-Coatlicue* in the Mother, *Guadalupe.*[34]

Tenderness, a sign of vulnerability, is so feared that it is showered on women with verbal abuse and blows. Men, even more than women, are fettered to gender roles. Women at least have had the guts to break out of bondage. Only gay men have had the courage to expose themselves to the woman inside them and to challenge the current masculinity. I've encountered a few scattered and isolated gentle straight men, the beginnings of a new breed, but they are confused, and entangled with sexist behaviors that they have not been able to eradicate. We need a new masculinity and the new man needs a movement.

Lumping the males who deviate from the general norm with man, the oppressor, is a gross injustice. *Asombra pensar que nos hemos quedado en*

[30]*chingar mujeres:* Fuck women.

[31]*la mujer:* The woman.

[32]*vieja:* Old woman.

[33]*puta/virgen:* Whore/virgin.

[34]*Coatlapopeuh-Coatlicue in the Mother, Guadalupe:* A reference to the dual identity (Indian/pagan and Spanish/Christian) of the Virgin of Guadalupe. Anzaldúa argues that "after the conquest, the Spaniards and their Church . . . desexed Guadalupe, taking Coatlalopeuh, the serpent/sexuality, out of her" (*Borderlands,* Chapter 3).

ese pozo oscuro donde el mundo encierra a las lesbianas. Asombra pensar que hemos, como femenistas y lesbianas, cerrado nuestros corazónes a los hombres, a nuestros hermanos los jotos, desheredados y marginales como nosotros.[35] Being the supreme crossers of cultures, homosexuals have strong bonds with the queer white, Black, Asian, Native American, Latino, and with the queer in Italy, Australia, and the rest of the planet. We come from all colors, all classes, all races, all time periods. Our role is to link people with each other—the Blacks with Jews with Indians with Asians with whites with extraterrestrials. It is to transfer ideas and information from one culture to another. Colored homosexuals have more knowledge of other cultures; have always been at the forefront (although sometimes in the closet) of all liberation struggles in this country; have suffered more injustices and have survived them despite all odds. Chicanos need to acknowledge the political and artistic contributions of their queer. People, listen to what your *jotería*[36] is saying.

The mestizo and the queer exist at this time and point on the evolu- 20
tionary continuum for a purpose. We are a blending that proves that all blood is intricately woven together, and that we are spawned out of similar souls.

Somos una gente[37]

> *Hay tantísimas fronteras*
> *que dividen a la gente,*
> *pero por cada frontera*
> *existe también un puente.*[38]
>
> —Gina Valdés[39]

Divided Loyalties

Many women and men of color do not want to have any dealings with white people. It takes too much time and energy to explain to the downwardly mobile, white middle-class women that it's okay for us to want to own "possessions," never having had any nice furniture on our dirt floors or "luxuries" like washing machines. Many feel that whites should help their own people rid themselves of race hatred and fear first. I, for one, choose to use some of my energy to serve as mediator. I think we need to allow

[35]*Asombra pensar que nos hemos quedado . . . :* It's astonishing to think that we have stayed in that dark well where the world locks up lesbians. It's astonishing to think that as feminist lesbians, we have closed our hearts to men, to our gay brothers, as disinherited and alienated as we are.

[36]*jotería:* Gayness.

[37]*Somas una gente:* We are one people.

[38]*Hay tantísimas fronteras . . . :* There are so many borders / dividing people / but through each border there / passes a bridge.

[39]Richard Wilhelm, *The I Ching or Book of Changes,* trans. Cary F. Baynes (Princeton, NJ: Princeton University Press, 1950), 98. [Author's note]

whites to be our allies. Through our literature, art, *corridos,*[40] and folktales we must share our history with them so when they set up committees to help Big Mountain Navajos[41] or the Chicano farmworkers or *los Nicaragüenses*[42] they won't turn people away because of their racial fears and ignorances. They will come to see that they are not helping us but following our lead.

Individually, but also as a racial entity, we need to voice our needs. We need to say to white society: we need you to accept the fact that Chicanos are different, to acknowledge your rejection and negation of us. We need you to own the fact that you looked upon us as less than human, that you stole our lands, our personhood, our self-respect. We need you to make public restitution: to say that, to compensate for your own sense of defectiveness, you strive for power over us, you erase our history and our experience because it makes you feel guilty — you'd rather forget your brutish acts. To say you've split yourself from minority groups, that you disown us, that your dual consciousness splits off parts of yourself, transferring the "negative" parts onto us. (Where there is persecution of minorities, there is shadow projection. Where there is violence and war, there is repression of shadow.) To say that you are afraid of us, that to put distance between us, you wear the mask of contempt. Admit that Mexico is your double, that she exists in the shadow of this country, that we are irrevocably tied to her. Gringo, accept the doppelganger[43] in your psyche. By taking back your collective shadow the intracultural split will heal. And finally, tell us what you need from us.

By Your True Faces We Will Know You

I am visible — see this Indian face — yet I am invisible. I both blind them with my beak nose and am their blind spot. But I exist, we exist. They'd like to think I have melted in the pot. But I haven't, we haven't.

The dominant white culture is killing us slowly with its ignorance. By taking away our self-determination, it has made us weak and empty. As a people we have resisted and we have taken expedient positions, but we have never been allowed to develop unencumbered — we have never been allowed to be fully ourselves. The whites in power want us people of color to barricade ourselves behind our separate tribal walls so they can pick us off one at a time with their hidden weapons; so they can whitewash and distort history. Ignorance splits people, creates prejudices. A misinformed people is a subjugated people.

Before the Chicano and the undocumented worker and the Mexican 25

[40] *corridos:* Ballads or narrative folk songs of Mexico.

[41] *Big Mountain Navajos:* Big Mountain is an area in New Mexico at the center of a Navaho and Hopi dispute over land rights and treaty conditions.

[42] *los Nicaragüenses:* The Nicaraguans.

[43] *doppelganger:* A double.

from the other side can come together, before the Chicano can have unity with Native Americans and other groups, we need to know the history of their struggle and they need to know ours. Our mothers, our sisters and brothers, the guys who hang out on street corners, the children in the playgrounds, each of us must know our Indian lineage, our afro-*mestisaje*,[44] our history of resistance.

To the immigrant *mexicano* and the recent arrivals we must teach our history. The 80 million *mexicanos* and the Latinos from Central and South America must know of our struggles. Each one of us must know basic facts about Nicaragua, Chile, and the rest of Latin America. The Latinoist movement (Chicanos, Puerto Ricans, Cubans, and other Spanish-speaking people working together to combat racial discrimination in the market place) is good but it is not enough. Other than a common culture we will have nothing to hold us together. We need to meet on a broader communal ground.

The struggle is inner: Chicano, *indio*,[45] American Indian, *mojado*,[46] *mexicano*, immigrant Latino, Anglo in power, working class Anglo, Black, Asian — our psyches resemble the bordertowns and are populated by the same people. The struggle has always been inner, and is played out in the outer terrains. Awareness of our situation must come before inner changes, which in turn come before changes in society. Nothing happens in the "real" world unless it first happens in the images in our heads.

[44]*afro-mestisaje:* Mixed-blood Latino people of African descent.
[45]*indio:* Indian (of Mexico/Central America).
[46]*mojado:* Wetback.

Engaging the Text

1. What does Anzaldúa mean by "*mestiza* consciousness"? Why does she think such a new consciousness is necessary? What risks and rewards does she associate with a *mestiza* consciousness?
2. The concept of the *mestiza*, like the myth of the melting pot, involves the coming together of two or more cultures. How does the idea of *mestiza* consciousness differ from the melting pot metaphor?
3. How does Anzaldúa define the concept of *machismo* in this essay? How does it connect to the idea of *mestiza* consciousness? Why, according to Anzaldúa, are homosexuals important to this new way of thinking?
4. In paragraph 7, Anzaldúa distinguishes between a western mode of thinking, which she considers narrow and inadequate, and a more comprehensive "divergent" mode of thought. Do you think a person trained in traditional western thought can or should learn to think differently?
5. Discuss the effects of Anzaldúa's frequent use of Spanish, her mix of prose and poetry, her references to Mexican/Indian deities and folktales, her movement between vivid image and broad generalization, and other distinctive elements of her essay.

Exploring Connections

6. What value might Anzaldúa's perspective have for a middle-class Jewish southerner? Write a letter from Anzaldúa to Adrienne Rich (p. 365) on being "split at the root."
7. Compare the idea of "recombinant culture" described by Lynell George (p. 422) with Anzaldúa's concept of "*mestiza* consciousness." Would Anzaldúa be likely to agree that the kind of cultural mixing experienced by the teens in George's essay actually involves a "new consciousness"?
8. Read James Weinrich and Walter Williams's "Strange Customs, Familiar Lives" (p. 295) and use it as the basis for exploring the notion, advanced by Anzaldúa, that homosexuals are the "supreme crossers of cultures" (para. 19).
9. Review Paula Gunn Allen's "Where I Come from Is Like This" (p. 312) and discuss the cultural, racial, and sexual borderlands that she inhabits as a woman of Native American and European descent. To what extent would you say that she displays the kind of "*mestiza* consciousness" Anzaldúa describes?

Extending the Critical Context

10. What advice do you think Anzaldúa would give to an American whose experience and family background are essentially monocultural?
11. Anzaldúa suggests that one option for the *mestiza* is "to disengage from the dominant culture, write it off altogether as a lost cause, and cross the border into a wholly new and separate territory" (para. 6). What would it mean to disengage from the dominant culture? Do you think this is possible?

Child of the Americas

Aurora Levins Morales

This poem concentrates on the positive aspects of a multicultural heritage, as Morales celebrates her uniqueness, her diversity, and her wholeness. It's an up-to-date and sophisticated reinterpretation of the melting pot myth and a possible illustration of Gloria Anzaldúa's "mestiza consciousness" *finding voice in poetry. As this autobiographical poem states, Aurora Levins Morales (b. 1954) was the child of a Puerto Rican mother and a Jewish father. She moved to the United States when she was thirteen and now writes, performs, and teaches in the San Francisco Bay Area. "Child of the Americas" is from the collection* Getting Home Alive *(1986), which she coauthored with her mother, Rosario Morales. Her mother has written that the book "began in long, budget-breaking telephone calls stretched across the width of this country . . . the phone line strung between us like a 3,000-mile umbilical cord from navel to navel, mine to hers, hers to mine, each of us mother and daughter by turns, feeding each other the substance of our dreams."*

I am a child of the Americas,
a light-skinned mestiza of the Caribbean,
a child of many diaspora,[1] born into this continent at a crossroads.

I am a U.S. Puerto Rican Jew,
a product of the ghettos of New York I have never known.
An immigrant and the daughter and granddaughter of immigrants.
I speak English with passion: it's the tongue of my consciousness,
a flashing knife blade of crystal, my tool, my craft.

I am Caribeña,[2] island grown. Spanish is in my flesh,
ripples from my tongue, lodges in my hips:
the language of garlic and mangoes,
the singing in my poetry, the flying gestures of my hands.
I am of Latinoamerica, rooted in the history of my continent:
I speak from that body.

I am not african. Africa is in me, but I cannot return.
I am not taína.[3] Taíno is in me, but there is no way back.
I am not european. Europe lives in me, but I have no home there.

I am new. History made me. My first language was spanglish.[4]
I was born at the crossroads
and I am whole.

[1]*diaspora:* Scattered colonies. The word originally referred to Jews scattered outside Palestine after the Babylonian exile; it is now used often to refer to African peoples scattered around the world.

[2]*Caribeña:* Caribbean woman.

[3]*taína:* Describing the Taino, an aboriginal people of the Greater Antilles and Bahamas.

[4]*spanglish:* Spanish and English combined.

Engaging the Text

1. Does this poem do more to challenge or to promote the myth of the melting pot? Explain.
2. Why does the poet list elements of her background that she scarcely knows ("the ghettos of New York" and Taíno)? How can they be part of her?
3. How do you interpret the last stanza? Rephrase its messages in more complete, more explicit statements.

Exploring Connections

4. To what extent does this poem display a "*mestiza* consciousness" as described by Gloria Anzaldúa (p. 434)? Do you see any important differences between these authors? Explain.
5. Feeling "split at the root" is an issue not only for Adrienne Rich (p. 365), but also for Gloria Anzaldúa (p. 434), Stephen Cruz (p. 460), Haunani-Kay Trask (p. 571), and many other writers/characters in this book. How does the speaker of this poem avoid the feeling of fragmentation or cultural schizophrenia?

Extending the Critical Context

6. Write your own version of "Child of the Americas," following Morales's structure but substituting ideas and images from your own heritage. Read it to the class.

Sources

Horatio Alger, *Ragged Dick.* Rpt. New York and London: Collier Macmillan, 1962.

Peter Baida, *Poor Richard's Legacy: American Business Values from Benjamin Franklin to Donald Trump.* New York: William Morrow, 1990.

J. Hector St. Jean de Crèvecoeur, *Letters from an American Farmer.* New York: Dolphin Books, 1961. First published in London, 1782.

Before Reading

- Working alone or in groups, make a list of people who best represent your idea of success. (You may want to consider public and political figures, leaders in government, entertainment, sports, education, or other fields.) List the specific qualities or accomplishments that make these people successful. Compare notes with your classmates, then freewrite about the meaning of success: What does it mean to you? To the class as a whole?
- Keep your list and your definition. As you work through this chapter, reread and reflect on what you've written, comparing your ideas with those of the authors included here.
- Write a journal entry that captures the thoughts of the man pictured in the photo at the beginning of this chapter. What feelings or attitudes can you read in his expression, his dress, and his body language? How do you think he got where he is today?

The New American Dreamers

Ruth Sidel

"The American Dream" — the notion that success will reward hard work — is one of the most important American myths. Certainly it is one of the oldest, most cherished, and most powerful; it has drawn immigrants to our shores and motivated generations of Americans to keep striving toward difficult goals. In the selection below, Ruth Sidel studies the myth's impact on young American women who "want it all," even though many of them face tremendous obstacles. Sidel (b. 1933) is an internationally recognized sociologist, author, and educator whose work has taken her from a community health center in the Bronx to Sweden, Chile, and China. She is currently a professor of sociology at Hunter College of the City University

5

Money and Success

The Myth of Individual Opportunity

Ask most people how they define the American Dream and chances are they'll say, "Success." The dream of individual opportunity has been at home in America since Europeans discovered a "new world" in the Western Hemisphere. Early immigrants like Hector St. Jean de Crèvecoeur extolled the freedom and opportunity to be found in this new land. His glowing descriptions of a classless society where anyone could attain success through honesty and hard work fired the imaginations of many European readers: in *Letters from an American Farmer* (1782) he wrote, "We are all animated with the spirit of an industry which is unfettered and unrestrained, because each person works for himself. . . . We have no princes, for whom we toil, starve, and bleed: we are the most perfect society now existing in the world." The promise of a land where "the rewards of [a man's] industry follow with equal steps the progress of his labor" drew poor immigrants from Europe and fueled national expansion into the western territories.

Our national mythology abounds with illustrations of the American success story. There's Benjamin Franklin, the very model of the self-educated, self-made man, who rose from modest origins to become a renowned scientist, philosopher, and statesman. In the nineteenth century, Horatio Alger, a writer of pulp fiction for young boys, became America's best-selling author with rags-to-riches tales like *Ragged Dick* (1867), *Struggling Upward* (1886), and *Bound to Rise* (1873). The notion of success haunts us: we spend millions every year reading about the rich and famous, learning how to "make a fortune in real estate with no money down," and "dressing for success." The myth of success has even invaded our personal relationships: today it's as important to be "successful" in marriage or parenthood as it is to come out on top in business.

But dreams easily turn into nightmares. Every American who hopes to "make it" also knows the fear of failure, because the myth of success inevitably implies comparison between the haves and the have-nots, the achievers and the drones, the stars and the anonymous crowd. Under pressure of the myth, we become engrossed in status symbols: we try to live in the "right" neighborhoods, wear the "right" clothes, eat the "right" foods. These emblems of distinction assure us and others that we are different, that we stand out from the crowd. It is one of the great paradoxes of our culture that we believe passionately in the fundamental equality of all, yet strive as hard as we can to separate ourselves from our fellow citizens.

Steeped in a Puritan theology that vigorously preached the individual's responsibility to the larger community, colonial America balanced the drive for individual gain with concern for the common good. To Franklin, the way to wealth lay in practicing the virtues of honesty, hard work, and thrift: "Without industry and frugality nothing will do, and with them every thing. He that gets all he can honestly, and saves all he gets . . . will certainly become RICH" ("Advice to a Young Tradesman," 1748). And Alger's heroes were as concerned with moral rectitude as they were with financial gain: a benefactor advises Ragged Dick, "If you'll try to be somebody, and grow up into a respectable member of society, you will. You may not become rich, — it isn't everybody that becomes rich, you know, — but you can obtain a good position and be respected." But in the twentieth century the mood of the myth has changed. Contemporary guides to success, like Robert Ringer's enormously popular *Looking Out for Number One* (1977), urge readers to "forget foundationless traditions, forget the 'moral' standards others may have tried to cram down your throat . . . and, most important, think of yourself — Number One. . . . You and you alone will be responsible for your success or failure." The myth of success may have been responsible for making the United States what it is today, but it also seems to be pulling us apart. Can we exist as a living community if our greatest value can be summed up by the slogan "Me first"?

This chapter examines how Americans define and are defined by the idea of success. The first half of the chapter investigates the power that the myth of success wields over our lives. In "The New American Dreamers," Ruth Sidel presents vignettes of young women who, despite the obstacles of race, gender, and class, continue to define success in terms of status and wealth. The stories of these young students, working women, and mothers are followed by the oral history of Stephen Cruz, a successful Mexican American engineer who questions the meaning of the American Dream after a series of disillusionments in his career. Gregory Mantsios's "Rewards and Opportunities" explores the forces that maintain the inequitable distribution of wealth, power, and opportunity in American society. Toni Cade Bambara's short story "The Lesson" dramatizes these inequities by presenting them through the eyes of a group of kids from Harlem who venture uptown to see how the rich live and spend. Jack Solomon's "Masters of Desire," the chapter's media selection, closes the first section by analyzing the way that advertisers exploit Americans' dreams of success and fears of failure to sell us everything from hamburgers to sports cars.

The next group of readings looks critically at the limits of the American Dream. In "The Great Boomer Bust" Katy Butler tells her own story as an example of the "downward mobility" that many young Americans face in the 1990s. Curtis Chang's "Streets of Gold" further complicates the myth by challenging the media-created stereotype of the successful Asian American. Next, Ellis Cose explains the "rage" that he and other highly successful African Americans continue to feel despite having lived lives that are models of the American success story. In "Number One!" African American journalist Jill Nelson offers a thought-provoking sketch of her father and the ambivalence he felt about making it in America.

The chapter closes with two positive rereadings of the meaning of success. Sucheng Chan's "You're Short, Besides!" profiles a woman who has resisted the definitions of race, gender, and physical ability imposed on her by a society obsessed with mythic images of success. In "Good Noise: Cora Tucker," Anne Witte Garland presents the story of an African American activist who measures success in terms of lives saved instead of dollars spent.

of New York. This selection is excerpted from one of her several books, On Her Own: Growing Up in the Shadow of the American Dream *(1990).*

> It's your life. You have to live it yourself . . . If you work hard enough, you will get there. You must be in control of your life, and then somehow it will all work out.
>
> — ANGELA DAWSON, high-school junior, southern California

She is the prototype of today's young woman — confident, outgoing, knowledgeable, involved. She is active in her school, church, or community. She may have a wide circle of friends or simply a few close ones, but she is committed to them and to their friendship. She is sophisticated about the central issues facing young people today—planning for the future, intimacy, sex, drugs, and alcohol — and discusses them seriously, thoughtfully, and forthrightly. She wants to take control of her life and is trying to figure out how to get from where she is to where she wants to go. Above all, she is convinced that if she plans carefully, works hard, and makes the right decisions, she will be a success in her chosen field; have the material goods she desires; in time, marry if she wishes; and, in all probability, have children. She plans, as the expression goes, to "have it all."

She lives in and around the major cities of the United States, in the towns of New England, in the smaller cities of the South and Midwest, and along the West Coast. She comes from an upper-middle-class family, from the middle class, from the working class, and even sometimes from the poor. What is clear is that she has heard the message that women today should be the heroines of their own lives. She looks toward the future, seeing herself as the central character, planning her career, her apartment, her own success story. These young women do not see themselves as playing supporting roles in someone else's life script; it is their own journeys they are planning. They see their lives in terms of *their* aspirations, *their* hopes, *their* dreams.

Beth Conant is a sixteen-year-old high-school junior who lives with her mother and stepfather in an affluent New England college town. She has five brothers, four older and one several years younger. Her mother is a librarian, and her stepfather is a stockbroker. A junior at a top-notch public high school, she hopes to study drama in college, possibly at Yale, "like Meryl Streep." She would like to live and act in England for a time, possibly doing Shakespeare. She hopes to be living in New York by the age of twenty-five, in her own apartment or condo, starting on her acting career while working at another job by which she supports herself. She wants to have "a great life," be "really independent," and have "everything that's mine — crazy furniture, everything my own style."

By the time she's thirty ("that's so boring"), she feels, she will need to be sensible, because soon she will be "tied down." She hopes that by then her career will be "starting to go forth" and that she will be getting good roles. By thirty-five she'll have a child ("probably be married beforehand"), be working in New York and have a house in the country. How will she manage all this? Her husband will share responsibilities. She's not going to be a "supermom." They'll both do child care. He won't do it as a favor; it will be their joint responsibility. Moreover, if she doesn't have the time to give to a child, she won't have one. If necessary, she'll work for a while, then have children, and after that "make one movie a year."

Amy Morrison is a petite, black, fifteen-year-old high-school sophomore 5
who lives in Ohio. Her mother works part-time, and her father works for a local art museum. She plans to go to medical school and hopes to become a surgeon. She doesn't want to marry until she has a good, secure job but indicates that she might be living with someone. She's not sure about having children but says emphatically that she wants to be successful, to make money, to have cars. In fact, originally she wanted to become a doctor "primarily for the money," but now she claims other factors are drawing her to medicine.

Jacqueline Gonzalez is a quiet, self-possessed, nineteen-year-old Mexican-American woman who is a sophomore at a community college in southern California. She describes her father as a "self-employed contractor" and her mother as a "housewife." Jacqueline, the second-youngest of six children, is the first in her family to go to college. Among her four brothers and one sister, only her sister has finished high school. Jacqueline's goal is to go to law school and then to go into private practice. While she sees herself as eventually married with "one or two children," work, professional achievement, and an upper-middle-class life-style are central to her plans for her future.

If in the past, and to a considerable extent still today, women have hoped to find their identity through marriage, have sought to find "validation of . . . [their] uniqueness and importance by being singled out among all other women by a man,"[1] the New American Dreamers are setting out on a very different quest for self-realization. They are, in their plans for the future, separating identity from intimacy, saying that they must first figure out who they are and that then and only then will they form a partnership with a man. Among the young women I interviewed, the New American Dreamers stand apart in their intention to make their own way in the world and determine their own destiny prior to forming a significant and lasting intimate relationship.

Young women today do not need to come from upper-middle-class homes such as Beth's or middle-class homes such as Amy's or working-class homes such as Jacqueline's to dream of "the good life." Even young women

[1] Rachel M. Brownstein, *Becoming a Heroine: Reading About Women in Novels* (New York: Penguin, 1984), p. xv. [Author's note]

with several strikes against them see material success as a key prize at the end of the rainbow. Some seem to feel that success is out there for the taking. Generally, the most prestigious, best-paying careers are mentioned; few women of any class mention traditional women's professions such as teaching or nursing. A sixteen-year-old unmarried Arizona mother of a four-and-a-half-month-old baby looks forward to a "professional career either in a bank or with a computer company," a "house that belongs to me," a "nice car," and the ability to buy her son "good clothes." She sees herself in the future as dating but not married. "There is not so much stress on marriage these days," she says.

Yet another young woman, a seventeen-year-old black unmarried mother of an infant, hopes to be a "professional model," have "lots of cash," be "rich," maybe have another child. When asked if a man will be part of the picture, she responds, "I don't know."

An eighteen-year-old Hispanic unmarried mother hopes to "be my own 10
boss" in a large company, have a "beautiful home," send her daughter to "the best schools." She wants, in her words, to "do it, make it, have money."

These young women are bright, thoughtful, personable. And they are quintessentially American: they believe that with enough hard work they will "make it" in American society. No matter what class they come from, their fantasies are of upward mobility, a comfortable life filled with personal choice and material possessions. The upper-middle-class women fantasize a life even more upper-middle-class; middle-class and working-class women look toward a life of high status in which they have virtually everything they want; and some young women who come from families with significant financial deprivation and numerous other problems dream of a life straight out of *Dallas, Dynasty,* or *L.A. Law.* According to one young woman, some of her friends are so determined to be successful that they are "fearful that there will be a nuclear war and that they will die before they have a chance to live their lives. If there is a nuclear war," she explained, "they won't live long enough to be successful."

Young women are our latest true believers. They have bought into the image of a bright future. Many of them see themselves as professional women, dressed in handsome clothes, carrying a briefcase to work, and coming home to a comfortable house or condo, possibly to a loving, caring husband and a couple of well-behaved children. How widespread is the dream? How realistic is it? What is the function of this latest American dream? What about those young women who cling to a more traditional dream? What about those who feel their dreams must be deferred? What about those with no dream at all? And what about those who "share the fantasy," as the Chanel No. 5 perfume advertisement used to say, but have little or no chance of achieving it?

Perhaps the most poignant example of the impossible dream is Simone Baker, a dynamic, bright, eighteen-year-old black woman from Louisiana. Simone's mother is a seamstress who has been off and on welfare over the years, and her father is a drug addict. Simone herself has been addicted to drugs of one kind or another since she was five. She has been in and out of drug-abuse facilities, and although she attended school for many years and was passed from grade to grade, she can barely read and write. When I met her in a drug rehabilitation center, she was struggling to become drug free so that she could join the Job Corps, finish high school, and obtain some vocational training. Her dream of the future is so extraordinary, given her background, that she seems to epitomize the Horatio Alger[2] myth of another era. When asked what she would like her life to be like in the future, Simone replies instantly, her eyes shining: "I want to be a model. I want to have a Jacuzzi. I want to have a *big*, BIG house and a BIG family—three girls and two boys."

"And what about the man?" I ask her.

"He'll be a lawyer. He'll be responsible, hardworking, and sensitive to my feelings. Everything will be fifty-fifty. And he'll take the little boys out to play football and I'll have the girls inside cooking. That would be a dream come true!"

Simone's dream is an incredible mixture of the old and the new — a Dick-and-Jane reader updated. And she's even mouthing the supreme hope of so many women in this age of the therapeutic solution to personal problems — that she'll find a man who is "sensitive" to her "feelings." She has lived a life far from the traditional middle class and yet has the quintessential image of the good life as it has been formulated in the last quarter of the twentieth century. But for Simone, it is virtually an impossible dream. One wishes that that were not so; listening to her, watching her excitement and hope at the mere thought of such a life, one gets caught up and wants desperately for it all to happen. The image is clear: the white house in the suburbs with the brass knocker on the front door, the leaves on the lawn in the fall, the boys playing football with this incredibly wonderful husband/father, and Simone sometimes the successful model, other times at home, cooking with her daughters. But we know how very unlikely it is that this particular dream will come true. And yet, maybe. . . .

How have young women come to take on the American Dream as their own? That this is a relatively new dream for women is clear. Until recent years women, for the most part, did not perceive themselves as separate, independent entities with their own needs and agendas. Women fit themselves into other people's lives, molded their needs to fit the needs of others. For the full-time homemaker the day began early enough to enable husband and children to get to work and school on time. Chores had to be done between breakfast and lunch or between lunch and the end of school. Dinnertime was when the man of the house returned from work. When a woman

[2]*Horatio Alger:* American author (1834–1899) of books for boys, now synonymous with the rags-to-riches dream.

worked outside of the home, her work hours were often those that fit into the schedules of other family members. Her needs were determined by the needs of others, as often her identity rested on her affiliation with them.

What some women seem to be saying now is that they will form their own identities, develop their own styles, and meet their own needs. They will be the central characters in their stories. They will work at jobs men work at, earn the money men earn; but many of them also plan at the same time to play all the roles women have traditionally played.

What has become clear in talking with young women throughout the country is that many of them are planning for their future in terms of their "public" roles as well as their "domestic" roles, that they are "laying claim to significant and satisfying work . . . as a normal part of their lives and laying claim also to the authority, prestige, power, and salary that . . . [that] work commands."[3] Historically, women have been confined primarily to the "domestic" sphere of life, particularly to child rearing and homemaking, and men, for the most part, have participated in the "public" sphere — that is, in social, economic, and political institutions and forms of association in the broader social structure. This dichotomy between "public" and "domestic" has led to "an asymmetry in the cultural evaluation of male and female that appears to be universal."[4] Margaret Mead[5] noted this asymmetry when she observed that "whatever the arrangements in regard to descent or ownership of property, and even if these formal outward arrangements are reflected in the temperamental relations between the sexes, the prestige values always attach to the activities of men."[6]

20 In New Guinea, women grow sweet potatoes and men grow yams; yams are the prestige food. In societies where women grow rice, the staple food, and men hunt for meat, meat is the most valued food.[7] Traditionally, the more exclusively male the activity, the more cultural value is attached to it. Because male activities have been valued over female activities and women have become "absorbed primarily in domestic activities because of their role as mothers,"[8] women's work of caring has traditionally been devalued. However, as political scientist Joan Tronto has pointed out, it is not simply the dichotomy between the public and the private that results in the devaluation of the female but the immense difference in power between the two

[3]Nadya Aisenberg and Mona Harrington, *Women of Academe: Outsiders in the Sacred Grove* (Amherst, MA: University of Massachusetts Press, 1988), p. 3. [Author's note]

[4]Michelle Zimbalist Rosaldo, "Women, Culture, and Society: An Overview" in *Women, Culture, and Society*, Michelle Zimbalist Rosaldo and Louise Lamphere, eds. (Stanford, CA: Stanford University Press, 1974), p. 19. [Author's note]

[5]*Margaret Mead:* Influential American anthropologist (1901–1978).

[6]Ibid. [Author's note]

[7]Ibid. [Author's note]

[8]Ibid., p. 24. [Author's note]

spheres.[9] So long as men have a monopoly on the public sphere and it in turn wields great power within society, women, identified with the private sphere, which is seen as relatively powerless, will be devalued.

Since the emergence of the women's movement in the 1960s, women in the United States as well as in many other parts of the world have been questioning the traditional asymmetry between men and women, seeking to understand its roots, its causes, and its consequences, and attempting to modify the male monopoly of power. Many strategies have developed toward this end: laws have been passed in an attempt to eliminate discrimination; groups have formed to elect more women to positions of power; those already in power have been urged to appoint more women to administrative roles; dominant, high-status, high-income professions have been pressured to admit more women to their hallowed ranks; and strategies to bring greater equity to male and female salaries have been developed.

Great stress has been placed on raising the consciousness of both women and men concerning this imbalance of power, but particular attention has been devoted to raising the consciousness of women. Discussion about the relative powerlessness of the non-wage-earning "housewife" has been widespread. Books and articles about the impoverishment of the divorced woman, the problems of the displaced homemaker, and the often desperate plight of the single, female head of household have been directed at women. During the 1970s and 1980s, the message suddenly became clear to many women: perhaps they are entitled to play roles formerly reserved for men; perhaps they would enjoy these challenges; perhaps they have something special to offer and can make a difference in the practice of medicine or law or in running the country. Moreover, it became clear that if women want power, prestige, and paychecks similar to those men receive, if they want to lessen the asymmetry between male and female, then perhaps they must enter those spheres traditionally reserved for men. If men grow yams, must women grow yams? If men hunt and women gather, must women purchase a bow and arrow? If men are in the public sphere while women are at home caring for children and doing the laundry, the consensus seems to say that women must enter the public sphere. If men are doctors and lawyers and earn great rewards while women are nurses and teachers and earn meager rewards, then women see what they obviously must do. If men have focused on doing while women have focused on caring, then clearly women must become doers.

It is not sufficient, however, to become a doer in a traditionally female occupation, for, as we know, these occupations are notoriously underpaid

[9]Joan C. Tronto, "Women and Caring: What Can Feminists Learn About Morality from Caring?" in *Body, Gender and Knowledge,* Alison Jagger and Susan Brodo, eds. (New Brunswick, NJ: Rutgers University Press, in press). See also Linda Imray and Audrey Middleton, "Public and Private: Marking the Boundaries," in *The Public and the Private,* Eva Gamarnikow et al., eds. (London: Heinemann, 1983), pp. 12–27. [Author's note]

and underesteemed. Women must become *real* doers in the arena that counts: they must learn to play hardball, or, as Mary Lou Retton[10] says in her breakfast-cereal advertisements, "eat what the big boys eat." For real power, status, money, and "success," it's law, medicine, and finance — also, possibly, acting, modeling, or working in the media, if one is very lucky.

An illustration of the current emphasis on male-dominated careers as the road to success for young women are the career goals of *Glamour* magazine's "Top Ten College Women '88." One woman hopes to become an astronaut; a second plans to work in the area of public policy, another to be a biologist, another to obtain a degree in business administration, yet another to obtain a degree in acting; and one young woman is currently working in journalism. One college senior is undecided between journalism and law, and the last three are planning to go to law school. These young women, according to *Glamour*, "possess the talents and ambition necessary to shape tomorrow's society." It is noteworthy that none of the women *Glamour* chose to honor are entering any traditionally female occupation or any "helping" profession — not even medicine. Don't nurses, teachers, and social workers "possess the talents and ambition necessary to shape tomorrow's society"? The word has gone out and continues to go out that the way to "make it" in American society and the way to "shape tomorrow's society" is the traditional male route.[11]

Once singled out, these young women play their part in spreading the 25
ideology of the American Dream. Three of the ten honorees appeared on NBC's *Today* show. When asked about the significance of their being chosen, one woman replied without hesitation that if you work hard, you can do whatever you want to do. This statement was greeted by smiles and nods; she had clearly given the right message.

In addition to wanting to break out of the mold of a secondary worker receiving inferior wages and benefits and having little authority or opportunity for advancement, women have been motivated to make real money and to acquire valued skills and some semblance of security because of their relatively recent realization that women, even women with children, may well be forced to care for themselves or, at the very least, to participate in providing for the family unit. Women have come to realize that whether because of divorce (which leaves women on the average 73 percent poorer and men on the average 42 percent richer), childbearing outside of marriage, the inability of many men to earn an adequate "family wage," or their remaining single — either through design or through circumstance — they must be prepared to support themselves and anyone else for whom they feel responsible.

But what of all that caring women used to do — for children, for elderly

[10]*Mary Lou Retton*: 1984 U.S. Olympic gold medalist in gymnastics (b. 1968).
[11]*Glamour* (August 1988), pp. 208–09. [Author's note]

parents, for sick family members, for the home? What about Sunday dinner, baking chocolate-chip cookies with the kids eating up half the batter, serving Kool-Aid in the backyard on a hot summer day? What about sitting with a child with a painful ear infection until the antibiotic takes effect, going with a four-year-old to nursery school the first week until the child feels comfortable letting you leave, being available when there's an accident at school and your second grader must be rushed to the emergency room? Who's going to do the caring? Who is going to do the caring in a society in which few institutions have been developed to take up the slack, a society in which men have been far more reluctant to become carers than women have been to become doers. Members of the subordinate group may gain significantly in status, in self-image, and in material rewards when they take on the activities and characteristics of the dominant group, but there is little incentive for members of the dominant group to do the reverse.

Above all, how do young women today deal with these questions? How do they feel about doing and caring, about power, prestige, and parenting? What messages is society giving them about the roles they should play, and how are they sorting out these messages?

A key message the new American Dreamers are both receiving and sending is one of optimism—the sense that they can do whatever they want with their lives. Many Americans, of course—not just young people or young women—have a fundamentally optimistic attitude toward the future. Historically, Americans have believed that progress is likely, even inevitable, and that they have the ability to control their own destinies. A poll taken early in 1988 indicates that while the American public was concerned about the nation's future and indeed more pessimistic about "the way things [were] going in the United States" than they had been at any other time since the Carter presidency in the late 1970s, they nonetheless believed that they could "plan and regulate their own lives, even while the national economy

and popular culture appear[ed] to be spinning out of control." As one would expect, those with higher incomes and more education are more optimistic than those with less; Republicans are more optimistic than Democrats or Independents; and, significantly, men are more hopeful than women. In looking toward the future, young men clearly dream of "the good life," of upward mobility and their share of material possessions. While young women historically have had far less control over their lives than men, for the past twenty-five years they have been urged to take greater control, both in the workplace and in their private lives, and they have clearly taken the message very much to heart.

Angela Dawson, a sixteen-year-old high-school junior from southern 30
California, sums up the views of the New American Dreamers: "It's your life. You have to live it yourself. You must decide what you want in high school, plan your college education, and from there you can basically get what you want. If you work hard enough, you will get there. You must be in control of your life, and then somehow it will all work out."

Engaging the Text

1. Who are the "New American Dreamers," and how do they differ from previous generations of Americans seeking success? What seems to be Sidel's attitude toward this group?
2. Sidel implies that many young dreamers will be disappointed, that their dreams are too good to come true. What specific obstacles, according to Sidel, may stand in the way of the dreamers' desires to "have it all"?
3. What advice do you think Sidel would give these young women? What advice about success, direct or indirect, have you actually received from parents, teachers, the media, or other sources?
4. Pick one of the women Sidel mentions (Beth Conant, Amy Morrison, Jacqueline Gonzalez, or Simone Baker); read about her hopes and then write an imaginary end to her story. Share these in class and discuss what the results reveal about your own attitudes toward success.
5. Sidel is writing here primarily about young women. What would you say about young men today and their dreams of success? Do men and women vary widely in their dreams or in their chances of achieving them?

Exploring Connections

6. Several selections earlier in the book feature people succeeding, striving for success, or preparing themselves for success; these include "The Achievement of Desire" (p. 61), "Para Teresa" (p. 74), "Looking for Work" (p. 145), "Nora Quealey" (p. 253), and "Child of the Americas" (p. 444). Compare and contrast one or more of these pieces with "The New American Dreamers." How is success portrayed in each selection? What roles do family, gender, or race play? How do the experiences in the poems and narratives compare to the dreams described in Sidel's piece?
7. Most of the women Sidel describes are still in high school. How might the

educational inequities in higher education identified by the Sadkers (p. 86) affect their chances to achieve their dreams?

8. Look at the cartoon on page 458 and create appropriate signs for one or more of the "New American Dreamers" Sidel describes. Then create a sign that reflects what you would be willing to spend your life working for.

Extending the Critical Context

9. Review the sketches above of Beth Conant, Amy Morrison, Jacqueline Gonzalez, and Simone Baker, paying particular attention to the kinds of questions these young women must have been asked. Then pair up with a classmate; interview each other and write a one- or two-paragraph sketch of your partner in imitation of Sidel's.
10. Sidel suggests that TV shows like *Dallas, Dynasty,* and *L.A. Law* played an important role in shaping the dreams of the women she interviewed. What current TV shows provide models of successful lifestyles? What values and attitudes are implied by these models?
11. Find and read some articles on "Generation X" in your library. Are the "New American Dreamers" part of Generation X? Compare and contrast Sidel's point of view with those of the other authors you read.

Stephen Cruz

Studs Terkel

The speaker of the following oral history is Stephen Cruz, a man who at first glance seems to be living the American dream of success and upward mobility. He is never content, however, and he comes to question his own values and the meaning of success in the world of corporate America. For a brief introduction to Studs Terkel (b. 1912) and his method of compiling oral histories, see the headnote to Terkel's "C. P. Ellis" (p. 388). This selection first appeared in Terkel's American Dreams: Lost and Found *(1980).*

He is thirty-nine.

"The family came in stages from Mexico. Your grandparents usually came first, did a little work, found little roots, put together a few bucks, and brought the family in, one at a time. Those were the days when controls at the border didn't exist as they do now."

You just tried very hard to be whatever it is the system wanted of you. I was a good student and, as small as I was, a pretty good athlete. I was well liked, I thought. We were fairly affluent, but we lived down where all the trashy whites were. It was the only housing we could get. As kids, we never understood why. We did everything right. We didn't have those Mexican accents, we were never on welfare. Dad wouldn't be on welfare to save his soul. He woulda died first. He worked during the depression. He carries that pride with him, even today.

Of the five children, I'm the only one who really got into the business world. We learned quickly that you have to look for opportunities and add things up very quickly. I was in liberal arts, but as soon as Sputnik[1] went up, well, golly, hell, we knew where the bucks were. I went right over to the registrar's office and signed up for engineering. I got my degree in '62. If you had a master's in business as well, they were just paying all kinds of bucks. So that's what I did. Sure enough, the market was super. I had fourteen job offers. I could have had a hundred if I wanted to look around.

I never once associated these offers with my being a minority. I was 5
aware of the Civil Rights Act of 1964, but I was still self-confident enough to feel they wanted me because of my abilities. Looking back, the reason I got more offers than the other guys was because of the government edict. And I thought it was because I was so goddamned brilliant. (Laughs.) In 1962, I didn't get as many offers as those who were less qualified. You have a tendency to blame the job market. You just don't want to face the issue of discrimination.

I went to work with Procter & Gamble. After about two years, they told me I was one of the best supervisors they ever had and they were gonna promote me. Okay, I went into personnel. Again, I thought it was because I was such a brilliant guy. Now I started getting wise to the ways of the American Dream. My office was glass-enclosed, while all the other offices were enclosed so you couldn't see into them. I was the visible man.

They made sure I interviewed most of the people that came in. I just didn't really think there was anything wrong until we got a new plant manager, a southerner. I received instructions from him on how I should interview blacks. Just check and see if they smell, okay? That was the beginning of my training program. I started asking: Why weren't we hiring more minorities? I realized I was the only one in a management position.

I guess as a Mexican I was more acceptable because I wasn't really black. I was a good compromise. I was visibly good. I hired a black secretary, which was *verboten*. When I came back from my vacation, she was gone. My boss fired her while I was away. I asked why and never got a good reason.

Until then, I never questioned the American Dream. I was convinced if you worked hard, you could make it. I never considered myself different.

[1] *Sputnik:* Satellite launched by the Soviet Union in 1957; this launch signaled the beginning of the "space race" between the United States and USSR.

That was the trouble. We had been discriminated against a lot, but I never associated it with society. I considered it an individual matter. Bad people, my mother used to say. In '68 I began to question.

I was doing fine. My very first year out of college, I was making twelve thousand dollars. I left Procter & Gamble because I really saw no opportunity. They were content to leave me visible, but my thoughts were not really solicited. I may have overreacted a bit, with the plant manager's attitude, but I felt there's no way a Mexican could get ahead here. 10

I went to work for Blue Cross. It's 1969. The Great Society[2] is in full swing. Those who never thought of being minorities before are being turned on. Consciousness raising is going on. Black programs are popping up in universities. Cultural identity and all that. But what about the one issue in this country: economics? There were very few management jobs for minorities, especially blacks.

The stereotypes popped up again. If you're Oriental, you're real good in mathematics. If you're Mexican, you're a happy guy to have around, pleasant but emotional. Mexicans are either sleeping or laughing all the time. Life is just one big happy kind of event. *Mañana.* Good to have as part of the management team, as long as you weren't allowed to make decisions.

I was thinking there were two possibilities why minorities were not making it in business. One was deep, ingrained racism. But there was still the possibility that they were simply a bunch of bad managers who just couldn't cut it. You see, until now I believed everything I was taught about the dream: the American businessman is omnipotent and fair. If we could show these turkeys there's money to be made in hiring minorities, these businessmen — good managers, good decision makers — would respond. I naively thought American businessmen gave a damn about society, that given a choice they would do the right thing. I had that faith.

I was hungry for learning about decision-making criteria. I was still too far away from top management to see exactly how they were working. I needed to learn more. Hey, just learn more and you'll make it. That part of the dream hadn't left me yet. I was still clinging to the notion of work your ass off, learn more than anybody else, and you'll get in that sphere.

During my fifth year at Blue Cross, I discovered another flaw in the American Dream. Minorities are as bad to other minorities as whites are to minorities. The strongest weapon the white manager had is the old divide and conquer routine. My mistake was thinking we were all at the same level of consciousness. 15

I had attempted to bring together some blacks with the other minorities. There weren't too many of them anyway. The Orientals never really got involved. The blacks misunderstood what I was presenting, perhaps I said it badly. They were on the cultural kick: a manager should be crucified for

[2]*The Great Society:* President Lyndon B. Johnson's term for the American society he hoped to establish through social reforms, including an antipoverty program.

saying "Negro" instead of "black." I said as long as the Negro or the black gets the job, it doesn't mean a damn what he's called. We got into a huge hassle. Management, of course, merely smiled. The whole struggle fell flat on its face. It crumpled from divisiveness. So I learned another lesson. People have their own agenda. It doesn't matter what group you're with, there is a tendency to put the other guy down regardless.

The American Dream began to look so damn complicated, I began to think: Hell, if I wanted, I could just back away and reap the harvest myself. By this time, I'm up to twenty-five thousand dollars a year. It's beginning to look good, and a lot of people are beginning to look good. And they're saying: "Hey, the American Dream, you got it. Why don't you lay off?" I wasn't falling in line.

My bosses were telling me I had all the "ingredients" for top management. All that was required was to "get to know our business." This term comes up all the time. If I could just warn all minorities and women whenever you hear "get to know our business," they're really saying "fall in line." Stay within that fence, and glory can be yours. I left Blue Cross disillusioned. They offered me a director's job at thirty thousand dollars before I quit.

All I had to do was behave myself. I had the "ingredients" of being a good Chicano, the equivalent of the good nigger. I was smart. I could articulate well. People didn't know by my speech patterns that I was of Mexican heritage. Some tell me I don't look Mexican, that I have a certain amount of Italian, Lebanese, or who knows. (Laughs.)

20 One could easily say: "Hey, what's your bitch? The American Dream has treated you beautifully. So just knock it off and quit this crap you're spreading around." It was a real problem. Every time I turned around, America seemed to be treating me very well.

Hell, I even thought of dropping out, the hell with it. Maybe get a job in a factory. But what happened? Offers kept coming in. I just said to myself: God, isn't this silly? You might as well take the bucks and continue looking for the answer. So I did that. But each time I took the money, the conflict in me got more intense, not less.

Wow, I'm up to thirty-five thousand a year. This is a savings and loan business. I have faith in the executive director. He was the kind of guy I was looking for in top management: understanding, humane, also looking for the formula. Until he was up for consideration as executive v.p. of the entire organization. All of a sudden everything changed. It wasn't until I saw this guy flip-flop that I realized how powerful vested interests are. Suddenly he's saying: "Don't rock the boat. Keep a low profile. Get in line." Another disappointment.

Subsequently, I went to work for a consulting firm. I said to myself: Okay, I've got to get close to the executive mind. I need to know how they work. Wow, a consulting firm.

Consulting firms are saving a lot of American businessmen. They're doing it in ways that defy the whole notion of capitalism. They're not allowing these businesses to fail. Lockheed was successful in getting U.S. funding guarantees because of the efforts of consulting firms working on their behalf, helping them look better. In this kind of work, you don't find minorities. You've got to be a proven success in business before you get there.

The American Dream, I see now, is governed not by education, oppor- 25
tunity, and hard work, but by power and fear. The higher up in the organization you go, the more you have to lose. The dream is *not losing.* This is the notion pervading America today: don't lose.

When I left the consulting business, I was making fifty thousand dollars a year. My last performance appraisal was: you can go a long way in this business, you can be a partner, but you gotta know our business. It came up again. At this point, I was incapable of being disillusioned any more. How easy it is to be swallowed up by the same set of values that governs the top guy. I was becoming that way. I was becoming concerned about losing that fifty grand or so a year. So I asked other minorities who had it made. I'd go up and ask 'em: "look, do you owe anything to others?" The answer was: "we owe nothing to anybody." They drew from the civil rights movement but felt no debt. They've quickly forgotten how it happened. It's like I was when I first got out of college. Hey, it's really me, I'm great. I'm great. I'm as angry with these guys as I am with the top guys.

Right now, it's confused. I've had fifteen years in the business world as "a success." Many Anglos would be envious of my progress. Fifty thousand dollars a year puts you in the one or two top percent of all Americans. Plus my wife making another thirty thousand. We had lots of money. When I gave it up, my cohorts looked at me not just as strange, but as something of a traitor. "You're screwing it up for all of us. You're part of our union, we're the elite, we should govern. What the hell are you doing?" So now I'm looked at suspiciously by my peer group as well.

I'm teaching at the University of Wisconsin at Platteville. It's nice. My colleagues tell me what's on their minds. I got a farm next-door to Platteville. With farm prices being what they are (laughs), it's a losing proposition. But with university work and what money we've saved, we're gonna be all right.

The American Dream is getting more elusive. The dream is being governed by a few people's notion of what the dream is. Sometimes I feel it's a small group of financiers that gets together once a year and decides all the world's issues.

It's getting so big. The small-business venture is not there any more. 30
Business has become too big to influence. It can't be changed internally. A counterpower is needed.

Engaging the Text

1. As Cruz moves up the economic ladder, he experiences growing conflict that keeps him from being content and proud of his accomplishments. To what do you attribute his discontent? Is his "solution" the one you would recommend?

2. Cruz says that the real force in America is the dream of "not losing." What does he mean by this? Do you agree?
3. What, according to Stephen Cruz, is wrong with the American Dream? Write an essay in which you first define and then either defend or critique his position.
4. Imagine the remainder of Stephen Cruz's life. Write a few paragraphs continuing his story. Read these aloud and discuss.

Exploring Connections

5. Write a brief profile of Stephen Cruz as you imagine him at age eighteen. Compare and contrast this with the profiles of the young women in "The New American Dreamers" (p. 450). What, if anything, distinguishes Cruz from the New American Dreamers?
6. Compare Stephen Cruz to Richard Rodriguez (p. 61), Gary Soto (p. 145), and Mike Rose (p. 33) in terms of their attitudes toward education and success.

Extending the Critical Context

7. According to Cruz, in 1969 few management positions were open to members of minority groups. Working in small groups, go to the library and look up current statistics on minorities in business (for example, the number of large minority-owned companies; the number of minority chief executives among major corporations; the distribution of minorities among top management, middle management, supervisory, and clerical positions). Compare notes with classmates and discuss.

Rewards and Opportunities: The Politics and Economics of Class in the U.S.[1]

Gregory Mantsios

Which of these gifts might a high school graduate in your family receive — a corsage, a savings bond, or a BMW? The answer indicates your social class, a key factor in American lives that many of us conspire to deny or ignore. The selection below makes it hard to deny class distinctions and their nearly universal influence on our lives. The statistics linking social class to everything from educational opportunities to health care are stag-

[1]The author wishes to thank Bill Clark for his assistance in preparing this selection. [Author's note]

gering, as are the gaps between rich and poor. For example, the richest Americans may accumulate more wealth in one day than you are likely to earn in ten years; meanwhile, there are two million poor people in New York City alone. Mantsios is the director of Worker Education at Queens College of the City University of New York. His essay appeared in Race, Class and Gender in the United States, *2nd ed. (1992).*

"[Class is] for European democracies or something else — it isn't for the United States of America. We are not going to be divided by class."
— GEORGE BUSH, 1988[2]

Strange words from a man presiding over a nation with more than 32 million people living in poverty and one of the largest income gaps between rich and poor in the industrialized world.[3] Politicians long before and long after George Bush have made and will continue to make statements proclaiming our egalitarian values and denying the existence of class in America. But they are not alone: most Americans dislike talking about class. We minimize the extent of inequality, pretend that class differences do not really matter, and erase the word "class" from our vocabulary and from our mind. In one survey, designed to solicit respondents' class identification, 35 percent of all those questioned told interviewers they had never thought about their class identification before that very moment.[4]

"We are all middle-class" or so it would seem. Our national consciousness, as shaped in large part by the media and our political leadership, provides us with a picture of ourselves as a nation of prosperity and opportunity with an ever expanding middle-class life-style. As a result, our class differences are muted and our collective character is homogenized.

Yet class divisions are real and arguably the most significant factor in determining both our very being in the world and the nature of the society we live in.

The Extent of Poverty in the U.S.

The official poverty line in 1990 was $12,675 for an urban family of four and $9,736 for a family of three. For years, critics have argued that the

[2]Quoted in George Will, "A Case for Dukakis," in *The Washington Post,* November 13, 1988, p. A27. [Author's note]

[3]The income gap in the United States, measured as a percentage of total income held by the wealthiest 20 percent of the population vs. the poorest 20 percent is approximately 11 to 1. The ratio in Great Britain is 7 to 1; in Japan, it is 4 to 1. (see "U.N. National Accounts Statistics." Statistical Papers, Series M no. 79. N.Y. U.N. 1985, pp. 1–11.) [Author's note]

[4]Marian Irish and James Prothro, *The Politics of American Democracy,* Englewood Cliffs, N.J., Prentice-Hall, 1965, p. 2, 38. [Author's note]

measurements used by the government woefully underestimate the extent of poverty in America.[5] Yet even by the government's conservative estimate, nearly one in eight Americans currently lives in poverty.

As deplorable as this is, the overall poverty rate for the nation effectively 5
masks both the level of deprivation and the extent of the problem within geographic areas and within specific populations. Three short years prior to George Bush's speech, the Physicians Task Force on Hunger in America declared that "Hunger is a problem of epidemic proportion across the nation." Upon completing their national field investigation of hunger and malnutrition, the team of twenty-two prominent physicians estimated that there were up to 20 million citizens hungry at least some period of time each month.

> Touring rural Mississippi the Task Force filed this report from one of the many such homes they visited:
>
> Inside the remnants of a house, alongside a dirt road in Greenwood, lived a family of thirteen people. Graciously welcomed by the mother and father, the doctors entered another world — a dwelling with no heat, no electricity, no windows, home for two parents, their children, and several nieces and nephews. Clothes were piled in the corner, the substitute location for closets which were missing; the two beds in the three-room house had no sheets, the torn mattresses covered by the bodies of three children who lay side by side. In the kitchen a small gas stove was the only appliance.
>
> No food was in the house. The babies had no milk; two were crying as several of the older children tried to console them. "These people are starving," the local guide told the doctors. Twice a week she collected food from churches to bring to the family. . . . Only the flies which crawled on the face of the smallest child seemed to be well fed. The parents were not; they had not eaten for two days. The children had eaten some dried beans the previous evening.
>
> — from *Hunger in America: The Growing Epidemic,*
> the PHYSICIANS TASK FORCE[6]

Nearly a quarter of the population of the state of Mississippi lives below the federal poverty level. Over a third of the population of Mississippi is so poor it qualifies for food stamps, although only 15 percent actually receive them.[7]

[5]See, for example, Patricia Ruggles, "The Poverty Line — Too Low for the 90's," in the *New York Times,* April 26, 1990, p. A31. [Author's note]

[6]Physicians Task Force on Hunger in America, *Hunger in America: The Growing Epidemic,* Wesleyan University Press, 1985, p. 27. [Author's note]

[7]Ibid. [Author's note]

The face of poverty in Greenwood, Mississippi, is not much different than that in other parts of the deep south and beyond. Appalling conditions of poverty are facts of life in the foothills of Appalachia, the reservations of Native America, the barrios of the Southwest, the abandoned towns of the industrial belt, and the ghettoes of the nation's urban centers. There are more than 2 million poor people in New York City alone, a figure that exceeds the entire population of some nations.

Today, the poor include the very young and the elderly, the rural poor and the urban homeless: increasingly, the poor also include men and women who work full time. When we examine the incidence of poverty within particular segments of the population, the figures can be both shameful and sobering:

- more than one out of every five children in the U.S. (all races) lives below the poverty line[8]
- 39 percent of Hispanic children and 45 percent of Black children in the U.S. live below the poverty line[9]
- one in every four rural children is poor[10]
- if you are Black and 65 years of age or older, your chances of being poor are one in three[11]
- roughly 60 percent of all poor work at least part-time or in seasonal work[12]
- 2 million Americans worked full-time throughout the year and were still poor[13]

Poverty statistics have either remained relatively constant over the years or have shown a marked increase in the incidence of poverty. The number of full-time workers below the poverty line, for example, increased by more than 50 percent from 1978 to 1986.[14]

The Level of Wealth

Business Week recently reported that the average salary for the CEO of 10
the nation's top 1,000 companies was $841,000.[15] As high as this figure is, however, it fails to capture the level of compensation at the top of the corporate world. Short-term and long-term bonuses, stock options and stock awards can add significantly to annual compensation. Take the following examples:

[8]Bureau of Census, "Statistical Abstract of the U.S. 1990," Department of Commerce, Washington, D.C., 1990, p. 460. [Author's note]

[9]Ibid. [Author's note]

[10]Ibid. [Author's note]

[11]Ibid. [Author's note]

[12]*U.S. News and World Report,* January 1, 1988, pp. 18–24. [Author's note]

[13]Ibid. [Author's note]

[14]Ibid. [Author's note]

[15]*Business Week,* October 19, 1990, p. 11. [Author's note]

- annual compensation in 1989, including short-term bonuses, for the Chief Executive Officer of UAL, came to $18.3 million; for the head of Reebok, compensation came to $14.6 million (in what was not a particularly hot year in the sneaker business).[16]
- annual compensation, including short-term and long-term bonuses and stock awards, for the head of Time Warner Inc. totaled $78.2 million; for the CEO of LIN Broadcasting, it came to a whopping $186 million.[17]

The distribution of income in the United States is outlined in Table 1.

Table 1 Income Inequality in the U.S.[18]

INCOME GROUP (FAMILIES)	PERCENT OF INCOME RECEIVED
Lowest fifth	4.6
Second fifth	10.8
Middle fifth	16.8
Fourth fifth	24.0
Highest fifth	43.7
(Highest 5 percent)	(17.0)

By 1990, according to economist Robert Reich, the top fifth of the population took home more money than the other four-fifths put together.[19]

Wealth, rather than income, is a more accurate indicator of economic inequality. Accumulated wealth by individuals and families runs into the billions, with the U.S. now boasting at least 58 billionaires, many of them multibillionaires. The distribution of wealth is far more skewed than the distribution of income. In 1986, the Joint Economic Committee of the U.S. Congress released a special report entitled "The Concentration of Wealth in the United States." Table 2 summarizes some of the findings.

Table 2 Distribution of Wealth in the U.S.[20]

FAMILIES	PERCENT OF WEALTH OWNED
The richest 10 percent	71.7
(The top 1/2 percent)	(35.1)
Everyone else, or 90 percent of all families	28.2

[16]Ibid., p. 12. [Author's note]

[17]*Business Week*, May 6, 1991, p. 90. [Author's note]

[18]U.S. Department of Commerce, "Statistical Abstract of the U.S. 1988," Washington, D.C., 1988, p. 428. [Author's note]

[19]Robert Reich, "Secession of the Successful," *New York Times*, January 20, 1991, p. M42. [Author's note]

[20]Joint Economic Committee of the U.S. Congress, "The Concentration of Wealth in the United States," Washington, D.C., 1986, p. 24. [Author's note]

It should be noted that because of the way the statistics were collected by the Congressional Committee, the figure for 90 percent of all other families includes half of the families who fall into the wealthiest quintile of the population. The "super rich," that is, the top one-half of one percent of the population, includes approximately 420,000 households with the average value of the wealth for each one of these households amounting to $8.9 million.[21]

> Most people never see the opulence of the wealthy, except in the fantasy world of television and the movies. Society pages in local newspapers, however, often provide a glimpse into the real life-style of the wealthy. A recent article in the *New York Times* described the life-style of John and Patricia Kluge.
>
> Mr. Kluge, chairman of the Metromedia Company, has an estimated worth of $5.2 billion. . . . The Kluges (pronounced Kloog-ee) have an apartment in Manhattan, an estate in the Virginia hunt country, and a horse farm in Scotland. . . .
>
> They are known in Washington and New York social circles for opulent parties. Mr. Kluge had the ballroom of the Waldorf done up like the interior of a Viennese belle epoque palace for Mrs. Kluge's forty-ninth birthday.
>
> Her birthday parties for him have been more intimate, friends say. Typically these involve only one or two other couples (once it was Frank and Barbara Sinatra) who take over L'Orangerie, a private dining room at Le Cirque that seats one hundred. The room was turned into an English garden for Mr. Kluge's seventieth birthday, with dirt covering the carpet, flowering plants, and trees. Hidden among the trees were nine violinists. The wine was a Chateau Lafite from 1914, the year of his birth. The birthday cake was in the shape of a $1 billion bill.[22]

The Plight of the Middle Class

The percentage of households with earnings at a middle-income level has been falling steadily.[23] The latest census figures show that the percentage of families with an annual income between $15,000 and $50,000 (approximately 50 percent and 200 percent of the median income) has fallen by nearly 10 percentage points since 1970.[24] While some of the households have moved upward and others have moved downward, what is clear is that the United States is experiencing a significant polarization in the distribution of

[21] Richard Roper, *Persistent Poverty: The American Dream Turned Nightmare,* Plenum Press, 1991, p. 60. [Author's note]

[22] *New York Times,* April 29, 1990, p. 48. [Author's note]

[23] Chris Tilly, "U-Turn on Equality," *Dollars and Sense,* May 1986, p. 84. [Author's note]

[24] Census, ibid., p. 450. [Author's note]

income. The gap between rich and poor is wider and the share of income earned by middle-income Americans has fallen to the lowest level since the census bureau began keeping statistics in 1946. More and more individuals and families are finding themselves at one or the other end of the economic spectrum as the middle class steadily declines.

Furthermore, being in the middle class is no longer what is used to be. Once, middle-class status carried the promise that one's standard of living would steadily improve over time. Yet 60 percent of Americans will have experienced virtually no income gain between 1980 and 1990. (Compare this to the income gains experienced by the wealthiest fifth of the population—up by 33 percent, and the wealthiest one percent of the population—up by 87 percent.)[25] One study showed that only one in five (males) will surpass the status, income, and prestige of their fathers.[26]

Nor does a middle-class income any longer guarantee the comforts it 15
once did. Home ownership, for example, has increasingly become out of reach for a growing number of citizens. During the last decade home ownership rates dropped from 44 percent to 36 percent among people in the 25–29 year old age-group and from 61 percent to 53 percent among those in their thirties.[27]

The Rewards of Money

The distribution of income and wealth in the U.S. is grossly unequal and becomes increasingly more so with time. The rewards of money, however, go well beyond those of consumption patterns and life-style. It is not simply that the wealthy live such opulent life-styles, it is that class position determines one's life chances. Life chances include such far-reaching factors as life expectancy, level of education, occupational status, exposure to industrial hazards, incidence of crime victimization, rate of incarceration, etc. In short, class position can play a critically important role in determining how long you live, whether you have a healthy life, if you fail in school, or if you succeed at work.

The link between economic status and health is perhaps the most revealing and most disheartening. Health professionals and social scientists have shown that income is closely correlated to such factors as infant mortality, cancer, chronic disease, and death due to surgical and medical complications and "misadventures."[28]

[25]"And the Rich Get Richer," *Dollars and Sense,* October 1990, p. 5. [Author's note]

[26]Richard DeLone, *Small Futures,* Harcourt Brace Jovanovich, 1978, pp. 14–19.

[27]Roper, ibid., p. 32. [Author's note]

[28]Melvin Krasner, *Poverty and Health in New York City,* United Hospital Fund of New York, 1989. See also U.S. Dept. of Health and Human Services, *Health Status of Minorities and Low Income Groups,* 1985; and Dana Hughes, Kay Johnson, Sara Rosenbaum, Elizabeth Butler, Janet Simons, *The Health of America's Children,* The Children's Defense Fund, 1988. [Author's note]

The infant mortality rate is an example that invites international as well as racial and economic comparisons. At 10.6 infant deaths per 1,000 live births, the U.S. places nineteenth in the world — behind such countries as Spain, Singapore, and Hong Kong; a statistic that is in and of itself shameful for the wealthiest nation in the world. When infant mortality only among Blacks in the U.S. is considered, the rate rises to 18.2 and places the U.S. twenty-eighth in rank — behind Bulgaria and equal to Costa Rica. The infant mortality rate in poverty stricken areas, such as Hale County, Alabama, is three times the national rate and nearly twice that of the nation of Malaysia (whose GNP per capita is one-tenth that of the U.S.).[29]

Table 3 Infant Mortality Rate Per 1,000 Births[30]

Total (national, all racial and ethnic groups)	10.6
Among Blacks only	18.2
In Hale County, Alabama	31.0

Analyses of the relationship between health and income are not always easy to come by. A recent study conducted in New York City, however, provided some important information. The study examined the difference in health status and delivery of health services among residents from different neighborhoods. The data provided allows for comparing incidents of health problems in neighborhoods where 40 percent or more of the population lives below the poverty line with those in other neighborhoods where less than 10 percent of the population lives below the poverty line. The study found that the incidence of health problems, in many categories, was several times as great in poorer neighborhoods. For example, death associated with vascular complications (from the heart or brain) occurred nearly twice as often in poor areas than in non-poor. Similarly, chances of being afflicted with bronchitis is 5 times as great in poor areas than in non-poor areas.[31] The study concluded, "The findings clearly indicate that certain segments of the population — poor, minority, and other disadvantaged groups — are especially vulnerable and bear a disproportionate share of preventable, and therefore unnecessary deaths and diseases."[32]

20 The reasons for such a high correlation are many and varied: inadequate nutrition, exposure to occupational and environmental hazards, access to

[29] Physicians Task Force, ibid.; Hughes et al., ibid.; and "World Development Report 1990," World Bank, Oxford University Press, 1990, pp. 232–233. [Author's note]

[30] Ibid. [Author's note]

[31] Krasner, ibid., p. 134 [Author's note]

[32] Ibid., p. 166. It should be noted that the study was conducted in a major metropolitan area where hospitals and health-care facilities are in close proximity to the population, rich and poor. One might expect the discrepancies to be even greater in poor, rural areas where access to health care and medical attention is more problematic. [Author's note]

health-care facilities, quality of health services provided, ability to pay and therefore receive medical services, etc. Inadequate nutrition, for example, is associated with low birth weights and growth failure among low-income children and with chronic disease among the elderly poor. It has also been shown that the uninsured and those covered by Medicaid are far less likely to be given common hospital procedures than are patients with private medical coverage.

The relationship between income and health is similar to that of income and rate of incarceration. One in four young Black men, age 20 to 29, are either in jail or court supervised (i.e., on parole or probation). This figure surpasses the number of Black men enrolled in higher education. The figure also compares negatively to that for white men where 1 in 16 are incarcerated in the same age-group.[33]

While it is often assumed that differences in rates of arrest and incarceration reflect differences in the incidents of crime, a recent study conducted in Pinellas County, Florida, found that most women prosecuted for using illegal drugs while pregnant have been poor members of racial minorities, even though drug use in pregnancy is equally prevalent in white middle-class women. Researchers found that about 15 percent of both the white and the Black women used drugs, but that the Black women were 10 times as likely as whites to be reported to the authorities and poor women were more likely to be reported than middle-class women. Sixty percent of the 133 women reported had incomes of less than $12,000 a year. Only 8 percent had incomes of more than $25,000 a year.

Differences in Opportunity

The opportunity for social and economic success are the hallmarks of the American Dream. The dream is rooted in two factors: education and jobs.

Our nation prides itself on its ability to provide unprecedented educational opportunities to its citizens. As well it should. It sends more of its young people to college than any other nation in the world. There are nearly 13 million Americans currently enrolled in colleges and universities around the country, a result of the tremendous expansion of higher education since World War II. The establishment of financial assistance for veterans and for the needy, and the growth of affordable public colleges all have had an important and positive effect on college enrollment. Most importantly from the point of view of a national consciousness, the swelling of college enrollments has affirmed our egalitarian values and convinced us that our educational system is just and democratic.

[33]*Washington Post,* February 27, 1990, p. A3, citing Marc Mauer, "Young Black Men and the Criminal Justice System: A Growing National Problem," The Sentencing Project January 1990. [Author's note]

Our pride, however, is a false pride. For while we have made great 25
strides in opening the doors of academe, the system of education in the United States leaves much to be desired and is anything but egalitarian.

More than a quarter of our adult population has not graduated from high school, nearly three quarters do not hold a college degree.[34] This is a record that does not bode well for the most industrialized and technologically advanced nation in the world. Perhaps more importantly, the level of educational achievement is largely class determined.

At least equal in importance to the amount of education received, is the quality of education. The quality of primary and secondary schools is largely dependent on geography and proximity to schools with adequate resources. Educational funding, and the tax base for it, are determined by residency and who can afford to live where. Schools in poorer districts are just not as likely to provide a high-quality education.

Student achievement in the classroom and on standardized tests is also class determined. Studies from the late 1970s showed a direct relation between SAT scores and family income. Grouping SAT scores into twelve categories from highest to lowest, researchers found that the mean family income decreased consistently from one group to the next as test scores declined. The study was done by examining the test results and family income of over 600,000 students![35] In other words, the higher the family income, the higher the test scores and vice versa.

Furthermore, for that segment of the population that does enter and complete a college education (approximately 18 percent of the population, including Associate degrees), the system is highly stratified. Precious few from poor and working-class families have gained access to the elite colleges. For the most part, these have remained the bastion of the wealthy, leaving the less prestigious two-year colleges almost exclusively the domain of the poor and the disadvantaged. The result is that colleges today are performing the same sorting function previously performed by high schools, where students are divided into vocational and academic tracks. The rate of participation in vocational programs at the college level is closely related to socioeconomic class, so that students from poorer backgrounds who do enroll in college are still being channeled into educational programs and institutions that are vocational in nature and that lead to less desirable occupations and futures.[36]

The "junior" colleges, whose growth once promised to serve as a step- 30

[34]The Chronicle of Higher Education, *The Almanac of Higher Education, 1989–1990,* The University of Chicago Press, 1989. [Author's note]

[35]Richard DeLone, ibid., p. 102. [Author's note]

[36]David Karen, "The Politics of Class, Race, and Gender," paper presented at Conference on "Class Bias in Higher Education," Queens College, Flushing, N.Y., November 1990. This does not deny the intrinsic value of vocational education, but points to the fact that poor and working class students are found in the sector of education that yields the smallest socioeconomic return. [Author's note]

ping stone for the disadvantaged and the underprepared to gain access to four-year liberal arts colleges have been transformed into "community" colleges which provide vocational programs and terminal degrees in fields that narrow occupational options. The effect is to limit opportunity and to provide what some critics have referred to as a "cooling out function" — the managing of ambitions of the poor and working class who might otherwise take the American dream seriously.[37]

Some might argue that intelligence and drive are more significant than education in determining a young person's future. A *New York Times* article, however, entitled "Status Not Brains Makes a Child's Future," neatly summed up the findings of a Carnegie Foundation study that examined the relationship between IQ scores and occupational success. Researchers compared economic success rates of individuals who had the same IQ. Their findings: even when IQ test scores were the same, a young person's ability to obtain a job that will pay in the top 10 percent of the income structure is 27 times as great if he or she comes from a wealthy background.[38]

Culture, the Media, and Ideology

If the U.S. is so highly stratified and if economic class makes such a difference, why is it, then, that we retain such illusions about an egalitarian[39] society? In part, it is because for many of us it is simply more comfortable to deny the class nature of our society and the rigid boundaries such a society suggests: we would rather consider our economic predicament, whatever our class standing, to be temporary and anticipate a brighter future in what we prefer to believe is a fluid and open opportunity structure. In part, it is also because we are constantly bombarded with cultural messages from the media and other sources that tell us that class in America, if it exists at all, does not really matter.

Both in entertainment and in relating the news of the day, the media convey important, albeit contradictory messages: classes do not exist, the poor and the working class are morally inferior, America is a land of great social and economic mobility, class is irrelevant.

TV sitcoms and feature films have traditionally ignored class issues. There have been relatively few serious portrayals of the poor or the working class in the history of film and television. Television, in particular, presents a view of America where everyone is a professional and middle class: daddy, it seems, always goes to the office, not to the factory.[40] There are notable

[37]Steven Brint and Jerome Karabel, *Diverted Dream: Community Colleges and the Promise of Educational Opportunity in America, 1890 to 1985*, Oxford University Press, 1989. [Author's note]

[38]Richard DeLone, ibid. [Author's note]

[39]*egalitarian:* Based on equal social, political, and economic rights and privileges.

[40]Barbara Ehrenreich, *Fear of Falling: The Inner Life of the Middle Class,* Pantheon, 1989, p. 140. [Author's note]

exceptions and these are of particular interest in that they usually present story lines that distort class realities even further.

Story lines about class do one of three things. First, they present and 35
reinforce negative class stereotypes. The poor are presented as hapless or dangerous and the working class as dumb, reactionary, and bigoted. Those not members of the professional middle class are to be laughed at, despised, or feared.[41] Second, they portray instances of upward mobility and class fluidity. These include rags-to-riches stories, Pygmalion tales,[42] and comic instances of downward mobility. Third, they stress that the people who think firm class lines exist come to discover that they are mistaken: everybody is really the same.[43] These are often rich girl/poor boy romances or their opposite.

Story lines about class make for good comedy, good romance, and in the last example, even good lessons in human relations. They also perform, however, a great disservice: "treating class differences as totally inconsequential strengthens the national delusion that class power and position are insignificant."[44]

A Structural Perspective

Vast differences in wealth have serious consequences and are neither justifiable nor a result of individual and personal deficiencies. People are poor because they have no money and no power to acquire money. The wealthy are rich because they have both.

The distribution of income and wealth occurs because a society is structured and policies are implemented in such a way to either produce or alleviate inequalities. A society can choose to minimize the gaps in wealth and power between its most privileged and its most disenfranchised. Government can serve as the equalizer by providing mechanisms to redistribute wealth from the top to the bottom. The promise of government as the great equalizer has clearly failed in the U.S. and rather than redoubling the efforts to redistribute wealth, traditional redistributive mechanisms, such as the progressive income tax, have declined in use in recent years. The tax rate for the wealthiest segment of the population, for example, steadily declined in spite of, or perhaps because of, the increasing concentration of wealth and power at the top. In 1944 the top tax rate was 94 percent, after World

[41] See Barbara Ehrenreich, ibid. [Author's note]

[42] *Pygmalion tales:* Tales in which a lower-class citizen is transformed into someone elegant and refined. In George Bernard Shaw's *Pygmalion* (1913), a British speech professor transforms a working girl; the musical version *My Fair Lady* (1956) is based on Shaw's play. In the original Greek myth, Pygmalion was an artist-king who fell in love with a beautiful statue, which the goddess Aphrodite then brought to life.

[43] Benjamin DeMott, *The Imperial Middle: Why Americans Can't Think Straight About Class,* William Morrow, 1990. [Author's note]

[44] DeMott, ibid. [Author's note]

War II it was reduced to 91 percent, in 1964 to 72 percent, in 1981 to 50 percent, in 1990 to 28 percent (for those with an annual income over $155,000).[45]

Nor is it the case that conditions of wealth simply coexist side-by-side with conditions of poverty. The point is not that there are rich and poor, but that some are rich precisely because others are poor, and that one's privilege is predicated on the other's disenfranchisement. If it were not for the element of exploitation, we might celebrate inequality as reflective of our nation's great diversity.

The great antipoverty crusader, Michael Harrington, tells of the debate 40
in Congress over Richard Nixon's Family Assistance Plan during the 1970s. If the government provided a minimum income to everyone, "Who," asked a southern legislator, "will iron my shirts and rake the yard?"[46]

The legislator bluntly stated the more complex truth: the privileged in our society require a class-structured social order in order to maintain and enhance their economic and political well-being. Industrial profits depend on cheap labor and on a pool of unemployed to keep workers in check. Real estate speculators and developers create and depend on slums for tax-evading investments. These are the injustices and irrationalities of our economic system.

What is worse is that inequalities perpetuate themselves. People with wealth are the ones who have the opportunity to accumulate more wealth.

The fortune of Warren Buffett is estimated to be approximately $4 billion dollars. He is one of 71 billionaires in the United States (their average holding is about $3 billion each).[47] Calculated below is the interest generated by Buffett's wealth at an 8 percent return.

Interest generated by $4 billion, at 8 percent return

$10 each second
$600 each minute
$36,000 each hour
$864,000 each day
$6,048,000 each week
$320,000,000 each year ($320 million)

In other words, Mr. Buffett makes more money in two days of nonwork than most people earn in a lifetime of work.

[45] Ironically those with an annual income between $75,000 and $150,000 pay a higher rate of 33 percent. [Author's note]

[46] Michael Harrington, *The New American Poverty*, Penguin, 1985, p. 3. [Author's note]

[47] *Fortune Magazine*, September 10, 1990, p. 98; *Forbes*, October 21, 1991, pp. 145–160. [Author's note]

It is this ability to generate additional resources that most distinguishes the nation's upper class from the rest of society. It is not simply bank interest that generates more money, but income producing property: buildings, factories, natural resources; those assets Karl Marx referred to as the means of production. Today, unlike the early days of capitalism, these are owned either directly or indirectly through stocks. Economists estimate that for the super rich, the rate of return on such investments is approximately 30 percent.[48] Economists have also designed a device, called Net Financial Assets (NFA), to measure the level and concentration of income-producing property. While Net Worth (NW), a figure that considers all assets and debts, provides a picture of what kind of life-style is being supported, the NFA figure specifically excludes in its calculation ownership of homes and motor vehicles. By doing so, the NFA figure provides a more reliable measure of an individual's life chances and ability to accumulate future resources. A home or a car are not ordinarily converted to purchase other resources, such as a prep school or college education for one's children. Neither are these assets likely to be used to buy medical care, support political candidates, pursue justice in the courts, pay lobbyists to protect special interests, or finance a business or make other investments. Net financial assets include only those financial assets normally available for and used to generate income and wealth.[49] Stock ownership, for example, is a financial asset and is highly concentrated at the top, with the wealthiest 10 percent of the population owning over 89 percent of the corporate stocks.[50] Since home ownership is the major source of wealth for those who own a house, removing home equity as well as car ownership from the calculations has a significant impact on how we view the question of equity.

- The median net household income in the U.S. is $21,744, net worth in the U.S. is $32,609, and the median Net Financial Assets is $2,599.
- While the top 20 percent of American households earn over 43 percent of all income, that same 20 percent holds 67 percent of Net Worth, and nearly 90 percent of Net Financial Assets.
- The median income of the top one percent of the population is 22 times greater than that of the remaining 99 percent. The median Net Financial Assets of the top one percent is 237 times greater than the median of the other 99 percent of the population.[51]

The ability to generate wealth on the part of this class of owners is truly staggering. It contrasts sharply with the ability of those who rely on selling their labor power. For those with income under $25,000, wage and salary income from labor comprised 90 percent of their total income.

[48] E. K. Hunt and Howard Sherman, *Economics,* Harper and Row, 1990, pp. 254–257. [Author's note]

[49] Melvin Oliver and Thomas Shapiro, "Wealth of a Nation," *The American Journal of Economics and Sociology,* April 1990, p. 129. [Author's note]

[50] The Joint Economic Committee, ibid. [Author's note]

[51] Oliver, ibid., p. 129. [Author's note]

There is also an entrepreneurial middle class in America that includes 45
farmers, shopkeepers, and others. The small entrepreneurs, however, are becoming increasingly marginal in America and their income-producing property hardly exempts them from laboring.

The wealthy usually work too: their property income, however, is substantial enough to enable them to live without working if they chose to do so.

People with wealth and financial assets have disproportionate power in society. First, they have control of the workplace in enterprises they own. They determine what is produced and how it is produced. Second, they have enormous control over the media and other institutions that influence ideology and how we think about things, including class. Third, they have far greater influence over the nations' political institutions than their numbers warrant. They have the ability to influence not only decisions affecting their particular business ventures, but the general political climate of the nation.

Spheres of Power and Oppression

When we look at society and try to determine what it is that keeps most people down — what holds them back from realizing their potential as healthy, creative, productive individuals — we find institutionally oppressive forces that are largely beyond their individual control. Class domination is one of these forces. People do not choose to be poor or working class; instead they are limited and confined by the opportunities afforded or denied them by a social system. The class structure in the United States is a function of its economic system — capitalism, a system that is based on private rather than public ownership and control of commercial enterprises and on the class division between those who own and control and those who do not. Under capitalism, these enterprises are governed by the need to produce a profit for the owners, rather than to fulfill collective needs.

Racial and gender domination are other such forces that hold people down. Although there are significant differences in the way capitalism, racism and sexism affect our lives, there are also a multitude of parallels. And although race, class, and gender act independently of each other, they are at the same time very much interrelated.

On the one hand, issues of race and gender oppression cut across class 50
lines. Women experience the effects of sexism whether they are well-paid professionals or poorly paid clerks. As women, they face discrimination and male domination, as well as catcalls and stereotyping. Similarly, a Black man faces racial oppression whether he is an executive, an auto worker, or a tenant farmer. As a Black, he will be subjected to racial slurs and be denied opportunities because of his color. Regardless of their class standing, women and members of minority races are confronted with oppressive forces precisely because of their gender, color, or both.

On the other hand, class oppression permeates other spheres of power and oppression, so that the oppression experienced by women and minorities is also differentiated along class lines. Although women and minorities find themselves in subordinate positions vis-à-vis white men, the particular issues they confront may be quite different depending on their position in the class structure. Inequalities in the class structure distinguish social functions and individual power, and these distinctions carry over to race and gender categories.

Power is incremental and class privileges can accrue to individual women and to individual members of a racial minority. At the same time, class-oppressed men, whether they are white or Black, have privileges afforded them as men in a sexist society. Similarly, class-oppressed whites, whether they are men or women, have privileges afforded them as whites in a racist society. Spheres of power and oppression divide us deeply in our society, and the schisms between us are often difficult to bridge.

Whereas power is incremental, oppression is cumulative, and those who are poor, Black, and female have all the forces of classism, racism, and sexism bearing down on them. This cumulative oppression is what is meant by the double and triple jeopardy of women and minorities.

Furthermore, oppression in one sphere is related to the likelihood of oppression in another. If you are Black and female, for example, you are much more likely to be poor and working class than you would be as a white male. Census figures show that the incidence of poverty and near-poverty (calculated as 125 percent of the poverty line) varies greatly by race and gender.

Table 4 Chances of Being Poor in America[52]

	WHITE MALE & FEMALE	WHITE FEMALE HEAD	BLACK MALE & FEMALE	BLACK FEMALE HEAD
Poverty	1 in 9	1 in 4	1 in 3	1 in 2
Near Poverty	1 in 6	1 in 3	1 in 2	2 in 3

In other words, being female and being nonwhite are attributes in our 55
society that increase the chances of poverty and of lower-class standing. Racism and sexism compound the effects of classism in society.

[52]"Characteristics of the Population Below the Poverty Line: 1984," from Current Population Reports, Consumer Income Series P-60, No. 152, Washington, D.C., U.S. Department of Commerce, Bureau of the Census, June 1986, pp. 5–9. [Author's note]

Engaging the Text

1. Explain the difference between wealth and income. Why is this such an important distinction to make?
2. Work out a rough budget for a family of four with an annual income of $12,675.

Be sure to include costs for food, housing, health care, transportation, and other unavoidable expenses. Do you think this would be a reasonable poverty line, or is it too low or too high?

3. Look past all the evidence Mantsios provides and make a list of his key claims about class in the United States. Discuss these briefly in class to identify areas of consensus and disagreement; in any controversial areas, consult Mantsios's evidence and weigh its adequacy and the author's logic.
4. Are the wealthy in the United States exploiting or oppressing those less fortunate? Are the disparities in wealth a necessary by-product of a free society? Is Mantsios's piece unpatriotic?
5. Mantsios says that government could redistribute wealth to reduce inequalities (para. 38). Clearly many wealthy Americans would oppose such steps. What do you believe most middle-class Americans would think, and why?

Exploring Connections

6. Review Ruth Sidel's "New American Dreamers" (p. 450). How might Mantsios rate the chances that Beth Conant, Amy Morrison, Jacqueline Gonzalez, and Simone Baker will achieve their dreams? To what extent would you agree?
7. Working in small groups, discuss which class each of the following would belong to and how this class affiliation would shape the life chances of each:
   - Anndee Hochman in "Growing Pains" (p. 150)
   - the narrator in "An Indian Story" (p. 225)
   - Gary Soto in "Looking for Work" (p. 145)
   - C. P. Ellis (p. 388)
   - Stephen Cruz (p. 460)
   - Miss Moore in "The Lesson" (p. 482)
8. Write an imaginary dialogue between Mantsios and Mike Rose (p. 33) about why some students, like Rose, seem to be able to break through social class barriers and others, like Ken Harvey, Dave Snyder, and Ted Richard, do not.

Extending the Critical Context

9. Skim through several recent issues of a financial magazine like *Forbes* or *Money*. Who is the audience for these publications? What kind of advice is offered, and what levels of income and investment are discussed?
10. Study the employment pages of a major newspaper in your area. Roughly what percentage of the openings would you consider upper class, middle class, and lower class? On what do you base your distinctions?
11. Mantsios claims that while TV reinforces negative class stereotypes, it generally depicts a world where class scarcely exists. Work together in small groups to survey a week's worth of TV programming. In general, how are upper-, middle-, and working-class Americans portrayed? To what extent does TV deny the power of class differences?
12. Watch the film *Trading Places* and critique its attitudes about wealth and poverty in the United States.

The Lesson

TONI CADE BAMBARA

"The Lesson" looks at wealth through the eyes of a poor Black girl whose education includes a field trip to one of the world's premier toy stores. The story speaks to serious social issues with a comic, energetic, and utterly engaging voice. Toni Cade Bambara (b. 1939) grew up in the Harlem and Bedford-Stuyvesant areas of New York City. Trained at Queens College and City College of New York in dance, drama, and literature, she is best known for her collections of stories, Gorilla, My Love *(1972) and* The Seabirds Are Still Alive and Other Stories *(1977), and for her novels,* If Blessing Comes *(1987) and* The Salt Eaters *(1980), winner of the American Book Award. This story is taken from* Gorilla, My Love.

Back in the days when everyone was old and stupid or young and foolish and me and Sugar were the only ones just right, this lady moved on our block with nappy hair and proper speech and no makeup. And quite naturally we laughed at her, laughed the way we did at the junk man who went about his business like he was some big-time president and his sorry-ass horse his secretary. And we kinda hated her too, hated the way we did the winos who cluttered up our parks and pissed on our handball walls and stank up our hallways and stairs so you couldn't halfway play hide-and-seek without a goddamn gas mask. Miss Moore was her name. The only woman on the block with no first name. And she was black as hell, cept for her feet, which were fish-white and spooky. And she was always planning these boring-ass things for us to do, us being my cousin, mostly, who lived on the block cause we all moved North the same time and to the same apartment then spread out gradual to breathe. And our parents would yank our heads into some kinda shape and crisp up our clothes so we'd be presentable for travel with Miss Moore, who always looked like she was going to church, though she never did. Which is just one of the things the grownups talked about when they talked behind her back like a dog. But when she came calling with some sachet[1] she'd sewed up or some gingerbread she'd made or some book, why then they'd all be too embarrassed to turn her down and we'd get handed out all spruced up. She'd been to college and said it only right that she should take responsibility for the young ones' education, and she not even related by marriage or blood. So they'd go for it. Specially Aunt Gretchen. She was

[1]*sachet:* A small bag filled with a sweet-smelling substance. Sachets are often placed in drawers to scent clothes.

the main gofer in the family. You got some ole dumb shit foolishness you want somebody to go for, you send for Aunt Gretchen. She been screwed into the go-along for so long, it's a blood-deep natural thing with her. Which is how she got saddled with me and Sugar and Junior in the first place while our mothers were in a la-de-da apartment up the block having a good ole time.

So this one day Miss Moore rounds us all up at the mailbox and it's puredee hot and she's knockin herself out about arithmetic. And school suppose to let up in summer I heard, but she don't never let up. And the starch in my pinafore scratching the shit outta me and I'm really hating this nappy-head bitch and her goddamn college degree. I'd much rather go to the pool or to the show where it's cool. So me and Sugar leaning on the mailbox being surly, which is a Miss Moore word. And Flyboy checking out what everybody brought for lunch. And Fat Butt already wasting his peanut-butter-and-jelly sandwich like the pig he is. And Junebug punchin on Q.T.'s arm for potato chips. And Rosie Giraffe shifting from one hip to the other waiting for somebody to step on her foot or ask her if she from Georgia so she can kick ass, preferably Mercedes'. And Miss Moore asking us do we know what money is, like we a bunch of retards. I mean real money, she say, like it's only poker chips or monopoly papers we lay on the grocer. So right away I'm tired of this and say so. And would much rather snatch Sugar and go to the Sunset and terrorize the West Indian kids and take their hair ribbons and their money too. And Miss Moore files that remark away for next week's lesson on brotherhood, I can tell. And finally I say we oughta get to the subway cause it's cooler and besides we might meet some cute boys. Sugar done swiped her mama's lipstick, so we ready.

So we heading down the street and she's boring us silly about what things cost and what our parents make and how much goes for rent and how money ain't divided up right in this country. And then she gets to the part about we all poor and live in the slums, which I don't feature. And I'm ready to speak on that, but she steps out in the street and hails two cabs just like that. Then she hustles half the crew in with her and hands me a five-dollar bill and tells me to calculate 10 percent tip for the driver. And we're off. Me and Sugar and Junebug and Flyboy hangin out the window and hollering to everybody, putting lipstick on each other cause Flyboy a faggot anyway, and making farts with our sweaty armpits. But I'm mostly trying to figure how to spend this money. But they all fascinated with the meter ticking and Junebug starts laying bets as to how much it'll read when Flyboy can't hold his breath no more. Then Sugar lays bets as to how much it'll be when we get there. So I'm stuck. Don't nobody want to go for my plan, which is to jump out at the next light and run off to the first bar-b-que we can find. Then the driver tells us to get the hell out cause we are there already. And the meter reads eighty-five cents. And I'm stalling to figure out the tip and Sugar say give him a dime. And I decide he don't need it bad as I do, so later for him. But then he tries to take off with Junebug foot still in the door so we talk about his mama something ferocious. Then we check out that we on Fifth Avenue[2] and everybody dressed up in stockings. One lady in a fur coat, hot as it is. White folks crazy.

“This is the place,” Miss Moore say, presenting it to us in the voice she uses at the museum. “Let's look in the windows before we go in.”

5 “Can we steal?” Sugar asks very serious like she's getting the ground rules squared away before she plays. “I beg your pardon,” say Miss Moore, and we fall out. So she leads us around the windows of the toy store and me and Sugar screamin, “This is mine, that's mine, I gotta have that, that was made for me, I was born for that,” till Big Butt drowns us out.

“Hey, I'm goin to buy that there.”

“That there? You don't even know what it is, stupid.”

“I do so,” he say punchin on Rosie Giraffe. “It's a microscope.”

“Whatcha gonna do with a microscope, fool?”

10 “Look at things.”

“Like what, Ronald?” ask Miss Moore. And Big Butt ain't got the first notion. So here go Miss Moore gabbing about the thousands of bacteria in a drop of water and the somethinorother in a speck of blood and the million and one living things in the air around us is invisible to the naked eye. And what she say that for? Junebug go to town on that “naked” and we rolling. Then Miss Moore ask what it cost. So we all jam into the window smudgin it up and the price tag say $300. So then she ask how long'd take for Big Butt and Junebug to save up their allowances. “Too long,” I say. “Yeh,” adds Sugar, “outgrown it by that time.” And Miss Moore say no, you never outgrow learning instruments. “Why, even medical students and interns and,” blah, blah, blah. And we ready to choke Big Butt for bringing it up in the first damn place.

“This here costs four hundred eighty dollars,” say Rosie Giraffe. So we pile up all over her to see what she pointin out. My eyes tell me it's a chunk of glass cracked with something heavy, and different-color inks dripped into the splits, then the whole thing put into a oven or something. But for $480 it don't make sense.

“That's a paperweight made of semi-precious stones fused together under tremendous pressure,” she explains slowly, with her hands doing the mining and all the factory work.

“So what's paperweight?” asks Rosie Giraffe.

15 “To weight paper with, dumbbell,” say Flyboy, the wise man from the East.

“Not exactly,” say Miss Moore, which is what she say when you warm or way off too. “It's to weigh paper down so it won't scatter and make your desk untidy.” So right away me and Sugar curtsy to each other and then to Mercedes who is more the tidy type.

[2]*Fifth Avenue:* The street in New York most famous for its expensive stores.

"We don't keep paper on top of the desk in my class," say Junebug, figuring Miss Moore crazy or lyin one.

"At home, then," she say. "Don't you have a calendar and a pencil case and a blotter and a letter-opener on your desk at home where you do your homework?" And she know damn well what our homes look like cause she nosys around in them every chance she gets.

"I don't even have a desk," say Junebug. "Do we?"

"No. And I don't get no homework neither," say Big Butt. 20

"And I don't even have a home," say Flyboy like he do at school to keep the white folks off his back and sorry for him. Send this poor kid to camp posters, is his speciality.

"I do," say Mercedes. "I have a box of stationery on my desk and a picture of my cat. My godmother bought the stationery and the desk. There's a big rose on each sheet and the envelopes smell like roses."

"Who want to know about your smelly-ass stationery," say Rosie Giraffe fore I can get my two cents in.

"It's important to have a work area all your own so that . . ."

"Will you look at this sailboat, please," say Flyboy, cuttin her off and 25
pointin to the thing like it was his. So once again we tumble all over each other to gaze at this magnificent thing in the toy store which is just big enough to maybe sail two kittens across the pond if you strap them to the posts tight. We all start reciting the price tag like we in assembly. "Handcrafted sailboat of fiberglass at one thousand one hundred ninety-five dollars."

"Unbelievable," I hear myself say and am really stunned. I read it again for myself just in case the group recitation put me in a trance. Same thing. For some reason this pisses me off. We look at Miss Moore and she lookin at us, waiting for I dunno what.

"Who'd pay all that when you can buy a sailboat set for a quarter at Pop's, a tube of glue for a dime, and a ball of string for eight cents? It must have a motor and a whole lot else besides," I say. "My sailboat cost me about fifty cents."

"But will it take water?" say Mercedes with her smart ass.

"Took mine to Alley Pond Park once," say Flyboy. "String broke. Lost it. Pity."

"Sailed mine in Central Park[3] and it keeled over and sank. Had to ask 30
my father for another dollar."

"And you got the strap," laugh Big Butt. "The jerk didn't even have a string on it. My old man wailed on his behind."

Little Q.T. was staring hard at the sailboat and you could see he wanted it bad. But he too little and somebody'd just take it from him. So what the hell. "This boat for kids, Miss Moore?"

[3]*Central Park:* A very large park in central Manhattan, New York City.

"Parents silly to buy something like that just to get all broke up," say Rosie Giraffe.

"That much money it should last forever," I figure.

"My father'd buy it for me if I wanted it."

"Your father, my ass," say Rosie Giraffe getting a chance to finally push Mercedes.

"Must be rich people shop here," say Q.T.

"You are a very bright boy," say Flyboy. "What was your first clue?" And he rap him on the head with the back of his knuckles, since Q.T. the only one he could get away with. Though Q.T. liable to come up behind you years later and get his licks in when you half expect it.

"What I want to know is," I says to Miss Moore though I never talk to her, I wouldn't give the bitch that satisfaction, "is how much a real boat costs? I figure a thousand'd get you a yacht any day."

"Why don't you check that out," she says, "and report back to the group?" Which really pains my ass. If you gonna mess up a perfectly good swim day least you could do is have some answers. "Let's go in," she say like she got something up her sleeve. Only she don't lead the way. So me and Sugar turn the corner to where the entrance is, but when we get there I kinda hang back. Not that I'm scared, what's there to be afraid of, just a toy store. But I feel funny, shame. But what I got to be shamed about? Got as much right to go in as anybody. But somehow I can't seem to get hold on the door, so I step away for Sugar to lead. But she hangs back too. And I look at her and she looks at me and this is ridiculous. I mean, damn, I have never ever been shy about doing nothing or going nowhere. But then Mercedes steps up and then Rosie Giraffe and Big Butt crowd in behind and shove, and next thing we all stuffed into the doorway with only Mercedes squeezing past us, smoothing out her jumper and walking right down the aisle. Then the rest of us tumble in like a glued-together jigsaw done all wrong. And people lookin at us. And it's like the time me and Sugar crashed into the Catholic church on a dare. But once we got in there and everything so hushed and holy and the candles and the bowin and the handkerchiefs on all the drooping heads, I just couldn't go through with the plan. Which was for me to run up to the altar and do a tap dance while Sugar played the nose flute and messed around in the holy water. And Sugar kept givin me the elbow. Then later teased me so bad I tied her up in the shower and turned it on and locked her in. And she'd be there till this day if Aunt Gretchen hadn't finally figured I was lying about the boarder takin a shower.

Same thing in the store. We all walkin on tiptoe and hardly touchin the games and puzzles and things. And I watched Miss Moore who is steady watchin us like she waitin for a sign. Like Mama Drewery watches the sky and sniffs the air and takes note of just how much slant is in the bird formation. Then me and Sugar bump smack into each other, so busy gazing at the toys, 'specially the sailboat. But we don't laugh and go into our fat-lady bump-stomach routine. We just stare at that price tag. Then Sugar run a finger over the whole boat. And I'm jealous and want to hit her. Maybe not her, but I sure want to punch somebody in the mouth.

"Watcha bring us here for, Miss Moore?"

"You sound angry, Sylvia. Are you mad about something?" Give me one of them grins like she tellin a grown-up joke that never turns out to be funny. And she's lookin very closely at me like maybe she plannin to do my portrait from memory. I'm mad, but I won't give her that satisfaction. So I slouch around the store bein very bored and say, "Let's go."

Me and Sugar at the back of the train watchin' the tracks whizzin by large then small then gettin gobbled up in the dark. I'm thinkin about this tricky toy I saw in the store. A clown that somersaults on a bar then does chin-ups just cause you yank lightly at his leg. Cost $35. I could see me askin my mother for a $35 birthday clown. "You wanna who that costs what?" she'd say, cockin her head to the side to get a better view of the hole in my head. Thirty-five dollars could buy new bunk beds for Junior and Gretchen's boy. Thirty-five dollars and the whole household could go visit Granddaddy Nelson in the country. Thirty-five dollars would pay for the rent and the piano bill too. Who are these people that spend that much for performing clowns and $1,000 for toy sailboats? What kinda work they do and how they live and how come we ain't in on it? Where we are is who we are, Miss Moore always pointin out. But it don't necessarily have to be that way, she always adds then waits for somebody to say that poor people have to wake up and demand their share of the pie and don't none of us know what kind of pie she talkin about in the first damn place. But she ain't so smart cause I still got her four dollars from the taxi and she sure ain't gettin it. Messin up my day with this shit. Sugar nudges me in my pocket and winks.

Miss Moore lines us up in front of the mailbox where we started from, 45
seem like years ago, and I got a headache for thinkin so hard. And we lean all over each other so we can hold up under the draggy-ass lecture she always finishes us off with at the end before we thank her for borin us to tears. But she just looks at us like she readin tea leaves. Finally she say, "Well, what did you think of F. A. O. Schwarz?"[4]

Rosie Giraffe mumbles, "White folks crazy."

"I'd like to go in there again when I get my birthday money," says Mercedes, and we shove her out the pack so she has to lean on the mailbox by herself.

"I'd like a shower. Tiring day," say Flyboy.

Then Sugar surprises me by saying, "You know, Miss Moore, I don't think all of us here put together eat in a year what that sailboat costs." And Miss Moore lights up like somebody goosed her. "And?" she say, urging Sugar on. Only I'm standin on her foot so she don't continue.

"Imagine for a minute what kind of society it is in which some people 50

[4] *F. A. O. Schwarz:* The name and the toy store are real. The store, in fact, has become a tourist attraction.

can spend on a toy what it would cost to feed a family of six or seven. What do you think?"

"I think," say Sugar pushing me off her feet like she never done before, cause I whip her ass in a minute, "that this is not much of a democracy if you ask me. Equal chance to pursue happiness means an equal crack at the dough, don't it?" Miss Moore is besides herself and I am disgusted with Sugar's treachery. So I stand on her foot one more time to see if she'll shove me. She shuts up, and Miss Moore looks at me, sorrowfully I'm thinkin. And somethin weird is going on, I can feel it in my chest.

"Anybody else learn anything today?" lookin dead at me. I walk away and Sugar has to run to catch up and don't even seem to notice when I shrug her arm off my shoulder.

"Well, we got four dollars anyway," she says.

"Uh hunh."

"We could go to Hascombs and get half a chocolate layer and then go 55
to the Sunset and still have plenty money for potato chips and ice-cream sodas."

"Uh hunh."

"Race you to Hascombs," she say.

We start down the block and she gets ahead which is O.K. by me cause I'm goin to the West End and then over to the Drive to think this day through. She can run if she want to and even run faster. But ain't nobody gonna beat me at nuthin.

Engaging the Text

1. What is the lesson Miss Moore is trying to teach in this story? How well is it received by Mercedes, Sugar, and the narrator, Sylvia? Why does the narrator react differently from Sugar, and what is the meaning of her last line in the story, "But ain't nobody gonna beat me at nuthin"?
2. Why did Bambara write the story from Sylvia's point of view? How would the story change if told from Miss Moore's perspective? From Sugar's? How would it change if the story were set today as opposed to twenty years ago?
3. The story mentions several expensive items: a fur coat, a microscope, a paperweight, a sailboat, and a toy clown. Why do you think the author chose each of these details?
4. In paragraph 44 Sylvia says, "Where we are is who we are, Miss Moore always pointin out. But it don't necessarily have to be that way." What does Miss Moore mean by this? Do you agree? What does Miss Moore expect the children to do to change the situation?

Exploring Connections

5. Write a dialogue between Miss Moore and Gregory Mantsios, author of "Rewards and Opportunities" (p. 465), in which they discuss Sylvia's future and her chances for success.

6. Compare Miss Moore with the matriarchs in "Envy" by Bebe Moore Campbell (p. 182). In particular, examine the goals they set, the behavior they expect, and their means of influencing the young women in their charge.
7. How might Sylvia's life be different if she attended a school like Central Park East Secondary School (CPESS), described in "Schools that Work" by George Wood (p. 121)? How well is Miss Moore compensating for what CPESS offers but Sylvia lacks? Does she accomplish anything that CPESS can't?
8. Compare Sylvia and Sugar's relationship here with that of Teresa and the speaker of the poem in "Para Teresa" (p. 74). Which girls stand the better chance of achieving success? Why?

Extending the Critical Context

9. For the next class meeting, find the most overpriced, unnecessary item you can in a store, catalog, TV ad or newspaper. Spend a few minutes swapping examples, then discuss the information you've gathered: are there any lessons to be learned here about wealth, success, and status?
10. The opening lines of "The Lesson" suggest that Sylvia is now a mature woman looking back on her youth. Working in groups, write a brief biography explaining what has happened to Sylvia since the day of "The Lesson." What has she done? Who has she become? Read your profiles aloud to the class and explain your vision of Sylvia's development.

Masters of Desire: The Culture of American Advertising

Jack Solomon

In The Signs of Our Time *(1988), the source of this selection, Jack Solomon (b. 1954) offers a crash course in the "semiotics" of American popular culture. Semiotics, or the study of signs, is concerned with the meanings one can "read" in almost every aspect of culture; semioticians work to discover and interpret the cultural myths and messages that lie hidden in the way we dress, the food we eat, the movie heroes we identify with. Here, Solomon analyzes how advertising exploits some of the most cherished values of American culture in order to sell pickup trucks, hamburgers, and beer. Solomon is an assistant professor of English at California State University, Northridge. In addition to scholarly articles on semiotics and literary theory, he has published* Discourse and Reference in the Nuclear Age *(1988) and co-edited an anthology,* Signs of Life in the USA *(1994).*

Amongst democratic nations, men easily attain a certain equality of condition; but they can never attain as much as they desire.
—ALEXIS DE TOCQUEVILLE

On May 10, 1831, a young French aristocrat named Alexis de Tocqueville arrived in New York City at the start of what would become one of the most famous visits to America in our history. He had come to observe firsthand the institutions of the freest, most egalitarian society of the age, but what he found was a paradox. For behind America's mythic promise of equal opportunity, Tocqueville discovered a desire for *unequal* social rewards, a ferocious competition for privilege and distinction. As he wrote in his monumental study, *Democracy in America:*

> When all privileges of birth and fortune are abolished, when all professions are accessible to all, and a man's own energies may place him at the top of any one of them, an easy and unbounded career seems open to his ambition. . . . But this is an erroneous notion, which is corrected by daily experience. [For when] men are nearly alike, and all follow the same track, it is very difficult for any one individual to walk quick and cleave a way through the same throng which surrounds and presses him.

Yet walking quick and cleaving a way is precisely what Americans dream of. We Americans dream of rising above the crowd, of attaining a social summit beyond the reach of ordinary citizens. And therein lies the paradox.

The American dream, in other words, has two faces: the one communally egalitarian and the other competitively elitist. This contradiction is no accident; it is fundamental to the structure of American society. Even as America's great myth of equality celebrates the virtues of mom, apple pie, and the girl or boy next door, it also lures us to achieve social distinction, to rise above the crowd and bask alone in the glory. This land is your land and this land is my land, Woody Guthrie's populist anthem tells us, but we keep trying to increase the "my" at the expense of the "your." Rather than fostering contentment, the American dream breeds desire, a longing for a greater share of the pie. It is as if our society were a vast high-school football game, with the bulk of the participants noisily rooting in the stands while, deep down, each of them is wishing he or she could be the star quarterback or head cheerleader.

For the semiotician, the contradictory nature of the American myth of equality is nowhere written so clearly as in the signs that American advertisers use to manipulate us into buying their wares. "Manipulate" is the word here, not "persuade"; for advertising campaigns are not sources of product information, they are exercises in behavior modification. Appealing to our subconscious emotions rather than to our conscious intellects, advertisements are designed to exploit the discontentments fostered by the American dream, the constant desire for social success and the material rewards that accompany it. America's consumer economy runs on desire, and advertising stokes the engines by transforming common objects — from peanut butter to political candidates — into signs of all the things that Americans covet most.

5 But by semiotically reading the signs that advertising agencies manufacture to stimulate consumption, we can plot the precise state of desire in the audiences to which they are addressed. In this [essay], we'll look at a representative sample of ads and what they say about the emotional climate of the country and the fast-changing trends of American life. Because ours is a highly diverse, pluralistic society, various advertisements may say different things depending on their intended audiences, but in every case they say something about America, about the status of our hopes, fears, desires, and beliefs.

Let's begin with two ad campaigns conducted by the same company that bear out Alexis de Tocqueville's observations about the contradictory nature of American society: General Motors' campaigns for its Cadillac and Chevrolet lines. First, consider an early magazine ad for the Cadillac Allanté. Appearing as a full-color, four-page insert in *Time,* the ad seems to say "I'm special — and so is this car" even before we've begun to read it. Rather than being printed on the ordinary, flimsy pages of the magazine, the Allanté spread appears on glossy coated stock. The unwritten message here is that an extraordinary car deserves an extraordinary advertisement, and that both car and ad are aimed at an extraordinary consumer, or at least one who wishes to appear extraordinary compared to his more ordinary fellow citizens.

Ads of this kind work by creating symbolic associations between their product and what is most coveted by the consumers to whom they are addressed. It is significant, then, that this ad insists that the Allanté is virtually an Italian rather than an American car, an automobile, as its copy runs, "Conceived and Commissioned by America's Luxury Car Leader — Cadillac" but "Designed and Handcrafted by Europe's Renowned Design Leader — Pininfarina, SpA, of Turin, Italy." This is not simply a piece of product information, it's a sign of the prestige that European luxury cars enjoy in today's automotive marketplace. Once the luxury car of choice for America's status drivers, Cadillac has fallen far behind its European competitors in the race for the prestige market. So the Allanté essentially represents Cadillac's decision, after years of resisting the trend toward European cars, to introduce its own European import — whose high cost is clearly printed on the last page of the ad. Although $54,700 is a lot of money to pay for a Cadillac, it's about what you'd expect to pay for a top-of-the-line Mercedes-Benz. That's precisely the point the ad is trying to make: the Allanté is no mere car. It's a potent status symbol you can associate with the other major status symbols of the 1980s.

American companies manufacture status symbols because American consumers want them. As Alexis de Tocqueville recognized a century and a half ago, the competitive nature of democratic societies breeds a desire for social distinction, a yearning to rise above the crowd. But given the fact that those who do make it to the top in socially mobile societies have often risen from the lower ranks, they still look like everyone else. In the socially immobile societies of aristocratic Europe, generations of fixed social conditions produced subtle class signals. The accent of one's voice, the shape of one's nose, or even the set of one's chin, immediately communicated social status. Aside from the nasal bray and uptilted head of the Boston Brahmin, Americans do not have any native sets of personal status signals. If it weren't for his Mercedes-Benz and Manhattan townhouse, the parvenu Wall Street millionaire often couldn't be distinguished from the man who tailors his suits. Hence, the demand for status symbols, for the objects that mark one off as a social success, is particularly strong in democratic nations — stronger even than in aristocratic societies, where the aristocrat so often looks and sounds different from everyone else.

Status symbols, then, are signs that identify their possessors' place in a social hierarchy, markers of rank and prestige. We can all think of any number of status symbols — Rolls-Royces, Beverly Hills mansions, even Shar Pei puppies (whose rareness and expense has rocketed them beyond Russian wolfhounds as status pets and has even inspired whole lines of wrinkle-faced stuffed toys) — but how do we know that something *is* a status symbol? The explanation is quite simple: when an object (or puppy!) either costs a lot of money or requires influential connections to possess, anyone who possesses it must also possess the necessary means and influence to acquire it. The object itself really doesn't matter, since it ultimately disappears behind the presumed social potency of its owner. Semiotically, what matters is the signal it sends, its value as a sign of power. One traditional sign of social distinction is owning a country estate and enjoying the peace and privacy that attend it. Advertisements for Mercedes-Benz, Jaguar, and Audi automobiles thus frequently feature drivers motoring quietly along a country road, presumably on their way to or from their country houses.

10 Advertisers have been quick to exploit the status signals that belong to body language as well. As Hegel[1] observed in the early nineteenth century, it is an ancient aristocratic prerogative to be seen by the lower orders without having to look at them in return. Tilting his chin high in the air and gazing down at the world under hooded eyelids, the aristocrat invites observation while refusing to look back. We can find such a pose exploited in an advertisement for Cadillac Seville in which we see an elegantly dressed woman out for a drive with her husband in their new Cadillac. If we look closely at the woman's body language, we can see her glance inwardly with a satisfied smile on her face but not outward toward the camera that represents our gaze. She is glad to be seen by us in her Seville, but she isn't interested in looking at *us!*

Ads that are aimed at a broader market take the opposite approach. If

[1]*Hegel:* G. W. F. Hegel (1770–1831), German philosopher.

the American dream encourages the desire to "arrive," to vault above the mass, it also fosters a desire to be popular, to "belong." Populist commercials accordingly transform products into signs of belonging, utilizing such common icons as country music, small-town life, family picnics, and farmyards. All of these icons are incorporated in GM's "Heartbeat of America" campaign for its Chevrolet line. Unlike the Seville commercial, the faces in the Chevy ads look straight at us and smile. Dress is casual; the mood upbeat. Quick camera cuts take us from rustic to suburban to urban scenes, creating an American montage filmed from sea to shining sea. We all "belong" in a Chevy.

Where price alone doesn't determine the market for a product, advertisers can go either way. Both Johnnie Walker and Jack Daniel's are better-grade whiskies, but where a Johnnie Walker ad appeals to the buyer who wants a mark of aristocratic distinction in his liquor, a Jack Daniel's ad emphasizes the down-home, egalitarian folksiness of its product. Johnnie Walker associates itself with such conventional status symbols as sable coats, Rolls-Royces, and black gold; Jack Daniel's gives us a Good Ol' Boy in overalls. In fact, Jack Daniel's Good Ol' Boy is an icon of backwoods independence, recalling the days of the moonshiner and the Whisky Rebellion of 1794. Evoking emotions quite at odds with those stimulated in Johnnie Walker ads, the advertisers of Jack Daniel's have chosen to transform their product into a sign of America's populist tradition. The fact that both ads successfully sell whisky is itself a sign of the dual nature of the American dream.

Beer is also pitched on two levels. Consider the difference between the ways Budweiser and Michelob market their light beers. Bud Light and Michelob Light cost and taste about the same, but Budweiser tends to target the working class while Michelob has gone after the upscale market. Bud commercials are set in working-class bars that contrast with the sophisticated nightclubs and yuppie watering holes of the Michelob campaign. "You're one of the guys," Budweiser assures the assembly-line worker and the truck driver, "this Bud's for you." Michelob, on the other hand, makes no such appeal to the democratic instinct of sharing and belonging. You don't share, you take, grabbing what you can in a competitive dash to "have it all."

Populist advertising is particularly effective in the face of foreign competition. When Americans feel threatened from the outside, they tend to circle the wagons and temporarily forget their class differences. In the face of the Japanese automotive "invasion," Chrysler runs populist commercials in which Lee Iacocca joins the simple folk who buy his cars as the jingle "Born in America" blares in the background. Seeking to capitalize on the popularity of Bruce Springsteen's *Born in the USA* album, these ads gloss over Springsteen's ironic lyrics in a vast display of flag-waving. Chevrolet's "Heartbeat of America" campaign similarly attempts to woo American motorists away from Japanese automobiles by appealing to their patriotic sentiments.

15 The patriotic iconography of these campaigns also reflects the general cultural mood of the early- to mid-1980s. After a period of national anguish in the wake of the Vietnam War and the Iran hostage crisis, America went on a patriotic binge. American athletic triumphs in the Lake Placid and Los Angeles Olympics introduced a sporting tone into the national celebration, often making international affairs appear like one great Olympiad in which America was always going for the gold. In response, advertisers began to do their own flag-waving.

The mood of advertising during this period was definitely upbeat. Even deodorant commercials, which traditionally work on our self-doubts and fears of social rejection, jumped on the bandwagon. In the guilty sixties, we had ads like the "Ice Blue Secret" campaign with its connotations of guilt and shame. In the feel-good Reagan eighties, "Sure" deodorant commercials featured images of triumphant Americans throwing up their arms in victory to reveal—no wet marks! Deodorant commercials once had the moral echo of Nathaniel Hawthorne's guilt-ridden *The Scarlet Letter;* in the early eighties they had all the moral subtlety of *Rocky IV,* reflecting the emotions of a Vietnam-weary nation eager to embrace the imagery of America Triumphant.

The commercials for Worlds of Wonder's Lazer Tag game featured the futuristic finals of some Soviet-American Lazer Tag shootout ("Practice hard, America!") and carried the emotions of patriotism into an even more aggressive arena. Exploiting the hoopla that surrounded the victory over the Soviets in the hockey finals of the 1980 Olympics, the Lazer Tag ads pandered to an American desire for the sort of clear-cut nationalistic triumphs that the nuclear age has rendered almost impossible. Creating a fantasy setting where patriotic dreams are substituted for complicated realities, the Lazer Tag commercials sought to capture the imaginations of children caught up in the patriotic fervor of the early 1980s.

Live the Fantasy

By reading the signs of American advertising, we can conclude that America is a nation of fantasizers, often preferring the sign to the substance and easily enthralled by a veritable Fantasy Island of commercial illusions. Critics of Madison Avenue often complain that advertisers create consumer desire, but semioticians don't think the situation is that simple. Advertisers may give shape to consumer fantasies, but they need raw material to work with, the subconscious dreams and desires of the marketplace. As long as these desires remain unconscious, advertisers will be able to exploit them. But by bringing the fantasies to the surface, you can free yourself from advertising's often hypnotic grasp.

I can think of no company that has more successfully seized upon the subconscious fantasies of the American marketplace — indeed the world marketplace — than McDonald's. By no means the first nor the only hamburger chain in the United States, McDonald's emerged victorious in the "burger wars" by transforming hamburgers into signs of all that was desirable in American life. Other chains like Wendy's, Burger King, and Jack-In-The-Box continue to advertise and sell widely, but no company approaches McDonald's transformation of itself into a symbol of American culture.

McDonald's success can be traced to the precision of its advertising. 20
Instead of broadcasting a single "one-size-fits-all" campaign at a time, McDonald's pitches its burgers simultaneously at different age groups, different classes, even different races (Budweiser beer, incidentally, has succeeded in the same way). For children, there is the Ronald McDonald campaign, which presents a fantasy world that has little to do with hamburgers in any rational sense but a great deal to do with the emotional desires of kids. Ronald McDonald and his friends are signs that recall the Muppets, *Sesame Street,* the circus, toys, storybook illustrations, even *Alice in Wonderland.* Such signs do not signify hamburgers. Rather, they are displayed in order to prompt in the child's mind an automatic association of fantasy, fun, and McDonald's.

The same approach is taken in ads aimed at older audiences — teens, adults, and senior citizens. In the teen-oriented ads we may catch a fleeting glimpse of a hamburger or two, but what we are really shown is a teenage fantasy: groups of hip and happy adolescents singing, dancing, and cavorting together. Fearing loneliness more than anything else, adolescents quickly respond to the group appeal of such commercials. "Eat a Big Mac," these ads say, "and you won't be stuck home alone on Saturday night."

To appeal to an older and more sophisticated audience no longer so afraid of not belonging and more concerned with finding a place to go out to at night, McDonald's has designed the elaborate "Mac Tonight" commercials, which have for their backdrop a nightlit urban skyline and at their center a cabaret pianist with a moon-shaped head, a glad manner, and Blues Brothers shades. Such signs prompt an association of McDonald's with nightclubs and urban sophistication, persuading us that McDonald's is a place not only for breakfast or lunch but for dinner too, as if it were a popular off-Broadway nightspot, a place to see and be seen. Even the parody of Kurt Weill's "Mack the Knife" theme song that Mac the Pianist performs is a sign, a subtle signal to the sophisticated hamburger eater able to recognize the origin of the tune in Bertolt Brecht's *Threepenny Opera.*

For yet older customers, McDonald's has designed a commercial around the fact that it employs a large number of retirees and seniors. In one such ad, we see an elderly man leaving his pretty little cottage early in the morning to start work as "the new kid" at McDonald's, and then we watch him during his first day on the job. Of course he is a great success, outdoing everyone else with his energy and efficiency, and he returns home in the evening to a loving wife and happy home. One would almost think that the ad was a kind of moving "help wanted" sign (indeed, McDonald's *was* hiring elderly employees at the time), but it's really just directed at consumers. Older viewers can see themselves wanted and appreciated in the ad—and perhaps be distracted from the rationally uncomfortable fact that many senior citizens take such jobs because of financial need and thus may be unlikely to own the sort of home that one sees in the commercial. But realism isn't the point here. This is fantasyland, a dream world promising instant gratification no matter what the facts of the matter may be.

Practically the only fantasy that McDonald's doesn't exploit is the fantasy of sex. This is understandable, given McDonald's desire to present itself as a family restaurant. But everywhere else, sexual fantasies, which have always had an important place in American advertising, are beginning to dominate the advertising scene. You expect sexual come-ons in ads for perfume or cosmetics or jewelry—after all, that's what they're selling—but for room deodorizers? In a magazine ad for Claire Burke home fragrances, for example, we see a well-dressed couple cavorting about their bedroom in what looks like a cheery preparation for sadomasochistic exercises. Jordache and Calvin Klein pitch blue jeans as props for teenage sexuality. The phallic appeal of automobiles, traditionally an implicit feature in automotive advertising, becomes quite explicit in a Dodge commercial that shifts back and forth from shots of a young man in an automobile to teasing glimpses of a woman—his date—as she dresses in her apartment.

The very language of today's advertisements is charged with sexuality. 25
Products in the more innocent fifties were "new and improved," but everything in the eighties is "hot!"—as in "hot woman," or sexual heat. Cars are "hot." Movies are "hot." An ad for Valvoline pulses to the rhythm of a "heat wave, burning in my car." Sneakers get red hot in a magazine ad for Travel Fox athletic shoes in which we see male and female figures, clad only in Travel Fox shoes, apparently in the act of copulation—an ad that earned one of *Adweek*'s "badvertising" awards for shoddy advertising.

The sexual explicitness of contemporary advertising is a sign not so much of American sexual fantasies as of the lengths to which advertisers will go to get attention. Sex never fails as an attention-getter, and in a particularly competitive, and expensive, era for American marketing, advertisers like to bet on a sure thing. Ad people refer to the proliferation of TV, radio, newspaper, magazine, and billboard ads as "clutter," and nothing cuts through the clutter like sex.

By showing the flesh, advertisers work on the deepest, most coercive human emotions of all. Much sexual coercion in advertising, however, is a sign of a desperate need to make certain that clients are getting their money's worth. The appearance of advertisements that refer directly to the prefabricated fantasies of Hollywood is a sign of a different sort of desperation: a desperation for ideas. With the rapid turnover of advertising campaigns mandated by the need to cut through the "clutter," advertisers may be hard pressed for new ad concepts, and so they are more and more frequently turning to already-established models. In the early 1980s, for instance, Pepsi-Cola ran a series of ads broadly alluding to Steven Spielberg's *E.T.* In one such ad, we see a young boy who, like the hero of *E.T.*, witnesses an extraterrestrial visit. The boy is led to a soft-drink machine where he pauses to drink a can of Pepsi as the spaceship he's spotted flies off into the universe. The relationship between the ad and the movie, accordingly, is a parasitical one, with the ad taking its life from the creative body of the film.

Pepsi did something similar in 1987 when it arranged with the producers of the movie *Top Gun* to promote the film's video release in Pepsi's television advertisements in exchange for the right to append a Pepsi ad to the video itself. This time, however, the parasitical relationship between ad and film was made explicit. Pepsi sales benefited from the video, and the video's sales benefited from Pepsi. It was a marriage made in corporate heaven.

The fact that Pepsi believed that it could stimulate consumption by appealing to the militaristic fantasies dramatized in *Top Gun* reflects similar fantasies in the "Pepsi generation." Earlier generations saw Pepsi associated with high-school courtship rituals, with couples sipping sodas together at the corner drugstore. When the draft was on, young men fantasized about Peggy Sue, not Air Force Flight School. Military service was all too real a possibility to fantasize about. But in an era when military service is not a reality for most young Americans, Pepsi commercials featuring hotshot fly-boys drinking Pepsi while streaking about in their Air Force jets contribute to a youth culture that has forgotten what military service means. It all looks like such fun in the Pepsi ads, but what they conceal is the fact that military jets are weapons, not high-tech recreational vehicles.

For less militaristic dreamers, Madison Avenue has framed ad cam- 30
paigns around the cultural prestige of high-tech machinery in its own right. This is especially the case with sports cars, whose high-tech appeal is so powerful that some people apparently fantasize about *being* sports cars. At least, this is the conclusion one might draw from a Porsche commercial that asked its audience, "If you were a car, what kind of car would you be?" As a candy-red Porsche speeds along a rainslick forest road, the ad's voice-over describes all the specifications you'd want to have if you *were* a sports car. "If you were a car," the commercial concludes, "you'd be a Porsche."

In his essay "Car Commercials and *Miami Vice*," Todd Gitlin explains the semiotic appeal of such ads as those in the Porsche campaign. Aired at the height of what may be called America's "myth of the entrepreneur," these commercials were aimed at young corporate managers who imaginatively identified with the "lone wolf" image of a Porsche speeding through the woods. Gitlin points out that such images cater to the fantasies of faceless corporate men who dream of entrepreneurial glory, of striking out on their own like John DeLorean[2] and telling the boss to take his job and shove it. But as DeLorean's spectacular failure demonstrates, the life of the entrepreneur can be extremely risky. So rather than having to go it alone and take

[2]*John DeLorean:* 1980s entrepreneur caught trying to finance his sports-car company by selling cocaine.

the risks that accompany entrepreneurial independence, the young executive can substitute fantasy for reality by climbing into his Porsche — or at least that's what Porsche's advertisers wanted him to believe.

But there is more at work in the Porsche ads than the fantasies of corporate America. Ever since Arthur C. Clarke and Stanley Kubrick teamed up to present us with HAL 9000, the demented computer of *2001: A Space Odyssey,* the American imagination has been obsessed with the melding of man and machine. First there was television's *Six Million Dollar Man,* and then movieland's *Star Wars, Blade Runner,* and *Robocop,* fantasy visions of a future dominated by machines. Androids haunt our imaginations as machines seize the initiative. *Time* magazine's "Man of the Year" for 1982 was a computer. Robot-built automobiles appeal to drivers who spend their days in front of computer screens — perhaps designing robots. When so much power and prestige is being given to high-tech machines, wouldn't you rather be a Porsche?

In short, the Porsche campaign is a sign of a new mythology that is emerging before our eyes, a myth of the machine, which is replacing the myth of the human. The iconic figure of the little tramp caught up in the cogs of industrial production in Charlie Chaplin's *Modern Times* signified a humanistic revulsion to the age of the machine. Human beings, such icons said, were superior to machines. Human values should come first in the moral order of things. But as Edith Milton suggests in her essay "The Track of the Mutant," we are now coming to believe that machines are superior to human beings, that mechanical nature is superior to human nature. Rather than being threatened by machines, we long to merge with them. *The Six Million Dollar Man* is one iconic figure in the new mythology; Harrison Ford's sexual coupling with an android[3] is another. In such an age it should come as little wonder that computer-synthesized Max Headroom[4] should be a commercial spokesman for Coca-Cola, or that Federal Express should design a series of TV ads featuring mechanical-looking human beings revolving around strange and powerful machines.

Fear and Trembling in the Marketplace

While advertisers play on and reflect back at us our fantasies about everything from fighter pilots to robots, they also play on darker imaginings. If dream and desire can be exploited in the quest for sales, so can nightmare and fear.

The nightmare equivalent of America's populist desire to "belong," for 35
example, is the fear of not belonging, of social rejection, of being different.

[3]*Harrison Ford's sexual coupling with an android:* This scene occurs in the science-fiction movie *Blade Runner.*

[4]*Max Headroom:* Computer-animated star of a series of commercials for Coca-Cola in the mid-1980s.

Advertisements for dandruff shampoos, mouthwashes, deodorants, and laundry detergents ("Ring Around the Collar!") accordingly exploit such fears, bullying us into consumption. Although ads of this type are still around in the 1980s, they were particularly common in the fifties and early sixties, reflecting a society still reeling from the witch-hunts of the McCarthy years. When any sort of social eccentricity or difference could result in a public denunciation and the loss of one's job or even liberty, Americans were keen to conform and be like everyone else. No one wanted to be "guilty" of smelling bad or of having a dirty collar.

"Guilt" ads characteristically work by creating narrative situations in which someone is "accused" of some social "transgression," pronounced guilty, and then offered the sponsor's product as a means of returning to "innocence." Such ads, in essence, are parodies of ancient religious rituals of guilt and atonement, whereby sinning humanity is offered salvation through the agency of priest and church. In the world of advertising, a product takes the place of the priest, but the logic of the situation is quite similar.

In commercials for Wisk detergent, for example, we witness the drama of a hapless housewife and her husband as they are mocked by the jeering voices of children shouting "Ring Around the Collar!" "Oh, those dirty rings!" the housewife groans in despair. It's as if she and her husband were being stoned by an angry crowd. But there's hope, there's help, there's Wisk. Cleansing her soul of sin as well as her husband's, the housewife launders his shirts with Wisk, and behold, his collars are clean. Product salvation is only as far as the supermarket.

The recent appearance of advertisements for hospitals treating drug and alcohol addiction have raised the old genre of the guilt ad to new heights (or lows, depending on your perspective). In such ads, we see wives on the verge of leaving their husbands if they don't do something about their drinking, and salesmen about to lose their jobs. The man is guilty; he has sinned; but he upholds the ritual of guilt and atonement by "confessing" to his wife or boss and agreeing to go to the hospital the ad is pitching.

If guilt looks backward in time to past transgressions, fear, like desire, faces forward, trembling before the future. In the late 1980s, a new kind of fear commercial appeared, one whose narrative played on the worries of young corporate managers struggling up the ladder of success. Representing the nightmare equivalent of the elitist desire to "arrive," ads of this sort created images of failure, storylines of corporate defeat. In one ad for Apple computers, for example, a group of junior executives sits around a table with the boss as he asks each executive how long it will take his or her department to complete some publishing jobs. "Two or three days," answers one nervous executive. "A week, on overtime," a tight-lipped woman responds. But one young up-and-comer can have everything ready tomorrow, today, or yesterday, because his department uses a Macintosh desktop publishing system. Guess who'll get the next promotion?

Fear stalks an ad for AT&T computer systems too. A boss and four junior 40
executives are dining in a posh restaurant. Icons of corporate power and

prestige flood the screen — from the executives' formal evening wear to the fancy table setting — but there's tension in the air. It seems that the junior managers have chosen a computer system that's incompatible with the firm's sales and marketing departments. A whole new system will have to be purchased, but the tone of the meeting suggests that it will be handled by a new group of managers. These guys are on the way out. They no longer "belong." Indeed, it's probably no accident that the ad takes place in a restaurant, given the joke that went around in the aftermath of the 1987 market crash. "What do you call a yuppie stockbroker?" the joke ran. "Hey, waiter!" Is the ad trying subtly to suggest that junior executives who choose the wrong computer systems are doomed to suffer the same fate?

For other markets, there are other fears. If McDonald's presents senior citizens with bright fantasies of being useful and appreciated beyond retirement, companies like Secure Horizons dramatize senior citizens' fears of being caught short by a major illness. Running its ads in the wake of budgetary cuts in the Medicare system, Secure Horizons designed a series of commercials featuring a pleasant old man named Harry — who looks and sounds rather like Carroll O'Connor[5] — who tells us the story of the scare he got during his wife's recent illness. Fearing that next time Medicare won't cover the bills, he has purchased supplemental health insurance from Secure Horizons and now securely tends his rooftop garden.

Among all the fears advertisers have exploited over the years, I find the fear of not having a posh enough burial site the most arresting. Advertisers usually avoid any mention of death — who wants to associate a product with the grave? — but mortuary advertisers haven't much choice. Generally, they solve their problem by framing cemeteries as timeless parks presided over by priestly morticians, appealing to our desires for dignity and comfort in the face of bereavement. But in one television commercial for Forest Lawn we find a different approach. In this ad we are presented with the ghost of an old man telling us how he might have found a much nicer resting place than the run-down cemetery in which we find him had his wife only known that Forest Lawn was so "affordable." I presume the ad was supposed to be funny, but it's been pulled off the air. There are some fears that just won't bear joking about, some nightmares too dark to dramatize.

The Future of an Illusion

There are some signs in the advertising world that Americans are getting fed up with fantasy advertisements and want to hear some straight talk. Weary of extravagant product claims and irrelevant associations, consumers trained by years of advertising to distrust what they hear seem to be developing an immunity to commercials. At least, this is the semiotic message I

[5]*Carroll O'Connor:* Star of *All in the Family,* an enormously popular TV comedy of the 1970s.

read in the "new realism" advertisements of the eighties, ads that attempt to convince you that what you're seeing is the real thing, that the ad is giving you the straight dope, not advertising hype.

You can recognize the "new realism" by its camera techniques. The lighting is usually subdued to give the ad the effect of being filmed without studio lighting or special filters. The scene looks gray, as if the blinds were drawn. The camera shots are jerky and off-angle, often zooming in for sudden unflattering close-ups, as if the cameraman was an amateur with a home video recorder. In a "realistic" ad for AT&T, for example, we are treated to a monologue by a plump stockbroker — his plumpness intended as a sign that he's for real and not just another actor—who tells us about the problems he's had with his phone system (not AT&T's) as the camera jerks around, generally filming him from below as if the cameraman couldn't quite fit his equipment into the crammed office and had to film the scene on his knees. "This is no fancy advertisement," the ad tries to convince us, "this is sincere."

An ad for Miller draft beer tries the same approach, recreating the effect 45
of an amateur videotape of a wedding celebration. Camera shots shift suddenly from group to group. The picture jumps. Bodies are poorly framed. The color is washed out. Like the beer it is pushing, the ad is supposed to strike us as being "as real as it gets."

Such ads reflect a desire for reality in the marketplace, a weariness with Madison Avenue illusions. But there's no illusion like the illusion of reality. Every special technique that advertisers use to create their "reality effects" is, in fact, more unrealistic than the techniques of "illusory" ads. The world, in reality, doesn't jump around when you look at it. It doesn't appear in subdued gray tones. Our eyes don't have zoom lenses, and we don't look at things with our heads cocked to one side. The irony of the "new realism" is that it is more unrealistic, more artificial, than the ordinary run of television advertising.

But don't expect any truly realistic ads in the future, because a realistic advertisement is a contradiction in terms. The logic of advertising is entirely semiotic: it substitutes signs for things, framed visions of consumer desire for the thing itself. The success of modern advertising, its penetration into every corner of American life, reflects a culture that has itself chosen illusion over reality. At a time when political candidates all have professional image-makers attached to their staffs, and the President of the United States is an actor who once sold shirt collars, all the cultural signs are pointing to more illusions in our lives rather than fewer — a fecund breeding ground for the world of the advertiser.

Engaging the Text

1. How, according to Solomon, does advertising exploit our dominant cultural myths? What central cultural paradox do U.S. advertisers exploit most frequently? Why?

2. Brainstorm a list of current status symbols. Why, according to Solomon, are they such an important feature of American life? What cultural function do they perform? In what sense can even your body language become a symbol of your social status?
3. What is the appeal of populist images in ads? What types of products are they most frequently associated with?
4. How do corporations like McDonald's manipulate the subconscious fears and desires of different groups of Americans in their carefully targeted advertising campaigns?

Exploring Connections

5. Solomon's analysis of status symbols and their power assumes that there is, in fact, a good deal of social mobility in U.S. culture. How might Gregory Mantsios (p. 465) critique this assumption? How might you explain the power of status symbols in a culture where social mobility is relatively restricted?
6. Gary Soto (p. 145) and Judith Ortiz Cofer (p. 278) both write about their childhood desires to be different than they were. Use Solomon's approach and, if possible, his terminology, to explicate the cultural signs and symbols that these writers mention in their narratives.
7. Review Holly Devor (p. 244), Michael Kimmel (p. 258), and James Weinrich and Walter Williams (p. 295) on the creation of gender categories. What gender categories does American advertising tend to create and perpetuate? How are gender roles defined within these categories?

Extending the Critical Context

8. Try your hand at a semiotic analysis of a print ad: What fears and fantasies does it appeal to in order to sell its product?
9. Working in small groups, survey a few hours of prime-time commercial TV and try to categorize the kinds of appeals that are made in the ads. How many, for example, offer imagery associated with status and success? With sexuality? With a need for community? How many touch on deep-seated fears? What conclusions can you draw from your survey results?
10. Solomon suggests that the mythic relationship between human beings and machines has changed dramatically over the last fifty years. Analyze the relationship suggested by movies like *Blade Runner*, *Total Recall*, or the *Terminator* or *Robocop* series.

The Great Boomer Bust

Katy Butler

According to Katy Butler, 1973 was the last good year for the middle class. Since then, a generation of Americans has learned the hard way that upward mobility is not a given, that they may never achieve the comfortable life their parents enjoyed. In this essay, which combines personal reminiscence with telling statistics, Butler shows how and why the American Dream may have eluded the baby boomer generation. She also explores the psychology of downward mobility in a society that has made success a key value. Butler (b. 1949) is a northern California–based writer and essayist whose subject matter is psychology, religion, and daily life. Her work has been published in the San Francisco Chronicle, *the* Washington Post, The New Yorker, Vogue, *and other publications. This selection first appeared in* Mother Jones.

Not long after we married, my husband and I flew to Connecticut to visit my parents. We carried our secondhand suitcases up to what was once my brothers' bedroom and dropped them on two beds pushed together to make one. The room was, as it always had been, scrupulously clean and white — but richer than I remembered. The beds had real box springs. A cashmere blanket lay folded at their base; on a nightstand, a red daylily from my mother's garden opened in a carafe of water. Outside the window, rain from a sprinkler fell on a long lawn sloping into the trees. Every room in the house — the spare bedrooms, the basement wood shop, my mother's darkroom, the kitchen smelling of herbs — every room whispered of surplus space and money and time. I took off my shoes and thought to myself, I will never live this way again.

I felt shame, resentment, confusion settling out in me. By the standards of their generation, my parents were only comfortably middle-class. Why, then, were they living so much better on one income than Bob and I, who, nearing forty, had no children and were living on two?

I could not blame my parents: they earned what they got. Immigrants from a pinched, postwar Britain, they came to the United States in the '50s when we were children, with little but my father's education. My mother sewed my clothes; my father worked hard and got promoted. Through the years, things got better: In the '60s, my father traded the bulbous, secondhand Buick that drove like a sofa for a new Rambler station wagon. In the '70s, he bought himself a Ford and my mother a Toyota. The $28,000 suburban house they built on a lake in the '60s — my mother tiled the bathroom and taped the Sheetrock — was sold in the '70s for a place with three bathrooms, four bedrooms, and a two-car garage. They had enough money to pay for my brothers' skiing, my college education, and a fattening retirement fund. I went to college in 1967 with a vague sense that my future would be much the same as my parents' past, only freer: I would marry, write or work in the mornings, and take care of my children in the afternoons.

By the '80s, my parents had raised three children and achieved all of the American dream on my father's income alone — and after 15 years in the full-time work force, I could not afford a child and had never owned a new car.

I couldn't have cared less about a new car. But it was an index of how 5
middle-class life had changed in the course of a single generation. And nowhere was the change more striking than in what each generation paid for housing and what they got for it. My parents paid $190 a month — on a 5 percent mortgage — for a four-bedroom house on an acre of land in Connecticut. Bob and I, with a combined income slightly lower than my father's, paid $1,500 a month — on a 9 percent mortgage — for a five-room bungalow slightly larger than my parents' deck. Yet we felt lucky to afford a house at all.

Every night during that visit, even as I reveled in my mother's homemade soups and slid between her clean, cool sheets, I thought bitterly of my downward mobility, not only in money, but in time. Bob and I both worked full-time and lived in time-poverty: our house in Mill Valley, California, was a launching pad, not a home. We commuted, ate Chinese takeout and microwaved burritos while standing in the kitchen, cleaned the house once in a blue moon, and sometimes went for days without an uninterrupted hour together.

On the last night of our visit with my parents, we all went to the movies. My mother and father got a senior citizen discount.

So it was with a sense of discontent that I returned home, got out of my unreliable but classy-looking old Mercedes, and opened the door to the tiny, cracked stucco house my husband and I bought for a paper fortune with help from our parents.

I looked at the weeds in the overgrown yard, the ink stain on the couch from a discount outlet, the dust in the corners, the mail-order catalogs and sweaters piled on the dining-room table. Our bedroom, I realized, was smaller than anywhere I had slept in childhood. On the deck were two Adirondack chairs I bought because the catalog said their arms were wide enough to hold a glass of lemonade on hot, lazy summer afternoons. I hadn't had a single glass of lemonade or a single lazy afternoon all summer; what I tried to buy was not a chair, but a memory of free time.

In the months after that visit East to what was once my home, I looked 10
at the lives of my friends as though through a set of hard, refracting prisms. With few exceptions, most of their parents had cobbled together some ver-

sion of the American dream: kids (the most expensive durable consumer good), education, houses, retirement accounts, and time to enjoy it all. My friends dressed and ate well, but most had only one or two elements of the dream we had laughed at in our twenties and now could not attain. We had to choose between kids, houses, and time. Those with new cars had no houses; those with houses, no children; those with children, no houses. A few lucky supercouples — a lawyer married to a doctor, say, with a combined income of more than $100,000 a year — had everything but time.

There were, of course, some notable exceptions to the disguised slide down: my women friends had careers and financial independence denied their mothers; a handful of others had made enough money in mail-order or computer software to afford comfortable houses, children, and leisure. But on the whole, I saw a generational dilemma perceived as individual failure. My friends in the baby-boom generation — so often accused of being unable to defer gratification — were deferring what their parents considered basic. They were smart and hardworking, but struggling, and ashamed to admit it even to each other.

It was the *shame* and pretense — in people I'd known since we were all in our twenties and poor — that puzzled me. Then, we'd all worn jeans and put our money into stereos; now my friends were gilding their downward mobility in a skin of glitz. One of my best friends had fallen in love, moved out of her rent-controlled flat in San Francisco, and taken (with the man she later married) a high-rent house, as nice as my parents', in the Berkeley Hills. I had gone there for dinner and Molly had met me at the door, tastefully dressed. Her table overlooked thousands of houses sparkling around the bay — like a lord's castle high above his subjects — and I had felt a little envious, almost intimidated.

It was only after she and her husband left town for new jobs that Molly told me that she'd been too deep in debt to buy a winter coat, so broke she'd stood in line at the phone company to pay the bill on cutoff day. I was shocked she hadn't trusted me enough to tell me, and something she'd said years before came drifting back, a piece of advice she had heard from her mother: "Never look poor, dear. Americans don't like poor people."

At the same time Molly made her confession, my former roommate Nancy — the daughter of a psychiatrist who had gone to school on the GI bill and bought his house with a VA loan — became truly poor. The father of her baby left her without child support; she was a technical writer, and her work dried up after her computer company lost a major contract. The safety net strung up in the 1930s did not help her: as a contract worker, she didn't qualify for unemployment compensation. Welfare turned her down because her rent was too high. "I think it's just as well," she told me at the time, still looking beautiful in clothes she'd bought before she lost her job. "I don't belong on welfare."

I lent her a little money with only the vaguest sense of her troubles. 15
Only recently, when she laid it all out for me, did I understand how bad it had been. "I couldn't afford to go to museums, but I went for walks. I breastfed for a long time, and that was a help," she said quietly. "Then I finally got a job and I was even worse off. I couldn't afford food, child care, and transportation to and from work. I saved money on food for myself. Thank God my son would eat tofu. I got up at four in the morning to do my overtime work — unpaid, of course — while my son was asleep. Sometimes I felt as if there really wasn't a place on the planet for someone like me. It makes one ashamed not to be able to buy light bulbs, food, toilet paper. I didn't like asking my friends for monetary assistance — I waited until I was desperate before I asked. I didn't want to be perceived as someone in that much trouble."

Meanwhile, the newspapers were full of stories about yuppies and blackened redfish and new restaurants. The cognitive dissonance hurt my head: Was I the only one who felt like a failure? Was it only *my* friends who were in trouble? Why was it so hard for me to say to a lunch companion, "Let's go somewhere cheaper"? Acquaintances were wearing $50 haircuts and $75 shoes.

A childless couple returned from a student year in Rome, got jobs, furniture, sophisticated clothes, and a nice apartment. They went bicycling in Virginia on vacation that year, staying at bed and breakfasts. They seemed to be doing just fine. Recently, Roger explained the secret of their success: they were $18,000 in credit-card debt, and he was leaving his nonprofit job for better-paying but more boring work in the computer industry to pay it off. "We both had grown-up jobs for the first time, and we thought we should be able to live like grown-ups," he said. "We'd struggled for a long time, and I was sick of this thing the Left has about not being desirous, of not wanting sex or money.

"I don't think you have to be unhappy to be on the Left," he went on. "I wanted to be able to pick up the tab for ten people, or take a cab when I wanted. I thought that part of being an adult was being able to go to a restaurant, look at the menu, and go in if you like the food, not because you're looking at the prices. A lot of it was playing grown-up and throwing the old plastic around. Then we realized we could have gone to Europe last year on our credit-card interest alone.

"We have nothing to show for it," he said. "We were in a lot of denial, and finally the denial broke." He asked for help from his father — a stockbroker in the Los Angeles suburbs who rarely takes a vacation — and was turned down. "My father's always telling me how much I'm going to inherit," said Roger, who resents the way money colors their relationship with the tones of prolonged adolescence. "He tells me that if we have a kid, the purse strings will open. I told him, you can't buy a grandchild."

I looked at him across the table, amazed that a friend of mine would 20
stake his sense of manhood on being able to pay a restaurant bill. "Man-

hood," once seen as the ability to fight and then as the capability to produce, had been redefined again, this time as the ability to consume. And Roger, like many of my friends, seemed willing to pay almost any price to appear as successful as his parents, even though the rules of the game had changed.

In the months that followed, as I clipped the *Wall Street Journal* and collected economic reports, I came to see that there was no way most of us could meet the expectations created in the late '40s and '50s, when having both a home and children was an attainable goal. Then, the economy was full of predictable middle-class rewards and hidden subsidies for young families.

In the '70s, as we came of age, the U.S. economy was entering a diguised but deepening depression whose burdens fell disproportionately on the young. The twin pillars of the middle-class dream — affordable housing and enough real income to support children — were crumbling without our knowing it. Germany and Japan reaped the fruits of their postwar industrial reconstruction, while U.S. products and farm goods lost their dominance in the world marketplace. Vietnam War debt and a bloated military budget — funded with borrowed money — fueled inflation. Real U.S. wages stopped growing and began to fall. Health-care costs grew. Meat went up, cheese went up, interest rates went up.

When the economy hit the skids, many older people were wearing safety belts. It was the young who went through the windshield. In 1973, 80 percent of those over thirty-five owned their own homes. But millions of baby boomers were arriving at the labor and housing markets to find starting wages stagnating and houses out of sight.

When productivity and profits declined and corporations squeezed unions and exported jobs to cheaper climes, it was younger workers who got the short end of two-tier wage contracts, failed to get good union jobs at all, or were paid minimum wages that did not keep pace with inflation.

25 When manufacturing declined and service industries grew, it was primarily younger workers who took the lower-paying new jobs. Between 1973 and 1986, the proportion of younger non-college-educated workers holding (usually better-paying) jobs in manufacturing dropped from one-third to less than one-quarter.

In our twenties, my friends and I hardly cared. We ate tofu and hung Indian bedspreads in rented apartments. We were young; it was a lark. But in our thirties, as we married or got sick of having places sold out from under us, we wanted to be grown-up, we wanted money, we wanted houses.

In 1973 — the last really good year for the middle class — the average thirty-year-old man could meet the mortgage payments on a median-priced home with about a fifth of his income. By 1986, the same home took twice as much of his income.

In the same years, the real median income of all families headed by someone under thirty fell by 26 percent. It was a loss virtually identical to the 27 percent drop in per-capita personal income between 1929 and 1933, the deepest years of the Depression. The Depression created a sense of shared misfortune and national crisis. But the stagflation of the '70s and '80s begot in its victims a sense of individual failure — and in its survivors, a sort of chumpish pride, as though they'd come up in the world by paying $100,000 for a house that would have cost their parents a fifth as much.

My friends, who spent much of their twenties marching and organizing on behalf of others, responded not by organizing politically but by making small personal adjustments. If the middle class was going to disappear, they would ape the rich, not the poor. They spent more on housing and less on charity and savings. (In 1981, young families saved less than 1 percent of their after-tax income, compared with 4 percent in 1973.) They took on more debt and paid it off more slowly. (In 1988, installment debt was at a record 16 percent of personal income, far above the 12 percent of the early 1980s). They took on this debt at an age when their parents were saving for retirement — perhaps on the unspoken assumption that their parents' deaths would eventually bail them out with a legacy. When pushed to the wall, they did with less: they gentrified slums and bought gimcrack condominiums in buildings with pretentious marbled lobbies and paper-thin walls.

30 Unable to meet the out-of-scale expectations created in the 1950s, they gave up on necessities and comforted themselves with cheap luxuries: flowers, Dove bars, Häagen-Dazs, Cuisinarts, dinners out. As people dispossessed from housing and family life have done before, they wore their fortunes on their backs or sunk them into their cars. Having unconsciously absorbed the cultural imperative to do better than our parents — and unable to do that in economic terms — my generation decided to be upwardly mobile in terms of taste, instead. In some ways, we created a culture more adapted to our realities; in other ways, we became a generation of wannabes. One year I gave my father a $200 gift certificate for custom-made shirts from the Custom Shop, and smiled when he ordered them in a cotton/polyester blend. I couldn't make as much money as he did, but at least, I thought, I knew how to spend it. The $200 that paid our parents' mortgages would only cover our car payments; but we bought Land's End instead of Sears, and learned to call noodles and coffee "fettuccine" and "cappucino."

Other adaptations involved fundamental changes in our family and personal lives. Women entered the full-time work force and stayed there: more than half of all women with children under a year old are working. People delayed marriage into their thirties (men tend not to marry until they earn a breadwinner wage — one reason why marriage rates are so low among young blacks); others postponed, or simply forgot about, having children.

Those friends of mine who had children despite the difficulties were forced to make sacrifices their parents were never asked to make. One of my closest friends, an art therapist married to a carpenter, has two young children. She had to return to work a month after each child was born. "I felt I had no choice at all, because of money," she told me. "There was no breathing time." One rainy morning a couple of years ago, she left the house with her three-month-old daughter on her chest in a Snugli, her four-year-old son in one hand, and an umbrella and her breakfast in the other. She was on the way to day care and work when she slipped on the steps and fell. She picked up the children, went back to the house, got in bed, and started to cry. "I just felt like I couldn't carry on anymore, and I tried to figure out what to do," she said. In the next six months, she collapsed physically with a series of infections and had to quit her job.

Faced with such examples, it's not surprising that many of the women I know have, sometimes reluctantly, foregone children. Unlike our mothers, we have been freed — by legalized abortion and changing customs — from obligatory motherhood. But for myself, the decision not to have children wasn't easily or freely made. For years I saved money toward marriage and family. I married late—at thirty-five—and two years later spent my birthday crying, feeling that my husband and I would never marshal the financial, physical, and emotional resources necessary to have a child while we both worked full-time. It wasn't a simple economic decision, and other factors played their part. But although I am sure there are other women crying secretly in other bedrooms, it was not the kind of thing I could talk to anybody about.

I have friends who cope by keeping up appearances — running up credit-card debt and pretending nothing has changed. But others face the truth about the way they live now with some dignity and grace. I recently went to dinner with Nancy, my old roommate, in her rent-controlled apartment in San Francisco's North Beach. She knows how to do well with nothing; we ate spaghetti and homemade applesauce by candlelight on an old picnic table in a courtyard where daisies grew in olive-oil cans. As we talked, her son circled the table on a tricycle. Nancy told me things were much better than they had been when her son was tiny, even though she still rises at four in the morning to get her work done. She still doesn't own a car, and she and her son leave the city about six times a year. At thirty-four, she owns only a refrigerator, a small Chinese carpet, an antique bench, and her mother's dinner dishes. "I don't feel poor," she said. "I feel as if I actually have luxuries." It turned out she meant taking cabs to work, sending the laundry out, and having the flat cleaned twice a month — tasks done in a previous generation by a wife whose cash income was not needed.

"You can talk about the economic problems of single mothers, but single 35
mothers exist because it's an option now, and it wasn't an option for my mother," she said earnestly. "I could get out of my relationship when I wanted to. Having a child is the most rewarding thing I've ever done. It changed my life for the better. I wouldn't go back. If I didn't have my son

to spend my money on, I'd be buying snazzy shoes or yuppiefied kitchen equipment. Instead, I'm seeing things I'd otherwise miss. I'm standing on the corner with him, waiting for the bus, looking at a seagull standing on top of a flagpole."

I went to dinner with my brother Peter in the flat he shares in San Francisco. He is thirty-six, a perpetual student, and lives on about a quarter of what I spend. There's always peace and quiet at his place, a sense of being an expected guest, an uncluttered awareness of the spaces between things. He knows how to use a pressure cooker and find things at Goodwill; when he wants to see a show, he works as an usher. When I arrived, the table was set and the lights turned low; there were wineglasses filled with mineral water, cloth napkins folded carefully at each place, and two stubs of candles glowing. When it was time, we sat down for homemade lentil soup, warm, fresh sourdough rye from the neighborhood bakery, salad and baked potatoes. I felt so well taken care of that I ate bread as though it was a rare food, tasting the grains against my palate instead of wolfing it down. There was a sort of Zen luxuriousness about the whole meal: we squeezed the maximum possible enjoyment out of the minimum possible consumption. My deepest needs—warmth, light, quiet, companionship—were satisfied. I didn't miss anything.

I thought of my own life—my constant conversations with myself about wanting a child, a new couch, a weekend cottage, a bigger house on a quieter street—and realized my discontent was cheating me of the life I *had.*

"If it's by choice and it's not overwhelming, having no money can be a way of entering more deeply into your life," my brother said, as he served me some more lentil soup.

Not long after that, I bought myself a new raincoat, a year's supply of shampoo, and a pressure cooker. I quit my job as a reporter to become a free-lance writer. I wrote to the direct-mail association and asked them to take me off the catalog lists. I sold my ancient, infuriating Mercedes and bought a dull but reliable used Honda. I bought a secondhand copy of *Laurel's Kitchen,* learned to cook beans, and started using my library card.

I decided that if the economy was going to deprive me of things I deeply 40
wanted, it would not also take my time.

I began facing the life I had, not the life I dreamed of having or thought I had the right to have. I turned off lights. I started to cut the link between consumption and pleasure, between consumption and self-worth. And that paved the way for some unexpected things. I recycled—because it saved money on garbage pickup—and ate less meat and more beans. I walked downtown instead of getting into the car. Having less money forced me to get to know my neighbors, and a network of borrowing emerged. My next-door neighbor Mack, a salesman, lost his job and borrowed my computer to type resumés; when my husband's car broke down, Mack lent us his. My husband Bob helped Jay, a carpenter, change his clutch; Jay brought us wood scraps for kindling and his wife Gloria fed us dinner. One weekend last fall, my husband and I came home from a walk and saw four of our neighbors standing outside Mack's house around a pyramid of lawn sod.

"Found it at the dump," said George, the young contractor who lives down the block. He picked up a roll of sod, laid it out in Mack's front yard, and jumped up and down to set it. "Some landscaper threw away a truck-load." Mack's wife Jan, who works as a flight attendant, laid out another roll, and in half an hour, the patch of dirt in front of her house was transformed into a carpet of green. Jan turned on the sprinkler.

"There's plenty left," said George. "Dig up your yard, and we'll do it too." They all carried their tools around the geraniums that serve as a hedge between our houses. My husband and I raked out wisps of yellow grass. "My grandfather owned this whole block in the '30s," said George over the clatter of rakes. He chopped out a root with his hoe. "There was a dairy farm behind your house, and a vineyard across the street." I cradled rolls of sod against my chest until I smelled like the riverbanks where I skinny-dipped as a child. Soon our weed patch was covered with a quilt of green, its nap running every which way. Jan knelt down with clippers and snipped along the edge of our walk as though cutting out the armhole of a dress. Mack brought out a six-pack. I squeezed lemons into a jug of iced water, and we sat around on the fresh new grass in the afternoon sunlight with no sense that anything needed to be repaid. I shut my eyes and felt no need to compare our block, held in its growing net of mutual favors and borrowings, with anything else I'd ever known.

Engaging the Text

1. What does Butler mean by "the great boomer bust"? What caused it, and what effects has it had on Butler, her friends and acquaintances, and her generation?
2. Butler describes a period of "cognitive dissonance" — when people she knew were struggling with expenses while the papers wrote about "yuppies and blackened redfish" (para. 16). Have you ever experienced the feeling that media depictions of "typical" American life-styles are at odds with your own experience? If so, how did you respond to the discrepancy?
3. Much of the anxiety that Butler expresses in this essay reflects the idea that "Americans don't like poor people" (para. 13). Do you agree with this view of American values?
4. How does Butler herself respond to the dilemmas posed by downward mobility? How would you characterize her attitude near the end of her essay?
5. Butler notes that one of her friends seems to define "manhood" as the ability to consume (para. 20). How common do you think it is for Americans — male or female — to measure their personal value in terms of what they can buy?

Exploring Connections

6. Compare and contrast Katy Butler's experience with that of Stephen Cruz (p. 460). How did their attitudes about the American Dream change? Why? How has this change influenced the way they chose to live?
7. Look at the cartoon below. How might its artist, Tom Tomorrow, respond to Katy Butler's essay?

Extending the Critical Context

8. Working in a small group, make a list of features that would define a middle-class household with two adults and two children. For example, what kind of house and cars might such a family have? What kind of vacation would they take? What should they be saving and spending for entertainment, food, education, and retirement? Do some quick research to estimate costs for this family, and then calculate how much annual income is necessary to support the kind of life you consider middle class.
9. Write a journal entry or essay about generational differences in your own family's history. Has your family experienced the downward mobility that Butler de-

THIS MODERN WORLD by TOM TOMORROW

scribes? Have living conditions, financial security, or leisure time been markedly different from one generation to another?

10. Butler notes that many young Americans attempt to deny their downward mobility by surrounding themselves with affordable status symbols like "flowers, Dove bars, Häagen-Dazs, Cuisinarts, [and] dinners out" (para. 30). What evidence do you see that Americans are using such "cheap luxuries" as a substitute for real economic success?

Streets of Gold: The Myth of the Model Minority

CURTIS CHANG

According to conventional wisdom, Asian Americans offer the latest, best evidence that the American Dream is alive and well. Publications like Time *and* Newsweek *have celebrated Asian Americans as a "super minority" that has adopted the Puritan work ethic and outshone even the Anglo majority in terms of education and financial success. In this essay, Curtis Chang probes the data used in such media reports and questions this new embodiment of the success myth. Since the educational achievement of Asians is an important component of the myth, the essay may prompt you to take a fresh look at the status of Asian American students on your campus. Chang was born in Taiwan and immigrated to the United States in 1971. This essay was written in 1987, when he was a freshman at Harvard; since graduating in 1990 Chang has taught in Harvard's government department and traveled to Soweto, South Africa, on a Michael C. Rockefeller Fellowship for Travel Abroad.*

Over 100 years ago, an American myth misled many of my ancestors. Seeking cheap labor, railroad companies convinced numerous Chinese that American streets were paved with gold. Today, the media portrays Asian-Americans as finally mining those golden streets. Major publications like *Time, Newsweek, U.S. News and World Report, Fortune, The New Republic,* the *Wall Street Journal,* and the *New York Times* have all recently published congratulatory "Model Minority" headline stories with such titles:

America's Super Minority
An American Success Story
A Model Minority

Why They Succeed
The Ultimate Assimilation
The Triumph of the Asian Americans

But the Model Minority is another "Streets of Gold" tale. It distorts Asian-Americans' true status and ignores our racial handicaps. And the Model Minority's ideology is even worse than its mythology. It attempts to justify the existing system of racial inequality by blaming the victims rather than the system itself.

The Model Minority myth introduces us as an ethnic minority that is finally "making it in America" (*Time,* July 8, 1985). The media consistently defines "making it" as achieving material wealth, wealth that flows from our successes in the workplace and the schoolroom. This economic achievement allegedly proves a minority can "lay claim to the American dream" (*Fortune,* Nov. 24, 1986).

Trying to show how "Asian-Americans present a picture of affluence and economic success" (*N.Y. Times Magazine,* Nov. 30, 1986), 9 out of 10 of the major Model Minority stories of the last four years relied heavily on one statistic: the family median income. The median Asian-American family income, according to the U.S. Census Survey of Income and Education data, is $22,713 compared to $20,800 for white Americans. Armed with that figure, national magazines have trumpeted our "remarkable, ever-mounting achievements" (*Newsweek,* Dec. 6, 1982).

Such assertions demonstrate the truth of the aphorism "Statistics are 5
like a bikini. What they reveal is suggestive, but what they conceal is vital." The family median income statistic conceals the fact that Asian-American families generally (1) have more children and live-in relatives and thus have more mouths to feed; (2) are often forced by necessity to have everyone in the family work, averaging *more* than two family income earners (whites only have 1.6) (Cabezas, 1979, p. 402); and (3) live disproportionately in high cost of living areas (i.e., New York, Chicago, Los Angeles, and Honolulu) which artificially inflate income figures. Dr. Robert S. Mariano, professor of economics at the University of Pennsylvania, has calculated that

> when such appropriate adjustments and comparisons are made, a different and rather disturbing picture emerges, showing indeed a clearly disadvantaged group. . . . Filipino and Chinese men *are no better off than black men with regard to median incomes.* (Mariano, 1979, p. 55)[1]

Along with other racial minorities, Asian-Americans are still scraping for the crumbs of the economic pie.

Throughout its distortion of our status, the media propagates two crucial

[1]The picture becomes even more disturbing when one realizes that higher income figures do not necessarily equal higher quality of life. For instance, in New York Chinatown, more than 1 out of 5 residents work more than 57 hours per week, almost 1 out of 10 elderly must labor more than 55 hours per week (Nishi, 1979, p. 503). [Author's note]

assumptions. First, it lumps all Asian-Americans into one monolithic, homogeneous, yellow skinned mass. Such a view ignores the existence of an incredibly disadvantaged Asian-American underclass. Asians work in low income and low status jobs 2 to 3 times more than whites (Cabezas, 1979, p. 438). Recent Vietnamese refugees in California are living like the Appalachian poor. While going to his Manhattan office, multimillionaire architect I. M. Pei's car passes Chinese restaurants and laundries where 72 percent of all New York Chinese men still work (U.S. Bureau of the Census, 1977, Table 7).

But the media makes an even more dangerous assumption. It suggests that (alleged) material success is the same thing as basic racial equality. Citing that venerable family median income figure, magazines claim Asian-Americans are "obviously nondisadvantaged folks" (*Fortune*, May 17, 1982). Yet a 1979 United States Equal Employment Opportunity Commission study on Asian-Americans discovered widespread anti-Asian hiring and promotion practices. Asian-Americans "in the professional, technical, and managerial occupations" often face "modern racism — the subtle, sophisticated, systemic patterns and practices . . . which function to effect and to obscure the discriminatory outcomes" (Nishi, 1979, p. 398). One myth simply does not prove another: neither our "astonishing economic prosperity" (*Fortune*, Nov. 24, 1986) nor a racially equal America exist.

An emphasis on material success also pervades the media's stress on Asian-Americans' educational status at "the top of the class" (*Newsweek on Campus*, April 2, 1984). Our "march into the ranks of the educational elite" (*U.S. News*, April 2, 1984) is significant because "all that education is paying off spectacularly" (*Fortune*, Nov. 24, 1986). Once again, the same fallacious assumptions plague this "whiz kids" image of Asian-Americans.

The media again ignores the fact that class division accounts for much of the publicized success. Until 1976, the U.S. Immigration Department only admitted Asian immigrants that were termed "skilled" workers. "Skilled" generally meant college educated, usually in the sciences since poor English would not be a handicap. The result was that the vast majority of pre-1976 Asian immigrants came from already well-educated, upper-class backgrounds — the classic "brain drain" syndrome (Hirschman and Wong, 1981, pp. 507–510).

The post-1976 immigrants, however, come generally from the lower, 10
less educated classes (Kim, 1986, p. 24). A study by Professor Elizabeth Ahn Toupin of Tufts University matched similar Asian and non-Asian students *along class lines* and found that Asian-Americans "did not perform at a superior academic level to non-Asian students. Asian-Americans were more likely to be placed on academic probation than their white counterparts . . . twice as many Asian American students withdrew from the university" (Toupin, 1986, p. 12).

Thus, it is doubtful whether the perceived widespread educational success will continue as the Asian-American population eventually balances out along class lines. When 16.2 percent of all Chinese have less than 4 years of schooling (*four times* that of whites) (Azores, 1979, p. 73), it seems many future Asian-Americans will worry more about being able to read a newspaper rather than a Harvard acceptance letter.

Most important, the media assumes once again that achieving a certain level of material or educational success means achieving real equality. People easily forget that to begin with, Asians invest heavily in education since other means of upward mobility are barred to them by race. Until recently, for instance, Asian-Americans were barred from unions and traditional lines of credit (Yun, 1986, pp. 23–24).[2] Other "white" avenues to success, such as the "old boy network," are still closed to Asian-Americans.

When *Time* (July 8, 1985) claims "as a result of their academic achievement Asians are climbing the economic ladder with remarkable speed," it glosses over an inescapable fact: there is a white ladder and then there is a yellow one. Almost all of the academic studies on the *actual returns Asians receive* from their education point to prevalent discrimination. A striking example of this was found in a City University of New York research project which constructed resumes with equivalent educational backgrounds. Applications were then sent to employers, one group under an Asian name and a similar group under a Caucasian name. Whites received interviews 5 times more than Asians (Nishi, 1979, p. 399). The media never headlines even more shocking data that can be easily found in the U.S. Census. For instance, Chinese and Filipino males only earned respectively 74 and 52 percent as much as their *equally educated* white counterparts. Asian females fared even worse. Their salaries were only 44 to 54 percent as large as equivalent white males' paychecks (Cabezas, 1979, p. 391). Blacks suffer from this same statistical disparity. We Asian-Americans are indeed a Model Minority—a perfect model of racial discrimination in America.

Yet this media myth encourages neglect of our pressing needs. "Clearly, many Asian-Americans and Pacific peoples are invisible to the governmental agencies," one state agency reported. "Discrimination against Asian-Americans and Pacific peoples is as much the result of omission as commission" (California State Advisory Committee, 1975, p. 75). In 1979, while the president praised Asian-Americans' "successful integration into American society," his administration revoked Asian-Americans' eligibility for minority small business loans, devastating thousands of struggling, newly arrived small businessmen. Hosts of other minority issues, ranging from reparations for the Japanese-American internment[3] to the ominous rise of anti-Asian violence, are widely ignored by the general public.

[2]For further analysis on the role racism plays in Asian-Americans' stress on education and certain technical and scientific fields, see Suzuki, 1977, p. 44. [Author's note]

[3]*reparations . . . internment:* During World War II, over one hundred twenty thousand Japanese Americans on the West Coast were sent to prison camps by order of the U.S. government; many lost their homes, businesses, and possessions because of this forced relocation.

The media, in fact, insist to the general populace that we are not a true 15
racial minority. In its attack on affirmative action, the *Boston Globe* (Jan. 14, 1985) pointed out that universities, like many people, "obviously feel that Asian-Americans, especially those of Chinese and Japanese descent, are brilliant, privileged, and wrongly classified as minorities." Harvard Dean Henry Rosovsky remarked in the same article that "it does not seem to me that as a group, they are disadvantaged. . . . Asian-Americans appear to be in an odd category among other protected minorities."

The image that we Asians aren't like "other minorities" is fundamental to the Model Minority ideology. Any elementary school student knows that the teacher designates one student the model, the "teacher's pet," in order to set an example for others to follow. One only sets up a "model minority" in order to communicate to the other "students," the blacks and Hispanics, "Why can't you be like that?" The media, in fact, almost admit to "grading" minorities as they headline Model Minority stories, "Asian-Americans: Are They Making the Grade?" (*U.S. News,* April 2, 1984). And Asians have earned the highest grade by fulfilling one important assignment: identifying with the white majority, with its values and wishes.

Unlike blacks, for instance, we Asian-Americans have not vigorously asserted our ethnic identity (a.k.a. Black Power). And the American public has historically demanded assimilation over racial pluralism.[4] Over the years, *Newsweek* has published titles from "Success Story: Outwhiting the Whites" (*Newsweek,* June 21, 1971) to "Ultimate Assimilation" (*Newsweek,* Nov. 24, 1986), which lauded the increasing number of Asian-White marriages as evidence of Asian-Americans' "acceptance into American society."

Even more significant is the public's approval of how we have succeeded in the "American tradition" (*Fortune,* Nov. 24, 1986). Unlike the Blacks and Hispanics, we "Puritan-like" Asians (*N.Y. Times Magazine,* Nov. 30, 1986) disdain governmental assistance. A *New Republic* piece, "America's Greatest Success Story" (July 15, 1985), similarly applauded how "Asian-Americans pose no problems at all." The media consistently compares the crime-ridden image of other minorities with the picture of law abiding Asian parents whose "well-behaved kids" (*Newsweek on Campus,* April 1984) hit books and not the streets.

Some insist there is nothing terrible about whites conjuring up our "tremendous" success, divining from it model American traits, then preaching, "Why can't you Blacks and Hispanics be like that?" After all, one might argue, aren't those traits desirable?

After decades of work by Asian American activists, Congress in 1988 ordered the government to pay $20,000 to each internee as partial recompense for these losses.

[4]A full discussion of racial pluralism vs. assimilation is impossible here. But suffice it to say that pluralism accepts ethnic cultures as equally different; assimilation asks for a "melting" into the majority. An example of the assimilation philosophy is the massive "Americanization" programs of the late 1800s which successfully erased Eastern European immigrants' customs in favor of Anglo-Saxon ones. [Author's note]

Such a view, as mentioned, neglects Asian-Americans' true and pressing needs. Moreover, this view completely misses the Model Minority image's fundamental ideology, an ideology meant to falsely grant America absolution from its racial barriers. 20

David O. Sears and Donald R. Kinder, two social scientists, have recently published significant empirical studies on the underpinnings of American racial attitudes. They consistently discovered that Americans' stress on "values, such as 'individualism and self-reliance, the work ethic, obedience, and discipline' . . . can be invoked, however perversely, to feed racist appetites" (Kennedy, 1987, p. 88). In other words, the Model Minority image lets Americans' consciences rest easy. They can think: "It's not our fault those blacks and Hispanics can't make it. They're just too lazy. After all, look at the Asians."[5] Consequently, American society never confronts the systemic racial and economic factors underlying such inequality. The victims instead bear the blame.

This ideology behind the Model Minority image is best seen when we examine one of the first Model Minority stories, which suddenly appeared in the mid 1960s. It is important to note that the period was marked by newfound, strident black demands for equality and power.

> At a time when it is being proposed that hundreds of billions be spent to uplift Negroes and other minorities, the nation's 300,000 Chinese Americans are moving ahead on their own — with no help from anyone else . . . few Chinese-Americans are getting welfare handouts — or even want them . . . they don't sit around moaning. (*U.S. News,* Dec. 26, 1966)

The same article then concludes that the Chinese-American history and accomplishment "would shock those now complaining about the hardships endured by today's Negroes" (*U.S. News,* Dec. 26, 1966).

Not surprisingly, the dunce-capped blacks and Hispanics resent us apple polishing, "well-behaved" teacher's pets. Black comedian Richard Pryor performs a revealing routine in which new Asian immigrants learn from whites their first English word: "Nigger." And Asian-Americans themselves succumb to the Model Minority's deceptive mythology and racist ideology.[6] "I made it without help," one often hears among Asian circles, "why can't they?" In a 1986 nationwide poll, only 27 percent of Asian-American stu-

[5]This phenomenon of blaming the victim for racial inequality is as old as America itself. For instance, Southerners once eased their consciences over slavery by labeling blacks as animals lacking humanity. Today, America does it by labeling them as inferior people lacking "desirable" traits. For an excellent further analysis of this ideology, actually widespread among American intellectuals, see *Iron Cages: Race and Culture in 19th-Century America* by Ronald T. Takaki. [Author's note]

[6]America has a long history of playing off one minority against the other. During the early 1900s, for instance, mining companies in the west often hired Asians solely as scabs against striking black miners. Black versus Asian hostility and violence usually followed. This pattern was repeated in numerous industries. In a larger historical sense, almost every immigrant group has assimilated, to some degree, the culture of anti-black racism. [Author's note]

dents rated "racial understanding" as "essential." The figure plunged 9 percent in the last year alone (a year marked by a torrent of Model Minority stories) (Hune, 1987). We "white-washed" Asians have simply lost our identity as a fellow, disadvantaged minority.

But we don't even need to look beyond the Model Minority stories themselves to realize that whites see us as "whiter" than blacks — but not quite white enough. For instance, citing that familiar median family income figure, *Fortune* magazine of May 17, 1982, complained that Asian-Americans are in fact "getting *more* than [their] share of the pie." For decades, when white Americans were leading the nation in every single economic measure, editorials arguing that whites were getting more than *their* share of the pie were rather rare.

No matter how "well behaved" we are, Asian-Americans are still ex- 25
cluded from the real pie, the "positions of institutional power and political power" (Kuo, 1979, p. 289). Professor Harry Kitano of UCLA has written extensively on the plight of Asian-Americans as the "middle-man minority," a minority supposedly satisfied materially but forever racially barred from a true, *significant* role in society. Empirical studies indicate that Asian-Americans "have been channeled into lower-echelon white-collar jobs having little or no decision making authority" (Suzuki, 1977, p. 38). For example, in *Fortune's* 1,000 largest companies, Asian-American nameplates rest on a mere half of one percent of all officers' and directors' desks (a statistical disparity worsened by the fact that most of the Asians founded their companies) (*Fortune,* Nov. 24, 1986). While the education of the upper-class Asians may save them from the bread lines, their race still keeps them from the boardroom.

Our docile acceptance of such exclusion is actually one of our "model" traits. When Asian-Americans in San Francisco showed their first hint of political activism and protested Asian exclusion from city boards, *The Washington Monthly* (May 1986) warned in a long Asian-American article, "Watch out, here comes another group to pander to." *The New Republic* (July 15, 1985) praised Asian-American political movements because

> unlike blacks or Hispanics, Asian-American politicians have the luxury of not having to devote the bulk of their time to an "Asian-American agenda," and thus escape becoming prisoners of such an agenda. . . . The most important thing for Asian-Americans . . . is simply being part of the process.

This is strikingly reminiscent of another of the first Model Minority stories:

> As the Black and Brown communities push for changes in the present system, the Oriental is set forth as an example to be followed — a minority group that has achieved success through adaptation rather than confrontation. (*Gidra,* 1969)

But it is precisely this "present system," this system of subtle, persistent racism that we all must confront, not adapt to. For example, we Asians gained our right to vote from the 1964 Civil Rights Act that blacks marched, bled, died, and in the words of that original Model Minority story, "sat around moaning for." Unless we assert our true identity as a minority and challenge racial misconceptions and inequalities, we will be nothing more than techno-coolies[7] — collecting our wages but silently enduring basic political and economic inequality.

This country perpetuated a myth once. Today, no one can afford to dreamily chase after that gold in the streets, oblivious to the genuine treasure of racial equality. When racism persists, can one really call any minority a "model"?

List of Sources

Azores, Fortunata M., "Census Methodology and the Development of Social Indicators for Asian and Pacific Americans," *U.S. Commission on Civil Rights: Testimony on Civil Rights Issues of Asian and Pacific Americans* (1979), pp. 70–79.

Boston Globe, "Affirmative Non-actions," Jan. 14, 1985, p. 10.

Cabezas, Dr. Armado, "Employment Issues of Asian Americans," *U.S. Commission on Civil Rights: Testimony on Civil Rights Issues of Asian and Pacific Americans* (1979), pp. 389–399, 402, 434–444.

California State Advisory Committee to the U.S. Commission on Civil Rights, *Asian American and Pacific Peoples: A Case of Mistaken Identity* (1975) (quoted in Chun, 1980, p. 7).

Chun, Ki-Taek, "The Myth of Asian American Success and Its Educational Ramifications," *IRCD Bulletin* (Winter/Spring 1980).

Dutta, Manoranjan, "Asian/Pacific American Employment Profile: Myth and Reality — Issues and Answers," *U.S. Commission on Civil Rights: Testimony on Civil Rights Issues of Asian and Pacific Americans* (1979), pp. 445–489.

Fortune: "America's Super Minority," Nov. 24, 1986, pp. 148–149; "Working Smarter," May 17, 1982, p. 64.

Gidra (1969), pp. 6–7 (quoted in Chun, p. 7).

Hirschman, Charles, and Wong, Morrison, "Trends in Socioeconomic Achievement Among Immigrant and Native-Born Asian-Americans, 1960–1976," *The Sociological Quarterly* (Autumn 1981), pp. 495–513.

Hune, Shirley, keynote address, East Coast Asian Student Union Conference, Boston University, Feb. 14, 1987.

Kahng, Dr. Anthony, "Employment Issues," *U.S. Commission on Civil Rights: Testimony on Civil Rights Issues of Asian and Pacific Americans* (1979), pp. 411–413.

Kennedy, David M., "The Making of a Classic, Gunnar Myrdal and Black-White Relations: The Use and Abuse of *An American Dilemma*," *The Atlantic* (May 1987), pp. 86–89.

Kiang, Peter, professor of sociology, University of Massachusetts, Boston, personal interview, May 1, 1987.

[7] *techno-coolies:* The original coolies were unskilled laborers from the Far East who were often paid subsistence wages in the United States.

Kim, Illsoo, "Class Division Among Asian Immigrants: Its Implications for Social Welfare Policy," *Asian American Studies: Contemporary Issues, Proceedings from East Coast Asian American Scholars Conference* (1986), pp. 24–25.

Kuo, Wen H. "On the Study of Asian-Americans: Its Current State and Agenda," *Sociological Quarterly* (1979), pp. 279–290.

Mariano, Dr. Robert S., "Census Issues," *U.S. Commission on Civil Rights: Testimony on Civil Rights Issues of Asian and Pacific Americans* (1979), pp. 54–59.

New Republic, "The Triumph of Asian Americans" (July 15–22, 1985), pp. 24–31.

The New York Times Magazine, "Why They Succeed" (Nov. 30, 1986), pp. 72+.

Newsweek: "The Ultimate Assimilation" (Nov. 24, 1986), p. 80; "Asian-Americans: A 'Model Minority' " (Dec. 6, 1982), pp. 39–51; "Success Story: Outwhiting the Whites" (June 21, 1971), pp. 24–25.

Newsweek on Campus: "Asian Americans, the Drive to Excel" (April 1984), pp. 4–13.

Nishi, Dr. Setsuko Matsunaga, "Asian American Employment Issues: Myths and Realities," *U.S. Commission on Civil Rights: Testimony on Civil Rights Issues of Asian and Pacific Americans* (1979), pp. 397–399, 495–507.

Sung, Betty Lee, *Chinese American Manpower and Employment* (1975).

Suzuki, Bob H., "Education and the Socialization of Asian Americans: A Revisionist Analysis of the 'Model Minority' Thesis," *Amerasia Journal,* vol. 4, issue 2 (1977), pp. 23–51.

Time, "To America with Skills" (July 8, 1985), p. 42.

Toupin, Dr. Elizabeth Ahn, "A Model University for A 'Model Minority,' " *Asian American Studies: Contemporary Issues, Proceedings from East Coast Asian American Scholars Conference* (1986), pp. 10–12.

U.S. Bureau of the Census, *Survey of Minority-Owned Business Enterprises* (1977) (as quoted in Cabezas, p. 443).

U.S. News & World Report: "Asian-Americans, Are They Making the Grade?" (April 2, 1984), pp. 41–42; "Success Story of One Minority Group in U.S." (Dec. 26, 1966), pp. 6–9.

Washington Monthly, "The Wrong Way to Court Ethnics" (May 1986), pp. 21–26.

Yun, Grace, "Notes from Discussions on Asian American Education," *Asian American Studies: Contemporary Issues, Proceedings from East Coast Asian American Scholars Conference* (1986), pp. 20–24.

Engaging the Text

1. In Chang's view, what are the key elements of the stereotype of Asian Americans as a model minority? Have you encountered these yourself? How pervasive do you believe they are in your school or community?
2. What is wrong with this positive image of Asian Americans, according to Chang? What assumptions does it make, and how do they mislead us about the situation of many Asian Americans?
3. Why has the myth of the model minority been so widely embraced, according to Chang? What does it do for the United States as a country? What is the effect of the model minority myth on other ethnic minorities?
4. Many scholars who question the image of the model minority are themselves

Asian Americans. Does this fact make their claims more or less persuasive? Explain.

5. Chang's essay analyzes news stories, interprets census data, and reports on work by other scholars, but it does not present any original research. What purpose do essays like this serve when all of the data they contain is already available elsewhere?

Exploring Connections

6. When Stephen Cruz (p. 460) became successful, he was seen not as a member of a model minority group but rather as a model member of a minority group. To what extent was his situation as a successful young Chicano engineer comparable to that of Asian Americans today?
7. Compare and contrast the idea of the "model minority" with the idea of a "scholarship boy" as defined by Richard Rodriguez (p. 61). On what assumptions does each concept rest? What expectations does each create? Why is each of these labels dangerous?

Extending the Critical Context

8. Discuss in small groups how you learned of the myth of the model minority. Was it through TV, family, reading? Be as specific as possible. Then try to draw some conclusions about how this type of cultural "knowledge" is taught.
9. Although the news media have been quick to extol the virtues of Asian Americans as models of achievement, representations of Asians and Asian Americans are scarce in most forms of mass entertainment. Survey movies, TV shows, music videos, song lyrics, and other forms of popular culture. How are Asian Americans represented, and how do these images compare with those implied by the myth of the model minority?

Tiptoeing Around the Truth

Ellis Cose

The "Truth" in Cose's title — the one Americans are tiptoeing around — is that upper- and middle-class African Americans are often frustrated, angry, and resentful despite their success as politicians, lawyers, executives, and the like. In this selection from his provocative book The Rage of a Privileged Class *(1993), Cose tells a number of stories that reveal the source of Black anger and the widespread desire, or necessity, to conceal it. Cose (b. 1951) has been a journalist for more than two decades and has worked for such major newspapers and magazines as the* Chicago Sun-Times, USA Today, *the* Detroit Free Press, Time, *and* Newsweek.

During the summer of 1991, I found myself in the presence of Robert Maxwell, the flamboyant and famously eccentric hulk of a British press lord. This was months prior to his death and subsequent revelations that he had looted his own companies; Maxwell, who had recently bought the money-hemorrhaging New York *Daily News,* was widely viewed not as a crook but as the paper's savior.

I was being recruited to come to the *News* as head of its editorial pages and chairman of its editorial board. As part of the process, orchestrated by editor James Willse, I was ushered into Maxwell's $4,000-a-day suite in the Waldorf-Astoria. Along with assorted senior executives seeking approval for various projects, Willse and I waited to be summoned. Eventually, we were shown into a makeshift office where the magisterial Maxwell sat behind a desk. He greeted us and then ignored me for several minutes as he interrogated Willse regarding my credentials and future responsibilities. Apparently satisfied, he signaled Willse to leave and began to pepper me with questions, most having to do with my background and my impressions of the *News.*

Suddenly he shifted focus. What statement would the *News* be making, he asked, by appointing me to the job? I knew where he wanted me to go, but I refused to bite. "You would be saying that you want a top-flight journalist running your editorial pages," I replied. He nodded but clearly judged the answer incomplete. Would the appointment make me, he wanted to know, the top-ranking black newspaperman in New York? I shrugged, saying it all depended on what one made of titles; maybe yes, maybe no. He indicated he was not quite satisfied, and posed the same question in a slightly different fashion. Again I gave an inconclusive answer, having decided — largely out of irritation — that if he wanted to make racial symbolism the center of the conversation he would have to do so on his own. Instead, Maxwell changed the subject, and shortly thereafter, with an imperial wave of the hand, abruptly ended the session.

Obviously, the very fact that I was offered the job meant that in this case my race had not worked against me. If anything, it had worked to my advantage. Certainly, it had not been immaterial.

For most blacks in America, regardless of status, political persuasion, or 5
accomplishments, the moment never arrives when race can be treated as a total irrelevancy. Instead, too often it is the only relevant factor defining our existence.

"A white man with a million dollars is a millionaire, and a black man with a million dollars is a nigger with a million dollars," New York's mayor, David Dinkins, told me over lunch in October 1992, attributing the aphorism to his friend Percy Sutton, the former Manhattan borough president. Dinkins quickly added that he wasn't sure Sutton was the source, and also made clear that the view expressed was not necessarily his own. Yet I suspected the statement captured a sentiment — and a resentment — that burned brightly in Dinkin's heart.

Only two weeks earlier several thousand members of his own police department had staged a raucous anti-Dinkins rally on City Hall's steps. In the course of the demonstration, a few of the cops had flaunted signs: "Dinkins, we know your true color — yellow-bellied," "Dump the Washroom Attendant," "No Justice, No Police." Jimmy Breslin, a *Newsday* columnist on the scene, reported that some of the protesters had shouted, "Now you got a nigger right inside City Hall. How do you like that? A nigger mayor."

Though I had not come to ask Dinkins about the police protest, I knew it weighed heavily on his mind. I also knew that as New York's first black mayor, he had been burdened with more than his share of symbolism. At a time when racial incidents (from verbal assaults to riots to beatings with baseball bats and clubs) exploded upon the city with sickening regularity, Dinkins was expected to be a racial healer — especially by whites, who had denied him a majority of their votes. At the same time, whites, as well as New York's menagerie of minorities, viewed virtually every Dinkins deed through a narrow racial prism.

Yet he was expected not to complain — and not to be bothered by the fact that many regarded him not as the mayor but as the *black mayor.* That very day, I had received a letter from a *Daily News* reader, which she had also sent to Dinkins. She doubted the mayor would read it, so requested that it be printed in the *News.* "It seems you are so concerned, because a police officer used the word 'nigger,' during their demonstration. . . . Why is it always racism when a black person is called nigger, but not when a white person is called a white bitch?" she wrote.

10 The woman's point seemed to be that Dinkins had no business being upset about being called a nigger, at least not as long as certain blacks felt free to call a white woman a bitch. Essentially she was holding Dinkins responsible for the behavior of those blacks, in a way she probably would never have considered holding a white mayor responsible. But she was also saying something more: that whatever reactions he might have to racism were inconsequential, certainly nothing she wanted to hear. And she was not alone.

"I have gone to great lengths to avoid any complaints about my personal circumstances as respects race," Dinkins confessed at one point. "Many is the reporter who has said to me, 'Do you think you're treated differently because you're black?' . . . And I leave it [to them to] . . . make the observation. 'Why do *you* think this happens or that happens?' " It was pointless to protest, or even to discuss the issues, because "there are people who want to seize upon such things" and accuse him of "playing the race card," or of introducing race to cover up his own alleged inadequacies. Instead of griping about how critics treat him, said Dinkins, "I've complained about how people treat the city. But I've never said it's because I'm black that you're treating me differently than you've treated this one, or would treat another."

He paused briefly and said, almost under his breath, "When I write my memoirs or something, I might be inclined to discuss it more fully. It's not in my interest to talk about my personal circumstances in that regard at this time. . . . I make no complaints." For an instant I thought he had exhausted the subject, but he went on, noting again that when reporters, especially white reporters, pressed him on the question, he made a practice of turning the tables and asking them why they had asked. If they thought he was being treated differently because of race, he wanted to know why the hell they didn't write that instead of trying to put him on the spot. And if they didn't have the courage to write the truth about their own observations, he certainly was not going to take the bait. "Nobody's going to acknowledge it. Nobody's going to admit it. If they think that [a black mayor is subjected to a double standard], they're not going to say it, unless they can tie it to somebody."

Never having asked the mayor whether he thought he was held to an unfair standard, I felt no need to defend those journalists who did. But I was fascinated by the agitation in his voice. Clearly, he was convinced that many people could not see beyond the color of his skin. And clearly he was right. The idea of cops, even enraged white cops, referring to a white mayor as a bathroom attendant, for instance, was absurd. Yet what he felt — and what in fact was true — was not something he permitted himself to say, certainly not on the record. For to speak frankly and honestly about race would be to anger (or perhaps "disaffiliate") those whites who preferred to believe that racism, by and large, had disappeared.

Asked whether it was possible to be honest about race, given that reality, Dinkins replied, "I think it's essential that you be honest about it — *to a degree.*" Certain things, he indicated, were none of the public's business; and he compared his refusal to discuss a possible double standard to his refusal to discuss the frequency of sex with his wife. To me, the comparison made absolutely no sense; while sex is a private affair, a mayor's relationship with the press and public is nothing of the sort. Still, I thought his reading of the degree of candor the public was willing to accept was essentially correct; for when race enters the discussion, more often than not truth slips away.

15 A few weeks before the conversation with Dinkins, I spent an evening with Basil Paterson, a Dinkins intimate who had served as a deputy mayor in the early part of Ed Koch's administration, was a former vice chair of the Democratic National Committee, and had been the 1970 Democratic candidate for lieutenant governor of New York. As a trailblazing black politician, Paterson had spent plenty of time pondering the art of survival in a predominantly white political system. He had concluded, he said, that "whites don't want you to be angry." So black politicians, in order to get along, often conceal their true feelings. "We're selective in our terminology. We waste a lot of time that ought to be devoted to candor."

Paterson's observation is clearly not true of all black politicians, or even of all those whose constituents are largely white. Some black officeholders behave in just the opposite manner, angrily blaming any misfortune — including being caught in illegal or immoral acts — on bigotry and racist conspiracies. Still, Paterson's words haunted me, for over and over, as I interviewed successful black people from various walks of life, I encountered very similar reactions. Many of these normally outspoken professionals were extremely reluctant to own up to or have attributed to them the anger they clearly felt. To acknowledge their race-related anger or frustration, they feared, would be to alienate (and perhaps provoke reprisals from) those whites whose goodwill was essential to their well-being.

One man, a ranking editor at a major newspaper, revealed that in the wake of the 1992 Los Angeles riots, he had thought of writing an article for his newspaper's magazine about anger among middle-class blacks. He had mentioned the idea to a colleague, who had advised him not to propose it. Even though the colleague thought the topic to be of critical importance, he also felt that writing about it would be dangerous to his friend's career. It would risk rousing the suspicions of powerful white editors who would conclude that he, the writer, was the one who was angry. And it was only a small step from being seen as an angry black man to being labeled a troublemaker. The writer decided to heed the advice, concluding that publishing an important article was hardly worth paying that price.

During an interview, a socially prominent partner in a major law firm passionately denounced racism and noted that many young minority lawyers bitterly complained of its effects, but he equivocated when asked whether it had affected him personally, preferring to keep his public anger focused on a generic grievance. At one point, the conversation turned to prestigious private clubs. He acknowledged that blacks were usually not welcome but added, "You just don't go to places that are not likely to admit you." As for himself, he said he took his pleasures where he could. While he certainly enjoyed his membership in the university-affiliated club that his status as an alumnus allowed him to join, he was not all that eager to join other clubs. Realizing that the answer was transparently disingenuous, he asked if he could say something not for attribution.

There were beautiful tennis courts in a private club a few minutes' walk from his suburban home, and though his white neighbors all belonged, he had never been asked to join. "That annoys me enormously," he admitted as indignation tightened his face. Then he relaxed and quickly added, as if to soften the statement, "We don't care much for those people, anyway."

The reluctance of many members of the black middle class to talk about 20
their anger out loud should not be confused with complacency. It is best understood as a painful adaptation to a society that does not want to hear that privileged members of a generally "underprivileged" group still harbor serious complaints. The problem with such silence is obvious. In the words of Edward Jones, the management consultant, "How the heck do we solve something we can't talk about?" Yet even he concedes that the truth "makes people uncomfortable."

Alvin Poussaint, associate professor of psychiatry at Harvard Medical School and a close advisor to Bill Cosby, sees black self-censorship as a simple tool of survival. "It's always a risk for a black person in a predominantly white corporation to express individual anger," he says, because whites tend not to understand what the anger is about. As a result they are likely to dismiss the complainer as a chronic malcontent or a maladjusted person who perhaps needs to be eased out.

The inability to talk about race in anything resembling honest terms compounds the very misunderstanding that renders silence necessary. For those blacks and whites who come into closest contact, it stands as a huge barrier to their ever truly accepting one another or finding common ground.

Senator Moynihan[1] believes Americans are in "kind of a denial of ethnicity." When he and Nathan Glazer wrote *Beyond the Melting Pot,* people were outraged at their examination of ethnic strife: "By and large the attitude was that 'if you want to talk about this stuff, you encourage it.' " Yet when I remarked on the dissatisfaction rampant within the black middle class, Moynihan dismissed it as essentially groundless. This "upper group" of blacks, he said, was "moving along very well" even though some remained "caught with the legacy of grievance which is inappropriate to their condition." "Those blacks with the jobs are perfectly capable of saying they're being persecuted," he added.

In mentioning Moynihan's observation to several solidly middle-class blacks, I found not one who accepted his pronouncement — even among those who said they had no complaints about their own treatment or situation.

Donald McHenry, former ambassador to the United Nations (a post 25
once held by Moynihan), said: "I don't agree that people are out of sync, if you will, with the level of their progress. One doesn't know how much further you could be along, how many other opportunities would be there." Indeed, many successful blacks know that if it were not for discrimination, they would have done much better. They know because they see others with no greater ability progress far beyond them; and they know that race is all that distinguishes them from their more successful white colleagues. "I think that even people who are in the middle class, or who are higher, still carry with them this resentment, this feeling that somehow they would be further along. How much further along would *I* be, I don't know. The difference between me and most is that I don't let it bother me."

Ron Brown, a psychologist whose San Francisco–based firm, Banks and Brown Inc., specializes in helping corporations manage and motivate multiethnic workforces, took a similar view. Time after time, he has encountered blacks who felt undermined in their work, or who watched less competent

[1] *Senator Daniel Patrick Moynihan:* (b. 1927) U.S. senator and social scientist.

whites pass them by. And while they suspected race may have played a role, they could never be sure, partly because the corporations refuse to acknowledge any such possibility. "There is a denial [by the corporation] of any racial factors, when your whole organizational experience tells you there are all kinds of racial factors. . . . So in most cases a lot of people don't even bring it up. . . . It doesn't ever get talked about." And eventually many black executives, once so motivated and raring to go, simply "shut down" in frustration. "If businesses knew that they were somehow coopting and suppressing and stifling thirty to forty percent of their brains, they might say, 'Well, we got to do something. Boy, you're walking around here with only one eye and half a brain working.' But they don't see it that way."

A senior partner in a major Washington law firm was even more emphatic: "Our rage is not basically just directed at [conditions in the workplace]," he said. "It's not just money. It's not just my house." It has to do with being totally and capriciously stripped of status at a moment's notice. It has to do, he said, with going into a store "where there's a white redneck who treats me like I make two cents and am uneducated," despite his degrees and high-powered job. "What needs to happen to Moynihan," he railed, is for him to wake up one day in an America that has decided, " 'We're going to kick the shit out of them [Irish-Americans] on every level except their salary and their job. You come to work, etcetera; but every other part of your life we're going to kick the shit out of you.' And then you may understand how it feels."

William Raspberry, a *Washington Post* columnist, told me: "African Americans are not yet at the point where we can react in political and social terms entirely as individuals. White people can pretty much react as individuals." If whites are not doing as well as they had hoped, said Raspberry, they can chalk it up to either bad luck or some personal failing, whereas blacks are much more likely to conclude that "a major part of . . . not doing well" relates to the color of their skin. And we don't dare become comfortable with our own situation as long as skin color still plays a major role in the prospects of people who look like us."

"People don't stop being angry just because they get money or get position," said Alvin Poussaint, the psychiatrist from Harvard, not as long as they face an unending stream of psychological slights. He knows black doctors who dress up to go shopping, simply to avoid being taken for shoplifters; and he knows major celebrities who feel excluded from the white old-boy Hollywood network where deals get made. "If you're black and middle-class . . . every day you're [going to get] a lot of crap. You're going to get angry."

Certainly, examples of angry celebrated blacks are easy to find. Film- 30
maker Spike Lee has become notorious for his vehement harangues against racism. But even among those who shy away from the role of black spokesperson and whose persona is anything but contentious or hostile, a sense of racial estrangement is palpable. Michael Morgan, the acclaimed classical conductor, told a writer for the *New York Times* in 1992: "I have a very nice

little career now, but I also know that sometimes that's because it has been to the advantage of an organization to have me, an African American, around. I see what others my age do, and that there are more star-studded careers that I have no doubt I would have if I were not black."

The people I interviewed about Moynihan's observation were obviously not a scientifically selected sample. It's possible they represent a fringe perspective or are all in the state of denial that Moynihan describes. I suspect, however, that something more is at work, that even if the depth of grievance is "inappropriate to their condition," the sense of injustice is not unfounded; and the plight is compounded by a society that in large measure insists that middle-class blacks have nothing to complain about.

Among successful blacks—and among many who belong to other ethnic minority groups as well — the number who spend much of their energy fighting desperation is alarmingly high, notwithstanding that we live in an age where legions of white men have concluded *they* are the group most discriminated against. That the pain of those blacks is generally invisible to whites in part reflects the fact that voicing it can carry consequences. Neither bosses nor colleagues much care for a crybaby—especially when they cannot understand what lies behind the tears.

In contrast, America easily understands, or thinks it does, the raw racial rage of the ghetto. Prose portraits of the nation's bullet-ridden slums have permitted even the most sequestered suburbanites to view an inner-city hell of drugs, squalid housing, and low expectations, where alienation thrives. When explosions come — as in South Central Los Angeles in 1992 or Miami's Liberty City in 1980 and 1989 — the cause is presumed to be clear. For those on the left, it lies in the wretchedness of inner-city life, in society's cold destruction of the human spirit. For those on the right, it stems from a poverty of values, from the inability and unwillingness of flawed people to take control of their lives and assume responsibility for their destiny. The explanations may be contradictory, but somewhere within or between them, most people believe, lies the secret to inner-city rage.

Rage among members of the black middle class is something different altogether. This is not a group that has any right to bellyache or wallow in self-pity—not if that right is won by dint of conspicuous suffering. After all, the economic and social status of many of its members is far higher than the level most Americans of any race have achieved.

At the celebrity super-rich level, the increased prominence of blacks has 35
been impossible to miss. Bill Cosby has become a fixture atop the *Forbes* list of the nation's highest-paid entertainers. In 1992, the magazine put the comedian's gross earnings for the most recent two years at $98 million. Talk-show host Oprah Winfrey came in at $88 million, and singers Michael Jackson and Prince at $51 million and $45 million, respectively.

But even well below that stratospheric level, many African Americans are doing quite nicely. According to U.S. Census figures, from 1967 to 1991 the proportion of black households earning $50,000 or more a year (in 1991 dollars) rose from 5.2 to 12.1 percent, or roughly 1.3 million households. The proportion earning $100,000 and up in those same years more than doubled, from .5 percent to 1.2 percent. Though the figures lagged far behind those for white households (27.5 percent with incomes of $50,000 and above in 1991, and 4.8 with incomes of at least $100,000), they obviously meant that the black upper middle class was growing.

In 1978, sociologist William Julius Wilson published an influential and important book, *The Declining Significance of Race.* Many read the title but not the tome and leapt to the conclusion that race no longer mattered in America. In fact, Wilson was saying nothing of the sort. He was making an argument a good deal more subtle, and also a good deal less exact. The "life chances of individual blacks have more to do with their economic class position than with their day-to-day encounters with whites," he concluded, citing a wealth of evidence that more blacks than ever were moving into white-collar jobs and skilled craft and foremen positions. He had little to say, however, about what happened once they got into those jobs, whether they moved up the ladder, or whether these privileged individuals ever managed to achieve their full potential.

The examination of such matters was not Wilson's purpose. His real concern was the black underclass, and the major point he set out to make was that the problems of that class could not be attributed to race alone, but were largely the consequence of certain economic developments. He was so disturbed that his short section on the black middle class received such disproportionate attention that he later published another book, *The Truly Disadvantaged,* which explicitly focused on the urban underclass. In it, he lambasted reviewers for their fixation on the middle-class section of his previous book: it "seemed that critics were so preoccupied with what I had to say about the improving condition of the black middle class that they virtually ignored my more important arguments about the deteriorating conditions of the black underclass."

The response to Wilson's remarks about the black middle class is hardly remarkable. America likes success stories. We also prefer to believe that our country—give or take a David Duke[2] or two—is well on the road to being color-blind. And since the predicament of the black underclass seems so hopeless, many find it comforting to concentrate on those who are doing well. Moreover, it is the black middle class, with its solid values and material attributes of success, that many deep thinkers have concluded may be the salvation of the down and out.

In a provocative 1988 article in *Esquire* magazine, Pete Hamill lamented 40
that there was "very little now that whites can do in a direct way for the maimed and hurting citizens of the Underclass." The way to the light, he argued, would have to be cleared by blacks who had made it into the middle

[2] *David Duke:* Former Ku Klux Klan leader (b. 1950) who ran for governor of Louisiana in 1991 and for president in 1992.

class. "I've come to believe that if there is to be a solution to the self-perpetuating Underclass, it must come from blacks, specifically from the black middle class. Blacks might have no other choice."

More recently political scientist James Q. Wilson has made a similar argument. "The best way to reduce racism real or imagined is to reduce the black crime rate," he says. "Decent black people" must assume major responsibility for transforming the lives of black infants so that crime rates will plummet. Those solidly responsible blacks "must accept, and ideally should develop and run, whatever is done."

The irony in such arguments is that the "decent black people" who will save America from the underclass, those paragons of middle-class virtue who will rescue the ghetto from violence, are themselves in a state of either silent resentment or deeply repressed rage. Taken as a group, they are at least as disaffected and pessimistic as those struggling at society's periphery. They consistently report more encounters with racial prejudice and voice stronger reservations about the country's success at delivering on the American dream. In a 1991 *Los Angeles Times* poll 58 percent of "affluent" blacks and 54 percent of college-educated blacks reported experiencing job- or education-related prejudice — higher numbers than were recorded for those who were poor and had no college education.

A May 1991 survey by the Gallup Organization asked, "Looking back over the last ten years, do you think the quality of life of blacks has gotten better, stayed about the same, or gotten worse?" Seventy percent of blacks with a college education felt things had gotten worse. Only 55 percent of those without a college education felt that way. Conversely, only 8 percent of the college-educated thought things had gotten better, compared to 18 percent of those without college.

In 1990, the Gallup Organization conducted a poll for *Newsday* in Long Island — its first ever of well-to-do suburban blacks — and discovered that two-thirds of those interviewed complained of discrimination. Three-fourths were convinced that realtors in the area steered blacks away from white neighborhoods. Respondents were significantly less satisfied with their lives than whites with substantially lower incomes. "Diane Colasanto, the Gallup vice president who prepared *Newsday*'s poll, said that because blacks are better off on Long Island than in most other areas she had expected that they would have more positive views," reported the paper.

When I spoke with Colasanto in 1992, she said she had not been sur- 45
prised at the results at all because some of her earlier work had also revealed "these feelings of separateness" among middle-class blacks. She had meant to communicate to *Newsday* her sense that the results were important, that they merited serious attention in part because they were so at odds with society's expectations.

Why would people who have enjoyed all the fruits of the civil rights revolution — who have Ivy League educations, high-paying jobs, and comfortable homes — be quietly seething inside? To answer that question is to go a long way toward explaining why quotas and affirmative action remain such polarizing issues; why black and white Americans continue to see race in such starkly different terms; and why solving America's racial problems is infinitely more complicated than cleaning up the nation's urban ghettos and educating the inhabitants — even assuming the will, wisdom, and resources to accomplish such a task.

Statistics tell only part of the story — though the part they tell is revealing. An analysis by Queens College of the City University of New York, for instance, shows that despite huge shifts in New York City's population, blacks and whites — regardless of income — remain as segregated now as ten years ago, and that for blacks race is a far more accurate indicator of where they are likely to live than economic class. Research by the Urban Institute indicates that in America's fifty largest metropolitan areas, 37 percent of blacks live in segregated neighborhoods, and that blacks experience discrimination 53 percent of the times they try to rent a home, and 59 percent of the times they look to buy one.

The inner sanctum of the corporate world remains largely segregated. Though the number of blacks earning high incomes has risen, only a handful have climbed near the top of the corporate structure. In 1989, Korn Ferry International replicated a 1979 survey of senior executives in Fortune 500 firms. In that ten-year interval, blacks went from .2 percent to .6 percent, and all minorities (blacks, Hispanics, and Asians) went from .5 percent to 1.3 percent.

In the real world such statistics are almost irrelevant, for rage does not flow from dry numerical analyses of discrimination or from professional prospects projected on a statistician's screen. It flows from the felt experiences of everyday life, from lessons learned in run-of-the-mill human encounters, from the struggles and disappointments of family members and peers. It comes from learning that one can never take the kindness — or the acceptance — of strangers for granted; from resentment at being judged at every turn, if only in part, for one's complexion instead of oneself.

Bill Bradley, U.S. senator from New Jersey, speaks of his career as a 50
professional basketball player as "those ten years I lived in a sort of a black world." As a result, Bradley told me, "I did see . . . things I would not have seen, and felt things that I would not have felt, had I not been in that group at that time on the road in America." For instance, he learned what it means never to be able to relax, never to know where the next insult or slight would come from. "And that is what's so depressing about it. You can't just [say], 'Well that's settled.' You want to get to a point [where you can drop your guard]." But that point, he indicated, never seemed to come.

What that means in the context of daily experience is being forced to bear what Isabel Wilkerson, Chicago bureau chief for the *New York Times*, calls "the incredible burden of living this dual life . . . and being constantly reduced to third-class citizenship and still expected to operate . . . with a smile on your face after one thing after another."

Asked for specific incidents, Wilkerson let go with a virtual catalog.

Once, upon arriving at the airport in Detroit, she found that she was running late for an interview. She raced through the terminal and was about to hop aboard an Avis bus when a man and a woman, both white, ran up behind her, announced they were with the Drug Enforcement Administration, and demanded that she step aside. She told them she couldn't afford to miss the bus, so they climbed on with her and watched her every move. Initially, she was "astonished and in kind of a daze" as it sunk in that she was suspected of carrying drugs. She was not too dazed to notice, however, that she was the only black person on the bus. As the agents stared at her, she found herself growing both angry and intensely embarrassed. "There was absolutely no reason for them to stop me except [that] I was black." When they tried to interrogate her, she took out her note pad and "ended up trying to do a little reverse psychology." She started asking them questions, mostly to help her keep her presence of mind. Still, as she realized the entire bus was staring, humiliation washed over her, and she wondered whether rape could be much worse. She was eventually let go without having to submit to a search, but she nonetheless found the experience "wrenching."

In another instance Wilkerson had to endure an interrogation from a secretary concerning her educational and professional credentials before being allowed to speak to an executive she was scheduled to interview. Though she was Chicago bureau chief, she had quickly learned not to trot out the title, since so many people refused to believe that she could possess the professional standing she claimed. Such things reminded her, said Wilkerson, that her status as a middle-class person was provisional, that "being a part of the middle-class professional society's world" was in many respects an "illusion."

This sense of the permanent vulnerability of one's status surfaced repeatedly in the interviews I conducted. Lynn Walker, a Ford Foundation executive, related how the residents of her co-op once resolved to determine which apartment dweller was misguidedly mixing construction debris in with the trash. Along with her white neighbors, she was picking through the garbage outside her building one morning, searching for evidence of ownership, when a white homeless person chanced upon the group of foragers. He paused, then walked directly up to Walker and helpfully advised her that he had already scoured the rubbish and found nothing worthwhile. For a moment she was confused, but she suddenly realized that though she was dressed for work, the man had taken her for a fellow homeless person. Later she laughed over the bizarre episode but observed that it had driven home for her how pervasive a role racial assumptions can play.

Knowing that race can undermine status, African Americans frequently 55
take aggressive countermeasures in order to avoid embarrassment. One woman, a Harvard-educated lawyer, learned to carry a Bally bag when going to certain exclusive shops. Like a sorceress warding off evil with a wand, she would hold the bag in front of her to rebuff racial assumptions, in the hope that the clerk would take it as proof that she could be trusted to enter. A prominent sociologist with a national reputation confessed to a similar frus-

tration. The saleswoman at a shop on New York's East Side refused to budge until his white girlfriend, who was already inside, asked, "Why aren't you letting him in?" When the woman finally opened the door, the sociologist was so enraged that he told her off and left.

My own wife, Lee, who is Puerto Rican, went apartment hunting by herself when we were considering moving. In one building after another, she got the distinct impression that she was being condescended to. A superintendent took one look at her and slammed the door, telling her not to disturb him while he was eating. When she called a listing and asked the

pleasant-sounding woman on the other end whether the apartment (advertised without an address) was in a good neighborhood, the woman responded, "Yes, it's a very good neighborhood. There are no black people here." On another occasion, she went to see a broker who insisted—despite our high income and Fifth Avenue address — on showing her one slum apartment after another. Only after she impressed on the woman that she was a lawyer and a prosecutor was she taken to a decent place—a studio so much smaller than the two- or three-bedroom apartment we had requested that the agent knew there was no possibility we would take it. Finally, in frustration, Lee gave up her search for the day. Later, her voice trembling with outrage, she declared, "Next time I go looking for an apartment, I'm taking somebody white along with me."

The pain and anger inflicted by such experiences do not quickly go away. Conrad K. Harper, a partner in the New York law firm Simpson Thacher & Barlett, recalls with precision the time, more than a decade and a half ago, when a broker called to tell him the deal had collapsed for a Westchester home he had planned to buy. He asked whether race was a factor and to his astonishment the broker confessed that it was. Harper sued, the broker testified in his behalf, and he eventually got his home. Yet despite the passage of time, says Harper, the experience "still makes me angry. At some level that particularly grates."

Reminders that one's humanity is automatically devalued because of race come in many forms—including what journalist Joseph Boyce calls the "black tax." A former Atlanta bureau chief of *Time* magazine, Boyce tells the story of his 1985 move to New York, where he was to become deputy bureau chief. Because Time Inc. had a policy of buying transferred employees' current homes at 105 percent of appraised value, it was in his interest to get a high appraisal. The first appraisal on his four-bedroom house came in significantly lower than expected, and Boyce, who is black, wondered whether his race was blinding the realtors to its true value, so he summoned another team of realtors. On the appointed day, he moved out and had his white secretary move in. She replaced the photographs of his beaming family with hers, and when the appraiser arrived she waltzed around the house as if she had lived there all her life. The result was an appraised value nearly 15 percent above the prior assessment. Though Boyce, now a senior editor at the *Wall Street Journal*, tells the tale with genuine humor, it is laced with weary resignation—a resignation born of the recognition that had he been a whit less clever his color, quite literally, would have cost him. And indeed still could.

As a consequence of the need for such constant alertness, even the most mild-mannered individuals sometimes find themselves boiling over with anger. Yet James Baldwin[3] had it wrong. To be black and "relatively conscious"

[3]*James Baldwin:* American novelist, dramatist, and essayist (1924–1987), perhaps best known for *The Fire Next Time* (1963).

in America is not necessarily to be in a perpetual state of rage. Few human beings of any race could survive the psychic toll of uninterrupted anger. Those who did would be in such a miserable state that they could scarcely cope with life, much less succeed at it. In successful individuals, especially those who are members of racial minority groups, even righteous rage tends to be leavened with humor and grace. What is constant is not anger but awareness, awareness that even the most pleasant interracial encounter can suddenly become awkward, ugly, or worse.

Engaging the Text

1. According to Cose, what economic, psychological, and political costs are associated with race? Why do many successful African Americans try to conceal their anger?
2. Cose writes that many Blacks he interviewed shared a "sense of the permanent vulnerability of one's status" (para. 54). What does he mean by this phrase? What causes this feeling?
3. Cose begins by summarizing his conversations with newspaper owner Robert Maxwell and New York City Mayor David Dinkins. What is the point of each of these stories, and why do you think Cose chose these to open "Tiptoeing Around the Truth"?
4. How would you describe Cose's methods as a writer in this excerpt? How has he gathered information, and how does he present it? What advantages and disadvantages do you see in his methods? What other approaches to this topic can you imagine?

Exploring Connections

5. Stephen Cruz (p. 460) was a successful Mexican American who nevertheless found himself dissatisfied. How closely do Cruz's circumstances and feelings resemble those of the African Americans Cose describes above?
6. Evaluate the ways that race can influence economic success, supporting your analysis with evidence from Studs Terkel's "Stephen Cruz" (p. 460), Curtis Chang's "Streets of Gold: The Myth of the Model Minority" (p. 513), and Ellis Cose's "Tiptoeing Around the Truth." How pervasive or important is the influence of race, in your view?
7. Write an imaginary dialogue between Cose and Shelby Steele (p. 411) about the reasons why successful African and other non-European Americans often feel silenced. How might they differ in their approaches to the task of improving communication between the races?
8. How might Cose interpret the actions and reactions of the characters in the Feiffer cartoon on page 534? What might the mask represent in this cartoon? What is Feiffer saying about ethnicity and success in America?

Extending the Critical Context

9. Make a list of all the middle- and upper-class African American characters you can think of in recent films and TV shows. To what extent do they reflect or challenge the experiences and attitudes Cose presents? How would you account for the image of successful African Americans portrayed in the media?

Number One!

Jill Nelson

In this brief excerpt from Volunteer Slavery: My Authentic Negro Experience *(1993), Jill Nelson paints an unforgettable portrait of her father. Head of an affluent Black family and a member of what Ellis Cose calls a "privileged class," Nelson's father made very sure his children didn't grow complacent about their social and economic position. Nelson (b. 1952) studied at the City University of New York and at Columbia and became a radical journalist; in 1986, "sick of committing class suicide in the name of righteousness," she accepted a position at the prestigious* Washington Post's Sunday *magazine, becoming the newsmagazine's first Black and first female writer. After a brief period with the* Post, *she quit her job because of the bias of the paper's managerial and editorial policies. Her work has appeared in numerous publications, including* Essence, Ms., USA Weekend, *and the* Village Voice.

That night I dream about my father, but it is really more a memory than a dream.

"Number one! Not two! Number one!" my father intones from the head of the breakfast table. The four of us sit at attention, two on each side of the ten-foot teak expanse, our brown faces rigid. At the foot, my mother looks up at my father, the expression on her face a mixture of pride, anxiety, and, could it be, boredom? I am twelve. It is 1965.

"You kids have got to be, not number two," he roars, his dark face turning darker from the effort to communicate. He holds up his index and middle fingers. "But number — " here, he pauses dramatically, a preacher going for revelation, his four children a rapt congregation, my mother a smitten church sister. "Number one!"

These last words he shouts while lowering his index finger. My father has great, big black hands, long, perfectly shaped fingers with oval nails so vast they seem landscapes all their own. The half moons leading to the cuticle take up most of the nail and seem ever encroaching, threatening to swallow up first his fingertips, then his whole hand. I always wondered if he became a dentist just to mess with people by putting those enormous fingers in their mouths, each day surprising his patients and himself by the delicacy of the work he did.

Years later my father told me that when a woman came to him with an 5
infant she asserted was his, he simply looked at the baby's hands. If they lacked the size, enormous nails, and half-moon cuticles like an ocean eroding the shore of the fingers, he dismissed them.

Early on, what I remember of my father were Sunday morning breakfasts and those hands, index finger coyly lowering, leaving the middle finger standing alone.

When he shouted "Number one!" that finger seemed to grow, thicken and harden, thrust up and at us, a phallic symbol to spur us, my sister Lynn, fifteen, brothers Stanley and Ralph, thirteen and nine, on to greatness, to number oneness. My father's rich, heavy voice rolled down the length of the table, breaking and washing over our four trembling bodies.

When I wake up I am trembling again, but it's because the air conditioner, a luxury in New York but a necessity in D.C., is set too high. I turn it down, check on Misu,[1] light a cigarette, and think about the dream.

It wasn't until my parents had separated and Sunday breakfasts were no more that I faced the fact that my father's symbol for number one was the world's sign language for "fuck you." I know my father knew this, but I still haven't figured out what he meant by it. Were we to become number one and go out and fuck the world? If we didn't, would life fuck us? Was he intentionally sending his children a mixed message? If so, what was he trying to say?

I never went to church with my family. While other black middle-class 10
families journeyed to Baptist church on Sundays, both to thank the Lord for their prosperity and donate a few dollars to the less fortunate brethren they'd left behind, we had what was reverentially known as "Sunday breakfast." That was our church.

In the dining room of the eleven-room apartment we lived in, the only black family in a building my father had threatened to file a discrmination suit to get into, my father delivered the gospel according to him. The recurring theme was the necessity that each of us be "number one," but my father preached about whatever was on his mind: current events, great black heroes, lousy black sell-outs, our responsibility as privileged children, his personal family history.

[1] *Misu:* Nelson's daughter.

His requirements were the same as those at church: that we be on time, not fidget, hear and heed the gospel, and give generously. But Daddy's church boasted no collection plate; dropping a few nickels into a bowl would have been too easy. Instead, my father asked that we absorb his lessons and become what he wanted us to be, number one. He never told us what that meant or how to get there. It was years before I was able to forgive my father for not being more specific. It was even longer before I understood and accepted that he couldn't be.

Like most preachers, my father was stronger on imagery, oratory, and instilling fear than he was on process. I came away from fifteen years of Sunday breakfasts knowing that to be number two was not enough, and having no idea what number one was or how to become it, only that it was better.

When I was a kid, I just listened, kept a sober face, and tried to understand what was going on. Thanks to my father, my older sister Lynn and I, usually at odds, found spiritual communion. The family dishwashers, our spirits met wordlessly as my father talked. We shared each other's anguish as we watched egg yolk harden on plates, sausage fat congeal, chicken livers separate silently from gravy.

We all had our favorite sermons. Mine was the "Rockefeller wouldn't 15
let his dog shit in our dining room" sermon.

"You think we're doing well?" my father would begin, looking into each of our four faces. We knew better than to venture a response. For my father, even now, conversations are lectures. Please save your applause—and questions—until the end.

"And we are," he'd answer his own query. "We live on West End Avenue, I'm a professional, your mother doesn't *have* to work, you all go to private school, we go to Martha's Vineyard in the summer. But what we have, we have because 100,000 other black people haven't made it. Have nothing! Live like dogs!"

My father has a wonderfully expressive voice. When he said dogs, you could almost hear them whimpering. In my head, I saw an uncountable mass of black faces attached to the bodies of mutts, scrambling to elevate themselves to a better life. For some reason, they were always on 125th Street, under the Apollo Theatre marquee. Years later, when I got political and decided to be the number-one black nationalist, I was thrilled by the notion that my father might have been inspired by Claude McKay's[2] poem that begins, "If we must die, let it not be like dogs."

"There is a quota system in this country for black folks, and your mother and me were allowed to make it," my father went on. It was hard to imagine anyone allowing my six-foot-three, suave, smart, take-no-shit father to do anything. Maybe his use of the word was a rhetorical device.

[2]*Claude McKay:* African American poet (1889–1948).

"Look around you," he continued. With the long arm that supported 20
his heavy hand he indicated the dining room. I looked around. At the eight-foot china cabinet gleaming from the weekly oiling administered by Margie, our housekeeper, filled to bursting with my maternal grandmother's china and silver. At the lush green carpeting, the sideboard that on holidays sagged from the weight of cakes, pies, and cookies, at the paintings on the walls. We were living kind of good, I thought. That notion lasted only an instant.

My father's arm slashed left. It was as though he had stripped the room bare. I could almost hear the china crashing to the floor, all that teak splintering, silver clanging.

"Nelson Rockefeller wouldn't let his dog shit in here!" my father roared. "What we have, compared to what Rockefeller and the people who rule the world have, is nothing. Nothing! Not even good enough for his dog. You four have to remember that and do better than I have. Not just for yourselves, but for our people, black people. You have to be number one."

My father went on, but right about there was where my mind usually started drifting. I was entranced by the image of Rockefeller's dog—which I imagined to be a Corgi or Afghan or Scottish Terrier—bladder and rectum full to bursting, sniffing around the green carpet of our dining room, refusing to relieve himself.

The possible reasons for this fascinated me. Didn't he like green carpets? Was he used to defecating on rare Persian rugs and our 100 percent wool carpeting wasn't good enough? Was it because we were black? But weren't dogs colorblind?

I've spent a good part of my life trying to figure out what my father 25
meant by number one. Born poor and dark in Washington, I think he was trying, in his own way, to protect us from the crushing assumptions of failure that he and his generation grew up with. I like to think he was simply saying, like the army, "Be all that you can be," but I'm still not sure. For years, I was haunted by the specter of number two gaining on me, of never having a house nice enough for Rockefeller dog shit, of my father's middle finger admonishing me. It's hard to move forward when you're looking over your shoulder.

When I was younger, I didn't ask my father what he meant. By the time I was confident enough to ask, my father had been through so many transformations — from dentist to hippie to lay guru — that he'd managed to forget, or convince himself he'd forgotten, those Sunday morning sermons. When I brought them up he'd look blank, his eyes would glaze over, and he'd say something like, "Jill, what are you talking about? With your dramatic imagination you should have been an actress."

But I'm not an actress. I'm a journalist, my father's daughter. I've spent a good portion of my life trying to be a good race woman and number one at the same time. Tomorrow, I go to work at the *Washington Post* magazine, a first. Falling asleep, I wonder if that's the same as being number one.

Engaging the Text

1. What lessons do you think Nelson's father meant to teach his children? Were these good lessons to teach? What do you think he meant by holding up his middle finger when he shouted, "Number one"?
2. Debate the father's assertion that "there is a quota system in this country for black folks" (para. 19). What does he mean by this? Do you think this is still true, was once true, or was never true?
3. What admirable traits and what flaws does Nelson reveal about her father? How has her attitude toward him changed over the years? Do you think he was a good father?
4. How do you interpret this line in Nelson's account: "It's hard to move forward when you're looking over your shoulder" (para. 25)?

Exploring Connections

5. Compare the explanation that Nelson's father offers to account for the relationship between successful African Americans and the white power structure with that offered by Ellis Cose in "Tiptoeing Around the Truth" (p. 522). How persuasive do you find their analyses?
6. Review Bebe Moore Campbell's "Envy" (p. 182) and compare what she learned about success from the women in her family with the lessons taught by Nelson's father. Which seem the most important or useful to you?

Extending the Critical Context

7. In this brief story, Nelson captures a single moment in her childhood that expresses her own eventual feelings about success. In an extended journal entry or as a short paper, write a story from your own life that captures the most important lesson you ever learned about the meaning of success.

You're Short, Besides!

Sucheng Chan

In this essay, Sucheng Chan analyzes her experiences as a "physically handicapped Asian American woman," showing how cultural myths about being disabled kept people from seeing her capacity for real achievement. Chan is a professor and the chair of Asian American studies at the University of California, Santa Barbara. She won the distinguished teaching award mentioned in her essay at UC Berkeley, where she received her Ph.D. and taught for ten years. She is author of the award-winning The Asian Ameri-

cans: An Interpretive History (1991) and, most recently, edited Hmong Means Free: Life in Laos and America *(1994). This essay first appeared in* Making Waves: An Anthology of Writing By and About Asian American Women *(1989).*

When asked to write about being a physically handicapped Asian American woman, I considered it an insult. After all, my accomplishments are many, yet I was not asked to write about any of them. Is being handicapped the most salient feature about me? The fact that it might be in the eyes of others made me decide to write the essay as requested. I realized that the way I think about myself may differ considerably from the way others perceive me. And maybe that's what being physically handicapped is all about.

I was stricken simultaneously with pneumonia and polio at the age of four. Uncertain whether I had polio of the lungs, seven of the eight doctors who attended me—all practitioners of Western medicine—told my parents they should not feel optimistic about my survival. A Chinese fortune teller my mother consulted also gave a grim prognosis, but for an entirely different reason: I had been stricken because my name was offensive to the gods. My grandmother had named me "grandchild of wisdom," a name that the fortune teller said was too presumptuous for a girl. So he advised my parents to change my name to "chaste virgin." All these pessimistic predictions notwithstanding, I hung onto life, if only by a thread. For three years, my body was periodically pierced with electric shocks as the muscles of my legs atrophied. Before my illness, I had been an active, rambunctious, precocious, and very curious child. Being confined to bed was thus a mental agony as great as my physical pain. Living in war-torn China, I received little medical attention; physical therapy was unheard of. But I was determined to walk. So one day, when I was six or seven, I instructed my mother to set up two rows of chairs to face each other so that I could use them as I would parallel bars. I attempted to walk by holding my body up and moving it forward with my arms while dragging my legs along behind. Each time I fell, my mother gasped, but I badgered her until she let me try again. After four nonambulatory years, I finally walked once more by pressing my hands against my thighs so my knees wouldn't buckle.

My father had been away from home during most of those years because of the war. When he returned, I had to confront the guilt he felt about my condition. In many East Asian cultures, there is a strong folk belief that a person's physical state in this life is a reflection of how morally or sinfully he or she lived in previous lives. Furthermore, because of the tendency to view the family as a single unit, it is believed that the fate of one member can be caused by the behavior of another. Some of my father's relatives told him that my illness had doubtless been caused by the wild carousing he did in his youth. A well-meaning but somewhat simple man, my father believed them.

Throughout my childhood, he sometimes apologized to me for having to suffer retribution for his former bad behavior. This upset me; it was bad enough that I had to deal with the anguish of not being able to walk, but to have to assuage his guilt as well was a real burden! In other ways, my father was very good to me. He took me out often, carrying me on his shoulders or back, to give me fresh air and sunshine. He did this until I was too large and heavy for him to carry. And ever since I can remember, he has told me that I am pretty.

After getting over her anxieties about my constant falls, my mother de- 5
cided to send me to school. I had already learned to read some words of Chinese at the age of three by asking my parents to teach me the sounds and meaning of various characters in the daily newspaper. But between the ages of four and eight, I received no education since just staying alive was a full-time job. Much to her chagrin, my mother found no school in Shanghai, where we lived at the time, which would accept me as a student. Finally, as a last resort, she approached the American School which agreed to enroll me only if my family kept an *amah* (a servant who takes care of children) by my side at all times. The tuition at the school was twenty U.S. dollars per month — a huge sum of money during those years of runaway inflation in China — and payable only in U.S. dollars. My family afforded the high cost of tuition and the expense of employing a full-time *amah* for less than a year.

We left China as the Communist forces swept across the country in victory. We found an apartment in Hong Kong across the street from a school run by Seventh-Day Adventists.[1] By that time I could walk a little, so the principal was persuaded to accept me. An *amah* now had to take care of me only during recess when my classmates might easily knock me over as they ran about the playground.

After a year and a half in Hong Kong, we moved to Malaysia, where my father's family had lived for four generations. There I learned to swim in the lovely warm waters of the tropics and fell in love with the sea. On land I was a cripple; in the ocean I could move with the grace of a fish. I liked the freedom of being in the water so much that many years later, when I was a graduate student in Hawaii, I became greatly enamored with a man just because he called me a "Polynesian water nymph."

As my overall health improved, my mother became less anxious about all aspects of my life. She did everything possible to enable me to lead as normal a life as possible. I remember how once some of her colleagues in the high school where she taught criticized her for letting me wear short skirts. They felt my legs should not be exposed to public view. My mother's response was, "All girls her age wear short skirts, so why shouldn't she?"

The years in Malaysia were the happiest of my childhood, even though

[1] *Seventh-Day Adventists:* A Protestant sect noted for their evangelical missionary work and their belief in the imminent and visible return of Christ, which would herald the coming of the Christian millennium.

I was constantly fending off children who ran after me calling, *"Baikah! Baikah!"* ("Cripple! Cripple!" in the Hokkien dialect commonly spoken in Malaysia). The taunts of children mattered little because I was a star pupil. I won one award after another for general scholarship as well as for art and public speaking. Whenever the school had important visitors my teacher always called on me to recite in front of the class.

A significant event that marked me indelibly occurred when I was 10
twelve. That year my school held a music recital and I was one of the students chosen to play the piano. I managed to get up the steps to the stage without any problem, but as I walked across the stage, I fell. Out of the audience, a voice said loudly and clearly, "Ayah! A *baikah* shouldn't be allowed to perform in public." I got up before anyone could get on stage to help me and, with tears streaming uncontrollably down my face, I rushed to the piano and began to play. Beethoven's "Für Elise" had never been played so fiendishly fast before or since, but I managed to finish the whole piece. That I managed to do so made me feel really strong. I never again feared ridicule.

In later years I was reminded of this experience from time to time. During my fourth year as an assistant professor at the University of California at Berkeley, I won a distinguished teaching award. Some weeks later I ran into a former professor who congratulated me enthusiastically. But I said to him, "You know what? I became a distinguished teacher by *limping* across the stage of Dwinelle 155!" (Dwinelle 155 is a large, cold, classroom that most colleagues of mine hate to teach in.) I was rude not because I lacked graciousness but because this man, who had told me that my dissertation was the finest piece of work he had read in fifteen years, had nevertheless advised me to eschew a teaching career.

"Why?" I asked.

"Your leg . . ." he responded.

"What about my leg?" I said, puzzled.

"Well, how would you feel standing in front of a large lecture class?" 15

"If it makes any difference, I want you to know I've won a number of speech contests in my life, and I am not the least bit self-conscious about speaking in front of large audiences. . . . Look, why don't you write me a letter of recommendation to tell people how brilliant I am, and let *me* worry about my leg!"

This incident is worth recounting only because it illustrates a dilemma that handicapped persons face frequently: those who care about us sometimes get so protective that they unwittingly limit our growth. This former professor of mine had been one of my greatest supporters for two decades. Time after time, he had written glowing letters of recommendation on my behalf. He had spoken as he did because he thought he had my best interests at heart; he thought that if I got a desk job rather than one that required me to be a visible, public person, I would be spared the misery of being stared at.

Americans, for the most part, do not believe as Asians do that physically handicapped persons are morally flawed. But they are equally inept at interacting with those of us who are not able-bodied. Cultural differences in the perception and treatment of handicapped people are most clearly expressed by adults. Children, regardless of where they are, tend to be openly curious about people who do not look "normal." Adults in Asia have no hesitation in asking visibly handicapped people what is wrong with them, often expressing their sympathy with looks of pity, whereas adults in the United States try desperately to be polite by pretending not to notice.

One interesting response I often elicited from people in Asia but have never encountered in America is the attempt to link my physical condition to the state of my soul. Many a time while living and traveling in Asia people would ask me what religion I belonged to. I would tell them that my mother is a devout Buddhist, that my father was baptized a Catholic but has never practiced Catholicism, and that I am an agnostic. Upon hearing this, people would try strenuously to convert me to their religion so that whichever God they believed in could bless me. If I would only attend this church or that temple regularly, they urged, I would surely get cured. Catholics and Buddhists alike have pressed religious medallions into my palm, telling me if I would wear these, the relevant deity or saint would make me well. Once while visiting the tomb of Muhammad Ali Jinnah[2] in Karachi, Pakistan, an old Muslim, after finishing his evening prayers, spotted me, gestured toward my legs, raised his arms heavenward, and began a new round of prayers, apparently on my behalf.

20 In the United States adults who try to act "civilized" towards handicapped people by pretending they don't notice anything unusual sometimes end up ignoring handicapped people completely. In the first few months I lived in this country, I was struck by the fact that whenever children asked me what was the matter with my leg, their adult companions would hurriedly shush them up, furtively look at me, mumble apologies, and rush their children away. After a few months of such encounters, I decided it was my responsibility to educate these people. So I would say to the flustered adults, "It's okay, let the kid ask." Turning to the child, I would say, "When I was a little girl, no bigger than you are, I became sick with something called polio. The muscles of my leg shrank up and I couldn't walk very well. You're much luckier than I am because now you can get a vaccine to make sure you never get my disease. So don't cry when your mommy takes you to get a polio vaccine, okay?" Some adults and their little companions I talked to this way were glad to be rescued from embarrassment; others thought I was strange.

Americans have another way of covering up their uneasiness: they become jovially patronizing. Sometimes when people spot my crutch, they ask

[2]*Muhammad Ali Jinnah:* Leading Indian politician (1876–1948) who opposed Hindu ideology and the methods of Gandhi for separate Muslim statehood; served as Pakistan's first governor general.

if I've had a skiing accident. When I answer that unfortunately it is something less glamorous than that, they say, "I bet you *could* ski if you put your mind to it!" Alternately, at parties where people dance, men who ask me to dance with them get almost belligerent when I decline their invitation. They say, "Of course you can dance if you *want* to!" Some have given me pep talks about how if I would only develop the right mental attitude, I would have more fun in life.

Different cultural attitudes toward handicapped persons came out clearly during my wedding. My father-in-law, as solid a representative of middle America as could be found, had no qualms about objecting to the marriage on racial grounds, but he could bring himself to comment on my handicap only indirectly. He wondered why his son, who had dated numerous high school and college beauty queens, couldn't marry one of them instead of me. My mother-in-law, a devout Christian, did not share her husband's prejudices, but she worried aloud about whether I could have children. Some Chinese friends of my parents, on the other hand, said that I was lucky to have found such a noble man, one who would marry me despite my handicap. I, for my part, appeared in church in a white lace wedding dress I had designed and made myself — a miniskirt!

How Asian Americans treat me with respect to my handicap tells me a great deal about their degree of acculturation. Recent immigrants behave just like Asians in Asia; those who have been here longer or who grew up in the United States behave more like their white counterparts. I have not encountered any distinctly Asian American pattern of response. What makes the experience of Asian American handicapped people unique is the duality of responses we elicit.

Regardless of racial or cultural background, most handicapped people have to learn to find a balance between the desire to attain physical independence and the need to take care of ourselves by not overtaxing our bodies. In my case, I've had to learn to accept the fact that leading an active life has its price. Between the ages of eight and eighteen, I walked without using crutches or braces but the effort caused my right leg to become badly misaligned. Soon after I came to the United States, I had a series of operations to straighten out the bones of my right leg; afterwards though my leg looked straighter and presumably better, I could no longer walk on my own. Initially my doctors fitted me with a brace, but I found wearing one cumbersome and soon gave it up. I could move around much more easily — and more important, faster — by using one crutch. One orthopedist after another warned me that using a single crutch was a bad practice. They were right. Over the years my spine developed a double-S curve and for the last twenty years I have suffered from severe, chronic back pains, which neither conventional physical therapy nor a lighter work load can eliminate.

25 The only thing that helps my backaches is a good massage, but the soothing effect lasts no more than a day or two. Massages are expensive, especially when one needs them three times a week. So I found a job that

pays better, but at which I have to work longer hours, consequently increasing the physical strain on my body—a sort of vicious circle. When I was in my thirties, my doctors told me that if I kept leading the strenuous life I did, I would be in a wheelchair by the time I was forty. They were right on target: I bought myself a wheelchair when I was forty-one. But being the incorrigible character that I am, I use it only when I am *not* in a hurry!

It is a good thing, however, that I am too busy to think much about my handicap or my backaches because pain can physically debilitate as well as cause depression. And there are days when my spirits get rather low. What has helped me is realizing that being handicapped is akin to growing old at an accelerated rate. The contradiction I experience is that often my mind races along as though I'm only twenty while my body feels about sixty. But fifteen or twenty years hence, unlike my peers who will have to cope with aging for the first time, I shall be full of cheer because I will have already fought, and I hope won, that battle long ago.

Beyond learning how to be physically independent and, for some of us, living with chronic pain or other kinds of discomfort, the most difficult thing a handicapped person has to deal with, especially during puberty and early adulthood, is relating to potential sexual partners. Because American culture places so much emphasis on physical attractiveness, a person with a shriveled limb, or a tilt to the head, or the inability to speak clearly, experiences great uncertainty—indeed trauma—when interacting with someone to whom he or she is attracted. My problem was that I was not only physically handicapped, small, and short, but worse, I also wore glasses and was smarter than all the boys I knew! Alas, an insurmountable combination. Yet somehow I have managed to have intimate relationships, all of them with extraordinary men. Not surprisingly, there have also been countless men who broke my heart—men who enjoyed my company "as a friend," but who never found the courage to date or make love with me, although I am sure my experience in this regard is no different from that of many able-bodied persons.

The day came when my backaches got in the way of having an active sex life. Surprisingly that development was liberating because I stopped worrying about being attractive to men. No matter how headstrong I had been, I, like most women of my generation, had had the desire to be alluring to men ingrained into me. And that longing had always worked like a brake on my behavior. When what men think of me ceased to be compelling, I gained greater freedom to be myself.

I've often wondered if I would have been a different person had I not been physically handicapped. I really don't know, though there is no question that being handicapped has marked me. But at the same time I usually do not *feel* handicapped—and consequently, I do not *act* handicapped. People are therefore less likely to treat me as a handicapped person. There is no doubt, however, that the lives of my parents, sister, husband, other family members, and some close friends have been affected by my physical condition. They have had to learn not to hide me away at home, not to feel embarrassed by how I look or react to people who say silly things to me, and not to resent me for the extra demands my condition makes on them. Perhaps the hardest thing for those who live with handicapped people is to know when and how to offer help. There are no guidelines applicable to all situations. My advice is, when in doubt, ask, but ask in a way that does not smack of pity or embarrassment. Most important, please don't talk to us as though we are children.

So, has being physically handicapped been a handicap? It all depends 30
on one's attitude. Some years ago, I told a friend that I had once said to an affirmative action compliance officer (somewhat sardonically since I do not believe in the head count approach to affirmative action) that the institution which employs me is triply lucky because it can count me as nonwhite, female, and handicapped. He responded, "Why don't you tell them to count you four times? . . . Remember, you're short, besides!"

Engaging the Text

1. How many ways has Chan been a success? How do you think she would define success? What role did her handicap play in her achievements?
2. Chan says many adults in the United States pretend not to notice visibly handicapped people. Is this a fair assessment of your own behavior? Have family members or others ever instructed you in "how to act" around physically challenged people? Has Chan's narrative changed in any way your attitude about people who face physical challenges?

Exploring Connections

3. Compare and contrast the stereotypes Chan faces with those described in Studs Terkel's "Stephen Cruz" (p. 460), Curtis Chang's "Streets of Gold: The Myth of the Model Minority" (p. 513), and Judith Ortiz Cofer's "The Story of My Body" (p. 278). What impact, if any, do such stereotypes have on Chan, Cruz, Ortiz Cofer, and the young people described by Chang?
4. Curtis Chang (p. 513) argues that the myth of the model minority has masked the difficulties faced by Asian Americans. Do you think there is a myth of the model handicapped person in American culture? If so, give a nutshell summary of this myth.

Extending the Critical Context

5. Do some research in *TV Guide* or your local video rental store to find one or more TV programs or films that include a physically challenged character. How are such characters portrayed? For example, is the "disability" invariably the focal point for that character, or is it just one part of a complex person?
6. Chan mentions that Asians generally have a stronger belief in connections between body, mind, and soul than Americans do. In small groups, discuss your own beliefs about one part of this issue: the power of the mind to heal the body.

Report to the class the range of beliefs within your group. Also try to determine whether these beliefs are influenced primarily by parents, by religion, by education, by personal experience, or by other factors.

Good Noise: Cora Tucker

Anne Witte Garland

When most people think about the American Dream, they don't visualize a factory job and a cluttered house right next to the railroad tracks. As you read this selection about community activist Cora Tucker, however, think about the connection of her life to core American values like democracy, progress, and individual rights. Author Anne Witte Garland is a free-lance writer covering environmental, public health, consumer, and women's issues. This selection comes from her 1988 book Women Activists: Challenging the Abuse of Power.

Cora Tucker's house is so close to the railroad tracks that at night when trains thunder by, the beds shake. The house and furniture are modest, and in the kitchen there's a lingering smell of the lard Cora cooks with. There are traces of Virginia red clay on the kitchen floor, and piled up on the bedroom floor are cardboard boxes overflowing with newspaper clippings and other papers.

Cora admits she doesn't like housekeeping anymore. The plaques and photographs hanging in the kitchen and living room attest to what she does enjoy; alongside religious pictures and photos of her children and grandchildren, there are several citizenship awards, certificates acknowledging her work in civil rights, and photos of her — a pretty, smiling black woman — with various politicians. One framed picture in the kitchen was handmade for Cora by some of the inmates in a nearby prison, whom Cora has visited and helped. In it, Old English letters made of foil spell out, "God grant me the serenity to accept the things I cannot change, the courage to change the things I can, and wisdom to know the difference." Cora has plenty of all three virtues, although "serene" probably isn't the first adjective a stranger would pin on her. But then, there isn't much that Cora would say she can't change, either.

Cora Tucker is something of an institution in Halifax County, Virginia, a rural county bordering North Carolina. In more than a dozen years, she has missed only a handful of the county board of supervisors' monthly meetings. Her name appears in the letters columns of the two daily newspapers several times a week—either signed onto her own letter or, almost as often, vilified in someone else's. She seems to know and be known by every black person on the street, in the post offices, and in stores and restaurants. And she is known by white and black people alike as having taken on many of the local, white-controlled institutions. Her main concern is simply fighting for the underdog, which she does in many ways — from social work–like visits to the elderly and invalids, to legal fights against racial discrimination, registering people to vote, and lobbying on issues like health care and the environment.

Cora was born in 1941 ten miles from where she lives now, near the Halifax county seat, in the small town of South Boston. Her father was a school teacher and later a railway porter. He died when Cora was three, and her mother and the nine children became sharecroppers on white men's farms. It was as a sharecropper, Cora says, that she learned how to do community organizing. She started by trying to help other sharecroppers to get things like better heating and food stamps. "I didn't call it 'organizing,' then," she says. "I just called it 'being concerned.' When you do sharecropping, you move around a lot. So I got to know everybody in the county, and to know what people's problems were.

"Sharecropping is the worst form of drudgery; it's slavery really. You 5
work on a man's farm, supposedly for half the profit on the crops you grow. That's what the contract says. But you pay for all the stuff that goes into the crop — seeds, fertilizer, and all. You get free housing, but most sharecroppers' housing is dilapidated and cold. It isn't insulated — it's just shacks, really. Sharecroppers are poor. I know of a family of twelve who grew fifteen acres of tobacco, and at the end of the year, they had earned just fifty dollars. And I know sharecroppers who needed food and applied for food stamps, but couldn't get them because they supposedly made too much money; the boss went to the food stamp office, and said they made such and such, so they couldn't qualify."

Cora went to work very young, planting and plowing with the others in the family. Her mother taught her to cook when she was six; Cora remembers having to stand on a crate to reach the kitchen counter. She was a curious and intelligent child who loved school and was unhappy when she had to stay out of school to clean house for the white woman on the farm where they lived.

Cora always adored her mother. Bertha Plenty Moesley was a "chief stringer"—a step in tobacco processing that involves picking the green tobacco leaves from the plants one at a time, and stringing them together three leaves to a stick, so that they can be hung to dry and cure. "My mama worked hard," Cora says. "She would plow and do all the things the men did. She was independent; she raised her children alone for eighteen years. When I was little, I felt so bad that she had to work that hard just so we could survive. There was welfare out there — all kinds of help, if only somebody had told her how to go about getting it. She had very little education, and didn't know to go down to the welfare office for help. As I got older, I was upset by that and made up my mind, when I was about eight or nine years old, that if I ever got grown, I'd make sure that everybody knew how to get everything there was to get. And I really meant it. I learned early how to get things done, and I learned it would take initiative to get what I wanted."

By the time Cora learned about welfare, her mother wouldn't take advantage of it. She was proud, and she told the children to have self-respect. "We didn't have anything else," Cora's mother says. "The kids had only themselves to be proud of." Cora took the advice to heart. There's a story she tells about growing up that has found a permanent place in community-organizing lore. In her high school, which was segregated at the time (Halifax County schools didn't integrate until 1969, under court order), Cora entered an essay contest on the topic of "what America means to me." She was taken by surprise when her bitter essay about growing up black in the South won a statewide award. But on awards night she was in for another surprise. The winners were to have their essays read, and then shake hands with the Virginia governor. Cora's mother was in the audience beaming, along with Cora's friends and teachers. But when her essay was read, Cora didn't recognize it — it had been rewritten, and the less critical sentiments weren't hers at all. She refused to greet the governor. "I disappointed everyone — my mother even cried."

The only person who supported her that night, she says, was a high school literature teacher, whom she credits as an important influence on her. "He spent a lot of time with me, encouraging me. Every time an issue came up that I felt strongly about, he'd have me write about it — letters to the editor that never got printed. He told me, 'Nobody can make you a second-class citizen but you. You should be involved in what's going on around you.' "

10 Instead, at seventeen she dropped out of high school to get married. As she describes it, the next several years were consumed with housekeeping and having children — six of them in rapid succession. She and her husband adopted a seventh. At first, Cora says, she threw herself enthusiastically into her new role. "I just wanted to be married. My father-in-law used to tease me about making myself so busy just being married. He'd say, 'You ain't going to keep this up for long.' But I'd say yes I would. Every morning, I put clean sheets on our beds — washed and ironed them. I ironed every diaper. I read all the housekeeping magazines; my house was immaculate. But I was beginning to find myself so bored, even then. My husband was farming then, sharecropping, and he'd get up early; I'd get up too, and feed him and the kids, and then do the cleaning. But when you clean every day, there just isn't that much to do, so I'd be finished by ten in the morning! I

joined a book club, so that I would get a book every month — but I would get bored in between. I would read the book in two days — I tried to savor it, but I couldn't make it last any longer. Then, when the kids started growing up and going to school, that would occupy me a little more. I'd feed them, then take them to school, and come back and clean and then start making lunch. But just as soon as my baby started school, I went out and got a job."

Halifax County has several textile and garment factories, and Cora went to work as a seamstress for one of the largest, a knit sportswear manufacturer. It was a fairly new operation, and the mostly women employees were expected to do everything, from lifting fabric bolts weighing forty or fifty pounds each, to sitting at sewing machines for eight hour stretches. There was no union; the county boasts in promotional material that less than 5 percent of the county's workforce is unionized. "Every time I used to talk to the girls there, my boss thought I was trying to get a union started. And I sure thought there *should* be a union; there were lots of health hazards, and people were always getting hurt. People got back injuries, two people even had heart attacks in the factory, because of the working conditions. I once got a woman to come down from Baltimore to talk about forming a union, but people got frightened because the bosses warned us that if there was any union activity, we'd lose our jobs."

Cora worked at the factory for seven years. The first thing she did with the money she was earning was to buy land for a house. "We had lived in places where we were so cold," she says. "We'd have no windows, and no wood. My dream was always to grow up and build me a house — my own house, out of brick. My husband never really wanted one; he was just as happy moving around. But after I had the babies and went to work at the factory, I told him I was going to build me a house. So the first year I worked, I saved a thousand dollars. The next year I saved another thousand, and then borrowed some from the company, to buy some land. Then I started saving again, for the house. But when I went to the FHA, they said I couldn't get a house without my husband's permission. At first, he said he wasn't going to have anything to do with it, so I said I'd buy a trailer instead. When he found out, he figured I might just as well put the money into a house, so he signed the papers. We built the house; it was the first time any of us had been inside a new house. I was crazy about it; we could sit down and say exactly where we wanted things. And while I was working, I bought every stick of furniture in it."

In 1976 Cora hurt her back and had to leave her job. Over the next few years she underwent surgery several times — first for her back, and then for cancer (for which she has had to have periodic treatments ever since). In the meantime, she had become active in the community. In the 1960s, she had participated in organizations like the National Association for the Advancement of Colored People, and another group called the Assemblies, but they moved too slowly for her tastes. ("They weren't really interested in taking on the power structure," she complains.) She had also organized her own letter-writing campaign in support of the federal Voting Rights Act to make it easier for blacks to vote. She had gone around to local churches, speaking to people and encouraging them to write to their representatives in Washington. She also took advantage of knowing women who ran beauty parlors—she provided the paper and pens, so that women could write letters while they sat under the hair dryers. "People would say to me, 'What good will it do?' But I think politicians have to be responsive if enough pressure can be brought to bear on them. You can complain, I can complain, but that's just two people. A politician needs to get piles of letters saying vote for this bill, because if you don't, you won't be in office much longer!" Cora was responsible for generating about five hundred letters supporting the voting law.

She takes voting very seriously. In 1977, she campaigned for a populist candidate for Virginia governor. She was undergoing cancer treatments at the time, but they made her tired, so she stopped the treatments in order to register people to vote. She had taught herself to drive, and personally rode around the county from house to house, filling her car with everyone there who was of voting age, driving them to the court house to register, and then home again. She's credited with having registered over one thousand people this way, and on election day, she personally drove many of them to the polling place.

While Cora was growing up, her mother's house was always filled with 15
people—besides her own family, several cousins lived with them, and aunts and uncles who had moved up north and came back to visit would stay with Cora's mother. Cora's own house was the same way — always filled with neighborhood teenagers, white and black. Cora became a confidante for the young people, and she encouraged them to read about black history, and to be concerned about the community. One of the things that upset the teenagers was the fate of a county recreation center. Halifax had no recreation facilities, and the county had applied for money from the federal Department of Housing and Urban Development (HUD) to build a center. When HUD awarded the county $500,000, however, the county turned it down because, as Cora puts it, there were "too many strings attached"—meaning it would have to be integrated. At home because of her back trouble and cancer, Cora took it on herself to help steer the teenagers' anger toward research into community problems. "When I heard about the recreation center, I went to the county board meeting and raised hell," she says. "But they went ahead and did what they wanted anyway. What I realized then was that if I had had all those kids come with me to the meeting, there would have been some changes. You need warm bodies — persons present and accounted for—if you want to get things done."

In 1975, Cora founded her own organization, Citizens for a Better America. CBA's first project was a study of black spending and employment patterns in the county. The study was based on a survey of three hundred people; it took two years to complete, with Cora's teenage friends doing much of the legwork. The findings painted a clear picture of inequality. Blacks made up nearly half the county population, and according to the survey, spent a disproportionate share of their salaries on food, cars, and furniture. But, as the study pointed out, there were very few black employees at the grocery stores where the money was spent, not a single black salesperson in the furniture stores, and no black salesperson at the auto dealerships. Blacks weren't represented at all on newspaper or radio station staffs.

Cora saw to it that the survey results were published in the local newspaper. The next step was to act on the results. The survey had uncovered problems with hiring practices and promotions of blacks in the school system, so Cora complained to the school board. After waiting in vain for the board to respond, CBA filed a complaint with what was then the federal Department of Health, Education, and Welfare. An HEW investigation confirmed the problems, and the agency threatened to cut off federal education funds to the county if the discrimination wasn't corrected. The county promised that the next principals it hired would be black.

CBA then took on other aspects of the county government. The survey had found that of all the county employees, only 7 percent were black — chiefly custodial workers or workers hired with federal Comprehensive Employment Training Administration (CETA) funds. Only one black person in the county government made over $20,000 a year. When the county refused to negotiate with Cora's organization about their hiring practices, CBA filed a complaint with the federal revenue sharing program. A Virginia state senator was successful in getting a federal investigation into the complaint stalled, but Cora went over his head, to the congressional Black Caucus and Maryland's black congressman, Parren Mitchell. Mitchell contacted Senator Edward Kennedy's office, which pressed to have the investigation completed. The findings confirmed CBA's, and the county was told to improve its hiring practices or stand to lose federal revenues.

CBA also initiated a boycott of local businesses that didn't hire minorities — Cora avoided the term "boycott," and instead called the action the "Spend Your Money Wisely Campaign." Leaflets were distributed listing the stores that hired black employees, and urging people, "Where Blacks are not HIRED, Blacks should not buy!"

20 Cora was developing a reputation. She started having frequent contact with the congressional Black Caucus, and would be called occasionally to testify in Washington on welfare issues. "They don't usually get people like me to testify; they get all these 'experts' instead. But every once in a while, it's good for them to hear from someone who isn't a professional, whose English isn't good, and who talks from a grassroots level."

It wasn't just in Washington that her reputation was growing, but back home, too. "I have a lot of enemies," she says. "There are derogatory things in the papers about me all the time. And the county government doesn't like me, because I keep going to all those board meetings and raising hell about what they do. When I go sometimes, they say, 'Yes, what do you want now, Ms. Tucker?' But I don't care what they think — I just tell them what I want. So a lot of the white power structure don't really like me. They think I'm a troublemaker, but I'm not really. I just believe what I believe in. Then there are black people too, who think that I want too much too soon. But when you think about it, black people have been in America 360-some years, so when is the time ever going to be right? The time doesn't *get* right; you make it right. So I'm not offended by what anybody says about me."

Sometimes the problem isn't just what people say; it's what they do. Cora has had many experiences with harassment. At first it was phone calls, from people threatening to burn her house down or telling her to "go back to Africa." Once she wrote a letter to the editor saying, "This is an open letter to all the people who call me and ask, what do you niggers want now? and hang up before I can tell them. . . .

"Blacks and poor people want to share in the economic progress of Halifax County, and when we get our children educated and motivated we would like them to come back to Halifax County and do something other than push mops and brooms. And a few of us would like our grandchildren to grow up near us, and if our children decide to make their home elsewhere it will be due to choice and not an economic necessity."

The harassment has taken other forms as well. Cora was followed and run off the highway one night, and had all four tires slashed one day when her car was parked in town. Once she was in the post office and a man recognized her, walked over, and spit on her; another time a car with out-of-state license plates pulled up next to her car as if to ask directions, and the man spat into her face. She came home from a meeting one night to find that someone had broken into her home and drenched her bed with gasoline. But Cora views the abuses with amazing equanimity: "If you stop doing things because somebody says something bad about you or does something to you," she says, "then you'll never get *anything* done."

And she wasn't making only enemies; she was also gaining a following. 25
One woman, who now works in the local legal aid office where Cora stops in frequently to get answers to legal questions, tells how she first met Cora. The woman had been born in Halifax, but had moved to New Jersey when she was a young girl. The civil rights movement progressed, and when the woman was finished with school, she moved back to Virginia, thinking that things there would be much better than they *had* been for blacks. But she found that any progress had been superficial only. When she started looking for work, she discovered that there were no blacks in responsible positions. She wore her hair in an Afro, and in hindsight thinks that it cost her jobs: at one point, it seemed she would be offered a position with the county, but when the man who was to be her boss saw her, he didn't give her the job.

Another prospective employer turned her down with the flat statement that he didn't want any union people around.

She became disillusioned, and was shocked at the complacency around her. About that time, she saw Cora Tucker's name in the paper. She was impressed, and started asking around about Cora. Not too long afterwards, she went to a community action program meeting, and noticed that Cora was scheduled to speak. "I was excited. I thought, finally, I'm going to meet a black person who's alive!" But she was initially disappointed. "I had pictured her as a towering woman — a fiery, eloquent speaker, like Barbara Jordan. Instead, there she was, short, and not that articulate."

But she quickly got drawn to Cora's strengths. "Cora wouldn't be happy at home, doing housekeeping," she says. "She's just not cut out for that. She's cut out for doing exactly what she's doing — getting out and raising hell about issues that affect people. She keeps pushing. When I get burned, I back off. But when Cora gets burned, she just blows out the fire and goes on."

Even people who don't like Cora give her credit: "I'm not a Cora Tucker fan," says one South Boston resident. "But I admit that she might just be the most informed person on political issues in this county." People credit Cora with having stamina and with inspiring others. An old friend of hers who runs a corner grocery says, "She keeps people fired up; she won't let us get lazy. It's because of her that I even watch the news!" One woman who was in school with Cora and now works for the county government says, "She was always making noise at school. We knew she'd grow up noisy. But it's *good* noise. When Cora talks, she knows what she's talking about."

And although Cora thinks she'll never be much of a public speaker, others disagree. One man who has worked with Cora for several years described a dinner ceremony sponsored by a human rights coalition in Richmond. "They had asked Cora to come and be a featured speaker. The woman who spoke before her gave this very polished speech. And then Cora got up, and gave her very unpolished speech. But it was moving to everyone in the room, because it was so much from the heart. It was the contrast of day and night between her and the previous speaker. What she had to say was so honest and down to earth, that people were very touched by it. And that's just the way she is."

30 Cora is very religious. "I believe in God, and in the providence of prayer. I go to church regularly." The churches in her area are still segregated; she attends the Crystal Hill Baptist Church, which, she points out with a chuckle, is brick-colored, while the white congregation down the road painted their brick church white. In an essay called "Halifax County and Blacks," under a subtitle "Things Blacks Must Do To Succeed," Cora once wrote, "First, blacks must go to church. The church is the backbone of black progress." Every summer for several years Cora has organized a "Citizenship Day of Prayer" on the lawn of the county courthouse in South Boston, which attracts

hundreds of people who probably wouldn't gather if the event were called a rally. At the event a list of grievances is always read off — including complaints about such things as how people are treated by the welfare system, unfair employment practices, or disproportionate suspensions of black pupils in the schools.

Problems like that — and what to do about them — are raised regularly at Citizens for a Better America meetings, held the fourth Friday of each month at a local funeral home. CBA has several hundred members, and with help from friends, Cora publishes a monthly one-page newsletter, which she decorates with American flag stickers and short religious sayings. The newsletter is a hodgepodge of useful information, including notices of food stamp law changes, regular updates on what the Virginia General Assembly is considering, board of supervisors' actions, community news, and news about other subjects that Cora is currently concerned with. One issue might have an essay on education, something on federal budget cutbacks and poor people, and a paragraph on the dangers of uranium mining. In 1986, when the federal government was considering southern Virginia, including part of Halifax County, as a possible site for a high-level nuclear waste dump, Cora and CBA fought back, using a section of the federal law requiring that the siting consideration take Indians and other minorities into account. Among other things, CBA found that blacks owned more farmland in Halifax County than in any other county in the country, and that historically, the first black-owned businesses and land in the country were on the site that would be affected by the nuclear waste dump.

Cora learns facts quickly; she can attend a meeting on the problems of family farmers one day, and the next, go to another meeting and be able to reel off facts and figures about farm foreclosures, the cost of fertilizers, trends in agribusiness, and the harmful effect of various pesticides. She reads constantly — newspapers, books, anything on an issue that interests her. "I save newspaper clippings — especially statements from politicians. That way, five years from now when they say, 'I'm definitely against that,' I can go back and say, 'But on such and such a date, you said *this*.'"

Cora stays extremely busy. Several years ago, she went back and got her graduate equivalency diploma, and took some courses at the community college. She thought she might want her degree: "I used to think I wanted to be a social worker. But I changed my mind, because you can't do as much inside the system as you can on the outside. There are so many people who become social workers, and then sit there with their hands tied. What people really need is somebody on the outside who's going to go and raise hell for them about laws and regulations."

Besides CBA gatherings, meetings of the county board of supervisors, and her usual rounds to the legal aid office and the county office building, Cora still visits elderly people, helps women without cars to do their shopping, reads and explains people's mail about food stamps and social security to them, and answers frequent letters. She takes every letter seriously. One, for instance, addressed simply to "Cora Tucker, Halifax, Virginia," read, "Dear Mrs. Tucker, Please don't let the county send us to be experimented on. We heard that they are going to take people on welfare to be experimented on." Cora remembered that there had been separate articles in the newspaper recently, on the "workfare" program to employ welfare recipients, and on a county decision to allow dogs from the animal pound to be used for medical experiments. Cora concluded that the person who wrote the letter had gotten the two issues confused—but she wasn't satisfied until she had called the county administrator and had gotten him to pledge to do a better job of explaining the issues publicly.

Cora's work goes far beyond Halifax. CBA itself has chapters in several 35
other places, including one started in Baltimore by one of Cora's sisters. In addition, when a new coalition group, Virginia Action, was started in the state in 1980, Cora was on the founding committee and was elected its first president. She also became active on the board of its national affiliate, Citizen Action. And in 1981, on top of everything else she was doing, this woman who as a girl had refused to shake the governor's hand was talked into running as a write-in protest candidate for governor by several black groups. She didn't get many votes, but her campaign was covered in the press, and she thinks that she raised issues about black people's concerns that otherwise would have been ignored.

Cora hasn't received much support in her work from her family, except from her mother. She and her husband are estranged, and her children haven't taken an active interest in Cora's work. Cora visits her mother often, in an old house several miles away that has woodburning stoves for heat, religious pictures in the downstairs room, and, hanging in the stairway, a plastic placemat depicting Martin Luther King's tomb. Cora's mother is clearly proud of her; she emphasizes what a smart girl Cora was, and is, and how courageous.

Others agree. As a man who works with Cora at Virginia Action puts it, "All of the issues Cora has taken on — like voting rights and employment discrimination — had been problems in Halifax County for decades. But nobody was willing to fight. And the reason was that it's very, very hard to be somebody going against the mainstream in a small rural community. It's a hell of a lot easier to play the role of the gadfly when you live in an urban environment, where you have your own community of friends, and you don't have to worry about the world. In a small rural community, your community *is* your world. And it's hard to fight the people you have to face every single day. Cora's able to do it because she's got guts. There's just nothing else to it but courage. In a small community those people writing nasty letters to the editor about you are people you're going to run into at the grocery, or whose kids go to school with yours. In addition, being black in a southern rural community, and being a woman, make it that much harder. She hasn't even had the active support of a large part of the black community—they feel threatened by her; she's stolen a lot of their fire. And she's always fighting back as opposed to the blacks who always cooperate with the white power structure. She just reached a point where she decided that slow-moving efforts weren't enough for the things that needed doing — things that were clear in her mind. She recognized the dangers that would be involved, but went ahead because she knew she was right."

Engaging the Text

1. How might Cora Tucker define success? To what extent has she achieved it?
2. What motivates Cora Tucker? How do you explain her courage and commitment? Can you think of any ways to encourage more people to emulate some of her virtues?
3. What has her experience taught Cora Tucker about "organizing"? What are her strategies for getting things done?
4. Do you think people in small towns or rural communities are better able than urban dwellers to influence political decisions that affect them? Why or why not?

Exploring Connections

5. The young women interviewed by Ruth Sidel in "The New American Dreamers" (p. 450) believe that material success is necessary for happiness and that they can "do whatever they want with their lives" as long as they work hard, make the right decisions, and stand on their own two feet. What alternative visions of success are offered by Cora Tucker, Sucheng Chan (p. 541), and Katy Butler (p. 503)?
6. Using evidence from Garland, Katy Butler (p. 503), and Toni Cade Bambara (p. 482), support or critique Gregory Mantsios's analysis of class in the United States (p. 465). Do you agree or disagree with his assertion that "people do not choose to be poor or working class; instead they are limited and confined by the opportunities afforded or denied by a social system" (para. 48).

Extending the Critical Context

7. Research grass-roots organizations like Citizens for a Better America in your community. Choose one and attend a meeting and interview members of the organization. Report to the class on its goals, strategies, accomplishments, and current objectives and challenges.
8. This chapter of *Rereading America* has been criticized by conservatives for undermining the work ethic of American college students. Rush Limbaugh, for example, claims that the chapter "presents America as a stacked deck," thus "robbing people of the ability to see the enormous opportunities directly in front of them." Do you agree? Write a journal entry in which you explain whether or how these readings have influenced your attitudes toward work and success.

6

Nature and Technology

The Myth of Progress

As it turned toward the Americas in the sixteenth and seventeenth centuries, Europe was shaking off a thousand years of feudalism. The old order, based on church authority and the power of kings, was giving way; in this climate of change, Europe saw America as a land where history could begin again. This "new world" offered itself as a fitting home for the innovative, freedom-loving, and ambitious. As the eminent American historian Frederick Jackson Turner wrote in 1893, "Since the days when the fleet of Columbus sailed into the waters of the New World, America has been another name for opportunity, . . . a gate of escape from the bondage of the past." America grew out of this astonishing optimism, this absolute belief in a better tomorrow.

But the dream of unlimited opportunity—the American dream of success—was possible only because of the vastness and richness of the land. Benjamin Franklin noted this around 1782 when he advised prospective European immigrants that America offered new opportunities to any "who, in their own Countries, where all the Lands are fully occupied, . . . could never have emerged from the poor Condition wherein they were born." Americans could dream of success because they had the unexploited natural wealth of a whole continent before them.

Thus, in the United States, the myth of progress has been linked to the western frontier. Many saw the westward movement (including the appropriation of American Indian lands and the conquest of Mexican territories) as the fulfillment of "Manifest Destiny." Western expansion was seen as part of a divine plan whose central aim was to "civilize" the land by making it fruitful and productive—supplying food for growing cities, coal and oil for burgeoning factories, iron ore for railroads and bridges. The 1845 *Emigrants' Guide to Oregon and California* epitomizes this faith in progress and the subjugation of nature:

> . . . the time is not distant when those wild forests, trackless plains, untrodden valleys, and the unbounded ocean, will present one grand scene, of continuous improvements, universal enterprise, and unparalleled commerce: when those vast forests, shall have disappeared, before the hardy pioneer; those extensive plains, shall abound with innumerable herds, of domestic animals; those fertile valleys, shall groan under the immense weight of their abundant products: when those numerous rivers, shall team with countless steam-boats, steam-ships, ships, barques and brigs; when the entire country, will be everywhere intersected, with turnpike roads, railroads and canals; and when, all the vastly numerous, and rich resources, of that now, almost unknown region, will be fully and advantageously developed. . . . And in fine, we are also led to contemplate the time, as fast approaching, when the supreme darkness of ignorance, superstition, and despotism, which now, so entirely pervade many portions of those remote regions, will have fled forever, before the march of civilization, and the blazing light, of civil and religious liberty; when genuine *republicanism,* and unsophisticated *democracy,* shall be reared up, and tower aloft, even upon the now wild shores, of the great Pacific; where they shall forever stand

forth, as enduring monuments, to the increasing wisdom of *man,* and the infinite kindness and protection, of an all-wise, and overruling *Providence.*"

The myth of progress, divinely sanctioned, gave the United States the justification it needed to seize the land and its resources. It did so by implying a sharp difference between the natural world and the world of human endeavor. Nature, according to the myth, is "other," and inferior to humans; land, rivers, minerals, plants, and animals are simply material made available for our use. And because our transformation of nature leads to "civilization," that use is ultimately justified.

Alongside the myth of progress, though, we find another myth — one that portrays nature as a spiritual resource and refuge from civilization. In his essay, "Nature" (1836), Ralph Waldo Emerson rhapsodized, "In the woods, we return to reason and faith. Standing on the bare ground, — my head bathed by the blithe air, and uplifted into infinite space . . . I am part or particle of God." Henry David Thoreau argued in *Walden* (1854) "our village life would stagnate if it were not for the unexplored forests and meadows which surround it. We need the tonic of wildness."

This countermyth inspired early conservationists like John Muir, who was instrumental in establishing the national park system, and it now drives much of the environmental movement. But the myth of progress has proved much more powerful: some of our most cherished parklands, including Yellowstone and Yosemite, were earmarked for preservation only after Congress determined that they had no commercial value. Even today, with widespread public concern about the environment, development commonly takes precedence over conservation; as recently as the late 1980s, Thoreau's wooded retreat, Walden Pond, was threatened by a condominium project.

This chapter invites you to reflect on the American definition of progress and the ways this cultural myth has molded our relationship to nature. The first half of the chapter explores the power and politics of cultural storytelling — in particular the way the history of progress has been told in the United States. In "Empire of Innocence," Patricia Nelson Limerick argues that the myth of progress enabled white Americans to reinvent western history by casting themselves, rather than the Indians they dispossessed or the land they exploited, as innocent victims. Haunani-Kay Trask's essay "From a Native Daughter" compares Native Hawaiian and mainland American versions of Hawaiian history — and shows that widely different attitudes toward the land inform the two accounts. Anita Gordon and David Suzuki's "How Did We Come to This?" examines more closely the attitudes underlying America's faith in science and in technology's ability to solve environmental problems. "Talking to the Owls and Butterflies," by Sioux medicine man John (Fire) Lame Deer and Richard Erdoes, forcefully challenges conventional assumptions about what constitutes a civilized life and offers "the Indian way" as an antidote to our technology-driven society. Leslie Marmon Silko's

"Storyteller" envisions an apocalyptic end to western-style progress in the Alaskan tundra.

The chapter's second half turns from rereading the meaning of progress to redefining our relation to the earth. Joyce Nelson's "The 'Greening' of Establishment PR" challenges us to reclaim our imaginations from the "pollution" of corporate eco-advertising. Next, Dave Foreman, one of the founders of Earth First!, rallies us to become eco-warriors in the battle against the anthropocentric thinking that has dominated American culture. Joni Seager's "The Eco-Fringe: Deep Ecology" critiques Earth First! and the deep ecology movement, charging that their calls for revolution mask traditional masculine values and attitudes. In "being property once myself," poet Lucille Clifton succinctly connects the ideas of racial, sexual, and environmental exploitation. The chapter closes with Cynthia Hamilton's "Women, Home, and Community: The Struggle in an Urban Environment." This account of how a group of inner-city women defeated plans to locate a giant incineration plant in their neighborhood affirms the power that average Americans have to resist even government-sponsored assaults on the planet.

Sources

Frank Bergon and Zeese Papanikolas, eds., *Looking Far West: The Search for the American West in History, Myth, and Literature.* New York: Meridian/New American Library, 1978.

Ralph Waldo Emerson, *Selected Writings.* New York: Signet/New American Library, 1965.

Leonard Pitt, *We Americans,* vol. 2, 3rd ed. Dubuque: Kendall/Hunt, 1987.

Laurence Shames, *The Hunger for More: Searching for Values in an Age of Greed.* New York: Times Books, 1989.

Henry David Thoreau, *Walden and "Civil Disobedience."* New York: Signet/New American Library, 1960.

Frederick Jackson Turner, "The Significance of the Frontier in American History." In *Annual Report for 1893,* American Historical Association, pp. 199–227.

Before Reading

- Working in small groups or as a class, brainstorm a list of words and ideas that you associate with the notion of progress. Evaluate your list: Does it primarily contain negative or positive terms? Then take a few minutes to freewrite on the meaning of technology in your life.
- Collect images from magazines, newspapers, or personal photos to make collages on the themes of nature and technology. Display these in class and discuss what they reveal about your attitudes toward natural and technological environments. As you work through the chapter, refer

back to these collages and compare the visions they offer to those of the writers you encounter here.

- Look again at the photo that opens this chapter and write a brief journal entry about what you think Doug Michels, the artist who created "Cadillac Ranch," was trying to say. Why do you suppose he decided to half-bury the cars instead of just lining them up? Why did he locate them in the desert and not in a cornfield or forest? Is there any significance to his choice of car? Overall, what does he seem to be saying about technology and its relation to the environment?

Empire of Innocence

PATRICIA NELSON LIMERICK

This excerpt from The Legacy of Conquest: The Unbroken Past of the American West *(1987) establishes a broad thesis about the American west and the "innocence" of its settlers. Limerick (b. 1951) is particularly skilled at seeing events from differing perspectives, and she sees in western history a complex moral landscape, peopled not by stereotypical cowboys and Indians but by extremely diverse groups, none of them in complete control of the events unfolding on the frontier. Widely acknowledged as a leader among the "new western historians," Limerick explodes mythic conceptions of western settlement as a triumphant narrative of progress and civilization. A frequent contributor to the* Journal of American History *and* American Historical Review, *Limerick has also written, coauthored, and coedited a number of volumes, including* Trails: Toward a New Western History *(1991). She teaches history at the University of Colorado, Boulder.*

To analyze how white Americans thought about the West, it helps to think anthropologically. One lesson of anthropology is the extraordinary power of cultural persistence; with American Indians, for instance, beliefs and values will persist even when the supporting economic and political structures have vanished. What holds for Indians holds as well for white Americans; the values they attached to westward expansion persist, in cheerful defiance of contrary evidence.

Among those persistent values, few have more power than the idea of innocence. The dominant motive for moving West was improvement and opportunity, not injury to others. Few white Americans went West intending to ruin the natives and despoil the continent. Even when they were trespassers, westering Americans were hardly, in their own eyes, criminals; rather, they were pioneers. The ends abundantly justified the means; personal interest in the acquisition of property coincided with national interest in the acquisition of territory, and those interests overlapped in turn with the mission to extend the domain of Christian civilization. Innocence of intention placed the course of events in a bright and positive light; only over time would the shadows compete for our attention. . . .

. . . Whether the target resource was gold, farmland, or Indian souls, white Americans went West convinced that their purposes were as commonplace as they were innocent. The pursuit of improved fortunes, the acquisition of property, even the desire for adventure seemed so self-evident that they needed neither explanation nor justification.

If the motives were innocent, episodes of frustration and defeat seemed inexplicable, undeserved, and arbitrary. Squatters defied the boundaries of Indian territory and then were aggrieved to find themselves harassed and attacked by Indians. Similarly, prospectors and miners went where the minerals were, regardless of Indian territorial claims, only to be outraged by threats to their lives and supply lines. Preemptors[1] who traveled ahead of government surveys later complained of insecure land titles. After the Civil War, farmers expanded onto the Great Plains, past the line of semiaridity, and then felt betrayed when the rains proved inadequate.

5 Western emigrants understood not just that they were taking risks but also that risks led to rewards. When nature or natives interrupted the progression from risk to reward, the Westerner felt aggrieved. Most telling were the incidents in which a rush of individuals — each pursuing a claim to a limited resource — produced their own collective frustration. In resource rushes, people hoping for exclusive opportunity often arrived to find a crowd already in place, blanketing the region with prior claims, constricting individual opportunity, and producing all the problems of food supply, housing, sanitation, and social order that one would expect in a growing city, but not in a wilderness.

If one pursues a valuable item and finds a crowd already assembled, one's complicity in the situation is obvious. The crowd has, after all, resulted from a number of individual choices very much like one's own. But frustration cuts off reflection on this irony; in resource rushes in which the sum of the participants' activities created the dilemma, each individual could still feel himself the innocent victim of constricting opportunity.

Contrary to all of the West's associations with self-reliance and individual responsibility, misfortune has usually caused white Westerners to cast themselves in the role of the innocent victim. One large group was composed of those who felt injured at the hands of nature. They had trusted nature,

[1]*preemptors:* People who seek to establish a right to land by being the first to occupy it.

and when nature behaved according to its own rules and not theirs, they felt betrayed. The basic plot played itself out with a thousand variations.

Miners resented the wasted effort of excavating sites that had looked promising and proved barren. Cattlemen overgrazed the grasslands and then resented nature's failure to rebound. Farmers on the Southern Plains used mechanized agriculture to break up the land and weaken the ground cover, then unhappily watched the crop of dust they harvested. City dwellers accumulated automobiles, gas stations, and freeways, and then cursed the inversion patterns and enclosing mountains that kept the automobile effluvia before their eyes and noses. Homeowners purchased houses on steep slopes and in precarious canyons, then felt betrayed when the earth's surface continued to do what it has done for millennia: move around from time to time. And, in one of the most widespread and serious versions, people moved to arid and semiarid regions, secure in the faith that water would somehow be made available, then found the prospect of water scarcity both surprising and unfair.

In many ways, the most telling case studies concern plants. When, in the 1850s, white farmers arrived in Island County, Washington, they had a clear sense of their intentions: "to get the land subdued and the wilde nature out of it," as one of them put it. They would uproot the useless native plants and replace them with valuable crops, transforming wilderness to garden. On one count, nature did not cooperate — certain new plants, including corn, tomatoes, and wheat, could not adapt to the local climate and soil. On another count, nature proved all too cooperative. Among the plants introduced by white farmers, weeds frequently did better than crops. "Weeds," Richard White notes, "are an inevitable result of any human attempt to restrict large areas of land to a single plant." Laboring to introduce valued plants, the farmer came up against "his almost total inability to prevent the entry of unwanted invaders." Mixed with crop seeds, exotic plants like the Canadian thistle prospered in the plowed fields prepared for them, and then moved into the pastures cleared by overgrazing. The thistle was of no interest to sheep: "once it had replaced domesticated grasses the land became incapable of supporting livestock."[2]

10 A similar development took place between the Rockies and the Sierras and Cascades. There, as well, "species foreign to the region, brought accidentally by the settlers, came to occupy these sites to the virtual exclusion of the native colonizers." With the introduction of wheat, "entry via adulterated seed lots of the weeds of wheat . . . was inevitable." One particular species—cheatgrass—took over vast territories, displacing the native bunch grasses and plaguing farmers in their wheatfields. There is no more effective way to feel authentically victimized than to plant a crop and then to see it

[2]Richard White, *Land Use, Environment, and Social Change: The Shaping of Island County, Washington* (Seattle: Univ. of Washington Press, 1980), 46, 68. [Author's note]

besieged by weeds. Farmers thus had their own, complicated position as injured innocents, plagued by a pattern in nature that their own actions had created.[3]

Yet another category of injured innocents were those who had believed and acted upon the promises of promoters and boomers. Prospective miners were particularly susceptible to reading reports of the gold strikes, leaping into action, and then cursing the distortions and exaggerations that had misled them into risking so much for so little reward. The pattern was common because resource rushes created a mood of such fevered optimism that trust came easily; people wanted so much to believe that their normal skepticism dropped away.

The authenticity of the sense of victimization was unquestionable. Still, there was never any indication that repeated episodes of victimization would reduce the pool of volunteers. Bedrock factors kept promoters and boomers supplied with believers: there *were* resources in the West, and the reports might be true; furthermore, the physical fact of Western distances meant, first, that decision making would have to rely on a chain of information stretched thin by the expanse of the continent and, second, that the truth of the reports and promises could not be tested without a substantial investment of time and money simply in getting to the site. One might well consume one's nest egg merely in reaching the place of expected reward.

Blaming nature or blaming human beings, those looking for a scapegoat had a third, increasingly popular target: the federal government. Since it was the government's responsibility to control the Indians and, in a number of ways increasing into the twentieth century, to control nature, Westerners found it easy to shift the direction of their resentment. Attacked by Indians or threatened by nature, aggrieved Westerners took to pointing accusingly at the federal government. In effect, Westerners centralized their resentments much more efficiently than the federal government centralized its powers.

Oregon's situation was a classic example of this transition. The earliest settlers were rewarded with Congress's Oregon Donation Act of 1850. Settlers arriving by a certain year were entitled to a generous land grant. This act had the considerable disadvantage of encouraging white settlement without benefit of treaties and land cessions from Oregon Indians. The Donation Act thus invited American settlers to spread into territory that had not been cleared for their occupation. It was an offer that clearly infringed on the rights of the Indians and that caused the government to stretch its powers thin. After the California gold rush, when prospectors spread north into the Oregon interior, a multifront Indian war began. Surely, the white miners

[3]Richard N. Mack, "Invaders at Home on the Range," *Natural History*, Feb. 1984, 43. [Author's note]

and settlers said, it is now the obligation of the federal government to protect us and our property.[4]

At this point, a quirk of historical casting brought an unusual man named 15
General John Wool into the picture. As the head of the Army's Pacific Division, General Wool was charged with cleaning up the mess that Oregon development had created. He was to control the Indians, protect the settlers, and end the wars. Here Wool's unusual character emerged: assessing this situation, he decided — and said bluntly — that the wars were the results of settler intrusion; he went so far as to propose a moratorium on further settlement in the Oregon interior, a proposal that outraged the sensitive settlers. Wool's personality did not make this difference of opinion more amicable. He was, in fact, something of a prig;[5] in pictures, the symmetrical and carefully waxed curls at his temples suggest that he and the Oregon pioneers might have been at odds without the troubles of Indian policy.[6]

Denounced by both the Oregon and the Washington legislatures, Wool's blunt approach did not result in a new direction in Indian affairs. The wars were prosecuted to their conclusions; the Indians, compelled to yield territory. But the Oregon settlers in 1857 knew what they thought of Wool. He was a supposed agent of the federal government, an agent turned inexplicably into a friend of the Indians and an enemy of the Americans.

It was not the first or the last time that white Americans would suspect the federal government and Indians of being in an unholy alliance. To the degree that the federal government fulfilled its treaty and statutory obligations to protect the Indians and their land, it would then appear to be not only soft on Indians but even in active opposition to its own citizens.

One other elemental pattern of their thought allowed Westerners to slide smoothly from blaming Indians to blaming the federal government. The idea of captivity organized much of Western sentiment. Actual white men, women, and children were at times taken captive by Indians, and narratives of those captivities were, from colonial times on, a popular form of literature. It was an easy transition of thought to move from the idea of humans held in an unjust and resented captivity to the idea of land and natural resources held in Indian captivity — in fact, a kind of monopoly in which very few Indians kept immense resources to themselves, refusing to let the large numbers of willing and eager white Americans make what they could of those resources. Land and natural resources, to the Anglo-American mind, were meant for development; when the Indians held control, the excluded whites took up the familiar role of injured innocents. The West, in the most common figure of speech, had to be "opened" — a metaphor based

[4]Dorothy O. Johansen and C. M. Gates, *Empire of the Columbia: A History of the Pacific Northwest,* 2d ed. (New York: Harper & Row, 1967), 250, 252. [Author's note]

[5]*prig:* One who adheres unthinkingly or smugly to rigid moral standards.

[6]Robert Utley, *Frontiersmen in Blue: The United States Army and the Indian, 1848–1865* (1967; Lincoln: Univ. of Nebraska Press, 1981), 178–200. [Author's note]

on the assumption that the virgin West was "closed," locked up, held captive by Indians.

As the federal government took over Indian territory, either as an addition to the public domain or as reservations under the government's guardianship, white Westerners kept the same sense of themselves as frustrated innocents, shut out by monopoly, but they shifted the blame. Released from Indian captivity, many Western resources, it seemed to white Americans, had merely moved into a federal captivity.

20 In 1979, the Nevada state legislature, without any constitutional authority, passed a law seizing from the federal government 49 million acres from the public domain within the state. This empty but symbolic act was the first scene in the media event known as the Sagebrush Rebellion, in which Western businessmen lamented their victimization at the hands of the federal government and pleaded for the release of the public domain from its federal captivity. Ceded to the states, the land that once belonged to all the people of the United States would at last be at the disposal of those whom the Sagebrush Rebels considered to be the *right* people — namely, themselves.[7]

Like many rebellions, this one foundered with success: the election of Ronald Reagan in 1980 and the appointment of James Watt as secretary of the interior meant that the much-hated federal government was now in the hands of two Sagebrush Rebels. It was not at all clear what the proper rebel response to the situation should be. In any case, the rebel claim to victimization had lost whatever validity it had ever had.

Reciting the catalog of their injuries, sufferings, and deprivations at the hands of federal officials, the rebels at least convinced Western historians of the relevance of their expertise. It was a most familiar song; the Western historian could recognize every note. Decades of expansion left this motif of victimization entrenched in Western thinking. It was second nature to see misfortune as the doings of an outside force, preying on innocence and vulnerability, refusing to play by the rules of fairness. By assigning responsibility elsewhere, one eliminated the need to consider one's own participation in courting misfortune. There was something odd and amusing about late-twentieth-century businessmen adopting for themselves the role . . . of the martyred innocents, trying to go about their business in the face of cruel and arbitrary opposition.

Even if the Sagebrush Rebels had to back off for a time, that did not mean idleness for the innocent's role. In 1982, Governor Richard Lamm of Colorado and his coauthor, Michael McCarthy, published a book defending the West — "a vulnerable land" — from the assault of development. "A new Manifest Destiny," they said, "has overtaken America. The economic imperative has forever changed the spiritual refuge that was the West." The

[7]"The Angry West vs. the Rest," *Newsweek,* Sept. 17, 1979, 31–40; "West Senses Victory in Sagebrush Rebellion," *U.S. News and World Report,* Dec. 1, 1980, 29, 30. [Author's note]

notion of a time in Western history when "the economic imperative" had not been a dominant factor was a quaint and wishful thought, but more important, Lamm and McCarthy thought, some Westerners now "refused" to submit to this change. "They — we — are the new Indians," Lamm and McCarthy concluded. "And they — we — will not be herded to the new reservations."[8]

In this breakthrough in the strategy of injured innocence, Lamm and McCarthy chose the most historically qualified innocent victims — the Indians facing invasion, fighting to defend their homelands—and appropriated their identity for the majority whites who had moved to the West for the good life, for open space and freedom of movement, and who were beginning to find their desires frustrated. Reborn as the "new Indians," Lamm's constituency had traveled an extraordinary, circular route. Yesterday's villains were now to be taken as today's victims; they were now the invaded, no longer the invaders. In keeping with this change, the *old* Indians received little attention in the book; as capacious as the category "injured innocent" had proven itself to be, the line had to be drawn somewhere.

Occasionally, continuities in American history almost bowl one over. 25
What does Colorado's utterly twentieth-century governor have in common with the East Coast's colonial elite in the eighteenth century? "Having practically destroyed the aboriginal population and enslaved the Africans," one colonial historian has said, "the white inhabitants of English America began to conceive of themselves as the victims, not the agents, of Old World colonialism." "The victims, not the agents" — the changes and differences are enormous, but for a moment, if one looks from Revolutionary leaders, who held black slaves as well as the conviction that they were themselves enslaved by Great Britain, to Governor Richard Lamm, proclaiming himself and his people to be the new Indians, American history appears to be composed of one, continuous fabric, a fabric in which the figure of the innocent victim is the dominant motif.[9]

[8]Richard D. Lamm and Michael McCarthy, *The Angry West: A Vulnerable Land and Its Future* (Boston: Houghton Mifflin, 1982), 4. [Author's note]

[9]Carole Shammas, "English-Born and Creole Elites in Turn-of-the-Century Virginia," in Thad Tate and David Ammerman, eds., *The Chesapeake in the Seventeenth Century: Essays on Anglo-American Society and Politics* (New York: W. W. Norton, 1979), 274. [Author's note]

Engaging the Text

1. According to Limerick, what was the settlers' dominant attitude toward the land and its resources? Find three or four quotations that illustrate this attitude.
2. What is a "resource rush"? Can you think of any modern examples, involving either land or some other desirable resource? (Hint: think globally as well as locally.)
3. Using specific examples, explain how settlers could come to consider themselves "injured innocents" when their hopes for success in the West were shattered or

compromised. What role does the notion of captivity play in this myth of innocence?

4. Limerick says in her concluding sentence that American history is "composed of one, continuous fabric, a fabric in which the figure of the innocent victim is the dominant motif." Brainstorm with classmates and list as many recent examples as you can in which a corporation, government body, or other group has unjustly assumed the role of innocent victim. Do you agree with Limerick that this role is a "dominant motif" in American life?

Exploring Connections

5. Review the discussion of self-reliance and the American West offered by Stephanie Coontz (p. 212). In what ways are the visions of western life offered by Limerick and Coontz consistent or inconsistent with those presented in recent "revisionist" western films like *Unforgiven* and *Posse?*
6. Shelby Steele (p. 411) asserts that, in the context of race relations, "innocence is power." Which of the historical incidents described by Limerick might be interpreted as struggles for power? What other motives, if any, can you see at work in these stories of "innocent victimization"?

Extending the Critical Context

7. All things considered, would it have been better to enforce General Wool's proposed moratorium on development in Oregon throughout the past century and a half? Why or why not?
8. Reread Limerick's discussion of the ways white settlers cast themselves as innocent victims of nature (paras. 7–10). Can you think of examples in your state in which people have "set themselves up" to become victims of earthquakes, floods, hurricanes, droughts, or other forces of nature? Under what circumstances do you think government should help people who have suffered financially at the hands of an unpredictable natural world?
9. Analyze a high school history text in terms of its treatment of conflicts between Native Americans and whites. Does the theme of "injured innocents" show up directly or indirectly? How might you account for any differences you find in these sources?

From a Native Daughter

Haunani-Kay Trask

Speaking of nineteenth-century Americans and birth control, a scholar recently said, "They didn't know much, and what they did know was wrong." The same could be said of the historians of Hawai'i. This selection comes from a scholar who is literally rewriting the history of Hawai'i. Trask explains how she learned radically different versions of history from her family and from missionary schools; having trusted her formal education for years, she eventually recognized that the colonists had distorted Hawaiian history in order to disrupt the islands' culture and appropriate their resources. This essay is an impassioned yet carefully reasoned assault on conventional interpretations of Hawai'i's past and peoples. Trask is a professor of Hawaiian studies and director of the Center for Hawaiian Studies at the University of Hawai'i at Mānoa. Her books include Eros and Power: The Promise of Feminist Theory *(1986),* From a Native Daughter: Colonialism and Sovereignty in Hawai'i *(1993), and* Light in the Crevice Never Seen *(1994). She also scripted and coproduced the award-winning film* Act of War: The Overthrow of the Hawaiian Nation.

> *E noi'i wale mai no ka haole, a,*
> *'a'ole e pau na hana a Hawai'i 'imi loa*
> Let the *haole* freely research us in detail
> But the doings of deep delving *Hawai'i*
> will not be exhausted.
> —KEPELINO, 19th-century Hawaiian historian

Aloha kākou. Let us greet each other in friendship and love. My given name is Haunaniokawēkiu o Haleakalā, native of *Hawai'i Nei.* My father's family is from the *'āina* (land) of Kaua'i, my mother's family from the *'āina* of Maui. I reside today among my native people in the community of *Waimānalo.*

I have lived all my life under the power of America. My native country, Hawai'i, is owned by the United States. I attended missionary schools, both Catholic and Protestant, in my youth, and I was sent away to the American mainland to receive a "higher" education at the University of Wisconsin. Now I teach the history and culture of my people at the University of Hawai'i.

When I was young the story of my people was told twice: once by my parents, then again by my school teachers. From my *'ohana* (family), I learned about the life of the old ones: how they fished and planted by the moon; shared all the fruits of their labors, especially their children; danced in great numbers for long hours; and honored the unity of their world in intricate genealogical chants. My mother said Hawaiians had sailed over thousands of miles to make their home in these sacred islands. And they had flourished, until the coming of the *haole* (whites).

At school, I learned that the "pagan Hawaiians" did not read or write, were lustful cannibals, traded in slaves, and could not sing. Captain Cook had "discovered" Hawai'i and the ungrateful Hawaiians had killed him. In revenge, the Christian god had cursed the Hawaiians with disease and death.

I learned the first of these stories from speaking with my mother and 5
father. I learned the second from books. By the time I left for college, the books had won out over my parents, especially since I spent four long years in a missionary boarding school for Hawaiian children.

When I went away I understood the world as a place and a feeling divided in two: one *haole* (white), and the other *kānaka* (native). When I returned ten years later with a Ph.D., the division was sharper, the lack of connection more painful. There was the world that we lived in — my ancestors, my family, and my people — and then there was the world historians described. This world, they had written, was the truth. A primitive group, Hawaiians had been ruled by bloodthirsty priests and despotic kings who owned all the land and kept our people in feudal subjugation. The chiefs were cruel, the people poor.

But this was not the story my mother told me. No one had owned the land before the *haole* came; everyone could fish and plant, except during sacred periods. And the chiefs were good and loved their people.

Was my mother confused? What did our *kūpuna* (elders) say? They replied: did these historians (all *haole*) know the language? Did they understand the chants? How long had they lived among our people? Whose stories had they heard?

None of the historians had ever learned our mother tongue. They had all been content to read what Europeans and Americans had written. But why did scholars, presumably well-trained and thoughtful, neglect our language? Not merely a passageway to knowledge, language is a form of knowing by itself; a people's way of thinking and feeling is revealed through its music.

I sensed the answer without needing to answer. From years of living in 10
a divided world, I knew the historian's judgment: *There is no value in things Hawaiian; all value comes from things haole.*

Historians, I realized, were very like missionaries. They were a part of the colonizing horde. One group colonized the spirit; the other, the mind. Frantz Fanon[1] had been right, but not just about Africans. He had been right about the bondage of my own people: "By a kind of perverted logic, [colonialism] turns to the past of the oppressed people, and distorts, disfigures, and destroys it" (1968:210). The first step in the colonizing process, Fanon had written, was the deculturation of a people. What better way to take our culture than to remake our image? A rich historical past became small and ignorant in the hands of Westerners. And we suffered a damaged sense of people and culture because of this distortion.

[1]*Frantz Fanon:* French West Indian psychiatrist, author, and political leader. Fanon (1925–1961) is perhaps best known for his psychoanalytic study of Black life in a white-dominated world, *Black Skin, White Masks.* His *Wretched of the Earth* called for an anticolonial revolution by peasants; he anticipated that such a struggle would produce a new breed of modern people of color.

Burdened by a linear, progressive conception of history and by an assumption that Euro-American culture flourishes at the upper end of that progression, Westerners have told the history of Hawai'i as an inevitable if occasionally bitter-sweet triumph of Western ways over "primitive" Hawaiian ways. A few authors—the most sympathetic—have recorded with deepfelt sorrow the passing of our people. But in the end, we are repeatedly told, such an eclipse was for the best.

Obviously it was best for Westerners, not for our dying multitudes. This is why the historian's mission has been to justify our passing by celebrating Western dominance. Fanon would have called this missionizing, intellectual colonization. And it is clearest in the historian's insistence that pre-*haole* Hawaiian land tenure was "feudal" — a term that is now applied, without question, in every monograph, in every schoolbook, and in every tour guide description of my people's history.

From the earliest days of Western contact my people told their guests that *no one* owned the land. The land — like the air and the sea — was for all to use and share as their birthright. Our chiefs were *stewards* of the land; they could not own or privately possess the land any more than they could sell it.

But the *haole* insisted on characterizing our chiefs as feudal landlords 15
and our people as serfs. Thus, a European term which described a European practice founded on the European concept of private property — feudalism — was imposed upon a people halfway around the world from Europe and vastly different from her in every conceivable way. More than betraying an ignorance of Hawaiian culture and history, however, this misrepresentation was malevolent in design.

By inventing feudalism in ancient Hawai'i, Western scholars quickly transformed a spiritually-based, self-sufficient economic system of land use and occupancy into an oppressive, medieval European practice of divine right ownership, with the common people tied like serfs to the land. By claiming that a Pacific people lived under a European system — that the Hawaiians lived under feudalism — Westerners could then degrade a successful system of shared land use with a pejorative and inaccurate Western term. Land tenure changes instituted by Americans and in line with current Western notions of private property were then made to appear beneficial to the Hawaiians. But in practice, such changes benefited the *haole,* who alienated the people from the land, taking it for themselves.

The prelude to this land alienation was the great dying of the people. Barely half a century after contact with the West our people had declined in number by eighty percent. Disease and death were rampant. The sandalwood forests had been stripped bare for international commerce between England and China. The missionaries had insinuated themselves everywhere. And a debt-ridden Hawaiian king (there had been no king before Western contact) succumbed to enormous pressure from the Americans and followed their schemes for dividing up the land.

This is how private property land tenure entered Hawai'i. The common people, driven from their birthright, received less than one percent of the land. They starved while huge *haole*-owned sugar plantations thrived.

And what had the historians said? They had said that the Americans "liberated" the Hawaiians from an oppressive "feudal" system. By inventing a false feudal past, the historians justify — and become complicitous in — massive American theft.

20 Is there "evidence" — as historians call it — for traditional Hawaiian concepts of land use? The evidence is in the sayings of my people and in the words they wrote more than a century ago, much of which has been translated. However, historians have chosen to ignore any references here to shared land use. But there *is* incontrovertible evidence in the very structure of the Hawaiian language. If the historians had bothered to learn our language (as any American historian of France would learn French) they would have discovered that we show possession in two ways: through the use of an "a" possessive, which reveals acquired status, and through the use of an "o" possessive, which denotes inherent status. My body (*ko'u kino*) and my parents (*ko'u mākua*), for example, take the "o" form; most material objects, such as food (*ka'u mea'ai*) take the "a" form. But land, like one's body and one's parents, takes the "o" possessive (*ko'u 'āina*). Thus, in our way of speaking, land is inherent to the people; it is like our bodies and our parents. The people cannot exist without the land, and the land cannot exist without the people.

Every major historian of Hawai'i has been mistaken about Hawaiian land tenure. The chiefs did not own the land: they *could not* own the land. My mother was right and the *haole* historians were wrong. If they had studied our language they would have known that no one owned the land. But was their failing merely ignorance, or simple ethnocentric bias?

No, I did not believe them to be so benign. As I read on, a pattern emerged in their writing. Our ways were inferior to those of the West, to those of the historians' own culture. We were "less developed," or "immature," or "authoritarian." In some tellings we were much worse. Thus, Gavan Daws (1968), the most famed modern historian of Hawai'i, had continued a tradition established earlier by missionaries Hiram Bingham (1848) and Sheldon Dibble (1909), by referring to the old ones as "thieves" and "savages" who regularly practiced infanticide and who, in contrast to "civilized" whites, preferred "lewd dancing" to work. Ralph Kuykendall (1938), long considered the most thorough if also the most boring of historians of Hawai'i, sustained another fiction — that my ancestors owned slaves, the outcast *Kauwā*. This opinion, as well as the description of Hawaiian land tenure as feudal, had been supported by respected sociologist Andrew Lind (1938).[2]

[2]See also Fornander (1878–85). Lest one think these sources antiquated, it should be noted that there exist only a handful of modern scholarly works on the history of Hawai'i. The most respected are those by Kuykendall (1938) and Daws (1968), and a social history of the twentieth century by Lawrence Fuchs (1961). Of these, only Kuykendall and Daws claim any knowledge of pre-*haole* history, while concentrating on the nineteenth century. However, count-

Finally, nearly all historians had refused to accept our genealogical dating of over one hundred generations in Hawai'i. They had, instead, claimed that our earliest appearance in Hawai'i could only be traced to A.D. 700. Thus at least seven hundred years of our history were repudiated by "superior" Western scholarship. Only recently have archeological data confirmed what Hawaiians had said these many centuries (Tuggle 1979).

Suddenly the entire sweep of our written history was clear to me. I was reading the West's view of itself through the degradation of my own past. When historians wrote that the king owned the land and the common people were bound to it, they were saying that ownership was the only way human beings in their world could relate to the land, and in that relationship, some one person had to control both the land and the interaction between humans.

And when they said that our chiefs were despotic, they were telling of their own society, where hierarchy always results in domination. Thus any authority or elder is automatically suspected of tyranny.

And when they wrote that Hawaiians were lazy, they meant that work 25
must be continuous and ever a burden.

And when they wrote that we were promiscuous, they meant that lovemaking in the Christian West is a sin.

And when they wrote that we were racist because we preferred our own ways to theirs, they meant that their culture needed to dominate other cultures.

And when they wrote that we were superstitious, believing in the *mana* of nature and people, they meant that the West has long since lost a deep spiritual and cultural relationship to the earth.

And when they wrote that Hawaiians were "primitive" in their grief over the passing of loved ones, they meant that the West grieves for the living who do not walk among their ancestors.

---

less popular works have relied on these two studies which, in turn, are themselves based on primary sources written in English by extremely biased, anti-Hawaiian Westerners such as explorers, traders, missionaries (e.g., Bingham [1848] and Dibble [1909]), and sugar planters. Indeed, a favorite technique of Daws's — whose *Shoal of Time* is the most acclaimed and recent general history — is the lengthy quotation without comment of the most racist remarks by missionaries and planters. Thus, at one point, half a page is consumed with a "white man's burden" quotation from an 1886 *Planter's Monthly* article ("It is better for the colored man of India and Australia that the white man rules, and it is better here that the white man should rule . . . ," etc., p. 213). Daws's only comment is "The conclusion was inescapable." To get a sense of such characteristic contempt for Hawaiians, one has but to read the first few pages, where Daws refers several times to the Hawaiians as "savages" and "thieves" and where he approvingly has Captain Cook thinking, "It was a sensible primitive who bowed before a superior civilization" (p. 2). See also — among examples too numerous to cite — his glib description of sacred *hula* as a "frivolous diversion," which, instead of work, the Hawaiians "would practice energetically in the hot sun for days on end . . . their bare brown flesh glistening with sweat" (pp. 65–66). Daws, who repeatedly displays an affection for descriptions of Hawaiian skin color, taught Hawaiian history for some years at the University of Hawai'i; he now holds the Chair of Pacific History at the Australian National University's Institute of Advanced Studies. [Author's note]

For so long, more than half my life, I had misunderstood this written 30
record, thinking it described my own people. But my history was nowhere present. For we had not written. We had chanted and sailed and fished and built and prayed. And we had told stories through the great blood lines of memory: genealogy.

To know my history, I had to put away my books and return to the land. I had to plant taro in the earth before I could understand the inseparable bond between people and *'āina.* I had to feel again the spirits of nature and take gifts of plants and fish to the ancient altars. I had to begin to speak my language with our elders and leave long silences for wisdom to grow. But before anything else, I had to learn the language like a lover so that I could rock within her and lay at night in her dreaming arms.

There was nothing in my schooling that had told me of this, or hinted that somewhere there was a longer, older story of origins, of the flowing of songs out to a great but distant sea. Only my parents' voices, over and over, spoke to me of a Hawaiian world. While the books spoke from a different world, a Western world.

And yet, Hawaiians are not of the West. We are of *Hawai'i Nei,* this world where I live, this place, this culture, this *'āina.*

What can I say, then, to Western historians of my place and people? Let me answer with a story.

A while ago I was asked to share a panel on the American overthrow of 35
our government in 1893. The other panelists were all *haole.* But one was a *haole* historian from the mainland who had just published a book on what he called the American anti-imperialists. He and I met briefly in preparation for the panel. I asked him if he knew the language. He said no. I asked him if he knew the record of opposition to our annexation to America. He said there was no real evidence for it, just comments here and there. I told him that he didn't understand and that at the panel I would share the evidence. When we met in public and spoke, I said this:

> There is a song much loved by our people. It was sung when Hawaiians were forbidden from congregating in groups of more than three. Addressed to our imprisoned Queen, it was written in 1898, and tells of Hawaiian feelings for our land against annexation. Listen to our lament:

Kaulana na pua a'o Hawai'i Kūpa'a mahope o ka 'āina Hiki mai ka 'elele o ka loko 'ino Palapala 'ānunu me ka pākaha	Famous are the children of Hawai'i Who cling steadfastly to the land Comes the evil-hearted with A document greedy for plunder
Pane mai Hawai'i moku o Keawe Kokua na hono a'o Pi'ilani Kāko'o mai Kaua'i o Mano Pau pu me ke one o Kakuhihewa	Hawai'i, island of Keawe, answers The bays of Pi'ilani [of Maui, Moloka'i, and Lana'i] help Kaua'i of Mano assists Firmly together with the sands of Kakuhihewa

'A'ole a'e kau i ka pūlima	Do not put the signature
Maluna o ka pepa o ka 'enemi	On the paper of the enemy
Ho'ohui 'āina kū'ai hewa	Annexation is wicked sale
I ka pono sīvila a'o ke kānaka	Of the civil rights of the Hawaiian people
Mahope mākou o Lili'ulani	We support Lili'uokalani
A loa'a 'e ka pono o ka 'āina	Who has earned the right to the land
Ha'ina 'ia mai ana ka puana	The story is told
'O ka po'e i aloha i ka 'āina	Of the people who love the land

This song, I said, continues to be sung with great dignity at Hawaiian political gatherings. For our people still share the feelings of anger and protest that it conveys.

But our guest, the *haole* historian, answered that this song, although beautiful, was not evidence of either opposition or of imperialism from the Hawaiian perspective.

Many Hawaiians in the audience were shocked at his remarks, but, in hindsight, I think they were predictable. They are the standard response of the historian who does not know the language and has no respect for its memory.

Finally, I proceeded to relate a personal story, thinking that surely such a tale could not want for authenticity since I myself was relating it. My *tūtū* (grandmother) had told my mother who had told me that at the time of annexation (1898) a great wailing went up throughout the islands, a wailing of weeks, a wailing of impenetrable grief, a wailing of death. But he remarked again, this too is not evidence.

And so, history goes on, written in long volumes by foreign people. 40
Whole libraries begin to form, book upon book, shelf upon shelf.

At the same time, the stories go on, generation to generation, family to family.

Which history do Western historians desire to know? Is it to be a tale of writings by their own countrymen, individuals convinced of their "unique" capacity for analysis, looking at us with Western eyes, thinking about us within Western philosophical contexts, categorizing us by Western indices, judging us by Judeo-Christian morals, exhorting us to capitalist achievements, and finally, leaving us an authoritative-because-Western record of their complete misunderstanding?

All this has been done already. Not merely a few times, but many times. And still, every year, there appear new and eager faces to take up the same telling, as if the West must continue, implacably, with the din of its own disbelief.

But there is, as there has been always, another possibility. If it is truly our history Western historians desire to know, they must put down their books, and take up our practices. First, of course, the language. But later, the people, the *'āina,* the stories. Above all, in the end, the stories. Historians must listen, they must hear the generational connections, the reservoir of sounds and meanings.

They must come, as American Indians suggested long ago, to understand 45
the land. Not in the Western way, but in the indigenous way, the way of living within and protecting the bond between people and *'āina.*

This bond is cultural, and it can be understood only culturally. But because the West has lost any cultural understanding of the bond between people and land, it is not possible to know this connection through Western culture. This means that the history of indigenous people cannot be written from within Western culture. Such a story is merely the West's story of itself.

Our story remains unwritten. It rests within the culture, which is inseparable from the land. To know this is to know our history. To write this is to write of the land and the people who are born from her.

Cumulative Bibliography

Bingham, Hiram (1848). *A Residence of Twenty-one Years in the Sandwich Islands.* 2nd ed. New York: Converse.

Daws, Gavan (1968). *Shoal of Time: A History of the Hawaiian Islands.* Toronto and New York: Macmillan.

Dibble, Sheldon (1909). *History of the Sandwich Islands.* Honolulu: Thrum.

Fanon, Frantz (1968). *The Wretched of the Earth.* New York: Grove, Evergreen Edition.

Fornander, Abraham (1878–85). *An Account of the Polynesian Race: Its Origin and Migrations and the Ancient History of the Hawaiian People to the Times of Kamehameha I.* 3 vols. Vol. 1. London: Trübner.

Fuchs, Lawrence (1961). *Hawaii Pono: A Social History.* New York: Harcourt, Brace and World.

Kame'eleihiwa, Lilikala (1992). *Native Land and Foreign Desires.* Honolulu: Bishop Museum Press.

Kuykendall, Ralph S. (1938). *The Hawaiian Kingdom, 1778–1854.* Honolulu: Univ. of Hawai'i Press.

Lind, Andrew (1938). *An Island Community: Ecological Succession in Hawaii.* New York: Greenwood.

Stannard, David (1989). *Before the Horror: The Population of Hawai'i on the Eve of Western Contact.* Honolulu: Social Science Research Institute, Univ. of Hawai'i.

Tuggle, H. David (1979). "Hawaii." In *The Prehistory of Polynesia.* Ed. Jesse D. Jennings. Pp. 167–99. Cambridge, Mass.: Harvard Univ. Press.

ENGAGING THE TEXT

1. What are the key mistakes *haole* historians have made, according to Trask? Why did they get things wrong?
2. Given the information presented in this selection, explain the Hawaiian understanding of land and natural resources prior to the arrival of white people and

discuss the subsequent legal, conceptual, and physical disruptions of the native way of life.

3. Whom do you trust more — Trask or the earlier historians? Why?

Exploring Connections

4. Compare the revised versions of U.S. history offered by Trask, Patricia Nelson Limerick (p. 564), and Ronald Takaki (p. 332). According to these authors, why did distortions of history arise, and how should they be corrected? Are their solutions compatible?
5. Like Trask, Paula Gunn Allen (p. 312) discovered that the truths of her family and the truths of scholars bore little resemblance to each other. Have you ever learned conflicting "truths" about an important issue? Write your own essay after reviewing Trask's and Allen's essays as models.

Extending the Critical Context

6. More than forty years after World War II, Japanese Americans who were sent to internment camps began receiving some compensation for the unjust and illegal treatment they had suffered. Assume that Trask's history is completely accurate, and debate whether the federal government ought to provide restitution to native Hawaiians (in the form of land or money).
7. Read about Hawai'i in one or more of the most recent encyclopedias you can find. Do they reflect any of Trask's thinking, or do they give the traditional versions she denounces? To extend the assignment, critique one or more of the encyclopedia entries in detail, showing how particular sentences hide, distort, or acknowledge the kind of information Trask provides.

How Did We Come to This?

Anita Gordon and David Suzuki

Is our love affair with technology killing us? Anita Gordon and David Suzuki argue that a misguided faith in our ability to "manage" nature scientifically is rapidly propelling us toward environmental disaster. Gordon, an award-winning documentary producer, also produces the weekly public radio series Quirks and Quarks, *hosted by Suzuki. Suzuki (b. 1936) teaches zoology at the University of British Columbia. He has devoted much of his professional life to making science accessible to the general public through his award-winning radio series, a weekly newspaper column, dozens of television programs, and six film documentaries. He has written and coauthored many books on science and the environment; this passage is taken from* It's a Matter of Survival *(1991), a book based on Gordon and Suzuki's five-part radio series of the same name.*

There's a strange phenomenon that biologists refer to as "the boiled frog syndrome." Put a frog in a pot of water and increase the temperature of the water gradually from 20°C to 30°C to 40°C . . . to 90°C and the frog just sits there. But suddenly, at 100°C (212°F), something happens: the water boils and the frog dies.

Scientists studying environmental problems, particularly the greenhouse effect, see "the boiled frog syndrome" as a metaphor for the human situation: we have figuratively, and in some ways literally, been heating up the world around us without recognizing the danger.

Psychologist Robert Ornstein, coauthor of *New World, New Mind,* points out that those people who have been sounding warnings receive the same response from us as would someone attempting to alert the frog to the danger of a rise in its water temperature from, say, 70° to 90°C (158° to 194°F). If the frog could talk, he would say, "There's no difference, really. It's slightly warmer in here, but I'm just as well off." If you then say to the frog, "If the heat keeps increasing at that rate, you will die," the frog will reply, "We have been increasing it for a long time, and I'm not dead. So what are you worried about?"

"Our situation is like the frog's," says Ornstein. Today, despite the fact that researchers using the most sophisticated atmospheric-monitoring equipment in the world are telling us that our future is at risk, we—as individuals and as governments—ignore or minimize the warnings.

5 The frog has a fatal flaw, explains Ornstein. Having no evolutionary experience with boiling water, he is unable to perceive it as dangerous. Throughout their biological evolution, frogs have lived in a medium that does not vary greatly in temperature, so they haven't needed to develop sophisticated thermal detectors in their skin. The frog in the pot is unaware of the threat and simply sits complacently until he boils.

Like the simmering frog, we face a future without precedent, and our senses are not attuned to warnings of imminent danger. The threats we face as the crisis builds—global warming, acid rain, the ozone hole and increasing ultraviolet radiation, chemical toxins such as pesticides, dioxins, and polychlorinated biphenyls (PCBs) in our food and water—are undetectable by the sensory system we have evolved. We do not feel the acidity of the rain, see the ultraviolet radiation projected through the ozone hole, taste the toxins in our food and water, or feel the heat of global warming except, as the frog does, as gradual and therefore endurable. Nothing in our evolutionary experience has prepared us for the limits of a finite world, one in which a five-degree climate change over a matter of decades will mean the end of life as we have known it on the planet.

How did we come to this? How did we plan our own obsolescence? The answer lies in millennia of human history, a surprisingly brief chapter in the chronicle of the planet. You can see just how brief if you use a standard calendar to mark the passage of time on Earth. The origin of the Earth, some 4.6 billion years ago, is placed at midnight January 1, and the present at midnight December 31. Each calendar day represents approximately 12 million years of actual history. Dinosaurs arrived on about December 10 and disappeared on Christmas Day. *Homo sapiens* made an appearance at 11:45 P.M. on December 31. The recorded history of human achievement, on which we base so much of our view of human entitlement, takes up only the last minute of that year.

The dinosaurs had a fortnight of supremacy on this planet before they were eradicated by some environmental catastrophe. We have had fifteen minutes of fame. And in that short period we have transformed the world. In fact, *Homo sapiens* has managed to extinguish large parts of the living world in a matter of centuries.

For the past million years, our biological makeup has changed very little: we are essentially the same creatures as those that emerged along the Rift Valley in Africa. But culturally we are a completely different genus. Where once we lived as part of the natural world, we now seek to conscript it in the service of our ends. And the result has been that we have altered the ecosphere in which we evolved into a form that cannot ensure our survival.

Compared to that of other mammals, human physical prowess is not 10
very impressive. We are not built for speed: a mature elephant can easily outrun the fastest sprinter in the world. We have no physical arsenal for self-defense — no claws, fangs, or horns. Our sensory acuity is limited: we can't see over great distances, as the eagle can, or at night like the owl; our hearing is not highly developed, as is the bat's; we can't sense ultraviolet light, like a bee. Indeed, our main survival strategy has been the development of a 1,600 gram (3.5 lb.) brain, capable of complex thought.

Out of that brain evolved a mind possessed of self-awareness, curiosity, inventiveness, memory. It enabled us to recognize patterns and cycles in the natural world — rhythms of day and night, seasonal changes, tides, lunar phases, animal migrations, plant successions — and to make out of this predictability a mode of existence for ourselves in what we saw as our natural environment. For millions of years our ancestors shared the grassy savannahs with other mammals and birds and plant life. We learned to "read" the alarms sounded by species more attuned to danger than we were. Other living things became our "early warning system."

Secure in our ability to rely on the natural world to troubleshoot for us, we began to shift from passively surviving to actively seeking to improve our quality of life. We made crude tools to facilitate hunting, and even our crudest ones were sufficient to make our early forebears deadly predators. The arrival of paleolithic peoples in North America across the Bering land-bridge[1] perhaps 100,000 years ago was followed by a north-south wave of extinction of species of large mammals.

Then, between 10,000 and 12,000 years ago, a major shift in human evolution took place—*Homo sapiens* became a farmer. We learned how to domesticate and cultivate plants and in doing so made the transition from nomadic hunter-gatherer to rooted agriculturalist. Once we knew how to ensure that we would have food, settlements grew up, and we started to exploit nature to serve our needs. We began to manage the planet, and the water in our pot heated up a few degrees.

Man the farmer was far more destructive than man the hunter. Early agriculture changed the landscape of the planet. While it fostered the rise of cities and civilizations, it also led to practices that denuded the land of its indigenous flora and fauna and depleted the soil of its nutrients and water-holding capacity. Great civilizations along the Indus and Nile rivers flourished and disappeared as once-fertile land was farmed into desert. We read the devastating signs as an indication that it was time to move on. We were few in number and the world was infinite.

15 The Industrial Revolution stoked the fire under our pot. The replacement of muscle power by machines, driven by wood and coal, then oil and gas, and finally nuclear fission, drowned out all warning signals under the roar and clatter of a culture heading inexorably toward the new Eden of growth and progress.

Once it took Haida Indians in the Queen Charlotte Islands[2] more than a year to cut down a single giant cedar. When the Europeans arrived with the technological know-how—the two-man saw and steel ax—the task was shortened to a week. Today, one man with a portable chain saw can fell that tree in an hour. It is that explosive increase in technological muscle power that has enabled us to attack the natural world and to bludgeon it into submission.

The massive application of technology by industry has been accompanied by an unprecedented increase in human population. With the conquest of the major causes of early death—sepsis, infectious disease, and malnutrition—world population numbers have exploded.

We are now the most ubiquitous large mammal on Earth, and armed with technological might, we have assumed a position of dominance on the planet. We have gained the ability to destroy entire ecosystems almost overnight, with dams, fires, clear-cut logging, agricultural and urban projects, and mining. And our self-awarded mandate to do so is predicated on the

[1]*the Bering land-bridge:* A narrow bridge of land that in prehistoric times connected present-day Alaska and Siberia; archeological evidence suggests that early humans crossed this land-bridge from Asia and migrated south, eventually populating North and South America.

[2]*the Queen Charlotte Islands:* Canadian islands located in Queen Charlotte Strait between the northeastern coast of Vancouver Island and mainland British Columbia.

assumption that we possess the knowledge to manage the environment, that nature is sufficiently vast and self-renewing to absorb the shocks we subject it to, and that we have a fundamental entitlement to nature's bounty. That has been our history, but the reality is different. Our machinery, based on fossil-fuel consumption, produces carbon dioxide in quantities that exceed the ability of the natural world to absorb it, as we inject almost six billion extra tons of carbon annually into the upper atmosphere, just from the burning of fossil fuels. As well as increasing naturally occurring compounds — methane, nitrous oxide, sulfur — the chemicals industry has introduced man-made compounds such as CFCs,[3] while the pulp and paper industry generates chloro-organics such as furans and dioxins.[4] Technology enables us to harvest previously unattainable "resources" in quantities far in excess of their regenerative capacity, and we pay no attention because, through the span of human history, we have considered those resources infinite and have believed that the human mind would always provide solutions to our problems. That belief has entrenched in us a mindless acceptance of certain truths and an equally mindless lack of comprehension of the consequences.

But history also tells us that both our ignorance of how the world works and our destructiveness have cast us in a dangerous role. There is a revealing story about all this that sounds like a parable, but unfortunately is true:

Once upon a time, there came into being an exotic land. Cut off from 20
the rest of the planet, it gave birth to a glorious but vulnerable world that was blanketed in softness. Deep-rooted, pliant grasses flourished in loose soil. If you had been there you could have plunged your hand inches into the rich earth. Everything that moved on the land moved gently, including strange animals that carried their young in pouches. Everything that trod the land had soft paws. And the land was benign and fruitful for all that lived there. Isolated through millions of years of time, the land was inviolate.

And so it was, for too many generations to count.

Then suddenly, almost in a moment, everything changed. Two hundred years ago the white man arrived on this strange alien continent and chose it for his own. The otherness of the landscape disturbed the newcomers, and they sought comfort in the creation of the familiar, transforming their surroundings to duplicate the memory of a place called home, a place called England. It was the beginning of a new era for this exotic world, one the Australian author and farmer Eric Rolls calls the time in which "they all ran wild."

Within six years of English settlers arriving with the animals and style of life they had known at home, Australia was an altered place; the soft native grasses had disappeared. The sheep and cattle trampled and ate them, and

[3]*CFCs:* Chlorofluorocarbons; chemical compounds responsible for damaging the ozone layer that protects the earth from exposure to cancer-causing ultraviolet rays.

[4]*chloro-organics . . . furans and dioxins:* Organic compounds containing chlorine which are the toxic by-products of industrial bleaching processes used in the pulp and paper industry.

in their wake tough, spiny crabgrasses that thrived in the newly hardened soil sprang up. But the sheep and cattle were only the beginning. In 1859, Thomas Austin, in a single instant of nostalgia, unleashed a scourge on Australia from which the country has never recovered. Lonely for home, Austin longed for the fun of the hunt, so he imported and released twenty-four English rabbits into the Australian countryside. The rabbits bred like rabbits and within ten years numbered in the millions on each property. One landowner, who in 1860 had a man arrested for poaching rabbits on his property, in 1863 hired one hundred men to rid his land of the beasts. The task was to prove impossible. In this rich country benignly free of predators, the rabbits ran wild, changing the landscape of Australia forever. Nothing could withstand their sheer numbers: they stripped the native shrubbery. Like hordes of locusts they began to eat their way across the continent, devouring undergrowth that had sustained a multitude of native animals.

In a desperate bid to contain the plague, Australians drew on the only technology they could. They built great wire rabbit fences—120 centimeters (4 ft.) high and 60 centimeters (2 ft.) into the ground—to check the advancing blight, but before construction of the fences was finished, the rabbits were across. It took until the 1950s for a solution to be found. When the virus myxomatosis was introduced to Australia, 99 percent of the rabbits succumbed—but even that wasn't enough. The 1 percent remaining developed an immunity, and today Australians are desperately trying, through genetic engineering, to develop stronger viruses in the lab to counter the resurgent millions.

As bad as they were, rabbits weren't the end. Practically every animal 25
that was introduced to Australia over the past two hundred years ran wild—pigs, donkeys, camels, to name a few. And plants such as the prickly pear, brought to create English gardens in the 1800s, overran the country in the 1900s. Through it all, Australians never learned the lessons of the ecosystem. In the 1930s, worried about insects devastating the sugar-cane crop, someone came up with the bright idea of importing the South American cane toad. No ordinary toad, this half-kilo (1 lb.) dinner-plate-size solution became a heavyweight problem in itself. The sugar-cane beetles flew. The toads stayed on the ground. The two did not meet and both flourished. Today the cane toad has occupied 500,000 square kilometers (193,065 sq. mi.) of the state of Queensland, and nothing can stop it.

Time and again over those fateful two hundred years, Australians have introduced a biological disaster. Today, Australia is a land transformed, or as the less charitable see it, grotesquely disfigured. The land has been overgrazed by 160 million sheep, 14 percent of all the sheep in the world. The precious topsoil is eroding fifty times faster today than it did before 1788. And Australians find themselves frantically trying to regreen a scorched earth.

Australia's story is in many ways universal. Out of ignorance, or in naive attempts to manage an unknown ecosystem, we have, often with the best of intentions, tipped the delicate natural balance. Faced with the great tapestry of life, we seem compelled to unravel it and remake it to portray our wilful and narrow worldview. Often we cast ourselves as fixers, and the destruction we cause is inadvertent. Too often, however, we act out of negligent self-interest.

On a desolate island in the Pacific Ocean stands one of the great mysteries of the world. Archeologists speculate about the origin of the bizarre statues that loom over Easter Island. Out in the middle of nowhere, about 3,200 kilometers (1,988 mi.) west of Chile, on an uninhabited island, are a thousand statues, each 18,000 kilograms (18 tons) of volcanic tufa[5] standing up to 4.5 meters (15 ft.) tall. Who carved them, and why? We may never know. The civilization that created them is gone, lost in history, but an English botanist has found that it may have been the architect of its own destruction.

The clue lies in what one finds on the island today. Just as strange as the massive statues that stand watch there is the fact that Easter Island, unlike its Pacific neighbors, is treeless. That wasn't always the case. From fossil pollen and some ancient fruit found on the island, botanist John Flenley deduced that a fruit palm had flourished there for thousands of years. By tracking the pollen record, he was able to pinpoint the decline of the tree species as beginning about 1,200 years ago and continuing for several hundred years until the tree became extinct. What cataclysm occurred that ended the millennia-long period during which the fruit palm thrived? The arrival of man.

30 Flenley believes that these ancient carvers arrived on the island and began to clear land for agriculture; they felled the trees to make canoes and levers for raising the statues, and for firewood; as many as 20,000 people were overusing what should have been a renewable resource. What nags at Flenley is that they were doing in microcosm exactly what we are doing to the planet today. But what nags at Flenley most is a terrible image of mindless destruction. Easter Island is so small that "if you stand on the peak of it, you can see almost all of it," says Flenley. "The man who felled the last piece of forest knew that he was felling the last piece of forest, but he did it anyway. What could he possibly have been thinking as he looked around the island, then cut down the very thing he depended on to survive?"

In 1990 the spirit of that Easter Islander hovers over the globe. And now we must ask ourselves, what can possibly be going through our minds as we threaten to destroy the very things we depend on to survive. On the western coast of North America stand the remnants of a once-magnificent temperate rain forest. Stretching from Alaska to California, these trees can trace their ancestry back more than 10,000 years. In the Carmanah Valley in British Columbia, one old giant, a Sitka spruce 90 meters (300 ft.) high and 3 meters (10 ft.) in diameter—perhaps the largest one living—towers

[5] *tufa:* Porous limestone.

over the surrounding trees. It began its life more than five hundred years ago, long before the modern chain saw that now threatens its relatives, long before the Industrial Revolution, before a white man stepped onto the shores of North America. All along the coast, these trees are in danger, targeted to be cut — to create jobs and profit and to fill the gaping maw of corporate greed. The coastal rain forest of British Columbia is given fifteen years before it is wiped out from logging. In Alaska's Tongass forest, the Sitka spruce were once prized as mainmasts for the clippers that cruised the world. Now you can buy one for the price of a cheeseburger. The U.S. forest service sells them for $1.60 apiece, mainly to Japan as pulp. Our natural heritage is being destroyed for short-term profit and short-term gain, some of it so quickly that we almost didn't even know it ever existed.

That's the way it was for Steller's sea cow. This 9 meter (30 ft.) long, 3,200 kilogram (3.1 ton) marine mammal lived unknown to man on one tiny group of islands in the northernmost Pacific Ocean. It flourished on the Commander Islands of Russia in great numbers until November 4, 1741, when the Dane Vitus Bering explored the area. The sea cow was named for the only naturalist who ever saw it alive, a German named Georg Wilhelm Steller, who wrote this account of it:

> These animals love shallow and sandy places along the seashore. With the rising tide they come in so close to the shore that not only did I on many occasions prod them with a pole but sometimes even stroked their backs with my hands. Usually entire families keep together, male and female, long-grown offspring and the little tender ones. They seem to have slight concern for their life and security, so that when you pass in the very midst of them with a boat, you can single out the one you wish to hook. When an animal caught on a hook began to move about somewhat violently, those nearest in the herd began to stir also and attempted to bring succor. To this end some of them tried to upset the boat with their backs while others tried to break the rope or strove to remove the hook from the wound by blows of their tails. It was a most remarkable proof of their conjugal affection that a male, having tried with all his might, but in vain, to free the female caught by a hook, and in spite of the beatings we gave him, nevertheless followed her to the shore, and that several times, even after she was dead, he shot unexpectedly up to her like a speeding arrow. Even early the next morning when we came to cut up the meat to bring it to the dugout, we found the male again near the female's body, and the same thing I observed on the third day, when I went up there myself for the sole purpose of examining the intestines.

Twenty-seven years after Steller's sea cow was discovered, the last one was butchered.

Today we live in an era of "last ones." We're told that elephants, rhinos, and tigers will exist only in zoos within our children's lifetime. Three hundred African elephants a day are killed — for trinkets. That senseless slaughter has gone on and will go on daily until all the elephants are sacrificed. In eight brief years, Africa's elephant population has been halved through poaching from 1.2 million to just over 600,000 — all to feed our consumer craving for ivory. The best projections say the elephants may last until the year 2030. The pessimistic scenario dates their demise at about 2010.

We create international laws like CITES (the Convention on International Trade in Endangered Species) to try to protect endangered species from ourselves. We mutilate animals on the verge of extinction in order to save them from our greed — for example, by cutting off the coveted horns of African rhinos so that the animals are no longer attractive to poachers. It is the unending demand for land for human use that destroys habitats and the combined forces of poverty and greed that fuel the relentless slaughter. What we don't destroy we seek to control. And through all of this we cling to the belief that science and technology are the tools that will allow us to manage the planet effectively.

Science, it has come to be believed, provides us with the knowledge and 35
the means to transform the planet into what we need, or simply want it to be. And when Science hesitates and stops to ponder, as Francis Bacon (1561–1626) did when he wrote that nature, to be commanded, must be obeyed, we dismissively call it Philosophy and plunge ahead anyway, driven by the momentum of past achievements, current needs, and a future guaranteed by our collective adherence to a body of *sacred truths.*

It is said that more than 90 percent of all scientists who have ever lived are still alive and publishing today. Twentieth-century science, especially since the end of the Second World War, has mushroomed, and science, when coopted by industry, medicine, and the military, has revolutionized every aspect of the way we live. An explosion in technological wizardry to aid scientists has created a sense that the knowledge gained permits us to understand and control all of nature. Experts in management of salmon, forests, and wildlife, and enforcers of quality control of air, water, and soil foster the illusion that we are capable, and entitled, to interfere in natural process.

In fact, that is a terrible delusion that anyone who understands the nature of scientific inquiry and insight understands. Scientific knowledge is fundamentally different from other ways of knowing and describing the world. A "worldview" is the sum total of a culture's insight, experience, and speculation. It is an integrated body of knowledge that incorporates values and beliefs as well as profound observational material in a holistic manner. Thus, in a worldview, the planets, a river, mountains, rocks, and so on are all interconnected, as are the past, present, and future.

Scientists examine the world in a very different way. The heart of the scientific approach is to focus on a single part of nature, whether a star, a plant, or an atom, and to try to separate and isolate it from all else. If one can bring it into the lab where it is carefully controlled, all the better. By controlling everything impinging on that fragment of nature and measuring everything within it, a scientist acquires knowledge — about that isolated fragment. But that information does not tell us about the whole, or about the interactions between the parts. Yet scientists today, with few exceptions, continue to examine the natural world in isolated fragments on the assumption that a sufficiently large inventory of pieces will yield a complete description. The picture we acquire is a vague sketch of the complex diversity that exists in nature.

Even if the reductionist assumptions were correct, it is the height of arrogance to think we are approaching a level of knowledge that enables us to manage a natural resource. Scientists don't even know the number of species on Earth because so little research money has been devoted to acquiring such a catalog. Rain-forest biologist E. O. Wilson puts it more graphically: "More money is spent in the bars of New York City in two weeks than is spent annually on tropical research." And even those who have devoted their lives to such study are severely hampered by the technical difficulties.

We know in detail about the basic life cycle and biology of only a handful 40
of plants and animals, and our understanding of the interaction of species in a diverse community is neglible. A decade ago, marine biologists based their understanding of ocean food chains and energy flow on plankton, the tiny plants and animals that can be trapped in fine-mesh nets. Then, *picoplankton,* single-celled organisms so small that they pass through the finest nets, were discovered. Today, picoplankton are thought to be so numerous that some scientists believe they are a major source of atmospheric oxygen. Yet ten years ago, we didn't even know they existed.

Perhaps one of the species most extensively studied has been the fruit fly *Drosophila melanogaster.* The center of attention for geneticists for eighty years, the fruit fly has cost hundreds of billions of dollars in research funds, consumed millions of person-years, and earned several Nobel Prizes. Yet even the most fundamental questions — how the insects develop from an egg through larva to adult — remain mysteries. It is astonishing, therefore, to hear foresters or fisheries experts confidently speak of managing natural "resources" about which they are far more ignorant than those fruit-fly geneticists are about *Drosophila.*

Science has not provided, and will not provide in the foreseeable future, the knowledge that we need to dominate and control nature. Every practicing scientist quickly realizes the enormity of our ignorance and that it is a perversion of the scientific enterprise to turn the small gains made in the past few decades into major triumphs of human knowledge. But that has not stopped us from doing so.

Inherent in our human conviction that we can manage the planet are ideas that seem so basic and true to societies around the world that they are never questioned — nature is infinite; the biblical injunction to go forth and multiply and dominate the Earth is the human mandate; pollution is the price of progress; growth is progress; all of nature is at our disposal. Yet it is these *sacred truths* that not only blind us to the reality of the environmental crisis but are the cause of it. We don't see that our current beliefs and values are right now compromising the very systems that keep us alive.

Like Samson blinded,[6] we are straining at the pillars of life and bringing them down around us.

[6] *Samson blinded:* The biblical hero Samson, captured and blinded by the Philistines, used his great strength to topple the supporting pillars of his enemies' house, destroying them and killing himself.

Engaging the Text

1. What distinction do Gordon and Suzuki draw between human biology and human culture? Why is this distinction significant in a discussion of the environment?
2. Gordon and Suzuki assert that our efforts to "dominate and control nature" have had consistently disastrous results. Review the historical examples and analogies they offer in support of their argument that humans have always had a destructive impact on the environment. How convincing do you find their analysis, and why?
3. According to Gordon and Suzuki, what are the "sacred truths" that blind us to the consequences of environmental destruction? What evidence have you seen that these beliefs are or are not widely shared?
4. What limitations do Gordon and Suzuki see in scientific approaches to understanding the natural world? Why do you think we rely so heavily on scientific knowledge in this culture?
5. What evidence do you see that people are becoming either more or less aware that "the planets, a river, mountains, rocks, and so on are all interconnected, as are the past, present, and future" (para. 37)? How would our lives and attitudes have to change in order to develop or recover the holistic worldview that Gordon and Suzuki favor?

Exploring Connections

6. Review Holly Devor's description of the behaviors and attitudes North Americans associate with male and female gender roles (p. 244). Are the attitudes and behaviors toward nature described by Gordon and Suzuki more consistent with traditionally "masculine" values or traditionally "feminine" values, or are they gender-neutral? Explain.
7. What is Judy Horacek, the artist of the following cartoon, saying about the consequences of human manipulation of nature? Write an imaginary conversation among Horacek, Gordon and Suzuki, and the "inventors" of blue roses and mini cows about the value of such curiosities.

Extending the Critical Context

8. Read a few articles about a current environmental debate in your community. Working in pairs or small groups, outline two possible resolutions to the issue, one based purely on proven scientific knowledge, the other based on a more

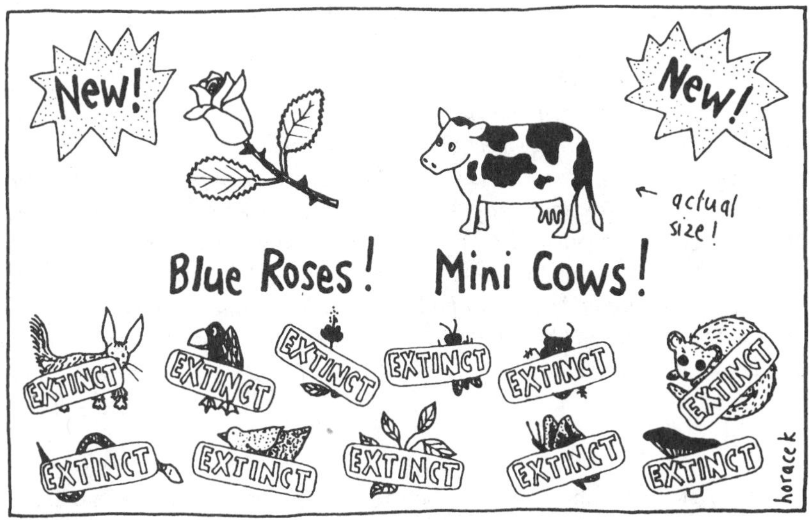

holistic assessment of the situation—including a consideration of noneconomic values and the impact your solution would have on interconnected communities, species, ecosystems, and generations. Present your alternatives to the class and discuss.

9. Is any species of plant or animal native to your area classified as endangered or threatened—that is, in danger of extinction? If so, what human developments, products, or behaviors threaten its existence? How much is known about its rôle in the ecosystem? What would have to change in order to ensure its survival?
10. As a class project, research the natural history of your region. How have the landscape, climate, and plant and animal life changed in the last thousand years? The last hundred years? The last ten years? What has been lost in the process? What, if anything, has been gained?

Talking to the Owls and Butterflies

JOHN (FIRE) LAME DEER AND RICHARD ERDOES

Fasten your intellectual seat belt. According to the speaker of this selection, a Sioux medicine man named John (Fire) Lame Deer (1900–1976), most Americans are doing just about everything wrong: in striving for progress, we have "declawed and malformed" ourselves and forgotten how to live. The passage is much more than a critique of Anglo civilization, however; it lends substance and detail to the idea of living in harmony with nature. Lame Deer has lived in both worlds, having been a painter and rodeo clown as well as a traditional healer and storyteller.

Richard Erdoes (b. 1912) was nearly sixty when he turned to serious writing from a career in magazine illustration and photography; the key event was meeting Lame Deer, when he was assigned by Life *magazine to paint and photograph a Sioux reservation. Lame Deer picked him to write the life story that became* Lame Deer, Seeker of Visions *(1972), from which this passage is excerpted. More recently, Erdoes has collaborated with Mary Crow Dog on her autobiography,* Lakota Woman *(1990), which received the 1991 American Book Award, and with Archie Fire Lame Deer (Lame Deer's son) on his memoir,* Gift of Power: The Life and Teachings of a Lakota Medicine Man *(1992).*

Let's sit down here, all of us, on the open prairie, where we can't see a highway or a fence. Let's have no blankets to sit on, but feel the ground with our bodies, the earth, the yielding shrubs. Let's have the grass for a mattress, experiencing its sharpness and its softness. Let us become like stones, plants, and trees. Let us be animals, think and feel like animals.

Listen to the air. You can hear it, feel it, smell it, taste it. *Woniya waken* — the holy air — which renews all by its breath. *Woniya, woniya waken* — spirit, life, breath, renewal — it means all that. *Woniya* — we sit together, don't touch, but something is there; we feel it between us, as a presence. A good way to start thinking about nature, talk about it. Rather talk to it, talk to the rivers, to the lakes, to the winds as to our relatives.

You have made it hard for us to experience nature in the good way by being part of it. Even here we are conscious that somewhere out in those hills there are missile silos and radar stations. White men always pick the few unspoiled, beautiful, awesome spots for the sites of these abominations. You have raped and violated these lands, always saying, "Gimme, gimme, gimme," and never giving anything back. You have taken 200,000 acres of our Pine Ridge[1] reservation and made them into a bombing range. This land is so beautiful and strange that now some of you want to make it into a national park. The only use you have made of this land since you took it from us was to blow it up. You have not only despoiled the earth, the rocks, the minerals, all of which you call "dead" but which are very much alive; you have even changed the animals, which are part of us, part of the Great Spirit, changed them in a horrible way, so no one can recognize them. There is power in a buffalo — spiritual, magic power — but there is no power in an Angus, in a Hereford.[2]

[1]*Pine Ridge:* Reservation established for the Oglala Sioux in 1978 following more than ten years of negotiation and fighting; site of the Wounded Knee massacre.

[2]*Angus, Hereford:* Breeds of cattle.

There is power in an antelope, but not in a goat or in a sheep, which holds still while you butcher it, which will eat your newspaper if you let it. There was great power in a wolf, even in a coyote. You have made him into a freak — a toy poodle, a Pekingese, a lap dog. You can't do much with a cat, which is like an Indian, unchangeable. So you fix it, alter it, declaw it, even cut its vocal cords so you can experiment on it in a laboratory without being disturbed by its cries.

5 A partridge, a grouse, a quail, a pheasant, you have made them into chickens, creatures that can't fly, that wear a kind of sunglasses so that they won't peck each other's eyes out, "birds" with a "pecking order." There are some farms where they breed chickens for breast meat. Those birds are kept in low cages, forced to be hunched over all the time, which makes the breast muscles very big. Soothing sounds, Muzak, are piped into these chicken hutches. One loud noise and the chickens go haywire, killing themselves by flying against the mesh of their cages. Having to spend all their lives stooped over makes an unnatural, crazy, no-good bird. It also makes unnatural, no-good human beings.

That's where you fooled yourselves. You have not only altered, declawed, and malformed your winged and four-legged cousins; you have done it to yourselves. You have changed men into chairmen of boards, into office workers, into time-clock punchers. You have changed women into housewives, truly fearful creatures. I was once invited into the home of such a one.

"Watch the ashes, don't smoke, you stain the curtains. Watch the goldfish bowl, don't breathe on the parakeet, don't lean your head against the wallpaper; your hair may be greasy. Don't spill liquor on that table: it has a delicate finish. You should have wiped your boots; the floor was just varnished. Don't, don't, don't . . ." That is crazy. We weren't made to endure this. You live in prisons which you have built for yourselves, calling them "homes," offices, factories. We have a new joke on the reservation: "What is cultural deprivation?" Answer: "Being an upper-middle-class white kid living in a split-level suburban home with a color TV."

Sometimes I think that even our pitiful tar-paper shacks are better than your luxury homes. Walking a hundred feet to the outhouse on a clear wintry night, through mud or snow, that's one small link with nature. Or in the summer, in the back country, leaving the door of the privy open, taking your time, listening to the humming of the insects, the sun warming your bones through the thin planks of wood; you don't even have that pleasure anymore.

Americans want to have everything sanitized. No smells! Not even the good, natural man and woman smell. Take away the smell from under the armpits, from your skin. Rub it out, and then spray or dab some nonhuman odor on yourself, stuff you can spend a lot of money on, ten dollars an ounce, so you know this has to smell good. "B.O.," bad breath, "Intimate Female Odor Spray" — I see it all on TV. Soon you'll breed people without body openings.

10 I think white people are so afraid of the world they created that they don't want to see, feel, smell, or hear it. The feeling of rain and snow on your face, being numbed by an icy wind and thawing out before a smoking fire, coming out of a hot sweat bath and plunging into a cold stream, these things make you feel alive, but you don't want them anymore. Living in boxes which shut out the heat of the summer and the chill of winter, living inside a body that no longer has a scent, hearing the noise from the hi-fi instead of listening to the sounds of nature, watching some actor on TV having a make-believe experience when you no longer experience anything for yourself, eating food without taste — that's your way. It's no good.

The food you eat, you treat it like your bodies, take out all the nature part, the taste, the smell, the roughness, then put the artificial color, the artificial flavor in. Raw liver, raw kidney — that's what we old-fashioned full-bloods like to get our teeth into. In the old days we used to eat the guts of the buffalo, making a contest of it, two fellows getting hold of a long piece of intestines from opposite ends, starting chewing toward the middle, seeing who can get there first; that's eating. Those buffalo guts, full of half-fermented, half-digested grass and herbs, you didn't need any pills and vitamins when you swallowed those. Use the bitterness of gall for flavoring, not refined salt or sugar. *Wasna* — meat, kidney fat, and berries all pounded together — a lump of that sweet *wasna* kept a man going for a whole day. That was food, that had the power. Not the stuff you give us today: powdered milk, dehydrated eggs, pasteurized butter, chickens that are all drumsticks or all breast; there's no bird left there.

You don't want the bird. You don't have the courage to kill honestly — cut off the chicken's head, pluck it and gut it — no, you don't want this anymore. So it all comes in a neat plastic bag, all cut up, ready to eat, with no taste and no guilt. Your mink and seal coats, you don't want to know about the blood and pain which went into making them. Your idea of war — sit in an airplane, way above the clouds, press a button, drop the bombs, and never look below the clouds — that's the odorless, guiltless, sanitized way.

When we killed a buffalo, we knew what we were doing. We apologized to his spirit, tried to make him understand why we did it, honoring with a prayer the bones of those who gave their flesh to keep us alive, praying for their return, praying for the life of our brothers, the buffalo nation, as well as for our own people. You wouldn't understand this and that's why we had the Washita Massacre,[3] the Sand Creek Massacre,[4] the dead women and

[3]*Washita Massacre:* The U.S. Army, led by Lt. Col. George Custer, attacked a Cheyenne camp at Washita River, now in Oklahoma, on November 27, 1868; the Cheyenne were resisting railroad construction.

[4]*Sand Creek Massacre:* On November 29, 1864, Colorado militiamen attacked an encampment of Southern Cheyenne at Sand Creek in southeastern Colorado, killing about a third of a band of five hundred. Many women and children were killed, mutilated, or tortured.

babies at Wounded Knee.[5] That's why we have Song My and My Lai[6] now.

To us life, all life, is sacred. The state of South Dakota has pest-control officers. They go up in a plane and shoot coyotes from the air. They keep track of their kills, put them all down in their little books. The stockmen and sheepowners pay them. Coyotes eat mostly rodents, field mice and such. Only once in a while will they go after a stray lamb. They are our natural garbage men cleaning up the rotten and stinking things. They make good pets if you give them a chance. But their living could lose some man a few cents, and so the coyotes are killed from the air. They were here before the sheep, but they are in the way; you can't make a profit out of them. More and more animals are dying out. The animals which the Great Spirit put here, they must go. The man-made animals are allowed to stay — at least until they are shipped out to be butchered. That terrible arrogance of the white man, making himself something more than God, more than nature, saying, "I will let this animal live, because it makes money"; saying, "This animal must go, it brings no income, the space it occupies can be used in a better way. The only good coyote is a dead coyote." They are treating coyotes almost as badly as they used to treat Indians.

15 You are spreading death, buying and selling death. With all your deodorants, you smell of it, but you are afraid of its reality; you don't want to face up to it. You have sanitized death, put it under the rug, robbed it of its honor. But we Indians think a lot about death. I do. Today would be a perfect day to die — not too hot, not too cool. A day to leave something of yourself behind, to let it linger. A day for a lucky man to come to the end of his trail. A happy man with many friends. Other days are not so good. They are for selfish, lonesome men, having a hard time leaving this earth. But for whites every day would be considered a bad one, I guess.

Eighty years ago our people danced the Ghost Dance, singing and dancing until they dropped from exhaustion, swooning, fainting, seeing visions. They danced in this way to bring back their dead, to bring back the buffalo. A prophet had told them that through the power of the Ghost Dance the earth would roll up like a carpet, with all the white man's works — the fences and the mining towns with their whorehouses, the factories and the farms with their stinking, unnatural animals, the railroads and the telegraph poles, the whole works. And underneath this rolled-up white man's world we would find again the flowering prairie, unspoiled, with its herds of buffalo and antelope, its clouds of birds, belonging to everyone, enjoyed by all.

I guess it was not time for this to happen, but it is coming back, I feel

[5]*Wounded Knee:* At Wounded Knee in South Dakota, Miniconjou Sioux led by Big Foot fought the Seventh U.S. Cavalry in December 1890. This battle, two weeks after Chief Sitting Bull was killed, ended the Ghost Dance War. Wounded Knee was also the site of a 1973 protest by the American Indian Movement.

[6]*Song My, My Lai:* My Lai was a Vietnamese hamlet, part of a village called Song My or Son My. In the most famous of Vietnam atrocities, American soldiers massacred several hundred Vietnamese civilians there on March 16, 1968.

it warming my bones. Not the old Ghost Dance, not the rolling-up — but a new-old spirit, not only among Indians but among whites and blacks, too, especially among young people. It is like raindrops making a tiny brook, many brooks making a stream, many streams making one big river bursting all dams. Us making this book, talking like this — these are some of the raindrops.

Listen, I saw this in my mind not long ago: in my vision the electric light will stop sometime. It is used too much for TV and going to the moon. The day is coming when nature will stop the electricity. Police without flashlights, beer getting hot in the refrigerators, planes dropping from the sky, even the President can't call up somebody on the phone. A young man will come, or men, who'll know how to shut off all electricity. It will be painful, like giving birth. Rapings in the dark, winos breaking into the liquor stores, a lot of destruction. People are being too smart, too clever; the machine stops and they are helpless, because they have forgotten how to make do without the machine. There is a Light Man coming, bringing a new light. It will happen before this century is over. The man who has the power will do good things, too — stop all atomic power, stop wars, just by shutting the white electro-power off. I hope to see this, but then I'm also afraid. What will be will be.

I think we are moving in a circle, or maybe a spiral, going a little higher every time, but still returning to the same point. We are moving closer to nature again. I feel it. . . . It won't be bad, doing without many things you are now used to, things taken out of the earth and wasted foolishly. You can't replace them and they won't last forever. Then you'll have to live more according to the Indian way. People won't like that, but their children will. The machine will stop, I hope, before they make electric corncobs for poor Indians' privies.

We'll come out of our boxes and rediscover the weather. In the old days 20
you took your weather as it came, following the cranes, moving south with the herds. Here, in South Dakota, they say, "If you don't like the weather, wait five minutes." It can be 100 degrees in the shade one afternoon and suddenly there comes a storm with hailstones as big as golf balls, the prairie is all white and your teeth chatter. That's good — a reminder that you are just a small particle of nature, not so powerful as you think. . . .

According to Sioux medicine man Pete Catches: "All animals have power, because the Great Spirit dwells in all of them, even a tiny ant, a butterfly, a tree, a flower, a rock. The modern white man's way keeps that power from us, dilutes it. To come to nature, feel its power, let it help you, one needs time and patience for that. Time to think, to figure it all out. You have so little time for contemplation; it's always rush, rush, rush with you. It lessens a person's life, all that grind, that hurrying and scurrying about. Our old people say that the Indians of long ago didn't have heart trouble. They didn't have that cancer. The illnesses they had they knew how to cure. But between 1890 and 1920 most of the medicines, the animal bundles, the pipes, the ancient, secret things which we had treasured for centuries, were lost and destroyed by the B.I.A.,[7] by the Government police. They went about tearing down sweat lodges, went into our homes, broke the pipes, tore up the medicine bags, threw them into the fire, burned them up, completely wiped out the wisdom of generations. But the Indian, you take away everything from him, he still has his mouth to pray, to sing the ancient songs. He can still do his *yuwipi* ceremony[8] in a darkened room, beat his small drum, make the power come back, make the wisdom return. He did, but not all of it. The elk medicines are gone. The bear medicine, too. We had a medicine man here, up the creek, who died about fifteen years ago. He was the last bear medicine man that I knew about. And he was good, too. He was really good. . . ."

As for myself, the birds have something to tell me. The eagle, the owl. In an eagle there is all the wisdom of the world; that's why we have an eagle feather at the top of the pole during a *yuwipi* ceremony. If you are planning to kill an eagle, the minute you think of that he knows it, knows what you are planning. The black-tailed deer has this wisdom, too. That's why its tail is tied farther down at the *yuwipi* pole. This deer, if you shoot at him, you won't hit him. He just stands right there and the bullet comes right back and hits you. It is like somebody saying bad things about you and they come back at him.

In one of my great visions I was talking to the birds, the winged creatures. I was saddened by the death of my mother. She had held my hand and said just one word: "pitiful." I don't think she grieved for herself; she was sorry for me, a poor Indian she would leave in a white man's world. I cried up on that vision hill, cried for help, stretched out my hands toward the sky and then put the blanket over myself — that's all I had, the blanket and the pipe, and a little tobacco for an offering. I didn't know what to expect. I wanted to touch the power, feel it. I had the thought to give myself up, even if it would kill me. So I just gave myself to the winds, to nature, not giving a damn about what could happen to me.

All of a sudden I hear a big bird crying, and then quickly he hit me on the back, touched me with his spread wings. I heard the cry of an eagle, loud above the voices of many other birds. It seemed to say, "We have been waiting for you. We knew you would come. Now you are here. Your trail leads from here. Let our voices guide you. We are your friends, the feathered people, the two-legged, the four-legged, we are your friends, the creatures, little tiny ones, eight legs, twelve legs — all those who crawl on the earth. All the little creatures which fly, all those under water. The powers of each one of us we will share with you and you will have a ghost with you always — another self."

[7]*the B.I.A.:* Bureau of Indian Affairs.

[8]*yuwipi ceremony:* A sacred ritual of healing, purification, and prayer using tiny sacred rocks gathered by medicine men from anthills for gourds and rattles.

That's me, I thought, no other thing than myself, different, but me all 25
the same, unseen, yet very real. I was frightened. I didn't understand it then. It took me a lifetime to find out.

And again I heard the voice amid the bird sounds, the clicking of beaks, the squeaking and chirping. "You have love for all that has been placed on this earth, not like the love of a mother for her son, or of a son for his mother, but a bigger love which encompasses the whole earth. You are just a human being, afraid, weeping under that blanket, but there is a great space within you to be filled with that love. All of nature can fit in there." I was shivering, pulling the blanket tighter around myself, but the voices repeated themselves over and over again, calling me "Brother, brother, brother." So this is how it is with me. Sometimes I feel like the first being in one of our Indian legends. This was a giant made of earth, water, the moon and the winds. He had timber instead of hair, a whole forest of trees. He had a huge lake in his stomach and a waterfall in his crotch. I feel like this giant. All of nature is in me, and a bit of myself is in all of nature.

Engaging the Text

1. Lame Deer's critique of modern life is wide-ranging and multifaceted. According to Lame Deer, what is wrong with whites' understanding of the following topics? Debate the wisdom and accuracy of his views.

the land	the animal world
sense of smell	death
eating	time

2. It's unlikely that most college students would give up pizza for buffalo guts or trade a dorm room, much less a luxury home, for a tar-paper shack. What is the value of reading a piece whose philosophy is so radically incompatible with the way American society functions?

Exploring Connections

3. Patricia Nelson Limerick (p. 564) claims that Americans are obsessed with their own innocence; Anita Gordon and David Suzuki (p. 580) liken human beings to slowly boiling frogs who deny their imminent danger; Lame Deer suggests that "white people are so afraid of the world they created that they don't want to see, feel, smell, or hear it" (para. 10). Do you agree with these writers that some or all of us are in a state of denial in relation to the environment? Explain.
4. Playing the role of Lame Deer, write a response to the question posed by the character in the cartoon that follows this selection.

Extending the Critical Context

5. Set aside your books and walk outside for a time, reflecting on what Lame Deer says. What do you see of nature where you live? What do you understand about the plants, animals, seasons, and stars? How far would you have to travel to sit in a place where you couldn't see signs of "civilization"?

Sidewalk Bubblegum ©1993 Clay Butler

6. The documentaries *Koyaanisqatsi* and *Powaqqatsi* take their titles from the Hopi for "life out of balance" and "life in transformation." Watch one or both of these films and discuss the critiques they suggest of modern technology and urban life. What do you think we might do to bring life into a better balance?

Storyteller

LESLIE MARMON SILKO

This is a strange and beautiful story. It portrays violence calmly; it sees the struggle of civilizations in terms of freezing metal; it speaks movingly of tradition, ignorance, betrayal, and revenge without using any of these words. The story unfolds gradually through a series of discrete scenes whose inter-

connections are not at first completely clear. In the end we see that every word and image was carefully chosen. The authenticity of this tale of revenge in the Arctic is so striking that you might think Silko was Alaskan, but she was born in Albuquerque, New Mexico, in 1948 and grew up at the Laguna Pueblo Reservation nearby. Winner of a prestigious MacArthur Foundation grant, Silko has published collections of poems and stories as well as two highly regarded novels, Ceremony *(1977) and* Almanac of the Dead *(1992). "Storyteller" is the title piece of a collection published in 1981. In reading the story, keep in mind that according to a traditional Eskimo poem, words once had the power to "come alive / and what people wanted to happen could happen — / all you had to do was say it."*

I

Every day the sun came up a little lower on the horizon, moving more slowly until one day she got excited and started calling the jailer. She realized she had been sitting there for many hours, yet the sun had not moved from the center of the sky. The color of the sky had not been good lately; it had been pale blue, almost white, even when there were no clouds. She told herself it wasn't a good sign for the sky to be indistinguishable from the river ice, frozen solid and white against the earth. The tundra rose up behind the river but all the boundaries between the river and hills and sky were lost in the density of the pale ice.

She yelled again, this time some English words which came randomly into her mouth, probably swear words she'd heard from the oil drilling crews last winter. The jailer was an Eskimo, but he would not speak Yupik to her. She had watched people in the other cells; when they spoke to him in Yupik he ignored them until they spoke English.

He came and stared at her. She didn't know if he understood what she was telling him until he glanced behind her at the small high window. He looked at the sun, and turned and walked away. She could hear the buckles on his heavy snowmobile boots jingle as he walked to the front of the building.

It was like the other buildings that white people, the Gussucks,[1] brought with them: BIA[2] and school buildings, portable buildings that arrived sliced in halves, on barges coming up the river. Squares of metal paneling bulged out with the layers of insulation stuffed inside. She had asked once what it was and someone told her it was to keep out the cold. She had not laughed then, but she did now. She walked over to the small double-pane window

[1]*Gussucks:* White people.
[2]*BIA:* Bureau of Indian Affairs.

and she laughed out loud. They thought they could keep out the cold with stringy yellow wadding. Look at the sun. It wasn't moving; it was frozen, caught in the middle of the sky. Look at the sky, solid as the river with ice which had trapped the sun. It had not moved for a long time; in a few more hours it would be weak, and heavy frost would begin to appear on the edges and spread across the face of the sun like a mask. Its light was pale yellow, worn thin by the winter.

She could see people walking down the snow-packed roads, their breath 5
steaming out from their parka hoods, faces hidden and protected by deep ruffs of fur. There were no cars or snowmobiles that day so she calculated it was fifty below zero, the temperature which silenced their machines. The metal froze; it split and shattered. Oil hardened and moving parts jammed solidly. She had seen it happen to their big yellow machines and the giant drill last winter when they came to drill their test holes. The cold stopped them, and they were helpless against it.

Her village was many miles upriver from this town, but in her mind she could see it clearly. Their house was not near the village houses. It stood alone on the bank upriver from the village, Snow had drifted to the eaves of the roof on the north side, but on the west side, by the door, the path was almost clear. She had nailed scraps of red tin over the logs last summer. She had done it for the bright red color, not for added warmth the way the village people had done. This final winter had been coming down even then; there had been signs of its approach for many years.

II

She went because she was curious about the big school where the Government sent all the other girls and boys. She had not played much with the village children while she was growing up because they were afraid of the old man, and they ran when her grandmother came. She went because she was tired of being alone with the old woman whose body had been stiffening for as long as the girl could remember. Her knees and knuckles were swollen grotesquely, and the pain had squeezed the brown skin of her face tight against the bones; it left her eyes hard like river stone. The girl asked once, what it was that did this to her body, and the old woman had raised up from sewing a sealskin boot, and stared at her.

"The joints," the old woman said in a low voice, whispering like wind across the roof, "the joints are swollen with anger."

Sometimes she did not answer and only stared at the girl. Each year she spoke less and less, but the old man talked more — all night sometimes, not to anyone but himself; in a soft deliberate voice, he told stories, moving his smooth brown hands above the blankets. He had not fished or hunted with the other men for many years although he was not crippled or sick. He stayed in his bed, smelling like dry fish and urine, telling stories all winter; and when warm weather came, he went to his place on the river bank. He sat with a long willow stick, poking at the smoldering moss he burned against the insects while he continued with the stories.

The trouble was that she had not recognized the warnings in time. She 10
did not see what the Gussuck school would do to her until she walked into the dormitory and realized that the old man had not been lying about the place. She thought he had been trying to scare her as he used to when she was very small and her grandmother was outside cutting up fish. She hadn't believed what he told her about the school because she knew he wanted to keep her there in the log house with him. She knew what he wanted.

The dormitory matron pulled down her underpants and whipped her with a leather belt because she refused to speak English.

"Those backwards village people," the matron said, because she was an Eskimo who had worked for the BIA a long time, "they kept this one until she was too big to learn." The other girls whispered in English. They knew how to work the showers, and they washed and curled their hair at night. They ate Gussuck food. She laid on her bed and imagined what her grandmother might be sewing, and what the old man was eating in his bed. When summer came, they sent her home.

The way her grandmother had hugged her before she left for school had been a warning too, because the old woman had not hugged or touched her for many years. Not like the old man, whose hands were always hunting, like ravens circling lazily in the sky, ready to touch her. She was not surprised when the priest and the old man met her at the landing strip, to say that the old lady was gone. The priest asked her where she would like to stay. He referred to the old man as her grandfather, but she did not bother to correct him. She had already been thinking about it; if she went with the priest, he would send her away to a school. But the old man was different. She knew he wouldn't send her back to school. She knew he wanted to keep her.

III

He told her one time that she would get too old for him faster than he got too old for her; but again she had not believed him because sometimes he lied. He had lied about what he would do with her if she came into his bed. But as the years passed, she realized what he said was true. She was restless and strong. She had no patience with the old man who had never changed his slow smooth motions under the blankets.

The old man was in his bed for the winter; he did not leave it except to 15
use the slop bucket in the corner. He was dozing with his mouth open slightly; his lips quivered and sometimes they moved like he was telling a story even while he dreamed. She pulled on the sealskin boots, the mukluks with the bright red flannel linings her grandmother had sewn for her, and she tied the braided red yarn tassles around her ankles over the gray wool

pants. She zipped the wolfskin parka. Her grandmother had worn it for many years, but the old man said that before she died, she instructed him to bury her in an old black sweater, and to give the parka to the girl. The wolf pelts were creamy colored and silver, almost white in some places, and when the old lady had walked across the tundra in the winter, she disappeared into the snow.

She walked toward the village, breaking her own path through the deep snow. A team of sled dogs tied outside a house at the edge of the village leaped against their chains to bark at her. She kept walking, watching the dusky sky for the first evening stars. It was warm and the dogs were alert. When it got cold again, the dogs would lie curled and still, too drowsy from the cold to bark or pull at the chains. She laughed loudly because it made them howl and snarl. Once the old man had seen her tease the dogs and he shook his head. "So that's the kind of woman you are," he said, "in the wintertime the two of us are no different from those dogs. We wait in the cold for someone to bring us a few dry fish."

She laughed out loud again, and kept walking. She was thinking about the Gussuck oil drillers. They were strange; they watched her when she walked near their machines. She wondered what they looked like underneath their quilted goosedown trousers; she wanted to know how they moved. They would be something different from the old man.

The old man screamed at her. He shook her shoulders so violently that her head bumped against the log wall. "I smelled it!" he yelled, "as soon as I woke up! I am sure of it now. You can't fool me!" His thin legs were shaking inside the baggy wool trousers; he stumbled over her boots in his bare feet. His toe nails were long and yellow like bird claws; she had seen a gray crane last summer fighting another in the shallow water on the edge of the river. She laughed out loud and pulled her shoulder out of his grip. He stood in front of her. He was breathing hard and shaking; he looked weak. He would probably die next winter.

"I'm warning you," he said, "I'm warning you." He crawled back into his bunk then, and reached under the old soiled feather pillow for a piece of dry fish. He lay back on the pillow, staring at the ceiling and chewed dry strips of salmon. "I don't know what the old woman told you," he said, "but there will be trouble." He looked over to see if she was listening. His face suddenly relaxed into a smile, his dark slanty eyes were lost in wrinkles of brown skin. "I could tell you, but you are too good for warnings now. I can smell what you did all night with the Gussucks."

She did not understand why they came there, because the village was 20
small and so far upriver that even some Eskimos who had been away to school would not come back. They stayed downriver in the town. They said the village was too quiet. They were used to the town where the boarding school was located, with electric lights and running water. After all those

years away at school, they had forgotten how to set nets in the river and where to hunt seals in the fall. Those who left did not say it, but their confidence had been destroyed. When she asked the old man why the Gussucks bothered to come to the village, his narrow eyes got bright with excitement.

"They only come when there is something to steal. The fur animals are too difficult for them to get now, and the seals and fish are hard to find. Now they come for oil deep in the earth. But this is the last time for them." His breathing was wheezy and fast; his hands gestured at the sky. "It is approaching. As it comes, ice will push across the sky." His eyes were open wide and he stared at the low ceiling rafters for hours without blinking. She remembered all this clearly because he began the story that day, the story he told from that time on. It began with a giant bear which he described muscle by muscle, from the curve of the ivory claws to the whorls of hair at the top of the massive skull. And for eight days he did not sleep, but talked continuously of the giant bear whose color was pale blue glacier ice.

IV

The snow was dirty and worn down in a path to the door. On either side of the path, the snow was higher than her head. In front of the door there were jagged yellow stains melted into the snow where men had urinated. She stopped in the entry way and kicked the snow off her boots. The room was dim; a kerosene lantern by the cash register was burning low. The long wooden shelves were jammed with cans of beans and potted meats. On the bottom shelf a jar of mayonnaise was broken open, leaking oily white clots on the floor. There was no one in the room except the yellowish dog sleeping in front of the long glass display case. A reflection made it appear to be lying on the knives and ammunition inside the case. Gussucks kept dogs inside their houses with them; they did not seem to mind the odors which seeped out of the dogs. "They tell us we are dirty for the food we eat — raw fish and fermented meat. But we do not live with dogs," the old man once said. She heard voices in the back room, and the sound of bottles set down hard on tables.

They were always confident. The first year they waited for the ice to break up on the river, and then they brought their big yellow machines up river on barges. They planned to drill their test holes during the summer to avoid the freezing. But the imprints and graves of their machines were still there, on the edge of the tundra above the river, where the summer mud had swallowed them before they ever left sight of the river. The village people had gathered to watch the white men, and to laugh as they drove the giant machines, one by one, off the steel ramp into the bogs; as if sheer numbers of vehicles would somehow make the tundra solid. But the old man said they behaved like desperate people, and they would come back again. When the tundra was frozen solid, they returned.

Village women did not even look through the door to the back room. The priest had warned them. The storeman was watching her because he didn't let Eskimos or Indians sit down at the tables in the back room. But she knew he couldn't throw her out if one of his Gussuck customers invited her to sit with him. She walked across the room. They stared at her, but she had the feeling she was walking for someone else, not herself, so their eyes did not matter. The red-haired man pulled out a chair and motioned for her to sit down. She looked back at the storeman while the red-haired man poured her a glass of red sweet wine. She wanted to laugh at the storeman the way she laughed at the dogs, straining against their chains, howling at her.

The red-haired man kept talking to the other Gussucks sitting around 25
the table, but he slid one hand off the top of the table to her thigh. She looked over at the storeman to see if he was still watching her. She laughed out loud at him and the red-haired man stopped talking and turned to her. He asked if she wanted to go. She nodded and stood up.

Someone in the village had been telling him things about her, he said as they walked down the road to his trailer. She understood that much of what he was saying, but the rest she did not hear. The whine of the big generators at the construction camp sucked away the sound of his words. But English was of no concern to her anymore, and neither was anything the Christians in the village might say about her or the old man. She smiled at the effect of the subzero air on the electric lights around the trailers; they did not shine. They left only flat yellow holes in the darkness.

It took him a long time to get ready, even after she had undressed for him. She waited in the bed with the blankets pulled close, watching him. He adjusted the thermostat and lit candles in the room, turning out the electric lights. He searched through a stack of record albums until he found the right one. She was not sure about the last thing he did: he taped something on the wall behind the bed where he could see it while he laid on top of her. He was shriveled and white from the cold; he pushed against her body for warmth. He guided her hands to his thighs; he was shivering.

She had returned a last time because she wanted to know what it was he stuck on the wall above the bed. After he finished each time, he reached up and pulled it loose, folding it carefully so that she could not see it. But this time she was ready; she waited for his fast breathing and sudden collapse on top of her. She slid out from under him and stood up beside the bed. She looked at the picture while she got dressed. He did not raise his face from the pillow, and she thought she heard teeth rattling together as she left the room.

She heard the old man move when she came in. After the Gussuck's trailer, the log house felt cool. It smelled like dry fish and cured meat. The room was dark except for the blinking yellow flame in the mica window of the oil stove. She squatted in front of the stove and watched the flames for a long time before she walked to the bed where her grandmother had slept. The bed was covered with a mound of rags and fur scraps the old woman had saved. She reached into the mound until she felt something cold and solid wrapped in a wool blanket. She pushed her fingers around it until she felt smooth stone. Long ago, before the Gussucks came, they had burned whale oil in the big stone lamp which made light and heat as well. The old woman had saved everything they would need when the time came.

In the morning, the old man pulled a piece of dry caribou meat from under the blankets and offered it to her. While she was gone, men from the village had brought a bundle of dry meat. She chewed it slowly, thinking about the way they still came from the village to take care of the old man and his stories. But she had a story now, about the red-haired Gussuck. The old man knew what she was thinking, and his smile made his face seem more round than it was.

"Well," he said, "what was it?"

"A woman with a big dog on top of her."

He laughed softly to himself and walked over to the water barrel. He dipped the tin cup into the water.

"It doesn't surprise me," he said.

V

"Grandma," she said, "there was something red in the grass that morning. I remember." She had not asked about her parents before. The old woman stopped splitting the fish bellies open for the willow drying racks. Her jaw muscles pulled so tightly against her skull, the girl thought the old woman would not be able to speak.

"They bought a tin can full of it from the storeman. Late at night. He told them it was alcohol safe to drink. They traded a rifle for it." The old woman's voice sounded like each word stole strength from her. "It made no difference about the rifle. That year the Gussuck boats had come, firing big guns at the walrus and seals. There was nothing left to hunt after that anyway. So," the old lady said, in a low soft voice the girl had not heard for a long time, "I didn't say anything to them when they left that night."

"Right over there," she said, pointing at the fallen poles, half buried in the river sand and tall grass, "in the summer shelter. The sun was high half the night then. Early in the morning when it was still low, the policeman came around. I told the interpreter to tell him that the storeman had poisoned them." She made outlines in the air in front of her, showing how their bodies laid twisted on the sand; telling the story was like laboring to walk through deep snow; sweat shone in the white hair around her forehead. "I told the priest too, after he came. I told him the storeman lied." She turned away from the girl. She held her mouth even tighter, set solidly, not in sorrow or anger, but against the pain, which was all that remained. "I never believed," she said, "not much anyway. I wasn't surprised when the priest did nothing."

The wind came off the river and folded the tall grass into itself like river waves. She could feel the silence the story left, and she wanted to have the old woman go on.

"I heard sounds that night, grandma. Sounds like someone was singing. It was light outside. I could see something red on the ground." The old woman did not answer her; she moved to the tub full of fish on the ground beside the work bench. She stabbed her knife into the belly of a whitefish and lifted it onto the bench. "The Gussuck storeman left the village right after that," the old woman said as she pulled the entrails from the fish, "otherwise, I could tell you more." The old woman's voice flowed with the wind blowing off the river; they never spoke of it again.

When the willows got their leaves and the grass grew tall along the river 40
banks and around the sloughs, she walked early in the morning. While the sun was still low on the horizon, she listened to the wind off the river; its sound was like the voice that day long ago. In the distance, she could hear the engines of the machinery the oil drillers had left the winter before, but she did not go near the village or the store. The sun never left the sky and the summer became the same long day, with only the winds to fan the sun into brightness or allow it to slip into twilight.

She sat beside the old man at his place on the river bank. She poked the smoky fire for him, and felt herself growing wide and thin in the sun as if she had been split from belly to throat and strung on the willow pole in preparation for the winter to come. The old man did not speak anymore. When men from the village brought him fresh fish he hid them deep in the river grass where it was cool. After he went inside, she split the fish open and spread them to dry on the willow frame the way the old woman had done. Inside, he dozed and talked to himself. He had talked all winter, softly and incessantly about the giant polar bear stalking a lone man across Bering Sea ice. After all the months the old man had been telling the story, the bear was within a hundred feet of the man; but the ice fog had closed in on them now and the man could only smell the sharp ammonia odor of the bear, and hear the edge of the snow crust crack under the giant paws.

One night she listened to the old man tell the story all night in his sleep, describing each crystal of ice and the slightly different sounds they made under each paw; first the left and then the right paw, then the hind feet. Her grandmother was there suddenly, a shadow around the stove. She spoke in her low wind voice and the girl was afraid to sit up to hear more clearly. Maybe what she said had been to the old man because he stopped telling the story and began to snore softly the way he had long ago when the old woman had scolded him for telling his stories while others in the house were trying to sleep. But the last words she heard clearly: "It will take a long time, but the story must be told. There must not be any lies." She pulled the blanket up around her chin, slowly, so that her movements would not be seen. She thought her grandmother was talking about the old man's bear story; she did not know about the other story then.

She left the old man wheezing and snoring in his bed. She walked through river grass glistening with frost; the bright green summer color was already fading. She watched the sun move across the sky, already lower on the horizon, already moving away from the village. She stopped by the fallen poles of the summer shelter where her parents had died. Frost glittered on the river sand too; in a few more weeks there would be snow. The predawn light would be the color of an old woman. An old woman sky full of snow. There had been something red lying on the ground the morning they died. She looked for it again, pushing aside the grass with her foot. She knelt in the sand and looked under the fallen structure for some trace of it. When she found it, she would know what the old woman had never told her. She squatted down close to the gray poles and leaned her back against them. The wind made her shiver.

The summer rain had washed the mud from between the logs; the sod blocks stacked as high as her belly next to the log walls had lost their square-cut shape and had grown into soft mounds of tundra moss and stiff-bladed grass bending with clusters of seed bristles. She looked at the northwest, in the direction of the Bering Sea. The cold would come down from there to find narrow slits in the mud, rainwater holes in the outer layer of sod which protected the log house. The dark green tundra stretched away flat and continuous. Somewhere the sea and the land met; she knew by their dark green colors there were no boundaries between them. That was how the cold would come: when the boundaries were gone the polar ice would range across the land into the sky. She watched the horizon for a long time. She would stand in that place on the north side of the house and she would keep watch on the northwest horizon, and eventually she would see it come. She would watch for its approach in the stars, and hear it come with the wind. These preparations were unfamiliar, but gradually she recognized them as she did her own footprints in the snow.

She emptied the slop jar beside his bed twice a day and kept the barrel 45
full of water melted from river ice. He did not recognize her anymore, and when he spoke to her, he called her by her grandmother's name and talked about people and events from long ago, before he went back to telling the story. The giant bear was creeping across the new snow on its belly, close enough now that the man could hear the rasp of its breathing. On and on in a soft singing voice, the old man caressed the story, repeating the words again and again like gentle strokes.

The sky was gray like a river crane's egg; its density curved into the thin crust of frost already covering the land. She looked at the bright red color of the tin against the ground and the sky and she told the village men to bring the pieces for the old man and her. To drill the test holes in the tundra, the Gussucks had used hundreds of barrels of fuel. The village people split open the empty barrels that were abandoned on the river bank, and pounded the red tin into flat sheets. The village people were using the strips of tin to mend walls and roofs for winter. But she nailed it on the log walls for its color. When she finished, she walked away with the hammer in her hand, not turning around until she was far away, on the ridge above the river banks, and then she looked back. She felt a chill when she saw how the sky and the land were already losing their boundaries, already becoming lost in each other. But the red tin penetrated the thick white color of earth and sky; it defined the boundaries like a wound revealing the ribs and heart of a great caribou about to bolt and be lost to the hunter forever. That night the wind howled and when she scratched a hole through the heavy frost on the inside of the window, she could see nothing but the impenetrable white; whether it was blowing snow or snow that had drifted as high as the house, she did not know.

It had come down suddenly, and she stood with her back to the wind looking at the river, its smoky water clotted with ice. The wind had blown the snow over the frozen river, hiding thin blue streaks where fast water ran under ice translucent and fragile as memory. But she could see shadows of boundaries, outlines of paths which were slender branches of solidity reaching out from the earth. She spent days walking on the river, watching the colors of ice that would safely hold her, kicking the heel of her boot into the snow crust, listening for a solid sound. When she could feel the paths through the soles of her feet, she went to the middle of the river where the fast gray water churned under a thin pane of ice. She looked back. On the river bank in the distance she could see the red tin nailed to the log house, something not swallowed up by the heavy white belly of the sky or caught in the folds of the frozen earth. It was time.

The wolverine fur around the hood of her parka was white with the frost from her breathing. The warmth inside the store melted it, and she felt tiny drops of water on her face. The storeman came in from the back room. She unzipped the parka and stood by the oil stove. She didn't look at him, but stared instead at the yellowish dog, covered with scabs of matted hair, sleeping in front of the stove. She thought of the Gussuck's picture, taped on the wall above the bed and she laughed out loud. The sound of her laughter was piercing; the yellow dog jumped to its feet and the hair bristled down its back. The storeman was watching her. She wanted to laugh again because he didn't know about the ice. He did not know that it was prowling the earth, or that it had already pushed its way into the sky to seize the sun. She sat down in the chair by the stove and shook her long hair loose. He was like a dog tied up all winter, watching while the others got fed. He remembered how she had gone with the oil drillers, and his blue eyes moved like flies crawling over her body. He held his thin pale lips like he wanted to spit on her. He hated the people because they had something of value, the old man said, something which the Gussucks could never have. They thought they could take it, suck it out of the earth or cut it from the mountains; but they were fools.

There was a matted hunk of dog hair on the floor by her foot. She thought of the yellow insulation coming unstuffed: their defense against the freezing going to pieces as it advanced on them. The ice was crouching on the northwest horizon like the old man's bear. She laughed out loud again. The sun would be down now; it was time.

The first time he spoke to her, she did not hear what he said, so she did 50
not answer or even look up at him. He spoke to her again but his words were only noises coming from his pale mouth, trembling now as his anger began to unravel. He jerked her up and the chair fell over behind her. His arms were shaking and she could feel his hands tense up, pulling the edges of the parka tighter. He raised his fist to hit her, his thin body quivering with rage; but the fist collapsed with the desire he had for the valuable things, which, the old man had rightly said, was the only reason they came. She could hear his heart pounding as he held her close and arched his hips against her, groaning and breathing in spasms. She twisted away from him and ducked under his arms.

She ran with a mitten over her mouth, breathing through the fur to protect her lungs from the freezing air. She could hear him running behind her, his heavy breathing, the occasional sound of metal jingling against metal. But he ran without his parka or mittens, breathing the frozen air; its fire squeezed the lungs against the ribs and it was enough that he could not catch her near his store. On the river bank he realized how far he was from his stove, and the wads of yellow stuffing that held off the cold. But the girl was not able to run very fast through the deep drifts at the edge of the river. The twilight was luminous and he could still see clearly for a long distance; he knew he could catch her so he kept running.

When she neared the middle of the river she looked over her shoulder. He was not following her tracks; he went straight across the ice, running the shortest distance to reach her. He was close then; his face was twisted and scarlet from the exertion and the cold. There was satisfaction in his eyes; he was sure he could outrun her.

She was familiar with the river, down to the instant the ice flexed into hairline fractures, and the cracking bone-sliver sounds gathered momentum with the opening ice until the sound of the churning gray water was set free. She stopped and turned to the sound of the river and the rattle of swirling ice fragments where he fell through. She pulled off a mitten and zipped the parka to her throat. She was conscious then of her own rapid breathing.

She moved slowly, kicking the ice ahead with the heel of her boot, feeling for sinews of ice to hold her. She looked ahead and all around herself; in the twilight, the dense white sky had merged into the flat snow-covered tundra. In the frantic running she had lost her place on the river. She stood still. The east bank of the river was lost in the sky; the boundaries had been swallowed by the freezing white. And then, in the distance, she saw something red, and suddenly it was as she had remembered it all those years.

VI

She sat on her bed and while she waited, she listened to the old man. 55 The man had found a small jagged knoll on the ice. He pulled his beaver fur cap off his head; the fur inside it steamed with his body heat and sweat. He left it upside down on the ice for the great bear to stalk, and he waited downwind on top of the ice knoll; he was holding the jade knife.

She thought she could see the end of his story in the way he wheezed out the words; but still he reached into his cache of dry fish and dribbled water into his mouth from the tin cup. All night she listened to him describe each breath the man took, each motion of the bear's head as it tried to catch the sound of the man's breathing, and tested the wind for his scent.

The state trooper asked her questions, and the woman who cleaned house for the priest translated them into Yupik. They wanted to know what happened to the storeman, the Gussuck who had been seen running after her down the road onto the river late last evening. He had not come back, and the Gussuck boss in Anchorage was concerned about him. She did not answer for a long time because the old man suddenly sat up in his bed and began to talk excitedly, looking at all of them—the trooper in his dark glasses and the housekeeper in her corduroy parka. He kept saying, "The story! The story! Eh-ya! The great bear! The hunter!"

They asked her again, what happened to the man from the Northern Commercial store. "He lied to them. He told them it was safe to drink. But I will not lie." She stood up and put on the gray wolfskin parka. "I killed him," she said, "but I don't lie."

The attorney came back again, and the jailer slid open the steel doors and opened the cell to let him in. He mentioned for the jailer to stay to translate for him. She laughed when she saw how the jailer would be forced by this Gussuck to speak Yupik to her. She liked the Gussuck attorney for that, and for the thinning hair on his head. He was very tall, and she liked to think about the exposure of his head to the freezing; she wondered if he would feel the ice descending from the sky before the others did. He wanted to know why she told the state trooper she had killed the storeman. Some village children had seen it happen, he said, and it was an accident. "That's all you have to say to the judge: it was an accident." He kept repeating it over and over again to her, slowly in a loud but gentle voice: "It was an accident. He was running after you and he fell through the ice. That's all you have to say in court. That's all. And they will let you go home. Back to your village." The jailer translated the words sullenly, staring down at the floor. She shook her head. "I will not change the story, not even to escape this place and go home. I intended that he die. The story must be told as it is." The attorney exhaled loudly; his eyes looked tired. "Tell her that she could not have killed him that way. He was a white man. He ran after her without a parka or mittens. She could not have planned that." He paused and turned toward the cell door. "Tell her I will do all I can for her. I will explain to the judge that her mind is confused." She laughed out loud when the jailer translated what the attorney said. The Gussucks did not understand the story; they could not see the way it must be told, year after year as the old man had done, without lapse or silence.

She looked out the window at the frozen white sky. The sun had finally 60
broken loose from the ice but it moved like a wounded caribou running on strength which only dying animals find, leaping and running on bullet-shattered lungs. Its light was weak and pale; it pushed dimly through the clouds. She turned and faced the Gussuck attorney.

"It began a long time ago," she intoned steadily, "in the summertime. Early in the morning, I remember, something red in the tall river grass. . . ."

The day after the old man died, men from the village came. She was sitting on the edge of her bed, across from the woman the trooper hired to watch her. They came into the room slowly and listened to her. At the foot of her bed they left a king salmon that had been split open wide and dried last summer. But she did not pause or hesitate; she went on with the story, and she never stopped, not even when the woman got up to close the door behind the village men.

The old man would not change the story even when he knew the end was approaching. Lies could not stop what was coming. He thrashed around on the bed, pulling the blankets loose, knocking bundles of dried fish and meat on the floor. The man had been on the ice for many hours. The freezing winds on the ice knoll had numbed his hands in the mittens, and the cold had exhausted him. He felt a single muscle tremor in his hand that he could not suppress, and the jade knife fell; it shattered on the ice, and the blue glacier bear turned slowly to face him.

Engaging the Text

1. What events take place in the story? You may want to break into several small groups to review the six sections of the story and establish the plot.
2. We get several glimpses of "the Gussucks" in the story. What do we learn of them in areas such as commerce, technology, sexuality, and law? How do the Gussucks interact with the natural world? What is the story's attitude about Gussuck technology?
3. Why doesn't the protagonist try to defend herself at the end of the story? What becomes of her?
4. Explain the connection between the grandfather's story of the polar bear and the main story told here. Support your explanation with specific references to the text. Be sure to consider the meaning of each story's ending.
5. How many stories are told within "Storyteller"? What seems to be the significance of storytelling itself in this culture?

Exploring Connections

6. Compare the portrayals of western technological society offered by Silko and John (Fire) Lame Deer (p. 591). What qualities do they associate with technological culture? What fates do they imagine for it?
7. Review the "innocent" reasons behind resource rushes as described by Patricia Nelson Limerick (p. 564). Then make up a specific hypothetical character who might have an innocent reason for going to the Arctic. Write a paragraph or two from this character's point of view about why she or he is heading north. Exchange paragraphs with a classmate and write a critique of each other's paragraphs from a broader perspective.
8. Drawing on the selections by Paula Gunn Allen (p. 312), Haunani-Kay Trask (p. 571), and Silko, discuss the power that stories have to shape our identities and ways of thinking.

Extending the Critical Context

9. John Boorman's film *The Emerald Forest* is set in the Amazon, yet it shares the apocalyptic environmental vision expressed in "Storyteller." Watch the film and compare the way it treats the conflict between nature and technology with the handling of the same theme in Silko's story. What is the appeal of such responses to technology?

The "Greening" of Establishment PR:[1] *Mind Pollution on the Rise*

Joyce Nelson

As the title of this passage suggests, Joyce Nelson is concerne dangers of intellectual as well as industrial pollution. In her view and the sleaze are produced by the same culprits — big busine interested in preserving the economic status quo. Nelson (I ecofeminist and writer who specializes in the politics of the Her books include The Perfect Machine: TV in the Nuc Sultans of Sleaze: Public Relations and the Media *(1989 passage was taken; and a retrospective collection of her* Road Kill: From Mediascape to Landscape *(1992).* ' *British Columbia.*

n
pr
co
tha

[Auth

[1] *PR:* Public relations.

On the cover of *The National Geographic* for December 1988 there is a double hologram depicting planet Earth. Beneath the image are the words, "As we begin our second century, the Geographic asks: Can Man Save This Fragile Earth?" Viewed from one angle, the holographic image shows the planet round and whole, with its North Pole tilted slightly down and towards the left, showing the North American continent, the USSR, Europe, and Scandinavia. Viewed from a different angle, the holographic image shows planet Earth breaking apart, with pieces flying off it like chunks of broken glass. Conceived as an "action hologram," it is a fascinating cover, suitable for an issue devoted (almost) entirely to "fragile Earth."

The back cover of the issue is also a double hologram made with the same special technology developed to create the front cover. The back cover depicts a McDonald's restaurant with a golden arches sign that reads "Over 10,000 Opened." Viewed from one angle, the restaurant is bathed in sunshine to depict daytime. Inside the building little human figures can be seen lined up at the counter. Viewed from a different angle, the restaurant (which, unlike the front-cover planet, does not change position) is seen at night. The sunlight has disappeared, but inside the building the lights are on and the little human figures are still lined up at the counter. The "action" in this double hologram is the change from day to night, from an exterior light source to an interior one. Underneath the image is a prominent quotation: "None Of Us Is As Good As All Of Us." Smaller ad copy beneath the quotation explains, "Whether applied to the issues of a growing business or a growing world, the words of McDonald's founder Ray Kroc are equally relevant."

The front and back covers of this issue of *The National Geographic* must be seen as a dialogue, a subtle communication from cover to cover, front to back, hologram to hologram, rather than as happenstance or accidental. Although the magazine's editorial office has assured me that McDonald's did not pay for the front-cover hologram, nonetheless the company's use of the same technology to create its back-cover institutional ad indicates that the presentation must be seen as a corporate response to the front cover's double hologram. Conceived as the reassuring counterpart to the disturbing image and question presented on the front of the magazine, and appearing as the "last word" in an issue devoted to environmental pillage, the McDonald's institutional hologram reveals the stunning finesse with which corporate public relations now operates.

One of the primary dictates of contemporary PR is that "a corporation ust sell itself as well as its product."[2] In this instance McDonald's has tched itself as an institution that is more stable than the planet itself. The rporate hubris involved in this back cover is a subtle, multilevelled effort t, coming from a major polluter, is breathtaking.

[2]Interview with Jerry Wattel, president of Hill and Knowlton, Autumn 1981, New York. r's note]

What is immediately noticeable is that there is no angle from which the 5
McDonald's restaurant can be seen to be breaking apart, with pieces flying off it, like planet Earth on the front cover. Apparently, although the Earth is endangered McDonald's is not. The supposed stability of the institution is reinforced by the fact that the depicted restaurant does not change position, as the Earth does on the front cover. As well, the "action" in the two covers is decidedly different in tone. On the front, the change in viewing angle yields a shock, a startling sight of the planet breaking apart. On the back cover, however, there is only a pleasurable surprise: the change of angle shows the passage of time from day to night, a familiar change that contributes to the aura of stability and reassurance being created around the corporate institution. . . .

The articles included in this issue of *The National Geographic* implicate many aspects of a Western life-style (both corporate and personal) based on planetary exploitation and environmental irresponsibility. In particular, "Population, Plenty, and Poverty," a lengthy article by ecologists Paul Ehrlich and Anne Ehrlich, makes vivid cross-cultural comparisons of the ways of living in six different countries. The section dealing with the United States is headed "Geared to Consumption" and reveals that per capita energy consumption in the country is forty times greater than in four of the other nations examined, Kenya, China, India, and Brazil, and more than twice as great as in the fifth country, Hungary. The U.S. section of the article even includes a full-page colour photograph of an American family seated in their car, gorging on McDonald's junk food. The corporate logo is clearly visible on the packaging for the french fries and soft drinks. It is precisely here that we can see the supreme corporate confidence and finesse at work in the back-cover ad.

McDonald's can tolerate an inside photograph that implicates it, in part because the company will have the last word, providing closure to our experience of the magazine and its two hundred pages of environmental information. That closure is an important aspect of "issues management," including the corporate "largesse" in helping to sponsor this particular issue of *The National Geographic.* A back-cover ad in the magazine costs far more than the $121,000 price tag for a one-page ad inside. And in this instance the holographic parallels from cover to cover imply McDonald's born-again environmentalism, at least at first glance.

Since one of the primary issues now confronting all corporate activity is the politics of the environment, the McDonald's holographic institutional ad might be seen as a kind of instructional primer, provided by founder Ray Kroc and his PR team to other "growing businesses," on just how to engage with the current challenge to business-as-usual.

The back cover neatly meets the challenge by showing us the McDonald's "world," an alternative to the front-cover depiction since it is stable, unthreatening, familiar, reassuring, unchanging. The institution has been around long enough to have become (or assume itself to be) a symbol of stability: serving us, reassuring us, providing a clean, well-lighted place where (as the hologram depicts) nothing more startling occurs than a change from day to night. It is a "world" that seems to exist entirely for our benefit, our pleasure. "You deserve a break today," the electronic ads have told us.

10 By contrast, the breaking world depicted on the front cover is threatening, unfamiliar, demanding. Indeed this disturbing image, as well as much of the information between the two covers, asks for nothing less than a radical change of life-style, a paradigm shift in both consciousness and consumer behaviour, if fragile Earth is to continue existing beyond its currently doomed prognosis. But McDonald's knows that our present concern is not yet enough to change our ways. In fact the evidence is there in its hologram, in the sign claiming "Over 10,000 Opened." We may read this issue of *The National Geographic* and contemplate the implications of the information therein, but it does not really penetrate to the core where real change occurs and then leads to profoundly different ways of living. It is in this sense that the corporate institution is unthreatened, can even play on our anxieties about "fragile Earth" and co-opt those concerns for its own purposes. Perhaps even more important, whatever we may know about McDonald's own thirty-year-long contribution to the depletion of the ozone layer, the elimination of the rain forests, and the mounting garbage problem, the corporation can point to us: for, after all, "We do it all for you."...

The escalating environmental crisis has knocked a huge "legitimacy gap" into the North American way of "life." This is a life-style addicted to fossil fuels and geared to an economy based on built-in obsolescence, disposable products, unlimited consumption, and a concept of "progress" that means defining the planet primarily as "natural resources" for human exploitation. It is becoming obvious that this way of life is no longer viable. Each crisis highlights the polarization taking place between radical and reformist environmental perspectives.

For example, the Exxon Valdez oil spill off the Alaskan coast in March 1989 resulted in a consumer boycott in which thousands cut up their credit cards and mailed them to Exxon's arrogant CEO,[3] Lawrence G. Rawl—who not only claimed the catastrophe was an "act of God" but also compared it favourably to Union Carbide's Bhopal disaster[4] because Exxon had "nobody dead."[5] The consumer boycott, as well as much of the media commentary accompanying the spill, avoided the larger issue at stake. Not only were there thirteen other oil spills in the three months preceding Valdez, but the whole

[3] *CEO:* Chief Executive Officer; head of a business or corporation.

[4] *Bhopal disaster:* In 1984 a massive leak at the Union Carbide chemical plant in Bhopal, India, released toxic fumes that killed close to 2,000 people and injured up to 300,000 more.

[5] See Andre Carothers, "A Nation Drunk on Oil," *Greenpeace,* July–August 1989, p. 2; and the editorial "Black Spring," *The Village Voice,* April 18, 1989, p. 3. [Author's note]

notion of "reforming" the oil industry's practices was also considered by many to be a cop-out. An editorial in Pollution Probe's[6] *Probe Post* stated:

> So what, then, is the answer to the question of how to stop such spills from happening, a question which so many people have debated in the media following the spills? Well, for those who rank the environment as one of their greatest concerns, the answer has nothing to do with creating new cleanup technology, nothing to do with testing ship captains for drugs or alcohol and nothing to do with oil-spill preparedness on the part of the army, coast guard, etc. The answer is simple: leave oil in the ground and take immediate and firm action to promote energy conservation and development of alternative energy sources. Environmentalists have been pointing out the hows and whys of such a shift in energy policy for years.[7]

The idea of "leaving oil in the ground" (and trees in the forest, minerals in the mountains, fish in the sea) has now become the crucial dividing line separating political perspectives. Since environmental concern is no longer a "lunatic fringe" issue (as it was once characterized), it has become a litmus test indicating the degree to which individuals and organizations, as well as politicians and corporations, have a stake in maintaining the status quo. Obviously, widespread radical change in the way we live our daily lives is a threat to both a power structure and an economy that need us to be diligent consumers. As a result, the "greening" of corporate and governmental personas is rapidly becoming the standard PR strategy in order to hold out the promise of "reform" and prevent radical change.

This is in itself a sign that more than twenty-five years of environmental action (dating from the 1962 publication of Rachel Carson's book *Silent Spring*) is bearing fruit in terms of public consciousness. A recent *Financial Post* article by Stephen Duncan, former Shell Canada PR manager of public affairs and government relations, provides hints of the fear which the establishment now holds toward environmental activism. Referring to the benefit concert organized by Ian Tyson[8] in June 1989 to stop the Oldman Dam project[9] in Alberta, Duncan writes:

> Environmental groups grow increasingly more sophisticated in elevating localized issues to the national agenda. And they do it with stunning efficiency: Tyson carried off his star-studded concert for a reported $3,000. He simply called in some Brownie points with his friends. In the polarization that is occurring, debates about job creation and growth are seemingly holding less appeal: the notion of sustainable development, more. Meanwhile the list of environmental victories and (usually) economic dislocation

[6] *Pollution Probe:* Toronto-based environmental group concerned with nuclear power and other polluting industries.

[7] Gail Richardson, "From the Editor," *Probe Post*, Spring 1989, p. 5. [Author's note]

[8] *Ian Tyson:* Canadian folksinger and environmental activist (b. 1933).

[9] *Oldman Dam project:* A megadam project that turned out to be an environmental disaster.

> continues to grow: the withdrawal of Uniroyal Chemical Ltd.'s Alar[10] spray and the shutdown of Rancho Seco,[11] the nuclear plant in Sacramento, both occurred within the past two weeks.[12]

While Duncan feels that "there is a lesson here" for politicians and corporations, it is a lesson that the establishment has been learning for several years. As a PR tactic, the "greening" of corporate and governmental personas has been used since at least the late 1970s, when a rash of health- and environment-threatening disasters (Three Mile Island,[13] Love Canal,[14] the Mississauga chlorine-train wreck,[15] increased acid rain) boosted public concern by a quantum leap.

One of the first companies to attempt this particular form of image-revamping also deserves the corporate bullshit award for the 1970s for its advocacy campaign that stated: "When you get right down to it, you'd be hard pressed to find any group of people who care as much about the environmental and economic well-being of Niagara Falls as the people at Hooker Chemical."[16] Having dumped 43.6 million pounds of waste solvents and pesticide residues into Love Canal from 1942 to 1953, Hooker nevertheless maintains to this day that the resulting toxic mess and health disaster were not its fault.[17]

15 As Love Canal became household terminology in the late 1970s, Hooker embarked on a nationwide PR campaign, complete with thousands of glossy pamphlets and a travelling two-man "truth squad," to convince the press and the public of its corporate social conscience. When that tactic failed, the company changed its name to Occidental Chemical, a subsidiary of Occidental Petroleum Corporation, chaired at the time by Armand Hammer.[18]

[10]*Alar:* Chemical once used to improve the appearance and shelf life of apples; it was subsequently found to be toxic and withdrawn from use following widespread public protests.

[11]*Rancho Seco:* Antinuclear activists won a major victory when Sacramento voters became the first in the United States to approve a referendum shutting down a functioning nuclear power plant.

[12]Stephen Duncan, "Environmentalists Are Beating Politicians at Their Own Game," *The Financial Post,* June 19, 1989, p. 14. [Author's note]

[13]*Three Mile Island:* A 1979 accident at the Three Mile Island nuclear power plant near Middletown, Pennsylvania, released dangerous levels of radiation; the incident undermined confidence in the safety of nuclear energy and inspired strenuous opposition to further development of nuclear facilities.

[14]*Love Canal:* Housing development built on the site of a former chemical waste dump near Niagara Falls, New York. Residents suffered severe health problems as a result of their exposure to toxic residues in the soil and water; the site was eventually declared an environmental disaster area and the residents relocated.

[15]*Mississauga chlorine-train wreck:* A multicar train derailment that spilled chlorine in the town of Mississauga, Ontario. The town had to be evacuated.

[16]Cited in Michael Brown, *Laying Waste: The Poisoning of America by Toxic Chemicals* (New York: Pocket Books, 1979), p. 100. [Author's note]

[17]Michael Brown, "A Toxic Ghost Town," *The Atlantic,* July 1989, p. 26. [Author's note]

[18]*Armand Hammer:* Wealthy American capitalist, formerly chairman of the board and CEO of Occidental Petroleum (1898–1990).

Public opinion polls conducted by the Ontario government in 1980 revealed that the people of the province felt strongly about the increasing pollution of the Ontario environment as well as the larger ecosystem. In a move characteristic for the time, the government put out a series of ads featuring vignettes of Ontario wilderness areas while an actor sitting in a canoe addressed the TV audience, saying: "I'm an engineer and I work all over the world. Ontario is the cleanest place that I know."[19] Trying to convince us that our perceptions were mistaken proved, however, to be increasingly untenable as the 1980s progressed. Confronted with firsthand evidence of dying lakes and forests, polluted drinking water, closed beaches, droughts and soil erosion, thermal inversions during urban summers, as well as news of fresh disasters like the pesticide leak at the Union Carbide factory in Bhopal, India, the death of the Rhine and the Black Forest,[20] drought and famines in Africa, and the nuclear accident at Chernobyl,[21] the majority of the population proved to have a significant "awareness level" (as the pollster would put it) of the whole environmental issue.

A nationwide attitudinal survey conducted by Angus Reid[22] in the summer of 1988 — the summer of the PCB fire at St.-Basile-le-Grand,[23] Quebec — revealed that 83 percent of Canadians ranked the environment as "very important," with 80 percent willing to spend more for consumer items that are environmentally safe. A whopping 89 percent believed that private industry does not contribute enough to solving environmental problems. Confronted with this environmentally aware public, corporations and governments began to take some unusual twists as part of a heightened effort to cover their assets. Like Hooker Chemical, McDonald's, and Nestlé's Carnation, they would like us to believe they "care."

In early 1988 the B.C. Council of Forest Industries initiated a paradigmatic example of PR "greening." Under attack for hideously irresponsible logging practices, the Council mounted a massive and expensive campaign to convince the public of its "sound forest stewardship and reforestation programs." The campaign included educational displays in shopping malls, huge posters at bus stops, ads inside buses, and colour supplements delivered

[19]Cited by Morris Wolfe in an interview, Autumn 1981, Toronto. [Author's note]

[20]*the death of the Rhine and the Black Forest:* Acid rain is destroying plant and animal life in the Rhine River and the Black Forest, two of Germany's most beautiful and famous natural assets.

[21]*Chernobyl:* Nuclear facility in Ukraine that in 1986 became the site of the world's worst nuclear accident. A reactor meltdown released clouds of radiation that contaminated soil, water, and crops throughout Europe and beyond. Thirty-one people died in the immediate aftermath; estimates of long-range cancer fatalities run as high as 100,000.

[22]*Angus Reid:* Canadian pollster.

[23]*PCB fire at St.-Basile-le-Grand:* A hazardous-waste storage facility in this Montreal suburb burned, blanketing the town in toxic smoke; polychlorinated biphenyls (PCBs) cause a variety of cancers and birth defects.

to most households in the province. As Kalevi Poeg reported, "There is even a $3,000 prize for high school students with the best essays on the theme: Why Clearcut Logging Is Beneficial for British Columbia."[24] The industry also developed a free educational package for B.C. classrooms, including a twenty-minute video presentation and twenty learning modules to "help secondary teachers and students understand our forest resources, the forest industry, and what they mean to our province."[25]

But the biggest irritant in the whole PR effort was the Council's "Forests Forever" ads: a $2 million pitch on billboards and TV and in the print media in which Council spokespeople say what a wonderful job they are doing in managing B.C. forests. At the end of each colour TV commercial there is a breathtaking shot of ancient trees bathed in cathedral light while a mellow male voice intones the words "Forests Forever."[26] The ads ran for over a year on CBC-TV despite protests by environmental groups; but when a counter-ad, "Mystical Forests," detailing the actual practices of the logging industry, was proposed by environmentalists and presented for CBC approval, it was turned down as "too controversial." Amidst the storm of protest that resulted from CBC's double standard, the network pulled the "Forests Forever" campaign off the air, but by then the commercial had already received a year's run on the public network. As Kalle Lasn and Bill Schmalz put it, the "Forests Forever" pitch "sounded great — and people believed it."[27]

This incident reveals, among other things, the prevailing ideology among 20
our media institutions. A message in support of the status quo is typically considered to be "neutral," "objective," and "noncontroversial," while a message that departs from the status quo position or criticizes it is considered to have a "point of view" and "bias.". . .

Co-opting nature icons for polluting products has been a time-tested strategy of marketing ever since the industry discovered "Marlboro Country," but in the late 1980s that tactic assumed new proportions. A sign of the times could be found in an ad campaign for Craven A cigarettes. Where once upon a time smokers were depicted enjoying the killer weed in great outdoors settings, the company now took a more aggressive stance by actually carving the corporate logo into the landscape. The ads showed smokers on a golf course where the putting green had been mowed into a huge circle containing the words "Craven A," or on a beach where a similar transformation was made of the sandy expanse. The message is like a staking of a

[24]Kalevi Poeg, "Money Talks," *Adbusters,* Summer 1989, p. 55. [Author's note]

[25]Quoted in ibid. [Author's note]

[26]Kalle Lasn and Bill Schmalz, "Forests Forever?," *Adbusters,* Summer 1989, p. 8. [Author's note]

[27]Ibid. [Author's note]

land claim, asserting the corporate place in the landscape, but also asserting the human "need" to rework and transform natural surroundings. In their attitudes towards nature the ads subtly stated that corporations have a right to alter the earth.

Where once car manufacturers were content to utilize animal totems merely in naming their vehicles, more recently the advertising goal was to completely anthropomorphize the product, making it seem like a new "species" and therefore worthy of human and animal rights. For instance, a 1988 ad for Saab in *Harrowsmith*[28] stated that the car was "an heir to the air"—subtly suggesting that automobiles too deserve their share of the available oxygen.

A Nissan Pathfinder ad claimed the vehicle was "half man, half beast," thereby denying all technological reality. Similarly the 1989 Audi ad, with its slogan "the hills are alive," transferred that ecological awareness to the car, making it seem like just another species roaming the planet. Ironically, in the January 2, 1989, edition of *Time,* whose cover story was devoted to the woes of "Endangered Earth," a Mercury Cougar ad made the claim that the car was "the next breed of cat," apparently meant to replace the actual animal species. The copy adopted a pseudo-evolutionary tone: "The breed begins. Again. Sleeker. Faster. More intelligent."

Attributing species status to polluting products like cars apparently allows them to frolic at will in nature. But sometimes advertisers actually proclaim human status for their products. The Hyundai ad for 1989 depicted a car apparently being delivered by stork. The "bundle of joy" will hold claim to its "parents'" loving care and attention no matter how naughty it is to the actual environment. Likewise, a Mercedes-Benz ad claimed that its product was "the automobile every sports sedan wants to be when it grows up."

But sometimes even human status isn't enough for consumer products. 25
Electronics and computer corporations often claim superspecies status for their technologies. A 1989 *Maclean's*[29] ad for Gold Star Electronics stated: "To err is human, so Gold Star tests with robots." Move over, humans, your claim to the planet is being usurped.

A November 7, 1988, ad in *Maclean's,* placed by the Canadian Nuclear Association lobby group, showed a family relaxing on the grassy slopes of a park with a nuclear power plant (the Pickering Generating Station) clearly visible in the background. At first one assumes that the ad copy accompanying such a photograph will be decidedly antinuclear, since the juxtaposition of this happy nuclear-family outing and the nuclear power plant is so ironic and bizarre; but the accompanying ad copy is all about the "safety" of nuclear power. Something that does not inherently belong in the landscape

[28]*Harrowsmith:* Bimonthly Canadian life-style magazine.

[29]*Maclean's:* Weekly Canadian newsmagazine similar to *Newsweek* or *Time.*

and is in fact a major polluter is made to seem like a "natural" feature of the scenic view.

. . . The paradox we face is that our life-style of luxury and "progress" — promulgated through the media over this century — increasingly reveals itself to be the prescription for planetary suicide. Moreover, that media system — which McLuhan referred to as the externalized nervous system of humanity — does not function to alert us to problems as soon as they are known, but instead is purposely controlled and used to keep us uninformed of critical problems, or misinformed about their causes and repercussions, and reassured that nothing needs to change.

But a growing number of people are beginning to reject the dominant life-style and "values" and are engaged in redefining the prevailing concepts of "rich" and "poor." Choosing and exploring a wide variety of paths based on voluntary simplicity and social activism, people are returning to their imaginations, ingenuity, and skills to find solutions for living their daily lives according to basic needs rather than created needs, and in harmony with the Earth. This return includes the relearning of older ways for doing things — an effort that is going to become even more crucial as the health hazards of electric power lines and even electric appliances are revealed.

After more than twenty years of controversy in the scientific field, this issue finally hit the mainstream in 1989, with articles in both *The New Yorker* and *Time* magazine discussing the effects of technologically-generated electromagnetic fields on human health, effects that may include suppression of the immune system, childhood leukemia, and other forms of cancer. As *Time* put it, the research implications "could be devastating. Appliances and electronic equipment would have to be redesigned, many homes rewired, and the nation's power-distribution system overhauled. Lawsuits, already on the rise, would surge as citizens filed claims to cover illness or property devaluation."[30] It is largely because of these repercussions that the issue has been kept out of the mainstream media for so long. In his three-part article for *The New Yorker* Paul Brodeur documents the extraordinary public-relations effort conducted by the utilities, other corporations, trade associations, and lobby groups to keep this issue under wraps.[31]

30 Similarly, the mounting garbage problem directly implicates our consumer culture. . . . Breaking away from both the fashion industry and the product industry based on built-in obsolescence and disposable items will involve a major shift in values, indeed in "wealth" itself. When people no

[30] Anastasia Toufexis, "Panic Over Power Lines," *Time,* July 17, 1989, p. 55. For a more detailed discussion of the issues, see Robert O. Becker, M.D., and Gary Selden, *The Body Electric: Electromagnetism and the Foundation of Life* (New York: William Morrow, 1985). [Author's note]

[31] Paul Brodeur, "Annals of Radiation: The Hazards of Electromagnetic Fields," parts 1–3, *The New Yorker,* June 12, 19, and 26, 1989. [Author's note]

longer define their worth and status in terms of owning the "latest," or the "newest," or the "most convenient," significant shifts in the entire economy will take place, especially in local efforts to meet local needs.

It is often said that "we can't go back to the past," an expression that usually means the modern multinationals-based economy is so completely dependent on maintaining the status quo that alternative or older ways of living would undermine it and throw it into chaos. Besides the fact that the global economy is already in chaos, the practices upon which it is based are politically, morally, and environmentally bankrupt. Indeed, that is why such a tremendous public-relations effort is put into maintaining the status quo — a redoubling of rhetoric and photo-ops, cosmetic "change," and meaningless gestures meant to keep us from using our own imaginations to find radical alternatives. It is well to remember that "radical" change means change "at the root." As Marc Ellis observes, that "*ground* from which momentous changes are nurtured and grow" has become "sterile and dry" and needs a "resurgence of imagination." Here, each one of us can play our part: we can begin by reclaiming our imaginations, which have been colonized by a century of PR geared to "regimenting the public mind." As a first step, that in itself would be a radical break.

Engaging the Text

1. What is the purpose of the extended analysis of the *National Geographic* cover and the McDonald's ad that opens the essay? Why are the placement and format of the ad in relation to the cover significant?
2. Nelson claims that "the escalating environmental crisis has knocked a huge 'legitimacy gap' into the North American way of 'life' " (para. 11). What does she mean by this?
3. What is the distinction between reformist and radical approaches to the environment according to Nelson?
4. Why does an environmentally aware public pose a threat to business interests? How do "green" commercials and PR campaigns attempt to counter that threat?
5. Nelson cites several polls indicating that most consumers would pay more for environmentally safe products. Have you ever paid more for a product because it's "green"? How often have you based a purchasing decision on one or more of the following considerations?
   - how much packaging the product uses
   - whether or not the product or the packaging is recyclable
   - whether or not the product or the packaging is biodegradable
   - whether or not the product or the packaging is made of recycled materials
   - whether or not the product contains toxic ingredients
   - whether or not the product contains or emits chemicals that damage the ozone layer

- whether or not the product has to be cleaned or maintained with hazardous chemicals
- whether or not the product generates radiation or an electromagnetic field
- how much pollution the product emits
- how energy-efficient the product is
- whether the company that makes the product has a good environmental record

6. Nelson suggests that in order to live more harmoniously with nature we must find ways to live "according to basic needs rather than created needs" (para. 28). Review your possessions and daily activities, and make a list of which ones satisfy basic needs and which do not. How much of your daily life is devoted to "needs" that have been created by marketers in order to sell products and services?

Exploring Connections

7. Compare Nelson's views of advertising to Jack Solomon's (p. 489). How does each writer assess the motives, methods, and psychological impact of advertising? Which analysis do you find more persuasive, and why?
8. Do you think the students described by Robin Templeton (p. 135) have successfully "reclaimed their imaginations" from commercial colonization by resisting the introduction of *Channel One* into their classrooms? Why or why not?

Extending the Critical Context

9. Analyze a print or TV ad that capitalizes on images from the natural world. What relationship does the ad assert or imply between nature and the sponsoring product or company? To follow up, find out what you can about the company's environmental record. Does the ad represent the kind of "mind pollution" Nelson condemns?
10. In paragraph 20 Nelson charges that the media typically treat opinions that support the status quo as " 'neutral,' 'objective,' and 'noncontroversial,' while a message that departs from the status quo position or criticizes it is considered to have a 'point of view' and 'bias.' " Look through several issues of a newspaper or news magazine to find evidence that supports or contradicts this claim.
11. Nelson recommends "decolonizing" our minds by imagining "radical alternatives" to wasteful consumption. Working in small groups, brainstorm as many radical alternatives to a specific environmental problem as you can. Compare notes with other groups and vote on which alternatives you'd be willing to try.

Putting the Earth First

DAVE FOREMAN

Dave Foreman (b. 1946) was once a reasonable man. A full-time lobbyist for the Wilderness Society, he worked to hammer out legislative compromises that would protect at least some of the remaining wilderness areas in the United States from development. But by 1981, convinced that mainstream environmentalists' reasonableness and willingness to compromise were bartering away our natural heritage, Foreman became a founding member of the now-defunct radical environmental group Earth First!, whose motto was "No Compromise in Defense of Mother Earth." In this passage from his 1991 autobiography, Confessions of an Eco Warrior, *Foreman outlines the guiding principles of Earth First! His other books include* Eco Defense: A Field Guide to Monkeywrenching *(ed. with Bill Haywood, 1987) and* The Big Outside: A Descriptive Inventory of the Big Wilderness Areas of the United States *(1992).*

> *These are the times that try men's souls; the summer soldier and the sunshine patriot will, in this crisis, shrink from the service of his country, but he that stands it now, deserves the love and thanks of man and woman.*
>
> — THOMAS PAINE

In July 1987, seven years after the campfire gathering that spawned Earth First!, I rose among the Ponderosa pines and scattered shafts of sunlight on the North Rim of the Grand Canyon and mounted a stage festooned with Earth First! banners and American flags. Before me sat several hundred people: hippies in tie-dyed shirts and Birkenstocks, rednecks for wilderness in cowboy boots and hats, middle-class hikers in waffle stompers, graybeards, and children. The diversity was impressive. The energy was overpowering. Never in my wildest dreams had I imagined the Earth First! movement would attract so many. Never had I hoped that we would have begun to pack such a punch. We were attracting national attention; we were changing the parameters of the debate about ecological issues; we had become a legend in conservation lore.

Yet, after seven years, I was concerned we were losing some of our clarity of purpose and blurring our focus. In launching Earth First!, I had said, "Let our actions set the finer points of our philosophy." But now I was concerned that the *what* of our actions might be overwhelming the *why*. For some of those newly attracted to Earth First!, action seemed to be its own justification. I felt a need to return to wilderness fundamentalism, to articulate what I thought were the principles that defined the Earth First! movement, that gave it a specific identity. The response to the principles I offered that day was so overwhelmingly positive that I elaborated on them in the *Earth First! Journal* later that fall. Here they are.

A Placing of Earth First in All Decisions, Even Ahead of Human Welfare if Necessary Our movement is called "Earth First!" not "People First!" Sometimes what appears to be in the short-term interest of human beings as a whole, a select group of human beings, or individual human beings is detrimental to the short-term or long-term health of the biosphere (and to the actual long-term welfare of human beings). Earth First! does not argue that native diversity should be preserved if it can be done without negatively impacting the material "standard of living" of a group of human beings. We simply state that native diversity should be preserved, that natural diversity a-building for three and a half billion years should be left unfettered. Human beings must adjust to the planet; it is supreme arrogance to expect the planet and all it contains to adjust to the demands of humans. In everything human society does, the primary consideration should be for the long-term health and biological diversity of Earth. After that, we can consider the welfare of humans. We should be kind, compassionate, and caring with other people, but Earth comes first.

A Refusal to Use Human Beings as the Measure by Which to Value Others An individual human life has no more intrinsic value than does an individual grizzly bear life. Human suffering resulting from drought and famine in Ethiopia is tragic, yes, but the destruction there of other creatures and habitat is even more tragic. This leads quickly into the next point:

*An Enthusiastic Embracing of the Philosophy of Deep Ecology or Bio- 5
centrism* This philosophy states simply and essentially that all living creatures and communities possess intrinsic value, inherent worth. Natural things live for their own sake, which is another way of saying they have value. Other beings (both animal and plant) and even so-called inanimate objects such as rivers and mountains are not placed here for the convenience of human beings. Our biocentric worldview denies the modern concept of "resources." The dominant philosophy of our time (which contains Judeo-Christianity, Islam, capitalism, Marxism, scientism, and secular humanism) is anthropocentrism. It places human beings at the center of the universe, separates them from nature, and endows them with unique value. EF!ers are in direct opposition to that philosophy. Ours is an ecological perspective that views Earth as a community and recognizes such apparent enemies as "disease" (e.g., malaria) and "pests" (e.g., mosquitoes) not as manifestations of evil to be overcome but rather as vital and necessary components of a complex and vibrant biosphere.

A Realization that Wilderness Is the Real World The preservation of wilderness is the fundamental issue. Wilderness does not merely mean backpacking parks or scenery. It is the natural world, the arena for evolution, the caldron from which humans emerged, the home of the others with whom we share this planet. Wilderness is the real world; our cities, our computers, our airplanes, our global business civilization all are but artificial and transient phenomena. It is important to remember that only a tiny portion of the history of the human species has occurred outside of wilderness. The preservation of wildness and native diversity is *the* most important issue. Issues directly affecting only humans pale in comparison. Of course, ecology teaches us that all things are connected, and in this regard all other matters become subsets of wilderness preservation — the prevention of nuclear war, for example — but the most important campaigns being waged today are those directly on behalf of wilderness.

A Recognition that There Are Far Too Many Human Beings on Earth There are too many of us everywhere — in the United States, in Nigeria; in cities, in rural areas; with digging hoes, with tractors. Although there is obviously an unconscionable maldistribution of wealth and the basic necessities of life among humans, this fact should not be used — as some leftists are wont to do — to argue that overpopulation is not the problem. It *is* a large part of the problem; there are far too many of us *already* — and our numbers continue to grow astronomically. Even if inequitable distribution could be solved, six billion human beings converting the natural world to material goods and human food would devastate natural diversity.

This basic recognition of the overpopulation problem does not mean that we should ignore the economic and social causes of overpopulation, and shouldn't criticize the accumulation of wealth in fewer and fewer hands, the maldistribution of "resources," and the venality of multinational corporations and Third World juntas alike, but simply that we must understand that great blue whales, jaguars, black rhinoceroses, and rain forests are not compatible with an exploding human population.[1]

A Deep Questioning of, and Even an Antipathy to, "Progress" and "Technology" In looking at human history, we can see that we have lost more in our "rise" to civilization than we have gained. We can see that life in a hunter-gatherer society was on the whole healthier, happier, and more secure than our lives today as peasants, industrial workers, or business executives. For every material "achievement" of progress, there are a dozen losses of things of profound and ineffable value. We can accept the pejoratives of "Luddite" and "Neanderthal" with pride. (This does not mean that we must immediately eschew all the facets of technological civilization. We are *of* it, and use it; this does not mean that we can't critique it.)

[1]Two excellent books on the population issue that are also sensitive to social and economic issues are William R. Catton, Jr.'s *Overshoot: The Ecological Basis of Revolutionary Change* (Urbana, Ill., and Chicago: University of Illinois Press, 1982) and *The Population Explosion*, by Paul and Anne Ehrlich (New York: Simon and Schuster, 1990). No one concerned with the preservation of biological diversity should be without these. [Author's note]

A Refusal to Accept Rationality as the Only Way of Thinking There is 10
room for great diversity within Earth First! on matters spiritual, and nowhere is tolerance for diversity more necessary. But we can all recognize that linear, rational, logical left-brain thinking represents only part of our brain and consciousness. Rationality is a fine and useful tool, but it is just that—a tool, one way of analyzing matters. Equally valid, perhaps more so, is intuitive, instinctive awareness. We can become more cognizant of ultimate truths by sitting quietly in the wild than by studying in a library. Reading books, engaging in logical discourse, and compiling facts and figures are necessary in the modern context, but they are not the only ways to comprehend the world and our lives. Often our gut instincts enable us to act more effectively in a crisis than does careful rational analysis. An example would be a patient bleeding to death in a hospital emergency room—you can't wait for all the tests to be completed. Your gut says, "Act!" So it is with Earth First!'s actions in Earth's current emergency.

A Lack of Desire to Gain Credibility or "Legitimacy" with the Gang of Thugs Running Human Civilization It is basic human nature to want to be accepted by the social milieu in which you find yourself. It hurts to be dismissed by the arbiters of opinion as "nuts," "terrorists," "wackos," or "extremists." But we are not crazy; we happen to be sane humans in an insane human society in a sane natural world. We do not have "credibility" with Senator Mark Hatfield or with Maxxam chairman Charles Hurwitz — but they do not have credibility with us! (We do have their attention, however.) They are madmen destroying the pure and beautiful. Why should we "reason" with them? We do not share the same worldview or values. There is, however, a dangerous pitfall here that some alternative groups fall into. That is that we gain little by being consciously offensive, by trying to alienate others. We can be strong and unyielding without being obnoxious.

The American system is very effective at co-opting and moderating dissidents by giving them attention and then encouraging them to be "reasonable" so their ideas will be taken seriously. Putting a critic on the evening news, on the front page of the newspaper, in a national magazine — all of these are methods the establishment uses to entice one to share their worldview and to enter the negotiating room to compromise. The actions of Earth First! — both the bold and the comic — have gained attention. If they are to have results, we must resist the siren's offer of credibility, legitimacy, and a share in the decision-making. We are thwarting the system, not reforming it. While we are therefore not concerned with political credibility, it must be remembered that the arguments and actions of Earth First! are based on the understandings of ecology. It is vitally important that we have biological credibility.

An Effort to Go Beyond the Tired, Worn-Out Dogmas of Left, Right, and Middle-of-the-Road These doctrines, whether blaming capitalism, communism, or the devil for all the problems in the world, merely represent internecine squabbles between different factions of humanism. Yes, multinational corporations commit great evil (the Soviet Union is essentially a state-run multinational corporation); there is a great injustice in the world; the rich are getting richer and the poor poorer — but all problems cannot be simplistically laid at the feet of evil capitalists in the United States, Europe, and Japan. Earth First! is not left or right; we are not even in front. Earth First! should not be in the political struggle between humanist sects at all. We're in a wholly different game.

An Unwillingness to Set Any Ethnic, Class, or Political Group of Humans on a Pedestal and Make Them Immune from Questioning It's easy, of course, to recognize that white males from North America and Europe (as well as Japanese males) hold a disproportionate share of responsibility for the mess we're in; that upper- and middle-class consumers from the First World take an excessive portion of the world's "resources" and therefore cause greater per capita destruction than do other peoples. But it does not follow that everyone else is blameless.

The Earth First! movement has great affinity with aboriginal groups 15
throughout the world. They are clearly in the most direct and respectful relationship with the natural world. Earth First! should back such tribes in the common struggle whenever possible without compromising our ideals. For example, we are supportive of the Dine (Navajo) of Big Mountain against relocation, but this does not mean we overlook the severe overgrazing by domestic sheep on the Navajo Reservation. We may be supportive of subsistence life-styles by natives in Alaska, but we should not be silent about clear-cutting old-growth forest in southeast Alaska by native corporations, or about the Eskimo Doyon Corporation's push for oil exploration and development in the Arctic National Wildlife Refuge. It is racist either to condemn or to pardon someone based on their ethnic background.

Similarly, we are inconsistent when we castigate Charles Hurwitz for destroying the last wilderness redwood forest, yet feel sympathy for the loggers working for him. Industrial workers, by and large, share the blame for the destruction of the natural world. They may be yoked by the big-money boys, but they are generally willing servants who share the worldview of their bosses that Earth is a smorgasbord of resources for the taking. Sometimes, in fact, it is the sturdy yeoman from the bumpkin proletariat who holds the most violent and destructive attitudes toward the natural world (and toward those who would defend it).[2] Workers are victims of an unjust economic system, but that does not absolve them of what they do. This is not to deny that some woods workers oppose the destruction of ancient forests, that

[2]A case in point involves the spotted owl, a threatened species dependent on ancient forests. These little owls are easily attracted by playing tapes of their call. Loggers in the Northwest are going into old-growth forests with tape recorders and shotguns to exterminate spotted owls. They feel that if they do so, they will eliminate a major reason to stop the logging of these pristine forests. [Author's note]

some may even be Earth First!ers, but merely that it is inappropriate to overlook abuse of the natural world simply because of the rung the perpetrators occupy on the economic ladder.

Some argue that workers are merely struggling to feed their families and are not delighting in destroying the natural world. They say that unless you deal with the needs of loggers to make a living, you can't save the forest. They also claim that loggers are manipulated by their bosses to express anti-wilderness viewpoints. I find this argument to be patronizing to loggers and other workers. When I read comments from timber fellers expressing hatred toward pristine forests and toward conservationists, it is obvious that they willingly buy into the worldview of the lumber barons. San Francisco's *Image Magazine* reports on a letter to the editor written by one logger: "Working people trying to feed their families have little time to be out in the woods acting like children and making things hard for other working people. . . . Anyone out there have a recipe for spotted owl? Food stamps won't go far, I'm afraid. And since they're always being shoved down my throat, I thought I'd like mine fried."[3] Bumper stickers proclaiming "Kill an owl. Save a logger" are rife in the Northwest. I at least respect the logger who glories in felling a giant tree and who hunts spotted owls enough to grant him the mental ability to have his own opinions instead of pretending he is a stupid oaf, manipulated by his bosses and unable to think for himself.

Of course the big timber companies do manipulate their workers with scare tactics about mill closings and wilderness lockups, but many loggers (or cat-skinners, oilfield workers, miners, and the like) simply hate the wild and delight in "civilizing" it. Even educating workers about ecological principles will not necessarily change the attitudes of many; there are basic differences of opinion and values. Conservationists should try to find common ground with loggers and other workers whenever possible, but the sooner we get rid of Marxist views about the noble proletariat, the better.

A Willingness to Let Our Actions Set the Finer Points of Our Philosophy and a Recognition that We Must Act It is possible to debate endlessly the finer points of dogma, to feel that every nuance of something must be explored before one can act. Too often, political movements become mere debating societies where the participants engage in philosophical masturbation and never get down to the vital business at hand. Others argue that you have no right to argue for environmental preservation until you are living a pure, nonimpacting life-style. We will never figure it all out, we will never be able to plan any campaign in complete detail, none of us will ever entirely transcend a polluting life-style — but we can act. We can act with courage, with determination, with love for things wild and free. We can't be perfect, but we can *act*. We are warriors. Earth First! is a warrior society. We have a job to do.

[3]Jane Kay, "Tree Wars," *San Francisco Examiner Image Magazine* (December 17, 1989). [Author's note]

An Acknowledgment that We Must Change Our Personal Life-Styles to Make Them More Harmonious with Natural Diversity We must eschew surplusage. Although to varying degrees we are all captives of our economic system and cannot break entirely free, we must practice what we preach to the best of our ability. Arne Naess, the Norwegian philosopher and originator of the term "deep ecology," points out that we are not able to achieve a true "deep ecology" life-style, but it is the responsibility of each of us to move in that direction. Most of us still need to make a living that involves some level of participation in "the system." Even for activists, there are trade-offs — flying in a jetliner to help hang a banner on the World Bank in Washington, D.C., in order to bring international attention to the plight of tropical rain forests; using a computer to write a book printed on tree pulp that will catalyze people to take action; driving a pickup truck down a forest road to gain access to a proposed timber sale for preventive maintenance. We need to be aware of these trade-offs, and to do our utmost to limit our impact. 20

A Commitment to Maintaining a Sense of Humor and a Joy in Living Most radicals are a dour, holier-than-thou, humorless lot. Earth First!ers strive to be different. We aren't rebelling against the system because we're losing in it. We're fighting for beauty, for life, for joy. We kick up our heels in delight in the wilderness, we smile at a flower and a hummingbird. We laugh. We laugh at our opponents — and, more important, we laugh at ourselves.

An Awareness that We Are Animals Human beings are primates, mammals, vertebrates. EF!ers recognize their animalness; we reject the New Age eco-la-la that says we must transcend our base animal nature and take charge of our evolution in order to become higher, moral beings. We believe we must return to being animal, to glorying in our sweat, hormones, tears, and blood. We struggle against the modern compulsion to become dull, passionless androids. We do not live sanitary, logical lives; we smell, taste, see, hear, and feel Earth; we live with gusto. We *are* Animal.

An Acceptance of Monkeywrenching as a Legitimate Tool for the Preservation of Natural Diversity Not all Earth First!ers monkeywrench, perhaps not even the majority, but we generally accept the idea and practice of monkeywrenching. Look at an EF! T-shirt. The monkeywrench on it is a symbol of resistance, an heir of the *sabot* — the wooden shoe dropped in the gears to stop the machine, from whence comes the word *sabotage.* The mystique and lore of "night work" pervades our tribe, and with it a general acceptance that strategic monkeywrenching is a legitimate tool for defense of the wild.

And Finally: Earth First! Is a Warrior Society In addition to our absolute commitment to and love for this living planet, we are characterized by our willingness to defend Earth's abundance and diversity of life, even if that defense requires sacrifices of comfort, freedom, safety, or, ultimately, our lives. A warrior recognizes that her life is not the most important thing in her life. A warrior recognizes that there is a greater reality outside her life that must be defended. For us in Earth First!, that reality is Earth, the evolutionary process, the millions of other species with which we share this bright sphere in the void of space.

Not everyone can afford to make the commitment of being a warrior. 25
There are many other roles that can — and must — be played in defense of Earth. One may not constantly be able to carry the burden of being a warrior; it may be only a brief period in one's life. There are risks and pitfalls in being a warrior. There may not be applause, there may not be honors and awards from human society. But there is no finer applause for the warrior of the Earth than the call of the loon at dusk or the sigh of wind in the pines.

Later that evening as I looked out over the darkening Grand Canyon, I knew that whatever hardships the future might bring, there was nothing better and more important for me to do than to take an intransigent stand in defense of life, to not compromise, to continue to be a warrior for the Earth. To be a warrior for the Earth regardless of the consequences.

Engaging the Text

1. How does biocentrism or deep ecology differ from other approaches to the environment? Why does Foreman reject less radical forms of environmentalism?
2. What is monkeywrenching? Under what circumstances, if any, do you think it is justified? Are some forms of monkeywrenching (i.e., damaging property, but not animals or humans) more acceptable than others? Why or why not?
3. Debate the following assertions made by Foreman:
   - An individual human life has no more intrinsic value than does an individual grizzly bear life. (para. 4)
   - Such apparent enemies as "disease" (e.g., malaria) and "pests" (e.g., mosquitoes) . . . [are] vital and necessary components of a complex and vibrant biosphere. (para. 5)
   - Life in a hunter-gatherer society was on the whole healthier, happier, and more secure than our lives today as peasants, industrial workers, or business executives. (para. 9)
   - We can become more cognizant of ultimate truths by sitting quietly in the wild than by studying in a library. (para. 10)
   - Industrial workers . . . are generally willing servants who share the worldview of their bosses that Earth is a smorgasbord of resources for the taking. (para. 16)
   - We must return to being animal, to glorying in our sweat, hormones, tears, and blood. (para. 22)

   Which of these statements, if any, do you find extreme or indefensible, and why?
4. Foreman argues that extremism is necessary, because "the American system is very effective at co-opting and moderating dissidents by giving them attention

and then encouraging them to be 'reasonable' so their ideas will be taken seriously" (para. 12). Do you agree? What kinds of evidence would you need to consider in order to determine the truth or falsehood of this statement?

Exploring Connections

5. Which of Foreman's attitudes toward humans, animals, and the earth would John (Fire) Lame Deer (p. 591) find compatible with his own? Which might he take issue with, and why?
6. Could the narrator of Leslie Marmon Silko's "Storyteller" (p. 599) be considered an eco-warrior? Why or why not?
7. What values and attitudes are being criticized in the cartoon on page 634? If the cartoonist's view is right, what obstacles stand in the way of putting the earth first?

Extending the Critical Context

8. Apply Foreman's principles to one or more environmental issues currently being debated in your community or state. What actions or positions are being considered? What actions or positions would Foreman support? Debate the merits of these options in class.
9. Foreman insists that "we must change our personal life-styles to make them more harmonious with natural diversity" (para. 20). Do a personal inventory to evaluate the impact of your life-style on the environment. During the course of a typical day:
   - What products and resources do you use (water, food, clothing, toothpaste, books, furniture, etc.), and what does it take to produce and transport these to you?
   - How much energy do you consume (by using lights, heat, cars, appliances, battery-powered gadgets, etc.), and what is required to produce it?
   - How much waste do you produce (product wrappers, junk mail, food scraps, paper tissues and towels, sewage, soapy water, etc.), and how is it disposed of?

   Compare notes with classmates and discuss which aspects of your life-styles would be easiest to change, which would be most difficult, and why.

The Eco-Fringe: Deep Ecology

Joni Seager

Readers who find the previous essay by Dave Foreman annoying will find plenty of moral support here. Joni Seager takes Foreman, Earth First!, and the deep ecology movement to task for everything from misanthropy to mixed metaphors. Are her criticisms just? You be the judge. Seager (b. 1954) teaches geography and women's studies at the University of Vermont. She has written for the Village Voice *and the* Women's Review of Books, *and during the Gulf War was a frequent commentator on environmental issues for CNN, NPR, and the BBC. Her books include* Embryos, Ethics, and Women's Rights: Exploring the New Reproductive Technologies *(1988);* The State of the Earth Atlas *(ed., 1990); and* Earth Follies: Coming to Feminist Terms with the Global Environmental Crisis *(1993), from which this selection was taken.*

For a hopeful moment in the mid-1980s, an environmental wave sweeping Europe and North America seemed to offer a new vision and a *counter-culture,* in the fullest sense of that word: "deep ecology" was an appealing, puzzling, and exotic environmental movement. Deep ecology was the pin set to burst the bubble of environmental hubris on which we build our human privilege. Its philosophers demanded that we ask probing questions of ourselves, of the nature of "being." Deep ecology represents an environmental *philosophy,* but at the same time it was a philosophy that actually spawned an activist wing with a distinct identity—deep ecology was not just an ideology, it was also a practice. The principles of deep ecology seemed

to offer a challenge to patriarchal attitudes toward nature; its practice suggested a potential challenge to patriarchal methods of environmental organizing. Deep ecology offered hope and a refreshing vision to people who were concerned about the environment but who were disillusioned with the bureaucratic, reformist, and presumably co-opted mainstream environmental groups.

The term "deep ecology" was coined in the early 1970s by a Norwegian philosopher, Arne Naess. Naess articulated an ecological approach that posed "deeper" questions about life on earth than mainstream environmentalists allowed themselves to ask.[1] The deep ecology he articulated was rooted in recasting the religious and philosophical interpretation of human relations with the natural world, starting with the necessity of shifting from human-centrism into biocentrism, a commitment to revaluing humanity's oneness with nature, and an appreciation of the intrinsic worth of all life forms.

Working from Naess's starting point, American deep ecologists in the 1980s elaborated an eight-point manifesto of "basic principles," among the most important of which are these: a reification of "biocentrism," which is a philosophy that nonhuman Life on Earth (capitals in original) has intrinsic value *in itself* independent of its usefulness to humans; that humans are too numerous and that a "substantial decrease" in human populations is required for the well-being of the earth; that humans must change their basic economic, technological, and ideological structures; and that everyone who subscribes to deep ecology has an obligation to try to implement these necessary changes.[2] The imperative to take direct action in defense of the earth is central to the philosophy of deep ecology. In the U.S., a loosely structured national group (with international affiliates) called "Earth First!" emerged as the organizational vehicle for translating the broad philosophical principles of deep ecology into an operational environmentalism. Although Earth First! disbanded in 1990, several EF! splinter groups remain in place as the organizational foci for the deep ecology philosophy.

Deep ecology is a big tent, under which many environmentalists gather — many of whom may disagree with one another on specific tactics or campaigns, but all of whom would broadly ascribe to the basic principles outlined above. As a Western environmental movement, deep ecology is also characterized by a distinctive tone and a particular set of associations:

[1] Arne Naess, "The Shallow and the Deep, Long-Range Ecology Movement: A Summary," *Inquiry*, Vol. 16, 1973. [Author's note]

[2] Bill Devall & George Sessions, *Deep Ecology: Living as If Nature Mattered* (Salt Lake City, UT: Peregrine Smith Books, 1985). Readers interested in exploring the literature of deep ecology might also read Rik Scarce, *Eco-Warriors: Understanding the Radical Environmental Movement* (Chicago: Noble Press, 1990); George Bradford, *How Deep Is Deep Ecology?* (Ojai, CA: Times Change Press, 1989); Michael Tobias, ed., *Deep Ecology* (San Marcos, CA: Avant Books, 1988; 2nd. revised printing); John Davis & Dave Foreman, eds., *The Earth First Reader* (Salt Lake City, Utah: Peregrine Smith Books, 1991). [Author's note]

- Deep ecology environmentalism is suffused with a ritualized vision of the Earth as Mother, and of the earth as an independent, self-regulating female organism.[3]
- Many deep ecologists celebrate an earth-centered "paganism"—the editions of the American deep ecology newspaper, *Earth First!*, for example, were designated by the names of Pagan holidays ("Brigid" for February, "Eostar" for March, etc.).
- Many Earth Firsters consider themselves a "tribe," and many of the American deep ecologists posit an affinity with indigenous, Native American ecological sensibilities.
- At heart, deep ecology is concerned with the preservation and protection of wilderness. Deep ecologists revere undisturbed wilderness as the pinnacle ecological state. Their militant defense of "Mother Earth" is rooted in an unflinching opposition to human attacks on wilderness. To the committed Earth Firster, the preservation of wilderness takes precedence over all human need.

5 Earth Firsters quickly established a high profile among environmentalists as guerilla-theater, lay-your-body-on-the-line afficionados. In Australia, Earth First! protesters buried themselves up to their necks in the sand in the middle of logging roads to stop lumbering operations; in the American Southwest, Earth Firsters handcuffed themselves to trees and bulldozers to prevent logging; in California, they dressed in dolphin and mermaid costumes to picket the stockholders' meeting of a tuna-fishing company. Earth First! actions were often choreographed with a beguiling sense of humor, and carried out with daring and panache—their most endearing and environmentally useful characteristics.

Deep ecology is not confined by a single script. It is meant to be defined through its actions as well as its philosophy.[4] If, then, the measure of deep ecology is to be taken in the actions of Earth First!-style environmentalists, the conclusions are troubling. Deep ecology, in practice, has been transformed into a paramilitary, direct action ecology force. Some of the tactics employed by Canadian, Australian, and American Earth First! contingents are questionable: for example, pouring graphite (or sand or sugar) into the fuel tanks of bulldozers and road-clearing equipment involved in logging and mining operations to seize the engines; or, more controversially, tree-spiking, a practice of hammering long nails into trees to "booby-trap" them (spiked trees are dangerous to cut, and most loggers won't work a forest that has been spiked.) While many Earth First! groups renounced the use of destructive tactics, others embraced a "no compromise" environmental fundamentalism.

The *practice* of deep ecology, as it defined itself over the decade of the

[3]This notion is loosely based on James Lovelock's "Gaia hypothesis." [Author's note]

[4]John Davis & Dave Foreman, eds., *The Earth First Reader* (Salt Lake City, Utah: Peregrine Smith Books, 1991). [Author's note]

1980s, suggests a peculiar mix of influences and archetypes — almost equal parts of survivalist paranoia, frontiersman bravado, anarchist politics, and New Age spiritual sensibility. With this profile, many observers have been tempted to dismiss deep ecology as the "lunatic fringe" of modern environmentalism — but it is a movement not to be easily dismissed. Deep ecology has become an important player on the American (and to a lesser extent, the European) environmentalist scene — because deep ecologists present themselves as the only viable alternative to mainstream environmentalism, because their direct action tactics have attracted considerable media attention, and because the controversy they engender has opened fractures in the American ecology community. They have achieved some measure of success. They have spun off fifty mostly autonomous Earth First! groups across the United States and overseas, created an international network of rain-forest activists, and have successfully halted or forestalled a number of ecologically irresponsible projects. As one observer notes, "The mainstream environmental groups have been caught running in place trying to regain the publicity and the place in the public imagination that Earth First! has seized from them. More respectable wilderness activists and ecologists . . . have been able to take much stronger positions than before as a result of Earth First!'s uncompromising presence. . . ."[5]

Further, deep ecology, at first blush, appears to offer a philosophy that speaks to feminist values. The call by deep ecologists for a major overhaul of the political, economic, and ideological system is a necessity that feminists have been arguing for years. Deep ecologists speak of the interconnectedness of life, a reverence for nature, a nonexploitative relationship with wilderness, a valuing of intuition over rational, "anthropocentric" linear thought — all essentially women-identified ideas.

Deep ecology is virtually the only wing of the environmental movement to make specific overtures to women in general and to feminists in particular. In the abstract, if not in the practice, deep ecologists are astute enough to recognize that it is not possible in the 1990s to make credible claims of a "radical" agenda without some nod to feminist analysis. A number of male deep ecologists argue that the philosophy and theory of deep ecology is in sympathetic harmony with feminism. Others, too, assume an affinity: Kirkpatrick Sale, a noted bioregionalist, for example, referred to deep ecology as "that form of environmentalism that comes closest to embodying a feminist sensibility," continuing by saying "I don't see anything in the formulation of deep ecology that contravenes the values of feminism or puts forward the values of patriarchy.[6]

[5]Brian Tokar, "Exploring the New Ecologies: Social Ecology, Deep Ecology and the Future of Green Political Thought," *Alternatives*, Vol. 15, No. 4, 1988. (*Alternatives* is an environmental magazine published from the University of Waterloo, Ontario). This article also appeared as "Ecological Radicalism," *Z Magazine* (Boston), 1988. [Author's note]

[6]Quoted in Janet Biehl, "Ecofeminism and Deep Ecology: Unresolvable Conflict?," *Green Perspectives*, 3. [Author's note]

Deep Machismo

One commentator, musing on deep ecology, noted, “Freely mixing 10 pseudo-scholarly tomes and spit-in-the-can barroom philosophy, there is something in Earth First! to offend just about anyone.[7] To this assessment, I would only add that women have been especially offended. Despite its surface overtures to feminists, the transformation of deep ecology into an environmental force has been characterized by deeply misogynistic proclivities. Macho rhetoric of the most conventional and offensive sort riddles the written record of deep ecologists. Their common practice of using women-identified terms as taunts, such as calling their critics “wimps,” “sops,” or “effetes,” panders to a blatant sexist and homophobic bias — as though the worst thing in the world is to be womanly! Edward Abbey, the recently deceased guru of the American Earth First! movement, nurtured a reputation as a crusty, take-no-guff curmudgeon — and as a misogynist. For instance, in a rebuff to Murray Bookchin, a critic of deep ecology, Abbey reveled in a well-worn combination of sexist stereotypes:

> And he [Bookchin] needn't worry that I will attack him . . . Fat old women like Murray Bookchin have nothing to fear from me. (What? “Fat old women?” Did I say that? Am I not only a fascist, a racist, a cultural chauvinist, but — God forbid — a male sexist pig as well?)[8]

Deep ecology is saturated with male bravado and macho posturing. The American Earth First! movement is particularly symptomatic of the masculinist ethos that suffused representations of deep ecology's philosophy. With very few exceptions, the self-styled leaders and spokespeople of Earth First! were all men, as was a considerable proportion of its membership (in contrast with all other environmental groups). Nonetheless, the sex ratio of Earth First! membership varies considerably among local affiliates and some local groups even have higher numbers of women than men. It is clear that Earth First! is attractive to women who want to participate in environmental change; it is not clear how feminist women within Earth First! reconcile their involvement with the deeply misogynistic face of the national and international branches of the movement. One feminist Earth Firster recently mused about the struggle to “feminize” Earth First!:

> I see no contradiction between deep ecology and ecofeminism, but Earth First! was founded by five men, and its principal spokespeople have all been male. As in all such groups, there have always been competent women behind the scenes. But they have been virtually invisible behind the public Earth First! persona of “big man goes into big wilderness to save big trees.” I certainly objected to this. Yet despite the image, the structure of Earth

[7] Brian Tokar, “Exploring the New Ecologies.” [Author's note]

[8] Correspondence from Edward Abbey in *Utne Reader*, March/April 1988, p. 7. [Author's note]

First! was decentralized and non-hierarchical, so we could develop any way we wanted.[9]

Moreover, Earth Firsters are not just men; they are "men's men." Dave Foreman, one of the founders of the American Earth First! movement, represented the tone and tenor of the group when he said that, "I see Earth First! as a warrior society."[10] The leaders of Earth First! reveled in an image of themselves as beer-swilling, ass-kicking, "dumb-cowboy rednecks" coming to the rescue of a helpless female—in this case, Mother Earth. Throughout most of the 1980s, the logo of the U.S. organization was a clenched fist encircled by the motto "No Compromise in Defense of Mother Earth"—a bewildering mixed metaphor if ever there was one.

American Earth Firsters often relied on antifeminist women as spokespersons for "the woman's" point of view (a tactic widely employed by other mostly male organizations, such as militaries and multinational corporations), to undercut feminist criticism. A 1989 article in *Earth First!* by a prominent Earth First! woman, for example, was a lengthy piece entitled "No, I'm Not an Eco-Feminist: A Few Words in Defense of Men," in which the author launched an attack on women, including such muddled nonsequiturs as "It's all over if men become feminists. Mothers and their children, alone, do not make a human society," and an even more bizarre rationalization for excluding women from decision-making roles:[11]

> In many tribes, a woman of childbearing age is excluded from the decision-making body; but when she has passed child bearing, she becomes the wise old woman. . . . There is good reason for this age differentiation. Many women are paranoid for two years after the birth of each child. . . . Such a person cannot make valid decisions for a group; but once this child-making period is over, such a person is a truly wise decision-maker. This [exclusion] is age-specific, not strictly sex-specific.

While deep ecologists represent themselves as forging a radical new relationship with nature, they give no credit to the women who broke this path for them. Deep ecologists speak reverently of rediscovering intuition in relating to nature; of breaking through the barriers of hierarchical thinking; of the necessity of viewing life on earth as an unbroken continuum; of celebrating the interwoven connectedness of us all—sensibilities that have been scorned by men for years as female-identified traits. But deep ecologists (mostly men) never say that. They exult as though they are the first to discover this cooperative, noninvasive, and holistic life philosophy. Sharon

[9]Judi Bari, "The Feminization of Earth First!" *Ms.*, May/June 1992. [Author's note]

[10]Quoted in Jim Robbins, "The Environmental Guerrillas," *Boston Globe Magazine*, March 27, 1988. [Author's note]

[11]Dolores LaChapelle, "No I'm Not an Ecofeminist: A Few Words in Defense of Men," *Earth First!* March 21, 1989. LaChapelle frequently is cast in the role of "token woman" for the deep ecology movement. She is the only woman, for example, included in a twenty-two-author anthology, edited by Michael Tobias, *Deep Ecology*. [Author's note]

Doubiago is one of a number of commentators who has taken the deep ecologists to task for this "oversight," in an uncompromising essay, "Mama Coyote Talks to the Boys":

> The deep ecology movement is shockingly sexist. Shocking because deep ecology consciousness is feminist consciousness. . . . But nowhere is this acknowledgment made. Instead, papers, books, and repeated efforts are made to establish a tradition to show the similarity of deep ecology consciousness with "intuitionists, mystics, and transcendentalists," with "the New Physicists," with Buddhism and traditional American Indian philosophies toward nature — all fields of study which are exotic, removed, and masculine.[12]

Moreover, the invocation of "native ways of being," which *is* acknowl- 15
edged as a source of inspiration, is distressingly shallow, often coming down to little more substance than a sentimentalized mythologizing of the "noble savage" — a view that can, and does, easily slip over into racist assumptions and simplistic misrepresentations of a complex culture to which few white Americans can really claim access.

Disregarding Difference

Despite their putative tilt toward feminism, deep ecologists are unwilling to include gender analysis in their analytical tool kit. Deconstructing and then *re*-constructing the human relationship to nature is absolutely central to deep ecology environmentalism. Yet, most deep ecologists are not interested in the social construction of attitudes toward nature, nor are they curious about the divergence in Western history (if not universally) of male and female attitudes toward wilderness and nature. Thus while there is an explicit criticism of destructive cultural attitudes toward nature, there is no apparent curiosity about the extent to which those "cultural" attitudes may be gender, race, or class specific.

And yet there is, now, a rich literature that explores the cultural and gender differences in human relationships to wilderness. Highly respected (and widely available) research by Annette Kolodny, for example, blazes a trail for gender-specific landscape/wilderness study.[13] Kolodny rewrites the history of the American frontier, establishing that images of "conquering the wilderness," "taming nature," "mastering the wild," and the like — images that North Americans take to be the standard fare of the European encounter with new lands, and images that continue to be the standard fare of popular culture — were, in fact, *male* fantasies and *male* imagery, and were

[12]Sharon Doubiago, "Mama Coyote Talks to the Boys," in Judith Plant, ed., *Healing the Wounds: The Promise of Ecofeminism* (Philadelphia, PA: New Society Publishers, 1989). [Author's note]

[13]Annette Kolodny, *The Lay of the Land* (Chapel Hill: University of North Carolina Press, 1975) and *The Land Before Her* (Chapel Hill: University of North Carolina Press, 1984). [Author's note]

not shared by their women counterparts in the wilderness. A recent study of women's attitudes toward nature and landscape in the American Southwest reinforces the argument made by Kolodny that, whereas European men saw the American West as a virgin land, ready to be raped and exploited, women typically regarded the landscape as "masterless." Rather than seeking conflict with the wilderness, women sought accommodation and reciprocity.[14] The conventional wisdom about the American wilderness experience is that "for most of their history, Americans [of European extraction] regarded the wilderness as a moral and physical wasteland, suitable only for conquest";[15]Kolodny's persuasive reply is that massive exploitation and alteration of the continent do not seem to have been part of women's fantasies.

Deep ecologists are attempting to reconfigure our contemporary ecological sensibilities by refuting this exploitative ethic of wilderness. But *whose* ethic needs reconstruction? It surely is important to understand that this exploitative ethic is neither universal nor shared across the cultural spectrum — if it can be generalized as the predominant ethic of any group at all (and this seems unlikely), it is only of white Euro-American men. But deep ecologists are not curious about the social construction of our contemporary environmental ethic, and beyond offering simplistic paeans about "women being closer to nature," they are certainly not interested in its gender construction. Men and women are painted with the same broad stroke, and are equally indicted by deep ecologists for "anthropocentric" attitudes to nature. This is one of the major points of departure between feminists and deep ecologists.[16]

The generalizations of deep ecologists blur distinctions not only of gender, but of race, class, and nationality too. Many deep ecologists portray the human race, as one species, as a sort of "cancer" on the earth that has devoured its resources, destroyed its wildlife, and endangered the biosphere. This sweeping misanthropy lacks social perspective — it is analytically unsound to make no distinction among peoples, nations, or cultures in assigning accountability for ecological destruction. Humanity is not an undifferentiated whole, and it is not credible to lay equal "blame" for environmental degradation on elites and minorities, women and men, the Third World and

[14]Vera Norwood & Janice Monk, eds., *The Desert Is No Lady: Southwestern Landscapes in Women's Writing and Art* (New Haven: Yale University Press, 1987). [Author's note]

[15]A quote from noted American historian Roderick Nash, *Wilderness and the American Mind* (New Haven: Yale University Press, 1967). Nash's book continues to be used as the standard source for understanding the American encounter with wilderness. Nash himself now appears to acknowledge the androcentric bias in his earlier work (see, for example, his article "Rounding Out the American Revolution," in the Michael Tobias anthology cited above), but he does not revise his basic presumptions about the nature of the American wilderness experience. [Author's note]

[16]See, for example, Janet Biehl, "Ecofeminism and Deep Ecology"; Murray Bookchin, "Social Ecology versus Deep Ecology," *Socialist Review*, 88/3, 1988; and Ynestra King, "Coming of Age with the Greens," *Z Magazine*, February 1988. [Author's note]

the First, the poor and the rich, the colonized and the colonizers.[17] Nonetheless, many American deep ecologists are insistent on this point. Dave Foreman, the U.S. Earth First! founder, explains the disinterest in social analysis: "We are not opposed to campaigns for social and economic justice. We are generally supportive of such causes. But Earth First! has from the beginning been a wilderness preservation group, not a class-struggle group."[18] Paul Watson, a well-known American ecoiconoclast, casts Foreman's sentiments in stronger language: "My heart does not bleed for the third world. My energies point toward saving one world, the planet Earth, which is being plundered by one species, the human primate. . . . All human political systems developed to date, be they right or left, are anthropocentric in philosophy and support the exploitation of the Earth."[19] In his germinal article, Arne Naess, the "father" of deep ecology, expressed concerns about inequalities within and between nations. But his concern with social cleavages and their impact on resource utilization patterns and ecological destruction appears to have gotten lost in the translation, because it is all but invisible in the later writings of deep ecologists.[20]

20 Even taking the deep ecology agenda as given, a number of critics point out that "class struggle" is inextricable from the struggle to preserve wilderness. An Indian environmentalist points out, for example, that the emphasis on wilderness preservation can be positively harmful when applied to the Third World: "Because India is a long settled and densely populated country in which agrarian populations have a finely balanced relationship with nature, the setting aside of wilderness areas has resulted in a direct transfer of resources from the poor to the rich.[21] The dilemma of wilderness vs. people is not an issue solely in the Third World (although it is in poor countries that the competing demands for land are often in sharpest relief). But wilderness advocates must at least come to terms with the analysis that suggests that efforts to protect wilderness in the Third World, particularly as they are orchestrated by Western environmentalists, may be received in those countries as just another example of imperialism, the same imperialism that pushes the poor and others into the wilderness in the first place.[22]

[17] A point made by Ynestra King, quoted in "Social Ecology vs. Deep Ecology," *Utne Reader,* Nov/Dec. 1988, p. 135. [Author's note]

[18] Dave Foreman & Nancy Morton, "Good Luck, Darlin', It's Been Great," in John Davis & Dave Foreman, eds., *The Earth First Reader.* [Author's note]

[19] Paul Watson in *Earth First!,* December 22, 1987, p. 20. [Author's note]

[20] Ramachandra Guha, "Radical American Environmentalism and Wilderness Preservation: A Third World Critique," *Environmental Ethics,* Vol. 11, Spring 1989, p. 72. [Author's note]

[21] Ibid., p. 75. [Author's note]

[22] David Johns, "The Relevance of Deep Ecology to the Third World: Some Preliminary Comments," *Environmental Ethics,* Vol. 12, Fall 1990, p. 238. [Author's note]

The "Population Problem"

It is their stance on population, "overpopulation," and overpopulation "solutions" that has most alienated women and short-circuited an intellectual alliance between feminists and deep ecologists. A deep belief of deep ecology is that there are "too many people" on the planet. "Substantial" and fast *reductions* in the human population (not just a stabilization of population growth rates), deep ecologists say, are essential for the survival of the earth.[23] Some deep ecologists have tried to put actual figures to these reductions— Arne Naess, for example, proposed that for the health of the planet, "we should have no more than 100 million people";[24] an Earth First! writer using the pseudonym "Miss Ann Thropy" suggested that the U.S. population would have to decline to 50 million.[25] (Given that the current population of the earth is just over 5 billion, and of the United States almost 300 million, it is clear that the reductions called for by deep ecologists are drastic and would require catastrophic action to implement.) Other deep ecologists have proposed a 90 percent reduction in human populations to allow a restoration of pristine environments, while still others have argued forcefully that a large portion of the globe must be immediately cordoned off from human beings.[26]

The logistics of achieving such population reductions don't daunt deep ecologists. Deep ecology spokespeople have proposed a number of solutions to the "population problem"—"solutions" that range along a short spectrum from tame, vague, and muddled at one end to racist, sexist, and brutish at the other end. At the tame end, some deep ecologists have issued vague calls for widespread birth control programs — which is neither new, nor radical, nor much different from the population policies of most mainstream environmental groups. There is no evidence of the much-vaunted feminist sensibility in the discussion of deep ecology population programs: women are once again rendered invisible, there is no linkage made between "population policies" and the daily lives of women around the world, nor is there any discussion or even acknowledgment of the fact that birth control policies inevitably bear disproportionately on Third World women. There is also no consciousness that, in issuing this call for population control, deep ecologists

[23]This call for severe population reductions has, surprisingly, recently been taken up by some representatives of the UK Green Party. A conference paper at the 1989 annual conference proposed a reduction of the population of the UK to "between 30 and 40 million." These population reductions, it was proposed, could be achieved through public education (to reverse attitudes that portray childless people as unfulfilled, for example) and through family planning. Victor Smart, "Greens Aim to Halve Population," *The Observer* (London), Sept. 17, 1989. [Author's note]

[24]Quoted in Bill Devall & George Sessions, *Deep Ecology*, p. 76. [Author's note]

[25]Miss Ann Thropy, "Population and AIDS," *Earth First!*, May 1, 1987. [Author's note]

[26]Ramachandra Guha, "Radical American Environmentalism," p. 72. [Author's note]

are preaching the same gospel as other men before them: that controlling female reproduction by technical means will solve the problems of "nature." Despite these "oversights" in the ideology of deep ecology population control, the call for birth control is not what has roused so much controversy.

Many of the other population solutions proposed by deep ecologists are not so benign. David Foreman, the Earth First! founder, proposes reducing the human population by halting life-saving medical interventions and aid for famine and disaster victims around the world. Speaking of the famines in Ethiopia, Foreman said, "The worst thing we could do in Ethiopia is to give aid. The best thing would be to just let nature seek its own balance, to let people there just starve.[27] This is an unconscionable and arrogant argument for a well-fed American to make, and is also based on the false premise that the famines in Ethiopia are somehow "natural." Mass starvation in Ethiopia derives not from a natural proclivity to famine, but from years of internal warfare, military spending bloated at the expense of social and environmental programs, corrupt governance, and regional environmental degradation.[28]

Edward Abbey, the guiding light of the American Earth First! movement, set off another firestorm of controversy by linking environmental population pressures with immigration policy. In the mid-1980s, Abbey started off by advocating that the United States close its borders to Central American and Latin American immigrants, and went on from there with an escalating racism that was only thinly wrapped in a concern for the environment. In a 1986 letter to *The Bloomsbury Review,* Abbey wrote:

> In fact, the immigration matter really *is* a matter of "we" versus "they" or "us" versus "them." What else can it be? There are many good reasons, any one sufficient, to call a halt to further immigration (whether legal or illegal) into the United States. One seldom mentioned, however, is cultural: the United States that we live in today, with its traditions and ideals, however imperfectly realized, is a product of northern European civilization. If we allow our country — *our* country — to become Latinized, in whole or in part, we shall see it tend toward a culture more like that of Mexico. In other words, we will be forced to accept a more rigid class system, a patron style of politics, less democracy and more oligarchy, a fear and hatred of the natural world, a densely overpopulated land base, a less efficient and far

[27] Quoted in Chris Reed, "Wild Men of the Woods," *The Independent* (UK), July 14, 1988. Similar sentiments were expressed in an article by Tom Stoddard, "On Death," and an accompanying editorial in *Earth First!*, February 6, 1986. [Author's note]

[28] For example, the Brundtland Commission on the Environment estimated that the Ethiopian government could have reversed the advance of desertification threatening its food supplies in the mid-1970s by spending no more than about $50 million a year to plant trees and fight soil erosion. Instead, the government in Addis Ababa pumped $275 million a year into its military machine between 1975 and 1985 to fight secessionist movements in Eritrea and Tigre. Figures cited in Michael Renner, "What's Sacrificed When We Arm," *World Watch Magazine*, Vol. 25, September/October 1989. [Author's note]

> more corrupt economy, and a greater reliance on crime and violence as normal instruments of social change.[29]

Abbey's racist remarks were never repudiated by Earth First!, and were celebrated and repeated by many.[30] Some Earth Firsters argued that allowing Central Americans to use the "overflow valve" of fleeing to the United States has two consequences: (a) it increases the U.S. population, and (b) it allows Central American governments to continue their irresponsible ways. Once again, there is no discussion of social context or historical reality: if people are fleeing Central America in increasing numbers, it is in some measure because large parts of the region have been rendered all but uninhabitable by U.S.-backed large landowners mismanaging the land and by U.S.-backed military destruction. Nor is there discussion of the century of U.S. intervention in and manipulation of the governments and economies of virtually every Central American country.

25 Racism lurks just beneath the surface of most discussions of "the population problem" in the deep ecology literature, and sometimes doesn't even lurk. Unfortunately, most deep ecologists have not taken on the issue of racism seriously, and instead of considering the issue anew, the anti-immigrant, and in particular anti-Hispanic, sentiment has been given considerable visibility in Earth First! literature.

By far the most controversial issue forwarded by a few deep ecologists was the suggestion that AIDS may be an environmental blessing in disguise. Because it has the potential to wipe out vast numbers of people worldwide, some deep ecologists suggest that AIDS will benefit the planet in the long run, and further, that it might be a disease "intentionally" introduced to lessen the human strain on the Earth's ecosystem. In a number of articles in 1987, writers in *Earth First!* put forward this amazing proposal, rousing an acrid cloud of controversy that has yet to disperse.[31]

> Barring a cure, the possible benefits of this [the AIDS epidemic] to the environment are staggering. If, like the Black Death in Europe, AIDS affected one-third of the world's population, it would cause an immediate respite for endangered wildlife on every continent.[32]

[29]Quoted in George Bradford, *How Deep Is Deep Ecology?* (Ojai, CA: Times Change Press, 1989, p. 32). [Author's note]

[30]See again, Tom Stoddard, *Earth First!,* February 1986; see also Miss Ann Thropy, "Overpopulation and Industrialism," originally published in *Earth First!,* 1987, reprinted in John Davis & Dave Foreman, eds. *The Earth First Reader.* [Author's note]

[31]The original essay putting forward this idea is Miss Ann Thropy, "Population and AIDS," *Earth First!,* May 1, 1987, p. 32. This was followed by a deluge of letters to the journal, and a very long article expanding the original argument by Daniel Conner, "Is AIDS the Answer to an Environmentalist's Prayer?" *Earth First!,* December 22, 1987. The question was picked up in the progressive press, where it has been circulating since. See, for example, Brad Edmondson, "Is AIDS Good for the Earth?" *Utne Reader,* Nov./Dec. 1987, and letters to *Utne Reader* on this topic for the following three years. [Author's note]

[32]Miss Ann Thropy, "Population and AIDS," p. 32. [Author's note]

The proponents of this view base their argument on linked assumptions, starting with a consideration of the disease itself. AIDS, they say, has particular and unusual characteristics that distinguish it from other infectious diseases, such as its long incubation period during which it cannot be detected, its ability to mutate, and its durability. The authors of the AIDS argument then link this with a discussion of the Gaia hypothesis.[33] If the earth is a self-regulating organism, they argue, then Gaia (the earth) might act like other living organisms that are capable of defending themselves against biological invasions. If humans have stressed the earth's biosystems to the breaking point, then Gaia might strike back with a deadly disease that reduces the human burden "she" carries. AIDS, they say, has the characteristics of a "designer" disease, and Gaia herself may be its designer. In the original article, Miss Ann Thropy expressed only glancing concern for those stricken with the disease: "None of this is intended to disregard or discount the suffering of AIDS victims. But one way or another, there will be victims of overpopulation. . . . To paraphrase Voltaire: if the AIDS epidemic didn't exist, radical environmentalists would have to invent one."

On Deep Being and Nothingness

There is a further profound philosophical rift between deep ecology and feminism. Deep ecology is premised on the necessity of breaking down barriers between human and nonhuman species. Deep ecologists exhort us to cultivate an ecological consciousness of total connectedness — to subsume our sense of self to a greater sense of oneness with all things, both sentient and insentient, around us.

For centuries women have been told that they have no singular identity. Women have always been subsumed by culture and by men, and denied independent existence. Selflessness, unbounded oneness, total connectedness, and denial of independent identity have been central to women's oppression. So, while it sounds ecologically ennobling to "think like a mountain,"[34] the male deep ecologist theorists who are promoting this notion refuse to acknowledge this historical and social context within which they are telling women to merge identities with the earth: they ask women, in effect, to once again embrace nonbeing.

It seems unpleasantly coincidental that at this historical moment, just as women and other oppressed groups are coming into self-subjectivity, deep

[33]A theory developed over the past twenty years by a British atmospheric scientist, James Lovelock, and an American microbiologist, Lynn Margulis, that the earth itself is akin to a single, living organism in that it has self-regulation capabilities and is self-monitoring. The Gaia hypothesis, initially discounted, is now enjoying a serious resurgence. Neither Lovelock nor Margulis have publically commented on the AIDS/Gaia link proposed by deep ecologists, but it is a proposal that distorts the original Gaia hypothesis. [Author's note]

[34]A term coined in the 1940s by an American naturalist, Aldo Leopold, and adopted by deep ecologists. A current shorthand for a sense of "oneness with nature." [Author's note]

ecologists are telling us that such self-presence and self-awareness are to be condemned.[35] The sublimation of identity urged by deep ecologists parallels in many ways the "relativism" of postmodernism — a trendy intellectual stance that has come under considerable criticism from feminist philosophers. Sandra Harding, for example, notes that "relativism appears as an intellectual possibility . . . for the dominating group at the point where the universality of their views is being challenged. Relativism is fundamentally a sexist response. . . ."[36] The revolutionary heart of the feminist movement is rescuing women from obscurity, acknowledging women as fully-embodied and well-defined beings in historical and contemporary culture, empowering women to develop a strong sense of self, to embrace their selfhood, to develop a self-conscious subjectivity. If anyone needs practice at selflessness, it is not women.[37]

Lost Promises

While deep ecologists have galvanized a renewed sense of environmen- 30
tal urgency and agency, the movement falls short of its claims as a radical challenge to the environmental status quo. With its macho-redneck style, its woman-hating rhetoric, its bordering-on-racism political stances, and its misanthropic bias, deep ecology is at the same time tediously old hat and frighteningly new. Ultimately, deep ecology represents an unfulfilled promise and a lost opportunity for women and men who were genuinely interested in transforming their relationship with the external world. Once again, it is male posturing that has poisoned an apparently promising coalition of feminist analysis and environmental philosophy.

[35] Nancy Hartsock was one of the earliest commentators to make this point in "Rethinking Modernism," *Cultural Critique*, Vol. 7, Fall 1987; and Janet Biehl, "Ecofeminism and Deep Ecology." [Author's note]

[36] On feminist critiques of postmodernism and of the relativism argument, see Frances Mascia-Lees, Patricia Sharpe, and Colleen Ballerino Cohen, "The Postmodernist Turn in Anthropology: Cautions from a Feminist Perspective," *Signs: Journal of Women in Culture & Society*, Vol. 15, No. 1, 1989; and Sandra Harding, "Introduction: Is There a Feminist Method?" in Sandra Harding, ed., *Feminism and Methodology* (Bloomington: Indiana University Press, 1987). [Author's note]

[37] Janet Biehl, "Ecofeminism and Deep Ecology." [Author's note]

Engaging the Text

1. Make a complete list of Seager's criticisms of deep ecology. Which of these, in your view, are the most serious or damaging, and why?
2. What problems or oversights in the environmental movement did deep ecology initially seem to address? What aspects of the movement does Seager still find attractive, and why?
3. Seager faults deep ecology for ignoring "distinctions not only of gender, but of race, class, and nationality too" (para. 19). Do you agree with her that

such distinctions are crucial to the analysis of environmental issues? Why or why not?

4. If all of Seager's criticisms of deep ecology are accurate and fair, is the idea of putting the earth first foolish or unworkable? What kinds of environmental activism does Seager appear to endorse?

Exploring Connections

5. How many of the problems Seager identifies with deep ecology are evident in the essay by Dave Foreman (p. 625)? What problems might Foreman point out in Seager's argument? Roleplay a debate between Seager and Foreman; then write a journal entry detailing your own responses to deep ecology.
6. Michael Kimmel (p. 258) summarizes the "four traditional rules of American manhood" as follows: "(1) No Sissy Stuff . . . (2) Be a Big Wheel . . . (3) Be a Sturdy Oak . . . (4) Give 'em Hell. . . ." Taking Dave Foreman's essay as an example, evaluate Seager's assertion that deep ecology is suffused by a "masculinist ethos."

Extending the Critical Context

7. Look up and read several issues of *Earth First!* magazine or something written by Edward Abbey. Based on your reading, do you think Seager paints a fair portrait of deep ecology?
8. Research methods of population control that have been implemented in India, China, and elsewhere. What ethical dilemmas are posed by such efforts? Are there any effective and humane ways to reduce the burden of human population on earth?

being property once myself

Lucille Clifton

"I am a Black woman poet, and I sound like one." Lucille Clifton's distinctive voice comes through even in this extremely short poem, which says more about people and nature in thirty-nine words than most politicians say in a lifetime. Clifton was born in 1936 in Depew, New York, and was educated at Fredonia State Teachers College and Howard University. She has published several books for children and six volumes of poetry and has won many prizes for her work. Clifton is currently Distinguished Professor of Humanities at St. Mary's College in Maryland. This poem originally appeared in Good Woman: Poems and a Memoir, 1969–1980 *(1987).*

being property once myself
i have a feeling for it,
that's why i can talk
about environment.
what wants to be a tree,
ought to be he can be it.
same thing for other things.
same thing for men.

Engaging the Text

1. Restate the poem's argument in your own words. What does it say about environment — and about people? (The poem is short enough that you may want to explain each phrase; for example, in what ways has the speaker been property herself?) After clarifying the poem's meaning, debate the points it makes.
2. Is a poem that can be read in less than a minute likely to be dismissed or easily forgotten? Discuss the effect of the extreme brevity of this poem.
3. Your instructor would probably not accept the grammar of lines 5 and 6 if you wrote something like this in an essay. What's the effect of this phrasing and of the informal style throughout the poem?

Exploring Connections

4. Do you think that Clifton would agree more with Dave Foreman's (p. 625) or with Joni Seager's (p. 633) assessment of deep ecology? Why?

Extending the Critical Context

5. As children we have all, in a sense, "[been] property once." Freewrite a page or two about a childhood memory of a moment or situation in which you felt owned. Follow up by trying to capture the experience in a poem.
6. Clifton has made several audio and video recordings, including a segment for the PBS series *The Power of the Word* (Bill Moyers, 1989). Check the holdings of your campus audio-video library and listen to at least one recording or watch at least one videotape of Clifton. Report to the class on what you learned and how it affects your reading of this poem.

Women, Home, and Community: The Struggle in an Urban Environment

CYNTHIA HAMILTON

In 1986 the Los Angeles City Council voted to build a mammoth waste incinerator in a poor inner-city neighborhood. To the council's surprise, the African American and Latino communities, led primarily by mothers and working women, fought and eventually defeated the project. Cynthia Hamilton documents their struggle against city hall in this essay, originally anthologized in Reweaving the World: The Emergence of Ecofeminism *(1990). Hamilton is director of the African and African American Studies Program at the University of Rhode Island. A political activist as well as a scholar, she has published widely on issues of race and environmental justice.*

In 1956, women in South Africa began an organized protest against the pass laws.[1] As they stood in front of the office of the prime minister, they began a new freedom song with the refrain "now you have touched the women, you have struck a rock." This refrain provides a description of the personal commitment and intensity women bring to social change. Women's actions have been characterized as "spontaneous and dramatic," women in action portrayed as "intractable and uncompromising."[2] Society has summarily dismissed these as negative attributes. When in 1986 the City Council of Los Angeles decided that a 13-acre incinerator called LANCER (for Los Angeles City Energy Recovery Project), burning 2,000 tons a day of municipal waste, should be built in a poor residential, Black, and Hispanic community, the women there said "No." Officials had indeed dislodged a boulder of opposition. According to Charlotte Bullock, one of the protestors, "I noticed when we first started fighting the issue how the men would laugh at the women . . . they would say, 'Don't pay no attention to them, that's only one or two women . . . they won't make a difference.' But now since we've been fighting for about a year the smiles have gone."[3]

Minority communities shoulder a disproportionately high share of the by-products of industrial development: waste, abandoned factories and warehouses, leftover chemicals and debris. These communities are also asked to

[1]*pass laws:* Statutes that regulated the travel of Black South Africans.

[2]See Cynthia Cockburn, "When Women Get Involved in Community Action," in Marjorie Mayo (ed.), *Women in the Community* (London: Routledge & Kegan Paul, 1977). [Author's note]

[3]All of the quotes from Charlotte Bullock and Robin Cannon are personal communications, 1986. [Author's note]

house the waste and pollution no longer acceptable in White communities, such as hazardous landfills or dump sites. In 1987, the Commission for Racial Justice of the United Church of Christ published *Toxic Wastes and Race*. The commission concluded that race is a major factor related to the presence of hazardous wastes in residential communities throughout the United States. Three out of every five Black and Hispanic Americans live in communities with uncontrolled toxic sites; 75 percent of the residents in rural areas in the Southwest, mainly Hispanics, are drinking pesticide-contaminated water; more than 2 million tons of uranium tailings are dumped on Native American reservations each year, resulting in Navajo teenagers having seventeen times the national average of organ cancers; more than 700,000 inner city children, 50 percent of them Black, are said to be suffering from lead poisoning, resulting in learning disorders. Working-class minority women are therefore motivated to organize around very pragmatic environmental issues, rather than those associated with more middle-class organizations. According to Charlotte Bullock, "I did not come to the fight against environmental problems as an intellectual but rather as a concerned mother. . . . People say, 'But you're not a scientist, how do you know it's not safe?' I have common sense. I know if dioxin and mercury are going to come out of an incinerator stack, somebody's going to be affected."

When Concerned Citizens of South Central Los Angeles came together in 1986 to oppose the solid waste incinerator planned for the community, no one thought much about environmentalism or feminism. These were just words in a community with a 78 percent unemployment rate, an average income ($8,158) less than half that of the general Los Angeles population, and a residential density more than twice that of the whole city. In the first stages of organization, what motivated and directed individual actions was the need to protect home and children; for the group this individual orientation emerged as a community-centered battle. What was left in this deteriorating district on the periphery of the central business and commercial district had to be defended — a "garbage dump" was the final insult after years of neglect, watching downtown flourish while residents were prevented from borrowing enough to even build a new roof.

The organization was never gender restricted but it became apparent after a while that women were the majority. The particular kind of organization the group assumed, the actions engaged in, even the content of what was said, were all a product not only of the issue itself, the waste incinerator, but also a function of the particular nature of women's oppression and what happens as the process of consciousness begins.

Women often play a primary part in community action because it is 5
about things they know best. Minority women in several urban areas have found themselves part of a new radical core as the new wave of environmental action, precipitated by the irrationalities of capital-intensive growth, has catapulted them forward. These individuals are responding not to "nature" in the abstract but to the threat to their homes and to the health of

their children. Robin Cannon, another activist in the fight against the Los Angeles incinerator, says, "I have asthma, my children have asthma, my brothers and sisters have asthma, there are a lot of health problems that people living around an incinerator might be subjected to and I said, 'They can't do this to me and my family.'"

Women are more likely than men to take on these issues precisely because the home has been defined and prescribed as a woman's domain. According to British sociologist Cynthia Cockburn, "In a housing situation that is a health hazard, the woman is more likely to act than the man because she lives there all day and because she is impelled by fear for her children. Community action of this kind is a significant phase of class struggle, but it is also an element of women's liberation."[4]

This phenomenon was most apparent in the battle over the Los Angeles incinerator. Women who had had no history of organizing responded as protectors of their children. Many were single parents, others were older women who had raised families. While the experts were convinced that their smug dismissal of the validity of the health concerns these women raised would send them away, their smugness only reenforced the women's determination. According to Charlotte Bullock:

> People's jobs were threatened, ministers were threatened . . . but I said, "I'm not going to be intimidated." My child's health comes first, . . . that's more important than my job.
>
> In the 1950s the city banned small incinerators in the yard and yet they want to build a big incinerator . . . the Council is going to build something in my community which might kill my child. . . . I don't need a scientist to tell me that's wrong.

None of the officials were prepared for the intensity of concern or the consistency of agitation. In fact, the consultants they hired had concluded that these women did not fit the prototype of opposition. The consultants had concluded:

> Certain types of people are likely to participate in politics, either by virtue of their issue awareness or their financial resources, or both. Members of middle or higher socioeconomic strata (a composite index of level of education, occupational prestige, and income) are more likely to organize into effective groups to express their political interests and views. All socioeconomic groupings tend to resent the nearby siting of major facilities, but the middle and upper socioeconomic strata possess better resources to effectuate their opposition. Middle and higher socioeconomic strata neighborhoods should not fall at least within the one mile and five mile radii of the proposed site.
>
> . . . although environmental concerns cut across all subgroups, people with a college education, young or middle aged, and liberal in philosophy are most likely to organize opposition to the siting of a major facility. Older

[4]Cockburn, "When Women," p. 62. [Author's note]

people, with a high school education or less, and those who adhere to a free market orientation are least likely to oppose a facility.[5]

The organizers against the incinerator in South Central Los Angeles are the antithesis of the prototype: they are high school educated or less, above middle age and young, nonprofessionals and unemployed and low-income, without previous political experience. The consultants and politicians thus found it easy to believe that opposition from this group could not be serious.

The intransigence of the City Council intensified the agitation, and the women became less willing to compromise as time passed. Each passing month gave them greater strength, knowledge, and perseverance. The council and its consultants had a more formidable enemy than they had expected, and in the end they have had to compromise. The politicians have backed away from their previous embrace of incineration as a solution to the trash crisis, and they have backed away from this particular site in a poor, Black and Hispanic residential area. While the issues are far from resolved, it is important that the willingness to compromise has become the official position of the city as a result of the determination of "a few women."

The women in South Central Los Angeles were not alone in their battle. 10
They were joined by women from across the city, White, middle-class, and professional women. As Robin Cannon puts it, "I didn't know we all had so many things in common . . . millions of people in the city had something in common with us — the environment." These two groups of women, together, have created something previously unknown in Los Angeles — unity of purpose across neighborhood and racial lines. According to Charlotte Bullock, "We are making a difference . . . when we come together as a whole and stick with it, we can win because we are right."

This unity has been accomplished by informality, respect, tolerance of spontaneity, and decentralization. All of the activities that we have been told destroy organizations have instead worked to sustain this movement. For example, for a year and a half the group functioned without a formal leadership structure. The unconscious acceptance of equality and democratic process resulted practically in rotating the chair's position at meetings. Newspeople were disoriented when they asked for the spokesperson and the group responded that everyone could speak for the neighborhood.

It may be the case that women, unlike men, are less conditioned to see the value of small advances.[6] These women were all guided by their vision of the possible: that it *was* possible to completely stop the construction of the incinerator, that it is possible in a city like Los Angeles to have reasonable growth, that it is possible to humanize community structures and services. As Robin Cannon says, "My neighbors said, 'You can't fight City Hall . . . and besides, you work there.' I told them I would fight anyway."

[5]Cerrell Associates, *Political Difficulties Facing Waste to Energy Conversion Plant Siting* (Los Angeles: California Waste Management Board, 1984), pp. 42–43. [Author's note]

[6]See Cockburn, "When Women," p. 63. [Author's note]

None of these women was convinced by the consultants and their traditional justifications for capital-intensive growth: that it increases property values by intensifying land use, that it draws new businesses and investment to the area, that it removes blight and deterioration—and the key argument used to persuade the working class — that growth creates jobs. Again, to quote Robin Cannon, "They're not bringing real development to our community. . . . They're going to bring this incinerator to us, and then say 'We're going to *give* you fifty jobs when you get this plant.' Meanwhile they're going to shut down another factory [in Riverside] and eliminate two hundred jobs to buy more pollution rights. . . . They may close more shops."

Ironically, the consultants' advice backfired. They had suggested that emphasizing employment and a gift to the community (of $2 million for a community development fund for park improvement) would persuade the opponents. But promises of heated swimming pools, air-conditioned basketball courts, and fifty jobs at the facility were more insulting than encouraging. Similarly, at a public hearing, an expert witness's assurance that health risks associated with dioxin exposure were less than those associated with "eating peanut butter" unleashed a flurry of derision.

The experts' insistence on referring to congenital deformities and can- 15
cers as "acceptable risks" cut to the hearts of women who rose to speak of a child's asthma, or a parent's influenza, or the high rate of cancer, heart disease, and pneumonia in this poverty-stricken community. The callous disregard of human concerns brought the women closer together. They came to rely on each other as they were subjected to the sarcastic rebuffs of men who referred to their concerns as "irrational, uninformed, and disruptive." The contempt of the male experts was directed at professionals and the unemployed, at Whites and Blacks — all the women were castigated as irrational and uncompromising. As a result, new levels of consciousness were sparked in these women.

The reactions of the men backing the incinerator provided a very serious learning experience for the women, both professionals and nonprofessionals, who came to the movement without a critique of patriarchy. They developed their critique in practice. In confronting the need for equality, these women forced the men to a new level of recognition—that working-class women's concerns cannot be simply dismissed.

Individual transformations accompanied the group process. As the struggle against the incinerator proceeded to take on some elements of class struggle, individual consciousness matured and developed. Women began to recognize something of their own oppression as women. This led to new forms of action not only against institutions but to the transformation of social relations in the home as well. As Robin Cannon explains:

> My husband didn't take me seriously at first either. . . . He just saw a whole lot of women meeting and assumed we wouldn't get anything done. . . . I had to split my time . . . I'm the one who usually comes home from work,

> cooks, helps the kids with their homework, then I watch a little TV and go to bed to get ready for the next morning. Now I would rush home, cook, read my materials on LANCER . . . now the kids were on their own . . . I had my own homework. . . . My husband still wasn't taking me seriously. . . . After about six months everyone finally took me seriously. My husband had to learn to allocate more time for baby sitting. Now on Saturdays, if they went to the show or to the park, I couldn't attend . . . in the evening there were hearings . . . I was using my vacation time to go to hearings during the workday.

As parents, particularly single parents, time in the home was strained for these women. Children and husbands complained that meetings and public hearings had taken priority over the family and relations in the home. According to Charlotte Bullock, "My children understand, but then they don't want to understand. . . . They say, 'You're not spending time with me.'" Ironically, it was the concern for family, their love of their families, that had catapulted these women into action to begin with. But, in a pragmatic sense, the home did have to come second in order for health and safety to be preserved. These were hard learning experiences. But meetings in individual homes ultimately involved children and spouses alike — everyone worked and everyone listened. The transformation of relations continued as women spoke up at hearings and demonstrations and husbands transported children, made signs, and looked on with pride and support at public forums.

The critical perspective of women in the battle against LANCER went far beyond what the women themselves had intended. For these women, the political issues were personal and in that sense they became feminist issues. These women, in the end, were fighting for what they felt was "right" rather than what men argued might be reasonable. The coincidence of the principles of feminism and ecology that Carolyn Merchant explains in *The Death of Nature* (San Francisco: Harper & Row, 1981) found expression and developed in the consciousness of these women: the concern for earth as a home, the recognition that all parts of a system have equal value, the acknowledgment of process, and, finally, that capitalist growth has social costs. As Robin Cannon says, "This fight has really turned me around, things are intertwined in ways I hadn't realized. . . . All these social issues as well as political and economic issues are really intertwined. Before, I was concerned only about health and then I began to get into the politics, decision making, and so many things."

In two years, what started as the outrage of a small group of mothers has transformed the political climate of a major metropolitan area. What these women have aimed for is a greater level of democracy, a greater level of involvement, not only in their organization but in the development process of the city generally. They have demanded accountability regarding land use and ownership, very subversive concerns in a capitalist society. In their organizing, the group process, collectivism, was of primary importance. It allowed the women to see their own power and potential and therefore allowed them to consolidate effective opposition. The movement underscored the role of principles. In fact, we citizens have lived so long with an unquestioning acceptance of profit and expediency that sometimes we forget that our objective is to do "what's right." Women are beginning to raise moral concerns in a very forthright manner, emphasizing that experts have left us no other choice but to follow our own moral convictions rather than accept neutrality and capitulate in the face of crisis.

The environmental crisis will escalate in this decade and women are 20
sure to play pivotal roles in the struggle to save our planet. If women are able to sustain for longer periods some of the qualities and behavioral forms they have displayed in crisis situations (such as direct participatory democracy and the critique of patriarchal bureaucracy), they may be able to reintroduce equality and democracy into progressive action. They may also reintroduce the value of being moved by principle and morality. Pragmatism has come to dominate all forms of political behavior and the results have often been disastrous. If women resist the "normal" organizational thrust to barter, bargain, and fragment ideas and issues, they may help set new standards for action in the new environmental movement.

Engaging the Text

1. Why, according to Hamilton, do minority women often bear the burden of industrial expansion? What other factors, in her opinion, make them natural leaders in opposing developments?
2. Why didn't the architects of the LANCER project worry about the women who were organizing against it? In what ways did the men who backed the project misjudge their opponents?
3. Explain in your own words what Hamilton means when she says that women have to resist "normal" methods of organization and strategies for addressing environmental issues. Why does she feel women need to "set new standards"?

Exploring Connections

4. Joyce Nelson argues that misleading advertising represents a kind of corporate "mind pollution" (p. 613). What other forms of mind pollution are practiced by proponents of the LANCER incinerator? How do the members of Concerned Citizens resist these attempts to manipulate them?
5. According to Hamilton, the success of the Concerned Citizens group illustrates "the coincidence of the principles of feminism and ecology" (para. 18). To what extent do the motives, organizational processes, and political strategies of this group embody the kind of feminist environmental activism called for by Joni Seager (p. 633)?
6. Review Patricia Hill Collins's discussion of "community othermothers" (p. 195) and Cora Tucker's life story (p. 549). Write an essay exploring the ways that Tucker and members of Concerned Citizens like Charlotte Bullock and Robin Cannon illustrate or extend Collins's definition of community othermothers.

Judging from their experiences, what are the risks and rewards associated with this role?

EXTENDING THE CRITICAL CONTEXT

7. Research the locations of dumps, toxic disposal sites, and toxin-producing industries in your area. Does your research confirm or challenge Hamilton's statement that "minority communities shoulder a disproportionately high share of the by-products of industrial development" (para. 2)?
8. Interview one or more environmental activists in your community. What environmental issues concern them the most? What obstacles do they face? What actions or campaigns have they been involved in? What strategies have they used, and how effective were they? Using Hamilton's essay as a model, write a paper detailing the activists' role in a particular environmental conflict and its outcome.

7

Liberty and Justice for All

The Myth of Freedom

America's belief in itself as "the land of the free" pervades our mythology: early in our schooling, we are taught that the Pilgrims came to America for religious freedom, that the colonists fought the Revolutionary War for freedom from England, and that the Union defeated the Confederacy to free the slaves. However, a deeper reading of history shows that the motives underlying each of these landmark events were far more complex. Indeed, America's relation to the ideal of freedom has never been uncomplicated.

It's hard to appreciate what America must have meant to religious dissenters like the Puritans in sixteenth-century Europe. Persecuted by what they saw as a corrupt and authoritarian church, the Pilgrims viewed America through the biblical stories of exile, enslavement, and liberation they had read in the Old Testament: they came to see themselves as the new "children of Israel," "the chosen people" destined to venture into the wilderness of a "New Eden." Just as Christ had come to redeem creation from sin, they saw themselves as his agents, freeing humanity from the sordidness and decadence of the "Old World." But the Pilgrims sought a very narrow kind of emancipation: they came to America in pursuit of religious — not personal — liberty; they sought freedom of worship, not the kind of individual liberty that has become the hallmark of American independence. Indeed, in the rigidity of their religious doctrines, the authoritarianism of their social structure, their distrust of difference, and their contempt for worldly pleasures, they seem an unlikely source of inspiration for the American creed of "Life, Liberty, and the pursuit of Happiness."

Some historians trace the American concept of freedom not to the Puritan settlements of New England but to the American Indian cultures the Puritans and other European settlers displaced. Beginning with Christopher Columbus, European explorers were amazed by the personal freedom enjoyed by the Native Americans they encountered: they could scarcely comprehend a life apparently unrestrained by rigid social distinctions, gender roles, financial obligations, religious doctrines, or state regulations. In a 1503 letter to Lorenzo de Medici, Amerigo Vespucci described these remarkable people who seemed to live in harmony with nature:

> The inhabitants of the New World do not have goods of their own, but all things are held in common. They live together without king, without government, and each is his own master. . . . There is a great abundance of gold, and by them it is in no respect esteemed or valued. . . . Surely if the terrestrial paradise be in any part of the earth, I esteem that it is not far distant from these parts.

Europeans raised in cultures dominated by the authority of monarchy, aristocracy, and the church were particularly impressed by the relative freedom of native children. American Indian families often encouraged their sons and daughters to develop a strong sense of independence and personal liberty. Iroquois children, for example, were taught to resist overbearing authority and were rarely punished severely; they were also taught that all tribal members — male, female, adult, and child — were equal and that possessions were to be shared by the entire community. Such attitudes contrasted sharply with those imported to the New World by the Pilgrims, who believed that a child's natural stubbornness and pride had to be broken down through education, discipline, and corporal punishment.

The examples of freedom and equality provided by societies like the Iroquois and the Huron sparked the European imagination and, as some scholars suggest, placed liberty at the top of the Western world's political agenda for the next four hundred years. To political philosophers like Jean-Jacques Rousseau, the "noble savage" was living proof that human beings were born free "in a state of nature" and that tyranny and slavery were the result of social corruption: if tyranny and injustice were not natural or god-given features of human life, then it would be possible—even necessary—for subjects to rebel against royal domination and reclaim their natural "inalienable" human rights. To political activists like Thomas Paine, the freedom and equality enjoyed within many American Indian cultures demonstrated that society could be organized without aristocracy, monarchy, and ecclesiastical authority. The first great advocate of both American independence and the abolition of slavery, Paine based many of his revolutionary ideas on his intimate knowledge of Iroquois customs and values.

The example of America's original inhabitants may have inspired the settlers to take up arms and fight for their own "natural" rights, but, as historian Howard Zinn has pointed out, the Revolutionary War had devastating consequences for Native Americans:

> What did the Revolution mean to the Native Americans, the Indians? They had been ignored by the fine words of the Declaration, had not been considered equal, certainly not in choosing those who would govern the American territories in which they lived, nor in being able to pursue happiness as they had pursued it for centuries before the white Europeans arrived. Now, with the British out of the way, the Americans could begin the inexorable process of pushing the Indians off their lands, killing them if they resisted. In short . . . the white Americans were against British imperial control in the East, and for their own imperialism in the West.

It is one of history's most profound ironies that America's war for independence, the first war ever fought in the name of individual liberty, hastened the destruction of the very societies that had inspired the modern myth of freedom.

America's ambivalence toward the principle of freedom also found expression in the nation's newly drafted Constitution. The American Revolution's idealization of freedom had made slavery appear hypocritical to some patriots; as Abigail Adams wrote during the war, "I wish most sincerely there was not a slave in the province; it always appeared a most iniquitous scheme to me to fight ourselves for what we are daily robbing and plundering from those who have as good a right to freedom as we have." Such feelings prevailed in Vermont, where slavery was outlawed a year after the colonies declared their independence. However, economic and political considerations took precedence over human rights as the Constitutional Convention debated the slavery issue in 1787.

Outright abolition was never discussed at the convention — it would have been politically unacceptable to the many delegates who owned slaves. The question that did arise was whether the United States should continue to allow the importation of Africans for slave labor. Several representatives argued that it was "inconsistent with the principles of the revolution and dishonorable to the American character to have such a feature in the Constitution." But delegates from the South contended that more slaves not only were essential for developing southern agriculture but also would provide economic benefits for the northern states. Thus, a document that sought to "secure the blessings of liberty to ourselves and our posterity" also legitimized the sale and ownership of one human being by another.

The ideal of freedom was compromised again when liberties explicitly protected by the Constitution were denied in practice. The First Amendment guarantee of free speech, for example, was not actively enforced until well into the twentieth century. Dissenters — abolitionists, political activists, labor organizers, feminists, and birth control advocates, among others — were frequently arrested, harassed, fined, denied permits, or otherwise prevented from speaking publicly. The problem was so widespread that, in 1915, a government-sponsored investigative committee reported that

> on numerous occasions in every part of the country, the police of cities and towns have either arbitrarily or under the cloak of a traffic ordinance, interfered with, or prohibited public speaking, both in the open and in halls, by persons connected with organizations of which the police or those from whom they receive their orders, did not approve. In many instances such interference has been carried out with a degree of brutality which would be incredible if it were not vouched for by reliable witnesses.

But while the United States has often failed to uphold the rights of all citizens, the ideals of liberty and self-determination set out in the Declaration and Constitution have inspired many to fight for — and sometimes win — their "inalienable rights." Popular movements throughout the nation's history have organized, marched, struck, sued, and practiced civil disobedience when established political channels failed them. A determined, seventy-five-year campaign by American feminists won women the vote in 1920, and systematic protests and court challenges by the labor movement in the 1930s gave us many of our current protections of free speech. Denied equal protection under the law, equal access to economic opportunity, equal education, and even an equal chance to vote, African Americans sought redress in the courts and on the streets of America for decades, eventually winning substantive legal reforms during the civil rights movement of the 1960s.

In spite of these victories, the struggle for freedom is far from over in

America. On college campuses across the nation, students and faculty are debating the need to regulate hate speech and other forms of racially or sexually offensive behavior. Conservatives and libertarians claim that speech codes violate their constitutional rights, while women and new-majority Americans see codes as their only protection against dehumanization and domination. Over the past few years, particularly vulnerable minority groups like gays and lesbians have experienced a backlash of prejudice and seen hard-won protections threatened by initiatives seeking to limit gay rights. Today, perhaps more than ever, America seems ambivalent about the myth of freedom. At times we seem to be foundering amid competing and often contradictory claims of individual rights. It's become nearly impossible to pick up a newspaper without encountering a story about victims' rights, children's rights, the rights of the unborn, animal rights, the right to privacy, the right to pray, freedom of speech, or freedom of the press. The clash of freedoms in contemporary America has even led some social critics to suggest that our devotion to liberty is transforming us into a selfish and dangerously fragmented society. According to "communitarians" like sociologist Amatai Etzioni, America has entered a period of "pervasive moral erosion": our inordinate respect for individual autonomy has led to a breakdown of our shared values and beliefs — "the social glue that helps hold the moral order together." And the communitarians aren't alone. Over the past decade, voices from both ends of the political spectrum — from conservative fundamentalists to radical new-age ecologists — have questioned whether America's experiment with freedom has gone too far and whether the principle of freedom itself may end in the destruction of our nation — or our planet.

This chapter invites you to examine the influence and limitations of the myth of freedom in contemporary American life. The first section focuses on personal visions of what it means — even what it feels like — to be free. The chapter opens with the *Declaration of Independence,* the first and best-known statement of American freedoms and rights. Pam Houston's "Selway" carries us from political to personal definitions of freedom; this dramatic short story relates the experiences of a young couple who arrive at very different views of freedom during a break-neck, white-water rafting trip. Next, attorney and activist Gerry Spence challenges us to consider how free we really are in his essay "Easy in the Harness." In "Charlie Sabatier," the oral history that follows, John Langston Gwaltney offers the harrowing story of a young man who discovers the price and the power of freedom after returning from Vietnam in a wheelchair. June Jordan's "Freedom Time" closes the first half of the chapter by asking if Americans in the 1990s aren't losing sight of what freedom really means.

The second half of the chapter probes some of the difficulties that arise in a society that recognizes conflicting freedoms and rights. In one of the chapter's two media selections, Bill McKibben takes a hard look at the way TV's celebration of freedom has undermined America's sense of community.

Our second media essay, Patricia J. Williams's "Hate Radio," carries the idea further by zeroing in on the anger and intolerance generated by talk show hosts like Howard Stern and Rush Limbaugh. In the editorial that follows, Richard Delgado and Jean Stefancic investigate the conflict between free speech and civil rights on America's college campuses. Stephen L. Carter's "Stuck with a Satanist?" considers a similar conflict of freedoms in the realm of religion and the right to worship.

The chapter closes with two selections that bear witness to the enduring power of freedom as an ideal in American life. "The Bridge Builder" offers the story of Kathleen Boatwright, a devout Christian and a lesbian who discovers the meaning of freedom through her relationships with church, God, and community. The chapter and the book close with Langston Hughes's impassioned appeal to make America a land that lives up to its finest myths:

> The land that never has been yet—
> And yet must be—the land where *every* man is free.

Sources

Lerone Bennett, Jr., *Before the Mayflower: A History of Black America,* rev. 5th ed. New York: Viking Penguin, 1984.

David Kairys, "Freedom of Speech." In *The Politics of Law: A Progressive Critique,* David Kairys, ed. New York: Pantheon Books, 1982.

Ralph Ketchem, ed., *The Anti-Federalist Papers and the Constitutional Convention Debates.* New York: Mentor Books, 1986.

Krishan Kumar, *Utopia and Anti-Utopia in Modern Times.* Oxford: Basil Blackwell, 1987.

Jack Weatherford, *Indian Givers: How the Indians of the Americas Transformed the World.* New York: Ballantine Books, 1988.

Howard Zinn, *A People's History of the United States.* New York: Harper and Row, 1980.

Before Reading

- Brainstorm a list of all the freedoms that are important to you, then rank them in the order of their importance. In small groups, compare your list with those of your classmates and discuss patterns or discrepancies that arise.
- Write about a time when freedom or a conflict of freedoms became an issue in your school or workplace. Describe the conflict and the effect it had on you. How was it resolved, and how did you feel about the resolution?
- What does the picture at the beginning of this chapter suggest to you about freedom? In what ways does the woman in this picture appear to be free—or not free? Write a journal entry about a time when you felt

the way she appears to feel. Describe the situation you were in. How free did you feel to express yourself or to take action in this situation? What, if anything, constrained you?

Declaration of Independence

THOMAS JEFFERSON

Drafted by Thomas Jefferson when he was only thirty-three years old, the Declaration of Independence was meant to announce and defend the colonies' decision to throw off British rule. But since its adoption by the Second Continental Congress on July 4, 1776, it has come to mean much more: its vision of responsive government and its insistence upon the fundamental equality of the governed have inspired democratic reforms for the past two hundred years —from the Bill of Rights *to the civil rights movement. Conceived as a revolutionary manifesto, the Declaration has become the preamble to the most durable of all American myths, the myth of individual liberty. As third president of the United States (1801–1809), Thomas Jefferson (1743–1826) promoted westward expansion in the form of the Louisiana Purchase and the Lewis and Clark Expedition. In addition to his political career he was a scientist, architect, city planner (Washington, DC), and founder of the University of Virginia; his writings fill fifty-two volumes.*

THE UNANIMOUS DECLARATION of the thirteen united STATES OF AMERICA.

When in the Course of human events, it becomes necessary for one people to dissolve the political bands which have connected them with another, and to assume among the powers of the earth, the separate and equal station to which the Laws of Nature and of Nature's God entitle them, a decent respect to the opinions of mankind requires that they should declare the causes which impel them to the separation. ——We hold these truths to be self-evident, that all men are created equal, that they are endowed by their Creator with certain unalienable Rights, that among these are Life, Liberty and the pursuit of Happiness. — That to secure these rights, Governments are instituted among Men, deriving their just powers from the consent of the governed. — That whenever any Form of Government becomes destructive of these ends, it is the Right of the People to alter or to abolish it, and to institute new Government, laying its foundation on such principles and organizing its powers in such form, as to them shall seem most likely to effect their Safety and Happiness. Prudence, indeed, will dictate that Governments long established should not be changed for light and transient causes; and accordingly all experience hath shewn, that mankind are more disposed to suffer, while evils are sufferable, than to right themselves by abolishing the forms to which they are accustomed. But when a long train of abuses and usurpations, pursuing invariably the same Object[1] evinces a design to reduce them under absolute Despotism, it is their right, it is their duty, to throw off such Government, and to provide new Guards for their future security. — Such has been the patient sufferance of these Colonies; and such is now the necessity which constrains them to alter their former Systems of Government. The history of the present King of Great Britain is a history of repeated injuries and usurpations, all having in direct object the establishment of an absolute Tyranny over these States. To prove this, let Facts be submitted to a candid world.—— He has refused his Assent to Laws, the most wholesome and necessary for the public good. —— He has forbidden his Governors to pass Laws of immediate and pressing importance, unless suspended in their operation till his Assent should be obtained; and when so suspended, he has utterly neglected to attend to them. —— He has refused to pass other Laws for the accommodation of large districts of people, unless those people would relinquish the right of Representation in the Legislature, a right inestimable to them and formidable to tyrants only. —— He has called together legislative bodies at places unusual, uncomfortable, and distant from the depository of their public Records, for the sole purpose of fatiguing them into compliance with his measures.—— He has dissolved Representative Houses repeatedly, for opposing with manly firmness his invasions on the rights of the people. —— He has refused for a long time, after such dissolutions, to cause others to be elected; whereby the Legislative powers, incapable of Annihilation, have returned to the People at large for their exercise; the State remaining in the mean time exposed to all the dangers of invasion from without, and convulsions within. —— He has endeavoured to prevent the population of these States; for that purpose obstructing the Laws for Naturalization of Foreigners; refusing to pass others to encourage their migrations hither, and raising the conditions of new Appropriations of Lands. —— He has obstructed the Administration of Justice, by refusing his Assent to Laws for establishing Judiciary powers. —— He has made Judges dependent on his Will alone, for the tenure of their offices, and the amount and payment of their salaries. —— He has

[1] *Object:* Goal, purpose.

erected a multitude of New Offices, and sent hither swarms of Officers to harass our people, and eat out their substance.—— He has kept among us, in times of peace, Standing Armies without the Consent of our legislatures. —— He has affected to render the Military independent of and superior to the Civil power.—— He has combined with others to subject us to a jurisdiction foreign to our constitution, and unacknowledged by our laws; giving his Assent to their Acts of pretended Legislation: — For Quartering large bodies of armed troops among us: — For protecting them, by a mock Trial, from punishment for any Murders which they should commit on the Inhabitants of these States: — For cutting off our Trade with all parts of the world: — For imposing Taxes on us without our Consent: — For depriving us in many cases, of the benefits of Trial by Jury: — For transporting us beyond Seas to be tried for pretended offences: — For abolishing the free System of English Laws in a neighbouring Province, establishing therein an Arbitrary government, and enlarging its Boundaries so as to render it at once an example and fit instrument for introducing the same absolute rule into these Colonies: — For taking away our Charters, abolishing our most valuable Laws, and altering fundamentally the Forms of our Governments: — For suspending our own Legislatures, and declaring themselves invested with power to legislate for us in all cases whatsoever. — He has abdicated Government here, by declaring us out of his Protection and waging War against us: — He has plundered our seas, ravaged our Coasts, burnt our towns, and destroyed the lives of our people. — He is at this time transporting large Armies of foreign Mercenaries to compleat the works of death, desolation and tyranny, already begun with circumstances of Cruelty & Perfidy scarcely paralleled in the most barbarous ages, and totally unworthy the Head of a civilized nation. — He has constrained our fellow Citizens taken Captive on the high Seas to bear Arms against their Country, to become the executioners of their friends and Brethren, or to fall themselves by their Hands. — He has excited domestic insurrections amongst us, and has endeavoured to bring on the inhabitants of our frontiers, the merciless Indian Savages, whose known rule of warfare, is an undistinguished destruction of all ages, sexes and conditions. In every stage of these Oppressions We have Petitioned for Redress in the most humble terms: Our repeated Petitions have been answered only by repeated injury. A Prince, whose character is thus marked by every act which may define a Tyrant, is unfit to be the ruler of a free people. Nor have We been wanting in attentions to our British brethren. We have warned them from time to time of attempts by their legislature to extend an unwarrantable jurisdiction over us. We have reminded them of the circumstances of our emigration and settlement here. We have appealed to their native justice and magnanimity, and we have conjured them by the ties of our common kindred to disavow these usurpations, which would inevitably interrupt our connections and correspondence. They too have been deaf to the voice of justice and of consanguinity. We must, therefore, acquiesce in the necessity, which denounces our Separation, and hold them, as we hold the rest of mankind, Enemies in War, in Peace Friends.

We, THEREFORE, the Representatives of the UNITED STATES OF AMERICA, in General Congress Assembled, appealing to the Supreme Judge of the world for the rectitude of our intentions, do, in the Name and by Authority of the good People of these Colonies, solemnly publish and declare, That these United Colonies are, and of Right ought to be FREE AND INDEPENDENT STATES; that they are Absolved from all Allegiance to the British Crown, and that all political connection between them and the State of Great Britain, is and ought to be totally dissolved; and that as Free and Independent States, they have full Power to levy War, conclude Peace, contract Alliances, establish Commerce, and to do all other Acts and Things which Independent States may of right do. —— And for the support of this Declaration, with a firm reliance on the protection of divine Providence, we mutually pledge to each other our Lives, our Fortunes and our sacred Honor.

ENGAGING THE TEXT

1. Paraphrase the opening of the Declaration, up to the phrase "former Systems of Government." Are the truths named here "self-evident"?
2. Outline the Declaration in three to five lines. What structure of argument is revealed here?
3. What attitudes toward women and Native Americans does the Declaration reveal?
4. How would you characterize the voice of this document? Read some of it aloud. What is its tone, and how, specifically, is that tone created?
5. Summarize the charges made against the king. Which address matters of individual freedoms? Economic freedoms? Colonial autonomy?

EXPLORING CONNECTIONS

6. Reread two or more of the following selections: Malcolm X's "Learning to Read" (p. 77), Ronald Takaki's "A Different Mirror" (p. 332), Wendy Rose's "Three Thousand Dollar Death Song" (p. 351), Janice Mirikitani's "We, the Dangerous" (p. 354), Gregory Mantsios's "Rewards and Opportunities" (p. 465), Patricia Nelson Limerick's "Empire of Innocence" (p. 564), or Haunani-Kay Trask's "From a Native Daughter" (p. 571). Drawing on these readings, write a response to the vision of freedom offered by Jefferson.

EXTENDING THE CRITICAL CONTEXT

7. Working in small groups, go to the library and compare the Declaration with the Constitution in terms of their tone, their approach to individual rights, and the notion of freedom they convey.

Selway

Pam Houston

Freedom may be one of the most important myths in American culture, but it's devilishly hard to define. Pressed to put freedom into words, we often fall back on negatives: freedom means not being controlled by the state or not having to think or act in officially approved ways. We have less trouble recognizing the feeling of freedom. For many Americans the experience of freedom beats in the rhythm of popular music, the getaway of a fast car, or the challenge of a sheer wall of granite. In the following short story by Pam Houston, a young woman searches for the limits of freedom—and the meaning of love — in the white water of a cresting river. This story of risk and relationship asks us to consider if men and women understand freedom in radically different ways. Houston (b. 1962) is a part-time river and hunting guide. "Selway" appeared in her award-winning short-story collection, Cowboys Are My Weakness *(1992).*

It was June the seventh and we'd driven eighteen hours of pavement and sixty miles of dirt to find out the river was at highwater, the highest of the year, of several years, and rising. The ranger, Ramona, wrote on our permit, "We do not recommend boating at this level," and then she looked at Jack.

"We're just gonna go down and take a look at it," he said, "see if the river gives us a sign." He tried to slide the permit away from Ramona, but her short dark fingers held it against the counter. I looked from one to the other. I knew Jack didn't believe in signs.

"Once you get to Moose Creek you're committed," she said. "There's no time to change your mind after that. You've got Double Drop and Little Niagara and Ladle, and they just keep coming like that, one after another with no slow water in between."

She was talking about rapids. This was my first northern trip, and after a lazy spring making slow love between rapids on the wide desert rivers, I couldn't imagine what all the fuss was about.

"If you make it through the Moose Creek series there's only a few more 5
real bad ones; Wolf Creek is the worst. After that the only thing to worry about is the takeout point. The beach will be under water, and if you miss it, you're over Selway Falls."

"Do you have a river guide?" Jack said, and when she bent under the counter to get one he tried again to slide the permit away. She pushed a small, multifolded map in his direction.

"Don't rely on it," she said. "The rapids aren't even marked in the right place."

"Thanks for your help," Jack said. He gave the permit a sharp tug and put it in his pocket.

"There was an accident today," Ramona said. "In Ladle."

"Anybody hurt?" Jack asked. 10

"It's not official."

"Killed?"

"The water's rising," Ramona said, and turned back to her desk.

At the put-in, the water crashed right over the top of the depth gauge. The grass grew tall and straight through the slats of the boat ramp.

"Looks like we're the first ones this year," Jack said. 15

The Selway has the shortest season of any river in North America. They don't plow the snow till the first week in June, and by the last week in July there's not enough water to carry a boat. They only allow one party a day on the river that they select from a nationwide lottery with thousands of applicants each year. You can try your whole life and never get a permit.

"Somebody's been here," I said. "The people who flipped today."

Jack didn't answer. He was looking at the gauge. "It's up even from this morning," he said. "They said this morning it was six feet."

Jack and I have known each other almost a year. I'm the fourth in a series of long-term girlfriends he's never gotten around to proposing to. He likes me because I'm young enough not to sweat being single and I don't put pressure on him the way the others did. They wanted him to quit running rivers, to get a job that wasn't seasonal, to raise a family like any man his age. They wouldn't go on trips with him, not even once to see what it was like, and I couldn't imagine that they knew him in any way that was complete if they hadn't known him on the river, if they hadn't seen him row.

I watched him put his hand in the water. "Feel that, baby," he said. 20
"That water was snow about fifteen minutes ago."

I stuck my foot in the water and it went numb in about ten seconds. I've been to four years of college and I should know better, but I love it when he calls me baby.

Jack has taken a different highwater trip each year for the last fifteen, on progressively more difficult rivers. When a river is at high water it's not just deeper and faster and colder than usual. It's got a different look and feel from the rest of the year. It's dark and impatient and turbulent, like a volcano or a teenage boy. It strains against its banks and it churns around and under itself. Looking at its fullness made me want to grab Jack and throw him down on the boat ramp and make love right next to where the river roared by, but I could tell by his face he was trying to make a decision, so I sat and stared at the river and wondered if it was this wild at the put-in what it would look like in the rapids.

"If anything happened to you . . ." he said, and threw a stick out in the middle of the channel. "It must be moving nine miles an hour." He walked up and down the boat ramp. "What do you think?" he said.

"I think this is a chance of a lifetime," I said. "I think you're the best boatman you know." I wanted to feel the turbulence underneath me. I wanted to run a rapid that could flip a boat. I hadn't taken anything like a risk in months. I wanted to think about dying.

25 It was already early evening, and once we made the decision to launch, there were two hours of rigging before we could get on the water. On the southern rivers we'd boat sometimes for an hour after dark just to watch what the moon did to the water. On the Selway there was a rapid that could flip your boat around every corner. It wasn't getting pitch dark till ten-thirty that far north, where the June dusk went on forever, but it wasn't really light either and we wouldn't be able to see very far ahead. We told ourselves we'd go a tenth of a mile and make camp, but you can't camp on a sheer granite wall, and the river has to give you a place to get stopped and get tied.

I worked fast and silent, wondering if we were doing the right thing and knowing if we died it would really be my fault, because as much as I knew Jack wanted to go, he wouldn't have pushed me if I'd said I was scared. Jack was untamable, but he had some sense and a lot of respect for the river. He relied on me to speak with the voice of reason, to be life-protecting because I'm a woman and that's how he thinks women are, but I've never been protective enough of anything, least of all myself.

At nine-fifteen we untied the rope and let the river take us.

"The first place that looks campable," Jack said.

Nine miles an hour is fast in a rubber raft on a river you've never boated when there's not quite enough light to see what's in front of you. We were taking on water over the bow almost immediately, even though the map didn't show any rapids for the first two miles. It was hard for me to take my eyes off Jack, the way his muscles strained with every stroke, first his upper arms, then his upper thighs. He was silent, thinking it'd been a mistake to come, but I was laughing and bailing water and combing the banks for a flat spot and jumping back and forth over my seat to kiss him, and watching while his muscles flexed.

30 My mother says I thrive on chaos, and I guess that's true, because as hard a year as I've had with Jack I stayed with it, and I won't even admit by how much the bad days outnumbered the good. We fought like bears when we weren't on the river, because he was so used to fighting and I was so used to getting my own way. I said I wanted selfless devotion and he took a stand on everything from infidelity to salad dressing, and it was always opposite to mine. The one thing we had going for us, though, was the sex, and if we could stop screaming at each other long enough to make love it would be a day or sometimes two before something would happen and we'd go at it again. I've always been afraid to stop and think too hard about what great sex in bad times might mean, but it must have something to do with timing,

that moment making love when you're at once absolutely powerful and absolutely helpless, a balance we could never find when we were out of bed.

It was the old southern woman next door, the hunter's widow, who convinced me I should stay with him each time I'd get mad enough to leave. She said if I didn't have to fight for him I'd never know if he was mine. She said the wild ones were the only ones worth having and that I had to let him do whatever it took to keep him wild. She said I wouldn't love him if he ever gave in, and the harder I looked at my life, the more I saw a series of men — wild in their own way — who thought because I said I wanted security and commitment, I did. Sometimes it seems this simple: I tamed them and made them dull as fence posts and left each one for someone wilder than the last. Jack is the wildest so far, and the hardest, and even though I've been proposed to sixteen times, five times by men I've never made love to, I want him all to myself and at home more than I've ever wanted anything.

"Are you bailing? I'm standing in water back here," he said, so I bailed faster but the waves kept on crashing over the bow.

"I can't move this boat," he said, which I knew wasn't entirely true, but it was holding several hundred gallons of water times eight pounds a gallon, and that's more weight than I'd care to push around.

"There," he said. "Camp. Let's try to get to shore."

He pointed to a narrow beach a hundred yards downstream. The sand looked black in the twilight; it was long and flat enough for a tent.

"Get the rope ready," he said. "You're gonna have to jump for it and find something to wrap around fast."

He yelled *jump* but it was too early and I landed chest-deep in the water and the cold took my breath but I scrambled across the rocks to the beach and wrapped around a fallen trunk just as the rope went tight. The boat dragged the trunk and me ten yards down the beach before Jack could get out and pull the nose of it up on shore.

"This may have been real fuckin' stupid," he said.

I wanted to tell him how the water made me feel, how horny and crazy and happy I felt riding on top of water that couldn't hold itself in, but he was scared, for the first time since I'd known him, so I kept my mouth shut and went to set up the tent.

In the morning the tent was covered all around with a thin layer of ice and we made love like crazy people, the way you do when you think it might be the last time ever, till the sun changed the ice back to dew and got the tent so hot we were sweating. Then Jack got up and made coffee, and we heard the boaters coming just in time to get our clothes on.

They threw us their rope and we caught it. There were three of them, three big men in a boat considerably bigger than ours. Jack poured them coffee. We all sat down on the fallen log.

"You launched late last night?" the tallest, darkest one said. He had curly black hair and a wide open face.

Jack nodded. "Too late," he said. "Twilight boating."

"It's up another half a foot this morning," the man said. "It's supposed to peak today at seven."

The official forest service document declares the Selway unsafe for boat- 45
ing above six feet. Seven feet is off their charts.

"Have you boated this creek at seven?" Jack asked. The man frowned and took a long drink from his cup.

"My name's Harvey," he said, and stuck out his hand. "This is Charlie and Charlie. We're on a training trip." He laughed. "Yahoo."

Charlie and Charlie nodded.

"You know the river," Jack said.

"I've boated the Selway seventy times," he said. "Never at seven feet. 50
It was all the late snow and last week's heat wave. It's a bad combination, but it's boatable. This river's always boatable if you know exactly where to be."

Charlie and Charlie smiled.

"There'll be a lot of holes that there's no way to miss. You got to punch through them."

Jack nodded. I knew Harvey was talking about boat flippers. Big waves that form in holes the river makes behind rocks and ledges and that will suck boats in and hold them there, fill them with water till they flip, hold bodies, too, indefinitely, until they go under and catch the current, or until the hole decides to spit them out. If you hit a hole with a back wave bigger than your boat perfectly straight, there's a half a chance you'll shoot through. A few degrees off in either direction, and the hole will get you every time.

"We'll be all right in this tank," Harvey said, nodding to his boat, "but I'm not sure I'd run it in a boat that small. I'm not sure I'd run it in a boat I had to bail."

Unlike ours, Harvey's boat was a self-bailer, inflatable tubes around an 55
open metal frame that let the water run right through. They're built for high water, and extremely hard to flip.

"Just the two of you?" Harvey said.

Jack nodded.

"A honeymoon trip. Nice."

"We're not married," Jack said.

"Yeah," Harvey said. He picked up a handful of sand. "The black sand 60
of the Selway," he said. "I carried a bottle of this sand downriver the year I got married. I wanted to throw it at my wife's feet during the ceremony. The minister thought it was pretty strange, but he got over it."

One of the Charlies looked confused.

"Black sand," Harvey said. "You know, black sand, love, marriage, Selway, rivers, life; the whole thing."

I smiled at Jack, but he wouldn't meet my eyes.

"You'll be all right till Moose Creek," Harvey said. "That's when it gets wild. We're gonna camp there tonight, run the bad stretch first thing in the morning in case we wrap or flip or tear something. I hope you won't think I'm insulting you if I ask you to run with us. It'll be safer for us both. The people who flipped yesterday were all experienced. They all knew the Selway."

"They lost one?" Jack said. 65

"Nobody will say for sure," Harvey said. "But I'd bet on it."

"We'll think about it," Jack said. "It's nice of you to offer."

"I know what you're thinking," Harvey said. "But I've got a kid now. It makes a difference." He pulled a picture out of his wallet. A baby girl, eight or nine months old, crawled across a linoleum floor.

"She's beautiful," I said.

"She knocks me out," Harvey said. "She follows everything with her finger; bugs, flowers, the TV, you know what I mean?" 70

Jack and I nodded.

"It's your decision," he said. "Maybe we'll see you at Moose Creek."

He stood up, and Charlie and Charlie rose behind him. One coiled the rope while the other pushed off.

Jack poured his third cup of coffee. "Think he's full of shit?" he said.

"I think he knows more than you or I ever will," I said. 75

"About this river, at least," he said.

"At least," I said.

In midday sunshine, the river looked more fun than terrifying. We launched just before noon, and though there was no time for sightseeing I bailed fast enough to let Jack move the boat through the rapids, which came quicker and bigger around every bend. The map showed ten rapids between the put-in and Moose Creek, and it was anybody's guess which of the fifty or sixty rapids we boated that day were the ones the forest service had in mind. Some had bigger waves than others, some narrower passages, but the river was continuous moving white water, and we finally put the map away. On the southern rivers we'd mix rum and fruit juice and eat smoked oysters and pepper cheese. Here, twenty fast miles went by without time to take a picture, to get a drink of water. The Moose Creek pack bridge came into sight, and we pulled in and tied up next to Harvey's boat.

"White fuckin' water," Harvey said. "Did you have a good run?"

"No trouble," Jack said. 80

"Good," Harvey said. "Here's where she starts to kick ass." He motioned with his head downriver. "We'll get up at dawn and scout everything."

"It's early yet," Jack said. "I think we're going on." I looked at Jack's face, and then Harvey's.

"You do what you want," Harvey said. "But you ought to take a look at the next five miles. The runs are obvious once you see them from the bank, but they change at every level."

"We haven't scouted all day," Jack said. I knew he wanted us to run alone, that he thought following Harvey would be cheating somehow, but I believed a man who'd throw sand at his new wife's feet, and I liked a little danger but I didn't want to die.

"There's only one way through Ladle," Harvey said. "Ladle's where they 85
lost the girl."

"The girl?" Jack said.

"The rest of her party was here when we got here. Their boats were below Ladle. They just took off, all but her husband. He wouldn't leave, and you can't blame him. He was rowing when she got tossed. He let the boat get sideways. He's been wandering around here for two days, I guess, but he wouldn't get back in the boat."

"Jesus Christ," Jack said. He sat down on the bank facing the water.

I looked back into the woods for the woman's husband and tried to imagine a posture for him, tried to imagine an expression for his face. I thought about my Uncle Tim, who spent ten years and a lifetime of savings building his dream home. On the day it was completed he backed his pickup over his four-year-old daughter while she played in the driveway. He sold the house in three days and went completely gray in a week.

"A helicopter landed about an hour ago," Harvey said. "Downstream, 90
where the body must be. It hasn't taken off."

"The water's still rising," Jack said, and we all looked to where we'd pulled the boats up on shore and saw that they were floating. And then we heard the beating of the propeller and saw the helicopter rising out over the river. We saw the hundred feet of cable hanging underneath it and then we saw the woman, arched like a dancer over the thick black belt they must use for transplanting wild animals, her long hair dangling, her arms slung back. The pilot flew up the river till he'd gained enough altitude, turned back, and headed over the mountain wall behind our camp.

"They said she smashed her pelvis against a rock and bled to death internally," Harvey said. "They got her out in less than three minutes, and it was too late."

Jack put his arm around my knees. "We'll scout at dawn," he said. "We'll all run this together."

Harvey was up rattling coffeepots before we had time to make love and I said it would bring us bad luck if we didn't but Jack said it would be worse than back luck if we didn't scout the rapids. The scouting trail was well worn. Harvey went first, then Jack, then me and the two Charlies. Double Drop was first, two sets of falls made by water pouring over clusters of house-sized boulders that extended all the way across the river.

"You can sneak the first drop on the extreme right," Harvey said. 95
"There's no sneak for the second. Just keep her straight and punch her through. Don't let her get you sideways."

Little Niagara was a big drop, six feet or more, but the run was pretty smooth and the back wave low enough to break through.

"Piece of cake," Harvey said.

The sun was almost over the canyon wall, and we could hear Ladle long before we rounded the bend. I wasn't prepared for what I saw. One hundred yards of white water stretched from shore to shore and thundered over rocks and logjams and ledges. There were ten holes the size of the one in Double Drop, and there was no space for a boat in between. The currents were so chaotic for such a long stretch there was no way to read which way they'd push a boat. We found some small logs and climbed a rock ledge that hung over the rapid.

"See if you can read this current," Harvey said, and tossed the smallest log into the top of the rapid. The log hit the first hole and went under. It didn't come back up. One of the Charlies giggled.

"Again," Harvey said. This time the log came out of the first hole and 100
survived two more before getting swallowed by the biggest hole, about midway through the rapid.

"I'd avoid that one for sure," Harvey said. "Try to get left of that hole." He threw the rest of the logs in. None of them made it through. "This is big-time," he said.

We all sat on the rock for what must have been an hour. "Seen enough?" Harvey said. "We've still got No Slouch and Miranda Jane."

The men climbed down off the rock, but I wasn't quite ready to leave. I went to the edge of the ledge, lay flat on my stomach, and hung over until my head was so full of the roar of the river I got dizzy and pulled myself back up. The old southern woman said men can't really live unless they face death now and then, and I know by men she didn't mean mankind. And I wondered which rock shattered the dead woman's pelvis, and I wondered what she and I were doing out here on this river when Harvey's wife was home with that beautiful baby and happy. And I knew it was crazy to take a boat through that rapid and I knew I'd do it anyway but I didn't any longer know why. Jack said I had to do it for myself to make it worth anything, and at first I thought I was there because I loved danger, but sitting on the rock I knew I was there because I loved Jack. And maybe I went because his old girlfriends wouldn't, and maybe I went because I wanted him for mine, and maybe it didn't matter at all why I went because doing it for me and doing it for him amounted, finally, to exactly the same thing. And even though I knew in my head there's nothing a man can do that a woman can't, I also knew in my heart we can't help doing it for different reasons. And just like a man will never understand exactly how a woman feels when she has a baby, or an orgasm, or the reasons why she'll fight so hard to be loved, a woman can't know in what way a man satisfies himself, what question he answers for himself, when he looks right at death.

My head was so full of the sound and the light of the river that when I climbed down off the bank side of the ledge I didn't see the elk carcass until I stepped on one of its curled hooves. It was a young elk, probably not dead a year, and still mostly covered with matted brown fur. The skull was picked clean by scavengers, polished white by the sun and grinning. The sound that came out of my mouth scared me as much as the elk had, and I felt silly a few minutes later when Harvey came barreling around the corner followed by Jack.

Harvey saw the elk and smiled. 105

"It startled me is all," I said.

"Jesus," Jack said. "Stay with us, all right?"

"I never scream," I said. "Hardly ever."

No Slouch and Miranda Jane were impressive rapids, but they were nothing like Ladle and both runnable to the left. On the way back to camp we found wild strawberries, and Jack and I hung back and fed them to each other and I knew he wasn't mad about me screaming. The boats were loaded by ten-thirty and the sun was warm. We wore life jackets and helmets and wet suits. Everybody had diver's boots but me, so I wore my loafers.

"You have three minutes in water this cold," Harvey said. "Even with a 110
wet suit. Three minutes before hypothermia starts, and then you can't swim, and then you just give in to the river."

Harvey gave us the thumbs-up sign as the Charlies pushed off. I pushed off right behind them. Except for the bail bucket and the spare oar, everything on the boat was tied down twice and inaccessible. My job was to take water out of the boat as fast as I could eight pounds at a time, and to help Jack remember which rapid was coming next and where we had decided to run it.

I saw the first of the holes in Double Drop and yelled, "Right," and we made the sneak with a dry boat. We got turned around somehow after that, though, and had to hit the big wave backwards. Jack yelled, "Hang on, baby," and we hit it straight on and it filled the boat, but then we were through it and in sight of Little Niagara before I could even start bailing.

"We're going twelve miles an hour at least," Jack yelled. "Which one is this?"

"Niagara," I yelled. "Right center." The noise of the river swallowed my words and I only threw out two bucketfuls before we were over the lip of Niagara and I had to hold on. I could hear Ladle around the bend and I was throwing water so fast I lost my balance and that's when I heard Jack say, "Bail faster!" and that's when I threw the bail bucket into the river and watched, unbelieving, as it went under, and I saw Jack see it too but we were at Ladle and I had to sit down and hold on. I watched Harvey's big boat getting bounced around like a cork, and I think I closed my eyes when the first wave crashed over my face because the next thing I knew we were out of the heaviest water and Harvey was standing and smiling at us with his fist in the air.

I could see No Slouch around the bend and I don't remember it or 115
Miranda Jane because I was kneeling in the front of the boat scooping armfuls of water the whole time.

We all pulled up on the first beach we found and drank a beer and hugged each other uncertainly, like tenants in an apartment building where the fires have been put out.

"You're on your own," Harvey said. "We're camping here. Take a look at Wolf Creek, and be sure and get to shore before Selway Falls." He picked up a handful of black sand and let it run through his fingers. He turned to me. "He's a good boatman, and you're very brave."

I smiled.

"Take care of each other," he said. "Stay topside."

We set off alone and it clouded up and started to rain and I couldn't 120
make the topography match the river map.

"I can't tell where we are," I told Jack. "But Wolf Creek can't be far."

"We'll see it coming," he said, "or hear it."

But it wasn't five minutes after he spoke that we rounded a bend and were in it, waves crashing on all sides and Jack trying to find a way between the rocks and the holes. I was looking too, and I think I saw the run, fifty feet to our right, right before I heard Jack say, "Hang on, baby," and we hit the hole sideways and everything went white and cold. I was in the waves and underwater and I couldn't see Jack or the boat, I couldn't move my arms or legs apart from how the river tossed them. Jack had said swim down to the current, but I couldn't tell which way was down and I couldn't have moved there in that washing machine, my lungs full and taking on water. Then the wave spit me up, once, under the boat, and then again, clear of it, and I got a breath and pulled down away from the air and felt the current grab me, and I waited to get smashed against a rock, but the rock didn't come and I was at the surface riding the crests of some eight-foot rollers and seeing Jack's helmet bobbing in the water in front of me.

"Swim, baby!" he yelled, and it was like it hadn't occurred to me, like I was frozen there in the water. And I tried to swim but I couldn't get a breath and my limbs wouldn't move and I thought about the three minutes and hypothermia and I must have been swimming then because the shore started to get closer. I grabbed the corner of a big ledge and wouldn't let go, not even when Jack yelled at me to get out of the water, and even when he showed me an easy place to get out if I just floated a few yards downstream. It took all I had and more to let go of the rock and get back in the river.

I got out on a tiny triangular rock ledge, surrounded on all sides by walls 125
of granite. Jack stood sixty feet above me on another ledge.

"Sit tight," he said. "I'm going to go see if I can get the boat."

Then he was gone and I sat in that small space and started to shake. It was raining harder, sleeting even, and I started to think about freezing to death in that space that wasn't even big enough for me to move around in and get warm. I started to think about the river rising and filling that space and what would happen when Jack got back and made me float downstream to an easier place, or what would happen if he didn't come back, if he died trying to get the boat back, if he chased it fifteen miles to Selway Falls. When I saw the boat float by, right side up and empty, I decided to climb out of the space.

I'd lost one loafer in the river, so I wedged myself between the granite walls and used my fingers, mostly, to climb. I've always been a little afraid of heights, so I didn't look down. I thought it would be stupid to live through the boating accident and smash my skull free-climbing on granite, but as I inched up the wall I got warmer and kept going. When I got to the top there were trees growing across, and another vertical bank I hadn't seen from below. I bashed through the branches with my helmet and grabbed them one at a time till they broke or pulled out and then I grabbed the next one higher. I dug into the thin layer of soil that covered the rock with my knees and my elbows, and I'd slip down an inch for every two I gained. When I came close to panic I thought of Rambo, as if he were a real person, as if what I was doing was possible, and proven before, by him.

And then I was on the ledge and I could see the river, and I could see Jack on the other side, and I must have been in shock, a little, because I couldn't at that time imagine how he could have gotten to the other side of the river, I couldn't imagine what would make him go back in the water, but he had, and there he was on the other side.

"I lost the boat," he yelled. "Walk downstream till you see it." 130

I was happy for instructions and I set off down the scouting trail, shoe on one foot, happy for the pain in the other, happy to be walking, happy because the sun was trying to come out again and I was there to see it. It was a few miles before I even realized that the boat would be going over the falls, that Jack would have had to swim one more time across the river to get to the trail, that I should go back and see if he'd made it, but I kept walking downstream and looking for the boat. After five miles my bare foot started to bleed, so I put my left loafer on my right foot and walked on. After eight miles I saw Jack running up the trail behind me, and he caught up and kissed me and ran on by.

I walked and I walked, and I thought about being twenty-one and hiking in mountains not too far from these with a boy who almost drowned and then proposed to me. His boots had filled with the water of a river even farther to the north, and I was wearing sneakers and have a good kick, so I made it across just fine. I thought about how he sat on the far bank after he'd pulled himself out and shivered and stared at the water. And how I ran up and down the shore looking for the shallowest crossing, and then, thinking I'd found it, met him halfway. I remembered when our hands touched across the water and how I'd pulled him to safety and built him a fire and dried his clothes. Later that night he asked me to marry him and it made me happy and I said yes even though I knew it would never happen because I was too young and free and full of my freedom. I switched my loafer to the other foot and wondered if this danger would make Jack propose to me. Maybe he was the kind of man who needed to see death first, maybe we would build a fire to dry ourselves and then he would ask me and I would say yes because by the time you get to be thirty, freedom has circled back on itself to mean something totally different from what it did at twenty-one.

I knew I had to be close to the falls and I felt bad about what the wrecked boat would look like, but all of a sudden it was there in front of me, stuck on a gravel bar in the middle of the river with a rapid on either side, and I saw Jack coming back up the trail toward me.

"I've got it all figured out," he said. "I need to walk upstream about a mile and jump in there. That'll give me enough time to swim most of the way across to the other side of the river, and if I've read the current right, it'll take me right into that gravel bar."

"And if you read the current wrong?" I said. 135

He grinned. "Then it's over Selway Falls. I almost lost it already the second time I crossed the river. It was just like Harvey said. I almost gave up. I've been running twelve miles and I know my legs'll cramp. It's a long shot but I've got to take it."

"Are you sure you want to do this?" I said. "Maybe you shouldn't do this."

"I thought the boat was gone," he said, "and I didn't care because you were safe and I was safe and we were on the same side of the river. But there it is asking me to come for it, and the water's gonna rise tonight and take it over the falls. You stay right here where you can see what happens to me. If I make it I'll pick you up on that beach just below. We've got a half a mile to the takeout and the falls." He kissed me again and ran back upriver.

The raft was in full sunshine, everything tied down, oars in place. Even the map I couldn't read was there, where I stuck it, under a strap.

I could see Jack making his way through the trees toward the edge of 140
the river, and I realized then that more than any other reason for being on that trip, I was there because I thought I could take care of him, and maybe there's something women want to protect after all. And maybe Jack's old girlfriends were trying to protect him by making him stay home, and maybe I thought I could if I was there, but as he dropped out of sight and into the water I knew there'd always be places he'd go that I couldn't, and that I'd have to let him go, just like the widow said. Then I saw his tiny head in the water and I held my breath and watched his position, which was perfect, as he approached the raft. But he got off center right at the end, and a wave knocked him past the raft and farther down the gravel bar. He got to his feet and went down again. He grabbed for a boulder on the bottom and got washed even farther away. He was using all his energy to stay in one place and he was fifty yards downriver from the raft. I started to pray then, to whomever I pray to when I get in real trouble, and it may have been a coincidence but he started moving forward. It took him fifteen minutes and strength I'll never know to get to the boat, but he was in it, and rowing, and heading for the beach.

Later, when we were safe and on the two-lane heading home, Jack told me we were never in any real danger, and I let him get away with it because I knew that's what he had to tell himself to get past almost losing me.

"The river gave us both a lesson in respect," he said, and it occurred to me then that he thought he had a chance to tame that wild river, but I knew I was at its mercy from the very beginning, and I thought all along that that was the point.

Jack started telling stories to keep himself awake: the day his kayak held him under for almost four minutes, the time he crashed his hang glider twice in one day. He said he thought fifteen years of highwater was probably enough, and that he'd take desert rivers from now on.

The road stretched out in front of us, dry and even and smooth. We found a long dirt road, turned, and pulled down to where it ended at a chimney that stood tall amid the rubble of an old stone house. We didn't build a fire and Jack didn't propose; we rolled out our sleeping bags and lay down next to the truck. I could see the light behind the mountains in the place where the moon would soon rise, and I thought about all the years I'd spent saying love and freedom were mutually exclusive and living my life as though they were exactly the same thing.

The wind carried the smell of the mountains, high and sweet. It was so 145
still I could imagine a peace without boredom.

ENGAGING THE TEXT

1. What do you learn about Jack and the narrator in the opening pages of the story? How would you describe their relationship?
2. What different kinds of freedom does the narrator contemplate in this story? How does each feel to her? Which actions or decisions in "Selway" do you attribute to the characters' desire for freedom?
3. How do Jack and the narrator initially regard the Selway? How and why do their views of the river and their adventure change? How do your own impressions of the characters and their adventure develop as the story progresses? Have they achieved any type of freedom?
4. Why does Harvey throw "black sand" from the Selway at his new wife's feet? What does he mean when he says, "You know, black sand, love, marriage, Selway, rivers, life, the whole thing" (para. 62)?
5. Write a paragraph continuing the story from the point it leaves off. What will happen to Jack and the narrator? Where will they be five years from the end of their adventure? Which one will be freer?
6. At one point, the narrator says that freedom had "circled back on itself to mean something totally different from what it did at twenty-one" (para. 132). What does freedom mean to her at age twenty-one? At age thirty-one? Do you think your concept of freedom will change over the next ten or fifteen years? If so, how?

7. According to the narrator, the meaning of freedom is different for men and women. Do you agree that men and women see freedom differently? Why or why not?

Exploring Connections

8. Like Thomas Jefferson (p. 664), the narrator of "Selway" is concerned with "Life, Liberty, and the pursuit of Happiness." How would each define these terms? Which of these definitions comes closest to the way you see life, liberty, and happiness?
9. How might Michael Kimmel (p. 259) explain Jack's relationship to the narrator and the river? Do you think Jack's behavior and attitudes represent those of most men?
10. Review the selections by John (Fire) Lame Deer (p. 591) and Paula Gunn Allen (p. 312) and write a brief critique of the attitudes expressed or implied in "Selway" about relations between men and women and between humans and nature.
11. Look at the following cartoon and describe the views of freedom suggested by Wiley's male and female characters. How do these gendered views of freedom compare to those expressed in "Selway"?

Extending the Critical Context

12. Houston uses the Selway as a complex image of freedom in this story. What does her depiction of the Selway at flood stage tell us about this view of freedom? Think of a few other images that capture the idea of freedom for you, and write a brief paper exploring them.
13. Houston suggests that freedom in American culture is intimately associated with risk. What evidence do you see in the media—or from your own experience—that risk, danger, and perhaps even death are linked with the idea of freedom in America?

Easy in the Harness: The Tyranny of Freedom

GERRY SPENCE

As one of America's most outspoken and successful trial lawyers, Gerry Spence has more than a passing acquaintance with issues of freedom. In 1979 Spence came to national attention when he took on and defeated one of the largest nuclear power companies in the United States; representing Karen Silkwood, a power-plant employee exposed to lethal doses of radiation, Spence won fame as a champion of individual rights and as a relentless critic of corporate excess. In this selection, Spence wonders if Americans understand the meaning of freedom and claims that genuine freedom is, in fact, too painful for most of us to bear. The author of several books on justice and injustice in American society, Spence (b. 1929) continues to practice law in Jackson Hole, Wyoming. "Easy in the Harness" originally appeared in From Freedom to Slavery: The Rebirth of Tyranny in America *(1994).*

"What is freedom?" an enlightened teacher asked her class.

"It's when you can leave home and go wherever you want, and do whatever you want, and your parents can't tell you what to do," a child replied.

"But what if you get hungry? Are you now free to starve?"

"I would go home," the child says.

We are not free. Nor have we ever been. Perfect freedom demands a 5
perfect vision of reality, one too painful for the healthy to endure. It requires that we be alive, alert, and exquisitely aware of our raw being. Faced with the pain of freedom, man begs for his shackles. Afraid of death, he seeks the stultifying boundaries of religion. Afraid of loneliness, he imprisons himself in relationships. Afraid of want, he accepts the bondage of employment. Afraid of rejection, he conforms to the commands of society. If our knowledge of freedom were perfect we would not choose it. Pure freedom is pure terror.

Freedom is like a blank, white canvas when no commitments, no relationships, no plans, no values, no moral restraints have been painted on the free soul. A state of perfect freedom is a state of nothingness. When we care for another, when we make room for another's wants and needs, we have lost an equal portion of our freedom, but in the bargain we are freed of loneliness. When we take on marriage and a family, we are bound by our vows, the law, and our moral commitments to spouse and child, but our bargain frees us of detachment and meaninglessness. When we live in the country we can drive our trucks across the prairies, but when we join a community we cannot drive our cars across our neighbors' lawns. We can abide by no moral values without being limited by them. We can belong to no clubs without agreeing to their rules, or to a neighborhood without recognizing the rights of our neighbors. When we become residents of a village, a state, or a nation, we must obey its laws. In short, when we join into any relationship our dues are always paid in freedom.

Robert Frost[1] understood freedom and expressed its essence in a typical Frostian metaphor: "Freedom is when you are easy in the harness." Easy in the harness. I used to sit behind a team of good horses, Star and Spiffy, and together we mowed the meadow hay. Their flanks foamed with sweat and after struggling for weeks at their tugs, sores developed on their necks from their rubbing collars. I remember a deep, sad look in the eyes of the horses. I liked to touch the horses, to feel their softer-than-velvet noses against my cheek. I liked their smell. I loved old Star and Spiffy.

I suppose that team of horses was mostly "easy in the harness." Willingly they would trudge up and down the field all day, their heads down, their tugs tight, their flanks digging like the pistons of engines, and at the end of the day when I lifted the wet harnesses from their backs they would run for the corral and lie down in the deep dust and roll, and roll again. Then they would get up and shake the dust from their backs and wait for me to open the corral gate to the pasture.

One spring when I returned to the ranch I found Star and Spiffy gone. Nobody wanted to talk about it. "They're just gone," the old rancher said.

"But where?" I asked. 10

"Gone," was all he would say, and the way he said it with such finality made it clear that was to be the end of it. Later I learned that each fall a horse buyer visited the neighboring ranches to buy the ranchers' worn-out nags. They brought a few cents a pound for dog meat. Some claimed the meat was shipped to Europe where horse meat was allegedly a delicacy, especially with the French, but I never confirmed it.

As I look back on it the horses were as easy in their harnesses as we. And their deaths were perhaps better than our own. I could see in my mind's eye the old team being shipped off, the eyes of the old horses as sad as ever. But it was only another ride to them. They were not being trucked to their execution. Their bellies were not gripped with fear. There was no sadness, no regrets. And as the truck rumbled down the highway toward the slaughterhouse, the fall air must have blown through their manes and made their old tired eyes water, and they must have felt joy.

Every day we spend our freedom like careless children with too many pennies. In exchange for acceptance by our friends we give up the right to say what we think. Being socially proper is more important than possessing a fresh, uncompromised soul. Being acceptable to our neighbors is often more important than being acceptable to ourselves. For nearly two hundred

[1] *Robert Frost:* American poet (1874–1963).

years slavery thrived in America over the silent protestations of decent citizens enslaved themselves by the tyranny of convention. The price of freedom is often rejection, even banishment.

I knew an old rancher who lived on the Wind River in Wyoming. People didn't have much good to say about old Jack. His chief crime was that he told the truth as he saw it and laughed at things we were all afraid to laugh at. Every once in a while I'd stop by to see him. He was usually in his garden. That day he was hoeing his corn, a special hybrid variety he had developed for our short growing season, and he was also locally famous for his high-altitude peas and potatoes.

"Well, what has God wrought today?" I asked, knowing full well my 15
question would engender a strong response.

"You talkin' 'bout *me*," he replied. "I'm my own god."

"Jack, aren't you afraid of going to hell for saying such irreligious things?"

"There ain't no hell 'cept on earth." He went on hoeing. His shirt was wet with good fresh summer sweat.

"Suppose God heard you say that," I said prodding him a little. "What if he condemned you to burn in hell for an eternity for such heresy?" I'd been introduced to such horrors as a child in Sunday school.

"No just god would condemn ya fer usin' the power of reason he give 20
ya," he said, "and the idea of hell is plumb unreasonable." He stopped, leaned on his hoe handle, and squinted at me. "Besides, who would want ta worship a god that would send yer ass to hell forever fer such a triflin' transgression as not believin' somethin' that is unreasonable? That would be no *just* god, and if he ain't just I don't want nothin' ta do with him."

The old boy was already well past eighty and he knew that by all odds his days were numbered. "How you been feeling, Jack?" I asked, trying to change the subject.

"Feel just perty perfect," he said. Then he went back to hoeing. "But I may not make it another winter."

The following spring I stopped by. He was on his hands and knees planting his garden.

"Well, Jack, I see you made it through another winter."

"Yep," he said. "See ya done the same." 25

"God willing," I said.

"God didn't have nothin' ta do with it," he said.

"How come you're so tough on God?" I asked.

"On accounta those kinda ideas hurt a lotta innocent folks," he said. He never looked up from his planting while he talked. He dropped the brown bean seeds about an inch apart in the shallow furrow. "Christ taught that love is the supreme law. But they got it all mixed up. I got a lotta neighbors that love God and hate each other. I say if yer gonna love, ya oughta love something ya can see, say, yer neighbor fer instance."

30 He had radical ideas for his time, for instance his views on birth control, about which he spoke often and freely. "This here earth is overrun with people. The multitudes is starving everywhere. Now when I can't feed no more cows on this little ranch I sure don't raise no more calves. There ain't no starvin' calves here," he said. He covered the seed with his old crooked fingers and tamped the fresh, moist soil over them with the heels of his hands. "So how come my cows has got better rights than people? What kind of a god would want ya to raise up kids ta starve?"

When he got to the end of the row he stood up, stretched his old stiff back, and looked at me for the first time. "Why them churchgoin' neighbors a mine claim to love the fetus in the womb. But as soon as the kid is born, they say it's all right if it's left ta starve. I never could figure out why little kids who never done nothin' ta nobody should be punished by bein' sentenced ta starve ta death fer no worse crime than being born in the first place." When he looked at me I never saw a kinder set of eyes. I never knew a more honest man. I never knew a man who was more free than old Jack. But I think Jack was lonely sometimes. And, to the wonder and secret disappointment of some of his neighbors who were put off by his harsh and unedited comments on religion, and who thought for sure he'd never make it another winter, he lived through a dozen more after that.

Sometimes when I think of old Jack I realize how unfree I am, how afraid, how timid and intimidated and how the bargains I make sometimes leave me feeling cheated, how I sometimes trade honest convictions for silence to gain acceptance by those around me. Yet, in the end, I doubt that my neighbors love me any more than Jack's loved him. They respected him, that much I know, and maybe Jack valued their respect more than their love. Yet respect and love are sometimes hard to separate.

Jack's neighbors all came to his funeral, and some who had been his most severe critics had tears in their eyes. I doubt that Jack would have been surprised. I think he knew.

They buried old Jack out behind his garden where he wanted, close to the creek. As they lowered the pine box into the ground I could hear his creaky old voice arguing away. "Why, Spence," he said, "we kick our dogs if they shit in the house, but we shit all over this beautiful planet like a herd a hogs sufferin' from terminal diarrhea. Baby owls are smarter'n that. Ya never seen a baby owl that ever fouled its nest. These human bein's ain't too smart a species."

35 And I thought, Well, Jack, your old bones won't pollute this little plot behind your garden, that's for sure. Next spring you'll turn into fresh buds on the cottonwood trees, and maybe you won't think that's too bad a place to be. Maybe that's eternity after all. Earth to earth.

"Beats hell outta hell," I could hear old Jack reply. And then I turned away before the neighbors could catch up with me to tell me all about how old Jack was. One thing I knew: old Jack was free. Always had been.

The notion of "being American" is heavily laden with ideas of freedom. Being American and being free are often thought synonymous. As Americans we envision Washington's battered patriots marching to the beat of the boy drummer. We see Washington crossing the Delaware. We think of the Constitution and the Bill of Rights, and remember the Civil War, Lincoln and the Gettysburg Address, the freeing of the slaves, the great world wars "to keep America free." We see the billowing smoke of the ships sinking at Pearl Harbor and our American heroes raising the flag at Iwo Jima. And we remember the marches of Martin Luther King, Jr. We believe we are free in the same way we believe in God. Freedom is an article of faith, not a fact, not a condition. True, the freedom we enjoy in America, when set against the freedom of peoples in other lands, is emblazoned like a single candle lighting the gloom.

Law and order and rules, although antithetical to freedom, provide us with safeguards by which we are free to live with reasonable safety among those who are stronger. But the strong impose themselves upon us nevertheless. Although our younger, stronger neighbor is not free to force us out of our homes, the bank can do so if we fail to pay it its tribute of green flesh. Although we argue we are free to labor where we please for whomever we please, unless we show up in the morning, unless like old Star and Spiffy, we take our places in our stanchions and consent to the harness, we will be free to join the depressed and desperate masses of the unemployed who become harnessed to yet another master — fear.

If we are American, we believe in an American religion called "free enterprise," the principal tenet of which holds that it is not only moral but divine to reserve for the corporate oligarchy substantially all the wealth — leaving to the people the blessed right to obtain whatever, if any, dribbles down. The religion called "free enterprise" holds that in exchange for corporate America's right to squash and squeeze from all below it, the next in power possess the right to squash and squeeze those below them, and so on down the line until there is nothing left but the empty dredges of humanity. Some of these we discard on the streets, where they are free to die of hunger, disease, and shame. Those who rebel are at last housed — in prisons. . . .

40 Today we are more concerned with extracting freedom from our enemies than in preserving our own. We wish into prison those who terrorize us in the streets and who break into our cars and homes. We wish the executioner's hand against those who kill our innocent without just cause. At last we wish to eliminate all those from our society who threaten us and frighten us and injure and kill us, and we seem willing to diminish or release our constitutional rights, indeed, our freedom, to be safer. In truth, we long for a more successful domestication of the human species.

I recall a certain white heifer at the ranch, a full-blown renegade. When she was disturbed in the slightest she would run bellowing and bawling and wildly kicking at everything and anything, including the air. To get her from one pasture to another took half a dozen good men on good horses half a day. I would have sent her to the butcher but for the fact that I had paid a pretty price for her one crazy afternoon at a fancy purebred sale that had been held in the lobby of the Hilton Hotel in Denver.

When her calf came, the calf was just like her. The little renegade wasn't more than a few days old when it kicked the old dog and broke his jaw. But for the fact that the calf in all other respects was quite a beautiful specimen and would bring a good price, I would have rid the ranch of her as well. But the calf's calf was even worse. Finally I realized I was breeding back to the wildebeest, and that unless I abandoned that bloodline, I would end up with an utterly unmanageable herd of cattle that would eventually do me in.

Domestication has been the specialty of man from the beginning. He domesticated the wolf into the dog, the wildcat into the lap pussy, the wild horse into the plow horse, the wildebeest into the Hereford and the Holstein. He has also been busily domesticating himself. As in the domestication of animals he has been selecting the most compliant members of his species and eliminating the least.

Today, America imprisons more people than any nation in the world. Those who occupy our prisons have been our noncomplying social deviants, whom we have removed from the reproductive cycle. In recent times we have become more willing to impose the death penalty against our own for a broader assortment of crimes. Facing proof that the death penalty has no deterring effect on crime whatsoever, we nevertheless encourage its imposition out of our true purpose, not to punish, not to prevent future crimes, but to further domesticate the species by eliminating those who are less compliant than we.

Something about servitude stills. Something about domestication stifles. 45
The wolf, now the poodle, no longer howls. The wild boar lies on its side in the hog pen and grunts. The wildebeest stands in her stall placidly chewing her cud while she's milked dry. Domestication of man and beast muffles the cry of freedom and suffocates the spirit of liberty.

As we continue to domesticate the species, we tend toward the creation of a mass of mankind that is as easily herded as a flock of dead-eyed sheep. This amorphous glob faithfully mumbles the liturgy demanded by the corporate oligarchy, which holds that it is moral to take first and most from the weakest and the poorest. The dogma also holds that it is laudable to create classes of people based on wealth, not virtue, that is to say, it makes no difference how miserly, how greedy, how uncaring and spiteful the individual may be, if he has wealth he is of a different and better class than the virtuous without wealth. This religion to which the people are bound delivers to the corporate oligarchy the prerogative to ply its enormous powers against the people in order to become yet more powerful. And so it has been throughout human history as man struggles for his freedom, fights and dies for it, but having once achieved it, squanders it or casts it aside as too naked, too frightening, too painful to long possess.

I think of the wars that have been fought, allegedly for freedom. More often the blood and suffering and death were sacrificed so that massively powerful moneyed interests might remain free to use us up in our harnesses. I think of the endless list of the dead who were said to have given their lives so that we might be free. But after the wars nothing much changed. As usual we arose every morning, slipped into our harnesses, plodded to our work, and believed we were free. Then we died.

We all wear our harnesses, and if we are easy in them, if we feel free, is not the illusion of freedom as satisfactory as freedom itself? Should we fret over our servitudes, petty or grand, when the fictions of freedom we embrace often serve as satisfactorily? Is not a shackled slave who cannot see or feel his chains as free as if he had no chains at all? Should we free the happy slave and cast him into the chaos and horrors of pure freedom? Indeed, have we not at last achieved the prediction of *Brave New World,*[2] in which Aldous Huxley observed that the "really efficient totalitarian state would be one in which the all-powerful executive of political bosses and their army of managers control a population of slaves who do not have to be coerced, because they love their servitude"? Huxley argued that, "To make them love it [their bondage] is the task assigned, in present-day totalitarian states. . . ." Ought we not consider the possibility that the *1984*[3] of George Orwell has come and gone and that his once chilling oracle is the culture of our time, one in which we do, in fact, love our bondage, one where, in fact, we happily accept the clichés, the images, the fables, and the fictions of freedom in the place of freedom itself?

Freedom, "that sweet bondage," as Shelley[4] called it, is a marvelous thing in small doses. Not to be afraid of our government is blessed. Not to be lied to, not to be cheated, not to be exploited and poisoned and hurt for corporate greed, not to be used up like old rags; to be heard, to be respected, to grow and to discover our uniqueness — these are the freedoms we most cherish, freedoms we, by reason of our occupancy of this earth, are entitled to enjoy.

Yet most of our freedoms lie within. As the poem goes, "Stone walls do 50
not a prison make, nor iron bars a cage." Most freedoms cannot be given, except as we give them to ourselves.

I think of old Jack who cherished his freedom above all. He is, at last, free, totally free, since freedom, by common definition, is a condition in which the individual may do what he wants, and since the dead have no

[2]*Brave New World:* A 1932 novel by Aldous Huxley portraying a future technocratic society in which life is completely controlled from cradle to grave.

[3]*1984:* A 1949 novel by George Orwell portraying life in an imagined totalitarian state.

[4]*Shelley:* Percy Bysshe Shelley (1792–1822), English Romantic poet also known for his radical politics, atheism, and advocacy of sexual freedom.

wants they are, are they not, totally free? Or perhaps as the Greeks argued, "Only Zeus is free."

And I also think of old Star and Spiffy, and of their freedom. Were I as successful, as free. Were I able to mow the meadows of my life and live by my own work as well. Were I able to remove the harness from within — such is freedom. And when finally the legs have given out, when the bones are old and brittle and crooked, and at last the shoulders too crippled to pull the load, I should hope that on the way to wherever it is that old horses and old men go I feel the wind through my hair, and that my eyes do not water from tears, but from having felt the joy of the trip, the trip to the last and only freedom.

Engaging the Text

1. What, according to Spence, is perfect freedom, and why is it so hard to bear?
2. Explain the point of the story Spence tells about Star and Spiffy. How does he feel about these horses and their fate? What does their story say about freedom?
3. Spence says that each American wears a "harness" within. What forces and institutions, according to Spence, impose this invisible harness? What other social forces or institutions would you add to this list? To what extent do you agree with Spence that "we long for a more successful domestication of the human species" (para. 40)?
4. What's particularly free about "old Jack"? Do you think it's inevitable that a genuinely free human being must also be offensive? Why?

Exploring Connections

5. How might Spence interpret the actions and reactions of Jack and the narrator in "Selway" (p. 668)? Which of these characters would he be more likely to sympathize with? Why?
6. Review two or more selections involving the following individuals or characters:

   Richard Rodriguez (p. 61)
   the narrator in "Para Teresa" (p. 74)
   Malcolm X (p. 77)
   Gary Soto (p. 145)
   Anndee Hochman (p. 150)
   Nora Quealey (p. 253)
   Judith Ortiz Cofer (p. 278)
   Paula Gunn Allen (p. 312)
   Adrienne Rich (p. 365)
   C. P. Ellis (p. 388)
   Stephen Cruz (p. 460)
   Sylvia in "The Lesson" (p. 482)
   Sucheng Chan (p. 541)

   Which of these individuals or characters seem the most free to you in Spence's sense of the word? Which seem most "domesticated"? Which challenge or complicate Spence's definition of what it means to be free?
7. Spence suggests that being free means being an outsider. How might Malcolm X (p. 77), Carmen Vázquez (p. 287), Paula Gunn Allen (p. 312), and/or Haunani-Kay Trask (p. 571) respond to this idea?

Extending the Critical Context

8. Make an inventory of the "deals," "bargains," or "trades" that you make with your friends, family, employer, school, and society every day. How do these implied agreements limit your freedom? What do you get in return for honoring them? Which of these "deals" impinge most on your freedom?
9. Write a profile of a person you've known who, as Jack does for Spence, symbolizes freedom for you. In this portrait, try to clarify how this person expresses her freeness and how her freedom has affected others.
10. Spence suggests that America is more concerned with the "illusion" of freedom than with its reality. Working in groups, survey a number of music videos and print ads for contemporary images of freedom. How is freedom portrayed in American culture? What costs or consequences are typically associated with it?

Charlie Sabatier

John Langston Gwaltney

Charlie Sabatier, speaker of the following monologue, offers a powerful example of the costs of freedom. A paraplegic veteran of the Vietnam War, Sabatier returned to the United States to become an activist for the disabled. This interview originally appeared in John Langston Gwaltney's The Dissenters *(1986). No stranger himself to the problems encountered by the physically challenged, Gwaltney (b. 1928) is a blind anthropologist who has made a career of studying the attitudes of marginalized groups; his first major book,* Drylongso *(1980), is a moving collection of first-person accounts of what it means to be a Black American. Gwaltney is currently a professor of anthropology at Syracuse University.*

Combat duty in Southeast Asia left Charlie Sabatier with a need for a wheelchair, but it is difficult for me to think of him as confined. The truth is, his mind is infinitely freer now than it was for most of his pre-Vietnam life. In that pre-Vietnam, South Texas existence, Charlie and I would probably not have had very much to do with one another. But in July of 1982 we met and talked in his suburban Boston home and he turned out to be civil, hospitable, direct, and a formidable raconteur. The talking and listening were facilitated by the array of thick sandwiches and cold beer he provided. Late in the afternoon of our day of talking and listening Charlie's wife, Peggy, phoned. He maneuvered his wheelchair out of the house they are remodeling, down the drive, and into his car and drove off to pick her up.

The May 1982 issue of the American Coalition of Citizens with Disabilities newsletter had carried a story about Charlie's successful battle with Delta Airlines over one of their policies regarding disabled persons. The story read, in part:

On March 17, 1982, in East Boston, Charles Sabatier fought with Delta Airlines over evacuation. Sabatier was arrested when he refused to comply with a Delta Airlines safety policy which stipulates that a disabled person must sit on a blanket while in transit so that he/she can be evacuated in case of emergency. . . . When Sabatier refused to sit on the blanket (which was folded), the flight was delayed, and Sabatier was eventually arrested for disorderly conduct.

The court in which he was charged was located in an inaccessible courthouse. Sabatier refused to be carried up the courthouse steps and was therefore arraigned on the steps. The location of the trial was then moved to an accessible courthouse. Charges against Sabatier were dismissed in court when the parties reached a pretrial settlement. Delta agreed to change its policy so that use of a blanket to evacuate persons will be optional and paid Sabatier $2,500.00 for legal fee expenses, $1.00 of which would be for punitive damages at Sabatier's request. Sabatier agreed not to sue Delta over the incident.

5 This blanket thing had happened to me at least a dozen times before, and in the last three years I've flown at least three dozen times. I mean, I've been *everywhere.* I've been to Seattle and Los Angeles and San Francisco and New Orleans and Chicago and any place you can name that's on the map, practically, any major city, I've been there in the last three years. I've been subjected to that probably ninety percent of the times I flew Delta or Eastern. I would protest. I would get on just like this time. I would get on out of the wheelchair and into this aisle chair that Delta, by the way, likes to call the "invalid" chair — I've even written them letters about that. You know, about how language means things. Like you don't call black people niggers and you don't call women broads and chick and honey and you don't call disabled people cripples and invalids. You know, I told 'em what an invalid meant. That that's somebody in a bed, totally helpless. I said, "I'm not totally helpless and stop calling me names." And I'd write them nice bureaucratic-type letters. Yeah, they write back all the time, bureaucratic-type things. They got a standard-type letter, I'm telling ya. They hire somebody, you know, whose only qualification is — can you write a bureaucratic meaningless letter? You know, at least a one-pager. That guy's probably paid twenty-five thousand dollars a year to answer people like me. And I never got anywhere by it, but that didn't stop me from writing them. I had to write to get it out of my system, I think. One of the things I contended was that the whole damn policy was arbitrary and capricious because it happened to me a dozen times before and I always talked my way off the blanket! I'd get in there and argue with 'em and talk about my rights and all this self-worth,

dignity, humiliation, and stigma and they'd go "Jesus Christ! Get him out of here. Forget about it." You know, "Just go sit down." They'd go, "Hey, we gotta take off, man!" So they'd say "Listen, forget it." And so that's what would happen. They would just forget about their dumb policy. And so I expected the same thing to happen this time. I mean, they're gonna subject me to this and I'll argue and get away with it. And this time I ran into a captain. The stewardess actually said forget it, and I went down—that's how I got into the seat. 'Cause this all happened at the door of the plane by the captain's cabin when I transferred from my chair to the aisle chair that gets me down the narrow aisle. And we argued and someone behind said, "Forget it." And so we went down. I got in the chair, got in the seat, had my seat belt on, they moved the chair out of the aisle and she comes down and says, "I'm sorry, the captain insists that you sit on the blanket." I said, "Look, you tell the captain what I told you. That I'm not about to sit on this blanket." And we went through this whole thing and I argued with every Delta person in probably the whole terminal over the course of about forty-five minutes and naturally, you know, this plane's going to Miami and everybody's saying, "Let's get going!" Yeah, I mean, it's not like it's wintertime and you're going to Minneapolis. They wanted to get going. Everybody's kinda wondering. I think the people on the plane, who saw me coming on, see, in this chair, they figured, this guy is sick or something and they were pretty nice. Well, finally the stewardess got irritated about this delay and she walks down the aisle and she used to like stoop down to talk to me but this time she comes down and just stands there and says, "Look, if you don't sit on the blanket, we're gonna have to de-board the plane and cancel the flight." Out loud, see? So everybody said, "Wait a minute, this guy's not sick. This delay's just 'cause he won't sit on a blanket." So some guy yells out, like about five rows behind me, "You mean to tell me that this delay is because this guy won't sit on a blanket?" And she says "Yes!" And he says, "Look, man, if I sit on a blanket, will you sit on a blanket?" And I said, "No. But if everybody sits on a blanket, I'll sit on a blanket." And he says, "Well, why do you have to sit on a blanket?" And she says, "It's for his safety." He says, "It's for your own good, do it." I said, "Look, seat belts are for people's safety. *Everybody* gets one. If blankets are for my safety, I want everybody to get one, Okay? If it's so good for my safety, it's so good for everybody else's. But if I'm the only one that has to do it, it's like puttin' a bag over an ugly man's head, you know? I mean, that's a stigma." So the guy says, "Okay, then we'll all sit on blankets." Everybody says, "Yeah!" So half these people started chanting, "We want blankets! We want blankets! We want blankets!" I kinda enjoyed it, 'cause I was getting some support finally. I was getting a kick out of it, but at the same time I was a little bit nervous. It was funny except for the fact that the State Police officer was comin' down the aisle at the same time they were chanting on the plane. So he says, "Either you sit on this blanket or I'm gonna have to arrest you." I said, "What charge? Where's the blanket charge?" He says, "Disorderly conduct." And that got me mad. Disorderly conduct? *These* are the people chanting "We want blankets," it's their conduct. I said, "If anybody's being disorderly, it's them. And it's this airline that's treating me like dirt who should be arrested." I said, "Besides, you don't work for the airline. You work for the State of Massachusetts, just like me. You shouldn't be arresting people that are violating some policy they have. This is not a Federal Aviation Administration regulation. And even if it was, it should be the feds making the arrest here, not you. You're out of your jurisdiction." Well, he didn't get ahold of all that and goes, "Oh well, I don't care. Look, these people are gonna have to get off, you're interrupting and costing them a lot of money. I'm going to arrest you. I'll worry about that later." I says, "You bet you will, 'cause I'm gonna sue you for false arrest. I got two attorneys sitting right here, right next to me, and I've got their cards and they've already said that I haven't done anything wrong and they're gonna be witnesses. You'd better write down your own witnesses 'cause you're gonna need 'em." I found out later that I was right. That I wasn't guilty of disorderly conduct.

But an ironic thing was that the guy who arrested me had a twelve-year-old son with multiple sclerosis who was in an electric wheelchair! When I was in his office taking care of the paperwork we were talking about his son and I said, "I'll tell you something. I feel better about taking a stand and doing this than I *ever* felt about my role in the war in Vietnam. I know that what I'm doing right here is right. I know right from wrong and I know that this policy humiliates people and irregardless of its intention to evacuate people in the event of a survivable crash, and that was even suspect if that was the real intention, it's categoric discrimination," I said. Because when they see me as a nonambulatory person they categorically discriminated against me because they have me stereotyped as being helpless. I have no problem about how they get me out of the plane, *if* they get me out. I've got a problem about how they treat me *before* the crash. They could put the blanket above the seat in the compartment, they could put it under the seat. Do they think I'm gonna sit there and twiddle my thumbs in the seat waitin' for the stewardess to come back and get me on the blanket? I weigh two hundred pounds! Give me a break! I'm gonna be out of that seat just like I got in it, 'cause I know that when people start headin' for the exits, they're not comin' back for their purse, right? I mean, they're gonna be in the aisle, right down back, and there's gonna be this big cluster of people around the doors jumpin' out and I'll be right behind 'em. There are like eighty-, ninety-year-old people who get on that plane with the help of a walker and their grandson and they help 'em sit down and they kiss 'em good-bye. I'm telling you, if there was a survivable crash, those people, because of arthritis and age, couldn't get out. They'd be more helpless in a situation than I would, but they're ambulatory, you see, so they don't have to sit on a blanket. I mean, I had 'em cold, it was just unbelievable. I could have brought paraplegics in there who can lift five hundred pounds. I mean, I can prove that paraplegics are not helpless people.

If I had been in that pilot's place, of course I wouldn't have done what he did. 'Course not, because I think I have more common sense than he had. I mean, I think I'd realize that if there was really a survivable crash, you're just gonna grab somebody and try to drag 'em out, no one's going to think about which one. I'll tell you something that I've always suspected. In their minds, they didn't just see me as a helpless person, they saw me as an incontinent person. They had probably had experiences of people who were paralyzed and incontinent and they're trying to protect the upholstery of their seats. That's not unusual, that paternalism. You know, I lobby all the time. I'll talk to people a half hour in their office — senators, congressmen — and on the way out I'll get patted on the back like I'm a little kid. I mean, even very high officials. They're so far out of tune with what's goin' on in the disabled movement and the women's movement, the black movement, I mean, they're just so engrossed, I guess, in doing their job, that they lose contact.

I've got a blind friend who we see every once in a while. One day I'm walking down the street with this guy — and he's got dark glasses and a white cane — and a guy pulls over and says to me, "Hey! Could you tell me how to get to the Prudential Building?" Well, I had been here only a year and a half and I know the major roads, but I don't know the names of the streets so my friend starts talkin' and tells the guy how to get there and the guy pulls off and like five feet later pulls over and asks somebody else, 'cause he says to himself, "Blind guys don't know where anything is." But my friend can get around that town as well as anybody else. If anybody's gonna memorize how to get around, he is. But yeah, that's not untypical of the nondisabled population.

One of the things that happens when you stigmatize people is, you see, if I can call people "niggers" in my mind, I don't think of these people as human beings. There's not equality, you know. They're not my peers. If I call a Vietnamese a gook, it's easier to kill him than Mr. Hung Yung or whatever his name would be, right? So we do it. Americans do it, everyone, man. We call people krauts, limeys, gooks, niggers, and handicapped. People are refusing to recognize people as people, as having human traits. It's easier to just stereotype a large group of people than it is to deal with the problems and the need.

10 We always deal with problems in this country either technologically or monetarily, and that's how this country has decided to deal with disabled people. Hey, I get my butt shot up in Vietnam, I come back here, they're not interested in what I'm gonna do, you know. They're not interested in my head problems about Vietnam or getting over all that trauma. It's later for that. We'll dump some money on you, just like, stay home. But if I say, "Look, later with your money. Stop subsidizing my life, just allow me equal opportunity to make my way in this life to the best that I can and all I want you to do is provide me accessible transportation so that I can get to and from my job, or make that post office that's two blocks away from here accessible so I can mail a letter and maintain my dignity while I'm doing it,

rather than have somebody go up and do it for me," they refuse to do that. They'll dump money on you though, so you can stay home.

I don't even know if I could really give an answer as to why I didn't sit on the blanket. I know good people, good friends of mine, who have sat on that blanket, and I consider them to be real advocates. They did it because, I guess, it was like the easiest course to take. Most people's lives, I think, probably are like water. Water runs to the easiest course and most people would prefer to go around a confrontation than actually confront somebody. Oh for sure I would have preferred that. I mean, nobody enjoys confrontation, really. I think you'd have to be sick to really enjoy confrontation. There's a lot that's gone on in my life that goes way back. There's building blocks, I guess, and you see things and it takes time. You are what you are today because of what you were yesterday and the day before. We are an accumulation.

I think by the time I got out of the army, I said to myself, "I'm gonna start making the decisions in my life." Because I was always saying, "I should have listened to myself." Well, I started really making decisions for myself for the first time when I was layin' in a bloody mess in Vietnam. It was the first time, okay? Up until then I'd always been doing these crazy things on the advice of other people. I grew up in a time where we saw too many John Wayne movies, okay? I was a World War II baby, I was born in July of forty-five and I grew up with all this Audie Murphy,[1] John Wayne type of thing. The good guy goes to war, gets a bullet in the shoulder, meets and marries the pretty nurse, and they live happily ever after. That was war to me — and besides, we always won. We were always the good guys and we were always moral and ethical and all that. That was the propaganda that I was fed all my life, through movies, television. When I was young, "Combat" was the big show. Vic Morrow, who just died, was the buck sergeant. I grew up in South Texas, my dad was a marine in World War II. I fell for it. I don't think that the movie industry really thought that they were propagandizing, but that's what it is. 'Cause you were subjected to only one side. I mean, the Nazis were always bad, every Nazi was bad, every bad guy had a foreign accent. The Japanese were the people who were always torturing people. My God, we'd never do a thing like that! Oh no! But I believed it. I mean, I was twenty years old and I believed it. I had *never learned* to question.

Actually I started questioning before I got shot but that changed my life completely. When I got shot I took a different road, I guess, from the one I might have taken. I probably would have come back from 'Nam and gone back to school and been workin' in a bank with a couple kids, probably divorced, I'm sure, that type of thing. But it's strange, you know. Being shot has made my life probably a lot more exciting. I would have probably lived a normal, average mundane kind of life. But it's like I entered a whole new field. I started learning real fast that disabled people were not considered the general population and I started wondering why.

[1]*Audie Murphy:* Most decorated American soldier of World War II (1924–1971).

I learned what things meant and the language and semantics got important to me. I was six foot two, a hundred seventy-five pounds, I'd never been disabled or in a hospital in my life. I had never seen anybody die before, then all of a sudden in a short period of time I'm killing people, people are trying to kill me, then I do get shot and almost killed. I get back and *then* I'm subjected to the worst bunch of crap I've ever seen in my life. I started being treated like dirt. It was ironic. Up until the time I got shot I was like Number One citizen. My country was spendin' *billions* of dollars for me. Thousands of dollars just to train me how to kill, thousands more dollars to send my halfway around the world to save us from "Communism." And they let it thrive ninety miles away! When I got in the army, that's when I started thinkin', wait a minute. Like I'm on this airplane and all of a sudden I realized, this is a one-way ticket! I'd been enslaved to keep this country "free." I'd been drafted for two years and if you don't think it's slavery, you just try to walk away from it! And so I said, okay, number one, I'm a slave, then I say, where am I? I'm goin' halfway around the world 'cause we had to pick a fight with some little Southeast Asian country to save the world from Communism! I had never even met a Vietnamese. I didn't even know what one *looked* like. I couldn't tell one from a Japanese and I'm going to go over there and kill these people? I thought, "This is ridiculous."

15 I was like twenty-one when I got there and the average age of everybody in 'Nam was nineteen. Which meant that the average age of the infantry, the guy on the line, was about seventeen and a half. And I just couldn't believe it. I just couldn't believe what was goin' on there. And we were goin' around in circles, you know, killin' people, and they were killin' us and it was like no war that we ever had. You never took ground, you never went north — you know, *that's* where the enemy is, Goddamn!

I think that we are a nation of dissenters. Our nation was created by dissenters. Anybody that's ever made a major change in this world has been someone who was a dissenter. It's been done by somebody, you know, who you would call an unreasonable person. It was George Bernard Shaw[2] who said the reasonable man looks at the world as it is and tries to adapt himself to suit the world. And the unreasonable man sees the world as it is and tries to change the world to suit himself. Therefore, said Shaw, all progress depends on the unreasonable man. I think that's absolutely true! And it's those dissenters that I think really are like a drumbeat ahead, you know, from the rest of the band. They are the people that are leading. Hey! If there were no dissenters, if there were no "unreasonable" people there'd just simply be the status quo. We'd still be goin' around as cave men. But somebody had to have a better idea. And it seems like every time somebody's got a better idea, the status quo is there to start callin' him names.

Like what I did. People would say, "Man, that was an unnatural thing

[2]*George Bernard Shaw:* Irish-born English playwright and critic (1856–1950).

to do." And it *is* unnatural, because thousands of people have sat on the damn blanket before me. I guess they didn't consider it unnatural. But I'm telling ya, people are going to *have* to start becoming more unnatural, if that's what you want to call it, more unreasonable; less tolerant with those greedy people.

I don't know what makes people principled dissenters. I'll tell ya, you're searching for somethin' and it's kinda like searching for something smaller than the atom. You *know* something's there, but it's those building blocks or the makeup or whatever that substance is that makes people good people or bad people. You know something's there, you're tryin' to search for it but I just don't think that we're there yet. I don't think we know what it is. I don't know. Everybody's different in their intellect, their ability. I'm no genius. I'm not really great with the books. I have to study real hard. I'm not super smart or anything, but I just think I was born with the right genes or something that just gave me good *common sense.* Good common sense to know right from wrong, good from bad and make good decisions in my life. And every once in a while we blow it.

I remember the first time I ever recognized discrimination in my life. I was on a bus and this great big, huge black lady gets on the bus and sits down and faces me and the bus driver stopped the bus and said, "I'm sorry, lady, you're gonna have to move to the back of the bus." And she says somethin' like, "Look I have a right to sit here. I don't have to sit back there. My feet are hurtin' me. I've been working all day. I don't want to walk back down there." Just like Rosa Parks.[3] And he says, "Look, that's the law! Either you sit in the back of the bus or this bus don't go anywhere." So she was at that tired, worn-out stage and says okay, I'm ready for a rest. So *she* was a principled dissenter as far as I'm concerned. First one I ever heard of. And she says, "Then you do what you have to do. I'm gonna sit here, I'm tired." So he got off the bus, went to the corner, and got this cop who was directin' traffic, and this cop come on and like put a handcuff on her and took her off the bus. Boy! I thought, what's goin' on here? I never realized, see, up until that time that black people had to sit in the back of the bus. I just thought, they wanted to sit there, that they liked it there. I guess I was about nine. I thought, well, I guess I'm always sittin' near white people 'cause I want to, but I never thought about goin' back there. I just never thought of it And then, all of a sudden, boom! I started thinking' about it. All the way when I was goin' home I was thinkin', what'd she do? I didn't see her do anything. I thought maybe she had pickpocketed or robbed a purse. I didn't know. Why did they take her off the bus? I didn't know anything about it. And so I went home and I said to my mother, "What happened? This lady was arrested. I don't understand. Why couldn't she sit there?" And my mother said, "That's just the way things are. They've always been like that

[3]*Rosa Parks:* The Black woman whose refusal to give up her seat to a white passenger initiated a bus boycott in Montgomery, Alabama, in 1955.

and that's the way they're always gonna be. Don't worry about it. Go outside and play." So I went outside and I remember sittin' on the porch for a long time and thinkin' about it, and *knowin'* that, now, I'm not getting the right answer here. Somethin's goin' on here, you know, like, even if it's always been that way and it's always goin' to be that way, well, why? Why is it that way? That's what I asked. I didn't get any answer to my question and back then that's probably the first time I started questioning like an adult would do. You know, I never thought of that again from that time on until after I got shot and I was in the VA hospital. The nurses were leavin' at four-thirty to go out and stand on the bus stop and take the bus and somebody said, "Why don't we go and take a bus and go down and have a drink with the nurses?" And everybody laughed. Ha. Ha. And there it went — boy! When that guy said that, I went back, back, seeing that person on the bus. And all of a sudden I went, "I don't believe this!" That's the first time that I had ever been discriminated against in my life!

20 I had been fortunate to live until that time as a white person in this racist society, and I'd never experienced any kind of discrimination, none. All of a sudden I realized — you know my life was so screwed up, it was like a big jigsaw puzzle and I had found one piece to start putting my life back together and I wanted to talk about it. Like, hey! There's a big puzzle out here and I know that if we can fit all the pieces together I'll understand everything that's happening to me. And that was the first significant piece of the puzzle I found out.

Listen, I'll tell you a story. This happened to me in New York. I came back from Los Angeles on TWA and I got to the terminal at Kennedy International and I was getting a transfer to Delta, okay? It had nothin' to do with the blanket, but another problem. Delta's terminal is in a separate terminal. It's about a half a mile around. And there's no curb cuts or anything. So I get there, it's midnight, and I get my bags on my lap and I'm goin' out and I figure I'll catch a cab around. So I ask a guy about cabs and he says, "Well, you're gonna have a hard time. Those cabbies have been sittin' in the line two hours and they want a big fare to go downtown." I says, "Well, I'll get one." So I went out and I told this lady who was the dispatcher. "I want a cab." She says, "Where ya goin'?" I said, "Delta Airlines." She says, "Nope! Nobody'll take ya!" So I say, "Look, then if I can't get over there, I want to go downtown, stay in a hotel overnight." She says, "Okay." Cab comes up, I get in, the guy puts my chair in the trunk and he says, "Where ya goin'?" "Delta Airlines." "Nope. I'm waiting here for a fare to go downtown." And I says, "Well, I ain't goin' downtown, I want to go to Delta Airlines." The dispatcher says, "You said you were goin' downtown." I said, "I changed my mind." He says, "Get out of the cab, I'm not goin' to take you over there. I've been sittin' here two hours." "No, I'm not going to get out." So *he* gets out and he takes my chair out of the trunk. I locked his doors. And he says, "Look, I'll call the police." And I said, "Call 'em. You call 'em and then I'll sue *you*." I says, "If you call 'em you're gonna be involved the whole damn night, you won't get another fare the whole night. Either you want to do that or take me to Delta. I don't know specifically what the law is here but I guarantee you you can't refuse to take me where I want to go. That's discrimination. Besides, if you don't take me to Delta, I'm not gonna letcha back in the cab!" And he says, "Look, man, don't make me break into my own cab!" I says, "I'm gonna tell ya, take me to Delta or I'm gonna crawl over this seat and drive this goddamned cab myself over there!" We went to Delta Airlines. That has happened to me, like, three times! I've locked the door. I'm just not gonna do that you know. And I know damn well ninety-nine percent of disabled people would *never* do anything like that because the movement is in its infancy stage. But we're getting there.

It *bugs* me that people in this country are always talkin' about civil rights, you know. When I think of rights, I think of something more — a civil right is something that is written in law and that's all bullshit anyway. We don't need any laws, we don't need any constitution, we don't need the Declaration of Independence. All we need to do is treat people with respect.

I grew up about twenty miles from this town called Alvin, Texas, and there used to be a sign out there — I was in junior high school the last time I saw it. I think since then they've had to take the thing down. It was a sign out in front of the town that said, "Nigger, don't let the sun set on your head." Not until I was twenty years old did I get out of South Texas. I'm not a racist. I might have been. I remember one time I pushed the button on the water fountain marked "white" and no water would come out of it, so I pushed the button marked "colored" and water came out, but I would not drink it. At that time we would think nothing about tellin' a racist joke — and laughing. Maybe that's a way of finding out who's a real racist. Something's happened to me. I don't think I've lost my sense of humor, I'm pretty funny, I laugh — we've been laughing here — but I just don't appreciate those kinds of jokes. The important thing was, I think, not just one incident, but I kept seeing incidents like that.

When I went into the army I was in Germany and I had never associated a whole lot with black people before, and suddenly I'm sleeping next to black people and showering with black people, drinkin' with black people and *fightin'* with black people. And I remember we were sittin' down on a cot and it was Christmastime and this one guy who was black got this big long bar of candy with these nuts all around it and he took this big bite out of it and handed it to me for me to get a bite of. Man! It was like somebody had handed me a piece of *shit* to take a bite of. Boy! Did that candy look good! But I hesitated you know, and he says, "Oh, forgit it!" And I said, "Hey, no, give it here." I still think of it and that was 1967 and Jesus! It makes you realize that, you know, they got me. They got a piece of me. There we were, havin' a good time, drinkin' beer and everything's great until I did somethin' like that, and I realized, well here I am, I'm a prejudiced ass. We grow though, we grow, hopefully.

What made me not like what was happening, those jokes, the water 25
fountain, what made me dislike that or understand that it's not right, I don't know. I think that's what you're really looking for. Why would somebody young and immature know in his soul and his heart and his mind that this is not right? Actually I did think about it a lot then. When I would see things like that happening, I would dwell on them. And I could look in the eyes of people when they were being done a number on and I could see it. I could see the hate, frustration, anger and I could see that what was happening here, this policy that would create that kind of reaction by somebody, is a policy that should be eliminated. We should have no policies that create that kind of tension in somebody, that kind of anxiety, that sense of disaster. I think I probably always felt that way. Not just for the racist-type things I saw, but as I grew up if I saw some kid being punished by his father or something, you know, when the punishment far surpassed what was just, if I saw somebody getting beat up on the playground, I was just the kind of person that would kind of go help the person.

I remember one time. It got me in really bad trouble. I was in eighth grade and I was a big kid. I was six feet tall and we had this one guy who was the only disabled person I'd ever met in my life. He had CP[4] and he couldn't talk very good and we were friends. Well, it had been rainin' on the playground and some kid threw him in this hole. Just for fun! Boy, I'll tell ya, when they threw this guy into the mud, it just made me sick and I ran over there to help him and these people were gonna throw *me* in the mud! And then we were both so muddy—it was raining like cats and dogs. And then when we were almost out of the hole, these kids kicked mud in our faces. So I told the kid, "I want to see you after school. I'll get you." And before I realized what I was sayin', I was talkin' to like one of the toughest guys in the school! And later I was sittin' in my class and my knees were almost shakin'. I'm thinkin', "I'm gonna get killed. What do I do now? If I back down now I'll be *dirt* for four years, all through high school." So I said, "Jeez, I gotta go get beat up." So I went over and met him at the drugstore. And I thought, "If I let this guy hit me, I'm gonna die, so I'm gonna get the first punch in anyway." So I walked out of this drugstore door, it was like eight steps down to the sidewalk and the glass door was framed in wood and it was closing behind this guy and he walked out and took that first step and I caught him in midair. I turned around and *smacked* this guy right in the face. I connected so good in his face that I could just feel the guy's nose crack. Blood went all over and he flew back and went right through the glass door. Just flew! And then all of a sudden I changed from being wimpo, like "I'm gonna get killed," to "Come on, man! Let's get going!" Yeah, I was *bad* you know. Next thing I knew, I was worried 'cause the guy wasn't wakin' up. And I'm goin', "Wheow! What power!" Next thing I know, they call the

[4] *CP:* Cerebral palsy, a condition caused by damage to the brain before or during birth, characterized by muscular uncoordination and speech disturbances.

police and I ran. No one squealed on me. I got away with the whole thing. I mean, the guy was so bad, if it had ever been a fair fight, I would have been dead. But the guy had some kind of respect for that kind of power and I just didn't. I had no respect for myself, see, 'cause I had sucker punched the guy, right? I hadn't really used any kind of power and after that he's thinkin' I'm this bad dude, don't mess with Sabatier, man. I had this great big reputation for nothin'. I said, "Thank God, nobody else'd pick a fight with me!" So I never really had much respect, I think, for strength as far as authority over other people. Maybe those kinds of things that happen throughout your life kinda teach that just because somebody has authority over you, has the power to do a number on you, doesn't make them the kind of person you have to respect. I don't think, when you fight, there's anything fair about it. When you fight, it's kinda like war — you win. The *only* thing that counts is to win. You defend yourself by destroying another person, that's all there is to it. I don't care what anybody says.

I enjoyed the fighting and I enjoyed being able to defend myself. That's a nice thing — to know that you can defend yourself. That you don't take much guff. That's good and every kid needs that, at least men in our society need that. It was just demanded when we were kids. If you grow up wimpy, brother! People are going to start stepping on you so you have to be able to take care of yourself. No one ever really got hurt. That's the thing women miss most, I think, the fact that there's nothin' like winnin' a fight. If you get in a fight and you win, boy! The feeling of success and victory and power — there's somethin' about it that is a *good* feeling. And that's why when we get to be adults we get into violence. We like the violence.

It's kinda strange what happened to me. Just killing somebody, you know, is something that you never get over, and when I left Vietnam I think I was more committed to learning as much as I could and trying to understand and be empathetic about people and I gained more respect for human life than I ever had before. I was put in a situation that had little respect for human life — either on our side or theirs. We had free fire zones and in the free-fire zone, anybody walking, you kill. You know, no respect. You don't ask any questions, in the free-fire zone you just kill 'em. And I think killin' somebody close up is more of an experience than doing a number on somebody in a bush that you don't see. You just fire at the bush or something and you walk by and you don't know what happened.

I had some really close experiences where I have actually killed somebody *very* close. And I killed a woman who was unarmed and *that* was somethin' I will *never* shake. We had set up this perimeter and we were there eleven days and every day we'd run out, search and destroy, and come back. Well, it just so happened that there were about thirty Vietcong who were digging these tunnels, and we had caught them out in the open and didn't know it and when we set up our perimeter it was right on top of them.

They hadn't dug the other entrance and so they were all closed in. They were like, after eleven days, tryin' to sneak out of the perimeter. They didn't have any food, they'd run out of water, and they were on their way out. And it was about four o'clock in the morning. I'd just got off guard duty and I was going to sleep and I heard this guy on this tank next to my armored personnel carrier. He started yelling, "Infantry, there's somebody in the perimeter. There's gooks in the perimeter!" And I said, "Okay, we'll go check it out." So I jumped up, I took a couple of guys from my squad and I went to the other side of this tank and he says, "There's somebody in the bomb crater. I killed two on the side of the bomb crater." We saw their bodies, they weren't moving and we could hear someone in the bomb crater. I had this tunnel light, this big flashlight that we used when we'd go through tunnels, and I shined it in the bomb crater and this guy's got these two big old bullet holes right on each side of his neck and he breathing, erh, arh, erh, arh, like that, and blood's burbling right out of the holes in his neck and he's *buck* naked and he's got a grenade in each hand and he's layin' on his back and the tanker yells, "Go get a medic." And I says, "There's no medic going to go down there. The guy's dyin', man," I says. "Besides, he's got grenades in his hands. What fool's goin' to go down there?" So the guy calls the medic and the medic wouldn't go down there and the guy ended up, like five minutes later he died. But I wouldn't have gone down there either. And so I said, "Look, let's fan out around this bomb crater." I'm right next to the bomb crater and there's a guy like two feet to my left and two feet to his left there's another and we're gonna walk around this bomb crater and then I realize, hey! I'm the guy that has the light! So I thought, I can use my power here, you know, I'm a sergeant. I could say, "Hey, psst, take this light." But they'd say, "Take *this*." So I didn't say that. I said to myself, "Wow! What am I gonna do?" So I held this light wa-a-ay out to my left and I could feel this guy's hand pushing it back over toward me, so I went way over to my right, where nobody was and I take one step and this gal jumped up in front of me on her knees and screamed out something, two or three words, and I just *instinctively* pulled the trigger on my M-16 and I just used up a whole ammo pack, twenty rounds, just destroyed her. Blood flew on me and she like flew forward and then backward and she hit me as I jumped down. I thought any second, after that, everybody's gonna open up and this guy's gonna start shootin' back or his friends will or something, but no one did. I jumped down and when I jumped down I jumped on her and I rolled off and I reached over. I was ready to fight this person, right? And of course she was dead and I grabbed her and when I grabbed her I thought, "Boy this is a little person," you know, "this is like grabbing my little niece or something." So, it was real quiet. We just lay there for a second or two and then I took the light and I said, "Let's take a look." And I put the light on her and she had her hair all up on top of her head and I cut this string that she had tied it with and boy! She had beautiful hair. It went all the way down, like past her knees.

Beautiful long black hair. And I searched her and she had this wallet, 30
the only thing in it was a picture of her and a guy that was probably her husband and two little kids and a razor blade, an old rusty razor blade. I don't know why she had that, but that's all that was in her wallet. So I took the picture. We went around and ended up killing three or four more people and capturing about eight others and the next morning, the sun came up and the CO[5] called me over and said, "What's the statistics here?" And I told him how many dead and how many captured and he says, "Was there a woman there?" And I said, "Yeah, there was a woman." And he said, "Was she armed?" And I says, "No, we didn't find any weapons." But hell, I didn't have time to say, "Hey, do you have a weapon?" There were bullet holes in her ankles, in her arms, in her face, it was terrible. So he says, "Well, who killed her?" And I says, "I did." And this fool, he's got one of these guys that we captured and he happened to be her husband. He's in his tent and he's having this conversation with this guy with the interpreter and the interpreter tells the guy that I'm the one that killed his wife. So right away, man, the guy comes *runnin'* at me, you know, his hands are tied behind his back, and I just threw him down on the ground. And the guy just went berserk, you know, crazy. I mean, he was like a chicken with its head cut off. He wasn't comin' at anybody, he just went runnin' into everything, throwing dirt up into the air and kicking and hollerin' and screamin' and like he'd lost his mind, which he did. So there I was, you know, and that night everybody's callin' me the woman killer. Like it's a big joke. You know, the woman killer, it's a joke. That was the heaviest thing that's ever happened to me. And so I think, Jesus, I don't know whatever happened to that guy. Whether he ever got his mind together. I don't know what happened to her kids. I don't know if they're dead or alive. Unbelievable! The next day we ended up gettin' in a big firefight and burning down by accident, by all the fire and ammo and everything, all these hooches[6] and stuff and the captain told me that that was the village that this lady lived in. So in a day I had killed an unarmed lady, seen her husband go crazy, and then burned down her village — and I'm the *good* guy! I'm the good guy? And I'm thinkin', "I've gotta get out of here." God, she wasn't even armed. She was diggin' a tunnel, you know, carrying water back and forth for these people and what are they doin? They're trying to get these foreigners out of their country, you know. That was us.

You know, I called them gooks. I used this term and everything. I played that game but I never, never really thought that I was going to be in a position — that's how stupid and naive I was — I never thought that *I* would really have to shoot somebody and that I would get shot. It was just stupid, just so stupid. I am convinced, I've talked to all those guys, you know, *none* of those people ever thought that they were actually gonna pull a trigger on

[5]*CO:* Commanding officer.

[6]*hooches:* G.I. slang for Vietnamese village houses.

somebody or that they would ever get killed. You know, what happens is that the country confused the war with the warriors. We lost the war, therefore the warriors are losers. We can make jokes about them. They're psychos, they're nuts, they're baby killers, they're losers! We are discriminated against as much as if we had been the ones over there being killed!

I thought a *lot* about that when I didn't have nothin' to do except think. I was always in the field and sneakin' all the time and walkin' down trails and thinking, what am I doing? If I get killed today, will I go to hell or heaven? Am I guilty or innocent? Am I a war criminal? Am I violating people's human rights? Would I appreciate them in my country doing this? I'd walk in people's hooches and I mean, we'd go through a village at four-thirty in the morning. We don't knock on the door, we walk through and they're sleeping with their wives and babies and they're scared, you know, and you see these people, their faces. I felt like I was the Gestapo[7] in World War II, walking in somebody's house without knocking on the door. 'Course that bothers me. I don't like doin' that. I'm not that kind of a person. But what am I gonna do? Refuse to go on a search-and-destroy mission? Jesus, so all I was hopin' to do was stay alive and get home and never find myself in that position again.

And so I *really* started thinking about all this right and wrong, good and bad and human rights, and what I would die for, what I wouldn't die for. And I came to the conclusion that there's just human rights. Human rights, not civil rights. And human rights are not conditional. Any commitment to a *conditional* human right is no commitment at all. And that's exactly what we got, we disabled people. Here's a President who says he's committed to social justice and all this business and at the same time it's being conditioned on your ability to get on the bus, or on your ability to see something. Things that really shouldn't matter. And so a commitment for conditional human rights to me is no commitment at all. Exactly none. And I'll do everything in my power to make sure that people understand that if you're gonna be committed toward something you can't talk commitment and in your actions do something else. You can't say you're in favor of affirmative action[8] and then go out and discriminate.

I mean all the people of the different populations should recognize things like that. Not many people look inward. They look outward to see where the problem is. They don't look in and say, "Yeah, I've wasted twenty people off the face of the earth and for what? You know, I'm guilty, okay, from there I'll make sure this never happens again and I'll try to stop it whenever I see it." You know, whenever I see that current of hate or that current of discrimination, or see that president or that mayor or the governor

[7]*Gestapo:* Secret police in Nazi Germany.

[8]*affirmative action:* Government policies aimed at redressing inequities caused by racism. Affirmative action programs have attempted to offer increased opportunity for education, employment, and career advancement to members of historically underrepresented groups.

or somebody making bad decisions, whenever I see it, I got to stand up and stop it. At least I owe those people, or their souls that! I have to. I figure, if *I* don't, who will? I owe it.

Engaging the Text

1. Sabatier places great value on learning to question one's assumptions; how and why does he learn to question his?
2. Do you agree with Sabatier and Shaw that "all progress depends on the unreasonable man" (para. 16)? Why or why not?
3. Debate Sabatier's assertion that "we don't need any laws, we don't need any constitution, we don't need the Declaration of Independence. All we need to do is treat people with respect" (para. 22).
4. Why does Sabatier say that his act of protest would strike many people as an "unnatural thing to do" (para. 17)? What forces or ideas in our culture make such actions seem "unnatural"?
5. How free is Charlie Sabatier at the beginning of his story? How would you explain his relationship to freedom at the story's end?

Exploring Connections

6. Compare Charlie Sabatier's attitudes toward freedom, risk, and responsibility with those of Jack and the narrator in "Selway" (p. 668). To what extent does Sabatier's story challenge the notion that freedom means different things to men and women?
7. Write an imaginary dialogue between Gerry Spence (p. 682) and Sabatier on the forces that harness us and keep us from being truly free.
8. Compare Sabatier's attitudes toward his disability and the challenges he faces with the attitudes expressed by Sucheng Chan in "You're Short, Besides!" (p. 541).
9. Compare the transformation that Sabatier experiences with that of C. P. Ellis (p. 388). What causes each to change? What does each learn?

Extending the Critical Context

10. Write a journal entry describing a time in your life when you began to question your own assumptions: What led you to re-evaluate your beliefs? How did you change as a result?
11. Watch Oliver Stone's *Born on the Fourth of July* (1989), the film version of paraplegic war veteran Ron Kovic's autobiography. How do Kovic's personal background, Vietnam experience, and subsequent transformation compare with Sabatier's? What do their stories tell us about the power of free individuals in America?
12. Interview someone you know who, like Sabatier, has made an individual protest against some injustice or unfairness. Then write an oral history, like Gwaltney's, using the person's own words to tell the story. Share your history in class and

see what conclusions you can draw from it and those of your classmates. Do you agree with Sabatier that "we are a nation of dissenters" (para. 16)?

Freedom Time

JUNE JORDAN

Does freedom come in colors? In the following essay, poet and activist June Jordan suggests that "white" conceptions of freedom may be very different from her own. She also warns that freedoms hard-won during the civil rights movement may be threatened in an America that's growing more divisive and bad-tempered by the day. A professor of African American studies at the University of California, Berkeley, Jordan (b. 1936) has authored several collections of poetry and political essays, including Living Room *(1985)* Naming Our Destiny *(1989),* Civil Wars *(1981),* On Call *(1985), and* Technical Difficulties *(1992).*

A million years ago, Janis Joplin was singing, "Freedom's just another word for nothing left to lose." I found that puzzling, back then. Or, "white."

To my mind, freedom was an obvious good. It meant looking at an apartment and, if you liked it, being able to put down a deposit and sign a lease. It meant looking for a job and, if you found something for which you qualified—on the basis of education and/or experience—being able to take that position. Freedom had to do with getting into college if your grades were good enough. Freedom meant you could register to vote and live to talk about it.

A lot of other Americans felt the same way, thirty years ago. And black and white, we sang militant songs and we tested public transportation and restaurants and universities and corporate hiring policies and nice, clean neighborhoods for freedom. And we rallied and we marched and we risked everything for freedom because we believed that freedom would deliver us into pride and happiness and middle-class incomes and middle-class safety.

Thirty years later and freedom is no longer a word that most folks remember to use, jokingly or otherwise. And the declining popularity of the word is matched by our declining commitment to protect, and to deepen, and to extend, the meanings of freedom in the United States.

Today we know that "black and white" does not adequately describe 5
anything real. Individual, economic, racial, ethnic, and sexual realities defy

such long-ago simplicity. "Black" has become Nigerian or Afro-Caribbean or Senegalese or African-American or Zulu. "White" has become Serbo-Croatian or Bosnian Muslim or Irish Republican or Italian-American or Greek or Norwegian. And, even as collective identities inside America have multiplied, our political presence here has intensified as well: women, Latino, Asian, Native, gay, lesbian, senior citizen, and so-called legal and illegal aliens. (As for the very popular concept of "aliens," you would think that, by now, anybody other than Native Americans or Chicanos/Mexicans would be pretty embarrassed to mouth such an obnoxious pejorative.)

But rather than recognize galvanizing intersections among us, too often we yield to divisive media notions such as women's rights, for example, threatening the rights of black folks or Chicanos. There is a dismal competition among Americans who should know better and who should join together for their own good. There is an acquiescence in the worst knavery of the mass media, as those top TV shows and those major weekly magazines inflame our egocentric and paranoid inclinations. In consequence, we are muddling through a terrifying period of atomization and bitterness and misdirected anger.

What the new emerging majority of these United States holds in common, at its core, is a need for freedom to exist equally and a need to become the most knowledgeable, happy, productive, interconnected, and healthy men and women that we can. Ours is a need for freedom that does not omit any racial, gender, ethnic, sexual, or physical identity from its protection. But unless we will, each of us, reach around all of these identities and embrace them even as we cherish our own, no one's freedom will be assumed.

In Margaret Atwood's novel *The Handmaid's Tale,* the reader comes upon this remarkable one-liner: "Nothing changes instantaneously: In a gradually heating bathtub, you'd be burned to death before you knew it." I think we're jammed inside that bathtub and the water's getting hot.

About five weeks ago, I was walking my dog, Amigo, along the rather quiet streets of North Berkeley when a young white man yelled something in my direction and asked me to stop. I stopped. He bolted in front of me and, excitedly, inquired whether I had seen "anything or anyone unusual." I said no, and waited to hear him out.

10 It seems that twice on that one day, somebody had "delivered" an anti-Semitic bound book of neo-Nazi filth to the lawn in front of his house. He, Eric, was the father of a newborn baby and his Jewish wife, he told me, was completely freaked out by these scary events.

"How about you?" I asked him. Eric shrugged, and kept repeating that he "didn't understand it" and "couldn't believe" that none of his neighbors had seen anything. We talked a little while and I gave Eric my name and telephone number, as well as the numbers of some active people who might rally, fast, against this hatefulness.

In subsequent weeks, Eric invited me (and Amigo) into his house to meet his wife and to see their new baby boy, but I never had the time. Or, I never made the time to visit them.

Shortly after the first delivery of neo-Nazi literature to my neighborhood, I got on a plane bound for Madison, Wisconsin. *The Progressive*[1] was putting on a benefit show and the editors arranged for me to join the celebration. Madison, Wisconsin, is a lot like North Berkeley except Madison gets cold, and stays cold, during the winter. Similar to my northern California habitat, there are abundant public indications of environmental concern and civility: sheltered bus stops, wheel-chair-accessible street crossings, bike lanes, public tennis courts, fabulous public libraries, a wonderful public university, and bookstores and backpackers all over the place.

I stayed with Dr. Elizabeth Ann Karlin during my visit to Madison. The morning after my arrival, Dr. Karlin and I sat at the dining table looking at newspapers, drinking coffee, and pushing bagels away from the butter and the cream cheese. At some point, Dr. Karlin stopped talking, and I glanced at her face: it was flushed, and she fell silent. Now her dogs were wild with barking and ferocious agitation.

I got up and went to the windows. Outside, two white men were march- 15
ing back and forth carrying placards that said, ABORTION, A BABY CAN LIVE WITHOUT IT, and LIBERTY AND JUSTICE FOR SOME.

Breakfast was over.

I located my press pass, my ballpoint pen, yellow pad, and I tied my sneaker shoelaces and went outside to interview these members of "Operation Rescue" and "Missionaries to the Pre-born." Why were they there?

"We're picketing Elizabeth Karlin's house because she kills babies in her Women's Medical Health Center."

I talked with Kermit Simpson and David Terpstra for more than two hours. It was eerie. It was familiar. They spoke about the futility of the courts, the brutality of the police, and their determination, regardless, to rescue "innocent babies" from "murder." It was familiar because their complaints and their moral certitude echoed the regular complaints and the moral certainty of the civil rights movement.

But these groups were white. These groups were right-wing religious 20
fundamentalists. And the only freedom they were concerned about was the freedom of the "unborn."

In fact, throughout our lengthy conversation, neither one of these men ever referred to any woman or anything female: "the baby" had to be saved from murder. That was the formulation. No woman's mind or body or feelings or predicament, at any moment, entered their consideration. What mattered was "the baby."

As I listened to David Terpstra, a good looking white man in his twen-

[1] *The Progressive:* A leftist newsmagazine.

ties, it occurred to me that he was the kind of person who might have shot and killed Dr. Gunn.[2] Certainly he would see no reason not to kill a doctor who "kills babies." David told me there are twenty-two warrants out for his arrest, and he keeps moving.

He has no wife and no children and nothing special besides his mission to save "the baby."

Inside Dr. Karlin's house, the day was ruined. Even if the sun had returned to the sky (which it refused to do), there was terror and dread palpable, now, in every room.

And where were the good people of Madison who love their civil lib- 25
erties and who hold Dr. Karlin in highest esteem as a warrior of our times and who used to understand that individual freedom depends upon a mass demand for its blessings and opportunities?

And what could I do for my friend, the doctor, before I got back on a plane, and left the scene of her clear and present danger?

The next weekend was a memorial reading for Tede Matthews, a gay white American who had managed the Modern Times bookstore in San Francisco, and who had died of AIDS in July. Tede Matthews had also distinguished himself as an activist for human rights in Central America. And he had helped many, many writers and poets to acquire a community of support. He was/he is much beloved. And he died of AIDS.

In the overflow audience of several hundred people who came to honor Tede Matthews's life and to establish a Tede Matthews fund for civil rights for gay men and lesbians in Central America and in the United States, there were many gay men and lesbians.

And I heard in my brain the helter-skelter of selective scripture that the Operation Rescue guys hurled into that Wisconsin silence. And I reflected on the tragedy of Tede Matthews's death, and the death of thousands upon thousands of young men whom we have loved and lost. And I wanted to rise from my seat in a towering, prophetic rage and denounce any scripture/any construct of divinity that does not cherish all of the living people on earth and does not grieve for the cruelties of daily life that afflict every one of us if basic freedom is denied.

But this was a memorial service. And Tede Matthews is no longer alive. 30

On my return to U.C. Berkeley, one of my students alerted me to a forthcoming issue of *Mother Jones*[3] that would trash women's studies in general and our department in particular. This student, Pamela Wilson, had been quoted out of context and she explained things to me. And she was mad.

[2] *Dr. Gunn:* A gynecologist killed outside his Florida clinic by an antiabortionist in 1993.
[3] *Mother Jones:* A magazine focusing on American culture.

The *Mother Jones* article proved to be a juicyfruit of irresponsible, sleazy journalism: a hatchet job with malice toward every facet of the subject under scrutiny and entitled, "Off Course."

Since its appearance, several other national publications have chimed in, applauding the "exposure" of "fraud" perpetrated upon students beguiled into taking courses that let them study themselves and sometimes sit in a circle of chairs.

The head of Women's Studies, Professor Evelyn Glenn, called a special departmental meeting. The faculty decided to respond to the attack, in writing, and on national public radio.

One student, Catherine Cook, has received hate mail from loquacious 35
bigots who believe that women's studies, along with ethnic studies, make it clear that public education is wasting taxpayer money. Furthermore, these "nonacademic" studies "debase" the minds of young Americans who, instead, should "get a job," and so forth.

As a matter of fact, this latest assault on freedom of inquiry and the pivotal role of public education within that categorical mandate, this most recent effort to roll things back to "the basics" of white men studies taught by white men with the assistance of books written by and about white men has upset our students. The young woman who received hate mail because she thought she had a right to pursue her (women's) studies had trouble breathing, and her hands shook, as she brought those items of hatred into our faculty meeting. Students in my class, Coming Into the World Female, seemed puzzled, at first, and then stunned, and now furious with brilliant energies as they prepare for a press conference, a mock women's studies class, and a demonstration that will take place just outside the entrance to the office building of *Mother Jones*.

The students voted to create those public reactions. They have spent hours and hours in solemn, wearisome research and composition. They believe that the truth of their intentions — and the truth of the necessity for women's studies and ethnic studies and African American studies — will become apparent to most of America if only they, the students, do all of this homework into the facts, and if only they give the design and the wording of their flyers maximal painstaking and meticulous execution.

They believe that there is a mainstream majority America that will try to be fair, and that will respect their courage, and admire the intelligence of their defense. They believe that there is a mainstream majority America that will overwhelm the enemies of public and democratic education. They believe that most of us, out here, will despise and resist every assault on freedom in the United States.

And I hope they're right. With all my heart, I hope so. But the water's boiling. And not a whole lot of people seem to notice, or care, so far.

Freedom is not "another word for nothing left to lose." And we are 40
letting it go; we are losing it. Freedom requires our steady and passionate devotion. Are we up to that?

Engaging the Text

1. Why does Jordan criticize the Janis Joplin song lyrics she uses to introduce this essay? Why do you think the idea expressed in this song strikes her as particularly "white"? Is it?
2. What did freedom mean to Jordan during the years of the civil rights movement? How did she view the purpose of freedom in those days? Has her view of freedom changed?
3. In the second half of the essay Jordan offers a series of examples meant to illustrate the weakening of freedom in contemporary America. In what ways is freedom challenged in the incidents involving Eric, Elizabeth Karlin, Tede Matthews, and the attack on her women's studies course? Can you think of any other incidents you have heard about recently that illustrate this danger?
4. Jordan shows some ambivalence about the two abortion protesters she talks to outside Elizabeth Karlin's home. What is her attitude toward these young men and their right to protest? Is her attitude consistent with her ideas about freedom in America?

Exploring Connections

5. Compare the visions of freedom presented by Jordan and Gerry Spence (p. 682). What concerns do they share about the current health of freedom in the United States? How compatible are their views of freedom? What aspects of Spence's idea of freedom might strike Jordan as particularly "white"? What aspects of Jordan's idea of freedom might strike Spence as just another bit of "harness"? Which view do you find more honest or attractive?
6. Review Carmen Vázquez's "Appearances" (p. 287), Ronald Takaki's "A Different Mirror" (p. 332), Katy Butler's "The Great Boomer Bust" (p. 503), and Ellis Cose's "Tiptoeing Around the Truth" (p. 522), and write an essay exploring Jordan's claim that "we are muddling through a terrifying period of atomization and bitterness and misdirected anger" (para. 6). What evidence, if any, do you see that America is becoming an increasingly angry and alienated nation?

Extending the Critical Context

7. Jordan claims that the media pose a threat to American freedom because they portray America as a country torn apart by "dismal competition" between a number of different factions. Working in groups, survey TV news programs over a few evenings. In general, how are relations between various American social, religious, economic, and ethnic groups portrayed? To what extent do your observations confirm or challenge Jordan's assertion?
8. Jordan suggests that we are in danger of losing the freedoms that were won during the 1960s and '70s. Make a list of freedoms that were gained or expanded during these years. Do you agree with Jordan that they are endangered by the media? Can you think of other forces that are placing these freedoms in jeopardy?

TV, Freedom, and the Loss of Community

Bill McKibben

To Bill McKibben, freedom is far from being an unqualified social good. From his perspective as an ecological advocate and lay minister, freedom is a double-edged sword that threatens to destroy our sense of community connection as it enhances our individual autonomy. A former staff writer for The New Yorker, *McKibben (b. 1960) is the author of* The End of Nature *(1989), an important work on global warming. This selection comes from his second collection of essays,* The Age of Missing Information *(1992). McKibben lives in the Adirondack Mountains where he is an avid hiker, a Sunday school teacher, and the treasurer of the local volunteer fire department.*

The light lasted a long time; as it was finally fading, I saw a pickup head down the part of the road visible from the ridge. I knew, by the size of the truck and the time of the day, who it was and what he'd been doing—he'd been working on an addition for a summer house down at the lake, working late, since it was the month with no bugs, no cold, and not much dark. Not many cars drive down the road—most of them I can identify. And my sense of the community is relatively shallow. A neighbor of mine used to man a nearby fire tower for the state. From the top he could look out and see the lake where he was born and grew up, and the long unnamed ridge where he learned to hunt whitetail deer. He could see the houses of four of his eight children, and his house, or at least the valley where it sat. His mother's house, too, and the old pastures where she ran a dairy, and the church where her funeral would take place the next year, a service led by his daughter who was a sometime lay preacher there. His whole world spread out before him. He'd been to New York City exactly once, to help someone move, and somehow he'd gotten his piled-high pickup onto the bus ramp at the Port Authority bus station, and all in all it wasn't quite worth it even for a hundred dollars a day. Why leave when you're as tied in as that—when you can see a puff of smoke and know by the location and the hour if it's so-and-so burning trash or a forest fire starting up. Why leave when you live in a place you can understand and that understands you. I was putting storm windows on the church last fall with a neighbor, an older man who'd lived here all his life. He suggested we crawl up into the belfry, where I'd never been. The boards up there were covered with carved initials, most of them dating from the 1920s or earlier—some were a hundred years old. My neighbor hadn't been up there for four or five decades, but he knew whom most of the initials belonged to and whether or not they'd ended up with the female initials carved next to them. "This is my brother's," he said. "And this is mine," he added, pointing to a "DA" carved before the Depression. He pulled a knife out of his pocket and added a fresh set, complete with the initials of his wife of fifty years.

"For most of human history," writes psychologist Paul Wachtel in his book *The Poverty of Affluence,* "people lived in tightly knit communities in which each individual had a specified place and in which there was a strong sense of shared fate. The sense of belonging, of being part of something larger than oneself, was an important source of comfort. In the face of the dangers and the terrifying mysteries that the lonely individual encountered, this sense of connectedness — along with one's religious faith, which often could hardly be separated from one's membership in the community — was for most people the main way of achieving some sense of security and the courage to go on."

"For most of human history." I have used this phrase before in this book, to try to make it clear just how different our moment is, just how much information we may be missing. In this case, the information is about "community." Many of us are used to living without strong community ties — we have friends, of course, and perhaps we're involved in the community, but we're essentially autonomous. (A 1990 survey found 72 percent of Americans didn't know their next-door neighbors.) We do our own work. We're able to pick up and move and start again. And this feels natural. It is, after all, how most modern Americans grew up. On occasion, though, we get small reminders of what a tighter community must have felt like. Camp, maybe, or senior year in high school. I can remember spring vacations when I was a teenager — the youth group from our suburban church would pile in a bus and head south for some week-long work project in a poor community. Twenty-four hours on a chartered Greyhound began to bring us together; after a week of working and eating and hanging out we had changed into a group. I can recall, too, the empty feeling when we got back to the church parking lot and our parents picked us up and we went back to the semi-isolation of suburbia — much of the fellow feeling just evaporated. I do not mean that a group of adolescents working together for a week somehow equaled a community — I do mean that there was something exhilarating about it. This twining together of lives, this intense though not always friendly communion. It seemed nearly natural. As if we were built to live that way.

"Community" is a vexed concept, of course — the ties that bind can bind too tight. Clearly, all over the world, people have felt as if they were liberating themselves when they moved to places where they could be anonymous, to the cities and suburbs that in the last seventy-five years have come to dominate the Western world. All of us have learned to luxuriate in privacy. But even just watching TV you can tell there's still a pull in the other direction, too. Fairfax Cable, on its Welcome Channel, promises you that "in our busy, fast-paced, congested world, cable TV is helping to revitalize the concept of community involvement" — in other words, they let each town in their service area operate a channel. Most of the time there is just a slow "crawl" of bulletin-board announcements, and it is from these that you can sense the desire and need for community, or at least for like-minded supportive people to whom you can turn in times of crisis. Thus there are innumerable announcements about hotlines and support groups — the child abuse hotline, the support group for mothers of AIDS patients, and so on. But in ordinary times how much community is there? The crawl of messages sheds some light on our aloneness, too. The town of Falls Church offers a service to all its elderly residents: a computer will call you at home once a day. If you don't answer, help is automatically summoned. Surely very few societies have ever needed such a thing — surely very few people lived such unaffiliated lives that their death could go unnoticed for a day.

5 Other functions nearly as central to the working of a community are automated too, and sold. For just ninety-five cents a minute, the 900 phone lines allow you to hear "real people" trading "confessions." That is, you can pay someone to let you gossip, or to gossip to you; eliminating communities doesn't eliminate their mild vices — it just makes them duller and costlier. New York's Channel 13, perhaps the most cerebral television channel in America, recently installed a 900 line so that people could call up after *MacNeil/Lehrer* or *Frontline* and chat with five other viewers for up to an hour — again only ninety-five cents a minute. Singles bars, once the classic symptom of modern loneliness, now involve too much contact, according to TV producer Rick Rosner; instead, you can stay at home and watch Rosner's new boy-meets-girl show, *Personals,* or maybe *Studs,* or *Love Connection,* "where old-fashioned romance meets modern technology." On May 3, a man appeared on *Love Connection* to say that the hips of the woman he had dated the night before — a lady sitting there in full view of the nation — were too large.

It's true that you can go altogether too warm and trembly at the idea of community solidarity. (The actor Alec Baldwin, for instance, told *Hollywood Insider* how "refreshing" he had found the three days he spent in prison while researching his role in a film called *Miami Blues.* "A lot of the guys in the joint lift weights and stuff," he said. "I don't like to do that, and the other option was a lot of them box. It was the best workout I ever had. There's no cruising girls at the juice bar and all that other health-club crap.") The idea that, say, small towns hum with peace and good cheer is nonsense — both *Good Morning America* and *Larry King Live* featured one tough mother from Crystal Falls, Michigan, who had gone undercover for the local cops and busted twenty-three of her friends and neighbors for selling drugs. She was not some church lady baking pies — she was mean. (On *Larry King Live,* a man phoned in to explain that *he* would teach his kids "responsible drug use." "What are you going to do, one nostril at a time?" she asked.) She left for the big city because her small-town neighbors were threatening to kill her kids.

Still, TV clearly understands that at least the *idea* of community ties attracts us. What is *Cheers* but an enclosed neighborhood where people depend on one another when the chips are down? "Where everybody knows your name. And they're always glad you came." No one moves away, no one can break up the kind of love that constantly makes jokes to keep from acknowledging that it is a kind of love. "You want to go where everybody knows your name." That's right — we do. That's why we loved *M*A*S*H,* another great TV community. But on TV, of course, while *you* know everybody's name, they've never heard of yours.

There were two Cosby episodes on this day, and both exploited this yearning. On the rerun, his former basketball coach returned to tell stories of Cliff as a youth; in the evening, it was his great-great-aunt, an ancient but vivacious lady who had taught the children of ex-slaves to read in a one-room schoolhouse. "Many of the kids had to walk twelve miles. And when they went home they had to work their farms till sundown." She told stories of the good old days, of courting, of chaperones — of community. The program ended in church, with Mavis Staples[1] singing a booming gospel number: "People, we all have to come together, 'cuz we need the strength and the power." It's a tribute to ties, to history—a meaningless tribute, of course, because it's all in the past tense and the present Cosbys need no one to help them lead their lives of muffled, appliance-swaddled affluence. The great-great-aunt represents a different, more primitive species, one that TV helped us "evolve" away from. But the sticky sentiment obviously plucks some strings in our hearts.

For every Hallmark card it mails to the idea of community, though, TV sends ten telegrams with the opposite meaning. Thinking of living in the same place your whole life, or even for a good long stretch of time? "No one said moving was easy. But Moving Means Moving Ahead," Allied Van Lines declares. When you reach your new home, of course, the TV will provide continuity — the same shows at the same times. And TV, of course, can provide you with people to be interested in, to gossip about — people you can take with you when you move. Not just TV actors but real-life people, like the Trumps.[2] An interesting episode of *Donahue* focused on gossips — he interviewed a woman who ceaselessly peeked out windows to find out what her neighbors were doing. The crowd was hostile — "Get a life," one lady shouted. But all day long the same demographic group that watches *Donahue* was watching, say, *Nine Broadcast Plaza,* where an "audiologist" and a "body language analyst" analyzed the videotape of an interview that Diane Sawyer had conducted the day before with Marla Maples, the other woman in the Trump divorce. On the tape, Marla grew flustered and inarticulate when asked "Was it the best sex you ever had?" The audiologist, despite "two independent scientific instruments," could only classify

[1]*Mavis Staples:* Gospel singer (b. 1940).
[2]*the Trumps:* Multimillionaire Donald Trump and his (now former) wife, Ivana.

her response as "inaudible," but the body language analyst thought she may have had better sex with someone else. Did she love Trump? Yes, the audiologist declared—definitely. "I don't think she knows what love is—she's too young," said the body language expert, who added that Maples was "lying through her teeth" when she said she didn't take cash from Donald. (*Nine Broadcast Plaza* also devoted time to a claim from Jessica Hahn that her encounter with Jim Bakker[3] involved "the *worst* sex I ever had.") That night on ABC, Sam Donaldson grilled Mr. Trump himself—he refused to talk about Marla or Ivana, but did say that his yacht was "the greatest yacht in the world," and that while he bought it for $24 million, he could *easily* sell it for $115 million. Who needs eccentric uncles or town characters when you've got the Trumps?

10 TV's real comment on community, though, is slyer and more potent than the ones I've described so far. Day after day on sitcom after talk show after cartoon after drama, TV actively participates in the savaging of an old order it once helped set in stone. TV history, as I've said, goes back forty years. At its dawn are the shows like *Ozzie and Harriet,* synonyms for the way things were. Every day we can watch Ozzie and Harriet and Beaver and the 1950s. They represent a certain sort of community. It is no longer a physical community, really—it's faceless suburbia. But there is still some sense of shared values, albeit white and patriarchal and square and repressive values, values largely worthy of being overthrown. And TV joined gleefully in this overthrow. Every day, over and over, we relive the vanquishing of that order in the name of self-expression and human liberation and fun. The greatest story of the TV age is the transition from the fifties to the sixties—the demolition of the last ordered American "way of life." And TV tells us this story incessantly.

It begins by repeating the old shows, and therefore the old verities. On *Father Knows Best,* Bud is trying out for the football team. To win the notice of the coach, he decides to date his daughter, a sweet and innocent girl. He makes the team—but of course he doesn't feel right, so he talks to his dad. "You got what you wanted, but you feel you didn't get it fairly," Pop says gravely. "Now your conscience is bothering you, and you'll figure some way to straighten it out." Which he does, quitting the team and genuinely falling in love with her. That plot seems so exceptionally familiar and yet so distant—the football team as the pinnacle of boyish desire, the formal courtship of the girl complete with long talks with her father. And especially the act of going to one's own parents to talk about such matters. It is resolutely unhip, almost as unhip as the *Leave It to Beaver* episode that begins with Eddie Haskell's[4] attempts to cheat on a history exam (a history exam with

[3] *Jim Bakker:* Televangelist involved in sexual and financial scandals in 1987.

[4] *Eddie Haskell:* Wally Cleaver's best friend on the 1950s *Leave It to Beaver* TV show.

questions on Clemenceau[5] and Lloyd George[6]) and ends as, reformed, he dutifully recites the first six countries to ratify the League of Nations[7] charter.

But TV doesn't simply offer us these shows as relics — consciously and unconsciously it pokes fun at them. Consider this promo for Nick at Nite's nonstop week of *Donna Reed Show* reruns: "This is Donna Reed, supercompetent mother of two and wife of one," says the announcer, who is imitating Robin Leach.[8] "She lives in this spectacular American dream house, which she cleans for her husband, the handsome Dr. Stone. Dinnertime at Chez Stone features meat, usually accompanied by potatoes, and takes place in this spotless dream kitchen!" Over pictures of people in gas masks and belching factories, the announcer says mockingly, "Out to save a world that's made a mess of things, she comes — mightly Hoover vacuum in hand. It's Donna Reed, sent from TV land to lead us politely into the new millennium."

Even when the ridicule is less explicit, it's fascinating to see the old order break down in front of your eyes each night. Over two hours on a single channel I watched a progression that began with Lucy trying desperately to get the handsome new teacher to ask her out on a date. Then came *That Girl!*, where Marlo Thomas was living alone in the city and faring well but still desperate for her parents to like her cooking. *Rhoda* was next — she went to the house of her husband's ex-wife to pick up the kids and they got roaring drunk. And finally, on *Phyllis*, most of the humor came from a cackling granny who loved to watch golf on TV because the golfers keep bending over and displaying their rear ends. In case you weren't getting the point, the shows were interspersed with ads like this one, for a videotape library of old TV shows: "The fifties — life seemed simpler then. Drive-ins, chrome-covered cars, and every Monday night there was *Lucy*."

This account of our liberation from the repressive mores of society is not an entirely new story (as the Zeffirelli version of *Romeo and Juliet* on Showtime made clear), but never has it been told so ceaselessly. Steve Vai had a tune in heavy rotation this week on MTV — it showed a young boy with a prim old lady for a teacher. He jumps up on the desk to play his guitar for show-and-tell, and the kids, liberated by the beat, tear the room apart; the teacher goes screaming out into the hall. The children watching this video have likely never known this sort of school, where learning is by rote and repression is the rule. And yet this mythical liberation survives, celebrated over and over again, as it will as long as the people who lived through that revolution are writing TV shows. (And perhaps as long as the

[5]*Clemenceau:* Georges Clemenceau (1841–1929), French statesman and premier of France from 1906 to 1909 and 1917 to 1920.

[6]*Lloyd George:* Lloyd David George (1863–1945), English statesman and prime minister from 1916 to 1922.

[7]*The League of Nations:* Predecessor of the United Nations, established in 1920.

[8]*Robin Leach:* Host of popular 1980s TV show *Lifestyles of the Rich and Famous.*

people who grew up watching those shows are writing them, and so on forever.)

Any revolution this constant and thorough breeds counterrevolt, or at 15
least uneasiness. Sometimes it is explicit, as with the conservatives who haunt the religious channels preaching "traditional family values." Usually, though, the uneasiness creeps in around the edges. On pay-per-view, *Field of Dreams* concerned a fellow, Ray Kinsella, who was a big wheel in the antiwar movement. He retains a fair amount of contempt for the stolid farmers around him, and his wife certainly stands up against book-burning bigots. But there's also a lot in the movie about his dad, who just wanted to play catch with him. Ray rejected all that family stuff in a huff and went off to college to protest — and now, more or less, he has to build a big stadium in the cornfield in order to get his daddy back. He'd gone a little bit too far back then.

Other, lesser movies made the same kind of point. HBO ran a fascinating film, *Irreconcilable Differences,* about a little girl who was suing her parents for divorce. They had been the classic sixties couple — they met as *semihippies* on a *road trip* across America. He'd written his thesis about *sexual overtones* in *early films.* She decided to dump her *Navy fiancé.* They drank *tequila* and listened to *James Taylor* and *cried* at films. And then they got rich writing movies on their own and fulfilled themselves in all sorts of predictable ways — divorces, bimbos, personal masseuses, big houses, fast cars. They were "doing their thing," "following their bliss." Which is why their daughter ends up explaining to the judge that she wants to go live with the Mexican housekeeper in her tiny bungalow, where the children sleep three to a bed. "I don't expect my mom to be a person who vacuums all day and bakes cookies for me when I get home from school, and I don't expect my dad to be some kind of real understanding person who wants to take me fishing all the time. But my mom and dad are just too mixed up for anyone to be around. I'm just a kid, and I don't know what I'm doing sometimes. But I think you should know better when you grow up." Their reconciliation comes in a cheap chain restaurant — utter normality as salvation.

This kind of reaction, though, has not really slowed the trend away from Ozzie and Harriet. One critic described Fox's *Married . . . With Children* as "antimatter to the Huxtables. . . . Sex (both the desire for and aversion to), the body at its grossest, stupidity, and familial contempt are the stuff of this sitcom." And yet, as CBS programmer Howard Stringer pointed out ruefully, more children were watching the program than any show on CBS. Therefore, he said, he was sending a signal to producers of comedy shows that they had an "open throttle" to change the network's image as "stuffy, stodgy, and old." He pointed with pride to an upcoming CBS pilot show that, in the words of the *Times,* "contains a provocative line of dialogue from a six-year-old girl." On *Leave It to Beaver,* Wally talks to his girlfriend on the phone in the living room in front of his parents and thinks nothing of it. By the *Brady Bunch,* the girls are giggling secretly over the princess phone. When you get to *One Day at a Time,* the children listen in as the mother talks to *her* boyfriend, who's trying to persuade her to come to a South Pacific island. "He's probably down there starving for your body, lusting for your lips," the daughter says. And *One Day at a Time* is already in reruns.

Ozzie and Harriet represented all sorts of things that needed to be overthrown, or at least badly shaken up — a world where women did what housework remained, where children never talked back, where appearance and conformity counted above all, where black people never showed their faces, where sex was dirty or absent, where God lived in some church, where America was the only country that counted. The problem is only that the rebellion against this world never ended, never helped create a new and better order to take its place. The American Revolution tossed out the tyrants and set up something fresh; the French Revolution tossed out tyrants and then looked for more tyrants.

The main idea that emerges from the breakup of this Donna Reed order is "freedom," or, more accurately, not being told what to do. You can listen to, say, sociologist Robert Bellah when he says "personal freedom, autonomy, and independence are the highest values for Americans," or you can listen to the crowd on one of the morning talk shows responding to the plight of a man whose XXXtasy hard-core pornography television service has been shut down by an Alabama sheriff. "It's just total censorship," someone in the studio audience said. "It all comes down to the same thing — our rights." "Everyone out there has to make their own decisions." The same kind of sentiments attended the 2 Live Crew controversy, which came to a head while I was working on this book. The Crew, you will recall, was the rap group that specialized in lyrics like "Suck my dick, bitch, and make it puke," and which finally found one cooperative Florida district attorney who rose to the bait and charged them with obscenity. As Sara Rimer reported in the *Times*, Luther Campbell, the group's leader, said he was worried that the six jurors, who included three women over age sixty and only one black, might be "too old, too white, and too middle-class" to "understand" his music. His worry was misplaced; after they quickly acquitted him, one juror said, "I thought it would've been cute if we could of come out with the verdict like we were doing a rap song," and another said the content of the lyrics had not affected her: "Those were their songs. They were doing their poetry in song."

The jurors made the right decision — "You take away one freedom and 20
pretty soon they're all gone," said one, and he was telling the truth. So were the people on *Nine Broadcast Plaza* — an Alabama sheriff shouldn't care what folks watch on their TVs. Tolerance is an unqualified good — a world where people of all races and all sexual orientations and both genders and all political persuasions can express themselves openly is so manifestly superior to the bigoted and repressed world we're leaving behind that they hardly bear comparison. And it's probably even useful to have occasional phenomena like 2 Live Crew to make us stand up once again and reassert our principles.

But tolerance by itself can be a cover for moral laziness. In a world with real and pressing problems, tolerance is merely a precondition for politics — it is not itself a meaningful politics. We try to pretend that "liberation" is enough because it's so much easier to eternally rebel: "Kicking against social repression and moral vapidity — that's an activity rock 'n' roll has managed to do better than virtually any other art or entertainment form," *Rolling Stone* boasted in a year-end editorial in 1990 that called for forming a "bulwark against those who would gladly muzzle that spirit . . . of insolent liberty." Good, fine, we all agree — "I thought it would've been cute if we could of come out with the verdict like we were doing a rap song." But is that all there is? Don't popular music and art and politics have a good deal more to do than "kick against social repression and moral vapidity"? Isn't it time to focus harder on substantive problems, such as, how do we build a society that doesn't destroy the planet by its greed, and doesn't *ignore* the weak and poor? (Not repress them, just ignore them.) I don't mean a lot of sappy records and TV shows with syrupy messages about saving dolphins — I mean popular art that fulfills the old functions of popular art, that reminds us of our connections with one another and with the places we live. An art that reminds us that our own lives shouldn't merely be free — that they should be of value to others, connected to others, and that if our lives are like that they will become finer. That's what a culture is. It's true that we don't need all the old "traditional" values — but as a society we desperately need *values*.

We need them because a culture primarily obsessed with "tolerance" as an end instead of a means is, finally, a selfish culture, a have-it-your-way world. A place where nothing interferes with desire, the definition of a perfect consumer society. Listen to Jerry Della Femina, the adman, on *Good Morning America*. He's excoriating Disney for not letting movie theaters show commercials with its films: "Disney is blackmailing the movie theaters. . . . It should be up to the audience. If you hate the commercial, boo and hiss. If you like the commercial, buy the product. That's the American way." Or listen to Marion Barry, who in 1990 was still the mayor of Washington but had already been indicted on any number of drug and malfeasance charges. The city Democratic committee was voting that night on a motion urging him not to run for re-election. "It amounts to a type of censorship," he told one network. "Our country was founded on the principle that all men have a right to life, liberty, and the pursuit of happiness. And I intend to pursue my happiness as I see fit." By the late news, he's Daniel Webster[9] — "I'd rather die losing and stand on principle." The principle is that no one should tell him what to do, never mind that his city was a grotesque shambles. That night, a woman stood up at the Democratic meeting to defend Barry: "We're not Hitler, and we can't say who should run and who should not run." This is tolerance replacing sense.

Though it's rarely mentioned on TV, the gay community in the wake of

[9]*Daniel Webster:* American statesman and orator (1782–1852).

the AIDS crisis provides an alternative example. Randy Shilts's eloquent history of the crisis, *And the Band Played On*, begins in San Francisco, where gay people had carved out an enclave of freedom and tolerance in a hostile world. And then, out of nowhere, not as a punishment but as a fact, came a strange disease. It was a proud community, and a community tolerant, even indulgent, of all desires. The emerging understanding of the disease—that it was sexually transmitted, that safety lay in limiting both partners and practices — conflicted sharply with that tolerant ethos. Some people said that closing the bathhouses or educating people about what not to stick where would force people back into the closet, interfere with their freedom, return them to the repressed past. But AIDS was a fact. Gradually — a little too gradually, probably—the gay community came as a group to embrace other values, to form a community that in its organized compassion, active caring, and political toughness is a model for every other community in America. A mature community. This does not mean that AIDS was a good thing. Far, far better it had never come, and life had gone on as before, and none of those tens of thousands had died. But AIDS was and is a fact, a shocking enough fact to force people into changing, into realizing that along with tolerance and liberation they now need commitment and selflessness.

By accepting the idea that we should never limit desire or choose from the options our material and spiritual liberations give us, we ignore similarly pressing facts about our larger community. In a different world perhaps we'd never need to limit our intake of goods, to slow down our consumption of resources, to stop and share with others. But we live in this world—a world approaching ecological disaster, riven by proverty. A world of limits, demanding choices. TV gives us infinite information about choice — it celebrates choice as a great blessing, which it is, and over the course of a single day it lays out a nearly infinite smorgasbord of options. As much as it loves choice, though, it doesn't actually believe in choosing. It urges us to choose *everything* — this and this and this as well. And it does nothing to help us create the communities that might make wise choices possible on a scale large enough to make a difference.

25 In this case, the mountain is useful mostly as a vantage point. It can offer scant advice about how humans should organize their lives together, but it does provide an aerial view; from up here on the ridge I can recognize each home by its kitchen lights, and see how they stand in relation to one another. And now the all-night light has switched on at the volunteer fire department, whose noon siren was about the only mechanical sound I heard all day.

No need, as I said, to romanticize small towns — they can be home to vicious feud and rankling gossip and small-minded prejudice and all the other things that made leaving them appear so liberating. But there are a few things to be said for them, and the volunteer fire department is one. A house fire is no joke—when you take the state qualifying course, they show you film after film of houses exploding with folks inside, just as in *Backdraft*. On this day, in fact, the Washington TV stations were covering a tragedy in a tiny Pennsylvania village, Hustontown. The firemen had been called to clean out a well for an old lady. It smelled funny, but they thought there was just a dead animal down there. The first man down suddenly lost consciousness — two more jumped down to get him. All three died from some gas that had collected there. The fiancée of one of the men sobbed hysterically on the porch of a nearby house — she'd begged him not to go, but "he told me it was his duty as a volunteer firefighter." His duty, that is, to friends, neighbors, community.

It may be more sensible, by some utilitarian calculation, to entrust your safety to trained professionals and to insurance companies — more reliable, perhaps, and in places of a certain size clearly necessary. But it comes at a cost in information. Abstracted from others, you begin to believe in your own independence, forgetting that at some level you depend on everyone else and they depend on you, even if it's only to pay taxes. (Pretty soon you don't want to pay taxes anymore.) "We place a high value on being left alone, on not being interfered with," says Bellah, the sociologist who has interviewed hundreds of Americans. "The most important thing is to be able to take care of yourself. . . . It's illegitimate to depend on another human being." And this belief is so lonely — it's something human beings have never had to contend with before.

Public television was airing a Bill Moyers interview with a businessman named James Autry. A former brand manager for Colgate, he was trained at Benton & Bowles advertising agency and now worked as the publisher of *Better Homes & Gardens.* He is also a poet. He took Moyers back to the Mississippi town where he'd grown up — where his father, Reverend Autry, had spent his life preaching at the local church in the piney woods. The son had left the South in part to escape its ugly, intolerant side — he didn't want all that went with being a white Southerner. But he'd started coming back in recent years — he sat in the graveyard next to his daddy's church and read a poem. "She was a McKinstry, and his mother was a Smith / And the listeners nod at what that combination will produce / Those generations to come of honesty or thievery / Of heathens or Christians / Of slovenly men or worthy. / Course his mother was a Sprayberry. . . ." And he said, this man who publishes *Better Homes & Gardens,* which convinces millions that a better home is a home with better furniture, "I've thought about my own sons. What are they connected to? Some house on Fifty-sixth Street in Des Moines? What will they remember?" And this is a hard and terrible question for all of us who grew up liberated.

Engaging the Text

1. What, according to McKibben, does a community offer its members? Write a brief journal entry about a time you felt you belonged to a community as McKibben defines it — whether a town, neighborhood, school, work situation, club, or other organization.

2. What evidence does McKibben offer to support the claim that America's sense of community is in decline? Do you agree with him? What examples can you think of that demonstrate the health or decay of America's sense of community?
3. McKibben portrays TV as playing a complex — almost a contradictory — role in relation to America's eroding sense of community. Using examples he provides, explain his analysis of the way that TV simultaneously exploits the myth of freedom and appeals to our need for social connection.
4. Toward the end of the essay, McKibben offers gay San Francisco as a model of a mature community. What qualities make this gay community such a positive example for McKibben? What other model communities can you think of?

Exploring Connections

5. Compare and contrast the concepts of freedom presented by Gerry Spence (p. 682), June Jordan (p. 706), and McKibben. How does each of these authors view freedom? What virtues and hazards does each associate with being free?
6. Discuss one or more of the following communities in light of McKibben's argument. For example, what do these communities offer their members? What does each demand or expect in return? To what extent do these examples challenge or confirm McKibben's account of the value of community life?
   - the schools featured in George Wood's "Secondary Schools, Primary Lessons" (p. 121)
   - the Native American tribes in Paula Gunn Allen's "Where I Come from Is Like This" (p. 312)
   - the network of mothers in Patricia Hill Collins's "Black Women and Motherhood" (p. 195)
   - the town C. P. Ellis grew up in (p. 388)
   - the new "melting pot" of Los Angeles in Lynell George's "Gray Boys, Funky Aztecs, and Honorary Homegirls" (p. 422)
   - the working-class women in Cynthia Hamilton's "Women, Home, and Community" (p. 650)
7. Drawing on McKibben's and Josh Ozersky's (p. 172) analyses of the state of American TV, write an essay on the impact of TV on American values and attitudes.

Extending the Critical Context

8. Watch an hour or so of MTV videos and analyze the messages that they convey about community and liberation. How well do your observations mesh with McKibben's claims about TV?
9. Would you consider your composition class a community? If not, why not? If so, what values and beliefs unite your classroom community? What responsibilities and duties does this community require of its members?
10. McKibben suggests that the media occasionally go through periods of "counterrevolution" when so-called traditional values and beliefs are glamorized at the

expense of more rebellious messages (para. 15). As a class, discuss the current state of the media in relation to the themes of community and liberation. Are TV shows and films currently highlighting what might be considered traditional values? Has there ever been a period when the media emphasized liberation at the expense of traditional values?

Hate Radio

PATRICIA J. WILLIAMS

America's fascination with in-your-face free speech has no better embodiment than talk radio: millions tune in daily to hear commentators like Howard Stern and Rush Limbaugh hold forth on everything from phone sex to the state of the union. But not every American is charmed by the new candor on the airwaves. In the following essay, Patricia J. Williams asks if the hatred vented on talk radio isn't preparing America for a renaissance of intolerance and bigotry. Williams (b. 1951) teaches law at Columbia University and is the author of The Alchemy of Race and Rights *(1991). This essay originally appeared in* Ms. *(March/April 1994).*

Three years ago I stood at my sink, washing the dishes and listening to the radio. I was tuned to rock and roll so I could avoid thinking about the big news from the day before — George Bush had just nominated Clarence Thomas to replace Thurgood Marshall on the Supreme Court. I was squeezing a dot of lemon Joy into each of the wineglasses when I realized that two smoothly radio-cultured voices, a man's and a woman's, had replaced the music.

"I think it's a stroke of genius on the president's part," said the female voice.

"Yeah," said the male voice. "Then those blacks, those African Americans, those Negroes — hey 'Negro' is good enough for Thurgood Marshall — whatever, they can't make up their minds [what] they want to be called. I'm gonna call them Blafricans. Black Africans. Yeah, I like it. Blafricans. Then they can get all upset because now the president appointed a Blafrican."

"Yeah, well, that's the way those liberals think. It's just crazy."

"And then after they turn down his nomination the president can say 5
he tried to please 'em, and then he can appoint someone with some intelligence."

Back then, this conversation seemed so horrendously unusual, so singularly hateful, that I picked up a pencil and wrote it down. I was certain that a firestorm of protest was going to engulf the station and purge those foul radio mouths with the good clean soap of social outrage.

I am so naive. When I finally turned on the radio and rolled my dial to where everyone else had been tuned while I was busy watching Cosby reruns, it took me a while to understand that there's a firestorm all right, but not of protest. In the two and a half years since Thomas has assumed his post on the Supreme Court, the underlying assumptions of the conversation I heard as uniquely outrageous have become commonplace, popularly expressed, and louder in volume. I hear the style of that snide polemicism everywhere, among acquaintances, on the street, on television in toned-down versions. It is a crude demagoguery that makes me heartsick. I feel more and more surrounded by that point of view, the assumptions of being without intelligence, the coded epithets, the "Blafrican"-like stand-ins for "nigger," the mocking angry glee, the endless tirades filled with nonspecific, nonempirically based slurs against "these people" or "those minorities" or "feminazis" or "liberals" or "scumbags" or "pansies" or "jerks" or "sleazeballs" or "loonies" or "animals" or "foreigners."

At the same time I am not so naive as to suppose that this is something new. In clearheaded moments I realize I am not listening to the radio anymore, I am listening to a large segment of white America think aloud in ever louder resurgent thoughts that have generations of historical precedent. It's as though the radio has split open like an egg, Morton Downey, Jr.'s[1] clones and Joe McCarthy's[2] ghost spilling out, broken yolks, a great collective of sometimes clever, sometimes small, but uniformly threatened brains—they have all come gushing out. Just as they were about to pass into oblivion, Jack Benny and his humble black sidekick Rochester get resurrected in the ungainly bodies of Howard Stern and his faithful black henchwoman, Robin Quivers. The culture of Amos and Andy[3] has been revived and reassembled in Bob Grant's radio minstrelry and radio newcomer Daryl Gates's[4] sanctimonious imprecations on behalf of decent white people. And in striking imitation of Jesse Helms's[5] nearly forgotten days as a radio host, the far Right has found its undisputed king in the personage of Rush Limbaugh—a polished demagogue with a weekly radio audience of at least twenty million, a television show that vies for ratings with the likes of Jay Leno, a newsletter

[1]*Morton Downey, Jr.:* 1980s talk show host famed for baiting guests and discussing incendiary topics.

[2]*Joe McCarthy:* Joseph R. McCarthy (1909–1957) U.S. senator and chairman of the infamous Senate subcommittee that investigated so-called un-American activities during the anticommunist hysteria of the 1950s.

[3]*Amos and Andy:* Popular 1950s TV series often seen as promoting racist stereotypes of African Americans.

[4]*Daryl Gates:* Former Los Angeles Police Department chief and host of his own conservative radio show.

[5]*Jesse Helms:* Conservative U.S. senator (b. 1921).

with a circulation of 380,000, and two best-selling books whose combined sales are closing in on six million copies.

From Churchill to Hitler to the old Soviet Union, it's clear that radio and television have the power to change the course of history, to proselytize, and to coalesce not merely the good and the noble, but the very worst in human nature as well. Likewise, when Orson Welles[6] made his famous radio broadcast "witnessing" the landing of a spaceship full of hostile Martians, the United States ought to have learned a lesson about the power of radio to appeal to mass instincts and incite mass hysteria. Radio remains a peculiarly powerful medium even today, its visual emptiness in a world of six trillion flashing images allowing one of the few remaining playgrounds for the aural subconscious. Perhaps its power is attributable to our need for an oral tradition after all, some conveying of stories, feelings, myths of ancestors, epics of alienation, and the need to rejoin ancestral roots, even ignorant bigoted roots. Perhaps the visual quiescence of radio is related to the popularity of E-mail or electronic networking. Only the voice is made manifest, unmasking worlds that cannot — or dare not? — be seen. Just yet. Nostalgia crystallizing into a dangerous future. The preconscious voice erupting into the expressed, the prime time.

10 What comes out of the modern radio mouth could be the *Iliad*,[7] the *Rubaiyat*,[8] the griot's[9] song of our times. If indeed radio is a vessel for the American "Song of Songs," then what does it mean that a manic, adolescent Howard Stern is so popular among radio listeners, that Rush Limbaugh's wittily smooth sadism has gone the way of prime-time television, and that both vie for the number one slot on all the best-selling book lists? What to make of the stories being told by our modern radio evangelists and their tragic unloved chorus of callers? Is it really just a collapsing economy that spawns this drama of grown people sitting around scaring themselves to death with fantasies of black feminist Mexican able-bodied gay soldiers earning $100,000 a year on welfare who are so criminally depraved that Hillary Clinton or the Antichrist-of-the-moment had no choice but to invite them onto the government payroll so they can run the country? The panicky exaggeration reminds me of a child's fear. . . . *And then, and then, a huge lion jumped out of the shadows and was about to gobble me up, and I can't ever sleep again for a whole week.*

As I spin the dial on my radio, I can't help thinking that this stuff must be related to that most poignant of fiber-optic phenomena, phone sex. Aural Sex. Radio Racism with a touch of S & M. High-priest hosts with the power and run-amok ego to discipline listeners, to smack with the verbal back of the hand, to smash the button that shuts you up once and for all. "Idiot!"

[6]*Orson Welles:* American actor and movie director (1915–1985).

[7]*Iliad:* Ancient Greek epic poem of Trojan war commonly attributed to Homer.

[8]*Rubaiyat:* Persian epic poem written by Omar Khayyám.

[9]*griot:* A singer of tales in African oral tradition.

shouts New York City radio demagogue Bob Grant and then the sound of droning telephone emptiness, the voice of dissent dumped out some trapdoor in aural space.

As I listened to a range of such programs what struck me as the most unifying theme was not merely the specific intolerance on such hot topics as race and gender, but a much more general contempt for the world, a verbal stoning of anything different. It is like some unusually violent game of "Simon Says," this mockery and shouting down of callers, this roar of incantations, the insistence on agreement.

But, ah, if you *will* but only agree, what sweet and safe reward, what soft enfolding by a stern and angry radio god. And as an added bonus, the invisible shield of an AM community, a family of fans who are Exactly Like You, to whom you can express, in anonymity, all the filthy stuff you imagine "them" doing to you. The comfort and relief of being able to ejaculate, to those who understand, about the dark imagined excess overtaking, robbing, needing to be held down and taught a good lesson, needing to put it in its place before the ravenous demon enervates all that is true and good and pure in this life.

The audience for this genre of radio flagellation is mostly young, white, and male. Two thirds of Rush Limbaugh's audience is male. According to *Time* magazine, 75 percent of Howard Stern's listeners are white men. Most of the callers have spent their lives walling themselves off from any real experience with blacks, feminists, lesbians, or gays. In this regard, it is probably true, as former Secretary of Education William Bennett says, that Rush Limbaugh "tells his audience that what you believe inside, you can talk about in the marketplace." Unfortunately, what's "inside" is then mistaken for what's outside, treated as empirical and political reality. The *National Review* extols Limbaugh's conservative leadership as no less than that of Ronald Reagan, and the Republican party provides Limbaugh with books to discuss, stories, angles, and public support. "People were afraid of censure by gay activists, feminists, environmentalists—now they are not because Rush takes them on," says Bennett.

U.S. history has been marked by cycles in which brands of this or that 15
hatred come into fashion and go out, are unleashed and then restrained. If racism, homophobia, jingoism, and woman-hating have been features of national life in pretty much all of modern history, it rather begs the question to spend a lot of time wondering if right-wing radio is a symptom or a cause. For at least 400 years, prevailing attitudes in the West have considered African Americans less intelligent. Recent statistics show that 53 percent of people in the United States agree that blacks and Latinos are less intelligent than whites, and a majority believe that blacks are lazy, violent, welfare-dependent, and unpatriotic.

I think that what has made life more or less tolerable for "out" groups have been those moments in history when those "inside" feelings were relatively restrained. In fact, if I could believe that right-wing radio were only about idiosyncratic, singular, rough-hewn individuals thinking those inside thoughts, I'd be much more inclined to agree with Columbia University media expert Everette Dennis, who says that Stern's and Limbaugh's popularity represents the "triumph of the individual" or with *Time* magazine's bottom line that "the fact that either is seriously considered a threat . . . is more worrisome than Stern or Limbaugh will ever be." If what I were hearing had even a tad more to do with real oppressions, with real white *and* black levels of joblessness and homelessness, or with the real problems of real white men, then I wouldn't have bothered to slog my way through hours of Howard Stern's miserable obsessions.

Yet at the heart of my anxiety is the worry that Stern, Limbaugh, Grant, et al. represent the very antithesis of individualism's triumph. As the *National Review* said of Limbaugh's ascent, "It was a feat not only of the loudest voice but also of a keen political brain to round up, as Rush did, the media herd and drive them into the conservative corral." When asked about his political aspirations, Bob Grant gloated to the Washington *Post,* "I think I would make rather a good dictator."

The polemics of right-wing radio are putting nothing less than hate onto the airwaves, into the marketplace, electing it to office, teaching it in schools, and exalting it as freedom. What worries me is the increasing-to-constant commerce of retribution, control, and lashing out, fed not by fact but fantasy. What worries me is the re-emergence, more powerfully than at any time since the institution of Jim Crow,[10] of a socio-centered self that excludes "the likes of," well, me for example, from the civic circle, and that would rob me of my worth and claim and identity as a citizen. As the *Economist* rightly observes, "Mr. Limbaugh takes a mass market—white, mainly male, middle-class, ordinary America—and talks to it as an endangered minority."

I worry about this identity whose external reference is a set of beliefs, ethics, and practices that excludes, restricts, and acts in the world on me, or mine, as the perceived if not real enemy. I am acutely aware of losing *my* mythic individualism to the surface shapes of my mythic group fearsomeness as black, as female, as left wing. "I" merge not fluidly but irretrievably into a category of "them." I become a suspect self, a moving target of loathsome properties, not merely different but dangerous. And that worries me a lot.

What happens in my life with all this translated license, this permission 20
to be uncivil? What happens to the social space that was supposedly at the sweet mountaintop of the civil rights movement's trail? Can I get a seat on the bus without having to be reminded that I *should* be standing? Did the civil rights movement guarantee us nothing more than to use public accommodations while surrounded by raving lunatic bigots? "They didn't beat this idiot [Rodney King] enough," says Howard Stern.

Not long ago I had the misfortune to hail a taxicab in which the driver was listening to Howard Stern undress some woman. After some blocks, I

[10]*Jim Crow:* Laws enacted in the post–Civil War South that mandated racial segregation.

had to get out. I was, frankly, afraid to ask the driver to turn it off — not because I was afraid of "censoring" him, which seems to be the only thing people will talk about anymore, but because the driver was stripping me too, as he leered through the rearview mirror. "Something the matter?" he demanded, as I asked him to pull over and let me out well short of my destination. (I'll spare you the full story of what happened from there — trying to get another cab, as the cabbies stopped for all the white businessmen who so much as scratched their heads near the curb; a nice young white man, seeing my plight, giving me his cab, having to thank him, he hero, me saved-but-humiliated, cabdriver pissed and surly. I fight my way to my destination, finally arriving in bad mood, militant black woman, cranky feminazi.)

When Yeltsin blared rock music at his opponents holed up in the parliament building in Moscow, in imitation of the U.S. Marines trying to torture Manual Noriega in Panama, all I could think of was that it must be like being trapped in a crowded subway car when all the portable stereos are tuned to Bob Grant or Howard Stern. With Howard Stern's voice a tinny, screeching backdrop, with all the faces growing dreamily mean as though some soporifically evil hallucinogen were gushing into their bloodstreams, I'd start begging to surrender.

Surrender to what? Surrender to the laissez-faire resegregation that is the metaphoric significance of the hundreds of "Rush rooms" that have cropped up in restaurants around the country; rooms broadcasting Limbaugh's words, rooms for your listening pleasure, rooms where bigots can capture the purity of a Rush-only lunch counter, rooms where all those unpleasant others just "choose" not to eat? Surrender to the naughty luxury of a room in which a Ku Klux Klan meeting could take place in orderly, First Amendment fashion? Everyone's "free" to come in (and a few of you outsiders do), but mostly the undesirable nonconformists are gently repulsed away. It's a high-tech world of enhanced choice. Whites choose mostly to sit in the Rush room. Feminists, blacks, lesbians, and gays "choose" to sit elsewhere. No need to buy black votes, you just pay them not to vote; no need to insist on white-only schools, you just well the desirability of black-only schools. Just sit back and watch it work, like those invisible shock shields that keep dogs cowering in their own backyards.

How real is the driving perception behind all the Sturm und Drang[11] of this genre of radio-harangue — the perception that white men are an oppressed minority, with no power and no opportunity in the land that they made great? While it is true that power and opportunity are shrinking for all but the very wealthy in this country (and would that Limbaugh would take that issue on), the fact remains that white men are still this country's most privileged citizens and market actors. To give just a small example, according to the *Wall Street Journal,* blacks were the only racial group to

[11] *Sturm und Drang:* "Storm and Passion": a Romantic German literary movement of the eighteenth century; here, something like impassioned posturing.

suffer a net job loss during the 1990–91 economic downturn at the companies reporting to the Equal Employment Opportunity Commission. Whites, Latinos, and Asians, meanwhile, gained thousands of jobs. While whites gained 71,144 jobs at these companies, Latinos gained 60,040, Asians gained 55,104, and blacks lost 59,479. If every black were hired in the United States tomorrow, the numbers would not be sufficient to account for white men's expanding balloon of fear that they have been specifically dispossessed by African Americans.

25 Given deep patterns of social segregation and general ignorance of history, particularly racial history, media remain the principal source of most Americans' knowledge of each other. Media can provoke violence or induce passivity. In San Francisco, for example, a radio show on KMEL called "Street Soldiers" has taken this power as a responsibility with great consequence: "Unquestionably," writes Ken Auletta in *The New Yorker,* "the show has helped avert violence. When a Samoan teenager was slain, apparently by Filipino gang members, in a drive-by shooting, the phones lit up with calls from Samoans wanting to tell [the hosts] they would not rest until they had exacted revenge. Threats filled the air for a couple of weeks. Then the dead Samoan's father called in, and, in a poignant exchange, the father said he couldn't tolerate the thought of more young men senselessly slaughtered. There would be no retaliation, he vowed. And there was none." In contrast, we must wonder at the phenomenon of the very powerful leadership of the Republican party, from Ronald Reagan to Robert Dole to William Bennett,

giving advice, counsel, and friendship to Rush Limbaugh's passionate divisiveness.

The outright denial of the material crisis at every level of U.S. society, most urgently in black inner-city neighborhoods but facing us all, is a kind of political circus, dissembling as it feeds the frustrations of the moment. We as a nation can no longer afford to deal with such crises by *imagining* an excess of bodies, of babies, of job-stealers, of welfare mothers, of over-reaching immigrants, of too-powerful (Jewish, in whispers) liberal Hollywood, of lesbians and gays, of gang members ("gangsters" remain white, and no matter what the atrocity, less vilified than "gang members," who are black), of Arab terrorists, and uppity women. The reality of our social poverty far exceeds these scapegoats. This right-wing backlash resembles, in form if not substance, phenomena like anti-Semitism in Poland: there aren't but a handful of Jews left in that whole country, but the giant balloon of heated anti-Semitism flourishes apace, Jews blamed for the world's evils.

The overwhelming response to right-wing excesses in the United States has been to seek an odd sort of comfort in the fact that the First Amendment is working so well that you can't suppress this sort of thing. Look what's happened in Eastern Europe. Granted. So let's not talk about censorship or the First Amendment for the next ten minutes. But in Western Europe, where fascism is rising at an appalling rate, suppression is hardly the problem. In Eastern and Western Europe as well as the United States, we must begin to think just a little bit about the fiercely coalescing power of media to spark mistrust, to fan it into forest fires of fear and revenge. We must begin to think about the levels of national and social complacence in the face of such resolute ignorance. We must ask ourselves what the expected result is, not of censorship or suppression, but of so much encouragement, so much support, so much investment in the fashionability of hate. What future is it that we are designing with the devotion of such tremendous resources to the disgraceful propaganda of bigotry?

Engaging the Text

1. What does Williams mean when she says that she hears the "snide polemicism" of talk radio everywhere in contemporary America? To what extent do you agree that "crude demagoguery" has infected the way Americans think and relate to each other?
2. How does Williams account for talk radio's popularity? Which of her explanations strikes you as the most plausible? Why? What other reasons can you offer?
3. What worries does Williams express about talk shows like Rush Limbaugh's? What, according to her, are such shows doing to America? Do you agree?
4. Williams mentions an incident in which she was forced to leave a cab because its driver was listening to Howard Stern "undress" a woman on the air. Should she have asked the cabdriver to turn the radio off? Should people in public places be allowed to listen to shows that may be racially or sexually offensive?

5. What is "laissez-faire segregation"? Is segregation acceptable if it is a matter of choice?
6. Although Williams criticizes talk radio, she offers little sense of what should be done to curb "the disgraceful propaganda of bigotry" it produces. What, if anything, should be done to address the excesses of shows like Howard Stern's and Rush Limbaugh's?

Exploring Connections

7. Drawing on June Jordan's "Freedom Time" (p. 706), Bill McKibben's "TV, Freedom, and the Loss of Community" (p. 712), and Williams's "Hate Radio," write a paper exploring the dangers that the mass media may pose in a democracy.
8. Review Gerry Spence's discussion of the risks entailed by real freedom in "Easy in the Harness" (p. 682), paying special attention to his observations on "old Jack" (para. 14). How might Spence interpret the "hate" Williams condemns on talk radio? How different are the opinions and the confrontational style of "old Jack" from those of talk radio stars like Howard Stern and Rush Limbaugh?
9. Imagine what TV show the characters are about to watch in the Callahan cartoon (p. 730) and write a sample of the language they are likely to hear. Who would be offended by it? Who would enjoy it? Why? Compare notes with your classmates and discuss.

Extending the Critical Context

10. Working in small groups, listen to an hour or more of "hate radio" hosted by any of the commentators Williams mentions. How many unsupported assertions are made during the show? How many derogatory labels or slurs are used? Overall, would you agree that such shows are providing America with "the disgraceful propaganda of bigotry"?

Regulation of Hate Speech May Be Necessary

Richard Delgado and Jean Stefancic

One of the paradoxes of life in a free society is that one citizen's freedom can be another's oppression. The Bill of Rights lays out our fundamental freedoms, but it is mute when those freedoms come into conflict. The past five years have witnessed growing tensions on American college campuses over the issue of speech codes—rules prohibiting the use of racial and ethnic slurs, verbal sexual harassment, and verbal assaults on gays and lesbians. This essay, which originally appeared in 1991 in The Chronicle of Higher Education, *probes the thinking behind these new campus regulations. Richard Delgado is a professor of law at the University of Colorado; Jean Stefancic is a research associate at the same school.*

Incidents of racial unrest on campuses in the past few years have prompted a number of colleges and universities to enact rules prohibiting slurs and disparaging remarks directed against individuals because of their race, ethnicity, religion, or sexual orientation. These rules raise thorny legal and educational issues.

People tend to react to such rules in one of two ways. Some frame the issue as a First Amendment problem: the rules limit speech, and the Constitution forbids official regulation of speech without a very good reason. If one takes that starting point, the burden shifts to colleges and universities to show that the interest in protecting people on campus from insults and name calling is compelling enough to overcome the presumption in favor of free speech. Further, there must be no less onerous way than regulations of accomplishing that objective. Some people will worry that the people enforcing the regulations may become censors, imposing narrow-minded restraints on campus discussion.

Others, however, frame the problem as one of protection of equality. They ask whether an educational institution does not have the power to protect core values emanating from the Fourteenth Amendment's guarantee to all citizens of equal protection of the laws. Cannot an institution enact reasonable regulations aimed at assuring equal personhood on campus? If one characterizes the issue *this* way, the defenders of racially scathing speech must show that their interest in protecting it is compelling enough to overcome the presumption of equal protection. Further, the interest in free speech must be advanced in the way that is least damaging to equality; those enforcing the regulations must be attuned to the nuances of insult and racial supremacy at issue.

The two sides invoke different narratives to rally support.

Protectors of the First Amendment see campus antiracism rules as parts 5
of a much longer story: the centuries-old struggle of Western society to free itself from superstition and enforced ignorance. They conjure up struggles against official censorship, book burning, witch trials, and communist blacklists. Compared to that richly textured, deeply stirring account, the interest of those who would protect a few (supersensitive?) individuals from momentary discomfort looks thin.

Those on the minority-protection side invoke a different, and no less powerful, narrative. They see a nation's centuries-long struggle to free itself from racial and other forms of tyranny, including slavery, lynching, Jim Crow laws,[1] and "separate but equal" schools. Arrayed against that richly textured historical account, the racist's interest in insulting a person of color face to face looks thin.

My view is that both stories are equally valid. Judges and university administrators have no easy way of choosing between them. Nothing in constitutional or moral theory requires one answer rather than the other. But, ultimately, judges and university administrators must *choose.*

Social science, case law, and the experience of other nations provide some illumination. The debate surrounding campus antiracism rules has proceeded largely in an empirical vacuum. Yet it involves several issues that have empirical components—questions that might be answered Yes or No. Can free speech continue to exist in a society that prohibits one of its forms? Will one type of regulation lead to another? Are laws limiting racist speech effective compared with other approaches to controlling racism? Although one must always be cautious in drawing conclusions from the experiences of other cultures, their experiences may nevertheless suggest answers to these questions.

Britain, for example, passed a Race Relations Act in 1965, which was amended in 1986, making it an offense to stir up hatred against any section of the public on the basis of color, race, ethnic, or national origins; to publish or distribute written matter that is threatening, abusive, or insulting; or to use in any public place or public meeting words that are threatening, abusive, or insulting. Only the attorney general can approve prosecutions under the law. Although the law still has critics, few people today advocate doing away with it altogether, and British courts have interpreted the act narrowly, so as to minimize conflict with free speech.

Like Britain, Canada has developed several measures to protect minor- 10
ities against racism. Its national criminal code has prohibited hate speech since 1970. Four types of hate speech are recognized as crimes—advocating genocide, public incitement of hatred, willful promotion of hatred, and spreading false news. Each of the offenses is subject to a number of defenses — all designed to protect free expression. Those, together with the requirement that the attorney general must approve any prosecutions, are designed to limit the likelihood of abuse. Although a few civil libertarians continue to express concern, criticism generally has been muted.

The Netherlands, France, Austria, Germany, Italy, Sweden, Norway, Australia, and New Zealand also have statutes or constitutional provisions prohibiting forms of hate speech, some of which go much further than any under discussion in the United States. Whether these have reduced the incidence of harassment is an open question. White supremacists have been prosecuted, and it seems likely that the laws have deterred other hate speech.

[1] *Jim Crow laws:* Laws enacted in the post–Civil War South that mandated racial segregation.

One must extrapolate cautiously from the experiences of other societies. Moreover, what holds true for a nation may not hold true for a university, whose peculiar interests may make anti-hate-speech legislation either more or less defensible. Still, it would be a mistake to ignore the experience of Canada, whose constitutional approach to regulation of speech resembles our own, or that of Britain, with whom we share a long common-law tradition. In these and other countries that have enacted anti-hate legislation, there appears to have been little of a snowball effect toward censorship. Thus, it is evidently possible to regulate the more vicious forms of racial hate speech, while remaining committed to free expression.

The debate about campus antiracism rules has proceeded in not only an empirical vacuum, but also in a theoretical one, blind to the insights of social scientists who have studied race and racism.

Social scientists have advanced several theories to explain the origins of racial bias, ranging from authoritarian personality traits to anxieties about economic dislocation and change that result in scapegoating, to humans' natural propensities to generalize and establish ingroups and outgroups. Indeed, more than one explanation may be essential to understand the complex phenomenon of racism. Unlike the etiology[2] of racism, however, there is relative agreement among many social scientists on how to control its expression.

The majority view among social scientists today on how to control racism 15
is probably the "confrontation theory," which holds that most people are ambivalent in matters of race and that much prejudice is situational — individuals express it because the environment encourages or tolerates it. Most who subscribe to this approach hold that laws and rules play a vital role in controlling racism. As the psychologist Gordon Allport has said, rules "create a public conscience and a standard for expected behavior that check *overt* signs of prejudice." Nor is the change merely cosmetic; studies have shown that in time, rules are internalized and the impulse to engage in racist behavior weakens.

Social scientists' current understanding of racial prejudice thus lends some support to campus antiracism rules. The mere existence of such rules may cause people to behave in a more egalitarian way, particularly when others may be watching. Further, a large body of literature shows that incessant racial categorization and biased treatment seriously impair the prospects and development of members of minority groups.

Case law also provides some help in analyzing the free-speech versus equal-dignity perspectives. The First Amendment appears to stand as a formidable barrier to campus rules prohibiting disparaging speech, yet during the past century, the courts have carved out or tolerated dozens of "exceptions" to free speech. They include speech that is used to form a criminal conspiracy, that disseminates an official secret, that is obscene, that libels or

[2]*etiology:* Cause or origin.

defames someone, that creates a hostile workplace, that violates a trademark or plagiarizes another's words, that constitutes "fighting words" likely to provoke violence, that defrauds a consumer, or that holds a judge, teacher, or military officer in disrespect.

Much speech then is unprotected. The question is whether the social interest in reining in racially offensive speech is as great as that which gives rise to these other "exceptional" categories and whether the use of racially offensive language has value as speech.

On the equal-protection side, one finds not only constitutional provisions, but also a myriad of federal and state statutes aimed at protecting the rights of minorities from discrimination in many areas of life. The equality principle is not without limits, however; government agencies cannot redress bias by means that encroach too much on the rights of whites or on other constitutional principles.

In the university sector, the Supreme Court held in 1983 in *Bob Jones* 20
University v. United States that universities may not discriminate in the name of religion. In *University of Pennsylvania v. EEOC* in 1990, it held that a university's desire to protect confidential tenure files did not insulate them from review in bias investigations. Both cases imply that the imperative against bias will at times prevail over other strong interests, such as freedom of religion or academic freedom.

How might we resolve the dilemmas raised by hate speech? Scholars in several fields have stressed that our understanding of reality is mediated by narratives or stories, interpretive structures that enable us to infuse separate events with meaning and coherence. The general term applied to this approach is "postmodernism." I believe hate speech is a way society "constructs" a stigmatized picture of minorities and that it may be regulated without violating the First Amendment. Indeed, regulation may be necessary to fully achieve equal protection of all of our citizens.

The first step is recognizing that racism is, in almost all its aspects, a class harm, the essence of which is subordination of one people by another. By "constructing" a shared cultural image of the victimized group as inferior, we enable ourselves to feel comfortable about the disparity in power and resources between ourselves and the stigmatized group. The shared picture also immobilizes the victims, particularly the young. Indeed, social scientists have seen evidence of self-hatred and rejection of their own identity in children of color as young as three.

Like water dripping on sandstone, ubiquitous and incessant negative racial depictions cause a pervasive harm that only the hardiest can resist. Yet the prevailing First Amendment paradigm predisposes us to treat racist speech as an individual harm, as though we only have to evaluate the effect of a single drop of water. This approach — corresponding to liberal, individualistic theories of self and society — systematically misperceives the experience of racism for both victim and perpetrator. This mistake is natural and corresponds to one aspect of our natures — our individualistic selves.

But we also exist as social beings; we need others to fulfill ourselves. In this group aspect, we require inclusion, equality, and equal respect. Constitutional narratives of equal protection and prohibition of slavery—narratives that encourage us to form and embrace collectivity and equal citizenship for all—reflect this second aspect of our existence.

When one group begins to coordinate the exercise of individual 25
rights so as to jeopardize seriously participation by a smaller group, the "rights" nature of the first group's actions acquires a different character and dimension. The exercise of an individual right now poses a group harm and must be weighed against this qualitatively different type of threat.

Not only does racist speech, by placing all the credibility with the dominant group, strengthen the dominant story, it also works to disempower minority groups by crippling the effectiveness of their speech in rebuttal. This situation makes free speech a powerful asset to the dominant group, but a much less helpful one to subordinate groups.

Unless society is able to deal with this incongruity, our constitutional equal protection guarantee and our complex system of civil rights statutes will be of little avail. At best, they will be able to obtain redress for episodic, blatant acts of individual prejudice and bigotry.

Could judges and legislators act on this idea that speech that constructs a stigmatized picture of a subordinate group stands on a different footing? One might argue that *all* speech constructs the world to some extent and that every spoken word could prove offensive to someone. Yet race—like gender—is different; our entire history and culture bespeak this difference. Judges easily could differentiate speech that subordinates blacks, for example, from speech that demeans factory owners or some other powerful group in our society.

The resurgent racism on our campuses has become a national embarrassment. Each separate racist act may seem harmless. But together they combine to crush the spirit of their victims and create an atmosphere at odds with our national values. Only by taking account of this group dimension can we capture the full power of racially scathing speech—and make good on our promises of equal citizenship to those who have so long been denied its reality.

Engaging the Text

1. What dilemma, according to Delgado and Stefancic, does the debate over speech codes present to campus authorities? What are the basic positions of each side in this debate?
2. What is the "confrontation" theory for controlling prejudice? What other ways can you think of to control, change, or discourage racist, sexist, and homophobic behavior?

3. Review the arguments Delgado and Stefancic provide to support the use of speech codes on campus. Which of these are most persuasive? Which seem weak or unconvincing? What additional arguments can you think of for or against the establishment of college speech codes?

Exploring Connections

4. Compare Delgado and Stafancic's objections to hate speech on campus with Patricia Williams's assessment of the damage done by hate radio (p. 724). Would Delgado and Stefancic be likely to extend the call for rules regulating hate speech to nationally broadcast radio shows? Why or why not?
5. What additional arguments might Myra Sadker and David Sadker (p. 86) and Carmen Vázquez (p. 287) provide for the direct control of sexist and homophobic speech on campus?

Extending the Critical Context

6. Research the history of existing speech and behavior codes on your campus. When, if ever, were codes first established and enforced? What types of speech or activity are currently regulated? How effective does your college's policy seem to be? What other strategies does or should your campus employ to discourage prejudice, sexism, and homophobia?
7. Research the "free speech" position on the issue of campus speech codes — for example, the position of the American Civil Liberties Union. What are the basic arguments against controlling speech on campus? How might Delgado and Stefancic respond to these counterarguments?
8. Working in small groups, discuss which, if any, of the following real-life situations should have been regulated by campus speech codes:
   - a campus address by a radical Nation of Islam representative who has a history of making anti-Semitic remarks
   - the establishment of a White Student Union
   - fraternity-sponsored "Fiji Island Parties" complete with Black makeup and pamphlets featuring racist stereotypes
   - the words "Death Nigger" written on a dorm door
   - a white professor teaching that the IQ of certain ethnic groups is lower than that of Euro-Americans
   - an African American professor teaching that Blacks are genetically superior to whites
   - a male student who says in class that "women just aren't as good in this field as men"
   - a white student who calls a group of African American female students "water buffaloes"
   - a student who puts a sign on a dorm door saying that the following people should be "shot on sight": "preppies, bimbos, men without chest hair, and homos"
   - a fraternity that publishes songbooks with violent, sexually explicit lyrics aimed at Latino/Chicano students and women

Stuck with a Satanist? Religious Autonomy in a Regulated Society

STEPHEN L. CARTER

The framers of the Constitution might not recognize today's multicultural America; nor would they be likely to comprehend the diversity of religious belief in the contemporary United States. We live in a land where one person's saint may be another's Satan — where the difference between sacrament and sacrilege may turn on one's point of view. In this selection, an expert on constitutional law argues that the rights of the religious in America have been largely ignored and that they deserve special "accommodation." Stephen L. Carter (b. 1954) is the William Cromwell Professor of Law at Yale University. He is the author of the controversial Reflections of an Affirmative Action Baby *(1991);* The Culture of Disbelief *(1993), the source of this selection; and* The Confirmation Mess: Cleaning Up the Federal Appointments Process *(1994).*

Suppose that you, a religious person, decide to rent out an apartment over your garage. Along comes a possible renter who seems to meet all your requirements, except that he lets slip, in casual conversation, that he is a Satanist. He tells you that he intends, while living in your apartment, to conduct certain rituals demanded by his faith. Now, it happens that your state's fair housing law prohibits religious discrimination, and you share the moral premises of that law. (The federal Fair Housing Act does not apply to rentals of single-family homes by their owners or rentals of rooms in such homes, or to buildings with fewer than five units if the owner actually occupies one of them.) On the other hand, you cannot, consistent with your own religion, allow Satanic rituals on your property. What do you do?

If you follow the law — a law you generally support — then you must allow on your property activities that your religion forbids. But if you reject the tenant because he happens to be a Satanist, you will be in violation of the law and could face a heavy fine. You might want to plead in defense your constitutional right to exercise your religion freely, asking for an accommodation of your beliefs, which means, in this case, an exception to a valid statute that applies to everybody else. But that would seem something of a long shot. The Supreme Court has made such a mess of the right to exercise one's religion freely that there is little chance the claim for an exemption would succeed. So you would, in the name of nondiscrimination, be stuck with the Satanist.

Of course you have an alternative. You could take the apartment off the market entirely. Or you could try. It might not work, because overcoming such devices as the withdrawal of a listing is the sort of thing any good lawyer can do in her sleep. Then, assuming you were to get away with it, you would have saved your religious beliefs, but at the cost of getting out of the market, which means losing income. If no exemption is forthcoming, your unattractive choice is between going to hell by renting to someone who will engage in activities you are religiously forbidden to allow on your property and not renting at all.

The dilemma is not entirely hypothetical. Consider a case that arose in California not long ago, when an unmarried couple found their application for an apartment refused because their potential landlords, John and Agnes Donahue, believed they would be "putting themselves in the position of eternal, divine retribution" if they allowed the sin of fornication, as they described it, on their property. Because housing discrimination on the basis of marital status is forbidden in California, the rejected applicants filed a complaint. The Donahues responded that their religious freedom was at stake.

5 The case poses precisely and painfully the liberal dilemma when religious liberty runs up against the regulatory ubiquity of the welfare state. In late twentieth-century America, nearly everyone seems to operate with the general presumption that the government can and should regulate in whatever areas suit its constituents' fancy — unless opponents can interpose a claim of constitutional right. And as federal constitutional rights go, the right to exercise religion freely is quite near the bottom of the totem pole. But the states are free under their own constitutions to protect more than the federal Constitution does, and a friend-of-the-court brief in the Donahue case, signed by religious organizations across the political spectrum, urged the California Supreme Court to demand that the state meet a heavy burden of justification before applying the antidiscrimination law to the Donahues — perhaps even the "compelling interest" test that the Supreme Court rejected when, in its 1990 decision in *Employment Division v. Smith,* it allowed punishment for Native Americans required to use peyote in their religious rituals.

The Donahue case, although many may find it especially poignant, is not unique. Antidiscrimination law is one of the cutting edges of the accommodation problem, not least because many religious traditions encourage or even require discrimination on grounds that we as a nation have rejected or are on the way to rejecting. Although few American religious traditions will admit any longer to relegating people of color to an inferior status — even the Mormons at last experienced a new revelation, that black members can be priests of the Inner Temple after all — there are many who understand the word of God as barring women from priesthood, notwithstanding that the equality of women is firmly established in secular law. And many more religions do not allow as ministers individuals who engage in homosexual activities, even as the gay and lesbian rights movement makes important secular inroads.

No one — yet — proposes state regulation of the ministry, but the organized churches are large and complicated operations, and most have many lay employees. Given the broad protections that exist in law against employment discrimination, the potential problems are obvious. Should a church be able to require that the gardener be a coreligionist? That the plumber take a religious oath? That the painter tithe[1]?

In general, the Supreme Court has seemed indecisive in the face of religious objections to statutes regarding employment practices. So, for example, the justices ruled in 1979 that the National Labor Relations Board cannot exercise jurisdiction over lay teachers in Catholic schools. Then, six years later, the Court ruled that the Labor Department can enforce minimum-wage laws on behalf of at least some employees of religious foundations. Now, that is another view, not quite consistent with the first. But at least the justices are in there punching.

When forbidden discrimination is the issue, even Supreme Court justices who might otherwise be considered accommodationists tread warily. In the best-known case, *Corporation of Presiding Bishop of the Church of Jesus Christ of Latter-Day Saints v. Amos* (1987), the Court upheld a provision of federal law exempting secular nonprofit activities of religious organizations from the general prohibition of discrimination on the basis of religion. The decision, though, was narrow, resting on the conclusion that the exemption was intended to avoid "significant governmental interference with the ability of religious organizations to defend and carry out their religious missions."

One might argue, as the legal scholar Kathleen Sullivan has done (see 10
"Religion and Liberal Democracy," *University of Chicago Law Review*, 59 [1992]), that what is at issue in these cases is a "religious opt-out from the redistributive programs of the welfare state." We are talking, after all, about employment rights that exist because of the statutes of the New Deal and the Second Reconstruction: the rights of employees to organize unions, to be paid a fair wage, and to be free to market discrimination. The same might be said of the California housing discrimination case mentioned earlier, even though the rights of unmarried couples there asserted are of more recent vintage. Thus, one might conclude, with Sullivan, that "[j]ust as religionists must pay for the secular army that engineers the truce among them, they must pay for the other common goods of the civil public order."

Now, even if one concedes the bemusing notion that a major task of the armed forces of the United States is to avert religious strife, there is still trouble in the welfare state paradise. If the religions are properly called upon to make the sacrifices that the law requires because the statutes in question all involve the provision of common goods, one might then conclude that

[1]*tithe:* To dedicate a set fraction of one's income to one's church.

the *Smith* case, sustaining the punishment of Native Americans for using peyote in worship as required by their religion, was rightly decided after all — a sacrifice that they must make in order to enable a common war on drugs. Sullivan, however, is certain that *Smith* is wrong, and that it represents discrimination against — indeed, a certain judicial "blindness" about — a minority religion, which it certainly does. Sullivan's distinction seems to be that *Smith* involves a judgment made by an adult about drug use, whereas the cases she comfortably considers examples of the welfare state in action involve the employment relationship, which is different.

One is tempted to respond, welfare state or none, that the employees are also adults, and may work for low pay for their religious organizations as willingly as the state employees in *Smith* used peyote in their rituals. But a different answer is also possible. Imagine that we are in the United States not of the late twentieth century but of the late nineteenth, when state laws required racial discrimination in many areas of life, and when, for example, religious groups that ran integrated schools in the South were threatened with prosecution. These statutes were defended — implausibly, but never mind — as improving the society. Would Sullivan really suggest that a religion should not be allowed to opt out of generally applicable secular regulations on education? One might answer that greater religious autonomy was needed in an oppressive American South of the nineteenth century than is needed in the liberal democracy we are said to enjoy today. But while I, like Sullivan, tend to be a supporter of regulatory government, many religions see the welfare state, for all its virtues, as oppressive of their liberties.

What is needed, in order to bring coherence to the problem of accommodation, is a richer understanding not of the nature of the welfare state, or, indeed, of government, but of the nature of the religions themselves, particularly the nature of religious autonomy. To gain that richer understanding, one must think not of the way the society looks at religions but of the way religions look at themselves. In the 1987 *Presiding Bishop* case, a separate opinion by Justice William J. Brennan, joined by Justice Thurgood Marshall, got the point right:

> For many individuals, religious activity derives meaning in large measure from participation in a larger religious community. Such a community represents an ongoing tradition of shared beliefs, an organic entity not reducible to a mere aggregation of individuals. Determining that certain activities are in furtherance of an organization's religious mission, and that only those committed to that mission should conduct them, is thus a means by which a religious community defines itself. Solicitude for a church's ability to do so reflects the idea that furtherance of the autonomy of religious organizations often furthers individual religious freedom as well.

What Brennan understood — and what the Court, and the literature, too often do not — was that religion is more than a matter of what an individual chooses to believe. Religions are communities of corporate worship, or, as one might say in this postmodern world, communities of sense and value, groups of believers struggling to come to a common understanding of the world. So when one speaks of autonomy, one is speaking not just of the individual, but also of the group.

15 The group, moreover, will often be engaged in what David Tracy[2] calls acts of resistance — interposing the group judgment against the judgment of a larger society. Worshiping together, endeavoring jointly to discern the will of God, if honestly done, will lead frequently to that result. When the state tries to block that process of discernment in a faith community, it is acting tyrannically by removing potential sources of authority and meaning different from itself. This, too, Brennan plainly understood in a way that the Court as a whole rarely has:

> The authority to engage in this process of self-definition inevitably involves what we normally regard as infringement on free exercise rights, since a religious organization is able to condition employment in certain activities on subscription to particular religious tenets. We are willing to countenance the imposition of such a condition because we deem it vital that, if certain activities constitute part of a religious community's practice, then a religious organization should be able to require that only members of its community perform those activities.

Brennan was concerned about what abuses this rule might invite, and he added a sensible caveat: "Religious organizations should be able to discriminate on the basis of religion only with respect to religious activities, so that a determination should be made in each case whether an activity is religious or secular." One can see Brennan's point: hiring a plumber to fix the sink in a parish hall is not the same thing as hiring a counselor to work in a religious program to fix dysfunctional families. Still, what Brennan does not say — but what his line of argument implies — is that the key "determination [of] whether an activity is religious or secular" must give considerable, if not decisive, weight to the religion's own vision of the distinction. If one does happen to encounter a religion that considers the repair of the sink God's work, one must not respond blithely — as the courts too often do — with, "Really? Well, we don't."

Translating this principle into law, one would say that the central acts of faith of a religious community — the aspects that do the most to produce shared meaning within the corporate body of worship — are entitled to the highest solicitude by the courts, and, therefore, when infringing on those central acts, the state must offer a very convincing reason. As the acts of faith that the state seeks to regulate or forbid become less central, the state's burden of justification grows less.

In terms of the cases, this would mean that before punishing an obviously central act such as the use of peyote by the Native American Church (the *Smith* case) or before destroying the land that makes a religious tradition possible (*Lyng v. Northwest Indian Cemetery Protective Association*, 1988),

[2]*David Tracy:* Catholic priest, writer, and educator (b. 1939).

the state would have to meet a very high burden of justification, perhaps even show a compelling interest, before it is allowed, through a seemingly neutral policy, to trespass upon the central faith-world of a religion. In those cases, it is not likely the burden could have been met, so the decisions are probably wrong.

The welfare-state cases — those involving employment or housing discrimination — might at first seem more difficult to resolve. After all (one might object), in *Smith* and *Lyng* the government is acting against people who simply want to worship, but the Donahues are trying to make money. If their religion will not let them make it by the rules the state has set out, can't they just put their money somewhere else? But the objection is a non sequitur. It in particular does not distinguish *Smith:* the reason the state of Oregon punished the Native Americans for using peyote was that they were state employees. Presumably, if they do not like the rule, they can work for somebody else.

More fundamentally, however, the objection misses the critical differ- 20
ence between living in a society that does much regulating and a society that does little. The First Amendment was written for a world in which regulation was expected to be rare and would almost never impinge on religious liberty. We live instead in a world in which regulation is everywhere, and the idea that the religious citizen can escape it, through a careful search, is a fantasy. Besides, even were escape easier, the problem remains that religious people might wind up finding it more costly to participate in the market than others who do not share their views. Of course these additional costs — such as the cost of not being able to discriminate — might be justifiable. The accommodation test here proposed would only demand that the state offer more than an ordinary justification for them.

It is not possible to resolve here all the many cases that might arise from pursuing this approach, so I will limit myself to making two points. First, it would be both a secular and a religious disaster were religions by the dozen suddenly to come forward claiming a free exercise right to engage in all the many forms of discrimination that secular politics has decided to forbid. However, it would also be a secular and religious disaster were we to rule out entirely the possibility that a few religions could come forward and meet the test I have proposed. Deciding when to allow exemptions would place a tremendous burden on the courts — but there is no reason that the hard work of protecting freedom should be easy.

Thus, resolution of the cases involving the minimum wage or labor-organizing rights for employees not directly connected with the central religious function of the church would require more searching inquiries than the Supreme Court generally likes to see the federal courts undertake. The case of the refusal of the Donahues to rent to an unmarried couple, however, may be a simple one. If, as the Donahues claim, their religious tradition teaches that they will be damned if they allow fornication on their property, it is hard to see why anything other than a compelling interest should allow the state to put them at risk.

Still, in crafting a sensible understanding of religious autonomy, the courts ideally should play only a minor role. The more important role is the one that society itself must play, in its politics and its rhetoric. As with every fundamental human right, the ultimate security of religious liberty lies not in judges' opinions but in citizens' commitments; it is vital that we ourselves, the people of the United States, before allowing our government to trespass on religious freedom, balance the depth of our moral commitment to the policy in question against the value of religious autonomy. If our commitment to the policy wins every time, then we really have become the majoritarian tyrants against whom Tocqueville[3] warned us a century and a half ago.

One of the reasons that the asserted political influence of religious groups is so feared is that some people believe that the religions, if politically empowered, might try to impose on the secular society their own versions of the good life. This is, of course, a real danger, although there is reason to doubt that more harm to individual freedom *necessarily* occurs when a religion seeks to impose its vision of the good life than when an entirely secular political movement does it. Indeed, it is not easy, in a nation committed to religious liberty, to understand why the risk that the religions might try to impose their religious visions of the good life on secular society is more to be avoided than the risk that the state and its powerful constituents might try to impose a secular vision of the good life on the religions.

[3]*Tocqueville:* See p. 142 for more about Alexis de Tocqueville.

Engaging the Text

1. Carter introduces this essay with the hypothetical case of the satanist tenant. Compare this hypothetical example to the actual case of the unmarried couple that follows (para. 4). How do you respond to each of these illustrations? Why do you think Carter opened his essay with the portrait of a satanist?
2. Why, according to Carter, must religious practice almost inevitably conflict with the practice, belief, and values of the larger secular society? To what extent is this true of most religions?
3. What is Carter's central argument for an expanded view of religious freedom? How would he determine which religious practices to accommodate? Does this strike you as a workable solution?
4. Summarize the last two paragraphs of Carter's essay. What is he saying about the nature of freedom and its relation to religion and the state in a democracy?

Exploring Connections

5. Drawing on both Carter and Bill McKibben (p. 712), write an essay in which you explore the idea that the myth of freedom is threatening the existence of community in American life.
6. Write an imaginary conversation between June Jordan (p. 706), Patricia Williams (p. 724), and Carter on the tension between individual freedom and social unity.

7. Richard Delgado and Jean Stefancic (p. 732) and Carter argue for extending the freedom of certain Americans at the expense of others. Compare the arguments they present for privileging these special groups. What values and assumptions underlie the cases they present? What vision of American society is implied in their positions?

Extending the Critical Context

8. Carter cites several cases involving American Indian religions in this essay, including *Employment Division v. Smith* (1990) and *Lyng v. Northwest Indian Cemetery Protective Association* (1988). Research news accounts dealing with these and other cases involving Native American religious practices and study the reasoning that has guided judges in their decisions. To what extent do these legal opinions support or challenge the arguments made by Carter?
9. Working in small groups, debate whether the individuals or groups in the following cases should be granted special accommodation to practice their religion as they see fit:
   - Individuals in a fundamentalist group refuse to pay taxes because the United States guarantees the right to abortion.
   - A Catholic parish fires teachers who are discovered to be gay or lesbian.
   - A religious school expels female students who become pregnant.
   - A church bars minority groups from assuming leadership roles.
   - A church bars women from assuming leadership roles.
   - A sect practices animal sacrifice as part of its weekly worship activities.
   - A Christian landlord refuses to rent to a rap musician because he believes that rap music is influenced by the devil.
   - A Christian landlord refuses to rent to an American Indian couple because she sees them as pagans.
   - A Rastafarian Jamaican American insists on smoking marijuana as part of her religious observance.

The Bridge Builder: Kathleen Boatwright

Eric Marcus

As the title of this personal history implies, freedom isn't always a matter of standing alone against the crowd: sometimes real freedom emerges from the relationships we build with new friends and communities. "The Bridge Builder" tells the story of Kathleen Boatwright, a devout Christian funda-

mentalist and mother of four who discovers freedom — and happiness — as she begins to explore her life as a lesbian. This selection originally appeared in Making History: The Struggle for Gay and Lesbian Equal Rights 1945–1990 *(1992), a collection of oral histories edited by Eric Marcus. A former associate producer for* CBS This Morning *and* Good Morning America, *Marcus (b. 1958) is the author of* The Male Couple's Guide *(1988) and* Is It a Choice? Answers to 33 of the Most Frequently Asked Questions about Gays and Lesbians *(1993).*

Invariably wearing a sensible Sears dress or skirt and jacket, Kathleen Boatwright doesn't look the part of a social activist, as she describes herself. But as vice president of the Western Region of Integrity, the gay and lesbian Episcopal ministry, Kathleen uses her conventional appearance, her status as a mother of four, her Christian roots, her knowledge of the scriptures, and her disarming personal warmth to wage a gentle battle for reform in the church she loves — and to change the hearts and minds of individuals within the church. According to Kathleen, "I see myself uniquely gifted to show people what we do to each other in ignorance."

Kathleen Boatwright's very difficult and painful journey from fundamentalist Christian, director of the children's choir at her local church, and pillar of her community to Episcopal lesbian activist began one day in August 1984, when Jean, a veterinary student at Oregon State University, walked through the door of Kathleen's church in Corvallis, Oregon.

The first time I met Jean, she was having a nice conversation with my fifteen-year-old daughter at our church. I was very impressed by the mature way in which she spoke to my daughter. Then, during the service, I sat in the front row and watched Jean sing. I was so enamored by her presence that she stuck in my mind. But then she left town and was gone until January the following year.

Come January, I was sitting in church and I looked across the room, and there was Jean, carrying her guitar, walking down the aisle with such determination. I had this incredible lump in my throat, and I said to myself, *Jean's back.* After the service, and despite my difficulty talking to new people, I just had to ask Jean where she had been. I had to talk to her.

5 I found out that she was back in Corvallis for five months to finish her degree. She didn't have a place to live. So I said to her, "Don't worry, my parents have always wanted to take in a college student. You're redheaded like Dad. They'll love it!" I went and dragged my mother away from where she was talking and I said, "You remember Jean, she's looking for a place to stay. Why don't you and Dad take her in and board her?"

From early on my parents encouraged the friendship because they saw how much Jean meant to me. Meeting her brought me to life in a way they hadn't seen before. They knew that I used to cry for hours on end when I was a child because no girls liked me at school. My mother would come in and rub my leg or pat my hand. I was extremely intelligent and bright, but I had low self-esteem because I wasn't able to find friendship. So my parents encouraged Jean to invite me to lunch or to take me for a drive or go horseback riding. They felt that her friendship was really wonderful for me. They were glad I was happy. For a while.

My husband didn't pay much attention — at first. He was a state policeman and had always been nonparticipatory, both as a parent and a spouse.

After four months of being friends, of having this wonderful platonic relationship, Jean had to go away for a month for her externship. While she was away she met a fundamentalist couple. Well, Jean sent me a postcard and said, "Something's going on. I'm playing with fire. I can't handle it. I've got to talk to you." My heart wrenched. What was going on?

When we were finally able to meet and talk, Jean explained to me how she and this fundamentalist woman started sharing in an intimate way. My response was to put my arm through hers and say, "Don't worry. We'll get it fixed." Jean couldn't be homosexual because it was wrong. Besides, if she was homosexual, then she would be leaving my life. And I think on a deeper level, I didn't want Jean exploring these things with anyone but me.

After her externship, Jean wanted to be more sensual with me. Her 10
attitude was, "Now I'm going to show *you*." She said, "I'll give you a back rub some night." So one night — after Bible study, no less — she was over at my house and said, "Why don't you lay down on the blanket on the floor and take off your blouse and bra and I'll rub your back?" And I was like, "Okaaay!" My husband was working all night, and this just seemed like a great setup. So this nice little Christian lady rubbed my back, and I said to myself, *Gee, this is it!*

All the little pieces, all the little feelings came together. Even comments my mother made to me over the years began to make sense. She'd say things like, "don't cut your hair too short." "You can't wear tailored clothes." It was then that I also realized that the neighbors I had grown up with were a lesbian couple, even though I had never thought about that before. I recalled the feeling of walking through the Waldenbooks bookstore, looking at *The Joy of Lesbian Sex* and longing for that kind of intimacy. It all came upon me at that moment, and I felt a real willingness to release myself to this person in a way I had never done before. Then the phone rang. It was my son from Bible college. I thought, *Oh, God, saved by the bell! I don't know where this would have gone.*

By the end of the month, Jean was graduating, taking her national boards, and trying to figure out what to do about her feelings toward me and what to do about the fundamentalist woman. It was Pentecostal hysteria.

Now don't forget, at this time I still had a husband and four kids. I had a nineteen-year-old son at a conservative Bible college. I had a sixteen-year-old daughter in the evangelical Christian high school, of which I was a board member. Two children were in parochial day school. My father was the worship leader at church. And I was still very bound to my parents for emotional support. I was the favorite child. And my grandparents lived in town.

Well, shit, I was in way over my head. I was really painted into a corner because there wasn't a single place I could turn for even questioning. So I started looking to some Christian sources. Some of the advice was so incredible, like, "If you feel homosexual tendencies, you can't have the person you have those feelings for over to your house in the evening." "You can never let a member of the same sex sit on your bed while you're chatting." "Meet only in a public place." I thought this advice was ridiculous, but I also thought it was my only option because my spiritual nature was more important than my physical nature. Intellectually and emotionally, I was so hungry and so turned on that I didn't know what to do with my feelings.

At this point, people pull the trigger, turn to the bottle, take drugs, leave town. But I didn't do any of those things because I was madly in love. If I had pulled the trigger, I wouldn't have been able to express the part of me I had discovered. I had found someone, someone who shared the same sort of values I had.

Everything reached a crisis point. I acknowledged to myself and to Jean that I was a lesbian and that I loved her. By this time we had already been sexually active. My husband began to get suspicious that someting was going on, and he and I went into counseling. Jean was leaving for a job in Colorado and told me that I couldn't go with her because she was a responsible woman and didn't want to destroy my family. And I still hadn't yet found the spiritual guidance that I needed.

I had to get away and do some soul-searching. I needed to figure out if there was any Christian support somewhere that said I could reconcile my love for Jean and my love for my faith. I didn't feel I could build a life of love if I rejected my faith. So I packed my bags and told my parents that I was leaving to go to stay with my great-aunt in Los Angeles for ten days. I told my husband, "I am going to get away and I'm going to think about a bunch of issues, and then I'm coming back."

For the first time in my entire life, at the age of thirty-six, I was by myself with my own agenda. I had left my husband, my children, my parents, my support structures; got in a car; and started driving to West Hollywood, where I knew there was a lesbian mayor and a gay community. So surely, I thought, there had to be a spiritual gay community.

In West Hollywood I found Evangelicals Together. It's not a church, just a storefront ministry to the gay community for people coming out of an evangelical Christian background. It's led by a former American Baptist minister who talked my language. He said to me, "In order to deal with your dilemma, you have to take a step back from your relationship with Jean. Lay her aside and ask yourself, *Who did God create me to be?*"

Through our sharing, and by looking from a different perspective at the 20
gospel and what Jesus had to say, I could embrace the theology that said, "God knew me before I was born. He accepted me as I was made to be, uniquely and wholly." Ultimately, in an obedience to God, you answer that call to be all that He has created you to be. I felt firmly and wholly that what I had experienced with Jean was no demonic possession, was not Satan tempting me with sins of lust, but an intimacy and a love that was beautiful and was God given. So now I had to figure out how to deal with it.

When you're my age, you're either going to go back to the way it's always been — go for the security you've always known — or take a chance. I felt that for the love I felt for Jean I was willing to risk all. Of course, having Jean there, I was hedging my bet a bit. I was jumping off a cliff, but I was holding somebody's hand.

Jean flew down a few days later to join me in Los Angeles. She agreed to commit to me and I to her. The first Sunday after we affirmed our relationship, we worshiped at All Saints' Episcopal Church in Pasadena because I was told that the Episcopals had the framework of faith I loved, as well as an ability to use reason in light of tradition and scripture.

It was God answering the cry of my heart to send me to that worshiping place. Jean and I had never been to an Episcopal church before. We went into this beautiful place with the largest Episcopal congregation west of the Mississippi River. We sat in the fourth row. It was just this incredible Gothic wonderful place. It was All Saints' Day at All Saints' Church. They played the Mozart Requiem with a full choir and a chamber ensemble, and a female celebrant sang the liturgy. We held hands and wept and wept. We could go forward because in the Anglican tradition, the Eucharist is open for everyone. God extends himself. There are no outcasts in the Episcopal church.

When I got back to town, I met with my husband at a counselor's office. I said, "Yes, you're right. I am gay and I'm going to ask for a divorce. I'm going to take this stand. I want to meet with my older children and my parents to talk about the decisions I've made." I felt at least I had a right to make my own decisions. I went to pick up my two youngest girls at my father's house. I went to open the door and I heard a flurry of activity, and the children saw me. "Oh, Mommy's home! Mommy's home!" And my dad stepped out on the front porch and pushed the children away and slammed the door. He took me forcibly by the arm and led me down the stairs and said, "You're never seeing your children again without a court order! Just go shack up with your girlfriend!" And he forced me down to the street.

It took going to court to see my two youngest children. They hadn't seen 25
me for two weeks. They asked, "Mommy, Mommy, what's wrong?" I leaned over and whispered in their ears, "Mommy loves you." My husband wanted to know, "What are you telling the children?" I had only a minute with them, then went downstairs, and my husband told me that he wanted me to come back, that he would be my brother, not my husband.

I tell you, my whole world came down upon my ears. I wasn't allowed to see my children. I was denied access to my residence. The church had an open prayer meeting disclosing my relationship with Jean. They tried to get Jean fired from her job. And when that didn't work, they called Jean's parents, who then tried to have her committed or have me arrested. My family physically disinherited me and emotionally cut me off. My older daughter, upon the advice of her counselor-pastor, shook my hand and said, "Thank you for being my biological mother. I never want to have anything to do with you again." After that, whenever she saw me in town, she hid from me. I saw her lay flat on the asphalt in the grocery store parking lot so I wouldn't see her. People I'd known all my life avoided me like I had the plague. I was surprised that Jean didn't just say, "Hey, lady, I'm out of here!"

Fortunately, I wasn't entirely without support. I went to Parents and Friends of Lesbians and Gays and I met some wonderful loving, Christian, supportive parents and gay children who said, "You're not sick. You're not weird. Everybody's hysterical." They offered any kind of assistance possible. Through their emotional support, I felt like it was possible to survive the crush.

Living in a small rural county in Oregon, I didn't know anything about women's rights, let alone gay rights. So it's not surprising that I bought into the lie that children of lesbians or gays are better off living with the custodial heterosexual parent. I believed my husband could provide a sense of normality that I could not. So I signed away my custodial rights and became a secondary parent. After being the primary-care parent for twenty devoted years, the judge only let me see the children two days a week.

By then I'd had enough. So I packed one suitcase and a few things in grocery sacks and left my family and children behind. Jean and I just rode quietly out of town in the sunset to her job in Denver, Colorado.

As you drive into Denver, you go over this big hill about fifteen miles from town. We stopped at a phone booth and called the local Parents FLAG president to ask if there was a supportive Episcopal parish in town. She said, "Yes, go to this place, look up this person." It was getting to be evening. It was clear, and we were going over the mountain. It was a whole new adventure. It was real closure to my past and a real opening toward my future. Still, the guiding force in my life was, "The church has the answers."

Jean and I called the church and found out when services were and asked if they had an Integrity chapter. Integrity is the Episcopal ministry to the gay and lesbian community. There was one, so two nights later we walked into our first Integrity meeting. There were twelve attractive men in their thirties and the rector. They were shocked to see two women because it's unusual for women to be in Integrity. The only thing dirtier than being a lesbian in a Christian community is being a Christian in the lesbian community because it brings in so many other issues besides sexual orientation, like women's issues and patriarchy and all that stuff.

Denver Integrity was an affirming congregation. We were out as a couple. We were healed of so many things through the unconditional love and acceptance of this parish of eighty people. The rector there encouraged me to become involved. Out of his own pocket he sent me to the first regional convention I went to, in 1987 in San Francisco. Now, I'm vice president of the Western Region for Integrity, and I'm on the national board of directors. I'm one of only maybe 125 women in Integrity's membership of about 1,500.

Integrity gives me a forum for the things I want to say, both as a lesbian woman and as a committed Christian. And because of my background and experience, I can speak to the church I love on a variety of issues that others cannot. I can say, "I call you into accountability. You are bastardizing children raised in nontraditional households. You're not affirming the people that love and guide them. You say you welcome us, but on the other hand you don't affirm us. You don't give us rites of passage and ritual and celebration like you do for heterosexual families."

The church needs to change. What we're asking for are equal *rites.* We're asking the church to bless same-sex unions. I'm asking for canonical changes that affirm my wholeness as a child of Christ who is at the same time in a loving committed relationship with a woman. We're also challenging the church to make statements asking the government to legitimize our relationships and give us the same sorts of tax breaks, pension benefits, et cetera. But most importantly, we need the church to get off the dime and start affirming gay and lesbian children's lives. I never want a girl to go through what I went through. I want to spare everybody right up front.

To get my point across when I go out and talk to groups as a represen- 35
tative of Integrity, I personalize the issue. I personalize my political activism by speaking to people as a person, as Kathleen Boatwright. People don't need to hear dogma or doctrine or facts or theology. They need to meet people.

Here's a great example. For the first time, the women of Integrity got seated at Triennial, which is this gigantic group of very traditional women who have a convention every three years. It used to be that while the men were making the decisions, the women held their own convention. With women's issues having changed so dramatically in the Episcopal church, that's no longer true. Now that women are allowed to serve in the House of Deputies and can be ordained into the priesthood, we've become full team members in the canonical process.

Triennial was made for me. Everybody wears their Sears Roebuck dress. Everybody is a mom. Everybody lived like I had lived for twenty years. I know how to network and how to deal with those women. But I also have a new truth to tell them that will have an impact on their lives in very special ways. Gays and lesbians are 10 percent of the population. Everybody is personally affected by that issue, including these women at Triennial.

During the convention, I attended a seminar given by conservative Episcopals who said gays and lesbians have confused gender identity. Later, we had an open meeting in which we talked about human sexuality. But no one talked about sexuality. Instead, we only talked about information on biological reproduction. After about forty minutes of hearing these women drone on, I stood up in my Sears Roebuck dress and said, "OK ladies, put on your seat belts because you're going to take a trip into reality. You won't want to hear it, but I need to say it because you need to know what people's lives are really like."

I talked to them about my journey. I talked to them about the misnomers, about "confused gender identity." I was wearing this circle skirt and I said, "As you can see from my appearance," and I curtsied, "I do not have a 'confused gender identity.' " Everybody who had been really stiff started laughing—and they started listening. The key is that I take risks. I risk being vulnerable. I risk sharing the secrets of my heart. We already know what the straight people feel in their hearts. But no one talks about how the lesbian or gay person feels in his or her heart.

For the next hour and a half, people talked about where they really live. They talked about their pregnant teenagers or the suicide attempts in their families. All those gut-level issues. But you have to have someone lead you to that. That's me—because I'm safe. I've also learned that instead of having all the answers, that God calls me to listen to people's pain, and not to judge it.

This one woman told me that she had been driving by her daughter's house for eight years and that her husband had never let her stop because her daughter was a lesbian. "But," she said, "I'm going to go home and I'm going to see her. My daughter's name is also Kathleen." Then she started to cry. She had never even told the women from her church about what had happened to her daughter. It's like the living dead for many Christian families. They just have a child who is lost prematurely in so many senses of the word.

Inevitably, everywhere I go I hear about parents who have made ultimatums. This one mother said, "I've never told anybody, but I said to my son, 'I wish you were dead.' And by forcing him into the closet, I fulfilled that prophecy. Three years later, he was dead." Then there was a woman who said to me, "Kathleen, I'm questioning my sexuality at seventy. Could you send me some information?"

I think in my heart that I represent the hidden majority of lesbian women because many, many are married or have been married, have children, and have too much to risk — like I've risked and lost — to come out. And those women who are out, who are much more political and aggressive, have seen enough successes happen, enough bridges built by my approach, that they're beginning to respect the fact that I can go through doors they never can.

The first time I spoke publicly to the leadership of the women of the church, I spoke along with another lesbian. She was politically correct and a strong feminist. *Feminist* was always a dirty word for me, so I've had to overcome a lot of my own bias. I said to her, "Please don't speak about politics. Don't brow beat these people. Stand up and say that you're a doctor, that you've never been in a committed relationship, that you're a feminist. Because I want to stand up and say, 'I've been a Blue Bird leader.' What that will say is that we represent the gamut of human experience, just like the heterosexual community. It's just our ability to develop intimate relationships with the same sex that makes us different."

45 People don't have to identify with my ideology. They identify with my person, and then the questions come from them. We don't have to tell them. They start asking us. People say to me, "What do you call your partner?" "You don't have any medical insurance?" To me that's the best sort of teaching process: answering questions rather than giving information.

My husband remarried; he married the baby-sitter. At Easter of 1987, I got a call informing me that he had removed my ten-year-old daughter from his house, accusing her of using "inappropriate touch" with his new stepsons. He wanted to unload the difficult child. Then he used that child as a weapon to try and deny me visitation for the younger one. The end result was that I had one child and he had one child. I filed suit against him without any hope or prayer of winning back custody of my other child.

I went to a lesbian minister to ask her about finding a lawyer to handle my case, and she said to me, "The best attorney in this town is Hal Harding, but he's your husband's attorney. Maybe that will prove to be a blessing." So I had to find another attorney.

As part of the custody proceedings, Jean and I eventually met with my husband's attorney. He took depositions and asked Jean and me really heartfelt questions. Then he advised his client — my ex-husband — to go ahead and have a psychological evaluation. The court had not ordered it and, in fact, would not order it because there was no precedent in that county. But my former husband agreed to go to the psychologist of his choice. That psychologist, a woman, took the time and energy to interview every person involved and recommended to the court that Jean and I become custodial parents. We now have custody of both children, sole custody. It was indeed a blessing.

We just added Jean's ninety-one-year-old grandmother to our family. So we are all-American lesbians living here in Greenacres, Washington. We are Miss and Mrs. America living together. The thing that we need in our life now that our faith doesn't give us is a community of supportive women. We have yet to find that place.

50 Not long ago, I went to the National Organization for Women lesbian rights agenda meeting and gave a workshop on spirituality for women, from the Christian perspective. And I took a deep breath in my Betty Crocker suit — if I ever write a book it's going to be *The Radicalization of Betty*

Crocker—and thought, *I wonder what the Assemblies of God girls would say now? From their perspective, I'm walking into the total pit of hell, and I'm bringing the very gift that they should be giving.* Who would have believed it?

Engaging the Text

1. What family, religious, and cultural bonds restrained Boatwright from acknowledging her sexuality? What were her options? How do you think she should have reacted when she realized that she was attracted to Jean? Why?
2. In what different ways does Boatwright's emerging lesbian identity change her and her life? What price does she pay?
3. How do Boatwright's attitudes toward the church develop during her story? How does her self-image change?
4. How do you interpret the title of this oral history? In what different senses is Boatwright a "bridge builder"?
5. From the information available about her past, write a brief character sketch of Boatwright, tracing the development of her personality from childhood through the occasion of this oral history.

Exploring Connections

6. Compare what freedom means to the couple in "Selway" (p. 668), Gerry Spence (p. 682), Charlie Sabatier (p. 690), and Kathleen Boatwright. What does freedom do to people in these stories? Where does it lead? Which of these visions strikes you as coming closest to the true meaning of freedom?
7. How might Kathleen Boatwright respond to Stephen Carter's assertion that religions are "communities of sense and value, groups of believers struggling to come to a common understanding of the world" (p. 739)? How might her experiences with organized religion complicate this view of religion as community? If she and Jean were rejected as prospective renters by the Donahues, how do you think Carter would assess the situation?

Extending the Critical Context

8. Several of the selections in this chapter refer to the "risk" associated with real freedom. Write a personal essay about the risks you feel are necessary in order to live a free life—or about a specific risk you once ran in order to be free.

Let America Be America Again

Langston Hughes

Our survey of American culture closes with a reflection on the power that the myth of freedom has to inspire hope, even in the face of despair. Written nine years into the Great Depression, "Let America Be America Again" (1938) offers a stinging indictment of the hypocrisy that Langston Hughes perceived everywhere in American life. Yet Hughes transcends his rage and dares to hope for America's future; in so doing he pays homage to ideals that retain their potency even in the 1990s. (James) Langston Hughes (1902–1967) was a major figure in the Harlem Renaissance—a flowering of African American artists, musicians, and writers in New York City in the 1920s. His poems, often examining the experiences of urban African American life, use the rhythms of jazz, spirituals, and the blues. Among the most popular of his works today are The Ways of White Folks *(1934), a collection of short stories, and* Montage of a Dream Deferred *(1951), a selection of his poetry.*

Let America be America again.
Let it be the dream it used to be.
Let it be the pioneer on the plain
Seeking a home where he himself is free.

(America never was America to me.)

Let America be the dream the dreamers dreamed—
Let it be that great strong land of love
Where never kings connive nor tyrants scheme
That any man be crushed by one above.

(It never was America to me.)

O, let my land be a land where Liberty
Is crowned with no false patriotic wreath,
But opportunity is real, and life is free,
Equality is in the air we breathe.

(There's never been equality for me,
Nor freedom in this "homeland of the free.").

Say who are you that mumbles in the dark?
And who are you that draws your veil across the stars?

I am the poor white, fooled and pushed apart,
I am the red man driven from the land.

I am the refugee clutching the hope I seek—
But finding only the same old stupid plan
Of dog eat dog, of mighty crush the weak.
I am the Negro, "problem" to you all.
I am the people, humble, hungry, mean—
Hungry yet today despite the dream.
Beaten yet today—O, Pioneers!
I am the man who never got ahead.
The poorest worker bartered through the years.
Yet I'm the one who dreamt our basic dream
In that Old World while still a serf of kings,
Who dreamt a dream so strong, so brave, so true,
That even yet its mighty daring sings
In every brick and stone, in every furrow turned
That's made America the land it has become.
O, I'm the man who sailed those early seas
In search of what I meant to be my home—
For I'm the one who left dark Ireland's shore,
And Poland's plain, and England's grassy lea,
And torn from Black Africa's strand I came
To build a "homeland of the free."

The free?
Who said the free? Not me?
Surely not me? The millions on relief today?
The millions who have nothing for our pay
For all the dreams we've dreamed
And all the songs we sung
And all the hopes we've held
And all the flags we've hung,
The millions who have nothing for our pay—
Except the dream we keep alive today.

O, let America be America again—
The land that never has been yet—
And yet must be—the land where *every* man is free.
The land that's mine—the poor man's, Indian's, Negro's, ME—
Who made America,
Whose sweat and blood, whose faith and pain,
Whose hand at the foundry, whose plow in the rain,
Must bring back our mighty dream again.

O, yes,
I say it plain,
America never was America to me,
And yet I swear this oath—
America will be!

ENGAGING THE TEXT

1. Explain the two senses of the word "America" as Hughes uses it in the title and refrain of the poem.
2. What different types of freedom does Hughes address in this poem?
3. According to Hughes, who must rebuild the dream, and why?
4. Why does Hughes reaffirm the dream of an ideal America in the face of so much evidence to the contrary?
5. Explain the irony of lines 40–41 ("And torn from Black Africa's strand I came / To build a 'homeland of the free.' ")
6. Examine the way Hughes uses line length, repetition, stanza breaks, typography, and indentation to call attention to particular lines of the poem. Why does he emphasize these passages?

EXPLORING CONNECTIONS

7. Review some or all of the poems in *Rereading America:*

   Melvin Dixon's "Aunt Ida Pieces a Quilt" (p. 234)
   Lucille Clifton's "being property once myself" (p. 648)
   Wendy Rose's "Three Thousand Dollar Death Song" (p. 351)
   Janice Mirikitani's "We, the Dangerous" (p. 354)
   Aurora Levins Morales's "Child of the Americas" (p. 444)
   Inés Hernández-Ávila's "Para Teresa" (p. 74)
   Langston Hughes's "Let America Be America Again" (p. 756)

   Then write an essay on poetry as a form of social action. What are the characteristics of this type of poetry? How does it differ from the poetry you have read before in school?

EXTENDING THE CRITICAL CONTEXT

8. Working in groups, "stage" a reading of the poem, using multiple speakers. Consider carefully how to divide up the lines for the most effective presentation. After the readings, discuss the choices made by the different groups in the class.
9. Working in pairs or in small groups, write prose descriptions of the two versions of America Hughes evokes. Read these aloud and discuss which description more closely matches your own view of the United States.

Acknowledgments

Paula Gunn Allen, "Where I Come from Is Like This" from *The Sacred Hoop* by Paula Gunn Allen. Copyright © 1986, 1992 by Paula Gunn Allen. Reprinted by permission of Beacon Press.

Jean Anyon, "From *Social Class and the Hidden Curriculum of Work*," edited, from the *Journal of Education*, vol. 162, no. 1 (Winter 1980). Reprinted by permission of the author and the *Journal of Education*.

Gloria Anzaldúa, "*La conciencia de la mestiza*/Towards a New Consciousness" from *Borderlands/La Frontera: The New Mestiza* © 1987 by Gloria Anzaldúa. Reprinted by permission of Aunt Lute Books, (415) 826-1300.

Toni Cade Bambara, "The Lesson" from *Gorilla, My Love* by Toni Cade Bambara. Copyright © 1972 by Toni Cade Bambara. Reprinted by permission of Random House, Inc.

Katy Butler, "The Great Boomer Bust." First published June 1989 in *Mother Jones*. Copyright © 1989 by Katy Butler. Reprinted by permission.

Bebe Moore Campbell, "Envy" from *Sweet Summer: Growing Up With and Without My Dad* by Bebe Moore Campbell. Copyright © 1989 by Bebe Moore Campbell. Reprinted by permission of The Putnam Publishing Group.

Stephen L. Carter, "Stuck with a Satanist? Religious Autonomy in a Regulated Society" excerpted from *The Culture of Disbelief* by Stephen L. Carter. Copyright © 1993 by Stephen L. Carter. Reprinted by permission of BasicBooks, a division of HarperCollins Publishers, Inc.

Sucheng Chan, "You're Short, Besides!" from *Making Waves* by Asian Women United. Copyright © 1989 by Asian Women United. Reprinted by permission of Beacon Press.

Lucille Clifton, "being property once myself" from *Good Woman: Poems and a Memoir 1969–1980* by Lucille Clifton. Copyright © 1987 by Lucille Clifton. Reprinted with the permission of BOA Editions, Ltd., 92 Park Avenue, Brockport, NY 14420.

Blythe McVicker Clinchy, Mary Field Belenky, Nancy Goldberger, and Jill Mattuck Tarule, "Connected Education for Women" from the *Journal of Education*, vol. 167, no. 3 (1985). Reprinted by permission of the *Journal of Education* and the authors.

Patricia Hill Collins, "Black Women and Motherhood" from *Black Feminist Thought: Knowledge, Consciousness, and the Politics of Empowerment* by Patricia Hill Collins. Reprinted by permission.

Stephanie Coontz, "We Always Stood on Our Own Two Feet: Self-reliance and the American Family" from Chapter 4 of *The Way We Never Were* by Stephanie Coontz. Copyright © 1992 by BasicBooks, a division of HarperCollins Publishers Inc. Reprinted by permission of BasicBooks, a division of HarperCollins Publishers, Inc.

Ellis Cose, "Tiptoeing Around the Truth" from Chapter 2 of *The Rage of the Privileged Class* by Ellis Cose. Copyright © 1993 by Ellis Cose. Reprinted by permission of HarperCollins Publishers, Inc.

Richard Delgado and Jean Stefancic, "Regulation of Hate Speech May Be Necessary" from the *Chronicle of Higher Education* (September 18, 1991). Reprinted by permission of the author.

Holly Devor, "Becoming Members of Society: Learning the Social Meanings of Gender" from pp. 43–45, 49–53 of *Gender Blending: Confronting the Limits of Duality* by Holly Devor. Copyright © 1989 by Indiana University Press, Bloomington, IN. Reprinted by permission of the author and Indiana University Press.

Melvin Dixon, "Aunt Ida Pieces a Quilt." Reprinted with the permission of the Estate of Melvin Dixon.

Dave Foreman, "Putting the Earth First" from *Confessions of an Eco-Warrior* by Dave Foreman. Copyright © 1991 by David Foreman. Reprinted by permission of Harmony Books, a division of the Crown Publishing Group.

Anne Witte Garland, "Good Noise: Cora Tucker" from *Women Activists: Challenging the Abuse of Power* by Anne Witte Garland, published by The Feminist Press at The City University of New York. Copyright © 1988 by The Center for the Study of Responsive Law. Reprinted by permission. All rights reserved.

Lynell George, "Gray Boys, Funky Aztecs and Honorary Homegirls." Copyright © Lynell George. Reprinted by permission.

Anita Gordon and David Suzuki, "How Did We Come to This?" from *It's a Matter of Survival* by Anita Gordon and David Suzuki. Copyright © 1990 by Anita Gordon and David Suzuki. Reprinted by permission of Harvard University Press and Stoddart Publishing Co. Limited, Don Mills, Ontario.

Ed Guerrero, "Slaves, Monsters, and Others" from *Framing Blackness: The African American Image in Film* by Ed Guerrero. Copyright © 1993 by Temple University. Reprinted by permission of Temple University Press.

John Langston Gwaltney, "Charlie Sabatier" from *The Dissenters: Voices from Contemporary America* by John Langston Gwaltney. Copyright © 1986 by John Langston Gwaltney. Reprinted by permission of Random House, Inc.

Cynthia Hamilton, "Women, Home, and Community: The Struggle in an Urban Environment" from *Reweaving the World,* edited by Irene Diamond and Gloria Feman Orenstein (Sierra Club Books). Reprinted by permission of the editors.

Inés Hernández-Ávila, "Para Teresa" from *Con Rázon, Corazón* by Inés Hernández-Ávila. Copyright © 1987 by Inéz Hernández-Ávila. Reprinted by permission.

Anndee Hochman, "Growing Pains: Beyond 'One Big Happy Family' " from *Everyday Acts and Small Subversions* by Anndee Hochman (Portland, OR: The Eighth Mountain Press, 1994). Copyright © 1994 by Anndee Hochman. Reprinted by permission of the publisher.

bell hooks, "Sexism and Misogyny: Who Takes the Rap?" from *Z Magazine,* February 1994, as excerpted from *Outlaw Culture: Resisting Representations* by bell hooks. Copyright © 1994 by bell hooks. Reprinted by permission.

Pam Houston, "Selway" from *Cowboys Are My Weakness* by Pam Houston. Copyright © 1992 by Pam Houston. Reprinted with the permission of W. W. Norton & Company, Inc.

Langston Hughes, "Let America Be America Again." Copyright 1938 by Langston Hughes. Copyright renewed 1965 by Langston Hughes. Reprinted by permission of Harold Ober Associates Incorporated.

Roger Jack, "An Indian Story" from *Dancing on the Rim of the World,* edited by Andrea Lerner (University of Arizona Press). Reprinted by permission.

June Jordan, "Freedom Time." Reprinted by permission from *The Progressive,* 409 East Main Street, Madison, WI 53703.

Michael S. Kimmel, "Clarence, William, Iron Mike, Tailhook, Senator Packwood, Spur Posse, Magic, . . . and Us." Copyright © 1993 by Michael S. Kimmel. Reprinted with permission.

Jamaica Kincaid, "Girl" from *At the Bottom of the River* by Jamaica Kincaid. Copyright © 1978, 1985 by Jamaica Kincaid. Reprinted by permission of Farrar, Straus & Giroux, Inc.

Maxine Hong Kingston, "Silence" from *The Woman Warrior* by Maxine Hong Kingston. Copyright © 1975, 1976 by Maxine Hong Kingston. Reprinted by permission of Alfred A. Knopf, Inc.

John (Fire) Lame Deer and Richard Erdoes, "Talking to the Owls and Butterflies" from *Lame Deer: Seeker of Visions.* Copyright © 1972 by John (Fire) Lame Deer and Richard Erdoes. Reprinted by permission of Simon & Schuster, Inc.

Patricia Nelson Limerick, "Empire of Innocence" from *The Legacy of Conquest: The Unbroken Past of the American West* by Patricia Nelson Limerick. Copyright © 1987 by Patricia Nelson Limerick. Reprinted with the permission of W. W. Norton & Company, Inc. Abridged with the permission of the author.

Karen Lindsey, "Friends as Family" from *Friends as Family* by Karen Lindsey. Copyright © 1981 by Karen Lindsey. Reprinted by permission of Beacon Press.

Gregory Mantsios, "Rewards and Opportunities: The Politics and Economics of Class in the U.S." from Paula S. Rothenberg's *Race, Class, and Gender in the United States: An Integrated Study* (1992). Reprinted by permission of the author.

Eric Marcus, "The Bridge Builder: Kathleen Boatwright" from *Making History: The Struggle for Gay and Lesbian Rights 1945–1990* by Eric Marcus. Copyright © 1992 by Eric Marcus. Reprinted by permission of HarperCollins Publishers, Inc.

Bill McKibben, "TV, Freedom, and the Loss of Community" from *The Age of Missing Information* by Bill McKibben. Copyright © 1992 by Bill McKibben. Reprinted by permission of Random House, Inc.

Janice Mirikitani, "We, the Dangerous" from *Awake in the River, Poetry and Prose* by Janice Mirikitani. Copyright © 1978 by Janice Mirikitani. Reprinted by permission of the author.

Aurora Levins Morales, "Child of the Americas" from *Getting Home Alive* by Aurora Levins Morales and Rosario Morales. Copyright © 1986 by Aurora Levins Morales. Reprinted by permission of Firebrand Books, Ithaca, NY.

Gloria Naylor, "The Two" from *The Women of Brewster Place* by Gloria Naylor. Copyright © 1980, 1982 by Gloria Naylor. Used by permission of Viking Penguin, a division of Penguin Books USA, Inc.

Jill Nelson, "Number One!" Reprinted courtesy of The Noble Press, Inc.

Joyce Nelson, "The 'Greening' of Establishment PR: Mind Pollution on the Rise" from *Sultans of Sleaze: Public Relations and the Media* by Joyce Nelson. Reprinted by permission of Between the Lines and Common Courage Press.

Michael Omi and Howard Winant, "Racial Formation" from *Racial Formation in the United States* (1986), by permission of the publisher, Routledge, NY.

Judith Ortiz Cofer, "The Story of My Body" from *The Latin Deli* by Judith Ortiz Cofer. Copyright © 1993 by Judith Ortiz Cofer. Reprinted by permission of The University of Georgia Press, Athens, GA.

Josh Ozersky, "TV's Anti-Families: Married . . . with Malaise." Appeared in *Tikkun* Magazine, vol. 6, no. 1 (January/February 1991). Copyright © 1991 by Josh Ozersky. Reprinted with permission of the author.

Vincent N. Parrillo, "Causes of Prejudice" from *Strangers to these Shores: Race and Ethnic Relations in the United States,* 3/e, by Vincent N. Parrillo. Copyright © 1990 by Macmillan College Publishing Company, Inc. Reprinted with the permission of Macmillan College Publishing Company, Inc.

Adrienne Rich, "Split at the Root: An Essay on Jewish Identity," slightly abridged, from *Blood, Bread, and Poetry, Selected Prose, 1979–1985,* by Adrienne Rich. Copyright © 1986 by Adrienne Rich. Reprinted by permission of the author and W. W. Norton & Company, Inc.

Richard Rodriguez, "The Achievement of Desire" from *Hunger of Memory* by Richard Rodriguez. Copyright © 1982 by Richard Rodriguez. Reprinted by permission of David R. Godine, Publisher.

Theodore Roethke, "My Papa's Waltz" from *The Collected Poems of Theodore Roethke* by Theodore Roethke. Copyright 1942 by Hearst Magazines, Inc. Used by permission of Doubleday, a division of Bantam Doubleday Dell Publishing Group, Inc.

Mike Rose, " 'I Just Wanna Be Average' " from *Lives on the Boundary: Struggles and Achievements of America's Underprepared* by Mike Rose. Copyright © 1989 by Mike Rose. Reprinted with permission of The Free Press, an imprint of Simon & Schuster.

Wendy Rose, "Three Thousand Dollar Death Song" from *Lost Copper* by Wendy Rose (Malki Museum Press). Copyright © 1980 by Wendy Rose. Reprinted by permission of the author.

Myra Sadker and David Sadker, "Higher Education: Colder by Degrees" from *Failing at Fairness: How America's Schools Cheat Girls* by Myra Sadker and David Sadker. Copyright © 1994 Myra Sadker and David Sadker. Reprinted with the permission of Charles Scribner's Sons, an imprint of Macmillan Publishing.

Jean Reith Schroedel, "Nora Quealey" from *Alone in a Crowd: Women in the Trades Tell Their Stories* by Jean Reith Schroedel. Copyright © 1985 by Temple University. Reprinted by permission of Temple University Press.

Joni Seager, "The Eco-Fringe: Deep Ecology" from *Earth Follies: Coming to Feminist Terms with the Global Environmental Crisis* (1993) by Joni Seager. Reprinted by permission of the publisher, Routledge, NY.

Ruth Sidel, "The New American Dreamers" from *On Her Own* by Ruth Sidel. Copyright © 1990 by Ruth Sidel. Used by permission of Viking Penguin, a division of Penguin Books USA Inc.

Leslie Marmon Silko, "Storyteller" from *Storyteller* by Leslie Marmon Silko, published by Seaver Books, New York, NY. Copyright © 1981 by Leslie Marmon Silko. Reprinted by permission.

Theodore Sizer, "What High School Is" from *Horace's Compromise* by Theodore Sizer. Copyright © 1984 by Theodore R. Sizer. Reprinted by permission of Houghton Mifflin Co. All rights reserved.

Jack Solomon, "Masters of Desire: The Culture of American Advertising" from *The Sign of Our Times* by Jack Solomon. Copyright © 1988 by Jack Fisher Solomon, Ph.D. Reprinted by permission of The Putnam Publishing Group/Jeremy P. Tarcher, Inc.

Gary Soto, "Looking for Work" from *Living up the Street: Narrative Recollections* by Gary Soto (Dell, 1992). Copyright © 1985 by Gary Soto. Used by permission of the author.

Gerry Spence, "Easy in the Harness: The Tyranny of Freedom" from the book *From Freedom to Slavery* by Gerry Spence. Copyright © 1993 by Gerry Spence. Reprinted with permission from St. Martin's Press, Inc., New York, NY.

Shelby Steele, "I'm Black, You're White, Who's Innocent?" from *The Content of Our Character* by Shelby Steele. Copyright © 1990 by Shelby Steele. Reprinted with special permission from St. Martin's Press, Inc., New York, NY.

Ronald Takaki, "A Different Mirror" from *A Different Mirror : A History of Multicultural America* by Ronald Takaki. Copyright © 1993 by Ronald Takaki. Reprinted by permission of Little, Brown and Company.

Robin Templeton, "Not for Sale" © 1993. Reprinted with permission of author and of publication (*Crossroads*).

Studs Terkel, "C. P. Ellis" and "Stephen Cruz" from *American Dreams: Lost and Found* by Studs Terkel. Copyright © 1980 by Studs Terkel. Reprinted by permission of Pantheon Books, a division of Random House, Inc.

Haunani-Kay Trask, "From a Native Daughter" from *The American Indian and the Problem of History*, edited by Calvin Martin. Copyright © 1987 by Haunani-Kay Trask. Reprinted by permission of Haunani-Kay Trask.

Carmen Vázquez, "Appearances" from Chapter 9 of *Homophobia: How We All Pay the Price* by Warren J. Blumenfeld. Copyright © 1992 by Warren J. Blumenfeld. Reprinted by permission of Beacon Press.

James D. Weinrich and Walter L. Williams, "Strange Customs, Familiar Lives: Homosexuality in Other Cultures," pp. 44–59 from *Homosexuality: Research Implications for Public Policy*, edited by J. C. Gonsiorek and J. D. Weinrich, © 1991. Reprinted by permission of Sage Publications, Inc.

Patricia J. Williams, "Hate Radio." Reprinted by permission of *Ms.* Magazine, © 1994.

George H. Wood, "Secondary Schools, Primary Lessons" from Chapter 2 of *Schools that Work* by George H. Wood. Copyright © 1992 by George H. Wood. Used by permission of Dutton Signet, a division of Penguin Books USA Inc.

Malcolm X, "Learning to Read" from *The Autobiography of Malcolm X* by Malcolm X, with the assistance of Alex Haley. Copyright © 1964 by Alex Haley and Malcolm X and copyright © 1965 by Alex Haley and Betty Shabazz. Reprinted by permission of Random House, Inc.

Art Acknowledgments

Chapter 1: Learning Power

"Skeptical Student" (p. 15) photograph by Charles Agel. © Charles Agel.

"Lesson 4: Wake Up! You'll Be Late For Your First Day of School" (p. 31) cartoon by Matt Groening. From *School Is Hell* © 1987 by Matt Groening. All rights reserved. Reprinted by permission of Pantheon Books, a division of Random House, Inc., NY.

"Life in School (Devious Little Weasels)" (p. 32) cartoon by Matt Groening. From *Love Is Hell* © 1986 by Matt Groening. All rights reserved. Reprinted by permission of Pantheon Books, a division of Random House, Inc., NY.

"A Girl's Education" (p. 109) cartoon by Garry Trudeau. *Doonesbury* copyright 1992 G. B. Trudeau. Reprinted with permission of Universal Press Syndicate. All rights reserved.

"Hey, Let's Hear It" (p. 138) cartoon by Rob Husberg. Copyright © 1992 Rob Husberg/The Scottsdale Progress.

Chapter 2: Harmony at Home

"African American Family Jogging" (p. 141) photograph by Jeffrey. From the book and traveling photographic exhibition, *Life in a Day of Black L.A.: The Way We See It,* produced by UCLA's Center for Afro-American Studies in association with Black Photographers of California: The Jogging Family © 1992 by Jeffrey.

"Roger Realizes . . ." (p. 152) cartoon by Andrew Struthers. Reprinted courtesy of Andrew Struthers © 1988.

"Dysfunctional Family Greeting Cards" (p. 173) cartoon by Jennifer Berman. Copyright © 1993 Jennifer Berman, P.O. Box 6614, Evanston, IL 60204-6614.

CHAPTER 3: WOMEN AND MEN IN RELATIONSHIP

"Delphinia Blue, Bree Scott-Hartland as" (p. 238) photograph by Carolyn Jones. From *Living Proof* (Abbeville Press, 1994). Copyright © 1992 by Carolyn Jones.

"Bad Housekeeping" (p. 257) cartoon by Roz Chast. Copyright © 1988 The New Yorker Magazine, Inc.

"Public Display of Affection" (p. 294) cartoon by Alison Bechdel. From *New, Improved! Dykes to Watch Out For* by Alison Bechdel (Firebrand Books, Ithaca, NY). Copyright © 1990 by Alison Bechdel.

CHAPTER 4: CREATED EQUAL

"Demonstrating for Peace and Unity, Los Angeles, 1992" (p. 328) photograph by Michael Justice. *Korean peace march* © Michael Justice/The Image Works.

"Black History, Women's History" (p. 350) cartoon by Barbara Brandon. *Where I'm Coming From,* copyright Barbara Brandon. Distributed by Universal Press Syndicate. Reprinted with permission. All rights reserved.

"Prejudice Workshop" (p. 387) cartoon by Judy Horacek. Reproduced with permission from *Life on the Edge* by Judy Horacek, published by Spinifex Press.

CHAPTER 5: MONEY AND SUCCESS

"Man with Rolls Royce" (p. 447) photograph by Steven Weirebe.

Affluence: Man in Cap by Rolls Royce © Steve Weinrebe/THE PICTURE CUBE.

"Will Work for Food" (p. 458) cartoon by Marian Henley. *Maxine* Comix © Marian Henley. Reprinted by permission of the artist.

"My Heart Bleeds" (p. 512) cartoon by Dan Perkins. Copyright © 1992 Tom Tomorrow. Reprint with permission of the artist.

"Why You Wearin' a Mask?" (p. 534) cartoon by Jules Feiffer. *Feiffer* copyright 1994 Jules Feiffer. Reprinted with permission of Universal Press Syndicate. All rights reserved.

CHAPTER 6: NATURE AND TECHNOLOGY

"Cadillac Ranch" (p. 560) photograph by Doug Michels. Copyright © 1974 by Ant Farm (Lord, Marquez, Michels). All rights reserved.

"Blue Roses! Mini Cows!" (p. 591) cartoon by Judy Horacek. Reproduced with permission from *Life on the Edge* by Judy Horacek, published by Spinifex Press.

"Quality Programming" (p. 599) cartoon by Clay Butler. *Sidewalk Bubblegum* © 1993 by Clay Butler.

"Honk If You Love the Environment" (p. 634) cartoon by Toles. *Toles* copyright 1990 The Buffalo News. Reprinted with permission of Universal Press Syndicate. All rights reserved.

CHAPTER 7: LIBERTY AND JUSTICE FOR ALL

"New Yorker Sticking Tongue Out, 1986" (p. 658) photograph by Bob Adelman. Copyright © Bob Adelman, 1986.

"Fix Your Own Damn Dinner" (p. 681) cartoon by Wiley. Copyright © 1994 The Washington Post Writers Group. Reprinted with permission.

"Offensive to Some, a Turn-on to Others" (p. 732) cartoon by John Callahan. Copyright © 1994. Reprinted by permission of John Callahan.

Index of Authors and Titles